US GAAP For Life Insurers

2ND EDITION

R. Thomas Herget
Editor

Frank Buck
Mark J. Freedman
Thomas R. Kochis
Daniel J. Kunesh
S. Michael McLaughlin
Edward L. Robbins
David Y. Rogers
Eric R. Schuering
Bradley M. Smith
John T. Zellner

Project Oversight Group
R. Thomas Herget
S. Michael McLaughlin
Shirley Hwei-Chung Shao

The material included in this book has been provided to assist actuaries and other professionals in understanding the principles of United States Generally Accepted Accounting Principles where they are unique or have specific applicability to life insurance companies.

Publication of this book has been a collaborative effort of actuaries and accountants with many years of relevant experience. Authors were selected based on their knowledge, experience, and communication skills. Work effort was shared in accordance with the authors' preferences and background. An elaborate quality management process included at least two reviews of each chapter as well as content and style editing. Principles and practices are characterized thoroughly and accurately to the best of the knowledge of the editor and authors.

This book presents a comprehensive analysis of the fundamentals of U.S. GAAP. However, it is not a substitute for a thorough review of the original pronouncements and supporting literature of the authoritative bodies.

Library of Congress Cataloging-in-Publication Data

U.S. GAAP for life insurers / R. Thomas Herget ... [et al.]. – 2nd ed.
p. cm.
Includes bibliographical references and index.
ISBN 0-938959-73-5
1. Insurance, Life—United States—Accounting. I. Herget, R. Thomas, 1950-

HG8848.U17 2006
657'.836030973—dc22 2005032321

Printed by Sheridan Books Inc., Ann Arbor, Michigan

Printed in the United States of America

Second Edition, Fifth Printing

Preface

Life insurers around the world prepare financial statements according to United States generally accepted accounting principles (GAAP). The sources for this authority are wide and varying. Thus, the Life Insurance Company Financial Reporting Section of the Society of Actuaries decided to create a single textbook for life insurers that would consolidate the principles and the sources underlying U.S. GAAP and that would provide instructive, enlightening examples of the use of these principles in practice.

US GAAP for Life Insurers is aimed at three audiences: the actuary who is new to GAAP and needs formal instruction, the seasoned accountant who wants to know what the actuary is doing, and the non-U.S. actuary or accountant who seeks instruction to establish U.S. GAAP financial statements.

Ten experienced practitioners were identified, contacted, and persuaded to serve as authors. They were selected on the basis of several criteria: 20 or more years of experience with GAAP, exposure to many companies in the industry, recognition as an authority, and proven communication capability. The authors were supported by the editor and a Project Oversight Group, bringing together a team of 12.

Much of the writing was accomplished in three face-to-face meetings of the author group. Convening for four-day periods in a conference room with personal computers but without cell phones, the authors wrote individually but frequently discussed and debated issues with the entire group.

Each author wrote two chapters and reviewed two chapters. Authors selected areas in which they could offer significant experience and expertise. The collaborative experience offered several benefits: the style of writing became more uniform; the depth of coverage for each topic converged; and a concerted effort was made to distinguish principles from practices. As a result, the reader will learn what should be done—rather than what has been done.

Two items could be addressed neither in detail nor with authority in this book because the associated pronouncements were not yet final or effective during the authors' writing period:

- Revised *SFAS No. 141*, "Business Combinations."
- *SOP 05-1*, "Accounting by Insurance Enterprises for Deferred Acquisition Costs in Connection with Modifications or Exchanges of Insurance Contracts."

This book does not explicitly address the concept of fair value, which is being deliberated by the FASB and international bodies.

After determining which topics were too fresh, indefinite, or obscure to address in the book, the authors focused on the best presentation of the selected topics. Thus chapters are arranged in a manner that optimizes the reader's time. Insurance products are treated thoroughly in dedicated chapters. However, to avoid excessive duplication, some common elements are treated in topic-dedicated chapters and not repeated in detail in subsequent product-dedicated chapters. For example, the chapters on objectives, authorities, expenses, shadow accounts, and reinsurance treat these common elements, and they are referenced, but not repeated, in the chapters that deal directly with insurance products.

Many textbooks present formulas in a singular style. In practice, however, a variety of styles are used. For example, some practitioners use capital letters, such as PVB for present value of benefits. Others use actuarial expressions, such as A_x^{Ben}, to express the same thing. Yet others no longer use either, relying on spreadsheet expressions relating only to prior rows and columns. All three conventions are used in this textbook. Note that commutation columns are not represented.

The authors, editor, and Project Oversight Group members spent 3,800 hours in less than a year to prepare the first edition book. At one point, the entire team was in a single room. A week later, more than half the team happened to be on four different continents. Nonetheless, the exchange of files and flow of ideas never diminished. The second edition also took a year to update; another 1,000 hours were invested by the authors and editor to produce the update.

To ensure the accuracy and consistency of the material presented, an elaborate quality management process was established and followed. Each author was assigned to review at least two other chapters. In addition, one author was designated as the verifier of formulas and numerical examples. An accountant was selected to review the chapters written by the CPA author.

After the author and the reviewer had agreed that a chapter was complete, the editor reviewed it. The chapter was then submitted, on a blind basis, to one or two reviewers to affirm that there were no ambiguities or omissions and that the text and the supporting examples were instructional. This layer of review provided very valuable input.

At this point, a technical editor, experienced with actuarial material, read each chapter to ensure that proper grammatical rules, textbook conventions, and mathematical protocols were being followed. A veteran practitioner then spent six days reading the entire text, adding more consistency and substance. Finally, yet another actuary read the entire book in print-ready status, ensuring proper form throughout.

The knowledge and support of quite a number of people were vital to the preparation of this book.

First and foremost, the authors deserve a standing ovation. The amount of effort they devoted to establishing, verifying, and putting into prose the numerous principles was simply enormous. The entire author team is entitled to step back and admire its work.

There was a tremendous amount of research, writing, discussion, debate, and confirmation. The authors are to be congratulated and thanked for the amazing number of hours they spent on this book in such a short period. Their names and qualifications are enumerated in the authors' Biographies.

Lois Chinnock, Michelle Smith, Patti Pape and Veronica Saldana coordinated all the meeting space, checking authors' accommodations and overseeing all the logistics for the meetings.

For the first edition, the many nuances of publishing were clarified by Michael Braunstein, Denise Rosengrant, Dick McKee, and Steve Gerhardt. For the second edition, the Society of Actuaries' director of publications Clay Baznik capably performed to coordinate printing and distribution. For both editions, artwork for the cover was provided by Lily Chow and Abby Herget.

Three people were very instrumental in converting the authors' actuarial expertise into prose suitable for reading and study. One was technical editor Barbara Simmons, ELS. Her many years of experience with actuarial material were evident and most valuable for the first edition. For the second round, Bob Barnett provided timely and valuable input. For both editions, assistant editor Tom Cook converted all the authors' drafts to create the final format. He had the ability and patience to decipher the most complex and obscure passages and legends. Few people other than Tom, Barbara, and Bob can spot the difference between a hyphen, an em dash, and a minus sign.

Project Oversight Group members Mike McLaughlin and Shirley Shao must be credited with adding a measure of democracy to the autocratic tendencies of the editor. Their independent viewpoints and persuasive suggestions elevated the quality of the text. Of course, this book wouldn't have been possible without the vision and prodding of Craig Raymond and Shirley Shao in their roles as Chair of the Society of Actuaries' Financial Reporting Section.

A very important contribution was the high degree of support for this textbook provided by the additional reviewers: Noel Abkemeier, John Adduci, John Agee, Steven Barclay, Ravi Bhandari, Lauren Bloom, Rick Browne, John Brumbach, Tom Campbell, Ginger Carter, Tom Corcoran, John Derrick, Donald Doran, Bud Friedstat, Tim Gaynor, Mike Grillaert, Jim Hawke, Laura Hay, Paul Hekman, Norm Hill, Bill Horbatt, Jim Housholder, Jeff Klanderman, Ken Klinger, Victor Kwong, Bob Lemke, Mike Leung, Shu Yen Liu, Lou Lombardi, Tricia Matson, Don Maves, Jim McDermott, Jim Milholland, David Montgomery, Brett Morris, Tom Nace, Donovan North, Bill Obert, Lynn Pogas, Art Roberts, Dave Rockwell, Dana Rudmose, Ted Schlude, Art Schneider, Gregg Schneider, Bill Shomaker, Ed Silins, Ken Smith, Peijian Sun, Ron Takemoto, Enrique Tejerina, Bob Thomas, Vincent Tsang, Marty Uhl, Robert Ward, David White, Ron Wittenwyler, Cindy Wu, and John Yanko.

Their independent perspectives and evaluations truly enhanced the quality of this text.

We sincerely hope that this second edition of *US GAAP for Life Insurers* will make a difference in your practice. We are very proud of our efforts and hope that the book will be a primary source that will enable you to understand and apply GAAP.

R. Thomas Herget

R. Thomas Herget, Editor
November 28, 2005
Chicago, Illinois

Contents

Preface iii
About the Authors xxi
Chapter 1 GAAP Objectives and their Implications to Life Insurers 1
Chapter 2 Authorities 17
Chapter 3 Expenses and Capitalization 35
Chapter 4 Traditional Life Insurance *(SFAS 60 & SFAS 97)* 81
Chapter 5 Traditional Life Insurance *(SFAS 120)* 123
Chapter 6 Universal Life Insurance 161
Chapter 7 Deferred Annuities 203
Chapter 8 Variable and Equity-Based Products 231
Chapter 9 Annuities in Payment Status 311
Chapter 10 Individual Health Insurance 321
Chapter 11 Credit Insurance 369
Chapter 12 Group Insurance, Large Case Pension Liabilities and Related Liabilities 381
Chapter 13 Investment Accounting 403
Chapter 14 Shadow Adjustments *(SFAS 115)* 441
Chapter 15 Accounting for Business Combinations 455
Chapter 16 Non-U.S. Products 491
Chapter 17 Reinsurance 523
Chapter 18 Other Topics 575
Chapter 19 Financial Statement Presentations 611
Appendix A Purchase Accounting 631
Appendix B Proposed Statement to Replace *SFAS 141* 665
Bibliography 669
Index 675

Detailed Contents

Preface ... iii
About the Authors ... xxi
Chapter 1 GAAP Objectives and their Implications to Life Insurers ... 1
1.1 Concepts ... 1
1.2 Desirable Accounting Information ... 4
1.2.1 Relevant Accounting Information ... 4
1.2.2 Reliable Accounting Information ... 5
1.3 Financial Statements ... 5
1.3.1 Basic Elements ... 5
1.3.2 Comprehensive Income ... 7
1.4 Recognition and Measurement of Financial Statement Elements ... 8
1.5 Emergence of Earnings for Life Insurers ... 9
1.5.1 Financial Statement Relationships ... 12
1.5.2 Fluctuations in Earnings ... 13
1.6 Measurement Methods, Estimates, and Materiality ... 13
1.7 Disclosures ... 15
1.8 Mutual Life Insurers ... 16
Chapter 2 Authorities ... 17
2.1 Historical Perspective: Regulatory Focus and the Needs of Investors ... 17
2.2 Standard Setters ... 18
2.2.1 American Institute of Certified Public Accountants ... 18
2.2.1.1 Accounting Research Bulletins ... 19
2.2.1.2 Accounting Principles Board Opinions ... 19
2.2.1.3 Practice Bulletins ... 19
2.2.1.4 Industry Audit Guides ... 20
2.2.1.5 Statements of Position ... 20
2.2.2 Financial Accounting Standards Board ... 23
2.2.2.1 Concept Statements ... 23
2.2.2.2 Statements of Financial Accounting Standards ... 23
2.2.2.3 FASB Interpretations ... 23
2.2.2.4 FASB Technical Bulletins ... 24
2.2.2.5 FASB Emerging Issues Task Force Issues ... 24
2.2.2.6 FASB Staff Positions ... 24
2.2.2.7 FASB Standards ... 24
2.2.2.8 EITF Abstracts ... 29
2.2.2.9 FASB Staff Position *(FAS 97-1)* ... 29
2.3 GAAP Hierarchy ... 29
2.3.1 Established Accounting Literature ... 29
2.3.2 Other Accounting Literature ... 30
2.3.3 Evolution of Authoritative Literature ... 30
2.3.4 Actuarial Standards of Practice ... 30
2.4 The Securities and Exchange Commission ... 31
2.5 Accounting by Analogy ... 32
2.6 Role of the Auditor ... 32
2.7 Congressional and Regulatory Involvement ... 32
Chapter 3 Expenses and Capitalization ... 35

3.1 Purpose ... 35
3.2 Background ... 35
3.2.1 Statements of Financial Concepts ... 35
3.2.2 Statements of Financial Accounting Standards ... 36
3.2.3 Terminology ... 37
3.3 Categorization Stipulated by *SFAS 60* ... 37
3.3.1 Deferrable Acquisition Costs ... 38
3.3.2 Nondeferrable Acquisition Costs ... 38
3.3.3 Direct Maintenance Costs ... 39
3.3.4 Investment Expenses ... 39
3.3.5 Future Utility Expenses ... 39
3.3.6 Overhead ... 39
3.4 Expense Categorization under other Pronouncements ... 39
3.4.1 *SFAS 91* ... 39
3.4.2 *SFAS 97* ... 40
3.4.3 *Practice Bulletin 8* ... 40
3.4.4 *SOP 95-1* ... 41
3.5 Line of Business and Category Analysis ... 41
3.5.1 Categorization ... 41
3.5.2 Percentage of Premium Expense Allocation ... 42
3.5.3 Allocations of Salary and Other Expenses ... 43
3.5.4 Distinction between Direct Maintenance and Overhead Expenses ... 43
3.5.5 Investment Expenses ... 44
3.5.6 Selection of Units of Measurement and Unitization of Expenses ... 44
3.5.7 Other Issues ... 47
3.6 Determination of Deferrability of Acquisition Costs ... 48
3.6.1 Commissions ... 49
3.6.2 Expenses Similar to Commissions ... 49
3.6.3 Home Office Expenses ... 50
3.7 Timing of Deferrability ... 51
3.7.1 True-up ... 51
3.7.2 Commission Timing ... 54
3.7.3 Anticipation of Future Deferrable Expenses ... 55
3.8 Recoverability Testing and Loss Recognition ... 56
3.8.1 Authority and Definitions ... 56
3.8.2 Level of Aggregation for Testing ... 57
3.8.3 Gross Premium Valuation Test and the Order of Adjustments to the Balance Sheet ... 58
3.8.4 Exclusion of Interest on Surplus from the Testing ... 60
3.9 Relation of GAAP Expense Assumptions to Pricing Expense Assumptions ... 62
3.10 Special Expense Issues ... 62
3.10.1 Internal Replacements ... 62
3.10.2 Reinsurance ... 63
3.10.3 Purchase Accounting ... 64
3.10.4 Discontinued Operations ... 65
3.11 Sales Inducements ... 66
3.11.1 Background ... 68
3.11.2 Capitalization and Amortization of Sales Inducements ... 68
3.11.2.1 Treatment of Type (1) – Immediate Sales Inducements ... 68
3.11.2.2 Treatment of Type (2) – Persistency Sales Inducements ... 69
3.11.2.3 Treatment of Type (3) – Enhanced Crediting Rate Sales Inducements ... 69
3.11.3 Transitional Rules ... 70
3.11.4 Interpretational Issues ... 70

3.11.4.1 Scope ... 70
3.11.4.2 Enhanced Crediting Rate as a Persistency Bonus for a Period of Years ... 71
3.11.4.3 Similar Contract Without a Sales Inducement ... 71
3.11.4.4 Computation of Sales Inducement Liabilities ... 71
3.11.4.5 Computation of Sales Inducement Assets ... 72
3.12 Worksheet Approaches to DAC Calculation ... 78
3.12.1 Static Worksheets ... 78
3.12.2 Dynamic Worksheets ... 79
Chapter 4 Traditional Life Insurance *(SFAS 60 & SFAS 97)* ... 81
4.1 Background ... 81
4.2 Product Features ... 82
4.3 Benefit Reserve Methodology ... 82
4.4 Expense Recognition ... 84
4.5 Selection of Assumptions ... 86
4.5.1 GAAP Assumption Eras ... 86
4.5.2 Provisions for Adverse Deviation ... 86
4.5.3 Investment Earnings Rate ... 89
4.5.4 Mortality and Morbidity Rates ... 89
4.5.5 Lapse Rates ... 90
4.5.6 Expenses ... 92
4.5.7 Taxes ... 92
4.6 Lock-In ... 92
4.7 Loss Recognition ... 93
4.8 *SFAS 60* Numerical Examples – 20 Year Endowment ... 95
4.9 *SFAS 60* Numerical Examples – 20 Year Term ... 106
4.10 Limited-Payment Contracts ... 109
4.11 *SFAS 97* Limited Pay Numerical Example ... 110
4.12 Participating Products ... 114
4.13 Indeterminate Premium Products ... 116
4.14 Implications of Reserve Formula Selection ... 118
4.14.1 Benefit Reserves ... 118
4.14.2 Expense Reserves ... 120
Chapter 5 Traditional Life Insurance *(SFAS 120)* ... 123
5.1 Introduction ... 123
5.2 Scope and Applicability ... 125
5.3 Overview of Accounting Model ... 128
5.4 Amortization Methods ... 130
5.5 Selection of Assumptions ... 133
5.5.1 Benefit Reserve Assumptions ... 133
5.5.1.1 Mortality ... 133
5.5.1.2 Interest ... 134
5.5.1.3 Method ... 134
5.5.2 Estimated Gross Margins Assumptions ... 134
5.5.2.1 Mortality ... 134
5.5.2.2 Interest ... 134
5.5.2.3 Dividend ... 135
5.5.2.4 Lapse Rates ... 136
5.5.2.5 Expenses ... 136
5.5.2.6 Grouping ... 136
5.5.3 Example ... 137
5.6 True-up and Unlocking ... 138
5.7 Realized Capital Gains ... 141

5.8 Recoverability and Loss Recognition ... 143
5.9 Policyholder Benefit Liabilities ... 146
5.10 DAC and Terminal Dividend Liabilities ... 148
5.11 Additional Considerations ... 150
5.11.1 Policy Riders ... 150
5.11.2 Reinsurance ... 152
5.12 Examples ... 152
5.12.1 Base Case ... 152
5.12.2 Dividend Fund Different Than Net Level Premium Reserve ... 152
5.12.3 Experience Different Than Best-Estimate Assumptions ... 155
5.12.4 Alternative Discount Rates ... 157
Chapter 6 Universal Life Insurance ... 161
6.1 Background ... 161
6.2 Applicability ... 162
6.3 Definition ... 163
6.3.1 Significance of Mortality and/or Morbidity Risks ... 163
6.3.2 Example of Significance Test ... 164
6.4 Typical Product Designs ... 165
6.5 Presentation of Results ... 166
6.6 Benefit Reserves ... 168
6.6.1 Account Balance Products ... 168
6.6.1.1 Additional Interest ... 168
6.6.1.2 Example of Additional Interest ... 168
6.6.1.3 Other Adjustments ... 170
6.6.2 Other Products ... 170
6.7 Capitalization and Amortization of Acquisition Expenses ... 171
6.7.1 Estimated Gross Profits (EGPs) ... 171
6.7.1.1 Mortality ... 171
6.7.1.2 Costs of Contract Administration ... 171
6.7.1.3 Investment Earnings ... 171
6.7.1.4 Surrender Charges ... 172
6.7.1.5 Other Assessments and Credits ... 172
6.7.1.6 Nondeferred Acquisition Costs ... 172
6.7.2 Expense Capitalization ... 173
6.7.3 Amortization of Deferred Acquisition Costs ... 173
6.7.4 Negative Gross Profits ... 175
6.7.5 Example of EGP Computation and Amortization of DAC ... 175
6.7.6 Selection of Assumptions and Unlocking ... 182
6.7.6.1 Selection of Assumptions ... 182
6.7.6.2 True-up for Actual Experience/Retrospective Unlocking ... 183
6.7.6.3 Assumptions and Prospective Unlocking ... 184
6.8 Deferral of Unearned Revenue ... 186
6.8.1 Definition ... 186
6.8.2 Example ... 187
6.9 Treatment of Bonuses and Other Special Benefits ... 188
6.10 Recoverability and Loss Recognition ... 189
6.11 Choice of Crediting Rate in DAC Amortization ... 189
6.12 "Profits followed by losses" ... 190
6.12.1 Insurance Benefit Feature ... 190
6.12.2 Definition of an Assessment ... 190
6.12.3 Interaction of an Unearned Revenue Liability with SOP Liability ... 191
6.12.4 Examples of Profits Followed by Losses Tests ... 192

6.13 Establishment of Liabilities under *SOP 03-1* 196
6.13.1 Example of Establishment of Liability and Impact on DAC 197
6.13.2 Examples of Interaction of *SOP 03-1* Liabilities and URL—"The circulatory issue". 200
Chapter 7 Deferred Annuities 203
7.1 Introduction 203
7.2 Types of Products 203
7.3 Accounting Model Classification 205
7.4 Benefit Reserves 208
7.4.1 *SFAS 97* for Investment Contracts 208
7.4.2 *SFAS 91* 209
7.4.3 Annuitization Benefits 209
7.5 Deferred Acquisition Costs, Front End Load and Deferred Sales Inducements 210
7.5.1 Deferred Acquistion Costs Considerations 210
7.5.2 Front End Load Considerations 210
7.5.3 Deferred Sales Inducements 211
7.6 DAC and DSI Amortization Under *SFAS 97* 211
7.6.1 Definition of Gross Profits 211
7.6.2 DAC/DSI Amortization Process 213
7.6.3 EGP and DAC Formulas 215
7.6.3.1 Definitions 215
7.6.3.2 Formulas 216
7.7 DAC Amortization Under *SFAS 91* 217
7.8 Accrual of Unearned Revenue Liability 218
7.9 Selection of Assumptions 218
7.10 Loss Recognition Tests 219
7.11 Examples 221
7.12 Presentation of Results 226
7.13 Special Accounting Considerations for Market-Value-Adjusted Annuities 228
7.13.1 Product Description 228
7.13.2 Accounting Issues 228
7.13.3 Example 229
Chapter 8 Variable and Equity-Based Products 231
8.1 Introduction 231
8.2 Variable Products 232
8.2.1 Product Descriptions 232
8.2.1.1 Variable Universal Life 232
8.2.1.2 Variable Deferred Annuities 233
8.2.1.3 Variable Payout Annuities 234
8.2.2 Contract Classification 234
8.2.2.1 Life Insurance 234
8.2.2.2 Deferred Annuities 235
8.2.2.3 Payout Annuities 237
8.2.3 Assumptions 238
8.2.3.1 Assumptions for DAC amortization 238
8.2.3.1.1 Contract Interest Rates for EGPs 239
8.2.3.1.2 Discount Rates 241
8.2.3.1.3 Mortality Rates 242
8.2.3.1.4 Other Assumptions 242
8.2.3.2 Assumptions Used for GMDB and GMIB Liability 243
8.2.3.3 Assumptions Used for GMAB and GMWB Liability 243
8.2.4 Methods 244
8.2.4.1 DAC Amortization 244

8.2.4.2 GMDB liability 247
8.2.4.3 Variable Universal Life no-lapse premium guarantee liability 248
8.2.4.4 GMIB liability 248
8.2.4.5 Liability for GMAB and GMWB 248
8.2.5 Examples 250
8.2.5.1 Variable Universal Life 250
8.2.5.2 Variable Deferred Annuities 258
8.2.5.3 Variable Payout Annuity 264
8.2.5.4 Alternative Contract Rate Assumptions 271
8.2.5.5 GMDB 276
8.2.5.6 GMAB 286
8.3 Equity-Indexed Annuities 289
8.3.1 Nature of Product 289
8.3.2 Accounting for Derivatives 290
8.3.3 Establishing GAAP Methodology for DAC and Reserves 291
8.3.4 Numerical Illustrations 294
8.3.4.1 Point to Point EIA Product 294
8.3.4.2 Annual Ratchet EIA Product 299
Chapter 9 Annuities in Payment Status 311
9.1 Background 311
9.2 Contract Classification 311
9.3 Investment Contracts 312
9.4 Limited Payment Contracts 317
9.5 Conversion of Policy-Year Factors to Calendar-Year Factors 319
Chapter 10 Individual Health Insurance 321
10.1 Characteristics of Health Insurance Business 321
10.1.1 Insurable Events 321
10.1.2 Contractual Terms 321
10.1.3 Benefits 322
10.1.4 Premiums 323
10.1.5 Premium Rate Increases 324
10.2 Types of Health Insurance Policies 325
10.3 Product Classification 328
10.4 Reserve Methods 330
10.4.1 Benefit Reserves 331
10.4.2 Maintenance Expense Reserves 332
10.4.3 Acquisition Expense Reserves 333
10.4.4 Unearned Premium Reserves 333
10.4.5 Deferred Profit Liability 333
10.4.6 Premium Deficiency Reserves 335
10.4.7 Claim Reserves 335
10.5 Benefit, Maintenance and DAC Reserve Formulas 335
10.5.1 Definitions 335
10.5.2 Formulas 336
10.5.3 High Lapse Rates 340
10.6 Selection of Assumptions 342
10.6.1 Mortality 344
10.6.2 Morbidity 344
10.6.3 Interest 345
10.6.4 Lapse rates 346
10.6.5 Expenses 346
10.6.6 Commissions 347

10.6.7 Taxes ... 348
10.6.8 Provisions for Adverse Deviation ... 348
10.6.9 Summary ... 351
10.7 Reserving after a Premium Increase ... 352
10.8 Recoverability and Loss Recognition ... 356
10.8.1 Recoverability ... 356
10.8.2 Loss Recognition ... 356
10.9 Claim Reserves ... 358
10.9.1 Requirement for Claim Reserves ... 358
10.9.2 Estimation of Claim Reserves ... 359
10.9.3 Components of Claim Reserves ... 359
10.9.4 Claim Reserves Based on Lag Tables ... 360
10.9.5 Claim Reserves Based on Pricing ... 361
10.9.6 Disability Income Benefit Claims ... 361
10.9.7 Claim Settlement Expenses ... 363
10.10 Reinsurance ... 364
10.11 Riders ... 364
10.11.1 Types of Riders ... 364
10.11.2 Reserving for Riders ... 365
10.11.3 Return of Premium Riders ... 366
Chapter 11 Credit Insurance ... 369
11.1 Description of Coverages ... 369
11.2 Overview of GAAP for Credit Insurance ... 370
11.3 Actuarial Calculations ... 370
11.3.1 Unearned Premium Reserves ... 370
11.3.2 Deferred Acquisition Costs ... 374
11.3.3 Recoverability and Loss Recognition ... 376
11.3.4 Claim Reserves and Loss Adjustment Expense Reserves ... 376
11.4 Reinsurance ... 379
Chapter 12 Group Insurance, Large Case Pension Liabilities and Related Liabilities ... 381
12.1 Group Life and Health Coverages ... 381
12.1.1 General Characteristics ... 381
12.1.2 Active Life and Unearned Premium Reserves ... 384
12.1.3 Expense Capitalization ... 384
12.1.4 Claim Reserves ... 385
12.1.5 Premium Deficiency Reserves ... 386
12.1.6 Reserve for Accrued Experience Refunds ... 388
12.1.7 Specific and Aggregate Stop-Loss Reinsurance ... 388
12.1.8 Other Considerations ... 389
12.2 Large Case Pension Liabilities and Related Liabilities ... 389
12.2.1 General Characteristics ... 389
12.2.2 GICs and Funding Agreements ... 390
12.2.3 Group Master Contract Pension Plans ... 391
12.2.4 Accounting for Liabilities ... 394
12.2.5 Deferred Acquisition Cost ... 397
12.2.6 Loss Recognition ... 400
12.2.7 Fair Value Accounting ... 400
12.2.8 Implications of *SFAS 133* ... 400
Chapter 13 Investment Accounting ... 403
13.1 Introduction ... 403
13.2 Typical Life Insurer Investments and Related Accounting Principles ... 403
13.3 Debt Securities ... 404

13.3.1 Bonds 407
13.3.2 Collateralized Mortgage Obligations 412
13.4 Preferred Stocks 418
13.5 Common Stocks 418
13.5.1 Unaffiliated Common Stock Investments 418
13.5.2 Affiliated Common Stock Investments 419
13.6 Mortgage Loans 420
13.7 Real Estate 421
13.8 Policy Loans 426
13.9 Partnerships 426
13.10 Short-Term Investments 426
13.11 Derivatives and Hedging Activities 427
13.12 Insurance Contract Analysis Under *SFAS 133* 428
13.12.1 Introduction 428
13.12.2 Guaranteed Investment Contracts 429
13.12.3 Synthetic GICs 429
13.12.4 Traditional Variable Annuity 430
13.12.5 Nontraditional Variable Annuity 432
13.12.6 Deferred Variable Annuity 432
13.12.7 Variable Annuity with Guaranteed Minimum Payments 434
13.12.8 Market Value Annuity 435
13.12.9 Equity-Indexed Life Insurance 435
13.12.10 Equity-Indexed Annuity 436
13.12.11 Foreign Currency Elements of Insurance Contracts 438
13.12.12 Modified Coinsurance and Similar Arrangements 438
Chapter 14 Shadow Adjustments *(SFAS 115)* 441
14.1 Background 441
14.2 Overview of *SFAS 115* Requirements 442
14.3 *EITF Topic D-41*, "Shadow Adjustments" 443
14.4 Shadow Calculations 448
14.5 Shadow Issues on Contracts Governed by *SFAS 97* and *SFAS 120* 451
14.5.1 Disregarding Historical Unrealized Gains and Losses 451
14.5.2 Ceilings and Floors on Amounts of Shadow DAC 452
14.6 Alternative Approach to Calculation of Shadow Amounts 452
14.7 Summary 453
Chapter 15 Accounting for Business Combinations 455
15.1 Key Decisions in *SFAS 141* and *SFAS 142* 456
15.1.1 Most Significant Decisions 456
15.1.2 Other *SFAS 141* Decisions 456
15.1.3 Other *SFAS 142* Decisions 456
15.2 Definition of a Business Combination 457
15.2.1 Definition 457
15.2.2 Determining Control 457
15.2.3 Reinsurance 458
15.3 Date of Acquisition 458
15.4 Reporting Units 459
15.4.1 Definition 459
15.4.2 Assigning Acquired Assets and Assumed Liabilities to Reporting Units 459
15.4.3 Importance of Carefully Defining Reporting Units 459
15.5 Acquisition Cost Allocation 460
15.6 Comparison of Acquisition Accounting with HGAAP 461
15.7 Policyholder Liabilities 463

15.7.1 General Approach ... 463
15.7.2 General Guidance on Reserve Methodology ... 463
15.7.3 Additional Comments on Methodology for Specific Products ... 465
15.7.3.1 Guaranteed Interest Contracts (GIC) ... 465
15.7.3.2 Certain Annuities ... 465
15.7.3.3 Single Premium Deferred Annuities (SPDA) ... 465
15.7.3.4 Universal Life ... 466
15.7.3.5 Universal Life with No Lapse Guarantees ... 466
15.7.3.6 Equity Indexed Annuities ... 466
15.7.3.7 Liabilities Required by *SOP 03-1* for MGDB, GMIB, Two-Tiered Annuities, and Sales Inducements ... 467
15.7.4 Group, Credit and Individual Health Coverage Considerations ... 468
15.7.5 Claim Reserves ... 468
15.7.6 Other Actuarial Liabilities ... 468
15.7.7 Special Issues Regarding Expense Assumptions ... 469
15.7.8 Reserve Formulas ... 469
15.8 Identifying Intangible Assets ... 469
15.8.1 Identifiable Intangible Assets ... 469
15.8.2 Examples of IIAs in Life Insurance Company Transactions ... 470
15.8.3 Negative Goodwill ... 471
15.9 Accounting for IIAs Other Than Goodwill ... 471
15.9.1 Determining the Useful Life of an Intangible Asset ... 472
15.9.2 Amortizable Intangible Assets ... 472
15.9.3 Nonamortizable Intangible Assets ... 473
15.9.4 Value of Business Acquired Asset ... 473
15.9.5 The Actuarial Appraisal Method ... 474
15.9.6 Appraisal Value Method Formulas for VOBA Determination ... 476
15.9.7 VOBA Amortization Procedure ... 477
15.9.8 Valuing IIAs Other Than VOBA ... 478
15.10 Accounting for Goodwill ... 479
15.10.1 Goodwill *SFAS 142* Requirement ... 479
15.10.2 Allocation of Goodwill ... 480
15.10.3 Reporting Unit Fair Value ... 480
15.10.4 Comparison With RU Carrying Value ... 481
15.10.5 Goodwill Impairment ... 481
15.10.6 Implementation Issues Related to Goodwill Accounting ... 482
15.10.7 Market Impact of Goodwill Accounting ... 484
15.11 Examples ... 484
15.12 Selecting Assumptions ... 487
15.13 Federal Income Tax Considerations ... 488
15.14 Post-Purchase Issues ... 488
15.15 Disclosures ... 489
Chapter 16 Non-U.S. Products ... 491
16.1 Background ... 491
16.2 Product Classification Issues ... 492
16.2.1 Flowchart ... 492
16.2.2 Applicability of *SFAS 120* for Participating Business ... 494
16.2.3 Applicability of *SFAS 60* for Participating Business ... 495
16.2.3.1 Restricted Distribution to Shareholders ... 495
16.2.3.2 Unrestricted Distribution to Shareholders ... 496
16.2.4 Products that Span Accounting Models ... 496
16.3 Impact of Tax Systems ... 497

16.4 Impact of Realized and Unrealized Investment Gains 502
16.5 Product Classification Considerations in Specific Markets 502
16.5.1 European Market in General 502
16.5.2 United Kingdom 503
16.5.2.1 Participating Business 503
16.5.2.2 Unit Linked Products 503
16.5.3 Germany 505
16.5.3.1 Life Business 505
16.5.3.2 Health Business 506
16.5.4 Switzerland 506
16.5.4.1 Participating Business 506
16.5.4.2 Group Pension Business 506
16.5.5 Italy 507
16.5.6 Asian Market in General 508
16.5.7 Japan 509
16.5.8 Korea 510
16.5.8.1 Korean Traditional Business 510
16.5.8.2 Korean Interest Sensitive Business 511
16.5.9 Singapore and Malaysia 511
16.5.10 Taiwan 512
16.5.11 China 513
16.5.12 Hong Kong 513
16.5.13 The Philippines 513
16.6 Practical Issues 514
16.7 Impact of *SOP 03-1* 516
16.7.1 Background 516
16.7.2 Definition of a Separate Account 516
16.7.3 Seed Money 517
16.7.4 Valuation of liabilities 517
16.7.4.1 Account Balance 517
16.7.4.2 Significance of Risk 518
16.7.4.3 Additional Liability for *SFAS 97*— universal life-type contracts 518
16.7.4.4 Contracts with Annuitization Benefits 519
16.7.4.5 Sales Inducements to Policyholders 520
16.7.5 Transition Rules 520
Chapter 17 Reinsurance 523
17.1 Uses of Reinsurance 523
17.2 Types of Reinsurance 524
17.2.1 Yearly Renewable Term 524
17.2.2 Coinsurance 525
17.2.3 Modified Coinsurance 525
17.2.4 Stop-Loss 526
17.2.5 Catastrophe 526
17.2.6 Assumption Reinsurance 526
17.3 Special Aspects of Reinsurance 526
17.3.1 Experience Rating 526
17.3.2 Recapture 527
17.4 GAAP Summary 527
17.5 Qualification as Reinsurance under *SFAS 113* 528
17.5.1 Short-Duration Contracts 528
17.5.2 Long-Duration Contracts 534
17.6 Accounting Requirements for Reinsurance Ceded 535

17.6.1 Short-Duration Contracts ... 535
17.6.2 Long-Duration Contracts ... 540
17.6.3 Examples ... 542
17.6.3.1 Coinsurance ... 542
17.6.3.2 Yearly Renewable Term ... 544
17.6.3.3 Modified Coinsurance ... 548
17.6.3.4 Post-Issue Reinsurance ... 551
17.6.3.5 Universal Life & Estimated Gross Profits ... 555
17.7 Accounting for Reinsurance under *SOP 03-1* ... 558
17.8 Accounting for Reinsurance under *SFAS 133* ... 562
17.8.1 *DIG B36* ... 562
17.8.2 Types of Credit Derivatives ... 563
17.8.3 Determining the Nature of an Embedded Derivative under *DIG B36* ... 564
17.8.4 Examples of Embedded Derivative Valuation ... 566
17.8.4.1 Total Return Swap with Floating Rate Leg ... 566
17.8.4.2 Total Return Swap with Fixed Rate Leg ... 569
17.8.4.3 Credit Default Swap ... 571
17.9 Accounting for Special Aspects of Reinsurance ... 573
17.9.1 Experience Rating ... 573
17.9.2 Recapture ... 574
17.10 Reinsurance Assumed ... 574
17.11 Recoverability and Loss Recognition ... 574
Chapter 18 Other Topics ... 575
18.1 Deferred Taxes ... 575
18.1.1 Differences Between Taxable Income and GAAP Income ... 575
18.1.2 *SFAS 109* ... 576
18.1.3 Glossary ... 577
18.1.4 The Asset and Liability Method ... 578
18.1.5 Temporary Differences ... 579
18.1.6 Recognition of Deferred Tax Assets and Liabilities ... 580
18.1.7 Measurement of Deferred Tax Assets and Liabilities ... 580
18.1.8 Recognition of Valuation Allowance on Deferred Tax Assets ... 581
18.1.9 *APB Opinion 23* Differences ... 582
18.1.10 Changes in Tax Laws or Rates ... 582
18.1.11 Alternative Tax Systems ... 583
18.1.12 Scheduling ... 583
18.1.13 Tax-Planning Strategies ... 583
18.1.14 Different Tax Jurisdictions ... 583
18.1.15 Purchase Business Combinations ... 584
18.1.16 Effective Date ... 584
18.1.17 Illustrative Application of *SFAS 109* ... 584
18.1.18 Summary of *SFAS 109* ... 587
18.2 Riders ... 589
18.2.1 Definition & Types ... 589
18.2.2 Classifications ... 590
18.2.3 Deferred Acquisition Costs ... 590
18.2.4 Benefit Reserves ... 590
18.2.5 Interdependency of Actuarial Assumptions ... 590
18.2.6 Loss Recognition and Recoverability ... 591
18.2.7 Reinsurance ... 591
18.3 Fair Value Reporting ... 591
18.3.1 Background ... 591

18.3.2 Fair Value and *SFAS 107* 592
18.3.3 *SFAS 133* and Fair Value 595
18.3.4 *SFAS 142* and Fair Value 597
18.4 Accounting for Demutualizations and Mutual Holding Company Formations 597
18.4.1 Background 597
18.4.2 Establishment of the Closed Block 598
18.4.3 Accounting for the Closed Block 599
18.4.4 Accounting for the Open Block 603
18.5 Surplus Notes 603
18.6 Materiality 604
18.6.1 Concept 604
18.6.2 Judgment 606
18.6.3 Quantitative Factors 606
18.6.4 Qualitative Factors 607
18.6.5 Responsibility 608
18.6.6 Professional Standards 609
Chapter 19 Financial Statement Presentations 611
19.1 Purpose 611
19.2 Company Description 611
19.3 Operating Environment 611
19.4 Product Segments 612
19.4.1 Participating Whole Life 612
19.4.2 Term Life Insurance 614
19.4.3 Universal Life 616
19.4.4 Variable Universal Life 618
19.4.5 Variable Annuity 620
19.4.6 Fixed Deferred Annuities 622
19.4.7 Equity-Indexed Annuity 624
19.4.8 Immediate Annuity 626
19.4.9 Disability Income 628
Appendix A Purchase Accounting 631
A.1 Introduction 631
A.2 Business Combination 631
A.3 The Pooling Method 632
A.4 The Purchase Method 633
A.4.1 Description of Concept 633
A.4.2 Initial PGAAP Balance Sheet 634
A.4.3 Comparison of PGAAP with HGAAP 635
A.5 Policyholder Liabilities 636
A.5.1 General Approach 636
A.5.2 Reserve Methods for *SFAS 60* and *SFAS 97* Limited-Pay 637
A.5.2.1 Historical Perspective 637
A.5.2.2 Methodology 637
A.5.3 Reserve Methods for Other *SFAS 97* Contracts 639
A.5.4 *SFAS 91* Reserve Methodology 639
A.5.5 *SFAS 120* Reserve Methodology 639
A.5.6 Other Actuarial Liabilities 640
A.5.7 Special Issues Regarding Expense Assumptions 641
A.5.8 Special Considerations for Group, Credit and Individual Health 641
A.5.9 Claim Reserves 642
A.6 The Value of Business Acquired Asset 643
A.6.1 Definition 643

A.6.2 Methods for Deriving the Initial VOBA Asset ... 644
A.6.3 VOBA Amortization Procedures ... 645
A.6.4 PGAAP Formulas ... 646
A.6.4.1 *SFAS 60* and *SFAS 97* LP ... 646
A.6.4.1.1 Definitions ... 646
A.6.4.1.2 Formulas ... 647
A.6.4.2 *SFAS 97* Universal Life-Type and Investment Contract ... 649
A.6.4.2.1 Definitions ... 649
A.6.4.2.2 Formulas ... 649
A.7 Treatment of Goodwill ... 651
A.7.1 Identification and Amortization ... 651
A.7.2 Goodwill Recoverability Issues ... 651
A.8 Tax Considerations ... 653
A.9 Post-Purchase Issues ... 653
A.10 Examples ... 654
A.10.1 *SFAS 60* ... 654
A.10.2 *SFAS 97* Limited-Pay ... 655
A.10.3 *SFAS 97* ... 656
A.10.4 Comparative Balance Sheets at the Purchase Date ... 657
A.10.4.1 Assumptions ... 659
A.10.4.2 Analysis of the Balance Sheets ... 660
A.10.5 Comparative Income Statements ... 661
A.11 Practice Variations ... 662
Appendix B Proposed Statement to Replace *SFAS 141* ... 665
B.1 Introduction ... 665
B.2 Purpose ... 665
B.3 Summary of Key Differences ... 666
Bibliography ... 669
Index ... 675

About the Authors

EDITOR

R. Thomas Herget, FSA, MAAA. Tom received a BA from the University of Illinois and is executive vice president at PolySystems in Chicago. His responsibilities include user needs identification, customer support, systems implementation, and project management involving life company financial reporting systems. Previously Tom held positions at CNA, Peat Marwick, and the Hartford. He has been a member of several AAA task forces on valuation and is a past chair and newsletter editor of the SOA's Financial Reporting Section Council. He formerly served on the SOA's Board of Governors.

AUTHORS

Frank Buck, FIA, FSA, MAAA. Frank has an MA from Queens' College in Cambridge and is currently a principal in the life actuarial practice of Deloitte, based in New York. He has recently returned from a three-year secondment to Deloitte Touche Tohmatsu in Hong Kong after leading the US Life Actuarial practice for Deloitte & Touche for a number of years. He has been the lead actuarial principal on many major life insurance clients for the firm. Frank previously worked at National Benefit Life and Coopers & Lybrand in the U.S., Manulife in Canada, and Equity & Law and Save & Prosper in the U.K. He is a past chair of the Financial Reporting Section Council of the SOA, was a member of the Life Committee of the Actuarial Standards Board and has recently been elected to the International Section Council of the SOA.

Mark J. Freedman, FSA, MAAA. Mark holds a BA in mathematics from the University of Pennsylvania. He is a consulting actuary and partner for Ernst & Young's Insurance and Actuarial Advisory Services in its Philadelphia office. His primary areas of experience are financial reporting, mergers and acquisition, and product development. Mark has been the chair of the Financial Reporting Section Council of the Society of Actuaries, the Society of Actuaries' representative on the Insurance Accounting Committee of the IAA committee on International Accounting Standards, and a member of the Life Operating Committee of the AAA Actuarial Standards Board.

Thomas R. Kochis, CPA. Tom earned a BSBA in accounting from Indiana University. He is a retired partner of KPMG LLP where he spent his entire professional career serving clients in the insurance industry. Some of these clients included Bankers Life & Casualty, CUNA Mutual, Employers Reinsurance Corporation, GenAmerica, Kemper National, the St. Paul Companies, and Unitrin. Tom has substantial experience in performance measurement at many life and casualty companies. He has also participated as a member of the resource and advisory groups to the NAIC's Codification and CMO committees.

Daniel J. Kunesh, FSA, MAAA. Dan has a BBA from the University of Wisconsin and an MSAS from Northeastern University. Dan is the Chief Actuary of China Life Insurance Company in Beijing. Previously, he was principal and consulting actuary in the Chicago office of Tillinghast–Towers Perrin, where he focused on the financial services area with an emphasis on U.S. and international GAAP accounting. Dan has previously worked at Kunesh, Montgomery & Associates, KPMG Peat Marwick LLP, the Franklin Life, and John Hancock. He has served as chair of the AAA's Committee on Life Insurance Financial Reporting. Dan is the co-author of the "Income-Based Reserves" study note, a comprehensive analysis of income-based accounting systems used for SOA Course 8.

S. Michael McLaughlin, FIA, FSA, MAAA. Mike holds a BSc in physics and mathematics from the University of the West Indies. Mike is global leader of the Actuarial and Insurance Solutions practice for Deloitte Consulting, LLP, based in Chicago. Previously he served as executive vice president & chief actuary at AXA Financial in New York. Mike has previously worked at Ernst & Young LLP, KPMG Peat Marwick LLP, Reserve Life, Lone Star Life, and British American Insurance Company. He is a prize-winning author, frequent speaker, and a member of the SOA's Board of Governors. Mike's main areas of interest are in product development, financial reporting, and company modeling.

Edward L. Robbins, FSA, MAAA. Ed holds a BS from Cornell University. He is senior actuary at Allstate Life Insurance Company. Ed was previously a principal at KPMG Peat Marwick. He has had significant experience in valuation, tax planning, and international operations. Ed has authored papers on tax, statutory, and GAAP issues. He served as vice president and member of the Board of Governors of the SOA. Ed currently serves as president-elect of the Society of Actuaries.

David Y. Rogers, FSA, MAAA. Dave holds a BS in mathematics from the University of Michigan. He leads the PricewaterhouseCoopers life actuarial practice. He has been working as an actuary in the financial reporting field for approximately 15 years, while at his current firm and at MetLife. Dave started his career as an actuary at CIGNA. He has been a member of the AAA's Committee on Life Insurance Financial Reporting and a member of the Financial Reporting Section Council. Dave is a frequent author and speaker on financial reporting matters in the life insurance industry.

Eric R. Schuering, ASA, MAAA. Eric received a BA from the University of Illinois. He focuses on life company actuarial consulting, audit support, and tax consulting for the Chicago office of PricewaterhouseCoopers, LLP. Eric has previously worked at Combined Insurance, CNA, and Metropolitan Life. He has served on the AAA's Committee on Life Insurance Financial Reporting.

Bradley M. Smith, FSA, MAAA. Brad holds a BS in actuarial science from the University of Illinois. He currently serves as chairman of Milliman Inc. and is a principal in its Dallas office. Brad practices in mergers/acquisitions, corporate restructurings, valuations, and product development. He formerly served as chief actuary at JCPenny Life. Brad has authored several papers on product profitability and pricing, has served on the SOA Board of Governors and as its director of publications.

John T. Zellner, FSA, FCA, MAAA. Jay holds a BBA from Georgia State University. He is an actuarial director in the Atlanta office of KPMG LLP and is the Southeastern and Latin American practice leader for U.S. actuarial financial consulting services. Jay has substantial experience in U.S. GAAP and financial projections including embedded value. Prior to joining KPMG in 1985, he worked for Forecast Consultants, Inc., Coopers and Lybrand, Tillinghast, and Life of Georgia. Jay has served on the AAA Committee on Life Insurance Financial Reporting.

The Project Oversight Group consisted of editor R. Thomas Herget, author S. Michael McLaughlin, and

Shirley Hwei-Chung Shao, FSA, MAAA, CEBS, CFA, ChFC, CLU. Shirley has an MS from University of Iowa and a BS from the National Cheng-Chi University. She is a vice president in the corporate actuarial area at Prudential Insurance of America and is involved with financial reporting, pricing, and asset-liability management. Shirley has been involved with various practice councils, task forces, and committees of the American Academy of Actuaries and American Council of Life Insurers. She is also a former chair of the SOA's Financial Reporting Section, has served on its Board of Governors, and has served as its vice president.

US

For
Life Insurers

GAAP

2ND EDITION

Chapter 1 GAAP Objectives and their Implications to Life Insurers

Generally Accepted Accounting Principles in the United States are the conventions, rules, and procedures that define accepted accounting practices at a particular time. These Generally Accepted Accounting Principles provide a standard by which business enterprises present and auditors opine on financial statements. Generally Accepted Accounting Principles include not only broad guidelines of general application but also detailed practices and procedures. Commonly referred to as GAAP, or U.S. GAAP, these conventions, rules, and procedures form a comprehensive basis of accounting.

1.1 Concepts

The United States has an open, free-enterprise economy. Privately-owned business enterprises conduct most of the country's productive activity. Government plays a role in monitoring and regulating, but it is private business enterprises that produce most goods and services for the benefit of other businesses or the ultimate consumer. Business enterprises require capital for their development, marketing, and productive activities. The capital is raised from financial institutions, private investors, and individual members of the public. Owners of capital will provide it for temporary or permanent use if they are satisfied that they will earn a satisfactory return in proportion to the apparent risk. Providers of capital expect to have information about the enterprise in which they are considering a loan or investment.

GAAP financial reporting is the process of providing appropriate, timely, and accurate information to providers of capital and other parties. GAAP financial reporting is not an objective in itself; it is the process, procedures, standards, numbers, and disclosures necessary to support the open, competitive, private sector of the American economy.

The primary information provided is in the form of financial statements. Financial statements provide financial information; the numbers are expressed in units of money. A single uniform currency is always used. If transactions have occurred in various foreign currencies, they must be converted to the currency of the financial statement. In the U.S., the currency is not adjusted for inflation; the effect of changing purchasing power over time is ignored. Non-monetary information must also be converted into monetary measures. Property, plant, and equipment are examples of non-monetary assets. Those assets must be converted into monetary measures, for example, depreciated value, for inclusion in financial statements.

Financial statements relate to a single enterprise. They are not used to measure the earnings or resources of a whole industry; similarly, they are not used primarily to measure the earnings or resources of small parts of an enterprise. When an enterprise comprises subsidiary companies, information on all subsidiaries combined is consolidated into a single financial statement. Separate rules apply for treating part ownership of other companies or assets. Segment reporting is the process of providing relevant information on parts of an enterprise that are relatively homogeneous within themselves yet different from other segments.

Financial statements provide summarized information about the enterprise, its resources (assets), claims against those resources (liabilities), and the transactions that influence those assets and liabilities. The information provided is not intended primarily as a determinant of the value of the enterprise, although it may be very useful in that regard. For publicly-owned companies, the value of the enterprise is determined by the operation of equity markets. Rather, the primary focus of U.S. GAAP financial statements is earnings and its components. Of course, earnings and the change in net assets of the enterprise are inextricably linked, as discussed further in Section 1.5.1.

The transactions reported in the financial statements are generally those that have already taken place. Future transactions are uncertain, even those transactions that company management intends to complete. In the case of life insurance, reported transactions include receipt of premiums and payment of expenses and claims. Claims that are likely to be incurred in the future are recognized and measured using actuarial methods.

Transactions are measured over a clearly defined period, typically quarterly or annually. This permits the performance of the enterprise and its management to be measured over a discrete period. More and more users are interested in performance over relatively shorter rather than longer periods. This is true despite the long-term nature of some contracts, particularly life and health insurance policies. Accurate determination or estimation of the financial effect in the current quarter of an insurance contract that may require 40 or 50 years for completion is an enduring challenge of financial reporting.

The receipt or disbursement of cash is only one element of a financial statement. Cash amounts may not accurately measure the value of a transaction. For example, a cash premium payment may be intended to provide for many years' worth of insurance. Inclusion of the entire cash amount without adjustment would overstate the importance of the payment in the current accounting period. Accrual accounting that refers to the process of making adjustments in financial statements to allocate revenue and expenses more appropriately to the measurement period. Reserves on life, health, and annuity contracts are non-cash transactions that are a special type of accrual adjustment. Other examples are deferred acquisition costs, the due premium asset, and the advance premium liability.

The profile of information to be provided in the financial statements is determined in accordance with U.S. GAAP. A body of literature created and maintained by rule-making authorities establishes the quantitative and qualitative information to be provided. Uniform standards are necessary because the users of the financial statements may have little or no ability to influence the company and its management to provide specific information. The users of the information may not even be known in advance. Conversely, standards benefit the company's management and directors because they need not respond to numerous individual requests for information that may be either expensive to provide or unavailable.

Financial statement information is intended to be relevant and reliable. *Statement of Financial Accounting Concepts No. 1*, "Objectives of Financial Reporting by Business Enterprises," states that the information should be useful to

> ... present and potential investors and creditors and other users in making rational investment, credit, and similar decisions. The information should be comprehensible to those who have a reasonable understanding of business and economic activities and are willing to study the information with reasonable diligence. (Paragraph 34)

The information is also intended to serve a broad range of purposes. Such financial reporting is called general purpose. There may be narrower purposes for which supplementary information beyond the standardized financial statements is needed. Examples of specialized purposes that U.S. GAAP financial statements are not intended to serve are statutory filings and determination of current federal income tax liability.

The information is intended to be consistent and comparable to that provided in prior periods and by other enterprises in similar situations. Measurement of performance over a period would be meaningless if the accounting principles changed during that time. Normally consistent accounting principles are used from period to period, and any appropriate changes are adequately described in notes to the financial statements, such that any lack of comparability can be understood. If a material error is discovered, it should be corrected in the current reporting period, and prior-period financial statements should be restated to maintain comparability.

Financial reporting includes not only financial statements but also other communications by the company, including conference calls with analysts, responses to queries from rule-makers, supplementary information provided to investors, and even press releases. Nevertheless, financial statements are the primary source of information about the enterprise broadly available to users.

Users of financial statements include providers of capital, whether in the form of equity or debt. Thus, users are financial institutions, investment banks, private lenders, commercial banks, individual investors, and brokers and dealers in financial instruments issued by the enterprise. Expert advisors to users of financial statements (for example, attorneys, actuaries, and accountants) are themselves users. Users can include any party with an interest in any of the assets or liabilities of the company, such as policyholders, or anyone who is party to any of the company's transactions. Users also can include the almost unlimited population of potential future investors, creditors, or parties to transactions with the company.

In their role of reviewing financial statements and other information, independent auditors are users. They are acting on behalf of other users to improve the quality and reliability of information provided. Other users, such as stock analysts and rating agencies, are similarly acting not only on their own account but also on behalf of other users.

The completion of the financial reporting process is the responsibility of company management. Company management can of course use the prepared financial statements or components of it for internal communication purposes. Company management, as well as its board of directors, is a special user because it presumably knows even more about the operations of the enterprise, its resources, claims, and transactions than can be summarized in the financial reporting process. In fact, management has the duty to provide narrative and tabular explanations of transactions or other matters that have an influence on the company that may not otherwise be evident through numerical information.

Potential capital providers make their own decisions on whether or not to provide capital based on many factors or sources of information. Available financial statements provide a primary source of information. However, the financial statements provide no guarantees for future outcomes or successful investment results.

The user needs to exercise appropriate diligence in interpreting the financial statements. Further, the user must decide whether past experience as reported in the financial statements is a reliable guide to future expectations.

The rule-making authorities are also important users of financial statements. They act to monitor and enforce compliance with applicable standards on behalf of providers of capital. For GAAP the accounting rule-makers are the Securities and Exchange Commission (SEC), the Financial Accounting Standards Board (FASB), and the American Institute of Certified Public Accountants (AICPA). The SEC is the ultimate regulator of public companies and has the ability to de-list a company's stock or halt its trading. The SEC issues pronouncements in various forms, including manuals, staff bulletins, and enforcement releases. The FASB issues standards, statements of concept, discussion papers, proceedings of the Emerging Issues Task Force (EITF), FASB staff positions (FSPs), and implementation guides, each with differing levels of authority. Through its committees, the AICPA issues professional standards, audit and accounting guides, bulletins and interpretations in various forms, and statements of position. The rule-making bodies are described in more detail in Chapter 2.

The FASB has issued a series of concept statements. These Statements of Financial Accounting Concepts (SFACs) are intended to articulate the basis on which financial accounting and reporting standards are to be based. The concepts themselves do not define GAAP but rather help to define its objectives. *SFAC No. 1*, "Objectives of Financial Reporting by Business Enterprises," states:

> ... The role of financial reporting in the economy is to provide information that is useful in making business and economic decisions, not to determine what those decisions should be. (Paragraph 33)

Other relevant concept statements include the following:

- *SFAC No. 2*, "Qualitative Characteristics of Accounting Information"
- *SFAC No. 5*, "Recognition and Measurement in Financial Statements of Business Enterprises"
- *SFAC No. 6*, "Elements of Financial Statements," which superseded *SFAC No. 3* and parts of *SFAC No. 2*
- *SFAC No. 7*, "Using Cash Flow Information and Present Values in Accounting Measurements."

Additional information on accounting concepts emerges frequently. The practitioner must continuously keep abreast of evolving requirements.

1.2 Desirable Accounting Information

Given that financial reporting is costly, why should it be performed? To say that it is required begs the question, why is it required? Financial reporting is required because it has value to the user's decision-making process and its value is greater than its cost. What are the factors that make financial statements useful enough to a broad array of users to justify its cost? Financial statements must provide information that is relevant and reliable.

1.2.1 Relevant Accounting Information

Relevant information must be timely. It must be an appropriate measure of the resource, claim, or effect of the transaction. Information that is otherwise perfectly accurate but is provided too late for a decision is not timely and is less valuable. Often, a trade-off between timeliness and accuracy or relevance and reliability exists.

To be relevant, the information must be consistent and comparable with other information. Consistent information is based on similar or identical measures to those used in prior periods. Comparable means equivalent to measures used in other enterprises. In making a decision about providing capital to one or other of several similar enterprises, the user may make an incorrect decision if the various enterprises do not provide comparable information. Comparability also implies that accounting information should be determined in a manner that is independent of the enterprise. For example, if a certain type of deposit contract is offered by both banks and insurance companies, but is reported according to different rules in the two enterprises, a user may be unable to make a correct decision. Similar economic results in the bank and the insurance company may be reported differently; conversely, different economic results may be reported similarly. For this reason, GAAP rule makers attempt, insofar as possible, to prescribe accounting rules without regard to the form of organization of the reporting entity. Of course, certain contracts or transactions, for example, insurance policies, are subject to industry-specific rules.

Information is relevant if it provides an appropriate level of detail. Relevant information should contain adequate detail to have value to an informed user, but not so much detail that it becomes confusing or difficult to use.

1.2.2 Reliable Accounting Information

Reliable information meets an objective standard of accuracy, which includes verifiability. Although perfect exactness cannot be achieved, the accuracy must be such that incorrect decisions would not result from using the information provided. The information must be materially accurate.

Reliability also implies that the information provided is free of bias. In other words, assets should be neither overstated nor understated relative to their true value. If presented with biased information, the user of the financial statement may be led to an incorrect decision about providing capital or entering into a transaction with the company. Similarly, liabilities should be neither overstated nor understated. In the case of life insurance reserves, conservatism is appropriate for certain lines of business. However, contingency reserves (provisions for unlikely or undefined purposes) do not meet the definition of a liability in GAAP financial reporting.

1.3 Financial Statements

1.3.1 Basic Elements

A financial statement comprises numbers and descriptions relating to the assets, liabilities, and transactions that result in changes to the assets and liabilities. These elements of the financial statement are defined in *SFAC No. 6*:

> Assets are probable future economic benefits obtained or controlled by a particular entity as a result of past transactions or events. (Paragraph 25)

If the probable future economic benefits decrease over time, provisions for losses may be necessary. In an extreme situation, the asset may no longer be recognized. Costs of maintaining or liquidating the asset are generally not recognized in financial statements until they are incurred.

Assets can be classified as tangible or intangible. Tangible assets include property, equipment, and financial instruments. Intangible assets include franchises, patents, goodwill, and deferred acquisition costs. *SFAC 6* states:

> Liabilities are probable future sacrifices of economic benefits arising from present obligations of a particular entity to transfer assets or provide services to other entities in the future as a result of past transactions or events. (Paragraph 35)

In contrast with comprehensive bases of accounting used in certain other countries, the definition of liabilities does not include deferred gains, allocations of equity, or general contingency reserves. Deferral of realized capital gains or losses is explicitly prohibited in *Statement of Financial Accounting Standards No. 97*, "Accounting and Reporting by Insurance Enterprises for Certain Long-Duration Contracts and for Realized Gains and Losses from the Sale of Investments:"

> Realized gains and losses shall not be deferred, either directly or indirectly. (Paragraph 28)

Statement of Financial Accounting Standards No. 5, "Accounting for Contingencies," provides more specific guidance on establishing liabilities for contingent events:

> An estimated loss from a loss contingency ... shall be accrued by a charge to income if both of the following conditions are met:
>
> a. Information available prior to issuance of the financial statements indicates that it is probable that an asset had been impaired or a liability had been incurred at the date of the financial statements. It is implicit in this condition that it must be probable that one or more future events will occur confirming the fact of the loss.
>
> b. The amount of loss can be reasonably estimated. (Paragraph 8)

In other words, a contingent liability must be probable and reasonably estimable. *SFAC No. 6* states:

> Equity or net assets is the residual interest in the assets of an entity that remains after deducting its liabilities. (Paragraph 49)

The equity is the ownership interest. It includes capital provided by the owners and accumulated earnings over time to the extent the company has retained them. Equity increases each year due to gains from operations and perhaps contributions from owners. Equity decreases if losses occur or dividends are paid out to owners. *SFAC No. 6* states:

> Comprehensive income is the change in equity of a business enterprise during a period from transactions and other events and circumstances from nonowner sources. It includes all changes in equity during a period except those resulting from investments by owners and distributions to owners. (Paragraph 70)
>
> Revenues are inflows or other enhancements of assets of an entity or settlements of its liabilities (or a combination of both) from delivering or producing goods, rendering services, or other activities that constitute the entity's ongoing major or central operations. (Paragraph 78)
>
> Expenses are outflows or other using up of assets or incurrences of liabilities (or a combination of both) from delivering or producing goods, rendering services, or carrying out other activities that constitute the entity's ongoing major or central operations. (Paragraph 80)

As discussed in more detail later, if an outflow or cost has future utility it would be recognized as an asset instead of an expense.

Gains and losses are defined as follows:

> Gains are increases in equity (net assets) from peripheral or incidental transactions of an entity and from all other transactions and other events and circumstances affecting the entity except those that result from revenues or investments by owners. Losses are decreases in equity (net assets) from peripheral or incidental transactions of an entity and from all other transactions and other events and circumstances affecting the entity except those that result from expenses or distributions to owners. (Paragraphs 82 and 83)

A complete financial statement includes assets and liabilities at the beginning and end of the period, earnings and comprehensive income for the period, and cash flows including capital transfers to or from owners during the period. Assets, liabilities, and equity are measured at a point in time. Earnings, comprehensive income, and capital transfers are measured over the period covered by the financial statements. A complete financial statement also includes descriptive comments, footnotes, and disclosures on important items.

The actuarial profession and the insurance industry routinely use the terms *reserve* and *surplus*. Generally Accepted Accounting Principles proscribes the use of the term *reserve* to describe a liability or deduction from an asset. While the actuary has been and will be schooled in the determination of *reserves*, that term does not appear in public documents. Further, the use of the word *surplus* to describe owners' equity has been discouraged and does not appear in FASB pronouncements except when referring to the legal notion of *policyholders' surplus*. Throughout this text, however, the terms *reserve* and *surplus* are used in the traditional actuarial sense.

1.3.2 Comprehensive Income

Earnings can be measured in different layers. For example, revenues less cost of goods sold is gross profit, an important measure of performance in some industries. Gross profit reduced by operating expenses is pre-tax net income. Pre tax net income less federal income tax is net income, which is the key GAAP measure of earnings. Net income includes realized capital gains and losses net of tax. Net income may reflect certain extraordinary items such as correction of a prior period error. Table 1-1 summarizes the key components of the income statement (this table is for illustrative purposes and is not intended to be complete).

Table 1-1
Components of the Income Statement

Revenues
Premiums
Policyholder charges
Investment income
Realized capital gains and losses
Expenses
Death claims
Surrenders and policyholder dividends
Expenses
Commissions
Change in reserves
Net income before tax
Federal income tax
Net income after tax
Extraordinary items
Net income after extraordinary items

Some companies prefer to use operating income for internal performance measurement purposes. Operating income is typically defined as net income after tax excluding realized capital gains and losses.

Net income of course is only part of the change in equity. In addition to net income, certain adjustments affect equity directly. These are items of other comprehensive income. Comprehensive income is defined by *SFAC No. 6*, paragraph 70 (see above). *SFAS 130*, "Reporting Comprehensive Income," elaborates:

> Comprehensive income ... describe(s) the total of all components of comprehensive income, including net income. ... The term other comprehensive income ... refer(s) to revenues, expenses, gains, and losses that under generally accepted accounting principles are included in comprehensive income but excluded from net income. (Paragraph 10)

Thus, comprehensive income represents all changes in equity other than owner-related transactions. Comprehensive income is then subdivided into net income and other comprehensive income (OCI). OCI includes the effects, under *Statement of Financial Accounting Standards No. 115*, "Accounting for Certain Investments in Debt and Equity Securities," of unrealized gains and losses. These items change equity without affecting net income. Table 1-2 summarizes changes in equity.

Table 1-2
Changes in Equity

Changes in Equity
Beginning of year equity
Comprehensive Income
Net income
Continuing operations
Discontinued operations
Extraordinary items
Other comprehensive income
Net unrealized capital gains and losses
Foreign currency translation
Pension liability adjustments
Owner transactions
Capital contributions
Shareholder dividends
End-of-year equity

The total change in equity comprises capital transfers and comprehensive income. Comprehensive income comprises net income and other comprehensive income. Comprehensive income is a more important measure to some users than net income.

Comprehensive income may be presented in financial statements in different ways, as a line below net income, in a comprehensive income statement, or as part of the summary of changes in equity.

1.4 Recognition and Measurement of Financial Statement Elements

The need for standardized and accurate measures implies the need for appropriate rules to recognize and measure financial statement elements.

Recognition means including an item in the financial statements in its appropriate treatment as an asset, liability, revenue, or expense. An outlay of cash can be either a cost that should be recognized as an expense, a dividend, a reduction in liabilities, or an investment that should be treated as an asset, depending on the facts and circumstances. A uniform set of criteria is applied to make the determination of whether and how such an item should be included in the financial statements.

An item needs to meet certain criteria to be recognized. In accordance with *SFAC No. 5*, the criteria are (i) definition, (ii) measurability, (iii) relevance, and (iv) reliability. An item needs to meet the definition of one of the financial statement elements (either an asset, liability, revenue, or expense) as outlined above. An item must be measurable in terms of a relevant attribute that is quantifiable with sufficient reliability. Relevance, as discussed above, means that information about the item is consistent, comparable, and meaningful in decisions to the informed user. Reliability, as discussed above, means that the information is accurate, verifiable and free of bias.

Recognition is a "yes or no" question. Either an item should be recognized or it should not. The answer is usually clear. For example, in other countries hidden reserves are used in financial statements to defer profits. The hidden reserve gives company management the ability to cushion losses in a bad year by reducing the hidden reserves. In U.S. GAAP such reserves are viewed as inappropriate because they are not liabilities and would distort earnings in a given accounting period. In any event, in most instances the criteria for recognition are easily applied.

Once a financial statement element is recognized, its attribute must be identified and that attribute must be measured. An attribute could be historical cost, market value, or present value of future cash flows. The appropriate attribute is determined by established GAAP guidance based on its presumed relevance to users.

The attribute is measured in monetary units (dollars or sometimes thousands of dollars) unadjusted for inflation. The nominal value of a dollar is not adjusted for its higher or lower purchasing power at a time other than the date of the financial statements. Foreign currencies are generally converted into U.S. dollars for assets and liabilities at the date of the balance sheet and for revenues and expenses at the time of the transaction.

The method of measuring the attribute depends on the circumstances. Historical cost is easy to determine based on the company's records. Historical cost may need to be adjusted for depreciation (for example, a computer system) or other amortization in value. Market value is obtained by reference to active, robust secondary markets (for example, the bid price for common stocks traded on a U.S. stock exchange). Market value is sometimes estimated by expert appraisal (for example, real estate values). Present values are estimated by using discounted cash flow methods. The inherent subjectivity in present value methods makes them the least preferred measurement method. However, for certain items, such as life insurance reserves, there may be no alternative to using present value methods.

1.5 Emergence of Earnings for Life Insurers

Any private business needs to keep track of its assets, liabilities, and transactions. Its resources are inherently limited. It needs to measure how much its net assets grow over time and the effects of certain kinds of transactions relative to others. The need for cash reckoning is obvious. Based on the criteria for financial reporting, it becomes equally clear that accrual accounting is necessary because not all transactions are completed as of the end of any single accounting period. Accrual adjustments correct for the fact that cash alone is not the appropriate measure for incomplete or long-term transactions. Each accrual adjustment is intended to measure an attribute of a liability, asset, revenue, or expense more appropriately than cash accounting alone.

The accounting rule-makers have attempted to prescribe methods that cause profits to emerge in proportion to the degree of completeness of the earnings process under the contract or in proportion to services rendered. Profits for insurers are recognized only as they are earned through the operation of the appropriate reserve accrual mechanism.

For insurers, accrual adjustments such as benefit reserves can be categorized as relating to past events or future events. Past events include premium receipts and incurral of claims and expenses. Future events include payment of benefits on claims not yet incurred or amounts payable but not yet due.

Accrual adjustments relating to past events include liabilities for advance or unearned premiums, unpaid claim liabilities, account deposits, accrued but unpaid policy dividends, and dividends on deposit. Premium-related liabilities arise because a portion of the cash premium may be attributable to future periods. The unpaid claim liability provides only for benefits already accrued but not yet settled, as distinct from benefits that may or will accrue in the future. Accrual adjustments may include certain assets, such as due premiums or equity in a portion of the unearned premium liability. Deferred policy acquisition costs are often a major adjustment item influencing the emergence of earnings.

Premium-related adjustments are intended to ensure that only premiums earned in the accounting period are treated as revenue. Thus, a liability is held in the amount of premiums attributable to a future period. The income statement reflects two elements: (i) cash received or returned and (ii) the change in related assets and liabilities. A premium that is due but not paid is held as an asset (an account receivable) as long as it appears that collection of the premium is likely.

The following example will illustrate this concept using dual entry accounting. The dual entry system was created on the concept that every transaction has a dual impact on an organization's financial position, operating results or both. The collection of a premium would increase the insurer's cash (financial position) and premium income (operating results).

The dual entry system provides each account with two sides. The terms *debit* and *credit* are used to refer to the two sides of an account; one side records the increases while the other side records the decreases. Increases in assets are recorded on the debit side of the account while decreases in assets are recorded on the right side. The opposite is true of liability and equity accounts. Increases in liability and equity accounts are recorded on the credit side and decreases are recorded on the debit side.

Consider two traditional life insurance policies, each with annual premiums of $100 due on October 1. As of December 31 one policy has paid its premium, but the other has not. The insurer shows cash received of $100. However, its income statement reflects revenue of $50, determined as follows:

Transaction	*Debit*	*Credit*	*Destination*
First policy:			
DR (debit) Cash received	100		Increase in cash assets
CR (credit) Premium income		100	Revenue account
DR Premium income	75		Increase in the UPR
CR Unearned premium reserve		75	Liability for portion attributable to next year
Second policy:			
DR Due premiums	100		Accounts receivable
CR Premium income		100	Takes the due premium into revenue
DR Premium income	75		Increase in the UPR
CR Unearned premium reserve		75	Liability for portion attributable to next year

For each of these policies, the premium income account will show $25 of earnings. This is true of the second policy despite the fact that no cash has yet been received. For each of these policies, a benefit reserve would be held (if appropriate for the type of policy) and the policies would both be considered *inforce*. For simplicity, no entries have been shown for benefit reserves or equity in the unearned premium.

The major accrual adjustment for most life insurers is the liability for future contractual benefits. This is the policy reserve, or benefit reserve. Benefit reserves provide for future claims not yet incurred. If a level gross premium is used to fund an increasingly costly benefit, the benefit reserve grows from the excess of the net benefit premiums over current incurred claims. After several years, the benefit reserve may reach a high level, even a multiple of the annual premium. The rate and pattern at which this reserve grows influences the pattern of profit emergence over time. Rules for establishing the benefit reserve have a major influence on the timing of profit emergence from life insurance policies and annuity contracts.

As life insurance products have evolved over the years, new accounting rules and clarification of existing rules have become necessary. For example, universal life insurance policies were introduced in the early 1980s. Existing accounting rules and actuarial models for traditional life insurance, specifically *Statement of Financial Accounting Standards No. 60*, "Accounting and Reporting by Insurance Enterprises," did not deal with these policies very well. Different methods and approaches were used for several years until authoritative guidance emerged. With *Statement of Financial Accounting Standards No. 97*, "Accounting and Reporting by Insurance Enterprises for Certain Long-Duration Contracts and for Realized Gains and Losses from the Sale of Investments," new benefit reserves were defined as the funds held by the company on behalf of the policyholder.

For universal life, deferred annuities and other non-traditional policies, premiums are not recognized as revenue. The income statement shows no unearned or due premiums, nor change in benefit reserves. Instead premiums are regarded as deposits and are directly credited to the appropriate balance sheet liability account representing funds held on behalf of the policyholder. Revenue on such policies comprises investment income, fees, and charges. The prescribed accounting principles for such policies cause profits to emerge in proportion to revenue as so defined. Other changes introduced by *SFAS 97* are discussed in more detail in later chapters.

Authoritative literature for GAAP for insurers has continued to evolve along product-specific lines. Traditional participating life insurance is governed mainly by *Statement of Financial Accounting Standards No. 120*, "Accounting and Reporting by Mutual Life Insurance Enterprises and by Insurance Enterprises for Certain Long-Duration Participating Contracts." Some investment-type annuity contracts are governed by *Statement of Financial Accounting Standards No. 91*, "Accounting for Nonrefundable Fees and Costs Associated with Originating or Acquiring Loans and Initial Direct Costs of Leases." Non-traditional policies are also affected by the new AICPA *Statement of Position (SOP) 03-1*, "Accounting and Reporting by Insurance Enterprises for Certain Nontraditional Long-Duration Contracts and for Separate Accounts."

It has not always been easy to agree on the appropriate attribute for measuring services being rendered in insurance policies. Is it insurance protection? Forced saving? Investment of assets? Tax deferral? Record keeping? Or some combination of these? The answers have varied. For traditional life and health insurance, the answer has been a combination of services best measured by the gross premium. For limited-payment life insurance, the answer has been not in proportion to premiums (which end at some point prior to expiry of the insurance coverage) but in relation to the insurance coverage provided. For universal life policies and deferred annuity contracts, the answer has been in proportion to gross profits (the excess of investment income and charges assessed for mortality and expenses over the cost of crediting interest, and paying claims and expenses). For participating policies issued in mutual companies, the answer has been in proportion to estimated gross margins relative to guaranteed reserve assumptions. For investment-type contracts, profits are allowed to emerge as a constant investment spread relative to the liability. The accounting pronouncements associated with each type of product are identified in Chapter 2.

Non-level expenses would have a large impact on emergence of earnings if no accrual adjustments were made. The best example is that certain costs incurred by the life insurer in issuing new policies have future value, namely, acquiring a stream of future profits. Such costs are not treated as a current expense; instead, they are recognized as an asset. This is the deferred policy acquisition cost asset. To the extent that $100 of cost (for example, commissions paid to the selling agent) is incurred, all or part has future value. This value is recognized as the deferred acquisition cost (DAC) asset. The DAC asset amortizes over time with a pattern of amortization that is proportional to revenues. DAC amortization for the accounting period is recognized as an expense in the income statement.

In this manner non-level benefits and acquisition costs are spread over many years in proportion to services. In the parlance of accounting concept statements, the attributes of the DAC and the benefit reserve are their future value or utility. Their future value or utility is the net present value of future expenses and benefits, respectively.

1.5.1 Financial Statement Relationships

The interrelationship of the income statement and balance sheet is described below. The first equation is a representation of the balance sheet in algebraic terms:

$$A = L + S,$$

where

A = assets
L = liabilities
S = surplus and capital, also referred to as owners' equity or net assets.

Surplus comprises retained earnings from prior years and net income from the current year. Capital comprises paid-in equity. Under GAAP debt and mezzanine instruments (a hybrid of debt and equity) are considered liabilities.

This second simple equation is a representation of the income statement:

$$NI = R - B - E - T$$

$$S_t = S_{t-1} + NI,$$

where

P = premiums
I = investment income
R = revenues, comprising premiums and investment income; $R = P + I$
B = benefits paid or payable under insurance policies and annuity contracts
E = expenses
T = taxes
NI = net income

Although simplistic, the equations show the change in equity due to net income in the absence of other capital transactions. Here, net income adds to the prior year capital and surplus.

Expressed another way, net income is the change in net assets. This is the relationship between the income statement and the balance sheet.

To influence the reporting of profits from the insurance policy in net income, the benefits paid are adjusted for benefits to be accrued in the future by passing the increase in reserves through the income statement. In the simple traditional policy example following, if premiums are $100 and the benefit reserves increase from $35 to $95, the profit to be reported is not $100 but only $40. The increase in the benefit reserves is recorded as follows:

Transaction	*Debit*	*Credit*	*Destination*
DR Reserve Increase	60		This shows $60 of policy benefit accrual adjustment
CR Reserves		60	This entry adds to the reserve liability account

Both the algebraic and the accounting presentation illustrate the same point. Profits, or net income reported, are reduced in the accounting period to the extent that the provision for benefit reserves has to be increased. The pattern of increasing or decreasing benefit reserves has an influence on net income. The choices of formulas, methods, and assumptions for determining benefit reserves influence reserve patterns and hence affect the timing of profit emergence.

1.5.2 Fluctuations in Earnings

Historically, GAAP financial reporting achieved a matching of revenues and expenses. However, GAAP accounting concepts are not necessarily intended to produce "smooth" earnings. GAAP earnings may be volatile, depending on the effect in the current accounting period of various transactions or external events. For example, a large transaction could have a very favorable or unfavorable impact in a particular year. GAAP accounting rules typically do not call for smoothing of such transactions. In fact, contingency reserves are expressly prohibited by *SFAS 5*, "Accounting for Contingencies":

> Some enterprises have in the past accrued so-called "reserves for general contingencies." General or unspecified business risks do not meet the conditions for accrual in paragraph 8, and no accrual for loss shall be made. (Paragraph 14)

Instead, predictable or estimable non-level costs or benefits are deferred and amortized into income in proportion to the appropriately defined revenues (premiums or gross profits, depending on the type of contract). Costs that are not deferrable acquisition costs (as described in Chapter 3) have an immediate impact on profits in the year in which they are incurred. Similarly, unusually high or low claim payments can have an impact on profits in the year in which they are incurred. Certain products experience fluctuations in profits arising from movement in interest rates or the equity markets.

1.6 Measurement Methods, Estimates, and Materiality

The information provided by financial reporting for life insurers often results from approximate, rather than exact, measures. The measures commonly involve numerous estimates, classifications, summaries, judgments, and allocations.

Benefit reserves and the deferred acquisition cost (DAC) asset represent future costs or benefits to be realized over time. Present values or other actuarial methods are needed to determine these items. Actuaries are familiar with the methods used to estimate future claims and expenses over a projection period of many years or decades. For each type of claim, past experience, pricing, or standard tables may be used. Assumptions are used for mortality, morbidity, persistency, interest rates, maintenance expenses, and other assumptions. The benefit reserve can be expressed either as the accumulation of past net premiums in excess of benefits incurred or as the present value of future benefits in excess of future net premiums. The derivation of these formulas follows standard actuarial conventions. Detail is provided in later chapters of this book. DAC is also estimated by using present value concepts but can be calculated using a variety of different mechanical approaches (worksheets, DAC factors, and other methods).

Since future events (such as death claims or expenses) are inherently unknowable, estimates of the value of such events using present value methods are appropriate. The alternative of waiting until insurance cash flows have emerged and measurable with certainty is impractical because the information so obtained would not be timely and hence not relevant.

This is a key trade-off in financial reporting. It is better to have approximately correct information on a timely basis than more accurate (even perfectly accurate) information too late to be valuable. Hence the use of estimates is common, appropriate, and inherent in financial statement presentations.

Given that estimates are used and given that any estimate is almost certain to be inaccurate if the attribute is subsequently exactly measured, the question arises, what is the appropriate level of precision in an estimate? The precision level is appropriate if the external users of the financial statement are able to make informed decisions about the allocation of capital to the enterprise. A minor inaccuracy discovered after the fact probably would have had no impact on a capital allocation decision. On the other hand, a major inaccuracy discovered after the fact could mean that a user of the financial statements would not have allocated capital or would have attempted to withdraw it. Estimates made for financial statements being prepared for subsidiaries or segment reporting may require greater precision. A tolerable error in consolidated financial statements may cause appreciable distortion in the smaller entity's financial statement information. The appropriate precision in making an estimate should be determined with its potential uses in mind. Greater precision may be necessary for other uses of the financial statement, such as internal use by company staff of line of business results.

Imprecision in estimation is tolerable within limits of materiality. Usually such imprecision need not be corrected after the fact. Instead, revised estimates are reported in subsequent accounting periods. Material mistakes or errors in applying accounting methodology are treated differently. Material mistakes and errors need to be corrected and normally would require restatement of previously issued financial statements, including disclosure of the corrections made.

One specific type of estimate sometimes made is the decision to ignore the impact of a certain transaction or financial statement element. The transaction or element in question may be small in size or uncertain as to occurrence. The decision on when this is permissible again should be based on the potential impact on the user of the financial statement. An impact that is so small as to have no influence on the decision is said to be immaterial. Immaterial items or immaterial inaccuracies in estimates are ignored on the basis that the cost of measurement, whether the expense or the delay involved, would reduce the relevance of the financial statements to a greater extent than the inaccuracy itself. The concept of immateriality is judgmental, and the accounting literature does not define ranges or tolerances explicitly. The company, together with its auditors, reaches its best judgment as to the immateriality of many financial statement elements. If the financial statements are to be regarded as a true and fair representation of the facts, then in the aggregate all items that were ignored plus the aggregated inaccuracies in all estimates must have no impact on the decisions of users of the financial statements. The concept and application of materiality is discussed in further detail in Chapter 18.

1.7 Disclosures

Financial statement elements that fail to satisfy the test for recognition may nonetheless be important. For example, a company may have an uncertain potential liability or a certain liability that cannot be quantified. The liability would not be recognized in the financial statement numbers. However, given its importance, its existence should be disclosed in narrative form. The footnotes and disclosures in financial statements are a part of the financial reporting process and have an impact on the decisions that may be made by users.

Another important disclosure is that required by *SEC Regulation S-K* regarding market risk disclosure. The financial statements represent a point estimate (for example, the best estimate of premiums due or unpaid claim liability). However, future events may influence these estimates. For example, equity markets and interest rates may change rapidly. The relevance of the point estimate numbers could dwindle rapidly if there were no acknowledgment or explanation of the impact of these changes. Specifically, the SEC requires quantitative and qualitative information on the impact of market risk on the financial statements. Quantitative disclosure can include one of three alternatives:

(i) Tabular presentation of information related to market risk sensitive instruments

(ii) Sensitivity analysis showing potential loss in future earnings resulting from selected hypothetical scenarios

(iii) Value at risk disclosures showing potential loss in future earnings resulting from changes in interest rates, currency exchange rates, and other relevant rates.

Qualitative information about market risk should include a list of the exposures, how they have changed, and how they are managed.

Other important disclosures include changes in accounting principles and disclosure of subsequent events. Accounting Principles Board *Opinion No. 20* addresses the reporting of changes in accounting principles and estimates. With rare exceptions, an accounting change is not reported by restating previously-issued financial statements. Instead, such changes are reflected in the current year's financial statements and disclosed. The Accounting Principles Board was a rule-making body predecessor to the FASB.

Statements on Auditing Standards 1, "Subsequent Events," provides guidance on reporting of significant events that occurred after the end of the reporting period but prior to the release of the audited financial statements. This deals with not only new events, but with new evidence on existing situations.

Footnotes of life insurers in GAAP financial statements also may include the following:

(i) Description of the company and its products
(ii) Summary of significant accounting policies
(iii) Details of invested assets
(iv) Details on other items such as leases, receivables and unpaid claim liabilities

(v) Sale or purchase transactions during the year
(vi) Reinsurance, stockholder dividends, stock repurchases, or other capital transactions
(vii) Changes to employee benefit plans
(viii) Reconciliation to statutory financial data

As mentioned above, these disclosures are part of the financial statements and are subject to similar standards of accuracy and verifiability as the numerical results.

The descriptions included in this chapter are not intended to replace authoritative literature. The actuary or accountant involved in preparing GAAP financial statements needs to remain aware of the constantly changing requirements for accounting and auditing GAAP financial statements prepared for life insurers.

1.8 Mutual Life Insurers

Prior to 1995, mutual and fraternal life insurers in the U.S. often did not prepare financial statements in accordance with GAAP. FASB *Interpretation 40* (released in 1995) made it clear that mutual and fraternal insurers had to comply with all applicable provisions of GAAP, except where explicitly exempted, in order to have their financial statements characterized as being in accordance with GAAP. *SFAS 120* eliminated certain exemptions that previously existed, for example, in *SFAS 60*. Since 1996, most mutual and fraternal insurers have prepared financial statements in accordance with GAAP. All life insurers of course must comply with statutory reporting requirements as well.

A few unique issues apply. Because there are no owners, there are no shareholder dividends or equity infusions into a mutual company. The change in equity from one year to the next does not involve owner transactions, despite the fact that policyholders can be regarded as owners of the entity. The policyholders are users of the GAAP financial statements, although in a few jurisdictions the company is required to provide statutory information to policyholders.

A hybrid form of organization, the mutual holding company, combines characteristics of both mutuals and stock companies. The parent company is mutual and is owned by its members, who are the policyholders of the insurance company. The mutual holding company owns, usually through an intermediate holding company, all or a majority of the equity of the stock life insurance company subsidiary. Consolidated GAAP financial statements for mutual holding companies sometimes include owner transactions, for example stockholder dividends from the subsidiary stock company to the mutual holding company.

Chapter 2 Authorities

2.1 Historical Perspective: Regulatory Focus and the Needs of Investors

Although the business of insurance in the United States began more than two centuries ago, the most significant advancements in the evolution of generally accepted accounting principles (GAAP) for insurance entities occurred in the early 1970s.

Prior to that time, financial reporting practices were driven primarily by the requirements of the regulatory bodies that governed the insurance companies. These practices came to be known as statutory accounting practices and are still known that way today. The evolution of statutory accounting practices has been significant as well, with what many believe has been significant convergence towards the current GAAP model.

The statutory accounting model has, over the years, served its purpose very well. Regulators charged with the responsibility of protecting policyholders designed the model with that duty in mind. The focus of statutory reporting has been on measuring the stability and strength of insurance companies. In other words, is the company solvent? How well equipped is it to meet its contractual obligations to policyowners, contractholders, and their beneficiaries not only today but the future?

This objective of statutory accounting is meaningful; however, in many ways it fell short of the needs of other groups of stakeholders. Owners, investors, and creditors have significant information needs that differ from those of the regulator or policyholder. This was one of the significant drivers of the early evolution of GAAP.

With the proliferation of publicly owned insurance companies in the 1950s and 1960s, the need for investor confidence in meaningful and consistent measurements of investment returns became more and more apparent. As recently as the 1960s, life insurance companies were exempt from certain filing requirements of the Securities Exchange Act of 1934 with the Securities and Exchange Commission (SEC). For those filings for which insurance companies were not exempt (Securities Act of 1933 filings), the statutory accounting model was accepted by the SEC. Yet many auditors were unwilling to express unqualified opinions on such financial statements, believing that they were at material variance from GAAP. Ultimately, the SEC required that filings be prepared on a GAAP basis.

This requirement prompted the life insurance industry and the accounting/auditing profession (as represented by the American Institute of Certified Public Accountants, the AICPA) to take action to resolve inconsistencies in practices and to codify the significant GAAP practices for life insurance companies. This resulted in the development of the first AICPA insurance industry audit guide, titled *Audits of Stock Life Insurance Companies* (commonly called the *Audit Guide*), in 1972.

This *Audit Guide* provided perspective on the life insurance business in general and on current prescribed and permitted statutory accounting practices. The *Audit Guide* also identified and discussed the significant variances between GAAP and statutory practices and provided guidance to auditors on appropriate audit procedures for the various accounts. Since then a significant number of authoritative pronouncements have directly or indirectly continued to form the basis for GAAP practices for life insurers. The following sections of this chapter describe the significant standard–setting bodies and provide an overview of the significant pronouncements that affect the life insurance industry.

2.2 Standard Setters

GAAP practices originated in the day-to-day accounting activities of practitioners attempting to record financial activity in accordance with the underlying objectives of GAAP for the recognition of assets, liabilities, revenue, and expenses as discussed in Chapter 1. In many cases, professionals account for certain types of transactions in an almost universally consistent manner even without formal written guidance. Therefore, the general practice of the profession has created accounting models that are "generally accepted."

Nonetheless, differences in accounting judgment sometimes arise. In many cases the principles adopted in practice for similar transactions may diverge onto two or more different pathways. To the extent that such divergence is significant and widespread, it soon becomes apparent that the GAAP objectives of consistency and comparability are not being achieved. In other words, the principle employed in practice in accounting for similar transactions is not universally "generally accepted." If such differences are unaddressed, variances persist and the value of financial reporting to the general public is less than optimal in the evaluation and analysis of the relative financial performance of entities engaging in similar businesses and/or transactions.

The need to address these situations has resulted in the evolution of standard-setting bodies or organizations that have assumed the responsibility of resolving significant inconsistencies in accounting practices as well as addressing the emerging issues that inevitably arise from changes in economic conditions and new types of financial instruments and transactions.

The following discussion will focus on the three primary standard setters:

- The American Institute of Certified Public Accountants (AICPA)
- The Financial Accounting Standards Board (FASB)
- The Securities and Exchange Commission (SEC)

Prior to 1973, the AICPA was the primary standard setter. In 1973 this responsibility was transferred to the FASB. The FASB is funded and governed by the Financial Accounting Foundation, a non-profit and independent organization. This Foundation is founded by the accounting profession, industry and others. The SEC has the regulatory authority to promulgate accounting standards for publicly-held companies (and has exercised that authority periodically) but generally relies on the AICPA and the FASB for such standard setting. As further discussed in Section 2.7 relating to recent congressional involvement in accounting, the FASB will become the sole standard setter in the future.

2.2.1 American Institute of Certified Public Accountants

The AICPA is the association representing the accounting and auditing professions. The AICPA has played a significant role in providing guidance to accountants and auditors in the conduct of their profession, including guidance on the proper application of accounting principles and practices. The following discussion describes the various vehicles by which the guidance was promulgated.

2.2.1.1 Accounting Research Bulletins

In the 1930s, in response to the needs discussed above, the AICPA formed committees to perform research and issue opinions. These opinions were published as Accounting Research Bulletins (ARBs) and were considered the authoritative literature of their day. The responsibilities of these committees were ultimately transferred to and assumed by the Accounting Principles Board of the AICPA in the late 1950s. Some of the guidance provided by the ARBs survives today although none of it is insurance industry-specific.

2.2.1.2 Accounting Principles Board Opinions

The Accounting Principles Board (APB) was formed in 1959 to assume the responsibility of resolving issues relating to GAAP and their application. The APB issued 31 opinions from 1962 through 1973. These APB Opinions, to the extent that they have not been superseded by other authoritative pronouncements, retain their status as authoritative guidance. As with the ARBs, the guidance provided in many cases may have good application to insurance entities. However, none is specific to the insurance industry.

The following APB opinions, if applicable to a particular insurance company's circumstances, provide significant guidance in applying GAAP to certain types of transactions. (Note: While APB Opinions No. 16 and No. 17 were superseded by *SFAS No. 141* and *No. 142*, respectively, they are still relevant to business combinations involving mutual insurance companies. See Section 2.2.2.7 for a discussion of a potential new standard which would modify and update *SFAS No. 141* and would also be applicable to business combinations involving mutual companies.)

- ***APB Opinion No. 16*** – **"Business Combinations."** This opinion provides guidance on how to account for the combination of businesses under two possible methods. The two methods are not alternatives. Based on the particular facts and circumstances of the combination, the transaction is considered either a *purchase* or a *pooling of interests*. If all the requirements are met, a pooling of interests results in the combination of the two businesses using the historical bases of accounting for the combined assets and liabilities that are being carried forward. In the case of a "purchase," the assets and liabilities of the acquired business are recorded at their fair value and any excess of the purchase price over the fair value of the net assets acquired is recorded as an intangible asset called goodwill. The goodwill then is subsequently amortized into earnings. Purchase accounting is more fully addressed in Chapter 15.

- ***APB Opinion No. 17*** – **"Intangible Assets."** This opinion covers the accounting for identifiable and unidentifiable intangible assets whether acquired or developed. This opinion has general theoretical application to the insurance industry in the areas of business combinations (goodwill and the value of business acquired) and the deferral and amortization of policy acquisition costs.

2.2.1.3 Practice Bulletins

The AICPA has issued a limited number of practice bulletins that provide additional practical guidance in relating narrow GAAP application circumstances. Two practice bulletins (PB) have direct applicability to the insurance industry:

- *Practice Bulletin No. 8* deals with application of *Statement of Financial Accounting Standards No. 97* to insurance enterprises. (See Chapters 6 and 7.)

- *Practice Bulletin No. 15* deals with the accounting by the issuers of surplus notes. (See Chapter 18.)

2.2.1.4 Industry Audit Guides

The AICPA has published audit guides for various industries, including guides for the insurance industry (both life and property and liability). Although these guides have been designed to provide guidance to certified public accountants in the conduct of their audits of insurance companies, they also serve as an excellent reference source for developing an understanding of the insurance industry and its unique accounting practices.

These audit guides are periodically updated to reflect and address changes in the accounting and auditing environments.

2.2.1.5 Statements of Position

The Accounting Standards Executive Committee of the AICPA (the AICPA's senior technical body) has issued Statements of Position (SOPs) on various accounting issues that, after clearance by the Financial Accounting Standards Board, have become sources of GAAP.

Although many of the SOPs have only general applicability to insurance enterprises, the following are specific to GAAP for life insurers.

- ***SOP No. 95-1*, "Accounting for Certain Insurance Activities of Mutual Life Insurance Enterprises."** Because of the lack of authoritative guidance on GAAP for mutual life insurers, the AICPA took on a project that resulted in the issuance of this SOP. It specifies the accounting for life insurance contracts that participated in the actual experience of the insurance enterprise through payment of dividends that are based on that experience and the relative contributions of the contracts to the cumulative actual experience. (See Chapter 5 for a detailed discussion.)

- ***SOP No. 97-3*, "Accounting by Insurance and Other Enterprises for Insurance-Related Assessments."** Insurance companies are subject to various assessments, in particular those coming from state guaranty funds resulting from the insolvencies of insurance companies.

  The accounting for such assessments had varied in practice from the cash basis method to various accrual basis methods. This SOP establishes that the accrual method is appropriate if it is probable that an assessment will be imposed and that the amount can be reasonably estimated.

- ***SOP No. 03-1*, "Accounting and Reporting by Insurance Enterprises for Certain Nontraditional Long-Duration Contracts and for Separate Accounts."**

Separate Accounts:

Companies divide their life insurance operations into two categories, those related to the separate accounts (if applicable) and those related to the general account.

SOP No. 03-1 defines two account types as follows:

Separate Account – A separate investment account established and maintained by an insurance enterprise under relevant state insurance law to which funds have been allocated for certain contracts of the insurance enterprise or similar accounts used for foreign originated products. Often for administrative purposes, separate account subaccounts with differing investment objectives are created within a single separate account.

General Account – All operations of an insurance enterprise that are not reported in the separate account(s).

The portion of the SOP dealing with separate accounts provides guidance as to,

a. How life insurance companies present separate accounts in the financial statements of the insurer. The assets of separate accounts meeting the criteria set forth in the SOP are valued at fair value and reported as a summary total in the balance sheet with a corresponding summary total for the liability to the contract holders.

b. How a life insurance company should account for an interest in one of its own separate accounts. If the sponsoring life insurance company maintains an interest in the assets of the qualifying separate account, the assets supporting that proportionate interest would be accounted for by using principles applicable to similar assets held in the company's general account. An exception to this accounting would exist if the life insurer's proportionate interest was less than 20 percent of the separate account and all of the underlying investments of the separate account were securities (as defined) or cash or cash equivalents. In this case, the insurance company can reflect its interest as an investment in equity securities classified as trading under the provisions of *SFAS No. 115*.

c. Proper gain or loss recognition on the transfer of assets from a general account to a separate account. Transfers to separate accounts from the general account should be accounted for at fair value and any gain or loss should be recognized if the risks and rewards related to these assets are transferred to the third party contractholders. The gain or loss would be reduced proportionately for the interest (if any) that the insurance company maintains in the separate account.

Nontraditional Long-Duration Contracts:

Prior to the issuance of *SOP No. 03-1* the primary authoritative literature relating the accounting for insurance policies and contracts for *SFAS No. 60* and *SFAS No. 97* (see Section 2.2.2.6). Since the time when those standards were issued, life insurance and annuity products have continued to evolve to include terms and provisions which are considered nontraditional and are also complex and varied. This SOP was written to address the appropriate accounting for these new features. Key provisions include:

- Determination of accrued account balances for insurance and investment contracts subject to *SFAS No. 97*. Generally the balance should be the highest contractually determinable balance without reduction for future fees or charges or possible surrender adjustment.

- *SFAS No. 97* states that contracts which do not contain significant mortality or morbidity risks should be accounted for as investment contracts. This SOP provides guidance on how to assess that significance.

- For universal life type products with insurance benefits, the insurance company will collect an amount each period which is intended to provide compensation for the insurance benefits expected to be provided. In many instances the amounts collected in the earlier years will exceed the expected benefits to be provided in those years while the benefits expected to be paid in later years may exceed amounts collected in those later years. The provisions of the SOP essentially result in the deferral of the income state impact of a portion of the amounts collected in the earlier years through the establishment of an additional liability. The same requirement applies to an assuming reinsurer of such benefits if the same or similar circumstances apply. The SOP points out that a reinsurer needs to make its own determination of the significance of mortality or morbidity risk in evaluating whether the reinsurer contract should be classified as an investment contract or an insurance contract. This determination may be different than that of the ceding company.

- Some products/contracts may include features that provide the contractholder with payout alternatives (annuity purchase guarantees for example) that could result in benefits exceeding the account balance. In these cases the insurance company should first determine if such features should be accounted for under the provisions of *SFAS No. 133* (see Section 2.2.2.7). If not, this SOP requires the establishment of an additional liability and describes the method to be used to calculate the liability. In the case of an arrangement to reinsure such additional benefits, both the ceding and assuming companies should consider the applicability of *SFAS No. 133* to the arrangement. If *SFAS No. 133* is not applicable, the same guidance above would apply to establishing an additional liability.

- Some products/contracts may provide for what is referred to as a "sales inducement." An example of a sales inducement could be an additional benefit that would be paid if a contractholder maintained the contract inforce for a specified period of time (persistency bonus). The SOP requires that this additional benefit be accrued as an additional liability over the period of time which the contract remains inforce. If these sales inducements require accrual as a liability, they potentially may be deferred and amortized similar to deferred acquisition costs if they meet the specific requirements of the SOP.

Proposed SOP – Deferred Acquisition Costs (DAC) on Internal Replacements:

Currently the AICPA is considering a new SOP addressing this topic. The current status of the proposed SOP is that the AICPA is responding to suggested changes and other comments received from the FASB as part of the clearance process. An "internal replacement" is defined by the proposed SOP as a modification in product benefits or features that occurs by amendment or rider to an existing contract or by the exchange of an existing contract for a new contract. The proposed guidance describes the accounting for replacements depending upon whether or not they are "substantially different" from the contract being replaced.

Substantially different –	the original contract is accounted for as being terminated and related account balances such as DAC should not continue to be deferred.
Not substantially different –	the replacement is accounted for as a continuation of the original contract where account balances such as DAC related to the original contract would carry over and continue to be deferred and amortized in connection with the replacement. The guidance also addresses the accounting for new sales inducements and acquisition cost incurred with replacements.

2.2.2 Financial Accounting Standards Board

In 1973 the Financial Accounting Standards Board was formed to become the primary accounting standard setter and continues in that capacity today. Under its purview, various pronouncements that have been issued continue to address the evolutionary aspects of financial accounting. These can be briefly summarized as follows.

2.2.2.1 Concept Statements

As discussed in Chapter 1, these statements are intended to provide the underlying concepts and principles upon which specific accounting and reporting standards will be set. However, in the hierarchy of GAAP, as discussed in Section 2.3, they are not included in the four categories of established accounting principles but are considered "other accounting literature," which may be considered in the absence of established principles.

2.2.2.2 Statements of Financial Accounting Standards

These FASB statements (SFASs) are the current primary standards of financial accounting reporting and address a wide variety of specific topics and issues. There is a due process for such standards. The public (companies, industry groups, accounting firms, and individuals) has the opportunity to comment upon and offer viewpoints, criticisms, or recommendations for improvement or support for the proposed standards. This period is referred to as the exposure period, and the draft pronouncements are known as exposure drafts. The length of the comment period can vary, but once the comments have been considered, the FASB finalizes the statement and issues it as a standard.

The standards include a background section that discusses the significant comments received and whether they were influential in the final construct of the standard. Depending upon the relative complexity of implementing a new standard and the significance of the potential impact on the financial statements, the transition guidance provides a time frame for implementation, whether implementation will be on a prospective or retroactive basis, and, in some cases, whether the effects of implementation may be reflected in the financial statements over an extended time. The transition guidance will also address whether or not the new standard supersedes all or parts of previous standards.

2.2.2.3 FASB Interpretations

Occasionally it becomes apparent through the practical application of the accounting literature that an "official" interpretation is needed. These FASB Interpretations (FIN) have been issued relating to prior APB Opinions and SFASs in response to this need.

2.2.2.4 FASB Technical Bulletins

These technical bulletins (FTBs) are designed to provide guidance in the application of the various standards and opinions where the guidance will not be costly to implement, will not be a significant change for a large number of companies, and does not result in a "novel" practice or contradiction to other fundamental principles.

2.2.2.5 FASB Emerging Issues Task Force Issues

The FASB's Emerging Issues Task Force (EITF) was formed in 1984 to identify, discuss, and resolve new issues using the existing literature as the foundation for its conclusions. The issues that are dealt with are numbered and titled. "Abstracts" summarize the issue and the results of the task force's deliberations including whether a "consensus" was reached. If the task force reaches a consensus, then that conclusion/guidance carries the weight of GAAP. The background discussions are not authoritative but help the reader understand the issue and the debate leading to the ultimate consensus. It should be noted that some issues are debated without a consensus being reached.

2.2.2.6 FASB Staff Positions

FASB Staff Positions (FSP's) were introduced in 2003 to provide a vehicle for more timely guidance for the application of FASB literature. FSP's are subject to an exposure and comment period of generally 30 days and are also subject to a discussion at an open public Board meeting before final approval. FSP's are numbered in such a manner to identify them with the Standards to which they relate. For example, the first FSP related to *SFAS No. 133* would be numbered *FSP FAS 133-1.*

The following FASB Standards, Interpretations, EITF Abstracts and FSP's have particular significance in the application of GAAP for life insurers. The discussion of these pronouncements is intended only as an overview. Subsequent chapters address the underlying concepts and their application in appropriate detail.

2.2.2.7 FASB Standards

***SFAS No. 5*, "Accounting for Contingencies" (1975).** This standard, while not industry specific, has significance for insurance enterprises because it provides the criteria for loss/liability accrual. In summary terms *SFAS 5* requires losses to be accrued when the loss is both probable and reasonably estimable. Practitioners oftentimes find themselves referring to the guidance of *SFAS 5* when analyzing whether a loss should be accrued or when an impairment of an asset should be recognized.

In earlier times in the United States when the strength of the balance sheet was the important focus in the preparation of financial statements, it was not uncommon for companies to record "cushions" or "contingency" reserves in the spirit of conservatism. *SFAS 5* specifically prohibits the use of such cushions and reserves because they can and have been used to "smooth" earnings in periods of volatile financial results. In some other countries such reserves are acceptable and may be known by names such as "equalization" reserves. The tension created by maintaining an appropriate balance between accurate income statement reporting and balance sheet conservatism at one point led the U.S. House Commerce Committee to ask a series of questions relating to *SFAS 5* including its provisions relating to contingency reserves. The FASB responded to the questions and reaffirmed the probable and estimable criteria of *SFAS 5* and the inappropriateness of the use of contingency reserves.

There is an exception to the general provisions of *SFAS 5*; this exception specifically relates to reserving for life insurance companies. As discussed in later chapters, *SFAS 60* provides for the concepts of margins for adverse deviation when reserves for life insurance policies are established.

***SFAS No. 60*, "Accounting and Reporting by Insurance Enterprises" (1982).** This standard is the primary authoritative source for guidance on GAAP for insurance companies. It not only brought together the existing specialized principles and practices but also established the basic accounting principles and reporting standards for revenue and expense recognition. This includes the deferral and subsequent amortization of policy acquisition costs, the financial statement carrying value of investments, and the treatment in the financial statements of realized and unrealized investment gains and losses. *SFAS 60*, as modified by *SFAS 97*, remains the primary source of guidance for proper expense treatment for insurers.

With respect to accounting for insurance policies and contracts, *SFAS 60* continues to be the authoritative guidance for traditional life insurance products. *SFAS 97*, discussed below, ultimately addressed the accounting for universal life insurance types of products and other contracts having significant investment characteristics.

Note that at the time *SFAS 60* was issued, mutual life insurers, because of their policyholder ownership structure, were exempted from following *SFAS 60* in the preparation of their financial statements. Even though it was a continuing subject of debate at that time, prescribed and/or permitted statutory accounting practices were also considered GAAP for mutual life insurers. In 1993, the FASB issued *FIN. No. 40*, which concluded that "statutory" was not GAAP for mutual life insurers. In 1995, the FASB issued *SFAS 120*, which established GAAP for mutual life insurers.

***SFAS No. 91*, "Accounting for Nonrefundable Fees and Costs Associated with Originating or Acquiring Loans and Initial Direct Costs of Leases" (1986).** While the title of this standard may not immediately bring the insurance industry to mind, it has significant applicability to the life insurance industry because it provides considerable guidance on accounting for fees and expenses related to financings as well as interest and amortization methods.

Many products issued by life insurers are in essence investment contracts and do not include significant insurance risk. Because of this, *SFAS 97* specifically states that such contracts should not be accounted for as insurance and that instead they should be accounted for consistent with the accounting for interest-bearing and other financial instruments. This is the insurance link to *SFAS 91*, the application of which is discussed in later chapters.

***SFAS No. 97,* "Accounting and Reporting by Insurance enterprises for certain Long-Duration Contracts and for Realized Gains and Losses from the Sale of Investments" (1987).** *SFAS 60* did not address the accounting for universal life-type contracts because universal life contracts were still quite new at the time. *SFAS 97* requires a deposit accounting model for the "premium" receipts related to such contracts. These receipts are not treated as revenue but are credited to the contractholders' account balances in the balance sheet, whereas fees earned by the insurance company for maintenance of the account and for the cost of true insurance protection are charged to the contractholders' balance and credited to "other revenues" in the income statement. Surrenders by contractholders are not treated as an expense but are handled as a withdrawal of funds from the balance sheet account balance. *SFAS 97* also provided for deferred acquisition costs and deferred revenue to be amortized in relation to the estimated gross profit stream of the underlying contracts as opposed to premiums, which are the base for traditional insurance products.

SFAS 97 also addressed the accounting for long-duration contracts that do not provide significant insurance protection, such as certain types of annuities. These types of contracts are described as investment contracts and are to be accounted for consistent with other interest-bearing financial instruments. As with universal life-type contracts, contractholder deposits and withdrawals are not considered revenues or expenses.

SFAS 97 also addressed the accounting for what are known as limited-payment contracts, in which the policyholder pays his/her premiums up front to some degree and receives insurance protection over an extended time. This standard requires that the gross premium received in excess of the amount required to provide for all benefits and expenses be deferred and recognized over the period that the insurance protection is provided.

SFAS 97 also amended *SFAS 60* by requiring that the realized investment gains and losses be reflected as an element of operating revenue on a pre-tax basis, whereas *SFAS 60* required such gains and loses to be recognized on a separate line in the income statement below operating income and on a net-of-tax basis. *SFAS 97* also prohibited any direct or indirect deferral of such gains or losses to future years.

***SFAS No. 113*, "Accounting and Reporting for Reinsurance of Short-Duration and Long-Duration Contracts" (1992).** Reinsurance can be thought of as insurance for an insurance company, whereby an insurance company transfers (cedes) some or all the risk associated with its policies and contracts to another insurer (the reinsurer). Such reinsurance arrangements are entered into for a variety of reasons, including the direct writer's (ceding company) desire to reduce its exposure to the effects of individually large losses, as a means of financing the commission expense strain on statutory surplus balances, and as a means of limiting losses that exceed desired aggregate retention.

Prior to the issuance of *SFAS 113*, insurers reported the amounts due to or from reinsurers on a net basis with the related insurance liabilities. This practice contradicted and was in conflict with other GAAP guidance that required gross presentations of receivables and payable unless there was a "right of setoff." *SFAS 113* changed existing practice to require that reinsurance balances be presented gross on the balance sheet.

In issuing *SFAS 113*, the FASB attempted to address the perception of deficiencies in reporting reinsurance and acknowledged that *SFAS 60* did not provide adequate guidance in light of the increasing significance and complexity of reinsurance transactions, some of which, despite their form, were, in substance, financing transactions and sometimes referred to as "surplus relief" reinsurance. *SFAS 113* established the criteria for an agreement to be accounted for as reinsurance and set the standards for such accounting and reporting.

***SFAS No. 115*, "Accounting for Certain Investments in Debt and Equity Securities" (1993).** Although this statement is not industry-specific, it has significant applicability to the life insurance industry. Prior to the issuance of *SFAS 115*, insurance enterprises accounted for investments in debt securities primarily on an amortized cost basis. In periods of rising interest rates, the fair values of such securities would decline, resulting in unrealized losses. Companies generally did not recognize such losses as realized because there may not have been any indication of permanent impairment and because of the company's explicit or implied intent to hold the securities to maturity. Some constituencies were concerned that the actual investment transaction practices of companies contradicted the intent to hold to maturity. Because of this, it was believed that the existing accounting model (amortized cost) was not resulting in a fair presentation of financial position.

This pronouncement was the subject of significant debate because its practical application had an additive impact on volatility within the balance sheet and because of the significant disconnect between the lack of corresponding accounting treatment for the liabilities that these investments were ultimately intended to fund.

SFAS 115 required entities to classify such investments into three categories and specified the accounting to be applied based on that classification, as follows:

- Held to maturity, carried at amortized cost
- Trading, carried at fair value with periodic changes in fair value recognized in earnings
- Available for sale, carried at fair value with periodic changes in fair value excluded from net income but included in other comprehensive income

***SFAS No. 120*, "Accounting and Reporting by Mutual Life Insurance Enterprises and by Insurance Enterprises for Certain Long-Duration Participating Contracts" (1995).** As previously discussed, prior to the issuance of *SFAS 120*, mutual life insurers were exempted from the accounting and reporting requirements of *SFAS 60, SFAS 97,* and *SFAS 113* because of their unique ownership structure. Basically, statutory accounting practices were considered GAAP. *SFAS 120* requires mutual life insurers to follow the provisions of *SFAS 60*, *SFAS 97*, and *SFAS 113* unless specific criteria are met that would require the insurers to use the concurrent guidance established by the AICPA's *SOP 95-1*. This SOP deals with the accounting for certain contracts that participate in the profits of mutual life insurers.

***SFAS No. 133,* "Accounting for Derivative Instruments and Hedging Activities" (1998) and *SFAS No. 138,* "Accounting for Certain Derivative Instruments and Certain Hedging Activities an amendment of FASB Statement No. 133" (2000).** With the proliferation of and increasing complexity of derivative instruments including derivative instruments which may be embedded in other contracts (such as equity-indexed annuities), it became apparent that the existing accounting literature did not provide sufficient guidance. Derivatives are also used frequently in hedging activities. Some derivatives were recognized off balance sheet, while others were not.

The general provisions of *SFAS 133* and *SFAS 138* require that all derivatives be recognized in the balance sheet as assets or liabilities and that they be measured at fair value. Specific conditions must be met for a derivative to be afforded hedge accounting treatment. Changes in the fair value of derivatives are generally to be reflected in earnings except to the extent that they are effectively functioning as a qualified hedge. Because these standards are very complex, a technical support group (the Derivatives Implementation Group [DIG] was constituted to deal with the many difficult implementation issues which subsequently surfaced. Decisions reached by the DIG, decisions resulting from FASB financial instrument projects and other implementation issues ultimately resulted in the issuance of *SFAS No. 149* which amends *SFAS No. 133* for these decisions. See Chapter 13 for further discussion of derivatives.

***SFAS No. 141*, "Business Combinations" (2001)**

Prior to the issuance of this Statement, accounting for business combinations was governed by APB Opinion No. 16 (see Section 2.2.1.2) which provided for two basic methods of accounting for business combinations based on the facts and circumstances surrounding a particular transaction. These methods are known as the "pooling of interests" method and the "purchase" method. In practice, similar transactions were sometimes accounted for using different accounting methods (pooling vs. purchase) which resulted in significant differences in financial statement results. In order to improve comparability and to provide financial statement users with information which would help them in their evaluation of the performance of a business combination investment, the FASB issued *SFAS No. 141*.

This Statement concluded that business combinations are acquisitions and, as such, the purchase accounting method should be the only method used. The Statement further requires that tangible assets meeting certain criteria be separately recognized. Previously, sometimes as a matter of accounting convenience, many such intangible assets had merely been subsumed as part of goodwill. These intangible assets generally have very different economic characteristics. Combining these different assets could result in financial statement distortions in periods subsequent to the combination.

SFAS No. 141 also requires disclosure of the reasons for the combination and expanded disclosures relating to goodwill and other intangible assets acquired in the transaction. While *SFAS No. 141* superseded APB No. 16 it did not change some of the provisions related to purchase accounting including:

- Cost determination of the acquired company,
- Allocation of that cost to the assets and liabilities acquired,
- Accounting for preacquisition contingencies and,
- Accounting for any contingent consideration in the transaction.

It should be noted that, as this text is being written, the FASB and the International Accounting Standards Board are considering issuing common Statements on business combinations which would improve consistency, relevance and international comparability in accounting for such transactions. The objective of this project is to issue Statements that would require business combinations to be accounted for at fair values at the transaction date with goodwill continuing to be accounted for as a residual. Currently some of the assets and liabilities of the acquired company are not revalued to fair values in the accounting for many business combinations. Because of this, the resulting financial information was less transparent and less relevant to financial statement users. The Statement which will result from this project will also be applicable to business combinations/acquisitions by mutual companies. It should also be noted that this project has not yet resulted in the issuance of an "exposure draft" and, as such, any tentative decisions/conclusions do not have authoritative weight.

SFAS No. 142, "Goodwill and Other Intangible Assets" (2001)

For goodwill and other intangible assets acquired in a business combination, this Statement provides the accounting guidance to be used for periods subsequent to acquisition date. *SFAS No. 141* addresses the accounting at the acquisition date. For other intangible assts not acquired in a business combination, this statement also provides the accounting for such assets at the date acquired and for periods subsequent thereto.

Significant provisions of the Statement include:

- Goodwill and other intangible assets with "indefinite useful lives" will no longer be amortized but will be periodically evaluated for possible impairment.

- The Statement further provides guidance on how to determine and measure any such impairment.

- Intangible assets with "finite useful lives" will continue to be amortized over their useful lives.

2.2.2.8 EITF Abstracts

There have been a number of Emerging Issues Task Force (EITF) Abstracts with direct applicability to the insurance industry. Some of these are primarily directed towards reinsurance issues affecting the property and liability industry and will not be addressed here. Those that affect life insurers are as follows:

- *EITF Issue No. 92-9,* "Accounting for the Present Value of Future Profits Resulting from the Acquisition of a Life Insurance Company," is discussed in Chapter 15.

- *EITF Topic No. D-41*, "Adjustments in Assets and Liabilities for Holding Gains and Losses as related to the Implementation of SFAS No. 115," is discussed in Chapter 14.

2.2.2.9 FASB Staff Position *(FAS 97-1)*

As of the time of writing this text there has only been a limited number of FSP's issued. Only one of these has specific applicability to the life insurance industry. This is *FSP FAS 97-1*, issued in June of 2004. This Staff Position provides guidance on situations for which certain provisions of *SFAS No. 97* require or permit the recognition/accrual of an unearned premium liability.

2.3 GAAP Hierarchy

Given all these types of authoritative literature, the reader might wonder which pronouncements carry the most weight and in what order the respective guidance should be applied. To answer this question, the AICPA has defined such a hierarchy in its *Statement on Auditing Standards No. 69.* There are two broad categories: established accounting literature and other accounting literature.

(As discussed in Section 2.7, the FASB will be taking steps to (1) move the GAAP hierarchy from "auditing standards" to FASB literature and (2) provide for two basic categories in the hierarchy – authoritative literature and non-authoritative literature. This process will likely take some time to accomplish.)

2.3.1 Established Accounting Literature

The established accounting literature category is broken down into four subcategories (a, b, c, d) and "other." Category a carries greater weight than category b and so on. SFASs and APB opinions are included in category a, while EITF Consensus and AICPA Practice Bulletins are considered category c. Entities preparing GAAP financial statements should be prepared to justify situations in which they have not followed the order and the guidance set forth in literature falling within categories a through d.

The following is an excerpt from *Statement on Auditing Standards No. 69* which summarizes the various categories in the hierarchy.

For financial statements of entities other than governmental entities:

- Category (*a*), officially established accounting principles, consists of Financial Accounting Standards Board (FASB) Statements of Financial Accounting Standards and Interpretations, Accounting Principles Board (APB) Opinions, and AICPA Accounting Research Bulletins.

- Category (*b*) consists of FASB Technical Bulletins and, if cleared by the FASB, AICPA Industry Audit and Accounting Guides and AICPA Statements of Position.

- Category (*c*) consists of AICPA Accounting Standards Executive Committee (AcSEC) Practice Bulletins that have been cleared by the FASB and consensus positions of the FASB Emerging Issues Task Force.

- Category (*d*) includes AICPA accounting interpretations and implementation guides ("Qs and As") published by the FASB staff, and practices that are widely recognized and prevalent either generally or in the industry.

2.3.2 Other Accounting Literature

In the absence of an authoritative pronouncement or other source of established accounting principles, the preparer of financial statements for entities other than governmental entities may consider other accounting literature, depending on its relevance in the circumstances. Other accounting literature includes, for example, FASB Statements of Financial Accounting Concepts (SFACs); AICPA Issues Papers; International Accounting Standards of the International Accounting Standards Committee; Governmental Accounting Standards Board (GASB) Statements, Interpretations, and Technical Bulletins; pronouncements of other professional associations or regulatory agencies; Technical Information Service Inquiries and Replies included in AICPA Technical Practice Aids; and accounting textbooks, handbooks, and articles. The appropriateness of other accounting literature depends on its relevance to particular circumstances, the specificity of the guidance, and the general recognition of the issuer or author as an authority. For example, FASB Statements of Financial Accounting Concepts would normally be more influential than other sources in this category.

The "other" category therefore would also include the Actuarial Standards of Practice issued by the Actuarial Standards Boards, which has been established by the American Academy of Actuaries.

2.3.3 Evolution of Authoritative Literature

As GAAP evolves, certain aspects of authoritative literature become obsolete or require amendment or interpretation. In many cases this "maintenance" of authoritative GAAP guidance does not result in complete rewrites or replacements of entire pronouncements but rather in partial changes resulting from the issuance of subsequent pronouncements.

2.3.4 Actuarial Standards of Practice

The American Academy of Actuaries is the organization representing the entire U.S. actuarial profession. The academy serves the U.S. actuarial profession, both nationally and internationally, by establishing, maintaining, and enforcing high professional standards of actuarial qualification, practice, and conduct.

To assist in this role, the academy has established the Actuarial Standards Board (ASB) as an independent entity. The ASB has the authority to approve exposure of proposed standards, to hold public hearings on them, and to adopt recommended standards of practice.

The ASB also provides continuous review of the existing Actuarial Standards of Practice (ASOPs) to determine whether they are in need of amendment, alteration, expansion, or elimination.

ASOP 10, "Methods and Assumptions for Use in Life Insurance Company Financial Statements Prepared in Accordance with GAAP," is the standard that sets out the considerations that bear on the actuary's professional work in preparing elements of financial statements prepared in accordance with GAAP.

While neither the academy nor the actuarial standards board can prescribe GAAP, their interpretations in areas not otherwise covered by authoritative literature are binding on actuaries in their professional capacity. While the ASOPs do permit deviation when properly disclosed, U.S. actuaries are required to follow the ASOPs in their practice under GAAP. Consequently, although neither the academy's nor the ASB's pronouncements have the status of authoritative GAAP literature, they are authoritative to the extent that an actuary wishes to practice under GAAP.

The ASOPs issued by the ASB are specifically written for U.S. practice. However, to the extent a foreign company wishes to follow US GAAP, the ASOPs offer good guidance to the company's actuary.

2.4 The Securities and Exchange Commission

In 1933, the U.S. Congress enacted the Securities Act of 1933 to regulate the securities markets. The act required registration of securities prior to their public sale and also required disclosure of certain financial and other data in order for investors to make informed decisions. The act also included provisions prohibiting false representations and disclosures. The enforcement of these laws became the responsibility of the Securities and Exchange Commission with the Securities Exchange Act of 1934.

While the FASB remains as the primary standard setter, the SEC can also be considered a GAAP standard setter for those companies that fall within its regulatory reach. The SEC, through its rules and regulations, prescribes the form and content of financial statements that are filed with it. In some cases the requirements are the same as those set forth by the FASB. In other cases the requirements may not be the same and may go beyond those of otherwise existing literature. The SEC's financial statement rules for insurance companies are set forth in "Regulation SX" Section 210.7. The SEC also periodically issues Staff Accounting Bulletins (SABs), which are intended to address specific accounting issues as they arise.

There are multiple situations in which companies are required to produce financial statements or other financial reporting information. These include:

- 10-K: submitted annually; includes comprehensive information such as earnings, cash flow, balance sheet, executive pay, litigation, and management discussion and analysis
- 10-Q: submitted quarterly; a shorter version of the 10-K
- 8-K: submitted whenever any development that is material to shareholders and the company; examples include a merger, acquisition, accounting problems or hiring and firing of key executives

- 13D: submitted whenever an individual or corporation acquires a 5% stake
- 14A: a proxy statement that includes details of issues to be voted on and background on management and Board of Directors

This information is intended to be publicly available for all.

2.5 Accounting by Analogy

As discussed earlier in this chapter, there are a significant variety of sources for determining appropriate application of GAAP to the financial statements of life insurers. This text attempts to provide not only a working understanding of GAAP for life insurers but also a comprehensive reference source. As a practical matter, however, the various accounting models do in fact change. The user of this text should periodically refer to the "Current Text" published annually by the FASB and review the insurance industry section to determine whether there have been any new pronouncements that could have an impact on the guidance in this text.

Also, in spite of the authors' attempts to be as comprehensive as possible, not all situations and factual circumstances can be addressed. Further, direct reference to the authoritative literature does not always provide conclusive, definitive answers. Practitioners have long known that accounting by analogy is necessary to arrive at the most appropriate and reasonable approach. In many cases there is a similar fact pattern in another industry for which authoritative literature has already been developed, or there are similar fact patterns for where the accounting practice/model has been well developed in general practice over time. These analogous scenarios often result in the development of practical solutions to accounting issues. At other times when existing literature is not applicable, common sense application of the GAAP concepts underlying financial accounting and reporting generally points the reader in the right direction.

2.6 Role of the Auditor

To many preparers and users of financial statements, the role of the auditor relative to GAAP practices is not clearly understood. Some have the mistaken belief that auditors are responsible for the preparation of financial statements, and others incorrectly believe that auditors somehow are the creators of GAAP. It is easy to understand how these notions arise given auditors' involvement with other interested preparers and users of financial statements in the evolutionary development of GAAP.

GAAP practices are defined through the pronouncements and practices described in the hierarchy of GAAP previously discussed. The preparer of financial statements is responsible for their conformity with GAAP. The auditor is responsible for expressing an opinion on the fair presentation of those financial statements in conformity with GAAP. Both parties must have an adequate understanding of GAAP in order to perform their respective functions. During an audit, the preparer and auditor confer many times to resolve practical issues in the application of GAAP to particular facts and circumstances. In general, any differences of opinion are resolved prior to the finalization and issuance of the financial statements. However, if differences of opinion remain and the amounts involved are material, the auditor is required to describe such differences of opinion in the audit reports.

2.7 Congressional and Regulatory Involvement

As this text is being written, the U.S. Congress is considering the proposed "Stock Option Accounting Reform Act." By virtue of this Act, Congress may insert itself into the standard setting process. The proposed Act would, among other things, establish accounting principles for stock options, a topic which has been debated in the accounting profession for many years. Whether or not the Reform Act is passed, it is interesting to note what may be the beginning of a further evolution of the standard setting process.

Congress has also recently gotten involved in accounting from another perspective. Accounting and accountants in general have received increased attention from those within the broad profession as well as from the general public. This focus has resulted from highly publicized accounting scandals at certain publicly traded companies. The concerns surrounding the integrity of financial reporting prompted the Federal government to step in and legislate certain governance requirements for public companies and their auditors.

This law known as the Sarbanes-Oxley Act of 2002 did not provide for any significant changes in the process for the development and maintenance of generally accepted accounting principles. This Act does, however, provide for the establishment of a "Public Company Accounting Oversight Board" whose duties include the oversight of auditors as well as those Company officials with responsibilities for financial reporting. The Oversight Board has certain reporting responsibilities to the Securities and Exchange Commission and is subject to the SEC's oversight.

This law grants broad authority to the Oversight Board to establish and enforce standards for auditors relating to auditing, quality control, ethics and independence. Other provisions of the Act were designed to preserve the independence of auditors and the independence of public company audit committee members and to reconfirm corporate responsibility for financial reporting and maintenance of adequate internal control systems.

Under the Sarbanes-Oxley Act, the management of a public company is required to assess the effectiveness of the company's internal control over financial reporting and report its conclusion in the company's annual report. In addition, the company's auditor is required to attest to management's assessment and also report its own conclusion. The existence of one or more material weaknesses will require management and the auditor to conclude that internal control over financial reporting is not effective. Such a conclusion, however, will not result in any sanctions or penalties from the SEC, provided the auditor issues an unqualified (clean) opinion on the financial statements.

The actuaries are part of the management team or auditor team in providing this assessment. The Sarbanes-Oxley Act requires the management and auditors to:

1. Focus on policies and procedures that pertain to reliable financial reporting: This will expand the actuaries' focus, which has been traditionally in the technical computations. Some examples of issues are lack of consistency of these policies and procedures, lack of segregation of duties, inadequate reconciliation and related actuarial analyses.

2. Build assessments based on a suitable and recognized framework. Nearly all companies use the framework developed by the Committee of Sponsoring Organizations (COSO) of the Treadway Commission.

3. Identify control deficiencies, if any, and determine if they are significant deficiencies or material weaknesses. Only the latter are required to be publicly reported.

4. Maintain sufficient documentation to support the assessment.

A substantial amount of work is needed to implement, which includes documenting internal controls, testing them for effectiveness and correcting any identified deficiencies. Management must also show awareness of the risks and commitment to strong controls.

The purpose of the discussion above is to emphasize the importance that is being placed on the fair and accurate reporting of financial information. For those involved in financial reporting it should be understood that integrity is not secondary to technical competence.

Also, and in accordance with the provisions of the Sarbanes-Oxley Act, the SEC conducted a study which resulted in a number of recommendations being made to the FASB which are intended to improve the financial reporting system in the United States. The FASB has indicated that it agrees with the recommendations and will attempt to address them. Some of the more significant recommendations for purposes of this textbook are discussed below.

The SEC recommended that there should be one standard setter. This will result in the FASB being the only entity responsible for establishing authoritative financial accounting and reporting standards. During a transition period the Accounting Standards Executive Committee of the AICPA (AcSec) will discontinue issuing Statements of Position (see Section 2.2.1.5). The AcSec will however continue to issue Accounting and Auditing Guides (see Section 2.2.1.4). These guides will be reviewed by the FASB Staff to make certain that the Guides do not result in the establishment of authoritative accounting and reporting guidance. Also, the FASB Board will now ratify EITF consensus decisions (see Section 2.2.2.5) before they are considered authoritative.

The SEC also recommended that, in issuing accounting standards, the FASB should move from rules-based standards to standards based on principles and objectives. Some current rules-based standards have significant complexity and have proven difficult to implement. The FASB will attempt to make its future standards more understandable which, it believes, will reduce implementation difficulties.

In response to another SEC recommendation, the FASB is taking steps intended to improve its conceptual framework (see Section 2.2.2.1) including a joint undertaking with the International Accounting Standards Board in this regard. This framework serves as the foundation for accounting standards. The SEC also suggested that the FASB should consider modifications to the existing GAAP hierarchy. The modifications would be necessary to address issues resulting from the move to one standard setter as well as to address the possible elevation of the Concept Statements within the hierarchy. Currently the Concepts Statements are included in the lowest level of the hierarchy.

These steps along with others should ultimately contribute to an improved financial reporting environment.

Chapter 3 Expenses and Capitalization

3.1 Purpose

This chapter:

- Provides a background discussing concepts and authoritative literature on how expenses are recognized and utilized

- Addresses which expenses are to be included in actuarial items such as benefit reserves, deferred acquisition costs, gross profits, gross margins, recoverability testing, and loss recognition

- Instructs the actuary how to gather actual expenses, by line of business and expense category, as well as how to translate and allocate these into unit expenses

- Explains recoverability and loss recognition

- Addresses special situations

3.2 Background

Expenses are an important element in quantifying GAAP assets and liabilities. The process of deriving expense assumptions as well as allocating and quantifying actual expenses has a significant influence on income recognition.

Different types of expense are recognized in a variety of ways under GAAP accounting. Expenses are generally recognized when cash is disbursed or liabilities are accrued. When appropriate, some of these expenses are deferred to future periods by capitalizing these costs as assets and subsequently amortizing them. While some costs are immediately recognized, other expenses are reallocated in time by means of distinct assets capitalized and later amortized or by establishing a reserve from current resources for later release.

3.2.1 Statements of Financial Concepts

Several FASB Statements of Financial Accounting Concepts (SFACs) refer to expenses. *SFAC 5*, "Recognition and Measurement in Financial Statements of Business Enterprises," stipulates:

Guidance for expenses and losses is intended to recognize:

- Consumption of benefit. Expenses are generally recognized when an entity's economic benefits are consumed in revenue-earning activities or otherwise or,

- Loss or lack of benefit. Expenses or losses are recognized if it becomes evident that previously recognized future economic benefits of assets have been reduced or eliminated, or that liabilities have been incurred or increased, without associated economic benefits.

SFAC 6, "Elements of Financial Statements," specifies:

- Expenses are outflows or other using up of assets or incurrences of liabilities (or a combination of both) from delivering or producing goods, rendering services, or carrying out other activities that constitute the entity's ongoing major or central operations. (Paragraph 80)

- Expenses represent actual or expected cash outflows (or the equivalent) that have occurred or will eventuate as a result of the entity's ongoing major or central operations. The assets that flow out or are used or the liabilities that are incurred 43 may be of various kinds-for example, units of product delivered or produced, employees' services used, kilowatt hours of electricity used to light an office building, or taxes on current income. Similarly, the transactions and events from which expenses arise and the expenses themselves are in many forms and are called by various names-for example, cost of goods sold, cost of services provided, depreciation, interest, rent, and salaries and wages-depending on the kinds of operations involved and the way expenses are recognized. (Paragraph 81)

One implication of the latter two paragraphs is that a cost does not become an expense until it is recognized in the financial statement of the company. An example is a deferrable acquisition cost (DAC). In an accounting sense, it is the amortization of that cost, and not the original cost itself, that becomes the expense. Similarly, a maintenance cost may not be recognized as an expense at the time the monies are expended. For example, the application of *SFAS 60* may cause level maintenance expenses on an increasing premium product to be reallocated in order to reflect these maintenance expenses proportionately to premium revenue, so that revenue and expense be matched. Since this would have a negative effect on the net GAAP liability, it might be a cause for additional recoverability testing. (Refer to Section 3.8 of this chapter for a discussion of recoverability testing and loss recognition.) Conversely, that same application of *SFAS 60* will cause limited pay life contracts to accrue a positive reserve in earlier years to pre-fund maintenance costs in the paid up years.

The concepts statements are written for all industries. The definition of "expense" in those statements includes embraces benefits paid to policyholders. The life insurance industry differs with respect to the scope implied by the definition of "expense." Consequently, this chapter deals with expenses other than benefit payments, such as sales compensation, policy acquisition costs, and expenses of maintaining the operation.

3.2.2 Statements of Financial Accounting Standards

As addressed in Chapter 2, various SFASs provide the primary GAAP guidance with respect to insurance contracts. Although detailed analyses are presented in subsequent chapters of this book, a summary is presented in this chapter to facilitate the understanding of the interaction between these standards.

SFAS 60 was the first SFAS designated specifically for life insurance companies. It covers all contracts except those that have been specifically reclassified by subsequent Standards. Thus, it forms the general set of GAAP guidance for nonparticipating traditional life, some participating traditional life, and individual health policies.

SFAS 97 covers most life insurance and annuity products with account values. Included here are universal life, variable universal life, and most fixed deferred annuities and variable annuities in the accumulation stage. *SFAS 97* also requires an additional liability for *SFAS 60* contracts for which premiums are payable for a shorter period than the coverage period. *SFAS 97* requires those contracts without significant mortality or morbidity risk to be accounted for similar to other debt instruments.

SFAS 91 addresses investment contracts as defined in *SFAS 97*. In general, this standard applies to amortization of DAC for guaranteed interest contracts, funding agreements, and deferred annuities with little or no surrender charges. The amortization of DAC for investment contracts as defined in *SFAS 97* is addressed through *Practice Bulletin 8* as using the interest method as defined in *SFAS 91* or the estimated gross profits as defined in *SFAS 97*.

SFAS 120 covers participating traditional life insurance policies of mutual life insurers if such participating business follows the actuarial contribution principle with respect to distribution of surplus. Stock life companies, at their option, can use *SFAS 120* for such contracts.

3.2.3 Terminology

The term DAC refers to the amount of capitalized expenses remaining on the balance sheet at any reporting date. In practice other terms are used to describe this asset. Several popular terms are unamortized acquisition costs (UAC), deferred policy acquisition costs (DPAC), and unamortized expense assets (UEA).

3.3 Categorization Stipulated by *SFAS 60*

The calculation of several types of benefit reserves (liabilities for future policy benefits) and all DAC requires the allocation of expenses into various categories. Paragraph 26 of *SFAS 60* suggests that maintenance expenses should be captured and reported within the benefit reserve. Although many companies present results in this fashion, some companies have segregated maintenance expenses and reported a separate reserve for this item.

Guidance for categorization of expenses can be found in several sources.

SFAS 60 stipulates:

> Costs incurred during the period, such as those relating to investments, general administration, and policy maintenance, that do not vary with and are not primarily related to the acquisition of new and renewal insurance contracts shall be charged to expense as incurred. (Paragraph 27)
>
> Acquisition costs are those costs that vary with and are primarily related to the acquisition of new and renewal insurance contracts. (Paragraph 28)

Further, the updated 1994 *Audits of Stock Life Insurance Companies* addressed another aspect of expenses. It specified:

> If an expenditure has substantial future utility, and is clearly associated with and recoverable from future revenue, it may be considered for separate deferral in line with practices followed in other industries. (Paragraph 8.38)

This essence of this paragraph existed in the original *Audit Guide*, the 1972 *Audits of Stock Life Insurance Companies*. The above paragraphs have served as the foundation for categorizing expenses for GAAP purposes. Thus, this chapter addresses total expenses in six mutually exclusive categories:

Table 3-1
Expense Categories Needed to Quantify Reserves and DAC Under GAAP

Expense Category	Asset or Liability Affected
1 Deferrable acquisition	DAC
2 Nondeferrable acquisition	None
3 Direct maintenance	Benefit reserve
4 Investment expenses	DAC & benefit reserve
5 Other deferrable-type expenses, where substantial future utility exists ("future utility expenses")	Unique asset
6 Overhead	None

Some costs will affect the benefit reserve or DAC; others could create a special capitalized asset. Many costs, such as overhead, simply become expenses for the period without affecting any benefit reserve or asset.

Proper expense categorization is important to ensure that correct amounts are being capitalized and that adequate provision is being made to maintain policies in the future.

3.3.1 Deferrable Acquisition Costs

Deferrable acquisition costs are defined in the *SFAS 60* paragraph 28 citation above, which uses the term "acquisition costs." The term "deferrable acquisition costs" signifies that the expenses are considered to vary with and primarily relate to the acquisition of new business. To acquire business a company may incur costs that do not vary directly with the acquisition of new business (for example, the costs to acquire or develop an illustration system) and therefore are not deferrable. Consequently, *deferrable acquisition costs* has become a frequently used term to describe the new business costs eligible for capitalization.

3.3.2 Nondeferrable Acquisition Costs

Nondeferrable acquisition costs are all other expenses associated with the new business function that do not vary with, or primarily relate to, the securing of new policies. Several examples are new ratebooks, dividend and reserve factor development for a new product, and institutional advertising used to promote the life insurance company in general. Expenses identified as nondeferrable acquisition costs are not capitalized and are costs in the period in which they are incurred. Commissions (in excess of ultimate renewal levels) on long-duration contracts and direct underwriting expenses clearly fit into the *deferrable acquisition cost* category. Commissions at the ultimate renewal level are considered nondeferrable and receive accounting treatment as maintenance expenses. Such ultimate renewal commissions are to be distinguished from those nondeferrable acquisition expenses that are not directly allocable to contracts, and which are expensed as incurred.

Later sections in this chapter give examples of company practices for distinguishing between deferrable and nondeferrable acquisition expenses.

3.3.3 Direct Maintenance Costs

Maintenance costs are defined in Appendix A of *SFAS 60* as "Costs associated with maintaining records relating to insurance contracts and with the processing of premium collections and commissions." This chapter uses the term "direct maintenance costs" to distinguish such costs from indirect costs, or *overhead.* Claim adjustment expenses, also as defined in Appendix A of *SFAS 60*, and termination expenses, as referred to in paragraph 26 of *SFAS 60*, are typically included in direct maintenance costs.

3.3.4 Investment Expenses

Investment expenses are defined in the Glossary of the *Audit and Accounting Guide* as "Expenses that are properly chargeable against investment income." Typically, these have included expenses of investment advisors, internal investment department expenses, and those transaction costs that cannot be capitalized into the cost of the asset being purchased.

3.3.5 Future Utility Expenses

Future utility expenses can occur if "substantial future utility exists" according to the 1972 and 1994 *Audit Guides.* While this category is not mentioned in *SFAS 60*, future utility expenses apply to all industries and are not unique to the life insurance industry.

AICPA *SOP 98-5*, "Reporting on the Costs of Start-Up Activities," addresses the concept of costs associated with substantial future utility. Its paragraph .05 defines such costs as "those one-time activities related to opening a new facility, introducing a new product or service, conducting business in a new territory, conducting business with a new class of customer, initiating a new process in an existing facility, or commencing some new operation." Its paragraph .12 provides guidance for the accounting of such costs: "Costs of start-up activities, including organization costs, should be expensed as incurred."

Certain computer hardware and software costs may qualify for capitalization. Explicit guidance for software is provided in AICPA *SOP 98-1,* "Accounting for the Costs of Computer Software Developed or Obtained for Internal Use."

3.3.6 Overhead

Overhead, sometimes referred to as indirect cost, is the residue resulting from the categorization of all expenses discussed in the first five categories.

3.4 Expense Categorization under other Pronouncements

The guidance in the previous section is based on *SFAS 60.* This section provides guidance on expense categorization for contracts that fall within the scope of other FASB standards.

3.4.1 *SFAS 91*

SFAS 91 can be used to account for expenses related to investment contracts. Although *SFAS 91* does not address insurance contracts, *SFAS 97* indicates that certain types of contracts issued by insurance companies are "investment contracts," thus placing them in the scope of *SFAS 91. SFAS 91* modifies the *SFAS 60* acquisition expense concept:

> Direct loan origination costs of a completed loan shall include only (a) incremental direct costs of loan origination incurred in transactions with independent third parties for that loan and (b) certain costs directly related to specified activities performed by the lender for that loan. (Paragraph 6)

For life insurance companies, this appears to be a more restrictive definition of deferrable expenses than that found in *SFAS 60*. *SFAS 91* speaks more to direct incremental costs with respect to the loan being made and appears to preclude the allocation of any "step-rated" variable policy acquisition costs.

3.4.2 *SFAS 97*

SFAS 97 states:

> This Statement establishes standards of financial accounting and reporting for three classes of long duration contracts ... and for reporting realized investment gains and losses. The accounting for long-duration contracts not otherwise addressed by this Statement is prescribed in Statement 60. (Paragraph 6)

Therefore, in general, the categorizations of expenses are identical for *SFAS 60* contracts and *SFAS 97* contracts. However, *SFAS 97* requires that percentage of premium expenses (commissions and premium taxes) must be separated between *deferrable acquisition costs* and *direct maintenance*. *SFAS 97* states:

> Estimated gross profit ... shall include estimates of the following elements: ... Amounts expected to be assessed for contract administration less costs incurred for contract administration (including acquisition costs not included in capitalized acquisition costs as described in paragraph 24) ... This Statement does not define the costs to be included in acquisition costs but does describe those that are not eligible to be capitalized under this Statement. ... Acquisition costs that vary in a constant relationship to premiums or insurance in force, are recurring in nature, or tend to be incurred in a level amount from period to period shall be charged to expense in the period incurred. (Paragraphs 23 and 24)

Thus, paragraphs 23 and 24 exclude from the deferrable category those acquisition costs that tend to be level or recurring, treating them instead in the same manner as direct maintenance expenses. Such expenses are thus considered in gross profits under *SFAS 97*, gross margins under *SFAS 120*, and in testing for recoverability and loss recognition.

3.4.3 *Practice Bulletin 8*

For flexible-premium universal life or deferred-annuity contracts, premium attrition causes commissions and premium taxes to decline after the first contract year but tend to become level at mature durations. The actuary should use judgment in determining at which point such expenses begin to levelize as a percentage of the revenue baseline (estimated gross profits). AICPA *Practice Bulletin 8* supports this concept: Paragraph 25 identifies contract administration costs to be included in the calculation of estimated gross profits as "policy-related acquisition costs that are not capitalized under FASB *Statement No. 97*, paragraph 24, such as ultimate renewal commission and recurring premium taxes." Assumptions for vesting of commissions (agent termination rates) are often used because they affect the estimated cash flows.

3.4.4 *SOP 95-1*

AICPA *SOP 95-1*, together with *SFAS 120*, provides guidance for participating policies of mutual life insurance companies when such policies follow the contribution principle of distribution of surplus. The goal of the contribution principle is for classes of policyholders to pay for their life insurance in a manner commensurate with the cost to the company of providing such insurance. The vehicle for accomplishing that is the policyholder dividend. *SOP 95-1* stipulates:

> This SOP uses the definition of acquisition costs contained in FASB Statement No. 60. ... Acquisition costs ... that vary in a constant relationship to premiums or insurance in force, that are recurring in nature, or that tend to be incurred in a level amount from period to period, should be charged to expense in the period incurred. (Paragraph 19)

This paragraph provides guidance virtually identical to the guidance provided by paragraphs 23 and 24 of *SFAS 97*.

In summary, *SFAS 60* forms the basis for expense categorization guidance for nearly all types of contracts. The one exception is investment contracts in which the eligibility of costs for capitalization is limited.

3.5 Line of Business and Category Analysis

In order to allocate costs into the six expense categories needed for GAAP, studies must be performed. This section describes the process and issues involved in performing such a study. This process and issues apply to every product, regardless of the FASB standard applicable.

- Line of business allocation. Usually, insurance products are grouped by common features and called lines of business. Expenses first need to be assigned to the product lines and then to the appropriate accounting model within each line of business. Some types of costs can be assigned directly at the policy level, such as commissions and premium tax. Some costs within a line of business may need to be allocated indirectly. An example is life insurance underwriting salaries that need to be allocated between policies in the *SFAS 97* model and those in the *SFAS 60* model. A holding company might establish lines of business that cross over subsidiaries if the lines contain similar policies administered together.

- Category determination. Costs need to be assigned to the appropriate category listed in Table 3-1. After such assignments, some costs are converted to a "unit" basis to conform to actuarial formula conventions that underlie DAC and benefit reserve calculations.

3.5.1 Categorization

The following tables illustrate a typical process used for categorizing costs. Table 3-2 illustrates an expense summary with categories typically found in a U.S. statutory financial statement. Some simplifying assumptions have been made. This enterprise has only one legal entity (the life insurance company itself) and only two lines of business (life insurance and health insurance). In addition, the description of expenses has been significantly consolidated.

The Table 3-2 type of presentation is not sufficient for GAAP line of business and category assignment purposes. Expenses generally need to be allocated by functional type. After these functional allocations are made, costs are then assigned to their GAAP category.

Table 3-2
Sample Life Insurance Company: Expenses, Taxes, Licenses & Fees

	Life	Health	Investment	Total
Expenses				
Salaries	$230,048	$417,828	$8,160	$656,036
Computer	86,268	91,163	1,080	178,510
Employee Benefits	57,512	106,356	1,800	165,668
Postage & Telephone	28,756	37,984	180	66,920
Other	172,536	106,356	780	279,672
Total	575,119	759,688	12,000	1,346,807
Taxes, Licenses & Fees				
Premium Tax	91,728	73,734	0	165,462
Examinations	44,878	21,914	1,820	68,612
Licenses	11,925	2,599	708	15,232
Social Security	7,236	7,083	679	14,998
Fees	14,472	11,166	0	25,638
Total	170,239	116,496	3,207	289,942
Total Expenses	745,358	876,184	15,207	1,636,749
Deduct Premium Tax	(91,728)	(73,734)	0	(165,462)
Total Expenses without Premium Tax	$653,630	$802,450	$15,207	$1,471,287

Table 3-3 illustrates the reconfiguration of expense information by function, line of business, and GAAP expense category.

Table 3-3
Sample Life: Expense Line of Business and Category Analysis: Allocation of Costs to Category

	Line of Business											
	Life Insurance					Health Insurance						
Function	Deferrable Acquisition	Nondeferrable Acquisition	Direct Maintenance	Overhead	Future Utility	Deferrable Acquisition	Nondeferrable Acquisition	Direct Maintenance	Overhead	Future Utility	Investment	Total Company
New Business	$80,806	$37,957	-	$24,892		$101,007	$22,446	-	$56,115	-	-	$323,223
Legal & Actuarial	-	-	26,935	67,378	-	-	-	33,669	84,173	-	-	212,155
Systems	26,935	6,005	32,935	32,887	18,265	48,670	5,669	63,669	22,446	-	8,978	266,459
Policyholder Service	-	-	89,785	31,425		-	-	112,231	39,281	-	6,229	278,951
Marketing	95,980	46,935	-	40,403	-	121,008	35,669	-	50,504	-	-	390,499
Total Company	$203,721	$90,897	$149,655	$196,985	$18,265	$270,685	$63,784	$209,569	$252,519	-	$15,207	$1,471,287

The total expenses considered for the line-of-business, category, and function analysis ($1,471,287) must reconcile to the total operating expenses in the company's financial statements. The grand totals in Table 3-3 equal the grand totals in Table 3-2 after removal of premium taxes.

The categorization shown in Table 3-3 is simplistic; most product lines are more detailed. A disability income or long term care line must identify claims adjustment expenses, and traditional life may need to split direct maintenance costs between premium-paying and paid up policies.

3.5.2 Percentage of Premium Expense Allocation

Premium taxes are usually removed from expense allocation studies because they can be directly assigned at the policy level. Premium taxes are generally stated as a percentage of premium in the reserve calculations. Commissions are also frequently stated as percentage of premium amounts in the reserve formulas.

3.5.3 Allocations of Salary and Other Expenses

Some items may need to be allocated to various functions and various categories. For example, an officer's salary may need to be allocated into the functions that he or she directly manages, such as underwriting, or sales and marketing. Such functional allocations must then be assigned to deferrable or nondeferrable expense.

Salaries are an important focus of expense allocation. Not only are salaries generally a high percentage of total expenses, but certain other major expense types, such as employee benefits, can be reasonably allocated in the same proportion as salaries. Other expenses, such as utility costs or rent, can be prorated by measures such as number of staff positions, number of policies in force, or as a percentage of premium income.

3.5.4 Distinction between Direct Maintenance and Overhead Expenses

Like the distinction between categories of deferrable and nondeferrable acquisition costs, the distinction between direct maintenance and overhead requires judgment. *SFAS 60* indicates that direct maintenance expenses may affect the balance sheet by stipulating:

> Expense assumptions used in estimating the liability for future policy benefits shall be based on estimates of expected nonlevel costs, such as termination or settlement costs, and costs after the premium-paying period. Renewal expense assumptions shall consider the possible effect of inflation on those expenses. (Paragraph 26)
>
> Costs incurred during the period, such as those relating to investments, general administration, and policy maintenance, that do not vary with and are not primarily related to the acquisition of new and renewal insurance contracts shall be charged to expense as incurred. (Paragraph 27)

These paragraphs imply that direct maintenance costs that are non-level (such as claims settlement expenses and expenses for limited-payment policies that will continue after the premium-paying period) affect the liability for future policy benefits (benefit reserve), while those that are a level percentage of revenue, such as premium collection expenses on non-limited-payment contracts, do not affect that liability.

Paragraphs 26 and 27 constitute a guide for traditional life and health plans falling under *SFAS 60.*

For products falling under *SFAS 97* or *SFAS 120*, level maintenance expenses can affect either the benefit reserve or the DAC, because these expenses generally are not a level percentage of the revenue baseline (premium income for *SFAS 97* limited-pay products, expected gross profits for *SFAS 97* fund products, and expected gross margins for *SFAS 120* products). General practice has been to include the entire direct maintenance costs in generating GAAP assets and liabilities. *SFAS 97* supports this conclusion in its definition of estimated gross profit. In paragraph 23, element (b), it speaks of "costs incurred for contract administration" as an element in the calculation of estimated gross profit. In addition, inclusion of the entire direct maintenance cost is consistent with loss recognition testing requirements discussed later in this chapter.

Chapter 2 catalogs the GAAP pronouncements pertinent to the life insurance industry. In general, the pronouncements themselves do not provide specific guidance in the area of expense determination.

Although the split between direct maintenance and overhead is judgmental, certain items are more clearly allocable than others. For example, the costs of collecting premiums, settling claims, handling cash surrenders, and processing policy changes clearly belong in direct maintenance costs. On the other hand, compensation of chief executives would generally not be considered direct maintenance and consequently would be allocated to overhead. In the categorization process, a company can allocate expenses "from the bottom up" (starting with inclusion of expenses that are clearly direct maintenance expenses), or "from the top down," starting with exclusion of expenses that are clearly overhead.

3.5.5 Investment Expenses

If investments are allocated to products within a line of business, the expenses associated with these assets can be directly assigned to a line of business. In general, investment expenses are expressed as a reduction of investment income. Investment income and expenses are usually expressed as a percentage of underlying assets. This percentage, rather than an actual dollar amount, is generally entered in the actuarial formulas for benefit reserves and DAC.

3.5.6 Selection of Units of Measurement and Unitization of Expenses

The actuary frequently needs to express deferrable costs and direct maintenance costs on a per-unit basis. The types of unit expressions are per policy, per current face amount, per unit issued, or percentage of premium. This section looks at practices used to convert a dollar amount of expense into a value per unit.

The maintenance expense reserve element of *SFAS 60* long-duration plans, the recurring expense element of *SFAS 97* and *SFAS 120,* and the deferrable costs under most standards are frequently expressed in terms of per-unit amounts. This unitization of expenses is the next step after the determination of expenses by line of business and category.

Judgment is used in determining the most appropriate unit of measure. Further breakdowns within line of business may be necessary, such as allocation of underwriting salaries to policies that naturally require more underwriting, such as at higher issue ages.

Table 3-4 illustrates common choices of measure for assumptions other than commissions and premium tax. It also displays the unitization of nondeferred acquisition costs. Although this category of expense never enters into the calculation of GAAP reserves and DAC, such unitization is valuable in initial GAAP conversions because it can be used to develop initial estimates of costs incurred many years in the past. Overhead, if need be, can also be expressed in terms of units.

Table 3-4
Commonly Employed Units of Measurement for Line and Category Analysis

Line of Business	Most Frequent Choice	Other Choices
Part 1	**Deferrable and Nondeferrable Non-Commission Acquisition Expenses**	
Traditional individual life	Policies issued	Amount of insurance issued Policies ***and*** life riders issued
Individual health	Policies issued	Annual premium issued Number of records issued
Universal life	Policies issued	First year entire premium First year target premium
Variable universal life	Policies issued	First year entire premium First year target premium
Individual deferred annuity	Policies issued	First year premium collected
Individual variable annuity	Policies issued	First year premium collected
Group pension	First-year premium collected	
Group life	First-year premium collected	
Group accident & health	First-year premium collected	
Guaranteed investment contracts & funding agreements	Initial premium	
Part 2	**Direct Maintenance Expenses other than Commissions and Premium Taxes**	
Traditional individual life	Average policies in force	Mean amount of insurance in force
Individual health	Average policies in force	Premiums collected
Universal life	Average policies in force	Premiums collected Mean account values Mean amount of insurance in force
Variable universal life	Average policies in force	Premiums collected Mean account values Mean amount of insurance in force
Individual deferred annuity	Average policies in force	Premiums collected Mean account values
Individual variable annuity	Mean policies in force	Premiums collected Mean account values
Group pension	Mean liabilities in force	
Group life	Premiums collected	
Group accident & health	Premiums collected	
Guaranteed investment contracts & funding agreements	Average liabilities in force	

Investment expenses are typically expressed as a percentage of underlying assets. Investment expenses can be compared to average cash and invested asset balances over the period, generating a unit expense expressed in terms of "basis points" on the assets. This approach to unit expenses enables investment expenses to be subtracted directly from the gross earned interest rate to obtain an earned interest rate net of investment expenses. Cash and invested assets are used instead of total assets, because certain assets such as DAC and due premiums are non-monetary. For separate account business, investment expenses are generally applied against average separate account fund values. In DAC and *SFAS 60* benefit reserves the interest assumption is generally net of investment expenses.

Sometimes it is appropriate to use more than one measure of expenses. Issue expenses might be unitized as follows. A per-policy-issue expense of $150 might cover the physical printing of the policy form and include allocations of agency expense. A per-unit issue expense assumption of $2.00 per $1000 might cover underwriting costs. Many companies use other allocation expressions, such as percentage of first-year commissions, percentage of cost of insurance charges, and per-surrender and per-death claim.

Underwriting department costs are usually converted to a "per application" basis. However, some policies will never be issued and fall into a "canceled not taken" condition. The actuary should be aware that, if underwriting costs are expressed on a "per-application" basis, the costs of underwriting canceled policies would not be carried into the DAC. Consequently, many companies convert underwriting costs to a "per policy issued" basis. Including these costs in the DAC gives a better reflection of the total costs necessary to issue policies.

In the case of claims adjustment expenses, a common unit for a disability income line is "per dollars of claims paid" in the period being measured.

Table 3-5 illustrates a method for converting the costs established in Table 3-3 through the unitization process to obtain unit costs by line and category.

Table 3-5

Sample Life: Conversion of Total Costs to Unit Costs by Line of Business and Category

	Line of Business										
	Life Insurance					Health Insurance					
	Deferrable Acquisition	Nondeferrable Acquisition	Direct Maintenance	Overhead	Future Utility	Deferrable Acquisition	Nondeferrable Acquisition	Direct Maintenance	Overhead	Future Utility	Investment
Expense (from Table 3-3)	$203,721	$90,897	$149,655	$196,985	$18,265	$270,685	$63,784	$209,569	$252,519	-	$15,207
Unit of Measurement In force	Policies Issued	Policies Issued	Mean Policies In force	Mean Policies In force	Policies Issued	Policies Issued	Policies Issued	Mean Policies In force	Mean Policies In force		Mean Assets
Amount	1,000	1,000	8,000	8,000	1,000	1,200	1,200	10,000	10,000		18,500,000
Unit Cost	$203.72	$90.90	$18.71	$24.62	$18.27	$225.57	$53.15	$20.96	$25.25		0.082%

During a conversion to GAAP, expense assumptions must be developed for earlier years because the DAC at conversion must be properly established and amortized. Table 3-6 demonstrates a methodology used to impute current expense assumptions and expressions to prior years. This technique can be effective if there have been no significant structural changes during this time.

Nondeferred acquisition costs must be quantified and expressed in terms of unit parameters to ensure that results in total are reasonable.

Table 3-6 presumes that a rigorous line of business and categorization analysis applies to a particular base or anchor calendar year. It presumes that the resulting unit costs can be extrapolated to produce reasonable results for a prior year, called the target year. The anchor year unit costs are applied to target year units of measurement to derive "implied expenses," the aggregate expenses incurred if unit costs were identical for those two particular years. A comparison of *actual* total company target year expenses with implied total company target year expenses allows the actuary to true up the target year unit costs. This approach automatically adjusts to changes in aggregate mix of business over time. However, due consideration must be given to major nonrecurring expenses and major structural changes in the enterprise.

Table 3-6
Sample Life: Extrapolation of Earlier Year's Costs Using Anchor Year to Target Year Approach

	Line of Business										
	Life Insurance					Health Insurance					
	Deferrable Acquisition	Nondeferrable Acquisition	Direct Maintenance	Overhead	Future Utility	Deferrable Acquisition	Nondeferrable Acquisition	Direct Maintenance	Overhead	Future Utility	Investment
(A) Unit Cost for Anchor Year	$203.72	$90.90	$18.71	$24.62	$18.27	$225.57	$53.15	$20.96	$25.25	-	0.082%
(B) Target Year Units of Measurement:											
– Description of Units	Policies Issued	Policies Issued	Mean Policies In force	Mean Policies In force	Policies Issued	Policies Issued	Policies Issued	Mean Policies In force	Mean Policies In force		Mean Assets
– Amounts of Units	800	800	8,200	8,200	800	850	850	8,700	8,700	-	7,900,000
(C) Implied Expenses = (A) × (B)	$162,977	$72,718	$153,396	$201,910	$14,612	$191,735	$45,180	$182,325	$219,692	-	$6,478
Ratio Analysis											
(D) Total of Row (C) $1,251,023											
(E) Actual Target Year Expenses $1,180,000											
(F) Ratio of (E) to (D) 94.32%											
(G) Final Unit Costs for Target Year = (A) × (F)	$192.16	$85.74	$17.64	$23.23	$17.23	$212.76	$50.14	$19.77	$23.82	-	0.079%

3.5.7 Other Issues

Certain deferrable expenses are incurred prior to the issue date of the policy. For example, the expenses of underwriting generally occur in the weeks prior to the policy's issue date. These two events can occur in different reporting periods. One method of handling expense timing is to delay explicit capitalization by recording such costs temporarily as prepaid expenses rather than as DAC. In the following period, once the corresponding policies are issued, the prepaid expense asset is released and the same amounts are then transferred into the DAC. This results in a better match of costs incurred with the policies that actually created the costs.

Although such a technique is not common, it does address the issue of matching the timing of deferrable expenses incurred with the timing of when the new issue first occurs.

Another issue common to most companies is called "backdating." A policy's stated issue date might be moved backwards several months to capture a more favorable premium rate. Thus, a policy may bear an issue date from a prior period, but its issue costs are incurred in the current period. Some companies attempt to restate the prior-period issue costs to accommodate this late entry; other companies correctly assign the issue expense to the current cohort of new issues. The reason that the latter practice is correct is that the expense was truly incurred in the current year.

Service agreements exist between legal entities, under which one party performs services for the other party. If the legal entities are related parties, then the effect of such service agreements is eliminated on consolidation. Thus for related parties service agreements are typically transparent. If the parties are not related or a separate GAAP opinion is required on one legal entity, then the service agreement should be examined as to the calculation of the reimbursement amounts. If such reimbursement amounts are commission-related (i.e., insurer A is using insurer B's field force), such commissions are clearly treatable as if insurer A were actually incurring those commissions directly. Expense reimbursements tied to production of business also clearly fall under the definition of deferrable acquisition cost, while expense reimbursements tied to average number of policies in force are clearly direct maintenance costs. Reimbursement for specific services rendered are treated as if the party serviced had incurred those costs directly. It should be noted that there may be differences in treatment between consolidated and stand-alone financial statements.

Life insurers frequently encounter large commitments that involve non-recurring expenses, such as an administrative systems conversion. Also, companies can be faced with the issue of expenses that are reasonably likely to increase or decrease in the future. While paragraph 26 of *SFAS 60* refers to the need to consider expense inflation, the standard is silent with respect to both (a) how to differentiate non-recurring expenses from recurring ones when performing expense allocations and (b) what to use as a guide when projecting future expenses. Although there is little formal guidance, the actuary should be consistent between years.

With respect to projected expense improvements, an entity in a startup operation should delineate "developmental expense" as an item of overhead and not capitalize it as a "future utility" expense. The company must clearly show that it is on a path to bring such expenses down to a reasonable level. This can be at a dollar level or expressed as a cost per unit.

Carving out developmental expenses from direct maintenance minimizes the distortion that would otherwise occur in the financial statements. Such distortion would accelerate earnings, because making projected direct maintenance expense reductions a component of the benefit reserve would tend to decrease the current benefit reserve on *SFAS 60* contracts. Similarly, under *SFAS 97* and *SFAS 120* contracts, making projected direct maintenance expense reductions a component of expected gross profits or expected gross margins would tend to unduly increase DPAC assets.

Life insurers frequently start new ventures and lines of business. In these situations, there is little or no prior experience from which to develop assumptions. In such situations, the initial maintenance and acquisition costs, when expressed on a unit basis, typically appear very high in the early years. A common technique has been to estimate the acquisition and direct maintenance expenses on a marginal basis. Another technique is to utilize pricing assumptions initially. As experience emerges, such expense assumptions should be monitored and refined as necessary.

Separate accounts deserve a brief mention. In the U.S., products whose total return performance is linked to the performance of a legally dedicated segment of assets are called variable products, and the legally segmented assets are referred to as a separate account. For companies with separate accounts there is the question of how to allocate costs between the general account and the separate account. Separate accounts introduce no new expense allocation concepts. The expenses associated with the product should "follow the product," wherever such expenses are incurred.

3.6 Determination of Deferrability of Acquisition Costs

This section discusses different types of expenses associated with acquiring new business and addresses their eligibility for capitalization. All expenses capitalized are subject to recoverability testing as addressed in Section 3.8.

3.6.1 Commissions

For short-duration contracts, the entire commission generally is capitalized. For long-duration contracts, the excess of initial commission over an ultimate level of commissions constitutes a deferrable expense, while the balance of the commission represents a direct maintenance expense. Renewal commissions in excess of the ultimate level are capitalized in renewal years. Excess commissions are generally determined by company commission rates, not absolute commission dollars.

There is seldom a question about the deferrability of excess commissions. One case to consider is the deferral of excess commissions on flexible-premium products governed by *SFAS 97*. This becomes an issue because the amount of and length of renewal premiums cannot be readily predicted. An early version of AICPA *Practice Bulletin 8* suggested that the "facts and circumstances" of each case would govern.

Commission advancing occurs with some frequency in the life insurance industry. For example, some distribution channels receive a full year's commission once a sale is completed even though the premium mode is not annual. The actuary needs to be aware of advancing and subsequent chargeback practices in establishing methodologies for determining DAC capitalization.

Agent financing occurs in many companies. Financing is usually in the form of loans to agents secured by the full faith and credit of the agent, by future commissions, or by some combination of the two. Agent financing costs are often capitalized. If they are in the nature of loans expected to be repaid, they are accounted for as receivables and not established as an element of DAC. Often these receivables include situations in which a full or partial commission on non-annual business has been annualized and paid in advance.

Fund-based sales compensation, sometimes called commission trailers, often exists on *SFAS 97* contracts. Beyond *SFAS 97* paragraph 24, which speaks to expenses that "tend to be incurred in a level amount from period to period," there is no specific guidance on whether trailer commissions should be categorized as recurring or as deferrable. However, since the trailer commissions are based on the account value (rather than a new premium) in renewal years, it is difficult to argue that trailer commissions vary with and are primarily related to the acquisition of new and renewal insurance contracts.

Some companies consider a commission vesting schedule when estimating future commissions. A vesting decrement assumption generally results in a declining commission schedule over time. This creates a larger portion of the initial commission that is in excess of the ultimate rate, which causes a higher initial DAC.

3.6.2 Expenses Similar to Commissions

Volume bonuses, sales contests, and sales conventions are other common forms of sales compensation. If based purely on new production, these costs are generally eligible for capitalization. They are capitalized as they are incurred.

More complex is the case in which sales-related costs are payable because of reaching target levels of renewal activity. These persistency bonuses are based on target renewal levels, either on renewal policy persistency for traditional policies or on renewal premium persistency on flexible premium contracts. The facts and circumstances would govern in each case. In practice, such amounts have been ascribed to all deferrable, all maintenance, or some combination. It is important that these anticipated costs are entered into the DAC and benefit reserve mechanics so that accurate recoverability and loss recognition can be performed.

Commission overrides for general agents, if expressed as specified percentages of premiums, are usually treated in the same way as commissions. In cases in which sales supervisors are paid on a salary-plus-bonus basis, the allocation becomes less clear and an analysis of their efforts and responsibilities should be considered. For example, functions such as agent training and agency recruitment are not generally considered deferrable, while certain agency administration duties such as sales lead creation, sales illustrations, and participation in the policy preparation and delivery process are considered deferrable costs.

Agency expense allowances and expense reimbursements that vary with production are generally deferrable. Recruiting and training allowances are considered developmental and usually are classified as nondeferrable acquisition costs.

Some sales forces are salaried, either fully or partially. Depending on the circumstances, such salaries could be considered a step-rated variable cost and thus deferrable. A step-rated variable cost is one in which, beyond a certain level of activity, an additional resource, such as an additional employee, would be needed. For example, an underwriter might be able to review 20 applications per day; a level of 21 applications would require an additional underwriter. These step-rated costs should be differentiated from the practice of putting newly hired agents on temporary salaries. The latter is generally perceived as a developmental cost and thus considered a nondeferrable acquisition cost.

3.6.3 Home Office Expenses

Certain home office expenses associated with marketing and selling are deferrable acquisition costs, while other such marketing and selling expenses are nondeferrable acquisition costs. Marketing and advertising expenses are generally not deferrable unless they are closely associated with production. For example, neither institutional advertising in a trade magazine nor an advertisement designed to attract salespeople is considered deferrable as a policy acquisition cost. However, an advertisement with a send-in form for the reader to inquire about or purchase life insurance could be viewed by some companies as deferrable.

Most underwriting expenses are deferrable. One issue is identifying the threshold of departmental supervision above which such expenses become nondeferrable or overhead. In general practice, the costs associated with the underwriters themselves, including salaries, benefits, allocations of rent, allocations of electricity, as well as costs associated with their immediate supervisors are deferrable. It is logical to extend this concept to administrative assistants who support those functions. With respect to certain other underwriting costs, such as paramedical, medical, and inspection procedures, such expenses are clearly deferrable.

Most policy issue expenses are deferrable. The physical assembly of the new policy form and its mailing are examples of this function. As with underwriting, the expenses connected with the policy issue staff and their immediate supervisors are generally considered deferrable.

Certain home office services in support of the policy issue function must be identified, allocated and categorized. Systems departments create commission statements and provide significant policy illustration and issue functions. They also track agent performance in connection with contests and conventions. Such functions generally are deferrable.

3.7 Timing of Deferrability

The actuary must ensure that the recognition of expenses inherent in reserve formulas and methods correlates with the recording of actual expenses in the company's financial statements. The following subsections address several methods and techniques commonly used to align expenses between actuarial formulas and the company's general ledger.

3.7.1 True-up

The amount of capitalization of deferrable acquisition costs should equal the deferrable acquisition costs incurred in the financial statement. *SFAS 60* states:

> Actual acquisition costs for long-duration contracts shall be used in determining acquisition costs to be capitalized as long as gross premiums are sufficient to cover actual costs. However, estimated acquisition costs may be used if the difference is not significant. (Paragraph 31)

This citation responds to the issue of whether a true-up is necessary. The actuary needs to establish that the amounts capitalized in the DAC are either equal or significantly close to those deferrable costs actually incurred.

Actuarial techniques for introducing capitalized costs into DAC generally follow one of two methods. One method is the direct input of actual, quantified dollars; the other method is the conversion and expression of actual dollar values to units for entry into actuarial reserve formulas.

The following discussion refers to the formulas used in reserve factors. However, all comments are applicable to reserves developed by using first principles and, to some extent, worksheets.

Reserve factors are more frequently used for *SFAS 60* and limited-pay *SFAS 97* life insurance products, not only because the assumptions are generally locked in at issue, but also because the basic benefits and guaranteed values do not change over time. *SFAS 97* and *SFAS 120* products are more conducive to the direct input of dollar amounts (rather than a per-unit assumption), primarily due to the dynamic nature of the periodic unlocking of assumptions. The unlocking process naturally calls for the replacement of the prior periods' expected values with those actually incurred, thus facilitating the use of actual expense numbers.

Paragraph 31 of *SFAS 60* suggests that the actuary demonstrate that (i) and (ii) are not significantly different:

(i) is the implied capitalization derived from the assumed per unit assumption used in the DAC reserve formula

(ii) is actual deferrable acquisition costs incurred.

In practice, several approaches are used to achieve and demonstrate this equality:

One approach is to re-enter deferrable cost assumptions periodically from recently performed expense categorization studies. If costs and new sales are relatively level, this updating may not need to occur frequently. As more companies have moved toward monthly reporting, the frequency of this parameter updating has accelerated.

Another approach to truing up implied capitalization to actual capitalization under a factor-type system has been to input modification factors that apply to certain policies based on a range of issue dates. A technique for this is as follows:

(1) Separate DAC development into two categories: (a) DAC derived from commissions and (b) DAC derived from other deferrable acquisition expenses. This split is needed because the commission scale needs to consider deferrable commissions incurred in renewal years, whose true-up should be independent of the true-up needed for item (b).

(2) For category (b), derive the DAC factors using hypothetical deferrable acquisition costs that produce borderline recoverability. Such borderline recoverability occurs when the total of GAAP net premiums for benefits and expenses equals 100% of gross premiums. In a mean or mid-terminal reserve formula, the initial term in the expense reserve formula includes all such category (b) expenses incurred at the moment the policy is issued. The technique described here places the maximum allowable category (b) expenses in that position. Table 3-7 shows that $5.05 per unit (column 14) is the maximum amount of category (b) expense that could be capitalized, based on the terms of the policy and the actuarial assumptions. Therefore, the DAC formula-based reserve is based on that $5.05 maximum amount and not on the actual amount of category (b) expenses incurred.

Table 3-7
Calculation of Maximum Expense (for Other Than Commissions) for a 5-Year Term Policy

Policy Year	(1) Investment Income Rate	(2) Mortality Rate/1000	(3) Lapse Rate	(4) Beginning of Year Survivorship & Discount Factor	(5) Gross Premium	(6) PV of Gross Premiums	(7) Commission Rate	(8) Maintenance Expense
1	7.00%	2.00	15.0%	1.00000	4.50	4.50	55.0%	0.30
2	7.00%	2.30	12.0%	0.79252	4.50	3.57	5.0%	0.31
3	6.50%	2.48	10.0%	0.65009	5.50	3.58	5.0%	0.31
4	6.50%	2.68	9.0%	0.54786	5.50	3.01	5.0%	0.32
5	6.50%	2.90	9.0%	0.46674	5.50	2.57	5.0%	0.32
				0.39754				
					Total	17.22		

Policy Year	(9) Resulting Reserves: Benefit & Maintenance Reserve	(10) Resulting Reserves: Commission DAC	(11) Present Values: Gross Premiums	(12) Present Values: Benefit & Maintenance Expenses	(13) Present Values: Commissions	(14) Maximum Present Value of Noncommission Acquisition Expense	(15) Maximum Noncommission DAC Terminal	(16) Maximum Noncommission DAC Mean
1	0.17	2.10	4.50	2.23	2.48		4.71	4.22
2	0.01	1.84	3.57	2.00	0.18		4.13	3.76
3	0.22	1.33	3.58	1.77	0.18		2.99	2.75
4	0.24	0.72	3.01	1.60	0.15		1.61	1.49
5	(0.00)	0.00	2.57	1.46	0.13		0.00	0.00
Total			17.22	9.06	3.11	5.05		
As % of Present Value of Gross Premiums				52.6%	18.1%	29.3%		

Legend:

(1), (2), (3) Given

(4) Annuity based on (1), (2), & (3)

(5) Given

(6) $= (4)_t \times (5)_t$

(7), (8) Given

(9) $= [(9)_{t-1} + 52.6\% \times (5)_t - (12)_t / (4)_t] \times (4)_t / (4)_{t+1}$

(10) $= [(10)_{t-1} - 18.1\% \times (5)_t + (13)_t / (4)_t] \times (4)_t / (4)_{t+1}$

(11) $= (4)_t \times (5)_t$

(12) $= (4)_t \times [(2)_t / (1 + (1)_t)^{0.5} + (8)_t]$

(13) $= (4)_t \times (7)_t \times (5)_t$

(14) This is the initial amount of maxiumum (DAC)
29.3% = 100% – 52.6% – 18.1%
Similarly, 5.05 = 17.22 – 9.06 – 3.11, present values from (6), (12) & (13)

(15) $= [(15)_{t-1} + 5.05$ (year one only) $- 29.3\% \times (5)_t] \times (4)_t / (4)_{t+1}$

(16) $= 0.5 \times [(15)_{t-1} + 5.05$ (year one only) $- 29.3\% (5)_t + (15)_t]$

(3) The product of the maximum deferrable amount times the units inforce will determine the maximum permissible category (b) expenses for the block studied. Table 3-8 demonstrates this process.

(4) The company's accounting department then provides the actual deferrable acquisition expenses.

(5) The ratio of actual deferrable acquisition expenses (item 4) to maximum deferrable acquisition expenses (item 3) is called the apportionment ratio, which is the ratio to be applied to the results from the unadjusted DAC. This ratio should not exceed 1.000, because that would cause overcapitalization, or recoverability problems.

Thus, this approach provides a built-in recoverability "ceiling" in the allowable DAC. In summary, Table 3-8 develops the factor to scale down from the theoretical maximum DAC to the DAC that reflects actual acquisition expenses incurred.

Table 3-8
Calculation of Current Period Apportionment Ratio for *SFAS 60* Term Products

(1) Plan of Insurance	(2) Face Amount Issued	(3) Maximum Cost Incurrable at Issue	(4) Maximum Noncommission Acquisition Expense	(5) Actual Noncommission Acquisition Expenses Incurred	(6) Apportionment Ratio
5-year term	500	5.05	$2,524		
7-year term	8,000	6.10	48,800		
10-year term	300	3.85	1,155		
12-year term	3,500	10.85	37,975		
15-year term	4,500	2.12	9,546		
Total	16,800		$100,000	$70,000	70%

$100,000 represents the maximum capitalizable noncommission expense to the line of business. This is referred to in the text as "maximum permissible operating deferrable acquisition expenses."

Legend:
(2) From new business report
(3) From Table 3-7, column (14) for 5-year term;
other plans of insurance would use similar calculation.
(4) = (2) × (3)
(5) From accounting department costs study
(6) = (5) / (4)

Table 3-9 illustrates the application of the apportionment ratio (calculated in Table 3-8) to the maximum DAC.

Table 3-9
Development of Noncommission DAC Using Apportionment Ratio for *SFAS 60* Term Products

(1) Plan	(2) Units In Force	(3) Mean Maximum DAC	(4) Unadjusted DAC	(5) Apportionment Ratio	(6) Final DAC
5-year term	450	4.22	$1,899.00		
7-year term	7,700	5.80	44,660.00		
10-year term	280	3.70	1,036.00		
12-year term	3,250	10.05	32,662.50		
15-year term	4,200	1.87	7,854.00		
Total for Issue Year	15,880		$88,111.50	70.00%	$61,678.05

Legend:
(2) From in force report
(3) From Table 3-7, column 16 for 5-year term
(4) = (2) × (3)
(5) From Table 3-8, column 6
(6) = (4) × (5)

The apportionment ratio in this example is applied to the entire in force. A company may want to refine this and have different ratios for different blocks of business.

One variation of this approach would be to establish DAC formulas using a constant number, such as $100 per policy issue cost. The company would then calculate and apply a ratio to the results that cause the actual deferrable amounts to be replicated. After this block is closed off for that issue year, the ratio would never change for that block. This variation allows for a more rapid calculation of initial DAC, but lacks the built-in recoverability ceiling of the approach described above.

3.7.2 Commission Timing

The timing of commission capitalization in the DAC must be consistent with recognition of commissions as a cost in the income statement.

For policies with a due premium, a commission would have been payable had the premium actually been paid. Thus, a liability is established for the cost of collecting this unpaid premium, as well as an asset established for due premium itself.

For policies using actuarial formulas to establish a DAC, there is generally a premium timing assumption inherent in the formula. If the formula presumes an annual premium (generally found in mean reserve formulas), it generally includes an annual commission. If non-annual premiums are paid, the resulting reserve formula overstates what has actually been incurred. Thus, a cost of collection liability is established based on the amount of gross deferred premiums.

If the actuarial mid-year reserve formula presumes no premium timing assumption (generally, a mid-terminal reserve), then an unearned premium is established. However, the commission for that premium has already been incurred. The amount of the commission correlating to the premium yet to be earned is reestablished as an asset. This is often called the equity in the unearned premium and is part of the total DAC.

For worksheet approaches, commissions are generally input directly from a general ledger into the worksheet. The actuary must be aware that first-year commissions on issues in a prior period will be part of the current total of first-year commissions. Thus, the worksheet, when established for the current-period issues, might contain some commissions attributable to prior-period issues. In general, as long as there is not a considerable increase or decrease in new business, this is not a significant concern.

3.7.3 Anticipation of Future Deferrable Expenses

Future deferrable expenses, such as heaped renewal commissions, must be anticipated and estimated in the DAC amortization calculation from the issue date forward. The DAC should be calculated with consideration for both past deferrable expenses and future deferrable expenses. One way of understanding this is to perceive the DAC as a loan balance. Such a loan balance increases as deferrable expenses are incurred and is paid off by a level percentage of revenues (such revenues being premiums under *SFAS 60*, estimated gross profits under *SFAS 97*, and estimated gross margins under *SFAS 120*). That level percentage of revenues will not be correct from the outset if all future "increments to the loan balance" are not counted. If all future deferrable expenses are not considered from the outset, the expense amortization premium (i.e., that level percentage of revenues) will be incorrectly calculated and will not provide for future deferrable expenses.

The amortization method used should anticipate and reflect deferrable expenses in the future, not only for creating an accurate DAC but also for demonstrating recoverability, for performing loss recognition testing and to facilitate the proper timing of profits.

Table 3-10 illustrates that only when such future deferrable expenses are properly anticipated in the calculations will profits be level as a percentage of the appropriate revenue. This table assumes experience emerges as expected.

This illustration is based on *SFAS 97* as applied to universal life insurance, which is addressed in Chapter 6. In addition, part 1 of Table 3-10 makes the example more mathematically elegant by substituting the earned rate for the discount rate. This enables the reader to better test profit emergence and recoverability. This substitution also causes GAAP earnings to emerge as a level percentage of the estimated gross profits, as illustrated in Column 10.

Table 3-10

***SFAS 97* Illustration of the Inclusion of Future Deferrable Expenses**

This is a demonstration and reinforcement that both historical and prospective deferrable expenses need to be included in the calculation of DPAC.

Assumes experience emerges exactly as expected, and future deferrable expenses are taken into consideration in the current DPAC.

20-year amortization period,
Valuation Date December 31, 2002

Part 1: Discount rate equals earned interest rate.
Discount Rate [i(d)]: 7.50%
Earned Interest Rate [i(e)]: 7.50%

Part 2: Discount rate equals credited rate.
Discount Rate: 6.00%
Earned Interest Rate: 7.50%

	(1)	(2)	(3)	(4)	(5)	(6)	(7)	(8)	(9)	(10)	(11)	(12)
			Present Values					Present Values				
Calendar Year	Expected Gross Profit (EGP)	Acquisition Costs	Gross Profit	Acquis. Costs	DAC	Net Profit	As % of EGP	Gross Profit	Acquis. Costs	DAC	Net Profit	As % of EGP
2000	300	1,100	289.35	1,100.00	927.17	86.66	28.887%	291.39	1,100.00	928.44	87.93	29.311%
2001	500	600	448.60	558.14	1263.23	144.44	28.887%	458.15	566.04	1261.74	141.58	28.316%
2002	600	200	500.76	173.07	1138.66	173.32	28.887%	518.66	178.00	1135.20	171.46	28.576%
2003	546	182	423.90	146.50	1024.49	157.72	28.887%	445.27	152.81	1019.26	156.22	28.612%
2004	497	166	358.84	124.02	919.71	143.53	28.887%	382.26	131.19	912.93	142.37	28.654%
2005	452	151	303.76	104.98	823.43	130.61	28.887%	328.17	112.62	815.30	129.77	28.702%
2006	411	137	257.14	88.87	734.79	118.86	28.887%	281.73	96.69	725.52	118.33	28.758%
2007	374	125	217.67	75.23	653.04	108.16	28.887%	241.86	83.00	642.84	107.92	28.824%
2008	341	114	184.26	63.68	577.48	98.43	28.887%	207.63	71.26	566.56	98.47	28.901%
2009	310	103	155.98	53.91	507.46	89.57	28.887%	178.25	61.17	496.03	89.88	28.990%
2010	282	94	132.04	45.63	442.39	81.51	28.887%	153.03	52.52	430.69	82.09	29.094%
2011	257	86	111.77	38.63	381.72	74.17	28.887%	131.37	45.09	369.98	75.01	29.215%
2012	234	78	94.61	32.70	324.94	67.50	28.887%	112.78	38.71	313.42	68.59	29.355%
2013	213	71	80.09	27.68	271.59	61.42	28.887%	96.82	33.23	260.55	62.76	29.520%
2014	193	64	67.80	23.43	221.24	55.89	28.887%	83.12	28.53	210.96	57.49	29.711%
2015	176	59	57.39	19.84	173.48	50.86	28.887%	71.36	24.49	164.27	52.70	29.933%
2016	160	53	48.58	16.79	127.92	46.28	28.887%	61.26	21.02	120.11	48.38	30.193%
2017	146	49	41.13	14.21	84.22	42.12	28.887%	52.59	18.05	78.17	44.46	30.495%
2018	133	44	34.81	12.03	42.04	38.33	28.887%	45.15	15.49	38.14	40.93	30.847%
2019	121	40	29.47	10.19	1.06	34.88	28.887%	38.76	13.30	-0.28	37.74	31.257%
2020	55	37	12.49	8.62	0.00	15.89	28.887%	16.66	11.42	0.00	17.32	31.497%
Total			3,850.43	2,738.14				4,196.28	2,854.62			
Amortization %			3A	71.113%				8A	68.027%			
Complement			3B	28.887%				8B	31.973%			

Legend:

(1) Given

(2) Given

(3) $= (1)_t \,/\, ((1 + i(d))^{t-0.6}$

(4) $= (2)_t \,/\, ((1 + i(d))^{t-0.5}$

(5) $(5)_1 = (2)_1 \times ((1 + i(d))^{0.5} - (3A) \times (1)_1$ $\quad (5)_t = [(5)_{t-1} \times (1 + i(d))] + (2)_t \times ((1 + i(d))^{0.5} - (3A) \times (1)_t$

(6) $(6)_1 = (1)_1 - (2)_1 \times ((1 + i(e))^{0.5} + (5)_1$ $\quad (6)_t = (1)_t - (2)_t \times ((1 + i(e))^{0.5} - [(5)_{t-1} \times (1 + i(e))] + (5)_t$

(7) $= (6)_t \,/\, (1)_t$

(8) $= (1)_t \,/\, ((1 + i(d))^{t-0.6}$

(9) $= (2)_t \,/\, ((1 + i(d))^{t-0.5}$

(10) $(10)_1 = (2)_1 \times ((1 + i(d))^{0.5} - (8A) \times (1)_1$ $\quad (10)_t = [(10)_{t-1} \times (1 + i(d))] + (2)_t \times ((1 + i(d))^{0.5} - (8A) \times (1)_t$

(11) $(11)_1 = (1)_1 - (2)_1 \times ((1 + i(e))^{0.5} + (10)_1$ $\quad (11)_t = (1)_t - (2)_t \times ((1 + i(e))^{0.5} - [(10)_{t-1} \times (1 + i(e))] + (10)_t$

(12) $= (11)_t \,/\, (1)_t$

3.8 Recoverability Testing and Loss Recognition

This section discusses recoverability testing, which is the process of establishing that amounts initially capitalized can be supported by future revenues. This section also addresses the fundamentals of loss recognition, which is the process of establishing the amount of DAC that has future utility and thus can be carried on the balance sheet.

3.8.1 Authority and Definitions

Paragraphs 32 through 37 of *SFAS 60* constitute a section entitled "premium deficiency." This section requires that, for a line of business for which future revenue is insufficient to provide for the future payment of benefits and expenses, the company needs to decrease the DAC asset and, if necessary, establish a liability for this deficiency. Financial reporting actuaries frequently use the terms "recoverability" and "loss recognition" when assessing "premium deficiency."

These two terms are discussed in the *Audit and Accounting Guide, Life and Health Entities*. Paragraph 10.39 speaks to the deferrability of an acquisition cost depending on its "recoverability." Paragraph 10.15 specifies, "The identification of acquisition costs requires considerable judgment; in making these judgments, due consideration should be given to the concepts of consistency, and recoverability." Paragraphs 10.42 through 10.48 speak to "loss recognition," the situation in which accumulated reserves together with future gross premiums will not be sufficient to cover future benefits and expenses and to also recover the unamortized DAC asset.

Recoverability testing determines whether an expense classifiable as an acquisition cost is deferrable from an economic perspective. It analyzes whether current-year issues are profitable from a GAAP perspective. Stated differently, it ascertains, as of the issue date, whether the present value of gross premiums equals or exceeds the present value of benefits, direct maintenance costs, and expenses classified as DAC. This is a more liberal test than that of pricing-basis profitability, because the latter basis includes overhead and nondeferrable acquisition expenses. For *SFAS 60* products, the initial recoverability testing will likely retain the provisions for adverse deviation in the study. Should costs appear not recoverable, the actuary may remove the margins to then re-test for recoverability.

The *Audit and Accounting Guide* specifies that recoverability testing be performed for policies issued in a given year:

> Recoverability tests are generally defined as profitability tests of a group of insurance contracts issued in a given year. Recoverability tests are performed only in the year of issue; thereafter, the year's issues may be merged with all other similar inforce contracts. (Paragraph 10.38)

Loss recognition tests for the existence of a probable loss on an entire line of business. Loss recognition can be viewed as prospective recoverability testing on an entire block of existing business. The actuary uses current best-estimate assumptions to determine if the net liability position (all liabilities less DAC) equals or exceeds the minimum liability requirement. This minimum requirement is arrived at via a gross premium valuation, which equals the present value of all remaining benefits and expenses less the present value of all remaining gross premiums, using current best-estimate assumptions.

There is no particular frequency with which loss recognition testing must be performed on an existing block. It is performed whenever the actuary suspects that a probable loss exists because of a change in experience.

3.8.2 Level of Aggregation for Testing

To define "probable loss," it is necessary to define the level of aggregation at which the future gains and losses are to be calculated. *SFAS 60* specifies:

> Contracts shall be grouped consistent with the enterprise's manner of acquiring, servicing, and measuring the profitability of its insurance contracts ...
> (Paragraph 32)

As indicated earlier, *SFAS 60* forms the general set of GAAP guidance for all contracts for which the other standards do not conflict with it. As a result, the above cited paragraph is applicable to all insurance contracts. The concept of consistency suggests that once the groupings are defined, these classifications are maintained.

The term "line of business" is frequently used to describe the contract groupings mentioned in paragraph 32.

Both recoverability testing and loss recognition testing are performed at an aggregate level for an entire line of business. Recoverability testing applies to a block of such business issued during the accounting period; loss recognition applies to the entire block of such business in force. Deficiencies in some contracts are offset by sufficiencies in other contracts; there is no requirement that every policy or cell within a line of business be recoverable on its own.

A company may certainly choose to perform recoverability testing at the plan level or at an even smaller grouping level. However, the lower the level of aggregation of testing, the more conservative the test, because there is less opportunity to offset nonrecoverable components with profitable components. Recoverability testing performed at the plan code or smaller level is useful, however, in helping to reveal the relative profitability of products currently being sold.

Paragraph 32 provides guidance for grouping contracts for loss recognition testing and recoverability testing. The following paragraphs provide a viewpoint and interpretations of the words used in that guidance.

"Manner of acquiring" suggests separating direct marketing business from agency-produced business. "Manner of acquiring" might imply a separation of a purchased block of business from the business sold by the company after the purchase. Group life and group health insurance would typically be combined; credit life and credit health insurance would typically be combined.

"Manner of servicing" would generally follow the "manner of acquiring" splits. Some practitioners view servicing as inseparable from acquiring. For example, if direct marketing is administered with agency business, or purchased business is administered with other business, some view that these blocks can be combined for loss recognition or recoverability purposes.

"Manner of measurement of profitability" would generally split blocks of business based on the guidance under which different contracts fall. This suggests a *SFAS 60* block would be tested independently from a *SFAS 97* block. However, some practitioners argue that if universal life can be administered with traditional life, the two could be combined for loss recognition and recoverability testing.

A contract whose applicable guidance changes (for example, a universal life-type contract that annuitizes) moves from the original line of business to the new line at such time for purposes of recoverability testing and loss recognition testing.

3.8.3 Gross Premium Valuation Test and the Order of Adjustments to the Balance Sheet

As *SFAS 60* indicates, "A probable loss ... exists if there is a premium deficiency relating to short-term or long-term contracts." The test compares a gross premium valuation (using current, best-estimate assumptions) with the GAAP net liabilities in the line of business. If the GAAP net liabilities are less than the gross premium valuation, a probable loss exists, and the premium deficiency at the valuation date is equal to the difference.

The gross premium reserve, as defined by *ASOP 22*, is

> The actuarial value of an insurance or annuity contract, calculated using best-estimate assumptions, of future cash flow disbursements minus future cash flow receipts. (Paragraph 2.5)

The gross premium valuation includes no assumption for federal income tax. Under GAAP, both benefit reserves and the DAC are established under pre-income-tax concepts. Taxes are provided for by *SFAS 109*, which provides the guidance for current and deferred tax provisions. This is addressed in detail in Chapter 18. Thus, the gross premium reserve tests done to support recoverability and loss recognition are performed on a pre-tax basis.

The recoverability and loss recognition guidance provided in *SFAS 60* applies to *SFAS 97* and *SFAS 120* contracts as well. *SFAS 91* contracts have different guidance.

When the recoverability test results in a premium deficiency, the order of adjustment for *SFAS 60*, *SFAS 97*, and *SFAS 120* products is as follows:

- If the block of business is an *SFAS 60* block, sufficient margins for deviation should be removed so that the premium deficiency is eliminated. *SFAS 97* and *SFAS 120* DAC assumptions do not have margins for adverse deviation, so this step would not be taken for products governed by those standards.

- If all such margins have been eliminated but a premium deficiency reserve still exists, acquisition expenses should be recategorized from deferrable to nondeferrable such that remaining deferrable costs are recoverable.

- Should any premium deficiency yet remain, a premium deficiency reserve is established such that the final net GAAP liability equals the gross premium reserve.

If a loss recognition test results in a premium deficiency, then the appropriate order of adjustment is similar to the above, that is:

- If the block of business is an *SFAS 60* block, sufficient margins for deviation must be removed to eliminate the premium deficiency. Because *SFAS 97* and *SFAS 120* contracts do not utilize margins for adverse deviation, this step does not apply to products governed by those standards.

- Once all such margins have been eliminated, the existing DAC asset is reduced to the point necessary to eliminate the balance of the premium deficiency.

- Should the DAC be entirely written down but a premium deficiency condition still exist, a premium deficiency reserve is established such that the final net GAAP liability equals the gross premium reserve.

In a loss recognition situation, assets are not decreased (nor liabilities increased) beyond the break-even point. Doing so would likely create positive earnings in the future, effectively overcorrecting for the future losses in the absence of this adjustment. For the same reason, the gross premium valuation for loss recognition testing is calculated without provisions for adverse deviation so that if future experience emerges as estimated, positive earnings would not have been created.

However, for *SFAS 60* products, should only some of the provision for adverse experience be removed, some future positive income would emerge if those best estimate assumptions were met. This would be through the release from risk of the remaining margins.

Once *SFAS 60* loss recognition has occurred and DAC has been reduced, the revised assumptions remain in place. At future valuation dates, even if emerging experience has proved more favorable, the premium deficiency reserve is not lowered nor is capitalization restored to the balance sheet.

Once probable losses are apparent and margins have been reduced or removed, such testing must continue to be performed at future valuation dates, inasmuch as further deteriorating experience will necessitate further adjustment. The exception is if experience later improves, thereby giving the actuary more cushion on the net GAAP liability compared to the gross premium reserve and, as a result, requiring less rigorous loss recognition testing. However, loss recognition testing must still be considered.

Many companies have approximated the future lifetime of policies as either 20 or 30 years after issue. While benefit reserves remain fully funded for the lifetime of the policy, the DAC is amortized to zero at this terminal duration. This approximation is not uncommon in worksheets and approaches supporting *SFAS 97* and *SFAS 120* products.

If a loss recognition or recoverability study is performed for policies whose DAC amortization is completed by 20 or 30 years, general practice permits the actuary to look at revenue from all future years on all policies, even those approaching (or already beyond) the end of the amortization period. This is because the actuary must use a best estimate of all future events at the time of the study.

Loss recognition and recoverability for *SFAS 91* contracts are addressed in AICPA *Practice Bulletin 8*, Questions 14 and 15. No margins for conservatism are permitted. Further, should recoverability or loss recognition mandate the removal of the DAC asset, a liability similar to a premium deficiency reserve above and beyond the contract value is not permitted.

3.8.4 Exclusion of Interest on Surplus from the Testing

An often-raised issue is whether interest on surplus (that is, interest on prior profits) plays a role in recoverability testing and loss recognition testing. Inspection of the components of a gross premium reserve (GPV) indicates that investment income on surplus is not used in recoverability or loss recognition testing.

The GPV is equal to the net GAAP liability minus the present value of future GAAP book profits if the discount rate used in the GPV calculation equals the earned interest rate. Book profits include interest on reserves but do not include interest on any retained surplus. Thus, using interest on surplus, either current or future, is precluded. This is demonstrated as follows:

Definitions:

BP_t	=	Book profit, year t
$PVFBP_t$	=	Present value of all future book profits as of year t
CF_t	=	Cash flows, year t, (premiums less benefits less expenses; investment income is not considered a cash flow for this purpose)
NGL_t	=	Net GAAP liability (the sum of all liabilities held less the sum of all associated actuarial assets (DAC)
i	=	Best estimate of current and future earned interest rates on invested assets, and $v = 1 / (1 + i)$
GPV_t	=	Gross premium valuation reserve, end of year t
n	=	Final year of coverage

$$BP_t = \left(NGL_{t-1}\right) \times (1+i) + CF_t - NGL_t$$

$$GPV_t = -\sum_{S=t+1}^{n} v^{s-t} \times CF_s$$

$$PVFBP_t = \sum_{S=t+1}^{n} v^{s-t} \times \left[\left(NGLs_1\right) \times (1+i) + CF_s - NGL_s\right]$$

$$= \sum_{S=t+1}^{n} v^{s-t} \times CF_s + \sum_{S=t+1}^{n} v^{s-t} \times \left[\left(NGL_{s-1}\right) \times (1+i) - NGL_s\right]$$

$$= \sum_{S=t+1}^{n} v^{s-t} \times CF_s + NGL_t$$

$$= NGL_t - GPV_t$$

Thus, $GPV_t = NGL_t - PVFBP_t$

In practice, the interest rate used for GPV has generally been level. However, a graded rate can be used if that is the actuary's best estimate. Also, the time horizon above is indicated by the year n. Frequently the GPV is performed until the end of time because all sources of revenue will need to be considered.

The actuary should consider the pattern of future GAAP book profits. If $PVFBP_t$ is positive but includes both positive and negative values of BP_t, there may be a time in the future when $PVFBP_t$ will be negative. If such is the case, then a liability should be established to provide for such future losses. It is appropriate to establish that liability over the period of future profits prior to the time such losses are expected to occur.

The fact that the GAAP book profit concept does not include interest on beginning-of-period surplus gives rise to the phenomenon that, when an interest-related investment gain occurs in a period of falling interest rates, the resulting transfer of assets into surplus may trigger loss recognition. U.S. statutory accounting provides for this phenomenon via the capitalization of such gains, tax-effected, into a liability (interest maintenance reserve) and amortization of that liability over the years after the sale until the instrument would otherwise have matured. No such liability exists under U.S. GAAP. Therefore the sale of an asset at its increased market value, theoretically an economically neutral action, could have a significant effect on the income statement.

A similar accounting loss can occur in a purchase situation (see Chapter 15), where assets must be marked to market at the purchase date. In a period of falling interest rates, a purchase can result in a need for loss recognition, inasmuch as a portion of the assets supporting the liabilities are in effect moved into surplus and thus cannot support the product line. For *SFAS 60* contracts, this problem can be ameliorated by an increase in the benefit reserve because of the decreased valuation interest rate, but under *SFAS 97*, where the benefit reserve is equal to the account value, no such amelioration occurs.

3.9 Relation of GAAP Expense Assumptions to Pricing Expense Assumptions

When establishing GAAP assumptions for a new product, the valuation actuary may turn to pricing assumptions to view the product's profitability. The same line of business and category expense analysis may serve as a source for baseline expense assumptions for both pricing and GAAP. If different expense analyses are used, an inconsistent allocation may make some products appear unrecoverable and others unduly profitable.

The pricing process can involve a different classification along line and category for several reasons: First, actual risk selection expenses vary significantly by issue age, by insurance amount, and by underwriting rigor. Guaranteed-issue policies and term conversions generally have little selection cost. A fully underwritten, high face amount policy issued to a 62-year-old in which the insurer has multiple risk classifications, on the other hand, would have a very high cost. The process of starting from a relatively simple line and category analysis and allocating it into such classifications is complex. Most actuaries are satisfied, for reporting under GAAP, if the weighted average of unit costs among the classifications is approximately equal to the aggregate unit cost from the simpler line and category analysis.

Another source of variation between pricing and valuation expense assumptions is the allocation of costs between base policies, supplemental benefits and life insurance riders. There are incremental expenses that are attributable to such benefits and riders. The line and category analysis should permit an accurate assessment of those costs.

With non-level-premium plans and certain other plans, the appropriate expense assumption also can vary by duration. One example is term insurance. For example, a company can have plans with varying level premium periods, such as 5, 10, 15, or 20 years, followed by an ultimate attained age rating structure. Another common term insurance example is n-year renewable term, a step-rated plan where the plan enters a new level premium period every n years. If these premiums increase significantly, the company is likely to experience two phenomena. First, a large portion of policyholders may terminate, creating significant additional policy service-handling costs. The actuary should be aware of the significant activity at the end of the 5th, 10th, 15th, etc., years. A second event may be a service campaign to retain policyholders. Again, the actuary should realize that this surge of activity corresponds only to certain durations.

The assignment of new plan codes for renewals or re-entries can cause additional concerns. If the company's administrative system assigns a new plan code, it usually assigns a new issue age and issue date to the policyholder. The actuary must match expense (as well as all other) assumptions appropriately with the plan code, issue age, and duration assignments of the administrative systems.

3.10 Special Expense Issues

3.10.1 Internal Replacements

A company's new product may be more attractive than an existing product; this can cause significant turnover from the old product to the new one.

An argument could be made that this turnover is a continuation of coverage rather than a surrender and new issue. The cost of such internal replacements is generally significantly less than the cost of issuing a new policy. *SFAS 97* stipulates:

> When surrender of a life insurance contract is associated with an internal replacement by a universal life-type contract, unamortized acquisition costs associated with the replaced contract and any difference between the cash surrender value and the previously recorded liability shall not be deferred in connection with the replacement contract. (Paragraph 26)

The standard defines the book loss with respect to the replaced contract as the algebraic sum of the DAC asset immediately prior to surrender and the excess of the cash surrender value over the benefit reserve on the replaced contract.

The conclusion of paragraph 26 is that this amount should not be carried over as a DAC asset on the new contract. The rationale used by the FASB is one of consistency with treatment of extinguishment of debt as discussed in *SFAS 97* paragraph 72.

Paragraph 26 was written during and in response to a significant revolution in insurance policy design in the United States during the 1980s. This era witnessed a large-scale replacement of traditional whole life and endowment plans by universal life plans.

AICPA *Practice Bulletin 8* further clarified this issue by indicating that paragraph 26 of *SFAS 97* was intended to apply only to the replacement of traditional insurance contracts by universal life-type contracts. However, it left unclear the treatment of remaining DAC balances on other types of replacements, stipulating:

> The accounting for other internal replacements should be based on the circumstances of the transaction.

Because this language is not precise, it opens the door for considering circumstances in which a stronger case for continuation of coverage can be made. If the measurement of profit continues under the same FASB standard, for example, from one *SFAS 97* product to another (instead of from a *SFAS 60* contract to a *SFAS 97* contract), perhaps sufficient circumstances exist for the carryover of the book loss on the old policy into the DAC on the new policy.

Whenever it is concluded that such carryover is appropriate, it is subject to the same recoverability testing as a company's deferrable acquisition cost category.

The reader should be aware that at the time of publication of this book there was a draft Statement of Position (SOP) on accounting for internal replacements. See Chapter 2 for a brief discussion of the accounting that would be required if this SOP becomes effective in its current draft form.

3.10.2 Reinsurance

Although reinsurance issues are addressed in depth in Chapter 17, several special reinsurance issues of capitalization are discussed in this chapter. Recoverability testing and loss recognition testing apply to the concepts discussed below. Recoverability testing and loss recognition testing on a block that is reinsured should be performed on a net retained basis.

Paragraph 39 of *SFAS 60* (which has been incorporated into paragraph 18 of *SFAS 113*) states that coinsurance allowances are treated as a negative amount to apply against the deferrable acquisition cost to obtain a net capitalized position. Conversely, the assuming party would treat the coinsurance allowances similarly to its other deferrable acquisition costs. The amount of the negative deferral is a function of the pattern of coinsurance allowances by policy duration.

Paragraph 39 also indicates that if the assuming company agrees to provide services (such as underwriting) on a class of contracts under a treaty "without reasonable compensation," then the present value of such excess future servicing costs is to be added to the deferrable acquisition cost of the assuming company to obtain the capitalizable amount.

The timing of DAC establishment and amortization may differ between the direct block and the reinsured block. Many reinsurance contracts for traditional life insurance remit premiums and credit expense allowances annually, regardless of the policyholder's true mode. Thus, for a newly issued policy on monthly mode, the direct DAC might contain only one month's commission, while the offsetting DAC on the ceded component might contain an entire annual expense allowance.

In the late 1990s, reinsurers started playing a more significant role in the support of term insurance in the United States. U.S. reinsurers would cede business to offshore affiliates, where local statutory reserving requirements were significantly less than the direct writers' requirements.

The direct writer could take credit for the full amount of its reserve ceded only if the offshore reinsurer could provide a letter of credit for the difference between the U.S reserve requirements and the reserves held on the assuming company's statutory balance sheet. In order to maintain this business, the assuming company would need to anticipate making payments for the costs of the letters of credit for the foreseeable future.

Paragraph 26 of *SFAS 60* sates that "Expense assumptions used in estimating the liability for future policy benefits shall be based on estimates of expected nonlevel costs." Thus, it is appropriate that costs to maintain such letters of credit be considered in the development of liabilities. Further, it appears that these costs, as they relate to actual experience, are appropriate for consideration in premium deficiency (loss recognition) testing as discussed in paragraph 35 of *SFAS 60*.

3.10.3 Purchase Accounting

Depending on a company's judgment, pre-purchase versus post-purchase portfolios can merit an additional dimension in the line of business and category expense analysis. This is especially true when the purchased company takes a different marketing direction from its pre-purchase years.

The purchased company generally has established an asset represented by the present value of future profits on its books (commonly called Value of Business Acquired, or VOBA). The future profits may be lowered in anticipation of paying all commissions in the future. These commissions will include first year commissions on business still in its first policy year, as well as heaped renewal commissions in later policy years. Such expenses, as cash outflows, should all be considered in the formula that defines the VOBA. Additionally, as such future first year deferred commissions and heaped renewal commissions are incurred after purchase, they should be deferred, notwithstanding the fact that they relate to pre-purchase business. The amortization pattern of such deferred commissions should follow the amortization pattern for the VOBA.

As an example, assume that a purchase occurred on January 1, 2000, and that a policy had been issued on December 1, 1999 with monthly premium frequency. Future first year commissions will continue to be paid on this policy for 11 months beyond the date of purchase. The actuary would capitalize these excess commissions as DAC.

With such treatment of capitalization and assuming that actual experience follows initial assumptions at purchase, future profits will be level as a percentage of the future revenue base (premiums in the case of *SFAS 60*, expected gross profits for *SFAS 97* and expected gross margins in the case of *SFAS 120*).

FASB *EITF 95-3* discusses the allocation of expenses to the purchase price.

For a detailed discussion of accounting for business combinations, refer to Chapter 15.

3.10.4 Discontinued Operations

AICPA *APB Opinion No. 30* (*APB 30*) deals with the effects of disposal of a segment of business. As paragraph 5 of this opinion indicates, some accountants believe that income statements are "more useful if the effects of events or transactions that occur infrequently are segregated from the results of the continuing, ordinary, and typical operations of an entity." The definition of "discontinued operation" includes a segment of the business that, even if still operating, is the subject of a formal plan for disposal. The measurement date for such disposal is the date on which management commits itself to a formal, official plan to dispose of a segment of business, whether by sale or by abandonment. This is a relatively rare event in the life insurance industry. The scope of discontinuance in a life insurance company environment would include a formal plan to close off the pursuit of new business in a line of business and simply maintain the existing block as it matures.

Once such a measurement date has occurred, then the financial results of continuing operations must be segregated from the financial results of each discontinued operation. This could result in certain complex expense allocation issues between lines of business, although *APB 30* stipulates:

> The fact that the results of operations of the segment being sold or abandoned cannot be separately identified strongly suggests that the transaction should not be classified as the disposal of a segment of the business. (Paragraph 13)

Prior to the promulgation of *SFAS 144* discussed below in this section, it could be presumed that a line of business, as defined in *SFAS 60*, was a "segment of the business" as that term was used in *APB 30*. Thus those allocation issues should be rare under *APB 30*, and virtually nonexistent under *SFAS 144*.

Paragraph 15 of *APB 30* indicates that if a loss is expected from disposal, it must be provided for at the measurement date, giving consideration to any estimated costs and expenses directly associated with the disposal (for example, the runoff of the block of business for operations subject to a formal plan of disposal). However, it also stipulates that future expected gains should not be recognized at the measurement date but should flow through later financial statements. Paragraph 18 of *APB 30* indicates that the assets that support the block must also be identified.

The preceding discussion leads to these interpretations:

- The minimum requirement to provide for future losses at the measurement date is analogous to the required gross premium valuation for *SFAS 60*, *SFAS 97* and *SFAS 120* policies used in loss recognition.

- Identification of the asset classes may require a change in expense assumptions going forward, inasmuch as a dedicated, "walled-off" set of assets is the most likely approach to the disposal process under this APB in many circumstances.

- It is necessary to fully allocate to the discontinuing segment those direct expenses incurred in connection with the discontinuance. Such direct expenses include items such as severance pay, additional pension costs, employee relocation expenses, and the like. This is in addition to unlocking of assumptions such as persistency, mortality, and so on, for the expected results post-measurement date.

- For a block of business in a runoff mode, there will eventually come a point at which a going-concern approach to expenses will no longer be reasonable. Provision will have to be made at the measurement date for dealing with expenses and benefits in those later years. This would not necessarily apply to closed blocks of business that are not being disposed of and are viewed as part of a ongoing, larger line of business.

SFAS 144, entitled, "Accounting for the Impairment or Disposal of Long-Lived Assets", additionally extends the provisions of *APB 30. SFAS 144* retains *APB 30* to report discontinued operations separately from continuing operations, and extends that reporting to the component of an entity that has been disposed of by:

- Sale
- Abandonment
- Distribution to owners or
- Classified as held for sale.

Deferred policy acquisition costs are excluded from the scope of *SFAS 144*. Moreover, it is believed by at least one major accounting firm that the value of business acquired (VOBA) arising from a business combination is similar in nature to a deferred policy acquisition cost and therefore also beyond the scope of *SFAS 144*. Therefore, *SFAS 144* only merits a brief discussion in this chapter.

Two definitions within *SFAS 144* deserve mention.

- An "asset group," for impairment calculation purposes, is the lowest level at which cash flows can be identified that are independent of cash flows of other asset groups.

- A "component of an entity" is defined in *SFAS 144* as an element that "comprises operations and cash flows that can be clearly distinguished operationally and for financial reporting purposes, from the rest of the entity". It appears that the term "discontinuing segment" is virtually synonymous with "component of an entity."

An asset group is a subset of a "component of an entity." Thus, some asset groups can deserve impairment, while other asset groups do not. The "Component of an entity" needs to be distinguished in the reporting process.

3.11 Sales Inducements

Statement of Position 03-1 (the *SOP*) provided new authoritative guidance for certain enhancements to contracts under the scope of *SFAS 97*, with such enhancements referred to therein as "Sales Inducements." Many Sales Inducements tend to be incurred in the first policy year, and their cost is recognized as an expense in the same manner as deferrable acquisition expenses. However, since the recipient is the policyholder, such expense is technically not a deferrable acquisition expense. The *SOP* covers sales inducements on both investment contracts and universal life-type contracts referred to in *SFAS 97.*

Typical forms of enhancements have included the following:

- *Initial Bonus Interest.* These take the form of an excess interest rate in the first contract year or in the year following a deposit. Generally the former is linked with surrender charge schedules that run from contract dates, whereas the latter is linked with surrender charge schedules that run from deposit dates, in order to protect the company from losses due to early surrenders.

- *Day-One Bonuses.* These enhancements take the form of immediate increments to account values at issue date or at time of deposit. As with initial bonus interest, surrender charges are timed to protect the company from losses due to early surrenders.

- *Dollar-Cost Averaging (DCA) Bonuses.* This is a special form of initial bonus interest, in that, if the deposit monies are committed to a pour-in into a separate account over time, such as monthly over 12 months, in order to dollar-average the investments, a bonus interest rate is paid on those monies while they remain in the general account.

- *Persistency Bonuses.* These take many forms, such as retroactive excess interest, returns of loads, and returns of cost of insurance (COI) charges.

All the above enhancements are benefits above and beyond the normal, periodic operations of the contracts. According to *SOP* Paragraphs 36 and 37, such enhancements are subject to the following criteria in order to be considered "Sales Inducements" for purposes of establishing dedicated assets and liabilities under GAAP:

a. Amounts are incremental to amounts the enterprise credits on similar contracts without sales inducements

b. Amounts are higher than the contract's expected ongoing crediting rates for periods after the inducement, as applicable

c. Amounts are recognized in the liability for benefits over the period through which the contract remains in force.

Sales inducements can be classified into three types, according to *SOP* Paragraph A49:

Type (1) – Immediate

Type (1) sales inducements are credited in the first contract year, such as Day-1 Bonuses and Initial Bonus Interest.

Type (2) – Persistency

Type (2) sales inducements are credited at some later date, contingent on the contractholder satisfying certain conditions until that time, such as a minimum cumulative premium payment criterion.

Type (3) – Enhanced crediting rate

Type (3) sales inducements are periodic enhancements taking place over a period of greater than one year.

3.11.1 Background

Prior to the *SOP*, there was no definitive guidance on how to account for sales inducements. From a purely economic perspective, Type (1) sales inducements mirror acquisition costs in terms of cost to the company, with the only difference being the nature of the party to whom the payment or crediting is made (the contractholder, in the case of a sales inducement). Similarly, Type (2) sales inducements are in the economic nature of a renewal year commission to an agent, which also would be an acquisition cost that would be subject to the general deferment process attributable to acquisition expenses, were it not for the nature of the party to whom the payment or crediting is made. As such, many companies were treating such costs similarly to, or even identically to, deferrable acquisition costs. That is, capitalizing and amortizing Type (1) costs and spreading Type (2) costs over the lifetime of the respective contracts according to expected gross profits (EGPs). Type (3) costs, on the other hand, were typically treated as elements of EGPs.

The *SOP* clarified that sales inducements are not acquisition costs, inasmuch as they are paid to the contractholder and not to a third party, per *SOP* Paragraph A52. Paragraph A50 of the *SOP* stipulates:

> Asset accumulation products accounted for under *FASB Statement No. 97* as investment products or universal life-type contracts are viewed as financial instruments. The insurance enterprise has a contractual obligation to deliver cash and the customer has a contractual right to receive cash. Paragraph 15 of *FASB Statement No. 97* requires that investment contracts issued by an insurance enterprise be accounted for in a manner consistent with the accounting for interest-bearing instruments.

SOP Paragraph A51 similarly stipulates in pertinent part:

> AcSEC believes instruments issued by financial institutions should be accounted for consistently, as noted in *FASB Statement No. 97,* paragraph 39: "While many investment contracts are issued primarily by insurance enterprises, the Board believes that similar financial instruments should be accorded similar treatment regardless of the form of the issuing enterprise."

The strong inference is that a universal life-type contract is such a similar financial instrument.

3.11.2 Capitalization and Amortization of Sales Inducements

3.11.2.1 Treatment of Type (1) – Immediate Sales Inducements

Capitalization is generally appropriate, subject to the following three criteria under *SOP* Paragraph 37:

> Sales inducements that (a) are recognized as part of the liability under paragraph 36…(b) are explicitly identified in the contract at inception, and (c) meet the criteria

> in the **following sentence** should be deferred and amortized using the same methodology and assumptions used to amortize capitalized acquisition costs. *[Emphasis added]*

The "following sentence," referred to above, stipulates that:

> The insurance enterprise should demonstrate that such amounts are (a) incremental to amounts the enterprise credits on similar contracts without sales inducements and (b) higher than the contract's expected ongoing crediting rates for periods after the inducement, as applicable; that is, the crediting rate excluding the inducement should be consistent with assumptions used in estimated gross profits, contract illustrations, and interest-crediting strategies.

The Sales Inducement Asset (SIA) should be separately recognized and accounted for and should not be included with the deferred acquisition cost. The amortization calculation should be consistent with the approach used for amortization of deferred acquisition costs under *SFAS 97*. *SOP* Paragraph A51 stipulates that for deferred annuities treated as universal life-type contracts, amortization should take place only over the accumulation period, inasmuch as the annuitization period is a separate contract, as stipulated in *SFAS 97* Paragraph 7.

In the income statement, the amortization should be included in benefit expense, pursuant to *SOP* Paragraph 37.

3.11.2.2 Treatment of Type (2) – Persistency Sales Inducements

This type is more complex than simply capitalizing and amortizing using the EGPs as the revenue baseline, due to the rules imposed by the *SOP*. The initial liability that would result from an EGP-based approach used to levelize the cost of renewal year commissions, for example, is not permitted under the *SOP* for sales inducements. Specifically, for the sales inducement liability (SIL) in advance of the persistency bonus, the accrual of the liability needs to be made "ratably" as a component of the account balance over the vesting period. A lapse decrement assumption is prohibited, according to *SOP* Appendix D, Paragraph D19. It is presumed that a death decrement assumption is also prohibited.

Both the SIL accruals and the bonus crediting are considered capitalizations for establishment of an asset, assuming the criteria for treatment as a Sales Inducement are met. Thereafter, amortization of that asset should be under the same methodology and assumptions as amortization of deferred acquisition costs, i.e., using the EGP stream as the revenue baseline.

3.11.2.3 Treatment of Type (3) – Enhanced Crediting Rate Sales Inducements

Type (3) sales inducements can begin in either the first year or a later year. If the sales inducement begins in the first year, the treatment governing the establishment of SOP assets and liabilities generally reverts to the Type (1) treatment described above in 3.11.2.1.

If the Type (3) sales inducement begins in a later year, the rules for Type (2) would appear to be applicable. For certain Type (3) sales inducements, depending on their incidence, it may be more appropriate to not accrue a liability and simply to reflect the increased interest credits in the EGPs.

3.11.3 Transitional Rules

The *SOP* is effective for fiscal years beginning after December 15, 2003. Thus the first quarter of 2004 was generally the effective date for which an insurer must recognize SIAs and SILs on its balance sheet, with the commensurate GAAP earnings and "Other Comprehensive Income" effects.

The *SOP* is to be applied prospectively only:

- Sales inducements incurred from the effective date forward fall under the guidance of the *SOP*.

- For any SIAs or SILs previously established as of the effective date (typically as of December 31, 2003), using methodology in compliance with the *SOP*, the practice should be continued.

- For any SIAs or SILs previously established as of the effective date, using methodology *not* in compliance with the *SOP*, those assets and liabilities should be established as is, as of the effective date, but amortized henceforth according to the *SOP*.

- Where an SIA or SIL has not previously been established as of the effective date, any future adjustment is prohibited.

- If future EGPs need to be unlocked as of the effective date, due to the application of the *SOP* as a whole (i.e., with respect to guidance other than with respect to sales inducements), a current SIA or SIL as of the effective date may change in value as a result. Such change needs to be categorized as a change in accounting principle and accounted for subject to *APB Opinion No. 20* or *EITF Topic No. D-41*.

- In addition, if previously categorized as deferred acquisition costs, the aggregate asset or liability must be separated into deferred acquisition costs versus SIAs or SILs.

3.11.4 Interpretational Issues

Interpretational issues have arisen in the attempt to apply the above authoritative guidance. The American Academy of Actuaries "Practice Note on Anticipated Common Practices Relating to [*SOP 03-1*]" (April 2005), referred to below as the Practice Note, speaks to several of those issues in a Question and Answer (Q & A) format. A summary of those issues follows.

3.11.4.1 Scope

SFAS 120, titled "Accounting and Reporting by Mutual Life Insurance Enterprises and by Insurance Enterprises for Certain Long-Duration Participating Contracts," as interpreted by *SOP 95-1*, appears to be covered in the scope of *SOP 03-1*, inasmuch as that *SFAS 120* is an amendment to *SFAS 60* and *SFAS 97*. However, termination dividend accrual, which one might consider to be analogous to persistency bonuses, are accorded specific treatment under *SFAS 120*, as analogous to a standalone renewal commission spread in incidence over the life of the contract to the date of such termination dividend.

Any item needing to be valued under *SFAS 133* is not a sales inducement. Additionally, any item giving rise to an unearned revenue liability under *SFAS 97* is not a sales inducement. For example, the Practice Note stipulates:

> Some actuaries, therefore, believe that refund of COIs for a UL, together with similar benefits of full or partial refund of other contract expense charges or leads, would be treated as unearned revenue under *SFAS 97* and not as sales inducements under the *SOP*. Other actuaries believe that, since a refund of COIs or similar benefits meet the criteria outlined for sales inducements in the SOP, they would appropriately be treated as such. (Q.50)

3.11.4.2 Enhanced Crediting Rate as a Persistency Bonus for a Period of Years

The Practice Note (Q.51) indicates that this is a facts-and-circumstances issue. If the enhancement is sufficiently large, it should be treated as a persistency bonus. If not, the enhancement should be treated as a component of EGP.

3.11.4.3 Similar Contract Without a Sales Inducement

The Practice Note (Q.54) stipulates, "Some actuaries believe comparison with a similar product offered by the company but without the sales inducement is a sufficient but not a necessary condition. They might note paragraph A54 of the *SOP*, which states:

> ...in cases where a similar product is not actively marketed and sold without the enhanced crediting rate, AcSEC believes the enterprise should demonstrate that the enhanced crediting rate is incremental to the effective crediting rate.

3.11.4.4 Computation of Sales Inducement Liabilities

The *SOP* requires amounts accrued but not yet credited to be included in the account balance. Since account balances are not generally credited with persistency bonuses until vesting thereof has been accomplished, an incremental liability must be established and added to the account balances for balance sheet recognition and income statement recognition.

Appendix D, Paragraph D19, of the *SOP* indicates with no additional elaboration that such liability accrual should be performed "ratably," with no allowance for surrender decrements. Several options as to the contribution to the liability are included in the Practice Note, as follows:

- A level percentage of the account balance
- A level percentage of the "assessments" (COI charges, investment spreads, and expense charges)
- A level percentage of death benefits.

There remains the issue of how to apply those level contributions to converge toward the final amount to be credited. Several methodologies are suggested. One approach that will accomplish such convergence is below, where the level deposit to the liability is derived.

$PV(Bon)_t$ = Present value at time t of the bonus to be credited at time n;

$Liab_t$ = Liability at time t;

AV_t = Account value at time t;

$PV(AV)_t$ = $\sum_{s=t+1}^{n} (v^{n-s}) \times (AV_s)$

Deposit to the Liability, expressed as a percentage of the Account Value, equals:

$$[PV(Bon)_t - Liab_t] / PV(AV)_t$$

Table 3-11 below illustrates that, if the assumptions are realized, the deposit becomes a level percentage of account value.

Table 3-11
Level Percentage of Account Value

	(1)	(2)	(3)	(4)	(5)	(6)	(7)	(8)	(9)
			At Issue Date						
Policy Dur_t	Account Value (BOY)	Estimated Persistency Bonus	$PV(Bon)_t$	$PV(AV)_t$	Deposit% @ time t	$Liab_t$(BOY)	Deposit	Interest	$Liab_t$(EOY)
1	1,000.00		327.76	54,556.66	0.601%	0	6.01	0.27	6.28
2	2,000.00		342.51	55,966.71	0.601%	6.28	12.02	0.82	19.12
3	3,000.00		357.92	56,395.22	0.601%	19.12	18.02	1.67	38.81
4	4,200.00		374.03	55,798.00	0.601%	38.81	25.23	2.88	66.93
5	5,600.00		390.86	53,919.91	0.601%	66.93	33.64	4.53	105.09
6	7,000.00		408.45	50,494.31	0.601%	105.09	42.05	6.62	153.77
7	9,000.00		426.83	45,451.55	0.601%	153.77	54.07	9.35	217.19
8	11,000.00		446.03	38,091.87	0.601%	217.19	66.08	12.75	296.02
9	13,000.00	200.00	466.11	28,311.00	0.601%	296.02	78.10	16.84	190.96
10	16,000.00	300.00	287.08	16,000.00	0.601%	190.96	96.12	12.92	-

Legend:
(1) Given
(2) Given
(3) For t = 0 to 8, $(2)_9 \times (v^{9-t}) + (2)_{10} \times (v^{10-t})$
For t = 9, $(2)_{10} \times (v)$
(4) $[(4)_{t+1}] \times (v) + (1)_t$
(5) $[(3) - (6)] / (4)$
(6) $(9)_{t-1}$
(7) $(1) \times (5)$
(8) $[(6) + (7)] \times (4.50\%)$
(9) $(6) + (7) + (8)$

Interest Assumption 4.50%
$v = 1/(1+i)$ 0.956937799

Accruals of such liabilities need to be added to account values and on a combined basis will thus be contained in the reserves for future policy benefits (benefit reserves). Increments in this liability, and the crediting of the persistency bonuses themselves, are to be included in benefit payments.

At such duration where there are no more future persistency bonuses, the accrued liability drops to zero, which serves as an offset for the actual amount of sales inducement actually credited to the account value.

3.11.4.5 Computation of Sales Inducement Assets

Some policy enhancements do not qualify as sales inducements, because they do not meet the criteria above. Additionally, the *SOP* stipulates that, in order to be able to establish an SIA, the sales inducement must be explicitly defined in the contract at inception, and not merely granted to the contractholder as an enhancement after the issue date. Thus, while a liability may need to be established for such nonqualifying enhancements, an asset may not be permitted.

For persistency bonuses, if an SIA is permitted by virtue of meeting the definition of Sales Inducement, such asset is capitalized and amortized in the same manner as amortization of a deferred acquisition cost. The capitalization element is calculated equal to the following:

(i) The increase in the accrued liability, plus
(ii) The persistency bonus actually paid or credited, less
(iii) Interest on the prior period liability.

The EGPs over which the SIA is amortized exclude the above three items, just as capitalization of expenses is excluded from the EGPs. The persistency bonuses illustrated are assumed to be paid both to terminating policyholders and to persisting policyholders once they have passed a specified anniversary.

Tables 3-12 through 3-15 illustrate the calculation of the SIA, given a fact pattern of persistency bonuses payable in years 9 and 10, together with a policy lifetime of 10 years.

Table 3-12 shows the development of the surviving account value, year by year. Table 3-13 simply provides a check on the surviving account value remaining over that period by rolling the account value forward at interest, deposits, and account values released by withdrawals.

Table 3-12
Total Benefit Reserve

Investment Income Rate, i	6.25%	**Deferrable Acquisition Expense (DAE):**	380.00
$v = 1/(1+i)$	0.94118	**Maintenance expense:**	10.00
Credited Interest Rate	4.50%		
$v = 1/(1+i)$	0.95694		

	(1)	(2)	(3)	(4)	(5)	(6)	(7)	(8)	(9)	(10)	(11)
									Survived Values, EOY		
Policy Dur_t	Termination Rate	Survivorship to Beg Year	Premium Deposit(BOY)	Acct Value Beg. of Yr	Interest Credited	Persistency Bonus	AV EOY	Liab_t (post-bonus)	Acct Value	Liab_t	Benefit Res
1	2.00%	1.00000	1,000.00	1,000.00	45.00		1,045.00	6.28	1,024.10	6.15	1,030.25
2	3.00%	0.98000	955.00	2,000.00	90.00		2,090.00	19.12	1,986.75	18.17	2,004.93
3	3.50%	0.95060	910.00	3,000.00	135.00		3,135.00	38.81	2,875.83	35.60	2,911.43
4	3.50%	0.91733	1,065.00	4,200.00	189.00		4,389.00	66.93	3,885.24	59.24	3,944.49
5	3.50%	0.88522	1,211.00	5,600.00	252.00		5,852.00	105.09	4,999.01	89.78	5,088.79
6	3.50%	0.85424	1,148.00	7,000.00	315.00		7,315.00	153.77	6,030.06	126.76	6,156.81
7	3.50%	0.82434	1,685.00	9,000.00	405.00		9,405.00	217.19	7,481.58	172.77	7,654.35
8	3.50%	0.79549	1,595.00	11,000.00	495.00		11,495.00	296.02	8,824.10	227.24	9,051.35
9	3.50%	0.76765	1,505.00	13,000.00	585.00	200.00	13,785.00	190.96	10,211.65	141.46	10,353.10
10	100.00%	0.74078	2,215.00	16,000.00	720.00	300.00	17,020.00	-	-	-	-

Legend:
(1) Given
(2) $(2)_{t-1} \times (1-(1)_{t-1})$
(3) Given
(4) $(4)_1 = (3)_1$
For $t > 1$, $(4)_t = (7)_{t-1} + (3)_t$
(5) $(4) \times (4.5\%)$
(6) Given
(7) $(4) + (5) + (6)$
(8) From Table 3-11, col. (9)
(9) $(7) \times (2)_{t+1}$
(10) $(8) \times (2)_{t+1}$
(11) $(9) + (10)$

Table 3-13
Check of Survived Account Value Rollforward

Policy Dur$_t$	(1) Termination Rate	(2) Survivorship to Beg Year	(3) Premium Deposit(BOY)	(4) Acct Value Beg. of Yr	(5) Interest Credited	(6) Persistency Bonus	(7) AV Released	(8) Acct Value End of Yr
1	2.00%	1.00000	1,000.00	1,000.00	45.00		20.90	1,024.10
2	3.00%	0.98000	935.90	1,960.00	88.20		61.45	1,986.75
3	3.50%	0.95060	865.05	2,851.80	128.33		104.30	2,875.83
4	3.50%	0.91733	976.96	3,852.78	173.38		140.92	3,885.24
5	3.50%	0.88522	1,072.00	4,957.25	223.08		181.31	4,999.01
6	3.50%	0.85424	980.67	5,979.68	269.09		218.71	6,030.06
7	3.50%	0.82434	1,389.02	7,419.07	333.86		271.35	7,481.58
8	3.50%	0.79549	1,268.81	8,750.38	393.77		320.05	8,824.10
9	3.50%	0.76765	1,155.31	9,979.41	449.07	153.53	370.37	10,211.65
10	100.00%	0.74078	1,640.83	11,852.47	533.36	222.23	12,608.07	-

Legend:
(1) Given
(2) $(2)_{t-1} \times (1-(1)_{t-1})$
(3) (2) × [Table 3-12, col (3)]
(4) $(8)_{t-1} + (3)_t$
(5) (4) × (4.50%)
(6) (2) × [Table 3-12, col (6)]
(7) (1) × [(4) + (5) + (6)]
(8) (4) + (5) + (6) – (7)

Table 3-14 illustrates the calculation of the EGPs using the "gross cash flows" (i.e., cash flows excluding deferrable acquisition costs, persistency bonus liability accruals, and persistency bonus credits).

Table 3-14
Gross Profit (Cash Flows minus Change in Account Value)

Policy Dur$_t$	(1) Surrender Charge Scale	(2) Surr. Values Paid	(3) Investment Income	(4) Premium Income	(5) Change in Reserve	(6) Maintenance Expenses	(7) EGP
1	0.07	19.44	62.50	1,000.00	1,024.10	10.00	8.96
2	0.06	57.76	122.50	935.90	962.65	9.80	28.19
3	0.05	99.09	178.24	865.05	889.07	9.51	45.62
4	0.04	135.28	240.80	976.96	1,009.42	9.17	63.89
5	0.03	175.87	309.83	1,072.00	1,113.77	8.85	83.34
6	0.02	214.33	373.73	980.67	1,031.05	8.54	100.48
7	0.01	268.64	463.69	1,389.02	1,451.52	8.24	124.30
8	0	320.05	546.90	1,268.81	1,342.53	7.95	145.18
9	0	370.37	623.71	1,155.31	1,234.01	7.68	166.96
10	0	12,385.83	740.78	1,640.83	(10,211.65)	7.41	200.01

Legend:
(1) Given
(2) [1 – (1)] × [Table 3-13, col (7)]. For $t = 10$, subtract [Table 3-13, $(6)_t$] to eliminate effect of 10th yr persistency bonus on surrender benefits.
(3) (6.25%) × [Table 3-12, col.(4)] × [Table 3-12, col (2)]
(4) Table 3-13, col (3)
(5) Table 3-12, $(9)_t - (9)_{t-1}$. For $t = 9$, subtract [Table 3-12, $(6)_t$] to eliminate effect of 9th yr persistency bonus on reserve.
(6) $10.00 × [Table 3-12, col (2)]
(7) (3) + (4) – (2) – (5) – (6)

Table 3-15 provides a check on the Table 3-14 EGPs using a source-of-earnings approach. That same table illustrates the calculation of the capitalization and amortization of the SIA.

Table 3-15
Gross Profits by Source, DAC Asset, and Persistency Bonus Asset (Sales Inducement Asset)

	(1)	(2)	(3)	(4)	(5)	(6)	(7)	(8)	(9)	(10)
								PB Asset Generation		
Policy Dur$_t$	Interest Margin	Surrender Charges	Expense Charges	EGP	Basic DAC Asset	Persistency Bonus	PB Liability	Capitalization	Pres.Value	PB Asset
1	17.50	1.46	10.00	8.96	392.28		6.15	6.15	5.89	3.03
2	34.30	3.69	9.80	28.19	394.77		18.17	11.74	10.75	5.08
3	49.91	5.22	9.51	45.62	388.00		35.60	16.61	14.56	6.01
4	67.42	5.64	9.17	63.89	371.10		59.24	22.04	18.48	6.03
5	86.75	5.44	8.85	83.34	342.98		89.78	27.87	22.36	5.11
6	104.64	4.37	8.54	100.48	304.37		126.76	32.94	25.30	3.24
7	129.83	2.71	8.24	124.30	251.22		172.77	40.31	29.62	0.34
8	153.13	-	7.95	145.18	184.44		227.24	46.69	32.83	(3.58)
9	174.64	-	7.68	166.96	102.94	153.53	141.46	57.52	38.71	(4.45)
10	207.42	-	7.41	200.01	(0.00)	222.23	-	74.41	47.91	(0.00)
Present Value of EGP at Crediting Rate:			706.54		**Present Value of PB Capitalization:**			246.41		
DAC Amortization Factor (*k* 1%)			53.78%		**PB Asset Amortization Rate (*k* 2%)**			34.88%		

Legend:

(1) [Table 3-14, col (3)] – [Table 3-13, col (5)]
(2) [Table 3-14, col (1)] × [Table 3-13, col (7)]
(3) \$10.00 × [Table 3-12, col (2)]
(4) (1) + (2) – (3)
(5) For $t = 1$, (DAE) × (1.045) – (k 1%) × (4)
For $t > 1$, $(5)_t = (5)_{t-1} \times (1.045) - (k\,1\%) \times (4)$
(6) Table 3-13, col (6)
(7) Table 3-12, col (10)
(8) $(7)_t - (1.045) \times (7)_{t-1} + (6)_t$
(9) $(8) / (1.045^t)$
(10) $(10)_{t-1} \times (1.045) + (8)_t - (k\,2\%) \times (4)_t$

There is a potentially significant set of negative SIA values in this fact pattern of coterminous persistency bonuses and SIA amortization periods.

A second study considers a fact pattern where the persistency bonus crediting takes place partway through the policy's lifetime and SIA amortization period. Table 3-16 illustrates the calculation of the SIL, where the persistency bonus is credited in years 4 and 5. Similarly to the Table 3-11 example, the liability decreases to zero when the last persistency bonus is paid or credited.

Table 3-16
Level Percentage of Account Value

Policy Dur_t	(1) Account Value (BOY)	(2) Estimated Persistency Bonus	(3) At Issue Date $PV(Bon)_t$	(4) At Issue Date $PV(AV)_t$	(5) Deposit% @ time t	(6) $Liab_t$(BOY)	(7) Deposit	(8) Interest	(9) $Liab_t$(EOY)
1	1,000.00		408.45	14,037.45	2.910%	-	29.10	1.31	30.41
2	2,000.00		426.83	13,624.14	2.910%	30.41	58.19	3.99	92.59
3	3,000.00		446.03	12,147.23	2.910%	92.59	87.29	8.09	187.97
4	4,200.00	200.00	466.11	9,558.85	2.910%	187.97	122.21	13.96	124.14
5	5,600.00	300.00	287.08	5,600.00	2.910%	124.14	162.94	12.92	-
6	7,000.00								
7	9,000.00								
8	11,000.00								
9	13,000.00								
10	16,000.00								

Legend:
(1) Given
(2) Given
(3) For t = 1 to 4, $(2)_4 \times (v^{4-t+1}) + (2)_5 \times (v^{5-t+1})$
For $t = 5$, $(2)_5 \times (v)$
(4) For $t = 5, (1)_5$. For $t < 5$, $[(4)_{t+1}] \times (v) + (1)_t$
(5) $[(3) - (6)] / (4)$
(6) $(9)_{t-1}$
(7) $(1) \times (5)$
(8) $[(6) + (7)] \times (4.50\%)$
(9) $(6) + (7) + (8)$

Investment Income Rate$_i$ 4.50%
$v = 1/(1+i)$ 0.956937799

Tables 3-17 through 3-20 contain a fact pattern identical to Tables 3-12 through 3-15 respectively, except that, as indicated above, the persistency bonuses are credited in years 4 and 5, instead of in years 9 and 10. Table 3-20 reveals that the SIA is now positive, which is due to the fact that, while the persistency bonuses are credited in years 4 and 5, the SIA is amortized over a longer period, 10 years.

Table 3-17
Total Benefit Reserve

Investment Income Rate$_i$	6.25%	**Deferrable Acquisition Expense:**	380.00
$v = 1/(1+i)$	0.94118	**Maintenance expense:**	10.00
Credited Interest Rate	4.50%		
$v = 1/(1+i)$	0.95694		

Policy Dur_t	(1) Termination Rate	(2) Survivorship to Beg Year	(3) Premium Deposit (BOY)	(4) Acct Value Beg. of Yr.	(5) Interest Credited	(6) Persistency Bonus	(7) AV EOY	(8) $Liab_t$ (post-bonus)	(9) Survived Values, EOY: Acct Value	(10) Survived Values, EOY: $Liab_t$	(11) Survived Values, EOY: Benefit Res
1	2.00%	1.00000	1,000.00	1,000.00	45.00		1,045.00	30.41	1,024.10	29.80	1,053.90
2	3.00%	0.98000	955.00	2,000.00	90.00		2,090.00	92.59	1,986.75	88.01	2,074.77
3	3.50%	0.95060	910.00	3,000.00	135.00		3,135.00	187.97	2,875.83	172.43	3,048.26
4	3.50%	0.91733	1,065.00	4,200.00	189.00	200.00	4,589.00	124.14	4,062.29	109.89	4,172.18
5	3.50%	0.88522	1,011.00	5,600.00	252.00	300.00	6,152.00	-	5,255.28	-	5,255.28
6	3.50%	0.85424	848.00	7,000.00	315.00		7,315.00	-	6,030.06	-	6,030.06
7	3.50%	0.82434	1,685.00	9,000.00	405.00		9,405.00	-	7,481.58	-	7,481.58
8	3.50%	0.79549	1,595.00	11,000.00	495.00		11,495.00	-	8,824.10	-	8,824.10
9	3.50%	0.76765	1,505.00	13,000.00	585.00		13,585.00	-	10,063.49	-	10,063.49
10	100.00%	0.74078	2,415.00	16,000.00	720.00		16,720.00	-	-	-	-

Legend:
(1) Given
(2) $(2)_{t-1} \times (1 - (1)_{t-1})$
(3) Given
(4) $(4)_1 = (3)_1$
For $t > 1$, $(4)_t = (7)_{t-1} + (3)_t$
(5) $(4) \times (4.5\%)$
(6) Given
(7) $(4) + (5) + (6)$
(8) From Table 3-16, col. (9)
(9) $(7) \times (2)_{t+1}$
(10) $(8) \times (2)_{t+1}$
(11) $(9) + (10)$

Table 3-18
Check of Survived Account Value Rollforward

Policy Dur$_t$	(1) Termination Rate	(2) Survivorship to BOY	(3) Premium Deposit (BOY)	(4) Acct Value BOY	(5) Interest Credited	(6) Persistency Bonus	(7) AV Released	(8) Acct Value EOY
1	2.00%	1.00000	1,000.00	1,000.00	45.00		20.90	1,024.10
2	3.00%	0.98000	935.90	1,960.00	88.20		61.45	1,986.75
3	3.50%	0.95060	865.05	2,851.80	128.33		104.30	2,875.83
4	3.50%	0.91733	976.96	3,852.78	173.38	183.47	147.34	4,062.29
5	3.50%	0.88522	894.96	4,957.25	223.08	265.57	190.61	5,255.28
6	3.50%	0.85424	724.40	5,979.68	269.09		218.71	6,030.06
7	3.50%	0.82434	1,389.02	7,419.07	333.86		271.35	7,481.58
8	3.50%	0.79549	1,268.81	8,750.38	393.77		320.05	8,824.10
9	3.50%	0.76765	1,155.31	9,979.41	449.07		365.00	10,063.49
10	100.00%	0.74078	1,788.98	11,852.47	533.36		12,385.83	-

Legend:
(1) Given
(2) $(2)_{t-1} \times (1 - (1)_{t-1})$
(3) (2) × [Table 3-17, col (3)]
(4) $(8)_{t-1} + (3)_t$
(5) (4) × (4.5%)
(6) (2) × [Table 3-17, col (6)]
(7) (1) × [(4) + (5) + (6)]
(8) (4) + (5) + (6) − (7)

Table 3-19
Gross Profit (Cash Flows minus Change in Account Value)

Policy Dur$_t$	(1) Surrender Charge Scale	(2) Surr. Values Paid	(3) Investment Income	(4) Premium Income	(5) Change in Reserve	(6) Maintenance Expenses	(7) EGP
1	0.07	19.44	62.50	1,000.00	1,024.10	10.00	8.96
2	0.06	57.76	122.50	935.90	962.65	9.80	28.19
3	0.05	99.09	178.24	865.05	889.07	9.51	45.62
4	0.04	135.28	240.80	976.96	1,009.42	9.17	63.89
5	0.03	175.87	309.83	894.96	936.72	8.85	83.34
6	0.02	214.33	373.73	724.40	774.77	8.54	100.48
7	0.01	268.64	463.69	1,389.02	1,451.52	8.24	124.30
8	0	320.05	546.90	1,268.81	1,342.53	7.95	145.18
9	0	365.00	623.71	1,155.31	1,239.39	7.68	166.96
10	0	12,385.83	740.78	1,788.98	(10,063.49)	7.41	200.01

Legend:
(1) Given
(2) [Table 3-18, col (1)] × [Table 3-18, col (4) + col (5)] × [1 − (1)]
(3) (6.25%) × [Table 3-17, col.(4)] × [Table 3-17, col (2)]
(4) Table 3-18, col (3)
(5) [Table 3-18, cols$\{(8)_{t-1} + (3)_t\}$] × (1.045) × [1 − (Table 3-18, col (1))] − [Table 3-18, col$(8)_{t-1}$]
(6) $10.00 × [Table 3-17, col (2)]
(7) (3) + (4) − (2) − (5) − (6)

Table 3-20
Gross Profits by Source, Bonus Asset & Total DAC Asset

	(1)	(2)	(3)	(4)	(5)	(6)	(7)	(8)	(9)	(10)
								PB Asset Generation		
Policy Dur_t	Interest Margin	Surrender Charges	Expense Charges	EGP	Basic DAC Asset	Persistency Bonus	PB Liability	Capitalization	Pres.Value	PB Asset
1	17.50	1.46	10.00	8.96	392.28		29.80	29.80	28.52	25.15
2	34.30	3.69	9.80	28.19	394.77		88.01	56.87	52.08	68.53
3	49.91	5.22	9.51	45.62	388.00		172.43	80.46	70.51	128.41
4	67.42	5.64	9.17	63.89	371.10	183.47	109.89	112.91	94.68	213.96
5	86.75	5.44	8.85	83.34	342.98	265.57	-	150.45	120.73	330.81
6	104.64	4.37	8.54	100.48	304.37		-	-	-	293.57
7	129.83	2.71	8.24	124.30	251.22		-	-	-	242.30
8	153.13	-	7.95	145.18	184.44		-	-	-	177.89
9	174.64	-	7.68	166.96	102.94		-	-	-	99.29
10	207.42	-	7.41	200.01	(0.00)		-	-	-	(0.00)
	Present Value of EGP at Crediting Rate:			706.536		Present Value of PB Capitalization:			366.51	
	DAC Amortization Factor (k1%)			53.78%		PB Asset Amortization Rate (k2%)			51.87%	

Legend:

(1) [Table 3-19, col (3)] – [Table 3-18, col (5)]
(2) [Table 3-18, col (1)] × [Table 3-19, col (1)] × [Table 3-18, col (4) + Table 3-18, col(5)]
(3) $10.00 × [Table 3-17, col (2)]
(4) (1) + (2) – (3)
(5) For $t = 1$, (DAE) × (1.045) – (k 1%) × (4)
For $t > 1$, $(5)_t = (5)_{t-1} \times (1.045) - (k\,1\%) \times (4)$
(6) Table 3-18, col(6)
(7) Table 3-17, col(10)
(8) $(7)_t - (1.045) \times (7)_{t-1} + (6)_t \times$ [Table 3-18, col(1)] × (1 – [Table 3-19, col(1)]) + $(6)_t$ × (1 – [Table 3-18, col(1)])
(9) $(8) / (1.045^t)$
(10) $(10)_{t-1} \times (1.045) + (8)_t - (k\,2\%) \times (4)_t$

3.12 Worksheet Approaches to DAC Calculation

Formulas for benefit reserves, including their maintenance components, and formulas for DAC for specific SFASs are covered in the following chapters. This section presents the features of the worksheet approach to capitalizing and amortizing DAC. The worksheet can be used for a variety of coverages and situations. Chapters 4 (traditional life) and 10 (individual health) address the development of formula-based reserves that are used for factor and first-principles reserve generation. To develop reserves, values are determined per unit and applied to the appropriate units in force on the valuation date. A comparable approach for DAC is known as a worksheet methodology.

The worksheet facilitates the exact period deferred acquisition expense to be applied. There is never a question about implied versus actual acquisition expense, as there can be under the formula-based methodology.

The worksheet approach operates well with respect to noncommission acquisition expenses. If a worksheet is used for commissions, the level of subsequent heaped renewal commissions must be estimated for each future duration. Depending on the amount of bonuses included in capitalized commissions in the first year, the relationship between the heaped levels and the first-year excess amount deferred can vary and consequently affect the DAC amortization.

The worksheet approach can be divided into two types, static and dynamic.

3.12.1 Static Worksheets

Table 3-21 illustrates the calculation process for the static worksheet approach. The expense to be deferred is introduced at the beginning of the table. A schedule using mortality and lapse rates is then used to develop an expected in force schedule at future dates. A terminal duration is selected, at which point the DAC will be amortized to zero.

Table 3-21
Static Worksheet for *SFAS 60* Product

Statement Date:	Dec. 31, 2000
Product:	Agency Term Insurance
Issue Year:	1998
Deferrable Non-commission Acquisition Expenses:	$31,000

Premium weights for years 1-5

Modeled Insurance Plan	per $1000	Premium Weighting	Initial Weighted Premium
5-Year Term	$2.25	18.50%	$0.42
10-Year Term	$3.12	42.00%	$1.31
15-Year Term	$5.15	39.50%	$2.03
Total		100.00%	$3.76

Premium weights for years 6-10

Modeled Insurance Plan	per $1000	Premium Weighting	Initial Weighted Premium
10-Year Term	$3.12	42.00%	$1.31
15-Year Term	$5.15	39.50%	$2.03
Total		81.50%	$3.34

(1) Policy Year	(2) Lapse Rate	(3) Mortality Rate/1000	(4) Beginning Year Survivorship Factor	(5) Weighted Premium per $1000	(6) Weighted Surviving Premium	(7) Premium Basis Amortization Table	(8) Premium Present Value	(9) Terminal DAC per $1.00 Acquisition Expense	(10) Mean DAC per $1.00	(11) Mean DAC
1	15.0%	0.800	1.000000	$3.76	$3.76	1.00000	1.00000	0.87375	0.84667	$26,246.73
2	12.0%	0.864	0.849200	$3.76	$3.19	0.84920	0.79737	0.76814	0.74433	$23,074.18
3	10.0%	0.933	0.746562	$3.76	$2.81	0.74656	0.65821	0.67529	0.65436	$20,285.07
4	8.5%	1.008	0.671209	$3.76	$2.52	0.67121	0.55566	0.59082	0.57250	$17,747.56
5	7.5%	1.088	0.613480	$3.76	$2.31	0.61348	0.47687	0.51189	0.49602	$15,376.76
6	7.0%	1.175	0.566801	$3.34	$1.90	0.50407	0.36791	0.44876	0.43485	$13,480.41
7	7.0%	1.269	0.526459	$3.34	$1.76	0.46819	0.32087	0.38839	0.37635	$11,666.92
8	7.0%	1.371	0.488939	$3.34	$1.64	0.43482	0.27981	0.33048	0.32023	$9,927.25
9	7.0%	1.481	0.454043	$3.34	$1.52	0.40379	0.24398	0.27473	0.26622	$8,252.78
10	7.0%	1.599	0.421587	$3.34	$1.41	0.37493	0.21272	0.22089	0.21404	$6,635.29
11	7.0%	1.727	0.391402	$2.03	$0.80	0.21171	0.11278	0.19476	0.18872	$5,850.34
12	7.0%	1.865	0.363328	$2.03	$0.74	0.19652	0.09830	0.16983	0.16457	$5,101.61
13	7.0%	2.015	0.337217	$2.03	$0.69	0.18240	0.08567	0.14599	0.14146	$4,385.35
14	7.0%	2.176	0.312933	$2.03	$0.64	0.16926	0.07465	0.12311	0.11929	$3,697.99
15	7.0%	2.350	0.290346	$2.03	$0.59	0.15705	0.06503	0.10107	0.09794	$3,036.14
16	7.0%	2.538	0.269340	$2.03	$0.55	0.14568	0.05665	0.07978	0.07731	$2,396.55
17	7.0%	2.741	0.249803	$2.03	$0.51	0.13512	0.04933	0.05913	0.05729	$1,776.09
18	7.0%	2.960	0.231632	$2.03	$0.47	0.12529	0.04295	0.03901	0.03780	$1,171.76
19	7.0%	3.197	0.214732	$2.03	$0.44	0.11615	0.03739	0.01933	0.01873	$580.67
20	7.0%	3.453	0.199014	$2.03	$0.40	0.10765	0.03254	0.00000	0.00000	($0.00)
			0.184396							
(8A)	Present Value of premiums given $1.00 initial premium in block						5.56869			
(8B)	Amortization Factor per $1.00 of Expense						17.958%			

Legend:

(1), (2), (3) Given

(4) $= [100\% - (1)_{t-1} - (2)_{t-1}] \times (4)_{t-1}$

(5) From premium weight tables above

(6) = (4) × (5)

(7) = (6) / 3.76

(8) $= (7) / 1.065^{(1)-1}$

(8A) = Sum of column (8)

(8B) = 1 / (8A)

(9)

$(9)_1 = [1 - (8B) \times (7)_1] \times 1.065$

$(9)_t = [(9)_{t-1} - (8B) \times (7)_t) \times 1.065$

(10) $= (9)_t / 1.065^{.5}$

(11) = (10) × 31,000

Assumes annual mode, lapses at end of year and 6.5% interest

An interest rate (6.5% in Table 3-11) is then introduced for present value calculations and also for determining accretions to DAC. Thus, DAC is increased with interest, just as it would under a formula-based approach. This approach is appealing in its simplicity. Its drawbacks are that the remaining DAC may be noticeably ahead or behind schedule based on how actual persistency emerges. Further, there is no convenient byproduct that establishes recoverability or facilitates loss recognition. Static worksheets should be used with care, and not used when actual inforce varies significantly from the assumed inforce.

3.12.2 Dynamic Worksheets

The first drawback of static worksheets is resolved by using a dynamic worksheet. This is illustrated in Table 3-22. The dynamic worksheet takes the static worksheet results and adjusts them by the ratio of actual to expected cumulative persistency. A worksheet for *SFAS 97* or *SFAS 120* products would utilize expected gross profits or expected gross margins in place of the gross premium as the amortization basis.

Chapter 4 Traditional Life Insurance *(SFAS 60 & SFAS 97)*

4.1 Background

This chapter covers the accounting applicable for nonparticipating traditional (in other words, non-interest-sensitive) fixed premium policies. The accounting for these types of products is generally dictated by *Statement of Financial Accounting Standard No. 60* (*SFAS 60*), "Accounting and Reporting by Insurance Enterprises," issued by the Financial Accounting Standards Board in June, 1982. *SFAS 60* became effective for fiscal years beginning after December 15, 1982 with earlier application encouraged. Prior to the issuance of *SFAS 60*, guidance for the appropriate accounting of these products was given by *Audits of Stock Life Insurance Companies* (generally referred to as the *Audit Guide*), issued by the American Institute of Certified Public Accountants in 1972. This reference was updated in 1994 for conforming changes. It was updated again in 2000 and retitled *AICPA Audit and Accounting Guide, Life and Health Insurance Entities*.

As stated in the original *Audit Guide*,

> Audit Guides do not require an effective date. However, because the restrictions on expression of reliance on actuaries, and the requirements for qualified, adverse or disclaimed opinions discussed in Part III will change practice which has heretofore been acceptable, such restrictions and requirements will not be effective with respect to auditors' reports on financial statements for periods ending before December 31, 1973. (Preface, page X)

Thus, guidance for the appropriate accounting of nonparticipating traditional fixed premium contracts has evolved since 1972.

The accounting methodology described in this chapter does not apply to traditional participating contracts in which policyholder dividends are determined by the company using the contribution principle. The appropriate accounting for these contracts is dictated by *SFAS 120,* "Accounting and Reporting by Mutual Life Insurance Enterprises and by Insurance Enterprises for Certain Long-Duration Participating Contracts" and *Statement of Position 95-1*, "Accounting for Certain Insurance Activities of Mutual Life Insurance Enterprises," and is described in Chapter 5.

The accounting for traditional policies with premium payment periods shorter than the period over which benefits to the policyholder are received, generally referred to as limited payment contracts, is detailed in *SFAS 97*, "Accounting and Reporting by Insurance Enterprises for Certain Long-Duration Contracts and for Realized Gains and Losses from the Sale of Investments," and will be covered in this chapter with respect to limited payment life insurance products.

When determining the methodology to be used for a particular policy covered under *SFAS 60,* the contract must first be classified as either a short-duration or a long-duration contract. The Standard states:

> Insurance contracts, for purposes of this Statement, shall be classified as short-duration or long-duration contracts depending on whether the contracts are expected to remain in force for an extended period. The factors that shall be considered in determining whether a particular contract can be expected to remain in force for an extended period are:

a. *Short-duration contract.* The contract provides insurance protection for a fixed period of short duration and enables the insurer to cancel the contract or to adjust the provisions of the contract at the end of any contract period, such as adjusting the amount of premiums charged or coverage provided.

b. *Long-duration contract.* The contract generally is not subject to unilateral changes in its provisions, ... and requires the performance of various functions and services (including insurance protection) for an extended period.
(Paragraph 7)

Examples of short-duration contracts include most property and liability insurance contracts and certain term life insurance contracts, such as credit life insurance. Group contracts are addressed in Chapter 12; credit life contracts are addressed in Chapter 11. The remainder of this chapter is devoted to the long-duration, traditional life insurance contracts.

4.2 Product Features

In the U.S., traditional life products have been popular for more than a century. Many variations of coverages and terms of traditional life insurance exist. Such variations include length of benefit period; level, increasing or decreasing face amount patterns; coterminous or limited pay premium period. The *SFAS 60* products addressed in this chapter include industrial (also known as debit) insurance as well as ordinary traditional life insurance.

Whole life contracts provide a fixed amount of death benefit over the life of the insured. Premiums are paid over various terms such as ten years, twenty years, to age 65 or for lifetime. Whole life contracts generally provide for nonforfeiture values such as cash values, reduced paid up insurance and extended term insurance.

Endowment contracts are similar to whole life contracts; in addition, they provide a living benefit, often the face amount, if the policyholder survives until the end of the coverage period. Some whole life and term products provide for small endowments during various points of the coverage; these living benefits have often been called "coupons."

Term life contracts provide for insurance over a specified time period. In general, term products do not have nonforfeiture values. The premiums are usually coterminous with the policy period. Term policies are written for relatively short periods (such as one, five, ten or fifteen years). They frequently have automatic or optional renewal features that extend coverage into another term period or offer the option to convert to whole life insurance.

4.3 Benefit Reserve Methodology

The accounting methodology used for short-duration contracts differs from that used in long-duration contracts. For short-duration contracts, *SFAS 60* states:

> Premiums from short-duration insurance contracts ordinarily shall be recognized as revenue over the period of the contract in proportion to the amount of insurance protection provided. A liability for unpaid claims (including estimates of costs for claims relating to insured events that have occurred but have not been reported to the insurer) and a liability for claim adjustment expenses shall be accrued when insured events occur. (Paragraph 9)

As stated earlier, credit insurance is typically classified as a short-duration contract, and the appropriate accounting for such contracts is addressed in Chapter 11.

For long-duration contracts, *SFAS 60* states:

> Premiums from long-duration contracts shall be recognized as revenue when due from policyholders. A liability for expected costs relating to most types of long-duration contracts shall be accrued over the current and expected renewal periods of the contracts. The present value of estimated future policy benefits to be paid to or on behalf of policyholders less the present value of estimated future net premiums to be collected from policyholders (liability for future policy benefits) shall be accrued when premium revenue is recognized. Those estimates shall be based on assumptions, such as estimates of expected investment yields, mortality, morbidity, terminations, and expenses, applicable at the time the insurance contracts are made. In addition, liabilities for unpaid claims and claim adjustment expenses shall be accrued when insured events occur. (Paragraph 10)

In determining the liability to be established for future benefits relating to long-duration contracts, *SFAS 60* stipulates:

> A liability for future policy benefits relating to long-duration contracts other than title insurance contracts shall be accrued when premium revenue is recognized. The liability, which represents the present value of future benefits to be paid to or on behalf of policyholders and related expenses less the present value of future net premiums (portion of gross premium required to provide for all benefits and expenses), shall be estimated using methods that include assumptions, such as estimates of expected investment yields, mortality, morbidity, terminations, and expenses, applicable at the time the insurance contracts are made. (Paragraph 21)

The liability discussed above is also referred to as the net GAAP reserve. The difference between the gross premium charged and the net premium used to calculate the net GAAP reserve is referred to as loading. The loading represents the portion of the gross premium that emerges as profit. The portions of the gross premium that support the payment of expenses (both acquisition and maintenance) are calculated by dividing the present value of acquisition or maintenance expenses by the present value of premiums calculated using a discount rate equal to the assumed net investment earnings rate. Likewise, the portion of the gross premium that supports the payment of policyholder benefits is calculated by dividing the present value of policyholder benefits by the present value of premiums calculated using a discount rate equal to the assumed net investment earnings rate. Therefore, assuming no loss recognition and consequent unlocking of assumptions, the net premium will remain a constant percentage of the gross premium for the duration of the contract. Thus, for a contract whose gross premiums are not level, the net premium for any given year is calculated by applying the appropriate percentage to the current year's gross premium.

In practice, some companies grade the net GAAP reserve to the statutory reserve at a later policy duration (such as thirty years) when only an insignificant, small percentage of contracts remain in force. When this occurs, the GAAP net premium is equal to the statutory net premium in durations subsequent to the grading. Therefore, the constant percentage relationship between the sum of the net GAAP benefit and expense premiums and the gross premium changes at the end of the grading period.

4.4 Expense Recognition

Insurance companies incur many different types of expenses, including agent/broker commissions, expenses associated with the underwriting and issuance of a new policy, state/local tax and premium tax expenses, expenses associated with the investment of assets, as well as direct maintenance and overhead expenses. A thorough discussion of each of these expenses is given in Chapter 3. A discussion of some of the accounting issues follows.

For both short and long-duration contracts, *SFAS 60* states:

> Costs that vary with and are primarily related to the acquisition of insurance contracts (acquisition costs) shall be capitalized and charged to expense in proportion to premium revenue recognized. Other costs incurred during the period, such as those relating to investments, general administration, and policy maintenance, shall be charged to expense as incurred. (Paragraph 11)

Acquisition expenses that may be deferred should only be deferred to the extent that deferral of such expenses would not create a loss in later years. This concept is referred to as recoverability.

The *Audit and Accounting Guide* states:

> Under generally accepted accounting principles, the costs attributed to the acquisition of contracts are deferred and amortized to match these costs with the related future revenue stream. Other costs are generally reported as expenses in the period incurred. (Paragraph 10.3)

> Under GAAP, commissions, allowances, and other costs that vary with and are primarily related to the acquisition of new and renewal business are generally deferred and amortized. (Paragraph 10.12)

> Regardless of the method used by a particular company to sell insurance, an acquisition expense should be deferred only if the expense both varies with and is primarily related to the production of business. (Paragraph 10.17)

> Issue costs which may be deferred are those expenses of the underwriting and contract issue departments that are primarily related to and vary with new business. (Paragraph 10.18)

Acquisition costs are defined in *SFAS 60* as follows:

> Acquisition costs are those costs that vary with and are primarily related to the acquisition of new and renewal insurance contracts. (Paragraph 28)

SFAS 60 states:

> Commissions and other costs (for example, salaries of certain employees involved in the underwriting and policy issue functions, and medical and inspection fees) that are primarily related to insurance contracts issued or renewed during the period in which the costs are incurred shall be considered acquisition costs. (Paragraph 28)

> Acquisition costs shall be capitalized and charged to expense in proportion to premium revenue recognized. (Paragraph 29)
>
> Actual acquisition costs for long-duration contracts shall be used in determining acquisition costs to be capitalized as long as gross premiums are sufficient to cover actual costs. However, estimated acquisition costs may be used if the difference is not significant. Capitalized acquisition costs shall be charged to expense using methods that include the same assumptions used in estimating the liability for future policy benefits. (Paragraph 31)

Unamortized acquisition costs, typically labeled deferred acquisition costs (DAC) or deferred policy acquisition costs (DPAC), are held as a deferred cost on the asset side (in other words, a negative reserve) of the company's balance sheet.

The *Audit and Accounting Guide* continues:

> A number of portions of a life insurance entity's costs, such as investment expenses, product development expenses, market research expenses, contract maintenance expenses, and general overhead, are not associated directly with acquiring business and are not appropriate for deferral. As is the case with other business enterprises, such expenses are charged to operations as incurred. (Paragraph 10.13)
>
> The expense portion of the gross premium must be adequate to provide for amortization of deferred costs and to cover level renewal expenses as well as nonlevel costs such as termination and settlement expenses. In addition, all renewal expense assumptions should take into account the possible effects of inflation on these expenses. (Paragraph 10.39)

Recognizing that the general level of inflation will affect an insurance company's cost structure in the future does not necessarily imply that the unit expenses used in the development of a product's net expense premium will grow with an assumed rate of inflation. Any economies of scale associated with the growth of the company as well as technological advances may partially, if not entirely, offset the effect of inflation on unit expenses. Likewise, use of a declining investment rate assumption may imply a reduced inflationary impact in the future, necessitating that any inflation assumption used in the development of unit expense factors be set consistently with the investment earnings rate assumption.

The use of an inflation assumption on maintenance costs *would* generate a maintenance expense reserve.

When the liability for future policyholder benefits is established, costs incurred in providing those benefits, such as termination or settlement costs should be considered.

SFAS 60 states:

> Expense assumptions used in estimating the liability for future policy benefits shall be based on ... costs after the premium-paying period. (Paragraph 26)

Thus, for limited payment policies a reserve for policy maintenance expenses projected to be incurred after the premium paying period should be established.

With respect to costs other than those that are acquisition related and those that are related to claims and policy benefits, *SFAS 60* states:

> Costs incurred during the period, such as those relating to investments, general administration, and policy maintenance, that do not vary with and are not primarily related to the acquisition of new and renewal insurance contracts shall be charged to expense as incurred. (Paragraph 27)

4.5 Selection of Assumptions

This section of the chapter deals with the many facets the actuary must consider when selecting assumptions for reserves.

4.5.1 GAAP Assumption Eras

In practice, companies have established GAAP eras in which the assumptions used in the determination of the liability for future policy benefits, as well as the amortization of DAC, remain appropriate. Typically, once assumptions deviate substantially from those that were assumed in the determination of the policy's gross premiums, the policy form is no longer sold. Rather, a different product with premiums determined by using revised assumptions reflective of the current environment is introduced and sold prospectively.

This transition is sometimes referred to as the issuance of a new "ratebook." While the "ratebook" concept applies more to products issued in the 1980s and earlier, companies frequently update their product portfolios. Thus, with respect to traditional nonparticipating fixed premium policies, GAAP eras often, but not always, coincide with changes in a company's "ratebook."

Nevertheless, if assumptions reflective of the current environment differ materially from those originally assumed and the company continues to issue the policy, a new GAAP era with revised assumptions is generally established.

4.5.2 Provisions for Adverse Deviation

When the assumptions used to determine the liability for future policyholder benefits and the amortization of deferred acquisition costs are set, a provision for adverse deviation should be included in the assumptions.

Only broad guidance is given in the literature as to the level of provision for adverse deviation in the assumptions for developing the net GAAP benefit and expense premiums. Therefore, given the same set of circumstances, it is likely that two actuaries would use different levels of provision for adverse deviation in each assumption (such as mortality, morbidity, investment rate, withdrawal, and expense), as well as different best estimate assumptions in developing GAAP net benefit and expense premiums. Of course, the reserve assumptions used will not affect the ultimate amount of profits that emerges from the block of business; ultimate profitability results from the actual cash flows that do emerge from the block. However, the reported emergence of profit will be affected by the use of different assumptions as will the distribution between profit that emerges as a level percentage of premium and profit that emerges as a release from risk of adverse deviation.

Thus, assuming that experience emerges as projected at issue on a best estimate basis, profit would emerge as a level percentage of premium (the difference between the gross premium and the sum of the net GAAP benefit and expense premiums), as well as a release from risk of adverse deviation (the profit emerging due to mortality, withdrawal, expense and investment rate actually earned versus that assumed in the development of the GAAP net benefit and expense premiums).

The Actuarial Standards Board's *Actuarial Standard of Practice No. 10*, "Methods and Assumptions for Use in Life Insurance Company Financial Statements Prepared in Accordance with GAAP" addresses issues surrounding assumptions to be used in the development of GAAP benefit/expense reserves and/or recoverability/loss recognition schedules as follows:

> *Risk of Adverse Deviation.* The risk that actual experience may differ from best-estimate assumptions in a manner that produces costs higher than assumed or revenues less than assumed.
>
> *Categories of Assumptions.* Two general types of actuarial assumptions are used in the preparation of GAAP financial statements. Best-estimate assumptions as of the financial statement date are required in certain instances. In others, assumptions that provide for the risk of adverse deviation are required. Relevant accounting standards call for best-estimate assumptions to be periodically reviewed and updated to reflect emerging experience, whereas assumptions with provision for risk of adverse deviation are subject to lock-in until a loss recognition situation arises.
>
> *Best-Estimate Assumptions.* In instances where GAAP requires best-estimate assumptions, the actuary should choose assumptions that, in his or her judgment, reflect the most likely outcome of events. Best-estimate assumptions selected by the actuary should be reasonable.
>
> *Provision for Risk of Adverse Deviation.* In certain instances GAAP requires a provision for the risk of adverse deviation in setting actuarial assumptions.
>
> *Degree of Risk.* In selecting assumptions that include provision for the risk of adverse deviation, the actuary should consider the degree to which the assumption is subject to such risk in total and at each future duration. Provision for the risk of adverse deviation should be reasonable in the actuary's judgment.
>
> *Relationship to Best-Estimates.* The actuary should select assumptions that include provision for the risk of adverse deviation that bear a reasonable relationship to the best-estimate assumptions. Under GAAP, the provision for the risk of adverse deviation should not increase the resulting GAAP net premium above the gross premium. The resulting GAAP net premium may be less than the gross premium, provided that due provision has been made for the risks of adverse deviation. Note that the GAAP net premium prior to provision for adverse deviation may be greater than the gross premium. The actuary should establish that the aggregate net GAAP liability determined using assumptions that include provision for the risk of adverse deviation equals or exceeds a similarly determined net liability determined using best-estimate assumptions without provision for the risk of adverse deviation.

The 1994 *Audit Guide* elaborates on reasons for including a margin for adverse deviation in the assumptions used to calculate benefit reserves and DAC as follows:

> In each accounting period, a company realizes actual experience with respect to these assumptions; in the process, a portion of the risk of adverse experience is removed.

> The process of assuming these risks and gradually being relieved from such risks represents an essential function or service performed by a life insurance company. The risks of adverse deviations from which the company is relieved during an accounting period, therefore, constitute an important measure of performance that should be recognized in determining the timing of the recognition of premium revenues and related costs. The inclusion of a provision for the risk of adverse deviations in arriving at reasonably conservative assumptions will cause some profits to emerge over the life of the contracts as risks are eliminated in that:
>
> 1. In the absence of adverse deviations in mortality, some profits will emerge in relation to the net amount at risk.
>
> 2. In the absence of adverse deviations in the investment yield, some profits will emerge in relation to invested funds or investment income.
>
> 3. In the absence of adverse deviations in withdrawal rates, some profits will emerge in relation to the excess of (a) the difference between the benefit reserve less unamortized acquisition expenses over (b) the related cash value.
>
> 4. In the absence of adverse deviations in estimated expenses, some profits will emerge in relation to expenses incurred.
>
> 5. Any profit in the premium in excess of provisions for adverse deviation will emerge in relation to premium revenues. Profits emerging as a level percentage of premiums give recognition to the importance of the sales effort as a source of profit. Margins allocated to this function, however, must not be at the expense of providing for the risk of adverse deviations in the mortality, investment yield, withdrawal, and expense assumptions. (Paragraph 8.16)
>
> The *Audit and Accounting Guide* states:
>
> ... assumptions, such as interest, mortality , withdrawals, and settlement expenses ... should also include a provision for adverse deviation. (Paragraph 8.61)

The following excerpts from the 1994 *Audit Guide* addressed provisions for adverse deviation. While these paragraphs were not reproduced in the *Accounting and Audit Guide*, they do provide insight to the actuary:

> In determining the provisions for risks of adverse deviation, it will be necessary to consider the individual assumptions; however, the provisions must be reasonable in relation to the total valuation premium. Conservatism in determining such provisions should also be considered in relation to the effect of the provision on recognition of profit. (Paragraph 8.85)
>
> ... the actuary's choice of assumptions to be used in connection with general purpose financial statements is disciplined by the principles of his profession. His responsibility to use assumptions which are "adequate and appropriate" is consistent with the concept, under generally accepted accounting principles, that actuarial assumptions be characterized by conservatism which is "reasonable and realistic." (Paragraph 8.06)

Once preliminary benefit and reserve factors have been calculated, the actuary should be aware of the emergence of profit for reasonableness under a range of plausible assumptions. This would assure that the inclusion of a provision for adverse deviation in the assumptions used in the benefit expense reserve calculation does in fact defer income to later durations.

A discussion of considerations to be taken into account when setting each of the assumptions follows.

4.5.3 Investment Earnings Rate

Many traditional life insurance products have a substantial investment component. The investment component builds up over a number of years and is typically guaranteed by the insurer, thus subjecting the company to the risk of not earning the investment return anticipated in the pricing of the product.

In practice, actuaries have typically reflected this risk by assuming a declining investment earnings rate in later policy durations for GAAP benefit reserves and DAC amortization schedules/expense reserves. Thus, if all other assumptions used to generate benefit/expense reserves and/or DAC amortization schedules are realized, profit will emerge as a level percentage of premium, as well as the difference between the investment earnings rate earned versus that assumed to be earned (in other words, release from risk of adverse deviation).

SFAS 60 gives the following guidance when setting the investment assumption:

> Interest assumptions used in estimating the liability for future policy benefits shall be based on estimates of investment yields (net of related investment expenses) expected at the time insurance contracts are made. The interest assumption for each block of new insurance contracts (a group of insurance contracts that may be limited to contracts issued under the same plan in a particular year) shall be consistent with circumstances, such as actual yields, trends in yields, portfolio mix and maturities, and the enterprise's general investment experience. (Paragraph 22)

The *Audit and Accounting Guide* states:

> In estimating yields for current contract issues, the entity considers its current and historical portfolio yields, trends in such yields, kinds of contracts, asset-liability relationships of yields and maturities, new money rates and cash flow projections for the particular mix of the investment portfolio, and general investment experience. Some entities may use a level interest assumption, while others use scaled down or graded interest assumptions since it is difficult to estimate yields so far into the future. Any anticipated effects of economic conditions on the interest assumption are also similarly applicable to the expense assumptions. Interest assumptions for FASB Statement No. 60 contracts must include a provision for adverse deviation. (Paragraph 8.107)

4.5.4 Mortality and Morbidity Rates

In practice, the mortality/morbidity assumptions used to calculate GAAP benefit reserves generally include a provision for adverse deviation, typically five to ten percent in excess of best-estimate assumptions. Doing so increases the net GAAP benefit premium and reduces the amount of profit in any year that emerges as a level percentage of premium and increases the amount of profit that emerges from the difference between the mortality/morbidity assumed in the development of benefit/expense reserves or DAC amortization schedules and the mortality/morbidity expected.

Mortality and morbidity experience expected at the time the insurance contract is written, including a provision for adverse deviation, should be used when establishing the liability for future policy benefits.

SFAS 60 states:

> The risk of antiselection (the tendency for lower terminations of poor risks) also shall be considered in making morbidity assumptions. (Paragraph 24)

Insured mortality experience has shown consistent improvement in the 1980s and 1990s. This improvement can be attributed to general improvement in the health habits of the population, advances in medicine, and improvements in the selection and classification of risks by underwriters. It is debatable whether levels of improvement seen historically will continue into the future. In practice, for life insurance coverage, it is rare that improvement in mortality levels is projected in the mortality assumed in the calculation of net GAAP benefit premiums. However, the reduction (or elimination) of an explicit provision for adverse deviation in the mortality assumptions used to calculate net GAAP benefit premiums may be justified if improvements in mortality experience are anticipated prospectively. The financial reporting actuary needs to be fully aware of the assumptions underlying any future improvement embedded in the pricing assumptions.

The *Audit and Accounting Guide* states:

> The mortality assumptions reflect realistic expectations of future results, considering historical experience. The life insurance entity may use tables developed from its internal experience, or may modify published tables that are consistent with its own expected results. (Paragraph 8.50) These assumptions should also include a provision for adverse deviation. (Paragraph 8.61)

For some *SFAS 60* products, such as increasing-premium term life insurance, it is challenging to establish the mortality assumption. Many actuaries believe that mortality, lapses, and premium increases are inextricably linked. In addition to the company's underwriting and marketing methods, factors such as product design, competition, and consumer attitudes can influence the actual mortality experience. When a scheduled premium increase arrives, some policyholders will find and qualify for lower premium policies from another carrier. Some policyholders will balk at frequent or large premium increases and simply drop all coverage. The groups of people who lapse for these reasons are usually expected to be better mortality risks. Consequently, the groups of insured lives that remain in force are expected to produce higher future mortality than the original pool of issues. The actuary should consider these potential effects when choosing mortality assumptions. Guidance for some possible techniques can be found in *Pricing a Select and Ultimate Renewable Term Policy* (Jeffrey Dukes and Andrew McDonald, 1980) and *Mortality and Lapse Assumptions in Renewable Term Insurance* (David Becker and Theodore Kitsos, 1985).

4.5.5 Lapse Rates

Lapse (also called termination or withdrawal) rates are used in the calculation of GAAP benefit/expense reserves or DAC amortization schedules. The actuary must inspect the lapse rates selected, because the profitability of some products (long term care, disability income, term life insurance) increases if lapse/termination rates in later policy durations increase. Higher lapses will increase the portion of the premium necessary to amortize DAC, thereby reducing the profitability of the product. Conversely, lower lapses will decrease the portion of the premium necessary to amortize DAC, thereby increasing the profitability of the product. This would argue for an increase in the lapse rates used to calculate GAAP benefit/expense reserves or DAC amortization schedules.

However, the benefit premium for products with little or no surrender benefits (long term care, disability income, term life insurance) that have level premiums supporting a policyholder benefit that has a risk of loss that increases with attained age/policy duration will generally decrease if lapse rates are increased. This is particularly true for lapses assumed at later policy durations.

Thus, adding a provision for adverse deviation by increasing lapse rates for all durations can actually increase the reported profit in early policy durations - an unintended and undesirable result. Because of this phenomenon, in practice best-estimate lapse rates may be appropriate in the calculation of GAAP benefit reserves, expense reserves and DAC amortization schedules. Alternatively, policy lapse rates may be increased in the early policy durations and lowered in the later policy durations. The actuary should test the net effect on the emergence of profitability before finalizing the lapse rate assumption.

The *Audit and Accounting Guide* states:

> Withdrawals affect anticipated premiums and death benefits; therefore, the liability computations should include provision for withdrawals, using anticipated withdrawal rates and contractual nonforfeiture benefits. (Paragraph 8.56) These assumptions should also include a provision for adverse deviation. (Paragraph 8.61)

With respect to policy terminations, *SFAS 60* states:

> Termination assumptions used in estimating the liability for future policy benefits shall be based on anticipated terminations and nonforfeiture benefits, using anticipated termination rates and contractual nonforfeiture benefits. Termination rates may vary by plan of insurance, age at issue, year of issue, frequency of premium payment, and other factors. If composite rates are used, the rates shall be representative of the enterprise's actual mix of business. Termination assumptions shall be made for long-duration insurance contracts without termination benefits because of the effects of terminations on anticipated premiums and claim costs. (Paragraph 25)

With respect to health products, it should be noted that for coverages which have increasing claim costs, it is not conservative to assume high lapse rates in renewal years.

After the actuary has chosen the lapse assumptions, he or she should verify that there are no anomalies at the end of the coverage period. Naturally, the combination of a lapse rate and the respective mortality should not cause the total decrement rate to exceed 100%. Further, if the combined decrement rate in total reaches 100% before the end of the coverage period, the actuary should reconsider the decrement scheme at the end of the table so that reserves are provided through the final duration of the contract.

4.5.6 Expenses

The reader should refer to Chapter 3 for guidance on expense categorization and selection of assumptions. Several observations on commission rate assumptions are discussed here.

Commissions on traditional life business are typically heaped, such as 100% in year one, 15% in year two, 7% in years three through ten and 2% thereafter. The level ultimate commission need not be deferred because it is already matched as a level percentage of premiums. However, it certainly should be considered in the expense net premium, which may be used for recoverability and loss recognition purposes.

Provisions for adverse deviation are not included in commission assumptions because they are capable of exact determination.

4.5.7 Taxes

Premiums on most traditional life business are subject to premium taxes in the various states. Because premium tax is a level percentage of the gross premium, no maintenance expense reserve is generated. However, as in the case of level maintenance expenses, there is a net premium that should be considered for recoverability and loss recognition purposes.

Federal income tax (FIT) is usually not considered in the reserving mechanism. Benefit reserves, maintenance reserves and DAC are calculated gross of FIT. A deferred tax asset or liability entry in the balance sheet is made to reflect the different timing of GAAP profits from taxable income. This subject is addressed in Chapter 18.

4.6 Lock-In

Assumptions used in the determination of the liability for future policyholder benefits and the amortization of DAC are locked in at the time the policy is issued.

The *Audit and Accounting Guide* states:

> For FASB Statement No. 60 long-duration contracts and FASB Statement No. 97 limited-payment contracts, GAAP requires that the original assumptions used when the contracts are issued be locked in and that those assumptions be used in all future liability calculations as long as the resulting liabilities are adequate to provide for the future benefits and expenses under the related contracts. (Paragraph 8.63)

Use of assumptions that are locked in at time of issue means that absent loss recognition, the same assumptions should be used forever in accounting for that particular block of business. In practice, benefit and expense "reserve factors" are developed per policy in force. These factors are developed using lapse rate assumptions that are locked in at the time the policy is issued. In subsequent accounting periods, these factors are applied to the actual number of units in force. Alternatively, GAAP benefit reserves may be recalculated each accounting period by using the locked in assumptions determined at issue. This recalculation, sometimes called "first principles," is equivalent to the application of reserve factors. This has emerged as a practice for many companies given the added speed of modern computing capabilities. A similar dynamic adjustment, reflecting the actual number of units in force (versus those projected to be in force based upon the locked in withdrawal assumptions) is sometimes made to DAC worksheets developed at the time of issue. None of these adjustments is considered to be in violation of the lock in concept detailed in *SFAS 60*.

4.7 Loss Recognition

Emerging experience different from that assumed at the issuance of the policy may result in a premium deficiency. As discussed in Chapter 3, *SFAS 60* states that a premium deficiency exists if:

> ... existing contract liabilities, together with the present value of future gross premiums, will not be sufficient (a) to cover the present value of future benefits to be paid to or on behalf of policyholders and settlement and maintenance costs relating to a block of long-duration contracts and (b) to recover unamortized acquisition costs. (Paragraph 35)

If a prospective loss is expected on a group of insurance contracts, a premium deficiency exists.

With respect to a premium deficiency for long-duration contracts, *SFAS 60* states:

> A premium deficiency shall be recognized by a charge to income and (a) a reduction of unamortized acquisition costs or (b) an increase in the liability for future policy benefits. If a premium deficiency does occur, future changes in the liability shall be based on the revised assumptions. No loss shall be reported currently if it results in creating future income. (Paragraph 36)

The *Audit and Accounting Guide* states:

> This deficiency represents a loss that, in conformity with GAAP, should be recognized immediately by a charge to earnings and either a reduction of unamortized acquisition costs or an increase in the liability for future policy benefits. Future annual reserve additions should be based on the revised assumptions. No charge should be made to record currently an indicated loss that will result in the creation of an apparent profit in the future. (Paragraph 10.46)
>
> Adjustments should always be made when losses first become apparent. (Paragraph 10.47)
>
> Although the computation can be made only by individual blocks of business, a provision for premium deficiency at a minimum should be recognized if the aggregate liability on an entire line of business is deficient. (Paragraph 10.47)

ASOP No. 10, "Methods and Assumptions for Use in Life Insurance Company Financial Statements Prepared in Accordance with GAAP" addresses loss recognition as follows:

> *Recognition of Loss*. GAAP requires the recognition of a loss when it is probable and can be reasonably estimated (SFAS No. 5, *Accounting for Contingencies*). This is further discussed in SFAS No. 60, SFAS No. 97, and SOP No. 95-1. If the actuary is asked to perform a loss recognition analysis, the actuary should use best-estimate assumptions.

The hierarchy of recognizing loss recognition on the balance sheet is elaborated in Chapter 3. Unamortized acquisition costs are decreased first. If such costs have been entirely written off and a premium deficiency still remains, the liability for future policy benefits is increased. In determining whether a premium deficiency exists, the actuary should use best-estimate assumptions. The level of reduction in unamortized acquisition costs or increase in the liability for policyholder benefits should not create future income. These best-estimate assumptions are then used in future periods in determining the level of unamortized acquisition costs and liability for future policyholder benefits and are locked in until an additional premium deficiency exists in the future.

SFAS 60 gives the following guidance in determining the appropriate grouping of policies to use when assessing whether a premium deficiency exists for either a long-duration contract or a short-duration contract:

> A probable loss on insurance contracts exists if there is a premium deficiency relating to short-duration or long-duration contracts. Insurance contracts shall be grouped consistent with the enterprise's manner of acquiring, servicing, and measuring the profitability of its insurance contracts to determine if a premium deficiency exists. (Paragraph 32)

The definitive guidance on grouping contracts for loss recognition is addressed in Chapter 3. Examples of such applications follow. Some companies look at all policies issued within a particular GAAP era (defined as when the assumptions for future policyholder benefits and amortization of deferred acquisition costs were set at the same time). Other groupings used in practice include policy forms within an issue year, line of business by issue year, or on an entire line of business basis.

The *Audit Guide*, in its Glossary, defines a "block of business" as:

> ... a group of policies as distinguished from a line of business. The term can be used in a narrow sense to refer to a particular group of contracts issued under the same plan in a particular year.

According to *SFAS 60*, paragraph 35, the amount of premium deficiency is determined as [(a) – (b)] – (c):

(a) present value of future payments for benefits and related settlement and maintenance costs, determined using revised assumptions based on actual and anticipated experience

(b) present value of future gross premiums, determined using revised assumptions based on actual and anticipated experience

(c) the liability for future policy benefits at the valuation date, reduced by unamortized acquisition costs

Note that the quantity [(a) – (b)] in the above is the gross premium reserve and that (c) is the GAAP net reserve being tested for deficiency. Of course, provisions for adverse deviation are removed from the assumptions for purposes of this test.

For recoverability, the issues of the most recent period are generally grouped together for analysis.

4.8 *SFAS 60* Numerical Examples – 20 Year Endowment

The following examples illustrate the development of GAAP benefit and expense reserves as well as the emergence of GAAP profits. The product is a level-premium, nonparticipating, guaranteed-cost 10-year endowment. Table 4-1 shows the best-estimate assumptions used in pricing the contract. Statutory reserves are illustrative only and do not affect the GAAP results.

Table 4-1
Per Policy Assumptions for Sample 10-Year Endowment Projected on a Best-Estimate Basis

(1)	(2)	(3)	(4)	(5)	(6)	(7)	(8)	(9)	(10)	(11)	(12)
Policy Year,	**Mortality Rate**	**Withdrawal Rate**	**Gross Premium**	**Face Amount**	**Per Policy Expense**	**Per Unit Expense**	**Commission Expense**	**Per Premium Expense**	**Investment Rate**	**Statutory Reserve**	**Cash Value**
0				1,000.00						0.00	0.00
1	0.00063	18.00%	95.00	1,000.00	35.00	1.00	80.00%	2.25%	7.00%	100.00	0.00
2	0.00076	12.00%	95.00	1,000.00	35.00	0.00	4.00%	2.25%	7.00%	200.00	100.00
3	0.00099	10.00%	95.00	1,000.00	35.00	0.00	4.00%	2.25%	7.00%	300.00	210.00
4	0.00114	9.00%	95.00	1,000.00	35.00	0.00	4.00%	2.25%	7.00%	400.00	320.00
5	0.00128	8.00%	95.00	1,000.00	35.00	0.00	4.00%	2.25%	7.00%	500.00	430.00
6	0.00140	7.00%	95.00	1,000.00	35.00	0.00	4.00%	2.25%	7.00%	600.00	540.00
7	0.00158	6.00%	95.00	1,000.00	35.00	0.00	4.00%	2.25%	7.00%	700.00	650.00
8	0.00178	5.00%	95.00	1,000.00	35.00	0.00	4.00%	2.25%	7.00%	800.00	760.00
9	0.00201	4.00%	95.00	1,000.00	35.00	0.00	4.00%	2.25%	7.00%	900.00	870.00
10	0.00224	100.00%	95.00	1,000.00	35.00	0.00	4.00%	2.25%	7.00%	1000.00	1000.00

Sample policy: Male, age 35
Premium mode: annual
Units of coverage: 100.000

Legend:
(1) Time, in years
(2) Mortality rate, applied at the middle of the year
(3) Withdrawal rate, applied at the end of the year
(4) Gross premium per year
(5) Face amount per policy unit
(6) Expense per policy, per year, beginning of year (maintenance expense)
(7) Expense per unit of face amount, per year, beginning of year (acquisition expense)
(8) Commission expense (as a percentage of premium)
(9) Expense as a percentage of premium (premium tax)
(10) Investment rate
(11) Statutory reserve per unit (at the end of the policy year)
(12) Cash value per unit (at the end of the policy year)

Table 4-2 displays the policy cash flows projected on a best estimate basis that, along with statutory reserves, produce book profit. The pre-tax profit margin is defined as the present value of pre-tax profits divided by the present value of premiums, all discounted at the assumed pre-tax investment earnings rate. The complement is the ratio of the present value of benefits and expenses divided by the present value of gross premiums, all discounted at the expected investment earnings rate.

Table 4-2
Statutory Book Profits for Sample 10-Year Endowment Projected on a Best-Estimate Basis

(1) Policy Year$_t$	(13) Projected In Force	(14) Premium Income	(15) Investment Income	(16) Maintenance Expense	(17) Acquisition Expense	(18) Commission Expense	(19) Premium Tax	(20) Mortality Expense	(21) Surrender Expense	(22) Increase in Reserve	(23) Book Profit
0	100,000										
1	81,948	9,500.00	106.42	35.00	100.00	7,600.00	213.75	63.00	0.00	8,194.83	(6,600.16)
2	72,060	7,785.09	1,080.38	28.68	0.00	311.40	175.16	62.28	982.63	6,217.11	1,088.20
3	64,790	6,845.67	1,453.86	25.22	0.00	273.83	154.03	71.34	1,511.76	5,024.92	1,238.45
4	58,891	6,155.01	1,760.37	22.68	0.00	246.20	138.49	73.86	1,863.81	4,119.65	1,450.70
5	54,111	5,594.67	2,012.07	20.61	0.00	223.79	125.88	75.38	2,023.27	3,498.80	1,639.01
6	50,252	5,140.51	2,227.29	18.94	0.00	205.62	115.66	75.75	2,042.52	3,096.15	1,813.16
7	47,163	4,773.98	2,419.93	17.59	0.00	190.96	107.41	79.40	1,956.75	2,862.40	1,979.41
8	44,725	4,480.45	2,600.96	16.51	0.00	179.22	100.81	83.95	1,788.99	2,765.96	2,145.97
9	42,849	4,248.85	2,779.23	15.65	0.00	169.95	95.60	89.90	1,553.29	2,784.71	2,318.97
10	0	4,070.70	2,962.30	15.00	0.00	162.83	91.59	95.98	42,753.49	(38,564.53)	2,478.64

Notes:
Premiums paid at the beginning of the year.
Commissions and expenses paid at the beginning of the year.
Death benefits paid at the middle of the year.
Withdrawals paid at the end of the year.

Legend:
(1) Time, in years
$(13)_t$ Projected face amount in force, $(13)_t = (13)_{t-1} \times \{[1 - (2)_t] \times [1 - (3)_t]\}$, $(13)_0 = (5)_0 \times$ units $= 1{,}000 \times 100.000$
$(14)_t$ Premium, $(14)_t = [13)_{t-1} / 1000] \times (4)_t$
$(15)_t$ Investment income, $(15)_t = (10)_t \times [(14)_t - (16)_t - (17)_t - (18)_t - (19)_t + (22)_1 + ... + (22)_{t-1}] - \{[1 + (10)_t]^{.5} - 1\} \times (20)_t$
(Assumes death benefits paid at mid year)
$(16)_t$ Maintenance expense (per policy expense), $(16)_t = \{[(13)_{t-1} / 1000] / 100\} \times (6)_t$ (Based on policy count, inforce divided by $(5)_t$ divided by units)
$(17)_t$ Acquisition expense (per unit expense), $(17)_t = [(13)_{t-1} / 1000] \times (7)_t$
$(18)_t$ Commission expense, $(18)_t = (14)_t \times (8)_t$
$(19)_t$ Premium tax (per premium expense), $(19)_t = (14)_t \times (9)_t$
$(20)_t$ Mortality expense (death benefits), $(20)_t = (13)_{t-1} \times (2)_t$
$(21)_t$ Surrender expense (withdrawals), $(21)_t = [(13)_{t-1} / 1000] \times [1 - (2)_t] \times (12)_t \times (3)_t$ (Assumes death before surrenders)
$(22)_t$ Increase in statutory reserve, $(22)_t = [(13)_t / 1000] \times (11)_t - [(13)_{t-1} / 1000] \times (11)_{t-1}$
$(23)_t = (14)_t + (15)_t - (16)_t - (17)_t - (18)_t - (19)_t - (20)_t - (21)_t - (22)_t$

Profit margin equals the present value of book profits divided by the present value of premium income = 9.23%

The pre-tax profit margin is dependent only on the level of ultimate reserve held (in this case, the endowment amount itself) and is independent of the reserves held in the intermediate years.

The calculated GAAP benefit and expense reserves are presented in Table 4-3. The GAAP profit projected to emerge assuming that the benefit and expense reserves are calculated using best estimate assumptions (no margin for adverse deviation) is a level percentage (the pre-tax profit margin) times the premium income (accumulated with interest to the end of the year).

Tables 4-4 through 4-6 present similar results assuming a provision for adverse deviation has been included in the investment rate and expense assumptions. These tables demonstrate that if experience emerges as assumed in the calculation of the reserves (i.e., actual experience that emerges is worse than expected), the pre-tax profit margin is reduced.

Table 4-3
Key GAAP Statistics for Sample 10-Year Endowment Projected on a Best-Estimate Basis

(1) Policy $Year_t$	(13) Projected In force	(24) Percentage of Premium	(25) Expense Reserve	(26) Benefit Reserve	(27) GAAP Book Profit
0	100,000		0.00	0.00	
1	81,948	9.23%	(7,599.64)	8,400.81	938.13
2	72,060	9.23%	(7,422.69)	16,672.50	768.78
3	64,790	9.23%	(7,048.82)	25,123.47	676.01
4	58,891	9.23%	(6,532.30)	33,925.45	607.81
5	54,111	9.23%	(5,860.70)	43,187.59	552.48
6	50,252	9.23%	(5,024.59)	53,021.20	507.63
7	47,163	9.23%	(4,018.79)	63,531.13	471.43
8	44,725	9.23%	(2,842.41)	74,817.85	442.45
9	42,849	9.23%	(1,499.64)	86,970.30	419.58
10	0	9.23%	0.00	0.00	401.98

Legend:

(1) Time, in years

$(13)_t$ Projected face amount in force, $(13)_t = (13)_{t-1} \times \{[1-(2)_t] \times [1-(3)_t]\}$; $(13)_0 = (5)_0 \times \text{units} = 1{,}000 \times 100.000$

$(24)_t$ GAAP book profit as a percentage of premium, $(24)_t = (27)_t \,/\, \{(14)_t \times [1+(10)_t]\}$

$(25)_t$ GAAP expense reserve, $(25)_t = \{(25)_{t-1} \times [(13)_{t-1}/(13)_0] - (16)_t - (17)_t - (18)_t - (19)_t + .2240 \times (14)_t\} \times [1+(10)_t] \,/\, [(13)_t/(13)_0]$

$(26)_t$ GAAP benefit reserve, $(26)_t = \{\{(26)_{t-1} \times [(13)_{t-1}/(13)_0] + .6837 \times (14)_t\} \times [1+(10)_t] - (21)_t - (20)_t \times [1+(10)_t]^{.5}\} \,/\, [(13)_t/(13)_0]$

$(27)_t$ GAAP book profit, $(27)_t = (23)_t + (22)_t - \{[(13)_t/(13)_0] \times [(25)_t + (26)_t] - [(13)_{t-1}/(13)_0] \times [(25)_{t-1} + (26)_{t-1})] +$
$(10)_t \times \{(25)_{t-1} \times [(13)_{t-1}/(13)_0] + (26)_{t-1} \times [(13)_{t-1}/(13)_0] - [(22)_1 + \ldots + (22)_{t-1}]\}$

GAAP benefit premium = 6,494.85 = $(4)_1$ × units × present value of columns (20) and (21) divided by the present value of column (14) discounted using the investment rate.

GAAP benefit premium percentage = 6,494.85 / [$(4)_1$ × units] = 68.37%.

GAAP expense premium = 2,128.39 = $(4)_1$ × units × present value of columns (16), (17), (18) and (19) divided by the present value of columns (14) discounted using the investment rate; includes acquisition and maintenance component.

GAAP expense premium percentage = 2,128.39 / [$(4)_1$ × units] = 22.40%.

Table 4-4
Per Policy Assumptions Sample 10-Year Endowment with Provision for Adverse Deviation

(1) Policy Year$_t$	(2) Mortality Rate	(3) Withdrawal Rate	(4) Gross Premium	(5) Face Amount	(6) Per Policy Expense	(7) Per Thousand Expense	(8) Commission Expense	(9) Per Premium Expense	(10) Investment Rate	(11) Statutory Reserve	(12) Cash Value
0				1,000.00						0.00	0.00
1	0.00063	18.00%	95.00	1,000.00	36.00	1.00	80.00%	2.25%	7.00%	100.00	0.00
2	0.00076	12.00%	95.00	1,000.00	36.00	0.00	4.00%	2.25%	6.90%	200.00	100.00
3	0.00099	10.00%	95.00	1,000.00	36.00	0.00	4.00%	2.25%	6.80%	300.00	210.00
4	0.00114	9.00%	95.00	1,000.00	36.00	0.00	4.00%	2.25%	6.70%	400.00	320.00
5	0.00128	8.00%	95.00	1,000.00	36.00	0.00	4.00%	2.25%	6.50%	500.00	430.00
6	0.00140	7.00%	95.00	1,000.00	36.00	0.00	4.00%	2.25%	6.50%	600.00	540.00
7	0.00158	6.00%	95.00	1,000.00	36.00	0.00	4.00%	2.25%	6.50%	700.00	650.00
8	0.00178	5.00%	95.00	1,000.00	36.00	0.00	4.00%	2.25%	6.50%	800.00	760.00
9	0.00201	4.00%	95.00	1,000.00	36.00	0.00	4.00%	2.25%	6.50%	900.00	870.00
10	0.00224	100.00%	95.00	1,000.00	36.00	0.00	4.00%	2.25%	6.50%	1,000.00	1,000.00

Sample policy: Male, age 35
Premium mode: annual
Units of coverage: 100.000

Legend:
(1) Time, in years
(2) Mortality rate, applied at the end of the year
(3) Withdrawal rate, applied at the end of the year
(4) Gross premium per year
(5) Face amount per policy unit
(6) Expense per policy, per year (maintenance expense)
(7) Expense per unit of face amount, per year (acquisition expense)
(8) Commission expense (as a percentage of premium)
(9) Expense as a percentage of premium (premium tax)
(10) Investment rate
(11) Statutory reserve per unit (at the end of the policy year)
(12) Cash value per unit (at the end of the policy year)

Table 4-5

Policy Year Results for Sample 10-Year Endowment with Provision for Adverse Deviation

(1) Policy $Year_t$	(13) Projected In force	(14) Premium Income	(15) Investment Income	(16) Maintenance Expense	(17) Acquisition Expense	(18) Commission Expense	(19) Premium Tax	(20) Mortality Expense	(21) Surrender Expense	(22) Increase in Reserve	(23) Book Profit
0	100,000										
1	81,948	9,500.00	106.35	36.00	100.00	7,600.00	213.75	63.00	0.00	8,194.83	(6,601.23)
2	72,060	7,785.09	1,064.89	29.50	0.00	311.40	175.16	62.28	982.63	6,217.11	1,071.89
3	64,790	6,845.67	1,412.27	25.94	0.00	273.83	154.03	71.34	1,511.76	5,024.92	1,196.14
4	58,891	6,155.01	1,684.88	23.32	0.00	246.20	138.49	73.86	1,863.81	4,119.65	1,374.56
5	54,111	5,594.67	1,868.31	21.20	0.00	223.79	125.88	75.38	2,023.27	3,498.80	1,494.66
6	50,252	5,140.51	2,068.16	19.48	0.00	205.62	115.66	75.75	2,042.52	3,096.15	1,653.49
7	47,163	4,773.98	2,247.04	18.09	0.00	190.96	107.41	79.40	1,956.75	2,862.40	1,806.02
8	44,725	4,480.45	2,415.14	16.98	0.00	179.22	100.81	83.95	1,788.99	2,765.96	1,959.69
9	42,849	4,248.85	2,580.68	16.10	0.00	169.95	95.60	89.90	1,553.29	2,784.71	2,119.97
10	0	4,070.70	2,750.68	15.43	0.00	162.83	91.59	95.98	42,753.49	(38,564.53)	2,266.59

Premiums paid at the beginning of the year.
Commissions and expenses paid at the beginning of the year
Death Benefits paid at the middle of the year
Withdrawals paid at the end of the year

Legend:

(1) Time, in years

$(13)_t$ Projected face amount in force, $(13)_t = (13)_{t-1} \times \{[(1-(2)_t] \times [1-(3)_t]\}$, $(13)_0 = (5)_0 \times$ units $= 1{,}000 \times 100.000$

$(14)_t$ Premium, $(14)_t = [(13)_{t-1} / 1000] \times (4)_t$

$(15)_t$ Investment income, $(15)_t = (10)_t \times [(14)_t - (16)_t - (17)_t - (18)_t - (19)_t + (22)_1 + \ldots + (22)_{t-1}] - \{[1 + (10)_t]^{.5} - 1\} \times (20)_t$ (assumes death benefits paid at mid year)

$(16)_t$ Maintenance expense (per policy expense), $(16)_t = \{[(13)_{t-1} / 1000] / 100\} \times (6)_t$ (based on policy count, in force divided by $(5)_t$ divided by units)

$(17)_t$ Acquisition expense (per unit expense), $(17)_t = [(13)_{t-1} / 1000] \times (7)_t$

$(18)_t$ Commission expense, $(18)_t = (14)_t \times (8)_t$

$(19)_t$ Premium tax (per premium expense), $(19)_t = (14)_t \times (9)_t$

$(20)_t$ Mortality expense (death benefits), $(20)_t = (13)_{t-1} \times (2)_t$

$(21)_t$ Surrender expense (withdrawals), $(21)_t = [(13)_{t-1} / 1000] \times [1-(2)_t] \times (12)_t \times (3)_t$ (assumes death before surrenders)

$(22)_t$ Increase in statutory reserve, $(22)_t = [(13)_t / 1000] \times (11)_t - [(13)_{t-1} / 1000] \times (11)_{t-1}$

$(23)_t = (14)_t + (15)_t - (16)_t - (17)_t - (18)_t - (19)_t - (20)_t - (21)_t - (22)_t$

Profit margin equals the present value of book profits divided by the present value of premium income = 7.91%

Table 4-6
Key GAAP Statistics for Sample 10-Year Endowment with Provision for Adverse Deviation

(1) Policy Year_t	(13) Projected In force	(24) Percent Premium	(25) Expense Reserve	(26) Benefit Reserve	(27) GAAP Book Profit
0	100,000		0.00	0.00	
1	81,948	7.91%	(7,612.70)	8,576.57	803.73
2	72,060	7.91%	(7,443.78)	17,032.92	658.02
3	64,790	7.91%	(7,072.57)	25,660.06	578.08
4	58,891	7.91%	(6,553.61)	34,609.17	519.27
5	54,111	7.91%	(5,869.60)	43,916.49	471.11
6	50,252	7.91%	(5,022.79)	53,744.33	432.87
7	47,163	7.91%	(4,009.32)	64,187.79	402.00
8	44,725	7.91%	(2,829.72)	75,337.73	377.29
9	42,849	7.91%	(1,489.64)	87,273.98	357.78
10	0	7.91%	0.00	0.00	342.78

Legend:

(1) Time, in years

$(13)_t$ Projected face amount in force, $(13)_t = (13)_{t-1} \times \{[1 - (2)_t] \times [1 - (3)_t]\}$, $(13)_0 = (5)_0 \times$ units $= 1{,}000 \times 100.000$

$(24)_t$ GAAP book profit as a percentage of premium, $(24)_t = (27)_t \,/\, \{(14)_t \times [1 + (10)_t]\}$

$(25)_t$ GAAP expense reserve, $(25)_t = \{(25)_{t-1} \times [(13)_{t-1} / (13)_0] - (16)_t - (17)_t - (18)_t - (19)_t + .2231 \times (14)_t\} \times [1 + (10)_t] \,/\, [(13)_t / (13)_0)]$

$(26)_t$ GAAP benefit reserve, $(26)_t = \{\, \{(26)_{t-1} \times [(13)_{t-1} / (13)_0] + .6978 \times (14)_t\} \times [1 + (10)_t] - (21)_t - (20)_t \times [1 + (10)_t]^{.5} \,\} \,/\, [(13)_t / (13)_0]$

$(27)_t$ GAAP book profit, $(27)_t = (23)_t + (22)_t - \{[(13)_t / (13)_0] \times [(25)_t + (26)_t] - [(13)_{t-1} / (13)_0] \times [(25)_{t-1} + (26)_{t-1})]\} +$
$(10)_t \times \{(25)_{t-1} \times [(13)_{t-1} / (13)_0] + (26)_{t-1} \times [(13)_{t-1} / (13)_0] - [(22)_1 + \ldots + (22)_{t-1}]\}$

GAAP benefit premium = 6,629.46 = $(4)_1$ × units × present value of columns (20) and (21) divided by the present value of column (14) discounted using the investment rate

GAAP benefit premium percentage = 6,629.46 / [$(4)_1$ × units] = 69.78%

GAAP expense premium = 2,119.39 = $(4)_1$ × units × present value of columns (16), (17), (18), and (19) divided by the present value of columns (14) discounted using the investment rate; includes acquisition and maintenance component

GAAP expense premium percentage = 2,119.39 / [$(4)_1$ × units] = 22.31%

Table 4-7 shows the GAAP results assuming best estimate assumptions are realized but GAAP benefit and expense reserves are calculated using margins for adverse deviation. Under this situation, profits emerge as an increasing percentage of premium over the life of the contract. Because the overall profit is independent of the level of intermediate reserves held, the present value of profits using the investment rate as the discount rate remains unchanged due to the change in the reserve methodology.

Table 4-7
Key GAAP Statistics for Sample 10-Year Endowment Projected on a Best-Estimate Basis with Margin for Adverse Deviation

(1) Policy $Year_t$	(13) Projected In force	(24) Percent Premium	(25) Expense Reserve	(26) Benefit Reserve	(27) GAAP Book Profit
0	100,000		0.00	0.00	
1	81,948	7.92%	(7,612.70)	8,576.57	804.80
2	72,060	8.01%	(7,443.78)	17,032.92	666.93
3	64,790	8.26%	(7,072.57)	25,660.06	605.39
4	58,891	8.70%	(6,553.61)	34,609.17	573.23
5	54,111	9.69%	(5,869.60)	43,916.49	580.29
6	50,252	10.18%	(5,022.79)	53,744.33	560.20
7	47,163	10.71%	(4,009.32)	64,187.79	547.06
8	44,725	11.27%	(2,829.72)	75,337.73	540.41
9	42,849	11.88%	(1,489.64)	87,273.98	540.03
10	0	12.53%	0.00	0.00	545.80

Legend:
(1) Time, in years
$(13)_t$ Projected face amount in force, $(13)_t = (13)_{t-1} \times \{[1-(2)_t] \times [1-(3)_t]\}$, $(13)_0 = (5)_0 \times$ units = 1,000 × 100.000
$(24)_t$ GAAP book profit as a percentage of premium, $(24)_t = (27)_t \ / \ \{(14)_t \times [1+(10)_t]\}$
$(25)_t$ GAAP expense reserve, calculated as detailed in Table 4-6, using expected assumptions for future experience per Table 4-5
$(26)_t$ GAAP benefit reserve, calculated as detailed in Table 4-6, using expected assumptions for future experience per Table 4-5
$(27)_t$ GAAP book profit, calculated as detailed in Table 4-6, using actual emerging experience per Table 4-2

Tables 4-8 through 4-10 illustrate results for the same contract with a severe reduction in the investment earning rate in years six and beyond. The GAAP results shown in Table 4-10 assume reserves calculated as in Table 4-6 (using a margin for adverse deviation but not reflecting the unexpected severe drop in the investment earnings rate). In this instance, losses would emerge in years seven and later. This is unacceptable under GAAP and necessitates a reduction in the DAC and possibly an increase in the benefit reserve held equal to the present value of the projected losses.

Table 4-8
Per Policy Assumptions for Sample 10-Year Endowment with Severe Reduction in Investment Earning Rate in Year Six and Beyond

(1) Policy Year$_t$	(2) Mortality Rate	(3) Withdrawal Rate	(4) Gross Premium	(5) Face Amount	(6) Per Policy Expense	(7) Per Thousand Expense	(8) Commission Expense	(9) Per Premium Expense	(10) Investment Rate	(11) Statutory Reserve	(12) Cash Value
0				1,000.00						0.00	0.00
1	0.00063	18.00%	95.00	1,000.00	35.00	1.00	80.00%	2.25%	7.00%	100.00	0.00
2	0.00076	12.00%	95.00	1,000.00	35.00	0.00	4.00%	2.25%	7.00%	200.00	100.00
3	0.00099	10.00%	95.00	1,000.00	35.00	0.00	4.00%	2.25%	7.00%	300.00	210.00
4	0.00114	9.00%	95.00	1,000.00	35.00	0.00	4.00%	2.25%	7.00%	400.00	320.00
5	0.00128	8.00%	95.00	1,000.00	35.00	0.00	4.00%	2.25%	7.00%	500.00	430.00
6	0.00140	7.00%	95.00	1,000.00	35.00	0.00	4.00%	2.25%	5.00%	600.00	540.00
7	0.00158	6.00%	95.00	1,000.00	35.00	0.00	4.00%	2.25%	5.00%	700.00	650.00
8	0.00178	5.00%	95.00	1,000.00	35.00	0.00	4.00%	2.25%	5.00%	800.00	760.00
9	0.00201	4.00%	95.00	1,000.00	35.00	0.00	4.00%	2.25%	5.00%	900.00	870.00
10	0.00224	100.00%	95.00	1,000.00	35.00	0.00	4.00%	2.25%	5.00%	1,000.00	1,000.00

Sample policy: Male, age 35
Premium mode: annual
Units of coverage: 100.000

Legend:
(1) Time, in years
(2) Mortality rate, applied at the end of the year
(3) Withdrawal rate, applied at the end of the year
(4) Gross premium per year
(5) Face amount per policy unit
(6) Expense per policy, per year (maintenance expense)
(7) Expense per unit of face amount, per year (acquisition expense)
(8) Commission expense (as a percentage of premium)
(9) Expense as a percentage of premium (premium tax)
(10) Investment rate
(11) Statutory reserve per unit (at the end of the policy year)
(12) Cash value per unit (at the end of the policy year)

Table 4-9
Policy-Year Results for Sample 10-Year Endowment with Severe Reduction in Investent Earning Rate in Year Six and Beyond

(1) Policy Year$_t$	(13) Projected In force	(14) Premium Income	(15) Investment Income	(16) Maintenance Expense	(17) Acquisition Expense	(18) Commission Expense	(19) Premium Tax	(20) Mortality Expense	(21) Surrender Expense	(22) Increase in Reserve	(23) Book Profit
0	100,000										
1	81,948	9,500.00	106.42	35.00	100.00	7,600.00	213.75	63.00	0.00	8,194.83	(6,600.16)
2	72,060	7,785.09	1,080.38	28.68	0.00	311.40	175.16	62.28	982.63	6,217.11	1,088.20
3	64,790	6,845.67	1,453.86	25.22	0.00	273.83	154.03	71.34	1,511.76	5,024.92	1,238.45
4	58,891	6,155.01	1,760.37	22.68	0.00	246.20	138.49	73.86	1,863.81	4,119.65	1,450.70
5	54,111	5,594.67	2,012.07	20.61	0.00	223.79	125.88	75.38	2,023.27	3,498.80	1,639.01
6	50,252	5,140.51	1,590.91	18.94	0.00	205.62	115.66	75.75	2,042.52	3,096.15	1,176.78
7	47,163	4,773.98	1,728.51	17.59	0.00	190.96	107.41	79.40	1,956.75	2,862.40	1,287.99
8	44,725	4,480.45	1,857.82	16.51	0.00	179.22	100.81	83.95	1,788.99	2,765.96	1,402.83
9	42,849	4,248.85	1,985.15	15.65	0.00	169.95	95.60	89.90	1,553.29	2,784.71	1,524.89
10	0	4,070.70	2,115.92	15.00	0.00	162.83	91.59	95.98	42,753.49	(38,564.53)	1,632.26

Premiums paid at the beginning of the year.
Commissions and expenses paid at the beginning of the year
Death Benefits paid at the middle of the year
Withdrawals paid at the end of the year

Legend:
(1) Time, in years
$(13)_t$ Projected face amount in force, $(13)_t = (13)_{t-1} \times \{[1-(2)_t] \times [1-(3)_t]\}$, $(13)_0 = (5)_0 \times$ units $= 1{,}000 \times 100.000$
$(14)_t$ Premium, $(14)_t = [(13)_{t-1} / 1000] \times (4)_t$
$(15)_t$ Investment income, $(15)_t = (10)_t \times [(14)_t - (16)_t - (17)_t - (18)_t - (19)_t + (22)_1 + \ldots + (22)_{t-1}] - \{[1 + (10)_t]^{.5} - 1\} \times (20)_t$ (assumes death benefits paid at mid year)
$(16)_t$ Maintenance expense (per policy expense), $(16)_t = \{[(13)_{t-1} / 1000] / 100\} \times (6)_t$ (based on policy count, inforce divided by $(5)_t$ divided by units)
$(17)_t$ Acquisition expense (per unit expense), $(17)_t = [(13)_{t-1} / 1000] \times (7)_t$
$(18)_t$ Commission expense, $(18)_t = (14)_t \times (8)_t$
$(19)_t$ Premium tax (per premium expense), $(19)_t = (14)_t \times (9)_t$
$(20)_t$ Mortality expense (death benefits), $(20)_t = (13)_{t-1} \times (2)_t$
$(21)_t$ Surrender expense (withdrawals), $(21)_t = [(13)_{t-1} / 1000] \times [1 - (2)_t] \times (12)_t \times (3)_t$ (assumes death before surrenders)
$(22)_t$ Increase in statutory reserve, $(22)_t = [(13)_t / 1000] \times (11)_t - [(13)_{t-1} / 1000] \times (11)_{t-1}$
$(23)_t = (14)_t + (15)_t - (16)_t - (17)_t - (18)_t - (19)_t - (20)_t - (21)_t - (22)_t$

Profit margin equals the present value of book profits divided by the present value of premium income = 5.06%

Table 4-10
Key GAAP Statistics for Sample 10-Year Endowment with Severe Reduction in Investment Earning Rate in Year Six and Beyond

(1) Policy $Year_t$	(13) Projected In force	(24) Percent Premium	(25) Expense Reserve	(26) Benefit Reserve	(27) GAAP Book Profit
0	100,000		0.00	0.00	
1	81,948	7.92%	(7,612.70)	8,576.57	804.80
2	72,060	8.01%	(7,443.78)	17,032.92	666.93
3	64,790	8.26%	(7,072.57)	25,660.06	605.39
4	58,891	8.70%	(6,553.61)	34,609.17	573.23
5	54,111	9.69%	(5,869.60)	43,916.49	580.29
6	50,252	0.99%	(5,022.79)	53,744.33	53.18
7	47,163	(0.62%)	(4,009.32)	64,187.79	(31.01)
8	44,725	(2.34%)	(2,829.72)	75,337.73	(110.08)
9	42,849	(4.19%)	(1,489.64)	87,273.98	(187.03)
10	0	(6.19%)	0.00	0.00	(264.45)

Legend:

(1) Time, in years

$(13)_t$ Projected face amount in force, $(13)_t = (13)_{t-1} \times \{[1 - (2)_t] \times [1 - (3)_t]\}$, $(13)_0 = (5)_0 \times$ units $= 1{,}000 \times 100.000$

$(24)_t$ GAAP book profit as a percentage of premium, $(24)_t = (27)_t \,/\, \{(14)_t \times [1 + (10)_t]\}$

$(25)_t$ GAAP expense reserve, calculated as detailed in Table 4-6, using expected assumptions for future experience per Table 4-5

$(26)_t$ GAAP benefit reserve, calculated as detailed in Table 4-6, using expected assumptions for future experience per Table 4-5

$(27)_t$ GAAP book profit, calculated as detailed in Table 4-6, using actual emerging experience per Table 4-9

Present value of projected losses using the projected investment rate (5.00%) as the discount rate at:
the end of year 6: $508.51
the end of year 7: $502.93
the end of year 8: $417.99
the end of year 9: $251.86

Table 4-11 presents the results assuming a partial DAC write-off occurs equal to the present value of future projected losses. This results in a large loss in year six and zero profits in subsequent years.

Table 4-11
Key GAAP Statistics for Sample 10-Year Endowment with a DAC Write-off Equal to the Present Value of Future Projected Losses

(1) Policy $Year_t$	(13) Projected In force	(24) Percent Premium	(25) Expense Reserve	(26) Benefit Reserve	(27) GAAP Book Profit
0	100,000		0.00	0.00	
1	81,948	7.92%	(7,612.70)	8,576.57	804.80
2	72,060	8.01%	(7,443.78)	17,032.92	666.93
3	64,790	8.26%	(7,072.57)	25,660.06	605.39
4	58,891	8.70%	(6,553.61)	34,609.17	573.23
5	54,111	9.69%	(5,869.60)	43,916.49	580.29
6	50,252	(8.44%)	(4,010.88)	53,744.33	(455.33)
7	47,163	0.00%	(2,942.94)	64,187.79	0.00
8	44,725	0.00%	(1,895.13)	75,337.73	0.00
9	42,849	0.00%	(901.87)	87,273.98	0.00
10	0	0.00%	0.00	0.00	0.00

Legend:
(1) Time, in years
$(13)_t$ Projected face amount in force, $(13)_t = (13)_{t-1} \times \{[1 - (2)_t] \times [1 - (3)_t]\}$, $(13)_0 = (5)_0 \times$ units $= 1{,}000 \times 100.000$
$(24)_t$ GAAP book profit as a percentage of premium, $(24)_t = (27)_t \,/\, \{(14)_t \times [(1 + (10)_t]\}$
$(25)_t$ GAAP expense reserve, through year 6, calculated as detailed in Table 4-6, using expected assumptions for future experience per Table 4-5
$(25)_t$ GAAP expense reserve, after year 6, calculated as detailed in Table 4-6, using expected assumptions for future experience per Table 4-5 + (absolute value of present value of prospective projected losses from Table 10 / $[(13)_t \,/\, (13)_0]$
$(26)_t$ GAAP benefit reserve, calculated as detailed in Table 4-6, using expected assumptions for future experience per Table 4-5
$(27)_t$ GAAP book profit, through year 6 calculated as detailed in Table 4-6, using actual emerging experience per Table 4-9
$(27)_t$ GAAP book profit, equals 0, years 7-10.

Present value of projected losses using the projected investment rate (5.00%) as the discount rate at:
the end of year 6: $508.51
the end of year 7: $502.93
the end of year 8: $417.99
the end of year 9: $251.86

4.9 *SFAS 60* Numerical Examples – 20 Year Term

Term insurance with premium increases can create reserves that appear unusual. This is due to a) an ultimate gross premium stream whose slope isn't correlated well with pricing mortality and b) the existence of extremely large lapse rates in the midst of the product's total life.

Table 4-12 illustrates the features of the policy. It then displays the benefit reserves, both terminal and mean, in the last two columns. The terminal reserve has been calculated after the consideration for lapsed policies.

Table 4-12
Per-Policy Assumptions and GAAP Benefit Reserves for 20-Year Non Level Premium Term Policy

(1) Policy Year$_t$	(2) Mortality Rate	(3) Withdrawal Rate	(4) Gross Premium	(5) Face Amount	(6) Interest Rate	(7) Cash Value	(8) Acquisition Per Premium Expense	(9) Acquisition Per Policy Expense	(10) Maintenance Per Premium Expense	(11) Maintenance Per Policy Expense	(12) GAAP Benefit Reserve (Terminal)	(13) GAAP Benefit Reserve (Mean)
1	0.000936	9.0%	138.00	50,000.00	4.50%	0.00	150.00%	100.00	5.00%	2.50	0.77	0.78
2	0.001376	9.0%	138.00	50,000.00	4.50%	0.00	0.00%	0.00	5.00%	2.50	1.17	1.17
3	0.001848	8.0%	138.00	50,000.00	4.50%	0.00	0.00%	0.00	5.00%	2.50	1.08	1.11
4	0.002200	8.0%	138.00	50,000.00	4.50%	0.00	0.00%	0.00	5.00%	2.50	0.58	0.65
5	0.002504	8.0%	138.00	50,000.00	4.50%	0.00	0.00%	0.00	5.00%	2.50	(0.32)	(0.20)
6	0.002776	7.0%	266.00	50,000.00	4.50%	0.00	0.00%	0.00	5.00%	2.50	0.03	0.14
7	0.003032	5.0%	266.00	50,000.00	4.50%	0.00	0.00%	0.00	5.00%	2.50	0.13	0.26
8	0.003312	5.0%	266.00	50,000.00	4.50%	0.00	0.00%	0.00	5.00%	2.50	(0.05)	0.09
9	0.003648	5.0%	266.00	50,000.00	4.50%	0.00	0.00%	0.00	5.00%	2.50	(0.62)	(0.45)
10	0.004064	95.0%	266.00	50,000.00	4.50%	0.00	0.00%	0.00	5.00%	2.50	(32.20)	(16.73)
11	0.009280	20.0%	1,476.00	50,000.00	4.50%	0.00	0.00%	0.00	5.00%	2.50	(32.04)	(28.39)
12	0.010656	20.0%	1,626.00	50,000.00	4.50%	0.00	0.00%	0.00	5.00%	2.50	(31.37)	(27.73)
13	0.012368	20.0%	1,782.00	50,000.00	4.50%	0.00	0.00%	0.00	5.00%	2.50	(30.38)	(26.77)
14	0.014160	20.0%	1,949.50	50,000.00	4.50%	0.00	0.00%	0.00	5.00%	2.50	(28.90)	(25.36)
15	0.016032	20.0%	2,124.50	50,000.00	4.50%	0.00	0.00%	0.00	5.00%	2.50	(26.74)	(23.34)
16	0.019024	20.0%	2,319.00	50,000.00	4.50%	0.00	0.00%	0.00	5.00%	2.50	(24.87)	(21.53)
17	0.021072	20.0%	2,526.00	50,000.00	4.50%	0.00	0.00%	0.00	5.00%	2.50	(21.92)	(18.80)
18	0.023312	20.0%	2,759.00	50,000.00	4.50%	0.00	0.00%	0.00	5.00%	2.50	(17.38)	(14.62)
19	0.025712	20.0%	3,023.00	50,000.00	4.50%	0.00	0.00%	0.00	5.00%	2.50	(10.40)	(8.25)
20	0.028336	20.0%	3,314.00	50,000.00	4.50%	0.00	0.00%	0.00	5.00%	2.50	0.00	1.19

Sample policy: Male, age 45, annual premium mode
Premium pattern: 5 year level, 5 year level, then 10 years of ART

Legend:
(1) Time, in years
(2) Annual mortality rate, applied at the middle of the month
(3) Annual withdrawal rate, applied at the premium due date
(4) Gross premium per year
(5) Face amount for the policy
(6) GAAP valuation interest rate
(7) Cash value for the policy (at the end of the policy year)
(8) Commission acquisition expense (as a percentage of premium)
(9) Non-commission acquisition expense per policy, per year, beginning of year
(10) Maintenance expense as a percentage of premium
(11) Maintenance expense per policy, per year, beginning of year
(12) GAAP benefit reserve per unit (at the end of the policy year); see column (18) for details
(13) Mean GAAP benefit reserve is Initial plus Terminal

Benefit Premium:	79.38
Acq. Premium:	35.05
Maint. Premium:	8.62
	123.04
Gross Premium:	138.00

The observer will note that the reserves start positive, then go modestly negative, then become significantly negative. While this phenomenon is entirely consistent with actuarial formulas commonly used for GAAP reserve calculations, these formulas do produce a negative liability. There is a school of thought that maintains that negative obligations cannot exist. Thus, a reserve so calculated should be floored at zero.

An inspection of rows 9 and 10 of Table 4-12 reveal that the terminal reserve jumps from –0.62 to –32.20. This is because the inforce is expected to be only 5% of its prior volume by the start of the 11th year. The mean reserve is between these values.

The reserves will be accurately expressed only if the actuary monitors the company's actual inforce during the critical moments before and after significant premium increases. Applying the mean reserve immediately in year ten will cause distortions, as the business will not lapse until the next premium-paying opportunity. Any use of a terminal reserve during this year will cause an overstatement of the reserve, as the policies will not have had any opportunity to lapse. The use of a "final" reserve will have a much better alignment between expected and actual inforce.

Actuaries must also be aware of company practices for retaining business inforce after a premium due date is missed. Companies commonly classify policies as active for 90 days after a premium is missed. Thus, in this example, an inflated reserve would be calculated for the first three months following the anniversary.

Table 4-12 focused on the benefit reserve. Table 4-13 illustrates the magnitude of the DAC and maintenance reserves, which will behave in a fashion similar to benefit reserves.

Table 4-13 also illustrates what happens on a monthly basis. Had this policy been on a monthly mode, the actuary needs to take care that the one-time excessive lapse at the end of the tenth year does not bleed in to the lapses expected during year ten.

Table 4-13

GAAP Reserves for 20-Year Non Level Premium Term Policy

(1) **Policy Year$_t$**	(14) **Policy Month$_m$**	(15) **Projected In Force**	(16) **DAC (Terminal)**	(17) **Expense Reserve (Terminal)**	(18) **Benefit Reserve (Terminal)**
1	12	45,457.41	312.59	(0.90)	38.61
2	12	41,309.32	319.16	(1.93)	58.28
3	12	37,934.35	323.31	(3.08)	53.77
4	12	34,822.82	328.15	(4.39)	29.07
5	12	31,956.77	333.76	(5.89)	(15.99)
6	12	29,637.30	299.96	(5.71)	1.37
7	12	28,070.07	256.42	(5.40)	6.69
8	12	26,578.24	208.45	(5.06)	(2.57)
9	12	25,157.22	155.55	(4.68)	(30.93)
10	**1**	**25,148.68**	**88.35**	**(3.88)**	**105.56**
10	**2**	**25,140.15**	**88.71**	**(3.89)**	**88.98**
10	**3**	**25,131.62**	**89.06**	**(3.91)**	**72.34**
10	**4**	**25,123.09**	**89.42**	**(3.93)**	**55.63**
10	**5**	**25,114.57**	**89.78**	**(3.94)**	**38.85**
10	**6**	**25,106.05**	**90.14**	**(3.96)**	**22.00**
10	**7**	**25,097.53**	**90.50**	**(3.97)**	**5.09**
10	**8**	**25,089.01**	**90.86**	**(3.99)**	**(11.89)**
10	**9**	**25,080.50**	**91.23**	**(4.00)**	**(28.94)**
10	**10**	**25,071.99**	**91.60**	**(4.02)**	**(46.06)**
10	**11**	**25,063.49**	**91.96**	**(4.04)**	**(63.25)**
10	**12**	**1,252.75**	**1,846.64**	**(81.07)**	**(1,610.06)**
11	**1**	**1,251.78**	**1,478.35**	**(65.45)**	**(803.41)**
11	**2**	**1,250.80**	**1,484.94**	**(65.74)**	**(845.92)**
11	**3**	**1,249.83**	**1,491.55**	**(66.03)**	**(888.62)**
11	**4**	**1,248.86**	**1,498.20**	**(66.33)**	**(931.51)**
11	**5**	**1,247.89**	**1,504.87**	**(66.62)**	**(974.60)**
11	**6**	**1,246.92**	**1,511.58**	**(66.92)**	**(1,017.87)**
11	**7**	**1,245.95**	**1,518.31**	**(67.22)**	**(1,061.34)**
11	**8**	**1,244.99**	**1,525.07**	**(67.52)**	**(1,105.00)**
11	**9**	**1,244.02**	**1,531.87**	**(67.82)**	**(1,148.86)**
11	**10**	**1,243.05**	**1,538.69**	**(68.12)**	**(1,192.91)**
11	**11**	**1,242.09**	**1,545.55**	**(68.42)**	**(1,237.16)**
11	**12**	**992.90**	**1,940.54**	**(85.91)**	**(1,602.01)**
12	12	785.85	2,016.92	(89.95)	(1,568.56)
13	12	620.91	2,069.03	(92.89)	(1,519.14)
14	12	489.69	2,085.48	(94.17)	(1,444.92)
15	12	385.47	2,052.28	(93.16)	(1,337.09)
16	12	302.51	1,948.56	(88.87)	(1,243.53)
17	12	236.91	1,744.08	(79.88)	(1,096.10)
18	12	185.11	1,395.47	(64.16)	(868.76)
19	12	144.28	841.63	(38.83)	(519.95)
20	12	0.00	(0.00)	0.00	0.00

Legend: Only the monthly calculations are described here

Monthly interest $I_{t,m} = 1 - (1 + (6)_t)$ ^ (1/12); Monthly mortality $q_{t,m} = 1 - (1 - (2)_t)$ ^ (1/12)

Monthly lapse $w_{t,m=12} = (1 - (2)_t) \times (3)_t$, $w_{t,m<>12} = 0$; Monthly premium $GP_{t,m=1} = (4)$, $GP_{t,m<>1} = 0$

(1) Time t, in years; (2) Time m, in months

(15) Projected face amount in force, $(15)_{t,m} = (15)_{(t,m)-1} \times [1 - q_{t,m} - w_{t,m}]$; $(15)_{0,0} = (5)_0 = 50{,}000$

(16) GAAP deferred acquisition cost, where $(t, m-1)$ should be read as $(t-1, 12)$ if $m = 1$

$(16)_{t,m} = -\{[-(16)_{t,m-1} + 0.25396 \times (GP)_{t,m} - (8)_t \times (GP)_{t,m} - (9)_t]\} \times [1 + I_{t,m}] / [1 - q_{t,m} - w_{t,m}]$

(17) GAAP expense reserve, where $(t, m-1)$ should be read as $(t-1, 12)$ if $m = 1$

$(17)_{t,m} = \{[(17)_{t,m-1} + 0.06247 \times (GP)_{t,m} - (10)_t \times (GP)_{t,m} - (11)_t]\} \times [1 + I_{t,m}] / [1 - q_{t,m} - w_{t,m}]$

(18) GAAP benefit reserve, where $(t, m-1)$ should be read as $(t-1, 12)$ if $m = 1$

$(18)_{t,m} = \{[(18)_{t,m-1} + 0.57519 \times (GP)_{t,m}] \times [1 + I_{t,m}] - w_{t,m} \times (7)t - q_{t,m} \times (5)_t \times I_{t,m} / LN(1 + I_{t,m})\} / [1 - q_{t,m} - w_{t,m}]$

GAAP benefit premium ratio 0.57519 = present value of death and surrender benefits divided by the present value of gross premiums

GAAP acquisition premium ratio 0.25396 = present value of acquisition expenses divided by the present value of gross premiums

GAAP maintenance premium ratio 0.06247 = present value of maintenance expenses divided by the present value of gross premiums

4.10 Limited-Payment Contracts

SFAS 97, "Accounting and Reporting by Insurance Enterprises for Certain Long-Duration Contracts and for Realized Gains and Losses from the Sale of Investments", defines the appropriate accounting for "limited-payment contracts that subject the insurance to mortality or morbidity risk over a period that extends beyond the period or periods in which premiums are collected and that have terms that are fixed and guaranteed."

SFAS 97 requires that:

> ... income from limited-payment contracts be recognized over the period that benefits are provided rather than on collection of premiums. (Summary, fifth paragraph)

It continues as follows:

> The period over which benefits are provided, as used in this Statement, includes the periods during which the insurance enterprise is subject to risk from policyholder mortality and morbidity and during which the insurance enterprise is responsible for administration of the contract. The benefit period does not include the subsequent period over which the policyholder or beneficiary may elect to have settlement proceeds disbursed. (Paragraph 9)

Insight into the methodology to be used is given by *SFAS 97* as follows:

> The collection of premium does not, however, represent the completion of an earnings process. Any gross premium received in excess of the net premium shall be deferred and recognized in income in a constant relationship with insurance in force (when accounting for life insurance contracts) or with the amount of expected future benefit payments (when accounting for annuity contracts). (Paragraph 16)

The Financial Accounting Standard Board's thought process is illuminated as follows:

> The Board concluded that limited-payment contracts with terms that are fixed and guaranteed are similar to other contracts addressed by Statement 60 in all respects except for the pattern of premium payment. The Board also concluded that income from insurance contracts is earned through the performance of contract services. The collection of a single premium or a limited number of premiums does not, in itself, represent the completion of an earnings process. The Board concluded that any amount of gross premium in excess of net premium, as those terms are defined in Statement 60, should be deferred and recognized over the period that services are provided. (Paragraph 42)

SFAS 97 states that:

> The provisions of Statement 60 dealing with loss recognition (premium deficiency), accounting for reinsurance, and financial statement disclosure shall apply to limited–payment and universal life-type contracts addressed by this Statement. (Paragraph 27)

SFAS 97 was effective for fiscal years beginning after December 15, 1988. The methodology described in *SFAS 97* was to be applied retrospectively through restatement of all previously issued financial statements. Alternatively, the cumulative effect of such adoption could have been presented in the year of adoption. In any event, all limited-payment contracts issued by an insurance enterprise, regardless of issue date, should be accounted for by using the methodology described in *SFAS 97*.

Limited-payment policies as defined by *SFAS 97* would include traditional nonparticipating single payment whole life contracts as well as traditional nonparticipating 10 and 20-payment whole life contracts and life paid-up-at-65 contracts that were very popular with the insurance-buying public in the 1950s through 1970s. This limited-payment methodology is not to be applied to single-premium universal life contracts such as those popular in the mid-1980s because the terms of these contracts were not fixed and guaranteed. Rather, these contracts would be accounted for by using the methodology defined in *SFAS 97* for universal life type contracts.

Absent adoption of *SFAS 97* for limited-payment contracts, applying *SFAS 60* methodology would result in a substantial portion of the total profits emanating from a limited-payment contract to be recognized in relation to premium revenues. In the extreme, a large portion of the profits projected to emerge over the life of a single payment contract would be reported at the time the policy was issued. This conflicts with the underlying premise of *SFAS 60* that profits are to be recognized over the life of the policy in relation to performance.

For limited-payment policies as defined by *SFAS 97*, premiums continue to be reported as revenues. Reserves are established based on assumptions of future experience including provisions for adverse deviation. Assumptions are locked-in. Deferred policy acquisition costs are amortized over the premium paying period by using assumptions consistent with the reserve assumptions.

In addition, *SFAS 97* requires that "any gross premium in excess of the net premium shall be deferred and recognized in income in a constant relationship with insurance in force."

This difference between the gross premium and the net premium represents the portion of total profits that would be recognized as a constant percentage of premiums under *SFAS 60* absent adoption of *SFAS 97*. Thus, for such limited-payment policies, profits will not emerge as a level percentage of premiums but as a level percentage of insurance in force as well as a release of the provision for adverse deviation.

4.11 *SFAS 97* Limited Pay Numerical Example

Table 4-14 illustrates the development of GAAP benefit and expense reserves as well as a deferred profit liability (DPL) established due to the limited premium payment period. The product is a level-premium nonparticipating guaranteed-cost, 3-pay, 10-year endowment. Table 4-14 shows the best-estimate assumptions used in pricing the contract. Statutory reserves are shown for illustrative purposes only and do not affect the GAAP results.

Table 4-14
Policy Level Assumptions for Sample 3-Pay 10-Year Endowment

(1) Policy Year,	(2) Mortality Rate	(3) Withdrawal Rate	(4) Gross Premium	(5) Face Amount	(6) Per Policy Expense	(7) Per Unit Expense	(8) Commission Expense	(9) Per Premium Expense	(10) Investment Rate	(11) Statutory Reserve	(12) Cash Value
0										0.00	0.00
1	0.0630%	18.00%	290.00	1,000.00	35.00	1.00	50.00%	2.25%	7.00%	300.00	0.00
2	0.0760%	12.00%	290.00	1,000.00	35.00	0.00	4.00%	2.25%	7.00%	600.00	450.00
3	0.0990%	10.00%	290.00	1,000.00	35.00	0.00	4.00%	2.25%	7.00%	900.00	900.00
4	0.1140%	4.00%	0.00	1,000.00	35.00	0.00	0.00%	0.00%	7.00%	910.00	910.00
5	0.1280%	4.00%	0.00	1,000.00	35.00	0.00	0.00%	0.00%	7.00%	920.00	920.00
6	0.1400%	4.00%	0.00	1,000.00	35.00	0.00	0.00%	0.00%	7.00%	930.00	930.00
7	0.1580%	4.00%	0.00	1,000.00	35.00	0.00	0.00%	0.00%	7.00%	940.00	940.00
8	0.1780%	4.00%	0.00	1,000.00	35.00	0.00	0.00%	0.00%	7.00%	960.00	960.00
9	0.2010%	4.00%	0.00	1,000.00	35.00	0.00	0.00%	0.00%	7.00%	980.00	980.00
10	0.2240%	100.00%	0.00	1,000.00	35.00	0.00	0.00%	0.00%	7.00%	1,000.00	1,000.00

Sample policy: Male, age 35
Premium Mode: Annual
Units of Coverage: 100.000

Legend:
(1) Time, in years
(2) Mortality rate, applied at the end of the year
(3) Withdrawal rate, applied at the end of the year
(4) Gross premium per year
(5) Face amount per policy unit
(6) Expense per policy, per year (maintenance expense)
(7) Expense per unit of face amount, per year (acquisition expense)
(8) Commission expense (as a percentage of premium)
(9) Expense as a percentage of premium (premium tax)
(10) Investment rate
(11) Statutory reserve per unit (at the end of the policy year)
(12) Cash value per unit (at the end of the policy year)

Table 4-15 shows the statutory book profits projected on a best estimate basis. The calculated benefit and expense reserves, as well as the DPL, are presented in Table 4-16.

The DAC is amortized over the premium-paying period, and a maintenance expense reserve is built up over the premium-paying period. Profit emerges as a level amount per thousand in force at the beginning of the year.

The GAAP benefit and expense reserves, as well as the DPL, should be calculated by using assumptions that include a margin for adverse deviation. This would result in profit that emerges partially as a level amount per thousand in force as well as a release from risk of adverse deviation.

The DPL is also known as an unearned revenue liability, unearned profit reserve, or unreleased profit reserve. The DPL should be established in addition to the benefit reserve to ensure a profit emergence in a constant relationship to the amount of insurance in force. Although not explicitly addressed in *SFAS 97*, the assumptions used to establish and release the DPL should be consistent with the *SFAS 60* assumptions used in the calculation of the benefit and expense reserves.

Table 4-15
Policy Year Results Sample 3-Pay 10-Year Endowment

(1) Policy $Year_t$	(13) Projected In force	(14) Premium Income	(15) Investment Income	(16) Maintenance Expense	(17) Acquisition Expense	(18) Commission Expense	(19) Premium Tax	(20) Mortality Expense	(21) Surrender Expense	(22) Increase in Reserve	(23) Book Profit
0	100,000										
1	81,948	29,000.00	957.71	35.00	100.00	14,500.00	652.50	63.00	0.00	24,584.50	(9,977.29)
2	72,060	23,765.02	3,276.34	28.68	0.00	950.60	534.71	62.28	4,421.85	18,651.34	2,391.90
3	64,790	20,897.32	4,393.68	25.22	0.00	835.89	470.19	71.34	6,478.96	15,074.76	2,334.64
4	62,127	0.00	4,077.61	22.68	0.00	0.00	0.00	73.86	2,355.65	(1,774.97)	3,400.39
5	59,566	0.00	3,953.24	21.74	0.00	0.00	0.00	79.52	2,283.35	(1,735.24)	3,303.86
6	57,103	0.00	3,831.70	20.85	0.00	0.00	0.00	83.39	2,212.74	(1,694.64)	3,209.36
7	54,732	0.00	3,712.90	19.99	0.00	0.00	0.00	90.22	2,143.68	(1,657.46)	3,116.47
8	52,449	0.00	3,596.69	19.16	0.00	0.00	0.00	97.42	2,097.98	(1,096.86)	2,478.99
9	50,250	0.00	3,519.69	18.36	0.00	0.00	0.00	105.42	2,051.88	(1,106.21)	2,450.23
10	0	0.00	3,442.06	17.59	0.00	0.00	0.00	112.56	50,137.67	(49,245.22)	2,419.47

Premiums paid at the beginning of the year.
Commissions and expenses paid at the beginning of the year
Death Benefits paid at the middle of the year
Withdrawals paid at the end of the year

Legend:
(1) Time, in years
$(13)_t$ Projected face amount in force, $(13)_t = (13)_{t-1} \times \{[1-(2)_t] \times [1-(3)_t]\}$, $(13)_0 = (5)_0 \times$ units $= 1{,}000 \times 100.000$
$(14)_t$ Premium, $(14)_t = (13)_{t-1} / 1000 \times (4)_t$
$(15)_t$ Investment income, $(15)_t = (10)_t \times [(14)_t - (16)_t - (17)_t - (18)_t - (19)_t + (22)_1 + \ldots + (22)_{t-1}] - \{[1+(10)_t]^{.5} - 1\} \times (20)_t$ (assumes death benefits paid at mid year)
$(16)_t$ Maintenance expense (per policy expense), $(16)_t = \{[(13)_{t-1} / 1000] / 100\} \times (6)_t$ (based on policy count, inforce divided by $(5)_t$ divided by units)
$(17)_t$ Acquisition expense (per unit expense), $(17)_t = [(13)_{t-1} / 1000] \times (7)_t$
$(18)_t$ Commission expense, $(18)_t = (14)_t \times (8)_t$
$(19)_t$ Premium tax (per premium expense), $(19)_t = (14)_t \times (9)_t$
$(20)_t$ Mortality expense (death benefits), $(20)_t = (13)_{t-1} \times (2)_t$
$(21)_t$ Surrender expense (withdrawals), $(21)_t = [(13)_{t-1} / 1000] \times [1-(2)_t] \times (12)_t \times (3)_t$ (assumes death before surrenders)
$(22)_t$ Increase in statutory reserve, $(22)_t = [(13)_t / 1000] \times (11)_t - [(13)_{t-1} / 1000] \times (11)_{t-1}$
$(23)_t = (14)_t + (15)_t - (16)_t - (17)_t - (18)_t - (19)_t - (20)_t - (21)_t - (22)_t$

Profit margin equals the present value of book profits divided by the present value of premium income = 11.09%

Table 4-16
Key GAAP Statistics for Sample 3-Pay 10-Year Endowment

(1) Policy Year$_t$	(13) Projected Face Amount In force	(29) Discounted Face Amount Inforce	(30) GAAP Profit	(31) Profit Per Unit	(32) Deferred Profit Liability	(24) Percent Premium	(25) Expense Reserve	(26) Benefit Reserve	(27) GAAP Book Profit
0	100,000	100,000			0.00				
1	81,948	76,587	1,609.35	16.09	1,832.55	0.11	(10,170.22)	23,795.03	3,441.90
2	72,060	62,940	1,318.83	16.09	3,462.57	0.11	(5,499.24)	44,978.48	2,820.58
3	64,790	52,888	1,159.69	16.09	5,025.48	0.11	180.50	65,173.72	2,480.22
4	62,127	47,396	1,042.69	16.09	4,334.57	0.00	162.36	68,809.81	0.00
5	59,566	42,469	999.84	16.09	3,638.15	0.00	142.13	72,821.13	0.00
6	57,103	38,050	958.62	16.09	2,934.20	0.00	119.57	77,252.94	0.00
7	54,732	34,084	918.99	16.09	2,220.61	0.00	94.41	82,153.92	0.00
8	52,449	30,526	880.83	16.09	1,495.22	0.00	66.34	87,538.53	0.00
9	50,250	27,333	844.09	16.09	755.80	0.00	35.00	93,465.15	0.00
10	0	0	808.70	16.09	0.00	0.00	0.00	0.00	0.00

Legend:

(1) Time, in years

$(13)_t$ Projected face amount in force, $(13)_t = (13)_{t-1} \times \{[1-(2)_t] \times [1-(3)_t]\}$, $(13)_0 = (5)_0 \times$ units $= 1{,}000 \times 100.000$

$(29)_t$ Discounted face amount in force, $(29)_t = (13)_t / [1+(10)_t]^t$

$(30)_t$ GAAP profit, $(30)_t = 15.04 \times (13)_{t-1} \times [1+(10)_t] / 1000$

$(31)_t$ GAAP profit per unit, $(31)_t = (30)_t \times (5)_1 / (13)_{t-1} = 15.04 \times [1+(10)_t]$

$(32)_t$ Deferred profit liability, $(32)_t = (32)_{t-1} \times [1+(10)_t] + (27)_t - (30)_t$

$(24)_t$ GAAP book profit as a percent of premium, $(24)_t = (27)_t / \{(14)_t \times [1+(10)_t]\}$

$(25)_t$ GAAP expense reserve, $(25)_t = \{(25)_{t-1} \times [(13)_{t-1} / (13)_0] - (16)_t - (17)_t - (18)_t - (19)_t + .2586 \times (14)_t\} \times [1+(10)_t] / [(13)_t / (13)_0]$

$(26)_t$ GAAP benefit reserve, $(26)_t = \{\, \{(26)_{t-1} \times [(13)_{t-1} / (13)_0] + .6305 \times (14)_t\} \times [1+(10)_t] - (21)_t - (20)_t \times [1+(10)_t]^{.5} \,\} / [(13)_t / (13)_0]$

$(27)_t$ GAAP book profit, $(27)_t = (23)_t + (22)_t - \{[(13)_t / (13)_0] \times [(25)_t + (26)_t] - [(13)_{t-1} / (13)_0] \times [(25)_{t-1} + (26)_{t-1})]\} +$
$(10)_t \times \{(25)_{t-1} \times [(13)_{t-1} / (13)_0] + (26)_{t-1} \times [(13)_{t-1} / (13)_0] - [(22)_1 + \ldots + (22)_{t-1}]\}$

GAAP benefit premium = 18,284.86 = $(4)_1$ × units × present value of columns (20) and (21) divided by the present value of column (14) discounted using the investment rate

GAAP benefit premium percentage = 18,284.86 / [$(4)_1$ × units] = 63.05%

GAAP expense premium = 7,498.41 = $(4)_1$ × units × present value of columns (16), (17), (18) and (19) divided by the present value of columns (14) discounted using the investment rate; includes acquisition and maintenance component

GAAP expense premium percentage = 7,498.41 / [$(4)_1$ × units] = 25.86%

Profit per unit = 15.04 = present value of column (27) discounted at the investment rate × $(5)_1$ / the sum of column (29)

4.12 Participating Products

As mentioned earlier, the accounting for participating products with policyholder dividends set using the contribution principle is dictated by *SFAS No. 120* "Accounting and Reporting by Mutual Life Insurance Enterprises and by Insurance Enterprises for Certain Long-Duration Participating Contracts and Statement of Position Accounting for Certain Insurance Activities of Mutual Life Insurance Enterprises 95-1," and is discussed in Chapter 5. Participating contracts in which dividends are not set using the contribution principle are accounted for by using the methodologies detailed in *SFAS 60.*

If profits emanating from participating policies are not limited by country law, state law, company charter, or policy form provision, policyholder dividends are assumed to be policyholder benefits that are a component of the GAAP benefit reserve. Thus, the level as well as slope of the policyholder dividends affect the GAAP benefit net premium as well as GAAP benefit reserve held. Policyholder dividend payments are an expense when incurred. In practice, the utilization of policyholder dividend options has not typically been reflected in the development of the GAAP benefit reserve; dividends are assumed to be paid immediately to the policyholder.

Limitations on the amount of profit from participating policies that can inure to the shareholders can exist due to various country laws, state laws, company charter, or policy form provision. In such a restricted environment, an additional liability, typically referred to as the undistributed participating policyholders' earnings account (UPPEA), is established to ensure that "profits" that will eventually be returned to policyholders through the payment of dividends in later policy durations are not reported as current income by the company. Consequently, in this restricted environment, policyholder dividends are generally not considered as an element in the calculation of the benefit reserve, because amounts to be set aside for future payments would be captured in the UPPEA.

The *Audit and Accounting Guide* states:

> If the contract does not meet the criteria in paragraph 5 of SOP 95-1 consider any restrictions on the amount of earnings of participating contracts that can inure to the benefit of the stockholders. Such restrictions may be imposed by law, charter, or contract, or they may be self-imposed as demonstrated by entity policy or practice. (Paragraph 8.80)

Actuarial Standard of Practice No. 10, "Methods and Assumptions for Use in Life Insurance Company Financial Statements Prepared in Accordance with GAAP" addresses this issue as shown below:

> *Participating Policies that are Subject to SFAS No. 60.* GAAP requires that only the portion of profits that inures to the benefit of stockholders is reflected in reported results. Profits that are attributable to participating policies and inure to the benefit of stockholders may be restricted (by law, regulation, company practice, or otherwise) or may be unrestricted. The actuary should use the appropriate methods and assumptions for each of these two circumstances.
>
> a. Restricted Stockholder Profits. Profits in excess of the amount inuring to the benefit of stockholders should be accumulated in a participating policyholder account. Assumptions, including provision for the risk of adverse deviation, may be established at a level consistent with those underlying gross premiums

or may be comparable to those used for the company's nonparticipating business. Policyholder dividends would generally be treated as disbursements of predividend profits, not as disbursements in the liability calculation.

b. Unrestricted Profits. Dividends should be treated as disbursements in the liability calculation. Assumptions may include a somewhat smaller provision for the risk of adverse deviation, given the flexibility provided by the dividend scale."

Table 4-17 illustrates one method of how an UPPEA would operate. The participating policyholders may be viewed as another type of shareholder. Each year, ten percent of the income generated leaves the participating line of business and goes over to the nonparticipating line of business. The UPPEA becomes the appropriate surplus dedicated to the participating line of business. Table 4-17 is pre-tax.

Table 4-17
Mechanics Pre-Tax of Undistributed Participating Policyholders' Earnings Account (UPPEA)

	YEAR				
Income Statement Participating Business	**1999**	**2000**	**2001**	**2002**	**2003**
(A) Revenue		3,000	3,500	4,000	4,150
(B) Expense (excluding policyholder dividends)		2,200	2,800	4,500	3,550
(C) Income before policyholder dividends		800	700	(500)	600
(D) Interest on prior Year End UPPEA		28	77	122	93
(E) Distributable to Shareholders		83	78	(38)	69
(F) Policyholder dividends awarded		45	60	75	40
(G) Contribution to the UPPEA		700	639	(415)	583
Balance Sheet Growth of UPPEA					
(H) Beginning of year amount		400	1,100	1,740	1,324
(I) Interest earned		28	77	122	93
(J) Contribution from the current year in add'n to interest		672	562	(537)	491
(K) End-of-year amount	400	1,100	1,740	1,324	1,908

Legend:
(A) Revenues include premium and investment income (other than investment income on the UPPEA).
(B) Expense includes claims, commissions, other expenses, increase in benefit reserve and decrease in DAC.
(C) = (A) – (B)
(D) $0.07 \times (K)_{t-1}$
(E) $0.10 \times [(C) + (D)]$
(F) Given
(G) $0.90 \times [(C) + (D)] - (F)$
(H) = $(K)_{t-1}$
(I) = $0.07 \times (H)_t$
(J) = (G) – (I)
(K) = (H) + (I) + (J)

Table 4-18 displays the same UPPEA calculation on an after-tax basis. The tax rate is assumed to be 35% with no tax loss carryforward credits. Solely for the purposes of illustration, the beginning UPPEA is 400.

Table 4-18
Mechanics of After-Tax Undistributed Participating Policyholders' Earnings Account (UPPEA)

	YEAR				
Income Statement Participating Business	**1999**	**2000**	**2001**	**2002**	**2003**
(A) Revenue		3,000	3,500	4,000	4,150
(B) Expense (excluding policyholder dividends)		2,200	2,800	4,500	3,550
(C) Income before policyholder dividends		800	700	(500)	600
(D) Tax rate		0.35	0.35	0.35	0.35
(E) After-tax income before dividends		520	455	(325)	390
(F) Interest on Prior Year UPPEA (AFIT)		18	39	57	44
(G) Distributable to Shareholders		54	49	(27)	43
(H) Policyholder dividends awarded		45	60	75	40
(I) Tax on policyholder dividends		16	21	26	14
(J) Contribution to UPPEA		455	406	(290)	365
Balance Sheet Growth of UPPEA					
(K) Beginning of year amount		400	855	1,261	971
(L) After-tax interest earned		18	39	57	44
(M) Contribution from the current year		437	367	(347)	321
(N) End of year amount	400	855	1,261	971	1,336

Legend:

(A) Revenues include premium and investment income (other than investment income on the UPPEA)
(B) Expense includes claims, commissions, other expenses, increase in benefit reserve and decrease in DAC
(C) = (A) – (B)
(D) Assume 35% all years
(E) = (C) × [1 – (D)]
(F) = $(N)_{t-1}$ × 0.07 × [1 – (D)]
(G) = 0.10 × [(E) + (F)]
(H) Given
(I) = (H) × (D)
(J) = (0.9) × [(E) + (F)] – (H) × [1 – (D)]
(K) = $(N)_{t-1}$
(L) = (F)
(M) = (J) – (L)
(N) = (K) + (L) + (M)

4.13 Indeterminate Premium Products

Indeterminate premium policies were developed by the life insurance industry in the late 1970s and early 1980s primarily in response to historically high investment rates in the United States. These policies are generally nonparticipating. "Indeterminate premium" refers to the fact that the premium can be reset prospectively to reflect a change in future assumptions from those that were originally used to price the product.

In the historically high-investment rate environment of the early 1980s, the premium rates for a traditional nonparticipating permanent product could be set at a lower level if the high investment rate was assumed to continue. Premiums for indeterminate premium policies developed during this period typically assumed that the high investment rate would continue for the life of the policy. The risk that interest rates would decline was passed partially to the policyholder, as the company retained the right to adjust future premium rates based upon conditions (interest rates, mortality levels) anticipated in the future.

Paragraph 13 of *SFAS 97* defines when a nonguaranteed premium contract should be accounted for by using universal life-type methodology. If such a contract does not include the features that would require universal life-type methodology, then it should be accounted for by using

SFAS 60 methodology. However, the concept of unlocking of assumptions generated rethinking of the lock-in concept. If the gross premium were adjusted prospectively due to changes in assumptions, could the assumptions that generate the reserves be changed as well?

Although no official accounting literature addressed this issue, actuarial literature and practices did emerge. *Actuarial Standard of Practice No. 10*, "Methods and Assumptions for Use in Life Insurance Company Financial Statements Prepared in Accordance with GAAP" addresses the accounting for indeterminate premium policies as follows:

> *Indeterminate Premium Policies*. Provided the policy is not, in substance, a UL-type policy, SFAS No. 60 is applicable to indeterminate premium policies. The premium flexibility associated with these policies may affect the application of SFAS No. 60, such as the use of a smaller provision for the risk of adverse deviation. The ability and willingness of the insurer to change premiums may be anticipated in performing loss recognition. Assumptions may be "unlocked" at gross premium change dates. If assumptions are adjusted, it should be done prospectively, without a change in the liability as of the valuation date.

The following formulas depict the indeterminate premium (also called prospective unlocking) method. In these formulas, *t* represents the reporting date.

RES_t = benefit reserve

PVB_t = present value of benefits using the locked-in assumptions
PVP_t = present value of net benefit premiums, again using the locked-in assumptions

PVB'_t = present value of benefits but using revised assumptions

Ann'_t = present value of an annuity but using revised assumptions and considering anticipated changes in future premium levels

GP'_t = the revised gross premium to be put into effect
NP'_t = the new valuation premium as a result of applying prospective unlocking

The reserve at the reporting date is:

$$RES_t = PVB_t - PVP_t$$

After the assumptions have been revised and new premiums been introduced, the following formula must be solved:

$$RES_t = PVB'_t - PVP'_t$$

Expanding the last term,

$$RES_t = PVB'_t - GP'_t \times level\%' \times Ann'_t$$

Once the level percentage (*level %'*) is determined using the preceding formula, it is applied to the new gross premium stream. The resulting new valuation net premiums, along with the revised present values of benefits, will be used in future valuations.

The same concepts apply to maintenance reserves and DAC. Should the total of the level percentages (*level%'*) that are used to generate the benefit, maintenance, and DAC exceed 100%, loss recognition testing should be performed.

A comprehensive discussion of the indeterminate premium methodology can be found in "GAAP for Non-Guaranteed Premium Life Insurance" (Cloninger, 1981)

4.14 Implications of Reserve Formula Selection

The tables in the preceding sections and their inherent formulas as expressed in the legend are crafted in terms of present values and are displayed by using policy-year-end values. In practice, different forms of reserve formulas are used, especially to accommodate the need to measure results on all days of the policy year.

This section addresses the many types of adjustments to standard formulas that the actuary should consider in financial reporting.

In order to focus on timing issues, this section provides an analysis based on a display of recursive formulas. These Fackler-type presentations permit the precise timing of events throughout the policy year to be more closely inspected.

As mentioned, actuarial reserve formulas are typically constructed by using annual assumptions. The formulas commence with the prior reserve, add any premiums at the start of the year, and deduct expenses incurred at the start of the year. This results in an initial reserve, a moment after the start of the policy year.

Throughout the year, events occur, such as death claims, maintenance expenses, and cash surrenders. Also throughout the year, the reserve grows with survivorship and interest. The value at the end of the policy year is generally called the terminal reserve.

These concepts are reflected in the development of reserve factors. While the actuary may visualize easiest in terms of reserve factors, these same formulas and concepts underlie reserves calculated using "first principles" as well as the elements of a static or dynamic worksheet.

The terminal reserve developed is an accurate depiction of the state of events as of the end of the policy year. However, interim values are needed because at any reporting date most policies are in the midst of a policy year.

4.14.1 Benefit Reserves

Using the following terms, all for policy year t, the recursive formula for a benefit terminal reserve can be written as:

$$TBR_t = [(TBR_{t-1} + NP_t) \times (1+i) - DB_t \times q^d \times (1+i)^{1/2} - CV_t \times (1-q^d) \times q^w] / (1-q^d) \times (1-q^w)$$

where

TBR_t = terminal benefit reserve per unit in force at the end of year t

NP_t = net premium (for either benefit or expense, as appropriate)

DB_t = death benefit per unit in force

CV_t = cash value per unit in force

i = interest rate

q^d = mortality rate

q^w = lapse rate

The terminal reserve at the point of issue, TBR_0, is defined as zero.

Because this formula's denominator adjusts for survivorship, the resulting reserve effectively anticipates that those who have died and those who have lapsed have been removed from the population.

This may not be the case under an annual mode policy. If the policy can lapse only on a premium due date, a lapsing policy would still be in force even on the 365th day of its policy year.

Lapse rates play a significant role in the development and growth of reserve factors. The lapse rate generally dwarfs the mortality rate when growth with survivorship is considered. In most U.S. practices, it is presumed that policies can lapse only on a premium due date.

This portion of the chapter refines the definition of a terminal reserve by introducing a term called a final reserve. This is the reserve a moment before the terminal; this is the reserve a moment before the lapses are assumed to occur. This final benefit reserve (FBR_t) can be expressed as:

$$FBR_t = [(TBR_{t-1} + NP_t) \times (1 + i) - DB_t \times q^d \times (1 + i)^{1/2}] \,/\, (1 - q^d)$$

This is similar to the formula for the terminal reserve except that all transactions involving a lapse have been removed.

The terminal reserve itself can be re-expressed in terms of the final reserve:

$$TBR_t = \{FBR_t - [CV_t \times (1 - q^d) \times q^w] \,/\, (1 - q^d)\} \,/\, (1 - q^w)$$

Actuaries generally use either a mean reserve basis or a midterminal reserve basis. The mean reserve concept considers the prior terminal, the receipt of the current-year premium, the incurral of costs at the beginning of the year, and a value for the end of the year. The midterminal concept considers the prior terminal, costs other than those directly related to premium collection, and a value for the end of the year.

For a benefit reserve, a mean reserve (MBR_t) for policy year t can be expressed as:

$$MBR_t = \tfrac{1}{2}(TBR_{t-1} + NP_t + TBR_t)$$

where the ending reserve is a terminal reserve, or

$$MBR_t = \tfrac{1}{2}(TBR_{t-1} + NP_t + FBR_t)$$

where the ending reserve is a final reserve.

When mean reserves are used for policies in which non-annual premiums have been paid, a deferred premium asset should be established to offset the annual mode assumption in the benefit reserve. The deferred premium is typically calculated on a seriatim basis reflecting the remaining modal premiums left to be paid between the valuation date and the next policy anniversary. Some companies approximate the GAAP net deferred premiums by applying net to gross ratios to gross deferred premiums.

In any mean or midterminal basis that uses a terminal reserve, the ending benefit terminal reserve should be adjusted so that it still includes any endowment payable at the end of the year and still includes a cash value at the final duration of the policy.

For a benefit reserve, a midterminal reserve ($midBR_t$) for policy year t can be expressed as:

$$midBR_t = \tfrac{1}{2}(TBR_{t-1} + TBR_t)$$

where the ending reserve is a terminal reserve, or

$$midBR_t = \tfrac{1}{2}(TBR_{t-1} + FBR_t)$$

where the ending reserve is a final reserve.

When midterminal reserves are used, an unearned premium liability should be established to reserve for the remaining premium element not reflected in the midterminal reserve formula. The unearned premium should be held on a net basis, although some companies hold the unearned premium on a gross basis.

4.14.2 Expense Reserves

The preceding concepts and formulas can be extended to the expense reserve, or DAC. Using these additional terms, all for policy year t, the recursive formula for an expense terminal reserve (an asset) can be written as:

$$TER_t = [TER_{t-1} + Pol_t + GP_t \times (Comm_t + PT_t) - NP_t] \times (1+i) / (1-q^d) \times (1-q^w)$$

where

TER_t = terminal expense reserve per unit in force at the end of year t

GP_t = gross premium

$Comm_t$ = commission percentage

PT_t = premium tax rate

Pol_t = policy expenses other than those directly a function of premium, incurred at the beginning of policy year t.

The expense terminal reserve at the point of issue, TER_0, is defined as zero.

As with benefit reserves, the "final" reserve concept exists with expense reserves. The final expense reserve, FER_t, can be expressed as:

$$FER_t \;=\; [TER_{t-1} + Pol_t + GP_t \times (Comm_t + PT_t) - NP_t] \times (1 + i) \,/\, (1 - q^d)$$

This is similar to the formula for the terminal reserve except that the impact of lapsation has been removed.

As with the terminal benefit reserve, the terminal expense reserve itself can be re-expressed in terms of the final reserve:

$$TER_t \;=\; FER_t \,/\, (1 - q^w)$$

As with benefit reserves, actuaries generally use either a mean reserve basis or a midterminal reserve basis. The mean reserve concept considers the prior terminal, the receipt of the current-year premium, the incurral of costs at the beginning of the year, and a value for the end of the year. The midterminal concept considers the prior terminal, costs other than those directly related to premium collection, and a value for the end of the year.

For an expense reserve, a mean reserve (MER_t) for policy year t can be expressed as:

$$MER_t \;=\; \tfrac{1}{2}[TER_{t-1} + Pol_t + GP_t \times (Comm_t + PT_t) - NP_t + TER_t]$$

where the ending reserve is a terminal reserve, or

$$MER_t \;=\; \tfrac{1}{2}[TER_{t-1} + Pol_t + GP_t \times (Comm_t + PT_t) - NP_t + FER_t]$$

where the ending reserve is a final reserve.

When mean reserves are used for policies in which non-annual premiums have been paid, a deferred premium asset should be established to offset the annual mode assumption in the expense reserve. Further, a cost of collection liability should be established to offset the percentage of premium expenses that the mean reserve formula considered paid.

The deferred premium is typically calculated on a seriatim basis, reflecting the remaining modal premiums left to be paid between the valuation date and the next policy anniversary. Some companies approximate the GAAP net deferred premiums by applying net-to-gross ratios to gross deferred premiums. The cost of collection liability (generally, the commissions and premium tax payable on gross deferred premiums) also is calculated on an exact or a grouped basis.

For an expense reserve, a midterminal reserve ($midER_t$) for policy year t can be expressed as:

$$midER_t \;=\; \tfrac{1}{2}(TER_{t-1} + Pol_t + TER_t)$$

where the ending reserve is a terminal reserve, or

$$midER_t \;=\; \tfrac{1}{2}(TER_{t-1} + Pol_t + FER_t)$$

where the ending reserve is a final reserve.

When midterminal reserves are used, an unearned premium liability should be established to reserve for the remaining premium element not reflected in the midterminal reserve formula. The unearned premium should be held on a net basis, although some companies hold the unearned premium on a gross basis. An equity in the unearned premium (EUP) asset should be established as an asset. This compensates for the fact that the percentage of premium expenses has been paid, but the premiums to which it relates have not yet been fully earned. The EUP asset (generally, the commissions and premium tax payable on gross unearned premiums) is calculated on either an exact or a grouped basis.

These mean and midterminal reserves can either be pure averages between endpoints or can be interpolated between endpoints, taking the valuation date into account.

Actuaries may not be familiar with the concept of the "final" aspect of a terminal reserve calculation. Its evolution and value can be seen by considering renewable term life insurance, a significant *SFAS 60* product. Term plans typically have step-rated premiums, where the premiums increase every five or ten years. Another variety is a level premium for a period of ten years followed by a schedule of attained age premium rates.

At the point of switch from the last premium in a segment to the next higher premium, companies have anticipated significantly higher lapses. Expected lapse rates in this period can range from 30% to 60%. If reserve factors are developed by using survivorship, which includes the full impact of these large lapses, the resulting benefit and expense reserves will be overstated if they are applied to an in force that still includes such policies. Thus, the use of the "final" reserve in the mean or midterminal formula has evolved. If the "final" reserve concept is not used in a situation with extraordinarily large lapses, reported earnings will not emerge as a level percentage of premium.

The above formulas display the basics of *SFAS 60* reserve calculations. Although the preceding discussion focused on annual calculations, the actuary could adapt these to a monthly or exact modal basis. Also, the actuary would need to enhance these formulas to include other elements as appropriate, such as maintenance costs, handling costs incurred at time of claim, endowments, coupons, regular dividends paid to policyholders, and terminal dividends paid to policyholders.

Chapter 5 Traditional Life Insurance *(SFAS 120)*

5.1 Introduction

Traditional participating life insurance contracts are life insurance contracts that are expected to pay dividends to policyholders. These contracts are usually the major component of the business in force at mutual life insurance companies, assessment enterprises, and fraternal benefit societies (together referred to as mutual life insurance enterprises).

For many years after the development of generally accepted accounting practices for the stockholder-owned insurance industry, the regulatory-basis (statutory) financial statements of mutual life insurance enterprises were prepared in accordance with generally accepted accounting practices. In 1993, the FASB issued *Interpretation 40*, "Applicability of Generally Accepted Accounting Principles to Mutual Life Insurance and Other Enterprises," which effectively prohibited describing statutory financial statements as being prepared in accordance with generally accepted accounting practices. As originally issued, *SFAS 60*, "Accounting and Reporting by Insurance Enterprises," specifically excluded mutual life insurance enterprises. *SFAS 97*, "Accounting and Reporting by Insurance Enterprises for Certain Long-Duration Contracts and for Realized Gains and Losses from the Sale of Investments," and *SFAS 113*, "Accounting and Reporting for Reinsurance of Short-Duration and Long-Duration Contracts," were both issued as applicable only to those entities to which *SFAS 60* applied and therefore also excluded mutual life insurance enterprises.

The exclusion of mutual insurance enterprises from the scope of all previous insurance-specific guidance led the AICPA to start a project to develop a generally accepted basis of accounting for any activities of mutual insurance enterprises for which there was no current guidance. That project culminated in the publication of AICPA *SOP 95-1*, "Accounting for Certain Insurance Activities of Mutual Life Insurance Enterprises." In 1995 the FASB issued *SFAS 120*, "Accounting and Reporting by Mutual Life Insurance Enterprises and by Insurance Enterprises for Certain Long-Duration Participating Contracts." *SFAS 120* extended the scope of *SFAS 60*, *SFAS 97*, and *SFAS 113* to contracts issued by mutual life insurance enterprises and identified AICPA *SOP 95-1* as the source of accounting guidance for certain participating life insurance contracts.

SFAS 60 addresses accounting for policyholder dividends attributable to participating insurance contracts issued by stock life insurance enterprises (*SFAS 60*, paragraphs 41-43.) The application of this guidance is discussed in Chapter 4. *SFAS 60* provides that policyholder dividends be accrued by using an estimate of the amount expected to be paid. It further describes separate methods of accounting for dividends that are attributable to policies with limitations on the amount of profits that may inure to the benefit of shareholders and for policies without such limitations. Participating contracts issued by mutual insurance enterprises make provision for dividends that are clearly without such limitations. However, the guidance in *SFAS 60* applicable to policyholder dividends not subject to these limitations is generally viewed as appropriate for dividend scales that are established at the issue of a contract but not actively managed. Dividends are actively managed if dividend scales are adjusted to reflect significant changes in experience on a reasonably timely basis. In drafting *SOP 95-1*, the AICPA considered the guidance in *SFAS 60* and determined that the participating contracts issued by mutual life insurance companies were sufficiently different from those addressed in *SFAS 60* that a new basis of accounting was necessary. In particular, the AICPA determined an actively managed dividend scale causes earnings to emerge in relation to margins rather than to the level of premiums received in that year. The *SFAS 60* accounting model uses premiums rather than margins as the basis for earnings recognition (for example, by amortizing DAC using a premium-based schedule.)

Similarly, *SFAS 97* provides guidance on the accounting for participating life insurance contracts that are in substance universal life contracts, as well as other contracts classified as universal life contracts. As addressed in detail later in this chapter, participating contracts that allow for policyholder flexibility in the timing or amount of premiums, provide for a stated account balance, or for which the insurer anticipates that changes in dividends or other credits will be based on changes in market conditions rather than on experience, are considered in substance universal life contracts. Earnings from participating insurance contracts issued by mutual life insurance enterprises that are not in substance universal life contracts tend to emerge in a manner similar to those of universal life-type contracts. However, because participating contracts have terms similar to conventional life insurance contracts, the provisions of *SFAS 97* were determined inappropriate for traditional participating contracts in their entirety.

In developing *SOP 95-1*, the AICPA recognized that the contracts being addressed had similarities to both the contracts covered in *SFAS 60* and those covered in *SFAS 97*. The accounting model developed in *SOP 95-1* borrows elements from both previous statements of financial accounting standards. In general, under the *SOP 95-1* model, earnings tend to emerge in relation to margins, comparable to the treatment provided for universal life-type contracts. The recognition in GAAP financial statements of premiums, benefits, and dividends, however, is comparable to the treatment provided conventional life insurance contracts under *SFAS 60*.

The accounting described in *SOP 95-1* is based on a model of how participating contracts are managed. Understanding this model will assist the reader in applying GAAP to situations or contractual features not specifically discussed here. In addition, the methods described in this chapter will be more easily understood with an appreciation of the generalized model from which they were developed.

The model assumes that a dividend fund exists to determine dividends. The dividend fund is a notional amount to which interest is credited and from which mortality and expense charges are assessed. (Note that if the dividend fund were an explicit amount and communicated to policyholders, the contract in question would be in substance a universal life-type contract.) Experience results more favorable than those implied in the development of the dividend fund are the source of dividends. Experience results in excess of the dividend fund that are not returned to the policyholders in the form of dividends are margins. In simple formula terms, let:

DF_t = the dividend fund for a policy at the end of period t
DI_t = interest credited to the dividend fund during period t
DP_t = gross premium credited to the dividend fund during period t
DE_t = expenses charged to the dividend fund during period t
DQ_t = mortality costs charged to the dividend fund during period t
Div_t = the dividend paid for period t
M_t = the margin to the enterprise for period t

Then:

$$DF_0 = 0 \quad (1)$$

and

$$DF_t = DF_{t-1} + DP_t + DI_t - DQ_t - DE_t \quad (2)$$

Under this construct, the dividend fund at the end of each period over the life of each contract is known. Define another set of dividend fund elements to be the comparable amounts that are determined on the basis of the experience of the company as the comparable elements primed (e.g., I_t' is the interest credited to the dividend fund at the dividend experience rate for period t, etc.) Then

$$DF_t' = DF_{t-1}' + DP_t' + DI_t' - DQ_t' - DE_t' \tag{3}$$

and

$$Div_t = (DF_t' - DF_t) - M_t \tag{3a}$$

In other words, any favorable experience results over and above those assumed in the progression of the dividend fund are either paid to the policyholder in the form of a dividend or retained by the company as a margin. Combining formulas (2) and (3) and solving for the dividend gives:

$$Div_t = (DP_t' - DP_t) + (DI_t' - DI_t) + (DQ_t - DQ_t') + (DE_t - DE_t') - M_t \tag{4}$$

Formula (4) is comparable to a standard three-factor dividend formula, with the addition of a premium term and an explicit charge for contributions to surplus, or earnings. Reconfiguring formula (4) gives a formula for the margin term as

$$M_t = (DP_t' - DP_t) + (DI_t' - DI_t) + (DQ_t - DQ_t') + (DE_t - DE_t') - Div_t \tag{5}$$

Formula (5) shows that the periodic contribution to surplus, or earnings, can be described in a format comparable to earnings by source, with the dividend representing a return of nonspecific earnings to the policyholder.

5.2 Scope and Applicability

SOP 95-1 applies to life insurance contracts issued by mutual life insurance enterprises that are expected to pay dividends to policyholders in accordance with the contribution principle. The specific language in the *SOP* is as follows:

> This *SOP* applies to all mutual life insurance enterprises, assessment enterprises, and fraternal benefit societies. This *SOP* also applies to stock life insurance subsidiaries of mutual life insurance enterprises. (Paragraph 4)
>
> This *SOP* applies to life insurance contracts that have both of the following characteristics:
>
> a. They are long-duration participating contracts that are expected to pay dividends to policyholders based on actual experience of the insurance enterprise.
>
> b. Annual policyholder dividends are paid in a manner that identifies divisible surplus and distributes that surplus in approximately the same proportion as the contracts are considered to have contributed to divisible surplus (commonly referred to in actuarial literature as the *contribution principle*). (Paragraph 5)

Paragraph 4 of *SOP 95-1* indicates that the guidance is applicable only to mutual life insurance enterprises, including stock insurance subsidiaries of mutual life insurance enterprises, because when the *SOP* was released in 1995, accounting guidance had already been established for all products issued by other life insurance companies (i.e., stockholder-owned life insurance companies.) *SFAS 120* permits stockholder-owned life insurance companies to adopt the provisions of *SOP 95-1* for any contracts in force that meet the provisions of the *SOP*. Use of the term *permit* in this context means that if a stockholder-owned life insurance company has contracts that meet the conditions for application of *SOP 95-1*, the accounting guidance in the *SOP* is *preferable* to that previously applied. As a result, a change from an approach described by *SFAS 60* to the approach described by the *SOP* would be permitted. However, in the normal course of events, an insurance enterprise could not switch from the approach described by the *SOP* to one described by *SFAS 60*.

Paragraph 5 of the *SOP* describes the specific contractual features necessary for the *SOP* to be applied. First, the contracts must be long-duration contracts; this excludes group term life insurance or any other contracts considered short duration. (Paragraphs 7 and 8 of *SFAS 60* provide guidance on determining whether a contract is short or long duration.) The contracts must be participating and must be expected to pay dividends based on "actual experience of the insurance enterprise." The *SOP 95-1* glossary of terms defines dividends to policyholders as:

> Non-guaranteed amounts distributable to policyholders of participating insurance contracts and based on actual performance of the insurance enterprise. Under various state insurance laws, dividends are apportioned to policyholders on an equitable basis. Dividends to policyholders include annual policyholder dividends and terminal dividends.

In the case in which dividends are paid but are not based on the actual experience of the insurance company, the contract fails to qualify for treatment under the *SOP*. As mentioned earlier, the basis for determining the dividend payment establishes the appropriate accounting treatment. A participating contract is accounted for under *SFAS 60* if dividends are not, for example, actively managed or as a universal life-type contract under *SFAS 97* if dividends are based on market interest rates rather than the on company's actual experience.

The second requirement for treatment under *SOP 95-1* is that annual policyholder dividends are paid in accordance with the contribution principle. *Annual policyholder dividends* are defined in the glossary of *SOP 95-1* as:

> Amount of dividends to policyholders calculated and paid each year, representing the policyholders' share of divisible surplus.

The distribution of divisible surplus in a manner consistent with the contribution principle is summarized as a system that distributes surplus to contracts in approximately the same proportion as the contracts are considered to have contributed to that surplus. Because the second requirement pertains to annual policyholder dividends, contracts with both annual and terminal dividends, in which the terminal dividend is used to balance equity among the policyholders, may not qualify for treatment under the *SOP*. In that instance, the company would have to demonstrate that annual policyholder dividends, on their own, were determined in accordance with the contribution principle.

A variety of actuarial methods are acceptable for determining annual policyholder dividends. In the U.S., there are normally regulatory requirements for mutual life insurance enterprises to pay dividends annually and to do so in an equitable manner. Equity is typically measured against the standard of the contribution principle. In other jurisdictions, these requirements may not exist, and significant judgement may need to be applied in evaluating whether the annual policyholder dividends are determined in accordance with the contribution principle. The model used in the *SOP* presumes that earnings emerge relative to margins net of policyholder dividends. If annual policyholder dividends are not paid in accordance with the contribution principle, application of the accounting model in the *SOP* could result in unusual and possibly inappropriate results.

SOP 95-1 is applicable to directly issued life insurance contracts with the participation features described in paragraph 5. Contracts that do not qualify as insurance contracts using the tests described in *SFAS 97*, paragraphs 7 and 8, are not accounted for using the provisions of *SOP 95-1* regardless of the nature of any participation feature. These contracts would be investment contracts and accounted for by using the applicable guidance discussed elsewhere in this book. Similarly, contracts classified as short-duration contracts would not be accounted for by using the provisions of *SOP 95-1*, regardless of their participation features. Long-duration participating life insurance contracts with premium payment periods different than the coverage period, also known as limited-payment contracts, would qualify for treatment under the *SOP* provided the contract would qualify without regard to the premium payment period.

Universal life contracts or long-duration participating life insurance contracts that are in substance universal life contracts are to be accounted for by using the provisions of *SFAS 97*. Determining whether a long-duration participating life insurance contract is in substance a universal life contract requires judgment and careful consideration of the terms of the contract. Guidance is provided in *SFAS 97*:

> A participating contract that includes any of the following features shall be considered a universal life-type contract:
>
> a. The policyholder may vary premium payments within contract limits and without consent of the insurer.
>
> b. The contract has a stated account balance that is credited with policyholder premiums and interest and against which assessments are made for contract administration, mortality coverage, initiation, or surrender, and any of the amounts assessed or credited are not fixed and guaranteed.
>
> c. The insurer expects that changes in any contract element will be based primarily on changes in interest rates or other market conditions rather than on the experience of a group of similar contracts or the enterprise as a whole. (Paragraph 12)

The presence of any one feature is sufficient to characterize the contract as universal life. The ability to vary premium payments would be present if the contract provided the policyholder with the unilateral right to change either the frequency or the amount of premium without affecting coverage. A provision that allows for using dividends, in part or in whole, to offset what would otherwise be contractually obligated premiums would not be considered as providing the policyholder the right to vary premium payments. Similarly, a feature that provides for the payment of premiums out of the policyholder's interest in the contract (the cash value) such as an automatic premium loan feature, would not be sufficient to qualify a participating contract as in substance a universal life contract.

The presence of a stated account balance is also not sufficient to qualify a participating contract as in substance a universal life contract. The contract must also provide that the amounts assessed or credited are not fixed and guaranteed. The maintenance of an account balance does not of itself trigger a universal life contract classification. The account balance must be stated, that is, provided or available, to the policyholder. The maintenance of an account balance for the internal use of the insurer, say as a dividend fund, would not be considered a stated account balance.

The third condition classifies contracts as in substance universal life contracts when changes in dividend or other contract elements are not based on the actual experience of the company. Because only those participating policies with annual policyholder dividends based on the actual experience of the company qualify for treatment under *SOP 95-1*, this third condition does not by itself disqualify a contract otherwise within the scope of the *SOP*. The third condition is used to determine whether a participating contract with dividends not paid on the basis of the company's actual experience should be accounted for as a universal life contract or a participating contract under the provisions of *SFAS 60*.

Participating health insurance contracts are generally considered outside the scope of *SOP 95-1*. References in the scope and applicability discussions of the *SOP* are to life insurance contracts.

Paragraph 4 of the *SOP* indicates that *SFAS 60* and *SFAS 97* should be applied to the activities of mutual life insurance enterprises except as noted in paragraph 5. Paragraph 5 of the *SOP* is specific to participating life insurance contracts. Judgment needs to be applied dealing with a participating life insurance contract with material health (or disability) benefits or a participating health insurance contract with material life insurance benefits. In addition to the referenced paragraphs of *SFAS 120*, paragraph 29 of *SOP 95-1* includes the following sentence:

> FASB Statement No. 120 requires that other insurance contracts of mutual life insurance enterprises, such as annuity contracts, group insurance contracts, disability contracts, universal life-type contracts, and pension guaranteed contracts should be accounted for under FASB Statement Nos. 60 and 97.

This suggests a strong bias for the exclusion of participating health insurance contracts from the provisions of *SOP 95-1*.

5.3 Overview of Accounting Model

The accounting model for participating life insurance contracts describes the recognition, in terms of timing and amount, of the various contractual cash flows. For participating life insurance contracts subject to the provisions of *SOP 95-1*, this model follows the accounting model of *SFAS 60* with the exception of:

1. The recognition of benefits through the policyholder benefit liabilities

2. The recognition of acquisition costs through the deferral and amortization of acquisition costs

3. Annual policyholder dividends

4. Terminal dividends.

The following points summarize the recognition of income statement elements for which the accounting models of *SFAS 60* and *SFAS 120* are the *same*:

- *Premiums.* Premium revenues are recognized when such amounts are due. Monthly premiums are therefore recognized monthly; annual premiums annually. Prepaid premiums are recognized as revenue with an appropriate accrual of a prepaid premium liability. The entire premium payment is recognized as revenue.

- *Expenses.* Policy maintenance expenses, nondeferrable acquisition costs, and all other expenses, with the exception of deferrable acquisition costs, are recognized when such amounts are incurred.

- *Benefits.* All benefits are recognized as incurred. Benefits are as specified in the contract and do not exclude any accumulated value in the contract.

The following points summarize the recognition of income statement elements for which the accounting models of *SFAS 60* and *SFAS 120* are *different*:

- *Policyholder Benefits.* Both *SFAS 60* and *SFAS 120* use a net level premium method to accrue policyholder benefit liabilities. However, the *SFAS 60* accounting model applies the net level premium method using assumptions based on anticipated experience at issue of the contract, whereas the *SFAS 120* model references only the guaranteed mortality and dividend fund interest assumptions. At the time of contract issue, dividend fund assumptions are normally more conservative than the experience-based assumptions underlying the *SFAS 60* policyholder benefit liability.

- *Annual Policyholder Dividends.* Under *SFAS 120*, policyholder dividends are recognized as such amounts are earned by the policyholder. For example, one-half the current-policy-year dividend (defined as the amount payable at the end of the policy year using the current dividend scale) would have been recognized (accrued as a liability) for a participating policy six months into a policy year. *SFAS 60* recognizes dividends as either an element of the policyholder benefits and therefore accrued based on net premiums, or through the accrual of a deferred dividend liability when profits inuring to shareholders are limited.

- *Acquisition Costs.* The identification and deferral of acquisition costs are generally consistent between the *SFAS 60* and *SFAS 120* accounting models; however, the recognition of deferred amounts is different. Under *SFAS 120*, the deferred acquisition costs associated with a book of contracts are amortized (recognized) based on a constant percentage of the present value, as of the contract's issue date, of the estimated gross margin amounts expected to be realized over the life of the book of contracts. The unrecognized (unamortized) amounts as well as the current amount recognized (amortized) are adjusted to reflect experience as it has occurred as well as current estimates of future experience.

- *Terminal Dividends.* Terminal dividends are recognized as a level amount relative to estimated gross margins, based on the amount expected to be paid. Both the amount expected to be paid and the pattern of recognition should reflect experience as it has occurred as well as current estimates of future experience. *SFAS 60* recognizes terminal dividends using the same methods as for annual policyholder dividends.

5.4 Amortization Methods

The *SFAS 120* accounting model establishes estimated gross margins (EGMs) as the primary basis for recognition of earnings from participating long-duration life insurance contracts. EGMs are equivalent to a special case of the margin as described by Formula (5), restated here for convenience.

$$M_t \quad = \quad (DP_t' - DP_t) + (DI_t' - DI_t) + (DQ_t - DQ_t') + (DE_t - DE_t') - Div_t \qquad (5)$$

In Formula (5) the unprimed elements represented the experience factors used in the development of the dividend fund and are fixed at issue. The primed elements represent the comparable amounts as actually experienced. Under *SFAS 120*, the dividend fund is assumed to be equivalent to the policyholder benefit liability computed by using a net level-premium method under certain specified assumptions (discussed in detail later.) Therefore, the unprimed elements in the formula for EGMs as defined by *SFAS 120* are derived from the assumptions underlying the net level-premium method policyholder benefit liability. As the primary basis for earnings recognition, EGMs are used to establish the recognition pattern (e.g., amortization) of acquisition costs and terminal dividends. The position of EGMs within the *SFAS 120* accounting model is comparable to that of estimated gross profits within the *SFAS 97* accounting model as defined therein.

As previously discussed, *SOP 95-1* requires that

> capitalized acquisition costs be amortized over the life of a book of contracts at a constant rate based on the present value of the estimated gross margin amounts expected to be realized over the life of the book of contracts. (Paragraph 21)

EGMs are defined in *SOP 95-1* as follows:

> Estimated gross margins, as the term is used in this *SOP*, should include estimates of the following:
>
> a. Amounts expected to be received from premiums, plus
>
> b. Amounts expected to be earned from investment of policyholder balances (that is, the net level premium reserve described in paragraph 15a), less
>
> c. All benefit claims expected to be paid, less
>
> d. Costs expected to be incurred for contract administration (including acquisition costs not included in capitalized acquisition costs), less
>
> e. Expected change in the net level premium reserve for death and endowment benefits, less
>
> f. Expected annual policyholder dividends, plus or less
>
> g. Other expected assessments and credits, however characterized
>
> Estimated gross margins should be determined on a best estimate basis, without provision for adverse deviation. (Paragraph 22)

The terms are defined as follows:

EGM_t	=	estimated gross margins for period t as defined by *SOP 95-1*
GP_t	=	amounts expected to be received in period t from premiums
I_t	=	amounts expected to be earned in period t from the investment of the net level premium reserve
B_t	=	benefit (death, surrender, and other) expected to be paid in period t
E_t	=	contract administration and policy-related acquisition costs that are not deferred and that are expected to be incurred in period t
Div_t	=	annual policyholder dividends expected to be incurred in period t
NLP_t	=	the net level premium reserve as of the end of period t as described in *SOP 95-1*
P_t	=	the expected increase in period t in the net level premium reserve due to premiums
IR_t	=	the expected increase in period t in the net level premium reserve due to interest
BR_t	=	the expected decrease in period t in the net level premium reserve due to benefits

(Note that the elements considered in paragraph 22(g), "other expected assessments and credits," are ignored in the remainder of this chapter.)

Then the following formulas can be developed:

$$EGM_t = GP_t + I_t - B_t - E_t - (NLP_t - NLP_{t-1}) - Div_t \quad (5a)$$

$$NLP_t = NLP_{t-1} + P_t + IR_t - Br_t \quad (5b)$$

Restating formula (5b) in terms of $NLP_t - NLP_{t-1}$, substituting into the first equation, and re-arranging yields the following formula (6), comparable to formula (5):

$$EGM_t = (GP_t - P_t) + (I_t - IR_t) + (BR_t - B_t) - E_t - Div_t \quad (6)$$

Formula (6) is an expression of estimated gross margins in terms of experience gains relative to the assumptions underlying the policyholder benefit liability, defined as the net level-premium reserve in *SOP 95-1*. The form of this formula can readily be compared to the expression for estimated gross profits, used as an amortization base in accounting for universal life-type contracts.

As defined in the accounting model, estimates of future gross margins are adjusted to reflect the reporting entity's current view. This method requires the amounts to be adjusted as estimates are changed, either through the use of a different assumption in the future or because experience has been different than what had been assumed, and frequently due to both. In these instances, the unamortized DAC balance and terminal dividend liability are adjusted to the amounts that would have resulted if the current estimate of gross margins had always been the estimate of gross margins. This assumes the use of actual results for past periods. This adjustment is made in the current period.

Continuing with the notation previously defined and limiting the example to deferred acquisition costs, let:

DE_t = deferrable expenses associated with a book of contracts in period t
$PV_t(\,)$ = the present value of the parenthetical element as of time t
${}_tEGM_{t+1}$ = gross margins, as defined by the *SOP*, expected in period $t + 1$ from a book of contracts, as projected at time t.

Primed notation indicates actual experience, and unprimed notation indicates assumed, or estimated, future experience. An amortization ratio as of point t, k_t, can then be defined as follows:

$$k_t = \left[PV_0\left(DE_{s>t}\right) + PV_0\left(DE'_{s=<t}\right)\right] / \left[PV_0\left({}_tEGM_{s>t}\right) + PV_0\left({}_tEGM'_{s=<t}\right)\right] \qquad (7)$$

By adopting the convention that the amortization ratio is constant over relatively short periods, then the amortization charge in (relatively short) period t is simply:

$$Amort_t = k_t \times {}_tEGM_t$$

In determining EGMs, a company may expect that in certain periods over the life of the contract, the EGMs may be negative. This situation is addressed in *SOP 95-1*, which includes the following sentence:

> If significant negative gross margins are expected in any period, then the present value of gross margins before annual dividends, estimated gross premiums, or the balance of insurance in force should be substituted as the base for computing amortization. (Paragraph 20)

The presence of negative estimated gross margins in any period involves first an evaluation of their significance and then, if they are significant, the selection of an alternative amortization base. Determining whether negative estimated gross margins are significant requires judgment. Considerations include the effect of the negative gross margins on the amortization pattern of deferred acquisition costs, the frequency and magnitude of the negatives, and the effect of alternatives on expected reported earnings. If the negative gross margins are not significant, they may be left in the amortization calculations or, alternatively, included as zero. If they are included as zeros, there must not be a significant effect on the expected amortization pattern. If there is, the conclusion about their significance should be re-evaluated.

If the negative expected gross margins are deemed to be significant, an alternative amortization base must be selected. This selection should be made with the objective of producing an amortization pattern for deferred acquisition costs and terminal dividend liabilities that fairly recognizes the costs of acquiring the contracts against the company's performance under those contracts. The accounting profession has determined that EGMs are the best measure of this performance, and therefore the selection of an alternative amortization base should attempt to match that pattern as closely as is reasonably practical within the alternatives identified by *SOP 95-1*. Once a an alternative amortization base has been selected and put into use, it should continue to be used over the life of the contracts for which it has been made. In general, considerations for EGMs are also applicable to the alternative amortization bases identified in paragraph 20 of *SOP 95-1*.

5.5 Selection of Assumptions

A variety of assumptions are called for in accounting for traditional participating life insurance contracts. The two main classes of assumptions are those underlying the policyholder benefit liability and those used in estimating future gross margins. A third possible set of assumptions are those used to evaluate a block of contracts for loss recognition. The assumptions underlying the policyholder benefit liability are established by reference to the contract for which the liability is being established. As a result, these assumptions are established at issue of the contract and do not change unless, in the rare circumstance, there is a post-issue contract modification. On the other hand, the assumptions used in estimating future gross margins need to be reviewed periodically and updated to reflect current estimates.

5.5.1 Benefit Reserve Assumptions

Policyholder benefit liabilities are based on the net level-premium method. The total liability for future policy benefits includes the net level premium reserve, the liability for terminal dividends, and any liability required as a result of loss recognition. (See *SOP 95-1*, paragraph 15.) As applied here, this method calls for the use of a mortality assumption and an interest assumption. These two assumptions are discussed in the *SOP*, and there is very little need to apply judgment in their determination. The *SOP* reads as follows:

> The net level premium reserve should be calculated based on the dividend fund interest rate, if determinable, and the mortality rates guaranteed in calculating the cash surrender values described in the contract. If the dividend fund interest rate is not determinable, the guaranteed interest rate used in calculating cash surrender values described in the contract should be used. If the dividend fund interest rate is not determinable and there is no guaranteed interest rate, the interest rate used in determining guaranteed nonforfeiture values should be used. Finally, if none of the above rates exists, then the interest rate used to determine minimum cash surrender values—as set by the National Association of Insurance Commissioners' (NAIC) model standard nonforfeiture law—for the year of issue of the contract should be used. Regardless of the rate used, net premiums should be calculated as a constant percentage of the gross premiums. (Paragraph 16)

5.5.1.1 Mortality

Paragraph 16 describes a hierarchy of bases for interest rate assumptions but only a single choice for the mortality assumption. In the United States, a guaranteed cash surrender value has been legally mandated for most traditional participating life insurance contracts. The mortality assumptions for these cash surrender values are contractually specified. Typically, these mortality assumptions are consistent with the mortality assumptions specified for regulatory minimum policy reserves. In the event that a contract does not contain guaranteed cash surrender values or that the values guaranteed do not involve a mortality assumption, it would be reasonable to refer to the mortality assumptions for the legally mandated policy reserves. If no such assumptions are required in the calculation, then it would seem reasonable to re-evaluate whether the contract is in fact a life insurance contract and within the scope of the *SOP*. To the extent policies are issued on a substandard basis, an additional liability should be determined for the additional expected costs and included in the net level premium reserve component of the liability for future policy benefits.

5.5.1.2 Interest

The hierarchy of interest rates for the interest assumption is considered to establish an ordering requirement. The dividend fund interest rate is determined at policy issuance and is the rate against which experience is measured to determine the interest portion of the dividend. If this rate cannot be determined, then the interest rate used to compute any guaranteed cash surrender values is used; this is referred to as the guaranteed interest rate. As a last resort, paragraph 16 refers to the NAIC minimum nonforfeiture interest rates. Although it may be unfortunate, the use of these rates in calculating the policyholder benefit liability may be required for contracts issued outside of the United States. Finally, in some instances, guaranteed cash surrender values are determined by using interest rates that vary by policy duration, usually one rate for the first 5 or 10 policy years and a second rate for the remainder of the policy's life. In these instances, it would be appropriate to use the guaranteed interest rates precisely and inappropriate to use a single intermediate rate.

5.5.1.3 Method

The *SOP* specifies that the net level premium method is used to determine the policyholder benefit liability. In applying this method, assumptions need to be made about the timing of payments of premiums and benefits. A discussion of these assumptions is not included in the *SOP*; however, they should be established for the consistency of the financial statements taken as a whole. For example, because premiums are recognized as revenue, there should be a related increase in the policyholder benefit liability. Similarly, for death benefits the liability should be reduced in the same period as a benefit is paid. The use of deferred-premium assets or other offsetting balance sheet adjustments, which are sometimes found in regulatory-based financial statements, should be avoided.

5.5.2 Estimated Gross Margins Assumptions

The assumptions used in estimating future gross margins are described in paragraph 22 of the *SOP*, which describes the elements of gross margins and then concludes with the sentence: "Estimated gross margins should be determined on a best estimate basis, without provision for adverse deviation." Best-estimate assumptions should be reasonable and realistic and should reflect the actuary's best judgment on the most likely future outcome for each assumption made. Best-estimate assumptions are discussed in a financial reporting context in *ASOP 10*, "Methods and Assumptions for Use in Life Insurance Company Financial Statements Prepared in Accordance with GAAP."

5.5.2.1 Mortality

EGMs must be based on best estimate mortality assumptions. Various sources should be considered in arriving at these assumptions, including but not limited to the dividend scale mortality assumption, pricing and the company's recent experience. The effect of underwriting and selection should be incorporated into the mortality rates used in the EGMs. Because expected mortality can be affected by policyholder lapses, the mortality and lapse assumptions should be evaluated in combination as well as independently. The effect of substandard mortality should be considered and reflected consistently with the method used in determining the net level premium reserve.

5.5.2.2 Interest

In addition to the dividend fund interest rate used in the calculation of the policyholder benefit liabilities, two additional significant interest rates are used in accounting for traditional participating life insurance contracts. An interest rate assumption is required for determining the amount expected to be earned from the investment of policyholder balances (the net level-premium reserve). This assumption would be based on the yield expected from the assets supporting these liabilities. It would include any estimates of future realized capital gains, although rare, as well as the yields expected on reinvested or new money. Another interest rate is used to discount future estimated gross margins.

This rate is described in paragraph 20 of the *SOP* as the expected investment yield. Investment yield is a defined term in the glossary of *SOP 95-1*. It is the "interest rate the company expects to earn on the assets supporting the policies, net of investment expense." The expected investment yield is also used to accrue interest on the unamortized balance of capitalized acquisition costs and the terminal dividend liability. It is generally expected that the rate used to estimate gross margins in the first year of a contract is the expected investment yield. This expectation is supported by the illustration provided in Appendix A of *SOP 95-1*. In that illustration, a single interest rate is used to determine amounts arising from the investment of policyholder balances and to discount estimates of future gross margins.

SOP 95-1 offers a choice in determining the rate used to discount estimates of future gross margins. The practitioner can either allow this rate to change to the current expected investment yield at each period or continue to use the expected investment yield determined at contract issue. However, once this choice is made, it must be applied consistently from period to period. If the expected investment yield is fixed, a difference between the expected investment yield used to estimate the interest component of gross margins and the rate used to discount gross margins would arise over time. If the rate or rates are allowed to change, they change only for the remaining life of the contract because the discount rates for prior periods are locked in. Therefore, under that approach, there may be a different discount rate for each historical period with the current estimate or estimates of discount rate or rates used for all future periods. The same rates would be used to accrue interest on unamortized or accrued balances.

The *SOP* does not appear to require that the investment yield be a single rate applicable to all prospective periods. In other words, the literature appears to allow for making estimates of current and future investment yields and then using that series of estimated rates to discount future estimate gross margins. One difficulty of this approach is the need for consistency between the dividend and investment terms used in the gross margin calculation. If future investment yields are initially projected as variable and the "fixed at issue" approach is used, then the initially projected series of investment yields would continue to be used for discounting gross margins and accruing interest to unamortized balances throughout the life of the contract.

5.5.2.3 Dividend

Estimates of future gross margins must include expected annual policyholder dividends. Gross margins do not include expected terminal dividends. The dividend scale in effect at policy issue would normally be expected to be the starting point for estimating future annual policyholder dividends. It may be necessary to estimate future changes in the initial dividend scale to reflect the effect of estimated future changes in the expected investment yield or other factors.

Estimated gross margins must incorporate the expected effect of elected dividend options. Participating insurance contracts usually provide for dividends to be used within the contract in a variety of ways at the election of the policyholder. Other than receiving dividends in cash, the common options are using dividends to reduce premium payments, to purchase paid-up insurance, to purchase one-year term insurance, or to leave the dividends on deposit at interest. How policyholders elect to use their dividends will have various effects on future expected gross margins. For example, using dividends to purchase one-year term insurance may generate an additional gross margin in the year of purchase, whereas using dividends to purchase paid-up insurance or leaving them to accumulate at interest may generate additional gross margins over a long period. In general, gross margins are not affected through either payment of dividends in cash or use of dividends to reduce premium payments. Best-estimate assumptions must be made about how policyholders are expected to use dividends in the future, including how such elections may change over time. The gross margins expected to be generated by these various elections should be incorporated into the gross margins used to amortize deferred acquisition costs or accrue a terminal dividend liability.

5.5.2.4 Lapse Rates

The assumed rates at which policies lapse and are surrendered need to be considered in estimating gross margins and should be current best estimates. These assumptions should be consistent with the other assumptions used in estimating gross margins; therefore, they need to be sensitive to the expected effect of assumed changes in policyholder dividends. When a policy is surrendered, a cash distribution representing the policyholder's surrender value in the contract is typically made. Thereafter, that contract does not affect gross margins. When a policy is lapsed, extended term insurance or reduced paid-up insurance may become effective. If these continuations of the original contract are themselves participating, the gross margins expected to be developed from these contract continuations should be incorporated into the gross margins used to amortize deferred acquisition costs or to accrue a terminal dividend liability. If these contract continuations are not participating, but the margins generated from these options are used to support the dividends paid to continuing participating policyholders, these margins should be considered as an other expected credit under *SOP 95-1* paragraph 22(g).

5.5.2.5 Expenses

Chapter 3 contains the needs, sources and rationale for expense assumption selection. The reader should refer to Chapter 3 for instruction on expense selection.

The expenses included in EGMs are "Costs expected to be incurred for contract administration (including acquisition costs not included in capitalized acquisition costs." These costs are the direct costs associated with maintaining the policies, including the costs of paying claims and otherwise providing service to policyholders. Policy-related costs that are incurred in acquiring new contracts but that are not eligible for capitalization should also be included in gross margins. Examples include nondeferrable commissions and recurring premium taxes.

5.5.2.6 Grouping

Policy-by-policy or group methods can be used for determining EGMs. Setting assumptions and determining experience results require grouping of similar contracts. Further, grouping is recommended, if not mandated, for recoverability testing and loss recognition, as discussed later. For premium deficiency testing (loss recognition), policies are grouped consistently with the way the company acquires, services, and measures the profitability of its contracts. This is described as a line of business and represents the minimum amount of grouping, or the maximum size group, generally considered reasonable for determining EGMs. Additional grouping may be convenient in order to improve the ability to establish assumptions or to perform the modeling necessary to evaluate EGMs. Establishing too fine a grouping can create issues about the credibility of experience results and unintended consequences in the financial statements. At a minimum, companies group contracts by issue year to ensure the ability to test the recoverability of acquisition costs deferred in a year. In addition, many companies further subdivide contracts based on product considerations to improve the matching of modeled results with the companies reported experience.

5.5.3 Example

In the sections that follow, various concepts are illustrated through a numerical example. Table 5-1 provides the assumptions that are used as the base-case scenario and the starting point for the determination of the effect of various experience fluctuations.

Table 5-1
Base Case Assumptions

Policyholder Benefit Liabilities				Expenses				Estimated Gross Margins for Experience			
Issue Age	Policy Year	Guaranteed Mortality	Dividend Fund Interest	Policy Year	Commissions % Premium	Deferrable Acquisition Per Policy	Maintenance Per Policy	Policy Year	Mortality	Surrender	Investment Yield
45	1	0.0045	5.00%	1	50.0%	65.00	2.50	1	0.0036	15.0%	7.00%
	2	0.0050	5.00%	2	20.0%	0.00	2.50	2	0.0040	10.0%	7.00%
	3	0.0055	5.00%	3	5.0%	0.00	2.50	3	0.0044	5.0%	7.00%
	4	0.0060	5.00%	4	5.0%	0.00	2.50	4	0.0048	5.0%	7.00%
	5	0.0065	5.00%	5	5.0%	0.00	2.50	5	0.0052	5.0%	7.00%
	6	0.0070	5.00%	6	2.0%	0.00	2.50	6	0.0056	5.0%	7.00%
	7	0.0075	5.00%	7	2.0%	0.00	2.50	7	0.0060	5.0%	7.00%
	8	0.0080	5.00%	8	2.0%	0.00	2.50	8	0.0064	5.0%	7.00%
	9	0.0085	5.00%	9	2.0%	0.00	2.50	9	0.0068	5.0%	7.00%
	10	0.0090	5.00%	10	2.0%	0.00	2.50	10	0.0072	5.0%	7.00%

Table 5-2 provides the specifics related to the policy form being modeled as well as the census information developed from the experience assumptions.

Table 5-2
Policy Form and Census Information

Policy Form: 10-year participating endowment
Issue age: 45
Face Amount: $1,000 level
Gross Premium: 95 per $1,000, level

Policy Year	(1) BOY	(2) Deaths	(3) Surrenders	(4) EOY
1	1,000.000	3.600	149.460	846.940
2	846.940	3.388	84.355	759.197
3	759.197	3.340	37.793	718.064
4	718.064	3.447	35.731	678.886
5	678.886	3.530	33.768	641.588
6	641.588	3.593	31.900	606.096
7	606.096	3.637	30.123	572.336
8	572.336	3.663	28.434	540.239
9	540.239	3.674	26.828	509.737
10	509.737	3.670	25.303	480.764

Legend:
(1) Beginning-of-year policies in force.
(2) Deaths during the year = experience mortality rate × (1).
(3) Surrenders during the year = experience surrender rate × [(1) – (2)], all for cash.
(4) End of year policies in force = (1) – (2) – (3).

As a participating endowment, the contract provides insurance coverage equal to the face amount over the 10-year policy period and then pays a lump sum to policyholders in force at the end of the 10-year period. Annual policyholder dividends are paid, but in the base case there is no terminal dividend. For simplicity, all periods are assumed to be one year and the policy is assumed to be issued at the beginning of the first accounting year.

The policy and census information provided in Table 5-2 combined with the experience and expense assumptions in Table 5-1 are used to develop the dividend fund and initial dividend scale in Table 5-3.

Table 5-3
Base Case Margins

Policy Year	(1) Gross Premiums	(2) Investment Income	(3) Commissions	(4) Issue Costs	(5) Maintenance Costs	(6) Death Claims	(7) Surrender Benefits	(8) Endowment Benefits	(9) Dividend Funds, EOY	(10) Dividends	(11) Margin
1	95.00	(1.40)	47.50	65.00	2.50	3.60	0.00	0.00	(24.60)	0.00	(0.40)
2	80.46	2.61	16.09	0.00	2.12	3.39	0.00	0.00	36.14	0.44	0.29
3	72.12	7.19	3.61	0.00	1.90	3.34	1.71	0.00	102.85	1.23	0.82
4	68.22	11.66	3.41	0.00	1.80	3.45	4.86	0.00	165.85	2.02	1.35
5	64.49	15.92	3.22	0.00	1.70	3.53	7.84	0.00	225.32	2.79	1.86
6	60.95	20.12	1.22	0.00	1.60	3.59	10.64	0.00	283.39	3.57	2.38
7	57.58	24.12	1.15	0.00	1.52	3.64	13.38	0.00	338.20	4.32	2.88
8	54.37	27.95	1.09	0.00	1.43	3.66	15.96	0.00	389.93	5.07	3.38
9	51.32	31.60	1.03	0.00	1.35	3.67	18.40	0.00	438.75	5.79	3.86
10	48.43	35.09	0.97	0.00	1.27	3.67	20.69	480.76	0.00	6.51	8.39

Legend:
(1) Premiums = \$95 × the number of policyholders in force at beginning of the year.
(2) Investment income = 7% × (prior year dividend fund plus premiums less all expenses) = 0.07 × (prior (9) + (1) – (3) – (4) – (5).
(3) Commissions = commission rates × gross premiums.
(4) Issue expenses = issue expense per-policy × number of policies issued (1,000).
(5) Maintenance expenses = per-policy maintenance expense factor × number of policies in force at beginning of year.
(6) Death benefits = face amount (\$1,000) × number of deaths for the year.
(7) Surrender benefits = surrender benefit per policy × number of surrenders during the year (cash surrender values are equal to 95% of prior year-end dividend fund). Surrenders are 100% cash (not reduced paid-up insurance or extended term insurance).
(8) Endowment benefits = Face amount (\$1,000) × number of policies in force at end of 10 years.
(9) Dividend funds, EOY = end-of-year dividend funds = prior (9) + (1) – (3) – (4) – (5) – (6) – (7) – (8) + 5% × [prior (9) + (1) – (3) – (4) – (5)] year 10 forced to zero.
(10) Dividends paid = 60% of the excess of investment income over interest required for dividend fund.
(11) Margin = margin earned against dividend fund = (1) + (2) – (3) – (4) – (5) – (6) – (7) – (8) – (10) – [(9) – prior (9)].

The assumptions underlying the dividend fund are identical to the experience assumptions, except for the interest component. The dividend fund accrues accumulated cash using an interest assumption of 5%. The dividend fund as of the end of the last year of the contract is assumed to be a permanent contribution to surplus. The margins are developed as the cash flows, less the increase in the dividend fund, accumulated at 7% interest. Dividends have been established as 60% of the excess of the estimated investment income (at 7%) over the interest accumulating in the dividend fund (at 5%). Benefits payable to surrendering policyholders are computed as 95% of the prior end of year per policy dividend fund, an amount assumed to extend minimum contractual requirements. The margins shown in Table 5-3 are those defined through Formula (5).

5.6 True-up and Unlocking

The *SOP* requires that EGMs be adjusted to reflect actual results as they are known. Therefore, as time passes, experience results are substituted for assumed results. This substitution can be done at the line-of-business level or at a lower level consistent with the company's method of grouping contracts for determining EGMs. The substitution can be accomplished by simply computing an experience EGM for the period and substituting it into the series of EGMs used as an amortization base. At the other end of the spectrum, experience can be translated into lapse, mortality, and interest factors that are then substituted for the applicable assumption set underlying the EGM computation. The *SOP* also requires that the assumptions used to estimate future EGMs be periodically evaluated and adjusted if estimates change.

True-up refers to the current-period effect on the amortization of deferred acquisition costs or accrual of terminal dividend liabilities of the difference between the actual gross margins and the estimated gross margins for the current period, with the amortization ratio held constant. *Unlocking* refers to the current-period effect on the amortization of DAC or accrual of terminal dividend liabilities of a change in the amortization ratio. *Unlocking* can arise as a result of the current-period true-up or a change in estimated future EGMs.

Limiting the analysis to deferred acquisition costs, let DAC_t represent the unamortized DAC at time t. Then:

$$DAC_t \quad = \quad DAC_{t-1} + Amounts\ Capitalized_t + Interest_t - Amort_t$$

Assuming that all amortization occurs at the end of each period and letting i_t equal the expected investment yield used to accrue interest to the unamortized balance of DAC in period t, then:

$$Interest_t \quad = \quad DAC_{t-1} \times i_t$$

Further, the DAC is amortized at a constant rate based on the present value of estimated gross margins. This rate is referred to as the amortization ratio, k, and is defined as:

$$k_t = [PV_0(DE_{s=>t}) + PV_0(DE'_{s<t})] \ / \ [PV_0({}_tEGM_{s=>t}) + PV_0({}_tEGM'_{s<t})] \qquad (7)$$

If the experience in period t is consistent with the assumptions used to develop the estimated gross margins for period t, then it would be expected that the amortization ratio would hold constant over period t. Because this is seldom the case, the reported amortization charge includes two additional terms. The first term reflects the amortization charge for differences between actual and expected experience in the period t. The second term reflects changes in the amortization ratio attributable to both differences in current experience as compared to expected and any changes in future expectations *(unlocking)*. Therefore, in the more complex and more common case, the amortization charge (that is, the decrease in DAC) in period t can be expressed as:

$$Amort_t = k_t \times {}_{t-1}EGM_t + [k_t \times {}_tEGM_t - k_{t+1} \times {}_{t-1}EGM_t)] + (1 + i_t) \times \{k_t \times PV_{t-1}({}_{t-1}EGM_{s>t-1}) - k_{t+1} \times PV_{t-1}({}_tEGM_{s>t-1})\} \qquad (8)$$

In Formula (8) an experience element that serves to increase actual gross margins in period t will increase the second, or *true-up* term (in square brackets [ ]) and will decrease the third, or *unlocking* term (in curly brackets { }). Although the effects combine to mitigate the impact on amortization due to experience different than expected, the degree to which they offset each other depends on a number of different factors. The amortization ratio and true-up and unlocking considerations discussed can be applied to any of the available amortization bases when a base other than estimated gross margins is required to be used.

Applying Formula (7) at contract initiation:

$$k_1 \quad = \quad PV_0(DE_{s>0}) \ / \ PV_0(EGM_{s>0}),$$

Assuming that deferrable acquisition costs are incurred at the beginning of the period,

$$k_1 \quad = \quad [DE_0 + PV_0(DE_{s=>1})] \ / \ PV_0(EGM_{s>0}), \text{ and then manipulating:}$$

$$DE_0 \quad = \quad k_1 \times PV_0(EGM_{s>0}) - PV_0(DE_{s=>1}).$$

With amortization occurring at the end of each period, DE_0 is equal to DAC_0 and the formula generalizes to:

$$DAC_t = k_{t+1} \times PV_t(EGM_{s>t}) - PV_t(DE_{s>t}) \quad (9)$$

In the simple case in which all the deferred acquisition costs are incurred in the first period, this is simply the formula case of the requirement that the DAC is amortized at a constant rate based on the present value of estimated gross margins. Assuming that all the DAC has been incurred by time t, the present value of future deferrable expenses can be ignored in Formula (9). This makes it easier to discuss the concepts of true-up and unlocking. Continuing:

$$DAC_t = DAC_{t-1} + i_t \times DAC_{t-1} - Amort_t$$

If experience over the period is as expected, then this formula can be restated to:

$$DAC_t = DAC_{t-1} + i_t \times DAC_{t-1} - k_t \times {}_tEGM_t$$

where ${}_tEGM_t$ is equal to ${}_{t-1}EGM_t$ because experience has been exactly as expected. At the end of period t, if future expectations have changed in periods $t + 1$ and beyond, the unamortized DAC at the beginning of period $t + 1$ needs to be adjusted to reflect the effect of the changed expectations. This adjustment can be computed from the formula:

$$Unlocking = k_t \times PV_t({}_{t-1}EGM_{s>t}) - k_{t+1} \times PV_t({}_tEGM_{s>t})$$

In this formula for the unlocking adjustment, k_{t+1} and ${}_tEGM_{s>t}$ reflect the revised expectations about the future. The terms k_t and ${}_{t-1}EGM_{s>t}$ do not. The first element in the formula is simply the unamortized DAC balance at the beginning of period $t + 1$ (or end of period t) if expectations for periods $t + 1$ and beyond have not been revised from the estimates made at the beginning of period t and the second element is the unamortized DAC balance at the beginning of period $t + 1$.

If experience over the period t is not as expected, even when there are changes expected beyond period t such that the amortization ratio will remain unchanged, a true-up adjustment to the amortization of DAC in period t would be needed. In this case, ${}_{t-1}EGM_t$, the gross margin expected in period t as of the beginning of period t, does not equal ${}_tEGM_t$, the gross margin experienced in period t, but k_t, the amortization ratio computed as of the beginning of period t, does equal k_{t+1}, the amortization ratio computed as of the beginning of period $t + 1$. The true-up adjustment can be expressed by using the following formula:

$$True\text{-}up = k_t \times ({}_tEGM_t - {}_{t-1}EGM_t)$$

If in a given period there is both a true-up and an unlocking adjustment, the allocation of the total amortization charge among its various components is judgmental. The issue is whether to treat the effect of the revised amortization ratio applied to the change in current period gross margins as an element of the true-up adjustment or the unlocking adjustment. Accounting literature does not require these elements to be disclosed and practice varies. Formula (7) and the analysis of Table 5-1 incorporate the effect of the revised amortization ratio applied to the change in current-period gross margins as part of the true-up adjustment. The following formula for amortization incorporates this effect into the unlocking component.

$$\begin{aligned} Amort_t = {} & k_t \times {}_{t-1}EGM_t + [k_t \times ({}_tEGM_t - {}_{t-1}EGM_t)] + \{{}_{t-1}EGM_t \times (k_t - k_{t+1}) \\ & + (1 + i_t) \times [k_t \times PV_{t-1}({}_{t-1}EGM_{s>t-1}) - k_{t+1} \times PV_{t-1}({}_tEGM_{s>t-1})]\} \end{aligned} \quad (8a)$$

Both unlocking and the process of true-up can cause an increase in the amount of unamortized DAC. For example, if prospective assumptions were unlocked and revised such that they produced more implied EGMs in the future, the amortization ratio would be reduced. Therefore, after introduction of such new prospective assumptions, the opening amount of unamortized DAC would be increased.

5.7 Realized Capital Gains

Realized capital gains are an element of gross margins. Therefore, realized investment gains affect the DAC amortization and the accrual of terminal dividend liabilities for traditional participating insurance contracts. If an amortization basis other than gross margins is being used, the effect of a realized capital gain on DAC amortization will need to be evaluated. A realized capital gain in period t would increase the I_t term in Formula (6). Further, a realized capital gain will increase future expected policyholder dividends if these gains are shared with the policyholder, increasing the dividend term of Formula (6) in future periods. This increase will be mitigated by lower future earned rates resulting from the interest environment responsible for the capital gain. Both changes would affect the amortization charge (or accrual of a terminal dividend liability) as described by Formula (8). Because of this interaction, it is important to establish which assets back the net level premium reserve so that as gains are realized on these assets, the DAC amortization and terminal dividend liability accrual can be appropriately adjusted.

Identifying the assets from the investment of the net level premium reserve associated with traditional participating life insurance contracts is generally not straightforward and also not addressed in the accounting literature. A variety of alternatives are reasonable and used in practice. Whatever approach is used, it should be consistent with the company's business practices, and it should be used consistently from period to period, with changes subject to normal disclosure requirements.

Accounting for investments requires that, for certain types of securities, unrealized gains or losses be recognized in the carrying value of those securities. Because of this, other balance sheet elements need to be adjusted to an amount that would result from the realization, in the current period, of the unrealized gains and losses recognized in the balance sheet. Such adjustments are made in the carrying values of DAC and terminal dividend liabilities associated with traditional participating life insurance contracts. Depending on the circumstances, it may also be necessary to reflect a liability for future expected losses (through the loss recognition requirements described in *SFAS 60*.) This treatment is discussed further in Chapter 7.

Table 5-4 illustrates the effect of a realized capital gain on the DAC amortization pattern.

Table 5-4
Impact of Realized Capital Gains on Amortization of Deferred Acquisition Costs

Period	(1) EGM	(2) BOY DAC	(3) Capitalization	(4) Interest	(5) Amortization	(6) Percentage	(7) EOY DAC
Original Schedule							
1	26.90	0.00	110.60	7.74	24.51	91.10%	93.83
2	27.32	93.83	14.48	7.58	24.89	91.10%	91.01
3	20.37	91.01	2.16	6.52	18.56	91.10%	81.13
4	19.63	81.13	2.05	5.82	17.88	91.10%	71.12
5	18.86	71.12	1.93	5.11	17.19	91.10%	60.98
6	18.05	60.98	0.00	4.27	16.45	91.10%	48.80
7	17.14	48.80	0.00	3.42	15.61	91.10%	36.61
8	16.21	36.61	0.00	2.56	14.77	91.10%	24.40
9	15.27	24.40	0.00	1.71	13.91	91.10%	12.20
10	14.33	12.20	0.00	0.85	13.05	91.10%	0.00
Investment Yield		7.0%					
Present Value		141.78		129.17			
Amortization Ratio		91.105%					
With Realized Capital Gains in Period 5							
1	26.90	0.00	110.60	7.74	22.84	84.89%	95.50
2	27.32	95.50	14.48	7.70	23.19	84.89%	94.49
3	20.37	94.49	2.16	6.77	17.29	84.89%	86.13
4	19.63	86.13	2.05	6.17	16.66	84.89%	77.69
5	**33.42**	77.69	1.93	5.57	28.37	84.89%	56.82
6	18.05	56.82	0.00	3.98	15.33	84.89%	45.48
7	17.14	45.48	0.00	3.18	14.55	84.89%	34.11
8	16.21	34.11	0.00	2.39	13.76	84.89%	22.74
9	15.27	22.74	0.00	1.59	12.96	84.89%	11.37
10	14.33	11.37	0.00	0.80	12.16	84.89%	0.00
Investment Yield		7.0%					
Present Value		152.16		129.17			
Amortization Ratio		84.891%					
As Reported							
1	26.90	0.00	110.60	7.74	24.51	91.10%	93.83
2	27.32	93.83	14.48	7.58	24.89	91.10%	91.01
3	20.37	91.01	2.16	6.52	18.56	91.10%	81.13
4	19.63	81.13	2.05	5.82	17.88	91.10%	71.12
5	**33.42**	71.12	1.93	5.11	21.34	63.87%	56.82
6	18.05	56.82	0.00	3.98	15.33	84.89%	45.48
7	17.14	45.48	0.00	3.18	14.55	84.89%	34.11
8	16.21	34.11	0.00	2.39	13.76	84.89%	22.74
9	15.27	22.74	0.00	1.59	12.96	84.89%	11.37
10	14.33	11.37	0.00	0.80	12.16	84.89%	0.00

Legend:

(1) Estimated gross margins for the period.
(2) Unamortized deferred acquisition costs at the beginning of the period.
(3) Acquisition costs capitalized in the period.
(4) Interest on DAC = 7.0% × [(2) + (3)].
(5) Amortization of DAC = amortization ratio × (1) [or (2) + (3) + (4) – (6)].
(6) Amortization as percent of EGM = (5) / (1).
(7) End of period DAC = (2) + (3) + (4) – (5).

The first schedule in Table 5-4 represents the original schedule of expected amortization charges. As originally scheduled, amortization is anticipated to be charged at the rate of approximately 91.10% of gross margins. The second schedule in Table 5-4 has been prepared as if experience has occurred exactly as expected up until period 5. In period 5, it is assumed that a capital gain is realized that increases the investment yield in that year by 5%, from 7% to 12%. This gain increased gross margins in that year by $14.56. For this illustration, this realized gain is not expected to cause any changes in dividend payments. Incorporating the realized capital gain into the gross margins reduces the amortization ratio by 6.21% to 84.89%. The third schedule in Table 5-4 provides the reported information over the ten periods these contracts are assumed to be in force. The amortization charge in the fifth year can be analyzed as follows:

Normal amortization: $17.19, equal to the initial expected amortization charge

True-up: $11.18, equal to the revised amortization ratio applied to the increased gross margins less the initial expected amortization charge

Unlocking: ($ 6.57) equal to the change in the beginning of period DAC from the first to the second schedule of Table 5-1 (including the change in the interest component)

Total $21.34

If it is expected that the gains realized are passed back to some degree to the policyholders through the dividends, expected future dividends would be increased and the revised amortization ratio would not change as significantly. If, as a result, the amortization ratio is unchanged, then the *unlocking* adjustment would be zero and the entire amortization adjustment would be attributable to *true-up*.

5.8 Recoverability and Loss Recognition

GAAP requires that amounts recorded as assets (including capitalized acquisition costs) have value. For capitalized acquisition costs, this is evaluated at contract inception by comparing the present value of the amounts to be capitalized to the present value of EGMs that will be used as the basis for amortizing the capitalized costs. This evaluation is referred to as recoverability testing. Further, ongoing evaluation of a book of contracts is needed to ensure that the amounts established on the balance sheet in recognition of a company's obligations under those contracts are sufficient to provide for those obligations. This ongoing evaluation of the balance sheet for a book of contracts is effectively loss recognition testing. Recoverability testing evaluates the amounts currently planned for capitalization relative to the margins expected from the contracts being issued in the current period and that gave rise to the capitalized costs. Loss recognition testing evaluates the unamortized balance in light of other amounts recorded on the balance sheet and relates to a book of contracts that may have been issued over several periods. The amortization ratio as calculated using estimated gross margins, k_0, is used for recoverability testing for traditional participating life insurance contracts. If this amortization ratio at contract inception is less than 100%, then it would normally be concluded that the amounts being capitalized (and used in the numerator of that ratio) are recoverable. Special circumstances, such as the use of an amortization base other than estimated gross margins or the presence of negative estimated gross margins at some point over the life of the contract, require additional analysis.

Because estimated gross margins are generally used both to amortize DAC and to accrue a liability for terminal dividends, both elements need to be considered in evaluating the recoverability of acquisition costs expected to be capitalized. In the case of a terminal dividend liability accrual, recoverability is expected if the sum of the amortization ratio related to capitalized acquisition costs and the amortization ratio related to the accrual of a terminal dividend liability is less than 100%.

If the amortization ratio (or sum of ratios) based on gross margins exceeds 100%, the amount of acquisition costs expected to be capitalized should be reduced by the amount necessary to bring the amortization ratio (or sum of ratios) to 100%. The amount by which expected capitalized acquisition costs are reduced would then be recorded as an expense in the current period. Note that nondeferred acquisition costs are not then considered in the EGMs expected in the year of issue. EGMs include "acquisition costs not included in capitalized acquisition costs." The acquisition costs included in gross margins are acquisition costs not eligible for capitalization rather than eligible amounts not capitalized, as would be the case in the event of a lack of recoverability. The acquisition costs not capitalized as a result of recoverability testing are excluded from gross margins. But for recoverability testing they would have been included in capitalized acquisition costs.

Loss recognition is defined as the process of evaluating whether the existing net liabilities, when combined with anticipated future revenues, is adequate to provide for future obligations. If the conclusion is that it is not adequate, the deficiency needs to be identified and recognized currently. This can be viewed as a deficiency in the amount of the existing provision or in the anticipated future revenues. As such it is sometimes referred to as a premium deficiency. *SOP 95-1* (paragraph 15c) requires that premium deficiency testing be performed in accordance with the methodology provided in *SFAS 60*. The *SOP* discusses the liability for future policy benefits and reads as follows:

> A liability for future policy benefits relating to participating life insurance contracts should be equal to the sum of –
>
> a. The net level premium reserve for death and endowment policy benefits
> b. The liability for terminal dividends
> c. Any probable loss (premium deficiency) as described in paragraphs 35 to 37 of *FASB Statement No. 60*. (Paragraph 15)

A premium deficiency must be recognized if, at a minimum, the deficiency exists on an entire line of business. A line of business is a grouping of insurance contracts consistent with a company's manner of acquiring, servicing, and measuring the profitability of its insurance contracts. A block of insurance contracts, at a minimum, is the same as a line of business; however, it is generally considered to be smaller. For traditional participating life insurance contracts, a block of contracts typically represents a single issue year of business and includes a variety of products with comparable premium payment periods and benefit periods. A line of business typically represents the combination of blocks of business from many issue years. The form of the test is described in paragraph 35 of *SFAS 60*. Effectively, it is a comparison of the sum of net balance sheet recognition of the company's obligations for a line of business and the expected future revenues from that business to the current best estimate of the costs associated with those obligations. The test is as follows:

> Present value of future payments for benefits and related settlement and maintenance costs, determined using revised assumptions based on actual and anticipated experience
>
> Less the present value of future gross premium, determined using revised assumptions based on actual and anticipated experience

Equals the liability for future policy benefits using the revised assumptions

Less the liability for future policy benefits at the valuation date, reduced by unamortized acquisition costs

Equals premium deficiency (Paragraph 35)

Should the test conclude that a premium deficiency exists, then a probable loss needs to be recognized. The amount to be recognized is the amount necessary to produce a zero net result in the test. The loss can be recognized either by a reduction in the unamortized DAC or through an increase in the policyholder benefit liabilities. This choice should be made based on the nature of the probable loss and its anticipated incidence, with the intention to recognize the loss in a manner that releases the additional provision at the same time as the expected additional losses are incurred.

Table 5-5 provides an example of a premium deficiency test for the example block of business. The test is done as of the end of the fifth year, shows that there is a "surplus" of $5.95; thus no premium deficiency needs to be recognized for this block of business. In practice, the premium deficiency test would be based on multiple issue years of contracts and possibly a broader grouping of products. However, regardless of the size of the line of business being tested, to the extent that DAC amortization is based on estimated gross margins, if the amortization ratio on the combined business is less than 100%, a premium deficiency would be unlikely. Note that the expected dividend payments are included in the determination of the liability for future policy benefits based on revised assumptions. The expected dividends used in this calculation should represent what would be expected to be paid based on the assumptions used in the gross premium and benefit estimates. Therefore, for a traditional participating life insurance contract, it may be assumed that dividends will be reduced to offset expected adverse experience, provided such a practice is consistent with the company's practices and other factors.

Table 5-5
Premium Deficiency Test

Present value of future payments for benefits and related settlement and maintenance costs, determined using revised assumptions based on actual and anticipated experience.	$452.64
Less the present value of future gross premium, determined using revised assumptions based on actual and anticipated experience	241.09
Liability for future policy benefits	211.55
Less the liability for future policy benefits at the valuation date, reduced by unamortized acquisition costs	217.51
Premium deficiency	$(5.95)

Period	(1) Gross Premiums	(2) Benefits	(3) Commissions	(4) Expenses	(5) Dividends	(6) Total Benefits & Expenses
6	60.95	14.24	1.22	1.60	3.57	
7	57.58	17.02	1.15	1.52	4.32	
8	54.37	19.62	1.09	1.43	5.07	
9	51.32	22.07	1.03	1.35	5.79	
10	48.43	505.12	0.97	1.27	6.51	
Present Value	241.09	421.17	4.82	6.34	20.31	452.64

Liability for future policy benefits	278.49
Unamortized DAC	60.98
Net	217.51

Legend:
(1) Gross premiums, paid at beginning of year.
(2) Benefits, paid at end of year.
(3) Commissions, paid at beginning of year.
(4) Maintenance (and settlement) expenses, paid at beginning of year.
(5) Dividends, paid at end of year.
(6) Sum of present values from columns (2) – (5).

Present values taken at 7.0% interest.

5.9 Policyholder Benefit Liabilities

SOP 95-1 requires the liability for policyholder benefits to be determined by using the net level-premium method and for the calculation to be performed using appropriate mortality and interest assumptions. In the accounting model for traditional participating life insurance contracts, the policyholder benefit liability functions in a manner comparable to the policyholder account balance in the accounting model for universal life-type contracts. The background discussion of *SOP 95-1* in fact describes identifying a proxy for the policyholder account balance as a principal consideration in arriving at the net level premium method liability. Five other possibilities were considered as candidates for the proxy to the policyholder account balance but were ultimately rejected. One of these was the dividend fund. However, many companies do not explicitly define the dividend fund or may not use a dividend fund approach in establishing policyholder dividends;

therefore this alternative was rejected in favor of the net level premium method using guaranteed mortality and the dividend fund interest rate.

The net level-premium method is a method for accruing a liability for future policyholder benefits. Under this method, the liability is accrued as a level proportion of the premiums paid by the policyholder. The method involves computing a net premium ratio. The net premium ratio is the level proportion of each and every gross premium payment that is necessary to provide the benefits under the contract. The method, as applied to life insurance contracts, considers only mortality and interest.

The first schedule in Table 5-6 [columns (1) – (11)] details the calculation of the net premium ratio. The present values of expected future death and endowment benefits are determined by using the mortality and interest assumptions defined for use in the net level premium reserve. These amounts are summed for the total present value of benefits. The present value of estimated gross premiums is likewise determined. The net premium ratio is then the present value of benefits divided by the present value of gross premiums, or in the example, 0.827990. The second schedule of Table 5-6 [columns (12) – (18)] uses the net premium ratio and the mortality and interest assumptions in the first schedule to compute net level premium reserves using an accumulation method. Before the first premium is paid under a policy, the net level premium reserve is defined to be zero. The net level-premium reserve at the end of each period thereafter is determined as the net level premium reserve at the end of the prior period, plus the net premium for the period, plus interest on the sum of the prior reserve and the net premium, less the current period cost of death and endowment benefits, all divided by the probability of survival from the beginning of the period to the end of the period. The net premium is determined as the product of the net premium ratio and the gross premium for the period. Because this is a per policy reserve, the probability of surviving to the beginning of the period is not a factor in the calculation. However, under the accumulation approach, the reserves accumulated for policies not surviving through the period effectively increase the per policy amounts accumulated for the survivors. This element of the calculation is reflected through dividing the accumulated amount by the proportion of policies starting the period (defined to be 100%) that survived to the end of the period.

Although the net level premium method using guaranteed mortality and dividend fund interest is mandated by *SOP 95-1*, the *SOP* also recognizes that there are policies that do not meet normal underwriting standards and for which the guaranteed mortality underlying the cash surrender values may not be a fair recognition of the true anticipated mortality costs. In these instances, additional amounts may be included in the net level premium reserve. The method for inclusion is unspecified, but should be consistent with the anticipated mortality characteristics and, to the extent appropriate, consistent with the net level premium method.

Table 5-6
Calculation of Net Level Premium Reserve for Death and Endowment Benefits

	(1)	(2)	(3)	(4)	(5)	(6)	(7)	(8)	(9)	(10)	(11)
Period	Mortality Rate	px	tpx	Interest	Discount Factor	Death Benefit	PV of Death Benefits	Endowment Benefits	PV of Endowment Benefits	Gross Premium	PV of Gross Premiums
1	0.0045	0.9955	0.9955	5.00%	0.95238	1000	4.2857	0.00	0.000	95.00	95.0000
2	0.0050	0.9950	0.9905	5.00%	0.90703	1000	4.5147	0.00	0.000	95.00	90.0690
3	0.0055	0.9945	0.9851	5.00%	0.86384	1000	4.7061	0.00	0.000	95.00	85.3511
4	0.0060	0.9940	0.9792	5.00%	0.82270	1000	4.8625	0.00	0.000	95.00	80.8397
5	0.0065	0.9935	0.9728	5.00%	0.78353	1000	4.9868	0.00	0.000	95.00	76.5283
6	0.0070	0.9930	0.9660	5.00%	0.74622	1000	5.0814	0.00	0.000	95.00	72.4103
7	0.0075	0.9925	0.9587	5.00%	0.71068	1000	5.1488	0.00	0.000	95.00	68.4795
8	0.0080	0.9920	0.9511	5.00%	0.67684	1000	5.1913	0.00	0.000	95.00	64.7294
9	0.0085	0.9915	0.9430	5.00%	0.64461	1000	5.2111	0.00	0.000	95.00	61.1539
10	0.0090	0.9910	0.9345	5.00%	0.61391	1000	5.2102	1,000.00	573.7044	95.00	57.7467
Total							49.1988		573.7044		752.3080
								Net Premium Ratio			**0.827990**

	(12)	(13)	(14)	(15)	(16)	(17)	(18)
Period	BOY NLP Reserve	Net Premium	Interest	Mortality Cost	Endowment Cost	Survivorship Factor	EOY NLP Reserve
1	0.000	78.659	3.933	4.500	0.000	0.996	78.445
2	78.445	78.659	7.855	5.000	0.000	0.995	160.763
3	160.763	78.659	11.971	5.500	0.000	0.995	247.253
4	247.253	78.659	16.296	6.000	0.000	0.994	338.237
5	338.237	78.659	20.845	6.500	0.000	0.994	434.062
6	434.062	78.659	25.636	7.000	0.000	0.993	535.103
7	535.103	78.659	30.688	7.500	0.000	0.993	641.763
8	641.763	78.659	36.021	8.000	0.000	0.992	754.479
9	754.479	78.659	41.657	8.500	0.000	0.992	873.722
10	873.722	78.659	47.619	9.000	991.000	0.991	0.000

(1) Probability of death in period t.
(2) Probablility of surviving period t, 1 – (1).
(3) Probability of surviving from issue to beginning of period $t + 1$, prior (3) × (2), initially 1.0.
(4) Interest rate applicable in period t.
(5) Interest discount factor to issue, prior (5) / [1 + (4)], initially 1.0.
(6) Death benefit amount payable to deaths in year t.
(7) Present value of expected death benefits at issue, (6) × (5) × (1) × prior (3).
(8) Endowment benefits payable to survivors to end of period t.
(9) Present value of expected endowment benefits at issue, (8) × (3) × (5).
(10) Gross premium payable by policyholders at beginning of period t.
(11) Present value at issue of expected gross premiums for period t, (10) × prior (3) × prior (5).
(12) End-of-prior-period net level-premium reserve, initially zero, thereafter, prior (18).
(13) Net premium in period t, net premium ratio × (10).
(14) Interest accrued to net level-premium reserve, [(12) + (13)] × (4).
(15) Mortality cost charged to net level-premium reserve, (6) × (1).
(16) Endowment costs charged to net level-premium reserve, (8) × (3).
(17) Survivorship factor to reflect mortality on net level-premium reserve per policy.
(18) End-of-period net level-premium reserve, [(12) + (13) + (14) – (15) – (16)] / (17).

5.10 DAC and Terminal Dividend Liabilities

Under generally accepted accounting practices, acquisition costs that are both variable and directly related to the activity of acquiring new and renewal insurance and annuity contracts are capitalized and then amortized into income over the life of the associated contracts. For traditional participating life insurance contracts, the amortization is determined relative to the present value of estimated gross margins. Estimated gross margins are defined in paragraph 22 of *SOP 95-1*, provided earlier in this chapter. Determination of the amount of acquisition costs to capitalize is addressed in Chapter 3.

Table 5-7 provides the calculation of estimated gross margins using the base case example previously described.

Table 5-7
Calculation of Unamortized Deferred Acquisition Costs

Period	(1) Expected Premiums	(2) Interest on NLP Reserve	(3) Interest on Cash Flow	(4) Benefits	(5) Administration Costs	(6) Nondeferred Acquisition Costs	(7) Increase in NLP Reserve	(8) Expected Dividends	(9) Expected Gross Margin	(10) Expected Investment Yield	(11) Discount Factor
1	95.00	0.00	6.34	3.60	2.50	1.90	66.44	0.00	26.90	7.00%	0.93458
2	80.46	4.65	5.37	3.39	2.12	1.61	55.61	0.44	27.32	7.00%	0.87344
3	72.12	8.54	4.81	5.05	1.90	1.44	55.49	1.23	20.37	7.00%	0.81630
4	68.22	12.43	4.55	8.31	1.80	1.36	52.08	2.02	19.63	7.00%	0.76290
5	64.49	16.07	4.31	11.37	1.70	1.29	48.86	2.79	18.86	7.00%	0.71299
6	60.95	19.49	4.07	14.24	1.60	1.22	45.83	3.57	18.05	7.00%	0.66634
7	57.58	22.70	3.84	17.02	1.52	1.15	42.98	4.32	17.14	7.00%	0.62275
8	54.37	25.71	3.63	19.62	1.43	1.09	40.30	5.07	16.21	7.00%	0.58201
9	51.32	28.53	3.43	22.07	1.35	1.03	37.77	5.79	15.27	7.00%	0.54393
10	48.43	31.18	3.23	505.12	1.27	0.97	(445.37)	6.51	14.33	7.00%	0.50835
Present Value at Issue											
Amortization Ratio											

Period	(12) Expected Gross Margin: Amount	(13) Expected Gross Margin: Present Value at Issue	(14) Deferrable Acquisiton Costs: Amount	(15) Deferrable Acquisiton Costs: Present Value at Issue	(16) BOY DAC	(17) Expected Gross Margin	(18) Amount Capitalized	(19) Interest	(20) Amount Amortized	(21) EOY DAC
1	26.90	25.14	110.60	110.60	0.00	26.90	110.60	7.74	24.51	93.83
2	27.32	23.86	14.48	13.54	93.83	27.32	14.48	7.58	24.89	91.01
3	20.37	16.63	2.16	1.89	91.01	20.37	2.16	6.52	18.56	81.13
4	19.63	14.97	2.05	1.67	81.13	19.63	2.05	5.82	17.88	71.12
5	18.86	13.45	1.93	1.48	71.12	18.86	1.93	5.11	17.19	60.98
6	18.05	12.03	0.00	0.00	60.98	18.05	0.00	4.27	16.45	48.80
7	17.14	10.67	0.00	0.00	48.80	17.14	0.00	3.42	15.61	36.61
8	16.21	9.43	0.00	0.00	36.61	16.21	0.00	2.56	14.77	24.40
9	15.27	8.31	0.00	0.00	24.40	15.27	0.00	1.71	13.91	12.20
10	14.33	7.28	0.00	0.00	12.20	14.33	0.00	0.85	13.05	0.00
Present Value at Issue		141.78		129.17						
Amortization Ratio				91.10%						

Legend:
(1) Gross premiums expected in period.
(2) Interest earned at expected investment yield on net level premium reserve at beginning of period.
(3) Interest earned on cash flow elements over period, expected investment yield × [(1) – (5) – (6)].
(4) Death, surrender, and endowment benefits expected to be paid in period.
(5) Administrative expenses expected to be incurred in period.
(6) Acquisition costs not capitalized in period (ultimate renewal commission rate applied to expected premiums).
(7) Increase in the net level-premium reserve expected for the period.
(8) Expected dividends in the period.
(9) Expected gross margins, (1) + (2) + (3) – (4) – (5) – (6) – (7) – (8).
(10) Expected investment yield in the period.
(11) Discount factor, initialized to 1.0 then, [prior (11)] / [1 + (10)].
(12) Expected gross margins, (9).
(13) Expected gross margins discounted to policy issue, (11) × (12).
(14) Deferrable acquisition costs in period, excess of commissions and issue expenses over (6).
(15) Deferrable acquisition costs in period discounted to policy issue, prior (11) × (14).
(16) Unamortized deferred acquisition costs at the beginning of the period, prior (21).
(17) Expected gross margins, (9).
(18) Deferrable acquisition costs, (14).
(19) Interest on unamortized deferred acquisition costs, (10) × [(16) + (18)].
(20) Amortization of deferred acquisition costs in period, amortization ratio × (17).
(21) End-of-year unamortized deferred acquisition costs, (16) + (18) + (19) – (20).

The first schedule in Table 5-7 [columns (1) – (9)] illustrates the calculation of estimated gross margins as of the issue date of the policy. The second schedule [columns (10) – (15)] is used to compute the amortization ratio as of the issue date, which in the example is 91.10%. The ratio is equal to the present value of expected DAC divided by the present value of estimated gross margins. The third schedule [columns (16) – (21)] provides the expected amount of unamortized DAC as of the beginning and end of each period and the progression of amortization over the life of the book of business.

The base-case example does not include a provision for terminal dividends. However, in order to illustrate how terminal dividends are addressed for traditional participating life insurance contracts, Table 5-8 provides an illustration using the base case example with the additional element of a terminal dividend.

Table 5-8
Calculation of Terminal Dividend Liability (TDL)

	(1)	(2)	(3)	(4)	(5)	(6)	(7)	(8)	(9)	(10)	(11)	(12)
			Expected Gross Margin		Terminal Dividends							
Period	**Expected Investment Yield**	**Discount Factor**	**Amount**	**Present Value at Issue**	**Amount**	**Present Value at Issue**	**BOY TDL**	**Expected Gross Margin**	**Terminal Dividends**	**Interest**	**Amount Accrued**	**EOY TDL**
1	7.00%	0.93458	26,903.82	25.14	0.31	0.29	0.00	26.90	0.31	0.00	1.45	1.15
2	7.00%	0.87344	27,319.36	23.86	0.35	0.31	1.15	27.32	0.35	0.08	1.48	2.35
3	7.00%	0.81630	20,370.66	16.63	0.25	0.20	2.35	20.37	0.25	0.16	1.10	3.37
4	7.00%	0.76290	19,628.64	14.97	0.31	0.24	3.37	19.63	0.31	0.24	1.06	4.35
5	7.00%	0.71299	18,863.17	13.45	0.37	0.27	4.35	18.86	0.37	0.30	1.02	5.30
6	7.00%	0.66634	18,054.99	12.03	0.43	0.28	5.30	18.05	0.43	0.37	0.98	6.22
7	7.00%	0.62275	17,137.33	10.67	0.47	0.29	6.22	17.14	0.47	0.44	0.93	7.11
8	7.00%	0.58201	16,208.89	9.43	0.51	0.30	7.11	16.21	0.51	0.50	0.88	7.97
9	7.00%	0.54393	15,271.36	8.31	0.55	0.30	7.97	15.27	0.55	0.56	0.82	8.80
10	7.00%	0.50835	14,326.21	7.28	10.19	5.18	8.80	14.33	10.19	0.62	0.77	0.00
Present Value at Issue				141.78		7.66						
TDL Accrual Rate						5.40%						

Legend:
(1) Expected investment yield in the period.
(2) Discount factor, initialized to 1.0 then, [prior (2)] / [1 + (1)].
(3) Expected gross margins.
(4) Expected gross margins discounted to policy issue, (2) × (3).
(5) Expected terminal dividends paid in period.
(6) Terminal dividends discounted to policy issue, (2) × (5).
(7) Beginning of year terminal dividend liability (TDL).
(8) Expected gross margins, (3).
(9) Terminal dividends, (5).
(10) Interest on beginning of year terminal dividend liability, (1) × (7).
(11) Amount of terminal dividend liability accrued during period, (8) × TDL accrual rate.
(12) End of period terminal dividend liability, (7) – (9) + (10) + (11).

Terminal dividend payments and the accrual of a terminal dividend liability are excluded from the calculation of expected gross margins. As a result, the expected gross margins used in Table 5-8 are the same as those used in Table 5-7 and equivalent to the base-case example. The terminal dividends used in the example in Table 5-8 are $2.00 per policy year (e.g., $10.00 in year 5) payable to all terminating policies (through surrender, death, or endowment.) Terminal dividend payments are charged against the accrued liability. The accrual of the liability is a charge to earnings. This produces a difference in the accrual formula for the terminal dividend liability as compared to the amortization of deferred acquisition costs. With the terminal dividend liability, amounts paid are an accrual in the liability; with DAC amortization, the amount of expenses being capitalized is an increase to the unamortized amount. Because these two items are in different balance sheet categories, this difference ultimately produces directionally the same effect on earnings.

5.11 Additional Considerations

5.11.1 Policy Riders

Frequently insurance contracts are sold with any number of a variety of benefits that are incidental to the base contract. These additional benefits are generally offered through riders to the base contract and are referred to as policy riders. Policy riders can be either participating or nonparticipating and do not necessarily involve life insurance. Common riders issued in the United States include the option to purchase additional insurance at specified points in time without underwriting, the waiver of premiums in the event of disability, and options to purchase through additional premiums, either single-premium paid-up insurance coverage or one-year term insurance. Riders are not specifically addressed in *SOP 95-1*. However, if viewed as a separate contract, they may have features that would cause them to fall within the scope of *SFAS 120* and *SOP 95-1*.

Each form of rider offered by the company needs to be considered against the scope provisions of *SOP 95-1*. In general, if the rider provides for policyholder dividends and is or can be attached to a traditional participating life insurance contract, then the rider is within the scope of *SOP 95-1*. Under these conditions, any acquisition costs associated with the rider need to be considered for capitalization. If amounts are capitalized, then they need to be amortized against the estimated gross margins associated with the rider. Because the rider is generally linked to the base contract and could not exist without the base contract, it is appropriate to consider the rider and the contract as a single unit, with the acquisition costs associated with the combined contract capitalized and amortized against the estimated gross margins. The result would be the same as if the rider and the contract were considered elements of the same block of business.

One type of insurance coverage often falling under *SFAS 120* involves a rider, attached to a whole life policy, that provides a combination of term insurance and paid-up additions (PUAs). The rider has a level premium and level benefit to the maturity age of the base whole life policy, but the amount of term insurance and PUAs fluctuates over the life of the policy. In addition, these plans often have dividends on both the base policy as well as the PUAs purchased with the rider premium. The rider applies all dividends to purchase PUAs. Without the PUAs purchased from the dividends, the face amount of the rider would decrease. In the earlier durations the amount of PUAs purchased from the rider premium is relatively higher and a smaller amount of term insurance is purchased. In the middle durations this relationship gradually shifts and a larger portion of the face amount of the rider becomes term insurance. Eventually, the PUAs purchased from the rider premium and the dividends start getting surrendered so that the cash value can be used to purchase enough term insurance to keep the rider face amount level.

Such a rider that involves a combination of term insurance and PUAs suggests GAAP treatment that integrates these rider records with the base policy. Because the base policy and the rider are intertwined, the commissions and other acquisition costs of the rider are capitalized along with the base policy commissions and other acquisition expenses. Amortization of the acquisition costs is based on the EGMs resulting from both the base policy and the rider.

Benefit reserves are developed separately for each type of coverage involved and then added together. There is a benefit reserve for the base policy, a benefit reserve for one-year-term insurance for the amount of term coverage, and a benefit reserve that is a net single premium for the total of the PUA face amounts.

The EGMs show the dividends as an expense item as well as an income item because they are used to purchase additional PUAs. Other income items include premiums from both the base policy and the rider. In later durations, the income component of the EGMs reflects the cash value resulting from the surrender of the PUAs to purchase term insurance. Similarly, the expense component of the EGMs shows PUAs being surrendered for this purpose.

If the rider does not fall within the scope of *SOP 95-1*, the capitalization and amortization of deferred acquisition costs should be handled in accordance with whatever accounting guidance is appropriate. For example, if the benefit offered through a rider is the waiver of premiums upon disability of the insured, then *SFAS 60* would likely describe the accounting method to be used. Under these conditions, the rider premiums and expenses, as determined under the appropriate accounting guidance, could be characterized as an element of paragraph 22g of *SOP 95-1*, "other assessment or credit." Alternatively, if the rider is detached from the base contract for accounting purposes, then it is not considered as part of the same block of business as the base contract.

5.11.2 Reinsurance

The treatment of reinsurance depends on the underlying contract (in this case traditional participating life insurance contracts) and the reinsurance contract. The treatment of reinsurance is addressed in Chapter 17, so it is not discussed extensively here. Reinsurance can affect the amount of amortization of DAC directly or indirectly. A direct effect would result from paying a ceding commission and using it to offset acquisition costs otherwise capitalized. An indirect effect would result from including the net cost of the reinsurance in estimated gross margins.

5.12 Examples

5.12.1 Base Case

Table 5-9 shows the anticipated reported results from the base case example.

Table 5-9
Base Case Pre-tax Profits

Period	(1) Gross Premiums	(2) Investment Income	(3) Benefits	(4) Commissions	(5) Expenses	(6) Increase in Liability for Benefits	(7) Decrease in DAC	(8) Dividends	(9) Pre-tax Profit
1	95.00	(1.40)	3.60	47.50	67.50	66.44	(93.83)	0.00	2.39
2	80.46	2.61	3.39	16.09	2.12	55.61	2.82	0.44	2.60
3	72.12	7.19	5.05	3.61	1.90	55.49	9.87	1.23	2.16
4	68.22	11.66	8.31	3.41	1.80	52.08	10.01	2.02	2.25
5	64.49	15.92	11.37	3.22	1.70	48.86	10.14	2.79	2.34
6	60.95	20.12	14.24	1.22	1.60	45.83	12.18	3.57	2.43
7	57.58	24.12	17.02	1.15	1.52	42.98	12.20	4.32	2.52
8	54.37	27.95	19.62	1.09	1.43	40.30	12.20	5.07	2.61
9	51.32	31.60	22.07	1.03	1.35	37.77	12.20	5.79	2.71
10	48.43	35.09	505.12	0.97	1.27	(445.37)	12.20	6.51	2.81

Legend:
(1) Premiums = \$95 × the number of policyholders in force at beginning of the year.
(2) Investment income from Table 5-4.
(3) Death, surrender, and endowment benefits (accumulated from Table 5-4).
(4) Commissions = Commission rates × gross premiums.
(5) Issue and administrative expenses paid (accumulated from Table 5-4).
(6) Increase in liability for future policy benefits (net level premium reserve).
(7) Decrease in unamortized deferred acquisition costs.
(8) Policyholder dividends.
(9) Pre-tax profits, (1) + (2) – (3) – (4) – (5) – (6) – (7) – (8).

In this example, investment income has been determined by using the expected investment yield applied to an assumed amount of invested assets. The assumed amount of invested assets is determined as the accumulated cash flows produced by the contracts. Simple timing assumptions have been applied as follows:

Cash flows occurring at beginning of year: premiums, commissions, expenses
Cash flows occurring at end of year: interest, benefits, dividends

5.12.2 Dividend Fund Different Than Net Level Premium Reserve

The net level-premium method policyholder benefit liability is used as the amount on which investment income is earned in developing estimated gross margins. If the dividend fund underlying the policyholder dividend determination is a different amount, there may be differences between the interest credit used in determining the dividend scale and the interest credit component of estimated gross margins. Therefore, even if a company uses the dividend fund method for establishing dividends, the dividends may not be a level proportion of estimated gross margins.

In the base-case example, the dividend fund is defined as accumulated cash flows based on the expected assumptions about mortality, surrender, and expenses, and a dividend fund interest rate of 5%. Dividends have been determined based on 60% of the difference between investment income and the amount credited to the dividend fund. Using a typical three-factor dividend formula, in this example it is assumed that the mortality and expense elements net to zero and the interest factor is paid out at 60% of the difference between earned interest and the amount credited to the dividend fund. Investment income has been calculated by using the expected investment yield applied to accumulated cash flows. An example of the earnings effect of replacing the dividend fund with the net level premium reserve is provided in Table 5-10.

In replacing the dividend fund with the net level premium reserve, the dividend scale was revised to be 50% of the excess of the expected investment yield applied to the net level-premium reserve over the dividend fund interest rate applied to the same base. This produces approximately the same present value of dividends under the two different scenarios.

The analysis shows that the change in dividend fund produces higher dividend payments in the early years of the contract relative to the base case. The higher dividends are largely offset by reduced DAC amortization, resulting in marginally higher early year profits in the base case as compared to the revised scenario. The "error" introduced in the accounting model by the substitution of the net level premium reserve for the dividend fund is largely offset by the increased amortization of deferred acquisition costs and ultimately has little effect.

Table 5-10
Impact of Replacing Dividend Fund with Net Level Premium Reserve

Period	(1) Gross Premiums	(2) Investment Income	(3) Benefits	(4) Commissions	(5) Expenses	(6) Increase in Liability for Benefits	(7) Decrease in DAC	(8) Dividends	(9) Profit	(10) Base Case Profit	(11) Revised Profit	(12) Difference	(13) Base Case Dividends	(14) Revised Dividends	(15) Difference	(16) Base Case DAC Change	(17) Revised DAC Change	(18) Difference
1	95.00	(1.40)	3.60	47.50	67.50	66.44	(94.62)	0.91	2.28	2.39	2.28	0.12	0.00	0.91	(0.91)	(93.83)	(94.62)	0.79
2	80.46	2.54	3.39	16.09	2.12	55.61	1.90	1.43	2.46	2.60	2.46	0.13	0.44	1.43	(1.00)	2.82	1.90	0.93
3	72.12	7.12	5.05	3.61	1.90	55.49	9.16	1.91	2.12	2.16	2.12	0.04	1.23	1.91	(0.68)	9.87	9.16	0.71
4	68.22	11.61	8.31	3.41	1.80	52.08	9.50	2.43	2.31	2.25	2.31	(0.06)	2.02	2.43	(0.41)	10.01	9.50	0.51
5	64.49	15.89	11.37	3.22	1.70	48.86	9.85	2.91	2.48	2.34	2.48	(0.14)	2.79	2.91	(0.12)	10.14	9.85	0.29
6	60.95	20.11	14.24	1.22	1.60	45.83	12.16	3.37	2.64	2.43	2.64	(0.21)	3.57	3.37	0.20	12.18	12.16	0.02
7	57.58	24.14	17.02	1.15	1.52	42.98	12.48	3.79	2.78	2.52	2.78	(0.26)	4.32	3.79	0.53	12.20	12.48	(0.28)
8	54.37	27.98	19.62	1.09	1.43	40.30	12.82	4.19	2.91	2.61	2.91	(0.30)	5.07	4.19	0.87	12.20	12.82	(0.61)
9	51.32	31.66	22.07	1.03	1.35	37.77	13.18	4.57	3.02	2.71	3.02	(0.31)	5.79	4.57	1.23	12.20	13.18	(0.98)
10	48.43	35.18	505.12	0.97	1.27	(445.37)	13.58	4.92	3.12	2.81	3.12	(0.30)	6.51	4.92	1.59	12.20	13.58	(1.38)

Legend:
(1) Premiums = $95 × the number of policyholders in force at beginning of the year.
(2) Investment income, at 7% on accumulated cash flows.
(3) Death, surrender, and endowment benefits (accumulated from Table 5-4).
(4) Commissions = Commission rates × gross premiums.
(5) Issue and administrative expenses paid (accumulated from Table 5-4).
(6) Increase in liability for future policy benefits (net level-premium reserve).
(7) Decrease in unamortized DAC.
(8) Policyholder dividends as redetermined from NLP reserve.
(9) Pre-tax profits, (1) + (2) – (3) – (4) – (5) – (6) – (7) – (8).
(10) Pre-tax profits from Table 5-9.
(11) Pre-tax profits from col. (9), Table 5-10.
(12) Effect on pre-tax profits, (10) – (9).
(13) Dividends from Table 5-9, col. (8).
(14) Dividends from Table 5-10, col. (8).
(15) Difference in dividends, (13) – (14).
(16) Base case DAC amortization from Table 5-9, col. (7).
(17) DAC amortization from Table 5-10, col. (7).
(18) Effect on DAC amortization, (16) – (17).

5.12.3 Experience Different Than Best-Estimate Assumptions

In the base-case, it is assumed that best estimate assumptions are used and that experience exactly follows these assumptions. Under normal circumstances, it is likely that experience will be different than the best-estimate assumptions underlying the estimated gross margins. In the following example, it is assumed that experience is the same as the base-case best estimates, but that the expected gross margins were determined using assumptions that, as experience unfolded, were slightly conservative.

In this example, expected gross margins are adjusted to be 95% of the base case. As experience unfolds at the best-estimate assumptions, the unamortized DAC is adjusted to reflect the actual gross margins (higher than the expected level) and to incorporate experience into the amortization ratio. The analysis shows the resulting year-by-year amounts. As might be expected, using assumptions in the amortization pattern that produce lower gross margins than actual experience has a tendency to delay the recognition of profits. The amortization ratios under this scenario incrementally decrease each year until they reach the base-case level in the final year.

The third schedule in Table 5-11 [columns (16) – (23)] shows the differences produced by the revised scenario in each element of the DAC carryforward. The normal amortization has been computed using the beginning of year amortization ratio applied to the expected gross margins, with the balance of the amortization categorized as "additional." Under this allocation method, normal amortization is somewhat lower than the base case amortization, but is offset by the effect of actual gross margins higher than expected in a combination of true-up and unlocking adjustments. As the block of business matures, these adjustments grow smaller and the force of the lower normal amortization produces profits higher than the base-case level.

Table 5-11
Impact of Actual EGM Exceeding Projected EGM

Period	(1) Gross Premiums	(2) Investment Income	(3) Benefits	(4) Commissions	(5) Expenses	(6) Increase in Liability for Benefits	(7) Decrease in DAC	(8) Dividends	(9) Profit	(10) Profit: Base Case	(11) Profit: Revised	(12) Profit: Difference
1	95.00	(1.40)	3.60	47.50	67.50	66.44	(92.78)	0.00	1.34	2.39	1.34	1.05
2	80.46	2.61	3.39	16.09	2.12	55.61	3.50	0.44	1.92	2.60	1.92	0.68
3	72.12	7.19	5.05	3.61	1.90	55.49	10.17	1.23	1.87	2.16	1.87	0.29
4	68.22	11.66	8.31	3.41	1.80	52.08	10.11	2.02	2.15	2.25	2.15	0.10
5	64.49	15.92	11.37	3.22	1.70	48.86	10.07	2.79	2.40	2.34	2.40	(0.07)
6	60.95	20.12	14.24	1.22	1.60	45.83	11.97	3.57	2.64	2.43	2.64	(0.21)
7	57.58	24.12	17.02	1.15	1.52	42.98	11.87	4.32	2.84	2.52	2.84	(0.33)
8	54.37	27.95	19.62	1.09	1.43	40.30	11.78	5.07	3.04	2.61	3.04	(0.43)
9	51.32	31.60	22.07	1.03	1.35	37.77	11.69	5.79	3.22	2.71	3.22	(0.51)
10	48.43	35.09	505.12	0.97	1.27	(445.37)	11.62	6.51	3.39	2.81	3.39	(0.58)

Period	(13) Amortization Ratio: Base Case	(14) Amortization Ratio: Revised	(15) Difference	(16) Interest on DAC: Base Case	(17) Interest on DAC: Revised	(18) Interest on DAC: Difference	(19) Normal Amortization: Base Case	(20) Normal Amortization: Revised	(21) Normal Amortization: Difference	(22) Additional Amortization	(23) Total
1	91.10%	95.01%	(3.91)%	7.74	7.74	0.00	24.51	24.51	0.00	(1.05)	(1.05)
2	91.10%	94.19%	(3.08)%	7.58	7.51	(0.07)	24.89	24.66	0.23	(0.83)	(0.68)
3	91.10%	93.62%	(2.51)%	6.52	6.40	(0.12)	18.56	18.23	0.33	(0.50)	(0.29)
4	91.10%	93.11%	(2.01)%	5.82	5.68	(0.14)	17.88	17.46	0.43	(0.38)	(0.10)
5	91.10%	92.66%	(1.56)%	5.11	4.97	(0.15)	17.19	16.69	0.50	(0.29)	0.07
6	91.10%	92.27%	(1.16)%	4.27	4.12	(0.14)	16.45	15.89	0.55	(0.20)	0.21
7	91.10%	91.92%	(0.81)%	3.42	3.29	(0.13)	15.61	15.02	0.59	(0.13)	0.33
8	91.10%	91.61%	(0.50)%	2.56	2.46	(0.11)	14.77	14.15	0.61	(0.08)	0.43
9	91.10%	91.34%	(0.23)%	1.71	1.63	(0.08)	13.91	13.29	0.62	(0.03)	0.51
10	91.10%	91.10%	0.00%	0.85	0.81	(0.04)	13.05	12.43	0.62	0.00	0.58

Legend:

(1) - (6) From corresponding column in Table 5-9.
(7) Decrease in DAC, as calculated in Table 5-7, but using amortization ratios from col. (14).
(8) From corresponding column in Table 5-9.
(9) Pre-tax profits, (1) + (2) – (3) – (4) – (5) – (6) – (7) – (8).
(10) Base case pre-tax profit from Table 5-9, col. (9).
(11) Revised pre-tax profits from Table 5-11, col. (9).
(12) Difference, (11) – (12).
(13) Base-case DAC amortization ratio from Table 5-7.
(14) Revised DAC amortization ratio, recalculated using 95% of base case EGM for future periods.
(15) Difference in DAC amortization ratios, (13) – (14).
(16) Base case interest on DAC, 7% of BOY amount from Table 5-7.
(17) Revised interest on DAC, 7% of revised DAC balance.
(18) Difference in interest component of DAC amortization, (16) – (17).
(19) Base case normal amortization, from Table 5-7, col. (20).
(20) Revised normal amortization using amortization ratios from col. (14).
(21) Difference in normal amortization, (19) – (20).
(22) Additional amortization, (7) + (17) – (20).
(23) Total effect on DAC amortization, (18) + (21) + (22).

5.12.4 Alternative Discount Rates

SOP 95-1 allows companies to use either the expected investment yield in effect at contract inception or the investment yield in effect in each year to discount estimated gross margins used as a basis for DAC annuitization. Thus far, all examples have been based on the fixed at issue approach. Table 5-12 provides an example of the alternative method, using the expected investment yield as it changes from year to year.

In this example, the expected investment yield increases by 0.25% in each year until it reaches an expected rate of 8.00%, and then decreases until it has reached its original level of 7.00%. This change from the base case affects cash flows due to changes in realized investment yields, changes in the dividends paid, and changes in the amount of accumulated cash flow on which interest is earned. The expected investment yield is assumed to be realized in actual results in each year. Because the dividend scales are linked to the investment spread, the dividends in each year are adjusted to reflect the changed expected investment yield. The resulting change in accumulated cash flows is then used as the basis for investment income.

The first schedule of Table 5-12 provides the estimated gross margins resulting from the revised investment yield assumption. In each year, the current investment yield is assumed to continue for all future years. Therefore, there is a revision to estimates of future expected gross margins in each year the expected investment yield changes. Once a year has passed, the actual gross margins are shown. For example, the initial estimated gross margins in the first year are $26.90. At the end of the first year, the expected investment yield in the second year is evaluated to be 7.25%. The second year estimated gross margins are then increased from $27.32 to $27.62. The first-year estimated gross margins are realized so they remain fixed at $26.90.

The second schedule of Table 5-12 provides the amortization ratios and DAC amounts resulting from the patterns of estimated gross margins provided in the first schedule of the table. In the second schedule, the discount rate applied to the estimated gross margins is fixed at the initial expected investment yield of 7.00%. This same rate is used to accrue interest on the unamortized DAC balance. Year-to-year changes in the amortization ratio are caused by changes in future expected gross margins arising from the increasing and then decreasing expected investment yields. The third schedule in Table 5-12 provides the profits arising from the expected investment yield scenario and using the initial investment yield in the computation of DAC amortization in all years.

Table 5-12
Analysis of Alternative Discount Rates Used in Establishing Deferred Acquisition Costs

First Schedule

Year	Expected Investment Yield	Gross Margins as Projected in Year 1	2	3	4	5	6	7	8	9	10
1	7.00%	26.90	26.90	26.90	26.90	26.90	26.90	26.90	26.90	26.90	26.90
2	7.25%	27.32	27.62	27.62	27.62	27.62	27.62	27.62	27.62	27.62	27.62
3	7.50%	20.37	20.69	21.02	21.02	21.02	21.02	21.02	21.02	21.02	21.02
4	7.75%	19.63	19.98	20.33	20.69	20.69	20.69	20.69	20.69	20.69	20.69
5	8.00%	18.86	19.24	19.61	19.99	20.37	20.37	20.37	20.37	20.37	20.37
6	7.75%	18.05	18.44	18.83	19.22	19.62	19.21	19.21	19.21	19.21	19.21
7	7.50%	17.14	17.53	17.92	18.32	18.72	18.31	17.88	17.88	17.88	17.88
8	7.25%	16.21	16.60	17.00	17.39	17.80	17.38	16.96	16.51	16.51	16.51
9	7.00%	15.27	15.66	16.05	16.44	16.84	16.43	16.01	15.57	15.11	15.11
10	7.00%	14.33	14.71	15.09	15.46	15.85	15.45	15.04	14.61	14.16	14.16

Second Schedule

Deferred Acquisition Cost Carryforward - Initial Investment Yield

Year	(1) Amortization Ratio	(2) BOY DAC	(3) Capitalized	(4) Interest	(5) Amortized	(6) Additional Amortization	(7) EOY DAC
1	0.91105	0.00	110.600	7.742	24.511	0.375	94.206
2	0.89712	94.206	14.483	7.608	24.780	0.671	92.188
3	0.88522	92.188	2.164	6.605	18.603	0.821	83.174
4	0.87514	83.174	2.046	5.965	18.104	0.906	73.988
5	0.86673	73.988	1.935	5.315	17.658	(0.946)	62.633
6	0.87370	62.633	0.00	4.384	16.782	(0.933)	49.302
7	0.87938	49.302	0.00	3.451	15.726	(0.836)	36.192
8	0.88369	36.192	0.00	2.533	14.591	(0.650)	23.484
9	0.88660	23.484	0.00	1.644	13.396	0.00	11.732
10	0.88660	11.732	0.00	0.821	12.554	0.00	0.00

Third Schedule

Profitability Using Initial Investment Yield as Discount Rate

Year	(1) Gross Premiums	(2) Investment Income	(3) Benefits	(4) Commissions	(5) Expenses	(6) Increase in Liability for Benefits	(7) Decrease in DAC	(8) Dividends	(9) Pre-tax Profit
1	95.00	(1.40)	3.60	47.50	67.50	66.44	(94.21)	0.00	2.77
2	80.46	2.70	3.39	16.09	2.12	55.61	2.02	0.49	3.44
3	72.12	7.70	5.05	3.61	1.90	55.49	9.01	1.54	3.23
4	68.22	12.93	8.31	3.41	1.80	52.08	9.19	2.78	3.58
5	64.49	18.26	11.37	3.22	1.70	48.86	11.35	4.19	2.05
6	60.95	22.40	14.24	1.22	1.60	45.83	13.33	4.94	2.19
7	57.58	26.04	17.02	1.15	1.52	42.98	13.11	5.47	2.37
8	54.37	29.19	19.62	1.09	1.43	40.30	12.71	5.81	2.60
9	51.32	31.87	22.07	1.03	1.35	37.77	11.75	5.96	3.27
10	48.43	35.37	505.12	0.97	1.27	(445.37)	11.73	6.68	3.39
								Sum:	28.89

Descriptions

First Schedule EGM as of the beginning of each year are shown. Historical results are locked in and future results are projected using the most recent investment yield assumption. The investment yield is shown in the first column.

Second Schedule The carryforward of the unamortized DAC balance. Columns (2) - (5) correspond to columns (16) - (19) of Table 5-7. Column (1) provides the amortization ratio developed from the EGM patterns shown in the first schedule and using a locked-in discount rate. Column (6) provides the additional amount of amortization arising from actual EGM different than projected.

Third Schedule Column definitions are the same as for Table 5-9. Investment income and dividends reflect the revised assumptions as to investment yield from first schedule. Decrease in DAC is determined using the amortization from the second schedule. Unamortized DAC balance is determined from the second schedule. EGM are as projected in first schedule.

The fourth and fifth schedules of Table 5-12 parallel the second and third schedules. In these last two schedules, DAC amortization is determined by using the current expected investment yield in all future years. The expected investment yield for past years is kept constant. For example, the rate used to discount estimated gross margins from the beginning of year 2 to the beginning of year 1 is always 7.00%. In this example, the profit pattern arising from allowing the discount rate to float is somewhat smoother than the locked-in approach. In each case, the total profits are the same. Figure 5-1 compares the pattern of profits arising from the two discount rate scenarios with the base-case scenario. As investment yields increase, profits increase over the base case amounts. As yields decrease, profits drop below the base-case scenario, even though the investment yields exceed those in the base-case scenario. This figure illustrates the leveraging effect of the DAC amortization methodology used for traditional participating life insurance contracts.

Table 5-12 (Continued)
Analysis of Alternative Discount Rates used in Establishing Deferred Acquisition Costs

Deferred Acquisition Cost Rollforward - Current Projected Investment Yield

Fourth Schedule	Year	(1) Amortization Ratio	(2) BOY DAC	(3) Capitalized	(4) Interest	(5) Amortized	(6) Additional Amortization	(7) EOY DAC
	1	0.91105	0	110.600	7.742	24.511	(0.021)	93.810
	2	0.90242	93.810	14.483	7.851	24.926	0.232	91.450
	3	0.89444	91.450	2.164	7.021	18.797	0.397	82.235
	4	0.88717	82.235	2.046	6.532	18.353	0.526	72.986
	5	0.88071	72.986	1.935	5.994	17.943	(0.637)	62.334
	6	0.88641	62.334	0	4.831	17.026	(0.709)	49.430
	7	0.89133	49.430	0	3.707	15.939	(0.695)	36.503
	8	0.89527	36.503	0	2.646	14.782	(0.579)	23.787
	9	0.89804	23.787	0	1.665	13.569	0	11.884
	10	0.89804	11.884	0	0.832	12.716	0	0

Profitability Using Current Projected Investment Yield as Discount Rate

Fifth Schedule	Year	(1) Gross Premiums	(2) Investment Income	(3) Benefits	(4) Commissions	(5) Expenses	(6) Increase in Liability for Benefits	(7) Decrease in DAC	(8) Dividends	(9) Pre-tax Profit
	1	95.00	(1.40)	3.60	47.50	67.50	66.44	(93.81)	0	2.37
	2	80.46	2.70	3.39	16.09	2.12	55.61	2.36	0.49	3.10
	3	72.12	7.70	5.05	3.61	1.90	55.49	9.22	1.54	3.03
	4	68.22	12.93	8.31	3.41	1.80	52.08	9.25	2.78	3.52
	5	64.49	18.26	11.37	3.22	1.70	48.86	10.65	4.19	2.75
	6	60.95	22.40	14.24	1.22	1.60	45.83	12.90	4.94	2.62
	7	57.58	26.04	17.02	1.15	1.52	42.98	12.93	5.47	2.55
	8	54.37	29.19	19.62	1.09	1.43	40.30	12.72	5.81	2.60
	9	51.32	31.87	22.07	1.03	1.35	37.77	11.90	5.96	3.12
	10	48.43	35.37	505.12	0.97	1.27	(445.37)	11.88	6.68	3.24
									Sum:	28.89

Descriptions

Fourth Schedule This schedule is the same as the second schedule except that the amortization ratios use a discount rate based on the most recent estimate of the investment yield.

Fifth Schedule This schedule is the same as the third schedule except that it is based on the DAC amortization shown in the fourth schedule.

Figure 5-1
Earnings Patterns

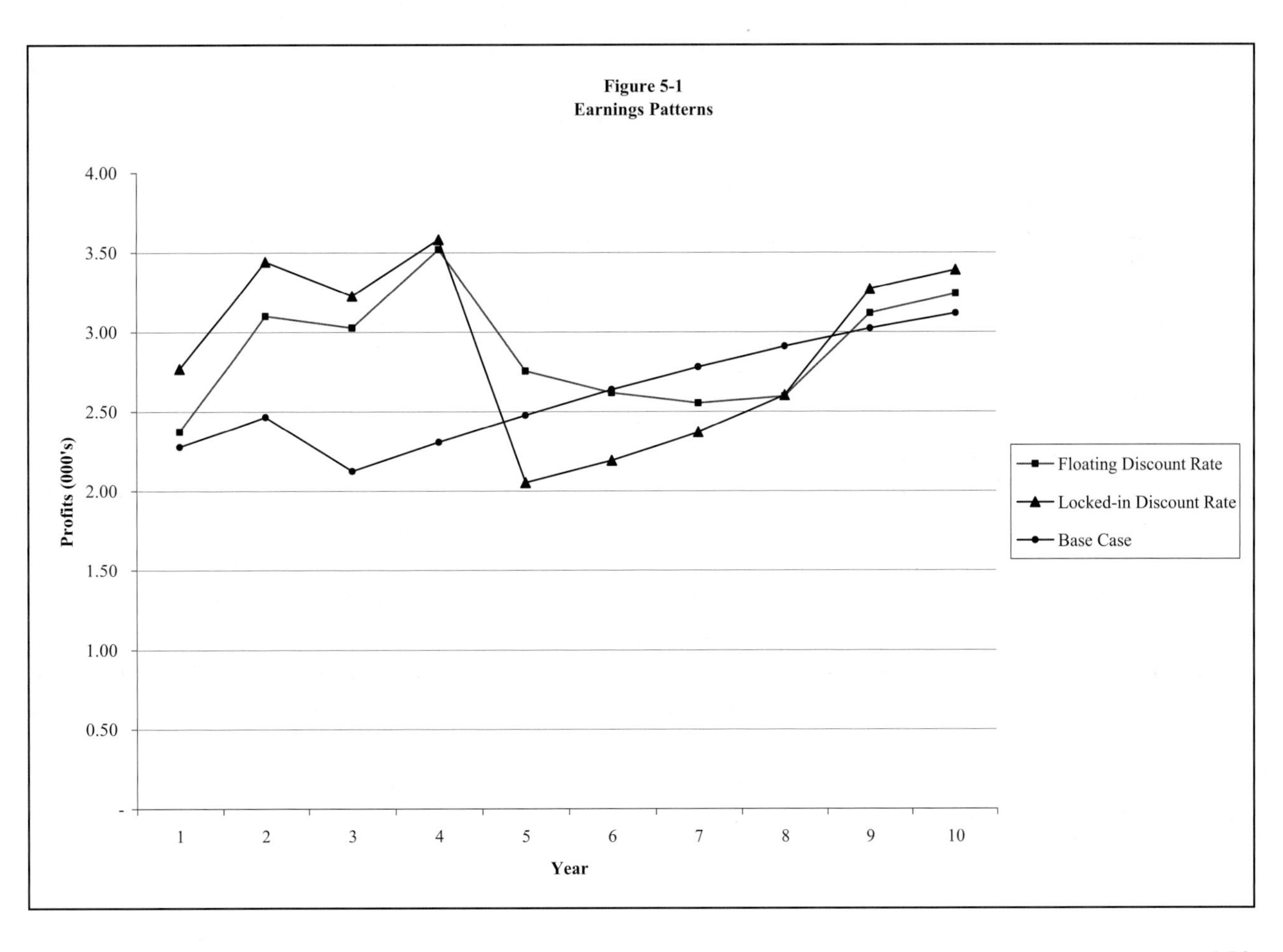

Chapter 6 Universal Life Insurance

6.1 Background

In the late 1970s, new insurance contracts were designed to address changing consumer needs. The marketplace was changing from one that was predominantly based on covering mortality risks to one that competed in the savings markets. In addition to universal life, there had been significant growth in the sale of annuities.

Paragraph 69 of *SFAS 60*, "Accounting and Reporting by Insurance Enterprises," recognized that the accounting for universal life contracts was being studied by the insurance industry, as well as by the accounting and actuarial professions. Traditional contracts were fixed, and assumptions for benefit reserve and deferred acquisition costs (DAC) calculations were locked in for administrative convenience. If experience followed the assumptions, profits emerged in proportion to premiums (except possibly in the first year).

SFAS 97, "Accounting and Reporting by Insurance Enterprises for Certain Long-Duration Contracts and for Realized Gains and Losses from the Sale of Investments," was issued in December 1987. Appendix A, "Background Information and Basis for Conclusions," states that:

> Most of the contracts to which Statement 60 applies have terms that are fixed and guaranteed. The purchaser of such a contract—having agreed to pay a fixed, usually level, premium in return for a guaranteed death benefit and schedule of cash value accumulations—cannot affect the individual elements of contract operation. Similarly, the insurer cannot unilaterally reduce the interest rate that is implicit in cash value increases or increase the amounts assessed for mortality, administration, and early termination that are inherent in the contract. (Paragraph 44)

Because new contracts were interest sensitive and premium payments were usually flexible, a more dynamic approach was needed to reflect changing market conditions. Appendix A to *SFAS 97* states that:

> The purchaser of a universal-life type of contract can often vary the amount and timing of premium payments, within limits set by the insurer, without the approval of the insurer..... . The insurer can often adjust the schedule of amounts assessed for contract services and the rate at which interest is credited to the policyholder balance. (Paragraph 45)

In September 1984, the American Academy of Actuaries released a discussion memorandum, *Accounting for Universal Life.* Also in 1984, the AICPA released an issues paper dealing with annuities, universal life, and nonguaranteed premium contracts, *Accounting by Stock Life Insurance Companies for Annuities, Universal Life Insurance and Related Products and Accounting for Nonguaranteed-Premium Contracts*, which led to the development of a new standard.

Paragraph 48 of Appendix A of *SFAS 97* mentions that some industry practitioners believed that "participating life insurance and nonguaranteed-premium life insurance contracts provide a measure of discretion to the insurance enterprise that is similar to that found in universal life-type contracts." It goes on to say:

Participating life insurance contracts usually contemplate the sharing of favorable experience relative to contract guarantees rather than the market-related adjustments that are characteristics of universal life-type contracts. The policyholder is thus granted a right that is not present in universal life-type contracts.

Conventional participating and nonguaranteed life insurance was not included in the scope of *SFAS 97*, unless the terms of a contract suggest that it is, in substance, a universal life-type contract. (See definition of universal life below.)

Since *SFAS 97* was introduced, there have been significant developments in the types of annuity and life insurance contracts offered for sale. Some of those products may combine fixed and variable features and may be sold as general account or separate account products. The features of these contracts are many and complex. They may be offered in different combinations, such that there are numerous variations of the same basic products being sold in the marketplace. Guaranteed minimum death and income benefits have become common features of variable annuities as well as different structures for charging for universal life and annuity contracts.

In addressing the appropriate accounting approach to these contracts, the AICPA also reviewed associated issues such as the definition of and accounting for separate accounts; sales inducements to contract holders; the significance of mortality and/or morbidity risks and the associated product classification; and accounting for certain death features, reinsurance, and annuitization features. The result was *Statement of Position 03-1* (*SOP 03-1*), "Accounting and Reporting by Insurance Enterprises for Certain Nontraditional Long-Duration Contracts and for Separate Accounts," issued July 7, 2003.

SOP 03-1 was primarily written to cover variable products. However, in paragraphs 26, 27, and 28, universal life-type contracts were included in its scope. Initially, there was more than one interpretation of the impact of paragraph 26. After the FASB staff issued a position paper (*FSP staff position FAS 97-a),* the AICPA subsequently issued guidance in the form of Technical Practice Aids (*TPAs*). *TPA 6300.05* to *6300.10* were posted on the AICPA website in September 2004. *TPA 6300.06* ("Definition of an Assessment") addressed paragraph 26 of *SOP 03-1.*

This chapter reflects the impact on the accounting for universal life-type products of *SOP 03-1* as clarified by *TPA 6300.05* to *6300.10.*

Addressing accounting for separate accounts is outside of the scope of this book.

6.2 Applicability

SFAS 97 established standards of accounting for universal life-type contracts, investment contracts, and limited-payment long-duration contracts that, in the absence of mention in *SFAS 97*, would otherwise fall under the scope of *SFAS 60*. It also amended *SFAS 60* to change the reporting of realized investment gains and losses. It was effective for fiscal years beginning after December 15, 1988, and required the restatement of prior-years financial statements to the extent practicable.

Practice Bulletin 8 was issued by the AICPA in 1990 to provide guidance, in the form of questions and answers, for insurance enterprises regarding the application of *SFAS 97*. It provides guidance in all the areas detailed above.

SOP 03-1 was issued by the AICPA in July 2003 to provide further guidance, which was clarified by *TPA 6300.05 to 6300.*10, issued in September 2004.

This chapter deals exclusively with fixed (general account) universal life-type contracts. Variable universal life contracts are described in Chapter 8.

6.3 Definition

Paragraph 10 of *SFAS 97* defines universal life-type contracts as long-duration contracts, providing either death or annuity benefits, with terms that are not fixed and guaranteed. This is in contrast to traditional participating and nonparticipating contracts.

Universal life-type contracts are those that include any of the following:

a. Contract assessments made by the insurer that are not fixed and guaranteed by the terms of the contract

b. Amounts that accrue to the benefit of the policyholder that are not fixed and guaranteed by the terms of the contract

c. Premiums that may be varied by the policyholder without the consent of the insurer.

Judgment is often required in determining whether a contract is universal life-type. In particular, paragraphs 12 and 13 describe some circumstances in which participating or nonguaranteed premium contracts should be accounted for as universal life, including any of the following features:

(1) The existence of an account balance for which any of the amounts assessed or credited is not fixed and guaranteed

(2) The expectation of the insurer that changes in any contract element would be based on changes in interest rates or other market conditions rather than group experience

(3) For participating contracts, the ability of the policyholder to vary premiums without the consent of the insurer.

6.3.1 Significance of Mortality and/or Morbidity Risks

SOP 03-1 states that contracts should be classified at inception as insurance or investment contracts based on the significance of mortality or morbidity risk. Contracts with nominal mortality or morbidity risk should be classified as investment contracts. All other contracts should be classified as insurance contracts.

The determination of insurance/investment classification described in *SOP 03-1* applies to both *SFAS 60* and *SFAS 97* contracts (however, the test is described using *SFAS 97* terms). The determination of significance is made by comparing the present value of "excess payments" to be made for all the contract's insurance benefit features to the present value of all amounts to be assessed against the policyholder (including investment margins, if such margins are included in estimated gross profits). Excess payments are benefit payments (including related claim adjustment expenses) to be made by the insurer in excess of the policyholder account balance. There is no specific threshold for defining significance, so some level of judgment is required in making such assessment.

The comparison described above must consider the frequency and severity of the benefits over a full range of scenarios that consider the volatility of assumptions. For universal life insurance, which is not subject to capital markets volatility, analysis over several deterministic scenarios, varying assumptions such as mortality and lapse, is typically considered sufficient. Once the comparison is performed, if the contract is an insurance contract with terms that are fixed and guaranteed, it would be classified as an *SFAS 60* insurance contract. If the contract has terms that are not fixed and guaranteed, it would be classified as an *SFAS 97* insurance contract.

It appears that most universal life contracts will include significant mortality risk, and therefore will be classified as insurance contracts. In addition, because the terms are not fixed and guaranteed, they will be *SFAS 97* insurance contracts.

For universal life-type contracts that are determined to have insufficient mortality/morbidity risk, *Practice Bulletin 8* says that, if revenues from other than investment are significant, the DAC should be amortized as described in *SFAS 97* universal life-type contracts. Thus all of this chapter will apply, except that the treatment under loss recognition will be different.

If there is insignificant mortality/morbidity risk and revenues from other than investment are also insignificant, *Practice Bulletin 8* references the guidance in *SFAS 91*.

6.3.2 Example of Significance Test

The following table shows an example of the significance test for a basic universal life contract. The result of the test indicates that the present value of excess benefits is approximately 33% of the total contract assessments, which indicates significant mortality risk. Therefore, the contract would be classified as an insurance contract.

Table 6-1
Example of a Significance Test

Contract Assumptions

Number of Policies	100	**Average Face Amount**	10,000	**Target Premium**	$25/1000

Year	COIs	Expected Mortality Rates	Expected Credited Rates	Expected Lapse Rates	Interest Spread	Expense Charges	Discount Rate
1	0.00077	0.0007	8%	3%	0.50%	$10/pol	8%
2	0.00088	0.0008	8%	3%	0.50%	$10/pol	8%
3	0.00099	0.0009	8%	3%	0.50%	$10/pol	8%
4	0.00110	0.0010	8%	3%	0.50%	$10/pol	8%
5	0.00121	0.0011	8%	2%	0.50%	$10/pol	8%
6	0.00132	0.0012	8%	1%	0.50%	$10/pol	8%
7	0.00143	0.0013	8%	1%	0.50%	$10/pol	8%
8	0.00154	0.0014	8%	1%	0.50%	$10/pol	8%
9	0.00165	0.0015	8%	1%	0.50%	$10/pol	8%
10	0.00176	0.0016	8%	100%	0.50%	$10/pol	8%

Year	(1) Premium	(2) Account Value EOP	(3) Total Death Benefits	(4) Excess Death Benefits	(5) COIs	(6) Interest Margins	(7) Other Assessments	(8) Total Assessments	(9) Discount Factor (8%)	(10) Persistency Factor	(11) "Significance Ratio"
1	25,000	26,171	689	671	738	125	985	1,848	0.962250	0.984530	
2	24,613	53,158	763	742	816	254	954	2,024	0.890973	0.954305	
3	23,858	80,607	832	783	861	385	925	2,171	0.824975	0.924913	
4	23,123	108,555	896	813	894	519	896	2,309	0.763865	0.896333	
5	22,408	138,456	955	831	914	655	869	2,438	0.707283	0.868547	
6	21,714	171,046	1,020	848	932	801	850	2,583	0.654891	0.850220	
7	21,256	205,338	1,093	862	948	962	841	2,750	0.606381	0.840698	
8	21,017	241,677	1,164	865	951	1,132	831	2,914	0.561464	0.831198	
9	20,780	280,194	1,233	856	941	1,312	822	3,075	0.519874	0.821722	
10	20,543	-	1,300	834	917	1,504	812	3,233	0.481365	0.812272	
PV				5,570	6,127	4,496	6,211	17,011			32.7%

Since Excess Benefits are 32.7% of Contract Assessments, mortality risk is significant and contract is an insurance contract.
Assumes premiums, interest credits, and expenses charges occur at start of year, deaths at mid year and surrenders at end of year.

Legend:
(1) Equals $25 × 1,000 × $(10)_{t-1}$
(2) Equals $[(2)_{t-1} + (1)]$ × (1 – mortality rate – lapse rate) × (1 + credited rate)
(3) Equals mortality rate × [1,000,000 × (10)]
(4) Equals mortality rate × [1,000,000 × (10) – $(2)_{t-1}$ × (1 + crediting rate) ^ 0.5]
(5) Equals COIs × [1,000,000 × (10) – $(2)_{t-1}$ × (1 + crediting rate) ^ 0.5]
(6) Equals 0.50% × ((1) + $(2)_{t-1}$)
(7) Equals $10 × 1,000 policies × (10)
(8) Equals (5) + (6) + (7)
(9) Equals $(9)_{t-1}$ / (1 + discount rate); Year 1 equals 1 / (1 + discount rate) ^ 0.5
(10) Equals $(10)_{t-1}$ × (1 – mortality rate – lapse rate); Year 1 equals (1 – mortality rate – lapse rate) ^ 0.5
(11) Equals (4) / (8)

6.4 Typical Product Designs

Premiums paid by the policyholder are treated as deposits by the insurance company and are accumulated in a notional fund. This fund is increased with interest at a rate declared by the company from time to time (the *credited rate*) and decreased with various charges. The notional value of this fund is the *account balance* (also known as *account value*, *fund value*, *fund balance*, or *accumulation fund*). If a policyholder wishes to terminate the contract, the full account balance may not be paid because a surrender charge may apply. The account value minus the surrender charge is called the *cash surrender value* (alternatively referred to as the *cash value* or the *surrender value*).

Partial surrenders are usually allowed. Sometimes partial surrenders of the account balance are allowed without a reduction in the insurance amount. Some policies, particularly single-premium policies, allow for a certain amount of withdrawals with no surrender charge.

Premiums may be fixed by the terms of the contract. Alternatively, many contracts allow the timing or amount of the premiums to be varied by the policyholder within wide parameters. A policy could be paid for by a single premium or on a regular or irregular basis. Many contracts specify a target premium, which, if paid and if all other assumptions are met, provides the illustrated benefits. However, the target premium is a guide and is not usually mandatory. Some companies send out a bill for the target premium, but, once again, it is optional to pay it.

Within the same product design, it is possible for one policyholder to be paying minimum premiums and effectively purchasing term insurance, whereas another policyholder could be accumulating a significant account balance. Many products allow extra dump-in premiums in addition to those regularly scheduled.

Some products impose a significant charge against the premium during the first year or two (front-end load products); some impose a level percentage load on every premium; and some rely on ongoing account balance charges (policy fees or contract administration charges, generally imposed monthly).

A mortality benefit is provided and normally is sufficient to qualify the product as life insurance under the Internal Revenue Code. The mortality benefit can be level (type A), can increase with interest or with the surrender value (type B), or can follow another pattern. A charge is made for mortality (the *cost of insurance*, or *COI*, charge). This charge is normally applied monthly to the excess of the mortality benefit over the account value. The rate of COI charges depends upon issue age, sex, and underwriting class and usually increases by attained age, although some products are designed with level or even decreasing charges. Some products also make other deductions such as expense charges.

There are many different product designs. Various combinations of these parameters are applied in practice. Early designs in the United States had front-end charges and little if any surrender charges. Later designs tended to have few front-end charges but high surrender charges.

Bonuses might be credited to the account value for other than interest. There could be a persistency bonus, which would increase the account value. Examples are a higher interest rate effective from outset if the policy stays in force 10 years or a refund of all COI charges if the policy stays in force 10 years. For single-premium policies, a higher-than-normal interest rate might be applied for the first or second year.

Interest-sensitive-whole-life (ISWL) is an example of a contract accounted for as universal life. ISWL in this context is a typical nonparticipating whole life plan, with cash values fixed at the outset, except that excess interest earnings are used to increase the policy values. This would often be achieved by accumulating the excess earnings in a side fund, which provides extra benefits.

Commission is paid to agents for acquiring and maintaining the business. For regular premiums, the commission rate is normally similar to the rates offered on traditional whole life products. For dump-in premiums, the commission rate is normally similar to the rates offered on single-premium products.

6.5 Presentation of Results

The retrospective deposit method must be used to account for universal life-type contracts. The footnote to paragraph 17a of *SFAS 97* states that "Accounting methods that measure the liability for policy benefits based on policyholder balances are known as retrospective deposit methods." Under this method, policy cash flows are accumulated to produce an account balance, similar to a bank deposit. The liability for future policy benefits (benefit reserve) is made equal to that account balance (plus other minor adjustments discussed below), which is diametrically opposed to the typical actuarial reserving method in which the benefit reserve equals the present value of future benefits and expenses less the present value of future valuation premiums.

The balance sheet presentation is similar to a *SFAS 60* balance sheet presentation. The benefit reserve for a fixed universal life-type contract is a liability of the general account of the insurance enterprise and must be included on the liability side of the balance sheet. Any unamortized deferred acquisition costs (DAC) must be included as an asset on the balance sheet. The benefit reserve may include an additional item on the liability side of the balance sheet, such as the unearned revenue liability (URL) (also called unearned revenue reserve), as defined below.

The income statement presentation for universal life-type contracts, however, is significantly different from other forms of insurance company income statements. In particular, paragraph 19 states that premiums are not reported as revenue on the income statement, and paragraph 21 states that payments to policyholders that represent the return of policyholder balances are not reported as expenses. Effectively, this means that under *SFAS 97* the income statement presentation appears similar to a bank deposit income statement presentation, under which deposits are generally accounted for as a liability increase and withdrawals as a liability decrease.

Revenue represents amounts assessed against the policyholders, such as COI charges, surrender charges, policy fees, and other charges. Revenue is reported in the period in which it is received, unless it can be demonstrated that the amounts are designed to compensate the insurer for services to be provided over more than one period. In this case, the revenue is deferred, reported as a URL, and amortized over the period benefited using the same assumptions and factors used to amortize capitalized acquisition costs. Amortization of URL is included in revenue.

Expense items in the income statement include benefit claims in excess of account balances, costs of contract administration, interest credited to policyholder balances, and amortization of capitalized acquisition costs.

An example of an income statement is in Table 6-2. The example contrasts the *SFAS 97* presentation with the *SFAS 60* presentation for the same universal life product.

Table 6-2
Comparison of Income Statement Presentation

	SFAS 60	*SFAS 97*
Revenues		
Premiums	1,000	
Universal life fee income		300
Net investment income	175	175
Earned deferred revenue	-	30
Total Revenues	1,175	505
Benefits and Other Deductions		
Death benefits	90	85
Surrender benefits	120	-
Interest credited to policyholder account balances	-	200
Increase in reserve	760	-
Bonus interest charge	-	15
Deferred policy acquisition costs amortized	40	40
Commission	20	20
Other operating costs and expenses	80	80
Total Benefits and Other Deductions	1,110	440
Earnings before income taxes	65	65
Income taxes	23	23
Net Earnings	42	42

6.6 Benefit Reserves

A liability for future benefits must be established on the balance sheet.

6.6.1 Account Balance Products

The retrospective deposit method is the appropriate accounting treatment for universal life-type contracts. For products with an explicit account balance, the basic benefit reserve liability is the account balance. No reduction is permitted for anticipated surrender charges or similar fees. In addition, any unamortized amounts of unearned revenues and any amounts assessed against policyholders that are refundable on contract termination must be held as liabilities. A further liability is required if any premium deficiency exists.

SOP 03-1 clarifies the definition of the accrued account balance referenced in paragraph 17a of *SFAS 97* as the sum of:

a. Deposit(s) net of withdrawals
b. Plus amounts credited pursuant to the contract
c. Less fees and charges assessed
d. Plus additional interest (for example, persistency bonus), and
e. Other adjustments.

Items a, b, and c have not changed since *SFAS 97* was issued. However, items d and e may be different from amounts held by some insurance companies.

6.6.1.1 Additional Interest

Additional interest represents amounts not yet credited to the policyholder balance, which must be accrued for as a liability.

Paragraph 20 of *SOP 03-1* states:

> Additional interest, if any, should be accrued through the balance sheet date at the rate that would accrue to the balance available in cash, or its equivalent, before reduction for future fees and charges, at the earlier of the date that the interest rate credited to the contract is reset or contractual maturity. The reset date is the date at which the existing contractually declared investment return expires.

Paragraph 36 of the *SOP* states "No adjustment should be made to reduce the liability for surrender charges, persistency, or early withdrawals."

The SOP does not prescribe a specific method for accruing the liability. Two methods used in practice are the straight line method and the interest method.

6.6.1.2 Example of Additional Interest

Table 6-3 below shows an example of how the additional interest liability could be established for a persistency bonus under both the straight line method and the interest method.

Table 6-3
Example of Persistency Bonus Liability

Contract Assumptions

Number of Policies	100	Target Premium	$25/100
Average Face Amount	10,000	Actual Annual Persistency	95%

Persistency Bonus: 5% of Account Value at end of Year 5

Basic Policy Illustration Assuming 100% Persistency

Year	Premium	Account Value EOP	Persistency Bonus	Actual Persistency	Assumed Interest Rate
1	25,000	26,250	-	0.9500	5%
2	25,000	53,813	-	0.9025	5%
3	25,000	82,753	-	0.8574	5%
4	25,000	113,141	-	0.8145	5%
5	25,000	152,300	7,252	0.7738	5%

Straight Line Method

Year	(1) Expected Reserve	(2) Actual Reserve	(3) Change in Reserve	(4) Benefits Paid	
1	1,450	1,378	1,378	-	
2	2,901	2,618	1,240	-	
3	4,351	3,731	1,113	-	
4	5,802	4,726	995	-	
5	-	-	(4,726)	5,612	

Interest Method

Year	(5) Expected Reserve	(6) Actual Reserve	(7) Change in Reserve	(8) Benefits Paid	
1	1,313	1,247	1,247	-	
2	2,691	2,428	1,181	-	
3	4,138	3,548	1,119	-	
4	5,657	4,608	1,060	-	
5	-	-	(4,608)	5,612	

Legend:

(1) Equals 7,252 × Year / 5 – (4)
(2) Equals (1) × Actual Persistency
(3) Equals $(2)_t - (2)_{t-1}$
(4) Equals Persistency Bonus × Actual Persistency
(5) Solved for amount such that Reserve accumulated at 5% equals 7,252 in Year 5
(6) Equals (5) × Actual Persistency
(7) Equals $(6)_t - (6)_{t-1}$
(8) Equals Persistency Bonus × Actual Persistency

The resulting deferral and amortization schedules are reproduced in Table 6-4.

Table 6-4
Deferral and Amortization of Persistency Bonus (Liability Uses Straight Line Method)

	(1)	(2)	(3)	(4)	(5)
Include Entire Change in Reserve in Deferrals					
Year	**Deferrals**	**EGPs**	**Amortization Ratio (k)**	**DAC Balance EOP**	**Amortization**
1	1,378	2,126		109	1,273
2	1,240	1,996		164	1,196
3	1,113	1,867		172	1,118
4	995	1,764		121	1,057
5	886	1,690		0	1,012
PV	4,735	7,907	59.9%		
Include Change in Reserve Gross of Lapses in Deferrals					
	(6)	(7)	(8)	(9)	(10)
Year	**Deferrals**	**EGPs**	**Amortization Ratio (k)**	**DAC Balance EOP**	**Amortization**
1	1,450	2,126		150	1,306
2	1,450	1,996		395	1,227
3	1,450	1,867		742	1,147
4	1,450	1,764		1,182	1,084
5	(190)	1,690		(0)	1,038
PV	4,858	7,907	61.4%		

Legend:
(1) Column (3) from Table 6-3
(2) Actual EGPs for DAC calculations
(3) PV of (1) divided by PV of (2)
(4) Equals $(4)_{t-1} \times 1.08 + ((1) - (2) \times (3)) \times 1.08 \wedge 0.5$
(5) Equals (2) × (3)
(6) Column (2) from Table 6-3
(7) Actual EGPs for DAC calculations
(8) PV of (6) divided by PV of (7)
(9) Equals $(9)_{t-1} \times 1.08 + ((6) - (7) \times (8)) \times 1.08 \wedge 0.5$
(10) Equals (7) × (8)

6.6.1.3 Other Adjustments

Other adjustments generally apply to variable and participating pension contracts, and therefore do not normally impact universal life insurance contracts.

Although not mentioned in *SFAS 97*, unearned COI charges are held as a liability by some companies.

6.6.2 Other Products

If the product does not have an explicit account balance, the benefit reserve is either an implicit account balance or, if that does not exist, the cash value available for the policyholder.

6.7 Capitalization and Amortization of Acquisition Expenses

As with traditional products, expenses that relate to the acquisition of new and renewal business must be capitalized and amortized. A full discussion of expenses and capitalization is given in Chapter 3. Paragraph 22 of *SFAS 97* says that the basis for amortization shall be estimated gross profits.

6.7.1 Estimated Gross Profits (EGPs)

Paragraph 23 defines estimated gross profit (EGP). It is made up of margins available from mortality and contract administration, investment earnings spreads, surrender charges, and other expected assessments and credits.

6.7.1.1 Mortality

The mortality margin is the excess of the amount charged for mortality (often referred to the COI) over the amount paid in benefit claims in excess of policyholder account balances. If the administration system does not provide the split of death benefits into account balances and the excess, reasonable estimates must be made.

Some contracts charge a level cost of insurance and some on a "reverse select and ultimate basis." The excess over the amount that would be charged if "normal" COI charges were made would be considered to be "compensation ... for services to be provided in future periods" and deferred and amortized as URLs as required by paragraph 20 of *SFAS 97*.

6.7.1.2 Costs of Contract Administration

The margin from contract administration is the excess of the amounts expected to be assessed for contract administration over expected costs of contract administration. AICPA *PB 8* clarifies the type of costs that should be included here:

Contract administration costs included in the calculation of EGP should consist of the following:

- Policy-related costs that are not primarily related to the acquisition of business, such as policy administration, settlement, and maintenance costs

- Policy-related acquisition costs that are not capitalized under FASB *Statement No. 97*, paragraph 24, such as ultimate renewal commission and recurring premium taxes. (Question 10)

More details about expenses are included in Chapter 3. Note that nondeferrable, non-policy related costs (for example advertising and marketing) should neither be included in estimated gross profits nor be capitalized.

6.7.1.3 Investment Earnings

The spread from investment earnings is the "Amounts expected to be earned from the investment of policyholders balances less interest credited to policyholders balances."

This implies that the insurance enterprise has the policyholder balance available for investment. In many regular premium universal life-type policies, 100% of the first-year premium and even some of the second-year premium may be needed for acquisition costs. For the purpose of calculating estimated gross profits, the total account balance is assumed to be invested, and acquisition costs are funded out of company surplus.

The "earned investment income should be based on the total expected yield from the investments" (AICPA *PB 8*, paragraph 28), which implies that expected realized gains and losses from investments should be estimated and included in estimated gross profits.

For bonds purchased at a discount or premium, the estimated earned investment income includes the amortization of the discount or premium in addition to the running yield. For equity-type investments, it includes an estimate of the future growth in the asset values.

The investment income both earned on and credited to policyholder balances may, in practice, be calculated by inputting interest rates in a spreadsheet and multiplying by the policyholder balance. Care must be taken, especially if different investment buckets attract different rates.

6.7.1.4 Surrender Charges

The total surrender charge expected to be collected each year upon policy termination is the difference between the total account balances for surrendered policies and the cash surrender values paid in each year. Some computer systems may need to be modified to compute actual charges made. Some systems track the amounts paid (surrender values), but not the account values released.

When future surrender charges are being estimated, the product design needs to be taken into account. If an amount of penalty-free withdrawal is permitted, an estimate must be made of the likely usage of this feature.

6.7.1.5 Other Assessments and Credits

Other assessments and credits are often included in the gross profits.

One example of an assessment caused by policy design is rider charges and the corresponding benefits paid. An example of an assessment created by an event that is not part of the policy design is reinsurance. The actuary would consider the effects of the excess of claim recoveries and ceding allowances over reinsurance premiums in the EGPs, both historically and prospectively. The treatment of reinsurance does vary in practice; one other method for reinsurance treats it as an *SFAS 60* offset.

Paragraphs 29 and 34 of *SOP 03-1* require that estimated gross profits be adjusted to reflect the recognition of the death and annuity liabilities established under paragraphs 28 and 33. This can lead to a circularity issue, which is addressed in section 6.13.2.1.

6.7.1.6 Nondeferred Acquisition Costs

Nondeferred acquisition costs are expensed in the year in which they are incurred. If they are policy-related, they affect gross margins. If they are not policy-related (such as advertising), they do not affect gross margins.

6.7.2 Expense Capitalization

Paragraph 24 of *SFAS 97* says that "This statement does not define the costs to be included in acquisition costs. ... Acquisition costs are addressed in paragraphs 28-31 of Statement 60." Those paragraphs in *SFAS 60* stipulate that "[C]osts that vary with and are primarily related to the acquisition of new and renewal insurance business ... shall be capitalized."

However, paragraph 24 of *SFAS 97* also states, "Acquisition costs that vary in a constant relationship to premiums or insurance in force, are recurring in nature, or tend to be incurred in a level amount from period to period shall be charged to expense in the period incurred." AICPA *PB 8*, Question 1 addresses this statement. Under *SFAS 60*, deferred acquisition costs are amortized over premiums. Deferring costs that are a level percentage of premium is mathematically equivalent, under *SFAS 60*, to expensing them in each period. The statement was necessary in *SFAS 97* to clarify the treatment of ongoing expenses, because the amortization basis is EGP and not premiums. Expenses that are a level percentage of premium must therefore be charged directly against EGP. Deferring them and amortizing them over EGPs would probably result in a different profit emergence.

Commissions paid in excess of an ultimate level amount are capitalized. Renewal commissions might exceed this ultimate level for many years.

Table 6-5 illustrates this point. It shows commissions and deferrable amounts for an illustrative commission scale for an interest-sensitive, fixed-premium universal life contract. The ongoing percentage of premium that is paid ultimately is not capitalized.

Even if premiums are flexible and, in the best estimate of the actuary and/or accountant, premiums at the longer durations will not be paid, the ultimate level commission rate (and premium tax rate) is considered a maintenance cost that should be charged to income in the period incurred. The excess of the commission rate over the ultimate rate is the appropriate amount considered an acquisition cost.

Table 6-5
Commission Rates and Deferrable Components

Year	Commission % of Premium	Deferrable Commission
1	50.0%	49.0%
2	20.0%	19.0%
3-10	5.0%	4.0%
11-15	2.5%	1.5%
Thereafter	1.0%	0.0%

If the first-year premium was $1,000, the commission payable under the above scale would be $500. The amount of commission capitalized would be $490. The difference, $10, would be included as an expense in the gross profits.

6.7.3 Amortization of Deferred Acquisition Costs

SFAS 97 states:

> Capitalized acquisition costs shall be amortized over the life of a book of universal life-type contracts at a constant rate based on the present value of the estimated gross profit amounts expected to be realized over the life of the book of contracts. The present value of estimated gross profits shall be computed using the rate of interest that accrues to policyholder balances (the *crediting rate*). (Paragraph 22).

At issue, projections of EGPs are made. The ratio of the present value of deferrable expenses to the present value of EGPs "computed using the rate of interest that accrues to policyholder balances" is calculated. This ratio represents the proportion of EGPs that is needed to amortize estimated deferrable expenses exactly, and in practice, this amortizing percentage is often referred to as the *k-factor*.

Subsequently, actual gross profits replace EGPs. Future projections are reviewed, and if experience differs or if expectations change, they should be revised. The actuary might have a different view about the future even if historical experience has not differed from expected. At subsequent reporting dates, the k-factor is recalculated as of outset using the then-current information.

When actual gross profits are computed, realized gains and losses must be included in investment earnings.

All changes in DAC are reported in the period. These changes in DAC could include a cumulative catch-up amount, which is described later under unlocking. Most financial reporting approaches for life insurance business combine the current events with future estimates. It is unique to U.S. GAAP to combine historic results back to the outset of the business with future estimates.

The amount of DAC at any time depends upon the relationship between future EGPs after that point and EGPs up to that point. Note that *SFAS 97* refers to actual gross profits from prior periods as EGPs. If, for example, it were deemed appropriate to change future assumptions, the DAC in force at the beginning of the year would automatically change. However, this change is reported in the current period; is not attributed to the prior period. This is discussed further in this chapter under unlocking. A simplified example is presented in Table 6-6.

Table 6-6

	Schedule 1 Original Expectation			Schedule 2 Actual to Year 3; Future Expectations Unchanged Revised Calculation			Schedule 3 Actual Reported Results		
	(1)	(2)	(3)	(4)	(5)	(6)	(7)	(8)	(9)
Policy Year	EGP	Capitalized Expenses	End of Year DAC	EGP	Capitalized Expenses	End of Year DAC	EGP	Capitalized Expenses	End of Year DAC
1	100	200	160	100	200	156	100	200	160
2	100		120	100		111	100		120
3	100		80	50		89	50		89
4	100		40	100		44	100		44
5	100		0	100		0	100		0

Schedule 1: PV @ 0% 500 200; k-factor = 200/500, 40%; $(3)_t = (3)_{t-1} + (2)_{t-1} - \text{k-factor} \times (1)_t$

Schedule 2: PV @ 0% 450 200; k-factor = 200/450, or 44%; $(6)_t = (6)_{t-1} + (5)_{t-1} - \text{k-factor} \times (4)_t$

Schedule 3: Rows 1 and 2: from Schedule 1; Rows 3, 4, and 5: from Schedule 2

Schedule 1 of Table 6-6 shows the original expectations. Schedule 2 reveals that while "actual" equaled "expected" for the first two years, the EGPs were only half of what was anticipated in year three. Schedule 3 displays the DAC that would be reported at each year-end.

In practice, a book of business for this purpose tends to be similar universal life-type business issued in a calendar year or calendar quarter. It is not normally subdivided by age or sex or underwriting class for capitalization and amortization purposes.

Materiality considerations affect the approach of some companies. In practice, if the amount of business expected to be in force at a certain duration is immaterial, DAC may be amortized until that period. This period depends upon the mortality and persistency assumptions. In the United States, 30 years is often used if it can be demonstrated that this will not materially distort the results.

SFAS 97 contains an explicit option for the interest-crediting rate in performing present value calculations and amortizing DAC and any URL. The interest rate used for the above present value calculations shall be, as stated in paragraph 25 of *SFAS 97*, "either the rate in effect at the inception of the book of contracts or the latest revised rate applied to the remaining benefit period." It is probably more common to use the latest revised rate, but both approaches are prevalent in the industry.

6.7.4 Negative Gross Profits

Paragraph 22 of *SFAS 97* states that "If significant negative gross profits are expected in any period, the present value of estimated gross revenues, gross costs, or the balance of insurance in force shall be substituted as a base for computing amortization." In practice, a commonly employed constraint has been that the amortization premium component is not allowed to be negative in any given financial statement period.

There is no specific authority on this issue, although there is a related requirement stipulated in *SFAS 97*, paragraph 22, that if significant negative gross profits are expected in any period, a different amortization base should be chosen. The requirement is similar to the requirement in *SOP 95-1*, paragraph 20, for contracts under the scope of *SFAS 120*. This requirement would frequently apply to a block of business that is recoverable but might incur a loss in one period or in a few periods. In general practice, the change in amortization basis is invoked only rarely because in many cases such action may result in distortions of and inconsistencies in the underlying accounting model resulting from what may be isolated and nonrecurring events. It is not unusual for life insurers to experience negative gross profits, for example, in a poor claims year. Specifically, it would not appear that it was the intent of the FASB to take a great portion of universal life-type contract portfolios out of the retrospective deposit model for such an isolated event. In addition, the term "expected" would be operative in that historical aberrations could be ignored if they were not expected to recur in the future.

When the stock market declined significantly in 2001 and 2002, many companies incurred large realized losses leading to negative gross profits. A number of companies decided that negative amortization could be appropriate provided the outstanding DAC (and VOBA, if any) was still recoverable and did not floor EGPs at zero. However, there is a constraint in the marketplace that the DAC cannot exceed the amounts deferred plus interest at the credited rate.

Three common practices have developed in situations where negative gross profits occur, but where they are not expected to recur in the future:

1. Floor EGPs at zero
2. Leave EGPs at the negative amount, but DAC is not allowed to exceed the original deferred amounts, or
3. Leave EGPs at the negative amount, but DAC is not allowed to exceed the original deferred amounts plus interest at the credited rate.

6.7.5 Example of EGP Computation and Amortization of DAC

The following tables show how the EGP and DAC amortization under a basic universal life contract can be computed.

Table 6-7 shows the basic policy provisions and initial assumptions for a universal life plan. Several assumptions have been made for convenience; the amortization period is 20 years and premium persistency is 100%.

Table 6-7
Characteristics of a Universal Life Block of Business

Sex	Male
Risk	Nonsmoker
Average Age	45
Number of Policies	400
Average Size	$250,000
Annual Premium	$2,250 for each $100,000
Interest	
Earned	8.00%
Credited	5.50%
Spread	2.50%
Expenses	
Deferred first year	$200 per policy
Deferred first year	20% of premium
Nondeferred first year	$50 per policy
Administrative, all years	$40 per policy, inflating at 2% annually
Premium tax	2.50%
Death claim cost	$250 per policy
Surrender cost	$25 per policy
Commission	
Year 1	86%
Year 2	10%
Years 3–10	5%
Years 11–15	2%
Years 16+	1%
Policy Persistency	
Lapses	
Year 1	12%
Year 2	10%
Year 3	9%
Year 4	8%
Year 5	7%
Year 6	6%
Year 7	5%
Year 8	4.5%
Year 9	4%
Year 10+	3%
Experience Mortality	45% of 1965/70 Select & Ultimate
Premium Persistency	100% all years
Policy Charges	$48 policy fee and 1% of premium

These assumptions lead to the policy values and projected cash flows in the following tables.

Table 6-8 displays the basic mechanics, death benefit, and cash value buildup for this plan. Table 6-9 shows the initial projection assumptions for this plan. Table 6-10 displays the cash flows resulting from the assumptions in Table 6-9

Note that the projected interest earned assumes that the reserve is the account value. In practice, different methods can be used to allocate investment income to a line of business.

Table 6-8
Basic Values for a Universal Life Policy
(Values per $100,000 Face Amount)

Year	(1) Premium	(2) Interest Credited	(3) Death Benefit	(4) COI Charge	(5) Loads & Policy Fees	(6) Interest Credited	(7) Account Value	(8) Surrender Charge	(9) Cash Value
1	2,250	5.50%	100,000	223	42	115	2,101	4,500	0
2	2,250	5.50%	100,000	230	42	231	4,310	4,100	210
3	2,250	5.50%	100,000	247	42	352	6,623	3,700	2,923
4	2,250	5.50%	100,000	251	42	479	9,059	3,300	5,759
5	2,250	5.50%	100,000	266	42	612	11,614	2,900	8,714
6	2,250	5.50%	100,000	278	42	752	14,296	2,500	11,796
7	2,250	5.50%	100,000	290	42	900	17,115	2,200	14,915
8	2,250	5.50%	100,000	308	42	1,054	20,069	1,900	18,169
9	2,250	5.50%	100,000	325	42	1,216	23,168	1,700	21,468
10	2,250	5.50%	100,000	338	42	1,386	26,425	1,500	24,925
11	2,250	5.50%	100,000	340	42	1,565	29,859	1,200	28,659
12	2,250	5.50%	100,000	355	42	1,754	33,465	900	32,565
13	2,250	5.50%	100,000	382	42	1,951	37,243	600	36,643
14	2,250	5.50%	100,000	394	42	2,159	41,216	300	40,916
15	2,250	5.50%	100,000	408	42	2,377	45,393	0	45,393
16	2,250	5.50%	100,000	407	42	2,606	49,801	0	49,801
17	2,250	5.50%	108,087	475	42	2,847	54,381	0	54,381
18	2,250	5.50%	117,606	567	42	3,096	59,118	0	59,118
19	2,250	5.50%	127,451	662	42	3,354	64,018	0	64,018
20	2,250	5.50%	137,635	774	42	3,620	69,072	0	69,072

Legend:
(1), (2) From Table 6-7.
(3) Larger of face amount and minimum qualifying death benefit.
(4) Monthly calculation applying COI rates to amount at risk.
(5) Policy fee and premium expense charges from Table 6-7.
(6) Monthly calculation of credited rate applied to account balance.
$(7)_t = (7)_{t-1} + (1)_t - (4)_t - (5)_t + (6)_t$
(8) Given.
(9) = (7) – (8), not to be less than zero.

Table 6-9
Initial Projection Assumptions for a Universal Life Policy

Year	(1) Mortality	(2) Lapse	(3) Interest Earned	(4) Interest Credited	(5) Expenses per Policy	(6) Expenses % Premium	(7) Commission	(8) In Force
					250.00	20.00%		1.0000
1	0.00080	12.00%	8.00%	5.50%	40.00	2.50%	86.00%	0.8792
2	0.00110	10.00%	8.00%	5.50%	40.80	2.50%	10.00%	0.7903
3	0.00143	9.00%	8.00%	5.50%	41.62	2.50%	5.00%	0.7181
4	0.00171	8.00%	8.00%	5.50%	42.45	2.50%	5.00%	0.6594
5	0.00194	7.00%	8.00%	5.50%	43.30	2.50%	5.00%	0.6119
6	0.00222	6.00%	8.00%	5.50%	44.16	2.50%	5.00%	0.5739
7	0.00253	5.00%	8.00%	5.50%	45.05	2.50%	5.00%	0.5437
8	0.00283	4.50%	8.00%	5.50%	45.95	2.50%	5.00%	0.5177
9	0.00311	4.00%	8.00%	5.50%	46.87	2.50%	5.00%	0.4954
10	0.00345	3.00%	8.00%	5.50%	47.80	2.50%	5.00%	0.4788
11	0.00391	3.00%	8.00%	5.50%	48.76	2.50%	2.00%	0.4626
12	0.00459	3.00%	8.00%	5.50%	49.73	2.50%	2.00%	0.4466
13	0.00538	3.00%	8.00%	5.50%	50.73	2.50%	2.00%	0.4308
14	0.00616	3.00%	8.00%	5.50%	51.74	2.50%	2.00%	0.4152
15	0.00693	3.00%	8.00%	5.50%	52.78	2.50%	2.00%	0.3999
16	0.00777	3.00%	8.00%	5.50%	53.83	2.50%	1.00%	0.3848
17	0.00848	3.00%	8.00%	5.50%	54.91	2.50%	1.00%	0.3700
18	0.00930	3.00%	8.00%	5.50%	56.01	2.50%	1.00%	0.3554
19	0.01022	3.00%	8.00%	5.50%	57.13	2.50%	1.00%	0.3411
20	0.01125	98.88%	8.00%	5.50%	58.27	2.50%	1.00%	0.0000

Legend:
(1) thru (7) from Table 6-7 except
$(2)_{20} = 1 - (1)_{20}$
$(8)_t = (8)_{t-1} \times (1 - (1)_t - (2)_t)$

Issue Age: 45
Average Size: 250,000

Table 6-10

Cash Flows Resulting from Projection Assumptions for a Universal Life Policy

Year	(1) Policies In Force	(2) Premium	(3) Commission	(4) Other Expenses	(5) Investment Income	(6) Deaths	(7) Surrenders	(8) Account Value
1	400.0	2,250,000	1,935,000	622,250	(27,722)	80,100	-	1,846,848
2	351.7	1,978,198	197,820	64,936	281,181	96,932	18,460	3,406,207
3	316.1	1,778,197	88,910	58,564	398,532	112,738	207,930	4,755,912
4	287.2	1,615,623	80,781	53,397	494,184	122,464	330,829	5,973,452
5	263.8	1,483,617	74,181	49,205	581,678	127,888	402,215	7,107,224
6	244.8	1,376,887	68,844	45,831	664,229	135,761	433,127	8,204,328
7	229.6	1,291,219	64,561	43,140	745,334	145,133	427,961	9,305,820
8	217.5	1,223,392	61,170	41,061	828,130	153,658	444,550	10,390,106
9	207.1	1,164,882	58,244	39,281	910,281	160,987	444,591	11,477,816
10	198.2	1,114,665	55,733	37,739	993,213	170,990	370,439	12,653,159
11	191.5	1,077,378	21,548	36,691	1,086,447	187,033	411,682	13,812,570
12	185.0	1,040,848	20,817	35,676	1,175,432	212,125	451,940	14,945,587
13	178.6	1,004,850	20,097	34,675	1,262,224	240,360	490,945	16,044,291
14	172.3	969,296	19,386	33,678	1,346,430	265,393	528,794	17,113,645
15	166.1	934,246	18,685	32,686	1,428,440	287,561	565,447	18,152,242
16	160.0	899,749	8,997	31,707	1,508,718	310,593	597,446	19,162,727
17	153.9	865,768	8,658	30,726	1,585,289	352,789	627,752	20,119,811
18	148.0	832,451	8,325	29,763	1,657,264	404,527	656,170	21,012,827
19	142.2	799,738	7,997	28,815	1,723,890	463,156	682,636	21,839,246
20	136.5	767,569	7,676	32,843	1,784,590	528,010	23,298,472	-
Present Value		14,789,070	2,547,395	1,044,983		1,848,259	8,414,538	

Legend:

$(1)_1$, $(2)_1$, (3)1, $(4)_1$ given

$(1)_t = (1)_{t-1} \times (1 - (1)_{t-1}^{\text{Table 6-9}} - (2)_{t-1}^{\text{Table 6-9}})$

$(2)_t = (2)_1 \times (1)_t / (1)_1$

$(3)_t = (2)_t \times (7)_t^{\text{Table6-9}}$

$(4)_t = (1)_t \times (5)_t^{\text{Table 6-9}} + (2)_t \times (6)_t^{\text{Table 6-9}}\ t > 1$

$(4)_t = (1)_t \times ((5)_t^{\text{Table 6-9}} + (5)_0) + (2)_t \times ((6)_t^{\text{Table 6-9}} + (6)_0)\ t = 1$

$(5)_t = ((2)_t - (3)_t - (4)_t + (8)_{t-1}) \times (3)_t^{\text{Table 6-9}} + (6)_t \times ((1 + (3)_t^{\text{Table 6-9}}) \wedge 0.5 - 1)$

$(6) = (1) \times (3)^{\text{Table 6-8}} \times (1)^{\text{Table 6-9}} \times$ average size /100000

$(7) = (1) \times (9)^{\text{Table 6-8}} \times (2)^{\text{Table 6-9}} \times$ average size /100000

$(8)_t = (7)_t^{\text{Table 6-8}} \times (1)_{t+1} \times 1000 / (1)_1$

In order to amortize capitalized acquisition expenses, EGPs are projected, which is shown in Table 6-11.

Table 6-11
Development of Estimated Gross Profits for a Universal Life Policy

Year	(1) Mortality Charges	(2) Mortality Cost	(3) Loads & Policy Fees	(4) Maintenance Expenses	(5) Interest Assumed	(6) Interest Credited	(7) Surrender Charges	(8) Estimated Gross Profit
1	223,053	78,362	41,700	94,750	167,790	115,356	252,072	396,147
2	201,892	92,744	36,663	84,718	295,019	202,825	360,472	513,758
3	194,921	105,324	32,956	76,346	404,299	277,956	263,173	435,723
4	180,455	111,509	29,943	69,553	500,079	343,804	189,566	375,177
5	175,195	113,264	27,496	64,041	587,301	403,769	133,855	342,773
6	170,419	116,689	25,518	59,600	669,792	460,482	91,792	320,750
7	166,174	120,762	23,931	56,052	750,987	516,304	63,126	311,100
8	167,719	123,431	22,674	53,295	833,691	573,163	46,489	320,684
9	168,102	124,456	21,589	50,929	915,802	629,614	35,205	335,700
10	167,480	126,767	20,658	48,885	998,884	686,733	22,293	346,931
11	162,728	132,420	19,967	47,464	1,090,174	749,494	17,238	360,728
12	164,354	142,736	19,290	46,084	1,179,973	811,231	12,490	376,056
13	170,434	152,879	18,623	44,724	1,267,510	871,413	8,039	395,590
14	169,852	158,541	17,964	43,371	1,352,623	929,928	3,877	412,476
15	169,213	160,093	17,315	42,029	1,435,429	986,858	-	432,977
16	162,761	159,617	16,675	40,704	1,516,068	1,042,297	-	452,887
17	182,824	179,491	16,046	39,384	1,593,360	1,095,435	-	477,919
18	209,953	205,900	15,428	38,087	1,666,128	1,145,463	-	502,059
19	235,273	235,826	14,822	36,812	1,733,896	1,192,054	-	519,299
20	264,044	268,959	14,226	40,519	1,796,231	1,234,909	-	530,114
						Present Value at 5.50% =		4,768,810

Legend:
EGP_t = Mortality margin + administrative cost margin + interest margin + surrender charges
$(8)_t = (1)_t - (2)_t + (3)_t - (4)_t + (5)_t - (6)_t + (7)_t$

The present value of the EGPs is calculated at the credited rate, which in this example is assumed to be a constant 5.5%. The next steps are to project expenses to be capitalized, calculate the initial k-factor, and amortize the deferred expenses, which are demonstrated in Table 6-13. The projected income statements arising from this example are shown in Table 6-12.

In practice, the investment income is the actual earned investment income and can be significantly different from the income assumed to be earned on the reserves, as shown in Table 6-13.

Table 6-12
Amortization of DAC for a Universal Life Policy

Year	(8) Estimated Gross Profit	(9) Expenses Capitalized	(10) Interest on DAC	(11) Expenses Amortized	(12) DAC	(13) Change in DAC	(14) Benefit Reserve
1	396,147	2,442,500	134,338	247,206	2,329,632	2,329,632	1,846,848
2	513,758	178,038	137,922	320,597	2,324,994	(4,638)	3,406,207
3	435,723	71,128	131,787	271,902	2,256,007	(68,987)	4,755,912
4	375,177	64,625	127,635	234,119	2,214,147	(41,860)	5,973,452
5	342,773	59,345	125,042	213,899	2,184,635	(29,512)	7,107,224
6	320,750	55,075	123,184	200,156	2,162,738	(21,897)	8,204,328
7	311,100	51,649	121,791	194,134	2,142,044	(20,694)	9,305,820
8	320,684	48,936	120,504	200,115	2,111,369	(30,675)	10,390,106
9	335,700	46,595	118,688	209,485	2,067,167	(44,202)	11,477,816
10	346,931	44,587	116,146	216,493	2,011,407	(55,760)	12,653,159
11	360,728	10,774	111,220	225,103	1,908,297	(103,110)	13,812,570
12	376,056	10,408	105,529	234,668	1,789,566	(118,731)	14,945,587
13	395,590	10,048	98,979	246,858	1,651,736	(137,830)	16,044,291
14	412,476	9,693	91,379	257,395	1,495,412	(156,323)	17,113,645
15	432,977	9,342	82,762	270,188	1,317,328	(178,084)	18,152,242
16	452,887	-	72,453	282,613	1,107,169	(210,160)	19,162,727
17	477,919	-	60,894	298,233	869,829	(237,339)	20,119,811
18	502,059	-	47,841	313,297	604,373	(265,456)	21,012,827
19	519,299	-	33,241	324,055	313,558	(290,815)	21,839,246
20	530,114	-	17,246	330,804	(0)	(313,558)	0
PV @ 5.5%	4,768,810	2,975,854		k-factor =	62.4%		

Legend:

(8) = (8) from Table 6-11

(9) Given

$(10)_t = i^{cred} \times ((10)_{t-1} + (9)_t)$ where icred = 5.5%

$(11)_t = \text{k-factor} \times EGP_t = \text{k-factor} \times (8)_t$

$DAC_t = DAC_{t-1} + \text{expenses capitalized}_t + \text{interest on } DAC_t - \text{expenses amortized}_t$

$(12)_t = (12)_{t-1} + (9)_t + (10)_t - (11)_t$

$(13)_t = (12)_t - (12)_{t-1}$

(14) = Benefit Reserve = Account Value; The benefit reserve is calculated by assuming monthly charges and credits. The present value of capitalized expenses and the EGP's is calculated at the credited rate, which is assumed to be a constant 5.5% in this example. The k-factor is the ratio of these present values. The interest on DAC in column (10) is calculated at the same 5.5% interest rate.

Table 6-13
Income Statement for a Universal Life Policy

	(15)	(16)	(17)	(18)	(19)	(20)	(21)	(22)	(23)	(24)
Year	Policy Charges	Investment Income	Total Income	Death Benefits in excess of Account Balance	Commission	Other Expenses	Interest Credited	Increase in DAC	Total Expenses	Profit
1	516,825	(27,722)	489,103	78,362	1,935,000	622,250	115,356	2,329,632	421,336	67,767
2	599,027	281,181	880,207	92,744	197,820	64,936	202,825	(4,638)	562,963	317,244
3	491,050	398,532	889,581	105,324	88,910	58,564	277,956	(68,987)	599,741	289,841
4	399,964	494,184	894,148	111,509	80,781	53,397	343,804	(41,860)	631,351	262,797
5	336,547	581,678	918,224	113,264	74,181	49,205	403,769	(29,512)	669,931	248,293
6	287,729	664,229	951,958	116,689	68,844	45,831	460,482	(21,897)	713,743	238,215
7	253,230	745,334	998,565	120,762	64,561	43,140	516,304	(20,694)	765,461	233,104
8	236,882	828,130	1,065,012	123,431	61,170	41,061	573,163	(30,675)	829,499	235,513
9	224,897	910,281	1,135,178	124,456	58,244	39,281	629,614	(44,202)	895,796	239,382
10	210,432	993,213	1,203,645	126,767	55,733	37,739	686,733	(55,760)	962,733	240,912
11	199,934	1,086,447	1,286,380	132,420	21,548	36,691	749,494	(103,110)	1,043,263	243,118
12	196,134	1,175,432	1,371,567	142,736	20,817	35,676	811,231	(118,731)	1,129,191	242,376
13	197,096	1,262,224	1,459,320	152,879	20,097	34,675	871,413	(137,830)	1,216,895	242,425
14	191,693	1,346,430	1,538,124	158,541	19,386	33,678	929,928	(156,323)	1,297,857	240,267
15	186,527	1,428,440	1,614,968	160,093	18,685	32,686	986,858	(178,084)	1,376,406	238,561
16	179,437	1,508,718	1,688,155	159,617	8,997	31,707	1,042,297	(210,160)	1,452,778	235,377
17	198,869	1,585,289	1,784,158	179,491	8,658	30,726	1,095,435	(237,339)	1,551,649	232,509
18	225,381	1,657,264	1,882,645	205,900	8,325	29,763	1,145,463	(265,456)	1,654,906	227,739
19	250,094	1,723,890	1,973,985	235,826	7,997	28,815	1,192,054	(290,815)	1,755,507	218,478
20	278,269	1,784,590	2,062,859	268,959	7,676	32,843	1,234,909	(313,558)	1,857,945	204,914

Legend:
(15) = (1) + (3) + (7) from Table 6-11
(16) = (5) from Table 6-10
(17) = (15) + (16)
(18) = (2) from Table 6-11
(19) = (3) from Table 6-10
(20) = (4) from Table 6-10
(21) = (6) from Table 6-11
(22) = (13) from Table 6-12
(23) = (18) + (19) + (20) + (21) – (22)
(24) = (17) – (23)

6.7.6 Selection of Assumptions and Unlocking

The actuary must select assumptions at the time the policy is written. Periodically, after issue, the actuary must re-evaluate the then-future assumptions being used in the amortization of the DAC.

6.7.6.1 Selection of Assumptions

At the time that interest-sensitive business is sold and at each reporting or valuation date thereafter, assumptions must be made about the then-future experience of the book of business. These assumptions include mortality, persistency (for the book of business), premium persistency (or what future premium pattern is expected), expenses, future investment earnings, and the future crediting strategy. Assumptions must also be made about any product features that could affect EGPs, for example, if partial withdrawals are permitted with no or reduced surrender penalty.

> As stated in *SFAS 97*, paragraph 23, each element of those assumptions, "shall be determined based on the best estimate of that individual element over the life of the book of contracts without provision for adverse deviation."

At outset, the pricing assumptions are often used as the best-estimate assumptions, provided any provisions for adverse deviation are removed. The financial reporting actuary must be aware of the provisions for conservatism in the set of pricing assumptions. For example, the actuary should have an understanding of the mortality classes as well as any mortality improvement inherent in the pricing tables. Subsequently, the experience of the block of business and general market conditions influence future best-estimate assumptions.

Because of the policyholder's ability to vary premium payments, historic patterns should be reviewed and used as a guide for the future. Economic trends can also influence whether a policyholder will continue premium payments or let the policy account balance decline as COI charges are used to maintain the policy in force.

In addition to the usual drivers of persistency, the ratio of the account value to the minimum balance needed to keep the policy in force may influence lapses. For example, if a policy is being maintained as similar to term insurance, it is likely to experience persistency similar to term insurance.

The reader should refer to Chapter 3 for guidance on expense categorization and selection of assumptions.

The interest crediting strategy can change over time and is strongly influenced by competition. A company actively selling new business needs to be able to demonstrate competitive historic interest crediting rates. Conversely, for a block of business in a run off mode, the motivation may be to try to maximize profits by increasing the spread. Prospective assumptions should reflect these expectations.

Premiums on most universal life business are subject to premium taxes in the various states. This will be part of the ongoing maintenance expense of the business and is an element in the EGP calculation.

Benefit reserves and DAC are calculated gross of FIT (federal income tax). FIT is usually not considered in the reserving mechanism. A deferred tax asset or liability entry is made in the balance sheet to reflect that the timing of GAAP profits differs from the timing of taxable income. This is addressed in more detail in Chapter 18.

6.7.6.2 True-up for Actual Experience/Retrospective Unlocking

At the end of each reporting period, the actual gross profit should be computed and used in lieu of the amount estimated for that period in the amortization of DAC. There is a new calculation covering the period from the original issue date to the end of the DAC amortization period using the new pattern of gross profits and deferrable expenses.

Each item in the EGPs described earlier needs to be replaced with emerging actual results. This often presents a practical difficulty because information is not always available on time. Death claims are frequently reported with a two- to three-month lag because investigations take time. Maintenance cost studies may not be available at the end of the reporting period. Other items, such as cash surrenders, premium tax, and investment earnings, are usually available on a timelier basis.

Realized capital gains and losses need to be included in investment earnings for a restatement of EGP for the period. In addition, a calculation of the unrealized gains and losses needs to be made for *SFAS 115* purposes. More details are provided in Chapters 13 and 14.

Replacing EGPs with actual historic gross profits, without changing future assumptions, is known as retrospective unlocking. As an example, suppose that experience exactly follows the expected assumptions in Table 6-6, except that the company realizes a capital gain in an equity investment in year six of $2 million. Assume that all other assumptions remain unchanged. (This manufactured example is not typical in the United States, however; it is more likely in areas where equity investments are common.)

The stream of estimated gross profits in Table 6-11 will be replaced by actual gross profits and in duration 6 will be $2 million higher. This will change the ratio of the present value of expected deferrable expenses to the present value of EGPs (the k-factor), and had this pattern been predicted, the DAC at the end of duration 5 would have been $337,296 higher. This change is known as retrospective unlocking. Note that the prior year balance is not restated. The change goes through income in duration 6.

The impact of the gain is somewhat offset by a greater amount of DAC amortization. The amount of amortization in year 6 in this example is $913,638, which is significantly greater than the original estimate of $21,897 (from Table 6-12). The revised amortization amounts are shown in Table 6-14.

6.7.6.3 Assumptions and Prospective Unlocking

At the end of each reporting period, in addition to replacing estimated gross profits with actual gross profits, the then-future assumptions must be reviewed and, if necessary, replaced with new assumptions. This change is known as prospective unlocking and also influences the DAC.

As an example, suppose that experience exactly follows the expected assumptions in Table 6-6, except that the company realizes a capital gain in a mix of equity and bond investments in year 6 of $2 million. Suppose that the bond gain has arisen from a reduction in interest rates of 150 basis points. Assume that all other assumptions remain unchanged. This implies that, although the future earnings rate has declined, the future credited rate has not changed. The effect is shown in Table 6-15.

This is a more usual change in practice. The k-factor of 63.1% is similar to the original 62.3%. However, the impact of prospective unlocking is the difference between the DAC at year six in Tables 6-14 and 6-15. This impact is $724,829.

Table 6-14

Retrospective Unlocking Using Realized Equity Capital Gain in Year 6

Year	(1) Mortality Charges	(2) Mortality Cost	(3) Loads and Policy Fees	(4) Maintenance Expenses	(5) Investment Earnings	(6) Interest Credited	(7) Surrender Charges	(8) Gross Profit	(9) Expenses Capitalized	(10) Interest on DAC	(11) Expenses Amortized	(12) DAC	(13) Change in DAC	(14) Change from Original DAC
1	223,053	78,362	41,700	94,750	167,790	115,356	252,072	396,147	2,442,500	134,338	189,551	2,387,286	2,387,286	57,654
2	201,892	92,744	36,663	84,718	295,019	202,825	360,472	513,758	178,038	141,093	245,826	2,460,590	73,304	135,596
3	194,921	105,324	32,956	76,346	404,299	277,956	263,173	435,723	71,128	139,245	208,488	2,462,475	1,885	206,468
4	180,455	111,509	29,943	69,553	500,079	343,804	189,566	375,177	64,625	138,990	179,517	2,486,573	24,098	272,426
5	175,195	113,264	27,496	64,041	587,301	403,769	133,855	342,773	59,345	140,025	164,013	2,521,931	35,358	337,296
6	170,419	116,689	25,518	59,600	2,669,792	460,482	91,792	2,320,750	55,075	141,735	1,110,449	1,608,293	(913,638)	(554,445)
7	166,174	120,762	23,931	56,052	750,987	516,304	63,126	311,100	51,649	91,297	148,857	1,602,381	(5,912)	(539,663)
8	167,719	123,431	22,674	53,295	833,691	573,163	46,489	320,684	48,936	90,822	153,443	1,588,696	(13,685)	(522,673)
9	168,102	124,456	21,589	50,929	915,802	629,614	35,205	335,700	46,595	89,941	160,628	1,564,605	(24,092)	(502,563)
10	167,480	126,767	20,658	48,885	998,884	686,733	22,293	346,931	44,587	88,506	166,002	1,531,695	(32,910)	(479,712)
11	162,728	132,420	19,967	47,464	1,090,174	749,494	17,238	360,728	10,774	84,836	172,604	1,454,700	(76,994)	(453,597)
12	164,354	142,736	19,290	46,084	1,179,973	811,231	12,490	376,056	10,408	80,581	179,938	1,365,752	(88,948)	(423,814)
13	170,434	152,879	18,623	44,724	1,267,510	871,413	8,039	395,590	10,048	75,669	189,285	1,262,185	(103,567)	(389,551)
14	169,852	158,541	17,964	43,371	1,352,623	929,928	3,877	412,476	9,693	69,953	197,364	1,144,467	(117,718)	(350,945)
15	169,213	160,093	17,315	42,029	1,435,429	986,858	-	432,977	9,342	63,460	207,174	1,010,095	(134,372)	(307,233)
16	162,761	159,617	16,675	40,704	1,516,068	1,042,297	-	452,887	-	55,555	216,700	848,950	(161,145)	(258,219)
17	182,824	179,491	16,046	39,384	1,593,360	1,095,435	-	477,919	-	46,692	228,678	666,964	(181,986)	(202,865)
18	209,953	205,900	15,428	38,087	1,666,128	1,145,463	-	502,059	-	36,683	240,228	463,419	(203,545)	(140,954)
19	235,273	235,826	14,822	36,812	1,733,896	1,192,054	-	519,299	-	25,488	248,478	240,429	(222,990)	(73,129)
20	264,044	268,959	14,226	40,519	1,796,231	1,234,909	-	530,114	-	13,224	253,653	(0)	(240,429)	0
						Present Value @	5.50% =	6,219,302	2,975,854			k-factor =	47.8%	

Legend:

(1)—(7) same as Table 6-11 except $(5)_6$ is now given

(8) = (1) – (2) + (3) – (4) + (5) – (6) + (7)

(9) same as Table 6-12

$(10)_t = i^{cred} \times ((10)_{t-1} + (9)_t)$, where $i^{cred} = 5.5\%$

The present value of capitalized expenses and the EGPs are calculated at the credited rate, which is assumed to be a constant 5.5% in this example. The k-factor is the ratio of these present values. The interest on DAC in column (11) is calculated at the same 5.5% interest rate.

$(11)_t$ = k-factor × EGP_t = k-factor × $(8)_t$

$DAC_t = DAC_{t-1}$ + Expenses Capitalized $_t$ + Interest on DAC_t – Expenses Amortized $_t$

$(12)_t = (12)_{t-1} + (9)_t + (10)_t - (11)_t$

$(14)_t = (13)_t$ – Table 6-10$(13)_t$

Table 6-15

Prospective Unlocking Using Realized Gain in Year 6 Offset by Reduced Future Investment Earnings

Year	(1) Mortality Charges	(2) Mortality Cost	(3) Loads and Policy Fees	(4) Maintenance Expenses	(5) Investment Earnings	(6) Interest Credited	(7) Surrender Charges	(8) Gross Profit	(9) Expenses Deferred	(10) Interest on DAC	(11) Expenses Amortized	(12) DAC	(13) Change in DAC	(14) Change from Original DAC
1	223,053	78,362	41,700	94,750	167,790	115,356	252,072	396,147	2,442,500	134,338	249,801	2,327,036	2,327,036	(2,596)
2	201,892	92,744	36,663	84,718	295,019	202,825	360,472	513,758	178,038	137,779	323,964	2,318,890	(8,147)	(6,104)
3	194,921	105,324	32,956	76,346	404,299	277,956	263,173	435,723	71,128	131,451	274,757	2,246,712	(72,178)	(9,295)
4	180,455	111,509	29,943	69,553	500,079	343,804	189,566	375,177	64,625	127,124	236,578	2,201,882	(44,829)	(12,264)
5	175,195	113,264	27,496	64,041	587,301	403,769	133,855	342,773	59,345	124,367	216,145	2,169,450	(32,433)	(15,185)
6	170,419	116,689	25,518	59,600	2,669,792	460,482	91,792	2,320,750	55,075	122,349	1,463,411	883,464	(1,285,986)	(1,279,274)
7	166,174	120,762	23,931	56,052	627,922	516,304	63,126	188,035	51,649	51,431	118,570	867,973	(15,490)	(1,274,071)
8	167,719	123,431	22,674	53,295	694,104	573,163	46,489	181,097	48,936	50,430	114,196	853,143	(14,830)	(1,258,225)
9	168,102	124,456	21,589	50,929	759,951	629,614	35,205	179,848	46,595	49,486	113,408	835,816	(17,327)	(1,231,351)
10	167,480	126,767	20,658	48,885	826,717	686,733	22,293	174,764	44,587	48,422	110,202	818,623	(17,193)	(1,192,784)
11	162,728	132,420	19,967	47,464	900,376	749,494	17,238	170,931	10,774	45,617	107,785	767,228	(51,395)	(1,141,069)
12	164,354	142,736	19,290	46,084	972,784	811,231	12,490	168,867	10,408	42,770	106,484	713,923	(53,305)	(1,075,643)
13	170,434	152,879	18,623	44,724	1,043,326	871,413	8,039	171,406	10,048	39,818	108,085	655,706	(58,218)	(996,030)
14	169,852	158,541	17,964	43,371	1,111,959	929,928	3,877	171,811	9,693	36,597	108,340	593,655	(62,050)	(901,757)
15	169,213	160,093	17,315	42,029	1,178,725	986,858	-	176,272	9,342	33,165	111,153	525,009	(68,646)	(792,319)
16	162,761	159,617	16,675	40,704	1,243,785	1,042,297	-	180,603	-	28,876	113,884	440,001	(85,009)	(667,168)
17	182,824	179,491	16,046	39,384	1,305,919	1,095,435	-	190,479	-	24,200	120,111	344,089	(95,911)	(525,740)
18	209,953	205,900	15,428	38,087	1,364,331	1,145,463	-	200,261	-	18,925	126,280	236,734	(107,355)	(367,639)
19	235,273	235,826	14,822	36,812	1,418,704	1,192,054	-	204,106	-	13,020	128,705	121,050	(115,684)	(192,508)
20	264,044	268,959	14,226	40,519	1,468,642	1,234,909	-	202,525	-	6,658	127,708	0	(121,050)	0
						Present Value @ 5.50% =		4,719,260	2,975,854			k-factor =	63.1%	

Legend:

(1)—(7) same as Table 6-11 except $(5)_t$ where $t > 5$

(8) = (1) – (2) + (3) – (4) + (5) – (6) + (7)

(9) same as Table 6-12

$(10)_t = i^{cred} \times ((10)_{t-1} + (9)_t)$, where $i^{cred} = 5.5\%$

The present value of capitalized expenses and the EGPs are calculated at the credited rate, which is assumed to be a constant 5.5% in this example. The k-factor is the ratio of these present values. The interest on DAC in column (11) is calculated at the same 5.5% interest rate.

$(11)_t$ = k-factor × EGP_t = k-factor × $(8)_t$

$DAC_t = DAC_{t-1}$ + expenses capitalized $_t$ + interest on DAC_t – expenses amortized $_t$

$(12)_t = (12)_{t-1} + (9)_t + (10)_t - (11)_t$

$(14)_t = (13)_t$ – Table 6-10$(13)_t$

In summary, the effects of unlocking in this example are as shown in Table 6-16.

Table 6-16
Summary of Effects of Unlocking

Duration	(1) DAC Original Projection	(2) DAC Retrospective Unlocking	(3) DAC Prospective Unlocking
5	2,184,635	2,521,931	2,169,450
6	2,162,738	1,608,293	883,464
From Table	6-12	6-14	6-15

This leads to the following:

DAC duration 5	2,184,635	$(1)_5$
Impact of Retrospective Unlocking	337,296	$(2)_5 - (1)_5$
Impact of Annual Events	(913,638)	$(2)_6 - (2)_5$
Impact of Prospective Unlocking	(724,829)	$(3)_6 - (2)_6$
DAC duration 6	883,464	$(3)_6$

6.8 Deferral of Unearned Revenue

6.8.1 Definition

SFAS 97 stipulates:

> Amounts assessed that represent compensation to the insurance enterprise for services to be provided in future periods are not earned in the period assessed. Such amount shall be reported as unearned revenue and recognized in income over the period benefited using the same assumptions and factors used to amortize capitalized acquisition costs. Amounts that are assessed against the policyholder balance as consideration for origination of the contract, often referred to as *initiation* or *front-end fees*, are unearned revenues. (Paragraph 20)

The first wave of universal life products designed in the United States usually employed a front-end load, which is a charge that is much higher than ongoing charges (often as much as 100% of a target premium) and which applied to premiums paid in the first and often the second policy years. These charges must be deferred and amortized in a manner similar to the DAC. Often the fees were designed to mirror acquisition costs, and the mathematical effect might be negated by the deferral and amortization of those acquisition expenses. Note that these are fees collected by the insurance enterprise and not expenses paid out, so that mathematically the unearned revenue liability (URL) is of opposite sign to the DAC.

Another area in which unearned revenue arises is if the COI charges do not follow a normal mortality pattern. Some universal life contracts have COI charges that are level or reducing. In this case, the excess over *normal* charges are commonly established as a URL and subsequently recognized in income during the period benefited.

The issuance of *SOP 03-1* raised certain questions regarding the circumstances under which a company should hold a URL for COI charges that do not follow a normal mortality pattern. Since the language of the *SOP* talked about the need for additional reserves only in the case of "profits followed by losses," there was some question as to whether a comparable threshold should apply for holding a URL. In response to this question, the FASB issued *FSP FAS97-a*, which clarifies that the need for a URL is not limited to situations in which the benefit pattern is expected to result in profits followed by losses. *FSP FAS97-1* states that the facts and circumstances of each situation should be considered in determining whether a URL is required.

6.8.2 Example

The COI charges per $1,000 amount at risk in Table 6-8 are based on the following pattern:

Duration	1	2	3	4	5	6	7	8
COI	2.28	2.40	2.64	2.76	3.00	3.24	3.48	3.84

Suppose the company decided to charge 3.00 per thousand for each of years 1 through 5. An appropriate treatment would be for the excess COI charge to be established as deferred revenue and amortized over the lifetime of the contract, which is demonstrated in Table 6-17.

Table 6-17
Amortization of Excess COI Charges

Year	(1) New Mortality Charges	(2) Original Mortality Charges	(3) Excess Mortality Charges	(4) Gross Profit	(5) Deferred Revenue Liability
1	293,490	223,053	70,438	396,147	59,771
2	252,366	201,892	50,473	513,758	98,588
3	221,501	194,921	26,580	435,723	117,477
4	196,147	180,455	15,692	375,177	128,143
5	175,195	175,195	-	342,773	124,308
6	170,419	170,419	-	320,750	120,960
7	166,174	166,174	-	311,100	117,736
8	167,719	167,719	-	320,684	114,029
9	168,102	168,102	-	335,700	109,642
10	167,480	167,480	-	346,931	104,656
11	162,728	162,728	-	360,728	98,959
12	164,354	164,354	-	376,056	92,461
13	170,434	170,434	-	395,590	84,986
14	169,852	169,852	-	412,476	76,564
15	169,213	169,213	-	432,977	67,027
16	162,761	162,761	-	452,887	56,334
17	182,824	182,824	-	477,919	44,258
18	209,953	209,953	-	502,059	30,751
19	235,273	235,273	-	519,299	15,954
20	264,044	264,044	-	530,114	0
		Present Value @ 5.5 %	151,416	4,768,810	
	Ratio	3.18%			

Legend:
$(1)_t = (2)_t \times \text{COInew}_t/\text{COIold}_t$
$(2)_t$ = Table 6-11, column $(1)_t$
(3) = (1) – (2)
The deferred revenue liability is determined in a similar way to DAC.
k1 = *npv* (excess charges)/*npv* (*EGPs)* at crediting rate
$(4)_t$ = Table 6-11, column $(8)_t$
$(5)_t = (5)_{t-1} \times (1 + i_t) + (3)_t \times (1 + i_t)\text{^}0.5 - \text{k1} \times \text{d}_t$
This calculation assumes that the excess mortality charges occur on average in the middle of the policy year.

6.9 Treatment of Bonuses and Other Special Benefits

There are many types of special bonuses and benefits that can be incorporated into a universal life-type contract. The most common types are as follows:

- Day-one bonuses (increased account value at inception of contract)
- Persistency bonuses (increased account value at the end of a stated period, typically several years)
- Enhanced interest rate bonuses (crediting interest, to the contract, at a rate in excess of what is currently being offered for other similar contracts for a limited period of time).

Bonuses at the outset are more common with single premium policies or in instances in which a lump sum is rolled over from another contract.

Persistency bonuses can take the form of a refund of all COI charges paid to date or a retroactive interest crediting rate increase if the policy stays in force for a period such as 10 years.

Paragraphs 6, 36, and 37 of *SOP 03-1* addressed these issues in the section "Sales Inducements to Contract Holders." They state that these special bonuses should be recognized as part of the liability for policy benefits. Paragraph 6 says sales inducements include an immediate bonus, a persistency bonus and an enhanced crediting rate or "bonus interest" during an initial contract period(s).

Paragraph 37 of the *SOP* states that the insurance enterprise must demonstrate that sales inducements are (a) incremental to amounts credited by the enterprise on similar contracts without sales inducements and (b) higher than the contract's expected crediting rates for the periods after the inducement and are explicitly recognized at the contract's inception. In that case, the inducement is deferred and amortized using the same methodology and assumptions used to amortize deferred acquisition costs. In addition, the change in liability for the sales inducement should be recognized as a component of benefit expense.

6.10 Recoverability and Loss Recognition

Recoverability of deferred policy acquisition costs and loss recognition analyses of the DAC asset for universal life contracts were not altered by *SFAS 97*. The principles of *SFAS 60* continue to apply for universal-life type contracts.

An expense should not be deferred if it cannot be recovered out of future income projected on a best-estimate basis. The DAC asset should be tested periodically to determine whether it is still recoverable. In both cases, the amount of DAC will be limited to the present value of future gross profits. As with *SFAS 60* products, loss recognition testing is performed on a block of business basis. It is not uncommon for all the in-force universal life business of a company to be aggregated for this purpose.

The discount rate used in recoverability testing and loss recognition should be the best estimate of the earned rate, not the crediting rate.

Once a recoverability problem has occurred, or a loss has been recognized, it is appropriate to use the earned rate to amortize any remaining DAC. The support for this is that the DAC is thereafter subject to a gross premium valuation in the nature of the requirements of paragraphs 32 to 37 of *SFAS 60*. As recoverability is demonstrated when the k-factor is less than or equal to 100% at the earned rate, once such a problem has occurred, the DAC is taken down so that the k-factor is exactly 100% at the earned rate, and a gross premium valuation approach is appropriate thereafter. Indeed, to change to the credited rate for DAC discounting and amortization once the DAC has been appropriately taken down would generate an apparent, yet specious, margin.

6.11 Choice of Crediting Rate in DAC Amortization

The interest rate used for the amortization of DAC and URL shall be, as stated in paragraph 25 of *SFAS 97*, "either the rate in effect at the inception of the book of contracts or the latest revised rate applied to the remaining benefit period." It is probably more common to use the latest revised rate, but both approaches are prevalent in the industry.

For simplicity's sake, the examples in this chapter have used the rate in effect at outset (5.5%).

6.12 "Profits followed by losses"

For contracts that are classified as insurance contracts, the next step is determining whether reserves are required under *SOP 03-1* as a result of the "profits followed by losses" test. Paragraph 26 of *SOP 03-1* states:

> If the amounts assessed against the contract holder each period for the insurance benefit feature are assessed in a manner that is expected to result in profits in earlier years and subsequent losses from the insurance benefit function, a liability should be established in addition to the account balance to recognize the portion of such assessments that compensates the insurance enterprise for benefits to be provided in future periods.

Additional guidance regarding the profits followed by losses test is provided in *TPA 6300.05* to *6300.10*. These were issued by the AICPA in September 2004 to address several questions raised by insurance companies regarding how *SOP 03-1* should be applied, including how insurance benefit features and amounts assessed against the contract holder should be defined and how to deal with situations in which there are losses in all years.

6.12.1 Insurance Benefit Feature

TPA 6300.05 states that the profits followed by losses test should be applied separately to the base mortality benefit feature and each additional insurance benefit feature. So, for example, if a UL contract included a no-lapse guarantee and a long term care rider, the profits followed by losses test would be applied separately to the base contract death benefit, the no-lapse guarantee benefit, and the long term care rider benefit.

A mortality or morbidity feature should be evaluated separately if any of the following are present:

- Explicit incremental charges
- Offered separately in the market place
- Described in the contract as a separate benefit, or
- The contract holder has a choice to accept or reject the additional benefit without rejecting the base contract.

However, this is not an exhaustive list of indicators suggesting separate evaluation.

6.12.2 Definition of an Assessment

TPA 6300.06 states that if an insurance benefit feature has an explicit fee, there is a rebuttable presumption that the explicit fee should be used for the profits followed by losses test, but that the presumption may be overcome if the substance of the agreement is not captured in the explicit terms of the contract. The support for this comes from paragraph 54 of *SFAS 97*, which contains comparable language. *TPA 6300.06* also states that it is unlikely that the presumption can be rebutted if "the assessment is explicitly incremental upon election of a separate insurance benefit feature and for which the policyholder has the choice to not pay if the election is not made."

TPA 6300.06 states that if there is no explicit fee or if the explicit fee does not capture the substance of the agreement, another method of determining assessments could be used.

An example of a situation in which it may be appropriate to use some alternative to the explicit fee is a universal life contract, which is profitable but where the pricing was done on an integrated basis and where the COI charges are insufficient on their own to cover the death benefits. In this case, the combined COI charges and appropriate investment or other margins should be used in the profits followed by losses test to determine if a reserve is needed for the base contract mortality benefit feature.

TPA 6300.06 provides a list of indicators that would imply that it is appropriate to allocate additional, implicit charges to the benefit feature as follows:

- Allocation is not inconsistent with documentation, if any, of pricing at contract inception
- Assessments are allocated considering the recovery of all costs of each product component
- Allocation does not contradict external information on the market value of an individual product component on a stand-alone basis, and
- Allocation method is applied consistently.

TPA 6300.06 states that it is presumed that a no-lapse guarantee on a universal life contract will result in profits followed by losses. Further, *TPA 6300.08* says that a liability should be held in situations in which the insurance benefit feature exhibits losses in all years.

6.12.3 Interaction of an Unearned Revenue Liability with SOP Liability

Paragraph 20 of *SFAS 97* states that "Amounts assessed that represent compensation to the insurance enterprise for services to be provided in future periods are not earned in the period assessed. Such amounts should be reported as unearned revenue." Under some universal life-type contracts, the ratio of mortality charges to expected mortality costs is higher in early durations than in later durations and many companies set up an unearned revenue liability for the excess charges. Paragraph 4 of *FSP FAS 97-a* agrees that, depending on the facts and circumstances, unearned revenue might exist.

FSP FAS97-a, in its paragraph 14, states:

> If a reporting enterprise has accrued an unearned revenue liability in accordance with paragraphs 17(b) and 20 of *Statement 97* that relates to a universal life-type insurance benefit liability, the amounts related to insurance benefits should be considered in determining the necessary insurance benefit liability under paragraph 26 of *SOP 03-1*.

In addition, paragraph 26 of *SOP 03-1* states:

> For contracts in which assessments are collected over a period significantly shorter than the period for which the contract is subject to mortality and morbidity risks, the assessment would be considered a front-end fee under *FASB Statement No. 97* and accounted for under paragraph 20 of *Statement No. 97*. The amounts recognized in income should be considered assessments for purposes of this paragraph.

Therefore, to the extent a company is holding a URL related to COI charges, the amortization of the URL should be taken into account in performing the profits followed by losses test.

6.12.4 Examples of Profits Followed by Losses Tests

The following tables show how the profits followed by losses test would be performed for two different UL contracts.

Table 6-18 illustrates a universal life policy with reverse select and ultimate COI charges with no secondary guarantees.

Table 6-18
Example of Profits Followed by Losses No Secondary Guarantee

Contract Assumptions

Number of Policies 100 | Average Face Amount 10,000 | Target Premium $25/1000

Year	COIs	Expected Mortality Rates	Expected Credited Rates	Expected Lapse Rates	Interest Spread	Expense Charges	Discount Rate
1	0.00176	0.0007	8%	3%	0.50%	$10/pol	8%
2	0.00165	0.0008	8%	3%	0.50%	$10/pol	8%
3	0.00154	0.0009	8%	3%	0.50%	$10/pol	8%
4	0.00143	0.0010	8%	3%	0.50%	$10/pol	8%
5	0.00132	0.0011	8%	2%	0.50%	$10/pol	8%
6	0.00121	0.0012	8%	1%	0.50%	$10/pol	8%
7	0.00110	0.0013	8%	1%	0.50%	$10/pol	8%
8	0.00099	0.0014	8%	1%	0.50%	$10/pol	8%
9	0.00088	0.0015	8%	1%	0.50%	$10/pol	8%
10	0.00077	0.0016	8%	100%	0.50%	$10/pol	8%

Only the Explicit Charge is Included in Assessments

Year	(1) Premium	(2) Account Value EOP	(3) Total Death Benefits	(4) Excess Death Benefits	(5) COIs	(6) Interest Margins	(7) Other Assessments	(8) Total Assessments	(9) Discount Factor (8%)	(10) Persistency Factor	(11) Profit / (Loss)*
1	25,000	26,171	689	671	1,687	125	985	2,797	0.962250	0.984530	1,016
2	24,613	53,158	763	742	1,530	254	954	2,738	0.890973	0.954305	788
3	23,858	80,607	832	783	1,339	385	925	2,649	0.824975	0.924913	557
4	23,123	108,555	896	813	1,162	519	896	2,577	0.763865	0.896333	349
5	22,408	138,456	955	831	998	655	869	2,521	0.707283	0.868547	166
6	21,714	171,046	1,020	848	855	801	850	2,506	0.654891	0.850220	7
7	21,256	205,338	1,093	862	729	962	841	2,531	0.606381	0.840698	(133)
8	21,017	241,677	1,164	865	612	1,132	831	2,575	0.561464	0.831198	(253)
9	20,780	280,194	1,233	856	502	1,312	822	2,636	0.519874	0.821722	(354)
10	20,543	-	1,300	834	401	1,504	812	2,717	0.481365	0.812272	(433)
PV				5,570	7,484	4,496	6,211	18,367			

** Profits followed by losses, therefore reserve is required*

Assumes premiums, interest credits, and expenses charges occur at start of year, deaths at mid year and surrenders at end of year

Based on Substance of Agreement, COIs and Interest Spread Included in Assessments

Year	(1) Premium	(2) Account Value EOP	(3) Total Death Benefits	(4) Excess Death Benefits	(5) COIs	(6) Interest Margins	(7) Other Assessments	(8) Total Assessments	(9) Discount Factor (8%)	(10) Persistency Factor	(11) Profit / (Loss) *
1	25,000	26,171	689	671	1,687	125	985	2,797	0.962250	0.984530	1,141
2	24,613	53,158	763	742	1,530	254	954	2,738	0.890973	0.954305	1,042
3	23,858	80,607	832	783	1,339	385	925	2,649	0.824975	0.924913	942
4	23,123	108,555	896	813	1,162	519	896	2,577	0.763865	0.896333	868
5	22,408	138,456	955	831	998	655	869	2,521	0.707283	0.868547	821
6	21,714	171,046	1,020	848	855	801	850	2,506	0.654891	0.850220	808
7	21,256	205,338	1,093	862	729	962	841	2,531	0.606381	0.840698	829
8	21,017	241,677	1,164	865	612	1,132	831	2,575	0.561464	0.831198	878
9	20,780	280,194	1,233	856	502	1,312	822	2,636	0.519874	0.821722	959
10	20,543	-	1,300	834	401	1,504	812	2,717	0.481365	0.812272	1,071
PV				5,570	7,484	4,496	6,455	18,435			

** All profits, so no reserve required*

Assumes premiums, interest credits, and expenses charges occur at start of year, deaths at mid year and surrenders at end of year

Legend:

(1) Equals $25 × 1,000 × $(10)_{t-1}$

(2) Equals $[(2)_{t-1} + (1)]$ × (1 – mortality rate – lapse rate) × (1 + credited rate)

(3) Equals mortality rate × [1,000,000 × (10)]

(4) Equals mortality rate × [1,000,000 × (10) – $(2)_{t-1}$ × (1 + crediting rate) ^ 0.5]

(5) Equals COIs × [1,000,000 × (10) – $(2)_{t-1}$ × (1 + crediting rate) ^ 0.5]

(6) Equals 0.50% × ((1) + $(2)_{t-1}$)

(7) Equals $10 × 1,000 policies × (10)

(8) Equals (5) + (6) + (7)

(9) Equals $(9)_{t-1}$ / (1 + discount rate); Year 1 equals 1 / (1 + discount rate) ^ 0.5

(10) Equals $(10)_{t-1}$ × (1 – mortality rate – lapse rate); Year 1 equals (1 – mortality rate – lapse rate) ^ 0.5

(11) Equals (5) – (4) in first example, (5) + (6) – (4) in second example

The contract assumptions are shown in the first section. The average expected assumptions would be set based on review of a range of scenarios as appropriate.

The next section shows the calculation of profits (losses) over the 10-year period. Results are shown separately for two different examples of the substance of the agreement. The first set of numbers shows the result if the substance of the contract based on its design and pricing intends for the COI charges to fully cover the death benefits; any other charges are designed to cover other expenses or profit margins. In this instance, because there are profits followed by losses, a reserve would be established. The last row of numbers shows the result if the explicit charge presumption is rebutted because the substance of the contract intends for the death benefits to be covered by a combination of COI charges and interest margins. In this instance, there are profits in all years and no reserve is required.

Table 6-19 illustrates a basic universal life contract with a no-lapse guarantee.

Table 6-19
Example of Profits Followed by Losses For Secondary Guarantee

Contract Assumptions

Number of Policies	100	Average Face Amount	10,000	Target Premium	$25/1000
No Lapse Guarantee Period	10 Years	Minimum Premium	$15/1000		

Year	COIs	Expected Mortality Rates	Expected Credited Rates	Expected Lapse Rates	Interest Spread	Expense Charges	Discount Rate	Premium Paid as a % of Target
1	0.00077	0.0007	8%	3%	0.50%	$10/pol	8%	100%
2	0.00088	0.0008	8%	3%	0.50%	$10/pol	8%	90%
3	0.00099	0.0009	8%	3%	0.50%	$10/pol	8%	85%
4	0.00110	0.0010	8%	3%	0.50%	$10/pol	8%	82%
5	0.00121	0.0011	8%	2%	0.50%	$10/pol	8%	80%
6	0.00132	0.0012	8%	1%	0.50%	$10/pol	8%	78%
7	0.00143	0.0013	8%	1%	0.50%	$10/pol	8%	75%
8	0.00154	0.0014	8%	1%	0.50%	$10/pol	8%	70%
9	0.00165	0.0015	8%	1%	0.50%	$10/pol	8%	67%
10	0.00176	0.0016	8%	100%	0.50%	$10/pol	8%	67%

Year	(1) Premium	(2) Account Value EOP	(3) Total Death Benefits	(4) Base Excess Death Benefits	(5) NLG Excess Death Benefits	(6) COIs	(7) Interest Margins	(8) Other Assessments	(9) Total Assessments	(10) Discount Factor (8%)	(11) Persistency Factor	(12) Base Benefit Assessments	(13) NLG Assessments	(14) Base Profit / (Loss)*	(15) NLG Profit / (Loss)*
												95.4%	4.6%		
1	25,000	26,171	689	671	-	738	125	985	1,848	0.962250	0.984530	704	34	33	34
2	22,152	50,581	763	742	-	816	242	954	2,012	0.890973	0.954305	778	37	37	37
3	20,279	74,165	832	785	-	864	354	925	2,143	0.824975	0.924913	824	40	39	40
4	18,961	97,457	896	809	10	901	466	896	2,263	0.763865	0.896333	860	41	51	31
5	17,927	121,985	955	812	32	928	577	869	2,374	0.707283	0.868547	886	43	74	11
6	16,937	148,355	1,020	809	59	955	695	850	2,500	0.654891	0.850220	911	44	102	(15)
7	15,942	175,436	1,093	822	70	982	821	841	2,644	0.606381	0.840698	937	45	114	(25)
8	14,712	203,019	1,164	814	94	999	951	831	2,781	0.561464	0.831198	953	46	139	(48)
9	13,923	231,602	1,233	805	111	1,008	1,085	822	2,914	0.519874	0.821722	961	46	156	(65)
10	13,764	-	1,300	777	138	1,006	1,227	812	3,045	0.481365	0.812272	960	46	183	(92)
PV				5,425	288	6,284	3,881	6,211	16,528						

No reserve required for base mortality benefit, reserve required for no lapse guarantee benefit
Assumes premiums, interest credits, and expenses charges occur at start of year, deaths at mid year and surrenders at end of year

Legend:

(1) Equals $25 × 1,000 × $(10)_{t-1}$
(2) Equals $[(2)_{t-1} + (1)]$ × (1 – mortality rate – lapse rate) × (1 + credited rate)
(3) Equals mortality rate × [1,000,000 × (10)]
(4) Equals mortality rate × [1,000,000 × (10) – $(10)_{t-1}$ × (1 + crediting rate) ^ 0.5]
(5) Death benefit for policyholders who died during the year and had a zero account value
(6) Equals COIs × [1,000,000 × (11) – $(2)_{t-1}$ × (1 + crediting rate) ^ 0.5]
(7) Equals 0.50% × ((1) + $(2)_{t-1}$)
(8) Equals $10 × 1,000 policies × (11)
(9) Equals (6) + (7) + (8)
(10) Equals $(9)_{t-1}$ / (1 + discount rate); Year 1 equals 1 / (1 + discount rate) ^ 0.5
(11) Equals $(10)_{t-1}$ × (1 – mortality rate – lapse rate); Year 1 equals (1 – mortality rate – lapse rate) ^ 0.5
(12) Equals ratio of 95.4% × (6). Ratio equals 100% less ratio for NLG assessments.
(13) Equals ratio of 4.6% × (6). Ratio equals PV of (5) / PV of (6)
(14) Equals (12) – (4).
(15) Equals (13) – (5)

The contract assumptions are shown in the first section. The average expected assumptions would be set based on review of a range of scenarios as appropriate.

The next section shows the calculation of profits (losses) over the 10-year period for each benefit feature separately, as required by the *SOP 03-1 TPA*. Because this contract does not have an explicit charge for the no-lapse guarantee, an implicit charge must be determined. This example assumes that the COI charges alone are intended to cover the base mortality benefit and the no-lapse guarantee. To determine an implicit charge for the no-lapse guarantee, a portion of the COIs is allocated. The allocation percentage is determined as the present value of future no-lapse guarantee benefits divided by the present value of the COIs. This ratio multiplied by each year's COIs equals the no-lapse guarantee charges. The remaining COI charges are allocated to the base mortality benefit.

Based on this allocation of charges, the base contract has profits in most years, and a very small level of losses in a few years. In such a case, it is common to view the losses as negligible, and therefore no reserve would be established.

For the no-lapse guarantees, as expected, there are profits followed by losses and a reserve would be required.

6.13 Establishment of Liabilities under *SOP 03-1*

For insurance contracts that exhibit a pattern of profits followed by losses, a liability must be held under *SOP 03-1*. Paragraph 26 of the *SOP* states:

> The amount of the additional liability should be determined based on the ratio (benefit ratio) of (a) the present value of total expected excess payments over the life of the contract, divided by (b) the present value of total expected assessments over the life of the contract. The benefit ratio may exceed one hundred percent, resulting in a liability that exceeds cumulative assessments. Total expected assessments are the aggregate of all charges, including those for administration, mortality, expense, and surrender, regardless of how characterized. For contracts whose assets are reported in the general account and that include investment margin in their estimated gross profits, the investment margin should be included with any other assessments for purposes of determining total expected assessments.

SOP 03-1 requires that the calculations of expected benefits and assessments be based on expected experience, taking into account a range of scenarios, rather than a single best estimate scenario. For universal life contracts, this may involve projecting benefits under a series of different interest rate scenarios or for various policyholder premium deposit levels. *SOP 03-1* also states that assumptions should be consistent with those used in determining estimated gross profits (EGPs) for purposes of amortizing DAC.

As described in section 6.12 above, amortization of any URL associated with COI charges should be included in assessments for purposes of calculating the reserve under paragraph 26.

SOP 03-1, in paragraph 28, states:

> The additional liability at the balance sheet date should be equal to:
>
> a. The current benefit ratio multiplied by the cumulative assessments

> b. Less the cumulative excess payments (including amounts reflected in claims payable liabilities)
> c. Plus accreted interest
>
> However, in no event should the additional liability balance be less than zero. The change in the additional liability should be recognized as a component of benefit expense in the statement of operations.

TPA 6300.07 deals with the level at which the calculation of the additional liability should be performed and states that the calculation of the additional liability should generally be performed at the same level at which DAC balances and associated DAC amortization ratios are calculated. It also states that a more detailed calculation level may be warranted based on specific facts and circumstances. This would apply to the level at which the benefit ratio and liability is calculated, as well as the level at which the zero floor is applied.

Comparable to the process described above for DAC, the SOP liability should be regularly updated to reflect actual historical experience (retrospective unlocking) and updated to assumed future experience (prospective unlocking). Paragraph 27 of *SOP 03-1* states:

> The insurance enterprise should regularly evaluate estimates used and adjust the additional liability balance, with a related charge or credit to benefit expense, if actual experience or other evidence suggests that earlier assumptions should be revised. In making such revised estimates, both the present value of total excess payments and the present value of total expected assessments and investment margins, should be calculated as of the balance sheet date using historical experience from the issue date to the balance sheet date and estimated experience thereafter.

SOP 03-1 also states that estimated gross profits used in determining DAC should be adjusted for the change in the liability.

6.13.1 Example of Establishment of Liability and Impact on DAC

Table 6-20 starts with the information set out for the example in Table 6-18 and shows how a reserve would be calculated.

Table 6-20
Example of Profits Followed by Losses No Secondary Guarantee

Contract Assumptions

Number of Policies 100 | Average Face Amount 10,000 | Target Premium $25/1000

Year	COIs	Expected Mortality Rates	Expected Credited Rates	Expected Lapse Rates	Interest Spread	Expense Charges	Discount Rate
1	0.00176	0.0007	8%	3%	0.50%	$10/pol	8%
2	0.00165	0.0008	8%	3%	0.50%	$10/pol	8%
3	0.00154	0.0009	8%	3%	0.50%	$10/pol	8%
4	0.00143	0.0010	8%	3%	0.50%	$10/pol	8%
5	0.00132	0.0011	8%	2%	0.50%	$10/pol	8%
6	0.00121	0.0012	8%	1%	0.50%	$10/pol	8%
7	0.00110	0.0013	8%	1%	0.50%	$10/pol	8%
8	0.00099	0.0014	8%	1%	0.50%	$10/pol	8%
9	0.00088	0.0015	8%	1%	0.50%	$10/pol	8%
10	0.00077	0.0016	8%	100%	0.50%	$10/pol	8%

Year	(1) Premium	(2) Account Value EOP	(3) Total Death Benefits	(4) Excess Death Benefits	(5) COIs	(6) Interest Margins	(7) Other Assessments	(8) Total Assessments	(9) Discount Factor (8%)	(10) Persistency Factor	(11) Profit / (Loss)*	(12) Benefit Ratio (BR):	(13) SOP Reserve	(14) Change in Reserve
1	25,000	26,171	689	671	1,687	125	985	2,797	0.962250	0.984530	1,016		184	184
2	24,613	53,158	763	742	1,530	254	954	2,738	0.890973	0.954305	788		291	107
3	23,858	80,607	832	783	1,339	385	925	2,649	0.824975	0.924913	557		336	45
4	23,123	108,555	896	813	1,162	519	896	2,577	0.763865	0.896333	349		330	(5)
5	22,408	138,456	955	831	998	655	869	2,521	0.707283	0.868547	166		287	(43)
6	21,714	171,046	1,020	848	855	801	850	2,506	0.654891	0.850220	7		219	(68)
7	21,256	205,338	1,093	862	729	962	841	2,531	0.606381	0.840698	(133)		139	(80)
8	21,017	241,677	1,164	865	612	1,132	831	2,575	0.561464	0.831198	(253)		63	(76)
9	20,780	280,194	1,233	856	502	1,312	822	2,636	0.519874	0.821722	(354)		9	(54)
10	20,543	-	1,300	834	401	1,504	812	2,717	0.481365	0.812272	(433)		(0)	(9)
PV				5,570	7,484	4,496	6,211	18,367						

** Profits followed by losses, therefore reserve is required*

Assumes premiums, interest credits, and expenses charges occur at start of year, deaths at mid year and surrenders at end of year

Legend:

(1) Equals $25 × 1,000 × $(10)_{t-1}$

(2) Equals $[(2)_{t-1} + (1)]$ × (1 – mortality rate – lapse rate) × (1 + credited rate)

(3) Equals mortality rate × [1,000,000 × (10)]

(4) Equals mortality rate × [1,000,000 × (10) × $(2)_{t-1}$ × (1 + crediting rate) ^ 0.5]

(5) Equals COIs × [1,000,000 × (10) – $(2)_{t-1}$ × (1 + crediting rate) ^ 0.5]

(6) Equals 0.50% × ((1) + $(2)_{t-1}$)

(7) Equals $10 × 1,000 policies × (10)

(8) Equals (5) + (6) + (7)

(9) Equals $(9)_{t-1}$ / (1 + discount rate); Year 1 equals 1 / (1 + discount rate) ^ 0.5

(10) Equals $(10)_{t-1}$ × (1 – mortality rate – lapse rate); Year 1 equals (1 – mortality rate – lapse rate) ^ 0.5

(11) Equals (5) – (4)

(12) Equals PV (4) / PV (8)

(13) Equals $(13)_{t-1}$ × 1.08 + [((12) × (8)) – (4)] × 1.08 ^ 0.5

(14) Equals $(13)_t$ – $(13)_{t-1}$

A 10-year projection of contract benefits and assessments is made and the corresponding reserve is calculated. The projected benefits and assessments are based on mean or best estimate projected amounts from a review of the results for a range of scenarios. The resulting benefit ratio is 15.8%, and the reserve at the end of year 1 is approximately $95.

Table 6-21 shows an example of the impact on DAC of the *SOP 03-1* liability.

Table 6-21
Impact of SOP Liability on DAC

DAC

	Year	(1) Account Value EOP	(2) Deferrals	(3) EGPs	(4) Amortization Ratio (k)	(5) DAC Balance EOP	(6) DAC Amortization
History	1	26,171	5,000	2,126		4,537	831
	2	53,158	-	1,996		4,089	780
	3	80,607	-	1,867		3,659	729
	4	108,555	-	1,764		3,235	689
Future	5	138,456	-	1,690		2,808	660
	6	171,046	-	1,658		2,359	648
	7	205,338	-	1,670		1,870	652
	8	241,677	-	1,710		1,325	668
	9	280,194	-	1,780		708	696
	10	-	-	1,883		-	736
	PV		5,000	12,797	39.1%		

SOP 03-1 Reserve and revised DAC Balance

	Year	(7) Account Value EOY	(8) Mean Benefits	(9) Mean Assessments	(10) Benefit Ratio	(11) SOP 03-1 Reserve	(12) Increase in Reserve	(13) Revised EGPs	(14) Revised DAC Balance
History	1	26,171	671	2,797		184	184	1,941	4,605
	2	53,158	742	2,738		291	107	1,889	4,200
	3	80,607	783	2,649		336	45	1,822	3,790
	4	108,555	813	2,577		330	(5)	1,770	3,368
Future	5	138,456	831	2,521		287	(43)	1,733	2,929
	6	171,046	848	2,506		219	(68)	1,726	2,456
	7	205,338	862	2,531		139	(80)	1,750	1,936
	8	241,677	865	2,575		63	(76)	1,786	1,360
	9	280,194	856	2,636		9	(54)	1,834	718
	10	-	834	2,717		(0)	(9)	1,893	0
	PV		5,570	18,367	30.3%			39.4%	

Legend:
(1) Column (2) from Table 6-20
(2) Actual deferrals for DAC calculations
(3) Column (8) – Column (4) from Table 6-20
(4) PV of (2) / PV of (3)
(5) Equals $(5)_{t-1} \times 1.08 + ((2) - (6)) \times 1.08$ ^ 0.5
(6) Equals (4) × (3)
(7) Equals (1)
(8) Column (4) from Table 6-20
(9) Column (8) from Table 6-20
(10) PV of (8) / PV of (9)
(11) Equals $(11)_{t-1} \times 1.08 + [((10) \times (9)) - (8)] \times 1.08$ ^ 0.5
(12) Equals $(11)_t - 11_{t-1}$
(13) Equals (3) – (12)
(14) Equals $(14)_{k-1} \times 1.08 + [(2) - ($Column (13) k factor $\times (13))] \times 1.08$ ^ 0.5

This shows the impact on DAC when the change in reserve is deducted from EGPs each year. This results in a higher k-factor and a longer deferral of the DAC.

6.13.2 Examples of Interaction of *SOP 03-1* Liabilities and URL—"The circulatory issue"

Table 6-22 shows the interaction of the *SOP* liability and URL for a universal life contract with a "reverse select and ultimate" COI pattern and no secondary guarantees.

Table 6-22
Example of Interaction of SOP Liability and Unearned Revenue Reserve

Contract Assumptions

Number of Policies 100 | Average Face Amount 10,000 | Target Premium $25/1000

Year	COIs	Expected Mortality Rates	Expected Credited Rates	Expected Lapse Rates	Interest Spread	Expense Charges	Discount Rate
1	0.00192	0.0007	8%	3%	0.50%	$10/pol	8%
2	0.00180	0.0008	8%	3%	0.50%	$10/pol	8%
3	0.00168	0.0009	8%	3%	0.50%	$10/pol	8%
4	0.00143	0.0010	8%	3%	0.50%	$10/pol	8%
5	0.00132	0.0011	8%	2%	0.50%	$10/pol	8%
6	0.00121	0.0012	8%	1%	0.50%	$10/pol	8%
7	0.00110	0.0013	8%	1%	0.50%	$10/pol	8%
8	0.00099	0.0014	8%	1%	0.50%	$10/pol	8%
9	0.00088	0.0015	8%	1%	0.50%	$10/pol	8%
10	0.00077	0.0016	8%	100%	0.50%	$10/pol	8%

Year	(1) Premium	(2) Account Value EOP	(3) Total Death Benefits	(4) Excess Death Benefits	(5) COIs	(6) COI Load	(7) Interest Margins	(8) Other Assessments	(9) Total Assessments	(10) Discount Factor (8%)	(11) Persistency Factor	(12) Earnings w/o Reserves
1	25,000	26,171	689	671	1,840	184	125	985	2,950	0.962250	0.984530	2,279
2	24,613	53,158	763	742	1,669	167	254	954	2,877	0.890973	0.954305	2,135
3	23,858	80,607	832	783	1,461	151	385	925	2,771	0.824975	0.924913	1,988
4	23,123	108,555	896	813	1,162	-	519	896	2,577	0.763865	0.896333	1,764
5	22,408	138,456	955	831	998	-	655	869	2,521	0.707283	0.868547	1,690
6	21,714	171,046	1,020	848	855	-	801	850	2,506	0.654891	0.850220	1,658
7	21,256	205,338	1,093	862	729	-	962	841	2,531	0.606381	0.840698	1,670
8	21,017	241,677	1,164	865	612	-	1,132	831	2,575	0.561464	0.831198	1,710
9	20,780	280,194	1,233	856	502	-	1,312	822	2,636	0.519874	0.821722	1,780
10	20,543	-	1,300	834	401	-	1,504	812	2,717	0.481365	0.812272	1,883
PV				5,570	7,856	451	4,496	6,211	18,739			13,169

Assumes premiums, interest credits, and expenses charges occur at start of year, deaths at mid year and surrenders at end of year

Reserves

METHOD 1: URR for front end load only

Year	(13) EGPs	(14) URR	(15) Change in URR	(16) Earnings	(17) Profit / (Loss)
1	2,095	114	114	2,165	1,055
2	1,968	224	110	2,025	817
3	1,837	332	107	1,881	571
4	1,764	293	(38)	1,803	388
5	1,690	255	(39)	1,728	205
6	1,658	214	(41)	1,699	48
7	1,670	170	(44)	1,714	(88)
8	1,710	120	(49)	1,759	(204)
9	1,780	64	(56)	1,836	(298)
10	1,883	-	(64)	1,948	(368)
PV or k	12,718	3.54%			

METHOD 2: No URR, SOP Only

Year	(18) Benefit Ratio (BR):	(19) SOP Reserve	(20) Change in Reserve	(21) Earnings
1		214	214	2,065
2		349	135	2,000
3		420	71	1,918
4		405	(15)	1,779
5		352	(53)	1,742
6		273	(79)	1,737
7		182	(92)	1,761
8		93	(89)	1,799
9		25	(68)	1,848
10		(0)	(25)	1,909
PV	29.73%			13,037

METHOD 3: URR for front end load and SOP reserve for COIs (3 iterations of URR)

	Iteration 2					Iteration 3					
Year	(22) Assessments (incl URR)	(23) Benefit Ratio	(24) SOP Reserve	(25) Revised EGPs	(26) Revised URR	(27) Assessments (incl URR)	(28) Benefit Ratio	(29) SOP Reserve	(30) Revised EGPs	(31) Revised URR	(32) Earnings
1	2,836		183	1,912	120	2,830		182	1,913	120	1,977
2	2,767		286	1,865	234	2,763		284	1,866	234	1,919
3	2,664		323	1,800	343	2,662		320	1,801	343	1,843
4	2,615		317	1,771	305	2,615		313	1,771	305	1,809
5	2,560		273	1,733	265	2,561		270	1,733	265	1,773
6	2,546		205	1,726	222	2,549		202	1,726	222	1,769
7	2,576		126	1,749	175	2,579		124	1,748	175	1,795
8	2,624		52	1,784	123	2,627		51	1,783	123	1,835
9	2,692		2	1,830	65	2,694		2	1,829	65	1,887
10	2,781		(0)	1,886	0	2,782		0	1,886	(0)	1,950
PV or k	18,641	29.88%		12,616	3.57%	18,637	29.89%		12,618	3.57%	

Legend:

(1) Equals \$25 × 1,000 × $(10)_{t-1}$
(2) Equals $[(2)_{t-1} + (1)]$ × (1 – mortality rate – lapse rate) × (1 + credited rate)
(3) Equals mortality rate × [1,000,000 × (10)]
(4) Equals mortality rate × [1,000,000 × (10) – $(2)_{t-1}$ × (1 + crediting rate) ^ 0.5]
(5) Equals COIs × [1,000,000 × (10) – $(2)_{t-1}$ × (1 + crediting rate) ^ 0.5]
(6) Equals COI load × [1,000,000 × (10) – $(2)_{t-1}$ × (1 + crediting rate) ^ 0.5]
(7) Equals 0.50% × ((1) + $(2)_{t-1}$)
(8) Equals \$10 × 1,000 policies × (10)
(9) Equals (9) – (4)
(10) Equals $(9)_{t-1}$ / (1 + discount rate); Year 1 equals 1 / (1 + discount rate) ^ 0.5
(11) Equals $(10)_{t-1}$ × (1 – mortality rate – lapse rate); Year 1 equals (1 – mortality rate – lapse rate) ^ 0.5
(12) Equals (9) – (4)
(13) Equals (12) – (6)
(14) Equals $(13)_{t-1}$ × 1.08 + [(6) – (URR k factor × (13)] × 1.08 ^ 0.5
(15) Equals $(14)_t - (14)_{t-1}$
(16) Equals (12) – (15)
(17) Equals (5) – (4) – (15)
(18) Equals PV (4) / PV (9)
(19) Equals $(19)_{t-1}$ × 1.08 + [((18) × (9)) – (4)] × 1.08 ^ 0.5
(20) Equals $(19)_t - (19)_{t-1}$
(21) Equals (12) – (20)
(22) Equals (9) – (15)
(23) Equals PV (4) / PV (22)
(24) Equals $(24)_{t-1}$ × 1.08 + [((23) × (22)) – (4)] × 1.08 ^ 0.5
(25) Equals (13) – $((24)_t - (24)_{t-1})$
(26) Equals $(26)_{t-1}$ × 1.08 + [(6) – (URR k factor × (25))] × 1.08 ^ 0.5
(27) Equals (12) – $((26)_t - (26)_{t-1})$
(28) Equals PV (4) / PV (27)
(29) Equals $(29)_{t-1}$ × 1.08 + [((28) × (27)) – (4)] × 1.08 ^ 0.5
(30) Equals (13) – $((29)_t - (29)_{t-1})$
(31) Equals $(31)_{t-1}$ × 1.08 + [(6) – (URR k factor × (30))] × 1.08 ^ 0.5
(32) Equals (12) – $((29)_t - (29)_{t-1})$ – $((31)_t - (31)_{t-1})$

The contract assumptions are shown in the first section. The next section shows the projection of contract benefits and assessments and the calculation of the earnings over the 10-year period assuming no URL and no *SOP 03-1* reserve. The projected benefits and assessments are based on mean or best estimate of a range of scenarios as appropriate.

The next section ("Pre-*SOP*") shows the impact on earnings if the front-end loading on the COIs is set up as a URL and amortized in proportion to EGPs. This was typically how such COI patterns were dealt with prior to the issuance of the *SOP*. The section also shows the resulting profit/loss pattern after taking into account the change in URL in assessments for the benefit feature. Because there are profits followed by losses after taking into account change in URL, an *SOP 03-1* reserve would still be required.

The final section ("Post-*SOP*") shows the impact on earnings if an *SOP 03-1* reserve is established in addition to the URL. In order to calculate the *SOP 03-1* reserves, the change in URL is added to the assessment base. Once the *SOP 03-1* reserve is established, the change in that reserve must be reflected in EGPs, which creates a circularity issue as discussed below. For purposes of this example, one additional iteration of the URL calculation was performed. The revised EGPs (after deducting the change in reserve) were used to determine a "final" URL amortization pattern. In practice, most companies would perform multiple iterations or use a convergence formula to derive appropriate estimates.

As discussed in 6.12.3, if a URL is established, the "profits followed by losses" test includes the change in URL. If "profits followed by losses" exist, a reserve is established and the change in that reserve becomes an element of the EGPs. This changes the amortization of URL, which changes the level of profits followed by losses, which changes the amount of reserve, which impacts the EGPs and so on.

Thus the calculation of the *SOP* liability is circular and many iterations may be needed to arrive at the appropriate amount. At the time of writing this book, it is not clear if approximate approaches are acceptable, and a solution has not been found if the results diverge.

Chapter 7 Deferred Annuities

7.1 Introduction

An annuity contract is a contract that provides for a series of payments to be made to the annuitant for a fixed period of time or over someone's lifetime. Payments either start immediately upon issuance of the contract or are deferred for a period of time or until the annuitant reaches a specific age. If deferred, the date that payments begin is either contractually provided for or optionally provided for, at the annuitant's discretion. The cost of an annuity contract (premium) can be paid in a single sum or periodically over a period of deferral before the annuity payments start.

Many optional forms of annuity contracts exist today. Annuity contracts in the income pay phase are often referred to as *payout annuities*. Contracts in a deferred accumulation phase are generally called *deferred annuities*. Income-pay annuities offer several payment options including *life annuity*, in which payments are contingent on the survival of one or more lives; *annuity certain*, in which payments are not contingent on survival of the annuitant; *certain and life*, in which payments are for a fixed period or until the death of the annuitant, if later; and *temporary*, in which payments are for a fixed period or until the death of the annuitant, if earlier.

Annuities can be classified as follows:

1. *By number of lives covered*, e.g., single life, joint life, and joint and last survivor

2. *By method of premium payment*, single, fixed periodic, flexible periodic, and lump-sum deposit from another policy or payment source (e.g., structured settlement)

3. *By manner in which annuity funds are invested*, in the company's general investment account or in a separate account (variable annuities)

4. *By when payments start*, immediately upon payment of a single premium or deferred to an age or date specified in the contract

5. *By nature of payments,* i.e., options on how annuity proceeds are distributed, including whether a refund feature exists and the duration of the benefit payout period.

This chapter deals only with deferred annuities (i.e., the accumulation phase) invested in the company's general investment account (hereinafter referred to as fixed deferred annuities). Variable annuities invested in a separate account and equity-indexed annuities are covered in Chapter 8, and income pay annuities (i.e., the payout phase) are discussed in Chapter 9.

7.2 Types of Products

Since the late 1970s, when interest rates increased significantly from prior levels, deferred annuity contracts have been very popular. Many different forms have come into existence over the years. The older forms of fixed deferred annuity contracts (sometimes called retirement annuities) were generally characterized by a fixed premium structure, high expense loads, and a fixed guaranteed interest rate and maturity structure (thus they were not unbundled). Some participated in excess investment income, credited at the discretion of the company.

Characteristics of fixed deferred annuities today include the following:

1. *Premium pattern.* Both single-premium deferred annuities (SPDAs) and flexible-premium deferred annuities (FPDAs) have been very popular.

2. *Load structure.* Common forms are front-end, back-end (surrender charges in early policy years), or a combination thereof. Back-end loads have been the most common. Some contracts have no loads.

3. *Surrender values.* The surrender value generally equals premiums received accumulated with credited interest less prior partial surrenders less a surrender charge. Surrender charges generally reflect the load structure; e.g., back-end-loaded contracts involve declining surrender charges over a number of policy years. Many products permit surrender of up to 10% to 15% of the fund value each year without a surrender charge. This is commonly referred to as the free partial withdrawal provision.

4. *Interest guarantee structure.* Interest may be guaranteed at current rates, based on company experience and competitive considerations, for a period of 1 year or less, subject to a guaranteed floor. Some contracts, especially SPDAs, have guaranteed a current rate for 3 or more years. Others have used a tiered approach in which different rates apply, depending on the size of the single premium or the fund value.

5. *Taxable nature.* Contracts may be tax-qualified (e.g., individual retirement accounts and other contracts qualifying under various sections of the *Internal Revenue Code*) or non-tax-qualified. Deposits (premiums) under tax-qualified contracts are generally tax deductible (in other words, not taxed as current income). Interest credited to both types of contracts is not taxed as long as it remains on deposit with the insurance company. All subsequent distributions (cash surrenders or annuity payments) are taxed as ordinary income to the extent each payment represents previously untaxed income.

Death benefits under most deferred annuity contracts during the accumulation phase are equal to the greater of the fund value (before surrender charges, less partial surrenders) and the premiums paid.

Some contracts contain a bail-out provision, which stipulates that if the actual rate credited falls below a set rate (often 1% to 3% below the current rate at contract issuance), surrender charges do not apply to funds withdrawn within a certain period of time.

Various other contract features have become popular over the years. Examples are as follows:

a. *Market-value-adjusted annuities.* These contracts are generally single-premium annuities in which the contract owner can lock in a guaranteed interest rate over a specified maturity period (typically 3 to 10 years) but if the contract is surrendered prior to maturity, the cash value is subject to a surrender charge plus a market value adjustment. If current rates increase during the guaranteed period, the market value adjustment is negative. If rates decrease, the market value adjustment is positive. The adjustment is generally defined by a formula in the contract.

b. *Annuities with sales inducements*. Some fixed deferred annuity contracts offer sales inducements as marketing incentives. These inducements may be offered in many forms, including an immediate bonus in the first year wherein extra dollars are added to the fund value (premium bonus), a persistency bonus credited to the contract holder's account after a specified period, or an enhanced crediting rate (bonus interest rate) of 1% to 5%, added to the base interest rate in the initial period(s) of the contract. Sales inducements became popular in the mid-1990s.

c. *Two-tiered annuities*. These contracts are also called dual-fund annuities, and the level of interest credited varies, depending on whether funds are applied to purchase an income pay annuity at a maturity date selected by the contract holder (annuitization). If the contract is surrendered for cash, a lower rate applies from the issue date of the contract (in addition to the application of a surrender charge, in some cases). If the contract annuitizes, a higher rate applies from the issue date and the amount applied to purchase the income pay annuity reflects this higher rate and no surrender charges.

Over time, considerable controversy has existed over the appropriate GAAP accounting treatment for contracts containing these features. AICPA *SOP 03-1*, "Accounting and Reporting by Insurance Enterprises for Certain Nontraditional Long-Duration Contracts and for Separate Accounts," issued July 2003 and effective in 2004 and later, clarified the accounting for sales inducements and two-tier annuities. The accounting for sales inducements is covered in Chapter 3. Section 7.4.3 discusses the GAAP reserve requirements for two tier annuities.

Fixed deferred annuities have been commonly used as savings vehicles, mainly because of the tax-deferred status of the inside buildup of interest on such contracts. Historically, few FPDAs and SPDAs have actually annuitized according to the terms of the contracts. This is true, even though most contracts specify a maturity date (or range of maturity dates) when the accumulated funds can be applied to purchase an income-pay annuity contract under a payment option provided for under the contract. Insurers usually allow the income to be purchased at current rates, if more favorable than the guaranteed purchase rates specified in the deferred annuity contract. Because of the long-term nature of these contracts, the guaranteed purchase rates are generally based on a conservative interest rate and mortality table.

7.3 Accounting Model Classification

A challenging aspect of GAAP for fixed deferred annuities is the selection of the appropriate accounting model to be applied to each contract type.

The older forms of fixed deferred annuities primarily issued before the 1987 release of *SFAS 97*, "Accounting and Reporting by Insurance Enterprises for Certain Long-Duration Contracts and for the Realized Gains and Losses from the Sale of Investments," were accounted for under *SFAS 60*, "Accounting and Reporting by Insurance Enterprises," in a manner similar to that for traditional life insurance, as described in Chapter 4. This is because premiums were fixed by contract and interest guarantees and benefits were bundled in a manner similar to other traditional life insurance products. Thus premium was considered to be revenue and reserves were calculated under the net premium method. Similarly, deferred acquisition costs were amortized in relation to premium revenue over the anticipated premium-paying period.

Most forms of fixed deferred annuities do not qualify for treatment under *SFAS 60* for two reasons:

1. The product features are unbundled, with excess interest credits, expense charges, and surrender charges explicitly defined by the contract.

2. Premiums are no longer fixed under FPDAs. Instead, premiums could be varied by the contract holder within contract limits and without the consent of the insurer.

Proper classification of fixed deferred annuity contracts exhibiting one or both of these two features require evaluation of the following issues:

1. Whether the accumulation and payout phases of the annuity contract are to be considered a single contract or two contracts, more specifically a deferred annuity contract in the accumulation phase and an income-pay annuity in the payment phase.

2. Whether the contract contains significant mortality guarantees.

3. Whether there are significant revenues from sources other than the investment of contract holder funds.

For the reasons outlined below, almost all U.S. fixed deferred annuity contracts have been subject to treatment as investment contracts under either *SFAS 97* or *SFAS 91*, "Accounting for Nonrefundable Fees and Costs Associated with Originating or Acquiring Loans and Initial Direct Cost of Leases."

Most deferred annuity contracts in the U.S. provide for the application of the available fund value, after a specified period of time or attainment of a minimum age, to annuitize the contract (establish an income stream) under one of the contract's settlement options, using the company's then current annuity purchase rates and subject to maximum guaranteed purchase rates specified in the contract. The option to annuitize is part of the deferred annuity contract, hence a single contract design. However, *SFAS 97* states that

> A contract provision that allows the holder of a long-duration contract to purchase an annuity at a guaranteed price on settlement of the contract does not entail a mortality risk until the right of purchase is executed. If purchased, the annuity is a new contract to be evaluated on its own terms. (Paragraph 7)

Under this definition, any mortality risk inherent in the guaranteed purchase rates does not apply until the contract holder actually decides to apply the proceeds of the deferred annuity contract to purchase an income-pay annuity. Further, the guidance in effect forces a two-contract approach to accounting.

Thus until recently (when *SOP 03-1* became effective, requiring consideration of any excess of the present value of annuitization benefits over the fund value at annuitization, as discussed later in this chapter), the accumulation phase of a deferred annuity contract had to be considered alone in the decision process, excluding the payout phase and any mortality risk inherent in the guaranteed purchase rates.

If a single contract approach were to apply, one of *SFAS 97* for limited-pay contracts, *SFAS 97* for investment contracts, or *SFAS 91* would apply. *SFAS 97* for limited-pay contracts would likely apply where the standard option contains life contingencies (e.g., a life annuity). *SFAS 97* for investment contracts or *SFAS 91* applies if the standard option excludes life contingencies. In such a case, *SFAS 97* for investment contracts applies if there are significant revenue sources other than from investment return and *SFAS 91* would apply if not. (See the discussion about AICPA *Practice Bulletin 8,* below.) If a two-contract approach is used, it is necessary to determine whether there are significant mortality guarantees in both the accumulation and payment phases.

Note that many non-U.S. fixed deferred annuity contracts explicitly require annuitization at a specific age or maturity date (within a range selected by the annuitant). Hence the payment phase continues under the same contract. Chapter 16 addresses the accounting model classification and the unique US GAAP accounting treatment of these products.

SFAS 97 states that "Long-duration contracts that do not subject the insurance enterprise to risks from policyholder mortality or morbidity are referred to ... as investment contracts" (Paragraph 7). In defining investment contracts, paragraph 15 references "significant insurance risk" without actually defining significant. The second footnote on page 3 of *SFAS 97* refers to the dictionary definition of *insignificant* as "having little or no importance; trivial." Many actuaries have attempted to define *significant* by stating that a contract has significant mortality risk if the present value of the expected life-contingent payments is at least 5% of the present value of all expected payments under the contract.

SOP 03-1 provides additional guidance to the process of determining significance. Paragraph 25 requires a comparison of the present value of expected excess insurance benefit payments (that is, insurance benefit amounts and related incremental claim adjustment expenses in excess of the account balance) with the present value of all amounts expected to be assessed against the contract holder. Contracts that include investment margin in "estimated gross profits" (see Section 7.6.1 below), should include such margin with all other assessments in the comparison. The analysis should consider both frequency and severity under a full range of scenarios that considers volatility inherent in the assumptions (considering historical investment returns, the volatility of those returns and expected future returns).

As indicated above, practitioners have generally disregarded the presence of guaranteed purchase options in a fixed deferred annuity contract as a significant mortality risk. Instead they have considered such risk as pricing risk.

> The risk that the guaranteed price of an annuity may prove to be unfavorable to the guaranteeing enterprise when the annuity is purchased is a price risk not unlike a guaranteed price of any commodity and does not create a mortality risk. (*SFAS 97* paragraph 40)

Only in the rare event when there are significant mortality guarantees during the accumulation phase would *SFAS 97* for universal life-type or limited payment contracts apply. Generally mortality guarantees in the accumulation phase (such as the return of premiums paid in excess of the cash surrender value upon death) create insignificant risk, as defined above, and treatment as an investment contract applies.

The third issue above in the classification decision process was raised in AICPA *Practice Bulletin 8*, released in 1990. Paragraph 7 indicates that investment contracts may follow the guidance of *SFAS 97* for universal life-type contracts if they "include significant surrender charges or ... yield significant revenues from sources other than the investment of contract holders' funds." Otherwise, the interest method described by *SFAS 91* applies. Again, *significance* is not defined, but it would be reasonable to apply the definition given earlier for defining significant mortality risk for this purpose. Thus, either *SFAS 97* for investment contracts or *SFAS 91* applies to most fixed deferred annuities issued in the U.S. (other than older fixed-premium contracts sold many years ago).

7.4 Benefit Reserves

The definition of benefit reserves for fixed deferred annuity contracts depends on the applicable accounting model.

7.4.1 *SFAS 97* for Investment Contracts

Fixed deferred annuity contracts subject to *SFAS 97* for investment contracts generally apply the guidance of *SFAS 97* for universal life-type contracts in defining reserves and the deferred acquisition cost (DAC) asset. *SFAS 97* states that the liability for policy benefits for universal life-type contracts shall equal the sum of:

a. The balance that accrues to the benefit of contract holders at the date of the financial statement (without reduction for any applicable surrender charges), often called the account value,

b. Any amounts that have been assessed to compensate the insurer for services to be performed over future periods (front-end loads or fees),

c. Any amounts previously assessed against contract holders that are refundable on termination of the contract, and

d. Any probable loss (premium deficiency) as described in paragraphs 35-37 of *SFAS 60*. (Paragraph 17)

For fixed deferred annuities, item a is generally the most significant policy liability, representing the accumulation of premiums received less permanent charges against the contract, at current interest rates credited by the company since contract issuance (called the retrospective deposit method).Note that for two-tier annuities, the account value is the amount that is available to the contract holder *in cash* before applicable surrender charges in the event of contract surrender prior to the annuitization date (hence the lower tier value). Item b relates to expense charges in the early contract years (on front-end loaded contracts) in excess of an ultimate level charge for servicing the contract and is often called an unearned revenue liability (URL). Item c seldom applies to deferred-annuity contracts, and item d does not apply to investment contracts (see Section 7.9). Items b and c (if applicable) are accrued in direct proportion to the level of *gross profits* defined by the contract (see Section 7.6 below).

Some fixed deferred annuity contracts offer contingent bonus features if the contract persists to a given duration (called persistency bonuses). The amounts are generally represented by extra credited interest, dating back to the original issue date. Paragraph 36 of *SOP 03-1* notes that persistency bonuses are a form of sales inducement and that a liability for the bonus must be accrued over the period in which the contract must remain in force for the contract holder to qualify for the bonus. Chapter 3, Section 3.11, provides detail as to how this liability is to be accrued and gives an example. Note paragraph 20 of *SOP 03-1* specifies that the required liability for persistency bonuses is to be considered a part of the accrued account value.

7.4.2 *SFAS 91*

Investment contracts subject to *SFAS 91* generally include deferred annuities with little or no surrender charges and no additional death benefit other than the account value. In addition, such contracts seldom have any front-end loads. In general, the policy liability is equal to the account value using the retrospective deposit method, as defined in Section 7.4.1 above. For contracts in which there is no explicit account value or if estimates of future experience are unlikely to require correction, a prospective method is prescribed, representing the present value of future contract cash flows at the assumed credited or contract rate. This latter method is sometimes called the interest method and uses best-estimate assumptions without provisions for adverse deviation to project the cash flows.

Presumably, future expected decrements (surrenders and deaths) can be anticipated in calculating the future cash flows for the interest method. However, the guidance is not clear whether future changes in the interest-crediting rate can be reflected in the present value calculation after the initial determination at contract issuance. In practice, some companies do and others do not. Failure to do so can lead to a liability that is substantially overstated or understated, depending on the company's current best estimate of future investment returns and crediting rates. If future crediting-rate estimates are substantially higher (lower) than the initial rate at contract issuance, the liability can be overstated (understated) in relation to the amount needed to pay claims as they come due.

7.4.3 Annuitization Benefits

Paragraph 31 of *SOP 03-1* specifies that an additional liability may be required for potential benefits in addition to the account balance that are payable only upon annuitization of a deferred annuity contract. These include annuity purchase guarantees, guaranteed maturity income benefits (GMIBs) and two-tier annuities. GMIBs only apply to variable annuities and are discussed in Chapter 6. An additional liability is required if the present value of expected annuitization payments at the expected annuitization date exceeds the expected account balance at that date.

To determine whether an additional liability is required for a given annuitization benefit, one must first compare the present value of expected annuitization payments to be made and related incremental claims adjustment expenses *at the expected date of annuitization* with the expected accrued account balance available in cash at that date (account balance for lower tier for two tier annuities). The discount rate to be used for this purpose is the estimated investment yield expected to be earned during the payout phase of the contract.

If the present value of payments exceeds the account balance at the expected annuitization date, a benefit ratio is calculated as the ratio of the positive excess to the present value of total expected assessments during the accumulation phase of the contract. If such excess is negative, no additional reserve is required. For fixed deferred annuities, expected assessments include all contract charges, including those for administration, mortality, expense and surrender, regardless of how characterized, plus total investment margin used in calculating estimated gross profits.

In calculating such excesses and total assessments for the benefit ratio, the company must use expected experience based on a range of scenarios that consider the volatility inherent in the assumptions rather than a single set of best-estimate assumptions. In selecting a set of scenarios, the actuary can use either a stochastic approach or a deterministic approach that is periodically generated afresh based on then current market conditions. However, calculation of the additional liability will generally use a single set of assumptions, consistent with those used in calculating estimated gross profits for purposes of amortizing deferred acquisition costs.

The benefit ratio and resultant additional liability must be regularly evaluated and updated for evolving experience. If actual experience and other evidence suggest that the earlier assumptions require revision, both the present value of total excess payments and the present value of expected assessments or investment margins must be calculated as of the balance sheet date using actual historical experience from date of issue to the balance sheet date and estimated experience thereafter. Each time the benefit ratio is reevaluated, a multiple scenario approach should be used.

Then at any given balance sheet date, the additional liability is defined as a + b – c:

a. The current benefit ratio multiplied by the cumulative assessments

b. Accreted interest

c. At time of annuitization, the cumulative excess payments determined at annuitization

The result cannot be less than zero. Note item c represents the amount that should be deducted at the actual date of annuitization. On the date of annuitization, the additional liability should equal zero and item c will be used in the calculation of the liability for the payout annuity.

In calculating the additional liability, paragraph 31 of *SOP 03-1* requires that the assumptions underlying the liability calculation are to be consistent with those used in calculating DAC. EGPs used in DAC amortization and URL release are to include the effect of the change in the additional liability. Many believe interest on assets supporting the liability should be a component of the investment margin component of EGP. See Chapter 12, Section 12.2.4, for an illustrative calculation of the additional annuitization liabilitiy.

7.5 Deferred Acquisition Costs, Front End Load and Deferred Sales Inducements

7.5.1 Deferred Acquistion Costs Considerations

Paragraph 8 of *Practice Bulletin 8* specifies that DAC related to investment contracts under *SFAS 97* should be reported as an asset in a manner consistent with the reporting of DAC for insurance contracts covered by *SFAS 97* (in other words, universal life-type contracts). While not explicitly stated in the guidance, the same treatment has been used for investment contracts subject to *SFAS 91*. In turn, paragraph 24 of *SFAS 97* states that acquisition costs for universal life-type contracts are the same as those addressed in paragraphs 28-31 of *SFAS 60*; i.e., costs that vary with and are primarily related to the acquisition of new and renewal insurance contracts qualify for deferral.

In general, for fixed deferred annuities, commissions and commission-related expenses are the primary acquisition costs, because little or no underwriting of risk is done. However, policy issue expenses that meet the two criteria of *SFAS 60* clearly qualify for deferral, as do all commissions and premium taxes on single-premium contracts.

Of course, the level of acquisition cost deferral may be limited by the recoverability test, described in Section 7.6.2.

7.5.2 Front End Load Considerations

For FPDAs with front-end loads (FEL), paragraph 20 of *SFAS 97* requires that the amount of such loads in excess of any ongoing service load be deferred as unearned revenue. In general, the ongoing service load is expressed as a constant percentage of premiums or as a flat percentage of the policyholder account value over the life of the contract. Front-end loads apply only to FPDAs subject to *SFAS 97* investment contract guidance. Such excess load revenue along with all other sources of contract revenue other than from investment income would have to be insignificant for *SFAS 91* to apply. Thus there is no unearned revenue liability associated with *SFAS 91* deferred annuities.

Note that DAC for deferred annuities subject to *SFAS 97* investment contract guidance amortizes in relation to estimated gross profits (EGP), as defined in Section 7.6 below. Similarly, any unearned revenue liability on *SFAS 97* investment contract business is released in relation to EGP revenue. DAC for deferred annuities subject to *SFAS 91* amortizes under the interest method, as defined in Section 7.7.

7.5.3 Deferred Sales Inducements

SOP 03-1 (in paragraphs 36 and 37) allow for the deferral of certain sales inducements as a deferred charge, much like DAC. Chapter 3, Section 3.11, outlines the criteria for deferral and gives the background underlying the AICPA's thinking in deciding that deferral is appropriate. It also outlines the guidance needed for capitalization and amortization of Deferred Sales Inducements (DSI) and provides an example. Note that amortization rules are very similar to those used for DAC. Also note that certain types of DSI require the accrual of a liability, as discussed in Section 7.4.1 and Chapter 3, Section 3.11. DSI is to be shown separately from DAC on the balance sheet.

7.6 DAC and DSI Amortization Under *SFAS 97*

The revenue defined for universal life-type contracts under *SFAS 97* also applies to investment contracts subject to *SFAS 97*. Thus fixed deferred annuities subject to the guidance of *SFAS 97* for investment contracts also use gross profits as revenue for amortizing DAC and DSI and accruing URL.

7.6.1 Definition of Gross Profits

Paragraph 23 of *SFAS 97* defines gross profits for universal life-type contracts. Such amounts are estimated at contract issuance (hence the term *estimated gross profits* or EGP). Paragraph 23 includes the following items in EGP:

a. Amounts expected to be assessed for mortality less benefit claims in excess of related policyholder balances

b. Amounts expected to be assessed for contract administration less costs incurred for contract administration

c. Amounts expected to be earned from the investment of policyholder balances less interest credited to policyholder balances

d. Amounts expected to be assessed against policyholder balances upon termination of a contract (sometimes referred to as surrender charges)

e. Other expected assessments and credits, however characterized.

These amounts are to represent the company's best estimates measured over the life of a book of contracts exhibiting similar characteristics, without provision for adverse deviation. Note that many companies will limit the period for calculating EGPs to a fixed period of years such as 10, 15, 20, 25, or 30 to avoid having to calculate small amounts with an insignificant effect in the later years for a given book of business. In general, each calendar year of issue is considered separately for this purpose.

For fixed deferred annuities, items b, c, and d are generally the most significant, particularly item c. Item a is generally insignificant or nonexistent unless riders with significant life-contingent benefits are made a part of the contract (the cost of which is charged against the contract holders' account balance each year). Item e includes things like contingent bonus accruals and the change in the additional liability for contracts that provide annuitization benefits.

In defining EGP, it is important to understand what *is* and what *is not* included in the calculation. DAC, DSI and deferred excess FEL are to be excluded, as well as the effect of income taxes. However, other acquisition costs that vary in a constant relationship to premiums or the account value, are recurring in nature, or tend to be incurred in a level amount from period to period should be charged to expense in the period incurred and included in the EGP determination. This includes premium taxes and ultimate level commissions on FPDAs.

Item b consists of contract-related costs that are not primarily related to the acquisition of business (such as contract administration, claim settlement, and maintenance costs) and contract-related acquisition costs that are not capitalized (for example, costs that fail the recoverability test and costs that fail to satisfy one or both criteria for deferral under paragraph 11 of *SFAS 60*). Non-contract-related expenses, however, are to be excluded from b (see paragraph 26 of *Practice Bulletin 8*). These include overhead costs and costs related to the acquisition of business that cannot be deferred, such as certain advertising and marketing costs. Chapter 3 discusses expense allocation procedures that can be used to appropriately allocate expenses for this purpose.

In calculating item c, consideration must be given to both investment return and realized capital gains and losses used in setting the earned rate and the credited rate assumptions underlying future EGP. Chapter 3 includes an example of how the earned rate can be calculated for this purpose. While *SOP 03-1* is silent on the issue, many believe that the earned interest and credited interest components of item c should include returns on assets supporting the account value related to day-one and enhanced interest bonuses and the additional liability for persistency bonuses and the periodic amounts credited thereto. This is believed to be true, even in cases where the bonus is not deferred. In the latter case (no deferral of the inducement), some also believe it is appropriate to include the sales inducement benefits in the EGPs on an incurred basis (i.e. paid plus change in sales inducement liability).

Practice varies regarding the accounting for capital gains and losses. In the answer to question 11 of *Practice Bulletin 8*, the AICPA stated that "Expected gains and losses from sales of investments ... should be included in the determination of EGP because earned investment income should be based on the expected total yield of the investments." Thus, projected realized gains and losses should be considered in estimating the future earned rate. Companies doing so will generally use a total return approach, averaged over all future years.

Further, estimated future investment earnings included in the EGP calculations should reflect expected earnings on new assets when assets previously supporting the line of business are sold. Thus companies making changes to their investment portfolios supporting a given line of business should also consider the potential effect on EGP.

Finally, if policy loans are expected to be a significant element of a product's operation, then the earned and credited interest assumptions of item c should consider the effect of such anticipated loans.

7.6.2 DAC/DSI Amortization Process

DAC and DSI under *SFAS 97* are amortized in proportion to EGP revenue each accounting period, over the period that such revenue is recognized (often limited to a fixed period of years, as noted earlier). Where a period shorter than the entire contract lifetime is used for amortization, the company must be prepared to demonstrate that most of the expected revenue from the business is earned in that shorter period. Section 7.6.3 provides a formulaic demonstration of the amortization process for DAC. DSI amortization would follow the same principles. Section 7.11 gives examples for various types of fixed deferred annuity contracts.

Many companies use a worksheet approach for amortizing DAC and DSI on fixed deferred annuities, combining the deferrable costs and EGP for aggregations of parts of the company's deferred annuity business that exhibit similar overall deferrable cost and gross profit patterns. The worksheets are defined by calendar year of issue. Some companies employ actuarial valuation systems that calculate DAC and DSI at a contract-by-contract (seriatim) level.

The amortization process can be expressed by using either a retrospective or prospective approach. The portion of EGP revenue initially needed for amortization at contract issuance (call it "k_0") equals the present value at issue of all future DAC or DSI divided by the present value of all future EGP.

For *SFAS 97* investment contracts, assumptions are not locked in. Instead, at the end of each accounting period, the EGP for the current accounting period is to be replaced by the company's actual experience for each element of gross profit (sometimes called actual gross profit or AGP). This procedure is called the true-up (or catch-up) process. In addition, the future best-estimate assumptions can be revised, if conditions warrant (i.e., if it is believed that there will be a long-standing or permanent shift in one or more of the elements of gross profits or gross margins). Note that this process can actually cause DAC or DSI to increase from one period to the next, a phenomenon called negative amortization. Such increases are possible, but in no event should the resulting DAC or DSI balance ever exceed the original amount of expense capitalization plus interest at the credited rate.

As a result, the "k_t" factor is revised in each accounting period that changes are made to the current and/or future EGP stream. Note that this recalculation is made as of the *original issue date* of the underlying business, replacing historic EGP with the company's actual experience over time (AGP) and restating future EGP with revised assumptions, as necessary. This has the effect of reflecting a portion of the cumulative amount (since policy issuance) of change in DAC or DSI each year in current period earnings and the rest in future earnings. Note that in calculating the actual investment return each accounting period, realized investment gains and losses incurred in the period are to be included as an element of EGP. Section 7.10 below provides examples of how the "k_t" factor is trued up to reflect actual experience and future assumption changes and the effect on current and future earnings.

If k_0 (summing for both DAC and DSI spreadsheets for common products) equals or exceeds 1 at policy issuance, a recoverability problem exists. (Note most companies will test for recoverability as k_0 approaches unity). In general, the k_0 factors are first recalculated, using the estimated earned rate rather than the estimated credited rate. This helps to confirm that earnings will be available if needed to recover deferred costs and maintain consistency with loss recognition concepts (see Section 7.9). If the recalculated k_0 factors (for DAC and DSI combined) still exceed unity, then the amount of DAC and DSI must be reduced until combined k_0 factors equal 1. Such reduction is reflected as a charge against earnings in the current accounting period. The process for handling recoverability problems is provided by *SFAS 60*.

If the present value of all EGP (after considering deferred FEL) is negative at contract issuance, then no DAC or DSI can be established. However, no additional reserve is required for *SFAS 97* investment contract business to make up any remaining deficiency (see paragraphs 35 and 36 of *Practice Bulletin 8*). Thus it is possible for GAAP losses to occur in all future years for deferred annuities subject to *SFAS 97*.

The actuary maintains some level of discretion when selecting the level at which recoverability analysis is performed. Some perform it at the product or worksheet level and others at a line-of-business level. At a product line of business level, care should be taken in combining products with and without a DSI asset. Seldom are adjustments made at a contract or model point level (e.g., for a given plan/issue age/issue year cell within the model), even by companies that use a seriatim valuation approach. In any event, the actuary should adhere to the general guidance in *SFAS 60*, which states

> Insurance contracts shall be grouped consistent with the enterprise's manner of acquiring, servicing and measuring the profitability of its insurance contracts to determine if a premium deficiency exists. (Paragraph 32)

If there are significant *negative* gross profits expected in one or more periods, "the present value of estimated gross revenues, gross costs or the balance of insurance in force shall be substituted as the base for computing amortization" (paragraph 22 of *SFAS 97*). Many companies encounter non-significant negative gross profits at some point for *SFAS 97* products.

However, over the years, companies have differed in their approaches for handling periods of negative gross profits. Many have set negative gross profits to zero; others have allowed such negatives to be included in the amortization schedule; still others aggregate such business with blocks that have positive gross profits to offset the negatives.

Some practitioners believe that alternative approaches such as those outlined in paragraph 22 of *SFAS 97* can invalidate the underlying consistency of the accounting model. Similarly aggregation techniques can mask profitability problems for the segments with negatives. Whatever method is used, the objective should be to effect an amortization pattern that reasonably reflects the revenue pattern of the underlying block of business and is supported by the overall profitability of the business in relation to the amount of DAC and DSI balances being amortized.

The interest rate used to calculate the "k_t" factor and to amortize DAC and DSI from period to period is either the crediting rate in effect at the inception of the contracts or the actual prior credited rates plus the latest revised rate applied to the remaining EGP period for *SFAS 97* investment contracts. Normally, use of the rate in effect at the inception of the contract causes the least volatility for fixed deferred annuities that invest assets in the company's general investment account. However, the greatest internal consistency will be obtained by combining actual past experience with the current best estimate of future credited rates. Once a definition of the interest rate pattern to be used for discounting EGP is selected, it must be used consistently in all future years. Note that in defining k_t factors, companies will aggregate business segments, such as all similar fixed deferred annuity policies issued in a given fiscal year.

Investment contracts that have both a URL and an additional liability for annuitization benefits create a problem in releasing the URL over time in that the two are interdependent. This interdependence arises because the URL is dependent on EGPs that are dependent on the additional insurance liability, and the additional insurance liability is dependent on assessments that are dependent on the URL. To get over this problem, a company can use an iterative approach similar to the following:

1. Calculate interim EGPs and URLs by first ignoring the additional insurance liability.

2. Deduct the change in interim URLs from collected assessments to get interim incurred assessments. Use these interim assessments to get an interim benefit ratio and an interim stream of additional insurance liabilities.

3. Use the interim stream of additional insurance liabilities to adjust the interim EGP stream calculated in step 1.

4. Use the adjusted EGP stream to adjust the URLs.

Some believe it may be adequate to simply eliminate the additional insurance liability from consideration when defining EGPs for the release of the URL, especially if the change in the additional liability is not that significant relative to other EGP components.

7.6.3 EGP and DAC Formulas

This section provides a general description of how to calculate EGP and the DAC amortization factor and how to apply the amortization procedure for a fixed deferred annuity subject to the *SFAS 97* investment contract accounting model. It is further assumed that all EGP is derived from investment margins, expense margins, and surrender charges and that all commission is expressed as a percentage of premium. Note that while DSI is excluded from this analysis, the same principles apply.

7.6.3.1 Definitions

These terms are used to define EGP and DAC calculations:

t	=	contract year or calendar year
n	=	number of years to end of revenue period
GP_t	=	expected gross premium collected in year t
m	=	number of premium payments per year
C_t	=	deferrable commission rate in year t
i_t	=	credited interest rate applicable in year t
I^E_t/AI^E_t	=	expected/actual interest earned in year t
I^C_t/AI^C_t	=	expected/actual interest credited in year t
E^A_t/AE^A_t	=	expected/actual costs incurred for contract administration in year t
E^C_t/AE^C_t	=	expected/actual contract charges for administration in year t
SC^E_t/SC^A_t	=	expected/actual surrender charges in year t
EGP_t	=	end-of-year value of EGP (revenue) in year t
AGP_t	=	end-of-year value of AGP in year t
DAE_0	=	deferred acquisition expense other than commission at issue date of contract
CAP_t	=	beginning-of-year value of capitalized acquisition costs in contract year t

= $DAE_0 + C_1 \times GP_1 \times (1 + i_1)^{-(m-1)/2m}$, in contract year 1
and
= $C_t \times GP_t \times (1 + i_t)^{-(m-1)/2m}$, in contract years 2 and later

DAC_t = DAC asset at end of policy year t

DAC^{CY}_t = DAC asset at end of calendar year t

k_t = amortization factor applicable to AGP or EGP in year t

7.6.3.2 Formulas

The formula for EGP is:

$$EGP_t = \left(I_t^E - I_t^C\right) + \left(E_t^C - E_t^A\right) + SC_t^E$$

To calculate DAC, an initial k_0 factor can be defined as follows:

k_0 = present value of all CAP_t divided by the present value of all future EGP revenue, at issue

$$= \sum\left[CAP_s / \prod\left(1 + i_p\right)\right] / \sum\left[EGP_s / \prod\left(1 + i_r\right)\right],$$

for $s = 1$ to n; $p = 0$ to $s-1$; and $r = 1$ to s. Note this assumes CAP_s is a beginning of year value and EGP_s is an end-of-year value.

Thereafter, actual experience replaces the estimates for all prior years (t) and future assumptions may be revised. Thus the k_t factor is recalculated each accounting period, measured from the original date of acquisition, as follows:

$$k_t = \sum\left[CAP_s / \prod\left(1 + i_p\right)\right] / \left\{\sum\left[AGP_v / \prod\left(1 + i_v\right)\right] + \sum\left[EGP_w / \prod\left(1 + i_w\right)\right]\right\},$$

for $s = 1$ to n; $p = 0$ to $s-1$; $v = 1$ to t; $w = t + 1$ to n.

The retrospective formula for DAC at the end of any given contract year (t) is as follows:

$$DAC_t = \left(DAC_{t-1} + CAP_t\right) \times \left(1 + i_t\right) - k_t \times AGP_t$$

The above formula can also be stated on a prospective basis as follows:

DAC_t = $k_t \times PV$ of future EGP revenues – PV of future deferrable costs.

To calculate DAC at the end of a calendar year, the following approximation can be used:

$$DAC^{CY}_t = 0.5 \times \left(DAC_{t-1} + DAC_t\right),$$

for the calendar year ending in contract year t. The formulas shown above apply at the amortization schedule level. They can be easily adjusted for the estimated timing of all transactions affecting the calculations. The goal in all cases is to calculate the outstanding DAC balance at the end of an accounting period (generally at the end of a calendar year or quarter).

Many actuaries develop amortization schedules from first principles, using an assumed average issue date and calendar year-based data from projection models that represent the deferred annuity plan's actual in force amounts underlying each amortization schedule. Where such projection models are used, the actuary should validate key model data with actual in-force values. Common data items included in a validation are account value, commissions, policy count, and premium. Others can be used.

7.7 DAC Amortization Under *SFAS 91*

For deferred annuities subject to *SFAS 91*, deferrable costs are to be amortized using the interest method, in accordance with the answer to question 2 of *Practice Bulletin 8*. The interest method "recognizes acquisition and interest costs as expenses at a constant rate applied to net policy liabilities."

As a practical matter, DAC under the interest method is generally defined as the difference between the policy liability, defined in Section 7.4.2 above, and a notional account value, calculated at a solved-for "break-even" interest rate. Calculation of the notional account value uses the same cash flows as for the policy liability. The break-even interest rate is calculated such that the policy liability at contract issuance exceeds the notional account value by the present value of estimated DAC, discounted at the assumed credited rate. All subsequent valuations use a similar approach to derive DAC. A notional account value is calculated using the original break-even interest rate and the remaining DAC becomes the difference between this notional account value and the policy liability at the valuation date.

Thus, for example, on a single premium deferred annuity to mature in 'n' years, with no lapses assumed,

$$PV_t = \text{policy value at the end of year } t$$

$$= PV_n \big/ \prod (1 + i_w); \text{ for } w = t + 1 \text{ to } n$$

Obtain the notional account value (NAV_t), using the same cash flows as those underlying PV_t, by first solving for the 'break-even' interest rate 'j', such that

$$NAV_0 = PV_0 - \sum CAP_s \big/ \prod (1 + i_z), \text{ for } s = 1 \text{ to } n \text{ and } z = 0 \text{ to } s-1.$$

Thereafter

$$NAV_t = (NAV_{t-1} - CAP_t) \times (1 + j_t), \text{ and}$$

$$DAC_t = (PV_t - NAV_t)$$

The interest method is generally used when the policy liability is calculated under the prospective method, as discussed in Section 7.4.2. In practice, contracts with an explicit account value will use a retrospective method, defining the account value as the policy liability. In this case, DAC is amortized in a manner similar to that defined in Section 7.6.2, using EGP defined to represent all future assumed investment spreads only. Over time, the amortization percentage is adjusted as experience (decrement rates, earned investment rate and credited rate) varies from expected, again in a manner consistent with that described in Section 7.6.2.

Investment contracts subject to *SFAS 91* are subject to loss recognition testing of DAC only. Hence no additional liability can be established for anticipated future losses. If the break-even interest rate defined above for the interest method exceeds the company's best estimate of what it expects to earn from the investment of contract holder funds at any time during the contract's lifetime, it may be necessary to write off all or a portion of the remaining DAC. Generally, the result is a break-even rate that does not exceed the best-estimate earned rate. However, if the break-even rate still exceeds the assumed earned rate after completely eliminating the deferrable acquisition costs, no additional reserve is required and losses will occur each year that the earned rate is less than the break-even rate.

Similarly under the retrospective method, if the amortization factor exceeds 1 at policy issuance or at any subsequent true-up date, DAC is reduced such that the amortization factor does not exceed 1. No additional reserve is required if the present value of EGP (or restated EGP, when experience changes) is negative.

The accounting for any product with DSI subject to *SFAS 91* would parallel the discussion above. Note that to date, most fixed deferred annuity products with sales inducements have included surrender charges such that *SFAS 97* for investment contracts applies rather than *SFAS 91*.

7.8 Accrual of Unearned Revenue Liability

Fixed deferred annuity contracts with front-end loads require deferral of all FELs in excess of level renewal service loads. *SFAS 97* paragraph 20 considers FEL to be "amounts assessed that represent compensation to the insurance enterprise for services to be provided in future periods." As such, they are not earned in the period assessed. As stated earlier, FEL are generally associated with deferred annuity contracts subject to the *SFAS 97* investment contract accounting model.

Recognition of the deferrable FEL results in the establishment of an unearned revenue liability (URL). The accrual and release of this liability take place in a manner similar to DAC under *SFAS 97* universal life-type contracts. Excess loads are deferred each accounting period as they are incurred (similar to the manner in which DAC are capitalized) and are released into earnings in proportion to AGP realized each period (again similar to the manner in which DAC is amortized).

A release rate factor is developed, similar to the k factor for DAC. The factor at issue represents the present value of future excess FEL divided by the present value of all future EGP, discounted at the assumed credited rate. The formulas for releasing the URL are similar to those for DAC shown in Section 7.6.3 and therefore are not repeated here. From period to period, the URL release rate factor must be recalculated to reflect the true-up of EGP to actual amounts earned and to reflect changes in future assumptions. In fact, this process is identical for both DAC amortization and URL release purposes. Note that in recoverability and loss recognition testing of DAC and DSI for each accounting period, the URL balance is added to the present value of all future EGP as revenue available to amortize the outstanding DAC and DSI balances.

The example in Table 7-2 (Section 7.11) shows how the URL is accrued and released.

7.9 Selection of Assumptions

The actuary must select appropriate assumptions at the time a fixed deferred annuity contract is issued and periodically thereafter as conditions change, leading to revised future expected gross profits.

At the time of sale and at each valuation date thereafter, assumptions must be made about the future experience of the book of business. For fixed deferred annuities, these include premium and contract persistency (for the book of business), maintenance expenses, future investment earnings, and the future crediting strategy. Mortality assumptions are also made but have little effect during the accumulation phase of a fixed deferred annuity contract. Assumptions must also be made about any product features that could affect EGP, for example, if partial withdrawals are permitted with no or reduced surrender penalty.

SFAS 97 states that each element of those assumptions "shall be determined based on the best estimate of that individual element over the life of the book of contracts without provision for adverse deviation." (paragraph 23) At contract issuance, pricing assumptions are often used as the best-estimate assumptions, removing any provisions for adverse deviation. The initial assumptions may also be influenced by recent company experience for similar in-force business. Subsequently, the experience of the block of business and general market conditions influence future best-estimate assumptions.

Because of the policyholder's ability to vary premium payments on FPDA, historic patterns should be reviewed and used as a guide for the future. Economic trends that influence investment returns in the marketplace may also influence premium payment and persistency patterns.

Chapter 3 addresses the needs, sources, and rationale for expense assumption selection. Refer to that chapter for instruction on expense selection and applications. Two of the most important assumptions for fixed deferred annuities are the assumed earned and credited interest rates. Estimates of the earned rate should take into account the company's investment strategy for the line of business, asset type and quality, asset duration, liquidity, and disintermediation risk. In addition, a provision should be made for default cost, by quality rating. The assumed rate will also be influenced by the company's reading of the factors that will have an effect on the current and future investment marketplace.

A company's interest crediting strategy can change over time and is strongly influenced by competition and the desire to maintain profitable spread from earned investment returns. A company actively selling new fixed deferred annuity business must be able to demonstrate competitive historic interest crediting rates to attract and retain business. Conversely, for a block of business in a runoff status, the motivation may be to try to maximize profits by increasing the spread. Prospective assumptions should reflect these expectations.

In some states, fixed deferred annuity premiums are subject to premium taxes. Where applicable, premium taxes are generally considered with other ongoing maintenance expenses and are an element in the EGP calculation.

Benefit reserves, DAC and the DSI asset are calculated gross of FIT (federal income tax); thus no tax assumption is required.

7.10 Loss Recognition Tests

Section 7.6.2 described the process for testing recoverability of DAC and the DSI asset in the year that *SFAS 97* fixed deferred annuity contracts are issued. As time passes and conditions change, experience will vary from the original assumptions underlying the EGP projections at issue. In fact, as Section 7.6.2 indicates, at each subsequent reporting date the EGP for the period just ended must be replaced by the AGP for the period. Similarly, future assumptions should be revised if it is believed that conditions affecting future EGP amounts (such as a change in interest rate environment) have changed significantly and such change is expected to be long lasting or permanent. This in turn affects the future gross profit estimates.

Adverse experience over a period of time reduces the AGP from expected levels and can lead to future assumption changes such that the recoverability of remaining DAC and DSI balances may be in doubt. This is confirmed in *Practice Bulletin 8*, which states

> 33. Question 14: Should DPAC related to investment contracts defined under FASB Statement No. 97 be written off if it is determined that the amount at which the asset is stated is probably not recoverable?
>
> 34. Answer 14: Yes. As stated in paragraph 87 in FASB Statement of Concepts No. 5, Recognition and Measurement in Financial Statements of Business Enterprises, "[a]n expense or loss is recognized if it becomes evident that previously recognized future economic benefits of an asset have been reduced or eliminated, or that a liability has been incurred or increased, without associated economic benefits." The DPAC asset should be reduced to the level that can be recovered. Further guidance is provided in paragraphs 35 and 36 of this practice bulletin.

Therefore, it is necessary to conduct periodic tests of recoverability.

The tests are relatively easy to perform, once current-period AGP and future assumption changes are determined. As stated in Section 7.6.2, the amortization factors (k_t) for DAC and DSI are recalculated each accounting period. If their sum increases and approaches 1, the indication is that may be inadequate future revenues to amortize the remaining DAC and DSI balances over the remaining period of amortization. In such case, the current DAC and DSI balances are reduced to cause the combined k_t factors to reach 1. This additional write-off of the DAC and DSI assets are charged to the current period's earnings. In conducting the test, some companies consider all future cash flows underlying EGP determination, even those beyond the remaining DAC and DSI amortization periods selected by the company.

Often a relatively small change in an assumption can have a large effect on future EGP. If the company overreacts to a negative trend in experience, the effect can be a large hit to earnings in the period of change. Accordingly, care must be taken in carefully evaluating experience variations and making assumption changes.

If the outstanding DAC and DSI asset balances are totally eliminated before the combined amortization factors reaches 1, no additional action is required under *SFAS 97* for investment contracts. This is in accordance with *Practice Bulletin 8*, which states

> 35. Question 15: Should the provisions of FASB Statement No. 60 concerning loss recognition (premium deficiency), by which an additional liability is established for anticipated losses on contracts, apply to investment contracts defined in FASB Statement No. 97?
>
> 36. Answer 15: No. Such loss recognition, as described in paragraph 34 above, is not permitted for investment contracts under FASB Statement No. 97.

Thus *SFAS 97* investment contracts never require a deficiency reserve. If future experience improves, thus increasing AGP and leading to more favorable future assumptions, the company cannot reinstate the DAC and DSI assets previously written off as a result of loss recognition testing.

Section 7.7 stated that fixed deferred annuity contracts that are subject to *SFAS 91* require no loss recognition testing at all. This is in accordance with *SFAS 91* guidance.

7.11 Examples

This section demonstrates the process of capitalizing and amortizing DAC and URL for a fixed deferred annuity contract. Note that the process for a DSI asset would be similar to that for DAC. A DSI example is given in Chapter 3, Section 3.11.4.

Tables 7-1 through 7-4 demonstrate the process for a 10-year single-premium deferred annuity that is subject to *SFAS 97* for investment contracts. The product has a 3% of premium front-end load, a surrender charge pattern of 5%, 5%, 4%, 3%, 1%, and 0 thereafter. At policy issuance, the assumed earned rate is 8% (after deduction of investment expenses) and the assumed credited rate is 6.5% in all years. The gross single premium is $100,000 with a commission rate of 7.5% and other DAC of $500. Maintenance expenses are $50 per policy, inflating at 3% per year. It is assumed that the company selects the credited rate at policy issuance as the DAC and URL discount rate. The surrender rate is assumed to be 8% in all years, with all remaining policies maturing for the cash value at the end of the 10-year period.

Table 7-1 provides the product's cash flows and estimated gross profits at the time the policy was issued. Table 7-2 develops the DAC and URL amortization schedules for all years, also at policy issuance. Also shown are the projected pre-tax GAAP profits for the policy.

Table 7-1
Cash Flows and EGP for a 10-Year Single-Premium Annuity

	Year									
	1	2	3	4	5	6	7	8	9	10
Cash Flows										
Premium	100,000									
Investment income	7,358	7,315	7,281	7,250	7,224	7,195	7,171	7,157	7,154	7,162
Commission	7,500									
Initial expenses	500									
Maintenance expense	50	47	45	43	40	38	36	34	33	31
Surrender benefits	7,851	7,693	7,617	7,540	7,540	7,463	7,312	7,164	7,020	6,878
Maturity benefits										79,094
Net cash flow	91,457	(425)	(381)	(333)	(357)	(306)	(177)	(42)	102	(78,841)
Earned rate	8.00%	8.00%	8.00%	8.00%	8.00%	8.00%	8.00%	8.00%	8.00%	8.00%
Credited rate	6.50%	6.50%	6.50%	6.50%	6.50%	6.50%	6.50%	6.50%	6.50%	6.50%
Surrender rate	8.0%	8.0%	8.0%	8.0%	8.0%	8.0%	8.0%	8.0%	8.0%	8.0%
Surrender charge	5.0%	5.0%	4.0%	3.0%	1.0%	0.0%	0.0%	0.0%	0.0%	0.0%
Front-end load	3,000									
Estimated Gross Profits										
(a) Earned interest on account balance	7,760	7,603	7,450	7,299	7,152	7,007	6,866	6,727	6,591	6,458
(b) Credited interest on account balance	6,305	6,178	6,053	5,931	5,811	5,693	5,578	5,466	5,355	5,247
(c) Investment spread	1,455	1,426	1,397	1,369	1,341	1,314	1,287	1,261	1,236	1,211
(d) Surrender charges	413	405	317	233	76	0	0	0	0	0
(e) Maintenance expenses	50	47	45	43	40	38	36	34	33	31
(f) Total EGP	1,818	1,783	1,669	1,559	1,377	1,276	1,251	1,227	1,203	1,180

Other Assumptions
Surrender rates include mortality.
All decrements occur at the end of the year.
Maintenance expenses occur in middle of year.
Item (a) is the assumed earned rate times the beginning-of-year account balance.
Item (b) is the assumed credited rate times the beginning-of-year account balance.
Item (d) is the end-of-year account balance times the surrender rate for the year times (1 minus the surrender charge percentage).
Item (f) is the investment spread plus surrender charges less maintenance expenses.

Table 7-2
DAC and URL Amortization (at Issue) for a 10-Year Single-Premium Annuity

	Year										
	0	**1**	**2**	**3**	**4**	**5**	**6**	**7**	**8**	**9**	**10**
(a) Estimated gross profits		1,818	1,783	1,669	1,559	1,377	1,276	1,251	1,227	1,203	1,180
(b) Present value of EGP	10,610										
(c) Deferrable expenses	8,000										
(d) DAC amortization percent	75.4%										
(e) Front-end load	3,000										
(f) URL amortization percent	28.3%										
(g) Interest on DAC		520	465	408	352	299	251	204	156	106	54
(h) DAC amortization		1,371	1,344	1,259	1,176	1,038	962	943	925	907	890
(i) DAC at EOY		7,149	6,269	5,418	4,595	3,855	3,144	2,405	1,636	835	0
(j) Interest on URL		195	174	153	132	112	94	77	59	40	20
(k) Release of URL in year		514	504	472	441	389	361	354	347	340	334
(l) URL at EOY		2,681	2,351	2,032	1,723	1,446	1,179	902	614	313	0
(m) GAAP reserve (account balance)		95,041	93,121	91,240	89,397	87,591	85,822	84,088	82,389	80,725	-
Pre-tax Shareholder Profit											
(o) Net cash flow in year		91,457	(425)	(381)	(333)	(357)	(306)	(177)	(42)	102	(78,841)
(p) Increase in DAC		7,149	(880)	(851)	(823)	(739)	(711)	(739)	(769)	(801)	(835)
(q) Increase in URL		2,681	(330)	(319)	(309)	(277)	(267)	(277)	(288)	(300)	(313)
(r) Increase in reserve		95,041	(1,920)	(1,881)	(1,843)	(1,806)	(1,769)	(1,734)	(1,699)	(1,664)	(80,725)
(s) Shareholder profit (pre-tax)		884	945	968	996	987	1,019	1,095	1,176	1,265	1,362

Legend:

Estimated gross profits, deferrable expense, front-end load, and net cash flows [items (a), (e), and (o)] are from Table 7-1.

Item (b) is the present value at the credited rate of all assumed EGP, measured from policy issuance.

Item (c) is the sum of deferrable commissions and initial expenses, from Table 7-1.

Items (d) and (f) represent the ratio of items (c) and (e) to item (b).

Items (g) and (j) are the credited interest rate times the beginning-of-year DAC balance (deferrable expense in the first year) and beginning-of-year URL balance (FEL in the first year), respectively.

Items (h) and (k) represent the EGP in the year times items (d) and (f), respectively.

Items (i) and (l) are the beginning-of year DAC and URL balances plus interest [items (g) and (j)] less amortization [items (h) and (k)], respectively.

Item (m) is the end-of-year account balance, accrued at the credited rate.

Item (o) comes from Table 7-1.

Items (p), (q) and (r) represent the change in items (i), (l) and (m) during the year.

Item (s) is item (o) plus item (p) less items (q) and (r).

Table 7-3 assumes that in the first two policy years, experience exactly equals the assumptions but in the third year, interest rates drop by 150 basis points (portfolio rate effect). However, the company decides to *not* drop the credited rate in the year, because it wishes to retain its policyholders and it believes earned rates will return to 8% in the future. In addition, surrenders in the year drop to 5%. This table demonstrates the effect of truing up the amortization schedules for both DAC and URL as a result of experience changes. Note the significant effect on profits in the third year.

Table 7-3
DAC and URL Amortization (Gross Profit Change in Year 3) for a 10-Year Single-Premium Annuity With No Change in Future Assumptions

	Year										
	0	**1**	**2**	**3**	**4**	**5**	**6**	**7**	**8**	**9**	**10**
(a) Estimated gross profits		2,074	1,783	153	1,610	1,422	1,317	1,292	1,267	1,243	1,219
(b) Present value of EGP	9,789										
(c) Deferrable expenses	8,000										
(d) DAC amortization percentage	81.7%										
(e) Front-end load	3,000										
(f) URL amortization percentage	30.6%										
(g) Interest on DAC		520	465	408	394	334	280	229	175	119	61
(h) DAC amortization		1,371	1,344	125	1,316	1,162	1,076	1,056	1,035	1,015	996
(I) True up in DAC balance in year				(487)							
(j) DAC at EOY		7,149	6,269	6,064	5,142	4,315	3,519	2,692	1,831	935	-
(k) Interest on URL		195	174	153	148	125	105	86	66	45	23
(l) Release of URL in year		514	504	47	493	436	404	396	388	381	373
(m) True up of URL balance in year				(183)							
(n) URL at EOY		2,681	2,351	2,274	1,928	1,618	1,320	1,009	687	351	-
(o) GAAP reserve (account balance)		95,041	93,121	94,215	92,312	90,447	88,620	86,830	85,076	83,357	-
Pre-tax Shareholder Profit											
(p) Net cash flow in year		91,457	(425)	1,110	(461)	(495)	(452)	(331)	(202)	(67)	(81,598)
(q) Increase in DAC		7,149	(880)	(205)	(922)	(828)	(796)	(827)	(860)	(896)	(935)
(r) Increase in URL		2,681	(330)	(77)	(346)	(310)	(299)	(310)	(323)	(336)	(351)
(s) Increase in reserve		95,041	(1,920)	1,094	(1,903)	(1,865)	(1,827)	(1,790)	(1,754)	(1,719)	(83,357)
(t) Shareholder profit (pre-tax)		884	945	(112)	866	852	877	943	1,014	1,091	1,175

Legend:
Total earned interest in year drops 150 basis points.
Company decides to not reduce the credited rate on assumption interest rates will return to 8%.
Surrender rate drops to 5% in year 3. Company assumes the rate returns to 8% in all remaining contract years.
Company decides to not change any other future assumptions from original schedule.
Discount rate for amortization left at the credited rate assumed at policy issuance.
See Table 7-2 for general description of key line items.
Items (a) and (b) reflect change in third year due to interest rate drop.
Items (d) and (f) are recalculated using the revised item (b), measured from original issue.
Items (g), (h), (k) and (l) all reflect the effect of the change in the earned interest rate in the third year. The effect of the change in the third year is shown in items (i) and (m).
Note the interest rate change does not affect the reserve because there was no change in the assumed credited rate.
Item (p) remains the same as in Table 7-1 for the first three years but reflects the subsequent changes in the earned rate and surrender rate noted above.
Items (q), (r) and (s) represent the change in items (j), (n) and (o) during the year.
Item (t) is item (p) plus item (q) less items (r) and (s).

Table 7-4 has the same fact situation as Table 7-3 except it is assumed that the company decides that the interest rate drop will be permanent or long-standing and accordingly it changes its future assumptions, in addition to truing up the third year gross profit to actual. The company decides to assume that only 6.5% will be earned in all future years (a drop of 1.5%) and that the credited rate will be dropped by 1.25% in all future years. Note the additional negative effect on fourth and subsequent year expected profits.

Table 7-4
DAC and URL Amortization (Gross Profit Change in Year 3)for a 10-Year Single-Premium Annuity When Future Assumptions Are Changed

	Year										
	0	1	2	3	4	5	6	7	8	9	10
(a) Estimated gross profits		2,074	1,783	153	1,372	1,176	1,065	1,032	1,000	969	939
(b) Present value of EGP	8,618										
(c) Deferrable expenses	8,000										
(d) DAC amortization percentage	92.8%										
(e) Front-end load	3,000										
(f) URL amortization percentage	34.8%										
(g) Interest on DAC		520	465	408	362	303	252	204	155	105	53
(h) DAC amortization		1,371	1,344	142	1,273	1,091	988	958	928	899	872
(I) True up in DAC balance in year				(959)							
(j) DAC at EOY		7,149	6,269	5,575	4,664	3,876	3,140	2,386	1,613	818	0
(k) Interest on URL		195	174	153	136	114	94	77	58	39	20
(l) Release of URL in year		514	504	53	477	409	371	359	348	337	327
(m) True up of URL balance in year				(360)							
(n) URL at EOY		2,681	2,351	2,091	1,749	1,454	1,177	895	605	307	0
(o) GAAP reserve (account balance)		95,041	93,121	94,215	91,228	88,336	85,536	82,825	80,199	77,657	-
Pre-tax sSareholder Profit											
(p) Net cash flow in year		91,457	(425)	1,110	(1,751)	(1,772)	(1,718)	(1,592)	(1,465)	(1,338)	(76,404)
(q) Increase in DAC		7,149	(880)	(694)	(911)	(788)	(736)	(754)	(773)	(795)	(818)
(r) Increase in URL		2,681	(330)	(260)	(342)	(296)	(276)	(283)	(290)	(298)	(307)
(s) Increase in reserve		95,041	(1,920)	1,094	(2,987)	(2,892)	(2,800)	(2,711)	(2,626)	(2,542)	(77,657)
(t) Shareholder profit (pre-tax)		884	945	(418)	666	627	622	648	677	708	742

Legend:
Interest rate drops 150 basis points in 3rd year. Decision is to change future earned rate assumption to 6.5% (4th year and later).
Company decides not to change credited rate in year 3 but drops future credited rate assumption by 125 basis points.
Surrenders drop to 5% in year 3. Returns to the original assumption of 8% thereafter.
Discount rate for amortization left at the credited rate assumed at policy issuance.
See Tables 7-2 and 7-3 for item descriptions. Note the decision to revise the future credited interest rate changes all future EGP from the original estimate.
This results in revised items (b), (d) and (f) and revised items (g) through (n) and (p) through (t) from the third year on.
Item (o), the reserve, changes from the fourth year on. The third year value remains unchanged because the credited rate is not changed until the fourth year.

Chapter 14 discusses required balance sheet adjustments to reflect the effect of unrealized gains or losses on certain marketable securities (shadow adjustments). The examples in Tables 7-3 and 7-4 ignore the shadow adjustments to DAC that would result when interest rates drop.

Table 7-5 demonstrates the process for a 10-year single premium deferred annuity subject to *SFAS 91*. The product has no front-end load and has surrender charges. The premium is $100,000 and the commission rate is 5.5%, with $500 of other DAC. The surrender charge grades from 4% to 0 after 4 years. The surrender rate is 10% in all years. Maintenance expense is $25 per policy inflating at 3% a year. The earned and credited rates are assumed to be 8% and 6.5%, respectively, in all future years. The break-even interest rate, the rate that causes the present value of all future cash flows (including policy maintenance costs but not overhead expense) to exactly break even to the company's cash position at policy issuance, is determined to be 7.4016%. Note that DAC is the difference between the account balance and the present value of future cash flows, using the break-even discount rate in all years.

Table 7-5
Example of a 10-Year Single-Premium Annuity Subject to *SFAS 91*

	Year									
	1	2	3	4	5	6	7	8	9	10
Cash Flows										
(a) Premium	100,000	0	0	0	0	0	0	0	0	0
(b) Investment income	7,520	7,256	6,999	6,747	6,501	6,261	6,033	5,817	5,612	5,419
(c) Commission	5,500	0	0	0	0	0	0	0	0	0
(d) Initial expenses	500									
(e) Maintenance expense	25	23	21	20	18	17	16	15	14	13
(f) Surrender benefits	10,224	9,902	9,589	9,285	8,989	8,616	8,259	7,916	7,587	7,272
(g) Maturity benefits	0	0	0	0	0	0	0	0	0	65,452
(h) Net cash flow	91,271	-2,669	-2,611	-2,558	-2,506	-2,372	-2,241	-2,114	-1,989	-67,318
Present Values (EOY)										
(I) Maintenance expense	115	101	87	74	61	49	37	24	12	0
(j) Benefits	90,525	87,324	84,198	81,146	78,163	75,332	72,649	70,110	67,712	0
(k) Net GAAP reserve*	90,640	87,425	84,286	81,220	78,224	75,381	72,686	70,135	67,724	0
* Calculated at the break-even rate of	7.4016%									
DAC Asset										
(l) Benefit reserve (account balance)	95,850	91,872	88,060	84,405	80,902	77,545	74,327	71,242	68,286	0
(m) Net GAAP reserve	90,640	87,425	84,286	81,220	78,224	75,381	72,686	70,135	67,724	0
(n) DAC (EOY)	5,210	4,448	3,774	3,185	2,678	2,164	1,641	1,107	561	0
(o) Increase in DAC asset	5,210	(762)	(674)	(588)	(507)	(514)	(523)	(534)	(546)	(561)
(p) Increase in benefit reserve	95,850	(3,978)	(3,813)	(3,654)	(3,503)	(3,357)	(3,218)	(3,085)	(2,957)	(68,286)
(q) Shareholder profit (pre-tax)	631	547	528	509	490	471	454	437	421	406

Legend:

(a) Single premium in year.
(b) Earned interest in year on assets equal to beginning-of-year assets plus cash flow in the year.
(f), (g) Surrender benefits are paid at the end of the year and equal 10% of the end-of-year account balance. All remaining contracts mature at the end of the tenth year for the tenth year account balance.
(i), (j) Items (i) and (j) represent the present value, at the break-even interest rate, of all future maintenance expenses and benefits, respectively.
(k) The net GAAP reserve is equal to the present value of future benefits and maintenance expenses.
(l) The benefit reserve is the account balance.
(n) The DAC asset is the difference between the account balance and the net GAAP reserve in all years.

Note that the decision to use *SFAS 91* is based upon a test that compares the present value of surrender charge revenue with the present value of total estimated gross profits, defined in the normal sense under *SFAS 97* and using the assumed crediting rate as the discount rate. In the example, this relationship was 9.5% and it was assumed that 'significance' (of revenue sources other than from investment return, see section 7.3) is defined by a 10% criterion. If a lower criterion for significance was used (say 5%), *SFAS 97* for investment contracts would be used.

7.12 Presentation of Results

The income statement presentation format for deferred annuities subject to *SFAS 97* for investment contracts and *SFAS 91* differs considerably from that used for U.S. statutory and *SFAS 60* reporting. It is generally believed that investment contracts should be reported in a format similar to that prescribed for *SFAS 97* universal life-type contracts (see Paragraphs 19–21).

Under U.S. statutory accounting and *SFAS 60*, premiums and investment income are reported as the primary elements of revenue; benefit payments and reserve changes are major components of expense. By contrast, premiums collected cannot be reported as revenue for *SFAS 97* universal life-type contracts. *SFAS 97* revenue comprises mainly investment income, amounts assessed against contract holders (typically investment management, expense, mortality and surrender charges), and deferred revenues earned in the period from the periodic release of any URL. As noted earlier, fixed deferred annuities seldom have significant COI charges so the primary revenue sources are investment income, surrender charges, expense charges, and earned deferred revenues.

Amounts assessed against contract holders that represent compensation to the insurance company for services to be provided in the future (for example, FEL) are not considered revenue in the period assessed. Instead they are accrued as a liability (the URL) and released proportionately into income as gross profits resulting from the business are earned.

Fixed deferred annuity expenses include benefit claims in excess of the account values for terminating contracts (by death or surrender), expenses of contract administration, interest credited to contract holder account values, the amortization of DAC, and the accrual of additional liabilities for persistency bonus features and annuitization benefits. Thus the increases in the contract holder's account value and the URL are not shown as expenses. Disclosure of select data in the financial statements is required for additional insurance benefits, annuitization benefits and other minimum guarantees, by type of benefit.

Table 7-6 compares key income statement items for an illustrative deferred annuity line of business under both *SFAS 60* and *SFAS 97* universal life-type contract formats. Note that the format for *SFAS 60* is merely illustrative, as the *SFAS 97* format would generally apply. "Claim costs" in the table comprises death benefits in excess of the account value released on death plus other insurance and annuitization benefits incurred in the accounting period. It is assumed that item 13 relates only to policy-related expenses.

Primary differences in formats relate to premiums, surrender benefits, reserve increases, and credited interest. Death benefits under *SFAS 97* are reduced by the account value released on death and are shown under "claim costs" under the *SFAS 97* format. Surrender benefits are not included under the *SFAS 97* format because they equal the amount of account value released on surrender, less the surrender charges specified under the contract, which are part of the earned contract charges in item 3. *SFAS 97* shows contract charges, deferred revenues earned in the period, and investment income as items of revenue. Interest credited to the account value in the year, accrued bonus expense, and DAC amortization are key items of expense. Commissions and other expenses are reduced by the amount of acquisition cost capitalization in the year.

Table 7-6
Comparative Income Statement Formats

Income Statement Item	*SFAS 60*	Reserve Calculation	Reclassification	*SFAS 97*
1. Premium income	150,000	(150,000)		
2. Investment income	67,500			67,500
3. Earned contract charges		7,500	9,500	17,000
4. Earned deferred revenues			3,200	3,200
5. Total revenue	217,500	(142,500)	12,700	87,700
6. Death Benefits	400	(300)	(100)	
7. Claim Costs			100	100
8. Surrender benefits	65,000	(74,500)	9,500	
9. Interest credited on account		50,600		50,600
10. Increase in reserves	118,300	(118,300)		
11. Accrued bonus expense			3,200	3,200
12. Commissions	200			200
13. Other general and administrative expenses	6,000			6,000
14. DAC and DSI amortization	199,400			9,400
15. Total benefits and expenses	199,300	(142,500)	12,700	69,500
16. Pretax income	18,200			18,200
17. Current taxes	4,200			4,200
18. Deferred tax expense	2,170			2,170
19. After-tax income	11,830			11,830

7.13 Special Accounting Considerations for Market-Value-Adjusted Annuities

7.13.1 Product Description

As stated in Section 7.2 above, market-value-adjusted-annuities allow companies to guarantee a competitive crediting rate of interest for a period of years (typically 3 to 10) in exchange for an additional surrender penalty, should interest rates rise during the guaranteed period. The theory is that to be able to offer a competitive rate, the company should invest in securities with a maturity structure that resembles the guarantee period. Further, the company should charge market value losses to customers who surrender their contracts prior to the end of the guarantee period. Over time, as surrender benefits are paid, assets will have to be sold at a gain or loss, depending on the level of interest rates at surrender.

The market value adjustment (MVA), defined by formula in the contract, is designed to cover realized capital losses (gains) when surrenders occur in periods when interest rates are higher (lower) than when the contract was issued. The formula generally bases the charge on one of two methods. One method is based on a comparison of the guaranteed rate at issue to the guaranteed rate applied to new contracts with a guarantee period equal to the time to the end of the guaranteed period. The other method is based on a comparison of a Treasury rate at issue to a Treasury rate for a time period until the end of the guaranteed period. The charge is intended to discourage additional surrenders during such period if interest rates have increased and to recover the company's realized capital losses on those surrenders that do take place. In some cases, the MVA charge is floored at zero, allowing the company to take into income all realized capital gains. However, most companies allow a partial payback of such gains to the contract holder.

7.13.2 Accounting Issues

Accounting issues relate to when and how such MVA adjustments and realized gains and losses should be included in the determination of EGP and what discount rate should be used when interest rates change. In defining EGP revenue at contract issuance, most companies do not anticipate future MVA adjustments and future realized gains and losses. In general, the credited rate is set equal to the guaranteed rate and the earned rate is set equal, for the duration of the guaranteed period, to the earned rate on the underlying assets at issue.

When interest rates rise such that the crediting rate on new business also increases and the MVA adjustment formula yields a positive charge, the company must decide whether to change future assumptions accordingly. Clearly the AGP calculation for the current period would reflect any MVA charges made and realized losses incurred. If interest rates are expected to continue at the higher level for the duration of the guaranteed period, then the future assumptions should reflect both the future expected MVA charges and realized capital losses on future surrenders.

The second issue relates to which interest rate to use in discounting future EGP when recalculating the DAC amortization factor each accounting period. In paragraph 25, *SFAS 97* outlines two possible approaches, "the [crediting] rate in effect at the inception of the book of contracts or the latest revised rate applied to the remaining benefit period." The logical choice would be the initial rate because it applies to the book of contracts for the entire guaranteed period.

7.13.3 Example

Tables 7-7 and 7-8 demonstrate a $100,000 10-year single premium market-value-adjusted annuity, for which the guaranteed crediting rate is a level 6% in all years and the earned rate is assumed to be 7.5%. The total decrement rate each year (including surrenders and mortality) is assumed to be 4.5%, with the contract maturing for its cash value at the end of the tenth year. Surrender charges apply, starting with 9% in the first year and grading down uniformly to 0 in the tenth year. The company has selected the initial crediting rate for discounting EGP and amortizing DAC for the entire contract period. Other assumptions are given in the example, including the MVA adjustment formula. Two illustrations are presented:

1. At policy inception, where it is assumed that the future interest rate environment will not change and no MVA charges or realized gains or losses will be incurred (Table 7-7).

2. Interest rates rise in the fifth year by 1.00% (Table 7-8). It is assumed that the company increases the crediting rate on new issues by 1.00%, and that the rates remain at the increased level for the duration of the contract guaranteed period.

Table 7-7
Example of a $100,000 Single-Premium Market-Value-Adjusted Annuity at the Inception of the Contract

(1)	(2)	(3)	(4)	(5)	(6)	(7)	(8)	(9)	(10)	(11)	(12)	(13)	(14)
						Estimated Gross Profits							
Duration	BOY Account Balance	Credited Interest	Earned Interest	AB Released on Surrender and Maturity	EOY Account Balance	Interest Spread	Surrender Charges	MVA Charges	Maintenance Expenses	Total	Interest on DAC	DAC Amortization	EOY DAC
1	100,000	6,000	7,500	4,770	101,230	1,500	429	-	100	1,829	300	724	4,576
2	101,230	6,074	7,592	4,829	102,475	1,518	386	-	101	1,804	275	714	4,136
3	102,475	6,149	7,686	4,888	103,736	1,537	342	-	102	1,777	248	703	3,681
4	103,736	6,224	7,780	4,948	105,012	1,556	297	-	104	1,749	221	692	3,210
5	105,012	6,301	7,876	5,009	106,303	1,575	250	-	105	1,721	193	681	2,721
6	106,303	6,378	7,973	5,071	107,611	1,595	203	-	106	1,691	163	669	2,215
7	107,611	6,457	8,071	5,133	108,934	1,614	154	-	108	1,661	133	657	1,690
8	108,934	6,536	8,170	5,196	110,274	1,634	104	-	109	1,629	101	645	1,147
9	110,274	6,616	8,271	5,260	111,631	1,654	53	-	110	1,596	69	632	584
10	111,631	6,698	8,372	118,328	-	1,674	-	-	112	1,563	35	619	(0)

(a) Present value of EGP at inception, 12,630
(b) Deferrable commission at 5%, 5,000
(c) Amortization factor (= b/a), 39.59%
(d) Earned rate, 7.5%
(e) Credited rate, 6.0%
(f) Lapse rate in all years, 4.50%
(g) All decrements occur at the end of the year.
(h) Maintenance expense(percent of the BOY account balance), 0.1%
(i) MVA charge: Max{0, number of years remaining × (i–ii)},
where i = annual effective credited interest rate for new contributions at time of withdrawal
ii = annual effective credited interest rate in effect for account balance being withdrawn

(15)	(16)	(17)	(18)	(19)	(20)	(21)	(22)	(23)	(24)	(25)
Pre-tax Income Statement										Inv. Assets
Duration	Premium	Investment Income	Capital G/L	Surrenders and Maturities	Change in Reserve	Commission	Maintenance Expense	Change in DAC	Pre-tax Income	Prior to Surrenders
1	100,000	7,118	-	4,341	101,230	5,000	100	4,576	1,023	94,900
2	-	7,318	-	4,442	1,245	-	101	(439)	1,090	97,576
3	-	7,526	-	4,546	1,260	-	102	(455)	1,162	100,349
4	-	7,742	-	4,651	1,276	-	104	(472)	1,239	103,225
5	-	7,966	-	4,759	1,292	-	105	(489)	1,322	106,211
6	-	8,198	-	4,868	1,308	-	106	(506)	1,411	109,312
7	-	8,440	-	4,979	1,324	-	108	(524)	1,505	112,535
8	-	8,692	-	5,092	1,340	-	109	(543)	1,607	115,887
9	-	8,953	-	5,207	1,356	-	110	(563)	1,716	119,376
10	-	9,226	-	118,328	(111,631)	-	112	(584)	1,833	123,010

Legend:
(17) = d × (25).
(20) represents the change in column (6).
(24) = (16) + (17) – (18) – (19) – (20) – (21) – (22) + (23)
(25) = (16) – (21) – (22) in the first year.
= [(25) + (17) + (18) – (19)] for the prior year, plus [(16) – (21) – (22)] for the current year, in years 2 on.

Table 7-8

Unanticipated Increase in Interest Environment in Fifth Duration for a $100,000 Single-Premium Market-Value-Adjusted Annuity

(1)	(2)	(3)	(4)	(5)	(6)	(7)	(8)	(9)	(10)	(11)	(12)	(13)	(14)	(15)	(16)	(17)
								Estimated Gross Profits								
Duration	BOY Account Balance	Credited Interest	Earned Interest	AB Released on Surrender and Maturity	EOY Account Balance	MVA Charge %	Realized Capital G/L	Interest Spread	Surrender Charges	MVA Charges	Maintenance Expenses	Total	Interest on DAC	DAC Amortization	Unlocking Effect	EOY DAC
1	100,000	6,000	7,500	4,770	101,230	0.00%	-	1,500	429	-	100	1,829	300	724		4,576
2	101,230	6,074	7,592	4,829	102,475	0.00%	-	1,518	386	-	101	1,804	275	714		4,136
3	102,475	6,149	7,686	4,888	103,736	0.00%	-	1,537	342	-	102	1,777	248	703		3,681
4	103,736	6,224	7,780	4,948	105,012	0.00%	-	1,556	297	-	104	1,749	221	692		3,210
5	105,012	6,301	7,876	5,009	106,303	5.00%	(185)	1,390	250	250	105	1,786	193	701	29	2,730
6	106,303	6,378	7,973	5,071	107,611	4.00%	(158)	1,437	203	203	106	1,736	164	681	0	2,212
7	107,611	6,457	8,071	5,133	108,934	3.00%	(126)	1,488	154	154	108	1,688	133	662	0	1,682
8	108,934	6,536	8,170	5,196	110,274	2.00%	(90)	1,544	104	104	109	1,643	101	645	0	1,139
9	110,274	6,616	8,271	5,260	111,631	1.00%	(48)	1,606	53	53	110	1,601	68	628	0	579
10	111,631	6,698	8,372	118,328	-	0.00%	-	1,674	-	-	112	1,563	35	613	0	(0)

(a) Present value of EGP at inception, 12,741
(b) Deferrable commission at 5%, 5,000
(c) Amortization factor (= b/a), 39.24%
(d) Earned rate, 7.5% New money rate goes up to 8.5% for years 5-10.
(e) Credited rate, 6.0% Credited rate on new policies goes up to 7% in years 5-10.
(f) Lapse rate in all years, 4.5%
(g) All decrements occur at the end of the year.
(h) Maintenance expense(percent of the BOY account balance), 0.1%
(i) MVA charge: Max{0, number of years remaining × (i–ii)], where
i = annual effective credited interest rate for new contributions at time of withdrawal
ii = annual effective credited interest rate in effect for account balance being withdrawn

Pre-tax Income Statement										Inv. Assets	Capital Gains and Losses					
(18)	(19)	(20)	(21)	(22)	(23)	(24)	(25)	(26)	(27)	(28)	(29)	(30)	(31)	(32)	(33)	(34)
Duration	Premium	Investment Income	Capital G/L	Surrenders and Maturities	Change in Reserve	Commission	Maintenance Expense	Change in DAC	Pre-tax Income	Prior to Surrenders	CF on 1000 10-yr Bond	Redemption Rate	EOY MV	Surrender Payments	BV of Assets for (32)	Capital G/L
1	100,000	7,118	-	4,341	101,230	5,000	100	4,576	1,023	94,900	75	7.50%	1,000	4,341	4,341	-
2	-	7,318	-	4,442	1,245	-	101	(439)	1,090	97,576	75	7.50%	1,000	4,442	4,442	-
3	-	7,526	-	4,546	1,260	-	102	(455)	1,162	100,349	75	7.50%	1,000	4,546	4,546	-
4	-	7,742	-	4,651	1,276	-	104	(472)	1,239	103,225	75	7.50%	1,000	4,651	4,651	-
5	-	7,966	(185)	4,508	1,292	-	105	(480)	1,396	106,211	75	8.50%	961	4,508	4,693	(185)
6	-	8,203	(158)	4,665	1,308	-	106	(517)	1,449	109,377	75	8.50%	967	4,665	4,823	(158)
7	-	8,449	(126)	4,825	1,324	-	108	(530)	1,536	112,650	75	8.50%	974	4,825	4,952	(126)
8	-	8,703	(90)	4,988	1,340	-	109	(544)	1,632	116,038	75	8.50%	982	4,988	5,078	(90)
9	-	8,966	(48)	5,155	1,356	-	110	(560)	1,737	119,553	75	8.50%	991	5,155	5,203	(48)
10	-	9,240	-	118,328	(111,631)	-	112	(579)	1,852	123,205	1075	8.50%	1,000	-	-	-

Legend:
(20) = d × (28)
(23) represents the change in column (6).
(27) = (19) + (20) + (21) – (22) – (23) – (24) – (25) + (26)
(28) = (19) – (24) – (25) in the first year.
= [(28) + (20) + (21) – (22)] for the prior year, plus [(19) – (24) – (25)] for the current year, in years 2 on.
(30) = new money rate in year (see d above).
(31) = present value of future cash flows at the redemption rate; this is the market value of the bond at the end of the year.
(33) = the book value of the assets needed to pay for surrender benefits in the year.

Note in the second illustration that the MVA charge exceeds the anticipated realized capital loss each year. This has a stabilizing effect on earnings from year to year, especially when interest rates are volatile and changing.

Chapter 8 Variable and Equity-Based Products

8.1 Introduction

Historically, the life insurance industry has issued contracts that provide the policyholder a guaranteed death benefit in exchange for the payment of a series of premiums. Embedded in many forms of these contracts is an implied return to the policyholder on the portion of the premium payments not required to provide for the expected cost of the death benefit and expenses. This savings element and the implied investment return thereon form the guaranteed cash surrender values paid or credited to policyholders upon their surrender of the contract.

Under this form of contract, the insurance company retains the investment risks associated with the assets supporting the savings element of the contract and provides a guaranteed return to the policyholder. Over time, customers have demanded greater returns in exchange for bearing the investment risks of the assets underlying the savings element of their contract, and insurance companies have responded to those demands. This trend has culminated in contracts through which customers bear substantially all the investment risk of the assets underlying the savings element of their contracts. Products that effectively provide for policyholders to bear substantially all the investment risk on all or a portion of the assets supporting the savings element of their premium payments are referred to as variable products. Outside of the United States, the label unit-linked is commonly used to describe these same products.

Variable product counterparts have been developed for virtually all types of products offered in the life insurance and annuity marketplace. Frequently, the accounting model used for the variable form of a product is the same as the accounting model used for the nonvariable form of the product. When this is the case, the actuary needs to extend the accounting model to incorporate the product's variable features. In some instances, the addition of a variable feature can change the accounting model required. One such example is payout annuities. In this case, the actuary needs to be able to clearly distinguish between contracts with variable features and those without and to separate the accounting elements associated with the variable products from those associated with the nonvariable products.

This chapter discusses the considerations involved in extending the accounting models to incorporate variable features and the additional considerations when an alternative accounting model is needed because of the addition of variable features. The chapters addressing the accounting for the nonvariable forms of these products should be referenced for additional information.

Equity-indexed products are special forms of guaranteed contracts that have variable-type features. In these cases, the policyholders are guaranteed an investment result on their account balance that is the greater of a minimum interest rate and a proportion of an equity-based index, such as the Standard & Poor's 500 (S&P 500). The indexing feature of these contracts generally is considered a derivative under generally accepted accounting principles. This chapter also explores the accounting treatments that have emerged for the equity-indexed annuity.

8.2 Variable Products

8.2.1 Product Descriptions

8.2.1.1 Variable Universal Life

Universal life contracts are insurance contracts with nonguaranteed features. As this product form has developed, the mix of features that are guaranteed versus those that are nonguaranteed has been broadened so that in the current marketplace, products are available with various levels of guarantees.

A variable universal life product is a universal life product that allows the policyholder to direct all or a portion of his or her account balance into an investment that passes the risks and rewards of holding that investment to the policyholder. A variable universal life contract does not provide a guarantee as to the investment performance of the policyholder's account balance. The investment performance of the account balance is an important element of the accounting model used for universal life contracts. The volatility introduced through the variable feature affects the liability, unearned revenue, and unamortized deferred acquisition cost accounts associated with the contract and therefore the earnings. But for this volatility, the accounting for a variable universal life contract is the same as that for a nonvariable universal life contract.

Because the accounting is the same for both variable and nonvariable universal life contracts, it is not necessary to determine whether the contract is in fact variable in order to establish the accounting for a variable universal life contract. It is of course necessary to appropriately account for the investment performance provided to the policyholders. This investment performance underlies the determination of the policyholder account balance and is an element in determining estimated gross profits (EGP) used to establish the pattern for the amortization of deferred acquisition costs (DAC) and unearned revenues.

In addition, but outside the scope of this chapter, in order to properly account for the invested assets held by or on behalf of the insurance company, it is necessary to determine who benefits from the risks and rewards of ownership of those assets. All or a part of the risks and rewards of ownership of assets supporting policyholder account balances associated with variable universal life contracts may be attributed to the policyholder. This, along with whether the entity holding the assets meets the requirement of "separate account" as defined under GAAP, could affect the the insurance company's accounting for these assets.

Features have been added to variable universal life-type contracts as a result of the variable aspect. In some instances, these features relate to the investment options offered to the policyholder. Included in this group would be features providing various levels of guarantees as to the performance of certain investment options. For example, an investment option could guarantee a minimum level of performance, be indexed, or offer a combination of both. In these instances, the accounting for the investments made to support the guarantee is determined by the appropriate guidance for investment accounting. The accounting for the policyholder account balance is determined by reference to the definition of the policyholder's value, or interest, in the contract. The EGP recognition would effectively be established by the difference. That is, the investment component of EGP would be the difference between the accounting recognition of the investment performance of the underlying assets and the accounting recognition of the change in the policyholder account balance due to investment performance.

Features that do not directly relate to the investment options offered the policyholder have also been added to universal life-type contracts. These features relate to such items as deposit flexibility, benefit riders, and the like. These non-investment-related features are outside the scope of this chapter and are fully addressed in Chapter 6. Variable universal life products tend to have no-lapse premium features similar to those in a universal life product. However, the risk inherent in this provision is equity-related instead of the interest rate-related risk in a universal life policy. Accounting for this provision will be discussed later in this chapter.

8.2.1.2 Variable Deferred Annuities

Deferred annuities are fully described in Chapter 7. A variable deferred annuity provides for the policyholder to direct all or a portion of his or her account balance into an investment that passes the risks and rewards of holding that investment to the policyholder. Variable deferred annuities are classified as investment contracts unless the contract provides for significant mortality or morbidity benefits. If significant mortality or morbidity benefits are provided, the deferred-annuity contract is classified as a universal life-type contract.

As with variable universal life contracts, it is not necessary to determine whether the deferred annuity contract is in fact variable in order to establish the appropriate accounting. It is of course necessary to appropriately account for the investment performance provided to the policyholders. This investment performance underlies the determination of the policyholder account balance and is an element in determining the pattern of amortization of DAC. In addition, the considerations related to accounting for the invested assets held by or on behalf of the insurance company also apply.

Because of its variable nature, a number of guarantees are available on annuities offered in the marketplace. The guaranteed minimum death benefit is the oldest and most common; most variable annuities sold in the US since 1990 have such a feature. Relatively recent additions include guaranteed minimum income, guaranteed minimum accumulation, and guaranteed minimum withdrawal benefits. Each of these benefit features has been added to provide an element of protection to policyholders from volatility in the equity markets.

Guaranteed Minimum Death Benefits. The typical nonvariable benefit is a return of policyholder's account balance in the event of termination due to death. In a variable annuity, the account balance moves according to the changes in the underlying assets. The guaranteed minimum death benefit (GMDB) protects the policyholder from the contingency that the account balance may be at a relatively low value at the time of death. Early forms of this feature simply provided a return of the policyholder's net deposits (deposits less partial withdrawals) on death. This form essentially provides a guarantee of principal in the event of death. As the benefit has evolved, it has been enriched in some product forms to provide a guaranteed death benefit equal to the greater of the policyholder's accumulated account balance as of the last policy anniversary (or some other date) and the net deposits. In other forms, a guaranteed accumulation interest rate is used to increase either the net deposit amount or the accumulated account balance used to determine the death benefit from the last reset date to the date of death.

Guaranteed Minimum Income Benefits. The guaranteed minimum income benefit (GMIB) provides that the policyholder's account balance at annuitization will be sufficient to purchase a minimum periodic payment amount under a standard payout annuity contract form, such as life income. These benefit features typically require the policyholder to hold the contract in the accumulation phase for a specified number of years before annuitizing.

Guaranteed Minimum Accumulation Benefits. The guaranteed minimum accumulation benefit (GMAB) provides the policyholder with an assurance that the variable annuity contract will, under the appropriate circumstances, provide a minimum guaranteed return that may be settled by the policyholder at a stated date.

Guaranteed Minimum Withdrawal Benefits. The guaranteed minimum withdrawal benefit (GMWB) guarantees that the policy will stay in force as long as a policyholder's annual withdrawals are less than a stipulated percentage of the single premium, regardless of the actual account balance. It has similarities to both a GMAB and GMIB, but it should be noted that it typically contains no mortality guarantee.

These features either enhance the mortality contingent element of the variable annuity contract or transfer back to the insurance company an element of the investment risk. These features must be carefully considered in order to establish the appropriate accounting for contracts that contain them.

8.2.1.3 Variable Payout Annuities

Variable payout annuities add a variable feature to the standard forms of payout annuities. The accounting for nonvariable forms of this contract is discussed in Chapter 9. Typically, at annuitization, the policyholder makes an election as to the expected long-term rate to be earned on the investments supporting the contract and the initial allocation of assets. Thereafter, the income benefit is indexed to the performance of the investments underlying the variable account. The premium rates used to convert a premium amount to a variable income benefit are determined by using a discount rate equal to the long-term rate elected by the policyholder from a relatively low range of choices (3% to 5%, for example.) The variable income benefit is then adjusted based on the performance of the variable account investments relative to the discount rate used for the conversion. The insurance company may be required to add or be allowed to subtract from the total amount of assets supporting a block of variable payout annuities as a result of mortality experience different from that assumed in determining the premium rates.

The remainder of this chapter discusses the considerations involved in classifying variable products for accounting purposes, establishing appropriate assumptions for the variable features, and applying the various accounting concepts to variable contracts.

8.2.2 Contract Classification

8.2.2.1 Life Insurance

The accounting model to be applied to a contract depends on the contract's features. Life insurance contracts may be either short-duration or long-duration contracts. The variable life insurance products discussed here are all long-duration contracts, and the addition of a variable feature to these contracts does not alter this conclusion. Traditional life insurance contracts can be either participating or nonparticipating and generally have terms that, but for the participating feature, are fixed and guaranteed. The addition of a variable feature to these contracts would prohibit them from being classified as traditional life insurance contracts. A traditional life insurance contract with variable features would be considered a universal life-type contract and accounted for by using the accounting model described in *SFAS 97*.

A universal life insurance contract already contains elements that are not fixed and guaranteed. The addition of variable features to a universal life contract simply modifies the investment component of the contract. For accounting purposes, a variable universal life-type contract is a special case of universal life contracts to which *SFAS 97* is applied in any event.

As discussed in Chapter 6, some product features contained in universal life contracts are accounted for under *SOP 03-1*. These include insurance benefit features that result in an expectation of profits followed by losses and sales inducements. This is also true for variable universal life contracts. In particular, the *AICPA Technical Practice Aid* – Section 6300 (*SOP 03-1 TPA*) clarifies that a liability must be held for VUL no-lapse premium guarantees in stating the following:

> There is a presumption that the minimum guaranteed death benefit of a variable annuity and the no-lapse guarantee mortality feature of a universal life or a variable universal life contract will result in profits in earlier years and losses in subsequent years. This pattern of profits followed by losses results from the design and capital markets risks of these benefit features. (Section 6300.06)

8.2.2.2 Deferred Annuities

Deferred-annuity contracts are typically accounted for as investment contracts. The presence of variable features in a deferred-annuity contract does not of itself alter this conclusion. However, certain of the features added to variable deferred-annuity contracts could alter this conclusion, depending on their significance. In particular, the GMDB feature may cause a variable deferred-annuity contract to be classified as a universal life-type contract. *SFAS 97* provides as follows:

> Long-duration contracts that do not subject the insurance enterprise to risks arising from policyholder mortality or morbidity are referred to in this Statement as investment contracts. A mortality or morbidity risk is present if, under the terms of the contract, the enterprise is required to make payments or forego required premiums contingent upon the death or disability (in the case of life insurance contracts) or the continued survival (in the case of annuity contracts) of a specific individual or group of individuals. A contract provision that allows the holder of a long-duration contract to purchase an annuity at a guaranteed price on settlement of the contract does not entail a mortality risk until the right to purchase is executed. If purchased, the annuity is a new contract to be evaluated on its own terms. (Paragraph 7)

The GMDB feature may require the company to make payments or forego surrender charges (considered "premiums" in the language of the preceding paragraph), "contingent upon the death" of the policyholder. *SFAS 133* does not apply to mortality and morbidity features because of the insurance exclusion in *SFAS 133*. Instead, *SOP 03-1* provides guidance on when and how to calculate a liability for these types of features.

If the mortality risk is nominal, the contract is classified as an investment contract and no additional liability is established for the insurance benefit feature until there is a triggering event (death).

If the mortality risk is other than nominal, the contract is classified as a universal life-type contract.

SOP 03-1 states:

> There is a rebuttable presumption that a contract has significant mortality risk where the additional insurance benefit would vary significantly in response to capital

> markets volatility. If the mortality or morbidity risk is other than nominal and the fees assessed or insurance benefits are not fixed and guaranteed, the contract should be classified as an FASB Statement No. 97 universal life-type contract by the insurance enterprise. (Paragraph 24)

SOP 03-1 provides further guidance in the calculations to be performed in order to assess the significance of mortality risk. This assessment is made once, at the inception of the contract and for existing in-force contracts at the adoption of *SOP 03-1*:

> The determination of significance of mortality or morbidity risk should be based on a comparison of the present value of expected excess payments to be made under insurance benefit features (that is, insurance benefit amounts and related incremental claim adjustment expenses in excess of account balance, herein referred to as the "excess payments") with the present value of all amounts expected to be assessed against the contract holder (revenue). (Paragraph 25)

If a universal life-type contract contains an insurance benefit feature that results in an expectation of profits in the early years followed by losses in the later years from that feature, a liability must be calculated for that feature under the guidance of *SOP 03-1*. Because of the nature of most current GMDBs, this expectation is met for variable contracts evaluated at inception. Therefore, a liability generally is calculated for GMDBs associated with any variable annuity contract classified as a universal life-type contract.

With a GMIB feature, the insurance company is guaranteeing that the combination of the premium available (the maturity value of the contract) and the purchase rates used to convert the premium into an income stream will produce at least a minimum periodic payment amount. Although the income stream may be life contingent, the presence of this feature will not affect the product classification of the variable annuity under *SOP 03-1* because the annuitization portion is considered a separate contract. This is addressed in the discussion section of *SFAS 97*:

> The Board concluded that the obligation to make payments that are contingent upon the death or continued survival of a specific individual or group is the essence of a mortality risk. The risk that the guaranteed price of an annuity may prove to be unfavorable to the guaranteeing enterprise when the annuity is purchased is a price risk not unlike a guaranteed price of any commodity and does not create a mortality risk. A mortality risk does not arise until the purchase provision is executed and the obligation to make life-contingent payments is present in an annuity contract. (Paragraph 40, in part)

In addition, neither the GMAB nor the GMWB feature would be considered to add mortality risk to a variable deferred-annuity contract. These benefits affect the degrees of pricing risk inherent in the variable deferred-annuity contract, but do not affect the mortality risk.

A variable annuity contract classified as universal life-type under GAAP requires the use of an EGP-based amortization schedule for DAC. As discussed in Chapter 7, AICPA Practice Bulletin 8 gives guidance on how DAC should be amortized for an investment contract. In practice, it is rare for a variable annuity to use the *SFAS 91* interest method for DAC amortization. Instead, the most common approach is also an EGP-based amortization schedule.

Derivative Implementation Group (*DIG*) Issue *B8* suggests that a GMAB provision within a variable annuity contract is an embedded derivative, since it is not clearly and closely related to the host contract. Therefore, the guarantee needs to b4e bifurcated and accounted for as a derivative if it meets the *SFAS 133* criteria of a derivative, including net settlement (i.e., it can be settled in cash). These criteria should equally apply to GMWB provisions.

GMIB provisions in variable annuity contracts generally do not meet the cash settlement criteria in *SFAS 133*. Therefore, they generally do not have to be bifurcated and valued under *SFAS 133*. Instead, *SOP 03-1* covers liabilities for GMIB provisions in variable annuity reinsurance contracts.

On the other hand, reinsurance treaties of GMIB coverage commonly cash settle at the annuitization date, which causes these reinsurance treaties to be accounted for under *SFAS 133* in whole or in part, depending generally on whether the reinsurance treaty provides only GMIB coverage. This potential accounting mismatch between the liability and the reinsurance asset is discussed in the basis for conclusions for *SOP 03-1* as follows:

> However, AcSEC observed that the GMIB liability recognized under the guidance in this SOP will not be measured at fair value and therefore would not necessarily offset the reinsurance asset. (Paragraph A41 in part)

8.2.2.3 Payout Annuities

Payout annuity contracts are generally classified either as investment contracts or as limited-payment contracts under *SFAS* 97. The considerations involved in determining the applicable accounting models are discussed in Chapter 9. The addition of a variable feature to a payout annuity otherwise classified as an investment contract does not affect that conclusion. However, the addition of a variable feature to a payout annuity contract otherwise classified as a limited-payment contract would affect its classification. *SFAS* 97 describes a limited-payment contract as follows:

> Long-duration insurance contracts with terms that are fixed and guaranteed, and for which premiums are paid over a period shorter than the period over which benefits are provided, are referred to in this Statement as limited-payment contracts. The period over which benefits are provided, as used in this Statement, includes the periods during which the insurance enterprise is subject to risk from policyholder mortality and morbidity and during which the insurance enterprise is responsible for administration of the contract. The benefit period does not include the subsequent period over which the policyholder or beneficiary may elect to have settlement proceeds disbursed. (Paragraph 9)

The variable feature of a payout annuity is not fixed and guaranteed and therefore would prohibit a variable payout annuity from being classified as a limited-payment contract. Limited-payment contracts without terms that are fixed and guaranteed are classified as universal life-type contracts. Because variable payout annuities do not have many of the features commonly found in universal life contracts, such as a stated account balance and explicit charges for mortality benefits, the application of the universal life-type accounting model to these contracts requires judgment and interpretation. The principal elements of the universal life-type accounting model as applied to a variable payout annuity are discussed in the following paragraphs.

Central to the accounting model for universal life-type contracts is the policyholder account balance. *SFAS* 97, paragraph 17(a), describes this amount as, "The balance that accrues to the benefit of policyholders at the date of the financial statements." In the case of a variable payout annuity, this amount is the present value of the expected income stream determined by using pricing-basis mortality and a discount rate equal to the rate elected by policyholder at annuitization.

In the accounting model for universal life-type contracts, EGPs are used as the basis for amortizing DAC. EGPs are described in *SFAS* 97 as:

> Estimated gross profit, as the term is used in paragraph 22, shall include estimates of the following elements, each of which shall be determined based on the best estimate of that individual element over the life of the book of contracts without provision for adverse deviation:
>
> a. Amounts expected to be assessed for mortality (sometimes referred to as the cost of insurance) less benefit claims in excess of related policyholder balances
> b. Amounts expected to be assessed for contract administration less costs incurred for contract administration (including acquisition costs not included in capitalized acquisition costs as described in paragraph 24)
> c. Amounts expected to be earned from the investment of policyholder balances less interest credited to policyholder balances
> d. Amounts expected to be assessed against policyholder balances upon termination of a contract (sometimes referred to as surrender charges)
> e. Other expected assessments and credits, however characterized. (Paragraph 23)

Mortality assessments are the expected benefit payments determined using the same mortality rates as used in the determination of the policyholder account balance less the amount by which annuity values are increased through survivorship. The mortality component of EGP would be determined as the excess of actual benefits paid over the amount of the mortality assessments and then reduced by the amount of required additions to the assets supporting the contract due to mortality experience different from the pricing basis. (If an amount is subtracted, then it increases the mortality component of EGP.) Contract administration assessments would be determined based on the purchase rate calculation. Typically, no surrender provisions exist. To the extent there are gains and losses, for example, relative to mortality experience, they would be considered either as an additional element of the mortality component [element (a)] or as an "Other expected assessment (gain) or credit (loss) in element (e) of this paragraph."

DIG Issue *B25* states that a certain annuity option within a variable payout annuity is an embedded derivative. For example, assume the annuity option is 10 year certain and life contingent thereafter. Then, the 10 year certain guarantee would be deemed an embedded derivative.

8.2.3 Assumptions

8.2.3.1 Assumptions for DAC amortization

The assumptions used for a variable product are the same as those for the comparable nonvariable product. However, consideration of a long-term interest rate assumption is required. To the extent that the variable product form entails benefit features not found on the nonvariable form, as with variable deferred annuities, or the variable product form is classified as a different type of product, as with certain variable payout annuities, there are additional considerations.

8.2.3.1.1 Contract Interest Rates for EGPs

In determining the EGP used to amortize the DAC associated with universal life-type contracts, the actuary must estimate the contract rate as described in *SFAS 97*, paragraph 22, as "the rate of interest that accrues to policyholder balances (sometimes referred to as the contract rate)."

This rate is then used (1) in estimating the amount of future policyholder account balances, and (2) as the rate credited to policyholder balances in the investment element of EGP.

In addition, the contract rate is generally used as the basis for determining the "amounts expected to be earned from the investment of policyholder balances" in the investment element of EGP associated with variable contracts. In most instances, the variable component of the liabilities is invested in accounts that provide for the insurance company to assess an asset-based fee. Therefore, the contract rate plus the amount of the fee becomes the basis for determining the amount expected to be earned from the investment of policyholder balances, and the contract rate alone is the rate credited to the policyholder balance. The investment element of EGP is the amount of the fee applied to the policyholder balance.

The investment results and hence the contract rate associated with the variable component of the policyholder account balance can be quite volatile, particularly when compared to the contract rate for nonvariable products. Actual results will almost always differ from the assumption used to determine EGP in any period. In developing the assumption to be used for the contract rate applied to the variable component of the liabilities in the future, there are a variety of alternatives.

One method is to estimate a single rate to be applied in all future periods and then rarely unlock this assumption, on the theory that the assumption is still a reasonable best estimate. For example, consider a situation where historical credited rates have always been 10% and the assumption for credited rates in all future years is also 10%. If the actual credited rate in the current year turns out to be 0%, but for future EGPs the 10% rate is still deemed to be appropriate, amortization is increased in the current year. This is because future EGPs as a percent of total EGPs are reduced from that assumed a year ago and the amortization factor (present value of deferrable expenses divided by the present value of EGPs) is increased.

Another technique, commonly called "mean reversion," considers recent investment results in establishing future credited rate assumptions. For example, assume that the best estimate of a long-term rate expected to be credited to policyholder balances is 10%. Further, assume that the expectation is that this will be the result over any 5-year period investment horizon. Finally, there must be an assumption made with respect to where the current year is within the investment horizon. The three scenarios illustrated in Figure 8-1 show the result of three possible assumptions with respect to this positioning within the investment horizon.

Figure 8-1 Variable Contract Rate Assumption				
		Assumed Rates		
Period	Credited Rate	Beginning	Middle	End
(5)	10.00%			
(4)	15.00%			
(3)	17.00%			
(2)	6.00%			
(1)	5.00%			
0	8.00%			
1		10.50%	15.50%	14.00%
2		10.50%	15.50%	10.00%
3		10.50%	10.00%	10.00%
4		10.50%	10.00%	10.00%
5		10.00%	10.00%	10.00%
6		10.00%	10.00%	10.00%
7		10.00%	10.00%	10.00%
8		10.00%	10.00%	10.00%
9		10.00%	10.00%	10.00%
10		10.00%	10.00%	10.00%

In this example, the *Credited Rate* column represents the actual rates credited to the variable portion of the policyholder account balances in past periods. The row for period 0 represents the period just ended. In the *Beginning* column, the assumed contract rate for future periods is established by assuming the most recent period is the first year of a 5-year period over which the average rate credited to the variable portion of the policyholder account is assumed to be 10.00%. In the *Middle* column, it is assumed that the most recent period is in the middle, or third year, of a 5-year period over which the average rate credited to the variable portion of the policyholder account averages 10.00%; and in the *End* column, the most recent period is assumed to be the fourth year of a 5-year period. Under this approach, as the actual contract rate on the variable portion of the policyholder account becomes known, the assumption for future periods (four, two, or one period, as appropriate) is reset such that the average rate over the assumed 5-year period is always 10.00%. In the *Beginning* column, the average of 8% in year 0 and 10.5% for years 1–4 is 10%. In the *Middle* column, the average of 6%, 5%, and 8% in years (2), (1), and 0, respectively, and 15.5% in years 1 and 2 is 10%. In the *End* column, the average of the actual rates in years (3) through 0 and 14% in year 1 is 10%.

In the example discussed earlier (10% historical credited rates, 10% assumed future returns, 0% actual return in a year), if a mean reversion technique is used, the 10% future return would be unlocked to a rate greater than 10%. Therefore, the additional DAC amortization, caused by the 0% actual return, will be partially mitigated by increasing the future return assumption. Shorter mean reversion periods result in less DAC amortization volatility.

Whatever specific method is applied, the contract rate should reflect the actuary's best estimate of the future with reference to the underlying investments. For example, if the mean reversion method produces future return assumptions that management would not consider a best estimate, the future assumptions must be changed. This has led many companies to put in caps and floors on future assumptions, while some companies have judgmentally reset the long-term assumption, the mean reversion horizon, or both, from time to time. The adjustment to DAC amortization caused by this kind of assumption "catch up" tends to be very large.

Some companies have applied a stochastic-type technique in analyzing future equity returns (and sometimes other elements of EGPs). This type of technique is described generally as follows:

1. A stochastic generator is used to derive a range of future investment return scenarios from which a distribution of the present value of future EGPs is obtained.

2. A corridor is developed around the mean of the present value of future EGPs, usually defined in relation to the standard deviation.

3. The prior period's estimate of the present value of future EGPs (excluding the current period's actual gross profit) is analyzed for reasonableness.

    a. If the prior period's present value of future EGPs is within the stipulated corrider, the prior period's estimated present value of future EGPs is not unlocked.
    b. If the prior period's present value of future EGPs is outside the stipulated corridor, the prior period's estimated present value of future EGPs is unlocked to the mean value of the distribution of results (or such other amount as represents management's new best estimate).

4. The DAC is calculated, using actual gross profits through the current period and the present value of future EGPs derived from the above algorithm.

Although the method is complex, it tends to produce stable DAC amortization in periods of small variations in equity returns. In that case, future EGPs will tend to stay within the stipulated corridor, so the present value of future EGPs will not change, and the only variation in DAC amortization from expectation will come from the difference in the current period's actual gross profits to the EGPs previously anticipated. But, if there are wide variations in equity returns, unlockings may be even larger than they would be under the other methods.

Some have argued that since the approach produces a distribution of the present value of future EGPs, the "best estimate" of the present value of future EGPs is, by definition, the mean value of the distribution. The counterargument is that the distribution of future results is only used for the analysis of whether the prior "best estimate" is still appropriate.

The contract interest rate used for payout annuity contracts classified as universal life-type contracts is determined by using the same approach as that for deferred variable annuity contracts.

8.2.3.1.2 Discount Rates

Under *SFAS 97*, the discount rate to be used for amortization of DAC for universal life-type contracts is equal to the credited rate. *SFAS 97* lists two options for determining the credited rate to be used for this purpose:

> The interest rate used to compute the present value of revised estimates of expected gross profits shall be either the rate in effect at the inception of the book of contracts or the latest revised rate applied to the remaining benefit period. The approach selected to compute the present value of revised estimates shall be applied consistently in subsequent revisions to computations of expected gross profits. (Paragraph 25, in part)

For variable contracts, it is common practice to use the "rate at inception" approach. The other approach tends to have frequently changing discount rates and even negative discount rates from time to time. Changing discount rates tends to exaggerate DAC volatility. When growth rates are high, not only do the EGPs rise but so does the amortization interest rate, causing more extreme unlocking. In the down markets, the opposite happens.

8.2.3.1.3 Mortality Rates

Mortality rate assumptions must be made to determine the EGPs used as a basis for amortizing DAC associated with universal life-type contracts. In addition, mortality rates will be a component used in determining the policyholder account balance associated with variable payout annuities classified as universal life contracts.

Mortality rates used to determine EGP are based on management's best estimate of future experience. For universal life contracts with variable features, the considerations involved in determining this assumption are the same as those used to determine the mortality assumption for universal life contracts without variable features, as discussed in Chapter 6. For a variable deferred annuity product with mortality features sufficient (not insignificant) to cause it to be classified as a universal life contract, the same considerations apply, but their application will affect the outcome. For example, one consideration is the underwriting criteria normally applied to insurance contracts with significant mortality exposures. The resulting selection will generally produce mortality experience better than average population mortality experience. This difference would be incorporated into the assumptions used to determine EGPs. For variable annuities, the mortality exposure is usually not sufficient to warrant underwriting, therefore mortality experience may not be as favorable as expected for universal life contracts. Typical mortality assumptions used for variable annuities classified as universal life-type contracts would be expected to approximate those experienced in unselected populations. In addition to being used to estimate the mortality component of EGPs, a mortality assumption may be used in determining future policyholder account balances.

Accounting for variable payout annuities requires a mortality assumption for determining EGPs and probably also for determining the policyholder account balance. The considerations applicable to the mortality assumption used in determining EGPs are effectively the same as those applied to variable deferred annuities. It is likely that the mortality rates themselves for payout annuities would be highly self-selected and better than deferred annuitant mortality. The mortality assumption used to determine the policyholder account balance should be consistent with the assumption used to convert the premium (or initial deposit) into the initial amount of periodic income.

8.2.3.1.4 Other Assumptions

In addition to mortality and interest rate assumptions, surrender and expense assumptions are required. The considerations used in developing expense assumptions for variable contracts are generally the same as those for the nonvariable forms of the contract. Variable contracts may include expense assessments for policyholder activity, in particular related to the movement of funds from one type of investment account to another type; this activity would not be present in nonvariable contracts. These charges should be estimated and used in determining EGPs. With variable payout annuities, if the basis used to convert the premium into the initial amount of periodic income included provision for expenses, the same basis should be used in the determination of expense charges for the EGPs.

8.2.3.2 Assumptions Used for GMDB and GMIB Liability

As previously discussed, *SOP 03-1* requires liabilities for GMDB and GMIB provisions. Assumptions required for both types of liabilities include variable fund growth rates, discount rates, and mortality and surrender during the deferral period.

SOP 03-1 states that (1) "expected experience should be based on a range of scenarios rather than a single set of best estimate assumptions," and (2) "the assumptions used, such as the interest rate, discount rate, lapse rate, and mortality, should be consistent with assumptions used in estimating gross profits for purposes of amortizing capitalized acquisition costs." (Paragraph 26, in part, for GMDB, and paragraph 31, in part, for GMIB)

Although strongly hinting at a stochastic approach, *SOP 03-1* is silent on how to (1) generate the range of scenarios, (2) use the results generated from the range of scenarios in the liability computation, and (3) ensure consistency with a scenario based approach for GMDB and GMIB liabilities and a deterministic type approach for DAC.

One common way of complying with this consistency requirement for variable fund growth rates is to set the mean returns used in a stochastic generator equal to the deterministic returns assumed for EGPs.

This logic would apply for mortality and surrender during the deferral period as well, if these assumptions vary by scenario. For example, some practitioners believe that surrenders will decrease as the equity market declines, because the GMDB or GMIB provision is more valuable. In that case, the average surrender rate in the GMDB or GMIB liability computation could be tied to that used for EGPs.

The discount rate assumed in the *SOP 03-1* liability calculation (for the deferral period) must be that used for DAC amortization in order to comply with this consistency requirement.

Assumptions specific to GMIB liabilities include annuitization election rates, the earned rate on general account assets during the annuitization period, and mortality during the annuitization period.

Although there is very little GMIB annuitization election data, it is common practice to assume annuitization will increase as the GMIB provision is more valuable. This will occur if either equities have performed poorly since the inception of the contract or if interest rates have decreased substantially.

For GMIB liabilities, sometimes a stochastic generator is used for not only generating variable component fund growth rates, but also for generating future interest rates. As discussed above, interest rates may influence policyholder behavior towards annuitization election. In addition, the assumed rate of return on assets backing the payout annuity must be used as the discount rate for the annuitization period.

8.2.3.3 Assumptions Used for GMAB and GMWB Liability

In valuing these product provisions under *SFAS 133*, assumptions needed include variable fund growth rates, discount rates, mortality and surrender rates, and benefit exercise patterns.

SFAS 133 requires a fair value calculation. Both fair value guidance (see Chapter 18, Section 3, for a discussion of FASB's exposure draft entitled "Fair Value Measurements") and industry practice are evolving in this arena towards the calibration of economic assumptions to those observable in the marketplace. Financial economic theory dictates that the inputs in determining the value of an option are the risk-free rate curve and the implied volatility curve. For the purpose of valuing a GMAB or GMWB feature, the interest rates (calibrated to the risk-free rate curve) are used not only in determining fund growth, but also in determining the discount rate. This is quite different from the guidance in *SOP 03-1* for GMDB and GMIB liabilities, which require a calibration of the fund growth assumption to a best estimate assumption used for determining EGPs and a calibration of the discount rate to that used for DAC amortization.

Risk-free rates are easily observable in the U.S. marketplace for most maturity lengths, but in some foreign countries there is no market for anything past 10 years. Implied volatility data, which can be derived by observing option prices, is not as readily available. For example, at the time of writing, implied volatility quotes on the Standards & Poor's 500 Index are available for quotes up to 10 years, but are unavailable for longer durations. Estimation techniques must be used when data is not available.

Mortality assumptions have the same considerations as discussed in determining EGPs. However, in determining surrender rates and benefit exercise patterns, policyholder behavior should also be taken into account. For example, some practitioners believe that surrenders will decrease as the equity market declines, because the GMAB or GMWB provision is more valuable. In addition, benefit utilization should increase, as the benefit becomes more "in the money."

This logic would apply for mortality and surrender during the deferral period as well, if these assumptions vary by scenario. For example, some practitioners feel that surrenders will decrease as the equity market declines, because the GMDB or GMIB provision is more valuable. In that case, the average surrender rate in the GMDB or GMIB liability computation could be tied to that used for EGPs.

8.2.4 Methods

8.2.4.1 DAC Amortization

In general, the methods used to develop the accounting for variable contracts of all types are consistent with the respective nonvariable contract forms. The exception is a variable payout annuity classified as a universal life contract. The rest of this section deals with payout annuities. While insurance companies have developed a variety of methods to price and administer these contracts, the following illustration uses a common approach (but adopts an annual annuity income for simplicity).

Let:

A	=	The initial deposit
x	=	Contract issue age
t	=	Time from contract initiation ($0 \leq t$)
i	=	Premium interest rate
p_{x+t}	=	Probability of survival from age $x + t$ to age $x + t + 1$
${}_tp_x$	=	Probability of survival from age x to age $x + t$
v	=	$1 / (1 + i)$

a_x = $\sum^{\infty}_{t=1} v^t\ {}_tP_x$, or the present value of a life annuity of 1 per annum issued to a person aged x.

Then, if a person aged x purchases a variable payout annuity with a premium payment of A, let:

P = Income units purchased
= (A – loading) / a_x.

Further, let:

uv_t = Accumulated investment performance of the variable account from issue date to time t

I_t = Investment income rate earned on the investments in the variable account for the period ending at time t

I_t = $(uv_t / uv_{t-1}) - 1$

uv_0 = 1.00.

Then, define an income unit value, IUV, to be the multiplier applied to the number of income units purchased to determine the current period income to be paid, representative of the investment performance of the variable account. If IA_t is the annual income payable at time t under the variable payout annuity contract, then

IA_0 = $P \times IUV_0$
= $P\ (IUV_0 = 1.00)$

and

IA_t = $P \times IUV_t$

IUV_t = $uv_t / (1 + i)^t$.

Under these definitions, to the extent investment performance exceeds the premium interest rate, the amount of annual income increases from one period to the next. To the extent investment performance is less than the premium interest rate, annual income decreases.

Now, a policyholder account balance can be defined:

$$PAB_t = IUV_t \times P \times a_{x+t} \qquad (1).$$

This policyholder account balance would be used as the principal element of the liability for a variable payout annuity. A roll forward of this account balance then generates the elements of *EGP* used to amortize any DAC.

Using the following formulas for sequential values of a_x and IUV_t:

$$a_{x+t+1} = [a_{x+t} - 1] / vp_{x+t}$$

$$= [a_{x+t} - 1] \times (1 + i) / p_{x+t}$$

$$IUV_{t+1} = IUV_t \times (uv_{t+1} / uv_t) / (1 + i)$$

$$= IUV_t \times (1 + I_{t+1}) / (1 + i)$$

the following formula for sequential values of the policyholder account balance emerges:

$$PAB_{t+1} = IUV_{t+1} \times P \times a_{x+t+1}$$

$$= \{IUV_t \times (1 + I_{t+1}) / (1 + i)\} \times P \times [a_{x+t} - 1] \times (1 + i) / p_{x+t}$$

$$= IUV_t \times (1 + I_{t+1}) \times P \times [a_{x+t} - 1] / p_{x+t}$$

$$= \{IUV_t \times P \times [a_{x+t} - 1] + IUV_t \times P \times I_{t+1} \times [a_{x+t} - 1]\} / p_{x+t}$$

$$= \{IUV_t \times P \times a_{x+t} - IUV_t \times P + I_{t+1} \times IUV_t \times P \times a_{x+t} - I_{t+1} \times IUV_t \times P\} / p_{x+t}$$

$$= \{PAB_t - IUV_t \times P + I_{t+1} \times (PAB_t - IUV_t \times P)\} / p_{x+t}.$$

Then:

$$PAB_{t+1} = PAB_t - IUV_t \times (1 + I_{t+1}) \times P + I_{t+1} \times PAB_t$$

$$+ [(1/p_{x+t}) - 1] \times \{PAB_t - IUV_t \times (1 + I_{t+1}) \times P + I_{t+1} \times PAB_t\} \quad (2).$$

Breaking equation (2) into its component parts for purposes of determining EGP could be done as follows:

Mortality assessments $= [(1 / p_{x+t}) - 1] \times \{PAB_t - IUV_t \times (1 + I_{t+1}) \times P + I_{t+1} \times PAB_t\}$

$- IUV_t \times (1 + I_{t+1}) \times P$

$= \{(PAB_t - IUV_t \times P) / p_{x+t} - PAB_t\} \times (1 + I_{t+1})$ (2a)

Interest credited $= I_{t+1} \times PAB_t$ (2b).

Under this approach, interest credited is easily determinable as the investment performance applied to the beginning of period policyholder account balance. Differences between the ending policyholder account balance and the value of the variable account would be attributable to the mortality component of EGP. At the individual policy level, these differences will arise from actual mortality experience for the policy being different from the average experience used in pricing. If the breakdown of Formula (2) above is used, the mortality component will also include investment performance on the net mortality assessment. An alternative would be to use the following breakdown:

Mortality assessments $= \{[PAB_t - IUV_t \times P] / p_{x+t} - PAB_t\}$ (3a)

Interest credited $= I_{t+1} \times \{[PAB_t - IUV_t \times P] / p_{x+t}\}$ (3b).

Formulas (3a) and (3b) allocate the investment performance attributable to benefit payments to the interest-credited component of EGP, whereas Formulas (2a) and (2b) allocate this element to the mortality assessment component.

In addition to variable payout annuities, methods may need to be developed for unearned mortality assessments attributable to any death benefit features added to variable deferred-annuity products. The recognition of this type of assessment is not specifically addressed in current accounting literature. In most instances, these assessments are made as a percentage of the liability, expressed as a number of basis points deducted from the investment performance. The services provided relate to the policyholder's exposure to loss of value in the event of death. While the mortality risk is relatively straightforward to evaluate, the exposure to loss of value depends on the investment performance of the variable element of the policyholder account balance and, over many scenarios, is zero. As a result, matching the recognition of these assessments to the performance of services requires using judgment. As a further complication, the method of recognition must address the possibility of no real exposure with average investment performance that produces account balances in excess of guaranteed death benefits. A range of practices has developed to deal with this. The most broadly used makes no attempt to match the revenues with the services and simply recognizes the assessments as they are deducted from the policyholder account balances and recognizes the death benefits as they are paid.

8.2.4.2 GMDB liability

In determining the "additional liability" under *SOP 03-1*, the current benefit ratio is first computed. The benefit ratio is defined as the present value of total expected excess payments, divided by the present value of total expected assessments over the life of the contract. For a variable annuity, the excess payments are defined as the death benefits in excess of the account value released at death and related incremental claim adjustment expenses. Variable annuity assessments are the aggregation of non-deferrable product loads (including the increase in unearned revenue liability), surrender charges, and asset-based fees. Interest margin contained in fixed-rate subaccounts of variable annuities as well as some or all of the investment management fees assessed within the variable account share prices are typically included as well.

The "additional liability," which may not be less than zero, is equal to the current benefit ratio multiplied by the cumulative assessments from the contract's issue date, less cumulative excess benefits from the issue date, plus accreted interest.

The "additional liability" is unlocked in an analogous manner to DAC unlocking under *SFAS 97*. The benefit ratio is readjusted at each reporting date as (1) experience emerges differently than previously expected, and (2) future expectations change.

Since the calculation considers benefits paid in the past on groups of contracts, there must be some element of grouping in the method. Different grouping methods would likely develop different liabilities, because of the existence of the additional liability's floor of zero.

The *SOP 03-1 TPA* provides guidance in this matter:

> It is presumed that the level of aggregation generally should be consistent with the level at which the entity's DAC amortization ratios and associated DAC balances are calculated. This is the level at which products with common features have been aggregated. It is not appropriate to combine DAC-level groups for aggregation purposes in paragraph 26 of SOP 03-1. Aggregation at a more detailed level than the level at which the entity's DAC amortization ratios and associated DAC balances are calculated may be warranted based on an individual entity's facts and circumstances including, but not limited to, the risk characteristics of the corresponding insurance benefit features, such as, variable annuities with a ratchet minimum guaranteed death benefit (MGDB) and variable annuities with a return of premium MGDB, or universal life products with and without secondary guarantees. (Section 6300.07)

SOP 03-1 does not provide guidance on how the current benefit ratio should be determined when multiple scenarios are used. In practice, three approaches have developed.

The first approach, which is consistent with the example published in *SOP 03-1*, specifies that excess benefits are either based on an adverse scenario determined judgmentally or as the average of the excess benefits in the multiple scenarios. Assessments are taken from those used in the deterministic EGP stream used to amortize DAC.

In the second approach, excess benefits are defined in the same manner as the first approach. But, assessments are either based on the same adverse scenario determined judgmentally or as the average of the assessments in the multiple scenarios.

In the third approach, the current benefit ratio is determined as the average of the benefit ratios determined in the multiple scenarios.

SOP 03-1, paragraph 29, states that, "the estimated gross profits used for the amortization of deferred acquisition costs should be adjusted to reflect the recognition of the liability in accordance with paragraph 28 of this SOP." This means the EGPs should be reduced by the change in the "additional liability." Some practitioners also adjust the EGPs for the interest earned on assets backing the "additional liability." While an interest adjustment would appear to be necessary to make the method conceptually correct, *SOP 03-1* is silent on this matter. In fact, the numerical example provided with *SOP 03-1* excludes such an interest adjustment.

8.2.4.3 Variable Universal Life no-lapse premium guarantee liability

The variable universal life no-lapse premium guarantee liability provision also is accounted for under *SOP 03-1*. The methodology is identical to that used for determining the "additional liability" for a universal life policy with no-lapse premium guarantees, as discussed in Chapter 6.

8.2.4.4 GMIB liability

The GMIB liability calculation is analogous to that used for the GMDB liability, except that total expected excess payments are viewed differently. For the GMIB liability, the excess payments are defined as of the annuitization date(s) and are equal to the present value of expected annuitization benefits and related incremental claim adjustment expenses, less the expected policyholder account balance. The discount rate used in the present value calculation is the estimated investment yield to be earned during the annuitization phase of the contract. (As previously discussed, the discount rate in the deferral period is the same as that used for the GMDB liability, i.e., it must be consistent with that used for DAC amortization.)

This calculation is also analogous to that used for the additional liability for two tiered annuities, as discussed in Chapter 7, and for guaranteed settlement options attached to all contracts classified as life insurance under GAAP.

8.2.4.5 Liability for GMAB and GMWB

The methodology for determining the liability for these contracts varies slightly, depending on whether the provision is a derivative or an embedded derivative. Generally, a stand-alone rider with specified fees would be considered a derivative, and if the product feature is contained within a variable annuity without specified fees for the product feature, it would be considered an embedded derivative.

Whether the product feature is a derivative or embedded derivative, *SFAS 133* requires that the liability be recorded at fair value. Assuming there is no market price for the derivative, an option pricing technique should be used. This involves using a Black-Scholes formula, which has limitations, because of the lack of policyholder behavior input, or a stochastic technique.

In practice, a stochastic technique generally is used. The liability for the derivative is equal to the average present value of benefits plus an option issuer's "required profit" less specified charges.

If the product feature does not have specified fees, the variable annuity contract is considered a hybrid instrument, consisting of an embedded derivative (the GMAB or GMWB provision) and a host (what the variable annuity would be like without the GMAB or GMWB provision).

The liability for the embedded derivative under *SFAS 133* is equal to the average present value of benefits plus required profit.

The liability for the host equals the account value less a "host offset." The value at issue of the "host offset" is equal to the embedded derivative value at issue. Going forward, this "host offset" is equal to the unamortized portion of the value of the host offset at issue.

The "required profit" component should be calibrated, if possible, to the marketplace. In the case of stand-alone benefit charges, a reasonable method of calibration is to ensure that the value of the initial derivative is zero, so that in total, the variable annuity does not generate a gain or loss at issue. In the case of a benefit without stand-alone charges, judgment must be used. However, it is not as critical an assumption in this case, as the "host offset" technique ensures that the contract breaks even at issue.

In theory, the "required profit" component should not be locked in, because market conditions might change. In practice, the component is rarely changed, unless observable market conditions indicate that such a change occurred. This might be noticed, for example, if the "required profit" for new issues of the identical product materially change from the prior year's issues.

The most common technique for establishing a runoff of the initial host offset in an embedded derivative is as follows:

1. Calculate the initial ratio of the host offset to the account value.
2. Lock in the future ratios of host offset to account value by grading the initial ratio to zero linearly over a reasonable amortization period.

Although the account value is listed in the financial statement in the separate account, the host offset is typically shown as an offset to a general account liability.

Under *SFAS 133*, there is no zero floor as there is in *SOP 03-1*, which means that a derivative or embedded derivative can either be a liability or asset. However, because the contract holder can typically surrender the GMAB or GMWB feature (along with the annuity contract) at any time, there are practical limits with respect to how large an asset value should be recorded for these features.

Although not explicitly stated in *SFAS 133*, the increase in all of the *SFAS 133*-related liabilities (i.e., derivative, embedded derivative, host offset) should be reflected in EGPs. However, determining the future movement of the *SFAS 133*-related liabilities is not entirely clear, since the

EGP assumptions are not necessarily consistent with those in *SFAS 133*. For example, best estimate fund growth assumptions are generally higher than risk-free rates.

Some practitioners also adjust the EGPs for interest earned on assets backing the *SFAS 133* liability items.

For example, assume that an insurer perfectly hedges its GMAB derivative. The purchased hedges are recorded at fair value under *SFAS 133*, just as the product feature is. As long as both derivative movements are brought into gross profits, there is no resulting impact on DAC.

8.2.5 Examples

8.2.5.1 Variable Universal Life

Tables 8-1 through 8-5 provide an example of accounting for a variable universal life contract. Contract-level assumptions and policy values are provided in Tables 8-1 and 8-2. It is assumed that premiums are front-ended, with the first year premium of $7,370 exceeding the ultimate renewal premium level of $670 per year by a factor of 11. The unit target premium is $67 per thousand, and the policy is assumed to have an initial death benefit of $100,000. Therefore, the first-year premium is 110% of target, and thereafter the premium is below target. Premiums are determined using the unit premium, the face amount and the expected premium persistency rates shown in Table 8-1. Commissions are paid at declining scale applied to the lesser of paid premium or target premium. First year premiums in excess of target generate a 4% commission. Under U.S. tax regulations, a minimum level of death benefit must be provided in order for a life insurance contract to qualify for certain tax advantages. Therefore, in the case of the example contract, there is a *Corridor Factor* [Table 8-2, column (4)] that describes the amount of the death benefit provided under the contract as a percentage of the account balance. In the base case example, the initial death benefit exceeds the death benefit as determined using the corridor factor and therefore the corridor factor does not enter into consideration in the base case.

Table 8-1
Variable Universal Life Contract
Base Case Assumptions

	Guarantees							
Issue Age	Policy Year	Loads Per Policy	Load % Premium	Load Per 1000	Guaranteed COI per 1000	Current COI per 1000	M&E Charge	Net Appreciation Rate
45	1	$120	2.50%	$0.15	$4.55	$3.64	1.25%	7.00%
	2	120	2.50%	-	4.92	3.94	1.25%	7.00%
	3	120	2.50%	-	5.32	4.26	1.25%	7.00%
	4	120	2.50%	-	5.74	4.59	1.25%	7.00%
	5	120	2.50%	-	6.21	4.97	1.25%	7.00%
	6	120	2.50%	-	6.71	5.37	1.25%	7.00%
	7	120	2.50%	-	7.30	5.84	1.25%	7.00%
	8	120	2.50%	-	7.96	6.37	1.25%	7.00%
	9	120	2.50%	-	8.71	6.97	1.25%	7.00%
	10	120	2.50%	-	9.56	7.65	1.25%	7.00%
	11	120	2.50%	-	10.47	8.38	1.25%	7.00%
	12	120	2.50%	-	11.46	9.17	1.25%	7.00%
	13	120	2.50%	-	12.49	9.99	1.25%	7.00%
	14	120	2.50%	-	13.59	10.87	1.25%	7.00%
	15	120	2.50%	-	14.77	11.82	1.25%	7.00%
	16	120	2.50%	-	16.08	12.86	1.25%	7.00%
	17	120	2.50%	-	17.54	14.03	1.25%	7.00%
	18	120	2.50%	-	19.19	15.35	1.25%	7.00%
	19	120	2.50%	-	21.06	16.85	1.25%	7.00%
	19	120	2.50%	-	21.06	16.85	1.25%	7.00%

Table 8-1 Continued
Variable Universal Life Contract
Base Case Assumptions

	Expenses							
Issue Age	Policy Year	Commission Target Premium	Total Commissions	Deferrable Commissions Below Target	Deferrable Commissions Above Target	Recurring Commissions	Deferrable Acquisition	Maintenance
45	1	$55.00	50.0%	49.0%	4.0%	1.0%	$65.00	$25.00
	2	58.00	5.0%	4.0%	0.0%	1.0%	-	25.00
	3	60.00	5.0%	4.0%	0.0%	1.0%	-	25.00
	4	62.67	5.0%	4.0%	0.0%	1.0%	-	25.00
	5	65.17	2.0%	1.0%	0.0%	1.0%	-	25.00
	6	67.67	2.0%	1.0%	0.0%	1.0%	-	25.00
	7	70.17	2.0%	1.0%	0.0%	1.0%	-	25.00
	8	72.67	2.0%	1.0%	0.0%	1.0%	-	25.00
	9	75.17	2.0%	1.0%	0.0%	1.0%	-	25.00
	10	77.67	2.0%	1.0%	0.0%	1.0%	-	25.00
	11	80.17	1.0%	0.0%	0.0%	1.0%	-	25.00
	12	82.67	1.0%	0.0%	0.0%	1.0%	-	25.00
	13	85.17	1.0%	0.0%	0.0%	1.0%	-	25.00
	14	87.67	1.0%	0.0%	0.0%	1.0%	-	25.00
	15	90.17	1.0%	0.0%	0.0%	1.0%	-	25.00
	16	92.67	1.0%	0.0%	0.0%	1.0%	-	25.00
	17	95.17	1.0%	0.0%	0.0%	1.0%	-	25.00
	18	97.67	1.0%	0.0%	0.0%	1.0%	-	25.00
	19	100.17	1.0%	0.0%	0.0%	1.0%	-	25.00
	20	102.67	1.0%	0.0%	0.0%	1.0%	-	25.00

Table 8-1 Continued
Variable Universal Life Contract
Base Case Assumptions

	Experience					Census			
Issue Age	Policy Year	Mortality	Surrender	Investment Yield	Premium Persistency	BOY	Deaths	Lapses	EOY
45	1	0.0027	12.0%	8.25%	110%	1,000.0000	2.7300	119.6724	877.5976
	2	0.0030	13.0%	8.25%	50%	877.5976	2.5906	113.7509	761.2560
	3	0.0032	7.0%	8.25%	40%	761.2560	2.4299	53.1178	705.7083
	4	0.0034	5.0%	8.25%	30%	705.7083	2.4305	35.1639	668.1139
	5	0.0037	5.0%	8.25%	20%	668.1139	2.4894	33.2812	632.3433
	6	0.0040	5.0%	8.25%	10%	632.3433	2.5458	31.4899	598.3076
	7	0.0044	5.0%	8.25%	10%	598.3076	2.6206	29.7844	565.9027
	8	0.0048	5.0%	8.25%	10%	565.9027	2.7028	28.1600	535.0399
	9	0.0052	5.0%	8.25%	10%	535.0399	2.7961	26.6122	505.6316
	10	0.0057	5.0%	8.25%	10%	505.6316	2.9003	25.1366	477.5947
	11	0.0063	5.0%	8.25%	10%	477.5947	3.0003	23.7297	450.8648
	12	0.0069	5.0%	8.25%	10%	450.8648	3.1001	22.3882	425.3764
	13	0.0075	5.0%	8.25%	10%	425.3764	3.1878	21.1094	401.0792
	14	0.0082	5.0%	8.25%	10%	401.0792	3.2704	19.8904	377.9183
	15	0.0089	5.0%	8.25%	10%	377.9183	3.3491	18.7285	355.8408
	16	0.0096	5.0%	8.25%	10%	355.8408	3.4332	17.6204	334.7872
	17	0.0105	5.0%	8.25%	10%	334.7872	3.5233	16.5632	314.7007
	18	0.0115	5.0%	8.25%	10%	314.7007	3.6235	15.5539	295.5234
	19	0.0126	5.0%	8.25%	10%	295.5234	3.7342	14.5895	277.1997
	20	0.0139	5.0%	8.25%	10%	277.1997	3.8486	13.6676	259.6835

Table 8-2
Variable Universal Life Contract
Base Case Policy-Level Experience

Issue Age	Policy Year	(1) Premium	(2) Unearned Loads	(3) Recurring Loads	(4) Corridor Factor	(5) Death Benefit	(6) Net Amount at Risk	(7) COI	(8) Variable Appreciation	(9) Account Balance	(10) M&E Charges
45	1	$7370	$15	$304	215%	$100,000	$92,949	$338	$470	$7,182	$84
	2	3,350	-	204	209%	100,000	89,671	353	698	10,674	125
	3	2,680	-	187	203%	100,000	86,833	370	896	13,693	160
	4	2,010	-	170	197%	100,000	84,467	388	1,060	16,205	189
	5	1,340	-	154	191%	100,000	82,608	410	1,189	18,170	212
	6	670	-	137	178%	100,000	81,297	436	1,279	19,545	228
	7	670	-	137	171%	100,000	79,921	467	1,373	20,985	245
	8	670	-	137	164%	100,000	78,482	500	1,471	22,490	263
	9	670	-	137	157%	100,000	76,977	536	1,574	24,060	281
	10	670	-	137	150%	100,000	75,406	577	1,681	25,698	300
	11	670	-	137	142%	100,000	73,769	618	1,793	27,407	320
	12	670	-	137	138%	100,000	72,060	661	1,910	29,189	341
	13	670	-	137	134%	100,000	70,278	702	2,031	31,051	363
	14	670	-	137	130%	100,000	68,416	744	2,159	32,999	386
	15	670	-	137	128%	100,000	66,467	785	2,292	35,040	409
	16	670	-	137	124%	100,000	64,427	829	2,432	37,176	434
	17	670	-	137	122%	100,000	62,291	874	2,578	39,414	460
	18	670	-	137	120%	100,000	60,053	922	2,732	41,757	488
	19	670	-	137	119%	100,000	57,710	972	2,892	44,210	516
	20	670	-	137	118%	100,000	55,257	1,023	3,060	46,781	547

Legend:

(1) Premium = $67.00 × face amount in thousands × premium persistency rate.
(2) Unearned load = Expense load per $1,000 face × face amount in thousands.
(3) Recurring loads = Expense load per policy + [Expense load % of premium × (1)].
(4) Corridor factor = Guaranteed minimum death benefit expressed as a percentage of account balance.
(5) Death benefit = Greater of face amount and account balance × (4).
(6) Net amount at risk = (5) – [Account balance + next premium – next unearned load – next recurring load].
(7) COI = Cost of insurance = (6) × current cost of insurance rate / 1,000.
(8) Variable appreciation = Net appreciation rate × [prior account balance + (1) – (2) – (3) – (7)].
(9) Account balance = Prior account balance + (1) – (2) – (3) – (7) + (8), Initially zero.
(10) M&E charges = M&E charge × [prior (9) + (1) – (2) – (3) – (7)].

The example contract includes annual recurring expense charges (loads) that are assessed on a per-contract basis and as a percentage of any premium payment. There is an additional load assessed on a per-1000 basis in the first year. This front-end load is unearned at collection and therefore results in the establishment of an unearned revenue liability (UER). Table 8-3 provides the base case expenses split between those that are deferrable and enter into the DAC calculation and those that are considered maintenance and are used in the computation of EGP. Table 8-4 provides the computation of the EGP for the base case and then the resulting amortization schedule for DAC (Table 8-5) and the recognition pattern for the UER (Table 8-6). The tables have been truncated at 20 years for this presentation and the present value of EGP amounts beyond 20 years are shown for completeness at the bottom of Tables 8-5 and 8-6.

Table 8-3
Variable Universal Life Contract
Base Case Expenses
($'s in 000's)

	(1)	(2)	(3)	(4)	(5)	(6)	(7)
Policy Year	**Premium**	**Deferrable Commission Below Target**	**Deferrable Commission Above Target**	**Recurring Commission**	**Deferrable Acquisition Expense**	**Deferrable Expenses**	**Maintenance**
1	$ 7,370.00	$2,695.00	$74.80	$73.70	$65.00	$2,834.80	$25.00
2	2,939.95	117.60	-	29.40	-	117.60	21.94
3	2,040.17	81.61	-	20.40	-	81.61	19.03
4	1,418.47	56.74	-	14.18	-	56.74	17.64
5	895.27	8.95	-	8.95	-	8.95	16.70
6	423.67	4.24	-	4.24	-	4.24	15.81
7	400.87	4.01	-	4.01	-	4.01	14.96
8	379.15	3.79	-	3.79	-	3.79	14.15
9	358.48	3.58	-	3.58	-	3.58	13.38
10	338.77	3.39	-	3.39	-	3.39	12.64
11	319.99	-	-	3.20	-	-	11.94
12	302.08	-	-	3.02	-	-	11.27
13	285.00	-	-	2.85	-	-	10.63
14	268.72	-	-	2.69	-	-	10.03
15	253.21	-	-	2.53	-	-	9.45
16	238.41	-	-	2.38	-	-	8.90
17	224.31	-	-	2.24	-	-	8.37
18	210.85	-	-	2.11	-	-	7.87
19	198.00	-	-	1.98	-	-	7.39
20	185.72	-	-	1.86	-	-	6.93

Legend:

(1) Premium = Table 8-2 Column (1) × Table 8-1 Census BOY.
(2) Table 8-1 Deferrable commissions below target × [Lesser of Table 8-1 target premium × face / 1,000 and Table 8-2 Premium] × Census BOY.
(3) Table 8-1 Deferrable commissions above target × [Greater of Table 8-2 premium – Table 8-1 target premium × face / 1,000 and zero] × Census BOY.
(4) Table 8-1 Recurring commission × (1).
(5) Table 8-1 Deferrable acquisition expenses × Table 8-1 Census BOY.
(6) (2) + (3) + (5).
(7) Table 8-1 Maintenance expense × Table 8-1 Census BOY.

Table 8-4
Variable Universal Life Contract
Development of Amortization Schedule
($'s in 000's)

Period	(1) Recurring Loads	(2) Maintenance Expenses & Recurring Commissions	(3) M&E Charges	(4) COI's	(5) Account Balance Release Death	(6) Death Benefits	(7) Account Balance Release Lapse	(8) Surrender Benefit	(9) EGP
1	$304.25	$98.70	$83.91	$338.34	$19.61	$273.00	$859.52	$859.52	$374.40
2	178.81	51.34	109.43	309.74	27.65	259.06	1,214.16	1,214.16	315.23
3	142.35	39.43	121.78	281.33	33.27	242.99	727.35	727.35	296.31
4	120.15	31.83	133.60	273.73	39.39	243.05	569.84	569.84	291.98
5	102.56	25.66	141.82	274.19	45.23	248.94	604.72	604.72	289.20
6	86.47	20.05	144.39	275.96	49.76	254.58	615.48	615.48	281.95
7	81.82	18.97	146.67	279.25	54.99	262.06	625.02	625.02	281.72
8	77.39	17.94	148.68	282.82	60.78	270.28	633.31	633.31	281.46
9	73.17	16.96	150.39	286.98	67.28	279.61	640.30	640.30	281.24
10	69.15	16.03	151.80	291.60	74.53	290.03	645.97	645.97	281.02
11	65.31	15.14	152.91	295.10	82.23	300.03	650.35	650.35	280.38
12	61.66	14.29	153.74	297.86	90.49	310.01	653.48	653.48	279.44
13	58.17	13.48	154.30	298.71	98.98	318.78	655.47	655.47	277.90
14	54.85	12.71	154.62	298.33	107.92	327.04	656.37	656.37	275.96
15	51.68	11.98	154.70	296.81	117.35	334.91	656.24	656.24	273.65
16	48.66	11.28	154.54	294.92	127.63	343.32	655.06	655.06	271.16
17	45.78	10.61	154.15	292.63	138.87	352.33	652.82	652.82	268.48
18	43.04	9.98	153.52	290.13	151.30	362.35	649.48	649.48	265.67
19	40.41	9.37	152.63	287.34	165.09	373.42	645.00	645.00	262.68
20	37.91	8.79	151.49	283.55	180.04	384.86	639.38	639.38	259.34

Legend:

(1) Table 8-2 Column (3) × Table 8-1 Census BOY.
(2) Table 8-3 Column (4) + Table 8-3 Column (7).
(3) Table 8-2 Column (10) × Table 8-1 Census BOY.
(4) Table 8-2 Column (7) × Table 8-1 Census BOY.
(5) Table 8-2 Column (9) × Table 8-1 Deaths.
(6) Table 8-2 Column (5) × Table 8-1 Deaths.
(7) Table 8-2 Column (9) × Table 8-1 Lapses.
(8) Table 8-2 Column (9) × Table 8-1 Lapses.
(9) [(1) – (2)] + (3) + {(4) – [(6) – (5)]} + [(7) – (8)].

Table 8-5
Amortization of Deferred Acquisition Costs

Discount Rate	7.00%
Present Value of Deferrable Expenses	$3,081.11
Present Value of EGP's	$3,713.81
Amortization Ratio	82.96%

Period	(10) EGP	(11) BOY DAC	(12) Capitalization	(13) Interest	(14) Amortization	(15) Percent	(16) EOY DAC
1	$374.40	$ -	$2,834.80	$198.44	$310.61	82.96%	$2,722.62
2	315.23	2,722.62	117.60	198.82	261.53	82.96%	2,777.51
3	296.31	2,777.51	81.61	200.14	245.83	82.96%	2,813.42
4	291.98	2,813.42	56.74	200.91	242.24	82.96%	2,828.83
5	289.20	2,828.83	8.95	198.64	239.93	82.96%	2,796.50
6	281.95	2,796.50	4.24	196.05	233.91	82.96%	2,762.87
7	281.72	2,762.87	4.01	193.68	233.72	82.96%	2,726.84
8	281.46	2,726.84	3.79	191.14	233.51	82.96%	2,688.27
9	281.24	2,688.27	3.58	188.43	233.33	82.96%	2,646.95
10	281.02	2,646.95	3.39	185.52	233.14	82.96%	2,602.72
11	280.38	2,602.72	-	182.19	232.62	82.96%	2,552.30
12	279.44	2,552.30	-	178.66	231.83	82.96%	2,499.12
13	277.90	2,499.12	-	174.94	230.56	82.96%	2,443.50
14	275.96	2,443.50	-	171.05	228.95	82.96%	2,385.60
15	273.65	2,385.60	-	166.99	227.03	82.96%	2,325.56
16	271.16	2,325.56	-	162.79	224.96	82.96%	2,263.39
17	268.48	2,263.39	-	158.44	222.74	82.96%	2,199.09
18	265.67	2,199.09	-	153.94	220.41	82.96%	2,132.62
19	262.68	2,132.62	-	149.28	217.93	82.96%	2,063.98
20	259.34	2,063.98	-	144.48	215.16	82.96%	1,993.30
PV 20+	$620.88						

Legend:

(10) From (9).
(11) Initially 0, then prior (16).
(12) Table 8-3 Column (6).
(13) Discount rate × [(11) + (12)].
(14) Amortization ratio × (10).
(15) (14) / (10).
(16) (11) + (12) + (13) – (14).

Table 8-6
Amortization of Unearned Revenue Liability

Discount Rate	7.00%
Present Value of Unearned Revenue	$15.00
Present Value of EGP's	$3,713.81
Amortization Ratio	0.40%

Period	(17) EGP	(18) BOY UER	(19) Capitalization	(20) Interest	(21) Amortization	(22) Percent	(23) EOY UER
1	$374.40	$ -	$15.00	$1.05	$1.51	0.40%	$14.54
2	315.23	14.54	-	1.02	1.27	0.40%	14.28
3	296.31	14.28	-	1.00	1.20	0.40%	14.09
4	291.98	14.09	-	0.99	1.18	0.40%	13.89
5	289.20	13.89	-	0.97	1.17	0.40%	13.70
6	281.95	13.70	-	0.96	1.14	0.40%	13.52
7	281.72	13.52	-	0.95	1.14	0.40%	13.32
8	281.46	13.32	-	0.93	1.14	0.40%	13.12
9	281.24	13.12	-	0.92	1.14	0.40%	12.90
10	281.02	12.90	-	0.90	1.14	0.40%	12.67
11	280.38	12.67	-	0.89	1.13	0.40%	12.43
12	279.44	12.43	-	0.87	1.13	0.40%	12.17
13	277.90	12.17	-	0.85	1.12	0.40%	11.90
14	275.96	11.90	-	0.83	1.11	0.40%	11.61
15	273.65	11.61	-	0.81	1.11	0.40%	11.32
16	271.16	11.32	-	0.79	1.10	0.40%	11.02
17	268.48	11.02	-	0.77	1.08	0.40%	10.71
18	265.67	10.71	-	0.75	1.07	0.40%	10.38
19	262.68	10.38	-	0.73	1.06	0.40%	10.05
20	259.34	10.05	-	0.70	1.05	0.40%	9.70
PV 20+	$620.88						

Legend:
(17) – (23) Comparable to Table 8-5 (10) – (16) except using unearned revenues instead of deferrable expenses.

Table 8-7 provides the expected pre-tax net income developed from the information in Tables 8-1 through 8-6.

Table 8-7
Variable Universal Life Base Case Example
Income Statement
($'s in 000's)

	Revenues					Expenses					
Period	(1) Loads	(2) M&E Charges	(3) COI	(4) Amortization of UER	(5) Total Revenues	(6) Death Benefits	(7) Commissions	(8) Expenses	(9) Amortization of DAC	(10) Total Expenses	(11) Pre-tax Income
1	319.25	83.91	338.34	(14.54)	726.95	253.39	2,843.50	90.00	(2,722.62)	464.27	262.68
2	178.81	109.43	309.74	0.26	598.24	231.41	147.00	21.94	(54.88)	345.47	252.78
3	142.35	121.78	281.33	0.20	545.66	209.72	102.01	19.03	(35.92)	294.84	250.82
4	120.15	133.60	273.73	0.19	527.66	203.66	70.92	17.64	(15.41)	276.82	250.85
5	102.56	141.82	274.19	0.20	518.76	203.71	17.91	16.70	32.34	270.65	248.11
6	86.47	144.39	275.96	0.18	506.99	204.82	8.47	15.81	33.63	262.73	244.26
7	81.82	146.67	279.25	0.19	507.94	207.07	8.02	14.96	36.03	266.07	241.87
8	77.39	148.68	282.82	0.20	509.09	209.49	7.58	14.15	38.57	269.80	239.30
9	73.17	150.39	286.98	0.22	510.76	212.34	7.17	13.38	41.31	274.20	236.56
10	69.15	151.80	291.60	0.23	512.78	215.50	6.78	12.64	44.23	279.14	233.63
11	65.31	152.91	295.10	0.25	513.57	217.80	3.20	11.94	50.43	283.36	230.20
12	61.66	153.74	297.86	0.26	513.52	219.53	3.02	11.27	53.17	286.99	226.53
13	58.17	154.30	298.71	0.27	511.45	219.79	2.85	10.63	55.62	288.90	222.55
14	54.85	154.62	298.33	0.28	508.08	219.12	2.69	10.03	57.90	289.74	218.34
15	51.68	154.70	296.81	0.29	503.48	217.56	2.53	9.45	60.04	289.58	213.90
16	48.66	154.54	294.92	0.30	498.42	215.68	2.38	8.90	62.17	289.14	209.29
17	45.78	154.15	292.63	0.31	492.87	213.46	2.24	8.37	64.30	288.38	204.49
18	43.04	153.52	290.13	0.32	487.01	211.04	2.11	7.87	66.47	287.49	199.52
19	40.41	152.63	287.34	0.33	480.71	208.33	1.98	7.39	68.64	286.34	194.37
20	37.91	151.49	283.55	0.34	473.29	204.82	1.86	6.93	70.68	284.29	189.00

Legend:

(1) [Table 8-2, column (2) + column (3)] × Table 8-1, BOY Census.
(2) Table 8-4, column (3).
(3) Table 8-4, column (4).
(4) Table 8-6, column (18) – column (23).
(5) (1) + (2) + (3) + (4)
(6) Table 8-4, column (6) – column (5).
(7) Table 8-3, column (2) + column (3) + column (4).
(8) Table 8-3, column (5) + column (7).
(9) Table 8-4, column (11) – column (16).
(10) (6) + (7) + (8) + (9).
(11) (5) – (10).

8.2.5.2 Variable Deferred Annuities

Tables 8-8 through 8-13 provide a base case example for a variable deferred annuity. In this example, the contract matures at the beginning of the seventeenth year, and all remaining policyholders are assumed to lapse at the end of the sixteenth year. The contract provides for an annual expense charge, or load, of $30. The variable investments carry a mortality and expense (M&E) charge of 1.65% of invested asset balances. Commissions are paid at 5% of all premiums paid in the first 10 contract years. Because the ultimate commission rate is zero, all the commissions are deferrable. There are assumed to be set-up costs of $125 per contract and ongoing maintenance expenses of $25 for each year the contract is in force. For simplicity, this example excludes the impact of a liability under *SOP 03-1*, as this point is covered in another example later in this chapter.

Table 8-8
Variable Annuity Contract
Base Case Assumptions

	Guarantees				Expenses					
Policy Year	Loads Per Policy	Surrender Charges	M&E Charge	Net Appreciation Rate	Policy Year	Total Commissions	Deferrable Commissions	Recurring Commissions	Deferrable Acquisition	Maintenance
1	$30	6.00%	1.65%	7.00%	1	5.0%	5.0%	0.0%	$125.00	$25.00
2	30	5.00%	1.65%	7.00%	2	5.0%	5.0%	0.0%	0	25.00
3	30	4.00%	1.65%	7.00%	3	5.0%	5.0%	0.0%	0	25.00
4	30	3.00%	1.65%	7.00%	4	5.0%	5.0%	0.0%	0	25.00
5	30	2.00%	1.65%	7.00%	5	5.0%	5.0%	0.0%	0	25.00
6	30	1.00%	1.65%	7.00%	6	5.0%	5.0%	0.0%	0	25.00
7	30	0.00%	1.65%	7.00%	7	5.0%	5.0%	0.0%	0	25.00
8	30	0.00%	1.65%	7.00%	8	5.0%	5.0%	0.0%	0	25.00
9	30	0.00%	1.65%	7.00%	9	5.0%	5.0%	0.0%	0	25.00
10	30	0.00%	1.65%	7.00%	10	5.0%	5.0%	0.0%	0	25.00
11	30	0.00%	1.65%	7.00%	11	0.0%	0.0%	0.0%	0	25.00
12	30	0.00%	1.65%	7.00%	12	0.0%	0.0%	0.0%	0	25.00
13	30	0.00%	1.65%	7.00%	13	0.0%	0.0%	0.0%	0	25.00
14	30	0.00%	1.65%	7.00%	14	0.0%	0.0%	0.0%	0	25.00
15	30	0.00%	1.65%	7.00%	15	0.0%	0.0%	0.0%	0	25.00
16	30	0.00%	1.65%	7.00%	16	0.0%	0.0%	0.0%	0	25.00

	Experience			Census				
Policy Year	Mortality	Surrender	Investment Yield	Premium Persistency	BOY	Deaths	Lapses	EOY
1	0.0036	1.0%	8.65%	100%	1,000.0000	3.6400	9.9636	986.3964
2	0.0039	2.0%	8.65%	50%	986.3964	3.8824	19.6503	962.8637
3	0.0043	2.0%	8.65%	50%	962.8637	4.0980	19.1753	939.5904
4	0.0046	3.0%	8.65%	50%	939.5904	4.3146	28.0583	907.2175
5	0.0050	4.0%	8.65%	50%	907.2175	4.5071	36.1084	866.6020
6	0.0054	5.0%	8.65%	50%	866.6020	4.6519	43.0975	818.8526
7	0.0058	15.0%	8.65%	50%	818.8526	4.7821	122.1106	691.9599
8	0.0064	15.0%	8.65%	50%	691.9599	4.4064	103.1330	584.4205
9	0.0070	15.0%	8.65%	50%	584.4205	4.0722	87.0522	493.2960
10	0.0076	15.0%	8.65%	50%	493.2960	3.7727	73.4285	416.0948
11	0.0084	15.0%	8.65%	50%	416.0948	3.4852	61.8914	350.7181
12	0.0092	15.0%	8.65%	50%	350.7181	3.2154	52.1254	295.3773
13	0.0100	15.0%	8.65%	50%	295.3773	2.9514	43.8639	248.5620
14	0.0109	15.0%	8.65%	50%	248.5620	2.7024	36.8790	208.9807
15	0.0118	15.0%	8.65%	50%	208.9807	2.4693	30.9767	175.5347
16	0.0129	100.0%	8.65%	0%	175.5347	2.2581	173.2766	-

Table 8-9 provides the progression of policy values using the base case net market appreciation assumptions. The contract provides a minimum death benefit of the greater of the account balance or accumulated premiums (less partial withdrawals) using an accumulation rate of 4.5%. Because the base case assumes net market appreciation at 7%, the minimum death benefit is not triggered in the base case. After an initial premium of $6,700, it is assumed that the policyholder makes deposits of half of that amount for each of the remaining contract years. Table 8-10 shows the expenses assumed in the base case for a block of contracts. The expenses are split between deferrable and nondeferrable, or maintenance, expenses.

Table 8-9
Variable Annuity Contract
Base Case Policy-Level Experience

	(1)	(2)	(3)	(4)	(5)	(6)	(7)	(8)	(9)	(10)
Policy Year	Premium	Unearned Loads	Recurring Loads	Guaranteed Minimum Death Benefit Return of Premium Accumulated at 4%	Death Benefit Account Balance	Death Benefit	Variable Appreciation	Account Balance	Cash Surrender Value	M&E Charges
1	$6,700	$ -	$30	$6,968	$7,137	$7,137	$467	$7,137	$6,709	$110
2	3,350	-	30	10,731	11,189	11,189	732	11,189	10,629	173
3	3,350	-	30	14,644	15,525	15,525	1,016	15,525	14,904	239
4	3,350	-	30	18,714	20,164	20,164	1,319	20,164	19,559	311
5	3,350	-	30	22,946	25,127	25,127	1,644	25,127	24,625	387
6	3,350	-	30	31,926	30,439	30,439	1,991	30,439	30,134	469
7	3,350	-	30	36,687	36,122	36,122	2,363	36,122	36,122	557
8	3,350	-	30	41,639	42,203	42,203	2,761	42,203	42,203	651
9	3,350	-	30	46,788	48,709	48,709	3,187	48,709	48,709	751
10	3,350	-	30	52,144	55,672	55,672	3,642	55,672	55,672	858
11	3,350	-	30	63,506	63,121	63,121	4,129	63,121	63,121	973
12	3,350	-	30	69,530	71,092	71,092	4,651	71,092	71,092	1,096
13	3,350	-	30	75,795	79,621	79,621	5,209	79,621	79,621	1,228
14	3,350	-	30	78,827	88,746	88,746	5,806	88,746	88,746	1,369
15	3,350	-	30	-	98,511	98,511	6,445	98,511	98,511	1,519
16	-	-	30	-	105,375	105,375	6,894	105,375	105,375	1,625

Legend:

(1) Premium, $(1)_t$ = \$6,700 × Table 8-8 premium persistency rate.
(2) Unearned loads, $(2)_t = 0$. This example has no unearned loads.
(3) Recurring loads, $(3)_t$ = Table 8-8 expense load per policy.
(4) Guaranteed minimum death benefit, $(4)_t = [(4)_{t-1} + (1)_t] \times (1.04)$.
(5) Death benefit account balance $(5)_t = (8)_t$. This is the death benefit ignoring the GMDB.
(6) Death benefit, $(6)_t = \max[(4)_t, (5)_t]$.
(7) Variable appreciation, $(7)_t$ = net appreciation rate of 7.00% × $[(8)_{t-1} + (1)_t - (2)_t - (3)_t]$.
(8) Account balance $(8)_t = (8)_{t-1} + (1)_t - (2)_t - (3)_t + (7)_t$, initially zero.
(9) Cash surrender value, $(9)_t = (8)_t \times$ [1 – Table 8-8 surrender charge %].
(10) M&E charges, $(10)_t$ = Table 8-8 M&E charge × $[(8)_{t-1} + (1)_t - (2)_t - (3)_t]$.

Table 8-10
Variable Annuity Contract
Base Case Expenses

	(1)	(2)	(3)	(4)	(5)	(6)
Policy Year	**Premium**	**Deferrable Commission**	**Recurring Commission**	**Deferrable Acquisition Expense**	**Deferrable Expenses**	**Maintenance Expenses**
1	$6,700.00	$335.00	-	$125.00	$460.00	$25.00
2	3,304.43	165.22	-	-	165.22	24.66
3	3,225.59	161.28	-	-	161.28	24.07
4	3,147.63	157.38	-	-	157.38	23.49
5	3,039.18	151.96	-	-	151.96	22.68
6	2,903.12	145.16	-	-	145.16	21.67
7	2,743.16	137.16	-	-	137.16	20.47
8	2,318.07	115.90	-	-	115.90	17.30
9	1,957.81	97.89	-	-	97.89	14.61
10	1,652.54	82.63	-	-	82.63	12.33
11	1,393.92	-	-	-	-	10.40
12	1,174.91	-	-	-	-	8.77
13	989.51	-	-	-	-	7.38
14	832.68	-	-	-	-	6.21
15	700.09	-	-	-	-	5.22
16	-	-	-	-	-	4.39

Legend:

(1) Premium, $(1)_t$ = Table 8-9, column $(1)_t$ × Table 8-8 census BOY.

(2) Deferrable commission, $(2)_t$ = Table 8-8 deferrable commission % × Table 8-9, column $(1)_t$ × Table 8-8 census BOY.

(3) Recurring commission, $(3)_1$ = Table 8-8 recurring commission % × Table 8-9, column $(1)_t$ × Table 8-8 census BOY.

(4) Deferrable acquisition expenses, $(4)_t$ = Table 8-8 deferrable acquisition expenses × Table 8-8 census BOY.

(5) Deferrable expenses, $(5)_t = (2)_t + (4)_t$.

(6) Maintenance expenses, $(6)_t$ = Table 8-8 maintenance expense × Table 8-8 census BOY.

The EGPs for the base case contract are developed in Table 8-11. Table 8-12 provides the expected amortization schedule for the DAC.

Table 8-11
Variable Annuity Contract
Development of Amortization Schedule

	(1)	(2)	(3)	(4)	(5)	(6)	(7)	(8)
Period	**Recurring Loads**	**Maintenance Expenses & Recurring Commissions**	**M&E Charges**	**Account Balance Release Death**	**Death Benefits**	**Account Balance Release Lapse**	**Surrender Benefit**	**EGP**
1	$30.00	$25.00	$110.06	$25.98	$25.98	$71.11	$66.84	$119.32
2	29.59	24.66	170.19	43.44	43.44	219.86	208.87	186.12
3	28.89	24.07	230.51	63.62	63.62	297.69	285.78	247.23
4	28.19	23.49	292.15	87.00	87.00	565.76	548.78	313.82
5	27.22	22.68	351.53	113.25	113.25	907.31	889.17	374.21
6	26.00	21.67	406.77	141.60	141.60	1,311.84	1,298.72	424.22
7	24.57	20.47	456.12	172.74	172.74	4,410.87	4,410.87	460.21
8	20.76	17.30	450.32	185.96	185.96	4,352.51	4,352.51	453.78
9	17.53	14.61	438.97	198.36	198.36	4,240.27	4,240.27	441.90
10	14.80	12.33	423.49	210.03	210.03	4,087.87	4,087.87	425.95
11	12.48	10.40	405.01	219.99	219.99	3,906.64	3,906.64	407.09
12	10.52	8.77	384.48	228.59	228.59	3,705.69	3,705.69	386.24
13	8.86	7.38	362.66	234.99	234.99	3,492.47	3,492.47	364.14
14	7.46	6.21	340.16	239.83	239.83	3,272.88	3,272.88	341.40
15	6.27	5.22	317.46	243.26	243.26	3,051.55	3,051.55	318.51
16	5.27	4.39	285.23	237.94	237.94	18,258.98	18,258.98	286.11

Legend:

(1) Recurring loads, $(1)_t$ = Table 8-9 column $(3)_t$ × Table 8-6 Census BOY.

(2) Maintenance expenses & recurring commissions, $(2)_t$ = Table 8-10 column $(3)_t$ + Table 8-10 column $(6)_t$.

(3) M&E charges, $(3)_t$ = Table 8-9 column $(10)_t$ × Table 8-8 Census BOY.

(4) Account balance release death, $(4)_t$ = Table 8-9 column $(8)_t$ × Table 8-8 deaths.

(5) Death benefits, $(5)_t$ = Table 8-9 column $(6)_t$ × Table 8-8 deaths.

(6) Account balance release lapse, $(6)_t$ = Table 8-9 column $(8)_t$ × Table 8-8 lapses.

(7) Surrender benefit, $(7)_t$ = Table 8-9 column $(9)_t$ × Table 8-8 lapses.

(8) EGP, $(8)_t = [(1)_t - (2)_t] + (3)_t + [(4)_t - (5)_t] + [(6)_t - (7)_t]$.

Table 8-12
Variable Annuity Contract
Amortization of Deferred Acquisition Costs

Discount Rate	7.00%
Present Value of Deferrable Expenses	$1,368.66
Present Value of EGP	$3,133.15
Amortization Ratio	43.68%

	(9)	(10)	(11)	(12)	(13)	(14)	(15)
Period	**EGP**	**BOY DAC**	**Capitalization**	**Interest**	**Amortization**	**Percentage**	**EOY DAC**
1	$119.32	-	$460.00	$32.20	$52.12	43.68%	$440.08
2	186.12	440.08	165.22	42.37	81.30	43.68%	566.37
3	247.23	566.37	161.28	50.94	108.00	43.68%	670.58
4	313.82	670.58	157.38	57.96	137.09	43.68%	748.84
5	374.21	748.84	151.96	63.06	163.47	43.68%	800.38
6	424.22	800.38	145.16	66.19	185.31	43.68%	826.41
7	460.21	826.41	137.16	67.45	201.04	43.68%	829.98
8	453.78	829.98	115.90	66.21	198.23	43.68%	813.87
9	441.90	813.87	97.89	63.82	193.03	43.68%	782.55
10	425.95	782.55	82.63	60.56	186.07	43.68%	739.67
11	407.09	739.67	-	51.78	177.83	43.68%	613.62
12	386.24	613.62	-	42.95	168.72	43.68%	487.85
13	364.14	487.85	-	34.15	159.07	43.68%	362.93
14	341.40	362.93	-	25.41	149.14	43.68%	239.20
15	318.51	239.20	-	16.74	139.13	43.68%	116.81
16	286.11	116.81	-	8.18	124.98	43.68%	0.00

Legend:

(9) EGP, $(9)_t$ = Table 8-11, column $(8)_t$.

(10) BOY DAC, $(10)_t = (15)_{t-1}$, initially 0.

(11) Capitalization, $(11)_t$ = Table 8-10 column $(5)_t$.

(12) Interest, $(12)_t$ = discount rate × $[(10)_t + (11)_t]$.

(13) Amortization, $(13)_t$ = amortization ratio × $(9)_t$.

(14) Percentage, $(14)_t = (13)_t / (9)_t$.

(15) EOY DAC, $(15)_t = (10)_t + (11)_t + (12)_1 - (13)_t$.

The results from Table 8-8 through 8-12 are then compiled to produce the expected net income in Table 8-13.

Table 8-13
Variable Annuity Contract
Income Statement

	Revenues					Expenses					
Period	(1) Loads	(2) M&E Charges	(3) Amortization of UER	(4) Surrender Charges	(5) Total Revenues	(6) Death Benefits	(7) Commissions	(8) Expenses	(9) Amortization of DAC	(10) Total Expenses	(11) Pre-tax Income
1	$30.00	$110.06	-	4.27	$144.32	-	$335.00	$150.00	($440.08)	$44.92	$99.40
2	29.59	170.19	-	10.99	$210.78	-	165.22	24.66	(126.29)	63.59	147.19
3	28.89	230.51	-	11.91	$271.30	-	161.28	24.07	(104.22)	81.13	190.17
4	28.19	292.15	-	16.97	$337.31	-	157.38	23.49	(78.25)	102.62	234.69
5	27.22	351.53	-	18.15	$396.89	-	151.96	22.68	(51.55)	123.09	273.80
6	26.00	406.77	-	13.12	$445.88	-	145.16	21.67	(26.03)	140.79	305.09
7	24.57	456.12	-	-	$480.68	-	137.16	20.47	(3.57)	154.06	326.63
8	20.76	450.32	-	-	$471.08	-	115.90	17.30	16.11	149.31	321.77
9	17.53	438.97	-	-	$456.51	-	97.89	14.61	31.32	143.82	312.68
10	14.80	423.49	-	-	$438.29	-	82.63	12.33	42.88	137.84	300.45
11	12.48	405.01	-	-	$417.49	-	-	10.40	126.05	136.46	281.04
12	10.52	384.48	-	-	$395.01	-	-	8.77	125.77	134.54	260.47
13	8.86	362.66	-	-	$371.52	-	-	7.38	124.92	132.30	239.22
14	7.46	340.16	-	-	$347.62	-	-	6.21	123.73	129.95	217.67
15	6.27	317.46	-	-	$323.73	-	-	5.22	122.39	127.62	196.12
16	5.27	285.23	-	-	$290.50	-	-	4.39	116.81	121.19	169.30
17	-	-	-	-	-	-	-	-	-	-	-
18	-	-	-	-	-	-	-	-	-	-	-
19	-	-	-	-	-	-	-	-	-	-	-
20	-	-	-	-	-	-	-	-	-	-	-

Legend:

(1) Loads, $(1)_t$ = [Table 8-9, column $(2)_t$ + Table 8-9, column $(3)_t$] × Table 8-8, BOY Census.
(2) M&E charges, $(2)_t$ = Table 8-11, column $(3)_t$.
(3) These contracts have no unearned revenue.
(4) Surrender charges, $(4)_t$ = Table 8-11, column $(6)_t$ – Table 8-11, column $(7)_t$.
(5) Total revenues, $(5)_t = (1)_t + (2)_t + (3)_t + (4)_t$.
(6) Death benefits, $(6)_t$ = Table 8-11, column $(5)_t$ – Table 8-11, column $(4)_t$.
(7) Commissions, $(7)_t$ = Table 8-10, column $(2)_t$ + Table 8-10, column $(3)_t$.
(8) Expenses, $(8)_t$ = Table 8-10, column $(4)_t$ + Table 8-10, column $(5)_t$ + Table 8-10, column $(6)_t$.
(9) Amortization of DAC, $(9)_t$ = Table 8-12, column $(10)_t$ – Table 8-12, column $(15)_t$.
(10) Total expenses, $(10)_t = (6)_t + (7)_t + (8)_t + (9)_t$.
(11) Pre-tax income, $(11)_t = (5)_t - (10)_t$.

8.2.5.3 Variable Payout Annuity

The variable payout annuity base case example is illustrated in Tables 8-14 through 8-24. The contract used is a single-premium immediate annuity. The assumed interest rate used in determining the initial premium is 6%. Mortality rates used in the premium are shown in Table 8-14 along with other assumptions.

Table 8-14
Variable Payout Annuity Contract
Assumptions

	Guarantees							Expenses				
Policy Year	Load % Premium	Income Units Purchased	Pricing Qx times 1000	M&E Charge	Net Appreciation Rate	Assumed Interest Rate AIR	Income Unit Value IUV	Policy Year	Total Commissions	Deferrable Commissions	Deferrable Acquisition	Maintenance
1	2.00%	17,337.54	1.92	1.00%	7.00%	6.00%	1.0094	1	7.0%	7.0%	$175.00	$25.00
2	-	17,337.54	2.15	1.00%	7.00%	6.00%	1.0190	2	-	-	-	25.00
3	-	17,337.54	2.41	1.00%	7.00%	6.00%	1.0286	3	-	-	-	25.00
4	-	17,337.54	2.67	1.00%	7.00%	6.00%	1.0383	4	-	-	-	25.00
5	-	17,337.54	2.96	1.00%	7.00%	6.00%	1.0481	5	-	-	-	25.00
6	-	17,337.54	3.25	1.00%	7.00%	6.00%	1.0580	6	-	-	-	25.00
7	-	17,337.54	3.54	1.00%	7.00%	6.00%	1.0679	7	-	-	-	25.00
8	-	17,337.54	3.85	1.00%	7.00%	6.00%	1.0780	8	-	-	-	25.00
9	-	17,337.54	4.16	1.00%	7.00%	6.00%	1.0882	9	-	-	-	25.00
10	-	17,337.54	4.47	1.00%	7.00%	6.00%	1.0984	10	-	-	-	25.00
11	-	17,337.54	4.80	1.00%	7.00%	6.00%	1.1088	11	-	-	-	25.00
12	-	17,337.54	5.13	1.00%	7.00%	6.00%	1.1193	12	-	-	-	25.00
13	-	17,337.54	5.47	1.00%	7.00%	6.00%	1.1298	13	-	-	-	25.00
14	-	17,337.54	5.83	1.00%	7.00%	6.00%	1.1405	14	-	-	-	25.00
15	-	17,337.54	6.23	1.00%	7.00%	6.00%	1.1512	15	-	-	-	25.00
16	-	17,337.54	6.67	1.00%	7.00%	6.00%	1.1621	16	-	-	-	25.00
17	-	17,337.54	7.19	1.00%	7.00%	6.00%	1.1731	17	-	-	-	25.00
18	-	17,337.54	7.79	1.00%	7.00%	6.00%	1.1841	18	-	-	-	25.00
19	-	17,337.54	8.50	1.00%	7.00%	6.00%	1.1953	19	-	-	-	25.00
20	-	17,337.54	9.33	1.00%	7.00%	6.00%	1.2066	20	-	-	-	25.00

	Experience			Census			
Policy Year	Mortality	Surrender	Investment Yield	BOY	Deaths	Lapses	EOY
1	0.0020	-	8.00%	1,000.0000	1.9672	-	998.0328
2	0.0022	-	8.00%	998.0328	2.2039	-	995.8289
3	0.0025	-	8.00%	995.8289	2.4571	-	993.3718
4	0.0027	-	8.00%	993.3718	2.7231	-	990.6487
5	0.0030	-	8.00%	990.6487	3.0008	-	987.6480
6	0.0033	-	8.00%	984.3623	3.5766	-	980.7857
7	0.0036	-	8.00%	980.7857	3.8700	-	976.9157
8	0.0039	-	8.00%	976.9157	4.1640	-	972.7517
9	0.0043	-	8.00%	972.7517	4.4597	-	968.2920
10	0.0046	-	8.00%	968.2920	4.7592	-	963.5328
11	0.0049	-	8.00%	958.4691	5.3751	-	953.0940
12	0.0053	-	8.00%	953.0940	5.6974	-	947.3966
13	0.0056	-	8.00%	947.3966	6.0456	-	941.3510
14	0.0060	-	8.00%	941.3510	6.4362	-	934.9149
15	0.0064	-	8.00%	934.9149	6.8866	-	928.0282
16	0.0068	-	8.00%	920.6162	8.0246	-	912.5916
17	0.0074	-	8.00%	912.5916	8.7285	-	903.8631
18	0.0080	-	8.00%	903.8631	9.5247	-	894.3384
19	0.0087	-	8.00%	894.3384	10.4129	-	883.9254
20	0.0096	-	8.00%	883.9254	11.3920	-	872.5335

The assumed initial deposit (or premium) is $25,000. An initial load of 2% is assessed, and the remaining $20,000 is used to purchase 17,337.54 income units, each worth $1.00 of annual life-contingent annuity payments. The income unit value determines the income benefit associated with the 17,337.54 income units. It is determined as the excess of accumulating the deposit at the net appreciation rate (7.00%) in this example over accumulating the deposit at the assumed interest rate of 6%, as previously described. Table 8-15 shows the first 20 years of contract values including the progression of expected annuity payments. Table 8-16 provides the expenses expected in the variable payout annuity base case.

Table 8-15
Variable Payout Annuity Contract
Base Case Policy-Level Experience

Policy Year	(1) Premium	(2) Unearned Loads	(3) Recurring Loads	(4) Annuity Benefit	(5) Mortality Assesment	(6) Interest Credited	(7) Account Balance	(8) M&E Charges
1	$250,000	$5,000	$ -	$17,501	$16,997	$17,150	$245,153	$2,450
2	-	-	-	17,666	17,100	17,161	245,214	2,452
3	-	-	-	17,833	17,200	17,165	245,179	2,452
4	-	-	-	18,001	17,298	17,163	245,044	2,452
5	-	-	-	18,171	17,394	17,153	244,803	2,450
6	-	-	-	18,342	17,489	17,136	244,450	2,448
7	-	-	-	18,515	17,585	17,112	243,977	2,445
8	-	-	-	18,690	17,681	17,078	243,374	2,440
9	-	-	-	18,866	17,779	17,036	242,631	2,434
10	-	-	-	19,044	17,878	16,984	241,737	2,426
11	-	-	-	19,224	17,978	16,922	240,681	2,417
12	-	-	-	19,405	18,078	16,848	239,451	2,407
13	-	-	-	19,588	18,179	16,762	238,033	2,395
14	-	-	-	19,773	18,279	16,662	236,416	2,380
15	-	-	-	19,960	18,375	16,549	234,590	2,364
16	-	-	-	20,148	18,463	16,421	232,549	2,346
17	-	-	-	20,338	18,537	16,278	230,290	2,325
18	-	-	-	20,530	18,595	16,120	227,816	2,303
19	-	-	-	20,724	18,633	15,947	225,130	2,278
20	-	-	-	20,919	18,650	15,759	222,239	2,251

Legend:

(1) Premium = $250,000.
(2) Unearned load, $(2)_t$ = Table 14 expense load % of premium × $(1)_t$.
(3) Recurring loads = none.
(4) Annuity benefit = Table 14 income units purchased × Table 14 IUV.
(5) Mortalilty assesment, $(5)_t = (4)_t$ – reserve adjustment due to expected deaths.
(6) Interest credited, $(6)_t$ = Table 14 net appreciation rate × $(7)_{t-1} + (1)_t - (2)_t - (3)_t$.
(7) Account balance $(7)_t = (7)_{t-1} + (1)_t - (2)_t - (3)_t - (5)_t + (6)_t$, initially zero.
(8) M&E charges, $(8)_t$ = Table 14 M&E charge % × $[(9)_{t-1} + (1)_t - (2)_t - (3)_t]$.

Table 8-16
Variable Payout Annuity Contract
Base Case Expenses

Policy Year	(1) Premium	(2) Deferrable Commission	(3) Recurring Commission	(4) Deferrable Acquisition Expense	(5) Deferrable Expenses	(6) Maintenance Expenses
1	250,000.00	17,500.00	-	175.00	17,675.00	25.00
2	-	-	-	-	-	24.95
3	-	-	-	-	-	24.90
4	-	-	-	-	-	24.83
5	-	-	-	-	-	24.77
6	-	-	-	-	-	24.69
7	-	-	-	-	-	24.61
8	-	-	-	-	-	24.52
9	-	-	-	-	-	24.42
10	-	-	-	-	-	24.32
11	-	-	-	-	-	24.21
12	-	-	-	-	-	24.09
13	-	-	-	-	-	23.96
14	-	-	-	-	-	23.83
15	-	-	-	-	-	23.68
16	-	-	-	-	-	23.53
17	-	-	-	-	-	23.37
18	-	-	-	-	-	23.20
19	-	-	-	-	-	23.02
20	-	-	-	-	-	22.81

Legend:

(1) Premium, $(1)_t$ = Table 8-1 column $(1)_t$ × Table 8-11 census BOY.

(2) Deferrable commission, $(2)_t$ = Table 8-14 deferrable commission % × Table 8-15 column $(1)_t$ × Table 14 census BOY.

(3) Recurring commission, $(3)_t$ = Table 8-14 recurring commission % × $(1)_t$.

(4) Deferrable acquisition expense, $(4)_t$ = Table 8-14 deferrable acquisition expenses × Table 8-14 census BOY.

(5) Deferrable expenses, $(5)_t = (2)_t + (4)_t$.

(6) Maintenance expenses, $(6)_t$ = Table 8-14 maintenance expense × Table 8-14 census BOY.

Table 8-17 illustrates the components of EGP for the base case variable payout annuity contract. In this case, the expense component of EGP includes only the maintenance expenses with no ongoing expense loads to offset it. The investment component comprises the M&E charges. The mortality component includes the mortality assessment which is the annual expected annuity benefits underlying the policyholder account balance progression reduced by the policyholder account balances released through death. Tables 8-18 and 8-19 use the EGP to develop the amortization of DAC and recognition of unearned revenue.

Table 8-17
Variable Payout Annuity Contract
Development of Amortization Schedule

Period	(1) Recurring Loads	(2) Maintenance Expenses & Recurring Commissions	(3) M&E Charges	(4) Mortality Assesment	(5) Account Balance Release Death	(6) Annuity Benefit	(7) Account Balance Release Lapse	(8) EGP
1	-	25.00	2,450.00	16,997.02	482.26	17,466.68	-	2,437.60
2	-	24.95	2,446.71	17,066.22	540.43	17,592.52	-	2,435.89
3	-	24.90	2,441.91	17,128.01	602.43	17,714.67	-	2,432.78
4	-	24.83	2,435.54	17,182.97	667.28	17,832.77	-	2,428.18
5	-	24.77	2,427.52	17,231.13	734.59	17,946.48	-	2,422.01
6	-	24.69	2,417.79	17,273.40	803.18	18,055.52	-	2,414.16
7	-	24.61	2,406.27	17,309.93	872.61	18,159.63	-	2,404.56
8	-	24.52	2,392.89	17,341.49	941.86	18,258.62	-	2,393.10
9	-	24.42	2,377.56	17,368.56	1,010.31	18,352.31	-	2,379.69
10	-	24.32	2,360.20	17,390.81	1,078.07	18,440.52	-	2,364.24
11	-	24.21	2,340.72	17,407.70	1,145.46	18,522.99	-	2,346.68
12	-	24.09	2,319.04	17,418.93	1,212.51	18,599.47	-	2,326.92
13	-	23.96	2,295.06	17,423.98	1,279.45	18,669.65	-	2,304.87
14	-	23.83	2,268.68	17,421.76	1,346.96	18,733.12	-	2,280.45
15	-	23.68	2,239.80	17,408.48	1,418.23	18,789.18	-	2,253.65
16	-	23.53	2,208.32	17,379.70	1,496.72	18,836.76	-	2,224.45
17	-	23.37	2,174.14	17,330.57	1,585.93	18,874.40	-	2,192.86
18	-	23.20	2,137.16	17,256.63	1,688.57	18,900.30	-	2,158.86
19	-	23.02	2,097.31	17,153.83	1,806.59	18,912.30	-	2,122.41
20	-	22.81	2,054.52	17,020.09	1,939.80	18,908.13	-	2,083.47

Legend:

(1) Recurring loads, $(1)_t$ = Table 8-15 column $(3)_t$ × Table 8-14 census BOY.
(2) Maintenance expenses & recurring commissions, $(2)_t$ = Table 8-16 column $(3)_t$ + Table 8-16 column $(6)_t$.
(3) M&E charges, $(3)_t$ = Table 8-15 column $(8)_t$ × Table 8-14 census BOY.
(4) Mortality assessment, $(4)_t$ = Table 8-15 column $(5)_t$ × Table 8-14 census BOY.
(5) Account balance release death, $(5)_t$ = Table 8-15 column $(7)_t$ × Table 8-14 deaths.
(6) Annuity benefit, $(6)_t$ = Table 8-15 column $(4)_t$ × Table 8-14 census EOY.
(7) Account balance release lapse, $(7)_t$ = Table 8-15 column $(7)_t$ × Table 8-14 lapses.
(8) EGP, $(8)_t = [(1)_t - (2)_t] + (3)_t + [(4)_t + (5)_t - (6)_t]$.

Table 8-18
Variable Payout Annuity Contract
Amortization of Deferred Acquisition Costs

Discount Rate	7.00%
Present Value of Deferrable Expenses	$17,675.00
Present Value of EGP's	$29,670.60
Amortization Ratio	59.57%

Period	(9) EGP	(10) BOY DAC	(11) Capitalization	(12) Interest	(13) Amortization	(14) Percentage	(15) EOY DAC
1	2,437.60	-	17,675.00	1,237.25	1,452.10	59.57%	17,460.15
2	2,435.89	17,460.15	-	1,222.21	1,451.08	59.57%	17,231.29
3	2,432.78	17,231.29	-	1,206.19	1,449.22	59.57%	16,988.25
4	2,428.18	16,988.25	-	1,189.18	1,446.48	59.57%	16,730.95
5	2,422.01	16,730.95	-	1,171.17	1,442.81	59.57%	16,459.31
6	2,414.16	16,459.31	-	1,152.15	1,438.13	59.57%	16,173.33
7	2,404.56	16,173.33	-	1,132.13	1,432.42	59.57%	15,873.04
8	2,393.10	15,873.04	-	1,111.11	1,425.59	59.57%	15,558.56
9	2,379.69	15,558.56	-	1,089.10	1,417.60	59.57%	15,230.06
10	2,364.24	15,230.06	-	1,066.10	1,408.40	59.57%	14,887.77
11	2,346.68	14,887.77	-	1,042.14	1,397.94	59.57%	14,531.98
12	2,326.92	14,531.98	-	1,017.24	1,386.17	59.57%	14,163.05
13	2,304.87	14,163.05	-	991.41	1,373.03	59.57%	13,781.44
14	2,280.45	13,781.44	-	964.70	1,358.48	59.57%	13,387.65
15	2,253.65	13,387.65	-	937.14	1,342.52	59.57%	12,982.27
16	2,224.45	12,982.27	-	908.76	1,325.12	59.57%	12,565.91
17	2,192.86	12,565.91	-	879.61	1,306.30	59.57%	12,139.22
18	2,158.86	12,139.22	-	849.75	1,286.05	59.57%	11,702.92
19	2,122.41	11,702.92	-	819.20	1,264.34	59.57%	11,257.79
20	2,083.47	11,257.79	-	788.04	1,241.14	59.57%	10,804.69
PV 20+	4,687.10						

Legend:

(9) EGP, $(9)_t$ = Table 8-17, column $(8)_t$.

(10) BOY DAC, $(10)_t = (15)_{t-1}$. Initially 0.

(11) Capitalization, $(11)_t$ = Table 8-16 column $(5)_t$.

(12) Interest, $(12)_t$ = discount rate × $[(10)_t + (11)_t]$.

(13) Amortization, $(13)_t$ = amortization ratio × $(9)_t$.

(14) Percentage, $(14)_t = (13)_t / (9)_t$.

(15) EOY DAC, $(15)_t = (10)_t + (11)_t + (12)_t - (13)_t$.

Table 8-19
Variable Payout Annuity Contract
Amortization of Unearned Revenue Liability

Discount Rate	7.00%
Present Value of Unearned Revenue	$5,000.00
Present Value of EGP's	$29,670.60
Amortization Ratio	16.85%

	(16)	(17)	(18)	(19)	(20)	(21)	(22)
Period	**EGP**	**BOY UER**	**Capitalization**	**Interest**	**Amortization**	**Percentage**	**EOY UER**
1	2,437.60	-	5,000.00	350.00	410.78	16.85%	4,939.22
2	2,435.89	4,939.22	-	345.75	410.49	16.85%	4,874.48
3	2,432.78	4,874.48	-	341.21	409.96	16.85%	4,805.73
4	2,428.18	4,805.73	-	336.40	409.19	16.85%	4,732.94
5	2,422.01	4,732.94	-	331.31	408.15	16.85%	4,656.10
6	2,414.16	4,656.10	-	325.93	406.83	16.85%	4,575.20
7	2,404.56	4,575.20	-	320.26	405.21	16.85%	4,490.25
8	2,393.10	4,490.25	-	314.32	403.28	16.85%	4,401.29
9	2,379.69	4,401.29	-	308.09	401.02	16.85%	4,308.36
10	2,364.24	4,308.36	-	301.59	398.42	16.85%	4,211.53
11	2,346.68	4,211.53	-	294.81	395.46	16.85%	4,110.88
12	2,326.92	4,110.88	-	287.76	392.13	16.85%	4,006.52
13	2,304.87	4,006.52	-	280.46	388.41	16.85%	3,898.57
14	2,280.45	3,898.57	-	272.90	384.29	16.85%	3,787.17
15	2,253.65	3,787.17	-	265.10	379.78	16.85%	3,672.50
16	2,224.45	3,672.50	-	257.07	374.86	16.85%	3,554.71
17	2,192.86	3,554.71	-	248.83	369.53	16.85%	3,434.01
18	2,158.86	3,434.01	-	240.38	363.80	16.85%	3,310.59
19	2,122.41	3,310.59	-	231.74	357.66	16.85%	3,184.66
20	2,083.47	3,184.66	-	222.93	351.10	16.85%	3,056.49
PV 20+	4,687.10						

Legend:

(16) EGP, $(16)_t$ = Table 8-17, column $(8)_t$.

(17) BOY UER, $(17)_t = (22)_{t-1}$. Initially 0.

(18) Capitalization, $(18)_t$ = Table 8-15 column $(2)_t$.

(19) Interest, $(19)_t$ = discount rate × $[(17)_t + (18)_t]$.

(20) Amortization, $(20)_t$ = amortization ratio × $(16)_t$.

(21) Percentage, $(21)_t = (20)_t \,/\, (16)_t$.

(22) EOY UER, $(22)_t = (17)_t + (18)_t + (19)_t - (20)_t$.

Table 8-20 provides the pre-tax income for the variable payout annuity base case.

Table 8-20
Variable Payout Annuity Contract
Income Statement

	Revenues					Expenses					
	(1)	(2)	(3)	(4)	(5)	(6)	(7)	(8)	(9)	(10)	(11)
Period	**Loads**	**M&E Charges**	**Mortality Assesment**	**Amortization of UER**	**Total Revenues**	**Annuity Benefit**	**Commissions**	**Expenses**	**Amortization of DAC**	**Total Expenses**	**Pre-Tax Income**
1	5,000.00	2,450.00	16,997.02	(4,939.22)	19,507.80	16,984.42	17,500.00	200.00	(17,460.15)	17,224.27	2,283.53
2	-	2,446.71	17,066.22	64.74	19,577.67	17,052.09	-	24.95	228.87	17,305.91	2,271.76
3	-	2,441.91	17,128.01	68.75	19,638.67	17,112.25	-	24.90	243.03	17,380.18	2,258.49
4	-	2,435.54	17,182.97	72.79	19,691.30	17,165.50	-	24.83	257.30	17,447.64	2,243.66
5	-	2,427.52	17,231.13	76.84	19,735.50	17,211.89	-	24.77	271.64	17,508.29	2,227.21
6	-	2,417.79	17,273.40	80.90	19,772.10	17,252.34	-	24.69	285.98	17,563.02	2,209.08
7	-	2,406.27	17,309.93	84.95	19,801.15	17,287.03	-	24.61	300.28	17,611.92	2,189.23
8	-	2,392.89	17,341.49	88.96	19,823.34	17,316.76	-	24.52	314.48	17,655.76	2,167.59
9	-	2,377.56	17,368.56	92.93	19,839.05	17,342.01	-	24.42	328.50	17,694.93	2,144.12
10	-	2,360.20	17,390.81	96.83	19,847.83	17,362.44	-	24.32	342.29	17,729.05	2,118.78
11	-	2,340.72	17,407.70	100.65	19,849.07	17,377.53	-	24.21	355.79	17,757.53	2,091.54
12	-	2,319.04	17,418.93	104.36	19,842.33	17,386.96	-	24.09	368.93	17,779.97	2,062.36
13	-	2,295.06	17,423.98	107.95	19,826.99	17,390.20	-	23.96	381.62	17,795.78	2,031.21
14	-	2,268.68	17,421.76	111.40	19,801.84	17,386.16	-	23.83	393.78	17,803.77	1,998.07
15	-	2,239.80	17,408.48	114.68	19,762.96	17,370.95	-	23.68	405.38	17,800.02	1,962.94
16	-	2,208.32	17,379.70	117.78	19,705.81	17,340.04	-	23.53	416.36	17,779.93	1,925.87
17	-	2,174.14	17,330.57	120.70	19,625.42	17,288.48	-	23.37	426.69	17,738.54	1,886.88
18	-	2,137.16	17,256.63	123.42	19,517.21	17,211.73	-	23.20	436.30	17,671.23	1,845.98
19	-	2,097.31	17,153.83	125.92	19,377.06	17,105.71	-	23.02	445.13	17,573.86	1,803.20
20	-	2,054.52	17,020.09	128.17	19,202.78	16,968.32	-	22.81	453.09	17,444.23	1,758.55

Legend:

(1) Loads, $(1)_t$ = [Table 8-15, column $(2)_t$ + Table 8-15, column $(3)_t$] × Table 8-14, BOY census.
(2) M&E charges, $(2)_t$ = Table 8-17, column $(3)_t$.
(3) Mortality assessment, $(3)_t$ = Table 8-17, column $(4)_t$.
(4) Amortization of UER, $(4)_t$ = Table 8-19, column $(17)_t$ – Table 8-19, column $(22)_t$.
(5) Total revenues, $(5)_t = (1)_t + (2)_t + (3)_t + (4)_t$.
(6) Annuity benefit, $(6)_t$ = Table 8-17, column $(6)_t$ – Table 8-17, column $(5)_t$.
(7) Commissions, $(7)_t$ = Table 8-16, column $(2)_t$ + Table 8-16, column $(3)_t$.
(8) Expenses, $(8)_t$ = Table 8-16, column $(4)_t$ + Table 8-16, column $(6)_t$.
(9) Amortization of DAC, $(9)_t$ = Table 8-18, column $(10)_t$ – Table 8-18, column $(15)_t$.
(10) Total expenses, $(10)_t = (6)_t + (7)_t + (8)_t + (9)_t$.
(11) Pre-tax income, $(11)_t = (5)_t - (10)_t$.

8.2.5.4 Alternative Contract Rate Assumptions

Earlier in this chapter, alternative approaches to estimating the future contract rates used in developing EGP for variable contracts were discussed. Table 8-20 illustrates the effect of one of these alternatives, under a specific scenario of actual investment appreciation rates, on the base case variable deferred annuity amortization and pre-tax operating income.

Table 8-21 provides the EGP and resulting DAC roll forward arising from the use of a *level prospective* approach to establishing future contract rate assumptions. Under this approach, the future contract rate assumption is independent of what has happened in the past. In the table, the contract rate assumptions used to determine EGP are shown for each of the first four years of experience. The EGPs that result from the assumptions are also provided. It is assumed that in all future years, the contract rate will be 7%. A 7% rate is also used to determine the present values of capitalized acquisition costs and EGPs to determine the amortization rate, and the discount rate is not adjusted from the value at contract inception. For past years, the actual earned contract rate is substituted for the 7% assumption, which creates a difference between the EGP originally estimated and actual amounts. These differences create an additional amount of DAC amortization shown in the DAC roll forward. The example assumes that in years 1–3, the actual earned rates are 12%, 10%, and 3%, respectively.

Table 8-21
Deferred Variable Annuity
DAC Amortization using "Level Prospective" Assumption

	EGP								DAC Rollforward						
	Year 1		Year 2		Year 3		Year 4		(1)	(2)	(3)	(4)	(5)	(6)	(7)
Period	Yield	EGP	Yield	EGP	Yield	EGP	Yield	EGP	BOY DAC	Capitalization	Interest	Amortization	Percentage	Additional	EOY DAC
1	7.00%	$119.32	12.00%	$119.52	12.00%	$119.52	12.00%	$119.52	-	$460.00	$32.20	$52.12	43.68%	($0.64)	$440.72
2	7.00%	186.12	7.00%	191.90	10.00%	192.21	10.00%	192.21	440.72	165.22	42.42	82.66	43.07%	(1.40)	567.10
3	7.00%	247.23	7.00%	253.19	7.00%	258.60	3.00%	258.13	567.10	161.28	50.99	110.15	42.59%	4.25	664.97
4	7.00%	313.82	7.00%	320.08	7.00%	325.77	7.00%	315.80	664.97	157.38	57.56	136.85	43.33%	-	743.06
5	7.00%	374.21	7.00%	380.64	7.00%	386.48	7.00%	376.24	743.06	151.96	62.65	163.04	43.33%	-	794.63
6	7.00%	424.22	7.00%	430.67	7.00%	436.53	7.00%	426.26	794.63	145.16	65.79	184.72	43.33%	-	820.86
7	7.00%	460.21	7.00%	466.53	7.00%	472.26	7.00%	462.21	820.86	137.16	67.06	200.29	43.33%	-	824.78
8	7.00%	453.78	7.00%	459.50	7.00%	464.68	7.00%	455.59	824.78	115.90	65.85	197.43	43.33%	-	809.11
9	7.00%	441.90	7.00%	447.06	7.00%	451.74	7.00%	443.53	809.11	97.89	63.49	192.20	43.33%	-	778.29
10	7.00%	425.95	7.00%	430.62	7.00%	434.85	7.00%	427.43	778.29	82.63	60.26	185.22	43.33%	-	735.95
11	7.00%	407.09	7.00%	411.30	7.00%	415.12	7.00%	408.42	735.95	-	51.52	176.99	43.33%	-	610.49
12	7.00%	386.24	7.00%	390.03	7.00%	393.48	7.00%	387.44	610.49	-	42.73	167.89	43.33%	-	485.33
13	7.00%	364.14	7.00%	367.56	7.00%	370.66	7.00%	365.22	485.33	-	33.97	158.27	43.33%	-	361.03
14	7.00%	341.40	7.00%	344.49	7.00%	347.28	7.00%	342.38	361.03	-	25.27	148.37	43.33%	-	237.94
15	7.00%	318.51	7.00%	321.28	7.00%	323.79	7.00%	319.38	237.94	-	16.66	138.40	43.33%	-	116.19
16	7.00%	286.11	7.00%	288.60	7.00%	290.86	7.00%	286.90	116.19	-	8.13	124.33	43.33%	-	-

Legend:

(1) BOY DAC = present value of column (2) as of current year less (5) × present value of EGP for appropriate year.

(2) Capitalization, $(2)_t$ = Table 8-10 column $(5)_t$.

(3) Interest, $(3)_t = 7\% \times [(1)_1 + (2)_t]$.

(4) Amortization, $(4)_t = (5)_t \times$ EGP for appropriate year and period.

(5) Percentage, $(5)_t$ = present value, at 7%, of all of column (2) / present value, at 7%, of appropriate EGP column.

(6) Additional, $(6)_t = (1)_t + (2)_t + (3)_t - (4)_t$ less $(1)_{t+1}$.

(7) EOY DAC, $(7)_t = (1)_t + (2)_t + (3)_t - (4)_t - (6)_t$.

Table 8-22 uses the same assumptions and methods as Table 8-21 with the one exception that future contract rates are estimated using a method that assumes each five-year period, beginning with the most recently completed year, will produce an average contract rate of 7%. For example, at the beginning of year two, the most recent contract rate was 12% and the next four years are each assumed to produce a contract rate of 5.75% such that the average over the five years is 7%. This method is referred to as the five-year average method.

Table 8-22
Deferred Variable Annuity
DAC Amortization using "Five Year Average" Assumption

	EGP								DAC Rollforward						
	Year 1		Year 2		Year 3		Year 4		(1)	(2)	(3)	(4)	(5)	(6)	(7)
Period	Yield	EGP	Yield	EGP	Yield	EGP	Yield	EGP	BOY DAC	Capitalization	Interest	Amortization	Percentage	Additional	EOY DAC
1	7.00%	$119.32	12.00%	$119.52	12.00%	$119.52	12.00%	$119.52	-	$460.00	$32.20	$52.12	43.68%	$0.44	$439.64
2	7.00%	186.12	5.75%	191.76	10.00%	192.21	10.00%	192.21	439.64	165.22	42.34	84.34	43.98%	(2.48)	565.34
3	7.00%	247.23	5.75%	250.80	6.25%	258.51	3.00%	258.13	565.34	161.28	50.86	111.53	43.14%	(3.22)	669.17
4	7.00%	313.82	5.75%	314.50	6.25%	323.78	8.00%	315.96	669.17	157.38	57.86	134.71	42.63%	-	749.71
5	7.00%	374.21	5.75%	371.18	6.25%	382.13	8.00%	379.40	749.71	151.96	63.12	161.75	42.63%	-	803.03
6	7.00%	424.22	7.00%	417.09	6.25%	429.55	8.00%	432.89	803.03	145.16	66.37	184.56	42.63%	-	830.00
7	7.00%	460.21	7.00%	453.23	7.00%	462.60	8.00%	472.50	830.00	137.16	67.70	201.45	42.63%	-	833.41
8	7.00%	453.78	7.00%	447.47	7.00%	455.94	7.00%	468.85	833.41	115.90	66.45	199.89	42.63%	-	815.87
9	7.00%	441.90	7.00%	436.19	7.00%	443.85	7.00%	455.52	815.87	97.89	63.96	194.21	42.63%	-	783.52
10	7.00%	425.95	7.00%	420.80	7.00%	427.72	7.00%	438.26	783.52	82.63	60.63	186.85	42.63%	-	739.93
11	7.00%	407.09	7.00%	402.44	7.00%	408.68	7.00%	418.19	739.93	-	51.80	178.29	42.63%	-	613.43
12	7.00%	386.24	7.00%	382.04	7.00%	387.67	7.00%	396.25	613.43	-	42.94	168.94	42.63%	-	487.43
13	7.00%	364.14	7.00%	360.36	7.00%	365.43	7.00%	373.16	487.43	-	34.12	159.10	42.63%	-	362.46
14	7.00%	341.40	7.00%	338.00	7.00%	342.57	7.00%	349.53	362.46	-	25.37	149.02	42.63%	-	238.81
15	7.00%	318.51	7.00%	315.45	7.00%	319.55	7.00%	325.82	238.81	-	16.72	138.91	42.63%	-	116.62
16	7.00%	286.11	7.00%	283.36	7.00%	287.05	7.00%	292.68	116.62	-	8.16	124.78	42.63%	-	-

Legend:

(1) BOY DAC = Present value of column (2) as of current year less (5) × present value of EGP for appropriate year.

(2) Capitalization, $(2)_t$ = Table 8-10 column $(5)_t$.

(3) Interest, $(3)_t = 7\% \times [(1)_t + (2)_t]$.

(4) Amortization, $(4)_t = (5)_t \times$ EGP for appropriate year and period.

(5) Percentage, $(5)_t$ = present value, at 7%, of all of column (2) / present value, at 7%, of appropriate EGP column.

(6) Additional, $(6)_t = (1)_t + (2)_t + (3)_t - (4)_t$ less $(1)_{t+1}$.

(7) EOY DAC, $(7)_t = (1)_t + (2)_t + (3)_t - (4)_t - (6)_t$.

The additional amortization shown in Table 8-22 is different in magnitude and, in the first year, in direction relative to the additional amortization shown in Table 8-21. In the first year, the combination of contract rates used to develop the 5-year average produces a lower estimated future policyholder account balance at the end of the 5-year period, resulting in lower estimate future EGP and therefore additional DAC amortization. In Table 8-21, the additional appreciation earned in the first year is assumed to be retained and accumulated at 7%; therefore future account balances are all estimated to be greater than those used in the prior-year estimates, which results in higher estimates of future EGP and therefore an amount of additional amortization that actually increases the unamortized DAC balance relative to what it otherwise would have been.

Tables 8-23 and 8-24 correspond to Tables 8-21 and 8-22 and show the pre-tax income expected to be produced through the combination of the higher assumed levels of market appreciation and the DAC amortization adjustments.

Table 8-23
Deferred Variable Annuity
Pre-Tax Operating Income Using "Level Prospective" Assumption

	Revenues					Expenses						
	(1)	(2)	(3)	(4)	(5)	(6)	(7)	(8)	(9)	(10)	(11)	(12)
Period	Loads	M&E Charges	Amortization of UER	Surrender Charges	Total Revenues	Death Benefits	Commissions	Expenses	Amortization of DAC	Total Expenses	Pre-tax Operating Income	Base Case Pre-tax Operating Income
1	$30.00	$110.06	-	$4.47	$144.52	-	$335.00	$150.00	($440.72)	$44.28	$100.24	$99.40
2	29.59	175.62	-	11.66	216.87	-	165.22	24.66	(126.38)	63.50	153.37	147.19
3	28.89	241.32	-	12.00	282.20	-	161.28	24.07	(97.87)	87.48	194.72	190.17
4	28.19	294.02	-	17.08	339.29	-	157.38	23.49	(78.10)	102.78	236.51	234.69
5	27.22	353.46	-	18.25	398.92	-	151.96	22.68	(51.57)	123.07	275.85	273.80
6	26.00	408.74	-	13.18	447.92	-	145.16	21.67	(26.22)	140.60	307.33	305.09
7	24.57	458.11	-	-	482.68	-	137.16	20.47	(3.92)	153.71	328.97	326.63
8	20.76	452.13	-	-	472.89	-	115.90	17.30	15.67	148.88	324.01	321.77
9	17.53	440.61	-	-	458.14	-	97.89	14.61	30.82	143.32	314.82	312.68
10	14.80	424.96	-	-	439.76	-	82.63	12.33	42.33	137.29	302.47	300.45
11	12.48	406.34	-	-	418.82	-	-	10.40	125.47	135.87	282.95	281.04
12	10.52	385.68	-	-	396.20	-	-	8.77	125.16	133.93	262.28	260.47
13	8.86	363.74	-	-	372.60	-	-	7.38	124.29	131.68	240.93	239.22
14	7.46	341.14	-	-	348.59	-	-	6.21	123.09	129.31	219.28	217.67
15	6.27	318.34	-	-	324.61	-	-	5.22	121.75	126.97	197.64	196.12
16	5.27	286.02	-	-	291.29	-	-	4.39	116.19	120.58	170.71	169.30
Sum											3,912.08	3,875.68

Legend:

(1) Loads, $(1)_t$ = [Table 8-9, column $(2)_t$ + Table 8-9, column $(3)_t$] × Table 8-8, BOY census.
(2) M&E charges reflect the alternative appreciation rates used in this example.
(3) These contracts have no unearned revenue.
(4) Surrender charges reflect the input of alternative appreciation rates used in this example.
(5) Total revenues, $(5)_t = (1)_t + (2)_t + (3)_t + (4)_t$.
(6) Death benefits. The death benefit is equal to the account balance released on death.
(7) Commissions, $(7)_t$ = Table 8-10, column $(2)_t$ + Table 8-10,column $(3)_t$.
(8) Expenses, $(8)_t$ = Table 8-10, column $(4)_t$ + Table 8-10, column $(6)_t$.
(9) Amortization of DAC, $(9)_t$ = Table 8-21, column $(1)_t$ − Table 8-21, column $(7)_t$.
(10) Total expenses, $(10)_t = (6)_t + (7)_t + (8)_t + (9)_t$.
(11) Pre-tax income, $(11)_t = (5)_t - (10)_t$.
(12) Base case pre-tax income, $(12)_t$ = Table 8-13, column $(11)_t$

Table 8-24
Deferred Variable Annuity
Pre-tax Operating Income Using "Five Year Average" Assumption

	Revenues					Expenses						
	(1)	(2)	(3)	(4)	(5)	(6)	(7)	(8)	(9)	(10)	(11)	(12)
Period	**Loads**	**M&E Charges**	**Amortization of UER**	**Surrender Charges**	**Total Revenues**	**Death Benefits**	**Commissions**	**Expenses**	**Amortization of DAC**	**Total Expenses**	**Pre-tax Operating Income**	**Base Case Pre-tax Operating Income**
1	$30.00	$110.06	-	$4.47	$144.52	-	$335.00	$150.00	($439.64)	$45.36	$99.16	$99.40
2	29.59	175.62	-	11.66	216.87	-	165.22	24.66	(125.71)	64.17	152.70	$147.19
3	28.89	241.32	-	12.00	282.20	-	161.28	24.07	(103.83)	81.52	200.68	$190.17
4	28.19	294.02	-	17.08	339.29	-	157.38	23.49	(80.53)	100.34	238.95	$234.69
5	27.22	353.46	-	18.25	398.92	-	151.96	22.68	(53.32)	121.32	277.61	$273.80
6	26.00	408.74	-	13.18	447.92	-	145.16	21.67	(26.97)	139.85	308.07	$305.09
7	24.57	458.11	-	-	482.68	-	137.16	20.47	(3.41)	154.22	328.46	$326.63
8	20.76	452.13	-	-	472.89	-	115.90	17.30	17.54	150.74	322.15	$321.77
9	17.53	440.61	-	-	458.14	-	97.89	14.61	32.35	144.85	313.28	$312.68
10	14.80	424.96	-	-	439.76	-	82.63	12.33	43.59	138.55	301.21	$300.45
11	12.48	406.34	-	-	418.82	-	-	10.40	126.50	136.90	281.92	$281.04
12	10.52	385.68	-	-	396.20	-	-	8.77	126.00	134.77	261.44	$260.47
13	8.86	363.74	-	-	372.60	-	-	7.38	124.97	132.36	240.25	$239.22
14	7.46	341.14	-	-	348.59	-	-	6.21	123.65	129.86	218.73	$217.67
15	6.27	318.34	-	-	324.61	-	-	5.22	122.19	127.42	197.19	$196.12
16	5.27	286.02	-	-	291.29	-	-	4.39	116.62	121.01	170.28	$169.30
Sum											3,912.08	$3,875.68

Legend:

(1) Loads, $(1)_t$ = [Table 8-9, column $(2)_t$ + Table 8-9, column $(3)_t$] × Table 8-8, BOY census.
(2) M&E charges reflect the alternative appreciation rates used in this example.
(3) These contracts have no unearned revenue.
(4) Surrender charges reflect the impact of alternative appreciation rates used in this example.
(5) Total revenues, $(5)_t = (1)_t + (2)_t + (3)_t + (4)_t$.
(6) Death benefits. The death benefit is equal to the account balance released on death.
(7) Commissions, $(7)_t$ = Table 8-10, column $(2)_t$ + Table 8-10,column $(3)_t$.
(8) Expenses, $(8)_t$ = Table 8-10, column $(4)_t$ + Table 8-10, column $(6)_t$.
(9) Amortization of DAC, $(9)_t$ = Table 8-22, column $(1)_t$ − Table 8-22, column $(7)_t$.
(10) Total expenses, $(10)_t = (6)_t + (7)_t + (8)_t + (9)_t$.
(11) Pre-tax income, $(11)_t = (5)_t - (10)_t$.
(12) Base case pre-tax income, $(12)_t$ = Table 8-13, column $(11)_t$

The results from Tables 8-23 and 8-24 are graphically displayed in Figure 8-2.

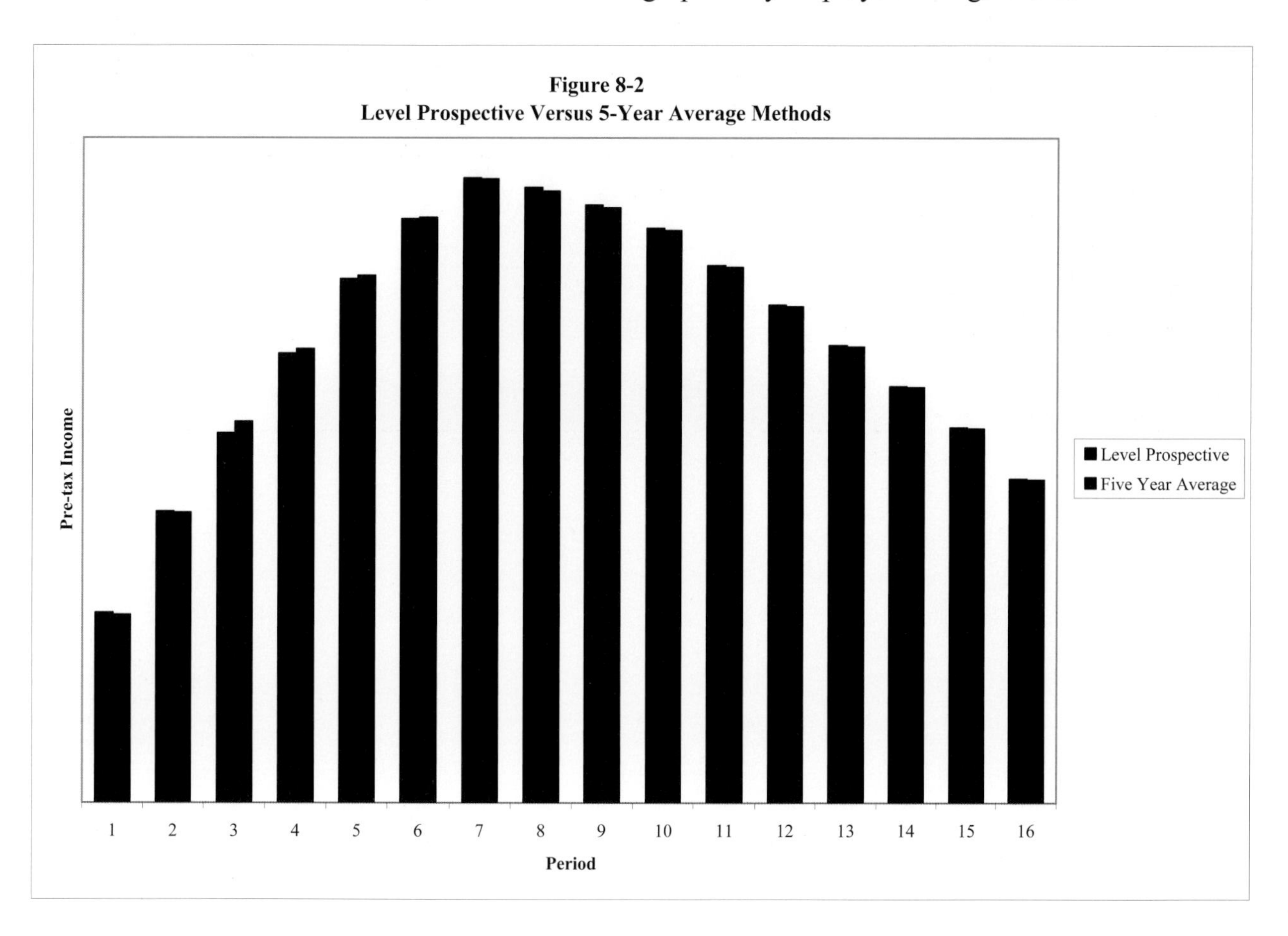

Figure 8-2
Level Prospective Versus 5-Year Average Methods

Both approaches produce approximately the same pattern of pre-tax income. The level prospective approach generally produces a more significant effect on pre-tax income in years when the actual contract rate is different from the assumed rate. However, the 5-year average approach will produce an assumption for the future year or years that is based on market trends reversing from the most recent year relative to the longer-term estimate. Therefore, if the market returns to the long-term estimate of performance, the 5-year average approach will produce an additional amount of amortization in that year whereas the level prospective approach will not. Note that the effect of the different approaches varies among the different variable product types based on the relative importance of investment results on future EGP. Further, actuaries have adopted a number of refinements to these basic methods, designed to produce a reasonable and appropriate DAC amortization pattern under a variety of scenarios.

Note what would have occurred if returns were bouncing around a lot more!

8.2.5.5 GMDB

Tables 8-25 through 8-33 provide a base case example for the calculation of a single premium variable deferred annuity GMDB liability and resulting DAC. In this example, the contract matures at the end of the tenth year. The variable investments carry a mortality and expense (M&E) charge of 1.50% of invested asset balances. Commissions are paid at 7% of the single premium. The death benefit is equal to the larger of the account value and premiums accumulated at 5% interest. The valuation date is at the end of the third year.

Table 8-25 lists the DAC assumptions. Because the valuation date is at the end of the third year, the assumptions listed for the first three years are based on historical experience and the assumptions for years 4 to 16 are best estimates as of the end of year 3.

Table 8-25
Variable Annuity GMDB Provision
Base Case DAC Assumptions

	(1)	(2)	(3)	(4)	(5)	(6)	(7)	(8)
Period	**Premium**	**M&E Charges**	**Surrender Charges**	**Deferrable Acquisition Expenses**	**Maintenance Per Policy**	**Mortality Rate**	**Surrender Rate**	**Gross Appreciation Rate**
1	20,000	1.50%	6.00%	7.00%	35	0.0036	1%	-2.00%
2	-	1.50%	5.00%	0.00%	35	0.0039	2%	5.00%
3	-	1.50%	4.00%	0.00%	35	0.0043	3%	4.00%
4	-	1.50%	3.00%	0.00%	35	0.0046	4%	8.00%
5	-	1.50%	2.00%	0.00%	35	0.0050	5%	8.00%
6	-	1.50%	1.00%	0.00%	35	0.0054	6%	8.00%
7	-	1.50%	0.00%	0.00%	35	0.0058	30%	8.00%
8	-	1.50%	0.00%	0.00%	35	0.0064	10%	8.00%
9	-	1.50%	0.00%	0.00%	35	0.0070	10%	8.00%
10	-	1.50%	0.00%	0.00%	35	0.0076	100%	8.00%

Table 8-26 lists the additional *SOP 03-1*-related assumptions. Analogous to the DAC assumptions, the first three years' assumptions are based on historical experience while the remaining years' assumptions are best estimates as of the end of year 3. Note that the average gross appreciation rate is equal to the gross appreciation rate used for EGPs.

Table 8-26
Variable Annuity GMDB Provision
Base Case SOP Specific Assumptions

	(9) Gross Appreciation Rate			(10) Average Gross Appreciation Rate
Period	**Scenario A**	**Scenario B**	**Scenario C**	
1	-2.00%	-2.00%	-2.00%	-2.00%
2	5.00%	5.00%	5.00%	5.00%
3	4.00%	4.00%	4.00%	4.00%
4	3.00%	9.00%	12.00%	8.00%
5	7.00%	-5.00%	22.00%	8.00%
6	-12.00%	18.00%	18.00%	8.00%
7	9.00%	4.00%	11.00%	8.00%
8	15.00%	9.00%	0.00%	8.00%
9	2.00%	7.00%	15.00%	8.00%
10	9.00%	2.00%	13.00%	8.00%

Table 8-27 shows the policy level development of the scenario-specific account balance and excess death benefit in force, which will be used in the *SOP 03-1* liability determination.

Similarly, Table 8-28 shows the policy level development of items, which will be used for EGP determination. Note that the account balance in Table 8-28 is based on the deterministic EGP assumptions, but the excess death benefit in force is based on the scenario-specific *SOP* liability assumptions, which is consistent with the numerical example provided with *SOP 03-1*.

Table 8-27
Variable Annuity GMDB Provision
Base Case Policy Level Experience for SOP 03-1 Additional Liability Calculation

	(1) Account Balance			(2) Premium +	(3) Death Benefit Account Balance			(4) Excess Death Benefit Inforce			(5)
Period	**Scenario A**	**Scenario B**	**Scenario C**	**5% Interest**	**Scenario A**	**Scenario B**	**Scenario C**	**Scenario A**	**Scenario B**	**Scenario C**	**Average**
1	19,300.00	19,300.00	19,300.00	21,000.00	21,000.00	21,000.00	21,000.00	1,700.00	1,700.00	1,700.00	1,700.00
2	19,975.50	19,975.50	19,975.50	22,050.00	22,050.00	22,050.00	22,050.00	2,074.50	2,074.50	2,074.50	2,074.50
3	20,474.89	20,474.89	20,474.89	23,152.50	23,152.50	23,152.50	23,152.50	2,677.61	2,677.61	2,677.61	2,677.61
4	20,782.01	22,010.50	22,624.75	24,310.13	24,310.13	24,310.13	24,310.13	3,528.11	2,299.62	1,685.37	2,504.37
5	21,925.02	20,579.82	27,262.82	25,525.63	25,525.63	25,525.63	27,262.82	3,600.61	4,945.81	-	2,848.81
6	18,965.14	23,975.49	31,761.19	26,801.91	26,801.91	26,801.91	31,761.19	7,836.77	2,826.42	-	3,554.40
7	20,387.53	24,574.88	34,778.50	28,142.01	28,142.01	28,142.01	34,778.50	7,754.48	3,567.13	-	3,773.87
8	23,139.85	26,418.00	34,256.83	29,549.11	29,549.11	29,549.11	34,256.83	6,409.26	3,131.11	-	3,180.13
9	23,255.54	27,870.98	38,881.50	31,026.56	31,026.56	31,026.56	38,881.50	7,771.02	3,155.58	-	3,642.20
10	24,999.71	28,010.34	43,352.87	32,577.89	32,577.89	32,577.89	43,352.87	7,578.18	4,567.55	-	4,048.58

Legend:

(1) Account Balance $(1)_t = ((1)_{t-1} + \text{Table 8-25 column } (1)_t) \times (1 + \text{Table 8-26 column } (9)_t - \text{Table 8-25 column } (2)_t)$.

(2) Premium + 5% Interest $(2)_t = ((2)_{t-1} + \text{Table 8-25 column } (1)_t) \times 1.05$.

(3) Death Benefit Account Balance = maximum $((1)_t, (2)_t)$.

(4) Excess Death Benefit Inforce $(4)_t = (3)_t - (1)_t$.

(5) Average Death Benefit Inforce $(5)_t$ = Average of $(4)_t$ Scenarios A, B, C.

Table 8-28 Variable Annuity GMDB Provision Base Case Policy Level Experience for DAC Calculation						
	(6)	(7)	(8)	(9)	(10)	(11)
Period	Premium	Variable Appreciation	M&E Charges	Account Balance	Cash Surrender Value	Excess Death Benefit Inforce
1	20,000.00	(400.00)	300.00	19,300.00	18,142.00	1,700.00
2	-	965.00	289.50	19,975.50	18,976.73	2,074.50
3	-	799.02	299.63	20,474.89	19,655.89	2,677.61
4	-	1,637.99	307.12	21,805.76	21,151.58	2,504.37
5	-	1,744.46	327.09	23,223.13	22,758.67	2,848.81
6	-	1,857.85	348.35	24,732.63	24,485.31	3,554.40
7	-	1,978.61	370.99	26,340.25	26,340.25	3,773.87
8	-	2,107.22	395.10	28,052.37	28,052.37	3,180.13
9	-	2,244.19	420.79	29,875.77	29,875.77	3,642.20
10	-	2,390.06	448.14	31,817.70	31,817.70	4,048.58

Legend:

(6) Premium $(6)_t$ = Table 8-25 column $(1)_t$.

(7) Variable Appreciation $(7)_t$ = Table 8-25 column $(8)_t \times ((9)_{t-1} + (6)_t)$.

(8) M&E Charges $(8)_t$ = Table 8-25 column $(2)_t \times ((9)_{t-1} + (6)_t)$.

(9) Account Balance $(9)_t = (9)_{t-1} + (6)_t + (7)_t - (8)_t$.

(10) Cash Surrender Value $(10)_t = (9)_t \times (1 -$ Table 8-25 column $(3)_t)$.

(11) Excess Death Benefit In Force $(11)_t$ = Table 8-27 column $(5)_t$.

Table 8-29 shows the development of the census.

Table 8-29 Variable Annuity GMDB Provision Census				
	(1)	(2)	(3)	(4)
Period	BOY	Deaths	Surrenders	EOY
1	1,000.0000	3.6000	9.9640	986.4360
2	986.4360	3.8471	19.6518	962.9371
3	962.9371	4.1406	28.7639	930.0326
4	930.0326	4.2781	37.0302	888.7243
5	888.7243	4.4436	44.2140	840.0666
6	840.0666	4.5364	50.1318	785.3984
7	785.3984	4.5553	234.2529	546.5902
8	546.5902	3.4982	54.3092	488.7828
9	488.7828	3.4215	48.5361	436.8252
10	436.8252	3.3199	433.5053	-

Legend:

(1) BOY $(1)_t = (4)_{t-1}$.

(2) Deaths $(2)_t = (1)_t \times$ Table 8-25 column $(6)_t$.

(3) Surrenders $(3)_t = ((1)_t - (2)_t) \times$ Table 8-25 column $(7)_t$.

(4) EOY $(1)_t = (1)_t - (2)_t - (3)_t$.

Table 8-30 shows how unadjusted EGPs (before incorporation of increase of *SOP 03-1* liability) are calculated, and Table 8-31 illustrates how the *SOP 03-1* liability is calculated. Note that for both calculations, assessments and maintenance expenses are based on the deterministic assumptions, but the excess death benefits are based on an average of the scenario specific assumptions. This is consistent with the numerical example provided with *SOP 03-1*. The liability, which must be posted to the financials at the end of year 3, is $13,653.

Table 8-30
Variable Annuity GMDB Provision
Development of Unadjusted EGPs

Period	(1) M&E Charges	(2) Surrender Charges	(3) Total Assessments	(4) Maintenance Expenses	(5) Excess Death Benefits Paid	(6) Unadjusted EGP
1	300,000	11,538	311,538	35,000	6,120	270,418
2	285,573	19,628	305,201	34,525	7,981	262,695
3	288,527	23,558	312,085	33,703	11,087	267,295
4	285,635	24,224	309,859	32,551	10,714	266,594
5	290,690	20,536	311,225	31,105	12,659	267,461
6	292,635	12,399	305,034	29,402	16,124	259,507
7	291,375	-	291,375	27,489	17,191	246,694
8	215,960	-	215,960	19,131	11,125	185,705
9	205,673	-	205,673	17,107	12,462	176,104
10	195,757	-	195,757	15,289	13,441	167,028

Legend:

(1) M&E Charges $(1)_t$ = Table 8-29 column $(1)_t$ × Table 8-28 column $(8)_t$.
(2) Surrender Charges $(2)_t$ = Table 8-29 column $(3)_t$ × (Table 8-28 column $(9)_t$ – Table 8-28 column $(10)_t$).
(3) Total Assesments $(3)_t = (1)_t + (2)_t$.
(4) Maintenance Expenses $(4)_t$ = Table 8-29 column $(1)_t$ × Table 8-25 column $(5)_t$.
(5) Excess Death Benefits Paid $(5)_t$ = Table 8-29 column $(2)_t$ × Table 8-28 column $(11)_t$.
(6) Unadjusted EGP $(6)_t = (3) - (4) - (5)$.

Table 8-31
Variable Annuity GMDB Provision
Development of GMDB Liability

Discount Rate	6.50%
Present Value of Excess Death Benefits Paid	$82,594
Present Value of Assessments	$2,035,999
Benefit Ratio	4.0567%

	(1)	(2)	(3)	(4)	(5)	(6)
Period	**Assessments**	**BOY Liability**	**Interest**	**Assessments × Benefit Ratio**	**Excess Death Benefits Paid**	**EOY Liability**
1	311,538	-	-	12,638	6,120	6,518
2	305,201	6,518	424	12,381	7,981	11,342
3	312,085	11,342	737	12,660	11,087	13,653
4	309,859	13,653	887	12,570	10,714	16,396
5	311,225	16,396	1,066	12,625	12,659	17,428
6	305,034	17,428	1,133	12,374	16,124	14,811
7	291,375	14,811	963	11,820	17,191	10,403
8	215,960	10,403	676	8,761	11,125	8,716
9	205,673	8,716	567	8,344	12,462	5,164
10	195,757	5,164	336	7,941	13,441	0

Legend:

(1) Assessments $(1)_t$ = Table 8-30 column $(3)_t$.
(2) BOY Reserve $(2)_t = (6)_{t-1}$.
(3) Interest $(3)_t = (2)_t \times$ discount rate.
(4) Assessments × Benefit Ratio $(4)_t = (1) \times$ Benefit Ratio.
(5) Excess Death Benefits Paid $(5)_t$ = Table 8-30 column $(5)_t$.
(6) EOY Reserve $(6)_t = (2)_t + (3)_t + (4)_t - (5)_t$.

Table 8-32 shows how EGPs are determined in order to compute the DAC, which is calculated in Table 8-33. Note in this example, interest on assets backing the *SOP 03-1* liability is not included, which is consistent with the numerical example provided with *SOP 03-1*. The DAC, which must be posted to the financials at the end of year 3, is $1,016,169.

Table 8-32
Variable Annuity GMDB Provision
Development of EGPs

Period	(1) Unadjusted EGP	(2) Increase in GMDB Liability	(3) EGP
1	270,418	6,518	263,900
2	262,695	4,824	257,871
3	267,295	2,311	264,984
4	266,594	2,743	263,850
5	267,461	1,032	266,429
6	259,507	(2,617)	262,124
7	246,694	(4,408)	251,103
8	185,705	(1,688)	187,392
9	176,104	(3,552)	179,655
10	167,028	(5,164)	172,192

Legend:

(1) Unadjusted EGP $(1)_t$ = Table 8-30 column $(6)_t$.
(2) Increase in GMDB Reserve $(2)_t$ = Table 8-31column $(6)_t$ – Table 8-31 column $(6)_{t-1}$.
(3) EGP $(3)_t = (1)_t - (2)_t$.

Table 8-33
Variable Annuity GMDB Provision
Development of DAC

Discount Rate	6.50%
Present Value of Deferrable Expenses	1,400,000
Present Value of EGP	$1,742,189
Amortization Ratio	80.3587%

Period	(1) EGP	(2) BOY DAC	(3) Capitilization	(4) Interest	(5) Amortization	(6) EOY DAC
1	263,900	-	1,400,000	91,000	212,067	1,278,933
2	257,871	1,278,933	-	83,131	207,222	1,154,842
3	264,984	1,154,842	-	75,065	212,938	1,016,969
4	263,850	1,016,969	-	66,103	212,027	871,046
5	266,429	871,046	-	56,618	214,099	713,565
6	262,124	713,565	-	46,382	210,639	549,307
7	251,103	549,307	-	35,705	201,783	383,229
8	187,392	383,229	-	24,910	150,586	257,553
9	179,655	257,553	-	16,741	144,369	129,926
10	172,192	129,926	-	8,445	138,371	0

Legend:

(1) EGP $(1)_t$ = Table 8-32 column $(3)_t$.
(2) BOY DAC $(2)_t = (6)_{t-1}$.
(3) Capitalization $(3)_t$ = Table 8-29 column $(1)_t$ × Table 8-28 column $(6)_t$ × Table 8-25 column $(4)_t$.
(4) Interest $(4)_t = ((2) + (3)) \times$ discount rate.
(5) Amortization $(5)_t = (1) \times$ amortization ratio.
(6) EOY DAC $(6)_t = (2)_t + (3)_t + (4)_t - (5)_t$.

8.2.5.6 GMAB

Tables 8-34 through 8-38 provide a base case example of a single premium variable deferred annuity with a GMAB provision. This example illustrates a method of calibrating the required profit margin at issue and how a liability valuation formula is derived. The GMAB rider benefit is a return of premium at the end of 10 years and the rider charges are specified.

Table 8-34 lists the best estimate non-economic assumptions, and Table 8-35 lists the economic assumptions, all as of the issue date. In this example, the average of the scenario-specific gross appreciation rate assumptions equals the risk-free forward interest rates, implying that the assumptions are market consistent. (In practice, the volatility of returns should also calibrate to the implied volatility observed in the market.)

Table 8-34
Variable Annuity GMAB Provision
Base Case Best Estimate Assumptions

Period	(1) Premium	(2) M&E Charges for Base Policy	(3) Charges for GMAB	(4) Mortality Rate	(5) Surrender Rate
1	20,000	1.50%	1.00%	0.0036	1%
2	-	1.50%	1.00%	0.0039	2%
3	-	1.50%	1.00%	0.0043	3%
4	-	1.50%	1.00%	0.0046	4%
5	-	1.50%	1.00%	0.0050	5%
6	-	1.50%	1.00%	0.0054	6%
7	-	1.50%	1.00%	0.0058	30%
8	-	1.50%	1.00%	0.0064	10%
9	-	1.50%	1.00%	0.0070	10%
10	-	1.50%	1.00%	0.0076	100%

Table 8-35
Variable Annuity GMAB Provision
Base Case GMAB Economic Assumptions

	(6)			(7)	(8)
	Forward Rate Curve	Gross Appreciation Rate		Average Gross	Risk-free
Period	Scenario A	Scenario B	Scenario C	Appreciation Rate	Forward Rate
1	2.25%	-4.75%	9.25%	2.25%	2.25%
2	-1.00%	-3.50%	12.00%	2.50%	2.50%
3	1.50%	3.50%	2.50%	2.50%	2.50%
4	-2.00%	4.00%	7.00%	3.00%	3.00%
5	1.25%	-9.25%	17.75%	3.25%	3.25%
6	-16.50%	13.50%	13.50%	3.50%	3.50%
7	4.75%	-0.25%	6.75%	3.75%	3.75%
8	11.00%	5.00%	-4.00%	4.00%	4.00%
9	-1.75%	3.25%	11.25%	4.25%	4.25%
10	3.50%	-1.50%	11.50%	4.50%	4.50%

Table 8-36 shows the policy level development of the scenario-specific account balance and maturity benefit, which will be used in the *SFAS 133* liability determination. The maturity benefit is equal to the excess of the single premium over the account balance and cannot be less than zero. Scenarios A and B are in the money; Scenario C is not.

Table 8-36
Variable Annuity GMAB Provision
Base Case Policy Level Experience

(1) Account Balance			(2)	(3) Maturity Benefit		
Scenario A	**Scenario B**	**Scenario C**	**Guaranteed Account Balance**	**Scenario A**	**Scenario B**	**Scenario C**
19,950.00	18,550.00	21,350.00	20,000.00	-	-	-
19,251.75	17,437.00	23,378.25	20,000.00	-	-	-
19,059.23	17,611.37	23,378.25	20,000.00	-	-	-
18,201.57	17,875.54	24,430.27	20,000.00	-	-	-
17,974.05	15,775.16	28,155.89	20,000.00	-	-	-
14,558.98	17,510.43	31,253.04	20,000.00	-	-	-
14,886.56	17,028.90	32,581.29	20,000.00	-	-	-
16,151.91	17,454.62	30,463.51	20,000.00	-	-	-
15,465.46	17,585.53	33,129.06	20,000.00	-	-	-
15,620.11	16,882.11	36,110.68	20,000.00	4,379.89	3,117.89	-

Legend:

Account Balance $(1)_t = ((1)_{t-1} + \text{Table 8-34 column } (1)_t) \times (1 + \text{Table 8-35 column } (6)_t - \text{Table 8-34 column } (2)_t - \text{Table 8-34 column } (3)_t)$.
Guaranteed Account Balance $(2)_t$ = Guaranteed Account Balance $(1)_t$ + Table 8-34 column $(1)_t$.
Maturity Benefit $(3)_{10}$ = maximium($(2)_{10}$ – (1)10),0).

Table 8-37 shows the development of the census.

Table 8-37
Variable Annuity GMAB Provision
Census

(1) BOY	(2) Deaths	(3) Surrenders	(4) EOY
1,000.0000	3.6000	9.9640	986.4360
986.4360	3.8471	19.6518	962.9371
962.9371	4.1406	28.7639	930.0326
930.0326	4.2781	37.0302	888.7243
888.7243	4.4436	44.2140	840.0666
840.0666	4.5364	50.1318	785.3984
785.3984	4.5553	234.2529	546.5902
546.5902	3.4982	54.3092	488.7828
488.7828	3.4215	48.5361	436.8252
436.8252	3.3199	433.5053	-

Legend:

BOY $(1)_t = (4)_{t-1}$.
Deaths $(2)_t = (1)_t \times$ Table 8-34 column $(4)_t$.
Surrenders $(3)_t = ((1)_t - (2)_t) \times$ Table 8-34 column $(5)_t$.
EOY $(1)_t = (1)_t - (2)_t - (3)_t$.

Table 8-38 shows how the liability calculation and calibration are done at issue.

Because the rider charges are specified, the GMAB is a derivative, which means that the liability for the derivative is equal to the average present value of [benefits plus an option issuer's "required profit" less specified charges].

In this example, the scenario-specific maturity benefits were discounted, using the scenario-specific gross appreciation rates, which are assumed equal to the scenario-specific risk-free forward interest rates. In practice, these are sometimes discounted, using the risk-free forward interest rate curve at issue.

The average present value of maturity benefits is $1,043,850.

The average present value of rider charges, discounted using the scenario-specific gross appreciation rates, is $1,399,124. This implies that the present value of required profit is $355,274. Since the rider charge is 1.00% of assets, the required profit charge is therefore 0.25% of assets.

Therefore, going forward, the *SFAS 133* liability equals the average present value of benefits less the average present value of specified charges plus the average present value of 0.25% charges for required profit. As mentioned earlier, the 0.25% charge should be unlocked if marketplace conditions change. At issue, the resulting liability is zero.

Table 8-38
Variable Annuity GMAB Provision
Calibration of Required Profit Margin

Scenario A	**Scenario B**	**Scenario C**	**Average**	
$1,886,407	$1,245,142	$0	$1,043,850	Present Value of Additional Maturity Benefits
$1,441,256	$1,428,747	$1,327,369	$1,399,124	Present Value of GMAB Rider Charges
			25.39%	Required Profit % of Charges
			1.00%	GMAB Charge
			0.25%	Required Profit Charge

(1)			(2)			(3)		
Gross Charges			**Additional Maturity Benefit**			**Discount Factor**		
Scenario A	**Scenario B**	**Scenario C**	**Scenario A**	**Scenario B**	**Scenario C**	**Scenario A**	**Scenario B**	**Scenario C**
						1.000	1.000	1.000
200,000	200,000	200,000				0.978	1.050	0.915
196,794	182,984	210,604				0.988	1.088	0.817
185,382	167,907	225,118				0.973	1.051	0.797
177,257	163,791	217,425				0.993	1.011	0.745
161,762	158,864	217,118				0.981	1.114	0.633
150,994	132,522	236,528				1.175	0.981	0.558
114,346	137,527	245,461				1.121	0.984	0.522
81,368	93,078	178,086				1.010	0.937	0.544
78,948	85,315	148,900				1.028	0.907	0.489
67,557	76,818	144,716	1,898,705	1,351,623	-	0.994	0.921	0.439

Legend:

Gross Charges $(1)_t$ = Table 8-37 $(1)_t$ × (Table 8-36 $(1)_{t-1}$ + Table 8-34 $(1)_t$) × Table 8-34 $(3)_t$.

Additional Maturity Benefit $(2)_{10}$ = Table 8-37 $(3)_{10}$ × Table 8-36 $(3)_{10}$.

Discount Factor $(3)_t$ = Discount Factor $(3)_{t-1}$ / (1 + Table 8-35 $(6)_t$).

Now assume another company issues the same product feature in a variable annuity with combined M&E fees of 2.50%, but without the charge for the GMAB feature separately identified.

In that case, the calculation at issue is as follows:

- The liability for the embedded derivative at issue is equal to the average present value of (benefits plus required profit). Assuming that required profit is identical with that from the other example, the liability is equal to $1,399,124.
- The liability for the host equals the account value less a "host offset." At issue, the "host offset" is $1,399,124.

Going forward, the embedded derivative liability is calculated identically and the "host offset" of $1,399,124 is amortized over time as discussed above.

8.3 Equity-Indexed Annuities

8.3.1 Nature of Product

Equity-indexed annuities became popular in the U.S. during the mid-1990s. In its simplest form, the equity-indexed annuity takes for its chassis the single-premium deferred-annuity product (SPDA). The equity-indexing feature of this product rides on top of the underlying SPDA. In the typical case, the amount of interest that would normally be credited to an SPDA contract is instead used to provide a call option to the insured. The company is the writer of this call option and the insured is the buyer. At the same time, the company will hedge its exposure to the written option by buying the same option or an equivalent set of derivatives in the derivatives markets. If there isn't a regular market for the derivatives needed by the company to hedge its exposure with the policyholder, the company may need to buy them from a specialty or boutique vendor.

Equity-indexed annuities may or may not come with minimum growth guarantees. In addition, equity indexed annuities will still need to meet the minimums required by the Standard Nonforfeiture Law. The current account balance and cash surrender value at any point in time may be the maximum of several values.

In order to manage the cost of the equity benefit, the insurer often designates either a cap or a participation rate to the actual growth rate of the index before applying it to the premium.

The following illustrates the principles of annual indexing:

Gross premium:	$1,000	
Participation rate:	70%	
Index on issue day:	1,200	
Index on first policy anniversary:	1,500	
Minimum policy value at first anniversary:	$ 927	($1.03 \times 0.9 \times 1000$)
Indexed contract value at first anniversary:	$1,175	$= 1{,}000 \times (1 + \{0.7 \times [(1{,}500 / 1{,}200) - 1]\})$

Many variations of this indexing exist. Some of these variations are as follows:

- A choice of index may be provided.
- The designated period may be changed; some contracts use up to nine years.
- A surrender charge may be applied to the indexed value if it is not annuitized.

- The death benefit may or may not include unrealized gains in the index at the time of death.
- Flexible premiums may be allowed.
- The equity indexing may be provided as a transfer option within a fixed or variable annuity.
- In order to prevent "all or nothing" scenarios resulting from a single day's market value, the index growth may be averaged of a period of weeks, days, or months (the"Asian" option).
- Periodically, the underlying floor may be reset to the current account value.
- There may be a blending of indexed and guaranteed values.
- Other index patterns may be used, such as the lowest value during the designated period or the highest value during the designated period. There may also be caps, floors, or asset fee adjustments to the amount of indexed benefit to be credited to the policyholder.

The assets used to support this contract usually consist primarily of bonds purchased to support the guarantee. Because the guarantee generally has a relatively low yield , the cost of the bonds is low compared with the cost of bonds needed to support a normal deferred annuity. The low cost of the underlying bonds leaves funds available to purchase call options to hedge the index risk. The contract participation rate, cap, or fee is adjusted as needed to control the cost of the options.

8.3.2 Accounting for Derivatives

In 1998 the FASB promulgated *SFAS No. 133*, "Accounting for Derivative Instruments and Hedging Activities," for financial reporting of derivatives. Included in the scope of the standard were not only derivative assets but also derivatives embedded in host contracts. A host contract is the underlying base contract (for example, a deferred annuity or a bond) to which a feature operating as a derivative is attached either by rider or by embedded language in the contract.

Equity-indexed annuities fall under the reporting requirements of *SFAS 133*. Chapter 2 of this book contains specific information on accounting for derivatives. Chapter 13 also has general guidance on analyzing insurance contracts under the requirements of *SFAS 133*.

Although not specifically mentioned as an example of a contract with an embedded derivative in *SFAS 133*, equity indexed annuities are addressed indirectly as part of description of variable annuity products (which are not subject to *SFAS 133*). Paragraph 200 supports the conclusion that equity-indexed annuities contain embedded derivatives as described in paragraph 12 of *SFAS 133*:

> if the product were an equity-index-based interest annuity ... the investment component would contain an embedded derivative (the equity index-based derivative) that meets all the requirements of paragraph 12 of this Statement for separate accounting. (Paragraph 200)

Other portions of *SFAS 133* that have particular relevance to equity indexed annuities include:

> An embedded derivative instrument shall be separated from the host contract and accounted for as a derivative instrument. (Paragraph 12)

> If an embedded derivative instrument is separated from its host contract, the host contract shall be accounted for based on … instruments of that type that do not contain embedded derivative instruments. (Paragraph 16)

In response to numerous questions from interested parties, a Derivatives Implementation Group (DIG) was formed. The DIG, sponsored by the FASB, was comprised of members from the financial services and the accounting industries and promulgated extensive guidance. There are several DIG Issues that relate to the accounting of equity-indexed annuities, and companies should consult the DIG pronouncements as well as the main text of *SFAS 133*. Some of the DIG Issues related to equity-indexed annuities will be described in the following paragraphs.

DIG B6, "Embedded Derivatives: Allocating the Basis of a Hybrid Instrument to the Host Contract and the Embedded Derivative," specifically defines the initial value of the host contract on a fund-type contract as the premium paid less the value of the embedded derivative. This requires that the initial reserve for an equity-indexed annuity be equal to the sum of the initial embedded derivative estimate and host contract value.

DIG B29, "Embedded Derivatives: Equity-Indexed Contracts with Embedded Derivatives," requires that the company value all forward-starting options that meet the definition of a derivative in *SFAS 133*. For annual ratchet-type products, only the current year's option values are known but *DIG B29* requires that companies still make a best estimate of the options that they are expecting to provide to the policyholders in all future policy years and include these in the value of the embedded derivative.

DIG B30, "Embedded Derivatives: Application of Statement 97 and Statement 133 to Equity-Indexed Annuity Contracts," states that a separate calculation of a *SFAS 97* account balance is no longer required and that the insurer should ignore any minimum liability that exceeds the sum of the embedded derivative and the host contract.

8.3.3 Establishing GAAP Methodology for DAC and Reserves

SFAS 133 provides requirements for the accounting of stand-alone derivatives and contracts containing embedded derivatives. Unless specifically addressed in *SFAS 133* or the DIG issues, it is assumed that any other existing GAAP accounting requirements must still be followed.

The first step in accounting for equity-indexed annuities is to determine the derivative embedded in the contract and to estimate its fair value. As specified in *DIG B29*, this embedded derivative value will include both the current period's derivative, for which the company will have stated the policyholders' share of the index growth as well as future period's derivatives, for which the company will generally not yet provided the terms of any policyholders' share of the index growth.

The derivatives embedded in an equity-indexed policy are generally assumed to be call options that expire in one year or in multiple years. The indexed benefits are only payable at the end of the stated term with no indexed benefits provide in the interim. These options are generally European-style options and therefore can only be exercised at the end of the option's term. Depending on the nature of the underlying policy guarantees, these options may have strike prices at the beginning of the option's term that equal the current index value or may have strike prices above the current index. Options that have strike prices equal to the current index value are sometimes referred to as in-the-money options; options that have strike prices in excess of the current index are sometimes referred to as out-of-the-money options.

Equity-indexed annuities providing index benefits that are credited on an annual basis are sometimes known as ratchet contracts and those where the index benefits are credited at the end of a durations longer than one year are sometimes known as point-to-point contracts.

The following example shows a 5-year point-to-point product that would require an out-of-the-money option at the beginning of the 5-year term. The strike price for the option would be determined as follows:

Gross premium:	\$1,000
Participation rate:	50%
Index on issue day:	1,500
Minimum policy value at fifth anniversary:	\$1,043 ($1.03^5 \times 0.9 \times 1{,}000$)
Strike Price for Five-Year Call Option:	\$1,630 = $[((1.043 - 1) / 0.5) + 1] \times 1{,}500$

Many companies are using versions of standard option pricing formulas, such as Black Scholes, to determine a fair value for the current period's embedded option liability on their EIA contracts. Depending on the nature of the indexed benefits, the Black Scholes formula may not be appropriate in all cases. For more complicated embedded options, companies may use modifications to the standard Black Scholes formula or may utilize more sophisticated option pricing models. In practice, the pricing models companies use to determine the value of any embedded derivative liabilities are frequently the same models they use to determine the fair value of any hedging assets purchased.

In addition to determining the fair value for the current period's option, a company must determine the value for all of the forward starting options. These options are the expected indexed benefits for future periods beyond the current option. Typically, companies have not established the terms of these future indexed benefits as of the date of valuation. Although there are no specific requirements under *SFAS 133* or the *DIGs* as to how companies should measure these benefits, these forward starting options still meet the definitions of a derivative under *SFAS 133* and therefore must be fair valued. *DIG B29* does state that "the forward starting options should be valued using the expected future terms."

In practice many companies are using a "budgeted" approach to establishing fair value of the forward starting options. The budgeted amount in any future year is usually the projected amount of interest spread that the company expects to have available to credit to policyholders.

The future policyholder benefits that these interest spreads are to cover can arise from policy guarantees or from indexed benefits.

The valuation of future budgeted amounts will therefore usually be the present value of expected future available interest spreads, based upon best estimate assumptions and discounted at the same interest rate as the current period's option value. In practice these present values are frequently based upon a single best estimate scenario. Companies may want to consider the use of more sophisticated scenario-based models when a fair value of expected results is not reasonably estimated with a single projected scenario.

Once a company has determined a value for the embedded derivative, it then must determine a value for the host contract. In simplest terms, the host contract is what is left over after the embedded derivative has been identified and valued. For an EIA contract, the host contract is composed of those expected policy liability cash flows that arise from the policy guarantees that are unrelated to the indexed (i.e., derivative) related benefits.

Once the embedded derivative is valued at issue, *DIG B6* states that the host contract will be the difference between the gross premium deposit and the fair value of the embedded derivative. Total *SFAS 133* liabilities at issue therefore equal the initial gross deposit.

DIG B6 also states that host contract shall "be accounted for under generally accepted accounting principles applicable to instruments of that type." *DIG B30* provides an example of a point-to-point equity indexed annuity contract in which the host contract is identified as a zero-coupon debt obligation.

In practice, most companies are using methodologies for valuing the host contract liabilities that assume the host contract is analogous to zero-coupon debt. For point-to-point contracts for which there are no future option periods expected under the policy, the host contract at any point in time may be determined with a breakeven interest rate that accretes the initial host contract value to the guaranteed benefit at the end of the option term. The host contract value at any point in time is then the present value of the expected guaranteed benefits at the breakeven interest rate.

In determining the fair value of the embedded derivative, it is reasonable to expect that the impact of future policy lapses will be recognized in the calculation. For the host contract, it isn't as clear that future lapses should be recognized since the host contract is not specifically called a fair value in *SFAS 133*. Some companies have used approaches to valuing the host contract that ignore the impact of lapses. The host contract approach that accretes an initial host contract value to the guaranteed benefit at the end of the option term for a point-to-point contract does not anticipate any future lapses. This approach to determining the host contract value without recognizing the impact of future lapses is used in Table 8-40.

For many practical situations, companies are determining the value of the host contract with methodology that does recognize expected future lapses. The calculations are still based upon a breakeven interest rate but that rate is determined so the present value of expected guaranteed cash flows in all durations is equal to the initial host contract value. This approach to determining the host contract with the recognition of future expected lapses is used in Tables 8-43 and 8-45.

There is no requirement that the *SFAS 133* liabilities be determined on a seriatim basis, and many companies use aggregated approaches. This is true for both the embedded derivative and the host contract valuations.

The discount rate for the embedded derivatives is typically based upon risk-free rates. However, there is no requirement to use risk-free rates for these valuations although it is most typical to value options that are exchange traded with a risk-free rate. There appears to be some diversity in practice as to what discount rate is used for the fair value of the embedded derivative liabilities. Regardless, at any point in time the discount rates should reflect current best estimates.

There is no specific guidance in *SFAS 133* or the DIG issues on how DAC for equity indexed annuities is to be accounted for but, without such guidance, *SFAS 97* would seem to apply in all other respects. Given that *SFAS 133* and *DIG B30* require that the GAAP liability no longer be the policyholder account balance but the sum of the embedded derivative and the host contract, it will not be possible to utilize an EGP based solely upon the spreads related to the policyholder's account balance.

The most reasonable approach to determining *SFAS 97* DAC amortization suggests that the change in the total *SFAS 133* liability must be reflected in the EGP. As long as hedge accounting is not claimed, the gains or losses on any hedging derivative assets that have matured or the company has disposed of should be reflected in the EGP; prior to maturity or disposition, changes in the reported GAAP fair value of these derivative assets should also be reflected in the EGP. Reflecting the change in GAAP liability in the EGP and the related derivative accounting adjustments would make the EGP for equity-indexed annuities analogous to the EGM used for amortizing DAC on participating life contracts.

8.3.4 Numerical Illustrations

8.3.4.1 Point to Point EIA Product

The following tables illustrate concepts and issues that the actuary should consider in generating DAC for point-to-point EIA contracts.

Table 8-39 illustrates basic features of a 5-year point-to-point EIA contract. Its first component shows contract features and forecast assumptions. In order to be conservative, this insurer has elected to hedge on the assumption that no policy terminations occur prior to maturity at the end of five years. In this example the company has therefore likely overhedged its derivative exposure to the options granted to the policyholder.

The Capital Markets section of Table 8-39 presents a single scenario of index changes for the purpose of illustrating the financial results. Assumptions used for Black-Scholes calculations are also presented. For purposes of the illustration, it has been assumed that the Black-Scholes parameters will not change over the 5-year period.

The final element of Table 8-39 lists policy features and assumptions. It illustrates the value of the embedded derivative calculation and its supporting asset hedge. It also shows calculation support for the derivation of future option values using the Black-Scholes method for this European option. The calculation begins with a calculation of the strike price for this policy. The derivation of this strike price is similar to the example shown in Section 8.3.3. Next, the Black-Scholes assumptions are used to generate a unit price for the embedded derivative. Finally, the unit price is scaled to the actual contract size. Under normal operations, the volatility, dividend, and risk-free rates would likely be different at each valuation date.

Table 8-39
Five Year Point-to-Point EIA Product Design and Pricing Assumptions

		Contract Duration					
		0	1	2	3	4	5
Contract Design and Pricing Assumptions							
(A)	Deposit	$100,000					
(B)	Policy load	10.00%					
(C)	Guaranteed interest rate	3.00%					
(D)	Maintenance expense	$50.00					
(E)	Acquisition cost as percentage of premium	5%					
(F)	Participation rate	50%					
(G)	Zero-coupon bond rate	7.00%					
(H)	Vesting	0.00%	0.00%	0.00%	0.00%	0.00%	100.00%
(I)	Percentage hedged	100.00%					
(J)	Mortality rate per 1,000		5.77	6.35	6.98	7.68	8.45
(K)	Lapse rate		1.00%	2.00%	3.00%	1.00%	0.00%
(L)	Contracts persisting	1.00000	0.98429	0.95848	0.92323	0.90698	0.89932
Capital Markets							
(M)	Index growth		(10%)	20%	(15%)	20%	10%
(N)	Index level	1,500	1,350	1,620	1,377	1,652	1,818
(O)	Implied volatility	22.0%	22.0%	22.0%	22.0%	22.0%	22.0%
(P)	Risk-free rate	6.00%	6.00%	6.00%	6.00%	6.00%	6.00%
(Q)	Dividend rate	1.25%	1.25%	1.25%	1.25%	1.25%	1.25%
Calculation of Black-Scholes Option Values							
(R)	Minimum guarantee as of year 5	104,335					
(S)	Guaranteed growth in index value	4.33%					
(T)	Strike price for liability option	1,630					
(U)	Time to expiry	5	4	3	2	1	0
(V)	D1	0.5597	0.2234	0.5483	(0.0813)	0.3878	
(W)	D2	0.0678	(0.2166)	0.1672	(0.3924)	0.1678	
(X)	Black-Scholes price	367.11	224.41	333.96	125.79	192.37	187.60
(Y)	Fair value of embedded derivative	12,237	7,480	11,132	4,193	6,412	6,253
(Z)	Fair value of hedge	12,237	7,480	11,132	4,193	6,412	6,253

Legend:

(A) to (H)	Policy features; (H) is applied to index account only.
(I)	Company hedges assuming no terminations prior to maturity
(J) and (K)	Experience assumptions
(L)	$= (L)_{t-1} \times [1 - (J)_t/1000] \times [1 - (K)_t]$; lapse rate is applied to survivors.
(M)	Assumptions for future index growth.
(N)	$(N)_t = (N)_{t-1} \times [1 + (M)_t]$; first index value, $(N)_0$, is the value of the index on the day the policy is issued.
(O) to (Q)	Assumptions
(R)	$= 90\% \times (A)_0 \times 1.03^5$; this is the guaranteed value at the end of the term.
(S)	$= (R)_0 / (A)_0 - 1$
(T)	$= (N)_0 \times [1 + (S)_0 / (F)_0]$; input to Black Scholes formula.
(U)	Time to maturity; first value is just after issue.
(V) and (W)	Components of Black-Scholes formula
(X)	Black-Scholes price for embedded option, initial index unit of $(N)_0$. Years 2-4 represent fair values; year 5 value is intrinsic value, i.e., index value less strike price.
(Y)	$= (A)_0 \times (F)_0 \times (X)_t / (N)_0$; Black-Scholes price/fair value scaled to actual contract size.
(Z)	$= (Y)_t \times (I)_0$; the price of options which hedge the floor of the benefit for policy; assumes benefit is hedged to extent of (I).

Table 8-40 continues with the same EIA product. This table displays values both before and after the application of decrements. The EGP is calculated directly with adjustments to reflect the differences between death and surrender benefits and the host contract released. This is equivalent to an approach in which the EGP is developed with an EGM approach (i.e., one in which the change in reserve is recognized in the EGP). The equivalence of these two approaches is demonstrated at the bottom of Table 8-40. In either case, all of the derivative-related gains and losses are reflected in the EGP. The discount rate used for the DAC calculations has been set equal to the earnings rates for the zero coupon bonds. In practice, other discounts rates may be utilized.

The net amount at risk selected for the deaths and surrenders is based on the excess of the available benefit over the value of the host contract. Further, for this illustration, the contractual guaranteed minimum value has been selected as the account that generates the interest spread.

Table 8-40
Policy Transactions, EGP and DAC for 5 Year Point to Point EIA Contract

		Contract Duration					
		0	1	2	3	4	5
Selected Items from Table 8-39							
(A)	Vesting	0.00%	0.00%	0.00%	0.00%	0.00%	100.00%
(B)	Index level	1,500	1,350	1,620	1,377	1,652	1,818
(C)	Fair value of hedge	12,237	7,480	11,132	4,193	6,412	6,253
Policy values before deaths and surrenders							
(D)	Guaranteed value	90,000	92,700	95,481	98,345	101,296	104,335
(E)	Index account before vesting	100,000	100,000	104,000	100,000	105,080	110,588
(F)	Index account after vesting						110,588
(G)	Host contract guaranteed annual growth rate	3.520%					
(H)	Value of host contract	87,763	90,852	94,050	97,360	100,787	104,335
(I)	Fair value of embedded derivative	12,237	7,480	11,132	4,193	6,412	6,253
(J)	Death benefit available		92,700	95,481	98,345	101,296	104,335
(K)	Surrender benefit available		92,700	95,481	98,345	101,296	104,335
EGP and DAC Calculation net of deaths and surrenders							
(L)	Value of host contract	87,763	89,424	90,145	89,886	91,412	93,830
(M)	Value of Embedded Derivative	12,237	7,363	10,670	3,871	5,816	5,624
(N)	Index account						99,454
(O)	Guaranteed value	90,000	91,243	91,517	90,796	91,874	93,830
(P)	Death benefit paid		535	596	658	718	799
(Q)	Surrenders Paid		922	1,868	2,808	928	
	Income						
(R)	Bond earned income		6,143	6,251	6,278	6,270	6,357
(S)	Gain on Hedge		(4,757)	3,652	(6,939)	2,220	(159)
	Expenses						
(T)	Interest credited on Host Contract		3,089	3,148	3,173	3,164	3,218
(U)	Increase in Value of Embedded Derivative		(4,874)	3,307	(6,799)	1,945	(192)
(V)	Death benefit in excess of Host Released		11	9	7	4	0
(W)	Surrender benefit in excess of Host Released		18	28	28	5	
(X)	Maintenance expense beginning of year		50	49	48	46	45
(Y)	Estimated Gross Profit		3,093	3,362	2,882	3,326	3,127
(Z)	Present value of EGP	13,671.30					
(AA)	DAC	5,000	4,119	3,095	2,196	1,089	
EGM presentation net of deaths and surrenders							
(BB)	Premium Income	100,000					
(CC)	Investment Income		1,386	9,903	(661)	8,489	6,198
(DD)	Benefits Paid		1,457	2,464	3,466	1,646	799
(EE)	Increase in Host Contract	87,763	1,662	720	(259)	1,526	2,418
(FF)	Increase in Value of ED	12,237	(4,874)	3,307	(6,799)	1,945	(192)
(GG)	Expenses		50	49	48	46	45
(HH)	EGM		3,093	3,362	2,882	3,326	3,127

Table 8-40 Continued
Policy Transactions, EGP and DAC for 5 Year Point to Point EIA Contract

Legend:	
(A)	From Table 8-39, (H).
(B)	From Table 8-39, (N).
(C)	From Table 8-39, (Z).
(D)	$(D)_t = (D)_{t-1} \times [1 + (C)_0$ from Table 8-39]; initial value $(D)_0 = (A)_0 \times [1 - (B)_0]$; (A), (B) and (C) are from Table 8-39.
(E)	$(E)_t = \text{Max}\,[(A)_0, (A)_0 \times \{1 + (F)_0 \times [(N)_t / (N)_0 - 1]\}]$; initial value $(F)_0 = (A)_0$; (A), (F) and (N) are from Table 8-39.
(F)	$= (E)_t \times (A)_t$.
(G)	$= \{[(R)_0 / (H)_0] \wedge (1/5)\} - 1$; $(R)_0$ is from Table 8-39.
(H)	$(H)_0 = (A)_0 - (Y)_0$; $(H)_t = (H)_{t-1} \times [1 + (G)_0]$ for $t = 1$ to 5. (A) and (Y) are from Table 8-39.
(I)	From Table 8-39, (Y).
(J)	$= (D)_t$.
(K)	$= (D)_t$.
(L)	$= (H)_t \times (L)_t$; (L) is from Table 8-39.
(M)	$= (I)_t \times (L)_t$; (L) is from Table 8-39.
(N)	$= (F)_t \times (L)_t$; (L) is from Table 8-39.
(O)	$= (D)_t - (L)_t$; (L) is from Table 8-39.
(P)	$= (J)_t \times (L)_{t-1} \times (J)_t / 1000$; (L) and second (J) are from Table 8-39.
(Q)	$= [(K)_t \times (L)_{t-1} \times (1 - J_t / 1000)] \times (K)_t$; (L) and second (K) are from Table 8-39.
(R)	$= [(L)_{t-1} + (M)_{t-1} - (C)_{t-1}] \times (G)_0$ where (G) is from Table 8-39.
(S)	$= (C)_t - (C)_{t-1}$.
(T)	$= (L)_{t-1} \times (G)_0$.
(U)	$= (M)_t - (M)_{t-1}$.
(V)	$= [(J)_t - (H)_t] \times (L)_{t-1} \times (J)_t / 1000$; (L) and second (J) are from Table 8-39.
(W)	$= [(K)_t - (H)_t] \times (L)_{t-1} \times (J)_t / 1000 \times (K)_t$; (L), (J) and second (K) are from Table 8-39.
(X)	$= (D)_0 \times (L)_{t-1}$ from Table 8-39.
(Y)	$= (R)_t + (S)_t - (T)_t - (U)_t - (V)_t - (W)_t - (X)_t$.
(Z)	Present value of the EGP (Y) at issue date discounted at earned rate $(G)_t$ less 200 basis points, where (G) is from Table 8-39.
(AA)	$= (AA)_{t-1} \times [1 + (G)_0 - 0.02] - (Y)_t \times (AA)_0 / (Z)_0$; $(AA)_0 = (A)_0 \times (E)_0$ where (A), (E) and (G) are from Table 8-39.
(BB)	= Table 8-39 $(A)_t$.
(CC)	$= (R)_t + (S)_t$.
(DD)	$= (P)_t + (Q)_t$.
(EE)	$= (L)_t - (L)_{t-1}$.
(FF)	$= (M)_t - (M)_{t-1}$; $(FF)_0 = I_0$.
(GG)	$= (X)_t$.
(HH)	$= (BB)_t + (CC)_t - (DD)_t - (EE)_t - (FF)_t - (GG)_t$.

Table 8-41 displays the resulting balance sheet and income statements for the product. For the sake of clarity, the bonds are assumed to be classified as held to maturity and are therefore reported at amortized cost. Their value has been diminished by cash needed to pay maintenance expenses, death claims, and surrenders.

Earnings are volatile because they are affected by the changing value of the index each year. The major contributing factor to this volatility is the unequal amounts in the early years of hedge and embedded options.

Table 8-41
Balance Sheet and Income Statement for 5 Yr Point to Point EIA Contract

		Contract Duration					
		0	**1**	**2**	**3**	**4**	**5**
Items from Table 8-39							
(A)	Deposit	100,000					
(B)	Zero-coupon bond rate	7.00%					
Items from Table 8-40							
(C)	Index account						99,454
(D)	Guaranteed value	90,000	91,243	91,517	90,796	91,874	93,830
(E)	Premium Income	100,000					
(F)	Investment Income for EGP		1,386	9,903	(661)	8,489	6,198
(G)	DAC	5,000	4,119	3,095	2,196	1,089	
(H)	Estimated Gross Profit		3,093	3,362	2,882	3,326	3,127
Balance Sheet							
	Assets						
(I)	Bonds held to maturity	82,763	87,046	90,623	93,449	98,295	104,327
(J)	Fair value of hedge	12,237	7,480	11,132	4,193	6,412	6,253
(K)	DAC	5,000	4,119	3,095	2,196	1,089	
(L)	Total assets	100,000	98,645	104,850	99,838	105,796	110,581
	Liabilities						
(M)	Value of host contract	87,763	89,424	90,145	89,886	91,412	93,830
(N)	Value of embedded derivative	12,237	7,363	10,670	3,871	5,816	5,624
(O)	Total liabilities	100,000	96,787	100,815	93,757	97,228	99,454
(P)	Equity		1,858	4,035	6,080	8,568	11,126
(Q)	Change in equity		1,858	2,177	2,045	2,488	2,558
Income Statement							
	Revenues						
(R)	Investment income on bonds	0	5,790	6,090	6,340	6,538	6,877
(S)	Gain on Hedge		(4,757)	3,652	(6,939)	2,220	(159)
(T)	Total revenues	0	1,033	9,742	(599)	8,758	6,718
	Expenses						
(U)	Interest credited on host contract	0	3,089	3,148	3,173	3,164	3,218
(V)	Death benefit in excess of Host Released		11	9	7	4	0
(W)	Surrender benefit in excess of Host Released		18	28	28	5	0
(X)	Maintenance cost	0	50	49	48	46	45
(Y)	Acquisition cost expense	0	881	1,024	899	1,107	1,089
(Z)	Increase in Value of Embedded Derivative		(4,874)	3,307	(6,799)	1,945	(192)
(AA)	Total expenses	0	(825)	7,565	(2,644)	6,270	4,160
(BB)	Net income	0	1,858	2,177	2,045	2,488	2,558

Table 8-41 Continued
Balance Sheet and Income Statement for 5 Yr Point to Point EIA Contract

Legend

(A)	From Table 8-39, (A).
(B)	From Table 8-39, (G).
(C)	From Table 8-40, (N).
(D)	From Table 8-40, (O).
(E)	From Table 8-40, (BB).
(F)	From Table 8-40, (CC)
(G)	From Table 8-40, (HH).
(H)	From Table 8-40, (Y).
(I)	$(I)_t = [(I)_{t-1} - (X)_t] \times [1 + (G)_0] - (P)_t - (Q)_t$; initial value $(I)_0 = (A)_0 \times [1 - (E)_0] - (Z)_0$ where (A), (E), (G) and (Z) come from Table 8-39; (X), (P) and (Q) from Table 8-40.
(J)	$= (C)_t$ from Table 8-40.
(K)	$= (G)_t$ from Table 8-41.
(L)	$= (I)_t + (J)_t + (K)_t$.
(M)	$= (L)_t$ from Table 8-40.
(N)	$= (M)_t$ from Table 8-40.
(O)	$= (M)_t + (N)_t$.
(P)	$= (L)_t - (O)_t$.
(Q)	$= (P)_t - (P)_{t-1}$.
(R)	$= [(I)_{t-1} - (X)_t] \times (B)_0$ where (X) is from Table 8-40.
(S)	$= (S)_t$ from Table 8-40.
(T)	$= (R)_t + (S)_t$.
(U)	$= (T)_t$ from Table 8-40.
(V)	$= (V)_t$ from Table 8-40.
(W)	$= (W)_t$ from Table 8-40.
(X)	$= (X)_t$ from Table 8-40.
(Y)	$= (AA)_{t-1} - (AA)_t$ from Table 8-40.
(Z)	$= (U)_t$ from Table 8-40.
(AA)	$= (U)_t + (V)_t + (W)_t + (X)_t + (Y)_t + (Z)_t$.
(BB)	$= (T)_t - (AA)_t$.

8.3.4.2 Annual Ratchet EIA Product

The following tables will illustrate how *SFAS 133* accounting can be applied to an annual ratchet product. They start with many of the same basic experience assumptions used in the point-to-point example in Section 8.3.4.1 and show results through the first five calendar years after issue. Tables 8-42, 8-43, and 8-44 are determined at the beginning of year 1 ($t = 0$). Tables 8-45, 8-46, and 8-47 are determined at the beginning of year 2 ($t = 1$) and reflect the impact of the first-year option benefits expiring in the money. Only a single deposit at issue is assumed for all of the tables.

Table 8-42 illustrates basic features of the ratchet EIA contract. The Capital Markets section shows the expected budgeted amounts (the amounts available to provide call options to the policyholders based upon pricing). Budgeted amounts are assumed to be fully available at the beginning of each year. Assumptions used for Black-Scholes calculations are also presented. At issue, the assumed participation rate of 41.15% has been scaled so that the initial option equals the budget.

The strike price for the option is equal to the initial index value. The at-the-money nature of the option reflects the fact that projected guaranteed benefits at the end of year 1 don't exceed the index value from the beginning of the year.

Table 8-42
Annual Ratchet EIA Product Design and Pricing Assumptions (Valuation Date t = 0)

		Contract Duration					
		0	1	2	3	4	5
Contract Design and Pricing Assumptions							
(A)	Deposit	$100,000					
(B)	Policy load	10.00%					
(C)	Guaranteed interest rate	3.00%					
(D)	Maintenance expense	$50.00					
(E)	Acquisition cost as percentage of premium	5%					
(F)	Participation rate	41.15%					
(G)	Zero-coupon bond rate	7.00%	7.00%	7.00%	7.00%	7.00%	7.00%
(H)	Mortality rate per 1,000		5.77	6.35	6.98	7.68	8.45
(I)	Lapse rate		1.00%	2.00%	3.00%	1.00%	0.00%
(J)	Surrender charge		10.00%	10.00%	10.00%	10.00%	10.00%
(K)	Contracts persisting (prior to maturity)	1.00000	0.98429	0.95848	0.92323	0.90698	0.89932
(L)	Maturity rate		0.00%	0.00%	0.00%	0.00%	100.00%
Capital Markets							
(M)	Option budget		4.50%	4.50%	4.50%	4.50%	4.50%
(N)	Index level	1,500					
(O)	Implied volatility	22.0%					
(P)	Risk-free rate	6.00%	6.00%	6.00%	6.00%	6.00%	6.00%
(Q)	Dividend rate	1.25%					
Calculation of Account, Guaranteed, and Option Values							
(R)	Index account	100,000	104,770	109,768	115,003	120,489	126,236
(S)	Guaranteed value	90,000	92,700	95,481	98,345	101,296	104,335
	BOY						
(T)	Strike price for annual hedge		1,500				
(U)	Time to expiry for annual hedge		1.0000000				
(V)	D1		0.33				
(W)	D2		0.11				
(X)	Black-Scholes price		164.03				
(Y)	Fair value of hedge		4,500	4,715	4,940	5,175	5,422
	EOY						
(Z)	Fair value of hedge		4,770	4,998	5,236	5,486	5,747

Legend:

(A) to (F) Policy features and assumptions.

(G) to (I) Experience assumptions.

(J) Annual Surrender Charge.

(K) $(K)_0 = 1$; For $t > 0$, $(K)_t = (K)_{t-1} \times [1 - (H)_t / 1000] \times [1 - (I)_t]$.

(L) to (Q) Assumptions

(R) $(R)_0 = (A)_0$; For t = 1–5, $(R)_t = (R)_{t-1} + (Z)_t$.

(S) $(S)_t = [1 - (B)_0] \times (A)_0 \times [1 + (C)_0]$ ^ t.

Beginning of Year Hedge Values

(T) $(T)_t = (O)_{t-1}$

(U) One-year hedge purchased at the beginning of the year.

(V) Black-Scholes Parameter D1 = $(V)_t = [ln[(N)_{t-1} / (T)_t] + [(P)_{t-1} - (Q)_{t-1} + (O)_{t-1}$ ^ 2 / 2] $\times (U)_t] / [(O)_{t-1} \times (U)_t$ ^ 0.5].

(W) Black-Scholes Parameter D2 = $(W)_t = (V_t) - (O)_{t-1} \times (U)_t$ ^ 0.5.

(X) $(X)_t = (N)_{t-1} \times \text{EXP}[-(Q)_{t-1} \times (U)_t] \times \text{NORMDIST}[(V)_t] - (T)_t \times \text{EXP}[-(P)_{t-1} \times (U)_t] \times \text{NORMDIST}[(W)_t]$.

(Y) For t = 1, $(Y)_t = (R)_{t-1} \times (F)_0 \times (X)_t / (N)_{t-1}$; For t = 2–5, $(Y)_t = (R)_{t-1} \times (M)_t$.

Year Hedge Values

(Z) $(Z)_t = (R)_{t-1} \times (M)_t \times [1 + (P)_t]$.

Table 8-43 shows the development of the embedded derivative and the host contract values. Guaranteed benefits for each year are calculated by multiplying total projected benefit cash flows by the ratio of beginning-of-the-year guaranteed values to beginning-of-the-year index account values. The derivative-based excess benefits are what remain of the total benefits after designating the guaranteed benefits. This is not the only approach that can be used to estimate these cash flows; other approaches are possible.

Table 8-43 also shows the development of projected margins for *SFAS 97* DAC amortization. This example shows the development of EGP with expected assumptions. In actual practice, differences between actual and expected experience would have to be recognized if an EGP-type approach is used to determine the margins for DAC amortization. The use of an EGM approach removes the need for these adjustments. The equivalent EGM calculations are also shown in Table 8-43.

The discount rate for the DAC calculations has been set equal to the long-term budget assumption of 4.5%. There may be other interpretations as to the appropriate discount for the determination of DAC.

Table 8-43
Policy Transactions, EGP and DAC for Annual Ratchet EIA Contract (Valuation Date t = 0)

		Contract Duration					
		0	1	2	3	4	5
Policy values before deaths and surrenders							
(A)	Guaranteed value	90,000	92,700	95,481	98,345	101,296	104,335
(B)	Index account	100,000	104,770	109,768	115,003	120,489	126,236
(C)	Fair value of hedge	4,500	4,770	4,998	5,236	5,486	5,747
(D)	Index credit		4,770	4,998	5,236	5,486	5,747
(E)	Death benefit available	100,000	104,770	109,768	115,003	120,489	126,236
(F)	Surrender benefit available	100,000	104,770	109,768	115,003	120,489	126,236
EGP and DAC Calculation net of deaths, surrenders, and maturities							
(G)	Index account (prior to maturity)	100,000	103,124	105,210	106,175	109,281	113,527
(H)	Guaranteed value (prior to maturity)	90,000	91,243	91,517	90,796	91,874	93,830
(I)	Death benefit paid		577	655	735	815	923
(J)	Account released on surrender		994	2,049	3,134	1,054	0
(K)	Maturity benefit paid		0	0	0	0	113,527
(L)	Guaranteed benefits paid		1,414	2,392	3,365	1,598	96,219
(M)	Excess benefits		157	312	504	271	18,231
(N)	Value of Embedded Derivative (VED)	14,686	15,410	16,023	16,481	17,199	0
(O)	Host contract interest rate	4.431%					
(P)	Host cash flow	85,314	(1,414)	(2,392)	(3,365)	(1,598)	(96,219)
(Q)	Value of host contract	85,314	87,680	89,172	89,758	92,137	0
	Income						
(R)	Non-hedge investment income		6,685	6,888	7,028	7,098	7,305
(S)	Gain on hedge		270	278	284	287	295
(T)	Surrender charge		99	205	313	105	0
	Expenses						
(U)	Interest credited on Host Contract		3,780	3,885	3,951	3,977	4,082
(V)	Adjusted Increase in Value of Embedded Derivative		881	925	961	989	1,032
(W)	Maintenance expense beginning of year		50	49	48	46	45
(X)	Estimated Gross Profit		2,343	2,512	2,666	2,478	2,441
(Y)	Present value of EGP	10,916					
(Z)	Deferrable Expenses	5,000					
(AA)	k-factor	45.806%					
(BB)	DAC	5,000	4,152	3,188	2,110	1,070	0
EGM presentation net of deaths, surrenders and maturities							
(CC)	Premium Income	100,000					
(DD)	Investment Income		6,955	7,166	7,312	7,385	7,600
(EE)	Benefits Paid		1,472	2,499	3,555	1,764	114,450
(FF)	Increase in Host Contract	85,314	2,366	1,492	586	2,379	(92,137)
(GG)	Increase in VED	14,686	724	613	458	718	(17,199)
(HH)	Maintenance expense beginning of year		50	49	48	46	45
(II)	EGM	0	2,343	2,512	2,666	2,478	2,441

Table 8-43 Continued
Policy Transactions, EGP and DAC for Annual Ratchet EIA Contract (Valuation Date t = 0)

Legend:

(A)	From Table 8-42, $(S)_t$.
(B)	From Table 8-42, $(R)_t$.
(C)	From Table 8-42, For $t = 0$, $(Y)_1$; For $t > 0$, $(Z)_t$.
(D)	$(D)_t = (B)_t - (B)_{t-1} - (A)_t$; $(A)_t$ is from Table 8-42.
(E)	$(E)_t = (B)_t$.
(F)	$(F)_t = (B)_t$.
(G)	$(G)_t = (B)_t \times (K)_t$; $(K)_t$ is from Table 8-42.
(H)	$(H)_t = (A)_t \times (K)_t$; $(K)_t$ is from Table 8-42.
(I)	$(I)_t = (E)_{t-1} \times (K)_{t-1} \times (H)_t / 1000$; $(K)_t$ and $(H)_t$ are from Table 8-42.
(J)	$(J)_t = (F)_{t-1} \times (K)_{t-1} \times [1 - (H)_t / 1000] \times (I)_t$; $(K)_t$, $(H)_t$ and $(I)_t$ are from Table 8-42.
(K)	$(K)_t = (G)_t \times (L)_t$; $(L)_t$ is from Table 8-42.
(L)	$(L)_t = [(I)_t + (J)_t + (K)_t] \times (H)_{t-1} / (G)_{t-1}$.
(M)	$(M)_t = [(I)_t + (J)_t + (K)_t] - (L)_t$.
(N)	$(N)_5 = 0$; For $t = 4$ to 0, $(N)_t = [(N)_{t+1} + (M)_{t+1}] / [1 + (P)_t]$; $(P)_t$ is from Table 8-42.
(O)	Internal rate of return based on Host Cash Flow $(P)_0$ through $(P)_5$.
(P)	For $t = 0$, $(P)_0 = (A)_0 - (N)_0 - (L)_0$; $(A)_0$ is from Table 8-42; For $t > 0$, $(P)_t = -(L)_t$.
(Q)	For $t = 0$, $(Q)_0 = (P)_0$; For $t > 0$, $(Q)_t = (Q)_{t-1} \times [1 + (O)_0] + (P)_t$.
(R)	$(R)_t = [(N)_{t-1} + (Q)_{t-1} - (C)_{t-1} \times (K)_{t-1}] \times (G)_0$; $(G)_0$ and $(K)_{t-1}$ are from Table 8-42.
(S)	$(S)_t = [(Z)_t - (Y)_t] \times (K)_{t-1}$; $(Z)_t$, $(Y)_t$ and $(K)_{t-1}$ are from Table 8-42.
(T)	$(T)_t = (J)_t \times (J)_t$; $(J)_t$ is from Table 8-42.
(U)	$(U)_t = (Q)_t \times (O)_0$.
(V)	$(V)_t = (N)_t - (N)_{t-1} + (M)_t$.
(W)	$(W)_t = (D)_0 \times (K)_{t-1}$; $(D)_0 \times (K)_{t-1}$ are from Table 8-42.
(X)	$(X)_t = (R)_t + (S)_t + (T)_t - (U)_t - (V)_t - (W)_t$.
(Y)	Present value of the EGP $(X)_t$ at issue date discounted at earned rate $(G)_t$ less 250 basis points; $(G)_t$ is from Table 8-42.
(Z)	$(Z)_t = (A)_t \times (E)_t$; $(A)_t$ and $(E)_t$ are from Table 8-42.
(AA)	$(AA)_0 = (Z)_0 / (Y)_0$.
(BB)	$(BB)_0 = (Z)_0$; For $t > 0$, $(BB)_t = (BB)_{t-1} \times [1 + (G)_t - 0.025] + (Z)_t - (AA)_0 \times (X)_t$; $(G)_t$ is from Table 8-42.
(CC)	$(CC)_t = (A)_t$; $(A)_t$ is from Table 8-42.
(DD)	$(DD)_t = (R)_t + (S)_t$.
(EE)	$(EE)_t = (I)_t + (J)_t + (K)_t - (T)_t$.
(FF)	$(FF)_t = (Q)_t - (Q)_{t-1}$.
(GG)	$(GG)_t = (N)_t - (N)_{t-1}$.
(HH)	$(HH)_t = (W)_t$.
(II)	$(II)_t = (CC)_t + (DD)_t - (EE)_t - (FF)_t - (GG)_t - (HH)_t$.

Table 8-44 displays the resulting balance sheet and income statements.

Table 8-44
Balance Sheet and Income Statement for Annual Ratchet EIA Contract (Valuation Date $t = 0$)

		Contract Duration 0	1	2	3	4	5
Items from Table 8-42							
(A)	Deposit	100,000					
(B)	Zero-coupon bond rate	7.00%	7.00%	7.00%	7.00%	7.00%	7.00%
Items from Table 8-43							
(C)	Index account	100,000	103,124	105,210	106,175	109,281	113,527
(D)	Guaranteed value	90,000	91,243	91,517	90,796	91,874	93,830
(E)	Premium Income	100,000					
(F)	Investment Income		6,955	7,166	7,312	7,385	7,600
(G)	DAC	5,000	4,152	3,188	2,110	1,070	0
(H)	Estimated Gross Profit	0	2,343	2,512	2,666	2,478	2,441
Balance Sheet							
	Assets						
(I)	Bonds held to maturity	90,500	95,310	99,568	103,129	108,792	2,066
(J)	Fair value of hedge	4,500	4,770	4,919	5,019	5,065	5,213
(K)	DAC	5,000	4,152	3,188	2,110	1,070	0
(L)	Total assets	100,000	104,231	107,675	110,257	114,927	7,279
	Liabilities						
(M)	Value of host contract	85,314	87,680	89,172	89,758	92,137	0
(N)	Fair value of embedded derivative	14,686	15,410	16,023	16,481	17,199	0
(O)	Total liabilities	100,000	103,090	105,196	106,239	109,336	0
(P)	Equity	0	1,141	2,479	4,018	5,591	7,279
(Q)	Change in equity		1,141	1,338	1,539	1,572	1,688
Income Statement							
	Revenues						
(R)	Investment income on bonds		6,331	6,677	6,979	7,233	7,623
(S)	Gain on Hedge		270	278	284	287	295
(T)	Surrender Charge		99	205	313	105	0
(U)	Total revenues		6,701	7,161	7,577	7,625	7,918
	Expenses						
(V)	Interest credited on host contract		3,780	3,885	3,951	3,977	4,082
(W)	Maintenance cost		50	49	48	46	45
(X)	Acquisition cost expense		848	964	1,078	1,040	1,070
(Y)	Increase in Value of Embedded Derivative		881	925	961	989	1,032
(Z)	Total expenses		5,560	5,823	6,038	6,052	6,229
(AA)	Net income		1,141	1,338	1,539	1,572	1,688

Table 8-44
Balance Sheet and Income Statement for Annual Ratchet EIA Contract (Valuation Date $t = 0$)

Legend:

(A)	From Table 8-42, $(A)_t$.
(B)	From Table 8-42, $(G)_t$.
(C)	From Table 8-43, $(G)_t$.
(D)	From Table 8-43, $(H)_t$.
(E)	From Table 8-43, $(CC)_t$.
(F)	From Table 8-43, $(DD)_t$.
(G)	From Table 8-43, $(BB)_t$.
(H)	From Table 8-43, $(X)_t$.
(I)	For $t = 0$, $(I)_0 = (A)_0 \times [1 - (E)_0] - (J)_0$; For $t = 1$, $(I)_t = (A)_t \times [1 - (E)_t] + (I)_{t-1} + (R)_t - (I)_t - (J)_t - (K)_t + (T)_t - (W)_t$ For $t > 1$, $(I)_t = (A)_t \times [1 - (E)_t] + (I)_{t-1} + (R)_t - (I)_t - (J)_t - (K)_t + (T)_t - (W)_t + (J)_{t-1} - (Y)_t \times (K)_{t-1}$ where $(E)_t$, $(Y)_t$ and $(K)_{t-1}$ are from Table 8-42; $(I)_t$, $(J)_t$, $(K)_t$ and $(T)_t$ are from Table 8-43.
(J)	For $t = 0$, $(J)_0 = (C)_0$; For $t > 0$, $(J)_t = (C)_t \times (K)_{t-1}$; $(K)_{t-1}$ is from Table 8-42; $(C)_t$ from Table 8-43.
(K)	$(K)_t = (G)_t$.
(L)	$(L)_t = (I)_t + (J)_t + (K)_t$.
(M)	$(M)_t = (Q)_t$ from Table 8-43.
(N)	$(N)_t = (N)_t$ from Table 8-43.
(O)	$(O)_t = (M)_t + (N)_t$.
(P)	$(P)_t = (L)_t - (O)_t$.
(Q)	$(Q)_t = (P)_t - (P)_{t-1}$.
(R)	For $t = 1$, $(R)_t = [(I)_{t-1} - (W)_t] \times (B)_t$; For $t > 1$, $(R)_t = [(I)_{t-1} - (W)_t + (J)_{t-1} - (Y)_t \times (K)_{t-1}] \times (B)_t$ where $(Y)_t$ and $(K)_{t-1}$ are from Table 8-43.
(S)	$(S)_t = (S)_t$ from Table 8-43.
(T)	$(T)_t = (T)_t$ from Table 8-43.
(U)	$(U)_t = (R)_t + (S)_t + (T)_t$.
(V)	$(V)_t = (U)_t$ from Table 8-43.
(W)	$(W)_t = (W)_t$ from Table 8-43.
(X)	$(X)_t = (G)_{t-1} - (G)_t$.
(Y)	$(Y)_t = (V)_t$ from Table 8-43.
(Z)	$(Z)_t = (V)_t + (W)_t + (X)_t + (Y)_t$.
(AA)	$(AA)_t = (U)_t - (Z)_t$.

Table 8-45 updates the information in Table 8-42 to the beginning of year 2 and reflects the impact of the first-year option benefit expiring in the money. The restated participation rate for the beginning of year two has been shown and is scaled to the value of the budget. Since the option budget and the assumptions used to price the option haven't changed from those used at the beginning of year 1, the restated participation rate is the same as the rate at the beginning of year one, or 41.15%.

Table 8-45
Annual Ratchet EIA Product Design and Pricing Assumptions (Valuation Date t = 1)

		Contract Duration					
		0	1	2	3	4	5
Contract Design and Pricing Assumptions							
(A)	Deposit	$100,000					
(B)	Policy load	10.00%					
(C)	Guaranteed interest rate	3.00%					
(D)	Maintenance expense	$50.00					
(E)	Acquisition cost as percentage of premium	5%					
(F)	Participation rate	41.15%	41.15%				
(G)	Zero-coupon bond rate	7.00%	7.00%	7.00%	7.00%	7.00%	7.00%
(H)	Mortality rate per 1,000		5.77	6.35	6.98	7.68	8.45
(I)	Lapse rate		1.00%	2.00%	3.00%	1.00%	0.00%
(J)	Surrender charge		10.00%	10.00%	10.00%	10.00%	10.00%
(K)	Contracts persisting (prior to maturity)	1.00000	0.98429	0.95848	0.92323	0.90698	0.89932
(L)	Maturity rate		0.00%	0.00%	0.00%	0.00%	100.00%
Capital Markets							
(M)	Index growth		10%				
(N)	Option budget			4.50%	4.50%	4.50%	4.50%
(O)	Index level	1,500	1,650				
(P)	Implied volatility	22.0%	22.0%				
(Q)	Risk-free rate	6.00%	6.00%	6.00%	6.00%	6.00%	6.00%
(R)	Dividend rate	1.25%	1.25%				
Calculation of Account, Guaranteed, and Option Values							
(S)	Index account	100,000	104,115	109,081	114,284	119,736	125,447
(T)	Guaranteed value	90,000	92,700	95,481	98,345	101,296	104,335
	BOY						
(U)	Strike price for annual hedge		1,500	1,650			
(V)	Time to expiry for annual hedge		1.0000000	1.0000000			
(W)	D1		0.33	0.33			
(X)	D2		0.11	0.11			
(Y)	Black-Scholes price		164.03	180.44			
(Z)	Fair value of hedge		4,500	4,685	4,909	5,143	5,388
	EOY						
(AA)	Strike price for annual hedge		1,500				
(BB)	Time to expiry for annual hedge		0.0000001				
(CC)	D1		1369.99				
(DD)	D2		1369.99				
(EE)	Black-Scholes price		150.00				
(FF)	Fair value of hedge		4,115	4,966	5,203	5,451	5,711

Legend:

(A) to (F) Policy features.

(G) to (I) Experience assumptions.

(J) Annual Surrender Charge

(K) $(K)_0 = 1$; For $t > 0$, $(K)_t = (K)_{t-1} \times [1 - (H)_t / 1000] \times [1 - (I)_t]$.

(L) to (R) Assumptions.

(S) $(S)_0 = (A)_0$; For $t = 1$, $(S)_t = \text{Max}[(S)_{t-1}, (S)_{t-1} \times [1 + (M)_t \times (F)_{t-1}]$; For $t = 2\text{–}5$, $(S)_t = (S)_{t-1} + (FF)_t$.

(T) $(T)_t = [1 - (B)_0] \times (A)_0 \times [1 + (C)_0] \wedge t$.

Beginning of Year Hedge Values

(U) $(U)t = (O)_{t-1}$.

(V) One-year hedge purchased at the beginning of the year.

(W) Black-Scholes Parameter D1 = $(W)_t = [ln[(O)_{t-1} / (U)_t] + [(Q)_{t-1} - (R)_{t-1} + (P)_{t-1} \wedge 2 / 2] \times (V)_t] / [(P)_{t-1} \times (V)_t \wedge 0.5]$.

(X) Black-Scholes Parameter D2 = $(X)_t = (W_t) - (P)_{t-1} \times (V)_t \wedge 0.5$.

(Y) $(Y)_t = (O)_{t-1} \times \text{EXP}[-(R)_{t-1} \times (V)_t] \times \text{NORMDIST}[(W)_t] - (U)_t \times \text{EXP}[-(Q)_{t-1} \times (V)_t] \times \text{NORMDIST}[(X)_t]$.

(DD) For $t = 1\text{–}2$, $(DD)_t = (S)_{t-1} \times (F)_0 \times (CC)_t / (O)_{t-1}$; For $t = 3\text{–}5$, $(DD)_t = (S)_{t-1} \times (N)_t$.

(EE) For $t = 1\text{–}2$, $(EE)_t = (U)_{t-1} \times (F)_1 \times (CC)_t / (O)_{t-1}$; For $t = 3\text{–}5$, $(EE)_t = (U)_{t-1} \times (N)_t$.

(Z) For $t = 1$, $(Z)_t = (S)_{t-1} \times (F)_0 \times (Y)_t / (O)_{t-1}$; For $t = 2\text{–}5$, $(Z)_t = (S)_{t-1} - (N)_t$.

End of Year Hedge Values

(AA) $(AA)_t = (O)_{t-1}$.

(BB) One-year hedge right before expiry.

(CC) $(CC)_t = [ln[(O)_t / (AA)_t] + [(Q)_t - (R)_t + (P)_t \wedge 2 / 2] \times (BB)_t] / [(P)_t \times (BB)_t \wedge 0.5]$.

(DD) $(DD)_t = (CC_t) - (P)_t \times (BB)_t \wedge 0.5$.

(EE) $(EE)_t = (O)_t \times \text{EXP}[-(R)_t \times (BB)_t] \times \text{NORMDIST}[(CC)_t] - (AA)_t \times \text{EXP}[-(Q)_t \times (BB)_t] \times \text{NORMDIST}[(DD)_t]$.

(FF) For $t = 1$, $(FF)_t = (S)_{t-1} \times (F)_{t-1} \times (EE)_t / (O)_{t-1}$; For $t = 2\text{–}5$, $(FF)_t = (S)_{t-1} \times (N)_t \times [1 + (Q)_t]$.

Table 8-46 shows the update of the embedded derivative, host contract, and DAC calculations at the beginning of year two. Except for the indexed benefits, other experience for the first duration is assumed to equal expected.

Table 8-46
Policy Transactions, EGP and DAC for Annual Ratchet EIA Contract (Valuation Date t = 1)

		Contract Duration					
		0	**1**	**2**	**3**	**4**	**5**
Policy values before deaths and surrenders							
(A)	Guaranteed value	90,000	92,700	95,481	98,345	101,296	104,335
(B)	Index account	100,000	104,115	109,081	114,284	119,736	125,447
(C)	Fair value of hedge	4,500	4,115	4,966	5,203	5,451	5,711
(D)	Index credit		4,115	4,966	5,203	5,451	5,711
(E)	Death benefit available	100,000	104,115	109,081	114,284	119,736	125,447
(F)	Surrender benefit available	100,000	104,115	109,081	114,284	119,736	125,447
EGP and DAC Calculation net of deaths, surrenders, and maturities							
(G)	Index account (prior to maturity)	100,000	102,479	104,552	105,511	108,598	112,817
(H)	Guaranteed value (prior to maturity)	90,000	91,243	91,517	90,796	91,874	93,830
(I)	Death benefit paid		577	650	730	810	917
(J)	Account released on surrender		994	2,037	3,115	1,047	0
(K)	Maturity benefit paid		0	0	0	0	112,817
(L)	Guaranteed benefits paid		1,414	2,392	3,365	1,598	96,219
(M)	Excess benefits		157	295	479	259	17,516
(N)	Value of Embedded Derivative (VED)	14,686	14,796	15,389	15,833	16,524	0
(O)	Host contract interest rate	4.431%					
(P)	Host cash flow	85,314	(1,414)	(2,392)	(3,365)	(1,598)	(96,219)
(Q)	Value of host contract	85,314	87,680	89,172	89,758	92,137	0
	Income						
(R)	Non-hedge investment income		6,685	6,890	6,986	7,055	7,260
(S)	Gain on hedge		(385)	277	282	285	293
(T)	Surrender charge		99	204	311	105	0
	Expenses						
(U)	Interest credited on Host Contract		3,780	3,885	3,951	3,977	4,082
(V)	Adjusted Increase in Value of Embedded Derivative		267	888	923	950	991
(W)	Maintenance expense beginning of year		50	49	48	46	45
(X)	Estimated Gross Profit		2,302	2,548	2,658	2,472	2,434
(Y)	Present value of EGP	10,891					
(Z)	Deferrable Expenses	5,000					
(AA)	k-factor	45.908%					
(BB)	DAC	5,000	4,168	3,186	2,109	1,069	0
EGM presentation net of deaths, surrenders and maturities							
(CC)	Premium Income	100,000	0	0	0	0	0
(DD)	Investment Income		6,300	7,166	7,268	7,340	7,553
(EE)	Benefits Paid		1,472	2,483	3,533	1,753	113,735
(FF)	Increase in Host Contract	85,314	2,366	1,492	586	2,379	(92,137)
(GG)	Increase in VED	14,686	110	593	444	691	(16,524)
(HH)	Maintenance expense beginning of year		50	49	48	46	45
(II)	EGM	0	2,302	2,548	2,658	2,472	2,434

Table 8-46 Continued
Policy Transactions, EGP and DAC for Annual Ratchet EIA Contract (Valuation Date t = 1)

Legend:

(A)	From Table 8-45, $(T)_t$.
(B)	From Table 8-45, $(S)_t$.
(C)	From Table 8-45, For $t = 0$, $(Z)_1$; For $t > 0$, $(FF)_t$.
(D)	$(D)_t = (B)_t - (B)_{t-1} - (A)_t$; $(A)_t$ is from Table 8-45.
(E)	$(E)_t = (B)_t$.
(F)	$(F)_t = (B)_t$.
(G)	$(G)_t = (B)_t \times (K)_t$; $(K)_t$ is from Table 8-45.
(H)	$(H)_t = (A)_t \times (K)_t$; $(K)_t$ is from Table 8-45.
(I)	$(I)_t = (E)_{t-1} \times (K)_{t-1} \times (H)_t / 1000$; $(K)_t$ and $(H)_t$ are from Table 8-45.
(J)	$(J)_t = (F)_{t-1} \times (K)_{t-1} \times [1 - (H)_t / 1000] \times (I)_t$; $(K)_t$, $(H)_t$ and $(I)_t$ are from Table 8-45.
(K)	$(K)_t = (G)_t \times (L)_t$; $(L)_t$ is from Table 8-45.
(L)	$(L)_t = [(I)_t + (J)_t + (K)_t] \times (H)_{t-1} / (G)_{t-1}$.
(M)	$(M)_t = [(I)_t + (J)_t + (K)_t] - (L)_t$.
(N)	$(N)_5 = 0$; For $t = 4$ to 1, $(N)_t = [(N)_{t+1} + (M)_{t+1}] / [1 + (Q)_t]$; $(Q)_t$ is from Table 8-45 $(N)_0 = (N)_0$ from Table 8-43.
(O)	Internal rate of return based on Host Cash Flow $(P)_0$ through $(P)_5$.
(P)	For $t = 0$, $(P)_0 = (A)_0 - (N)_0 - (L)_0$; $(A)_0$ is from Table 8-45; For $t > 0$, $(P)_t = -(L)_t$.
(Q)	For $t = 0$, $(Q)_0 = (P)_0$; For $t > 0$, $(Q)_t = (Q)_{t-1} \times [1 + (O)_0] + (P)_t$.
(R)	$(R)_t = [(N)_{t-1} + (Q)_{t-1} - (C)_{t-1} \times (K)_{t-1}] \times (G)_0$; $(G)_0$ and $(K)_{t-1}$ are from Table 8-45.
(S)	$(S)_t = [(FF)_t - (Z)_t] \times (K)_{t-1}$; $(FF)_t$, $(Z)_t$ and $(K)_{t-1}$ are from Table 8-45.
(T)	$(T)_t = (J)_t \times (J)_t$; $(J)_t$ is from Table 8-45.
(U)	$(U)_t = (Q)_t \times (O)_0$.
(V)	$(V)_t = (N)_t - (N)_{t-1} + (M)_t$.
(W)	$(W)_t = (D)_0 \times (K)_{t-1}$; $(D)_0 \times (K)_{t-1}$ are from Table 8-45.
(X)	$(X)_t = (R)_t + (S)_t + (T)_t - (U)_t - (V)_t - (W)_t$.
(Y)	Present value of the EGP $(X)_t$ at issue date discounted at earned rate $(G)_t$ less 250 basis points; $(G)_t$ is from Table 8-45.
(Z)	$(Z)_t = (A)_t \times (E)_t$; $(A)_t$ and $(E)_t$ are from Table 8-45.
(AA)	$(AA)_0 = (Z)_0 / (Y)_0$.
(BB)	$(BB)_0 = (Z)_0$; For $t > 0$, $(BB)_t = (BB)_{t-1} \times [1 + (G)_t - 0.025] + (Z)_t - (AA)_0 \times (X)_t$; $(G)_t$ is from Table 8-45.
(CC)	$(CC)_t = (A)_t$; $(A)_t$ is from Table 8-45.
(DD)	$(DD)_t = (R)_t + (S)_t$.
(EE)	$(EE)_t = (I)_t + (J)_t + (K)_t - (T)_t$.
(FF)	$(FF)_t = (Q)_t - (Q)_{t-1}$.
(GG)	$(GG)_t = (N)_t - (N)_{t-1}$.
(HH)	$(HH)_t = (W)_t$.
(II)	$(II)_t = (CC)_t + (DD)_t - (EE)_t - (FF)_t - (GG)_t - (HH)_t$.

Table 8-47 shows the restated balance sheets and income statements. The balance sheet at $t = 1$ and the income statement for year 1 are actual. The items for the remaining periods are projected.

Table 8-47
Balance Sheet and Income Statement for Annual Ratchet EIA Contract (Valuation Date t = 1)

		Contract Duration					
		0	1	2	3	4	5
Items from Table 8-45							
(A)	Deposit	100,000					
(B)	Zero-coupon bond rate	7.00%	7.00%	7.00%	7.00%	7.00%	7.00%
Items from Table 8-46							
(C)	Index account	100,000	102,479	104,552	105,511	108,598	112,817
(D)	Guaranteed value	90,000	91,243	91,517	90,796	91,874	93,830
(E)	Premium Income	100,000					
(F)	Investment Income		6,300	7,166	7,268	7,340	7,553
(G)	DAC	5,000	4,168	3,186	2,109	1,069	0
(H)	Estimated Gross Profit	0	2,302	2,548	2,658	2,472	2,434
Balance Sheet							
	Assets						
(I)	Bonds held to maturity	90,500	95,310	98,914	102,450	108,075	2,013
(J)	Fair value of hedge	4,500	4,115	4,888	4,987	5,033	5,180
(K)	DAC	5,000	4,168	3,186	2,109	1,069	0
(L)	Total assets	100,000	103,593	106,988	109,546	114,177	7,194
	Liabilities						
(M)	Value of host contract	85,314	87,680	89,172	89,758	92,137	0
(N)	Fair value of embedded derivative	14,686	14,796	15,389	15,833	16,524	0
(O)	Total liabilities	100,000	102,476	104,562	105,591	108,661	0
(P)	Equity	0	1,117	2,427	3,955	5,517	7,194
(Q)	Change in equity		1,117	1,310	1,528	1,562	1,677
Income Statement							
	Revenues						
(R)	Investment income on bonds		6,331	6,633	6,933	7,185	7,572
(S)	Gain on Hedge		(385)	277	282	285	293
(T)	Surrender Charge		99	204	311	105	0
(U)	Total revenues		6,046	7,114	7,527	7,575	7,866
	Expenses						
(V)	Interest credited on host contract		3,780	3,885	3,951	3,977	4,082
(W)	Maintenance cost		50	49	48	46	45
(X)	Acquisition cost expense		832	982	1,077	1,040	1,069
(Y)	Increase in Value of Embedded Derivative		267	888	923	950	991
(Z)	Total expenses		4,929	5,804	5,999	6,013	6,189
(AA)	Net income		1,117	1,310	1,528	1,562	1,677

Table 8-47 Continued
Balance Sheet and Income Statement for Annual Ratchet EIA Contract (Valuation Date t = 1)

Legend:

(A)	From Table 8-45, $(A)_t$.
(B)	From Table 8-45, $(G)_t$.
(C)	From Table 8-46, $(G)_t$.
(D)	From Table 8-46, $(H)_t$.
(E)	From Table 8-46, $(CC)_t$.
(F)	From Table 8-46, $(DD)_t$.
(G)	From Table 8-46, $(BB)_t$.
(H)	From Table 8-46, $(X)_t$.
(I)	For $t = 0$, $(I)_0 = (A)_0 \times [1-(E)_0] - (J)_0$; For $t = 1$, $(I)_t = (A)_t \times [1-(E)_t] + (I)_{t-1} + (R)_t - (I)_t - (J)_t - (K)_t + (T)_t - (W)_t$ For $t > 1$, $(I)_t = (A)_t \times [1-(E)_t] + (I)_{t-1} + (R)_t - (I)_t - (J)_t - (K)_t + (T)_t - (W)_t + (J)_{t-1} - (Z)_t \times (K)_{t-1}$ where $(E)_t$, $(Z)_t$ and $(K)_{t-1}$ are from Table 8-45; $(I)_t$, $(J)_t$, $(K)_t$ and $(T)_t$ are from Table 8-46.
(J)	For $t = 0$, $(J)_0 = (C)_0$; For $t > 0$, $(J)_t = (C)_t \times (K)_{t-1}$; $(K)_{t-1}$ is from Table 8-45; $(C)_t$ from Table 8-46.
(K)	$(K)_t = (G)_t$.
(L)	$(L)_t = (I)_t + (J)_t + (K)_t$.
(M)	$(M)_t = (Q)_t$ from Table 8-46.
(N)	$(N)_t = (N)_t$ from Table 8-46.
(O)	$(O)_t = (M)_t + (N)_t$.
(P)	$(P)_t = (L)_t - (O)_t$.
(Q)	$(Q)_t = (P)_t - (P)_{t-1}$.
(R)	For $t = 1$, $(R)_t = [(I)_{t-1} - (W)_t] \times (B)_t$; For $t > 1$, $(R)_t = [(I)_{t-1} - (W)_t + (J)_{t-1} - (Z)_t \times (K)_{t-1}] \times (B)_t$ where $(Z)_t$ and $(K)_{t-1}$ are from Table 8-46.
(S)	$(S)_t = (S)_t$ from Table 8-46.
(T)	$(T)_t = (T)_t$ from Table 8-46.
(U)	$(U)_t = (R)_t + (S)_t + (T)_t$.
(V)	$(V)_t = (U)_t$ from Table 8-46.
(W)	$(W)_t = (W)_t$ from Table 8-46.
(X)	$(X)_t = (G)_{t-1} - (G)_t$.
(Y)	$(Y)_t = (V)_t$ from Table 8-46.
(Z)	$(Z)_t = (V)_t + (W)_t + (X)_t + (Y)_t$.
(AA)	$(AA)_t = (U)_t - (Z)_t$.

Chapter 9 Annuities in Payment Status

9.1 Background

"Annuity" is derived from the Latin word *annus*, meaning year, and hence connotes an annual payment. A broader definition of an *annuity*, however, is a periodic payment to commence at a stated or contingent date and to continue throughout a fixed period or for the duration of a designated life or lives.

Annuities in payment status emanate from many sources, including:

- Sale of single premium immediate annuities
- Application of policy benefits arising from a life insurance or deferred annuity contract to settlement options embedded in those contracts
- Purchase of an annuity by a defendant in a lawsuit to fund a structured settlement
- Purchase of an annuity to fund state lottery prizes, which are frequently paid over a number of years (such as 20).

Continued payment of annuity benefits may depend on the continued survival of the annuitant(s). These annuities are life contingent and should be accounted for by using the methodology described in *SFAS 97* for limited payment contracts.

Annuities not having a significant component of life-contingent payments are considered to be investment contracts for GAAP accounting purposes. These annuities should be accounted for by using methodologies consistent with those used to account for comparable products offered by other financial services institutions. *SFAS 97* states:

> ... the Board believes that similar financial instruments should be accorded similar treatment regardless of the nature of the issuing enterprise. Therefore, the Board concluded that the accounting for investment contracts issued by insurance enterprises should be consistent with the accounting for interest-bearing and other financial instruments. (Paragraph 39)

No further direction as to the appropriate accounting for these contracts is given in *SFAS 97*. This chapter examines the accounting for each of these types of contracts.

9.2 Contract Classification

Annuities having no mortality or morbidity risk (as defined in the *SFAS 60* Glossary) are investment contracts. However, many annuities issued by insurance companies combine payments that are certain (those that are not contingent upon the continued survival of the individual annuitant(s)) along with payments that are contingent upon the continued survival of the annuitant(s) (life contingent payments). In addition, many life insurance and deferred annuity contracts contain guaranteed settlement options, giving the policyowner the option to apply policy proceeds to purchase a payment annuity at a guaranteed purchase price. The existence of the option to apply policy proceeds to purchase a payment annuity does not constitute sufficient mortality risk to result in the classification of the policy as an insurance contract. *SFAS 97* states:

Annuity contracts may require the insurance enterprise to make a number of payments that are not contingent upon the survival of the beneficiary, followed by payments that are made if the beneficiary is alive when the payments are due (often referred to as *life-contingent payments*). Such contracts are considered insurance contracts under this Statement and Statement 60 unless:

(a) the probability that life-contingent payments will be made is remote, or

(b) the present value of the expected life-contingent payments relative to the present value of all expected payments under the contract is insignificant. (Paragraph 8)

SFAS 97 continues:

The risk that the guaranteed price of an annuity may prove to be unfavorable to the guaranteeing enterprise when the annuity is purchased is a price risk not unlike a guaranteed price of any commodity and does not create a mortality risk. A mortality risk does not arise until the purchase provision is executed and the obligation to make life-contingent payments is present in an annuity contract. A nominal mortality risk-a risk of insignificant amount or of remote probability-is not sufficient to permit that a contract be accounted for as an insurance contract. (Paragraph 40)

The determination of whether life-contingent payments to be made constitute a "nominal mortality risk" is a matter of judgment. Table 9-1 illustrates the present value of life-contingent payments as a percentage of the present value of total payments to be made under annuity contracts issued with different certain periods at various issue ages. As the certain period and issue age increase, the present value of payments that are life contingent decreases as a percentage of the present value of total payments anticipated to be made under the contract. Interpretation of what constitutes a "nominal mortality risk" has differed from company to company. However, it is generally accepted that a contract whose life contingent payments exceed 5 to 10% of the present value of all payments anticipated under the contract contains more than a "nominal mortality risk" and therefore should be accounted for as a limited payment insurance contract.

Table 9-1
Percentage of Life-Contingent Payments*

Issue Age	**Years Certain and Life Thereafter**		
	10	**20**	**30**
45	51.5%	25.3%	11.1%
65	38.9%	13.8%	4.5%

*Male 1996 U.S. Annuity 2000 Table 5% Interest

Determination of whether a particular contract is an investment contract or a limited-payment insurance contract should be done on a contract-by-contract basis. However, some companies have grouped contracts with similar characteristics (for example, certain period/issue age) together when classifying policies for accounting purposes. In practice, once a contract is assigned to an accounting basis, it remains in that classification for its lifetime.

9.3 Investment Contracts

SFAS 97 gives little detail as to the appropriate method for accounting for investment contracts. It states:

Amounts received as payments for such contracts shall not be reported as revenues. Payments received as payments for such contracts shall be reported as liabilities and accounted for in a manner consistent with the accounting for interest-bearing or other financial instruments. (Paragraph 15)

SFAS 91, "Accounting for Nonrefundable Fees and Costs Associated with Originating or Acquiring Loans and Initial Direct Costs of Leases", issued in December 1986, gives some insight into the concepts appropriate to account for annuities in payment status.

SFAS 91 specifies that:

> ... loan origination fees shall be recognized over the life of the related loan as an adjustment of yield. ... loan fees, certain direct loan origination costs, and purchase premiums and discounts on loans shall be recognized as an adjustment of yield generally by the interest method based on the contractual terms of the loan. (Paragraph 5)

The first step in applying Constant Yield Method to account for a payment annuity that has been classified as an investment contract is to project the anticipated cash flows (for example, premiums, expenses, and policyholder benefits) utilizing best-estimate assumptions (with no explicit margin for adverse deviation). The next step is to solve for the interest rate that results in a present value of future cash flows equal to the net proceeds at issue. The net proceeds are generally the consideration received less any commission or other acquisition costs. The present value of cash flows, using this solved-for interest rate, is held as the net GAAP reserve [that is, benefit reserve plus maintenance expense reserve minus deferred acquisition costs (DAC)]. The splitting of this net reserve between benefit reserve, maintenance expense reserve, and DAC is discussed later in this chapter. This Constant Yield Method has also been referred to as the Prospective Deposit Method in insurance accounting circles.

The example presented in Table 9-2 illustrates such an approach to the accounting for a 10-year certain annuity. Premium income and acquisition expense are assumed to occur at policy issue, and maintenance expense and policy benefits are assumed to be paid at the end of each year. The present value of the cash flows is equal to zero using a discount rate equal to 5.33%. Therefore, the net reserve at the end of each year is equal to the present value of the prospective net cash flows discounted at 5.33%.

Table 9-2
Example of Use of Constant Yield Method for Accounting for a 10-Year Certain Annuity

(1) Policy Year t	(2) Premium (BOY)	(3) Acquisition Expense (BOY)	(4) Policy Benefits (EOY)	(5) Maintenance Expense (EOY)	(6) Net Cash Flow	(7) Net Reserve at 5.33%	(8) Maintenance Expense + Benefit Resv at 4.28%	(9) Benefit Reserve at 4.28%	(10) Maintenance Expense Reserve at 4.28%	(11) Implied DAC	(12) Investment Income at 7.00%	(13) GAAP Profit	(14) GAAP Profit Alternative Calculation
0	1,000.00	50.00	0.00	0.00	950.00	950.00	1,000.00	960.00	40.00	50.00			
1			120.00	5.00	(125.00)	875.62	917.77	881.06	36.71	42.15	66.50	15.88	15.88
2			120.00	5.00	(125.00)	797.28	832.03	798.75	33.28	34.75	61.29	14.64	14.64
3			120.00	5.00	(125.00)	714.76	742.62	712.92	29.70	27.86	55.81	13.33	13.33
4			120.00	5.00	(125.00)	627.85	649.39	623.41	25.98	21.54	50.03	11.95	11.95
5			120.00	5.00	(125.00)	536.30	552.17	530.08	22.09	15.86	43.95	10.49	10.49
6			120.00	5.00	(125.00)	439.88	450.79	432.75	18.03	10.90	37.54	8.96	8.96
7			120.00	5.00	(125.00)	338.32	345.07	331.26	13.80	6.75	30.79	7.35	7.35
8			120.00	5.00	(125.00)	231.35	234.83	225.43	9.39	3.48	23.68	5.65	5.65
9			120.00	5.00	(125.00)	118.68	119.87	115.08	4.79	1.20	16.19	3.87	3.87
10			120.00	5.00	(125.00)	0.00	0.00	0.00	0.00	0.00	8.31	1.98	1.98

BOY = Beginning of year
EOY = End of year

Legend:

(1) Time, in years
(2) Policyholder premium, paid at the beginning of the policy year
(3) Policy acquistion costs, paid at the beginning of the policy year
(4) Policyholder benefits, paid at the end of the policy year
(5) Policy maintenance costs, paid at the end of the policy year
(6) Net cash flow, $(6)_t = (2)_t - (3)_t - (4)_t - (5)_t$
(7) Net benefit reserve = present value of future benefit payments calculated at 5.33%
(8) Maintenance expense reserve + benefit reserve = present value of future benefit and maintenance expense payments calculated at 4.28%
(9) Benefit reserve = present value of future benefit payments calculated at 4.28%
(10) Maintenance expense reserve = present value of future maintenance expense payments calculated at 4.28%
(11) Implied DAC, $(11)_t = (8)_t - (7)_t$
(12) Investment Income, $(12)_t = 0.07 \times (7)_{t-1}$
(13) GAAP profit, $(13)t = (12)t - (4)t - (5)t - (7)t + (7)t-1$
(14) Alternative calculation of GAAP profit to validate (13), $(14)_t = (0.07 - 0.0533) \times (7)_{t-1}$

It is generally accepted that the net GAAP liability can be split into an asset piece and a liability piece for balance sheet presentation. This can be done by calculating the present value of the maintenance expenses and policyholder benefit payments only. The interest rate used to discount the maintenance expenses and the policyholder benefits is the rate that equates the present value of the maintenance expenses and the benefit payments with the premium paid. A 4.28% interest rate equates the present value of maintenance expenses and the benefit payments with the gross premium in the example illustrated in Table 9-2. Absent significant changes in the projected cash flows, this rate, as well as the rate used to calculate the net reserve, will remain constant for the life of the contract and is used to calculate the present value of projected policyholder benefits prospectively in the determination of the benefit reserve. Likewise, the maintenance expense reserve is set equal to the present value of the projected maintenance expenses discounted at this solved for rate (4.28% in the example). Once the benefit reserve, maintenance expense reserve, and the net GAAP reserve are calculated, the DAC balance (a balance sheet asset) is equal to the benefit reserve plus the maintenance expense reserve minus the net GAAP reserve.

Income statement presentation of results is to be consistent with investment products sold by other financial institutions. Therefore, premiums are not booked as revenue but are recorded as deposits. In addition, policyholder benefits are not a deduction to income, merely a return of deposit. Increase in policyholder benefit reserves is not a deduction to income in the income statement presentation. The following is an algebraic transformation of GAAP income to the appropriate income statement presentation.

P_t	=	GAAP profit in year t
I_t	=	Investment income in year t
B_t	=	Policyholder benefits in year t
E_t	=	Maintenance expense in year t
R_t	=	Net benefit, maintenance expense, and acquisition expense reserve at end of year t
BR_t	=	Benefit reserve at end of year t
DAC_t	=	Deferred acquisition costs at end of year t
ER_t	=	Maintenance expense reserve at end of year t
EE_t	=	Expected maintenance expense in year t
n	=	Solved for net benefit, maintenance expense, and acquisition expense reserve interest rate
r	=	Solved for net benefit and maintenance expense reserve interest rate
i_t	=	Investment earnings rate in year t

$$P_t = I_t - B_t - E_t - R_t + R_{t-1}$$

where

$$I_t = i_t \times R_{t-1}$$
$$R_t = BR_t + ER_t - DAC_t$$

By assuming benefits paid are equal to benefits anticipated in the benefit reserve calculation, then:

$$BR_t = BR_{t-1} \times (1 + r) - B_t$$

Therefore,

$$P_t = I_t - B_t - E_t - (BR_{t-1} \times (1 + r) - B_t) + BR_{t-1} - ER_t + ER_{t-1} + DAC_t - DAC_{t-1}$$

$$= I_t - E_t - r \times BR_{t-1} - [ER_t - ER_{t-1}] + [DAC_t - DAC_{t-1}]$$

This results in the appropriate income statement presentation as shown below.

Investment Income
minus Maintenance Expense
minus Required/Credited Interest
minus Increase in Maintenance Expense Reserve
plus Increase in Deferred Acquisition Costs
equals Pre-tax GAAP Profit

If the actual maintenance expense incurred, E_t, equals the expected maintenance expense, EE_t, used in the calculation of the maintenance expense reserve, then the profit that emerges is equal to the investment income earned on assets supporting the net reserve at the beginning of the period minus the required interest on the benefit and maintenance expense reserve plus the increase in DAC.

$$Er_t = ER_{t-1} \times (1 + r) - EE_t$$

assuming

$$Ee_t = E_t$$

$$Er_t = ER_{t-1} \times (1 + r) - E_t$$

$$P_t = I_t - E_t - [ER_{t-1} \times (1 + r) - E_t] + ER_{t-1} - r \times BR_{t-1} + [DAC_t - DAC_{t-1}]$$

$$= I_t - r \times ER_{t-1} - r \times BR_{t-1} + [DAC_t - DAC_{t-1}]$$

In addition, assuming benefits paid and maintenance expense incurred are equal to those anticipated in the reserve calculation, it can be demonstrated that profits emerge as the difference between investment income earned and the required interest on the net GAAP reserve.

$$P_t = I_t - E_t - B_t - [R_t - R_{t-1}]$$

where $R_t = R_{t-1} \times (1 + n) - B_t - E_t$

$$P_t = I_t - E_t - B_t - [R_{t-1} \times (1 + n) - B_t - E_t - R_{t-1}]$$

$$= I_t - n \times R_{t-1}$$

and $I_t = i_t \times R_{t-1}$

so $P_t = i_t \times R_{t-1} - n \times R_{t-1}$

$$= (i_t - n) \times R_{t-1}$$

SFAS 97 presents a few additional ramifications when accounting for investment contracts. It states:

> The provisions of Statement 60 dealing with loss recognition (premium deficiency) ... shall apply to limited-payment and universal life-type contracts addressed by this Statement. (Paragraph 27)

The omission of investment contracts from this paragraph leads to the conclusion that the concept of loss recognition does not apply when accounting for these contracts.

According to *Practice Bulletin 8*, issued by the AICPA in November 1990, DAC related to investment contracts defined under *SFAS 97* should be written off if it is determined that it is not recoverable from future profits. It states:

> As stated in paragraph 87 in FASB Statement of Concepts No. 5, Recognition and Measurement in Financial Statements of Business Enterprises, [a]n expense or loss is recognized if it becomes evident that previously recognized future economic benefits of an asset have been reduced or eliminated, or that a liability has been incurred or increased, without associated economic benefits. (Paragraph 34)

The DAC asset should be reduced to the level that can be recovered. However, according to paragraph 36 of *Practice Bulletin 8*, once the DAC has been written off, the deferral of a future loss cannot be avoided by increasing the benefit reserve, because loss recognition is not a concept recognized in the accounting for investment contracts as it is for insurance contracts. Absent DAC recoverability issues, realized capital gains and losses do not affect the DAC amortization for annuities in payment status classified as investment contracts because, DAC is not being amortized over the policy's gross profits. Rather, the Constant Yield Method is used, which is unaffected by the level of investment income. Likewise, there are no shadow DAC issues, which emerge due to the amortization of DAC over the gross margins produced by the contracts.

Because the link between the accounting for investment contracts and the methodologies prescribed in *SFAS 60* has been cut, it seems reasonable that the concept of lock-in of assumptions no longer is applicable for these contracts. This conclusion is reinforced by the fact that lock-in no longer applies when accounting for universal life contracts using the retrospective deposit method (*SFAS 97*, paragraph 25), which appears to be the appropriate method for accounting for single and flexible-premium deferred-annuity investment contracts. However, this issue is largely academic with respect to investment contracts in payment status, because benefit payments are by definition substantially fixed; changes in the investment rate earned and the maintenance expense incurred in a particular accounting period affect net income directly in that period. In addition, *SFAS 91* (paragraph 18c) under certain circumstances allows but does not mandate changes in the constant effective yield.

9.4 Limited Payment Contracts

Once it has been determined that enough mortality risk exists within an annuity contract in payment status (for example, in excess of 5 to 10% of the present value of annuity payments are contingent upon the survival of one or more of the annuitants), the contract should be accounted for as described in *SFAS 97* by using the methodology for limited-payment contracts. Specifically, the methodology described in *SFAS 60* and in the AICPA Audit and Accounting Guide, "Life and Health Insurance Entities," New Edition as of June 15, 2000, should be used. *SFAS 60* requires that premiums be recognized as revenue. Likewise, the liability for policy benefits is computed on the same basis as for other long-duration contracts. For policies in which premiums continue throughout the duration of the contract, net income emerges partially as a level percentage of premium and partially as a release from risk due to assumptions used in the calculation of benefit and expense reserves (DAC) that incorporate a margin for adverse deviation. *SFAS 97* states:

> The Board concluded that limited-payment contracts with terms that are fixed and guaranteed are similar to other contracts addressed by Statement 60 in all respects except for the pattern of premium payment. The Board also concluded that income from insurance contracts is earned through the performance of contract services. The collection of a single premium or a limited number of premiums does not, in itself, represent the completion of an earnings process. The Board concluded that any amount of gross premium in excess of net premium, as those terms are defined in Statement 60, should be deferred and recognized over the period that services are provided. (Paragraph 42)

SFAS 97 also states:

> The collection of premium does not, however, represent the completion of an earnings process. Any gross premium received in excess of the net premium shall be deferred and recognized in income in a constant relationship with insurance in force

(when accounting for life insurance contracts) or with the amount of expected future benefit payments (when accounting for annuity contracts). (Paragraph 16)

Therefore, for annuities in payment status with more than an insignificant amount of mortality risk, the initial premium is considered revenue; acquisition expenses are capitalized and then amortized over the premium paying period (the entire amortization is usually instantaneous); benefit and maintenance expense reserves are established by using assumptions reflecting the company's expectations including an appropriate margin for adverse deviation; and any excess of the gross premium collected over the sum of the acquisition expense incurred plus the initial benefit and maintenance expense reserve established is capitalized as a deferred profit liability (DPL).

This DPL is then amortized in proportion to the expected annuity payments to be made. Table 9-3 illustrates a simplified example assuming experience emerges exactly as assumed in the development of the reserves (in other words, no profit emerges due to the release of margins for adverse deviation).

Table 9-3
Limited-Payment Contract

(1) Policy Year t	(2) Premium (BOY)	(3) Acquisition Expense (BOY)	(4) Policy Benefits (EOY)	(5) Maintenance Expense (EOY)	(6) Benefit Reserve at 7.00%	(7) Maintenance Expense Reserve at 7.00%	(8) Deferred Profit Liability	(9) Investment Income at 7.00%	(10) GAAP Profit	(11) Alternative GAAP Profit
0	1,000.00	50.00	0.00	0.00	819.19	35.12	95.69			
1			140.00	5.00	736.53	32.58	86.04	66.50	16.35	16.35
2			140.00	5.00	648.09	29.86	75.70	59.86	16.35	16.35
3			140.00	5.00	553.46	26.95	64.65	52.76	16.35	16.35
4			130.00	5.00	462.20	23.83	53.99	45.15	15.19	15.19
5			120.00	5.00	374.56	20.50	43.75	37.80	14.02	14.02
6			110.00	5.00	290.77	16.94	33.97	30.72	12.85	12.85
7			100.00	5.00	211.13	13.12	24.66	23.92	11.68	11.68
8			90.00	5.00	135.91	9.04	15.88	17.42	10.51	10.51
9			80.00	5.00	65.42	4.67	7.64	11.26	9.34	9.34
10			70.00	5.00	0.00	0.00	0.00	5.44	8.18	8.18

BOY = Beginning of year
EOY = End of year

Legend:
$(8)_0$ = Initial deferred profit liability = 1000 – 50 – 819.19 – 35.12 = 95.69
Profit per annuity payment = $(8)_0 / (6)_0$ = 95.69/819.19 = 11.68%
(1) Time, in years
(2) Policyholder premium, paid at the beginning of the policy year
(3) Policy acquistion costs, paid at the beginning of the policy year
(4) Policyholder benefits, paid at the end of the policy year
(5) Policy maintenance costs, paid at the end of the policy year
(6) Benefit reserve = present value of future benefit payments calculated at 7.00%
(7) Maintenance expense reserve = present value of future maintenance expense payments calculated at 7.00%
(8) Deferred profit liability = $(8)_{t-1} \times 1.07 - (10)_t$ (beginning at policy year 1)
Alternatively, $(8)_t = 11.68\% \times (6)_t$
(9) Investment income, $(9)_t = 0.07 \times \{(6)_{t-1} + (7)_{t-1} + (8)_{t-1}\}$
(10) GAAP profit, $(10)_t = (9)_t - (4)_t - (5)_t - (6)_t + (6)_{t-1} - (7)_t + (7)_{t-1} - (8)_t + (8)_{t-1}$
(11) Alternative GAAP profit calculation, $(11)_t = 11.68\% \times (4)_t$

Because these contracts have mortality risk, they are considered insurance products for which the methodologies and concepts detailed in *SFAS 60* apply. As such, the assumptions used in the development of the benefit reserve, maintenance expense reserve, and deferred profit liability are determined at issue and are locked in as long as the business is expected to remain profitable prospectively. This means that the reserves will continue to be calculated by using the assumptions (mortality, expense, interest) determined at the time of issue.

Assumptions used in these calculations should include a margin for adverse deviation. Critical assumptions for these types of policies include the mortality and investment earnings assumption. Grading the investment earnings rate down over a number of years from the new money rate available at the time of issue to a lower ultimate rate is an acceptable method of incorporating a provision for adverse deviation in the investment earnings rate assumption. It is important to recognize that incorporating a margin for adverse deviation in the mortality assumption entails reducing the expected mortality rather than increasing it. This can be accomplished, at least partially, by projecting mortality improvement over the lifetime of the contract. The accounting for these contracts is subject to loss recognition. If the present value of pre-tax GAAP profits using best estimate assumptions discounted at the pre-tax investment earnings rate is negative, the liability held should be increased by the amount of the deficiency (by the amount of the negative present value of pre-tax profits). Specifically, benefit reserves and maintenance expense reserves would be recalculated by using best-estimate assumptions and reduced by the amount of the deferred profit liability.

9.5 Conversion of Policy-Year Factors to Calendar-Year Factors

GAAP benefit, deferred profit, maintenance expense reserves, as well as DAC are typically calculated on a policy-year basis for annuities in payment status. However, financial statements are prepared throughout the year, necessitating the calculation of factors at a time other than policy-year end. For the type of policies discussed in this chapter, determination of reserve factors on dates other than policy-year ends is typically done through interpolation.

Alternatively, an exact calculation of the present values of the projected payments (using the applicable discount rates) can be made as of each valuation date. Table 9-4 illustrates the differences between an exact calculation of the reserve value as of the valuation date versus an interpolation of the terminal reserve values. Assuming a reasonably uniform distribution of projected payments throughout the policy year, very little distortion in the reserve values is created by doing a direct interpolation of the terminal reserve factors as shown in the example presented in Table 9-4. However, an exact calculation should be made for contracts with benefit payments that are less uniform throughout the policy year. In some circumstances, companies have taken the interpolation of terminal reserve factors a step further. Assuming a uniform distribution of issues throughout the calendar year, these companies take the average of applicable terminal reserves for all policies, ignoring the relationship for any individual policy. This is typically acceptable and will not create a substantial distortion if the block is sufficiently large and the assumption of uniform distribution of issues throughout the year is reflective of the in-force business.

Table 9-4
Exact Calculation Versus Interpolation of Reserve Values

(1) Valuation Date / Payment Date	(2) Month t	(3) Projected Payments	(4) Exact Reserve @ 5.00%	(5) Interpolated Terminal Reserves	(6) Difference	(7) Difference As a Percentage Reserve
December 31, 2000	0		10,641.93	10,641.93	0.00	0.00%
January 31, 2001	1	100.00	10,586.27	10,584.98	1.29	0.01%
February 28, 2001	2	100.00	10,530.38	10,528.03	2.35	0.02%
March 31, 2001	3	100.00	10,474.26	10,471.07	3.18	0.03%
April 30, 2001	4	100.00	10,417.90	10,414.12	3.78	0.04%
May 31, 2001	5	100.00	10,361.31	10,357.17	4.14	0.04%
June 30, 2001	6	100.00	10,304.48	10,300.22	4.26	0.04%
July 31, 2001	7	100.00	10,247.42	10,243.27	4.15	0.04%
August 31, 2001	8	100.00	10,190.11	10,186.31	3.80	0.04%
September 30, 2001	9	100.00	10,132.57	10,129.36	3.21	0.03%
October 31, 2001	10	100.00	10,074.79	10,072.41	2.38	0.02%
November 30, 2001	11	100.00	10,016.77	10,015.46	1.31	0.01%
December 31, 2001	12	100.00	9,958.51	9,958.51	0.00	0.00%
Present Value of Continuing Future Payments at 5%	13	10,000.00				

Legend:

(1) Date of valuation and date of benefit payment

(2) Time, measured in months

(3) Payments to policyholder

(4) Reserve determined using an "exact calculation," i.e. present value of future benefit payments $(4)_t = [(4)_{t+1} + (3)_{t+1}] / (1 + 0.05 / 12)$ where $(4)_{13} = 0$

(5) Reserve determined by interpolation between beginning and end of year terminal reserves $(5)_t = (10{,}641.93 \times (12 - t) + 9{,}958.51 \times t) / 12$

(6) Difference between methods in calculated reserve, $(6)_t = (4)_t - (5)_t$

(7) Difference between methods in calculated reserve as a percentage of "exact calculated" reserve, $(7)_t = (6)_t / (4)_t$

Chapter 10 Individual Health Insurance

10.1 Characteristics of Health Insurance Business

Health insurance policies cover morbidity risks. Morbidity is the collective term for risks relating to poor health—including acute and chronic conditions—and injuries. Disability means a chronic health condition in which the insured person is not able to perform certain normal functions, such as earning an income. In this chapter the terms health insurance, and accident & health (A&H) insurance, are used interchangeably.

Many standard morbidity tables are in existence, based on experience on hospital confinement, surgical costs, nursing home confinement, disability incidence and termination, accidental death, and cancer benefits. A morbidity table shows claim costs per unit of benefit, with variation by age (or age group), sex, risk class, benefit characteristics, and other variables.

In the U.S. insurance regulatory environment, individual health insurance policies are issued mainly by life insurers, although similar contracts are sometimes offered by property-casualty insurers.

10.1.1 Insurable Events

Insurable events are frequent enough that reliable statistics can be compiled, but not so frequent that they are predictable at an individual level. Events include sickness, temporary, or permanent disability, and accidental injury or death. The insurance policy provides financial reimbursement under its contractual terms upon occurrence of an insured event. The reimbursement may be more or less closely correlated with the actual expenses and damages suffered.

A single policy may provide benefits for a wide variety of events or may be more narrowly specified. Riders are commonly used to add enhanced or supplemental coverages to a basic policy. Many policies permit additional coverages to be added after the original issue date, subject to underwriting or other constraints.

10.1.2 Contractual Terms

Individual A&H policies provide benefits only during their contract term (with limited exceptions for deferred benefits). The contract term begins on the policy effective date and ends at the contractual expiry date or earlier death. The typical expiry date is insured age 65, consistent with statutory requirements for guaranteed renewable contracts. The policy of course may lapse for nonpayment of premiums.

Older policies were issued for a one-year term, similar to many property-casualty contracts, and certain conditions were attached to subsequent renewal terms. Current terminology is still based on this annual renewable concept. Renewability refers to the extension of the contract beyond the initial and successive one-year terms.

- *Guaranteed renewable.* The insurer may not cancel the policy under any circumstances. Subject to certain conditions (e.g., regulatory approval or adverse morbidity experience), the premium rates may be increased.

- *Noncancelable* (also *noncan* or *noncancelable and guaranteed renewable*). The insurer may not cancel the policy and may not increase premiums for any reason.

- *Collectively renewable.* The insurer may not cancel an individual policy under any circumstances. The insurer may cancel policies in similar rating classes. In some cases, regulatory approval is necessary.

- *Conditionally renewable.* The insurer may not cancel an individual policy except for certain contractually specified reasons. This is sometimes called nonrenewable for stated reasons only (NRSRO). A specified reason may not include health condition of the insured. An acceptable condition for renewability may include residence in a state or continuance in an occupation group.

- *Optionally renewable.* The insurer may cancel an individual policy at any renewal date (in some cases, at any premium payment date). This is sometimes referred to as commercial business. This type of individual policy is less common than it was, partly because of the temporary nature of the coverage and the potential for abuse.

- *Short-term medical.* This type of policy provides medical coverage for a short period of time (e.g., 90 days) and is intended for use by college students or workers between jobs. The policy may provide for one or two renewals.

Guaranteed renewable policies are perhaps the most common contract form for medical insurance coverages. Noncan is still preferred for the most select disability income risks. The shorter and less liberal contract renewability provisions are not as popular with the public or regulators.

Cancellation and nonrenewal have different meanings. Both refer to actions that may be taken by the insurer. Cancellation means that the contract may be canceled by the insurer at any premium due date or on the policy anniversary. Nonrenewal usually means that the company must meet its obligations through the next policy anniversary. A contract that is canceled as of its issue date is called rescinded.

Under federal law and the laws of some states, a trust can be formed to provide employee benefits. Examples include VEBAs (Voluntary Employer Benefit Associations) and the so-called Missouri Trusts, named for the state in which this form of contract became popular. Certificates are offered to individuals in accordance with a group master contract, but the sale, administration, and claim settlement processes are very similar to those of individual policies. In some cases it is difficult for the purchaser of the policy to identify that the policy is really a group insurance certificate. The advantage of this form of contract to the insurer is reduced regulation of rates by the state insurance departments. For GAAP reserving purposes, however, these contracts are so similar to individual contracts that they should be reserved accordingly. Similarly, franchise and association group business, although nominally sold under a master contract, may be so similar by the terms of the individual certificates to individual policies that individual policy reserve methods should be used.

10.1.3 Benefits

Benefits paid under A&H insurance policies are mainly of two types: indemnity and expense. Indemnity benefits pay a contractually agreed amount upon occurrence of a specified event, for example, $300 per day of hospital confinement. Expense benefits attempt to match actual economic losses associated with an event such as actual costs of a surgery. Expense benefits are less predictable as to amount than indemnity benefits.

Medical expense benefits increase over time due to cost inflation. Medical inflation has exceeded the general rate of inflation for decades and seems to fluctuate more widely and rapidly. Medical inflation rates during the 1990s have varied between 5 and 20%, with lower and higher values sometimes seen, depending on the type of benefit. The effect of benefit inflation over time frames as short as 1 year can be dramatic. Any discussion of medical benefits must include consideration of the effects of inflation.

Limits on benefits are used to reduce the insurer's exposure and to make certain coverages more affordable. Limits include deductibles, co-payments, and maximum limits. A deductible tries to eliminate frequent, less costly events that are not true insurable events. The intent is to exclude minor budgetable expenses and reduce the insurer's administrative costs. A co-payment is a relatively small sharing in the cost of each claim by the insured, for example, $5 per prescription drug payment. A benefit maximum controls the amount of benefit, thus limiting the insurer's exposure to inflation or excessive utilization. It may apply per claim, annually, or over the lifetime of the contract.

Deductibles and co-payments have the side effect of exaggerating inflation on insured costs. This deductible leverage effect is a major reason that insured medical cost inflation typically exceeds general medical cost inflation. Even in an overall benign inflation environment such as the late 1990s, medical cost trends can rise sharply and severely affect profitability.

Table 10-1
Effect of 6% Inflation on Medical Claim Costs

	Medical Claim Costs		
	Year 1	**Year 2**	**Year 3**
Raw Cost	1,000.00	1,060.00	1,123.60
Deductible	250.00	250.00	250.00
Insured Costs	750.00	810.00	873.60
Inflation in Insured Costs		8.0%	7.9%

A&H benefit costs to an insurer are also subject to utilization trends. Total claim costs on medical benefits are the product of utilization rate and unit costs. Utilization trends are an important, separate trend factor. They tend to vary in cycles as new services and techniques replace older ones.

Disability income (DI) benefits are analogous to indemnity benefits and are typically expressed as a stated amount of monthly benefit. Thus they are not susceptible to cost inflation. However, the incidence of disablement may rise, and the duration of payment may continue longer than expected while the insured remains disabled. The degree of disablement may be difficult to judge objectively; hence the insurer may have to pay benefits on marginal claims. Elimination and benefit periods (for example, 90 days and to age 65, respectively) limit the insurer's exposure.

DI policies are uniquely subject to moral hazard. The policyholder's degree of inability to perform the duties of his or her occupation due to pain, lack of mobility, or depression can be difficult or impossible to measure objectively, even by experts. Thus malingering or outright fraud occurs more frequently with DI than with other coverages for which the continuance of a claim and its associated costs (e.g., hospitalization) can be measured with much greater accuracy.

10.1.4 Premiums

Morbidity risks typically increase with age. To the extent level premiums are used to fund increasing benefits in advance, a benefit reserve is required.

Premiums can be structured to increase with attained age, similar to annual renewable term rates, or can be level over the contract term. Both structures are in common use. Premiums typically run for the same term as benefits are payable; limited payment premiums are rare for forms other than long term care.

The premium structure is an integral part of the reserving process. When level premiums are used to fund an increasing risk, a significant level of benefit reserves is generated. When premiums increase annually in approximate proportion to increasing morbidity, benefit reserves tend to be smaller.

Level premiums are appropriate for indemnity benefits that are not subject to cost inflation. The level premium pre-funds claim costs that increase with age, similar to the case of a level term life insurance policy. Annually increasing or step-rated premiums are more appropriate for medical expense benefits. Such benefits increase over time both due to age and inflation. The compounded rate of increase may be relatively high especially when accumulated over several years. The level premium needed to pre-fund such benefits may be unacceptably high.

10.1.5 Premium Rate Increases

Adjustment of premium rates for changing experience over time is a complex subject. Benefits may increase over time with the aging of the insured, with inflation of benefit unit costs, and with increasing benefit utilization. Medicare supplement benefits can increase due to government requirements (which in turn relate to cost inflation). Increasing claim costs are not the only risk. Maintenance and administrative expenses can increase above expectations, for example, due to inflation. Interest rates can decline below the levels expected in pricing.

Persistency is also a risk. Antiselective lapsation occurs because the healthiest insured persons are more likely to lapse their coverage voluntarily than the least healthy. Thus the overall morbidity level of a block of policies deteriorates with time. Morbidity increases due to aging should rarely trigger rate increases per se, because such increases are (or should be) able to be anticipated. However, antiselective lapsation can also leave an insurer with a book of business that ages more rapidly than expected, as younger insured persons lapse their coverage more frequently than older ones.

If experience deteriorates, the insurer's anticipated profit margin is reduced. At some point it becomes necessary to increase rates. The actuary needs to be aware of regulatory requirements for rate filings that vary by state. Many states require prior approval of rate increases. Other states require filing for information purposes only. When regulatory approval is required, the state regulators may disapprove all or part of the company's requested rate increase because of public policy issues, differing judgments on future experience assumptions, or other reasons.

Under the A&H model law approach as promulgated by the National Association of Insurance Commissioners (NAIC), policies must be priced as a group such that a minimum anticipated loss ratio requirement is met. After experience deteriorates, future expectations must exceed a minimum anticipated loss ratio and experience overall from issue must likewise exceed a minimum. In accordance with these requirements, to the extent that the experience has deteriorated to the point at which a block of business is experiencing losses, those past losses usually cannot be recouped through the rate increase process. At best, future rate increases will return the contract to its initially targeted level of profitability or, in some cases, break even.

The minimum anticipated loss ratios required vary by type of coverage, renewability, and size of policy as measured by annualized premiums.

Regulators may be suspicious of rate increases occurring within a very few years of a block of policies being sold. If they think initial premium rates were deliberately underpriced, they may be reluctant to permit rate increases. In many cases regulators would also be reluctant to permit rate increases to correct pricing errors on the grounds that such risks are appropriately borne by the insurer.

Regulators may also be reluctant to approve rate increases on very small blocks of policies. There is a preference for pooling of experience over a wider range of generally similar policies for two reasons. First, experience on smaller blocks of policies is more volatile than that on larger blocks. Second, there have been perceived abuses of the practice of introducing new policy series at periodic intervals. As new policy series are issued, the older policy series experience rising loss ratios mainly due to aging rather than deteriorating experience. Rate increase requests based on rising loss ratios in closed blocks may be disapproved by regulators.

This chapter does not deal with the algebra of determining the appropriate rate increase. However, in concept, if premiums are purportedly level, they pre-fund future increasing benefits. If morbidity develops adversely, a new equation must be solved in which higher future morbidity is funded by higher future premiums. Past losses may not be recouped. The state regulators will want to understand the approach taken to ensure that past losses are not being recouped and that future profit margins will be no greater than when the policy was originally priced. They want to be sure that any accumulated value is not ignored in determining future premiums. The statutory active life reserve is regarded as value accumulated by the policyholder available to fund future benefits. Consequently health insurers often find it difficult to increase rates to the extent desired.

Even when rates are increased, they may be ineffective due to antiselective lapsation. In a block of policies the least healthy individuals will still find it economic to pay a higher premium. A single health insurance claim may exceed the annual premium by a large multiple. A modest rate increase (e.g., 15–20%) will have little effect on an unhealthy life, who still stands to benefit from retaining the coverage. On the other hand, the healthiest individuals may be able to buy new insurance policies elsewhere or may not feel the need for the coverage at all. As a consequence, they may refuse to pay a higher premium and permit their policies to lapse. This antiselective lapsation becomes more pronounced with higher rate increases. Thus the effectiveness of a rate increase is reduced, and in fact loss ratios may not decline very much after a rate increase. This phenomenon can still be observed even after several rate increases as more individual policyholders experience deteriorating health with increasing age. In extreme cases a spiral of increasing loss ratios can be observed. A block of business with a high loss ratio may take a very long time to return to profitability, if ever.

The difficulty of increasing rates and the limited effectiveness of increasing rates translates into high pricing risk on individual A&H policies. On this type of business the actuary should take a conservative view of the probability of increasing profit margins in the future. This view is relevant to the discussion of recoverability and loss recognition in Section 10.8.

10.2 Types of Health Insurance Policies

Health insurance policies are issued in a wide variety of forms.

Medical coverages are issued in two markets, under age 65 and age 65 and over. Age 65 and over is often referred to as the senior market. Under age 65 policies include major medical expenses, hospital indemnity, and supplementary coverages. Major medical policies reimburse for hospital, medical, surgical, pharmaceutical, laboratory and X-ray, and perhaps other medical services. Deductibles apply, typically annually per family member with an overall out-of-pocket limit. Co-payments (e.g., 80% reimbursement) and maximums limit the benefit paid. Individual major medical policies are purchased in many cases by people who do not have access to group coverages. Group coverages tend to be cheaper than individual policies due to lower sales and administrative costs; on the other hand, individual coverages are underwritten. Also, group coverages are usually not age rated while individual policies are.

Indemnity policies pay a stated amount, for example, $200 per day of hospital confinement, or an amount in accordance with a surgical schedule. Other services are not reimbursed by the policy unless listed, for example, ambulance, emergency room, X-rays, laboratory charges, and drugs. Exclusions due to certain causes are common, either contractually or as a result of the issue and underwriting process. Indemnity benefits are typically used to supplement more comprehensive coverages.

There are other specialized and more limited contracts, including specified disease coverage (e.g., cancer), student accident, and accidental death & dismemberment policies. These limited contracts serve specialized purposes, including mass markets, high schools and colleges, and worksite distribution methods.

Medical savings account policies were created by the Health Insurance Protection and Availability Act (HIPAA) in 1997. A tax-deferred savings account can be used to pay for medical costs, provided a high deductible medical policy also exists to cover major expenses. The law permitted only a limited number of such contracts to be issued out of concern that their popularity would lead to a loss of tax revenue. As of 2000, the concept has not proved very popular.

DI policies provide a fixed monthly benefit while the insured is disabled. Most contracts pay for disability due to either accident or sickness; some supplementary coverages are limited to accidental injury causes. The benefit commences after an elimination period (e.g., 90 days) and continues for a maximum term (e.g., to age 65). Disability is defined in the contract, but a typical provision is

> Total Disability and Totally Disabled mean that because of Sickness or Accidental Bodily Injury (i) the Insured is unable to perform the important duties of the Insured's Occupation and is not engaged in any other gainful occupation, and (ii) the Insured is under regular care and treatment by a Physician. The company will waive the requirement of regular care and treatment by a Physician in determining any benefits under the policy, if future or continued care appropriate to treating the condition causing disability is no longer necessary.

DI contracts are rated separately by individual issue age, sex, benefit and elimination period, and importantly, occupation class. The typical market is employed workers, perhaps ages 30 to 50. The market is classified by occupation categories. The lowest risk (most select) occupations are commonly denoted AAAA, while the highest risk occupations are classified as A, B, or C. Policies sold to the most select occupations are typically noncancelable, while those sold to the higher risk occupations are typically guaranteed renewable and thus subject to rate increases if experience deteriorates over time.

DI morbidity varies over a wide range. Claim costs increase markedly with age. Claim costs also vary with sex, with male claim costs tending to increase more steeply with age.

Claim costs are defined as the expected present value of future benefits at each attained age. In Figure 10-1 claim costs are shown for males and females at attained ages 20 through 64 at the best risk class, occupation class AAAA, from the 1985 CIDA table. The benefit is subject to a 90-day elimination period payable to age 65 but not less than 2 years.

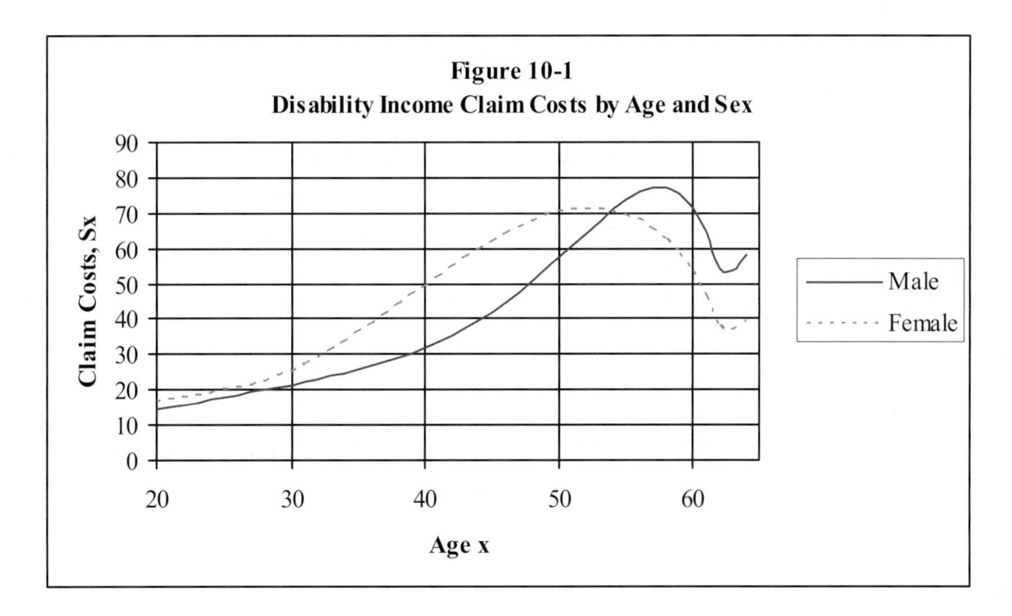

Figure 10-1
Disability Income Claim Costs by Age and Sex

Disability incidence rates vary widely as the elimination period increases from 0 to 30 days. Disability termination (i.e., end of disablement due to death or recovery) rates vary widely with the definition of disability. For example, if disability is defined as the inability to perform the duties of one's own occupation, then a professional in a highly specialized practice might continue to be regarded as disabled although his or her disability is relatively slight. A skilled surgeon might be considered permanently disabled under this type of contractual provision due to the onset of arthritis, although he or she may be able to teach, consult, work in business, or perform many other jobs with ease.

DI morbidity also varies widely by occupation class. The white collar professions (attorneys, accountants, senior executives) tend to be at low risk of accidental injury. The effect of permanent conditions (e.g., ruptured disks or knee injuries) may have no effect whatsoever on job performance or income. The blue collar professions are at much higher risk. Tradespersons who work with their hands, with power tools, or in demanding physical environments are more subject to injury and perhaps chronic illnesses.

Income replacement policies provide a special type of disability benefit that attempts to reimburse actual economic losses associated with the condition of disability. The income replacement policy pays benefits in proportion to income actually lost while disabled due to sickness or injury. It combines into one benefit provision the features of the basic disability benefit plus the partial and residual benefits. While attractive in concept, the measurement of loss of earnings can be complicated, especially in the case of self-employed professionals such as physicians.

Business overhead policies are a special type of DI contract used to cover costs incurred or revenues lost by a business while a key owner or manager is disabled.

Long-term-care (LTC) policies provide a fixed daily benefit while the insured is confined in a nursing home (but not a hospital) or receiving home health care services or both. Benefits are subject to a waiting period, typically 90 or 100 days, and a limit, typically 2 or 3 years. The type of facility (skilled, intermediate, or custodial) and the level of home care (nurses, aides, or therapists) are options available to the insured at the time the policy is applied for. Other options include an inflation adjustment and guaranteed purchase options. Premiums are issue age based, and most policies are guaranteed renewable for life. Typical issue ages are 55 to 75. HIPAA prescribes conditions for certain policies to be considered qualified LTC contracts; premiums on qualified contracts are tax deductible (subject to rules applicable to medical expenses), while benefits are not taxable income.

Medicare supplement policies serve the special needs of seniors (beginning at age 65 and certain disabled persons at younger ages). These policies supplement the gaps in coverage provided by Medicare and provide benefits to cover the Part A (hospital) deductible, hospital co-payments, Part B (medical) deductible, and prescription drugs. In an attempt to simplify a complex set of benefits, the NAIC has promulgated standardized combinations of benefits.

Each year the Health Care Financing Administration calculates an increased Part A deductible in proportion to hospital cost inflation. Other Medicare benefits (e.g., hospital reimbursement for the first 60 days, 50% for the 61st through 90th day, and reducing thereafter) are proportional to the Part A deductible. The increased exclusion implies the need for a higher supplemental benefit from private insurance. Many Medicare supplement policies provide for automatic increases in benefit on January 1 of each year, synchronous with the changes in Medicare. Premium increases associated with benefit increases are usually necessary but generally are subject to regulatory approval. The annual benefit increases and corresponding premium increases must be considered in reserving, as discussed in Section 10.7.

All Medicare supplement policies are guaranteed renewable for life.

10.3 Product Classification

While most accounting guidance is generic to all types of entities, *SFAS 60*, "Accounting and Reporting by Insurance Enterprises," is specific to insurance companies; it states:

> This Statement establishes accounting and reporting standards for the general-purpose financial statements of stock life insurance enterprises, property and liability insurance enterprises, title insurance enterprises, mutual life insurance enterprises, assessment enterprises, and fraternal benefit societies. (Paragraph 6)

The exclusion of mutual life insurance enterprises and fraternal benefit societies in earlier versions of *SFAS 60* has been superseded by *SFAS 120*, "Accounting and Reporting by Mutual Life Insurance Enterprises and by Insurance Enterprises for Certain Long Duration Participating Contracts," effective for most companies beginning in 1996. Mutual and fraternal insurers are required to comply with *SFAS 60* and all other GAAP pronouncements for audited financial statements.

There are still a few participating A&H insurance contracts in force, although very few are currently issued. Among in-force participating policies, most no longer pay dividends. Participating A&H policies issued in either stock or mutual life insurance companies would be governed by *SFAS 60*.

SFAS 120 applies to participating life insurance contracts whether issued by mutual or stock companies, although under paragraph 6 stock companies may optionally apply *SFAS 60*. Under the provisions of *SFAS 120*, costs and profits are matched in level proportion to gross margins (including mortality, interest, and expense margins) built into the contract. It is possible to construct a similar reserving method for A&H business.

All health insurance policies issued by life insurers are covered by *SFAS 60*, either as long-duration or short-duration contracts. This standard states:

> Insurance contracts, for purposes of this Statement, shall be classified as short-duration or long-duration contracts depending on whether the contracts are expected to remain in force for an extended period. The factors that shall be considered in determining whether a particular contract can be expected to remain in force for an extended period are:
>
> (a) Short-duration contract. The contract provides insurance protection for a fixed period of short duration and enables the insurer to cancel the contract or to adjust the provisions at the end of any contract period, such as adjusting the amount of premiums charged or coverage provided.
>
> (b) Long-duration contract. The contract generally is not subject to unilateral changes in its provisions, such as a non-cancelable or guaranteed renewable contract, and requires the performance of various functions and services (including insurance protection) for an extended period. (Paragraph 7)

In this chapter, the words *policy* and *policies* are used interchangeably with *contract* and *contracts* respectively.

SFAS 97 makes clear that it does not apply to health insurance:

> This Statement does not apply to the following types of long-duration insurance contracts:
>
> (a) Contracts with terms that are fixed and guaranteed and for which premiums are collected over the same period that benefits are provided.
>
> (b) Contracts that provide benefits related only to illness, physical injury, or disability. (Paragraph 14)

There is a possible exception. The AICPA *Practice Bulletin 8* clarifies the intent of paragraph 14.b in Question 9 and the response to Question 9. Accounting for long-duration insurance contracts that provide benefits related only to illness, physical injury, or disability, but that also have characteristics and benefits falling under *SFAS 97*, such as significant cash surrender benefits and limited-payment or universal life-type provisions, should be guided by the concepts of *SFAS 97*. Thus universal health policies or limited-pay health contracts should be treated similarly to life insurance contracts with similar provisions.

For classification purposes, short duration usually means one year or less. However, some policies such as credit life or disability, which may extend over 3 to 4 years (for example, in connection with a car loan), are also considered short duration. Extended period means more than 1 year. A contract that is likely to renew for several years is clearly a long-duration contract.

If there are restrictions on the insurer's ability to change rates or cancel coverage, then the insured person owns certain guarantees or representations. This extends the coverage beyond the short-duration concept and confirms the likelihood of renewal for several years. Therefore the company can expect the contract to remain in force for an extended period. *SFAS 60* gives a specific example:

> Accident and health insurance contracts may be short-duration or long-duration depending on whether the contracts are expected to remain in force for an extended period. For example, individual and group insurance contracts that are noncancelable or guaranteed renewable (renewable at the option of the insured), or collectively renewable (individual contracts within a group are not cancelable), ordinarily are long-duration contracts. (Paragraph 8)

Contract renewability provisions have an important bearing on GAAP benefit reserves. All guaranteed renewable and noncancelable policies should be considered long-duration contracts that need reserves for future benefits. These benefit reserves are sometimes called active life reserves or contract reserves. Collectively and conditionally renewable contracts usually should be considered long duration, unless they clearly expire without a renewability option within 3 or 4 years after issue.

Optionally renewable (OR) contracts are normally treated as short-duration contracts because the insurer can unilaterally cancel or nonrenew them. The contracts typically are in effect for only a few years, and the premiums are not intended to cover costs that increase with inflation or attained age. In other words pre-funding of future years' benefits is not a feature of these contracts. These policies do not necessarily require benefit reserves even if they are usually renewed.

10.4 Reserve Methods

This section describes reserve methods that provide for future incurred policyholder benefits and nonlevel expenses and includes a discussion of unearned premium reserves. Unpaid claim reserves or liabilities are not addressed in this section.

Health policy reserves follow the same theoretical basis as life insurance reserves. Premiums are recognized as revenue when due, in accordance with *SFAS 60*. However, part of the current year's premiums may be required to fund benefits payable in future periods. The reserve mechanism holds back a portion of premiums that otherwise would be reported as profits. If the policy is guaranteed renewable, as mentioned above, the reserve provides for claims that may be incurred many years into the future. Benefit reserves can grow large relative to premiums if the premium is level while morbidity costs increase over the lifetime of the policy. An unearned premium reserve provides for accruing of premiums for a future accounting period. Unlike life insurance, health insurance policies typically do not have nonforfeiture benefits (for example, cash surrender values).

This section discusses issues of reserving of policies as established at initial issue date of the policy. As mentioned later, this initial reserving mechanism stays the same for an extended time unless and until experience changes significantly. Evidence that experience has changed significantly would be premium rate increases, where permitted, or indication that future profits have disappeared. Issues of reserving after morbidity or other experience may have deteriorated are discussed later.

10.4.1 Benefit Reserves

Actuarial principles call for reserves based on either of two approaches: (a) an accumulation of past net premiums in excess of tabular morbidity cost (the retrospective approach) or (b) the excess of the present value of future benefits over the present value of future net premiums (the prospective approach). The two approaches are algebraically identical. If retrospective and prospective assumptions are identical, these two approaches produce the same numeric result.

For either approach, an actuarial projection is necessary. The actuary projects future benefits from the initial date of issue of the contract. The projection period should cover the maximum term of the contract, for example, to age 65, or lifetime, as appropriate. A GAAP valuation net premium is calculated that begins on the inception date of the contract and continues in a uniform proportion to the gross premium to the end of the premium payment term. The premium payment term typically coincides with the contract term.

For the retrospective approach, the benefit reserve is the accumulation of past net premiums minus past tabular claim costs, accrued at the valuation rate of interest. For the prospective approach, the benefit reserve at any policy date is the present value of future benefits less the present value of future net premiums.

It is customary to use assumptions that are realistic or somewhat conservative. These choices of actuarial assumptions are discussed in more detail later. However, the net level premium method spreads or allocates nonlevel costs, whether benefit costs or expenses, in level proportion to expected premiums. Expected premiums are based on future gross premiums reflecting assumed mortality and persistency. If actual experience emerges identical to the assumptions, profits also emerge in level proportion to gross premiums. To the extent that conservative valuation assumptions are used, reserves are higher in earlier years; as actual experience emerges better than valuation assumptions, profits are released. Thus profits emerge partly in level proportion to gross premiums and partly in proportion to release from risk.

In reserving at issue of the contract, the actuary should consider the premium payment term and the level of scheduled gross premiums. Usually the premium payment term and the term of the contract are the same. As mentioned above, most long-duration A&H policies involve increasing morbidity costs that are pre-funded. To keep premium costs low, it is usually desirable to use a longer rather than a shorter premium payment term. Hence gross premiums payable for the same period for which benefits are provided are common. In instances in which morbidity costs decline with advancing attained age (e.g., maternity and certain accident benefits), limited-payment premiums are sometimes found.

Gross premiums are not necessarily level. Step-rated premiums are used for certain policies to improve affordability at younger attained ages. As an example, certain major medical benefit policies are issued with 5-year step rates, in which premiums increase at the fifth policy anniversary, the tenth, fifteenth, and so on. In other cases, annual increasing premiums are used. The expected increasing gross premium scale should be reflected in the reserve formula.

It is assumed here that premium rate increases caused by deteriorating experience are not anticipated at issue. To the extent that benefit cost inflation is anticipated, it should be reflected in the structure and pricing of the policy. Similarly, benefit cost inflation should be reflected in the expected morbidity assumptions (discussed in more detail below).

As will be shown by formula, benefit reserves are calculated as a factor per policy, which then is aggregated to a total portfolio number for an entire book of business. The factors are calculated based on typical assumptions and applied to an inventory of the in-force business by computer. Factor approaches are commonly used for *SFAS* 60 reserves; factor approaches could similarly be used for DAC balances. Advantages of factor methods include a high degree of automation and automatic correction for persistency that is better or worse than originally expected.

Factors can be calculated in advance and stored for later application in computer systems. Alternatively, reserves can be calculated "on the fly" from first principles. This term is used to mean calculation of the reserve from basic formulas and assumptions. The term reserve mechanism means the use of factors, worksheets, or calculation from first principles.

As an alternative, instead of factors, a worksheet approach can be used. A worksheet develops DAC or reserves for a book of business in the aggregate. DAC factors can be converted into an unamortized percentage relative to first-year initial capitalized expenses. Then the worksheet is used at each successive financial reporting period to determine the new unamortized balance based on the percentage times the initial capitalized amount. Successive issue years require additional worksheets. Advantages of factor methods include explicit identification of deferred expenses and a more open process of calculation. Disadvantages may include the more approximate modeling that is usually inherent in these methods and the need to manually adjust for persistency different from initial expectations.

Worksheet approaches are rarely used for benefit reserves.

Benefit reserves, DAC, and other reserves (such as unearned premium, deferred profit liability and premium deficiency reserves) need to be adjusted to the exact value as of the financial reporting date rather than their value as of policy anniversaries. Formulas for interpolating reserves between anniversaries are provided in Section 10.5.

Some contracts are constructed such that gross premiums are approximately proportional to claim costs over the contract term. If gross premiums are closely proportional to claim costs, there is little if any pre-funding of benefits; hence zero benefit reserves are appropriate. This approximation is sometimes seen as an expedient practice. However, the actuary should consider the appropriateness of the approximation in each case. For example, although premiums and ultimate claim costs may be proportional, underwriting selection can result in much lower morbidity and perhaps mortality experience during the first several policy years. Benefit reserves associated solely with select morbidity may be surprisingly high—perhaps of the order of 50–150% of the benefit net premium. (Table 10-6 gives an example of the effect of selection factors on reserves.)

10.4.2 Maintenance Expense Reserves

Benefit reserves should provide for the cost of future unaccrued expenses associated with policyholder benefits; this includes policy maintenance expenses. Benefit reserves may include an adjustment for associated maintenance expenses, or a separate maintenance expense reserve may be calculated. Classification of expenses among acquisition, maintenance, and overhead expenses may be performed through a cost study as described earlier in Chapter 3. Oftentimes maintenance costs are allocated as a level percentage of premium. Such level expenses do not generate a reserve under *SFAS 60* because the costs are already matched to premiums without a reserve mechanism. However, the allocation of costs as a level percentage of premium is not always appropriate. In the case of A&H business significant costs are associated with processing and adjudicating claims. Thus a portion of maintenance expenses may best be allocated in proportion to claims. This would seem particularly important with DI business because disability incidence rates rise rapidly with age and claims occurring at older ages may be more complicated. If maintenance expenses are allocated as a level proportion of benefits, the increasing pattern of claim settlement expenses with age will result in a significant maintenance expense reserve.

10.4.3 Acquisition Expense Reserves

Acquisition expenses are incurred mainly at or near the inception of the contract. Typically these are commissions and up-front administrative costs of the underwriting and new business departments. Commissions are typically higher in the first year, or the first several years, than ultimately. The excess over ultimate commissions is normally the amount deferred. Underwriting for DI business can be costly because it involves both medical and financial considerations. Such acquisition costs are deferred and amortized in level proportion to gross premiums over the expected lifetime of the contract. Deferrable expenses are treated more fully in Chapter 3. Nonlevel (declining) expenses produce a negative reserve (an asset).

The capitalization and deferral of nonlevel acquisition expenses achieve a spreading of the costs in proportion to gross premiums over the term of coverage. Certain nonlevel expenses are not spread, as discussed more fully elsewhere; acquisition expenses that do not meet the *SFAS 60* criteria for deferral (namely attribution and variability) affect profits in the year in which they are incurred.

In the case of expense reserves, any expenses that are a level proportion of premium are automatically matched to the gross premium. Typically they require no reserve. If such level expenses are included in reserve formulas, the formulas produce zero reserves. Thus there is no need to exclude level expenses in the reserve calculation. In fact, it is better to include such expenses so that the correct net premium is calculated. The gross premium has to fund all commissions, all expenses, and all benefits in all years, plus provide for a profit margin as well. Thus all expenses including level expenses should be included in the calculation of the net premium and reserves.

10.4.4 Unearned Premium Reserves

The unearned premium reserve (UPR) is a liability held to set aside the portion of premiums received and reported as income that must be allocated to future periods. The UPR splits premium revenue into past and future components. Hence the name unearned: although a premium has been received, for example, a quarterly premium, as of the financial reporting date the insurance company has not yet performed its duties under the contract associated with that premium. All premiums due in the future are considered in the benefit reserves.

Just as the gross premium is divisible into portions needed to cover policy benefits, maintenance expenses, acquisition expenses, and profits, the unearned premium is similarly allocated. Each reserve element (benefit, maintenance, and DAC) should include its net portion of the unearned premium. Another approach is to use the gross unearned premium. The use of gross unearned premium is more common for group policies and individual policies for which no benefit reserve is held. The gross unearned premium is a slightly larger liability than the sum of the net unearned premiums, to the extent the gross premium includes a profit margin.

10.4.5 Deferred Profit Liability

As mentioned above, few A&H contracts involve limited-payment premium terms. Of course, a few riders do. Under *SFAS 97*, profits from limited-payment contracts cannot be spread solely in relation to premiums. Profits from the insurance contract are not earned proportionately to the earning of premiums because profit recognition would be complete, or mostly complete, before all contract services (i.e., policyholder benefits) have been provided. *SFAS* 97 states:

> Limited-payment contracts subject the insurer to risks arising from policyholder mortality and morbidity over a period that extends beyond the period or periods in which premiums are collected. For those contracts, the liability for policy benefits shall be established in accordance with the provisions of Statement 60. The collection of premium does not, however, represent the completion of an earnings process. Any gross premium received in excess of the net premium shall be deferred and recognized in income in a constant relationship with insurance in force (when accounting for life insurance contracts) or with the amount of expected future benefit payments (when accounting for annuity contracts). The Board concluded that limited-payment contracts with terms that are fixed and guaranteed are similar to other contracts addressed by Statement 60 in all respects except for the pattern of premium payment. The Board also concluded that income from insurance contracts is earned through the performance of contract services. The collection of a single premium or a limited number of premiums does not, in itself, represent the completion of an earnings process. The Board concluded that any amount of gross premium in excess of net premium, as those terms are defined in Statement 60, should be deferred and recognized over the period that services are provided. (Paragraph 16)

Profits calculated as the excess of the present value of gross premiums over future benefits and expenses (i.e., future net premiums) are deferred. The deferred profit liability changes over time such that it releases in uniform proportion to benefits provided. *Practice Bulletin 8* addresses limited-payment contracts:

> Question 3: Should the deferred profit liability (excess of gross premiums over net premiums), if any, on limited-payment contracts be amortized in relation to the discounted amount of insurance in force (or expected future benefit), and should interest accrue to the unamortized deferred profit liability balance?
>
> Answer 3: Yes. The deferred profit liability should be amortized in relation to the discounted amount of the insurance in force or expected future benefit payments, and interest should accrue to the unamortized balance. The use of interest in the amortization is consistent with the determination of the deferred profit using discounting.

Other aspects of *SFAS 60* rules remain the same, including the need for benefit reserves and DAC calculated in the same way as for non-limited-payment contracts.

Note that for guaranteed renewable A&H contracts, although the premiums are not guaranteed, the provisions of *SFAS 97* would apply. This is consistent with Question 6 of *Practice Bulletin 8*:

> Question 6: Does paragraph 16 of FASB Statement No. 97, which addresses limited-payment contracts, apply to limited-payment participating and limited-payment nonguaranteed-premium contracts that are not, in substance, universal life-type contracts?

Answer 6: Yes. These contracts are limited-payment contracts under paragraph 9 of FASB Statement No. 97 and are not excluded under paragraph 11 because they are not conventional forms of participating or nonguaranteed-premium contracts.

The formula mechanism is such that the excess of the gross premium over the net premium each year is incremented to a reserve. The reserve is decremented as a level proportion of expected morbidity benefits, using the same assumptions as appropriate for benefit reserves.

10.4.6 Premium Deficiency Reserves

Premium deficiency reserves may be required for benefits for which the present value of future benefits and expenses exceeds future gross premiums. In other words, a provision must be made when future losses are anticipated. This requirement applies to partial-year periods, not just multiyear periods. This requirement also applies to short term and group coverages, although it is more significant when gross premiums are guaranteed for longer periods.

A premium deficiency reserve would be established when the gross premium reserve exceeds the sum of the benefit reserve, the unearned premium reserve, the claim reserve and the deferred profit liability, less DAC.

10.4.7 Claim Reserves

Claim reserves or claim liabilities are the provision for the unpaid portion of claims already incurred as of the valuation date, regardless of whether they have been actually reported. Section 10.9 is devoted to claim reserves.

10.5 Benefit, Maintenance and DAC Reserve Formulas

10.5.1 Definitions

GP	=	gross premium
x	=	issue age
t	=	policy duration
$S_{[x]+t}$	=	policy claim costs per unit of in-force coverage
ME_t	=	maintenance expenses
DE_t	=	deferrable acquisition expenses
BNP_x	=	benefit net premium
$MENP_x$	=	maintenance expense net premium
$DENP_x$	=	deferrable acquisition expense net premium

Profit margin = $GP_x - BNP_x - MENP_x - DENP_x$

The profit margin is available to cover overhead expenses and provide for profits. Other terms are defined as follows:

i	=	valuation interest rate
v^t	=	$1 / (1 + i)^t$
q^d	=	mortality rate
q^w	=	withdrawal rate
${}_1p_x$	=	probability of surviving inforce one year = $(1 - q_x^{\,d})\,(1 - q_x^{\,w})$
${}_tp_x$	=	probability of surviving inforce to year $t = \prod_{s=1}^{t} (1 - q_{x+s-1}^{\,d})\,(1 - q^{w}_{x+s-1})$

${}_tBV$	=	benefit reserve, policy year t
${}_tMEV$	=	maintenance expense reserve, policy year t
${}_tDAC$	=	unamortized deferred acquisition cost asset, policy year t.

10.5.2 Formulas

The benefit net premium is defined as the net premium, proportional to gross premiums in all years, whose present value equals the present value of the benefits.

$$BNP = \sum v^t \times {}_tp_x \times B_t \Big/ \sum v^t \times {}_tp_x$$

The general Fackler formula for benefit reserves describes terminal reserves in terms of beginning reserves, gross premiums, benefits, and maintenance expenses:

$$\left({}_{t-1}BV + BNP\right)(1+i) = {}_tBV\left(1-q^d\right)\left(1-q^w\right) + S_{[x]+t}$$

Given that ${}_0BV = 0$, this can be rearranged into the typical prospective reserve formula:

$${}_tBV = \sum_{t=0} v^t \times {}_tp_x \times S_{[x]+t} - \sum_{t=0} v^t \times {}_tp_x \times BNP$$

The above formula describes reserves at the end of each policy year, based on policies expected to be in force at that time, i.e., terminal reserves.

The prospective formula is equivalent to the retrospective formula:

$${}_tBV = \sum_{t=0} BNP \times (1+i)^t \Big/ {}_tp_x - \sum_{t=0} S_{[x]+t} \times (1+i)^t \Big/ {}_tp_x$$

Similar formulas apply to maintenance expense reserves.

These formulas apply to per unit of benefit in force. Reserve factors are most commonly calculated per unit of benefit (e.g., \$100 of monthly DI benefit or \$100 per day of hospital confinement indemnity) per policy in force at the end of the policy year. It is commonly assumed that reserve factors are linear; thus morbidity risks are assumed to be proportionally greater for \$200 of benefit as for \$100. Note that this is an approximate assumption. In the case of life insurance, risks for large face amounts are not proportional to those for smaller face amounts. The actuary should consider the appropriateness of applying large multiples to standard morbidity tables.

If identical algebraic derivations are used for acquisition expenses, the formulas produce negative reserves. Deferrable acquisition expenses are high in earlier policy years and decline to zero within a few years. This negative reserve is presented as an asset in the balance sheet. This can be understood as a prepaid expense that will be recouped with a portion of the gross premium, assuming of course that the gross premium is adequate to pay for all benefits and expenses. If experience deteriorates unduly, the availability of the gross premium to recover all acquisition expenses comes into doubt. In that event a portion of the DAC asset may need to be written off.

Financial reporting of course does not occur on policy anniversaries. At the date of financial reporting, in-force policies will fall between policy anniversaries and between premium payment dates. To report reserves accurately, adjustments need to be made for the exact duration of the policy and the exact timing of payment of benefits and expenses. For reporting purposes, terminal reserves are usually interpolated in some fashion. Reserves are generally calculated on a mid-terminal or mean basis. Several examples follow.

For policies issued on July 1, i.e., at the mid point of the calendar year, the midterminal reserve used at December 31 is:

$$_{t-1/2}BV = \tfrac{1}{2}\left(_{t-1}BV + {}_{t}BV\right)$$

This midterminal reserve is midway between the prior and next terminal reserves. In addition, the modal premium received is only partly earned. For policies issued on July 1 with annual premiums, the unearned benefit net premium as of December 31 is:

$$\tfrac{1}{2}BNP_x$$

For policies with non-annual premium mode the unearned portion is less than an annual net premium. A common approximation is that issue dates are spread uniformly throughout the year. In that event the unearned premium is one-half of the modal premium.

For policies issued on July 1, i.e., at the midpoint of the calendar year, the mean reserve used at December 31 is:

$$_{t-1/2}BV = \tfrac{1}{2}\left(_{t-1}BV + BNP_x + {}_{t}BV\right)$$

This mean reserve is midway between the prior and next terminal reserves. In addition, future modal premiums have not been received. Thus, a deferred net premium must be established to counter the overstatement in the reserve. For policies issued on August 15 with monthly premiums, the deferred net benefit premium as of December 31 is:

$$\tfrac{7}{12} \times BNP_x$$

Corresponding formulas are used for maintenance expense reserves and maintenance expense net premiums.

The formulas above can be used for all policies, regardless of issue date, provided that policies are issued uniformly throughout the year and lapses occur uniformly throughout the year. Those assumptions are not always valid. For example, supplementary accident policies sold to college students tend to be issued more heavily during sales campaigns at the beginning of the academic year. For policies issued on October 1, the formula for an exact interpolated midterminal reserve as of December 31 is:

$$_{t-3/4}BV = \tfrac{3}{4}\,{}_{t-1}BV + \tfrac{1}{4}\,{}_{t}BV$$

The formula for the mean reserve would be:

$$_{t-3/4}BV = \tfrac{3}{4}\left(_{t-1}BV + BNP_x\right) + \tfrac{1}{4}\,{}_{t}BV$$

Similarly, it may not be valid to assume that issue dates are uniformly spread throughout the month. If policies are all issued on the first day of the month, the unearned premium at month end is zero. This is a fairly common practice for group insurance but is less common for individual insurance.

While statutory reserves use mean or midterminal reserves, GAAP calculations are often based on a more exact interpolation. Computer systems used for reserving may have the capability of determining the interpolated reserve and unearned premium seriatim (policy by policy) based on exact issue dates.

Analogous formulas are used for deferred acquisition costs (DAC or DPAC). The deferrable acquisition expense net premium and DAC formulas are shown below:

$$DENP = \sum_{t=0} v^t \times {}_tp_x \times DE_t \Big/ \sum_{t=0} v^t \times {}_tp_x$$

$${}_tDAC = \sum_{t=0} DENP \times (1+i)^t \big/ {}_tp_x - \sum_{t=0} DE_t \times (1+i)^t \big/ {}_tp_x$$

With DAC it is important to begin the calculations or summations at time 0, which is the time at which the largest initial acquisition costs tend to be incurred. Interpolated DAC numbers in the first year have to reflect not only terminal DAC numbers but also deferrable acquisition expense.

Thus the midterminal DAC balance is:

$${}_{t-1/2}DAC = \tfrac{1}{2}\left({}_{t-1}DAC + DE_{t-1} + {}_tDAC\right)$$

where only noncommission expenses are considered in DE_{t-1}.

So a midterminal DAC reserve for policies in their first year is the mean of zero (the prior terminal reserve), first-year noncommission deferrable acquisition expenses, and first-year terminal DAC balance. In addition to the above, not only must the unearned expense premium be established, but a provision made for commissions already incurred must be made. An "equity in the unearned premium (EUEP)" is established as an asset. The EUEP is generally the product of the gross unearned premium and the commission plus premium tax rates.

The formula for a mean DAC balance is:

$${}_{t-1/2}DAC = \tfrac{1}{2}\left({}_{t-1}DAC + DE_{t-1} - DENP_x + {}_t\%Prem + {}_tDAC\right)$$

In this situation, ${}_t\%Prem$ represents all percentage-of-premium expenses associated with the collection of the premium and DE_{t-1} represents the noncommission deferrable expenses.

Should the policyholder be paying a mode other than annual, a deferred expense premium must be established as an asset. Further, the costs associated with collecting this deferred premium must be established as a liability, or they must directly offset the DAC. This cost of collection liability item is generally calculated as the product of the gross deferred premium and the sum of commission and premium tax rates.

The sum of the prior-year terminal value plus the deferrable acquisition expenses deferred at the very beginning of the policy year is called the initial (as opposed to terminal) balance. Interpolation to a more exact issue date would fall between the initial and terminal DAC balances.

For a policy issued on October 1 and valued as of December 31, the interpolated midterminal DAC would be:

$$_{t-3/4}DAC = \tfrac{3}{4}\left({}_{t-1}DAC + DE_{t-1}\right) + \tfrac{1}{4}\,{}_{t}DAC$$

Tables 10-2 and 10-3 show formulas and numerical results for calculation of benefit and maintenance expense reserves and DAC. DAC is shown in this example as a negative acquisition expense reserve.

Table 10-2
Example of Valuation Assumptions for Reserve and DAC

(1) Policy Year, t	(2) Interest Rate	(3) Mortality Rate	(4) Lapse Rate	(5) Claim Costs	(6) Maintenance Expenses	(7) Acquisition Expenses	(8) Gross Premium	(9) Projected In Force
0								100.00%
1	7.0%	0.00214	30.0%	142.50	74.08	276.76	748.00	69.85%
2	7.0%	0.00237	25.0%	263.63	76.53	127.16	748.00	52.26%
3	7.0%	0.00262	20.0%	418.00	78.98	52.36	748.00	41.70%
4	7.0%	0.00290	17.5%	486.40	81.50	52.36	748.00	34.30%
5	7.0%	0.00319	15.0%	552.90	83.95	52.36	748.00	29.07%
6	7.0%	0.00354	15.0%	619.40	86.40	0.00	748.00	24.62%
7	7.0%	0.00394	15.0%	699.20	89.34	0.00	748.00	20.84%
8	7.0%	0.00441	15.0%	780.90	92.35	0.00	748.00	17.64%
9	7.0%	0.00494	15.0%	860.70	95.29	0.00	748.00	14.92%
10	7.0%	0.00547	15.0%	942.40	98.30	0.00	748.00	12.61%
11	7.0%	0.00600	15.0%	1022.20	101.24	0.00	748.00	10.66%
12	7.0%	0.00658	15.0%	1067.80	102.92	0.00	748.00	9.00%
13	7.0%	0.00724	15.0%	1115.30	104.67	0.00	748.00	7.59%
14	7.0%	0.00802	15.0%	1160.90	106.35	0.00	748.00	6.40%
15	7.0%	0.00894	15.0%	1208.40	108.10	0.00	748.00	5.39%
16	7.0%	0.00994	15.0%	1254.00	109.78	0.00	748.00	4.54%
17	7.0%	0.01098	15.0%	1311.00	111.88	0.00	748.00	3.82%
18	7.0%	0.01208	15.0%	1368.00	113.98	0.00	748.00	3.20%
19	7.0%	0.01320	15.0%	1425.00	116.08	0.00	748.00	2.69%
20	7.0%	0.01441	15.0%	1482.00	118.18	0.00	748.00	2.25%
21	7.0%	0.01575	15.0%	1539.00	120.28	0.00	748.00	1.88%
22	7.0%	0.01730	15.0%	1588.40	122.10	0.00	748.00	1.57%
23	7.0%	0.01905	15.0%	1637.80	123.92	0.00	748.00	1.31%

Legend:
Premiums and expenses are assumed incurred at the beginning of the policy year.
Claims and deaths occur at the midpoint of the year; lapses occur at the end of the policy year.
Decrements occur at the end of the year.
Maintenance expenses comprise 8.5% of premium and 3.7% (except 7.4% year one; 4.9% year two) of tabular claim costs.
Acquisition expenses by year are 37% of premium, 17, 7, 7, 7 and zero after the fifth year.
Annual gross premiums are level from issue age 42 through age 65.

In the example in Table 10-3 profits emerge as a level percentage of premiums. Illustrated later (in Tables 10-8 and 10-9) is the effect of including in the reserve assumptions provisions for adverse deviations in experience. This example is illustrative. The assumptions used are not necessarily appropriate for any specific situation.

Table 10-3
Example of Policy-Year Results for Reserve and DAC

(1) Policy Year$_t$	(10) Premium Income	(11) Investment Income	(12) Claims	(13) Maintenance Expenses	(14) Acquisition Expense	(15) Benefit Reserve	(16) Maintenance Expense Reserve	(17) Acquisition Expense Reserve	(18) Cash Flows	(19) Increase in Reserve	(20) Book Profit	(21) Profit as Percentage of Premium
0						0.00	0.00	0.00				
1	748.00	22.97	142.50	74.08	276.76	456.41	12.45	(251.36)	277.63	151.92	125.71	15.71%
2	522.48	31.03	184.14	53.46	88.82	911.44	25.92	(380.19)	227.09	139.28	87.81	15.71%
3	390.93	35.59	218.46	41.28	27.37	1264.95	39.09	(428.96)	139.42	73.72	65.70	15.71%
4	311.93	36.68	202.84	33.99	21.83	1600.92	51.77	(479.52)	89.95	37.52	52.42	15.71%
5	256.59	36.53	189.67	28.80	17.96	1897.56	63.18	(529.40)	56.70	13.58	43.12	15.71%
6	217.41	36.61	180.03	25.11	0.00	2191.96	74.51	(526.45)	48.88	12.34	36.54	15.71%
7	184.14	35.66	172.13	21.99	0.00	2467.69	85.16	(522.94)	25.68	(5.27)	30.95	15.71%
8	155.91	33.86	162.76	19.25	0.00	2717.99	94.85	(518.74)	7.75	(18.45)	26.20	15.71%
9	131.94	31.46	151.81	16.81	0.00	2938.93	103.44	(513.71)	(5.23)	(27.40)	22.17	15.71%
10	111.59	28.67	140.59	14.67	0.00	3120.69	110.56	(507.62)	(15.00)	(33.75)	18.75	15.71%
11	94.33	25.64	128.92	12.77	0.00	3255.37	115.91	(500.17)	(21.71)	(37.56)	15.85	15.71%
12	79.70	22.63	113.78	10.97	0.00	3372.61	120.63	(491.03)	(22.41)	(35.81)	13.39	15.71%
13	67.30	19.82	100.35	9.42	0.00	3465.88	124.48	(479.76)	(22.64)	(33.95)	11.31	15.71%
14	56.79	17.22	88.14	8.07	0.00	3531.77	127.33	(465.85)	(22.20)	(31.75)	9.54	15.71%
15	47.89	14.83	77.36	6.92	0.00	3561.26	128.84	(448.60)	(21.57)	(29.61)	8.05	15.71%
16	40.34	12.63	67.63	5.92	0.00	3547.29	128.75	(427.12)	(20.58)	(27.36)	6.78	15.71%
17	33.95	10.60	59.50	5.08	0.00	3464.29	126.11	(400.23)	(20.03)	(25.74)	5.71	15.71%
18	28.54	8.71	52.19	4.35	0.00	3293.42	120.21	(366.42)	(19.29)	(24.09)	4.80	15.71%
19	23.96	6.97	45.65	3.72	0.00	3010.27	110.14	(323.70)	(18.44)	(22.47)	4.03	15.71%
20	20.10	5.35	39.83	3.18	0.00	2583.46	94.72	(269.53)	(17.55)	(20.93)	3.38	15.71%
21	16.84	3.85	34.65	2.71	0.00	1972.38	72.46	(200.62)	(16.66)	(19.49)	2.83	15.71%
22	14.09	2.48	29.92	2.30	0.00	1133.50	41.71	(112.67)	(15.65)	(18.02)	2.37	15.71%
23	11.77	1.21	25.77	1.95	0.00	0.00	0.00	0.00	(14.74)	(16.72)	1.98	15.71%
Net Premium						435.64	82.21	112.67				

Legend (columns (2) through (9) come from Table 10-2):

$(10)_t$ = Premium Income $= (8)_t \times (9)_{t-1}$

$(11)_t$ = Investment Income $= (2)_t \times \{(10)_t - (13)_t - (14)_t + (9)_{t-1} \times [(15)_{t-1} + (16)_{t-1} + (17)_{t-1}]\} - (12)_t \times HY_t$

where HY_t is one half-year interest $= [1 + 0.5 \times (2)_t] \times [(1 - 0.5 \times (3)_t)] - 1$

$(12)_t$ = Claims $= (5)_t \times (9)_{t-1}$

$(13)_t$ = Maintenance expenses $= (6)_t \times (9)_{t-1}$

$(14)_t$ = Acquisition expenses $= (7)_t \times (9)_{t-1}$

Net premium for benefits, BNP = present value of column (12), including half year of interest, divided by present value of column (10)

Net premium for maintenance expenses, MENP = present value of column (13) divided by present value of column (10)

Net premium for acquisition expenses, AENP = present value of column (14) divided by present value of column (10)

$(15)_t$ = Benefit reserves $= \{[(15)_{t-1} + BNP] \times [1 + (2)_t] - (5)_t \times (1 + HY_t)\} / [(1 - (3)_t) \times (1 - (4)_t)]$

$(16)_t$ = Maintenance expense reserves $= [(16)_{t-1} + MENP - (6)_t] \times [1 + (2)_t] / [(1 - (3)_t) \times (1 - (4)_t)]$

$(17)_t$ = Acquisition expense reserves $= [(17)_{t-1} + AENP - (7)_t] \times [1 + (2)_t] / [(1 - (3)_t) \times (1 - (4)_t)]$

$(18)_t$ = Cash flows $= (10)_t + (11)_t - (12)_t - (13)_t - (14)_t$

$(19)_t$ = Increase in reserves $= [(15)_t + (16)_t + (17)_t] \times (9)_t - [(15)_{t-1} + (16)_{t-1} + (17)_{t-1}] \times (9)_{t-1}$

$(20)_t$ = Book profit as of end of policy year $= (18)_t - (19)_t$

$(21)_t$ = Profit as a percentage of premium $= [(20)_t / (10)_t] / (1 + (2)_t)$

Profit as a percentage of premium is level because expected and valuation assumptions are the same.

10.5.3 High Lapse Rates

A feature of many A&H policies that differs from most life policies is high lapse rates. This may be due to the method of marketing policies or their relatively high cost. In any event, first-year lapse rates may fall into the range of 20 to 50%, or even higher in some situations. Renewal lapse rates are somewhat lower but may be high relative to lapse rates common with life insurance.

Reserve factors are applied to actual in-force policies to determine benefit reserves to be held. This is a dynamic adjustment process: if lapses are higher or lower than expected, the reserves held are automatically scaled up or down to the appropriate extent. This dynamic adjustment works well if actual and expected lapses are fairly low and relatively similar in magnitude.

With A&H policies, lapse rates are higher and more difficult to predict. This poses a challenge in developing reserve factors. In Table 10-4, reserve factors were first calculated assuming 30% first-year lapses. Actual first-year lapse experience was 35%. Total reserves reflect actual in-force policies; hence there is no overstatement of the volume of business in force. However, if reserve factors had been calculated with the correct lapse assumption, the factors would have been higher and reserves would have been slightly higher.

Table 10-4
Analysis of First Year Lapse Rate Effect on Reserve Factors

	(1)	(2)	(3)	(4)	(5)	(6)	(7)
Year	**Assumed Lapses**	**Reserve Factors**	**Reserve Factors Using 35% First Year Lapse**	**Actual In force Remaining**	**Calculated Reserve**	**Reserve Should Be**	**Ratio**
1	30%	456.41	481.47	64.86%	296.03	312.28	105%
2	25%	911.44	938.57	48.53%	442.33	455.49	103%
3	20%	1264.95	1293.15	38.72%	489.82	500.74	102%
4	18%	1600.92	1629.68	31.85%	509.95	519.11	102%
5	15%	1897.56	1926.19	26.99%	512.14	519.86	102%

The lock-in concept prohibits recalculation of reserve factors in light of actual experience. It is intended that deviations from expected experience are reflected each year in GAAP net income. On the other hand, this example shows that expected experience should be determined as accurately as possible to avoid unduly large deviations.

One method that is sometimes used to minimize this deviation effect is the use of "final reserves" instead of terminal reserves. The preceding formulas addressed terminal reserve factors. The terminal reserve can be thought of as the reserve at the end of the policy year for policies then in force. Policies that have lapsed at the end of the policy year are not included as in force. As shown above, there may be a high number of lapses, especially in early policy durations. The final reserve is the reserve at the end of the policy year for policies in force prior to decrementing for those year end lapses.

As noted above, the general Fackler formula for benefit reserves describes terminal reserves in terms of beginning reserves, gross premiums, benefits, and maintenance expenses:

$$\left({}_{t-1}BV + BNP\right)(1+i) = {}_{t}BV\left(1-q^{d}\right)\left(1-q^{w}\right) + S_{[x]+t}$$

These terms can be rearranged as such:

$${}_{t}BV = \left({}_{t-1}BV + BNP\right)(1+i) - S_{[x]+t} \Big/ \left[\left(1-q^{d}\right)\times\left(1-q^{w}\right)\right]$$

The final reserve would be the terminal reserve a moment before the policy lapse, or

$${}_{t}BV^{\text{Final}} = \left({}_{t-1}BV + BNP\right)(1+i) - S_{[x]+t} \Big/ \left(1-q^{d}\right)$$

The ending value of a midterminal or mean reserve can be based on either the ending terminal or final reserve. A midterminal or mean reserve factor using the final as an endpoint is numerically smaller than a factor based on terminals. This type of factor in many cases is more consistent with the policy count from the in-force database. The in-force database typically reflects lapses not at the moment they are effective but rather some time after the end of the grace period, when it finally becomes clear that the required premium has not been paid. Some policies that will eventually lapse are treated as in force; thus it would be appropriate to use a reserve factor per policy consistent with the count of policies in force.

In instances in which lapse rates are high, the approximate assumption that lapses occur uniformly throughout the policy year may be invalid. For example, a policy with 35% lapse rate for the first policy year may experience lapses by quarter as shown in Table 10-5.

Table 10-5
Skewness Due to Lapses

	Policies That Lapse	Remaining in force
At issue		100
In First quarter	15	85
Second quarter	10	75
Third quarter	6	69
Fourth quarter	4	65

Actual policies in force at the midpoint of the year are 75, not the average of the beginning- and end-of-year values (i.e., $\frac{1}{2} \times (100 + 65) = 82.5$ policies). This skewing of lapsation during the year is more pronounced when lapse rates are high and in the first one or two policy durations.

This phenomenon is equivalent to underestimating lapses in the first half of the year. As shown in the example in Table 10-4, underestimating lapses could result in an understatement of the reserve. A refined formula for reserve factors or interpolated reserves may be necessary.

Application of reserve factors or calculation of reserves from first principles is easily performed with mainframe or personal computer systems. Standard packages are available for this purpose. A potentially significant practical issue for the actuary is that health insurance policies often comprise many benefits that need to be aggregated.

10.6 Selection of Assumptions

Cash accounting consists of tracking actual cash flows that move into and out of a company's accounting records. Accrual accounting makes adjustments to match the cash proceeds to the services performed in that accounting period. Perhaps the simplest example of an accrual adjustment is the unearned premium reserve, which matches premium revenues to the accounting period. A second example of an accrual adjustment is the claim reserves, which match benefit costs to the current accounting period for claims already incurred but not completely settled. The valuation mechanism, including the methods and assumptions used, cause the spreading of nonlevel costs, including benefit costs and expenses. Benefit reserves and DAC change between accounting periods to a degree that is intended to match the appropriate amount of benefit costs and deferrable acquisition expenses to the accounting period.

As mentioned above, *SFAS 60* methods seek to match income and expenses to services performed under the insurance contract in proportion to gross premiums earned. This is accomplished through the net level reserve mechanism, with formulas as shown in Section 10.5. The choice of assumptions, though, is critical. For a perfect match of profits to premiums, the valuation assumptions would need to be the same as those actually experienced. This is an impossibility in practice. However, to the extent that reasonably accurate assumptions as to future experience can be made, they should form the basis of *SFAS 60* valuation assumptions. This choice is a critical determinant of emergence of earnings. *SFAS 60* states:

> A liability for future policy benefits ... shall be accrued when premium revenue is recognized. The liability, which represents the present value of future benefits to be paid to or on behalf of policyholders and related expenses less the present value of future net premiums (portion of gross premium required to provide for all benefits and expenses), shall be estimated using methods that include assumptions, such as estimates of expected investment yields, mortality, morbidity, terminations, and expenses, applicable at the time the insurance contracts are made. The liability also shall consider other assumptions relating to guaranteed contract benefits, such as coupons, annual endowments, and conversion privileges. The assumptions shall include provision for the risk of adverse deviation. Original assumptions shall continue to be used in subsequent accounting periods to determine changes in the liability for future policy benefits (often referred to as the "lock-in concept") unless a premium deficiency exists (paragraphs 35-37). Changes in the liability for future policy benefits that result from its periodic estimation for financial reporting purposes shall be recognized in income in the period in which the changes occur. (Paragraph 21)

SFAS 60 valuation assumptions need to be based on, although not necessarily equal to, best-estimate assumptions with a provision for adverse deviation. In this way, the reserve mechanism is conceptually soundly rooted in the net level reserve mechanism with profits emerging mostly in proportion to premiums. Providing for the risk of adverse deviation causes the *SFAS 60* valuation assumptions to be conservative relative to best estimates. *SFAS 60* is unusual in the use of conservative assumptions, in that elsewhere in the GAAP literature best estimate assumptions are required. As described elsewhere, profits emerge partly in proportion to gross premiums and partly in proportion to the release of margins in the valuation assumptions.

SFAS 60 valuation assumptions are locked in from the date of issue. This requirement is unusual in the GAAP literature. Elsewhere, best estimates are used as of each valuation date (e.g., in claim reserves, *SFAS 97* lines of business, and valuation of non-insurance liabilities and assets). One perspective on the lock-in concept assumes that best-estimate assumptions can be set at issue and that experience variations thereafter will represent fluctuations around the best estimate. Lock-in avoids the need to frequently true up best-estimate assumptions due to minor variations in experience. Minor variations in morbidity, for example, relative to best estimate expectations, would flow through into profits without being dampened or spread by the reserve mechanism. Elsewhere in the GAAP literature (e.g., in *SFAS 97*) frequent true-ups of valuation assumptions are necessary.

Lock-in refers to original assumptions. *SFAS 60* states:

> ... Original assumptions shall continue to be used in subsequent accounting periods to determine changes in the liability for future policy benefits (often referred to as the "lock-in" concept) unless a premium deficiency exists. (Paragraph 21)

This is done to preserve the original earnings pattern in proportion to gross premiums; minor variations in experience come through income each year as they occur. Eventually, if large permanent changes in experience occur, as evidenced by disappearance of profit margins and the need for premium deficiency reserves, then changes to the original assumptions are necessary. Premium rate increases are considered by some actuaries to represent prima facie evidence that expectations have changed and assumptions should be unlocked, although premium rate increases preferably are made before profit margins disappear completely. Reserving after a premium rate increase is discussed in section 10.7.

10.6.1 Mortality

Health insurance policies terminate on death of the insured without paying a death benefit. On the other hand, injuries and sicknesses may precede death; thus benefits may be triggered by events immediately preceding death. This type of benefit is covered by the policy, but usually no specific adjustment needs to be made in pricing because the morbidity tables and statistical data used include such data. However, the policy term ends at death thus mortality needs to be considered in the reserving process.

Populations of health insureds are not selected for low mortality by the sales and underwriting process as with life insurance. However, the process does select individuals in good health who presumably would experience better mortality than the population at large. Thus mortality tables used for valuation assumptions are consistent with insured populations although perhaps not as select as individual life insurance mortality.

Although select mortality assumptions may be appropriate for underwritten coverages, lapse rates especially in early policy years are typically much higher than mortality rates. Thus a high level of refinement in mortality assumptions is often unnecessary, especially with coverages that cease at attained age 65.

10.6.2 Morbidity

Morbidity assumptions for *SFAS 60* valuation are usually derived from pricing morbidity assumptions. This is a challenging area for most kinds of A&H policies. Standard tables are available from industry or professional sources, or a company's own experience may be a guide. Provisions for adverse deviation (PAD) should be included.

Morbidity varies widely from one company to another, even for apparently similar blocks of business. Differences in experience arise because of geography, local medical practices, occupations in the insured population, environmental risk, and other factors. A major source of variation is the sales and marketing process and underwriting. If policies are sold to higher risk groups, the resulting morbidity experience may be markedly worse for the entire lifetime of the block of business. In an effort to increase the volume of business, the sales force may be less than selective in its efforts. In certain cases, if underwriting screens are low, the sales force may be attracted to poorer risks, which may make the sales process easier. The actuary needs a clear understanding of the marketing and sales process, as well as the associated underwriting practices and procedures, in order to establish morbidity assumptions.

The underwriting and policy issue process has a large effect on morbidity. While the impact is hard to quantify, a detailed application form including a full medical questionnaire coupled with underwriting action to decline or exclude certain coverages can reduce morbidity claim costs by a large fraction. Again, to the extent a rigorous pricing process has been followed, the actuary can base valuation assumptions on pricing assumptions, with a PAD.

The use of selection factors in morbidity should be considered. Guaranteed issue policies may exhibit little if any select experience in the early years, but a fully underwritten DI or major medical policy may have lower morbidity in the first several years. Policy provisions have an effect also; certain exclusions and limitations apply in the first two years.

Policy exclusions avoid major antiselection, but unrelated or vaguely related medical or physical conditions could imply that a substandard risk remains substandard even with benefit exclusions in place. Policy exclusions usually do not affect benefit reserves—the exclusion does not improve expected morbidity but rather returns expected morbidity to a level presumably identical to other similar policies without the substandard risk.

The effect of underwriting selection is difficult to measure accurately but has an important effect on reserves. As illustrated in Table 10-6, underwriting selection was assumed to reduce claim costs by 50% in the first year, 25% in the second year, and to have no effect thereafter. Although the use of selection factors reduces the benefit net premium, it may increase the required reserves sharply, particularly in the early policy years. This is because the selection factor increases the slope of the claim cost curve.

Table 10-6
Effects of Selection on Benefit Reserve

Policy Year	No selection	With selection
1	325.76	456.41
2	678.14	911.44
3	1022.36	1264.95
4	1353.54	1600.92
5	1651.33	1897.56
6	1947.10	2191.96
7	2224.46	2467.69
8	2476.72	2717.99
9	2699.99	2938.93
10	2884.59	3120.69
11	3022.74	3255.37
12	3144.23	3372.61
13	3242.74	3465.88
14	3315.10	3531.77
15	3352.61	3561.26
16	3348.63	3547.29
17	3278.13	3464.29
18	3123.00	3293.42
19	2859.71	3010.27
20	2458.09	2583.46
21	1879.06	1972.38
22	1081.10	1133.50
23	0.00	0.00
Net Premium	488.04	435.64

Table 10-6 displays a medical policy that is issued at age 42. Premiums are step-rated with one increase after 5 years. The first column shows reserves and benefit net premiums assuming no underwriting selection. The second column shows reserves and benefit net premiums calculated assuming a 50% reduction in first-year claim costs due to underwriting selection and a 25% reduction in the second year.

In the case of life insurance, underwriting selection appears to last for many years. In the case of A&H business, absent specific experience, the longevity of the effect is usually considered to last for only a few years.

10.6.3 Interest

As with life insurance, pricing and reserving for long-duration A&H contracts is heavily influenced by the effect of compound interest. Unlike life insurance, there are seldom cash values and less accumulation of benefit reserves over time. Hence there is often a lesser effect of interest rates on the performance of the company and morbidity experience. A static level interest rate assumption is often used. As with any product line, the actuary should understand the company's investment policy and make a determination about the likely best-estimate for future interest rates. The interest rate assumption is an expected earned rate with PAD. The direction of the adverse deviation is a negative spread relative to expected interest earnings. Adjustments for capital gains would be unusual; instead a total return assumption related to an overall portfolio earned rate is typical. Again, depending on the type of policy, refinement in the interest rate assumption may be less important than refinement of the morbidity assumption.

The appropriate level of PAD is discussed in more detail in a section 10.6.8.

The level of precision appropriate in choosing the interest assumption varies. For annually increasing or step rated policies, large benefit reserves do not accrue and interest does not become a major profit factor. On the other hand, for longer term, level-premium coverages such as noncancelable DI or long term care, interest is an important assumption. Investment income spreads earned on a large block of benefit reserves (as well as claim reserves in some cases) may be available to offset a significant amount of deteriorating morbidity experience. For that reason some actuaries prefer to use a very conservative valuation interest rate on such business. If the interest margin is important, the interest rate assumption may appropriately be based on a broader approximation of earned interest rates. In some cases an accurate asset model is used to project investment income for greater precision in setting interest rates.

10.6.4 Lapse rates

SFAS 60 reserves reflect assumed future lapses based on realistic expectations. The resulting GAAP reserves are usually lower than otherwise. Lapse rates (the complement of persistency rates) for A&H business are usually higher than those for traditional life insurance policies.

Lapse rates are typically based on pricing assumptions or experience studies. Many companies find lapse rates higher in early policy durations than in later durations and higher at younger issue ages than older issue ages.

Special considerations apply because of the high lapse rates often experienced with A&H business. For example, reserve factors can change dramatically based on lapse rates. The reserve mechanism should anticipate not only the application of high lapse rates in reserve determination but also the effect of lapse experience that varies from assumptions.

When lapse rates are in the range of 10 to 15% annually, it is common to ignore the variations during the policy year. On the other hand, first-year lapse rates for supplementary coverages may fall in the range of 40 to 60%. Such high lapse rates may also be non-uniformly distributed across the policy year. Improved valuation accuracy may be appropriate in certain circumstances to adjust lapse rates to a non-uniform monthly rate.

A certain percentage of policies issued by the insurance company are not accepted by the applicant, even for a month; these are "not-takens." In other situations an application is rejected (declined) by the insurance company because of high insurance risk (e.g., a combination of high morbidity risk conditions). In these cases, premiums are not collected, or if collected, the premiums are refunded. No special assumptions are required in reserving for not-taken or declined policies. These policies are regarded as never having been in force.

10.6.5 Expenses

Chapter 3 discussed the categories, sources and rationale for expense assumption selection. The reader should refer to Chapter 3 for instruction on expense assumption selection. This section deals with expense elements that are pertinent to individual health insurance.

As with other product types, overhead, corporate and executive expenses that do not tie directly to the A&H line of business are excluded from the reserve mechanism. Examples of this type of expense are the legal and actuarial departments. Although both functional areas are important, their costs are not usually directly associated with acquisition or maintenance of a book of business. In the case of A&H business, however, litigation is so common in the management of the line of business that a portion of legal costs may appropriately be considered maintenance expense.

Allocating maintenance costs as a level percentage of premium may or may not be completely appropriate for A&H business. A&H claims are much more frequent than claims under life insurance. Depending on the type of coverage, a significant percentage of the business in force will have claims in a given year. For example, Medicare supplement business may experience claims on 60% of insureds each year. It is appropriate to allocate costs associated with claim adjudication and settlement in proportion to tabular morbidity. This implies a rising pattern of expenses; thus a significant maintenance expense reserve will develop. Maintenance costs also apply to claims that are in course of settlement. This is particularly clear in the case of DI claims that require ongoing monitoring of the claimant's condition. Hence there needs to be a reserve for settlement expenses on claims already incurred, as well as expenses on claims to be incurred in the future.

A difficult expense-related assumption is future inflation. Expense inflation is likely to remain a feature of the economy indefinitely, although it may rise and fall to different levels. Thus many actuaries include an inflation assumption whose general order of magnitude would fall in the range of 2 to 6%. This assumption, like all others, should be based on some level of study, either as to experience, pricing, or comparable industry experience. It should also be consistent with other related assumptions such as interest rates and growth rates. If the company is growing, it may be able to achieve economies of scale. However, this assumption should not be made without actual evidence of growth. If productivity improvements are likely to occur, the effect would offset inflation. In those cases it may be appropriate to assume level or even declining unit expenses.

It is appropriate to include PADs in maintenance expense assumptions. The appropriate level of PAD would depend on the company's experience and its expectations primarily as to future expense inflation.

10.6.6 Commissions

Commissions on individual A&H business are typically heaped, as displayed in Table 10-7.

Table 10-7
Commission Schedule as a Percentage of Premium

Year	Total Commission	Excess Commission
First year	40%	35
Second year	25	20
Years 3 to 5	15	10
Years 6 to 10	10	5
Thereafter	5	-

In this example, the excess commissions that are deferrable are shown in the second column. The deferral of commissions offsets the expense incurred by the company in paying the commission, hence achieving the matching of nonlevel commission costs to a level proportion of gross premiums. The level ultimate commission need not be deferred because it is already matched as a level percentage of premiums.

Note that if total commissions as shown in column 1 are deferred, the resulting DAC factors would be no different that if only excess commissions are deferred. The factor calculation process would determine a higher acquisition expense net premium, 5% higher to be exact. Thus the reserve mechanism would call for capitalizing a higher expense (for example, 40% instead of 35% of premium), but amortization would likewise be 5% higher. The distinction is important when the total net premium is being calculated. If DAC is being determined by a worksheet (see Chapter 3), the amortization calculations and the amounts actually entered into the worksheet should be consistent (that is to say, both consistently should include or exclude ultimate commissions).

As elaborated on in Chapter 3, commissions and overrides paid to field sales management should be included in total commissions. Production incentive bonuses are difficult to quantify in advance, but they certainly are attributable to and variable (although perhaps not proportionate) with new business. As such, they are eligible deferrable expenses. Similarly, agent conventions that reward high production of new business are eligible deferrable expenses.

PAD is not included in commission assumptions because commissions are capable of exact determination.

10.6.7 Taxes

Premiums on most A&H business are subject to premium taxes in the various states. Hence premium tax is appropriately reflected in pricing these products. Premium tax is not a major issue in reserving because it is a level percentage of the gross premium. Hence no maintenance expense reserve is necessary. As in the case of level maintenance expenses, although there is no reserve, there is a net premium.

Federal income tax (FIT) is not considered in the reserving mechanism. Benefit and maintenance expense reserves and DAC are calculated before FIT. A separate deferred tax asset or liability entry in the balance sheet is made to reflect the different timing of GAAP profits from taxable income. Typically GAAP profits are lower than taxable income in the early policy years. Many additional considerations apply in the determination of deferred taxes and are addressed further in Chapter 18.

10.6.8 Provisions for Adverse Deviation

PAD modifies profit emergence. Under *SFAS 60* reserve methods, profits do not emerge exactly in proportion to premiums. Conservative assumptions cause net premiums and reserves to be higher, thus holding back profits to be released in later policy durations.

Judgment is necessary to determine the appropriate amount of PAD. Of course, the PAD may not become so large that the net premium exceeds the gross premium.

PAD does not have to be included in every valuation assumption. In fact, that would likely result in unduly conservative assumptions, perhaps with little profit emerging in proportion to gross premiums and most profit emerging as the PADs release. It is possible to demonstrate that if PADs are included such that the net premium equals the gross premium, no profit will emerge in proportion to premiums and instead all profits will emerge in proportion to the PADs. This approach is sometimes called the source-of-earnings approach.

The PAD generally should be greatest when the level of confidence in the assumption is least. This in itself may be hard to identify, but expense assumptions should be able to be set in advance with reasonable accuracy. Most expenses are subject to management control. Interest rates are completely outside of management's control, but may have a modest effect on pricing or reserving. Mortality is relatively predictable and modest in its effect on reserves. Morbidity is usually very uncertain and may deserve the largest PAD.

Providing a PAD for lapse rates is a challenging endeavor. The actuary must inspect the lapse rates selected, because of the varying impact it has on profitability. Higher lapse rates in later years may increase profitability due to fewer claims being incurred. Higher lapses, however, will increase the portion of the premium necessary to amortize DAC, thereby reducing the profitability of the product. Conversely, lower lapses will decrease the portion of the premium necessary to amortize DAC, thereby increasing the profitability of the product.

Thus, adding a provision for adverse deviation by increasing lapse rates for all durations can actually increase the reported profit in early policy durations—an unintended and undesirable result. Because of this phenomenon, in practice best-estimate lapse rates may be appropriate in the calculation of GAAP reserves. The actuary should test the net effect on the emergence of profitability before finalizing the lapse rate assumption.

Ideally, conservative assumptions should be based on best-estimate assumptions plus an explicit PAD. This is preferable to determining an overall assumption that is known or intended to be conservative, but where the degree of conservatism is uncertain.

Table 10-8 illustrates a simple example of profit emergence. Claim costs reflect a guaranteed renewable disability income policy issued at age 42. The pricing interest rate is 7% and mortality is based on the 1965-70 table. Lapse rates begin at 30% in the first year and decline to 15% in the fifth year and thereafter. Expenses reflect commissions, and issue and maintenance expenses. Maintenance expenses are 8.5% of premiums plus approximately 3.7% of claims. These assumptions are not necessarily representative of any company's pricing assumptions.

Table 10-8 shows book profit each year expressed as a percentage of the gross premium. In the first column valuation assumptions are chosen equal to pricing (that is, without PAD). This is the same example shown in Tables 10-2 and 10-3. These assumptions are for illustration only and would not normally be appropriate under *SFAS 60.* The second column shows the effect of a 10% reduction to valuation mortality and lapse rates in all policy years. The third column shows the effect of a 10% increase in valuation morbidity rates. The fourth column shows the effect of a 100-basis-point reduction in valuation interest rates. The fifth column shows the effect of the latter two PADs combined.

Table 10-8
Effect of PAD on Profits (Profits Expressed as a Percentage of Gross Premium)

Year	(1) No PAD	(2) Mortality and Lapse Rate Reduction	(3) Morbidity Only Increase	(4) Interest Only Reduction	(5) Morbidity and Interest Increase
1	15.71%	14.02%	11.72%	14.60%	10.48%
2	15.71%	14.99%	13.29%	14.89%	12.39%
3	15.71%	15.46%	15.28%	15.33%	14.88%
4	15.71%	15.86%	16.16%	15.75%	16.22%
5	15.71%	16.00%	17.02%	16.13%	17.51%
6	15.71%	16.61%	17.88%	16.47%	18.74%
7	15.71%	17.19%	18.91%	16.86%	20.20%
8	15.71%	17.72%	19.96%	17.24%	21.66%
9	15.71%	18.19%	20.99%	17.57%	23.06%
10	15.71%	18.58%	22.04%	17.87%	24.44%
11	15.71%	18.88%	23.06%	18.12%	25.73%
12	15.71%	19.14%	23.65%	18.30%	26.52%
13	15.71%	19.36%	24.25%	18.47%	27.30%
14	15.71%	19.53%	24.83%	18.60%	28.03%
15	15.71%	19.63%	25.44%	18.70%	28.74%
16	15.71%	19.64%	26.02%	18.75%	29.37%
17	15.71%	19.52%	26.74%	18.75%	30.10%
18	15.71%	19.23%	27.47%	18.67%	30.72%
19	15.71%	18.72%	28.19%	18.47%	31.23%
20	15.71%	17.94%	28.91%	18.14%	31.58%
21	15.71%	16.81%	29.63%	17.64%	31.74%
22	15.71%	15.24%	30.25%	16.92%	31.56%

The effect of PAD on benefit reserves is shown in Table 10-9.

Table 10-9
Effect of PAD on Reserves

Year	(1) No PAD	(2) Mortality and Lapse Rate	(3) Morbidity Only Increase	(4) Interest Only Reduction	(5) Morbidity and Interest Increase
1	456.41	475.84	502.05	472.85	520.14
2	911.44	944.78	1002.59	943.98	1038.38
3	1264.95	1311.47	1391.44	1311.14	1442.25
4	1600.92	1659.64	1761.01	1659.02	1824.92
5	1897.56	1969.24	2087.32	1964.90	2161.39
6	2191.96	2274.48	2411.15	2267.39	2494.13
7	2467.69	2558.74	2714.46	2549.80	2804.78
8	2717.99	2815.13	2989.79	2805.25	3085.78
9	2938.93	3039.61	3232.82	3029.73	3332.70
10	3120.69	3222.45	3432.76	3213.36	3534.70
11	3255.37	3355.98	3580.91	3348.30	3683.13
12	3372.61	3469.56	3709.87	3464.31	3810.74
13	3465.88	3556.47	3812.47	3554.71	3910.18
14	3531.77	3613.06	3884.95	3615.95	3977.54
15	3561.26	3630.23	3917.39	3638.89	4002.78
16	3547.29	3600.90	3902.02	3616.40	3978.04
17	3464.29	3499.98	3810.72	3522.89	3875.17
18	3293.42	3309.60	3622.76	3339.81	3673.79
19	3010.27	3007.00	3311.29	3043.32	3347.65
20	2583.46	2563.52	2841.80	2603.05	2863.35
21	1972.38	1942.77	2169.61	1980.04	2178.04
22	1133.50	1107.43	1246.85	1133.36	1246.70

Overall profitability is not affected by PAD in the reserve. Ultimate profits are based on the excess of premiums and investment income over claims and expenses. However, a steeper increase in reserves in the early years defers the emergence of profits. PAD has this effect because valuation net premiums increase and the present value of future benefits increases.

The effects can also be explained by formula. The combined benefit, maintenance, and deferrable expense terminal reserve is ${}_tV$, and similarly the combined net premium is P_x. The recursive terminal reserve formula is:

$$\left({}_tV + P_x - ME_t - DE_t\right)(1+i) = S_{[x]+t} + {}_1p_x \times {}_{t+1}V$$

In the following formula, primed symbols are used to denote actual experience. Unprimed symbols represent valuation assumptions. The formula for profit in year t, G_t, is:

$$G_t \quad = \quad GP_x(1+i') - \left(ME'_t + DE'_t\right)(1+i') - (1+i'/2)S'_{[x]+t} - \left({}_1p'_x \times {}_{t+1}V - (1+i')\,{}_tV\right)$$

In other words, profits in year t equal gross premiums plus investment income less expenses, claims, and the increase in combined reserves.

By substituting for ${}_tV$ and rearranging terms, profits can be expressed as follows:

$$
\begin{aligned}
G_t = & \left(GP_x - P_x\right) \\
& + \left(ME_t - ME_t'\right) + \left(DE_t - DE_t'\right) \\
& + \left(S_{[x]+t} - S_{[x]+t}'\right) + i'\left({}_tV + GP_x - ME_t' - DE_t' - \tfrac{1}{2} S_{[x]+t'}\right) \\
& - i \times \left({}_tV + P_x - ME_t - DE_t - \tfrac{1}{2} S_{[x]+t}\right) \\
& + \left(q^{w'} - q^{w}\right) \times {}_tV
\end{aligned}
$$

In words, profits equal a level percentage of premium plus the differences between actual experience and valuation assumptions. Because valuation assumptions include PADs, it is expected that profits will include a component represented by the release over time of the PADs.

More information on the effect of PADs can be found in "Life Insurance Earnings and the Release from Risk Policy Reserve System" (Horn, 1971), and in "A Comparison of Alternate Generally Accepted Accounting Principles (GAAP) Methodologies for Universal Life" (McLaughlin, 1987).

10.6.9 Summary

As implied in the formula development section, the same assumptions must be used for reserves and DAC. Otherwise the appropriate pattern of earnings emergence do not occur. Of course, DAC is not dependent on morbidity assumptions, just as benefit reserves are not dependent on acquisition costs (e.g., commissions). However, mortality, persistency, and interest rate assumptions are common to both and should be identical.

It is sometimes difficult to establish consistency between assumptions if different mechanisms are used for reserves and DAC. It is fairly common to have factors or first principles calculations applied seriatim to determine reserves while DAC is calculated for large blocks of policies aggregated into a spreadsheet. Tables of lapse rates are entered into the reserve factor calculation programs; these tables can vary by age, sex, and other variables. In the aggregated worksheet, a weighted average lapse rate is applied. If there is an implicit or explicit inconsistency between the reserve and DAC assumptions, the reserve mechanism will fail to produce profits as a level percentage of premium (plus release of PAD).

SFAS 60 valuation assumptions need to be supportable. The external audit of the financial statements is an important part of the value of GAAP financial statements. The audit implies that the work performed by the company's accountants and actuaries is reliable and reproducible. The actuaries should document adequate support for all valuation assumptions. Ideally this is in the form of a summary of standard tables, experience studies, industry studies, or pricing assumptions.

When a block of A&H business is acquired, the purchaser needs to establish a reserve method consistent with rules for GAAP purchase accounting. Chapter 15 covers purchase accounting in detail.

10.7 Reserving after a Premium Increase

In reserving after experience has deteriorated, new considerations apply. For this discussion, it is presumed that the business remains profitable or potentially profitable. If future losses appear likely, loss recognition (discussed later) must be performed.

Medical business or other A&H business subject to inflation of benefit costs is significantly exposed to C2 (premium adequacy) risk. In fact, such blocks of business may be re-rated not once but several times. If that situation is likely to occur due to the nature of the benefits, the policy probably should be priced with an increasing premium structure, not on a level premium basis. If gross premiums are closely proportional to claim costs, there is little if any pre-funding of benefits; hence benefit reserves will be close to zero. Benefit reserves may arise nonetheless due to underwriting selection; in that event the benefit reserves will likely increase to a maximum then decline back to zero within a few policy durations.

If a level-premium basis is used, the pre-funding implicit in the early years needs to be taken into account with each re-rate. Further, the morbidity assumptions should reflect the actuary's best estimate as to future cost inflation. While the estimate may not be accurate, it would be preferable to assuming zero inflation. This may appear to be a pricing matter, yet this issue becomes important under loss recognition where it is necessary to have premium increase and benefit inflation assumptions that are realistic and internally consistent. If increasing premiums are projected, the assumptions should reflect the reality (the difficulty) of increasing premiums in proportion to deteriorating experience.

Assume for the moment that experience has deteriorated but not to the point that losses are indicated. The company makes the decision to increase premium rates to restore original profit margins. New assumptions must be considered; there are several viewpoints. Under a strict application of the lock-in concept, all reserve and DAC factors continue unchanged. The increased premium will cover the increased morbidity; thus some variation from initial pricing profit targets will take place, to the extent that the extra premium does not exactly match the extra morbidity. This answer is not unreasonable and is the one most commonly seen. Table 10-10 is an example of this situation. For a sample A&H policy, the table shows profits that emerge each policy year as a percentage of premium. The first column assumes no PAD; in other words valuation assumptions are equal to pricing assumptions. The profits are a level percentage of premium (except if there were first-year nondeferrable acquisition expenses). The second column shows profits with PAD in the valuation assumptions. In this example the valuation interest rate was reduced by 1% and the morbidity assumption was increased by 10%. Expected profits are deferred to some extent to later policy durations. Column 3 shows the effect of experience deterioration. This is represented by a 5% increase in claim costs that occurs suddenly and permanently in year 3. In actuality, of course, experience would change more gradually over time. Profits reduce in all future years. Column 4 displays the effect of a premium increase of 5% in year 4. This example ignores the reality of antiselective lapsation. Profits are restored although not to the original pricing level.

Table 10-10
Effect of Rate Increases on Profits (Book Profits Expressed as Percentage of Premium)

Year	(1) Profits without PAD	(2) Profits with PAD	(3) Profits after Experience Deterioration	(4) Profits after Rate Increase
1	15.71%	10.48%	10.48%	10.48%
2	15.71%	12.39%	12.39%	12.39%
3	15.71%	14.88%	14.88%	14.88%
4	15.71%	16.22%	13.08%	13.08%
5	15.71%	17.51%	13.94%	17.71%
6	15.71%	18.74%	14.74%	18.80%
7	15.71%	20.20%	15.69%	19.71%
8	15.71%	21.66%	16.63%	20.60%
9	15.71%	23.06%	17.51%	21.44%
10	15.71%	24.44%	18.36%	22.25%
11	15.71%	25.73%	19.14%	22.99%
12	15.71%	26.52%	19.64%	23.46%
13	15.71%	27.30%	20.12%	23.92%
14	15.71%	28.03%	20.55%	24.34%
15	15.71%	28.74%	20.96%	24.73%
16	15.71%	29.37%	21.31%	25.05%
17	15.71%	30.10%	21.67%	25.40%
18	15.71%	30.72%	21.93%	25.65%
19	15.71%	31.23%	22.08%	25.79%
20	15.71%	31.58%	22.07%	25.78%
21	15.71%	31.74%	21.87%	25.59%
22	15.71%	31.56%	21.38%	25.13%

In this example, reserve assumptions are locked in and reserves are unchanged through the experience deterioration and subsequent premium rate increase.

On the other hand, given a permanent deterioration in experience, expectations for future experience have changed fundamentally. Whereas, for example, original pricing anticipated experience at 100% of a standard morbidity table, some years later after inflation has had an effect, the new expectations are for experience at 120% of the standard table. Perhaps in this hypothetical example the company could increase gross premiums by 15%.

SFAS 60 states explicitly:

> Original assumptions shall continue to be used in subsequent accounting periods to determine changes in the liability for future policy benefits (often referred to as the "lock-in concept") unless a premium deficiency exists. (Paragraph 21)

It seems arguable that the incremental premium and benefits constitute an incremental benefit to the basic policy. For example, if a new rider is added to a hospital indemnity policy, additional reserves are needed. Suppose the base policy covers $200 per day and five years later the insured adds coverage for an additional $50 per day. The lock-in principle would not apply. Instead, an additional benefit reserve would begin to accrue on the date the new rider is issued. The benefit reserve would be based on the anticipated benefits, premiums, and future experience. By analogy the incremental medical benefit that has arisen may require additional reserves. Although not common in practice, this approach is consistent with actuarial guidance and does not violate the lock-in principle. Thus increased reserves would begin to accrue at the date of change in which higher future morbidity is reflected. A new net premium would be determined reflecting new expectations of future morbidity and the availability of the benefit reserve. From the date of change reserves would accrue consistent with the higher morbidity assumption and higher net premium.

Practical issues arise and will vary in effect depending on the mechanics of the valuation process. For example, morbidity deterioration occurs gradually, not just on a given date. The effective date of new morbidity assumptions cannot be set exactly. Rate increases take effect on a specific date, but a given calendar date will fall in different policy durations, depending on the issue date of the policy. Thus different calculations would be needed depending on issue year. Rate increases may take effect on policy anniversaries or next premium due date, depending on the circumstances; theoretically the reserve method should reflect the timing appropriately. Further, rate increases may vary as to amount and timing in different states. Approximations and simplifying assumptions are appropriate and are commonly used to deal with these practical issues.

This approach to reserving for incremental benefits and an approach to dealing with the practical issues is discussed in more detail in "GAAP for Non-Guaranteed-Premium Life Insurance" (Cloninger, 1981).

Medicare supplement policies are an important type of individual coverage. As Medicare deductibles increase, benefits increase in approximate proportion and premiums usually increase automatically in proportion. The increases need to be reflected in the reserve mechanism. While some actuaries believe that the lock-in concept requires benefit reserves and DAC to remain unchanged, it does not appear that the lock-in concept was intended to apply to structural policy changes. By analogy with the hospital indemnity example above, it seems clear that the incremental benefits require incremental reserves.

Different actuarial approaches are justifiable. One approach is to make an estimate at issue of the probable future increases in premiums and benefits. This approach produces appropriate reserves to the extent that actual benefit changes are approximately consistent with assumptions. Under this approach it seems that the lock-in principle should apply. A second approach is to blend into a new morbidity table and net premium at the date of change. In this approach there would be no discontinuity in reserves at the date of change, but the reserve would begin to increase at a more rapid rate. This latter approach is discussed in more detail in two relevant papers, "GAAP for Non-Guaranteed-Premium Life Insurance" (Cloninger, 1987) and "GAAP for Medicare Supplement Policies" (Raws, 1990). Raws' paper discusses the approaches mentioned in this section as well as other alternative approaches that may or may not be appropriate under current accounting guidance.

The approach taken will effect how well benefits, expenses, and premiums match and consequently the emergence of profits from the business. The actuary should investigate the various approaches in advance to fully understand their effect under a range of possible outcomes. Failure to do so invites the possibility of surprises in gains or losses arising from the book of business.

To illustrate this point, using the example from Table 10-10, a very different profit pattern would have been noted under different approaches. In Table 10-11, the first two columns recapitulate Table 10-10, first showing the profits that emerge if experience and valuation assumptions do not vary, and second, the profits if experience varies but reserves remain locked in. The last two columns indicate the profits if the changes had been either (i) anticipated in advance and reflected in the reserving mechanism, or (ii) not anticipated in advance, but reflected in reserves as of the date premiums changed.

Table 10-11
Effect of Valuation Approach on Profits (Profits Expressed as Percentage of Premium)

Year	(1) No Changes in Experience	(2) Changes in Experience, but Reserves Locked in	(3) Changes Anticipated and Reserved in Advance	(4) Changes Reflected in Reserves When They Occur
1	10.48%	10.48%	9.49%	10.48%
2	12.39%	12.39%	11.42%	12.39%
3	14.88%	14.88%	13.93%	14.88%
4	16.22%	13.08%	15.61%	13.08%
5	17.51%	17.71%	17.37%	16.42%
10	24.44%	22.25%	24.03%	23.09%
15	28.74%	24.73%	28.40%	27.47%
20	31.58%	25.78%	31.32%	30.43%

The last two columns indicate the profits if the changes had been either (i) anticipated in advance and reflected in the reserving mechanism or (ii) not anticipated in advance but reflected in reserves as of the date premiums changed.

The effect on reserves is displayed in Table 10-12:

Table 10-12
Medicare Supplement Benefit Reserves under Different Valuation Approaches

Year	(1) No Changes in Experience	(2) Changes in Experience, but Reserves Locked in	(3) Changes Anticipated and Reserved in Advance	(4) Changes Reflected in Reserves when They Occur
1	520.14	520.14	533.45	520.14
2	1038.38	1038.38	1069.66	1038.38
3	1442.25	1442.25	1495.47	1442.25
4	1824.92	1824.92	1871.19	1824.92
5	2161.39	2161.39	2224.72	2178.69
6	2494.13	2494.13	2574.37	2528.62
7	2804.78	2804.78	2900.88	2855.46
8	3085.78	3085.78	3196.31	3151.29
9	3332.70	3332.70	3456.04	3411.50
10	3534.70	3534.70	3668.70	3624.72
11	3683.13	3683.13	3825.22	3781.94
12	3810.74	3810.74	3960.04	3917.60
13	3910.18	3910.18	4065.46	4024.05
14	3977.54	3977.54	4137.42	4097.28
15	4002.78	4002.78	4165.43	4126.85
16	3978.04	3978.04	4141.33	4104.66
17	3875.17	3875.17	4035.65	4001.36
18	3673.79	3673.79	3827.09	3795.77
19	3347.65	3347.65	3488.27	3460.66
20	2863.35	2863.35	2984.31	2961.36
21	2178.04	2178.04	2270.48	2253.41
22	1246.70	1246.70	1299.82	1290.19
23	0.00	0.00	0.00	0.00

This example reflects 5% increases in morbidity in year 4 and premiums in year 5. The effect on profits and reserves is relatively small in this example. The effect would be much greater if larger changes occurred, especially if they occurred several years in succession. Hence the actuary needs to examine reserve mechanisms very carefully if rate increases occur.

If gross premiums are attained-age-rated, then little or no pre-funding of future benefits is anticipated and benefit reserves may be immaterial. The need to blend benefit reserves when rates increase would not exist.

10.8 Recoverability and Loss Recognition

Recoverability and loss recognition refer to the concept that the intangible DAC asset (or VOBA for acquired business) must be supportable out of future profits. Future gross premiums less expenses together with benefit reserves must be adequate to provide for contractual obligations including future expenses. If the asset is not supportable, it must be reduced and a loss taken immediately when the loss is recognized as likely and its amount can reasonably be estimated. Recoverability refers to the test performed at issue. Loss recognition refers to the test performed after issue on a line of business or group of policies.

10.8.1 Recoverability

Recoverability establishes whether the DAC asset initially posted is recoverable from the profits associated with the business to which it is attributed. Rather than being evaluated individually, usually all new business issued in a given year is considered together, although sometimes different blocks are examined separately. One method for demonstrating recoverability is the gross premium valuation. A second, simpler method is to examine the net-to-gross premium ratio using valuation assumptions. Valuation assumptions are established as realistic with some PAD. The net premiums for benefits and maintenance and acquisition costs should total some amount less than gross premiums. This test is typically performed in the aggregate, if factors are available, or on a sample basis. As mentioned before, the net premium must include all expenses, not just excess commissions. Of course, overhead and nondeferrable acquisition expenses are not included when the net premium is determined.

If the net premium exceeds the gross premium, it would be appropriate to recalculate the net premium after removing some or all of the PADs. If this process results in the net premium equaling the gross premium, these assumptions define the maximum level of PAD in the valuation assumptions taken in the aggregate. These are the valuation assumptions that should be used going forward. In this situation no profits emerge in proportion to premiums. All profits emerge as the PADs are released.

If the net premium still exceeds the gross even with all PADs removed, the amount of acquisition expense that is deferred must be reduced. This is done in stages, with less and less of the first-year deferrable expenses capitalized; then second year; and so on. When the net premium equals the gross premium, the reserve method is then defined, using the realistic assumptions (i.e., no PADs) and only partial deferral of acquisition costs.

If no acquisition costs whatsoever are deferrable because the net premium still exceeds the gross, a premium deficiency reserve must be established. This is the present value of the deficient premiums.

10.8.2 Loss Recognition

In addition to recoverability at issue, the DAC asset must at all times be recoverable out of profits or premiums on the block of business with which it is associated. In other words, the present value of future gross premiums must exceed the present value of future benefits and maintenance expenses by a margin that equals or exceeds the unamortized DAC balance.

As a practical matter, an approximate GPV is often performed using valuation assumptions rather than realistic assumptions. If the test is failed, then as above the PADs should be removed (hence lower future morbidity and higher interest earnings are reflected). This may be sufficient to pass the test, in which case the revised assumptions (i.e., excluding PAD) become the valuation assumptions from that point forward. If the test is still failed, the unamortized DAC balance must be reduced to the point that is recoverable, using realistic assumptions as the valuation assumptions from that point forward.

If the situation is so extreme that all DAC must be eliminated, then as mentioned above a premium deficiency reserve must be established.

Many A&H lines of business are subject to morbidity inflation, antiselective lapsation, moral hazard, and other risks. Unfortunately, once experience begins to deteriorate, it is likely to continue. For this reason a GPV or an equivalent loss recognition test must be performed periodically.

For blocks of business for which loss recognition has occurred, a new form of lock-in is applied. The current realistic assumptions continue to be used if experience should subsequently improve. In other words, once the DAC asset has been written down or eliminated, it may not be re-established if experience improves. In that event profits would emerge from the block of business. If (as is more likely) experience continues to deteriorate, loss recognition would again become necessary.

One of the many difficult issues with loss recognition is the problem of determining when deterioration in morbidity experience is permanent. Many kinds of A&H business, including DI, are subject to fluctuations in experience. It may be difficult to distinguish an experience deterioration from a temporary fluctuation; there is no hard-and-fast rule. If an experience deterioration continues over more than one year, the actuary may be well advised to consider it permanent. In general, deterioration in morbidity experience is permanent due to antiselective lapsation. For more information, refer to "Cumulative Anti-Selection Theory," (Bluhm, 1982).

In attempting to establish realistic assumptions, the actuary may inadvertently use conservative assumptions. This would constitute a more severe test than the GPV and would result in a larger than appropriate DAC write-off. If DAC is written off based on a conservative test, profits may emerge out of the block of business in later years. This is an unintended and inappropriate result; conservatism should be avoided. Experience should be monitored and a new GPV performed every year if appropriate. This is consistent with the *SFAS 5* requirement to use best estimates in reserving.

On the other hand, the actuary should not be overly optimistic. Consider a case study in which a block of major medical business experiences high loss ratios for several years. It appears obvious that the business is unprofitable and that all or most of the DAC being carried on the line of business should to be written off. However, the company's actuaries perform a gross premium valuation assuming that premium rate increases would exceed medical cost inflation trend by a few percent points per annum. Also, the loss ratios decrease gradually. On a present value basis with a long projection period, a profit margin appears.

In reality it would be extremely difficult or impossible to increase premium rates so rapidly that they restored original pricing margins prospectively. Regulatory approval is necessary, time delays are inevitable, and antiselective lapsation on an unprofitable line of business makes it very difficult to restore profits once loss ratios exceed a breakeven level.

With respect to loss recognition, recoverability, and premium deficiency reserving, the definition of a line of business is not always clear. *SFAS 60* paragraph 37 calls for premium deficiency reserve to be established on an entire line of business in the aggregate, at a minimum. Smaller policy groups would also be allowed. A block of similar policies all issued in the same year is subject to recoverability testing at issue, but there is no clear requirement that each year of issue should subsequently prove profitable. Likewise, a line of business may be subject to many rating dimensions or risk categories, including issue age, sex, occupation class, and other risk factors. The usual interpretation is that groups of policies with similar characteristics should be aggregated for loss recognition testing. Thus all DI policies issued by a company would be studied separately from the medical expense business issued by the same company. Although the company and its marketplace are the same, the risks and characteristics of the two lines of business are very different. Policies with different renewability provisions may be different enough that they should be segregated for loss recognition testing purposes.

In general, a narrower definition of a line of business results in a more conservative reserve method.

SFAS 60 paragraph 37 also requires that premium deficiency reserves be established to cover temporary losses, even if a line is not deficient in the aggregate. In other words, passing a gross premium valuation test may not be sufficient because the GPV is performed on a total present value basis. If a line of business shows losses for a few years but gains later on, the total present value of future profits may nonetheless be positive. In this situation a premium deficiency reserve is required to provide for those future losses.

10.9 Claim Reserves

A&H policies pay a wide variety of benefits. There is a time lag of a few days to many years between the occurrence of the insured contingent event and the final settlement of its obligation by the insurance company. When the benefit is paid under a policy, the company's books record the cash paid as an expense. As of the financial reporting date the company must record a liability to provide for claims incurred under its policies but not yet settled. In this manner incurred claims for a given accounting period are matched to the premiums received in the same period.

10.9.1 Requirement for Claim Reserves

The requirement for claim reserves is explicitly stated in *SFAS 60*:

> A liability for unpaid claim costs relating to insurance contracts other than title insurance contracts, including estimates of costs relating to incurred but not reported claims, shall be accrued when insured events occur. (Paragraph 17)

The unpaid claims liability provides for all claims incurred during the accounting period that have been neither settled in cash nor paid. The company of course is unaware of the exact amount to be paid in the future; the final amount is unknown for claims reported and still pending. There are some incurred claims that have not yet been communicated to the insurer.

In this chapter the terms claim reserve and unpaid claims liability are used interchangeably.

SFAS 60 clarified and made specific the provisions of *SFAS 5*, "Accounting for Contingencies." Note that *SFAS 60* requires provision for adverse deviation in the assumptions chosen for benefit reserves. It makes no such requirement for claim reserves. *SFAS 5* defines the recognition and measurement of a liability for a future contingent event. Contingent future events can be probable, possible, or remote. This statement applies to most liabilities other than policy benefit reserves.

SFAS 5 says:

> An estimated loss from a loss contingency ... shall be accrued by a charge to income ... if both of the following conditions are met: a. ... it is probable that an asset had been impaired or a liability had been incurred at the date of the financial statements. ... b. The amount of loss can be reasonably estimated. (Paragraph 8)

Future payments on past incurred claims are probable and their amount can be reasonably estimated. *SFAS 5*, paragraph 4f, mentions future claims as a specific example of a liability. The amount can be reasonably estimated based either on historical records of claim payments or pricing assumptions. Although the process of setting claim reserves is inherently approximate, usually a single best estimate can be made. In some cases, only a range can be identified. The fact that an estimate would cover a range rather than a single point estimate does not imply that a reserve should not be carried.

10.9.2 Estimation of Claim Reserves

FASB Interpretation No. 14, "Reasonable Estimation of the Amount of a Loss: An interpretation of FASB Statement No. 5," indicates how an estimate should be made:

> When some amount within the range appears at the time to be a better estimate than any other amount within the range, that amount shall be accrued. When no amount within the range is a better estimate than any other amount, however, the minimum amount in the range shall be accrued. (Paragraph 3)

The appropriate claim reserve number is the best estimate of the obligation. Of course, actual experience will differ to a greater or lesser extent. Any such difference will have an effect in a subsequent accounting period. But prior-year financial statements are not restated; *SFAS 60*, states:

> Changes in estimates of claim costs resulting from the continuous review process and differences between estimates and payments for claims shall be recognized in income of the period in which the estimates are changed or payments are made. (Paragraph 18)

Claim reserves are intended for GAAP to be best estimates. There is no explicit requirement for conservatism (PAD) as there is in *SFAS 60* benefit reserves. In practice, some actuaries include a PAD either explicitly or implicitly by setting reserves toward the higher end of a range. Such PADs are not required and, if material, may be inappropriate.

10.9.3 Components of Claim Reserves

Claim reserves comprise (i) reported but unpaid claims (also referred to as *pending* or *in course of settlement*) and (ii) incurred but not reported (IBNR). DI claims that have been reported and for which payments are being made are usually called *open*. The term IBNR is often misused to refer to the entire unpaid claim liability.

The relative magnitude of the two components is a function of the type of risk and precision in benefit amount, the behavior of the policyholder, administrative timing, and many other issues. Smaller claims, or indemnity-benefit-related claims, are generally less complicated and tend to be reported and settled more quickly. Larger claims, expense benefits, or disability-benefit-related claims may be more complex to adjudicate and will exhibit longer reporting and settlement lags. Claims for which there is a high deductible or long waiting period may be subject to very long reporting lags that tend to increase the IBNR component of the liability. Disability income claims may be paid out over many years or even decades. For these claims the reported but unpaid portion of the liability tends to be large.

No liability is carried for claims that have been denied. Reasons for denial include ineligibility of the insured or the type of expense under contract terms. However, most companies would hold a liability for denied claims that are in dispute or being contested by the claimant.

10.9.4 Claim Reserves Based on Lag Tables

Medical benefits claims are typically settled within 12 to 24 months. In this situation lag tables are used to estimate the claim reserve. The term *lag table* is interchangeable with methods called *development*, *completion factor* or *claim triangle*. The claim reserve is the estimated amount of future payments to be made on claims already incurred. The initial working assumption is that future payment patterns will be similar to the recent past. Past claim payments are sorted according to the date incurred and the date paid. For medical business the grouping is monthly. For longer term claims (e.g., certain property/casualty lines of business) larger groupings such as quarterly or annual are used. The claim data can be examined to predict the percentage completion of payout based on payments to date on past incurred claims.

Many special adjustments may be necessary in predicting or estimating future claim payments. If contractual provisions have changed for recent policy issues, future payments may not follow historic patterns. Similarly, changes in administrative systems can have large temporary or permanent effects on the speed with which claims are processed. Historic patterns may indicate average claim payment lags very different than future patterns. Unless adjustments are made claim reserve estimates will be incorrect.

Special treatment is also necessary for large claims, whether reinsured or not. One or very few large claims can have a distorting effect on lags for most other claims. In some cases companies estimate reserves for very large claims on a case-by-case basis (hence *case reserves*). In this situation care is needed to avoid duplication of the claim reserve provision. This chapter does not cover claim reserve methods in any further detail; instead, only GAAP-specific issues are covered.

The data summarized by most companies can be sorted by incurred date, reported date, and paid date. If the lag table is based on the period from incurral to payment, the reserve calculated is the total unpaid claim liability, i.e., IBNR plus pending. This is perhaps the most common approach. GAAP reporting does not require separate presentation of IBNR and pending claims reserves; hence they are often calculated together. In some situations it is preferable to calculate the pending claim reserve seriatim, for example, for very large claims or very high deductible benefits. In such situations the IBNR would be calculated separately from pending claim reserves. This can be done using lag table methods provided the data are summarized by incurred and reported (as opposed to paid) date.

10.9.5 Claim Reserves Based on Pricing

For new blocks of business experience may be insufficient for lag table methods. In a typical situation, A&H claims require 12 months or more to be fully reported and paid; lag study methods would need 2 or 3 years of payment data for stable conditions to be reached such that credible reserve estimates may be made. For the first 2 or 3 years of a new block of business, other methods of estimation are appropriate. Such methods are commonly based on pricing. If pricing predicts a given loss ratio, the claim reserve would be set at the predicted loss ratio less actual cash claims paid. In this manner the company reports no more or less profit than anticipated in pricing.

When this method is used, the anticipated pricing loss ratio by policy duration should be reflected. Loss ratios are typically lower in the first few years than ultimately, due to either underwriting selection or the presumption of good health at the outset of the policy and antiselective lapsation over time.

10.9.6 Disability Income Benefit Claims

A number of special issues apply to disability income claims. These claims may pay out over a very long period, for example, from 90 days after the date of disability through age 65. As a result, (i) not all benefit payments accrue as of the claim incurral date; (ii) disability continuance tables are used instead of lag tables; (iii) the reserve is discounted for interest; and (iv) individual consideration is given to claimants.

In a typical DI claim, an accidental injury or diagnosis of a disease occurs on a clearly identifiable date. The claim incurral date is defined as first day of disablement to ensure that the disability continuance tables are used correctly in calculating the unpaid claim liability. Of course, if the policy provides for a 90-day elimination period, no contractual liability is incurred if the insured person recovers on the 89th day.

Most DI benefits are non-retroactive. For those that are, the benefit cost on the incurral date would include (in this example) 3 months of benefit. The insurer has an obligation to pay future monthly benefits contingent on the insured person remaining disabled. An estimate of the value of that obligation is made beginning at that point in time and for future periods as long as disablement continues.

The appropriate liability is based on a disability continuance table. The 1985 Commissioners Individual Disability table (85CIDA) is a statutory valuation table rather than a pricing table. It contains a built in provision for adverse deviation. It would be entirely appropriate for a company to use its own experience for GAAP purposes to the extent the underlying experience is credible. Disability tables are constructed from disability incidence and continuance rates. Incidence rates reflect the likelihood of the onset of disablement per 100,000 active lives at each attained age. Continuance rates reflect the likelihood of remaining disabled per 100,000 disabled lives at each attained age. Disability continues until terminated either by recovery or death. Disablement terminates rapidly in the first few days after onset because many disabilities arise due to relatively minor accidents or sickness. Disability terminations due to recovery tend to slow down over time, while terminations due to death increase with advancing age. A longer elimination period has a major effect in reducing DI claim costs due to the early recoveries.

An interesting phenomenon occurs due to the very rapid rates of recovery in early durations of disablement, followed by very slow rates of recovery among those who have been disabled for long periods. Among a group of 1000 persons disabled after 7 days, many will recover in the next

30 days. The present value of future benefits (or present value of amounts not yet due, PVANYD) reflects a very short average lifetime. Among a group of 1000 persons disabled after 3 years, many of those are permanently disabled; hence the determination of PVANYD reflects a long average lifetime. Thus the PVANYD changes with duration since the onset of disablement. It remains relatively low for the first few weeks or months, rises to a maximum after a few years, then declines as the end of the benefit period approaches. Figure 10-2 provides an example.

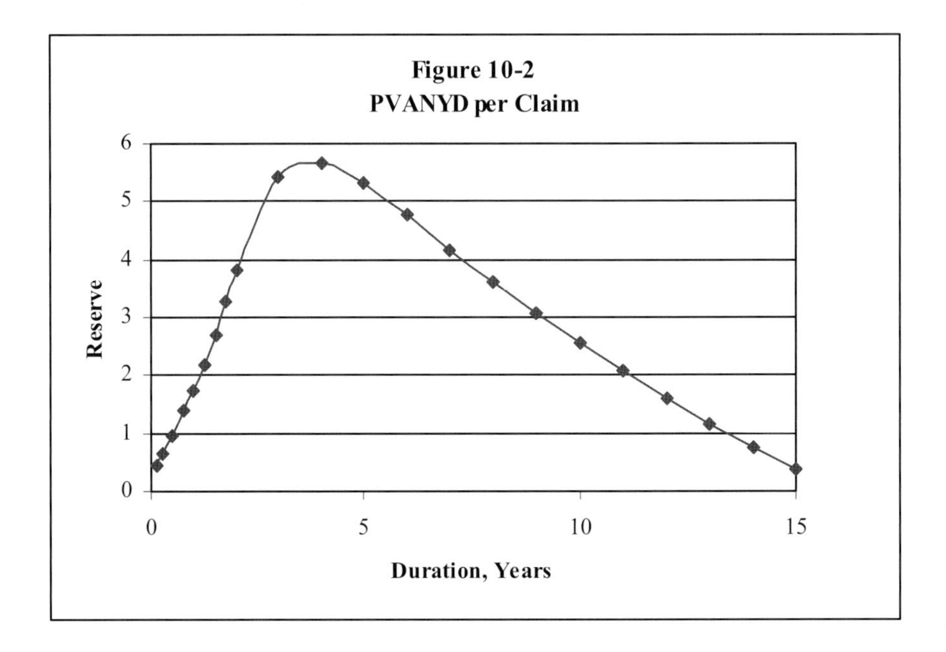

The unpaid claim liability for DI policies is primarily the present value of future benefit payments (also called PVANYD). The liability could include benefit amounts relating to past periods that have not yet been paid due to delays in reporting or processing. The PVANYD calculation is a projection of the value of an annuity in which payments are expected to continue while the insured remains disabled.

DI claims, especially those still open a year or more after disablement, are reserved by using disability continuance tables. Continuance tables indicate how many individuals remain disabled after various time intervals of continuing disablement. Actuaries should ensure that, if standard tables are used, appropriate adjustments are made to reflect expected company experience. Disablements within the first year or two may be reserved using nontabular methods, for example, based on the average multiple of monthly payments anticipated.

Unlike most other claim reserves, PVANYD is discounted at interest. *SAB 62* defines claim reserve discounting by property-casualty companies. This guidance also has been applied to life insurance companies. *SAB 62* indicates that there will be no objection to discounting claim reserves under the following circumstances:

> Discounting liabilities for unpaid claims and claim adjustment expenses at the same rates that it uses for reporting to state regulatory authorities with respect to the same claims liabilities, or
>
> Discounting liabilities with respect to settled claims under the following circumstances: (1) The payment pattern and ultimate cost are fixed and determinable on an individual claim basis, and (2) The discount rate used is reasonable based on the facts and circumstances applicable to the registrant at the time the claims are settled. (Page 3)

Thus DI claim reserves and claim adjustment expense reserves appropriately may be discounted, either at the statutory rate or at a "reasonable" rate. Discounting of medical claims, which are mostly paid off in less than one year, is not a common practice. It would likely have a very minor effect and, depending on the circumstances, may not be permissible under *SAB 62*. A portfolio earned investment rate as of the claim incurral date would be a reasonable rate, and this is the most common approach. It could be reasoned that a current investment rate is appropriate and should be used to ensure that the claims reserve is "best estimate," although this approach is rarely seen.

In addition to reported claims, there may be unreported DI claims as of the end of the accounting period. The company should make an estimate of IBNR claims based on reasonable assumptions including past experience as to the reserve required. The reserve will comprise payments that will have accrued as of the reporting date as well as the PVANYD.

For policies on which claim reserves are held (disabled lives), the underlying policy contract normally remains in force. In many cases the basic policy has a premium waiver rider that pays the premiums necessary for the policy to remain in force. In any event, if the policy remains in force, benefit reserves are still held to provide for future incurred claims. It is acknowledged that for total and permanent disability where the policy benefit period runs to age 65 or for lifetime, it would be unlikely that a new claim would be incurred. However, disability incidence rates are typically based on data for all policies in force, whether active or disabled. A benefit reserve held for only those policies with truly active lives may be inadequate.

10.9.7 Claim Settlement Expenses

The cost of paying claims is a substantial part of an insurer's administrative costs. Such costs are referred to as claim settlement expenses or loss adjustment expenses (LAE). As mentioned above, benefit reserves should provide for future benefits and the expenses of settling such claims. Benefit costs to be incurred in the future should be provided for, regardless of whether the claims have been incurred. Similarly, claim reserves should provide not only for unpaid claims, regardless of whether reported, but also the associated costs of settling those claims. The requirement for a reserve for expenses of settling claims is established in *SFAS 60*:

> A liability for all costs expected to be incurred in connection with the settlement of unpaid claims (claims adjustment expense) shall be accrued when the liability for unpaid claims is accrued. (Paragraph 20)

These costs are defined to include:

> ... costs associated directly with specific claims paid or in the process of settlement, such as legal and adjusters' fees. Claim adjustment expenses also include other costs that cannot be associated with specific claims but are related to claims paid or in the process of settlement, such as internal costs of the claims function. (Paragraph 20)

LAE expenses may be allocated or unallocated. These reserves are commonly estimated by measuring claim adjustment expenses over an observation period of 1 to 3 years relative to claim payments made in the same period. The LAE ratio is then applied to the claim reserve to derive the LAE reserve estimate.

LAE for DI policies are typically calculated as a percentage of the unpaid claim reserves; hence they are implicitly discounted also.

10.10 Reinsurance

Reinsurance is commonly used to transfer risk of loss in the event of large claims. Reinsurance is rare with supplementary coverages but is common with comprehensive major medical policies or long-term disability policies. Comprehensive major medical policies may provide coverage up to $2 million or more; DI policies with $10,000 of monthly benefit could pay benefit amounts of $2 million or more for a disablement lasting 20 years. The direct writing insurer often will seek reinsurance coverage.

Reinsurance coverage typically is excess of loss coverage. Coinsurance of medical coverages is rare. DI reinsurance may use extended wait provisions in which the reinsurer applies what is in effect a very long elimination period (e.g., 5 years) before coverage takes effect. There would commonly be a coinsurance element (e.g., 25%) to the limit of the benefit period.

Expense allowances should be established as an unearned revenue liability in accordance with *SFAS 113*. Expected reinsurance benefits on future claims are calculated similarly to benefit reserves and held as an asset. The calculation should reflect the contractual benefits reinsured (e.g. deductibles, co-payments, maximums, and waiting periods). Assumptions chosen should be consistent with the corresponding assumptions used for the direct business. Similar morbidity tables should be used unless there is evidence to support different experience for the reinsured benefit amounts.

If the amounts are immaterial, the direct writing company's DAC and reserves may be shown net of reinsured amounts.

Reinsurance recoveries on incurred claims are held as a receivable asset. These are sometimes calculated on a lag table basis. On the other hand, reinsurance is typically used for very large and hence relatively infrequent claims. It is possible to establish reinsurance recoveries for these claims on a case-by-case basis.

Reinsurance is covered in more detail in Chapter 17.

10.11 Riders

A&H policies can include riders that tailor contractual benefits to the insured person's specific needs. Riders can be issued at the initial policy effective date or later, subject to underwriting or other conditions. Examples of riders include benefit increase riders, accidental death, and premium waiver.

10.11.1 Types of Riders

Benefit increase riders are added to increase benefits on indemnity-type policies. Hospital confinement policies pay a fixed benefit amount that may become inadequate if medical cost inflation persists. As an example, a rider may provide an additional $50 per day of hospital confinement benefit for an additional premium. The rider becomes part of the policy.

Accidental death benefits (ADB) or accidental death and dismemberment (ADD) riders provide fixed amounts (the principal sum) of coverage payable on the death or loss of a limb or eyesight. Typical principal sums range from $25,000 to $100,000 or more.

The waiver-of-premium rider provides for payment of premiums on behalf of the policyholder while he or she is disabled.

DI policies offer many optional riders. Examples are partial disability, residual disability, cost-of-living riders, and Social Security supplements.

Residual disability benefits are partial benefits intended to allow the disabled policyholder to return to work part time or on a trial basis following a period of disability. The residual benefit provision eliminates the disincentive of completely losing benefits under the policy when the policyholder returns to work. Otherwise, a disabled policyholder may postpone returning to active work until recovery is absolutely complete for fear of losing benefits or a relapse. Some actuaries price this benefit very inexpensively on the grounds that it encourages earlier return to work for many policyholders; thus benefits paid under the provisions of this optional benefit are believed to be offset in part by lower benefits paid under the provisions of the basic policy.

Partial disability riders allow for payment of partial benefits while the policyholder is partially disabled without the condition of prior total disablement. Thus a sickness or injury may force a policyholder to work only part time thus losing part of his or her income. As with the residual disability rider, the part of the maximum benefit paid is proportional to lost earnings.

An attractive feature on many disability income policies is the cost-of-living adjustment (COLA) rider. Benefits increase each year during disablement by a stated amount (e.g., 5 percent) or proportionate to the consumer price index.

Social Security supplement riders integrate payment of benefits with those paid by the Social Security Administration (SSA). SSA benefits are sizable enough that over-insurance would exist in many cases but for the integration of basic policy benefits. Thus part of the monthly benefit to which the policyholder is entitled when disabled is contingent on SSA benefits not being paid. This benefit is of course less expensive than the noncontingent benefit. SSA benefits are more difficult to qualify for than private insurance because the condition of disablement is defined strictly:

> ... individual has a disability so severe as to be unable to engage in any Substantial Gainful Activity; medically determinable physical or mental condition, expected to continue for at least 12 months or to result in prior death.

Also the elimination period is 5 months or more. Thus there is a chance that SSA will not pay although the insurer is paying.

10.11.2 Reserving for Riders

The main reserving challenge for A&H riders is identification of the appropriate morbidity for benefit reserves. Rider design can be creative and unique hence standard tables may not be available. Pricing assumptions with a provision for adverse deviation are appropriate to use but are not always available or accurate.

Other assumptions should be consistent with those for the base policy, including interest rate, mortality, and persistency.

Rider expenses may be unique. Expenses allocated on a per-policy basis are not applicable to riders, but commissions and certain administrative expenses are applicable. Appropriate reserving for riders is important, because they may be a significant source of profit to the insurance company.

Reserving for premium waiver riders on DI policies usually involves the benefit reserve factors for the base policy. The reserve for the premium waiver is a proportional increase to the reserve for the monthly benefit. Some premium waiver riders are retroactive, while most DI benefits are not; a minor increase to the reserve would be appropriate. Reserving for riders is covered in more detail in Chapter 18.

10.11.3 Return of Premium Riders

This type of rider includes return-of-premium riders, cash value riders, and cash surrender riders. They are collectively referred to as ROP riders. Other than from ROP riders, most A&H policies have no cash surrender or other nonforfeiture benefits.

Many different ROP rider designs are possible. In most cases they provide for a return of cumulative premiums paid—both rider and base policy premiums—after 10 to 25 years. The return of premiums normally does not include interest. On surrender before the end of the rider term a partial benefit is payable, based on a scale that runs from 0 to 100%. Ten-year riders may include a restart provision in which a new period begins every 10 years. ROP riders provide for a carve-out of benefits paid under the base policy. In other words, benefits under the rider are reduced by the amount of health insurance benefits paid under the policy. The idea behind ROP riders is to encourage policy persistency, to discourage minor claims, and to provide a nonforfeiture benefit. ROP riders may be attached to DI or other types of A&H policies.

The ROP rider premium is usually expressed as a percentage of the base policy premium. The increase in premium over the base policy is substantial, in some cases 100% of the base premium, depending on the terms of the rider. However, the policyholder is virtually guaranteed some benefit regardless of health.

Accurate pricing of the ROP rider is complex. The rider may attach to different types of policies and actual experience may vary from that expected. For both of these reasons the actual benefit carve-out under the rider may vary over a wide range. In other words, the ROP rider may pay different benefits even when attached to policies with identical premiums and expected loss ratios because different morbidity tables (for example, DI versus hospital indemnity) have different slopes by attained age.

Different types of benefit also have different distributions of claims by size. This has ROP rider implications too. Average claim costs cannot be used in estimating the benefit carve-out. Average claim costs are made up of certain policies with no claims whatsoever, certain policies with claims between zero and the sum of premiums paid, and other policies with claims that exceed all premiums. The last category contributes heavily to average claim costs, yet the ROP benefit never falls below zero. In pricing the rider, the benefit stream is greater than predicted by average claim costs. Each of the three scenarios must be considered to derive a weighted average ROP benefit payout.

Reserving involves similar issues. Benefit reserves must be based on the expected payout of ROP claims, which include base policy premiums. The expected payout benefit is similar to a pure endowment at the end of the rider term in an amount equal to a multiple of cumulative premiums paid, typically without interest, less prior claims. Prior claims, as mentioned above, depend on the underlying base coverage and are complex to model. Further, the valuation assumption for prior claims paid will inevitably vary from actual experience. Reflecting actual prior claims is not a violation of the lock-in principle and is preferred to an approach that does not reflect actual experience.

Because of the complexity of modeling different streams or alternatives, simplified approaches are commonly used. For example, ROP benefit reserves can be calculated in two stages, first, assuming no carve-out of prior claims (which is very conservative), and second, deducting actual prior-claim payments on the corresponding policies. The deduction should not exceed cumulative premiums on a seriatim basis. The net effect should be conservative because it ignores potential claim offsets in future years.

Although it is beyond the scope of this book, many states have specific statutory reserving requirements for ROP riders.

Chapter 11 Credit Insurance

11.1 Description of Coverages

Credit insurance includes insurance coverage sold in conjunction with consumer credit loan transactions. The purpose of these coverages is to ensure that the borrower can meet the obligations to repay the outstanding loan balance in cases in which death, disability, or unemployment of the borrower might make this difficult or impossible. Ultimately, credit insurance protects the financial interests of both the lender and the borrower.

Credit insurance is frequently written to accompany loans for automobile and other large consumer purchases such as appliances. Consumers also purchase credit insurance coverage to insure repayment of the balance on their credit cards. Many loans, such as car loans, specify the repayment period and amount at the inception of the contract.

Other loan or credit arrangements, such as for credit cards, are more open-ended and may provide for repayment periods or amounts that cannot be specified at contract inception. For credit cards, the repayment period is a fixed time (usually 40 months or less) measured from the current credit card statement date, and the minimum payment is defined by the terms of the borrower's credit card.

Basic credit insurance coverage sold by life insurance companies insures a policyholder for death or disability. For both types of coverage, the amount of insurance coverage at any time is usually a function of the outstanding loan balance (i.e., "net" coverage) or the remaining loan payments (i.e., "gross" coverage). There are other credit-related coverages, generally provided by riders to the standard credit life or credit disability insurance. An example is critical illness coverage, which pays off all or a portion of a loan insured with credit life when the insured has a specified medical condition, usually cancer. Critical illness benefits are analogous to accelerated benefits riders attached to traditional life and universal life contracts. Insurers may offer bundled credit coverage including certain property and casualty benefits such as unemployment together with death or disability benefits.

Credit life insurance generally pays off the borrower's remaining balance on a loan or credit card upon death. As a result, the amount of life insurance provided varies over time. For loans with specific repayment periods and amounts, the amount of life insurance frequently is net coverage and decreases according to a loan amortization schedule. Otherwise, the amount of the life insurance on a gross coverage basis and is the sum of the remaining loan payments.

For credit card coverage, the amount of credit life coverage is generally the current credit balance, which varies with the borrower's buying and repayment practices. Although not common, some credit life policies have provided for level death benefits at all policy durations.

Credit disability insurance pays a limited number of monthly payments to the lender on a loan or credit card if the insured becomes disabled. For loans with specific repayment periods, the payment made by the insurer is the monthly payment owed by the borrower to the lender. For credit cards, the payment made by the insurer is usually the minimum monthly balance as specified by the credit card terms. As long as the insured remains disabled, the insurer continues to make the monthly payments to the lender until the loan is extinguished or some shorter fixed time elapses. Those credit disability policies that pay the disability for only a fixed period of time are called critical period contracts.

Insurance companies typically collect premiums for credit coverage on a single pay or monthly premium basis. Single-pay contracts provide for a refund if a borrower prepays a loan prior to its contractual term. The payment of a refund terminates any remaining term of the insurance contract.

Property and casualty companies also issue credit insurance coverages to borrowers. These include warranty, credit disability and unemployment. In addition, banks and other lending institutions provide similar credit related coverages directly to borrowers as part of a loan transaction. These banking products are referred to as debt cancellation products. Typical debt cancellation products provide accidental death, unemployment and disability coverage. The rest of this chapter will not discuss the accounting for these other credit and debt cancellation products, although the GAAP accounting for the property and casualty credit products is covered by the same standards that apply to credit life and accident coverages. The GAAP accounting for the debt cancellation coverages is governed by the standards applying to finance companies.

11.2 Overview of GAAP for Credit Insurance

GAAP for credit insurance contracts is governed by the requirements of *SFAS 60*, "Accounting and Reporting by Insurance Enterprises." Credit insurance contracts are generally classified as short-duration contracts under *SFAS 60* because they provide "for insurance protection for a fixed period of short duration" (paragraph 7). The underlying accounting principle of *SFAS 60* is that accounting benefits, expenses, and profits should be recognized as a level percentage of premium revenues over the life of a book of business.

For short-duration contracts such as credit, *SFAS 60* does not have a requirement to calculate policy reserves but does have a requirement to recognize premium "as revenue over the period of the contract in proportion to the amount of insurance protection provided" (*SFAS 60*, paragraph 9). Instead of policy reserves, *SFAS 60* requires that unearned premium reserves for credit insurance. Unearned premium reserves allow premium revenue to be recognized in proportion to the expected amounts of benefits. In contrast, a policy reserve provides for benefits and policy maintenance expenses in proportion to premium revenues. Regardless of the approach (unearned premium or policy reserves), the goal is to recognize benefits, expenses and profits as a level percentage of premium revenues.

In calculating GAAP unearned premium reserves for credit contracts, the effect of interest is ignored. There is no provision for the risk of adverse deviation. Although many single-pay credit contracts have refund-of-premium provisions, they are ignored in the calculation of unearned premium reserves. Because unearned premiums are released at the time of a refund, there may be an accounting gain or loss due to the difference between the refund amount and the reserve. Finally, the unearned premium reserves reported for credit contracts are based upon collected gross premiums.

11.3 Actuarial Calculations

11.3.1 Unearned Premium Reserves

As stated above, *SFAS 60* requires an unearned premium reserve for credit coverage. However, the guidance does not specify the methods to be used in determining the unearned premium reserves. For credit life, the AICPA *Audit and Accounting Guide* provides additional guidance on how premium revenues (and unearned premium reserves) should be recognized:

> Premiums from short-duration contracts ordinarily are recognized as revenue over the contract term or period of risk, if different, in proportion to the amount of insurance protection provided. (Paragraph 7.18)

This has been interpreted as requiring the use of the "rule of 78" method to calculate GAAP unearned premium reserves for single-pay credit life contracts, and, in practice, this has usually been the case. For monthly-premium credit life contracts, the unearned premiums are based upon a mid-month assumption or are calculated to the day.

Calculating unearned premium reserves with a rule of 78 pattern assumes that the coverage in each period decreases on a straight-line basis from the beginning of the contract until the end. A formula for a rule of 78 unearned premium can be derived as follows, where:

G = Gross single premium
t = Time left to run (in months)
n = Term of coverage (in months).

Unearned premium with t (complete) months left to run is:

$$G\left[\sum_{s=1}^{t} s \Big/ \sum_{s=1}^{n} s\right] = G\left[t(t+1)/n(n+1)\right]$$

If a mid-month assumption is chosen for months left to run, then the unearned premium for $t - 0.5$ months left to run becomes:

$$G\left[t^2/n(n+1)\right]$$

An example of the rule of 78 for single pay gross credit life coverage is presented in Table 11-1.

Table 11-1
Development of Unearned and Earned Premium
Single Premium Credit Life Plan Using Rule of 78 Earnings Pattern

(1) Policy Month	(2) Months to Run	(3) Premium (BOM)	(4) Remaining Coverage (BOM)	(5) Unearned Premium (BOM)	(6) Earned Premium	(7) Percentage of Total Premium Earned
0	12	10	1200	10.00		
1	11		1100	8.46	1.54	15
2	10		1000	7.05	1.41	14
3	9		900	5.77	1.28	13
4	8		800	4.62	1.15	12
5	7		700	3.59	1.03	10
6	6		600	2.69	0.90	9
7	5		500	1.92	0.77	8
8	4		400	1.28	0.64	6
9	3		300	0.77	0.51	5
10	2		200	0.38	0.38	4
11	1		100	0.13	0.26	3
12	0		0	0.00	0.13	1

Legend:
BOM = beginning of month
EOM = end of month
(1) Time in months
(2) Number of months left to run of coverage
(3) Policyholder gross premium, paid at beginning of year
(4) Remaining coverage on a gross basis
(5) Unearned premium at beginning of month based upon rule of 78 = $(3)_0 \times [(2)_t \times \{(2)_t + 1\}] / [(2)_0 \times \{(2)_0 + 1\}]$
(6) Earned premium = BOM unearned premium less EOM unearned premium = $(5)_{t-1} - (5)_t$
(7) Percentage of total premium earned during month = $(6)_t / (3)_0$

For credit disability, paragraph 7.18 from the *Audit and Accounting Guide* cited above suggests that premium revenues should be recognized in reasonable relationship to the anticipated claims. In practice for single-pay credit disability contracts, this has usually been interpreted as requiring the use of the mean of the rule of 78 and the pro-rata methods to calculate GAAP unearned premium reserves. An insurer should be able to support the pattern used. For monthly-premium credit disability contracts, the unearned premiums are based upon mid-month assumptions or calculated to the day.

Calculating unearned premium reserves with a pro-rata pattern assumes that the coverage in each period is the same. A formula for a pro-rata unearned premium can be derived as follows, where:

G = Gross single premium
t = Time left to run (in months)
n = Term of coverage (in months).

The pro-rata unearned premium basis with t (complete) months left to run is:

$$= G\left[\sum_{s=1}^{t} 1 \Big/ \sum_{s=1}^{n} 1\right] = G\left[t/n\right]$$

If a mid-month assumption is chosen for months left to run, then the pro-rata unearned premium for $t - 0.5$ months left to run becomes:

$$= G\left[(t - 0.5)/n\right]$$

The mean of the rule of 78 and the pro-rata (based upon complete months to run) is equal to

$$0.5\left\{G\left[t(t+1)/n(n+1)\right]\right\} + 0.5\left\{G\left[t/n\right]\right\}$$

The mean of the rule of 78 and the pro-rata (based upon mid-month assumption) is equal to

$$0.5\left\{G\left[t^2/n(n+1)\right]\right\} + 0.5\left\{G\left[(t - 0.5)/n\right]\right\}$$

An example of the mean of the rule of 78 and pro-rata for single pay credit disability is shown in Table 11-2.

Table 11-2
Development of Unearned and Earned Premium
Single Premium Credit Disability Plan Using Mean of Rule of 78 and Pro-rata Earnings Pattern

(1) Policy Month	(2) Months to Run	(3) Premium (BOM)	(4) Remaining Coverage (BOM)	(5) R78 Unearned Premium	(6) PR Unearned Premium	(7) Unearned Premium (BOM)	(8) Earned Premium	(9) Percentage of Total Premium Earned
0	12	30	1200	30.00	30.00	30.00		
1	11		1100	25.38	27.50	26.44	3.56	12
2	10		1000	21.15	25.00	23.08	3.37	11
3	9		900	17.31	22.50	19.90	3.17	11
4	8		800	13.85	20.00	16.92	2.98	10
5	7		700	10.77	17.50	14.13	2.79	9
6	6		600	8.08	15.00	11.54	2.60	9
7	5		500	5.77	12.50	9.13	2.40	8
8	4		400	3.85	10.00	6.92	2.21	7
9	3		300	2.31	7.50	4.90	2.02	7
10	2		200	1.15	5.00	3.08	1.83	6
11	1		100	0.38	2.50	1.44	1.63	5
12	0		0	0.00	0.00	0.00	1.44	5
	Average Coverage		650					

Legend:
BOM = Beginning of Month
EOM = End of Month
(1) Time in months
(2) Number of months left to run of coverage
(3) Policyholder premium, paid at beginning of year
(4) Remaining coverage on a gross basis; average coverage = sum of remaining coverage divided by 12
(5) Unearned premium at beginning of month based upon Rule of 78 = $(3)_0 \times [(2)_t \times \{(2)_t + 1\}] / [(2)_0 \times \{(2)_0 + 1\}]$
(6) Unearned premium at beginning of month based upon pro-rata = $(3)_0 \times [(2)_t] / [(2)_0]$
(7) Unearned premium based upon the mean of the Rule of 78 and pro-rata = $0.5 \times [(5)_t + (6)_t]$
(8) Earned Premium = BOM unearned premium less EOM unearned premium = $(7)_t - (7)_{t-1}$
(9) Percent of total premium earned during month = $(8)_t / (3)_0$

If the expected pattern of claims is not matched by an earnings pattern based upon the mean approach, then a more appropriate pattern based upon expected claims experience should be used. A company should be prepared to demonstrate that its own experience supports the use of a different earnings pattern for premiums. Once an earnings pattern has been established for a block of business, that pattern is locked-in at issue and used throughout the remaining lifetime of the block. Although *SFAS 60* only describes the lock-in principle for the liability for policyholder benefits for long duration contracts, it is accepted practice that this principle also applies to the unearned premium reserve for short duration contracts accounted for under *SFAS 60*.

For those policy benefits provided by rider, the gross premium (if any) associated with that rider is included with the gross premium used to determine the unearned premium reserve for the base policy coverage for credit life or disability.

11.3.2 Deferred Acquisition Costs

SFAS 60 permits the capitalization and amortization of acquisition costs for credit contracts. For most credit insurance contracts the primary acquisition cost is commissions. In general little or no underwriting is performed on credit insurance, and as a result, there are usually minimal underwriting expenses to capitalize. Premium taxes are usually included in the acquisition expenses to be amortized.

Paragraph 29 of *SFAS 60* requires that "acquisition costs shall be capitalized and charged to expense in proportion to premium revenues recognized." For single-pay contracts, this is accomplished by determining total acquisition costs at issue as a percentage of the gross single premium. For each subsequent reporting period, the remaining unamortized acquisition cost asset is equal to this percentage times the remaining unearned premium reserve. Because of the method used to determine this unamortized acquisition cost asset, it is sometimes referred to as the "equity in the unearned premium reserve." The amount of expense amortization recognized in each period after issue is equal to the level acquisition cost percentage calculated at issue times the premium earned in the period. Examples of a deferred acquisition cost asset are shown for a single pay credit life contract Table 11-3 and for a single pay credit disability contract in Table 11-4.

It is not typical to capitalize and amortize acquisition costs on monthly premium policies beyond the equity in the unearned premium reserve that would be calculated with the unearned monthly premium. Commissions are generally level for these contracts, and the contract term is generally short, usually a month.

Table 11-4
Development of DAC and GAAP Profit
Single Premium Credit Disability Plan Using Mean of Rule of 78 and Pro-rata Earnings Pattern

(1) Policy Month	(2) Months to Run	(3) Premium (BOM)	(4) Remaining Coverage (BOM)	(5) Acquisition Expense (BOM)	(6) Unearned Premium (BOM)	(7) Earned Premium	(8) DAC (BOM)	(9) Disability Benefits (EOM)	(10) Maintenance Expense (EOM)	(11) Investment Income at 7.00%	(12) GAAP Profit
0	12	30	1200	10	30.00		10.00				
1	11		1100		26.44	3.56	8.81	1.11	0.71	1.2	1.8
2	10		1000		23.08	3.37	7.69	1.05	0.67	1.1	1.6
3	9		900		19.90	3.17	6.63	0.99	0.63	0.9	1.4
4	8		800		16.92	2.98	5.64	0.93	0.60	0.8	1.3
5	7		700		14.13	2.79	4.71	0.87	0.56	0.7	1.1
6	6		600		11.54	2.60	3.85	0.81	0.52	0.5	0.9
7	5		500		9.13	2.40	3.04	0.75	0.48	0.4	0.8
8	4		400		6.92	2.21	2.31	0.69	0.44	0.3	0.7
9	3		300		4.90	2.02	1.63	0.63	0.40	0.2	0.5
10	2		200		3.08	1.83	1.03	0.57	0.37	0.1	0.4
11	1		100		1.44	1.63	0.48	0.51	0.33	0.1	0.3
12	0		0		0.00	1.44	0.00	0.45	0.29	0.0	0.2
Average Coverage			650								

Legend:
BOM = beginning of month
EOM = end of month
(1) Time in months
(2) Number of months left to run of coverage
(3) Policyholder premium, paid at beginning of year
(4) Remaining coverage on a gross basis
(5) Acquisition costs, paid at beginning of year
(6) UPR based upon the mean of the rule of 78 and pro-rata (from Table 11-2)
(7) Earned premium = BOM unearned premium – EOM unearned premium = $(6)_{t-1} - (6)_t$
(8) DAC = UPR × (acquisition expense/single premium) = $(7)_t \times (5)_0 / (3)_0$
(9) Disability benefits at end of month = the sum of 1/2 of the remaining coverage at BOM and 1/2 of the average coverage times 1.2/1000 per month
(10) Maintenance expense = 0.2 × earned premium
(11) Investment income = interest × (BOM unearned premium less BOM DAC) = $0.07 \times [(6)_t - (8)_t]$
(12) GAAP profit = $(7)_t + (8)_t - (8)_{t-1} - (9)_t - (10)_t + (11)_t$
This display ignores the effect of refunds

Table 11-3
Development of DAC and GAAP Profit
Single Premium Credit Life Plan Using Rule of 78 Earnings Pattern

(1) Policy Month	(2) Months to run	(3) Premium (BOM)	(4) Remaining Coverage (BOM)	(5) Acquisition Expense (BOM)	(6) Unearned Premium (BOM)	(7) Earned Premium	(8) DAC (BOM)	(9) Death Benefits (EOM)	(10) Maintenance Expense (EOM)	(11) Investment Income at 7.00%	(12) GAAP Profit
0	12	10	1200	4	10.00		4.00				
1	11		1100		8.46	1.54	3.38	0.29	0.31	0.4	0.7
2	10		1000		7.05	1.41	2.82	0.26	0.28	0.3	0.6
3	9		900		5.77	1.28	2.31	0.24	0.26	0.2	0.5
4	8		800		4.62	1.15	1.85	0.22	0.23	0.2	0.4
5	7		700		3.59	1.03	1.44	0.19	0.21	0.2	0.4
6	6		600		2.69	0.90	1.08	0.17	0.18	0.1	0.3
7	5		500		1.92	0.77	0.77	0.14	0.15	0.1	0.2
8	4		400		1.28	0.64	0.51	0.12	0.13	0.1	0.2
9	3		300		0.77	0.51	0.31	0.10	0.10	0.0	0.1
10	2		200		0.38	0.38	0.15	0.07	0.08	0.0	0.1
11	1		100		0.13	0.26	0.05	0.05	0.05	0.0	0.1
12	0		0		0.00	0.13	0.00	0.02	0.03	0.0	0.0

Legend:
BOM = Beginning of Month
EOM = End of Month
(1) Time in months
(2) Number of months left to run of coverage
(3) Policyholder premium, paid at beginning of year
(4) Remaining coverage on a gross basis
(5) Acquisition costs, paid at beginning of year
(6) Unearned premium at beginning of month based upon Rule of 78 (from Table 11-1)
(7) Earned Premium = BOM unearned premium – EOM unearned premium = $(6)_{t-1} - (6)_t$
(8) DAC = UPR × acquisition costs / single premium = $(6)_t \times (5)_0 / (3)_0$
(9) Death benefits at end of month = remaining coverage at BOM times 0.24/1000 per month
(10) Maintenance expense = 0.2 × earned premium
(11) Investment Income = interest × (BOM unearned premium less BOM DAC) = $0.07 \times [(6)_t - (8)_t]$
(12) GAAP profit = $(7)_t + (8)_t - (8)_{t-1} - (9)_t - (10)_t + (11)_t$
This display ignores the effect of refunds

11.3.3 Recoverability and Loss Recognition

The accounting requirements for assessing recoverability or loss recognition for short-duration contracts such as credit insurance are different than the requirements for contracts defined as long duration contracts under *SFAS 60*. The test for recoverability or loss recognition on short duration contracts is defined in *SFAS 60* as follows (where it is referred to as a premium deficiency):

> A premium deficiency shall be recognized if the sum of expected claim costs and claim adjustment expenses, expected dividends to policyholders, unamortized acquisition costs, and maintenance costs exceeds related unearned premiums. (Paragraph 33)

Premium deficiency tests for short duration contracts are usually done with undiscounted values, although *SFAS 60* does not prohibit the use of present value measures. However, if an insurer chooses to use discounted values in determining a premium deficiency, it will have to disclose the practice in the GAAP financial statements (see *SFAS 60*, paragraph 60e).

Recoverability refers to assessing a premium deficiency at issue and loss recognition to the same process at times subsequent to issue. Insurers need to be able to demonstrate that they have no premium deficiencies in either case. If a premium deficiency exists on a short duration contract, *SFAS 60* requires:

> ... a premium deficiency shall be first be recognized by charging any unamortized acquisition costs to expense to the extent required to eliminate the deficiency. If the premium deficiency is greater than the unamortized acquisition costs, a liability shall be accrued for the excess deficiency. (Paragraph 34)

If an additional liability is accrued for the excess deficiency as described, it should be released in a manner consistent with the recognition of earned premium.

Other aspects of the testing and recognition of recoverability and loss recognition may be relevant to GAAP for credit insurance. However, they are not discussed in this chapter. For more detail, consult Chapter 3.

11.3.4 Claim Reserves and Loss Adjustment Expense Reserves

Credit insurance is subject to the requirements of *SFAS 60* for claim reserves and loss adjustment expense (LAE) reserves. The requirement for claim reserves is stated in *SFAS 60*:

> A liability for unpaid claim costs relating to insurance contracts other than title insurance contracts, including estimates of costs relating to incurred but not reported claims, shall be accrued when insured events occur. (Paragraph 17)

In this chapter the term claim reserve shall be used in lieu of liability for unpaid claim costs.

The requirement for LAE reserves is stated in *SFAS 60*:

> A liability for all costs expected to be incurred in connection with the settlement of unpaid claims (claim adjustment expenses) shall be accrued when the liability for unpaid claims is accrued. (Paragraph 20)

SFAS 60 clarified and made specific the provisions of *SFAS 5*, "Accounting for Contingencies." Both claim reserves and LAE reserves are loss contingencies under the definitions of *SFAS 5*. FASB *Interpretation 14*, "Reasonable Estimation of the Amount of a Loss: An Interpretation of FASB Statement No. 5," provides guidance on how loss contingencies should be estimated:

> When some amount within the range appears at the time to be a better estimate than any other amount within the range, that amount shall be accrued. When no amount within the range is a better estimate than any other amount, however, the minimum amount shall be accrued. (Paragraph 3)

For claim and LAE reserves, Paragraph 3 requires that best estimate values be accrued for GAAP. No margin for adverse deviation is required.

Claim reserve estimates can be viewed as having two components, reported but unpaid (also referred to as pending) and incurred but not reported (IBNR). However, there is no requirement that claim reserves be split in this fashion for GAAP, and, in practice, claim reserves are frequently estimated in total.

In practice, credit life claim reserves are generally developed for both pending and IBNR. Pending claim reserves are usually the sum of all reported and approved claims. The benefits payable for each claim are determined by the terms of the insurance contract and, for most credit life claims are equal to the outstanding balance on the insured loan or credit card at the time of the insured's death.

IBNR claims for credit life are generally estimated by trending the experience from prior periods. For example, one common technique is to divide the IBNR claims (as reported subsequently) for some prior time by some exposure or inforce base at that time. A typical exposure or inforce base might be total face amount in force or total claims paid in the prior year. By analyzing the trend in these ratios over time, a reasonable estimate can be developed for the current period by multiplying the trended ratio times the current in force or exposure amount.

Lag methods are sometimes used to estimate credit life claim reserves. These methods require that prior claim history be tracked by date of incurral and by date of payment and, accordingly, the method is only credible for large blocks of business with a significant claims history. When credit life claim reserves are estimated with a lag method, the resulting claim reserve estimate includes both the pending and the IBNR. If it is necessary to split a lag estimate for credit life into pending and IBNR, it is normally accomplished by subtracting an estimate of the pending claims from the total lag estimate; the results an estimate of the IBNR reserve.

Credit disability claims are generally paid in installments. As a result, credit disability claim reserves are commonly estimated with lag methods. As already mentioned, lag methods require that prior claim history be tracked by date of incurral and by date of payment. The resulting claim reserve liability estimate includes an estimated amount for both the pending and IBNR claims.

Credit disability claim reserves are sometimes developed with separate estimates for pending and IBNR. When this is done, the pending reserves are usually estimated with a disability table. However, there is no industry table for credit disability. In most practical situations, an industry table for individual disability is used instead. The most current individual disability table is the 1985

CIDA. The 1964 CDT table has also been used, and a company's own experience can be used to develop a disability table for claim reserves estimation. *SFAS 60* states:

> The liability for unpaid claims shall be based on the estimated ultimate cost of settling the claims ... using past experience adjusted for current trends, and any other factors that would modify past experience. (Paragraph 18)

Such other factors that might modify past experience would include seasonality, regional unemployment experience, the impact of lump sum settlements and a shifting risk profile, such as the lengthening of auto loans from 3 year to 4 to 5 year periods.

The use of industry disability tables does not guarantee that claim reserves based upon those tables will provide appropriate claim reserves for any particular company. To demonstrate adequacy companies must continue to monitor the appropriateness of both the methods and assumptions used to determine claim reserves. This monitoring can be performed by a number of different approaches. Many involve the recasting of prior period claim reserve estimates in light of actual historical experience.

Because of the installment nature of credit disability claims, estimating IBNR tends to be more difficult for credit disability than it is for credit life. Trending experience on IBNR claims from prior periods is delayed until the payment of those earlier IBNR claims is substantially completed. As a result, IBNR can be estimated with methods more elaborate (and judgmental) than those used for credit life IBNR. One method that can be used to estimate credit disability IBNR is to first estimate the number of expected IBNR claims and then to multiply that estimated count by an estimate of the average claim. Other approaches have been based upon expected loss ratios.

Companies frequently use tabular methods to estimate pending reserves when claim reserves must be split and reported for a large number of separate entities, for example, when separate financial statements are reported for each writing agent. In these cases, adequacy of total claim reserves can be tested with a lag method. Any differences between total claim reserve estimated with a lag method and the total reserves based upon a tabular approach for pending and a separate approach for IBNR are usually reflected in an overall adjustment to the IBNR reserves.

SFAS 60 does not specifically address the discounting of credit life and health claim reserves. However, SEC *Staff Accounting Bulletin (SAB) 62* (Section N) does address the issue of discounting claim reserves for property-casualty companies. The guidance in Section N has also been applied to life insurance companies. In particular, *SAB 62* indicates that there will be no objection by the SEC to a company discounting claim reserves under the following circumstances:

> Discounting liabilities for unpaid claims and claim adjustment expenses at the same rates that it uses for reporting to state regulatory authorities with respect to the same claim liabilities, or
>
> Discounting liabilities with respect to settled claims under the following circumstances:
>
> (1) the payment pattern and ultimate cost are fixed and determinable on an individual claim basis, and
>
> (2) the discount rate used is reasonable based upon the facts and circumstances applicable to the registrant at the time the claims are settled. (Page 3)

SAB 62 permits the discounting of claim reserve liabilities for settled claims when the future costs are fixed and determinable. This would support discounting of pending credit disability claim reserves because claims to be paid are fixed amounts paid on an installment basis. *SAB 62* would permit the discounting of pending credit life claim reserves, but in practice this is rarely done because the effect is immaterial due to the generally short payment lag for credit life claims.

In choosing an interest rate to discount claim reserve liabilities, *SAB 62* permits the use of the rate being used to discount statutory reserves or a reasonable rate based on the company's circumstances at the time the claims are settled. For credit disability this could be an interest rate based upon those assets deemed to support the claim liabilities at the time claim payments begin.

When pending credit disability claim reserves are discounted, the reserve estimate is generally based upon a disability table. In practice, credit disability claim reserves are not usually discounted when lag methods are used. However, the language of *SAB 62* would not seem to prohibit this practice.

LAE reserves are required for credit insurance contracts by *SFAS 60*, which defines claim adjustment expenses to include:

> ... costs directly with specific claims paid or in the process of settlement, such as legal and adjusters' fees. Claim adjustment expenses also include other costs that cannot be associated with specific claims but are related to claims paid or in the process of settlement, such as internal costs of the claims function. (Paragraph 20)

For credit coverage, LAE reserves are generally estimated by adding all the appropriate expenses over a recent time (frequently 1 to 3 years) and dividing by the claim payments made during the same time. The resulting LAE ratio is then multiplied by the current claim reserve balance to derive the LAE reserve estimate. The method used to calculate the LAE ratio just described tends to overstate the LAE liability if a large part of the LAE expenses are incurred when a claim is first established. If this is the case, suitable adjustments are made to the LAE ratio calculation.

11.4 Reinsurance

Standard forms of reinsurance are used with credit insurance coverages. However, many credit insurers have profit sharing arrangements with the organizations (producers) who sell the credit insurance contracts that involve the establishment of producer-owned insurance companies. In these sorts of arrangements, the direct writer will generally enter into a coinsurance treaty that will cede most of the business sold by the producer to the producer-owned company. The direct writing company will then retain only a small of amount of risk. The direct writing company may still provide many of the administrative functions for the reinsurer and will be reimbursed for these functions as part of the expense allowances paid by the reinsurer under the terms of the reinsurance treaty. See Chapter 17 for detail on accounting for reinsurance.

Chapter 12 Group Insurance, Large Case Pension Liabilities and Related Liabilities

Group contracts are sold to employers or other representatives of groups of individuals rather than to the individuals themselves. As with individual policies, group contracts can cover either insurance risk or aid in asset accumulation. Insurance risks are mortality, morbidity, and disability. Asset accumulation is provided through group pension contracts (including group annuities and Immediate Purchase Guarantee contracts) and guaranteed investment contracts. Individuals pay premiums or make contributions to the contract; the employer or group contractholder may make such payments on their behalf. These are the group plans discussed in this chapter.

Group UL and 401(k) plans are not covered in this chapter. Under these contracts, individual accounts are tracked for members of the group. They are similar to individual coverages; the chief exception is group billing arrangements. Financial reporting for these contracts is similar to financial reporting for the corresponding individual contract.

12.1 Group Life and Health Coverages

12.1.1 General Characteristics

Group life and health insurance is issued through a master policy to the policyholder. The policyholder can be an employer, a multiemployer trust, a credit union, another creditor type, an association formed for a purpose other than obtaining insurance, or some other discretionary group. A certificate of coverage is issued to each insured.

Group life and health insurance covers a wide variety of products. The permissible types of group insurance are typically dictated by the laws of the state in which the group master policy is issued. A typical large carrier of group life and health will often provide up to four general categories of coverage, as follows:

(i) Group life insurance, including the following types (not all-inclusive)

- Group term life insurance for active employees
- Group term life insurance for retired employees
- Group paid-up life insurance purchased for active employees
- Group survivorship income
- Accidental death and dismemberment
- Waiver of premium on total and permanent disability

(ii) Group disability insurance, including the following types (not all-inclusive)

- Short-term disability
- Long-term disability

(iii) Group medical, dental, and vision insurance

(iv) Group long term care insurance.

Group term life insurance on active lives is the most common form of group life insurance. It is put into effect via group underwriting, using simplified criteria such as an actively-at-work requirement at the enrollment date and face amounts of insurance based on a uniform multiple of monthly salary.

Premiums are generally monthly, although quarterly, semiannual, and annual frequencies are sometimes utilized. At the beginning of each contract year, a census of the group is taken. Attained-age premium rates are applied to the corresponding face amounts of coverage by attained age to produce a weighted average premium rate per $1,000 of total face amount. The weighted average monthly premium rate for the group is then applied to the total face amount. Each individual pays the same premium rate per $1,000.

Large groups are usually experience rated. Experience rating can be regarded as profit sharing. It takes both retrospective and prospective forms. Retrospective experience rating takes the form of a dividend or a rate credit against the premium currently payable based on the experience of the prior contract year. Prospective rating is the calculation of the prospective premium rate for the contract year about to begin. Often the retrospective rate credit is credited to a premium stabilization fund, which earns interest, and against which excess claims over a stipulated percentage of premium can be charged.

Experience rating can utilize notional experience accounts that can be positive or negative. An experience account for a group case generally takes the form of an accumulating notional fund, to which premiums and interest are added, and claims, expense charges, profit charges and refunds (or dividends) are subtracted. Depending on the terms of the contract, claims may include the increase in unpaid claim liability. In this situation adjustments are contractually permitted if the actual claim payout differs from the liability accrued.

It is possible for an experience account to be in a negative (or deficit) position. If the contract holder cancels the policy while in deficit, the insurer is subject to a loss. For this reason it is common for all coverages in a group contract to be combined for experience rating. For example, life coverage may show gains, while health or disability coverages show losses. Aggregating these experience refund accounts reduces the insurer's risk.

Small groups may or may not be experience rated. Experience for small groups fluctuates more than for large groups; thus the experience refund may be very volatile. For small groups some pooling of experience is common. For the smallest groups, fixed rates may apply with no experience refund.

Group life insurance is almost always offered to spouses, children, and other dependents. Employee coverage is sometimes subsidized with an employer contribution to the premiums. Dependent coverage is usually not subsidized.

Group life insurance is often extended to retired employees, typically in reduced amounts. It can be via simple additions to the employee census for a period or in the form of deposits to special contingency funds established over time from which group term life insurance premiums for retired employees are paid. Again, typical premium frequency is monthly. Retired life reserves are not treated in this chapter.

Group paid-up life insurance is another form of advance provision for life insurance on retired lives. It is no longer a common form of group life insurance and is not dealt with in this chapter.

Group survivorship income is group term life insurance in a form other than a lump sum. When a group life insured dies, an income is payable to the spouse during his or her lifetime, often only until remarriage.

Accidental death coverage pays an amount over the basic sum insured in the event of accidental death. The amount of coverage is usually the same as or less than the basic group term life coverage. Dismemberment is generally offered with this coverage at a fixed percentage of the accidental death face amount.

Waiver-of-premium benefit is a common additional benefit to the basic group term life insurance coverage. On proof of total and permanent disability, group life premiums are waived for the duration of such disablement (until recovery or death) even after the group master policy terminates.

Comprehensive group medical, dental, and vision insurance coverage declined in popularity in the 1990s in favor of managed care benefits or self-insured (administrative services only) plans. Under managed care, monthly premium payments go through the plan to the provider of health-care services. The provider is at risk for excessive utilization of medical services. Under self-insured plans, the employer is at risk for excessive utilization of medical services. A health insurer provides administrative services, such as eligibility and claim settlement. Under partially self-insured plans, the employer is at risk for certain claims but has various forms of annual stop-loss insurance coverage on individuals (specific stop-loss) and/or on groups (aggregate stop-loss). Specific and aggregate stop loss reinsurance are discussed in Section 12.1.7.

Group long-term-care insurance is a product popular with retirement communities and with employer groups. Group Medicare Supplement coverage is issued to associations and retirement communities. The economics and administration of these certificates are more closely akin to that of individual policies and should be so treated under GAAP.

The following two variations of the typical group merit mention:

- Group insurance is not restricted to large groups (generally considered to be 50 or more lives). Small-group coverage is common. Small-group plans tend to be less customized to the group and typically are subject to individual underwriting.

- In addition, some groups are groups in name only. For example, group "wrapper" master policies with individual certificates are close to individual policies in terms of economic performance and contract conditions. Association group policies, franchise policies, and some group trust policies may fall into this category. The wrapper may provide for group billing only. The administration and financial reporting for the certificates is closely akin to that of individual policies.

The discussions that follow deal with the large group life and health policy that is renewable annually with the consent of both parties, usually at renegotiated rates. Small-group insurance GAAP accounting would by-and-large follow the accounting approaches mentioned below for large groups. The group "wrapper" master policies should be dealt with from a GAAP treatment perspective as if each certificate were an individual policy.

12.1.2 Active Life and Unearned Premium Reserves

The group life and health insurance contract is a short-duration contract. As such, generally, there is no advance funding of future claims or expenses, and no liability for future policy benefits exists. There may be situations in which limited underwriting selection occurs. In that event, the actuary may wish to consider whether a provision should be made.

Gross unearned premiums are held as a liability for active lives in the group. *SFAS 60* states:

> Premiums from short-duration contracts ordinarily shall be recognized as revenue over the period of the contract in proportion to the amount of insurance protection provided. (Paragraph 13)

Example 12.1
Unearned Premium Calculation

Premium mode	Quarterly
Modal premium	\$600.00
Case anniversary	November 1, 2000
Statement date	December 31, 2000
Unearned premium	\$600 × 30/90 = \$200.00

Simple proportionality is the calculation rule.

Thus, because the risk over the premium coverage period tends to be level, an unearned premium reserve is generally held such that the premium is earned ratably over the period for which the premium is collected. This results in straight-line premium recognition over such period.

In the common case of monthly premium frequency in which premiums are due and payable on the first day of each month, no unearned premium is held. To be consistent with this treatment, any premium paid in advance of the due date should be recognized fully as a liability for advance premiums until the due date.

12.1.3 Expense Capitalization

Acquisition expenses are generally low compared to individual life insurance acquisition expenses. This is partly because underwriting is relatively simple and partly because compensation to the sales force is usually not a heaped commission as with individual life insurance. Also, acquisition and maintenance expenses tend to recur in level amounts over time.

To the extent such acquisition expenses exist, they should be determined as appropriate in the guidance as presented in Chapter 3. To properly match acquisition expenses with revenue, such acquisition expenses should be timed with earned premiums. *SFAS 60* stipulates:

> If acquisition costs for short-duration contracts are determined based on a percentage relationship of costs incurred to premiums from contracts issued or renewed for a specified period, the percentage relationship and the period used, once determined, shall be applied to applicable unearned premiums throughout the period of the contracts. (Paragraph 30)

Thus, for example, if acquisition expense is equal to 15% of premiums collected, then a deferred policy acquisition cost (DPAC) of 15% of unearned gross premiums should be established as an asset. Obviously, in the case cited above of monthly premium business due on the first day of the month, no DPAC would be established in instances in which no unearned premium has been established.

Example 12.2
Calculation of DPAC

Use data from Example 12.1:

Unearned premium	$200.00
Acquisition expense percentage	15%
DPAC = 15% of 200.00 =	$ 30.00

Chapter 3 refers to expenses that may have future utility, a concept that applies in group insurance occasionally. AICPA *SOP 98-5*, "Reporting on the Costs of Start-Up Activities," addresses the concept of costs associated with substantial future utility. Its paragraph .05 defines such costs as "those one-time activities related to opening a new facility, introducing a new product or service, conducting business in a new territory, conducting business with a new class of customer, initiating a new process in an existing facility, or commencing some new operation." Its paragraph .12 provides guidance for the accounting of such costs: "Costs of start-up activities, including organization costs, should be expensed as incurred."

12.1.4 Claim Reserves

SFAS 60 refers to claim cost recognition in paragraphs 17 though 20 and, in doing so, speaks to the liabilities required to be held in order to recognize such cost. The following components of unpaid claims are mentioned as required to be established:

- Incurred but not reported claims (IBNR) (paragraph 17)
- Unpaid claims in excess of IBNR (paragraph 17)
- Claim adjustment expenses (CAE), when unpaid claims are accrued, including "internal costs of the claims function" (paragraph 20).

Methodology must be based on the estimated ultimate cost of settling the claims (including the effect of inflation and other societal and economic factors, per paragraph 18). There is no explicit requirement to include a provision for adverse deviation.

Methodology for determination of estimated unpaid claims is not specified beyond the above. However, depending on the product, there are four general approaches to determination of the unpaid claims amount, varying by product type:

- For group life and accidental death and dismemberment claims, the process is relatively simple. Death claims usually are relatively few, are reported quickly, and are clearly defined as to the amount of benefit. Unpaid claims are easily inventoried. IBNR is generally established based on historical studies. CAE is generally not held except at times in the case of resisted claims or those not yet approved. Survivorship benefits follow this approach, except that the commuted value of such benefits is used in place of the face amount in the development of these liabilities.

- For long-term disability income, a table of disability termination rates is used and periodically updated. Reserve factors are developed from those termination rates and a suitable interest rate, to be applied to the monthly indemnity amounts. The IBNR is generally based on such tabular factors modified for company experience, as is the liability for claims in course of settlement.

- For group life waiver-of-premium benefit, factors are generally applied based on standard tables of net single premiums for disabled lives. Such factors are used, with differing modification factors, for claims approved, claims in course of settlement, and IBNR, based on historical studies.

- For all other coverages mentioned above, except for short-term disability at times, a reserve development, or lag table, approach is used, similarly to the approach used for loss reserves in property/casualty insurance. The unpaid claims liability is typically not broken out between IBNR and the balance of the unpaid claims liability.

For short-term disability, either a tabular method or a reserve development approach tends to be used.

Because this is short-term coverage, the lock-in principle does not apply. It is appropriate to update assumptions to reflect changing best estimates as experience emerges, even on in-force disabled blocks of business.

In the situation in which a new contract is issued, there may not be enough experience to apply lag tables. The actuary may determine unpaid claim reserves based on pricing loss ratios. In the example shown in Example 12.3, a new type of contract has been issued for a period of less than one year. In this example, the incurred loss ratio exactly equals the pricing assumption.

Example 12.3
Claim Reserve Calculation Using Pricing Assumption Loss Ratio

Earned premiums during the year	$1,000,000
Pricing loss ratio	75%
Cash claims paid to date	$100,000
Apparent loss ratio	10%
Unpaid claim liability	$650,000
Incurred claims to date	$750,000

12.1.5 Premium Deficiency Reserves

Recoverability testing is appropriate for group life and health. The test performed compares the total of the loss ratio, the maintenance expense ratio, and the acquisition expense ratio to 100% of the premium. If the loss ratio total indicates that the product is profitable, then any DPAC asset held is recoverable. In the case of a recoverability problem, the first step is to write down the DPAC so that the ratio becomes 100%. The next step, once DPAC is eliminated, is to test whether the maintenance expense plus the loss ratio is over 100%. To the extent that there remains an excess over 100%, it is necessary to establish a premium deficiency reserve for such excess. As mentioned above, DPAC is not common on true group business.

Example 12.4
Recoverability Testing with Positive Results

Use data from Example 12.1:

Unearned premium	=	\$200.00. No guarantees thereafter.
Loss ratio	=	60%
Acquisition expense	=	15%
Maintenance expense	=	17%
Total	=	92%

Recoverability is demonstrated.

A premium deficiency reserve funds any projected losses in advance. This applies to the entire premium guarantee period, even if it extends beyond the current contract year.

Example 12.5
Recoverability Testing with Need to Write Down DPAC

Identical to Example 12.3, but loss ratio = 75%

Combined ratio = 75% + 15% + 17% = 107%

Write down DPAC to 8% (which is the 15% DAC less the 7% premium deficiency) of unearned premium

Example 12.6
Recoverability Testing, with Need to Eliminate DPAC and Establish Premium Deficiency Reserve

Identical to Example 12.3, but loss ratio = 95%

Combined ratio = 95% + 17% = 112%

Premium deficiency reserve = 12% of unearned premium

Note, if guarantees extend to future premiums, the premium deficiency reserve is increased by 12% of those future premiums plus future acquisition expense on those future premiums.

Investment income may exist in substantial amounts on unpaid claim liabilities or unearned premium reserves. If needed, companies have used such investment income in determining recoverability. The premium deficiency reserve testing as shown in the above examples has not considered the use of investment income.

12.1.6 Reserve for Accrued Experience Refunds

A liability must be held for the accrued portion of the experience refund based on the experience of the group contract year to date. Thus, at the statement date a partial year's worth of experience refund is held where experience shows a gain. This is true despite the fact that an experience refund is not fully accrued until the contract year expires.

As mentioned earlier, the experience refund is affected by the amount of incurred claims, which is affected in turn by the level of unpaid claim liability. In the case of a fully experience-rated contract, the insurer bears little if any risk. An increase or inaccuracy in the unpaid claim liability is offset by the accrued experience refund. Of course, the actuary should use the same unpaid claim liability in the financial statements as in the determination of the accrued experience refund. Alternatively, the experience refund reserve could be restated to reflect the level of claim reserves reported in the financial statement.

Generally, an asset is not established for cases where the accrued experience refund is in a deficit position. Because the contractholder does not owe the amount of the deficit position to the life insurer, the company should not consider it an asset. The deficit position would not be an asset unless there was an enforceable right of collection.

Interesting issues arise when an insurer carries many group contracts or many coverages within a single contract. Some contracts may be in a surplus position, while others are in a deficit position. It seems preferable to carry liabilities for accrued experience refunds for those cases in surplus, but not to offset the liability for assumed recovery of deficits. An appropriate exception to this rule is the situation in which many group contracts are associated with a family of companies. In this case if the insurer has the right of offset of deficits against surpluses, the experience refund liability should reflect the offsets.

12.1.7 Specific and Aggregate Stop-Loss Reinsurance

Specific and aggregate stop-loss reinsurance (S&A) is a special type of policy generally provided to employers. It is called reinsurance, but it is group insurance sold directly to self-insuring employers.

Specific stop-loss coverage insures medical claims above a specific limit, typically $5,000 to $25,000 per claim, or more. Smaller claims are self-insured by the employer, using an insurer or third-party administrator in an administrative capacity only. The enabling legislation for these employer self-insured plans is the Employee Retirement Income Security Act (ERISA); hence the basic self insurance coverage is not regulated as insurance. Individual claims over the specific attachment point are covered by the insurer. The incurral period is a 12-month policy year. The time period during which claim payments are recorded is 15 months beginning coincident with the policy year and ending 3 months after it. This provision limits the insurer's exposure to late reporting of claims and encourages the renewal of the coverage. Such a provision would be characterized as "12/15" coverage—other provisions may include 12/12 or 12/18.

Aggregate stop-loss coverage is an overlaid coverage. If the employer's aggregate benefits net of specific stop-loss insurance exceed a predetermined level, or "attachment point," the reinsurer pays the excess. The attachment point is commonly a multiple, such as 125%, of expected claims. The combination of specific and aggregate stop-loss coverage protects the employer from risks due either to very large claims or high frequency of claims.

The insurer charges a rate each year that is intended to provide for benefits, expenses, and profits. The rate increases each year in accordance with inflation. Specific stop-loss rates typically increase rapidly with inflation due to the leverage effect of the high deductible. An explanation of this phenomenon is included in Chapter 10, Table 10-1.

Reserving issues are similar to those of other groups with some special considerations, including high rate inflation, relatively fast reporting of claims, and the difficulty of predicting claims under aggregate coverage.

12.1.8 Other Considerations

Group medical coverages are provided by an employer to the employee and dependents. In some situations, for example, a working spouse with group coverage of his or her own, overlapping coverages may exist. Group contracts typically provide coverage for the primary insured(s) and take a secondary payor role for the spouse. Where overlapping coverages exist, claim settlement can be complex. Recoveries by one insurer from another may occur several months or more after the original claim. Subrogation, or coordination-of-benefits, payments should be considered in determining claim liabilities for both reported and unreported claims.

Long-term disability coverages may provide for offsets with Social Security disability benefit payments. The interaction can be complex, with different elimination and benefit periods. The actuary should reserve for the full group contractual benefit, less an offset for the expected coordinated benefits from the government.

Group insurance is not commonly reinsured. However, where reinsurance exists, all appropriate reporting entries should be made, including unearned premium reserves, active life reserves, premium deficiency reserves, DAC equity in the unearned premium, and unpaid claim liabilities, in accordance with *SFAS 113*, "Accounting and Reporting for Reinsurance of Short-Duration and Long-Duration Contracts."

12.2 Large Case Pension Liabilities and Related Liabilities

12.2.1 General Characteristics

Much of the size of the life insurance industry, as measured by assets, is attributable to large case pension funding and similar contracts. These contracts are characterized by large deposits, typically in millions of dollars, from pension plans, municipalities, and other government agencies, as well as others seeking the high rates of return coupled with strong guarantees available from life insurers.

Large case pension liabilities can be categorized into two broad classes:

- Guaranteed investment contracts (GICs) and funding instruments, under which a pension plan administrator or other large institutional investor seeks an investment with a reasonable yield and the safety of an insurance company contract. Most of these products are essentially pure investment contracts under the *SFAS 97* and *SOP 03-1* definitions, because they contain neither significant mortality guarantees nor sources of profit other than interest margins. A major exception is the case where there are no funding assets on the balance sheet of the insurance company, such as in synthetic GICs, which are discussed below.

- Group master pension contracts, with certificates for the participants.

The attractive features of large case pension plans relative to individual pension plans are similar to those of group insurance relative to individual plans:

- Simplicity of administration.
- Mitigation of antiselection at time of annuitization. For a typical group pension contract, there is a mix of both healthy and unhealthy lives annuitizing, and thus the pricing of life annuities can afford to be more liberal.
- More efficient investment of the supporting assets, due to both the size of the funds involved and the experience-rating nature of the contracts.

12.2.2 GICs and Funding Agreements

Historically, many of these deposits come from entities that are not taxpayers, such as pension plans and municipalities. These types of contracts, unlike life insurance and annuities, do not enjoy special status under the Internal Revenue Code. The investment income (cash value build up) is not tax-deferred. As a result, they do not offer tax advantages when compared to competing products of banks, mutual funds, or others. Despite this fact, a significant portion of new deposits is from business enterprises that are taxpayers.

This type of product is popular because it enjoys favorable accounting treatment for the depositor. The depositor carries the contract as an asset at its amortized cost rather than market value, which reduces the volatility on its balance sheet.

These products come in many varieties and, because state insurance laws generally do not require that the forms be filed and approved by regulators, can be tailored to fit a particular client situation. The products fall into a few general types.

The most common type is the fixed-rate GIC, which guarantees the principal value of the deposit and a rate of interest to the end of a specified period. Other forms guarantee principal and provide an indexed return. Term periods vary, with three to five years being common.

Other arrangements, frequently referred to as funding agreements, provide similar guarantees of principal but operate on a much shorter-term period with respect to crediting rates, frequently less than a year and sometimes in days or months. Such funding arrangements are expected to roll into renewal periods and to be on deposit with the insurer for a total period that ultimately may be similar to those of GICs. Funding agreements generally relate to assets that pension plan sponsors or other depositors do not expect to need in the foreseeable future. With the short guarantee periods and with an appropriate investment strategy, interest rates can be kept current with market interest rates for short-term financial instruments. Crediting rates are frequently expressed as spreads to London Inter-Bank Overnight Rates (LIBOR).

A third form is simply a guarantee issued relative to a specified, appropriately structured set of assets held in trust, with ownership retained by the client. The guarantee is intended to provide the advantages of a GIC without obligating the insurance company to take over ownership and administration of the investments. These contracts are commonly referred to as "synthetic GICs." Insurers are naturally very restrictive about the nature of the investments held in trust and the anticipated cash flows.

Other contract features relate to flexibility regarding additional deposits and withdrawals. Contracts sold to 401(k) plans generally allow additional deposits as plan participants make additional contributions to their accounts. 401(k) plans exist under the eponymous section of the Internal Revenue Code. They permit savings to be invested tax-free until withdrawal, subject to certain conditions. Similarly, these accounts allow a certain amount of benefit-responsive withdrawals according to the pension plan's need to fund participant withdrawals. These contract provisions are generally structured to keep these additional deposits and withdrawals within the bounds that an insurer can tolerate to manage its asset/liability risk.

A key feature of GICs and funding agreements relates to premature contract terminations. Some contracts do not allow cash surrenders; the deposits are available only when the contract matures. More commonly, contracts provide cash surrenders with a market value adjustment. A typical surrender value would be the lesser of book value or market value. The usual surrender provisions notwithstanding, contracts may allow for surrender at book value if the insurer's ratings are lowered. Such provisions arose because the rating of the insurance company is an important consideration in the selection of an insurer.

From the insurer's perspective, the contracts represent deposits for which the insurer provides the stipulated investment performance. As such, the insurer's obligation is to the pension plan, municipality, or institutional depositor. The funds may ultimately be allocated, for example, to 401(k) plan participants, but the allocation is not a responsibility of the insurer under the contract. The insurer may or may not play a role in the plan administration. For example, under a GIC related to a 401(k) contract, the participants do not have individual deposits with the insurer. Rather, their contributions to the 401(k) plan are commingled and deposited with the insurer. The GIC is an asset of the 401(k) plan.

The contracts described above are all obligations of the general account of the insurer. Some variations on the GIC and funding agreements involve separate accounts, which put the contract holder at risk for investment results. Some variable contracts, particularly some forms found in Canada, provide guaranteed floors to the values at specified dates or even minimum accumulation rates over a period of time.

12.2.3 Group Master Contract Pension Plans

Group pension contracts generally fall into five general categories (with some outliers): (1) Deferred Pension Annuity Contracts; (2) Deposit Administration Contracts; (3) Pension Fund Administration Contracts; (4) Pension Participating Contracts; and (5) Terminal Funding Contracts.

Deferred Pension Annuity Contracts are basically group annuity contracts in which the premium amounts and annuity benefits are calculated to provide an annuity coverage equal to the pension plan benefit. Investment, mortality, and expense risk is transferred completely and permanently to the life insurer with each deposit, subject to the rights of the master contract holder to cancel and surrender. Premiums are paid on a periodic basis in an amount sufficient to increase the annuity benefit equal to the increase in pension under the pension plan with each according increase in the annuitant's creditable service. There is normally an accounting entry for each individual annuitant on an allocated basis. Deferred Pension Annuity Contracts are primarily designed for the immediate purchase of benefits. Certain benefits, such as past service and supplemental benefits, are usually purchased at retirement by a lump sum payment. In sum, these contracts have the following characteristics:

- All funds are used to purchase annuities.
- Retirement benefits are funded through units of single premium deferred annuities.
- Immediate purchase of benefits.
- Past service and supplemental benefits may be purchased at retirement by lump sum.
- Insurer accumulates a contingency reserve and controls the rate at which actuarial gains (re: guaranteed rates) are credited to the plan, which usually reduces the premium.
- Optional unallocated fund (with interest) to support lump sum purchases.
- Contract holder directs distribution between annuities and unallocated fund.
- No liquidation provision in the event of termination. Typically goes to a non-participating form of annuity in the event of termination

Deposit Administration (DA) Contracts have a deposit fund into which all contributions are placed. These contracts are designed to provide the plan sponsor with the ability to purchase guaranteed annuities for retirees and to maintain unallocated funds to which interest is credited at guaranteed rates and from which guaranteed expense fees are withdrawn by the insurer. The unallocated funds are maintained not only for the purchase of annuities but also for other benefits under the pension plan. Under a DA contract, the purchase of all plan benefits is delayed until retirement. Other payments, such as disability benefits and refunds of employee contributions, are generally disbursed from the contract's unallocated fund. Some contracts may provide for the purchase of disability benefits. When a member retires, money to purchase the benefits is withdrawn from this fund and an annuity contract is purchased. Because the interest rates and annuity purchase rate guarantees are generally conservative, the insurance company typically pays an experience refund to the deposit fund. Experience rating is done using the entire contract fund. Some DA contracts provide that part or all of the employer contributions to the plan may be invested in separate accounts rather than in the deposit fund. In sum, these contracts have the following characteristics:

- Insurer guarantees principal and interest and a set of guaranteed annuity purchase rates for monies in general investment account.
- Insurer guarantees expenses.
- Annuities are purchased at retirement from an unallocated fund.
- Contract holder directs unallocated funds to a general or separate account.
- Insurer accumulates a contingency reserve and controls rate at which actuarial gains are credited to the plan—usually credited to contract.
- Benefits are purchased at retirement.
- Unallocated fund used for other payments (e.g., disability benefits, refunds of employee contributions).
- Withdrawals from DA fund via installment payments (5–10 years) require no market value adjustment.
- Lump sum payments require adjustment to reflect current market value and value is paid in full discharge of insurer's liabilities. If withdrawal requests are considerable from all contract holders, insurer may have cash flow clause permitting delay of payment of cash.
- Experience rating based on entire DA fund, excluding any Separate Account monies.

Thus group DA pension plans are pension contracts that provide for the employer to contribute to an interest-bearing account (DA Fund), from which immediate annuities are payable at retirement.

Pension Fund Administration Contracts, also referred to as Pension Fund Investment Contracts, or Investment Facility Contracts (PICs), are designed to allow the plan sponsor to avail itself of the insurance company's payment services without having to pay for mortality guarantees. Benefits may be provided under a PIC contract but they are usually not guaranteed and are usually not maintained. Any benefits and employee contribution refunds are disbursed from the contractual fund. PIC contracts provide for the purchases of annuities for benefits at discontinuance at the contract holder's discretion. This contract contains amendment, termination, and cash-out provisions similar to deposit administration contracts.

- Policyholder may use general account and separate account investment facilities of unallocated fund.
- May purchase annuities for retired employees or utilize other insurer services.
- No guarantee of principal and interest or general account monies.
- Schedule of annuity purchase rates.

Pension Participating Contracts (Immediate Participation Guarantee, or IPG, Contracts) are designed to allow the plan sponsor to avail itself of the insurance company's mortality, interest, and expense guarantees, payment capabilities, and investment expertise at the same time the contract holder participates directly in the contract's experience with respect to mortality, expenses, and interest. Like a DA contract, an IPG contract has a deposit account into which employer contributions are paid. Pension benefits provided under an IPG contract are paid directly from the fund monthly as they become due while the contract is in force rather than by purchasing an annuity. The basis for annuity purchase rates is guaranteed, but annuities are not usually purchased at retirement unless the contract is discontinued. Because the insurer guarantees that a retirement benefit will be provided, a required minimum balance is maintained by the contract holder and appropriate statutory reserves are held by the insurer. Retirement benefits, as well as disability payments and refunds of employee contributions, are treated as disbursements from the contractual fund. If the contract discontinues, retirement annuities are purchased for all retired lives. This contract contains amendment, termination, and cash-out provisions similar to DA contracts. In sum, IPG contracts have the following characteristics:

- Guaranteed annuity gross premium rates (significant only in the event of termination).
- Unallocated account invests in general account or separate accounts.
- Guarantee of principal and interest is optional for the general account portion of unallocated fund.
- Minimum balance maintained by the insurer in order to guarantee retirement benefits.
- Direct participation of contract holder in contract's experience (mortality, expenses, and interest).
- All expenses charged to unallocated account or direct billed.
- Periodic valuations performed to ensure sufficiency fund for plan benefit payments.
- Benefits paid directly from fund during contract's existence.

A terminal funding (or pension plan closeout) case arises because the employer wishes to divest itself of all pension plan obligations under his current plan, and it turns the agreed-upon monies over to the insurance company. The insurance company takes on the obligations for individuals currently retired and receiving income, plus the obligations for those actively employed individuals with currently vested future pension benefits. Terminal funding typically utilizes a nonparticipating single premium group annuity contract designed to take over the liability of a terminating pension plan. For retired lives, the contract is simple. For a single premium, the insurer will take over benefit payment as of a given date. In the case of terminated vested lives, where a life-contingent, deferred annuity benefit is involved, the contract must provide many of the pre-retirement benefits provided by the plan. These usually include early retirement benefits using plan factors (usually subsidized when compared to the insurer's normal retirement date annuity purchase rates), death benefits, spouse's benefits, and alternative optional forms of income. The contract is usually issued to the trustee or employer, and certificates are issued to the individual annuitants or employees.

12.2.4 Accounting for Liabilities

As can be seen, one common attribute of these contracts is that, other than purchased immediate life annuities and vested deferred life annuities, which generally fall under the scope of *SFAS 60* and are covered in Chapter 9, the liabilities do not expose the insurance company to significant mortality or morbidity risk. Rather, they are classified as investment contracts under guidance found in *SFAS 97*. For the simpler forms in the general account, the accounting for the obligation is fairly simple. The insurance company's liability is classified as policyholders' deposits and carried at the nominal account value. For other contracts the accounting is not as simple. As discussed below, GICs held in separate accounts can present some challenges. The related assets and liabilities are recorded along with other separate account items rather than with policyholders' deposits. Typically, separate account liabilities equal separate account assets, unless there is seed money in the separate account.

There is no specific GAAP guidance for the valuation of synthetic GIC liabilities; hence, practices vary in the industry. One approach is to accumulate a portion of the fees each year as a provision for future benefits, with the release of the provision over time as contracts mature or as it becomes apparent that the provision is more than sufficient for the likely outcome. Perhaps the most common approach is to hold no reserve. This approach presumes that the likelihood of a claim is remote and that the fees represent profit and contingency charges, which should be recognized and realized in the period in which received. Should the situation arise in which a loss situation had been identified, the appropriate liability could be accrued at that time.

When there are performance guarantees, the value of the liabilities may not be limited to the value of assets. As a general practice, the guarantees have traditionally not affected the valuation of liabilities when they have been "out of the money." When "in the money," additional liabilities have often been held. A contract is "in the money" when the value of the investments is below the floor guarantee and the policyholder has the right to surrender for an amount greater than the variable account value or when the variable account value is below the guaranteed minimum accumulation value. The simplest approach has been to value the additional liability as the excess of the floor over the asset value. Another possibility was to calculate the option-adjusted value of the contract and record the liability as the greater of the variable account value or the option-adjusted value. Option-adjusted value refers to a present value that reflects not only the single most likely future scenario, but also many other scenarios in which the contract holder exercises various rights and options. The additional liability is a liability of the general account, and the expense of providing the liability is charged to income through increase in reserves. The promulgation of *SOP 03-1*, effective in 2004, has formalized requirements as described below.

Some group pension contracts may entail annuitization guarantees in excess of the lump sum cashout benefits. Under *SOP 03-1*, the AICPA Accounting Standards Executive Committee (AcSec) concluded that *SFAS 97*, Paragraph 7, could be interpreted to apply only to testing for mortality risk and "not to preclude recognition of a liability." The guidance from the SOP, Appendix A, Paragraph A.39, prohibits accounting as if annuitization were elected, but "acknowledges existence of price risk inherent in the annuitization option."

Also under consideration was whether annuitization options, as elective benefit options, should be accounted for as written options. This approach was rejected in favor of a ratable approach to generation of the annuitization liability, as described in Paragraphs 31 to 33 of the SOP. That is, the value of elective annuitization options at any statement date should be calculated as follows:

Calculate a Benefit Ratio, equal to (i) divided by (ii), where:

(i) equals present value of excesses of annuitization rights over projected account values
(ii) equals present value of "assessments," defined as all administrative, mortality, and surrender charges, regardless of characterization, plus investment margins.

The Liability equals (i) – (ii), below:

(i) (Accumulated Assessments) × (Benefit Ratio), accreted at interest
(ii) Accumulated Excess Payments (i.e., payments for annuitization benefits in excess of account values), ascertained at times of annuitization.

Just as for Estimated Gross Profits (EGPs) as defined in *SFAS 97*, the benefit ratio should be regularly reviewed and adjusted where experience deems appropriate. For a detailed discussion of accounting for annuitization guarantees in excess of account values, please see the detailed illustration in Table 12-1 below. This table is simplistic in that, in spite of the *SOP 03-1* requirement that multiple scenarios must be run in support of generation of this liability, it assumes only one scenario, which can be presumed for illustrative purposes to be an average of those multiple scenarios.

In Tables 12-1 and 12-2, the annuitization option liability is calculated in several steps:

- In Part I, the contract history and the present value of excess annuitizations (column 15) are calculated.
- In Part II, the present value of "assessments" pursuant to the SOP is calculated (column 19). A Benefit Ratio (*BR*%) is calculated as column 15 divided by column 19.

In Part II, the Liability (L_t) is then calculated recursively, as:

$(L_{t-1}) \times (1 + i) + (BR\%) \times (\text{Assessments}_t) - (\text{Expected Excess Annuitizations}_t)$,

where

i is the credited interest rate (the same rate as that used for discounting and amortization of deferrable acquisition costs).

Table 12-1
Annuitization Liability
Part I. Account Value and Annuitization Cost Development

Investment Income Rate (i)	5.75%
$v = 1/(1+i)$	0.94563
Credited Interest Rate	4.50%
$v = 1/(1+i)$	0.95694
Maintenance expense	10.00

	(1)	(2)	(3)	(4)	(5)	(6)	(7)	(8)
Policy	**Surrender**	**Annuitization**	**Survivorship**	**Premium**	**Acct Value**	**Interest**	**Account Value End of Yr**	
Dur_t	**Rate**	**Election Rate**	**to Beginning Year**	**Deposit (BOY)**	**Beginning of Year**	**Credited**	**AV EOY**	**Survived**
1	2.00%		1.00000	1,000.00	1,000.00	45.00	1,045.00	1,024.10
2	3.00%		0.98000	955.00	2,000.00	90.00	2,090.00	1,986.75
3	3.50%		0.95060	910.00	3,000.00	135.00	3,135.00	2,875.83
4	3.50%		0.91733	1,065.00	4,200.00	189.00	4,389.00	3,885.24
5	3.50%		0.88522	1,211.00	5,600.00	252.00	5,852.00	4,999.01
6	25.00%		0.85424	1,148.00	7,000.00	315.00	7,315.00	4,686.57
7	3.50%		0.64068	1,685.00	9,000.00	405.00	9,405.00	5,814.70
8	3.50%		0.61826	1,595.00	11,000.00	495.00	11,495.00	6,858.11
9	3.50%		0.59662	1,505.00	13,000.00	585.00	13,585.00	7,821.37
10	3.50%		0.57574	2,215.00	15,800.00	711.00	16,511.00	9,173.26
11	3.50%	5.00%	0.55558	500.00	17,011.00	765.50	17,776.50	9,054.14
12	3.50%	5.50%	0.50933	500.00	18,276.50	822.44	19,098.94	8,870.94
13	3.50%	6.00%	0.46447	500.00	19,598.94	881.95	20,480.89	8,629.08
14	3.50%	6.00%	0.42132	500.00	20,980.89	944.14	21,925.03	8,379.36
15	100.00%	0.00%	0.38218	500.00	22,425.03	1,009.13	23,434.16	

	(9)	(10)		(11)	(12)	(13)
Policy	**Annuitization Value***			**Excess Ann. Value**		**Cost of**
Dur_t	**Per Inforce**	**Survived**		**Per Inforce**	**Survived**	**Annuitization**
1						
2						
3						
4						
5						
6						
7						
8						
9						
10						
11	18,665.32	9,569.39		888.82	455.69	22.78
12	20,053.88	9,410.67		954.95	448.13	24.65
13	21,504.93	9,187.51		1,024.04	437.50	26.25
14	23,021.28	8,929.43		1,096.25	425.21	25.51
15	24,605.86	4,399.16		1,171.71	209.48	

*Calculated at investment income rate.

Legend:

- (1) Given.
- (2) Given.
- (3) $(3)_1 = 1$. For $t > 1$, $(3)_t = (3)_{t-1} \times (1 - (1)_1) \times (1 - (2)_1)$.
- (4) Given.
- (5) $(5)_t = (5)_{t-1} + (6)_{t-1} + (4)_t$.
- (6) (Credited Interest Rate) $\times (5)_t$.
- (7) (5) + (6)
- (8) $(7)_t \times (3)_{t+1}$.
- (9) Assume annuitization value based on scenarios = $1.05 \times (7)_t$.
- (10) $1.05 \times 0.5 \times ((8)_{t-1} + (8)_t)$.
- (11) (9) – (7).
- (12) $(10) - 0.5 \times ((8)_{t-1} + (8)_t)$.
- (13) $(12) \times (2)$.

Table 12-2
Annuitization Liability
Part II. Development of Annuitization Liability

	(14)	(15)	(16)	(17)	(18)	(19)	(20)
Policy	**Election Cost**		**Expense**	**Investment**	**Total Assessments**		**Liability**
Dur,	**Expected**	**Present Value**	**Charges (EOY)**	**Margins**	**Expected**	**Pres Val**	
1			10.00	12.50	22.50	21.53	1.49
2			9.80	24.50	34.30	31.41	3.83
3			9.51	35.65	45.15	39.57	6.99
4			9.17	48.16	57.33	48.08	11.10
5			8.85	61.97	70.82	56.83	16.29
6			8.54	74.75	83.29	63.96	22.54
7			6.41	72.08	78.48	57.67	28.75
8			6.18	85.01	91.19	64.13	36.08
9			5.97	96.95	102.92	69.25	44.52
10			5.76	113.71	119.47	76.93	54.43
11	22.78	14.04	5.56	118.14	123.69	76.22	42.29
12	24.65	14.53	5.09	116.36	121.45	71.62	27.58
13	26.25	14.81	4.64	113.79	118.43	66.83	10.42
14	25.51	13.78	4.21	110.50	114.71	61.94	(7.03)
15			3.82	107.13	110.95	57.33	0.00
Totals		57.16				863.28	
					Benefit Ratio (*BR*%)	6.621%	

Legend:
(14) (13).
(15) (14) / (1.045^t).
(16) (\$10.00) × $(3)_t$.
(17) (6) × (3) × ((0.0575 / 0.045) – 1).
(18) (16) + (17).
(19) (18) / (1.045^t).
(20) $(20)_{t-1}$ × (1.045) + (BR%) × (18) – (14).

Notes: Interest used for discounting is the credited interest rate.
The above is based on the results of multiple scenarios.
Final liability forces negatives to zero. Thus $(20)_{14} = 0$.

The interest-effected change in the annuitization liability would then become an element in the Estimated Gross Profit (EGP) used for discounting and amortizing deferrable acquisition costs.

That is, the following would be subtracted from the EGP for a given period t.

$$L_t - (1 + i) \times L_{t-1},$$

where

i is the investment income (earned) rate pre-tax.

12.2.5 Deferred Acquisition Cost

In general, large case pension plans and similar contracts have very low acquisition costs, especially as compared to other insurance contracts. Nonetheless, certain expenses, such as broker's commissions, can be clearly identified as acquisition costs and warrant deferral and amortization. The guidance found in *SFAS 97* related to DAC for investment contracts is limited. *SFAS 97* states simply that investment contracts should be accounted for like similar contracts with other financial institutions. Other financial institutions do not have significant acquisition costs and hence do not have DAC.

More specific guidance is found in AICPA *Practice Bulletin 8*, "Application of FASB Statement No. 97 (*PB 8*), Accounting and Reports by Insurance Enterprises for Certain Long

Duration Contracts and for Realized Gains Losses on the Sale of Investments, to Insurance Enterprises," which specifically addresses deferred acquisition costs and makes reference to *SFAS No. 91*, "Accounting for Non-refundable Fees and Costs Associated with Originating Loans and Initial Direct Cost of Leases."

According to *PB 8*, the approach to DAC depends on whether the investment contract includes significant surrender charges or has significant revenue from sources other than the interest margins. When an investment contract includes significant surrender charges or has significant revenues other than interest margin, treatment of DAC should be consistent with that for universal-life type contracts (the "UL method"). Otherwise, the DAC treatment should be consistent with that described in *SFAS 91* for loan origination fees. Under this approach the net liability (reserve less DAC) builds to the maturity value at the effective crediting rate. The reserve accumulation rate is the level rate at which the net proceeds, the deposit less deferrable costs, accumulates to the maturity value. This method is referred to as the interest method. Under either method, DAC amortization should anticipate terminations (surrenders) and is updated for deviations in actual experience from assumptions. DAC is reported as an asset, even if the insurer's approach is to calculate a net reserve.

These two approaches are shown in Tables 12-3 and 12-4 for a 3-year traditional GIC with no cash surrender option. Table 12-3 displays the results of the UL method.

Table 12-3
DAC on 3-Year GIC Using the UL Method

(1) Policy Year	(2) Year-End Fund Value	(3) Mid-Year Fund Value	(4) Basis Point Spread	(5) Gross Margin	(6) Deferrable Costs	(7) End-of-Year DAC	(8) End-of-Year Net Liability Position
0	10,000				25		
1	10,700	10,344	0.35	36.20		17.83	10,682
2	11,449	11,068	0.35	38.74		9.54	11,439
3	12,250	11,843	0.35	41.45		0.00	12,250
(5a) present value of gross margins				101.507331			
(6a) amortization factor					0.2462876		

Legend:
Assumptions:

Deposit = \$10,000 — Interest earned rate = 7.45%
Credited rate = 7% annually — Acquisition costs = 25 basis points
Maturity value = \$12,250 — Annual maintenenace costs = 10 basis points

(2) $= (2)_{t-1} \times 1.07$.
(3) $= (2)_{t-1} \times 1.07^{\wedge 0.5}$.
(4) $= 7.45 - 7.00 - 0.10$.
(5) $= (3) \times (4) / 100$.
(5a) = present value of (5) at credited rate.
(6) = 25 in year 1 only.
(6a) $= (6)_0 / (5a)$.
(7) $= [(7)_{t-1} \times 1.07] - [(6a) \times (5)_t]$ where $(7)_0 = (6)_0$.
(8) $= (2) - (7)$.

The interest method is displayed in Table 12-4.

Table 12-4
DAC on 3-Year GIC Using the Interest Method

(1) Policy Year	(2) Deposit	(3) Acquisition Costs	(4) Net Proceeds	(5) Maturity Value	(6) Value Accumulated at Discount Rate	(7) Gross Liability	(8) DAC
0	10,000	25	9,975		9,975.00	10,000	25.00
1					10,682.03	10,700	17.97
2					11,439.18	11,449	9.82
3				12,250	12,250.00	12,250	0.00
(5a) Discount rate				0.0708806			

Legend:
Assumptions:
Deposit = $10,000   Interest earned rate = 7.45%
Credited rate = 7% annually   Acquisition costs = 25 basis points
Maturity value = $12,250   Annual maintenenace costs = 10 basis points

(2), (3) Given.
(4) = (2) – (3).
(5) From Table 12-3, column (2).
(5a) = interest rate i such that $(4)_0 \times (1+i)^{\wedge 3} = (5)_3$.
$(6)_t$ = $(6)_{t-1} \times [1 + (5a)]$ where $(6)_0 = (4)_0$.
(7) From Table 12-3, column (2).
(8) = (7) – (6).

The interest method and the UL method can be seen to produce materially the same result in the simple case in which there are no surrender charges and maintenance costs are small. Although the interest method emphasizes the effective level crediting rate, the DAC should be calculated and recorded as an asset.

The use of either the UL method or the interest method raises some related questions with respect to DAC unlocking. When the UL approach is used, unlocking principles apply consistently with paragraph 25 of *SFAS 97*. *PB 8* requires that, under the interest method, the rate of DAC amortization should be adjusted for changes in the incidence of surrenders. However, that does not address other changes, such as changes in spread. When the company's investment strategy is such that the spread is not fixed, it can vary from expectations. The guidance seems to imply that when the interest method is used, the DAC would not be unlocked for such variances.

The significance of surrender charges is subject to different interpretations. Is the surrender charge significant to the contract or are the expected surrender charge revenues significant to the revenue stream? Under the first view, the UL approach may be applied, even if termination rates are expected to be low and surrender charge revenues are expected to be insignificant.

DAC calculations for variable contracts require projecting variable account fees, which provide the basis of amortization. With swings in market values of separate account assets, the ability to project revenues is much more difficult, and unlocking issues become exaggerated when compared to unlocking for general account products. For example, if the anticipated growth rate is 8% and the fund has growth of 20% for the year, should unlocking anticipate that future growth will be at the original 8% or that it will be lower, averaging 8% over the life? Or is something in between more appropriate? A related question under the UL method is whether the DAC amortization discount rate should be fixed or if it should change with unlocking. The answers to these questions can materially affect amortization, and policies should be chosen only after analysis of the alternatives, including sensitivity testing.

Shadow adjustments, discussed at length in Chapter 14, are applicable to Deferred Acquisition Costs on group pension contracts as on other products. Recent new guidance, namely *SFAS 133* and *SOP 03-1* have changed the results for experience-rated group pension contracts. For a detailed discussion of Shadow adjustments on experience-rated group pension contracts, please refer to Chapter 3, Section 3.11.

12.2.6 Loss Recognition

As discussed in previous chapters on annuities and other types of investment contracts, loss recognition principles are applied to the extent that DAC can be written off when it is not recoverable. Beyond DAC write-off, the rules do not allow accrual of any additional liability for anticipated losses.

12.2.7 Fair Value Accounting

U.S. GAAP requires certain disclosures relating to the fair value of financial instruments. Guidance is found in *FASB Statement No. 107*, "Disclosures of about Fair Value of Financial Instruments." The rules make exceptions for insurance contracts but not for investment contracts. Insurers therefore must disclose the fair value of their GICs and similar contracts. Because there is not an observable market for these contracts, there is no quoted market value. Under the guidance, companies must find the most appropriate value. The fair value of GICs and related contracts is not well defined and practices vary. The most common solutions fall under the three major categories:

- *Fair value equals the nominal account value.* One approach is to assert that the value of deposit contracts is the accumulated value of deposits. This approach seems to consider that GICs are analogous to deposits of other financial institutions, specifically demand deposits of banks and savings and loans. In general, terms of GICs with respect to surrender provisions and market value adjustments make this a dubious conclusion. However, it is consistent with the conclusion that GICs are not marked to market on the depositor's balance sheet.

- *Surrender value.* When viewed as individual contracts, the argument can be made that each contract has a settlement value equal to its current surrender value, taking into account market value adjustments and other applicable charges. This value is typically readily available and is probably the most common valuation basis for fair value disclosures.

- *Discounted cash flows.* Consistent with general guidance for fair value disclosures, when the value is not otherwise determinable, a company should project and discount the contract cash flows. This approach is particularly appropriate when the fair value calculation is based on the portfolio of contracts, rather than contract by contract. The discounting is typically at rates that reflect crediting rates for new issues of similar contracts. This approach has an implicit spread, such that the fair-value measure provides margins for future profits and contingencies.

12.2.8 Implications of *SFAS 133*

Companies applying principles of *SFAS 133* should consider to what extent GICs and similar contracts are derivatives or contain embedded derivatives. It appears likely that features of many of these contracts could bring *SFAS 133* into play. Performance guarantees, index features, market value adjustments, and other aspects possess characteristics of derivatives. As investment contracts,

GICs, unlike conventional insurance contracts, are not exempt from application of *SFAS 133*. Applying *SFAS 133* causes companies to define accounting policies for the fair value measure of their contracts or of some of their features. Especially, separate account contract liabilities where guarantees may cause lump sum payments in excess of account values may be "hybrid instruments" under *SFAS 133*, i.e., host contracts with embedded derivatives.

The application of *SFAS 133* is discussed in detail in Chapter 8, primarily Section 8.3.

Chapter 13 Investment Accounting

13.1 Introduction

The operations of an insurance entity can be categorized into underwriting, investment and benefits paying/reserving operations. When the public thinks of an insurance entity, the benefits operations and underwriting processes are usually the first to come to mind. The investment operations are rarely contemplated because they are largely invisible to the typical policyholder. The public's contact with an insurance company is generally through the payment of premiums or the receipt of benefits. Not much thought may be devoted to what happens to the funds between the time premiums are remitted and the time when benefits are paid. The reality, however, is that all three functions are interrelated and are integral components of the overall financial success of an insurance company.

An insurance entity evaluates risk and determines the price at which it will take on those risks (underwriting), optimizes the return on the cash flows from premiums and deposits (investing) until the time comes for the funds to be used to satisfy benefit liabilities (benefit operations). A positive cash flow ultimately benefits the insurance company owners, whether they are the shareholders in a stock company or the policyholders in a mutual company.

The interrelationships and dependencies between the functions are important. For example, the underwriting function, in the long term, cannot price its products in anticipation of the higher yields that might be available from riskier investments if the investment policy is not reflective of such an appetite for risk. Likewise, in the evaluation of the adequacy of benefit reserves and related cash flow tests, the meaningfulness of the conclusions drawn is dependent upon how well the assumptions correlate with realistic expectations of current and future investment results.

Insurance products can be sophisticated and complex. Likewise, the investments vehicles available to meet overall cash flow and income objectives can be sophisticated and complex. In the U.S., asset accumulation products are prominent in the life insurance industry. A significant element of asset accumulation product profitability is the difference between what the insurance company earns on its invested assets and the rate of return credited to the contractholder. This difference, known as the *spread*, is under constant pressure due to the competitive environment from both within and outside of the insurance industry. All this leads life insurers to evaluate new and different investment vehicles that may help increase spreads and profitability.

Thus, the evolution of insurance products has resulted in an ever-increasing importance of the investing function. Not only is the selection and management of investments important, but the accounting for such investments is critical. The life company needs to know when it has earned investment income and must periodically reassess the amount and timing of future principal and interest payments. The balance of this chapter is devoted to a discussion of the investment vehicles typically employed by a life insurance company and the related application of generally accepted accounting principles.

13.2 Typical Life Insurer Investments and Related Accounting Principles

While the focus of this text is GAAP, it is still useful to understand some of the statutory factors that may influence the investment decisions and policies of an insurance company. Life insurance enterprises are regulated entities, and the state of domicile is the primary regulator. Each state has laws, rules, and regulations that address the types and quantities of investments that an insurance enterprise may invest in. These investment restrictions are designed to provide protection to the policy and contractholders by requiring diversification and by encouraging, directly and indirectly, higher quality investments. There are statutory penalties for lack of diversification and riskier investment practices. The penalties can range from provisions for additional statutory reserves (asset valuation reserves) and increased risk-based capital (RBC) requirements to potential nonrecognition as assets (nonadmitted status).

Life insurance companies typically invest in the following broad categories of investments:

- Debt Securities
  - Bonds
  - Collateralized Mortgage Obligations
- Preferred Stocks
- Common Stocks
  - Unaffiliated
  - Affiliated
- Mortgage Loans
- Real Estate
- Policy Loans
- Partnerships
- Short-Term Investments
- Derivatives.

The values of assets under GAAP are reported by using the following prescribed methodologies unless an allowance for potential impairment losses needs to be provided. Such losses could be credit-related or due to other than temporary declines in the fair value of the asset. The consideration for loss provision is made on a security-by-security basis (or for a block of similar investments). The provision would be based on the expected losses to be incurred on the specific portfolio being evaluated. GAAP loss recognition requires that losses be both probable and measurable before they are accrued in the financial statements. GAAP also requires that such losses be charged to earnings.

The following sections provide further background information and the basic GAAP accounting principles for these investment types.

13.3 Debt Securities

Debt securities are those investments that represent a debtor/creditor relationship between the issuer and holder, respectively, of the security. These securities are commonly referred to as bonds and can be issued by a wide variety of entities including governmental agencies and units as well as corporations. *SFAS 115* is the primary authoritative literature for such investments.

This classification also includes other financial instruments that have been securitized by underlying asset groups. A common investment in this subcategory of debt securities is the collateralized mortgage obligation (CMO) and derivations thereof, such as interest only strips (IOs) and principal only strips (POs).

Also included in this classification are those preferred stocks that, because of their terms, more closely resemble debt rather than equity. Such preferred stocks are either mandatorily redeemable or redeemable at the option of the owner.

Debt securities are popular investments for life insurance companies because their ultimate cash flows and inherent yields are relatively predictable. Such predictability facilitates and enhances the asset/liability matching process, which is a critical process in the management of a life insurance company.

The key accounting considerations for debt securities are proper:

- Recording at acquisition
- Income recognition while the security is held
- Gain or loss recognition upon sale or maturity of the investment
- Carrying value while the security is being held.

At acquisition, debt securities are recorded in the general ledger at their cost. The cost of a debt security may be more or less than the amount that will ultimately be repaid at maturity. This disparity is generally reflective of a difference in the current interest rate environment as compared to the contractual rate of return promised by the terms of the debt security. For example, a bond with a stated rate of 6% will trade at a discount in an environment in which similar investments return 8% yields. Conversely, that same bond would trade at a premium in a 4% environment. Any premium (the excess of cost over face value/par value of the security) that is paid or discount (the excess of face value/par value of the security over cost) that is received is reflected as an element of the cost of the investment. Premiums and discounts can also result from changes in the credit quality of the security. Securities that carry variable interest rates generally do not trade at significant premiums or discounts because the terms of such instruments are designed to be responsive to changing interest rate scenarios.

GAAP requires that premiums and discounts be factored into the income recognition process while a security is held. GAAP income on a debt security is generally equal to the periodic contractual interest payments or accruals plus any accretion of discount or less any amortization of premium. The periodic amortization or accretion is equal to the amount needed to result in a constant effective yield over the period from the acquisition date to the maturity date or, if callable, to the earlier call date.

The amortization of premium or accretion of discount ultimately results in the adjusted cost being equal to the par value/face value at maturity or the call date if earlier with no gain or loss being recognized.

The carrying values of debt securities on a GAAP basis are governed by the provisions of *SFAS 115*. As described in Chapter 2, investors in debt securities must classify the investments into one of three categories.

- Securities that are held to maturity (HTM)
- Securities that are held for trading purposes (Trading)
- Securities that are available for sale (AFS).

Companies may have investments in portfolios of all three different types but the vast majority of insurance company debt security investments are classified as available for sale. GAAP accounting rules generally prohibit the subsequent reclassification of a HTM security to another category without tainting the classification of the remaining HTM securities and jeopardizing the balance sheet stability which many see as the primary advantage or benefit of such classification.

HTM securities are carried at amortized cost while Trading and AFS securities are carried at fair value. Fair values are generally obtained from published sources which monitor current market prices or from pricing models which calculate the values based on the fair values of similar investments with similar attributes (rates, maturities, credit ratings, etc.). Changes in the fair values are recognized in earnings in the case of Trading securities and in "other comprehensive income" (shareholders' or policyholders' equity) in the case of AFS securities. For securities classified as Trading and AFS, the general ledger will continue to reflect the amortized cost of such investments. When periodic GAAP financial statement are prepared, valuation adjustments are made to bring the carrying value up or down to the fair value with corresponding adjustments to "income" or "other comprehensive income" for trading and AFS securities, respectively.

If the fair value of an HTM or AFS security is below the cost of such security, then the holder of such security is required to evaluate whether or not this situation is a temporary phenomenon. This situation can result from changes in the interest rate environment or other factors which do not call into question the ultimate recoverability of the asset. If, however, the decline in value is deemed to be other than temporary, then a write-down of the security along with a related income statement charge is appropriate.

In March of 2004, a consensus was reached by the FASB's Emerging Issues Task Force regarding such writedowns. The guidance under *EITF Issue No. 03-1*, "The Meaning of Other-Than-Temporary Impairment and Its Application to Certain Investments" sets forth criteria to be analyzed in the determination of when a loss should be recorded. The process to be followed is depicted by the decision tree below.

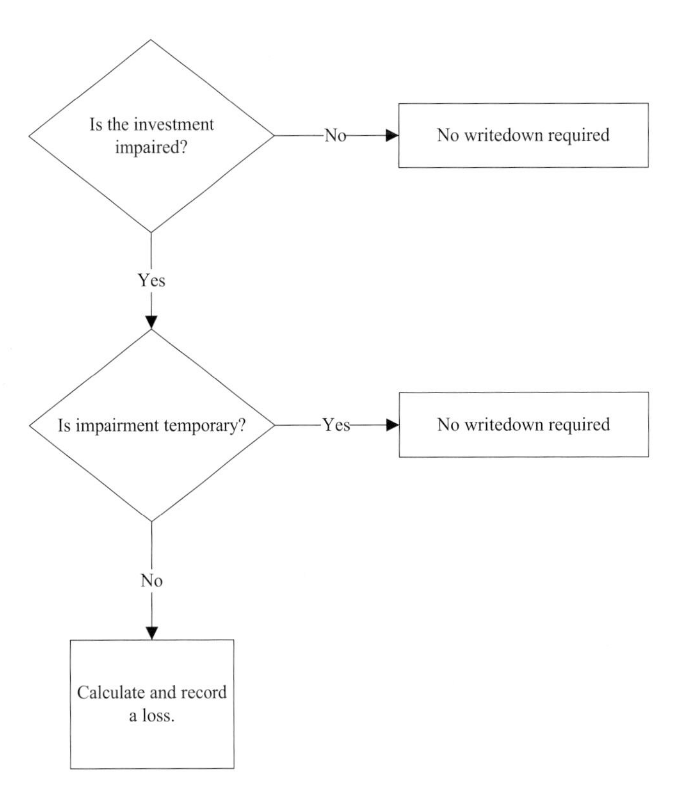

Impairment occurs when the fair value of an investment falls below its carrying value (amortized cost). For typical HTM and AFS securities held by insurance companies, fair value can be determined by reference to quoted market prices.

EITF No. 03-1 also sets forth the criteria for evaluating if an impairment is to be considered temporary. This determination is dependent upon whether the impaired investment's recovery is tied to increases in market prices (market dependent for this discussion) or results from the ultimate collection of amounts due from debt securities (collection dependent for this discussion).

Market dependent	An impairment is considered to be temporary if the investor has the ability and intent to hold the investment during a reasonable forecasted recovery period.
Collection dependent	An impairment is considered to be temporary if it is probable than an investor would recover the cost of the investment through collection of the amounts due. This implies a positive evaluation that the investor has the ability and intent to hold the investment to maturity or until a forecasted recovery in fair value.

These determinations require significant judgments and potential accumulation of evidence supporting those judgments. Cash flow projections may be required to support "ability to hold" judgments. Sales of similar securities at losses may contradict "intent to hold" judgments. The duration of an impairment may impact judgments regarding "reasonable periods of time" for recovery. Other factors affecting these determinations could include consideration of credit ratings of debt issuers, changes in fair values of investments subsequent to the balance-sheet date, changes in the economic and regulatory environments, an investee's forecasts regarding its performance as well as investment analysts' forecasts. If the determination is that the decline in fair value is temporary, the company should be prepared to convincingly support its judgments.

If an impairment is ultimately determined to be "other than temporary," a loss should be recorded equal to the difference between its cost and its fair value which also establishes a new cost basis for the investment.

In connection with the implementation of *EITF No. 03-1* a controversy arose regarding "collection dependent" securities that are impaired solely because of changes in the interest rate environment. The issue centers around the "intent to hold" criteria. Some companies have sold such securities at losses and argue that such sales do not constitute evidence that contradicts their assertion that they have the intent to hold other similarly impaired securities until recovery or collection. Others take the view that such sales "taint" all such securities and that writedowns should therefore be taken. As this text is being written, the EITF is addressing this issue and may defer the effective date of Consensuses issued *EITF No. 03-1* until additional guidance can be developed.

The following is a presentation of the accounting for two typical types of debt securities, bonds and collateralized mortgage obligations.

13.3.1 Bonds

The cash flows underlying a bond generally are comprised of a series of interest payments (sometimes called coupons) on the principal amount outstanding and a payment of principal at the end of the term period. Accounting entries for a bond are illustrated under several scenarios in the following four tables. For these illustrations, the bond pays a coupon semiannually. The coupon rate has been quoted as a nominal interest rate so that an 8% coupon bond pays $40 of interest semiannually for a par value of $1,000.

Table 13-1 illustrates the cash flows and accounting entries for a five year bond with par value of $1,000 and coupon rate 8%. It was purchased for $1,000, thus generating an effective yield rate at purchase of 8%.

Table 13-1
Cash Flows and Accounting Entries for a Bond Purchased at Par

(A) Point in Time	0	0.5	1	1.5	2	2.5	3	3.5	4	4.5	5
(B) Investment	$1,000	$0	$0	$0	$0	$0	$0	$0	$0	$0	$0
(C) Cash Flow	$0	$40	$40	$40	$40	$40	$40	$40	$40	$40	$1,040
(D) Interest Income	$0	$40	$40	$40	$40	$40	$40	$40	$40	$40	$40
(E) Amortized Cost at End of the Period	$1,000	$1,000	$1,000	$1,000	$1,000	$1,000	$1,000	$1,000	$1,000	$1,000	$0

Legend:

(B) Investment = The outlay to acquire the bond, $1,000.

(C) Cash flow = Semiannual coupon + principal at end of the period.

(D) Interest income = Prior amortized cost × yield rate / 2 = $(E)_{t-1} \times 0.08 / 2$.

(E) Amortized cost at end of the period = amortized cost at beginning of period less amortization and principal payments during the period = $(E)_{t-1} - 0$. (Note that there is no amortization or accretion since the bond was purchased at par value.)

	Ledger Entries for Above Bond					
	Bond Investment		Bond Interest Income		Cash	
Point in Time	Debit	Credit	Debit	Credit	Debit	Credit
0.00	$1,000					$1,000
0.50				$40	$40	
1.00				$40	$40	
1.50				$40	$40	
2.00				$40	$40	
2.50				$40	$40	
3.00				$40	$40	
3.50				$40	$40	
4.00				$40	$40	
4.50				$40	$40	
5.00		$1,000		$40	$1,040	
Source for Ledger Entries	Row B	Row C		Row D	Row C	Row B

When a bond is acquired at a premium or at a discount, the periodic interest payments need to be adjusted (by amortization of the premium or discount) to result in the effective yield implied in the cost of the bond at its acquisition.

When a bond is purchased at a premium, the yield rate at purchase is less than the coupon rate. Amortization of the premium accomplishes the financial reporting objective of a constant effective yield. The amortization of premium would be recorded as a credit in the bond investment account and a debit in the bond interest income account. Table 13-2 illustrates such a bond. The same 5-year bond with par value of $1,000 and coupon rate 8% has been purchased for $1,041.58, generating an effective yield rate of 7%.

Table 13-2

Cash Flows and Accounting Entries for a Bond Purchased at a Premium

(A) Point in Time	0	0.5	1	1.5	2	2.5	3	3.5	4	4.5	5
(B) Investment	$1,041.58	$0.00	$0.00	$0.00	$0.00	$0.00	$0.00	$0.00	$0.00	$0.00	$0.00
(C) Cash Flow	$0.00	$40.00	$40.00	$40.00	$40.00	$40.00	$40.00	$40.00	$40.00	$40.00	$1,040.00
(D) Coupon	$0.00	$40.00	$40.00	$40.00	$40.00	$40.00	$40.00	$40.00	$40.00	$40.00	$40.00
(E) Interest Income		$36.46	$36.33	$36.20	$36.07	$35.93	$35.79	$35.64	$35.49	$35.33	$35.17
(F) Amortization of Premium		$3.54	$3.67	$3.80	$3.93	$4.07	$4.21	$4.36	$4.51	$4.67	$4.83
(G) Amortized Cost at End of the Period	$1,041.58	$1,038.04	$1,034.37	$1,030.57	$1,026.64	$1,022.58	$1,018.37	$1,014.01	$1,009.50	$1,004.83	$0.00

Legend:

(B) Investment = The outlay to acquire the bond, $1,041.58.

(C) Cash flow = semiannual coupon plus principal at end of the period.

(D) Coupon = par value × coupon rate / 2 = 1000 × 8% / 2.

(E) Interest income = prior amortized cost (G) × yield rate at purchase / 2 = $(G)_{t-1} \times 0.07 / 2$.

(F) Amortization of premium = coupon – interest income = $(D)_t - (E)_t$.

(G) Amortized cost at end of the period = amortized cost at beginning of period less amortization and principal payments during the period = $(G)_{t-1} - (F)_t$.

Ledger Entries for Above Bond

	Bond Investment		Bond Interest Income		Cash	
Point in Time	**Debit**	**Credit**	**Debit**	**Credit**	**Debit**	**Credit**
0.00	1,041.58					1,041.58
0.50		3.54	3.54	40.00	40.00	
1.00		3.67	3.67	40.00	40.00	
1.50		3.80	3.80	40.00	40.00	
2.00		3.93	3.93	40.00	40.00	
2.50		4.07	4.07	40.00	40.00	
3.00		4.21	4.21	40.00	40.00	
3.50		4.36	4.36	40.00	40.00	
4.00		4.51	4.51	40.00	40.00	
4.50		4.67	4.67	40.00	40.00	
5.00		*1,004.83	4.83	40.00	1,040.00	
Source for Ledger Entries	Row B	Row F	Row F	Row D	Row C	Row B

* Includes $1,000 principal repayment at end of year 5.

When a bond is purchased at a discount, the yield rate at purchase is higher than the coupon rate. Thus, the coupon alone is insufficient to reflect the return on investment. Consequently, the amount of the discount is periodically accreted into investment income to achieve the effective yield rate. This accretion of discount is recorded as a debit in the bond Investment account and a credit in the bond interest income account.

Table 13-3 illustrates the same 5 year bond with par value of $1,000 and coupon rate 8%. It has been purchased for $960.44, thus generating an effective yield rate of 9%.

Table 13-3
Cash Flows and Accounting Entries for a Bond Purchased at a Discount

(A) Point in Time	0	0.5	1	1.5	2	2.5	3	3.5	4	4.5	5
(B) Investment	$960.44	$0.00	$0.00	$0.00	$0.00	$0.00	$0.00	$0.00	$0.00	$0.00	$0.00
(C) Cash Flow	$0.00	$40.00	$40.00	$40.00	$40.00	$40.00	$40.00	$40.00	$40.00	$40.00	$1,040.00
(D) Coupon	$0.00	$40.00	$40.00	$40.00	$40.00	$40.00	$40.00	$40.00	$40.00	$40.00	$40.00
(E) Interest Income		$43.22	$43.36	$43.52	$43.67	$43.84	$44.01	$44.19	$44.38	$44.58	$44.78
(F) Accretion of Discount		$3.22	$3.36	$3.52	$3.67	$3.84	$4.01	$4.19	$4.38	$4.58	$4.78
(G) Amortized Cost at End of the Period	$960.44	$963.66	$967.02	$970.54	$974.21	$978.05	$982.06	$986.26	$990.64	$995.22	$0.00
(H) Fair Value at End of the Period	$960.44	$963.66	$967.02	$970.54	$949.24	$1,000.00	$964.54	$972.77	$1,000.00	$1,000.00	$0.00
(I) Other Comprehensive Income		$0.00	$0.00	$0.00	($24.97)	$46.92	($39.47)	$4.03	$22.85	($4.58)	($4.78)
(J) Balance of Bond Valuation Adjustment Account	$0.00	$0.00	$0.00	$0.00	($24.97)	$21.95	($17.52)	($13.49)	$9.36	$4.78	$0.00

Legend:
(B) Investment = The outlay to acquire the bond, $960.44.
(C) Cash flow = Semiannual coupon plus principal at the end of the period.
(D) Coupon = par value × coupon rate / 2 = 1000 × 8% / 2.
(E) Interest income = Prior amortized cost × yield rate at purchase / 2 = $(G)_{t-1}$ × 0.09 / 2.
(F) Accretion of discount = interest income – coupon = $(E)_t - (D)_t$.
(G) Amortized cost at end of the period = amortized cost at beginning of period plus accretion of discount less principal payments during the period = $(G)_{t-1} + (F)_t$.
(H) Fair value did not change from amortized cost during the first three periods; then, changes occur.
(I) Other comprehensive income = change in the unrealized capital gain/loss = $(J)_t - (J)_{t-1}$.
(J) Balance of bond valuation adjustment account = Difference between fair value and amortized cost = $(H)_t - (G)_t$.

The bond in Table 13-3 has been classified as Available for Sale. This mandates that the investment be recorded at its fair value. The preceding table identifies the elements necessary for reporting other comprehensive income and for the bond valuation account.

Table 13-4 displays the accounting entries for the preceding bond.

Table 13-4
Ledger Entries for the Bond Purchased at a Discount in Table 13-3

Point in Time	Bond Investment		Bond Interest Income		Cash		Other Comprehensive		Bond Valuation Adjustment	
	Debit	Credit	Debit	Credit	Debit	Credit	Debit	Credit	Debit	Credit
0.00	$960.44					$960.44				
0.50	$3.22			$43.22	$40.00					
1.00	$3.36			$43.36	$40.00					
1.50	$3.52			$43.52	$40.00					
2.00	$3.67			$43.67	$40.00		$24.97			$24.97
2.50	$3.84			$43.84	$40.00			$46.92	$46.92	
3.00	$4.01			$44.01	$40.00		$39.47			$39.47
3.50	$4.19			$44.19	$40.00			$4.03	$4.03	
4.00	$4.38			$44.38	$40.00			$22.85	$22.85	
4.50	$4.58			$44.58	$40.00		$4.58			$4.58
5.00	$4.78	$1,000.00		$44.78	$1,040.00		$4.78			$4.78
Source for ledger entries All from Table 13-3	Rows (B) and (F)	Row (C)		Row (E)	Row (C)	Row (B)	Row (I)		Row (I)	

Balance Sheet Consequences of Above Entries

Point in Time	Amortized Cost of Bond	Balance of Bond Valuation Adjustment Account*	Financial Statement Carrying Value
0.00	$960.44	0.00	$960.44
0.50	$963.66	0.00	$963.66
1.00	$967.02	0.00	$967.02
1.50	$970.54	0.00	$970.54
2.00	$974.21	(24.97)	$949.25
2.50	$978.05	21.95	$1,000.00
3.00	$982.07	(17.52)	$964.54
3.50	$986.26	(13.49)	$972.77
4.00	$990.64	9.36	$1,000.00
4.50	$995.22	4.78	$1,000.00
5.00	$0.00	0.00	$0.00
Derivation:	Cumulative Sum of Bond Investment Debits	Cumulative Bond Valuation Account Debits and Credits	Sum of the Columns to the Left

* This balance is offset in the equity section of the balance sheet in an account called "accumulated other comprehensive income."

If a security is sold prior to its call or redemption, any difference between the sale proceeds and the amortized cost of the security is recognized as a realized gain or loss. Realized gains and losses are recognized separately within a GAAP income statement and may not be deferred directly or indirectly.

13.3.2 Collateralized Mortgage Obligations

Another type of debt security for GAAP accounting purposes is the collateralized mortgage obligation (CMO). There are three primary authoritative sources for CMO accounting: *EITF 89-4*, "Accounting for a Purchased Investment in a Collateralized Mortgage Obligation Instrument or in a Mortgage-Backed Interest-Only Certificate," *SFAS No. 91,* "Accounting for Nonrefundable Fees and Costs Associated with Originating or Acquiring Loans and Initial Direct Costs of Leases," and *EITF 93-18*, "Recognition of Impairment for an Investment in a Collateralized Mortgage Obligation Instrument or in a Mortgage-Backed Interest-Only Certificate." CMOs represent a pool of mortgage loans that have been securitized. CMOs pass on to the investor payments that correspond to the cash flows of the underlying mortgage loans; as principal and interest payments are being made on the mortgage loans, similar payments are passed on to the investors. CMOs are packaged in groupings of cash flows, generally related to the sequence of the cash flows; these groupings are referred to as tranches. The later or residual tranches carry more of the risk of default within the underlying loan portfolio but can be structured to present an opportunity for greater return to the investor because of this risk.

As long as a CMO is appropriately collateralized and is in a tranche that carries minimal default risk, the accounting is very similar to that for a corporate bond. This difference is in the manner in which any premium or discount is amortized. Premiums and discounts on CMOs result from economic characteristics similar to those of bonds. If the pool of mortgages carries an average interest rate greater than the current market rate, a premium may be paid. Conversely, if the pool's stated rate of return is below the current market rate, then the securities may sell at a discount. The difference in amortization arises because bonds generally have a fixed maturity date or a date when the bond may be called. Mortgage loans, however, tend to prepay because the mortgagors often move and sell their homes prior to the mortgage reaching maturity. This type of prepayment is somewhat predictable given the long-term history of large numbers of mortgage loans.

A more unpredictable factor affecting prepayments, however, is the interest rate environment in general. In an environment of declining interest rates, mortgage loan rates may also decline, and if these declines are significant enough, they will result in the refinancing of mortgage loans. The rate at which this prepayment phenomenon occurs is known as the prepayment speed. When a CMO is purchased, the buyer is anticipating a certain prepayment speed, which gives the investor the ability to calculate an estimated effective yield over the expected duration of the CMO. The accounting then follows the model discussed previously for bonds. To the extent that prepayment speeds deviate from the initial expectations, the amortization period may lengthen or shorten and the effective yield is also affected. Under GAAP (*SFAS 91*, paragraph 19), the investor is required to use the benefit of hindsight and periodically assess whether or not actual experience has deviated from the assumptions for purposes of premium or discount amortization. This approach is known as the retrospective method. The investor is required to revise the estimated effective yield given the actual experience since acquisition of the CMO and the best estimate of the future experience. The investor is thus required to recalculate a revised book value of the CMO as if this information (the revised effective yield) was available at the acquisition date. Any difference is booked as a *true-up* and is credited or charged to investment income. Such reassessment should occur at least annually but may be necessary more frequently if the economic conditions are affecting the assumptions for premium or discount amortization.

The following tables demonstrate the nature of and accounting for a CMO tranche with fairly predictable principal payments, such as a planned amortization class (PAC) tranche.

Table 13-5 demonstrates the accounting in which the tranche is acquired at par and there are no deviations from expected prepayment patterns or amounts. The principal amount is $1,000,000 and the stated interest rate is 6%. Because the security was purchased for $1,000,000, its effective yield rate at purchase is 6%. For this and subsequent tables, principal and interest pay at the end of the year; the amortized cost shown is calculated immediately after the principal and interest payment.

Table 13-5
Cash Flows for a CMO Purchased at Par
Classified as Held to Maturity

		Assumptions at Purchase			
(1)	(2)	(3)	(4)	(5)	(6)
Year	Investment	Principal Pay Down Schedule	Interest Payment	Interest Income	Amortized Cost at End of Period
0	$1,000,000.00	$0.00	$0.00		$1,000,000.00
1	$0.00	$0.00	$60,000.00	$60,000.00	$1,000,000.00
2	$0.00	$0.00	$60,000.00	$60,000.00	$1,000,000.00
3	$0.00	$0.00	$60,000.00	$60,000.00	$1,000,000.00
4	$0.00	$0.00	$60,000.00	$60,000.00	$1,000,000.00
5	$0.00	$100,000.00	$60,000.00	$60,000.00	$900,000.00
6	$0.00	$100,000.00	$54,000.00	$54,000.00	$800,000.00
7	$0.00	$100,000.00	$48,000.00	$48,000.00	$700,000.00
8	$0.00	$100,000.00	$42,000.00	$42,000.00	$600,000.00
9	$0.00	$100,000.00	$36,000.00	$36,000.00	$500,000.00
10	$0.00	$100,000.00	$30,000.00	$30,000.00	$400,000.00
11	$0.00	$100,000.00	$24,000.00	$24,000.00	$300,000.00
12	$0.00	$100,000.00	$18,000.00	$18,000.00	$200,000.00
13	$0.00	$100,000.00	$12,000.00	$12,000.00	$100,000.00
14	$0.00	$100,000.00	$6,000.00	$6,000.00	$0.00

Legend:
(2) Investment $1,000,000 is given.
(3) Results of best-estimate forecasting.
(4) Interest payment = remaining principal × interest rate = [$1,000,000 less cumulative (3)] × 0.06.
(5) Interest income = amortized cost at the end of the prior year × yield rate at purchase = $(6)_{t-1} \times 0.06$.
(6) Amortized cost at end of period = amortized cost at beginning of period less amortization and principal payments during the period = $(6)_{t-1} - (3)_t$. (Note that there is no amortization or accretion since the CMO was purchased at par value.)

Ledger Entries for Above CMO

	CMO Investment		CMO Interest Income		Cash	
Year	Debit	Credit	Debit	Credit	Debit	Credit
1	$1,000,000.00	$0.00		$60,000.00	$60,000.00	$1,000,000.00
2		$0.00		$60,000.00	$60,000.00	
3		$0.00		$60,000.00	$60,000.00	
4		$0.00		$60,000.00	$60,000.00	
5		$100,000.00		$60,000.00	$160,000.00	
6		$100,000.00		$54,000.00	$154,000.00	
7		$100,000.00		$48,000.00	$148,000.00	
8		$100,000.00		$42,000.00	$142,000.00	
9		$100,000.00		$36,000.00	$136,000.00	
10		$100,000.00		$30,000.00	$130,000.00	
11		$100,000.00		$24,000.00	$124,000.00	
12		$100,000.00		$18,000.00	$118,000.00	
13		$100,000.00		$12,000.00	$112,000.00	
14		$100,000.00		$6,000.00	$106,000.00	
Source	(2)	(3)		(5)	(3) + (4)	(2)

Table 13-6 looks at the same security but in a different environment. The principal amount of $1,000,000 and stated interest rate of 6% remain the same. However, the security was purchased at a premium for $1,072,946.19, thus generating an effective yield rate at purchase of 5.00%.

Table 13-6
Cash Flows and Accounting Entries for a CMO Purchased at a Premium
Classified as Held to Maturity

Assumptions at Purchase

(1) Year	(2) Investment	(3) Principal Pay-Down Schedule	(4) Interest Payment	(5) Interest Income	(6) Amortization of Premium	(7) Amortized Cost at End of Period
0	$1,072,946.19	$0.00	$0.00	$0.00	$0.00	$1,072,946.19
1	$0.00	$0.00	$60,000.00	$53,647.31	$6,352.69	$1,066,593.50
2	$0.00	$0.00	$60,000.00	$53,329.68	$6,670.32	$1,059,923.18
3	$0.00	$0.00	$60,000.00	$52,996.16	$7,003.84	$1,052,919.33
4	$0.00	$0.00	$60,000.00	$52,645.97	$7,354.03	$1,045,565.30
5	$0.00	$100,000.00	$60,000.00	$52,278.27	$7,721.73	$937,843.57
6	$0.00	$100,000.00	$54,000.00	$46,892.18	$7,107.82	$830,735.74
7	$0.00	$100,000.00	$48,000.00	$41,536.79	$6,463.21	$724,272.53
8	$0.00	$100,000.00	$42,000.00	$36,213.63	$5,786.37	$618,486.16
9	$0.00	$100,000.00	$36,000.00	$30,924.31	$5,075.69	$513,410.47
10	$0.00	$100,000.00	$30,000.00	$25,670.52	$4,329.48	$409,080.99
11	$0.00	$100,000.00	$24,000.00	$20,454.05	$3,545.95	$305,535.04
12	$0.00	$100,000.00	$18,000.00	$15,276.75	$2,723.25	$202,811.79
13	$0.00	$100,000.00	$12,000.00	$10,140.59	$1,859.41	$100,952.38
14	$0.00	$100,000.00	$6,000.00	$5,047.62	$952.38	$0.00

Legend:

(2) Investment $1,072,946.19 is given.
(3) Results of best-estimate forecasting.
(4) Interest payment = remaining principal × interest rate = [$1,000,000 less cumulative (3)] × 0.06.
(5) Interest income = amortized cost at end of the prior year × yield rate at purchase (5%) = $(7)_{t-1} \times 0.05$.
(6) Amortization of premium = interest payment – interest income = $(4)_t - (5)_t$.
(7) Amortized cost at end of period = amortized cost at beginning of period less amortization and principal payments during the period = $(7)_{t-1} - (3)_t - (6)_t$.

Ledger Entries for Above CMO

Year	CMO Investment Debit	CMO Investment Credit	CMO Interest Income Debit	CMO Interest Income Credit	Cash Debit	Cash Credit
1	$1,072,946.19	$6,352.69		$53,647.31	$60,000.00	$1,072,946.19
2		$6,670.32		$53,329.68	$60,000.00	
3		$7,003.84		$52,996.16	$60,000.00	
4		$7,354.03		$52,645.97	$60,000.00	
5		$107,721.73		$52,278.27	$160,000.00	
6		$107,107.82		$46,892.18	$154,000.00	
7		$106,463.21		$41,536.79	$148,000.00	
8		$105,786.37		$36,213.63	$142,000.00	
9		$105,075.69		$30,924.31	$136,000.00	
10		$104,329.48		$25,670.52	$130,000.00	
11		$103,545.95		$20,454.05	$124,000.00	
12		$102,723.25		$15,276.75	$118,000.00	
13		$101,859.41		$10,140.59	$112,000.00	
14		$100,952.38		$5,047.62	$106,000.00	
Source	(2)	(3) + (6)		(5)	(3) + (4)	(2)

Table 13-7 demonstrates the accounting treatment in which actual prepayments and future expectations of principal payments deviate from the original assumptions.

In Table 13-7, a $50,000 principal payment was received at the end of year three. This prepayment triggered a reassessment of future cash flows. The resulting actual and revised projected future cash flows, when compared to the original purchase price of $1,072,946.19, resulted in a revised yield rate of 4.902676%. Determination of this yield rate at the acquisition date creates a discontinuity in reported values as of the date of evaluation. The requirement of *SFAS 91* to use this hindsight and to revise future assumptions also requires that the amortized cost of the investment be *trued up* to the amount that would have resulted had the current assumptions been used at the acquisition date. This *true-up* is recorded as a charge or credit to income at the point of determination.

There is no restatement of prior year reported amounts. Rather, there is simply a true-up recorded, not dissimilar to the concepts related to true-ups of deferred acquisition costs required by *SFAS 97* (covered in detail in Chapters 6 and 7).

Table 13-7 presents the first three years of accounting entries.

Table 13-7
Revised Assumptions at the End of Year 3 for the Premium CMO Acquired in Table 13-6 Classified as Held to Maturity

(1) Year	(2) Investment	(3) Principal Pay-Down Schedule	(4) Interest Payment	(5) Interest Income	(6) Amortization of Premium	(7) Amortized Cost at End of Period
0	$1,072,946.19	$0.00	$0.00	$0.00	$0.00	$1,072,946.19
1	$0.00	$0.00	$60,000.00	$52,603.07	$7,396.93	$1,065,549.26
2	$0.00	$0.00	$60,000.00	$52,240.42	$7,759.58	$1,057,789.69
3	$0.00	$50,000.00	$60,000.00	$51,860.00	$8,140.00	$999,649.68
4	$0.00	$50,000.00	$57,000.00	$49,009.58	$7,990.42	$941,659.27
5	$0.00	$100,000.00	$54,000.00	$46,166.50	$7,833.50	$833,825.77
6	$0.00	$100,000.00	$48,000.00	$40,879.77	$7,120.23	$726,705.54
7	$0.00	$100,000.00	$42,000.00	$35,628.02	$6,371.98	$620,333.55
8	$0.00	$100,000.00	$36,000.00	$30,412.94	$5,587.06	$514,746.50
9	$0.00	$100,000.00	$30,000.00	$25,236.35	$4,763.65	$409,982.85
10	$0.00	$100,000.00	$24,000.00	$20,100.13	$3,899.87	$306,082.98
11	$0.00	$100,000.00	$18,000.00	$15,006.26	$2,993.74	$203,089.23
12	$0.00	$100,000.00	$12,000.00	$9,956.81	$2,043.19	$101,046.04
13	$0.00	$100,000.00	$6,000.00	$4,953.96	$1,046.04	$0.00

Legend:
(2) Investment $1,072,946.19 is given.
(3) Results of best-estimate forecasting, triggered by receipt of $50,000 principal in year three.
(4) Interest payment = remaining principal × interest rate = [$1,000,000 less cumulative (3)] × 0.06.
(5) Interest income = amortized cost at end of the prior year × the revised yield rate (4.9%) = $(7)_{t-1} \times 0.049$.
(6) Amortization of premium = interest payment – interest income = $(4)_t - (5)_t$.
(7) Amortized cost at end of period = amortized cost at beginning of period less amortization and principal payments during the period = $(7)_{t-1} - (3)_t - (6)_t$.

Ledger Entries for Above CMO with Change in Experience and Future Assumptions

Year	CMO Investment Debit	CMO Investment Credit	CMO Interest Income Debit	CMO Interest Income Credit	Cash Debit	Cash Credit
1	$1,072,946.19	$6,352.69		$53,647.31	$60,000.00	$1,072,946.19
2		$6,670.32		$53,329.68	$60,000.00	
3		$7,003.84		$52,996.16	$60,000.00	
3 (Principal)		$50,000.00			$50,000.00	
3 (True-up)*		$3,269.65	$3,269.65			
Source	(2)	Table 13-6		Table 13-6	(3) + (4)	(2)

*Original cumulative interest income at the end of year 3 = $159,973.14 Source: $(5)_1 + (5)_2 + (5)_3$ from Table 13-6
revised cumulative interest income at the end of year 3 = $156,703.49 Source: $(5)_1 + (5)_2 + (5)_3$ from above
cumulative catch-up at the end of year 3 = ($3,269.65)

In the previous three tables, the investment was considered as held to maturity. Table 13-8 provides the additional accounting entries as if the security were classified as available for sale.

Table 13-8
Cash Flow and Accounting Entries for a CMO Purchased at a Premium
Revised Assumptions at the End of Year Three
Classified as Available for Sale

(1) Year	(2) Investment	(3) Principal Pay-Down Schedule	(4) Interest Payment	(5) Interest Income	(6) Amortization of Premium	(7) Amortized Cost at End of Period	(8) Financial Statement Carrying Value (Fair Value)	(9) Other Comprehensive Income	(10) Balance of Bond Valuation Adjustment Account
0	$1,072,946.19	$0.00	$0.00	$0.00	$0.00	$1,072,946.19	$1,072,946.19	$0.00	$0.00
1	$0.00	$0.00	$60,000.00	$52,603.07	$7,396.93	$1,065,549.26	$1,068,450.00	$2,900.74	$2,900.74
2	$0.00	$0.00	$60,000.00	$52,240.42	$7,759.58	$1,057,789.69	$1,055,262.00	($5,428.42)	($2,527.69)
3	$0.00	$50,000.00	$60,000.00	$51,860.00	$8,140.00	$999,649.68	$1,001,509.00	$4,387.00	$1,859.32
4	$0.00	$50,000.00	$57,000.00	$49,009.58	$7,990.42	$941,659.27			
5	$0.00	$100,000.00	$54,000.00	$46,166.50	$7,833.50	$833,825.77			
6	$0.00	$100,000.00	$48,000.00	$40,879.77	$7,120.23	$726,705.54			
7	$0.00	$100,000.00	$42,000.00	$35,628.02	$6,371.98	$620,333.55			
8	$0.00	$100,000.00	$36,000.00	$30,412.94	$5,587.06	$514,746.50			
9	$0.00	$100,000.00	$30,000.00	$25,236.35	$4,763.65	$409,982.85			
10	$0.00	$100,000.00	$24,000.00	$20,100.13	$3,899.87	$306,082.98			
11	$0.00	$100,000.00	$18,000.00	$15,006.26	$2,993.74	$203,089.23			
12	$0.00	$100,000.00	$12,000.00	$9,956.81	$2,043.19	$101,046.04			
13	$0.00	$100,000.00	$6,000.00	$4,953.96	$1,046.04	$0.00			

Legend:

(1) – (7) Identical to Table 13-7.

(8) Fair values as of the reporting date.

(9) Change in the unrealized capital gain/loss = $(10)_t - (10)_{t-1}$.

(10) Difference between fair value and amortized cost = $(8)_t - (7)_t$.

Accounting entries for CMO investment, CMO interest income, and cash accounts are found in Table 13-7.

Accounting Entries to Reflect Fair Value Adjustments

Year	Other Comprehensive		Bond Valuation	
	Debit	Credit	Debit	Credit
1		$2,900.74	$2,900.74	
2	$5,428.42			$5,428.42
3		$4,387.00	$4,387.00	

Some CMOs are referred to as principal only (PO) or interest only (IO) strips. These CMOs are structured to pass on only the cash flows related to the underlying principal payments or interest payments, respectively. POs are generally sold at discounts that, as principal prepayments are made, will result in a yield being earned. Again, as prepayment speeds change, the expected yields will change requiring the application of the retrospective method previously discussed.

IOs are different. The purchase price for an IO generally reflects the investor's estimate of the present value (at an expected effective yield) of the future cash flows resulting from the interest payments. IOs carry a risk of loss relating to the principal that generates the interest payments. Prepayment speeds can accelerate to the point at which there are insufficient interest payments or cash flows to recover the cost of the investment. Therefore, the investor is required to periodically (as of each reporting date) reassess recoverability. Recoverability is evaluated based on an analysis of expected future cash flows, discounted at a risk-free rate of return, using assumptions that represent the current best estimate. If the analysis results in an amount that is less than the amortized book value, then the security is considered impaired and is to be written down to fair (market) value. This becomes the new cost basis that serves as the basis for calculation of the yield to be used on a going-forward (prospective) basis.

Note that CMOs that have been purchased at significant premiums also have exposure to loss of principal in increasing prepayment scenarios. The CMO may prepay so quickly that there is insufficient time for the otherwise favorable interest payments to recover the additional cost of the investment. Such circumstances require periodic recoverability analysis to determine whether or not a write-down is appropriate.

13.4 Preferred Stocks

Preferred stocks which by their terms have characteristics similar to those of debt instruments are accounted for as fixed maturity (debt) securities. Otherwise, these securities are considered equity securities and based upon the intended purpose of the investment, are classified as either a *trading* security or an AFS security. Cost is not subsequently adjusted unless the security is impaired (cost, to some extent, is estimated to be unrecoverable). These preferred stocks are carried at their fair value in the balance sheet. Any unrealized gain or loss, represented by the difference between cost and fair value and the change therein, from reporting date to reporting date is recognized in earnings for trading securities and in other comprehensive income (equity) for AFS securities.

The dividend income received and/or accrued is recognized as income as it is earned, which is generally on the date that the investor becomes entitled to receive such distribution. Because these are equity securities, there is no premium or discount that needs to be amortized.

13.5 Common Stocks

The accounting for common stocks is generally dictated by the ownership percentage the investment represents.

13.5.1 Unaffiliated Common Stock Investments

For holdings of less than 20% of the outstanding stock of a company, the guidance of *SFAS 115* applies. Such investments are carried in the financial statements at their fair values with unrealized gains or losses reflected in earnings for *trading* securities, or in other comprehensive income for AFS securities. Dividend distributions are generally recognized as they are earned, generally when such dividends are declared and payable to the stockholders of record on a specific date known as the ex-dividend date.

13.5.2 Affiliated Common Stock Investments

This category of common stock investments includes investees (20% to 50% ownership interest) and subsidiaries (greater than 50% ownership interest).

Investees are carried at the cost incurred to acquire the investment plus or minus cumulative undistributed comprehensive income. Unrealized gains or losses are not reflected in the financial statements, and net income as well as other comprehensive income is recognized on the *equity* method. The equity method requires the investor to calculate its pro-rata share of after-tax earnings and other comprehensive income and recognize such earnings and other comprehensive income in the investors' financial statements. Assume the following set of facts for ABC Company's 40% investment in Company XYZ.

Company XYZ's results for fiscal year ending 200X

Net Income	$	2,000
Other Comprehensive Income:		
• Net unrealized gain		400
• Foreign exchange		–100
		300
Comprehensive Income	$	2,300
Dividends Declared and Paid	$	400

ABC Company would make the following entries to record its 40% share of the investees' year 200X results:

Dr. Investment in investee	$	920
Cr. Equity in the net income of investee	$	800
Cr. Equity in the other comprehensive income of investee	$	120

With respect to the dividends received, they are credited directly to the accumulated cost of the investee. In the case above, the entry which would be recorded by ABC Company is shown below;

Dr. Cash	$	160
Cr. Investment in investee	$	160

For an investment in a subsidiary (ownership is greater than 50%), the financial statements of such subsidiary are consolidated with the financial statements of the parent company. Such accounting results in the combination of the various financial statement line items of the parent and subsidiary companies as if they were one company. Consolidation requires the identification and elimination of all material intercompany balances and transactions from the financial statements.

In cases in which the ownership percentage is not 100%, a minority interest calculation is made whereby the minority stockholders' share of net income and other comprehensive income is determined and subtracted from the consolidated results and added to the accumulated minority interest balance. Such minority interest balance is intended to represent the minority stockholders' interest in the net assets of the subsidiary and is therefore presented on the balance sheet between total liabilities and the stockholders' equity section (commonly referred to as the mezzanine). Dividends between the subsidiary and the parent are eliminated in the consolidation process, whereas dividends paid to the minority shareholders are charged directly to the minority interest balance in the balance sheet.

13.6 Mortgage Loans

Mortgage loan investments represent loans secured by interests in underlying real estate. Because of statutory investment limitations, most mortgage loan investments of insurance companies tend to be first mortgages.

Mortgage loans are recorded and carried at the unpaid principal balance adjusted for any unamortized premiums or discount (see Section 13.3 for a discussion of premiums and discounts). Premiums and discounts are amortized by using methods that result in a constant effective yield to maturity. Insurance companies should perform annual evaluations of the recoverability or collectibility of such assets. If the ultimate collectibility of 100% of an individual mortgage loan or the overall portfolio of loans in doubtful, then the insurance company should establish a reserve for the best estimate of the uncollectible amount. This amount is generally reflected as a contra account in the general ledger and combined (netted against) the unpaid principal balances when periodic financial statements are prepared.

The following is an example of accounting for a mortgage loan.

Table 13-9
Cash Flows and Accounting Entries for a Mortgage Loan
\$10,000 mortgage; stated interest rate is 12% compounded annually; payments made at the end of each year. Loan Term: 7 years

(A) Point in Time	0	1	2	3	4	5	6	7
(B) Investment	$10,000.00	$0.00	$0.00	$0.00	$0.00	$0.00	$0.00	$0.00
(C) Mortgage Payment	$0.00	$2,191.18	$2,191.18	$2,191.18	$2,191.18	$2,191.18	$2,191.18	$2,191.18
(D) Interest on Outstanding Balance	$0.00	$1,200.00	$1,081.06	$947.84	$798.64	$631.54	$444.38	$234.77
(E) Principal Reduction	$0.00	$991.18	$1,110.12	$1,243.33	$1,392.53	$1,559.64	$1,746.79	$1,956.41
(F) Outstanding Balance	$10,000.00	$9,008.82	$7,898.70	$6,655.37	$5,262.84	$3,703.20	$1,956.41	$0.00

Legend:
(B) The outlay to acquire the mortgage, $10,000.
(C) = $10,000 / immediate annuity at 12% (4.5638).
(D) $= 0.12 \times (F)_{t-1}$
(E) $= (C)_t - (D)_t$
(F) $= (F)_{t-1} - (E)_t$

Ledger Entries for Above Mortgage Loan

Point in Time	Mortgage Investment		Mortgage Interest Income		Cash	
	Debit	Credit	Debit	Credit	Debit	Credit
0	$10,000.00					$10,000.00
1		$991.18		$1,200.00	$2,191.18	
2		$1,110.12		$1,081.06	$2,191.18	
3		$1,243.33		$947.84	$2,191.18	
4		$1,392.53		$798.64	$2,191.18	
5		$1,559.64		$631.54	$2,191.18	
6		$1,746.79		$444.38	$2,191.18	
7		$1,956.41		$234.77	$2,191.18	
Source for ledger entries	Row B	Row E		Row D	Row C	Row B

13.7 Real Estate

Insurance companies acquire real estate generally for two reasons:

- Ownership versus leasing of the company's operational facilities
- Investment purposes.

In the case of real estate that is used in the company's operations, the asset is carried at its cost adjusted for depreciation over the estimated useful life of the property. This useful life generally does not exceed 40 years. There are a variety of depreciation methods, from straight line to various accelerated methods. Ordinarily, as long as the company intends to continue to use such real estate in support of its operations, no adjustments are required for declines in the market value of such assets.

Investment real estate is also carried at depreciated cost. The revenue and expenses resulting from the operations of the property are generally reflected as a component of net investment income. Investors are periodically required to evaluate the recoverability of their real estate investments. Such assessments can be made by obtaining independent appraisals or by preparing discounted cash flow analyses, which serve as indicators of a company's ability to recover its investments. If such appraisal or valuation analysis indicates a recoverability issue, the company should write down the assets to its best estimate of the amount ultimately recoverable.

The accounting for real estate sales transactions can be very complex and result from provisions in the literature that were developed over the years to deal with the extremely complex transactions entered into by entities specializing in such real estate transactions. The primary issue is if and when profit should be recognized on a sale. *SFAS No. 66*, "Accounting for Sales of Real Estate," is the primary authoritative literature. This statement provides a decision tree that helps to establish the proper timing and extent of revenue recognition. This decision tree is reproduced in Figures 13-1 and 13-2. Further analysis of this highly complex subject area extends beyond the scope of this textbook.

Figure 13-1
Retail Land Sales

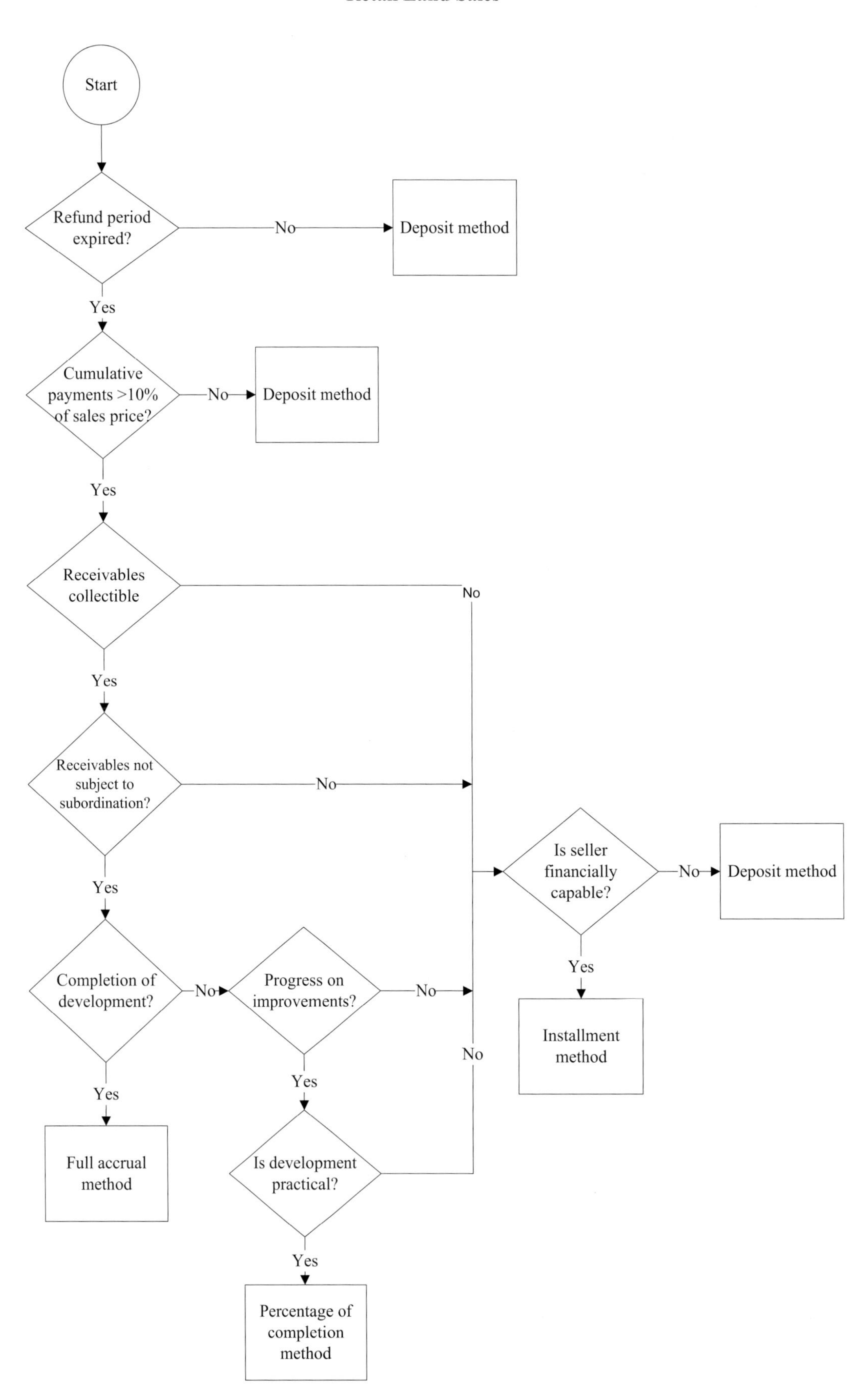

Figure 13-2
Sales of Real Estate Other than Retail Land Sales

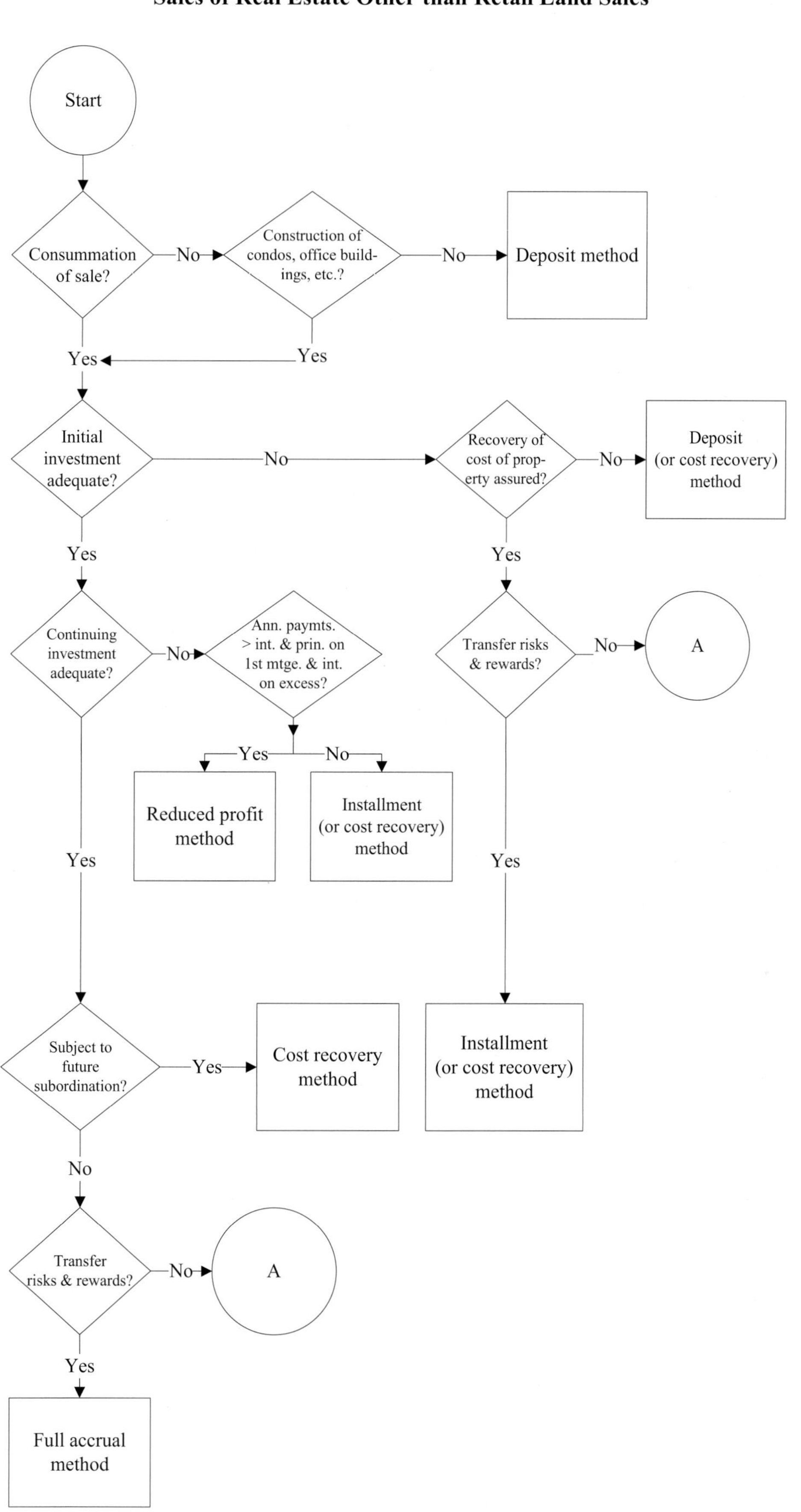

Figure 13-2 (Continued)
Sales of Real Estate Other than Retail Land Sales

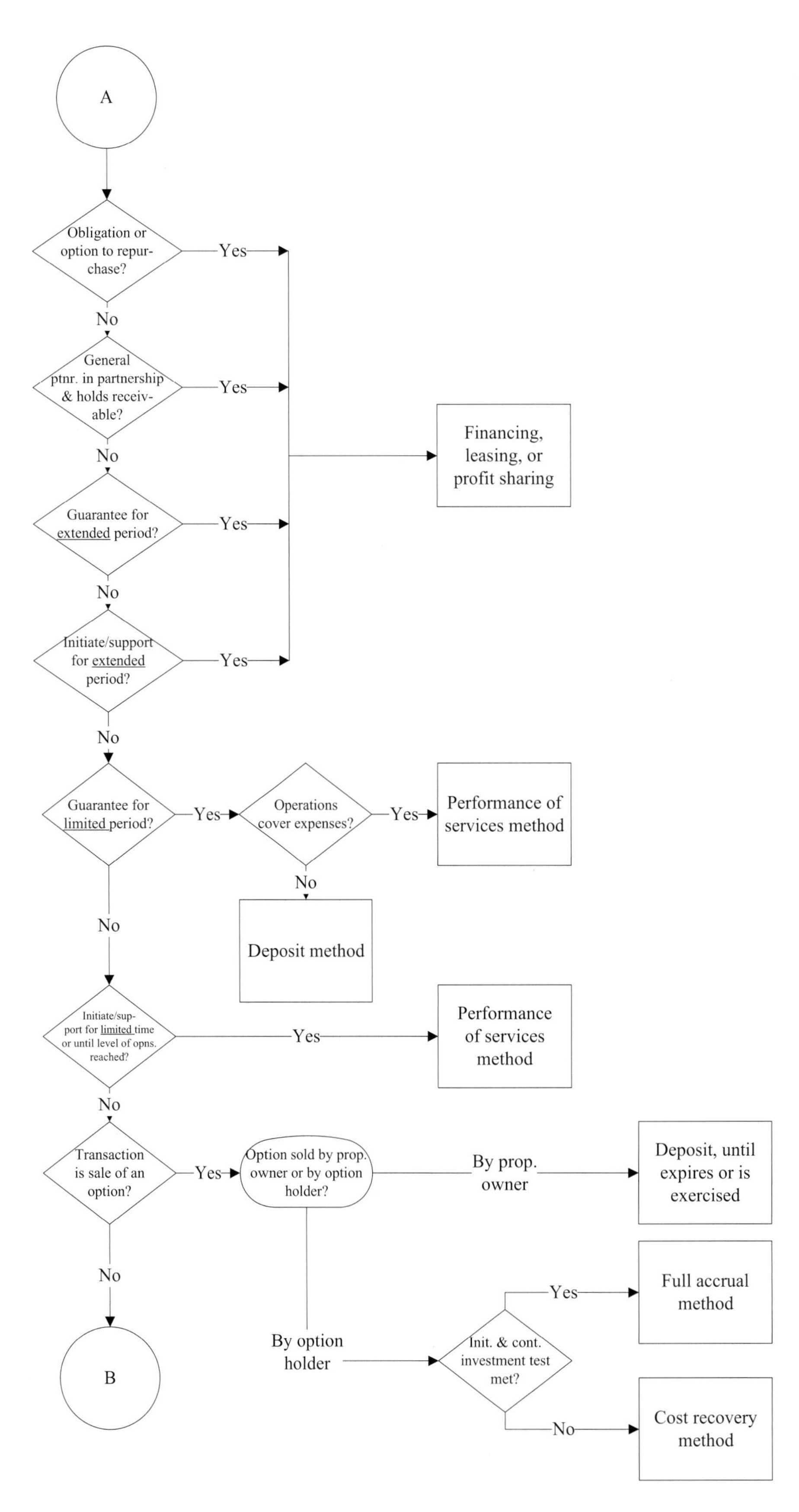

Figure 13-2 (Continued)
Sales of Real Estate Other than Retail Land Sales

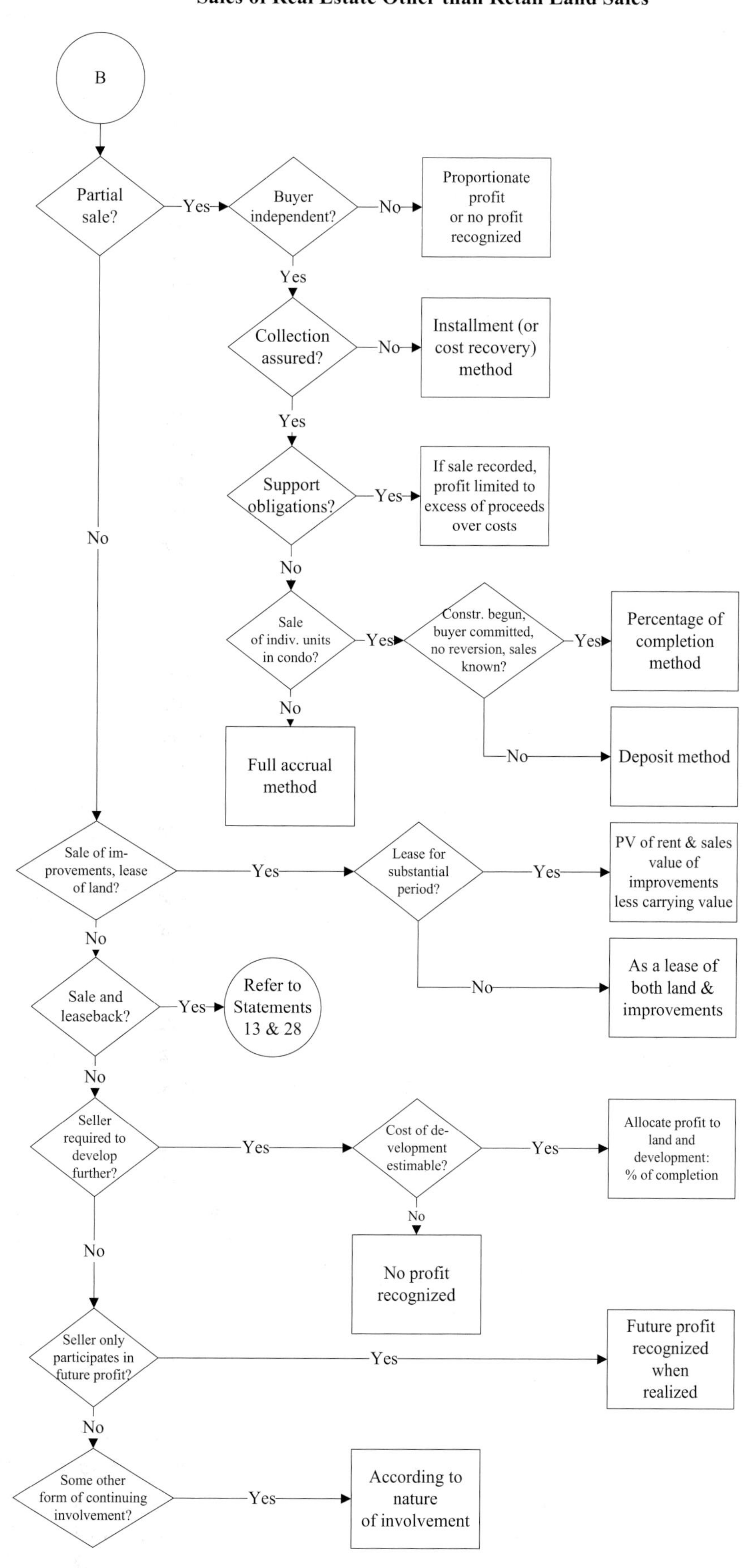

For relatively simple transactions, the general requirements for full gain recognition from a real estate sale as set forth in *SFAS 66* are as follows:

- The net proceeds from the sale are reasonably assured.
- The seller has no further significant obligations to be satisfied after the sale to earn the profit.

If these general requirements are not met, some or all of the profit on the sale should be deferred until the requirements are satisfied.

13.8 Policy Loans

Many of the products sold by life insurance companies provide for the accumulation of cash values that are ultimately payable to the policyholder in the event that the contract is canceled. The policyholder may also have the option to borrow funds from the insurance company. These loans, which are secured by the surrender value of the policies, are known as policy loans. Such loans typically carry interest rates that are favorable to the policyholder and still provide for an appropriate return to the insurance company so it can meet its obligations under the policies.

Policyholders may also elect to have the insurance company *automatically* process policy loans to pay any past-due premiums that may be payable. Typically policy loans are not granted for amounts in excess of the accumulated cash surrender value of the policy or contract.

Policy loans are carried in the balance sheet as invested assets at the unpaid balance of the loans. In some cases interest payments are made at the beginning of the period and in some cases, at the end. The earning of interest, however, is over the period that the loan is outstanding with appropriate accruals of unearned interest or interest receivable made to accomplish such earnings process.

13.9 Partnerships

Partnership investments and investments in joint ventures by life insurers are generally accounted for by using the equity method of accounting (see Section 13.5.2). For such investments that represent less than a 20% interest, some companies have used a cost basis to record their investment interest. However, the SEC has taken the position that partnership investments that constitute as little as 3%-5 % interest should be accounted for on the equity method as required by AICPA *Statement of Position No. 78-9*, "Accounting for Investments in Real Estate Ventures."

SOP 78-9 requires equity method accounting unless the investment interest is so minor that the investor has no real influence or control over the operation.

13.10 Short-Term Investments

Short-term investments are common for life insurance companies. Short term investments generally have maturities of less than 1 year and are used by insurance companies to manage their short-term liquidity and cash needs.

Because they are short-term, there are typically no significant differences between amortized cost and fair value. Accordingly, such investments are generally carried at amortized cost.

13.11 Derivatives and Hedging Activities

Life insurance companies as part of their overall asset/liability matching programs may invest in derivatives in order to hedge and reduce the uncertainties and financial statement and/or economic risks and impacts associated with changes in certain variables. Such uncertainties could include changes in the overall interest rate environment or uncertainties relating to movements in the fair value of equity securities. These changes in variables which are outside of the control of the insurance company can also have significant impacts on contractholder decisions regarding their investment in interest sensitive products or products whose returns are tied to other indices such as equity indexed annuities. For example, in an increasing interest rate environment, contractholders may seek alternative investments if crediting rates aren't adjusted to their satisfaction. Resultant surrenders may also trigger the need for the insurance company to liquidate investments which may also be suffering from interest rate-related declines in fair values. Such sales would trigger realized capital losses which would be reflected in earnings.

There are a variety of derivative products which can be used to minimize such risks and uncertainties. Such use is generally referred to as a hedging activity. Some companies have also invested in derivatives on a speculative basis in order to hopefully achieve higher rates of investment return. These types of speculative investment activities have generally been limited by insurance companies' internal investment policies as well as external regulatory-imposed investment limitations.

As the use of derivatives became more widespread in the 1990s, it became apparent that there was very little in the way of authoritative accounting and disclosure guidance that users and preparers of financial statements could look to. In 1998, after a lengthy process, the FASB issued *SFAS 133,* "Accounting for Derivative Investments and Hedging Activities." It is effective for all fiscal quarters in years beginning after June 15, 2000 which, for insurance companies, means this standard will be effective for the year ended December 31, 2001.

The standard is comprehensive and very complex. It is so complex that the FASB created a special team called the Derivatives Implementation Group (DIG). The DIG has the responsibility to study implementation and practice issues and advise the FASB on those issues.

The DIG's resolutions remain tentative until the FASB clears them. In June 2000 the FASB issued *SFAS No. 138*, "Accounting for Certain Derivative Instruments and Certain Hedging Activities an Amendment of FASB Statement No. 133." This statement addressed some specific issues causing difficulty for a widespread group of entities implementing *SFAS No. 133*, as well as incorporating the guidance, as appropriate, arising from the DIG process. In April of 2003 the FASB issued *SFAS No. 149* which further amends and clarifies accounting for derivatives (including derivatives imbedded in other contracts) and hedging activities. This amendment of *SFAS No. 133* incorporates additional guidance resulting from decisions reached during the DIG process and other financial instrument projects as well as from implementation issues encountered relating to the definition of a derivative.

This extraordinary implementation process is reflective of the complexity of derivatives and the related accounting for and reporting thereof. The discussion which follows is intended to provide a general conceptual overview.

SFAS No. 133 provides a definition of derivatives by describing their essential characteristics. Typical derivatives used by insurance enterprises include swaps, options, forwards, futures, caps, floors and collars. Derivatives that meet the definitions of assets or liabilities should be recognized as such in the financial statements. They should also be measured at fair value. Changes in the fair value of derivative instruments are to be recognized in earnings as the changes occur. If the derivative qualifies as a hedge, then the accounting for the changes in fair value may vary depending upon the risk being hedged. The FASB, however, decided to limit hedge accounting to certain transactions meeting specific criteria and established strict documentation requirements related to such transactions. The limitations resulted in three general groupings: fair value, cash flow, and foreign currency hedges.

- Fair value hedges are used to reduce or eliminate the risk of changes in fair values due to fixed rates or prices. Gains or losses on such derivative hedging instruments, as well as gains and losses on the related hedged item, are recorded in earnings. To the extent that the gains and losses do not completely offset then the difference effectively results in a gain or loss being reflected in earnings. This difference is known as the ineffective portion of the hedge.

- Cash flow hedges are used to reduce or eliminate the rish of changes in cash flows due to variable rates or prices. To the extent that the derivative is effective at offsetting the cash flows or the hedged item, then the effective portion of the gain or loss on the derivative is accumulated in "other comprehensive income" and subsequently transferred to earnings when the hedged item impacts earnings. The ineffective portion of the gain or loss from the derivative is recognized in earnings immediately.

- Foreign currency hedges are used to reduce or eliminate the risks from changes in fair values, cash flows or net investments in foreign operations resulting from changes in foreign exchange rates. Fair value and cash flow hedges receive the same accounting treatment as described above. For a derivative hedging the foreign currency exposure related to a net investment in a foreign operation, any gain or loss is reported in "other comprehensive income" as a part of the cumulative translation adjustment, but only to the extent that the derivative is effective as a hedge. The ineffective portion is recognized in earnings immediately.

The standard goes on to specifically exclude certain types of transactions or instruments such as certain insurance contracts (traditional life and property/casualty insurance policies) from the scope of the pronouncement. *SFAS 133* also addresses derivatives which may be embedded in host contracts. Life insurers will need to carefully evaluate their product offering to determine if there are such embedded derivatives and, if so, perform the appropriate research to ensure that these contracts are appropriately accounted for in accordance with the provisions of *SFAS No. 133*.

In summary, this complex standard requires a significant commitment from the entities it affects. Significant resources may be required to assess the standard's impact, train the appropriate personnel, and develop and maintain new accounting and/or information systems. The standard may also change the way the entity looks at its risk management objectives and strategies.

13.12 Insurance Contract Analysis Under *SFAS 133*

13.12.1 Introduction

Generally, contracts of the type that are within the scope of *SFAS 60*, "Accounting and Reporting by Insurance Enterprises"; *SFAS 97*, "Accounting and Reporting by Insurance Enterprises for Certain Long-Duration Contracts and for Realized Gains and Losses from the Sale of

Investments"; and *SFAS 113*, "Accounting and Reporting for Reinsurance of Short-Duration and Long-Duration Contracts" are not subject to the requirements of *SFAS 133*, regardless of whether they are written by insurance enterprises.

A contract is not subject to the requirements of *SFAS 133* if it entitles the holder to be compensated only if, as a result of an identifiable insurance event (other than a change in price), the holder incurs a liability or there is an adverse change in the value of a specific asset or liability for which the holder is at risk.

Traditional life insurance contracts are not subject to the requirements of *SFAS 133* because the payment of benefits is the result of an identifiable insurable event (the death of the insured), not changes in a variable. Similarly, traditional property and casualty contracts are not subject to the requirements of the standard because the payment of benefits is the result of an identifiable insurable event (for example, theft or fire) rather than changes in a variable.

However, certain entities enter into contracts that combine derivative instruments with insurance products or nonderivative contracts. The following sections analyze common types of contracts that are likely to fall within the scope of *SFAS 133* and its related statements *SFAS 138* and *SFAS 149*.

In connection with *SFAS 133*, the FASB established the Derivatives Implementation Group for the purpose of addressing implementation issues. Since 1998, the FASB staff, through the DIG process, has provided guidance on over 150 implementation issues. These issues and future additions may be referenced by accessing the FASB website at www.fasb.org.

13.12.2 Guaranteed Investment Contracts

In a traditional guaranteed investment contract (GIC), the issuer of the contract takes deposits from a benefit plan (or other institutional investor) and purchases fixed income investments that are held in its general account. The benefit plan is a creditor of the issuing company and, therefore, has credit risk, although generally the issuing company has a high credit-quality rating. The issuer is contractually obligated to repay the principal and specified interest guaranteed to the benefit plan. The benefit plan's provisions typically permit the participant to withdraw funds at book value for specified reasons, such as loans, hardship withdrawals, and transfers to other investment options offered by the plan. A benefit-responsive GIC contains provisions that mirror the plan's participant-directed withdrawal/transfer provisions. Therefore, the issuer is at risk that interest rates could increase, thereby reducing the price of the fixed-income investments backing the GIC liability, while those investments may have to be sold at a loss to cover withdrawals. From the issuer's perspective, traditional GICs are accounted for in accordance with *SFAS97* in a manner similar to other financial instruments. In addition, traditional GICs neither meet the characteristics of a derivative nor typically have embedded derivative components within the scope of the standard.

13.12.3 Synthetic GICs

A synthetic GIC is a contract that simulates the performance of a traditional GIC through the use of financial instruments. A key difference between a synthetic GIC and a traditional GIC is that the policyholder (such as a benefit plan) owns the assets underlying the synthetic GIC. Those assets may be held in a trust owned by the policyholder and typically include government securities, private and public mortgage-backed securities, other asset-backed securities, and investment-grade corporate obligations. To enable the policyholder to realize a specific known value for the assets if it needs to liquidate them, synthetic GICs use a wrapper contract that provides market and cash flow risk protection to the policyholder. In a synthetic GIC, the issuer, in effect, sells a put option to the policyholder. For many synthetic GICs, the option premium is in the form of a fee charged on the outstanding contract book value.

Synthetic GICs fall into several broad structural categories, including buy and hold, actively managed, and fixed-rate/fixed maturity. In each of these, the holder's exposure to variable cash flows is transferred to the issuer of the contract. In addition, payments under synthetic GICs are not limited to identifiable insurable events (the holder does not need to incur a loss to receive compensation under the contract). As a result, the guarantee of cash flows on the underlying assets by the issuer constitutes a derivative (e.g., the issuer is selling a put option to the holder of the GIC) and, as a result, the issuer accounts for the synthetic GIC, in its entirety, as a derivative under *SFAS 133*. The fair value of the derivative must take into account all contractual terms of the synthetic GIC. See *DIG Issue A16* for further reference.

The accounting guidance for the holder of a synthetic GIC depends on the type of entity holding the instrument and the type of synthetic GIC. Paragraph 10(g) of *SFAS 133* excludes from the requirements synthetic GICs that are fully benefit-responsive and held by defined-contribution plans, including both health and welfare pension plans. AICPA *Statement of Position 94-4*, Application of Fair Value and Contract Value Reporting for Defined Contribution Plan Investments (*SOP 94-4*), instead provides the accounting guidance for these instruments. Based on paragraph 4 of *SOP 94-4*, defined-contribution plans, including both health and welfare pension plans, holding a fully benefit-responsive synthetic GIC should separately value and disclose the assets underlying the synthetic GIC and the wrapper contract. The wrapper contract should be valued at the difference between the fair value of the underlying assets and the contract value attributable by the wrapper contract to those assets.

A fully benefit-responsive contract provides a liquidity guarantee by a financially responsible third party of principal and previously accrued interest for liquidations, transfers, loans, or hardship withdrawals initiated by plan participants exercising their right to withdraw, borrow, or transfer funds under the terms of the ongoing plan. Access to funds is not substantially restricted by plan provisions. For all other holders of synthetic GICs, as well as for those holders noted above when the synthetic GIC is not fully benefit-responsive, *SFAS 133* applies.

Under *SFAS 133*, a wrapper contract is generally a freestanding derivative because it was issued after the issuance of the underlying assets and by a party other than the issuers of the assets. The derivative contract would be marked to fair value with changes in value reflected in earnings. The fair value of the derivative contract must take into account all contract terms of the synthetic GIC. The underlying assets would continue to be accounted for at fair value by the policyholder.

Paragraph 10(g) of *SFAS 133* also excludes insurance contracts accounted for under paragraph 4 of *SFAS 110*, Reporting by Defined Benefit Pension Plans of Investment Contracts; paragraph 12 of *SFAS 35*, Accounting and Reporting by Defined Benefits Pension Plans, as amended; and paragraph 5 of *SOP 94-4*.

13.12.4 Traditional Variable Annuity

Traditional variable annuity products are investment contracts as contemplated in *SFAS 60* and *SFAS 97*. An annuity contract is a contract that provides for fixed or variable periodic payments made from a stated or contingent date and continuing for a specified period. A variable annuity contract is an annuity in which the payment amounts are specified in units, rather than in dollars.

When a payment is due, the amount of the unit is determined based on the value of the investments in an annuity fund.

Similar to variable life insurance products, in a variable annuity contract, even though the insurance company owns the investments, policyholders direct the investment account asset mix among a variety of mutual funds that include equities, bonds, or both, and assume the risks and rewards on investment performance. The insurance company generally maintains the funds in separate accounts.

A traditional variable annuity product generally includes several attributes. Policyholders' payments, after deducting specified sales and administrative charges, are used to purchase units of a separate investment account (a separate account). The policyholder directs the allocation of the account value among various investment options (typically various mutual funds) and the policyholder bears the investment risk (i.e., the account value is based entirely on the performance of the directed investments). Units may be surrendered for their current value in cash, although there often is a small surrender charge, or the units may be applied to purchase annuity income. The issuer guarantees mortality and maximum expense charges; amounts are deducted periodically from the separate account to cover these charges. If the contract is a deferred annuity contract, it may provide a death benefit during the accumulation period under which the policyholder may receive the greater of the sum of premiums paid or the value of total units to the credit of the account at time of the policyholder's death.

A traditional variable annuity product is not within the scope of *SFAS 133* and contains no embedded derivatives that warrant separate accounting under the standard, provided the following conditions are met:

- The variable annuity contract is established, approved, and regulated under special rules applicable to variable annuities (such as state insurance laws, securities laws, and tax laws).
- The assets underlying the contract are insulated from the general account liabilities of the insurance company (the policyholder is not subject to insurer default risk to the extent of the assets held in the separate account).
- The policyholder's premium is invested in contract-approved separate accounts at the policyholders direction.
- The insurer invests in the assets on which the account values are based.
- If applicable, the policyholder may redirect investment among the contract-approved investment options.
- The account values are based entirely on the performance of those directed investments.
- All investment returns are passed through to the policyholder (including dividends, interest, and gains/losses).

- The policyholder may redeem the contract at any time; however, it may be subject to surrender charges, and
- If applicable, the policyholder has voting rights in certain separate account structures.

DIG Issue B7 provides further reference.

Although the liability to policyholders is not specifically required to be re-measured at fair value with changes reported in earnings under existing GAAP, current accounting practice for traditional variable annuity contracts is to record a liability that is generally equal to the total of the market value of the assets backing the variable investment options held in the separate account for the policyholders.

13.12.5 Nontraditional Variable Annuity

Enterprises have developed a wide range of variable annuity contracts with nontraditional features. Nontraditional features of traditional variable annuity contracts result in a sharing of investment risk between the issuer and the holder. Nontraditional variable annuity contracts provide for a minimum guarantee of the account value at a specified date. This minimum may be guaranteed through a minimum accumulation benefit or a guaranteed account value floor. For example, the floor guarantee might be that, at a specified anniversary date, the contract holder would be credited with the greater of (1) the account value, as determined by the separate account assets, or (2) all deposits that are made, plus three percent interest compounded annually. While these nontraditional variable annuity contracts have distinguishing features, they possess a common characteristic the issuer and the policyholder share the investment risk associated with the assets backing the contract. In contrast to traditional variable annuity contracts, the investment risk is, by virtue of the nontraditional product features, allocated between the two parties and not borne entirely by one of the parties (the holder in the case of a traditional variable annuity contract) to the contract. The sharing of risks makes nontraditional variable annuities hybrid instruments.

The host contract in a nontraditional variable annuity contract would be considered a traditional variable annuity, as described above. Nontraditional features, such as a guaranteed investment return through a minimum accumulation benefit or a guaranteed account value floor, would need to be analyzed to determine whether they are embedded derivatives. Specifically, features, such as a guaranteed investment return through a minimum accumulation benefit or a guaranteed account value floor, that are included in variable annuity contracts would not meet the clearly and closely related requirement in paragraph 12(a) of *SFAS 133* and must be accounted for separately if they meet the other requirements in paragraph 12.

13.12.6 Deferred Variable Annuity

An annuity contract whose benefit payments have not yet commenced is referred to as a deferred annuity. Deferred annuities have two phases. The first is the accumulation phase, during which payments received by the insurance enterprise are accumulated and earn either a fixed or variable return. Much like a savings account, the cash surrender value may be withdrawn. The second phase is the payout phase, during which annuity payments are made to the annuitant under one of various options chosen by the policyholder at annuitization, including the following:

- Life-contingent payments (payable for life of the annuitant)

- Payments for a period-certain (e.g., a 10-year period-certain annuity for 10 years to the annuitant or the annuitants beneficiary or estate), or

- Period-certain-plus-life-contingent payments (e.g., a life-and-10-year-certain annuity pays the annuity benefit for the greater of the annuitants life or 10 years).

At the end of the accumulation period, some deferred annuity contracts allow the policyholder to elect an immediate payout of the account value. A minimum guarantee offered in conjunction with a variable annuity that is provided prior to annuitization is discussed in section 13.12.5, second paragraph. The remainder of this section relates solely to the interaction of certain features within a deferred variable annuity contract and the standard during the accumulation period. See DIG Issue B25 for further reference.

At the end of the accumulation period, some deferred annuity contracts provide the policyholder with the option to annuitize at a guaranteed minimum annuity interest rate. That is, at the date of annuitization, the fixed periodic annuity payments would be determined using the current accumulated account value at the date of annuitization and the higher of the minimum guaranteed interest rate and currently offered annuity interest rates.

During the accumulation phase of the deferred annuity contract, the guarantee of a minimum interest rate to be used in computing periodic annuity payments if and when a policyholder elects to annuitize does not require separate accounting under paragraph 12 of *SFAS 133* because the criterion in paragraph 12(c) is not met. That is, the embedded option does not meet the definition of a derivative instrument because it does not meet the net settlement criteria in paragraphs 6(c) and 9 because settlement of the option can be achieved only by an investment of the account balance in a payout annuity contract in lieu of electing an immediate payout of the account value. In addition, if a provision existed whereby the policyholder could withdraw all or a portion of its account balance during the payout phase, an embedded derivative still would not exist during the accumulation period because the economic benefit of the guaranteed minimum interest rate would be obtainable only if an entity were to maintain the annuity contract through its specified maturity date.

Some deferred variable annuities, in exchange for the issuer's right to charge a fee, may provide a guaranteed minimum amount available to annuitize after a specified period in addition to a guaranteed minimum annuity interest rate. These benefits are often referred to as guaranteed minimum income benefits, or GMIBs. The payment alternatives have the effect of modifying the account value at the end of the accumulation period. The provision that guarantees a minimum account value that is available to annuitize if and when a policyholder elects to annuitize fails to meet the definition of a derivative during the accumulation phase because it cannot be net-settled. The policyholder realizes the benefit of the minimum account value by annuitizing and receiving the economic benefit over the payout term. However, if the policyholder is able to withdraw all or a portion of the guaranteed account balance during the payout (annuitization) period, or the payout (annuitization) period is set to an unrealistically short period, such as one year, this right is equivalent to net settlement, and the guarantee (or the portion of the guarantee that is withdrawable, if applicable) is an embedded derivative only during the accumulation period.

When an entity reinsures a GMIB benefit, the reinsurer typically pays the insurance company a lump sum amount, rather than paying a stream of payments over the life of the policyholder, when the policyholder elects the GMIB benefit. As a result, the lump sum payment represents net settlement. Consequently, when reinsured, the GMIB benefits meet the definition of a derivative.

Instead of providing a guaranteed minimum account value at annuitization, some deferred annuities provide for a variable-payout annuity option with a minimum guarantee on the periodic annuity payments made during the payout phase. That is, once the payout phase has begun, the periodic annuity payments may be variable (i.e., benefits will vary with investment performance of underlying funds, a formula, or an index, such as the S&P 500 Index), but with a provision that each periodic payment will be at least equal to a specified minimum amount. An embedded derivative does not exist during the accumulation phase of such a deferred variable annuity contract because the policyholder cannot net-settle the contract. This is because the only way the policyholder can obtain the benefit of the floor payment guarantee is over the life of the variable-payout annuity.

13.12.7 Variable Annuity with Guaranteed Minimum Payments

A variable annuity contract (including a deferred annuity during the payout phase) can contain a minimum guarantee on the periodic annuity payments. The term of the annuity payments may be period-certain, solely life-contingent, or period-certain-plus-life-contingent. Some contracts offer annuities with partial withdrawal features during the payout phase. The accounting treatment for the contractual provision for guaranteed minimum periodic payments depends on the payout option in the variable-payout annuity contract.

For the period-certain variable-payout annuity, the guaranteed minimum periodic payment is, during the payout phase, an embedded derivative that is required to be separated under paragraph 12 of *SFAS 133*. This conclusion is based on the assessment that the guaranteed payment floor is not considered clearly and closely related to the host contract, a traditional variable-payout annuity contract. However, a solely life-contingent variable-payout annuity contract with features described above that meets the definition of an insurance contract under paragraph 8 of *SFAS 97* would not be subject to the requirements of *SFAS 133* provided there are no withdrawal features.

For a period-certain-plus-life-contingent variable-payout annuity contract, the embedded derivative related only to the period-certain guaranteed minimum periodic payments would be required to be separated under paragraph 12 of *SFAS 133*, whereas the embedded derivative related to the life-contingent guaranteed minimum periodic payments would not be separated under paragraph 12. Separate accounting for the embedded derivative related only to the period-certain guaranteed minimum periodic payments would be required even if the period-certain-plus-life-contingent annuity, in its entirety, meets the definition of an insurance contract under *SFAS 97*'s paragraph 8 and has no withdrawal features. See DIG Issue B25 for further reference.

The separate accounting for the embedded derivative is required even though *SFAS 133* generally does not intend for a contract both to meet the definition of a derivative in its entirety, but be excluded in paragraphs 10 and 11 of *SFAS 133*, and to be considered a hybrid instrument that contains an embedded derivative that requires separate accounting.

A hybrid instrument is a contract that does not in its entirety meet the definition of a derivative instrument in *SFAS 133*, paragraphs 6 through 9, but contains explicit or implicit terms that affect some or all of the cash flows under the contract similarly to the way in which the terms of a derivative instrument affects its cash flows. A hybrid instrument consists of a host contract and one or more embedded components. A common example of a hybrid instrument is a debt instrument that contains a put option, call option, conversion option, or a combination thereof. In general, an instrument cannot be a hybrid instrument if it meets the definition of a derivative in its entirety but is explicitly excluded from the scope of *SFAS 133* by paragraphs 10 or 11.

A contract that is a derivative in its entirety and that qualifies for the normal purchases and sales exception is not evaluated further under paragraph 12 for an embedded derivative. *SFAS 133* did not intend for a contract both to meet the definition of a derivative in its entirety and be considered a hybrid instrument that contains an embedded derivative that requires separate accounting. The normal purchases and normal sales exception is written narrowly to permit only a subset of contracts with specific characteristics to qualify. If a contract has characteristics that extend beyond those described in paragraph 10(b), the application of the exception is not permitted and the contract, in its entirety, must be accounted for as a derivative.

13.12.8 Market Value Annuity

A market value annuity (MVA) accounted for as an investment contract under *SFAS 97* provides for a return of principal plus a fixed rate of return if held to maturity, or alternatively, a market-adjusted value if the surrender option is exercised by the contract holder before maturity. The market-adjusted value typically is based on current interest crediting rates being offered for new MVA purchases. As an example of how the market-adjusted value is calculated, the formula typically takes the contractual guaranteed amount payable at the end of the specified term, including the applicable guaranteed interest, and discounts the future cash flow to its present value using rates currently being offered for new MVA purchases with terms equal to the remaining term to maturity of the existing MVA. As a result, the market value adjustment may be positive or negative, depending on market interest rates at each period end. In a rising interest rate environment, the market adjustment may be such that less than substantially all principal is recovered on surrender.

An MVA is essentially a debt host contract with an embedded put option. The embedded put option allows the holder to redeem the contract for its fair value on the redemption date. Because the embedded put option has interest rates as its underlying and the host contract is a debt instrument, the embedded put option is considered clearly and closely related to the debt host contract, unless it contains a leverage feature as discussed in paragraph 13 and 61(a) of *SFAS 133*. Paragraph 13(a) indicates that an embedded derivative would not be considered clearly and closely related to the host contract if the hybrid instrument can contractually be settled in such a way that the investor (holder) would not recover substantially all of its initial recorded investment. Although, in a rising interest rate environment, the investor has the potential to lose a substantial portion of principal if the option is exercised, paragraph 13(a) applies only if the investor (holder) does not have a choice of selecting settlement. Because the embedded put option is exercisable by the holder, it is considered clearly and closely related to the debt host contract, assuming all other criteria in paragraphs 13 and 61(a) are met. See DIG Issues B5 and B9 for further reference.

13.12.9 Equity-Indexed Life Insurance

Equity-indexed life insurance contracts combine term life insurance coverage with an investment feature, similar to universal life contracts. The death benefit amount is selected by the policyholder; with a choice to include or exclude the account value in the benefit (Option A/B). Charges for the cost of insurance and administrative costs are assessed periodically against the account. The policyholder's account value, maintained in the insurance company's general, not separate, account is based on the cumulative deposits credited with positive returns based on the S&P 500 Index or some other equity index. An essential component of the contract is that the cash surrender value is also linked to the index. Accordingly, the policy's cash surrender value also is linked to an equity index. The death benefit amount also may depend on the cumulative return on the index.

Equity-indexed life insurance contracts are accounted for as universal life (UL) insurance contracts under *SFAS 97*. For those contracts, the customer's account value (the investment component of a UL contract) is credited with a return linked to an equity index (e.g., the S&P 500 Index) rather than an interest rate established by the insurer, as is done with typical UL contracts.

If the contract holder is entitled to the change in value of the index only if he or she dies, which is an insurable event as described in paragraph 10(c) of *SFAS 133*, the embedded derivative should not be separated from the host contract. However if the contract holder can access the equity linked surrender value by cashing out, without dying, the requirements in paragraph 12 need to be considered to determine whether the embedded derivative should be separated. In essence, because the host universal life insurance contract is a debt host, the equity-indexed option is not considered clearly and closely related to the host debt instrument. See DIG Issue B10 for further reference.

13.12.10 Equity-Indexed Annuity

An equity-indexed annuity (EIA) contract is a deferred fixed annuity contract with a guaranteed minimum interest rate plus a contingent return based on some internal or external equity index, such as the S&P 500 Index. The guaranteed contract value generally is designed to meet certain regulatory requirements. Commonly, the contract holder receives no less than 90 percent of the initial deposit, compounded annually at 3 percent, which establishes a floor value for the policy. EIAs typically have minimal mortality risk and, therefore, are classified as investment contracts under *SFAS 97*. EIAs often do not have specified maturity dates; therefore, the contracts remain in the deferral (accumulation) phase until the customer either surrenders the contract or elects annuitization. Customers typically can surrender the contract at any time, at which time they receive their account value, as specified in the contract, less any applicable surrender charges. The account value is defined in the policy as generally the greater of the policyholder's initial investment plus the equity-indexed return or a guaranteed floor amount (calculated as the policyholder's initial investment plus a specified annual percentage return).

Two popular designs for EIA products are:

- *The periodic ratchet design.* In the annual version, the customer receives the greater of the appreciation in the equity index during a series of one-year periods (ending on each policy anniversary date) or the guaranteed minimum fixed rate of return over that period.

- *The point-to-point design.* The customer receives the greater of the appreciation in the equity index during a specified period (e.g., five or seven years, starting on the policy issue date) or the guaranteed minimum fixed rate of return over that period.

For many products of either design, the contract holder receives only a portion of the appreciation in the S&P 500 Index (or other index, as applicable) during the specified period (a participation rate) and/or has an upper limit on the amount of appreciation that will be credited during any period (a cap rate). For the annual ratchet design, the prospective participation and cap rates for each one-year period often are at the discretion of the issuer. They may be reset on future policy anniversary dates subject to contractual guarantees. Flexibility on the part of the issuer to establish new cap and participation rates, coupled with uncertainty around the customer's account value (which establishes the notional amount of the option) and strike price (which is determined by the level of the index on subsequent anniversary dates) make several of the terms of the forward-starting options unknown at the annuity contract's inception. However, those flexible terms can be viewed as a bundle of options.

Holders of equity-indexed annuity products traditionally have recognized those contracts on their balance sheets as structured notes in accordance with *EITF Issue 96-12* and have recognized the interest credited to the contracts as interest income. Under *EITF Issue 96-12*, a structured note is carried on the balance sheet in a manner similar to an *SFAS 115* debt security. That is, it would be classified as either an available-for-sale security, and carried at fair value with changes in fair value recorded in other comprehensive income, or a held-to-maturity security carried at historical cost. Because the contracts are not carried at fair value with changes in fair value recorded currently in earnings, the paragraph 12(b) separation exception in *SFAS 133* for such contracts is not met.

Furthermore, the embedded equity-indexed return portion of the annuity contract is not considered clearly and closely related to the annuity host contract, and it meets the definition of a derivative. As a result, the embedded derivative portion of the contract (the equity-indexed return) is required to be separated from the host contract and accounted for as a derivative under *SFAS 133*. Even though these equity-indexed annuity products are in the accumulation phase until the customer either surrenders the contract or elects annuitization, the embedded equity-indexed return feature meets the net-settlement criteria because the customer can obtain the account value, which includes the equity-indexed return, at any point in time (annuitization is not required to obtain the equity-indexed return).

From the insurer's perspective, both the option component of an EIA product that specifies a point-to-point design and the option component of an EIA product that specified a periodic ratchet design meet the definition of a derivative and require separate accounting under *SFAS 133*, paragraph 12. The option component in the periodic ratchet design results in a series of forward-starting options on an equity index over the duration of the contract and must be accounted for as one compound derivative. Valuing that derivative will be difficult because the issuer retains the ability to establish new caps and participation rates. In addition, the uncertainty of the account value (notional amount) and strike price makes the terms of the forward-starting options unknown before the options start date. Therefore, the key issue with respect to the periodic ratchet design feature is the proper valuation of the series of forward starting options. The valuation of the options requires management to use a significant amount of judgment in estimating the future equity index to which the equity-indexed return feature relates. Also, the derivative should be valued based on expected future terms; however, the value should not be less than the minimum amount specified in the contract. See *DIG Issue B29* for further reference.

When separating the option component of an EIA product, the issuer would determine that the hybrid instrument consists of a fixed annuity host and an embedded written equity option. As stated above, the embedded equity option should be accounted for under the provisions of *SFAS 133*. The fixed annuity component should be accounted for under the provisions of *SFAS 97* that require debt instrument accounting.

On receipt of premium for an EIA, the issuing company should consider allocating a portion of the premium to the embedded written option using the with-and-without method (i.e., the fair value of the option is assigned to the embedded derivative). The remainder of the consideration would be assigned to the fixed annuity host contract. Both credited interest and changes in the fair value of the embedded equity option would be recognized in earnings.

For example, the host contract would be accreted annually to the minimum account value at the end of the contract using an effective yield method. As a result, a separate calculation of an *SFAS 97* account value of the aggregate contract no longer is required because the derivative is carried at fair value in accordance with *SFAS 113* and the host contract is recorded following the guidance for an *SFAS 97* investment contract. The insurer would ignore any minimum liability that exceeds the sum of the embedded derivative separately accounted for and the host debt instrument that is accounted for by applying the debt model. See DIG Issue B30 for further reference.

13.12.11 Foreign Currency Elements of Insurance Contracts

Insurance contracts that provide coverage for various types of property and casualty exposure commonly are executed between U.S.-based insurance companies and multinational corporations that have operations outside the U.S. The contracts may be structured to provide for payment of claims in the functional currency of the insurer or in the functional currency of the entity experiencing the loss. The contract will typically specify the exchange rate to be used in calculating loss payments. Because the insurance company does not record a claim liability until losses are incurred in accordance with *SFAS 60*, no foreign-currency-denominated liability exists (that would otherwise be subject to *SFAS 52* as contemplated by paragraph 15 of *SFAS 113*) during the period between the inception of the insurance contract and the loss occurrence date. Therefore, the insurance contract must be assessed to determine whether it contains an embedded foreign currency derivative under paragraph 12.

The scope exception in *SFAS 133*'s paragraph 15 may be applied during the period between the inception of the contract and the loss occurrence date, by analogy, to an insurance contract in which losses are denominated in either (a) the functional currency of one of the parties to that contract or (b) the local currency of the country in which the loss is incurred. See DIG Issue B28 for further reference.

13.12.12 Modified Coinsurance and Similar Arrangements

It is not uncommon for reinsurance arrangements to be conducted on a funds-withheld basis. Examples would include modified coinsurance and similar arrangements. Under funds-withheld arrangements, all or a portion of the reinsurance premiums are maintained by the ceding company, invested and used to pay reinsurance losses. Generally, because the reinsurer is foregoing the opportunity to invest the premium, the ceding company pays the reinsurer a yield on the funds withheld. The yield is usually based on a specified portion of the ceding company's return on either its general account assets or a specified block of those assets (such as a specific portfolio of its investment securities).

When the ceding company and the reinsurer enter into this type of arrangement, the reinsurer recognizes a funds-withheld receivable from the ceding insurer as well as a liability representing reserves for the insurance coverage assumed under the arrangement. In essence, the amount of the reinsurer's receivable (and the ceding company's payable) is the ceding company's statutory reserve, whereas the amount of the reinsurer's liability (and the ceding company's receivable) is the reserve under generally accepted accounting principles.

The ceding company's funds-withheld payable and the reinsurer's funds-withheld receivable include an embedded derivative feature that is not considered clearly and closely related to the host contract. The yield on the payable and receivable in the host contract is based on a specified proportion of the ceding company's return on either its general account assets or a specified block of those assets (such as a specific portfolio of the ceding company's investment securities). The risk exposure of the ceding company's return on its general account assets or its securities portfolio is not considered clearly and closely related to the risk exposure arising from the overall creditworthiness of the ceding company, which also is affected by other factors.

Consequently, the economic characteristics and risks of the embedded derivative feature are not considered clearly and closely related to the economic characteristics and risks of the host contract and, accordingly, the criterion in paragraph 12(a) of *SFAS 133* is met. The embedded derivative feature generally will require bifurcation. However, the criteria in paragraphs 12(b) and 12(c) must be considered before concluding that the embedded derivative feature should be bifurcated and accounted for separately. The nature of the embedded derivative feature and the host contract should be determined based on the facts and circumstances of the individual contract. See DIG Issue B36 for further reference.

Chapter 14 Shadow Adjustments *(SFAS 115)*

14.1 Background

Chapter 13 describes the detailed requirements of *SFAS 115* with respect to invested assets. After reviewing those requirements, this chapter addresses the consequences of *SFAS 115* on deferred acquisition costs (DAC) and similar items. These calculations are commonly referred to as *shadow adjustments*. Shadow adjustments can affect DAC, value of business acquired (VOBA), unearned revenue liability (URL), premium deficiency reserves, loss recognition, policyholder liabilities, claim reserves, and deferred tax assets and liabilities. Recently, with the promulgation of *SOP 03-1*, other assets and liabilities can be affected, such as any asset or liability item created pursuant to that SOP that accumulates or amortizes over estimated gross margins or estimated gross profits (EGP's).

SFAS 115 was published in May 1993. Its primary emphasis was a change of the balance sheet with respect to certain debt and equity instruments. The required treatment under *SFAS 115* resulted in a general shift from amortized value to "fair value," except for unsecuritized loans, such as individual mortgages, and certain bonds that are expected to be held to the maturity date. Equity instruments with readily determinable fair values were also to be recognized on balance sheets at fair value.

This pronouncement was primarily driven by the financial problems of the United States savings and loan industry during the 1980s. As many actuaries and accountants are aware, public policy over time had driven that industry into a textbook case of adverse asset/liability mismatch: long duration, negative convexity assets (mortgages) versus demand liabilities (savings accounts).

As yield curves became more volatile, practices developed in that industry to cosmetically enhance balance sheets. "Gains trading" was an example of such practices, whereby assets whose market value was above book value were being sold, while assets whose market value was below book value were being held.

A major problem that the life insurance industry had with *SFAS 115* was that the assets were being revalued to fair value while the liabilities were not. Because life insurance industry liabilities are generally long term, yield curve changes can cause significant volatility in the balance sheet assets while leaving the balance sheet liabilities unaffected from one statement date to the next. This can lead to a distorted presentation, leading away from the underlying economics and possibly confusing the user of the financial statements. A life insurance company, even with its assets and liabilities perfectly matched, could yet undergo significant changes in GAAP book value as yield curves change over time.

The FASB understood very well the problems that this new standard would create if liabilities were not also adjusted to fair value. However, the complexities of such liability fair value calculations and the division of opinions from industry experts convinced the FASB to move to solve the perceived immediate problem before all refinements could be put in place. The board did remain concerned about what it termed *mixed-attribute* financial statements (i.e., some items at historical value, others at fair value).

14.2 Overview of *SFAS 115* Requirements

As mentioned in Chapter 13, *SFAS 115* addresses the accounting and reporting for certain investments in debt securities and equity securities. *SFAS 115* subdivides all such monetary assets coming within its scope into three categories: held to maturity (HTM), available for sale (AFS), and trading (TR). Similarly, *SFAS 115* subdivides investments in equity securities that have readily determinable fair values into two categories: AFS and TR.

On the balance sheet, TR investments are held at fair value, while HTM assets are held at amortized value. AFS holdings are reported at fair value, but in two parts: the book value and the market value/book value difference, such difference being charged or credited to a separate component of shareholder equity. That difference is referred to in *SFAS 115* as unrealized holding gains and losses (UHG&Ls).

Unrealized gains and losses on AFS assets are not recognized in the income statement; unrealized gains and losses on HTM assets are not recognized in either the income statement or the balance sheet. The exception to this is in the event of other-than-temporary impairments (per *SFAS 115*, paragraph 16). For a full discussion of the treatment of other-than-temporary impairments for AFS and HTM securities see Chapter 13.

Realized gains and losses on AFS holdings are recognized in the income statement; this is not so for unrealized gains and losses. Changes in UHG&Ls on AFS investments, other than for accrual of discount or amortization of premium, are recognized through "Other Comprehensive Income."

Other comprehensive income (OCI) is defined in *SFAS 130*, paragraph 10, as comprehensive income other than net income [GAAP earnings]. *SFAS 130* is titled, "Reporting Comprehensive Income" and requires such reporting in the financial statement, separated between GAAP earnings and OCI. According to *SFAS 130*, "comprehensive income" is defined in Statement of Financial Accounting Concepts No. 6 as:

> the change in equity [net assets] of a business enterprise during a period from transactions and other events and circumstances from nonowner sources. It includes all changes in equity during a period except those resulting from investments by owners and distributions to owners. (Paragraph 70)

The predominant approach in the life insurance industry has been to minimize the number of assets categorized as HTM. Though a larger percentage of AFS assets generally cause more potential volatility in GAAP equity, the additional investment flexibility tends to drive companies toward categorizing almost all their fixed debt instrument assets as AFS.

SFAS 115 restricts the life insurer's ability to dispose of HTM securities without calling into question the asserted intent to hold to maturity. Only a few types of events can trigger a permitted disposition, thus limiting an entity's investment flexibility. Also, the transfer rules of *SFAS 115* are such that a company can freely transfer any AFS into the HTM category at any time. It is the only transfer among the three defined asset categories that is not designated as "rarely to be invoked."

As indicated above, *SFAS 115* is one of the most contentious of the FASB pronouncements. As a result of the possible distortions caused by this pronouncement on the balance sheet, many stockholder analysts have chosen to illustrate some of their computations, such as return on equity, both before and after the effects of *SFAS 115*, in order to clarify its unaffected versus its affected results.

As discussed below, the shadow DAC, the shadow VOBA and the shadow URL adjustments are generally offsets to the gross UHG&Ls in the separate component of shareholder equity (in addition to the deferred tax offset). Thus, since the advent of *EITF Topic D-41*, "Shadow Adjustments," the volatility of the separate component is generally dampened from when the SFAS was first published.

The separate component of shareholder equity (accumulated "Other Comprehensive Income," pursuant to *SFAS 130*) is subject to more adjustments than simply the UHG&Ls. A deferred tax rate is applied to that component to generate a deferred tax asset or liability, to the extent there is no equivalent value in the conceptual tax basis balance sheet. Such deferred tax results in an offset to such separate component. It is a net liability when the separate component before tax is a positive adjustment to the instrument's book value; it is an asset when the separate component before tax is a negative such adjustment. However, as with any deferred tax asset, it is subject to reduction (a valuation allowance) if the nonrecovery of such deferred tax asset is more likely than not. The primary other adjustments to the separate component of shareholder equity are the shadow adjustments.

14.3 *EITF Topic D-41*, "Shadow Adjustments"

An issue arose during late 1993 in the accounting profession. If an asset was to be categorized pursuant to *SFAS 115*, the effect on equity for financial statement purposes was *as if* that asset had been sold on the last day of the accounting period. Yet, if that asset had actually been sold for a realized gain or loss, certain other balance sheet items would likely also have been affected. For example, for long-duration life insurance liabilities falling under *SFAS 97* and *SFAS 120*, the revenue basis for amortization of DAC and VOBA is "gross profits" and "gross margins," respectively, which would incorporate realized investment gains and losses. For life insurance contracts, realized gains in an environment of falling interest rates could result in future losses, thus necessitating a premium deficiency reserve. It appeared logical that such unrealized gains and losses should also be treated as if the gains and losses were recognized in the related actuarial calculations. The resultant effect would also be recognized as a component of "Other Comprehensive Income." Because of the mechanics of how changes in gross profits or gross margins affect the DAC or the VOBA, the inclusion of these corollary adjustments would also help mitigate the volatility introduced by *SFAS 115*.

The following discusses why the resulting mathematics of recognizing adjustments to DAC, VOBA, and URL mitigates the volatility caused by the basic operations of *SFAS 115*.

For example, consider the effect if the accounting were allowed to treat unrealized gains on AFS securities as if they had actually been realized on the last day of the financial period:

- Such extra gross profit or gross margin would cause increased amortization during the period
- It could be anticipated that, to the extent such gains are caused by changes in the yield curve, such future gross profits or gross margins will be lower than previously anticipated, because the company would be investing in the future into a lower yield curve without reducing credited rates or dividends.

Both of these phenomena would cause gross profits to be more front-ended, thus causing more rapid amortization of DAC, VOBA, and URL.

This effect would be symmetrical in the opposite direction in the case of unrealized holding losses.

Another shadow adjustment example is caused when interest-related capital gains occur. If future reinvestment rates are sufficiently lower; this could potentially necessitate premium deficiency reserves.

A third example applies to companies that unlock discount rates on claim reserve liabilities, based on their new view of prospective book yields on assets backing these liabilities. Interest-related realized capital gains or losses would tend to cause this discount rate to be unlocked.

A fourth example applies to contracts that contain experience accounting. In this case, the policyholder liability held by the insurer is a function of realized (but not unrealized) gains and losses.

In summary, the issue was whether to consider all the effects of a gain or loss. To do so, the collateral effects of UHG&Ls, as if such gains and losses had been realized, must be taken into account. Such collateral effects are primarily the adjustments to the DAC, the VOBA, and the other items mentioned above. The issue of collateral effects to realized gains and losses was addressed in late 1993 and early 1994 by the EITF.

The logic of such collateral effect was not lost on the SEC. In January 1994, after resisting such adjustments to the DAC and VOBA, the SEC agreed on limited adjustment of those assets and liabilities, with the difference going into the separate component of shareholder equity. This was articulated in *EITF Topic D-41*, released January 20, 1994. The collateral effects on DAC and VOBA values, based on the change to these values *as if* the assets in question had been sold on the statement date and gains and losses were realized, are commonly called "shadow" adjustments. Thus, in addition to UHG&Ls, the separate component of shareholder equity now includes:

- Shadow DAC adjustment
- Shadow VOBA adjustment
- Shadow URL adjustment
- Shadow premium deficiency reserve and shadow loss recognition adjustment
- Shadow policyholder liability adjustment
- Shadow claim reserve adjustment
- Deferred taxes on the entire such separate component of shareholder equity.

In this chapter, the shadow DAC *adjustment* is the difference between the primary DAC balance (the DAC asset in the balance sheet for GAAP income statement purposes) and the shadow DAC balance (the DAC balance *as if* the UHG&Ls had been recognized). Equivalent terminology would govern for the VOBA and URL. The DAC that does appear on the published balance sheet is the shadow DAC, not the primary DAC.

In July 1994, the language of *EITF Topic D-41* was changed to make the process symmetric; that is, the process would be followed consistently for unrealized holding losses versus unrealized holding gains.

Some contracts issued by life insurance companies contain "experience accounting." In this context, experience accounting implies that realized gains and losses do affect the amount of the policyholder liability. In the case of contracts that contain experience accounting, *EITF Topic D-41*, in its fifth paragraph, explicitly states:

> Certain policyholder liabilities also should be adjusted to the extent that liabilities exist for insurance policies that, by contract, credit or charge the policyholders for either a portion or all of the realized gains or losses of specific securities classified as available-for-sale.

Consider, for example, a group pension contract or group variable universal life contract that contains a contractual formula for interest crediting to all or part of the funds administered for the contractholder by the insurance company. Consider also that such formula includes a provision for recognizing realized investment gains and losses in the crediting of such interest. In that case, *EITF Topic D-41* would require the assumption that all UHG&Ls on AFS assets were realized on the statement date, resulting in shadow adjustments to the account value and to the DAC and VOBA (caused by the shadow adjustment to the account value as well as by the resultant "shadow effect" on gross profits).

The shadow adjustment to the account value would typically offset the UHG&Ls to a significant extent, thus minimizing the shadow adjustment in the DPAC or VOBA. The actuary should always confirm that the shadow adjustment does not exceed the UHG&Ls in aggregate.

This contractual criterion from *EITF Topic D-41* would extend to contracts where there is a legal or regulatory obligation to pay a specified amount of participation, typically expressed as a minimum participation to be paid to policyholders. Certain states and some countries specify such legal requirements. The existence of these legal requirements for participating policies forms another area where shadow policyholder liability adjustments might appear to be appropriate.

Until recently, this policyholder liability adjustment was thus another potential additional adjustment to the separate component of shareholder equity required by *SFAS 115*, but this adjustment to contracts with contractual experience rating formulas has been substantially eliminated.

Effectively *SFAS 133* and *SOP 03-01* both bring such policyholder liability to their values as if the underlying assets had been sold, thus eliminating the need for an incremental shadow adjustment to that liability. The details are below:

- If the experience refund under the contract is subject to *SFAS 133* and is thus a hybrid instrument under that pronouncement, i.e., a host contract with an embedded derivative, there is little or no need for a shadow adjustment with respect to the experience refund. To illustrate, let us assume an underlying asset pool, which in part supports the experience refund. The experience refund liability is bifurcated pursuant to *SFAS 133* into the following two components:

  - "Host contract" (i.e., assuming unrealized gains and losses were not realized)
  - A swap (for example, total return swap with a floating rate leg).

  The concept under such a derivative is that the company would pay a floating rate to the counterparty and receive back a value equal to the total return on the contract. At the point of purchase of each of the underlying assets in the pool and the corresponding swaps on the refund liability, there is no additional value, positive or negative. But at the point, for example, where an unrealized gain exists that is partly or wholly allocable to the experience-rated contract, the swap on the refund liability has a positive value that brings the experience-rated contract portion of the total pool to fair value, effectively eliminating the need for any shadow adjustment.

- If the contract is not subject to *SFAS 133*, then *SOP 03-1* applies. Under Paragraph 21 of *SOP 03-1*, "the amount of other adjustments described in paragraph 20 of this SOP [to the accrued account balance] should be based on the fair value of the referenced pool of assets at the balance sheet date, even if the related assets are not recognized at fair value..." Therefore there is no incremental shadow adjustment necessary in such case.

It should be noted that, given that the preponderance of assets held by life insurance companies are classified as "Available for Sale," changes to the underlying asset values would go through Other Comprehensive Income, whereas changes to the accrued experience refund liability would go through GAAP earnings. Thus there is a mismatch between the two sides of the balance sheet.

The above-mentioned contractual criterion from *EITF Topic D-41* generally does not extend to the more commonly sold universal life and deferred annuity contracts, where the adjustment of credited interest rates as a result of realized gains and losses is not contractual. However, it would be appropriate, for purposes of shadow DAC and Shadow VOBA adjustments, to make assumptions as to future interest credited on such contracts if such realized gains and losses were to be taken on the statement date and would have a different result on credited interest rates from that if such AFS assets were to be held to a later date. This would provide consistency with the fundamental principles espoused in *EITF Topic D-41*.

As an illustration of the dynamics of the *SFAS 97* shadow DAC calculation, consider the following formula presentation. For purposes of formula simplicity, it makes the following assumptions:

- Realization of the investment gain or loss is a profit-neutral event over the amortization period. This is generally true for interest-related capital gains on bonds, for example. Thus the DAC amortization percentage (the k-factor) does not change on such realization.

- All effects of realization of investment gain or loss would terminate prior to the end of the amortization period.

- There is no shadow adjustment to the account value.

- The issue date is January 1st of the calendar year.

Definitions, where the subscript "t" refers to year:

EGP_t = Estimated gross profit, assuming unrealized gains and losses are not recognized

EGP'_t = Estimated gross profit, assuming unrealized gains and losses are recognized

IGL_t = Unrealized investment gains and losses as if they were realized ("*as if* realized" gains and losses)

DAC_t	=	Deferred acquisition cost (primary DAC) (one can substitute VOBA or URL and achieve the same result.)
DAC'_t	=	Shadow DAC
$Am\%$	=	Amortization percentage (This is the present value of deferrable expenses at the issue date divided by the present value of gross profits at the issue date.)
DAE_t	=	Deferrable acquisition expenses
v	=	$1 / (1 + i)$, where i is the interest rate used for discounting and amortization
n	=	Length of DAC amortization period.

Primed figures are the new figures assuming the *SFAS 115* assets have been sold and the corresponding gains and losses realized. All summation signs assume that s goes from $t + 1$ to n.

If we assume that taking the realized gain is a profit-neutral activity from a time-valued perspective, then:

$$PV(EGP)_t = \sum v^{(s-t)} (EGP)_s \quad (14.1)$$

$$= IGL_t + \sum v'^{(s-t)} (EGP')_s$$

Therefore, $IGL_t = \sum v^{(s-t)} (EGP_s) - \sum'^{(s-t)} (EGP'_s) \quad (14.2)$

$$DAC_t = Am\% \times \{\sum v^{(s-t)} (EGP_s)\} - \sum v^{(s-t)} \times DAE_s \times (1 + i) \quad (14.3)$$

$$DAC'_t = Am\% \times \{\sum v'^{(s-t)} (EGP'_s)\} - \sum v'^{(s-t)} \times DAE_s \times (1 + i') \quad (14.4)$$

Assume $v = v'$. This is reasonable because many companies lock in the discount rate at issue. In addition, for *SFAS 97* products, because the credited rate (not the earned rate) is used for discounting and amortization, it is not likely to change due to a profit-neutral event.

Therefore, $DAC'_t - DAC_t = (Am\%) \times \{\sum v'^{(s-t)} (EGP'_s) - \sum v^{(s-t)} (EGP_s)\} \quad (14.5)$

Combining equations (14.1) and (14.5),

$$DAC'_t - DAC_t = (Am\%) \times (IGL_t) \quad (14.6)$$

This difference, often referred to as the "Shadow DAC Adjustment" is negative when there is a gain and positive when there is a loss.

The resulting conclusion is that the shadow DAC adjustment should be close to the product of the amortization percentage multiplied by the UHG&L amount at the statement date. This is a valuable concept in any review of reasonableness of the shadow DAC adjustment for interest-related unrealized capital gains on bonds.

The shadow DAC adjustment related to other types of unrealized capital gains (such as common stock gains) can be more complicated, because the amortization percentage might change in the case of these types of gains.

Shadow VOBA, shadow URL, and certain of the new liabilities and assets created pursuant to *SOP 03-1* would be calculated in a manner identical to that for shadow DAC. The above analysis would be equivalent for those asset and liability items. The above analysis would also be equivalent for *SFAS 120* business except that the EGPs would be replaced with EGMs, estimated gross margins, as defined in *SOP 95-1*.

Those claim reserves that use an interest element in their derivation, such as disability income, could require a shadow adjustment. Although many companies in the U.S. do not adjust their claim reserves interest rate assumptions periodically, a case can be made for adjusting the interest under the concept that a revised interest rate is the "best estimate" at that time. If a company does dynamically adjust the claim reserves for shifts in interest rate assumptions, then, in fact, a shadow claim reserve adjustment would be appropriate. This calculation would be highly dependent on the company's practices in setting these claim reserves in the first place.

14.4 Shadow Calculations

Since the publication of *EITF Topic 92-9*, which provided guidance with respect to purchase accounting (see Chapter 15), the amortization methodology structure is the same for VOBA, DAC, and URL. Thus the discussion below is limited to the calculation of the shadow DAC on contracts falling under the scope of *SFAS 97* or *SFAS 120*.

To calculate the shadow DAC balance, recalculate the DAC *as if* the realization of those UHG&Ls had taken place on the statement date ("*as if* realized" gains and losses). That would entail the same modeling approach, methodology, and assumptions as those used for the original [primary] DAC used in the GAAP income statement, with the addition of the following:

- The direct effect of the "*as if* realized" gain or loss on gross profits (or gross margins) in the current period just closed

- The direct effect of such "*as if* realized" gain or loss on future gross profits (or gross margins) with respect to future interest earned

- Any effect of such "*as if* realized" gains and losses on liabilities for future policy benefits where there is a contractual linkage or where different treatment of policyholder liabilities would be expected if actually realized gains and losses were to be advanced to the statement date (for example, the effect of the "*as if* realized" gain or loss on future interest crediting or other experience credits). This does tend to have an offsetting effect on gross profits (or gross margins) to the above "*as if* realized" gains or losses.

Table 14-1 displays the development of primary DAC. Note that the amortization factor (am%) is 54.02%.

Table 14-1
Development of Primary DAC

(1) Calendar Year	(2) Estimated Gross Profits_t	(3) Deferrable Expenses_t	(4) PV of $1 end of year 6.00%	(5) PV of Estimated Gross Profits_t	(6) PV Deferrable Expenses_t	(7) Primary DAC Asset_t
1999	1,500.00	5,000.00	0.9434	1,415.09	5,000.00	4,489.70
2000	1,400.00	1,500.00	0.8900	1,246.00	1,415.09	5,592.80
2001	1,316.00	0.00	0.8396	1,104.94	0.00	5,217.46
2002	1,237.04	0.00	0.7921	979.85	0.00	4,862.26
2003	1,162.82	0.00	0.7473	868.92	0.00	4,525.84
2004	1,093.05	0.00	0.7050	770.56	0.00	4,206.93
2005	1,027.47	0.00	0.6651	683.32	0.00	3,904.30
2006	965.82	0.00	0.6274	605.97	0.00	3,616.83
2007	907.87	0.00	0.5919	537.37	0.00	3,343.40
2008	853.40	0.00	0.5584	476.53	0.00	3,083.00
2009	802.19	0.00	0.5268	422.59	0.00	2,834.64
2010	754.06	0.00	0.4970	374.75	0.00	2,597.37
2011	708.82	0.00	0.4688	332.32	0.00	2,370.31
2012	666.29	0.00	0.4423	294.70	0.00	2,152.60
2013	626.31	0.00	0.4173	261.34	0.00	1,943.42
2014	588.73	0.00	0.3936	231.75	0.00	1,741.99
2015	553.41	0.00	0.3714	205.52	0.00	1,547.56
2016	520.20	0.00	0.3503	182.25	0.00	1,359.40
2017	488.99	0.00	0.3305	161.62	0.00	1,176.81
2018	459.65	0.00	0.3118	143.32	0.00	999.11
2019	432.07	0.00	0.2942	127.10	0.00	825.65
2020	406.15	0.00	0.2775	112.71	0.00	655.79
2021	381.78	0.00	0.2618	99.95	0.00	488.90
2022	358.87	0.00	0.2470	88.63	0.00	324.37
2023	337.34	0.00	0.2330	78.60	0.00	161.60
2024	317.10	0.00	0.2198	69.70	0.00	0.00
Total				11,875.39	6,415.09	
Amortization Percentage (AM%)					54.02%	

Legend:

(1) Policy anniversary is January 1 of the specified calendar year.

(2) Estimated gross profits as defined in *FAS 97*, actual historical profits through valuation year 2010, future projected via model.

(3) Deferrable acquisition expenses, determined by the company.

(4) Present value of $1 at end of the calendar year assuming a 6% credited interest rate.

(5) Present value of the estimated gross profits in column $(2)_t$, $(5)_t = (2)_t \times (4)_t$.

(6) Present value of the deferrable expenses in column $(3)_t$, $(6)_t = (3)_t \times (4)_t \times (1 + 6\%)$. where the deferrable expenses are assumed to occur at the policy anniversary date and the amortization percentage = total (6) / total (5).

(7) Primary DAC asset, $(7)_t = [(7)_{t-1} + (3)_t] \times (1 + 6\%) - [54.02\% \times (2)_t]$.

Table 14-2 displays the calculation of the shadow DAC. A $100 unrealized capital gain exists as of the valuation date. The actuary has recast future margins to be slightly lower. The interest credited to the policyholder will be the same as before, but the proceeds of the gain, had they been realized, would have been reinvested at a lower rate, thus lowering future margins.

Table 14-2
Development of Shadow DAC

(1) Calendar Year	(2) Estimated Gross Profits$_t$	(3) Deferrable Expenses$_t$	(4) PV of $1 end of year 6.00%	(5) PV of Estimated Gross Profits$_t$	(6) PV Deferrable Expenses$_t$	(7) Shadow DAC Asset$_t$	(8) Shadow DAC Adjustment
1999	1,500.00	5,000.00	0.9434	1,415.09	5,000.00	4,488.80	
2000	1,400.00	1,500.00	0.8900	1,246.00	1,415.09	5,591.02	
2001	1,316.00	0.00	0.8396	1,104.94	0.00	5,214.79	
2002	1,237.04	0.00	0.7921	979.85	0.00	4,858.69	
2003	1,162.82	0.00	0.7473	868.92	0.00	4,521.36	
2004	1,093.05	0.00	0.7050	770.56	0.00	4,201.52	
2005	1,027.47	0.00	0.6651	683.32	0.00	3,897.97	
2006	965.82	0.00	0.6274	605.97	0.00	3,609.53	
2007	907.87	0.00	0.5919	537.37	0.00	3,335.13	
2008	853.40	0.00	0.5584	476.53	0.00	3,073.72	
2009	802.19	0.00	0.5268	422.59	0.00	2,824.32	
2010	854.06	0.00	0.4970	424.44	0.00	2,531.91	(65.46)
2011	700.00	0.00	0.4688	328.19	0.00	2,305.27	
2012	655.00	0.00	0.4423	289.71	0.00	2,089.36	
2013	617.00	0.00	0.4173	257.45	0.00	1,881.05	
2014	576.00	0.00	0.3936	226.74	0.00	1,682.41	
2015	538.00	0.00	0.3714	199.79	0.00	1,492.41	
2016	508.00	0.00	0.3503	177.97	0.00	1,307.23	
2017	475.00	0.00	0.3305	156.99	0.00	1,128.78	
2018	444.00	0.00	0.3118	138.44	0.00	956.40	
2019	416.00	0.00	0.2942	122.37	0.00	788.81	
2020	391.00	0.00	0.2775	108.50	0.00	624.69	
2021	365.00	0.00	0.2618	95.56	0.00	464.78	
2022	343.00	0.00	0.2470	84.71	0.00	307.17	
2023	320.00	0.00	0.2330	74.56	0.00	152.55	
2024	299.00	0.00	0.2198	65.72	0.00	0.00	
Total				11,862.29	6,415.09		
Amortization Percentage (AM%)					54.08%		

Legend:

(1) Policy anniversary is January 1 of the specified calendar year.

(2) Estimated gross profits as defined in FAS 97, actual historical profits through 2009
valuation year 2010 profits of $854.06 include unrealized gains of $100
future profits projected via model assuming unrealized gains were realized at valuation.

(3) Deferrable acquisition expenses, determined by the company.

(4) Present value of $1 at end of the calendar year assuming a 6% credited interest rate.

(5) Present value of the estimated gross profits in column $(2)_t$, $(5)_t = (2)_t \times (4)_t$.

(6) Present value of the deferrable expenses in column $(3)_t$, $(6)_t = (3)_t \times (4)_t \times (1 + 6\%)$
where the deferrable expenses are assumed to occur at the policy anniversary date
and the amortization percentage = total (6) / total (5).

(7) Shadow DAC Asset, $(7)_t = [(7)_{t-1} + (3)_t] \times (1 + 6\%) - [54.08\% \times (2)_t]$.

(8) Shadow DAC Adjustment, $(8)_t = (7)_{valuation\ year}$ [from Table 14-2] $-$ $(7)_{valuation\ year}$ [from Table 14-1]

The slight difference between the primary DAC am% of 54.02% and the shadow DAC am% of 54.08% indicates that, while this could be a profit-neutral event, the actuary will need to estimate the impacts in the future of this event.

Table 14-3 displays the calculations necessary to record the impacts of shadow DAC on shareholders' equity.

Table 14-3
Entries Needed for Comprehensive Income within Shareholders' Equity

(1) **Shareholders' Equity Component**	(2) **Debit**	(3) **Credit**
Unrealized Holding Gains and Losses	100.00	
Shadow DAC Adjustment		65.46
Deferred Tax on Balance @ 35%		12.09
Other Comprehensive Income		22.45

Legend:
(1) Component definition within shareholders' equity.
(2) Debit amount, unrealized gains on assets classified as "available for sale."
(3) Shadow DAC adjustment from column (8) of Table 14-2
Deferred tax is calculated assuming a 35% tax rate, where
Deferred tax = 35% × [(2) – (3 – shadow DAC adjustment)]
Other comprehensive income = \$100.00 – \$65.46 – \$12.09

Beyond *EITF Topic No. D-41*, there is no definitive guidance from the FASB or the AICPA on calculation of the shadow DAC.

The realization of investment gains and losses due to the shift of the yield curve generally would cause future investment earnings rates to move in the opposite direction. For example, investment gains resulting from a downward shift in the yield curve would reasonably result in an assumption that future interest rates earned on the portfolio would decline. This is a major issue in the emergence of shadow loss recognition adjustments under, for example, *SFAS 60* blocks of business. A major interest-driven investment gain may result in future losses on a *SFAS 60* block because of the lower investment income rates the company will now earn, causing future GAAP book losses and the consequent need to recognize losses by establishing an additional liability. Thus, if the actuary must assume that an unrealized holding gain was realized on the statement date, the collateral effect may well be a future loss.

14.5 Shadow Issues on Contracts Governed by *SFAS 97* and *SFAS 120*

This section of the chapter deals with two special issues, prior unrealized gains and losses and ceilings/floors on shadow DAC.

14.5.1 Disregarding Historical Unrealized Gains and Losses

The Shadow DAC, as well as the primary DAC, grows as follows:

(i) Prior balance, plus
(ii) New capitalization, plus
(iii) Unlocking (or "breakage") between the DAC as of the end of the prior period and the DAC as of the beginning of the current period as a result of historical

trueups of experience and/or changes of prospective assumptions (which could be positive or negative), plus

(iv) Interest accretion, minus

(v) The amortization premium (as a percentage of gross profit or gross margins).

Just as with primary DAC, there is no constraint on period-end shadow DAC based on the period-beginning amount of shadow DAC. Quoting the pertinent part of *EITF Topic D-41*:

> [*SFAS 97* DAC] ... should be adjusted to reflect the effects that would have been recognized had the unrealized holding gains and losses actually been realized.

The actuary can infer from this statement that the UHG&Ls used in prior shadow DAC calculations should be ignored for purposes of calculating the current shadow DAC, as if no prior adjustments had ever occurred. To assume otherwise (to assert that we must be constrained in some manner by the prior- year shadow DAC balance) would create severe potential anomalies. Indeed, such a year-by-year constraint on the shadow DAC would actually exacerbate unrealized losses rather than offsetting them. Thus, no fluctuation in market versus book value from the issue date until the statement date is presumed. Only at the statement date are such unrealized gains or losses are assumed to be realized.

In summary, realized gains and losses can be compared with unrealized holding gains and losses on AFS assets, with respect to their treatment in the financial statements as follows:

- Investment gains, once *realized*, form a permanent part of the gross profit schedule for the amortization period. Tables 14-1 and 14-2 already include all historical realized gains and losses through the statement date.

- On the contrary, UHG&Ls exist for only one moment for purposes of affecting financial statements. That is, for shadow adjustment purposes, only those unrealized holding gains and losses as of the current statement date are used, all prior UHG&L inventories being ignored.

14.5.2 Ceilings and Floors on Amounts of Shadow DAC

Under the gross profit and gross margin true up processes defined in *SFAS 97* and *SFAS 120s* references to *SOP 95-1*, realized capital losses could cause negative DAC amortization. Although there is no definitive FASB or SEC guidance on this item, the constraint often used in practice is that cumulative DAC amortization from issue cannot be negative. This implies that the DAC cannot be larger than the capitalized expenses plus interest.

Companies applying this type of limitation would apply it consistently for the shadow DAC calculation.

Also, the shadow DAC asset should generally remain a positive amount. If unrealized capital gains would have been so great as to eliminate future profits, the DAC (as well as the shadow DAC) would be reduced to zero and loss recognition would be considered.

14.6 Alternative Approach to Calculation of Shadow Amounts

As indicated above, Table 14-2 illustrates the theoretical approach to calculation of the shadow DAC or shadow VOBA in the case of a block of *SFAS 97* or *SFAS 120* contracts.

Although this textbook focuses on principles rather than practice, there are areas in which commonly used approximations are appropriate for discussion. One approach to approximating the shadow DAC balance involves a methodology that utilizes the formula stipulated in Section 14.3. The approach is in two steps:

a. Ascertain the portion of UHG&Ls attributable to the *SFAS 97* and *SFAS 120* portfolios.

b. Multiply that portion of UHG&Ls by negative one times the weighted average DAC, VOBA, and URL amortization percentage on the *SFAS 97* and *SFAS 120* portfolios to obtain the corresponding shadow adjustment.

Further detail on this approach may be found in the following two articles in the Financial Reporter (Society of Actuaries): "Dealing with the New Shadow DAC" (Robbins, 1994) and "Implementation Issues of the Shadow DAC" (Robbins, 1995).

Because this is an approximation, it is up to the actuary to ascertain the relative validity of this pragmatic approach and the materiality of the error involved. Two examples in which this approximation may not be appropriate are as follows:

a. Unrealized capital gains on common stocks, depending upon a company's philosophy for passing these gains to policyholders

b. Unrealized interest-related capital gains on assets backing any block of business for which the remaining DAC amortization period is short.

14.7 Summary

SFAS 115 compels the actuary to perform a series of complex calculations. There is one thought that the actuary could always retain to help guide these calculations. The actuary could contemplate a simple question: if the UHG&Ls were suddenly realized on the valuation date, how would any item determined by the actuary (reserves, DAC, VOBA, and the like) be affected by such a realization? Then the calculation proceeds accordingly in the form of a shadow adjustment.

Chapter 15 Accounting for Business Combinations

Merger and acquisition are significant activities in the insurance business sector. U.S. GAAP accounting rules for business combinations strive for consistency and transparency so that reported information for similar transactions can be comparable and relevant.

Prior to June 2001 the principle guidance was provided by the Accounting Principles Board (predecessor to the FASB) *Opinion 16*, "Business Combinations," and *Opinion 17*, "Intangible Assets," issued in 1970. Since then, a host of interpretive documents were released by the FASB and the AICPA, along with EITF issues papers and SEC Staff Accounting Bulletins and Accounting Series Releases. The fact that APB 16 allowed two different methods of accounting for business combinations—the "pooling of interests" method, described in Appendix A, section A.3, and the purchase method, described in Appendix A, section A.4.1 and later in this chapter, led to diversity in practice.

Similarly, actuarial guidance has not been particularly definitive. Even though AAA *Interpretation 1-D* (see Appendix A, section A.5.2.2, for guidance on methodology) has been rescinded, practitioners still use many of its principles. In addition, actuarial guidance is contained in *EITF 92-9* (see Appendix A, sections A.6.1 through A.6.3, for guidance on measuring and amortizing the "value of business acquired" intangible asset.)

Concern over increased acquisition activity and the inconsistencies caused by the different results of the two permissible methods of accounting for otherwise similar transactions lead the FASB, in the mid-1990s, to initiate a special project to redefine the accounting for business combinations. Their activities lead to the release of two definitive new standards in June 2001, thus replacing *APB Nos. 16* and *17* and most of the subsequent interpretative guidance. The release of these new accounting standards ended Phase I of the FASB's business combinations project. Phase II involves the efforts of both the FASB and the International Accounting Standards Board (IASB). The release of additional accounting standards, designed to improve consistency, relevance, and international comparability, could be a result of their joint deliberations. See Chapter 2, section 2.2.2.7, and Appendix B for further discussion about Phase II.

SFAS 141, "Business Combinations," and *SFAS 142,* "Goodwill and Other Intangible Assets," changed the previously defined accounting and reporting guidance for business combinations. These are summarized in Section 15.2 and discussed in greater detail in later sections of this chapter. *SFAS 141* and *SFAS 142* became effective for all qualifying new business combinations after June 30, 2001. *SFAS 142* became effective at the start of the fiscal year beginning after December 15, 2001, for goodwill and intangibles on the books as of June 30, 2001.

Appendix A is a reprint of Chapter 15, "Purchase Accounting," included in the first volume of this textbook, released in 2000. It is repeated here because many life insurance companies continue to have significant business segments on their books related to business combinations entered into prior to the release of the new accounting standards. Hence, the prior rules still apply to most accounting and reporting aspects of these earlier acquisitions (other than for goodwill and intangible assets). The intent of this chapter is to supplement the content of Appendix A and to discuss the significant aspects of the accounting for business combinations that have changed, both as a result of new literature and evolving practice. This chapter will periodically cross reference the reader to Appendix A for accounting aspects that have not changed.

15.1 Key Decisions in *SFAS 141* and *SFAS 142*

15.1.1 Most Significant Decisions

The most significant impacts made by the FASB in *SFAS 141* and *SFAS 142* relate to scope issues and the accounting for intangible assets, including goodwill, arising from purchase business combinations. *SFAS 141* prohibits use of the pooling-of-interests accounting method for business combinations "initiated" after June 30, 2001. A transaction is "initiated" upon the earlier of (a) the date that the major terms of a plan of combination, including the exchange ratio in a stock-for-stock deal, are announced or otherwise formally made known to the shareholders and (b) the date that the shareholders are notified in writing of an exchange offer. Prior poolings remain unaffected. Only the purchase method can be used going forward.

SFAS 142 changes the accounting for goodwill from the amortization method to an impairment-only approach for all transactions subject to the purchase method. Hence goodwill from transactions initiated after June 30, 2001 is no longer amortized but is subject to impairment testing at least annually. Goodwill that remained on the books from prior transactions stopped amortizing after the start of the fiscal year following December 15, 2001 (January 1, 2002, for calendar-year companies) and became subject to the same impairment test rules applicable to future transactions.

15.1.2 Other *SFAS 141* Decisions

According to *SFAS 141,* a *business combination* occurs when a company acquires net assets that constitute a business or the equity interests of one or more other companies and obtains control. Section 15.2 provides additional details of the Statement's scope limitations and how "control" is to be measured.

SFAS 141 recognizes goodwill as an asset in the financial statements and initially defines goodwill as the excess of the cost of an acquired entity over the fair value of the net assets acquired (the acquired tangible and intangible assets other than goodwill less assumed liabilities). The Statement also discusses negative goodwill and how it is to be treated in the financial statements going forward, which is covered in Section 15.8.3.

SFAS 141 also defines intangible assets as assets that lack physical substance. Quite obviously goodwill satisfies this definition. An acquired intangible asset shall be recognized as an asset *apart from goodwill* if either of two criteria is satisfied:

1. It arises from contractual or other legal rights, or
2. It is separable; that is, capable of being separated or divided from the acquired entity and sold, transferred, licensed, rented, or exchanged.

Acquired intangible assets that fail these criteria are to be included with goodwill. This is covered further in Section 15.9.

15.1.3 Other *SFAS 142* Decisions

As stated earlier, goodwill is no longer amortized but is subject to impairment testing. According to *SFAS 142*, *SFAS 121*, "Accounting for the Impairment of Long-Lived Assets and for Long-Lived Assets to be Disposed of," no longer applies to goodwill. Instead, a rather complicated two-step fair value-based approach is defined to test for impairment losses at a "reporting unit" level (see Sections 15.10.4 and 15.10.5 for additional details). Hence there can no longer be any "enterprise goodwill." Equity method goodwill (goodwill related to investments accounted for by the equity method) also is no longer amortized and is subject to impairment testing in accordance with paragraph 19(b) of *APB 18*, "The Equity Method of Accounting for Investments in Common Stock."

SFAS 142 specifies that the acquiring entity must assign the acquired assets and assumed liabilities of the acquired entity at a reporting unit level, as well as any goodwill resulting from the transaction. "Reporting unit" is defined in paragraphs 30 and 31 of the Statement and is discussed in Section 15.4. The criteria for assigning assets (including goodwill) and liabilities are defined in paragraphs 32 through 35 of the Statement.

SFAS 142 also specifies that intangible assets other than goodwill must be evaluated to determine if they have a finite useful lifetime. If they do, they are subject to amortization and impairment testing in accordance with *SFAS 121* (subsequent to the release of *SFAS 142*, *SFAS 121* was superseded by *SFAS 144*). If not, they are not amortized and must be tested for impairment in a manner similar to goodwill. Section 15.9.2 discusses this in greater detail.

Both *SFAS 141* and *SFAS 142* broadly expand the disclosure requirements in the financial statements. These are discussed further in Section 15.15.

15.2 Definition of a Business Combination

15.2.1 Definition

SFAS 141 defines a business combination as occurring when a company acquires net assets that comprise a business (as described by *EITF 98-3*, "Determining Whether a Nonmonetary Transaction Involves Receipt of Productive Assets or of a Business") or equity interests of one or more other companies and obtains control over the company or companies. Included are all unaffiliated two-party and multiparty combinations, including transactions where all companies transfer their net assets or the owners of those companies transfer their equity interests to a newly formed company (referred to as "roll-ups" or "put-togethers") and exchanges (of one business for another). Excluded are joint ventures, not-for-profit organizations, the acquisition of some or all of the equity interests held by minority shareholders of a subsidiary, and transfers of the net assets or exchange of shares between companies under common control.

The Statement also applies to the combination of mutual enterprises, but the effective date has been deferred until interpretive guidance on how to apply the purchase method to such transactions is finally released, under Phase II of the FASB's business combinations project. (See Appendix B for additional details.)

15.2.2 Determining Control

All business combinations are required to use the purchase method of accounting. Therefore, an "acquiring enterprise" must be defined in all cases. This can be difficult to do, especially in stock-for-stock transactions when the combining companies are similar in value. In identifying which enterprise is the acquirer, all pertinent facts must be considered. *SFAS 141* provides that consideration should be given to the following:

1. The relative voting rights in the combined company after the combination,
2. The existence of any large minority voting interests in the combined company when no owner or organized group of owners has a significant voting interest,

3. The composition of the board of directors of the combined company,
4. The composition of the senior management of the combined company,
5. The terms of the share-for-share exchange; in other words, the company that pays a premium over the market value of the shares of the other is the acquirer.

Considerable judgment may be required in a final decision.

15.2.3 Reinsurance

A common strategy for growth in the life insurance industry is to acquire blocks of business through indemnity or assumption reinsurance. Indemnity arrangements are more common because they avoid the legal complexities of contract novation, which are required of an assumption arrangement. The question that often arises is whether such a reinsurance transaction meets the definition of a "business combination" and hence qualifies for accounting under the purchase method.

SFAS 141 is silent on the treatment of reinsurance as a business combination. However, *EITF 98-3* provides guidance in the determination of whether a transferred set of assets constitute a business, stating that "a business is a self-sustaining integrated set of activities and assets conducted and managed for the purpose of providing a return to investors." Most practitioners believe that if all of the elements necessary to sustain normal operations of the reinsured block of business are transferred, the transferred set is a business and the acquisition would follow *SFAS 141* accounting. If not, they believe that *SFAS 60, 91, 97,* or *120* as appropriate would apply.

Generally, there would be no goodwill involved with such a transaction, unless intangible value is also transferred, such as an active distribution system associated with the business, in which case there would be either a distribution-system intangible asset or goodwill.

15.3 Date of Acquisition

Paragraphs 48 and 49 of *SFAS 141* provide guidance for selecting the date of acquisition. The guidance is carried forward, without reconsideration, from *APB 16*. This date ordinarily is deemed to be the date assets are received and other assets are given, liabilities are assumed or incurred, or equity interests are issued. This date is significant because the initial carrying value of the acquired entity is determined from an allocation of the purchase price based on the fair value of the assets and liabilities as of the acquisition date. In addition, it is the date from which the results of the acquiring and acquired entities are presented on a consolidated basis.

Normally, the acquisition date is the closing date or the date on which consideration is exchanged between parties. Another date, such as the end of an accounting period falling between the initiation and consummation of the business combination may be designated, if certain conditions are satisfied, as outlined in paragraph 48.

Where regulatory approvals are required, an earlier date than the date approval is received can be used as long as the conditions in paragraph 48 are met. Otherwise, if regulatory approval is uncertain, the acquisition date would probably not precede the date approval is actually received.

In business combinations where shareholder approval is required, most observers believe that it would be difficult to meet the condition that effective control of the acquired entity was transferred before obtaining that approval. Therefore, the acquisition date should not precede the approval date.

Phase II of FASB's business combinations project revisits its guidance on how to determine the date of acquisition (See Appendix B).

15.4 Reporting Units

15.4.1 Definition

SFAS 142 introduces the concept of a reporting unit (RU) for purposes of allocating assets and liabilities acquired in a business combination and for allocating goodwill. Paragraph 30 defines a reporting unit as an operating segment (as defined in *SFAS 131*) or one level below an operating segment (referred to as a component). A component of an operating segment can be classified as a RU if the component is a business for which discrete financial information is available and for which segment management reviews and makes decisions, based on the operating results of such component. If, however, two or more components of an operating segment have similar economic characteristics, they shall be aggregated and treated as one RU. As an example, a life insurer might combine fixed annuities, variable annuities, and immediate annuities into one "annuity" operating segment, but might prepare separate financial statements for each of the three annuity subcomponents. Therefore, each subcomponent could be considered a RU. There may be a range of interpretations from company to company in defining RUs.

15.4.2 Assigning Acquired Assets and Assumed Liabilities to Reporting Units

As discussed later in section 15.10.2, goodwill must be assigned to one or more RUs of the acquiring entity. For the purposes of testing goodwill for impairment (see sections 15.10.3 through 15.10.5), acquired assets and assumed liabilities shall be assigned to a RU as of the acquisition date if both of the following criteria are met:

1. The asset will be used in or the liability relates to the operations of the RU, and
2. The asset or liability will be considered in determining the RU's fair value.

The two criteria must also be met by corporate assets or liabilities, such as a pension obligation that will be included in the determination of the RU's fair value.

Some assets or liabilities may be used in or relate to the operations of more than one RU. The method used to allocate such assets or liabilities to a RU must be reasonable and supportable and applied consistently. For example, if more than one RU benefit from such asset or liability, the allocation can be made according to the benefit received by each of the RUs or in relation to the fair value of each RU.

15.4.3 Importance of Carefully Defining Reporting Units

It is important that an acquiring entity give careful thought to the process of selecting appropriate RUs and allocating acquired assets and assumed liabilities to those RUs. In many cases, the buyer will allocate portions of the acquired entity to one or more of its *existing* RUs. Remaining portions of the acquired business may either be assigned to newly-defined RUs or folded into one or more of the segments or components previously used by the acquired entity.

As provided for in paragraph 36 of *SFAS 142*, the acquiring company may wish to reorganize and redefine its RU structure after a major acquisition to best represent the planned future operations of the combined company. Such reorganization may be necessary to take advantage of the synergies offered by the business combination. The strategic realignment of a company's RU structure can result in making available the internally generated goodwill of the acquiring company's existing business in future goodwill impairment tests.

15.5 Acquisition Cost Allocation

Paragraphs 35 through 38 of *SFAS 141* provide the basis for allocating the acquisition cost to the assets acquired and the liabilities assumed based upon their respective fair values at the date of acquisition. In large part, this was carried forward from *APB No. 16*. Such allocation is to include the fair value estimates of all intangibles other than goodwill. Goodwill then becomes the residual.

Paragraph A.4.2 of Appendix A outlines the general guidance for assigning fair value estimates to individual acquired assets and assumed liabilities, as specified in paragraphs 37 and 38 of *SFAS 141*. In addition to the guidance given in these paragraphs, certain other adjustments are made to the acquired company's initial balance sheet, previously reported on a historic GAAP (HGAAP) basis. These are as follows:

1. Deferred acquisition costs (DAC) are replaced by the value of the business acquired asset, VOBA (sometimes called the present value of future profits or "PVP" asset), an amortizable intangible asset (see sections 15.9.4 through 15.9.7 for further discussion).
2. Other deferred costs, intangibles, and prepaid expenses appearing on the acquired company's HGAAP balance sheet are eliminated to the extent there is no future benefit to the acquiring company.
3. HGAAP reserves for future policyholder benefits are replaced by reserves restated on a fair value basis (see sections 15.7.1 through 15.7.3); and
4. HGAAP deferred income tax assets or liabilities are recalculated using temporary timing differences, applicable as of the acquisition date.

Certain asset items like reinsurance accounts receivable and accrued investment income can be carried forward, adjusted for collectibility.

APB 16 and *SFAS* 141 were written for general application to all entities and industries. In many cases, the formal guidance does not adequately address the complexities associated with the accounting for life insurance companies. As a result, considerable judgment and analysis may be required in selecting the appropriate accounting methodology for assigning fair value estimates to individual acquired assets and liabilities of a business combination.

In addition, some of the guidelines of *APB No. 16* are inconsistent with the notion of true fair value. For example, some companies have applied the *APB 16* guidance for fair value estimation by using acquirer-specific assumptions rather than market-driven assumptions. While the FASB recognized these inconsistencies in *SFAS 141*, paragraphs B99 and B100, they decided to defer consideration until Phase II of the business combinations project.

Similarly, paragraph 40 of *SFAS 141* carries forward without reconsideration the provisions of *SFAS 38*, "Accounting for Preacquisition Contingencies of Purchased Enterprises," on how to account for preacquisition contingencies; in other worcds, whether or not to carry an amount in the acquisition cost if it can be estimated. Currently, changes in the amount of a preacquisition contingency during the allocation period are accounted for as adjustments to the purchase price. Subsequent changes are recognized in earnings in the period of change. The allocation period is the time required to identify and measure the fair value of the assets acquired and liabilities assumed and is limited to one year from the acquisition date.

Paragraph 39 of *SFAS 141* states that intangible assets that meet certain criteria (as outlined in Section 15.1.2 above) are to be estimated on a fair value basis, apart from goodwill. The VOBA asset is one of the most significant intangible assets for life insurance companies and is discussed in sections 15.9.4 through 15.9.7. Other intangible assets apart from goodwill identified in life insurance company business combinations are discussed in sections 15.8.2 and 15.9.8.

15.6 Comparison of Acquisition Accounting with HGAAP

Table 15-1 provides a comparison of acquisition accounting under the purchase method with HGAAP in areas of interest to actuaries involved in the accounting for a business combination. The primary involvement of actuaries in the initial conversion efforts and subsequent reporting for a business combination include the determination of the initial fair value estimate of the VOBA asset and other intangible assets (along with subsequent amortization, where applicable), the determination of post-acquisition DAC asset amounts, the restatement of initial policyholder liabilities to an estimated fair value basis (along with subsequent reserve changes), goodwill impairment testing of goodwill and non-amortizable other intangible assets, expense recoverability analysis, and loss recognition testing. Actuaries will also generally be involved in preparing GAAP financial projections that include acquisition accounting values for planning, budgeting, and other purposes.

Table 15-1
General Comparison of HGAAP and Acquisition Accounting

	HGAAP	Acquisition Accounting
Accounting models	*SFAS 60*, *91*, *97*, and *120*.	*SFAS 60*, *91*, *97*, and *120*.
Basis for applying models	Product level.	Product level.
Asset valuation	For income statement purposes, asset values generally based on cost at the acquisition of the asset. For balance sheet purposes, SFAS 115 requires market values for most bonds and equities.	Fair value at purchase date for all assets; becomes cost basis going forward for income statement purposes.
Policyholder reserves – basis and assumptions at issue / date of acquisition	NLP basis, based on best estimate assumptions at issue plus PAD (*SFAS 60* and *97* LP); AV (*SFAS 97* products with AV); NLP basis, based on dividend basis assumptions (*SFAS 120*).	Fair value at purchase date for all liabilities; generally, for *SFAS 60* and 97 LP, approximated by using NLP basis, based on best estimate assumptions at acquisition date plus PAD (usually similar to HGAAP assumptions for new issues); for other products, generally equals NLP basis plus fair value adjustment for non-market consistent product provisions.
Policyholder reserves – basis and assumptions after issue / date of acquisition	Same as basis at issue.	For *SFAS 60* and *97* LP, same as basis and assumptions at acquisition; for other products, same as HGAAP, except fair value adjustment at purchase generally amortized into net income.
Basis of establishing DAC asset	Based on *SFAS 60* deferability criteria.	Only for post-purchase business and future deferrable costs on acquired in force, based on *SFAS 60* deferrability criteria.
Basis of establishing VOBA asset	None.	Commonly established by actuarial appraisal technique, using market based assumptions and discount rate as of acquisition date.
Discount rate for DAC / VOBA amortization	GAAP earned rate for *SFAS 60*, *97* LP and *120*; assumed credited rate for *SFAS 97*; break-even rate for *SFAS 91*.	Usually similar to that for DAC on new business issued at acquisition date.
Basis for DAC / VOBA amortization	Premium for SFAS 60 using assumptions consistent with reserves; expected gross profits / margins for SFAS 97 and 120, using best estimate assumptions; liability cash flows for SFAS 91 using best estimate cash flows.	Same as HGAAP.
Other intangible assets (other than VOBA)	None.	Recognized apart from goodwill if SFAS 141 paragraph 39 criteria are met; SFAS 142 Appendix A provides list; those with useful life are amortized; impairment is tested under SFAS 144; others are treated like goodwill and not amortized
Goodwill	None.	Excess of purchase price over net assets acquired, including VOBA and other intangible assets, at purchase; not regularly amortized but subject to annual impairment testing.
Deferred FIT	Yes, based on timing differences between HGAAP and tax basis.	Yes, based on timing differences between acquisition accounting and tax basis.

15.7 Policyholder Liabilities

15.7.1 General Approach

SFAS 141 requires that all liabilities assumed in a business combination, including policyholder liabilities, be recorded at fair value. At least in theory, this was also the case under *APB 16*, where the underlying liability assumptions were to be those appropriate to other marketplace participants or, if unavailable, those specific to the acquiring entity. Unfortunately, neither *APB 16* nor *SFAS 141* provide any definitive guidance as to methodology. As a result, a variety of methods have evolved over the years for life insurance liabilities.

In practice, a general guiding principle has been that the same rules that define HGAAP also apply to acquisition accounting regarding product classification, reserve methodology, and the inclusion of provisions for adverse deviation (PAD). At purchase, the reserve for future policyholder benefits may require restatement depending on the product type, the underlying applicable accounting model, and the nature of the reserve.

For example, in order to obtain a fair value estimate of reserves as of the date of acquisition, as required by *APB 16* in paragraph 87, restatement is required of products subject to *SFAS 60* and *SFAS 97* limited-pay contracts. However, in practice, companies selling universal life-type contracts and investment contracts subject to *SFAS 97* have carried over from HGAAP the policyholder account value (AV) as the fair value estimate of the reserve. While over the years, the AV had been commonly accepted as an acceptable estimate of fair value at the acquisition date, it is becoming frequent that a discounting-type approach is applied to reflect the difference between a policyholder's credited rate and a market-based crediting rate on new business.

For *SFAS 91* products, the practice has been to hold a reserve equal to either the account value (if one exists) or the discounted value of future benefit and maintenance expense cash flows at the assumed credited rate or the contract rate at time of acquisition. The basic reserve for *SFAS 120* products has generally been the same net level premium (NLP) reserve defined for HGAAP reporting. This practice has evolved, too, to a more market-based approach, as discussed above.

15.7.2 General Guidance on Reserve Methodology

General purpose accounting standards seldom provide industry-specific guidance for calculating financial statement liabilities or other items. As stated, *SFAS 141* and *APB 16* were silent on reserve methodology for life insurance products. Various actuarial releases, particularly *Interpretation 1D*, entitled "Purchase Accounting" (American Academy of Actuaries, 1977), have provided some specific guidance.

Sections A.5.2.1 and A.5.2.2 of Appendix A describe the general reserve guidance available from the American Academy of Actuaries. Section A.5.2.2 describes two commonly followed approaches for *SFAS 60* products and for *SFAS 97* limited-pay contracts – the defined initial reserve (DIR) method and the defined valuation premium (DVP) method. These sections of Appendix A should be read in their entirety to gain a clear understanding of the *Interpretation 1D* guidance for traditional life insurance product types and how these two methods are calculated.

The topic of valuing policyholder liabilities under fair value is still in its early stages of development. It is unclear whether a fair value reserve should allow for PAD in the assumptions or other margins to compensate the acquiring insurer for assuming the risks inherent in the assumed contracts. One can expect more definitive guidance in the future as new methods unfold and the topic is fully developed. Nevertheless, to date, most companies have included PAD in the assumptions for *SFAS 60* and *97* for limited-pay contracts; the methodologies outlined in Appendix A have continued to be used virtually unchanged from prior years.

Appendix A, sections A.5.3, A.5.4, and A.5.5, provide a general description of current and prior reserve practices for other *SFAS 97* contracts (universal life-type and investment contracts), *SFAS 91* contracts, and *SFAS 120* participating contracts respectively. The reader should be aware that the proposed AICPA Statement of Position referenced in section A.5.5 on the accounting for closed blocks did get finalized in *Statement of Position (SOP) 00-3*, "Accounting by Insurance Enterprises for Demutualizations and Formations of Mutual Insurance Holding Companies and for Certain Long-Duration Participating Contracts." *SOP 00-3* addresses restrictions on stockholder income imposed by closed blocks in states where they are required. Favorable deviations in closed block performance from that assumed in the original closed block funding must be made available for future distribution only to closed block policyholders, not to shareholders. As favorable experience emerges, to avoid the acceleration of shareholder income and to recognize restrictions on distributions, a policyholder dividend obligation (PDO) must be maintained.

The SOP requires an actuarial calculation to project net level premium reserves and closed block assets from the date that the closed block was established to the time when closed block assets are depleted. Projected closed block assets that are classified as available for sale (AFS) under *SFAS 115* would *exclude* the fair value adjustment required by *SFAS 115*. Going forward, the Shadow PDO sets up a liability for a portion of unrealized capital gains. The actuarial calculation is based on best-estimate assumptions at the date of demutualization and is locked-in. The projected net closed block liability (the NLP reserves less the closed block assets) forms the basis for a *glidepath* of future earnings. The glidepath is used for the post-demutualization determination of the PDO. At any future valuation date, the PDO will emerge as the excess (if any) of the glidepath net closed block liability over the actual net closed block liability. The PDO can only be positive or zero. If the closed block is charged with federal income tax, the excess would be an after-tax PDO, which must be grossed up to a pre-tax basis for balance sheet purposes.

Existing HGAAP DAC assets of the closed block business are eliminated at demutualization. Some practioners feel that the PDO should also be eliminated as a separate liability at the date of acquisition and should be carried over as a fair value adjustment to the NLP reserve. Similar liabilities should be accrued to honor any future bonus or terminal dividend obligations. On the acquisition date, all closed block assets are revalued at fair value. This becomes the new cost basis going forward. Generally, any net increase (decrease) in closed block assets resulting from fair value restatement is treated as a corresponding decrease (increase) in the actual net closed block liability. Hence, under such approach, the NLP reserve is increased (decreased) accordingly.

An interesting question relates to whether the glidepath can be unlocked and reset at the date of acquisition. A literal reading of *SOP 00-3* would imply that the glidepath is permanently locked in. However, the closed block assets, not the mechanics of the glidepath, determine the amounts that are ultimately paid to policyholders. The glidepath is intended to control the speed of DAC amortization and shareholder income accrual.

Since, under acquisition accounting, DAC is replaced by VOBA, invested assets are written to market value, reserves are restated to fair value, and a new group of shareholders emerge, the purchase represents a "new beginning." Therefore, the benefits of retaining the original glidepath seem less certain; many feel that unlocking the glidepath at the date of acquisition is proper.

15.7.3 Additional Comments on Methodology for Specific Products

A number of concerns have been raised about how reserves should be calculated under acquisition accounting for a host of different product types. This section lists some of these products and concerns and outlines current practices. In light of *SFAS 141's* explicit requirement that fair values be used for liability accounting in purchase situations, care must be taken that any estimation procedure clearly represents a fair value estimate.

15.7.3.1 Guaranteed Interest Contracts (GIC)

GICs are investment contracts that include little or no life insurance risk. Most cannot be surrendered before a scheduled maturity date. The underlying interest rate is often fixed by contract. Hence, they are generally classified as *SFAS 91* investment contracts. They are sold either on a group or individual basis.

Even though an explicit account value may be available, a discounted cash flow approach is often used to calculate the fair value reserve. Companies taking this approach will generally use the current (at acquisition) new money credited rate as the cash flow discount rate.

15.7.3.2 Certain Annuities

Certain annuities are interest-only contracts, generally without early surrender privileges, paid over a predetermined period of time. As such, they are classified as *SFAS 91* investment contracts. A fair value estimate of reserves will involve discounting future contract cash flows (promised benefits plus policy maintenance costs) using a current interest rate like the *SFAS 91*-type internal rate of return appropriate for new issues of similar contracts.

15.7.3.3 Single Premium Deferred Annuities (SPDA)

SPDAs are generally investment contracts that can either be classified under *SFAS 97* (contracts involving significant surrender charge, the usual case) or *SFAS 91* (those with no surrender charges). As stated earlier, historically, many practitioners have accepted the contract's account value as the estimated fair value reserve upon purchase. Many claim this is based upon the belief that it is the account value, before applicable surrender charges, that is available upon surrender of the policy at any time (in essence, an exit value) and that the exit value comprises a reasonable fair value estimate, especially in light of a company's ability to reset credited rates.

SFAS 141's insistence that all liabilities must be based upon fair value, combined with the recent flurry of activity to define fair value for insurance liabilities may lead to the use of a discounting-type approach, similar to that described above. If that becomes the case or if a company now wishes to employ a discounting-type approach, a paramount issue is the determination of the interest rate used for discounting.

Some believe it should be based on risk-free returns. However, most believe the crediting rates for other similar SPDA products being sold at the acquisition date are a more appropriate answer. This result would cause the reserve to degenerate to the account value if the product had just been issued prior to the valuation date, assuming that the economic environment had not changed. The selection of an appropriate rate, however, is no easy choice. For variable SPDAs, there would be no fair value adjustment because the contractual crediting rate is directly tied to the performance of the underlying asset pools of the segregated separate account and such rate would also apply to new policyholders.

In a declining interest rate environment, the crediting rate on the acquired inforce block may actually lag the change in new money credited rates on new issues. The acquiring entity will likely continue to credit rates, post-purchase, that exceed the current new money market rates until they reset or possibly longer, depending upon the promises made in the filings to regulators, agents, or others. In this case, the use of new money crediting rates could very well increase the reserve from its pre-acquisition level (the account value).

In some cases, guaranteed provisions in products have changed over the years. As an example, the guaranteed minimum interest rate included in products currently being sold may differ from those included in the acquired inforce block. This difference in guarantees should also be fair valued. This has rarely been done in practice.

15.7.3.4 Universal Life

Universal life products are generally subject to *SFAS 97 UL* guidance. Similar to SPDAs, current interest is credited to the policyholder's account value (or the actual performance on the underlying asset pools of a variable UL contract). However, unlike SPDAs, most acquisitions have used the account value as the fair value estimate of the reserve required at acquisition.

Most general investment account UL contracts credit interest on a portfolio basis. Many practitioners believe that because most companies writing UL business also use a portfolio basis, the portfolio rate being credited to the acquired block of policyholders is already a market-driven rate. Hence, continued use of the account value is indeed an appropriate estimate of fair value, as long as COI and other contractual provisions are also market consistent. If a market-driven risk-free rate were to be required under fair value accounting, the same observations noted above for SPDAs would also apply.

Additionally, the same issue noted above for SPDAs regarding changes in the guaranteed provisions of the contracts also applies to UL.

15.7.3.5 Universal Life with No Lapse Guarantees

Typically, UL contracts that provide a no lapse guarantee stipulate that as long as prescribed minimum premiums are paid, the contract will not lapse even if the account value balance is depleted. AICPA *SOP 03-1*, "Accounting and Reporting by Insurance Enterprises for Certain Nontraditional Long-Duration Contracts and for Separate Accounts," requires that a reserve for this contingency be held in addition to the policyholder account value. The principles of the DIR and DVP methods (described in Appendix A) can be applied to establish an acquisition reserve consistent with requirements of the SOP and as a reasonable estimate of fair value as of the acquisition date.

15.7.3.6 Equity Indexed Annuities

Equity indexed annuities (EIAs) are a special case of investment contracts that contain embedded derivatives as defined by *SFAS 133*, "Accounting for Derivative Instruments and Hedging Activities." The embedded derivative that ties investment performance under such contracts to a stated index is already fair valued under HGAAP, in accordance with *SFAS 133*. Therefore, it is only necessary to fair value liabilities of the host contract. The same considerations apply here as those discussed earlier for SPDAs or any other general investment account deferred annuity contracts.

15.7.3.7 Liabilities Required by *SOP 03-1* for MGDB, GMIB, Two-Tiered Annuities, and Sales Inducements

Most variable annuity contracts issued in the twenty first century in the U.S. include some form of policy guarantees in the accumulation phase to improve marketability, such as a minimum guaranteed death benefit (MGDB) and a guaranteed minimum income benefit (GMIB). *SOP 03-1* states that if mortality risk during the accumulation phase is significant, the contract is to be classified as a universal life-type contract and an additional reserve may be required for the guarantee. This reserve is held in addition to the reserve for the basic contract, generally the account value.

For variable annuities with significant mortality risk in the accumulation phase, if the pattern of expected periodic contract holder assessments for insurance benefit features less expected claims results in profits followed by losses, an additional MGDB reserve is required based on the excess of a uniform percentage (the benefit ratio) of the contract holder assessments less the accumulated value of actual claims, using the credited rate underlying DAC amortization.

Also for variable annuities, the GMIB risk arises when the estimated value of guaranteed income at annuitization exceeds actual fund performance. The required additional GMIB liability during the accumulation phase becomes the excess of the present value of expected guaranteed annuity benefits at the expected date of annuitization over the expected account value balance, using the same *methodology of ratio to assessments* described for MGDB, discounted from the assumed annuitization date to the valuation date at the assumed credited rate used in DAC amortization.

Both the MGDB and GMIB additional liabilities are kept current through the required use of multiple scenarios of projected fund performance each year to adjust the benefit ratio and direct reflection of actual claims paid to date (a stochastic approach can be used). However, some would not consider this reserve to represent fair value at acquisition because it is not based on a *SFAS 133*-type approach, using risk-neutral assumptions.

Two-tiered annuity contracts typically have two account value balances, a lower tier available upon surrender and a higher tier available upon annuitization. *SOP 03-1* specifies that the basic benefit reserve is the account value of the lower tier. An additional liability is required for the excess of the present value of annuity benefits guaranteed at annuitization, purchased with the expected higher-tier account value, over the expected lower-tier account value at annuitization, discounted to the valuation date using the credited rate assumption underlying DAC amortization. A similar additional liability may be required for insurance and investment contracts that contain guaranteed annuity purchase rates. The reserve is to be calculated using a benefit ratio approach similar to the one described above for the MGDB benefit; the same comments regarding fair value apply. Since two-tiered annuities (and other contracts that contain guaranteed annuity purchase rates) are usually general investment account products, a fair value estimate of the basic benefit reserve (benefits excluding annuitization) can be calculated in a similar manner as discussed for SPDAs.

SOP 03-1 also addresses sales inducements, including various forms of day one or other front-end bonus interest credits and persistency bonuses (bonus interest credited if the policy remains in force for a contractually stated period of time). The liability for day one and other front-end bonuses is generally included with the basic policy benefit reserve (the account value) and accordingly fair considerations are the same as for other deferred annuity contracts. The liability for persistency bonuses is to accrue over the period that the contract must remain in force to receive the bonus. *SOP 03-1* also defers the liability accruals in certain circumstances and establishes a sales inducement asset.

No guidance is provided by *SOP 03-1* for the accounting for business combinations. Clearly the need for a liability for future persistency bonus accruals exists. In theory, this would be fair value as of the acquisition date. In practice, the HGAAP liability might be considered a reasonable proxy for fair value. The HGAAP sales inducement asset, which is similar to DAC, is eliminated.

15.7.4 Group, Credit and Individual Health Coverage Considerations

This topic is covered in some detail in Section A.5.8 of Appendix A. Long-duration contracts such as individual disability and health coverage will follow the general principles described earlier (Sections 15.7.1 and 15.7.2) for life insurance business subject to *SFAS 60*. Fair value estimates of the reserve would likely continue to use best-estimate assumptions appropriate as of the date of acquisition generally applicable to the acquiring entity, but to the extent possible, consideration should be given to general market conditions.

For short-duration business, the gross unearned premium reserves should theoretically be replaced as of the date of acquisition with a market unearned premium reserve, where a market premium reflects current pricing. Some believe that the apparent small difference between a gross unearned premium and a market unearned premium reserve is generally immaterial to the total transaction and therefore not quantified.

15.7.5 Claim Reserves

Section A.5.9 of Appendix A provides details of the accounting for claim reserves in a purchase situation. *SFAS 141* requires that fair value be used at the acquisition date for all receivables and payables. A literal interpretation would suggest that the claim liability assumptions used for short-duration product benefits, expenses, and profit allowances should be those a market participant would use, not necessarily those specific to the acquiring entity.

While there is no authoritative guidance on the topic, some believe that claim reserves for short-duration products whose liabilities are not normally discounted (for example, certain property/casualty coverages) should be recorded as the undiscounted value of future claim payments and claim settlement expenses, based upon management's best estimate. Then a contra-liability would also be recorded for the difference between the undiscounted reserve and a fair value reserve that reflects the impact of such things as a risk-free discount rate, a risk premium in the underlying risk assumptions, and an adjustment for the credit standing of the acquiring entity.

Notwithstanding these theoretical approaches to estimate fair value, most transactions have generally used the approach outlined in Section A.5.9 of Appendix A and have reflected the acquiring company's best-estimate assumptions.

15.7.6 Other Actuarial Liabilities

Section A.5.6 of Appendix A provides details on how to treat certain other actuarial liabilities that appear on the acquired company's HGAAP balance sheet prior to acquisition. This guidance continues to apply. With the emphasis on the use of fair value estimates for all liabilities at the time of purchase, the practitioner should be prepared to demonstrate that any estimation procedure used provides a result that generally adheres to fair value principles.

Section 15.7.3 already addressed this topic for persistency bonuses paid on certain deferred annuities and other contracts providing such benefits. Any deferred profit liability (DPL) on single premium and limited-pay traditional coverage on the HGAAP balance sheet should be eliminated. Unearned revenue liability (URL) amounts on the HGAAP books of an acquired company at purchase likely exist because many contracts use a front-end load pricing scheme. As stated in Appendix A, such amounts are generally eliminated upon acquisition. A new URL accrues post-acquisition for any residual excess front-end load on the acquired business.

15.7.7 Special Issues Regarding Expense Assumptions

The guidance given in section A.5.7 of Appendix A on expenses is still applicable. Most practitioners agree that under a fair value accounting approach, use of company-specific expense assumptions remains reasonable, although it could be subject to challenge.

15.7.8 Reserve Formulas

Section A.6.4 of Appendix A outlines standard formulas for the calculation of reserves under acquisition accounting, the initial and post-purchase VOBA asset, any post-purchase DAC asset, and the deferred profit liability (DPL). Formulas are given for *SFAS 60* and *SFAS 97* limited-pay contracts and for *SFAS 97* universal life-type and investment contracts. Sections 15.9.1 and 15.9.6 provide additional discussion regarding formulas for the VOBA asset.

15.8 Identifying Intangible Assets

SFAS141 defines intangible assets as assets that lack physical substance. Goodwill clearly meets this definition. Paragraph 43 defines goodwill as "the excess of the cost of the acquired entity over the net of the amounts assigned to assets acquired and liabilities assumed." In this definition, all amounts are determined on a fair value basis. The assets acquired include certain identifiable intangible assets.

15.8.1 Identifiable Intangible Assets

According to *APB 16,* intangible assets resulting from a purchase business combination should be accounted for apart from goodwill if they are readily apparent and their values are readily estimable. *SFAS 141* clarified the conditions for identifying such assets and defined in general terms the basis for their initial recognition and valuation. As stated in section 15.1.2, such treatment apart from goodwill requires satisfaction of at least one of two criteria:

1. It arises from contractual or other legal rights.
2. It is separable; that is, capable of being separated or divided from the acquired entity and sold, transferred, licensed, rented, or exchanged.

Regarding the second criterion, it is irrelevant whether management ever intends to separate the intangible. Further, the intangible is still treated as separable if it is capable of being separated in combination with a related contract, asset, or liability. Such an example is a captive agency force tied directly to a given book of acquired inforce business that may be sold by the acquiring entity, post acquisition. The FASB does not consider a company's assembled workforce of at-will employees to be an identifiable intangible asset.

15.8.2 Examples of IIAs in Life Insurance Company Transactions

Appendix A of *SFAS 141* provides implementation guidance for recognition of intangible assets apart from goodwill. It also provides a list of examples. The following lists identifiable intangible assets (IIAs) associated with life insurance company acquisitions:

1. ***Value of business acquired (VOBA).*** VOBA is the most common and generally the most significant IIA in a life insurance company transaction. It represents the present value of the profits inherent in the acquired inforce business. VOBA is discussed in greater detail in sections 15.9.4 through 15.9.7.

2. ***Distribution systems.*** The concept here is to include distribution channels that are likely to generate new and renewal business under existing agency contracts. For example, the value of new individual business expected to be written by existing agents of a captive agency force would likely fall into this category, as well as group renewals of existing group representatives. The value depends upon the strength of the contractual relationship with the acquired entity. Hence, greater value might be attributable to a captive agency force than to independent agents under contract or other marketing organizations or affinity groups. Similar considerations might apply to a direct marketing channel tied to the company or to an outside organization under contract with the insurer for pre-arranged direct marketing campaigns.

3. ***Service contracts/outsourcing of costs.*** The cost of or revenues generated by such contracts might require valuation as an intangible asset depending upon the terms of the contract. Consideration needs to be given to whether such terms are at, above, or below current market rates.

4. ***Service agreements.*** These are situations where the acquired company has entered into third-party contracts for various insurance services, like claims administration. If such agreements are transferred to the buyer, they should be considered and fair valued.

5. ***Trade names and trademarks.*** Usually they are protected by a legal right and therefore meet the recognition criteria as an asset under *SFAS 141.*

6. ***Customer relationships.*** While infrequent relative to business combinations, insurance companies sometimes enter into purchase agreements to acquire customer records and files from other insurers with the objective of renewing policies in future periods (for example, group) or soliciting new business. It is generally believed these types of relationships support the separability criterion of paragraph 30 of *SFAS 141.*

7. ***Customer lists and marketing information.*** To the extent such data can lead to new business, consideration should be given to their value as an intangible asset.

8. ***Provider contracts.*** These are generally related to health insurance-related contracts with third parties.

9. ***Reinsurance contracts.*** Whenever the terms of a significant reinsurance contract do not represent current market rates, a fair value approach should be used.

10. ***State licenses***. While it may not be management's intent to ever sell these licenses, the possibility of such a sale would appear to indicate that they meet the separability criterion and have value.

11. ***State approved insurance products***. An example such as a Medicare supplement or similar product, unique to the market and difficult for other companies to copy, could have more value than, say, a state-approved individual term insurance product.

Prior to the release of *SFAS 141* and *142*, VOBA, state licenses and possibly trademarks, trade names and certain service agreements were, for the most part, the only intangible assets from the preceding list that were recognized on the post-purchase balance sheet. The criteria of *SFAS 141* led to the identification and recognition of more intangible assets since the release of the standard in 2001.

15.8.3 Negative Goodwill

Negative goodwill is the amount by which the fair value of assets acquired, net of the liabilities assumed in a business combination, exceeds the purchase price. The acquiring company must reduce proportionately the purchase price allocated to all of the acquired assets, with certain exceptions, for the amount of the negative goodwill, but not below zero. The exceptions, listed below, are not reduced because it is believed they have a more reliably determinable fair value and a lower risk of measurement error:

- Financial assets,
- Acquired assets that the company intends to dispose of in the near term,
- Deferred taxes,
- Prepaid pension assets,
- Other current assets.

SFAS 141 changes the accounting for negative goodwill from prior guidance, in that any remaining negative goodwill after the above allocation is recognized immediately as an extraordinary gain in the period of the acquisition.

Some business combinations involve contingent considerations resulting in an additional purchase price being paid at a future date when the contingency is resolved. In such case, the recognition of any negative goodwill must be deferred, as a liability, up to the maximum amount of contingent consideration issuable. When the contingency is finally resolved, the contingent consideration realized is added to the original purchase price. Any residual negative goodwill is accounted for as described above. It is possible to have to allocate a portion of the negative goodwill twice in situations involving contingent considerations. This situation is likely to change as a result of Phase 2 of the FASB's Business Combinations project. See Appendix B for further details.

15.9 Accounting for IIAs Other Than Goodwill

This section deals with the initial and ongoing valuation aspects of the accounting for identifiable intangible assets other than goodwill, which includes necessary periodic testing for the recoverability or impairment of such assets. Particular emphasis will be placed on the VOBA asset because of its significance to the initial balance sheet after the acquisition.

Identifiable intangible assets acquired in a business combination are to be recorded at estimated fair value. For this purpose, paragraph 37 of *SFAS 141* defines fair value as the amount at which an asset can be bought or sold in a current transaction between a willing buyer and a willing seller, other than in a forced sale or liquidation.

A number of valuation methods can be used to estimate fair value. Because the FASB guidance is silent as to specific methodology, it is left up to the company to select an appropriate methodology that complies with the general principles of fair value accounting. As stated earlier, a common method used by insurance companies is the discounted cash flow approach. Regardless of the methodology selected, marketplace-participant assumptions should be used unless they are not available without undue cost and effort. In such case, buyer-specific assumptions may be used.

15.9.1 Determining the Useful Life of an Intangible Asset

SFAS 142 states that the accounting for an intangible asset depends on whether its useful life is determinable. Useful life is defined as the period over which an asset is expected to contribute directly or indirectly to future cash flows. The most common example of an intangible asset with a determinable useful life is the VOBA asset. The policies that are valued all have a determinable lifetime and estimable cash flows.

Intangible assets with a determinable useful life are amortized; those with an indefinite useful life are not but are subject to impairment testing. Generally, indefinite is viewed as extending beyond the foreseeable horizon. Where a precise finite life cannot be determined, a best estimate can be used. *SFAS 142* requires that the following be considered when estimating useful life:

- Legal, regulatory, or contractual provisions,
- Legal, regulatory, or contractual provisions that allow for renewal or extension without substantial additional cost,
- The effects of obsolescence, demand, competition, and other economic factors (such as known technological advances),
- The expected useful life of related assets or groups of assets,
- The expected use of the asset by the company,
- The level of maintenance costs required to obtain the expected future economic benefits for the asset.

An intangible asset can move from indefinite useful life status to determinable status over time as conditions change. In such event the asset then becomes amortizable.

While the FASB does provide for intangible assets with an indefinite useful life, it believes most intangible assets acquired in an acquisition will have a finite useful life (see paragraph B56 of *SFAS 142*). Of the list of possible insurance company identifiable intangible assets listed in section 15.8.2, only state licenses and possibly certain trademarks would likely be deemed to have indefinite useful lives.

15.9.2 Amortizable Intangible Assets

Amortization of the recorded fair value of intangible assets at acquisition is to take place in proportion to the economic benefits consumed. Generally, an undiscounted basis is used. The method should be systematic and rational. In many cases, a straight-line method is considered appropriate, especially when the pattern of consumption cannot be reliably determined. Section 15.9.7 describes how the VOBA asset is to be amortized.

The useful life of an intangible asset is to be reevaluated each reporting period, with any changes in estimated useful life being accounted for prospectively over the revised remaining useful life. A company should stop amortizing prospectively if it is determined that the intangible asset now has an indefinite useful life.

SFAS 142 also specifies that amortizable intangible assets are to be reviewed annually for impairment in accordance with *SFAS 121*. Subsequent to the issuance of *SFAS 142* in 2001, *SFAS 144* was released, superseding most of the applicable provisions of *SFAS 121*. Hence, *SFAS 144* provides the necessary guidance for impairment testing of most intangible assets, except for the VOBA asset, which was scoped out of *SFAS 144*. Sections 15.10.4 and 15.10.5 discuss impairment testing of the VOBA asset.

If one of the triggering events outlined in *SFAS 144* occurs, the recoverability of the intangible asset must be evaluated. Assuming the asset is to be held and used, it is considered impaired if the carrying value is less than the undiscounted cash flows. In that case, the intangible asset is written down to its fair value. A write-down for the excess is recorded through operations and the adjusted carrying amount (fair value at impairment) becomes its new accounting basis. Reversal of a previously recorded impairment is prohibited.

15.9.3 Nonamortizable Intangible Assets

Intangible assets with indefinite useful lives are not amortized. They are subject to impairment testing on an annual basis or more frequently if events or circumstances indicate that the asset may be impaired. *SFAS 142* does not permit use of an undiscounted cash flow recoverability test for nonamortizable intangible assets, on the presumption that the cost basis of an asset with an indefinite life normally would prove to be recoverable on an undiscounted cash flow basis. Rather, the test is a comparison of the asset's fair value with its current carrying value. Any excess is recognized as an impairment loss in the financial statements as a charge to operations. As with amortizable intangible assets, such losses cannot be reversed and the adjusted carrying amount becomes its new accounting basis.

15.9.4 Value of Business Acquired Asset

The existing U.S. GAAP accounting model is partly based on the matching of costs (benefits and expenses) with revenues over time in deriving net income. An important component of that matching concept involves the capitalization and amortization of acquisition expenses. *SFAS 60* describes the methodology to be used for most traditional life insurance contracts. It requires that acquisition expenses be capitalized and amortized against future premium. Likewise, profit should emerge as a level percentage of premium plus a release of built-in margin for adverse deviation. *SFAS 97* describes the methodology to be used for many investment contracts and universal life-type contracts. It requires that acquisition costs be capitalized and amortized in proportion to estimated gross profits. Therefore, actual profits should emerge as a level percentage of estimated gross profits.

In the case of business acquired via the purchase of a company or a block of business, deferrable acquisition costs are associated with the *purchase transaction* rather than the original costs of issuing the acquired policies. The intangible asset created by capitalizing these acquisition costs is the "value of business acquired (VOBA) asset" and is based on the fair value of the acquired inforce business. Both in effect and in fact, the VOBA asset replaces the HGAAP DAC asset on the balance sheet.

Over the years, a number of different approaches have been taken to define the initial VOBA asset at purchase. These variations in practice have been an area of controversy among actuaries and accountants. Section A.6.1 of Appendix A gives an historical perspective to the concept of a VOBA asset. Section A.6.2 of Appendix A outlines some of the various methods used historically to calculate the initial VOBA asset amount. Another method, called "the actuarial appraisal method," has also been used in business combinations involving life insurance companies. A key advantage of this method is that it reflects how typical market participants currently analyze transactions, including target surplus, discount rates, and the actuarial assumptions selection process. Many believe it comprises the most reliable estimate of fair value for the VOBA asset at purchase. Section 15.9.5 discusses the value of an appraisal in a purchase transaction and more fully describes how the actuarial appraisal method is used to define the initial VOBA asset.

In most cases, the VOBA intangible asset is classified as having a finite life under *SFAS 142*. It could be argued that for certain group pension contracts that do not involve a fixed maturity date, an indefinite life may be more appropriate, resulting in an asset that does not have to be amortized. Such decision depends upon how close the contract is to an asset management agreement, which some practitioners feel should be classified as an indefinite life contract.

Section A.6.4 of Appendix A provides formulas for the development of the VOBA asset for a number of calculation methods. Additional formulas for the appraisal value method are given in section 15.9.6. Regardless of how the initial estimate of the VOBA asset is determined, it is amortized in the same manner as defined for the DAC asset—as a constant percentage of revenue defined for the underlying business—using the GAAP rate as the discount rate. Also similar to DAC, the adequacy of future revenues is monitored in periodic loss recognition testing of the VOBA balance.

Some practitioners feel that VOBA does not meet the definition of an intangible asset. Under this approach, the fair value reserve would presumably be lower to reflect the fact that there is no VOBA asset.

15.9.5 The Actuarial Appraisal Method

To understand why the actuarial appraisal method is an appropriate fair value estimate of the value of an acquired block of inforce life insurance contracts, one must comprehend the mechanics of a life insurance company acquisition. In reality, it is rare that the purchase price exactly equals the actuarial appraisal value. An actuarial appraisal value is derived from a projection of future distributable earnings (to shareholders) derived from both the inforce business and business expected to be sold in the future. Hence, an appraisal value reflects the economic value determined for each block's profit potential under a set of assumptions, deemed to be most likely or best estimates. Distributable earnings are defined as after-tax statutory book profits less the change in required or target surplus (defined below) plus investment income earned on assets backing target surplus.

The value of any enterprise is a matter of informed judgment. The purchase or sale price is determined by the parties involved based on their respective evaluations of all relevant factors. These factors include but are not limited to:

- The perspective of the buyer or the seller and the level of confidence felt with respect to the assumptions underlying the projected profits,
- The desired risk rate of return (the acquiring company's hurdle rate),

- The degree of urgency attached to the sale or acquisition,
- Significant tax or other consequences, unique to the proposed transaction, which can have an effect upon fair market value,
- The economies of scale associated with maintaining additional inforce policies, which are unique to each acquiring company,
- Any perceived special opportunities for buyer or seller.

An actuarial appraisal normally calculates the value of both the company's inforce business and projected new business expected to be sold post-acquisition. The VOBA asset relates only to the inforce business of the acquired company; in other words, to the value embedded in the business in force at the date of acquisition. The value of future new business generally constitutes a major component of intangibles, other than VOBA, resulting from the transaction.

Risk discount rates, used in determining the present value of projected statutory profits and distributable earnings, are critical determinants of the values presented. If the resulting present value is viewed as a price to be paid to purchase the business (in addition to the initial amount of target surplus) and profits emerge as projected (the actual experience conforms to expected), the discount rate is the effective annual rate of return on the investment. However, constraints imposed by GAAP accounting standards (particularly *EITF 92-9*, discussed in section 15.9.7) result in a return on GAAP equity that does not necessarily equal the risk discount rate used in the determination of the purchase price or actuarial appraisal value of the acquired book of business, even when experience emerges exactly as projected. This is illustrated by the pattern of ROE that is projected to emerge in the simplified example in section 15.11 and in the examples included in section A.10 of Appendix A.

An actuarial appraisal value (embedded value) of a block of business is an estimate of its economic value under a set of assumptions. It is equal to the present value of the projected after tax statutory profits minus its cost of capital. To understand the concept of cost of capital, it is necessary to understand why capital and surplus is needed to operate a life insurance company.

In order to ensure continued solvency, an insurance company needs to maintain a certain level of statutory surplus to absorb fluctuations in financial results as well as the strain associated with producing new business. The level of surplus required to ensure continued statutory solvency is called "target surplus." While there is general agreement with respect to the need to hold target surplus within the insurance industry, opinion varies as to what is an appropriate level. This is determined by a number of variables, including:

- Type of inforce business,
- Valuation basis of the reserves on inforce business,
- Level of new business produced,
- Statutory strain associated with the production of new business,
- Type of assets held supporting the statutory reserves,
- Rating agency expectations to sustain/attain desired rating.

Rating agencies (for example, A. M. Best, Standard & Poor's, Moody's, and Fitch) and state insurance departments monitor the level of a company's statutory surplus. If a company wishes to receive or sustain a favorable rating it must have statutory surplus consistent with its level and type of business. Many companies may choose to incur the cost of holding additional surplus in order to maintain a particular rating, thus potentially enhancing their marketing effort.

The cost of capital is calculated as the present value of after-tax statutory profits plus the initial target surplus minus the present value of distributable earnings, using the company's risk discount rate. As stated above, distributable earnings equal after- tax statutory profits minus the increase in target surplus plus after-tax investment income on assets supporting the target surplus held. The cost of holding target surplus is zero if one uses the after-tax investment rate as the discount rate. However, it increases as the discount rate increases. Specifically the cost of capital increases as the difference increases between the risk discount rate used (the hurdle rate/desired rate of return on the transaction) and the after-tax investment earnings rate.

In summary, defining the initial VOBA asset as the embedded value of the acquired inforce business, resulting from the application of the appraisal value method, is believed by many to constitute an appropriate fair value estimate of the intangible asset. This is particularly true if the underlying assumptions reflect best-estimate expectations in arms-length negotiations between contracting parties. It reflects investor expectations for a return (the risk discount rate or hurdle rate) and target surplus, an amount needed to satisfy regulators and rating agencies going forward.

Section 15.11 includes a simplified example of the accounting for the purchase of a company that uses the appraisal value method to estimate the VOBA asset.

15.9.6 Appraisal Value Method Formulas for VOBA Determination

As stated in section 15.9.5, the actuarial appraisal method is one technique used to help develop the fair value of a block of acquired business as of the date of acquisition (the initial VOBA asset). The estimate starts with the actuarial appraisal value used to develop the purchase price paid for the business, which equals the present value of projected after-tax statutory profits discounted at the acquiring company's hurdle rate (its desired rate of return) minus its cost of capital (discussed in section 15.9.5).

Since actuarial appraisals are typically based upon statutory reserves, most (but not all) practitioners believe that an adjustment is needed to reflect the difference between the GAAP benefit reserve and the statutory reserve as of the acquisition date.

The actuarial appraisal value represents an after-tax value. However, most (but not all) practitioners believe that the VOBA asset should reflect a pre-tax value, because it is a temporary difference in the calculation of the deferred tax liability. This is analogous to the accounting for the DAC asset. Hence, another adjustment is needed to increase the value of the VOBA asset by the amount of the deferred tax liability that is established on the GAAP balance sheet. (See formula 1 below.)

Since an increase in VOBA also increases the deferred tax liability established, the following equations can be used to calculate the adjustments to VOBA necessary to reflect the value of the deferred tax established.

(1) Let $VOBA = PVATP - COC + GBR - SR + DFIT$

where

PVATP is the present value of after-tax statutory profit discounted at its acquiring company's risk discount rate;

COC is the company's cost of holding target surplus;

GBR is the GAAP benefit reserve held at the time of acquisition;

SR is the statutory reserve held at the time of acquisition;

DFIT is the GAAP deferred tax liability established at the time of acquisition.

DFIT′ is the GAAP deferred tax liability established at the time of acquisition excluding the impact of income tax on the VOBA asset.

(2) Then $DFIT = DFIT' + \text{tax rate} \times VOBA$.

From this, it follows that:

(3) $VOBA = PVATP - COC + GBR - SR + DFIT' + \text{tax rate} \times VOBA$, and

(4) $VOBA = (PVATP - COC + GBR - SR + DFIT') / (1 - \text{tax rate})$.

15.9.7 VOBA Amortization Procedure

The VOBA asset is an intangible asset that must be amortized over its estimated useful lifetime in proportion to the revenues generated by the underlying insurance contracts, in accordance with the applicable U.S. GAAP accounting model. *SFAS 142* does not include the concept of accreting interest on an intangible asset. However, the VOBA asset is subject to *EITF 92-9,* which states that interest should accrete on the VOBA balance.

EITF 92-9 draws three crucial conclusions:

1. The GAAP interest rate underlying the deferred acquisition cost (DAC) must be used in defining the amortization stream.

2. Normal HGAAP accounting guidance for *SFAS 97* business regarding the periodic true up of assumptions for actual experience as it evolves and future assumptions unlocking continue to apply in defining a post-acquisition amortization pattern.

3. The VOBA asset is subject to both recoverability and loss recognition testing in accordance with *SFAS 60* and *97* rules, in the same manner that DAC is.

While *EITF 92-9* was released before *SFAS 120*, it is widely believed that the above criteria apply in a manner similar to *SFAS 97* products.

EITF 92-9 forbids the use of a risk rate of return in VOBA amortization. As noted in section 15.9.5, the most common method for defining the initial value of the VOBA asset is with the use of the appraisal value method, which uses a risk discount rate to present value future statutory cash flows. Accordingly, future profits under acquisition accounting will not flow in accordance with the desired risk rate of return for acquisitions because *EITF 92-1* requires use of the GAAP rate used in DAC amortization. This generally hastens the amortization process and delays profit recognition in the early years after the purchase date. Section A.10 of Appendix A provides examples of VOBA amortization and pre-tax earnings effect under varying methods of defining the initial VOBA asset.

Generally *SFAS 144* applies for guidance on recognition and measurement of an impairment loss on amortizable intangible assets. However, the VOBA asset was scoped out of *SFAS 144*, and therefore *EITF 92-9*, in conjunction with *SFAS 60*, *97*, and *120*, dictate amortization and impairment methodology, regardless of how the initial asset was determined. Therefore, the VOBA asset should be tested for loss recognition in the same manner that the DAC asset is, under each of the applicable accounting standards.

15.9.8 Valuing IIAs Other Than VOBA

Section 15.8.2 lists a series of identifiable intangible assets that are can be associated with a life insurance company business combination. This section comments on methods often used to value some of these assets.

1. ***Distribution systems***. Value relates to present value of profits inherent in business expected to be written by agents and other distributors currently under contract, discounted at a higher rate to reflect the uncertainty inherent in estimating agent retention and new business production. Amortization might be similar to that used for VOBA or may use a straight-line approach, given the level of uncertainty in the estimates. Some practitioners feel that the useful life is the period that written business is expected to remain in force, while others feel the time period should be limited to the expected tenure of the agents.

2. ***Service contracts/outsourcing of costs***. Value should be measured over the remaining period of the contract and would likely be amortized on a straight line basis over the same period.

3. ***Service agreements***. Agreements expected to be transferred to the purchaser should value expected fee revenue less expenses to provide the service over the expected period that such agreements are expected to remain in effect. Most likely straight line amortization over the same period would apply.

4. ***Trade names/trademarks***. These may be considered finite or indefinite, depending upon their nature and significance. Some trademarks expire, others can be renewed indefinitely. Valuation must somehow reflect the additional cash flows expected to be generated by the trade name or trademark, which can be very difficult to do.

5. ***Customer relationships***. Value must somehow reflect the level of renewal or new business expected to result from such relationships and then the underlying cash flows resulting from such business. The amortization period should reflect the expected period of retaining these relationships and the retention of the underlying business generated.

6. ***Reinsurance contracts***. Value can be measured over the period that such contracts are expected to remain in force and management's intent to retain such contracts. Such value may already be factored into the determination of the future profits underlying the VOBA asset. Amortization is likely to be by the straight-line method.

7. ***State licenses***. This is an intangible with an infinite useful life. The fair value of such licenses can sometimes be obtained from brokers dealing in company shells. Such values tend to vary over time, depending upon the nature of the license and which states are involved.

Efforts should be made to avoid double counting of intangible value. For example, the initial value of the VOBA asset may include profits that result from other intangibles, such as reinsurance contracts (noted above) or trade names.

15.10 Accounting for Goodwill

SFAS 142 dramatically changed the accounting methodology for goodwill and requires substantial new disclosures regarding acquired intangible assets, which for an insurance company is primarily VOBA and goodwill. Prior to *SFAS 142*, goodwill was amortized on a straight-line basis over a fixed period, often 40 years. Under paragraph 18 of *SFAS 142*, goodwill is not amortized but is subject to an annual impairment test. The impairment test is done by reporting unit (RU) and is analyzed on a fair value basis. The *SFAS 142* requirements apply to existing goodwill and identifiable intangible assets, from prior transactions, as well as all future transactions. *SFAS 142* became effective for fiscal years beginning after December 15, 2001, with additional requirements for acquisitions after June 30, 2001.

While the pooling-of-interests method of accounting was common in other industries, most life insurance acquisitions used the purchase method. *SFAS 142* was, in part, an offset to the expected adverse effect that the *SFAS 141* elimination of pooling was expected to have on subsequent mergers and acquisitions

If negative goodwill exists as of the acquisition date, the amount of the negative is first offset against certain assets, with any residual reported as an extraordinary gain in the accounting period that the acquisition took place. Section 15.8.3 provides more details.

15.10.1 Goodwill *SFAS 142* Requirement

Unlike *APB 17,* which treated goodwill as a wasting asset and required amortization, *SFAS 142* prohibits amortization. Replacing the amortization requirement, however, is an annual impairment test. After defining the reporting units and allocating goodwill to the RUs at the acquisition date, the ongoing steps involved in accounting for goodwill and testing for impairment are:

1. Determine the fair value of each RU.

2. Compare the fair value of each RU with the carrying value of that RU.

3. If the carrying value of a RU is less than the fair value of that RU, goodwill impairment is deemed not to exist and no additional steps are necessary. If the carrying value of the RU exceeds the fair value of that RU, test for impairment in steps 4–6.

4. Determine the implied fair value of goodwill (IGW) for the RU, which equals the fair value of the RU minus the fair value of net assets of the RU, *excluding* goodwill.

5. The carrying value of goodwill (CGW) minus IGW equals the amount of the impairment reduction.

6. The revised carrying value of goodwill (CGWR), after an impairment reduction, equals IGW.

The reporting unit was defined in section 15.4. All of the remaining steps are now discussed in more detail.

15.10.2 Allocation of Goodwill

All goodwill acquired in a business combination (whether from a previous transaction or from a current transaction) must be allocated to one or more reporting units. The allocation of goodwill from prior transactions was based on the unamortized goodwill balance as of the beginning of the fiscal year that *SFAS 142* became effective (generally January 1, 2002). Goodwill should be assigned to the RUs that are expected to benefit from the synergies of the combination.

The methodology used to allocate goodwill to the various RUs should be reasonable, supportable, and consistently applied. The basic approach to assigning goodwill to a RU should be consistent with the manner (fair value) in which goodwill is determined in a business combination. The fair value, in effect, represents a "purchase price" to be paid for the RU. If the purchase price exceeds the net assets assigned to the RU, the excess is the RU's goodwill.

For a new acquisition, the process for determining the goodwill for each RU is fairly straightforward. For companies that have goodwill related to acquisitions completed prior to *SFAS 142* or from multiple acquisitions, the process was more difficult during the transitional phase in 2002, but still should have been done on a basis that was reasonable, supportable, and consistent with a post June-2001 acquisition.

15.10.3 Reporting Unit Fair Value

Determining the fair value of each reporting unit is the essence of the *SFAS 142* requirements. The fair value of a RU is the amount for which the RU could be sold in a transaction between willing parties. The best evidence of fair value is quoted market prices in an active market. However, quoted market prices for life insurance business are typically unavailable. In such case, the best information available should be used. Methodologies that can be used to determine the fair value of a RU include prices of similar assets and liabilities; other valuation techniques, such as a P/E multiple; and present value techniques, such as an actuarial appraisal approach, which might include published embedded values of the target insurance company's inforce business (embedded values exclude the value of new business).

In determining the fair value of insurance company RUs, present value techniques are widely used. *SFAS 142* requires that if a present value approach is used, future cash flow estimates should be consistent with the objective of measuring fair value and the assumptions used (including the discount rate) should be consistent with those used by marketplace participants. The determination of what constitutes a valid set of marketplace assumptions involves judgment and could involve a range of possible answers.

15.10.4 Comparison With RU Carrying Value

The first step in the goodwill impairment test is to compare the carrying value of a RU (including its allocated goodwill) with its fair value. If fair value exceeds the carrying value, goodwill of the RU is not considered to be impaired and no additional analysis is required. If, however, the carrying value of the RU exceeds fair value, a second step is needed to determine the amount of the impairment, if any.

The second step calculates the implied fair value of RU's goodwill. The fair value of goodwill cannot be determined directly, but can only be determined as a residual amount. *SFAS 142* defines a method for estimating the fair value of GW for the purpose of determining an impairment loss. This estimate is referred to as the implied fair value of GW (IGW).

The IGW is determined in the same way that goodwill is determined in a business combination. The fair value of a RU is allocated to all of the assets and liabilities of the RU based on the assumption that the fair value was the price paid for the RU in a business combination, effective on the reporting date. The excess of the fair value of the RU over the fair value of the net assets allocated to the RU (all as of the reporting date) is the implied fair value of goodwill for the unit. The "net assets" include allocated identifiable intangible assets. This process of determining IGW is only for the purpose of quantifying the amount of goodwill impairment.

The excess of a RU's carrying value over its fair value is not necessarily the amount of the required GW impairment write-off. The fact that the carrying value exceeds the fair value only means that the second step of the impairment test must be completed. The result of the impairment test process is that the carrying value of a RU is allowed to be greater than its fair value (even though this result may be unusual), for accounting periods subsequent to the initial acquisition.

The following example illustrates this nuance. Assume that the fair value of a reporting unit is $900 and its carrying value is $1,000. According to *SFAS 142*, an impairment test would be required since the carrying value exceeds the fair value, in this case by $100. Assume that the carrying value is composed of $100 of goodwill and $900 of other net assets. Assume that the fair value of the other net assets is $850. Thus, the implied fair value of GW is the fair value of the reporting unit ($900) minus the fair value of the other net assets ($850), which is $50. Therefore, the goodwill impairment is the carrying value of goodwill ($100) minus the implied goodwill ($50), or $50. Thus, the carrying value of GW would be decreased by the $50 impairment, which is less than the difference between the carrying value of the reporting unit ($1,000) and the fair value of the reporting unit ($900), or $100.

In another example, assume the fair value of a reporting unit is $999 and its carrying value is $1,000. Assume this total deficiency of $1 consists of a VOBA sufficiency (the fair value of VOBA is in excess of the carrying value of VOBA) of $50 and a GW insufficiency of $51. Then the carrying value of GW would need to be decreased by the $51 impairment, even though the VOBA sufficiency almost outweighs the GW insufficiency.

15.10.5 Goodwill Impairment

The amount of goodwill impairment for a RU is equal to the RU's goodwill carrying value minus its implied fair value. Obviously, the impairment loss cannot exceed the goodwill carrying value prior to the write-down. The revised carrying value of goodwill for the RU becomes the IGW. Once a goodwill impairment loss is recorded, it cannot be reversed later.

The goodwill impairment test is to be performed annually, although in certain circumstances more frequent testing may be required or less frequent testing may be allowed. The impairment testing may be performed at any time during the year, but must be performed at the same time every year. Not all RUs have to be tested at the same time during the year.

A previous detailed fair value analysis of GW can be carried forward to the next year without further testing if the following three conditions hold:

1. The assets and liabilities of a RU have not changed significantly since the previous fair value determination.

2. A substantial margin existed between the fair value and the carrying value.

3. The likelihood that the carrying value exceeds the fair value is remote, based on an analysis of the events that have occurred or circumstances that have changed since the last fair value determination.

If events have occurred since the last fair value analysis that would more likely than not reduce the fair value of GW below its carrying value, an interim impairment test must be performed. Examples of events that could trigger an interim test include:

1. An adverse change in the legal or business climate,

2. Adverse regulatory action,

3. Unanticipated competition,

4. Loss of key personnel,

5. Expectation that a RU, or significant portion thereof, will be sold.

15.10.6 Implementation Issues Related to Goodwill Accounting

There are a number of implementation issues that companies must address to comply with *SFAS 142*. These include defining RUs, allocating existing goodwill to the various RUs, determining the method of calculating RU fair value, setting up a systematic procedure for calculating RU fair value on an ongoing basis, and determining the timing of the fair value tests during each fiscal year for the various RUs. Since *SFAS 142* does not provide guidance in addressing these issues, companies have some flexibility. Once a company makes decisions regarding these issues, however, they are locked into consistent treatment prospectively.

FASB's logic in assigning goodwill at the RU level was based on the belief that companies manage their business at this level. Section 15.4 defined a RU and stressed the importance of determining RUs.

SFAS 142 does not allow internally generated goodwill to be carried in the financial statements but does allow for it to act as a cushion in a goodwill impairment test. Goodwill created by each acquisition does not have to be supported by that acquisition, but could be cushioned by a prior acquisition or other excesses within the RU. An example of this situation would be two acquisitions where goodwill at acquisition was based on expected new production. If the shortfall in future new business expected from one deal was more than offset by additional future new business from the other (or from other sources within the RU, such as synergies resulting from a business combination or other internally generated growth), the RU would not have a goodwill impairment issue. Therefore, considerations of this type can become a part of sound business judgment when allocating future acquired businesses among existing or new RUs.

It is possible for the acquisition of a block of business related to one RU to create additional GW for another RU. As an example, a life insurance block of business with new business capabilities is acquired. Going forward, the distribution system is expected to sell both life insurance and annuities. In this case, a portion of the purchase price could be allocated to the annuity RU, which would increase the annuity RU goodwill (and possibly other intangibles) by a like amount. However, if the additional new annuity production were not expected at the time of acquisition (and the purchase price was not allocated), the annuity RU would grow a cushion, prospectively, once the synergies of this business combination were recognized in determining the fair value of the annuity RU.

To comply with *SFAS 142* the company must establish a systematic procedure to periodically calculate the fair value of each RU. The same tools that are used in embedded value analysis or cash flow testing process can be used for this task. Cash flow testing does not take new business into account, so these models would have to be expanded and segmented to handle analysis by the RU. Additional procedures will also have to be put into place to facilitate disclosures of VOBA and the other identifiable intangible assets.

Another *SFAS 142* compliance task is determining the fair value of each RU. Even if all of the models required to do the necessary analysis were available, this task is difficult because it is inherently subjective. The best evidence of fair value would be the market price in an actively traded market, but this may only be available for a company that is publicly traded and that has only one RU. Even in this case, a quoted market value need not be the only basis for fair value determination. Since most companies will not fall into this category, other valuation techniques, such as the prices of similar assets and liabilities, price to earnings ratios, and present value techniques will be necessary. Since the standard became effective in 2002, present value techniques have been heavily relied upon to determine RU fair values for life insurance companies. *SFAS 142* states "the estimate of fair value shall be based on the best information available." Whatever approach is adopted is expected to be used for future RU fair value calculations unless a better method becomes available.

SFAS 142 defines two types of present value techniques, as described in *FASB Concepts Statement No. 7,* "Using Cash Flow Information and Present Value in Accounting Measurements." Excerpts are included in Appendix E of the *SFAS 142.* As stated earlier, if present value techniques are being used, the assumptions should be consistent with the objectives of measuring fair value and with the assumptions used by other marketplace participants.

FASB Concepts Statement No. 7 distinguishes between a traditional present value approach and an expected value approach. A traditional approach refers to the approach typically used in actuarial appraisals. It uses an investor's rate of return as the discount rate, incorporates all of the uncertainties associated with the projected cash flows and embodies a risk-free rate to arrive at a result. The expected value approach uses a risk-free rate of return as the discount rate. For the latter approach to be meaningful, realistic probabilities of all projected cash flows are necessary. The expected value approach might be more appropriate for stochastic projections, where greater confidence might be placed on stochastically projected cash flows. The FASB states a preference for the expected value approach but does not require that it be used in lieu of the traditional present value approach. Historically, since most life insurance company analyses of value have relied on the traditional present value approach for purchasing blocks of business and companies, as discussed in section 15.9.4, the technique is believed to be a reasonable approach for *SFAS 142* fair value determinations.

Finally, the timing of the RU fair value analysis within the fiscal year must be determined. While not stipulated, all RU fair values could be tested at the same time, if desired. The RU fair value analysis must be done in the same accounting period each year for a given RU.

15.10.7 Market Impact of Goodwill Accounting

Many practitioners believe that *SFAS 142* offers an advantage to companies deciding to grow through acquisition as compared with companies that grow internally. Acquired goodwill is treated as an asset that increases equity and lowers the price to book value ratio, which internally generated goodwill does not do. While this was also true under *APB 17*, the prior accounting standard, goodwill was amortized as an expense against future income, which is no longer the case under *SFAS 142*.

Some practitioners believe that *SFAS 142* can lead companies to price new acquisitions more aggressively. They point to the *SFAS 142* advantages of no longer having to amortize goodwill and to the opportunity to use internally generated goodwill and other cushions to offset possible impairment write-offs. Even if the purchase price is not higher, future earnings will be enhanced if more value is allocated to goodwill and less to VOBA and other amortizable intangible assets. Allocating more value to goodwill can, however, increase the possibility of a future goodwill impairment loss. Companies will need to continue to monitor the relationship between goodwill carried and total equity.

In theory, *SFAS 142* should have no effect on the value of a company, because the level of goodwill should not affect cash flows. However, if a company's stock price stays the same after an acquisition, then its P/E ratio will decrease because earnings are higher in the absence of goodwill amortization. On the other hand, if the company's P/E ratio stays the same, the stock price will rise due to higher earnings, reflecting no goodwill amortization.

A potential negative effect of *SFAS 142* is the possibility of greater earnings volatility. While acquirers generally view the elimination of goodwill amortization positively, the possibility of a periodic goodwill write-off (even if infrequent) does still exist, adding to earnings volatility.

15.11 Examples

Section A.10 of Appendix A provides a series of examples that demonstrate the concepts of this chapter, as follows:

1. The acquisition accounting reserve and VOBA asset for a non par 10-year endowment product (*SFAS 60*), showing income statement and balance sheet development (Appendix A section A.10.1).

2. Development of the VOBA asset and DPL for a *SFAS 97* limited-pay plan, showing the balance sheet and income statement development (Appendix A section A.10.2).

3. Development of the VOBA asset and goodwill for a *SFAS 97* universal life product, showing income statement development (Appendix A section A.10.3).

4. Initial acquisition accounting balance sheet, in comparison with HGAAP and statutory basis, with positive and negative initial goodwill and deferred tax implications (Appendix A section A.10.4).

5. Comparative 3-year pro forma acquisition accounting income statement and balance sheet, measured from date of purchase at the company level (Appendix A section A.10.5).

The intent of these examples is to demonstrate how acquisition accounting works under different situations.

This section also includes another simplified example of the actuarial aspects of accounting used in the purchase of a life insurance company. The acquired company has one line of business: universal life. The price paid for the company reflects the value of the existing universal life business, the value of new universal life business to be written, and the value of adjusted capital and surplus, as shown in Table15-2. It assumes there are no intangibles other than VOBA and goodwill.

Table 15-2
Summary of Values – using a 10% Risk Discount Rate

Description	Value (in thousands)
Total adjusted capital and surplus	$75,741
Value of inforce business (PV of after-tax profits after reflecting the cost of capital)	156,514
Value of new business (PV of after-tax profits after reflecting the cost of capital	111,283
Assumed purchase price	$343,538

Once the purchase price has been determined, a simplified set of balance sheets for the company to be acquired can be produced (see Table 15-3). The statutory invested assets shown on the balance sheet are the assets transferred with the company plus any surplus contribution and minus any pre-close or post-close shareholder dividend. The statutory benefit reserve is the sum of the reserves from all lines of business. In this example, statutory capital and surplus is assumed to exactly equal the buyer's estimate of target surplus for the inforce business. This implies that any excess capital and surplus existing in the acquired company was distributed to shareholders prior to closing the transaction.

On the balance sheet of the acquired company at acquisition, invested assets are held equal to the market value of the statutory invested assets. In this simplified example, the statutory book value of the assets is assumed to be exactly equal to market value on the acquisition date. Benefit reserves are restated under acquisition accounting by line of business. GAAP equity represents the purchase price paid plus any capital contribution less any pre-close dividend necessary to have statutory capital and surplus equal to the desired level of target surplus.

The value of the VOBA asset is calculated using the actuarial appraisal method (described in sections 15.9.5 and 15.9.6). This method is based on the present value of distributable earnings using a discount rate consistent with the determination of the purchase price, adjusted for GAAP/statutory reserve differences and adjusted to reflect a pre-tax valuation. VOBA is defined by formula 4 outlined in section 15.9.6.

The deferred tax liability is calculated by taking 35% of the difference between the GAAP and tax items on the balance sheet, other than goodwill. Deferred FIT = 0.35 × [(GAAP assets, excluding goodwill – tax assets) – (GAAP liabilities – tax liabilities)]. Goodwill is the balancing item and is subject to the impairment rules discussed in section 15.10.

The tax balance sheet in this example assumes invested assets are valued at their statutory values (which in this example equals the GAAP values being held). Tax reserves are used. The tax basis VOBA amount is the tax basis purchase price offset by the initial tax basis "proxy DAC" (as defined by Internal Revenue Code Section 848), which is typically zero in a stock transaction. It may be positive in either the acquisition of a block of business or in a stock transaction where the parties elect to treat the transaction for tax purposes as an asset purchase. This example is a stock purchase and assumes the election is not made. Therefore, the value of the tax basis VOBA asset is zero. DAC on the tax balance sheet is the initial proxy DAC balance resulting from the transfer of business in an asset purchase or the proxy DAC balance carried over from the acquired company in a stock purchase.

Table 15-3 is a simplified acquisition accounting balance sheet, along with comparable statutory and tax values. Other assets and other liabilities are assumed to be zero.

Table 15-3
Comparative Balance Sheets for Acquired Company (in thousands)

Balance sheet item	**Statutory**	**GAAP**	**Tax**
Assets			
Invested assets	$1,758,871	$1,758,871	$1,758,871
Other assets	0	0	0
VOBA asset	0	369,337	0
DAC	0	0	37,113
Goodwill	0	111,283	0
Total assets	1,758,871	2,239,491	1,795,984
Liabilities			
Benefit reserves	1,683,130	1,866,853	1,617,771
Other liabilities	0	0	0
Deferred income taxes	0	29,100	0
Subtotal	1,683,130	1,895,953	1,617,771
Equity	75,741	343,538	178,213
Total liabilties & equity	1,758,871	2,239,491	1,795,984
VOBA (pre-tax value)	*$369,337* [1]	*Purchase price*	*$343,538*

[1] Equal to (156,514 + 1,866,853 – 1,683,130 – 100,168) / (1 – 0.35), using formula 4 of section 15.9.6. The DFIT' component of this formula (–100,168) is calculated as 35% of (1,617,771 – 1,866,853 – 37,113). It is negative because it is an asset.

The inforce business of the acquired company consists of universal life, which is subject to *SFAS 97* for universal life-type contracts. In the example, the VOBA asset is amortized over a 30-year projection period (a proxy for the life of the business) as a level percent of gross profits. The projected gross profits and VOBA amortization schedule are shown in Table 15-4.

Goodwill is held constant over the projection period on the presumption that no impairment will emerge. For future universal life business, a DAC asset is established and amortized in accordance with *SFAS 97* principles such that GAAP book profits emerge as a level percentage of estimated gross profits.

The projected pre-tax GAAP net income includes projected GAAP gross profits plus the change in the DAC and VOBA assets plus investment income on additional invested assets (other than those supporting projected reserves).

Shareholder dividends equal to statutory distributable earnings are assumed to be paid at the end of each year, thus keeping the company's statutory surplus level at its desired target surplus.

Table 15-4 illustrates GAAP net income along with GAAP equity and return on equity (ROE) for the example. ROE is the ratio of after-tax GAAP net income to GAAP equity at the beginning of the year. The 10-year weighted ROE is the sum of after-tax GAAP net income divided by the sum of beginning of year GAAP equity. As one can see, this 10-year weighted ROE generally approximates the discount rate (10 percent) used in the determination of the purchase price for the company.

Table 15-4
Projection Results (in thousands)

	Gross Profits										
	Exiting Business	New Business	Other Investment Income*	EOY VOBA	Deferred Expense	DAC (EOY)	Pre-tax Net Income	After-tax Net Income	Dividend (EOY)	GAAP Equity (EOY)	ROE %
1	74,248	10,913	(6,479)	342,698	113,087	105,984	44,941	29,212	1,298	371,452	8.5
2	71,507	31,820	(8,912)	316,263	124,395	214,438	52,039	33,825	1,694	403,583	9.1
3	68,306	61,968	(11,020)	290,345	134,347	318,102	62,654	40,725	4,199	440,109	10.1
4	64,671	92,576	(12,527)	265,262	142,408	414,571	73,698	47,903	10,790	477,222	10.9
5	61,622	122,368	(13,621)	240,678	150,952	504,536	84,796	55,118	19,254	513,085	11.5
6	58,346	148,929	(14,498)	216,771	150,952	581,261	94,644	61,518	31,286	543,318	12
7	54,562	170,591	(15,131)	193,916	150,952	647,340	102,295	66,492	40,489	569,321	12.2
8	50,037	188,730	(15,558)	172,665	150,951	704,586	108,252	70,364	47,747	591,937	12.4
9	43,978	204,644	(15,842)	154,121	150,952	754,052	112,749	73,287	52,800	612,423	12.4
10	37,750	218,596	(15,993)	138,558	150,952	796,662	116,448	75,691	56,456	631,658	12.4

* Other investment income is negative because the difference between GAAP and statutory reserves exceeds the target surplus being held during the projection years shown.

15.12 Selecting Assumptions

SFAS 141 and *142* require the value of acquired assets and assumed liabilities obtained in a business combination to be determined on a fair value basis as of the date of acquisition.

As stated several times throughout this chapter, use of a discounted cash flow approach may be considered the most appropriate methodology for calculating these values. An important concept underlying fair value determination is the use of marketplace-participant assumptions, wherever feasible. With life insurance business, such assumptions are seldom reliably available. As outlined in paragraph B174 of *SFAS 141,* if marketplace information needed to select assumptions "is not available without undue cost and effort, the entity should use its own assumptions." Whatever basis is used for assumption selection, the assumptions should be reliably estimable and well documented.

Marketplace-participant assumptions might be available for assumptions like estimates of useful life for certain identifiable intangible assets, the level of future contract renewals, benefits that may arise from acquisition-related synergies, and perhaps risk-free interest rates. It is generally agreed for life insurance contracts that most non-economic assumptions are not reliably estimable from available marketplace data and that buyer-specific assumptions are probably required. Such assumptions should be based upon the buyer's best estimate of future experience and should reflect to the extent possible planned post-acquisition activities regarding the combined operations. These actions may include consolidating operating functions (impacts level of future expense levels), communications with the acquired entities existing policyholders (affects future lapse patterns), and claims practices (affects level of claim reserves).

15.13 Federal Income Tax Considerations

Section A.8 of Appendix A discusses various income tax considerations regarding acquisition accounting. Those considerations still largely apply under *SFAS 141* and *SFAS 142*. For tax purposes, business combinations are classified as nontaxable or taxable.

In a nontaxable business combination, the acquiring company carries over the acquired company's tax basis of assets and liabilities ("carryover basis"). The resultant values assigned for financial statement purposes to the acquired assets and assumed liabilities will frequently differ from the tax basis. In these cases, a deferred tax asset or liability is required for the tax effects of such basis differences.

In a taxable business combination, the purchase price is allocated to the acquired assets and assumed liabilities for tax purposes. The resultant tax basis of the assets and liabilities are stepped up to fair value at the date of acquisition ("step-up basis"). Although the assigned values for both financial statement and tax purposes will generally be the same, some of the values may differ in certain circumstances and a deferred tax or liability would be required for the tax effects of the differences.

15.14 Post-Purchase Issues

Section A.9 of Appendix A outlines some of the issues related to the ongoing reporting for a business combination involving a life insurance company. Section 15.10.6 outlines some of the post-acquisition issues relating to goodwill accounting.

Of particular importance is what to do with the fair value reserve estimates post-acquisition. Going forward, reserves should be consistent with HGAAP principles. Therefore, any excess of fair value over HGAAP has to be amortized into net income over time, similar to the way it is amortized on the invested asset side. For example, the difference between a bond's fair value at acquisition and par value is ratably amortized into income over the remaining period to maturity.

In many cases, this will occur as a natural process defined by the reserving method. Take for example non-participating traditional life insurance using the defined initial reserve method. Under this approach, fair value is defined by a specific pre-determined reserve level and a net valuation premium is solved for, given the new best-estimate assumptions appropriate as of the acquisition date.

In other cases, the fair value reserve may not be changed from its PGAAP level. An example is the continued use of the account value for certain interest-sensitive products subject to *SFAS 97.* However, where a fair value-type reserve replaces the account value on such products, the difference should be amortized into income over the time when a policyholder starts receiving market credited rates. Hence, the fair value estimate would grade into the full account value over this period.

Another example relates to the additional mortality reserve under *SOP 03-1* for variable annuity contracts. Consider the reserve for a MGDB provision of such contracts. Define "x" as the fair value reserve at acquisition. The initial benefit ratio, "k," would be defined as: [present value of future benefits using best-estimate assumptions minus x] divided by the present value of future assessments using best estimate assumptions. Thereafter, the post-acquisition reserve for this benefit on acquired business would be the reserve at the end of the prior reporting period plus interest plus "k" times the assessments incurred in the current period less actual benefits paid in the current period (subject to a floor of zero). Of course, the reserve continues to be subject to retrospective unlocking as experience assumptions change over time.

15.15 Disclosures

SFAS 141 significantly increases the disclosure requirements of a business combination in the financial statements.

In the period in which a material business combination is completed, required disclosures include:

1. Information about the acquired company (name, description, percentage acquired, reason for the acquisition, and factors that contributed to the purchase price),

2. The cost of the company and information about equity interests issued or issuable, the value assigned to those interests, and the basis for determining that value,

3. A condensed balance sheet disclosing the amount assigned to each major asset and liability of the acquired company at the acquisition date,

4. Information about contingent payments, options, or commitments specified in the acquisition agreement,

5. Where purchase price allocations cannot be finalized due to pre-acquisition contingencies, reasons therefore and, in subsequent periods, the nature and amount of any material adjustments to the initial allocation,

6. For intangible assets subject to amortization, the total amount assigned, the amount assigned to each major intangible asset class, any significant residual value, and the weighted average amortization period in total and by major intangible asset class,

7. For intangible assets *not* subject to amortization, the total amount assigned and the amount assigned to each major intangible asset class, and

8. For goodwill, the total amount, the amount expected to be deductible for tax purposes, and the amount by reportable segment (if *SFAS 131* applies).

If the combined company is a public business enterprise, the notes to the financial statements must include the following supplemental information, on a pro forma basis, for the period in which the business combination occurs:

1. Operating results for the current and prior periods as if the business combination had been completed at the start of the period,

2. Information including revenue, income before extraordinary items, the cumulative effect of accounting changes, net income, and earnings per share, and

3. The nature and amount of material, nonrecurring items.

If a material business combination is completed after the balance sheet date but before the financial statements are issued, the company must still disclose the above items (but not the supplemental pro forma information in the notes to the financial statements), unless it is not practical to do so.

The *SFAS 142* disclosures regarding goodwill and other intangibles are also substantial. The aggregate amount of goodwill and intangible assets must be presented as separate line items in the balance sheet. Regulation S-X, Rule 5-02, requires separate presentation for each class of intangible asset that is in excess of five percent of total assets.

Disclosure requirements for goodwill and other identifiable intangible assets *not* subject to amortization include:

1. The total carrying amount at the end of each financial reporting period,

2. The change in the carrying amount of each item during the period, including the aggregate amount of goodwill and intangible assets acquired, the amount of impairment losses recognized, and the amounts of goodwill and intangible assets included in the gain or loss on disposal of a RU (or portion thereof), and

3. For each goodwill and intangible asset impairment loss:

    a. A description of the facts and circumstances related to the impairment,

    b. The amount of the loss and the method used to determine fair value of the RU, and

    c. If the impairment loss is an estimate that has not been finalized, a discussion of the reasons and, in subsequent periods, the amount of any material adjustment to the estimate.

Required disclosures for other intangible assets subject to amortization include:

1. The gross carrying amount and accumulated amortization for each major class of identifiable intangible asset,

2. The aggregate amortization expense for the current accounting period, and

3. An estimate of aggregate amortization expense for each of the next five years.

Chapter 16 Non-U.S. Products

16.1 Background

At the end of the 20th century, the financial services industries have been consolidating and becoming more global. In both the United States and other countries, regulation has facilitated expansion. Increasingly, companies have been making acquisitions in other countries. These activities require capital. The leading financial marketplace is the United States, which is regulated by the Securities and Exchange Commission (SEC).

The SEC requires public companies domiciled in the United States to file both quarterly and annual financial statements prepared in accordance with the Generally Accepted Accounting Principles of the United States (U.S. GAAP). For foreign companies that register with the SEC, annual filings of local financial statements are required where the SEC has determined that the "home country" accounting framework is acceptable. A reconciliation to U.S. GAAP is a required disclosure (unless the filing itself is in compliance with U.S. GAAP). Interim filings are also required if needed by the country of origin, although these may not require a reconciliation to U.S. GAAP. Even though the SEC may not require foreign companies to file more than annually, competitive and analyst pressures contribute to the decision of many foreign registrants to produce semi-annual financials, at a minimum. Foreign companies can experience some difficulties in meeting the earlier reporting requirements for U.S. GAAP as these dates may precede the required filing dates for the company's local financial statements.

U.S. companies with foreign subsidiaries must prepare U.S. GAAP financial statements for those subsidiaries and include the results in the consolidated return. While some approximations may be used, it is critical that such approximations are made to a high enough standard to obtain an unqualified audit opinion in light of Staff Accounting Bulletin 99 on materiality. Any approximations must be well documented and quantified wherever possible.

At the time of writing this book, the International Accounting Standards Committee ("IASC") is preparing an international approach to accounting for life insurance contracts. It is at the stage of discussing various issues. Realistically, it will be a number of years before standards are set and accepted by the member organizations. Until those standards are finalized and accepted by the SEC, U.S. GAAP will continue to be required as the basis for financial statements filed in the United States. The SEC has delegated much of the mechanics of implementation to the accounting profession, particularly to the FASB.

U.S. GAAP is designed for the U.S. marketplace. The FASB sets methods and standards for reporting traditional participating and non-participating life, health, and annuity contracts and interest-sensitive life and annuity contracts sold both on an individual and group basis in the regulatory and tax environment of the United States. In other countries, different market, tax, and regulatory conditions give rise to contracts that may not easily fit into the U.S. reporting framework.

Local basis accounting for non-U.S. companies, similar to U.S. statutory accounting, tends to be driven by the desire for a strong balance sheet. It is not uncommon to establish contingency reserves that may be released when they are needed. Some of these contingency reserves are commonly referred to as "equalization" or "global" reserves because they exist primarily to smooth year-on-year profits. In the U.S., GAAP tends to be driven more by the earnings in a reporting period. Arthur Leavitt, former Chairman of the Securities and Exchange Commission, has said that "good accounting standards produce financial statements that report events in the period in which they occur, not before, and not after. … there are no 'rainy day' reserves, no deferral of loss recognition, and actual volatility is not 'smoothed away' to create an artificial picture of steady and consistent growth." Non-U.S. companies have to be aware of this difference in approach.

For those non-domestic companies filing U.S. GAAP financial statements, there are a number of points to consider in complying with U.S. GAAP. This chapter describes several non-U.S. products and discusses considerations that must be taken into account when addressing U.S. GAAP issues.

16.2 Product Classification Issues

16.2.1 Flowchart

Different accounting standards are used for insurance contracts depending upon the type of contract. These standards have been described in detail in earlier chapters. The first step in deciding how to report the financial results of a block of business is to classify the underlying contracts according to the appropriate financial accounting statement. Chart 16-1 shows a series of questions that must be addressed in order to decide which statement applies. These questions are no different from those that a U.S. company would ask itself. However, product classification in the U.S. is relatively straightforward since U.S. GAAP was written with U.S. products in mind.

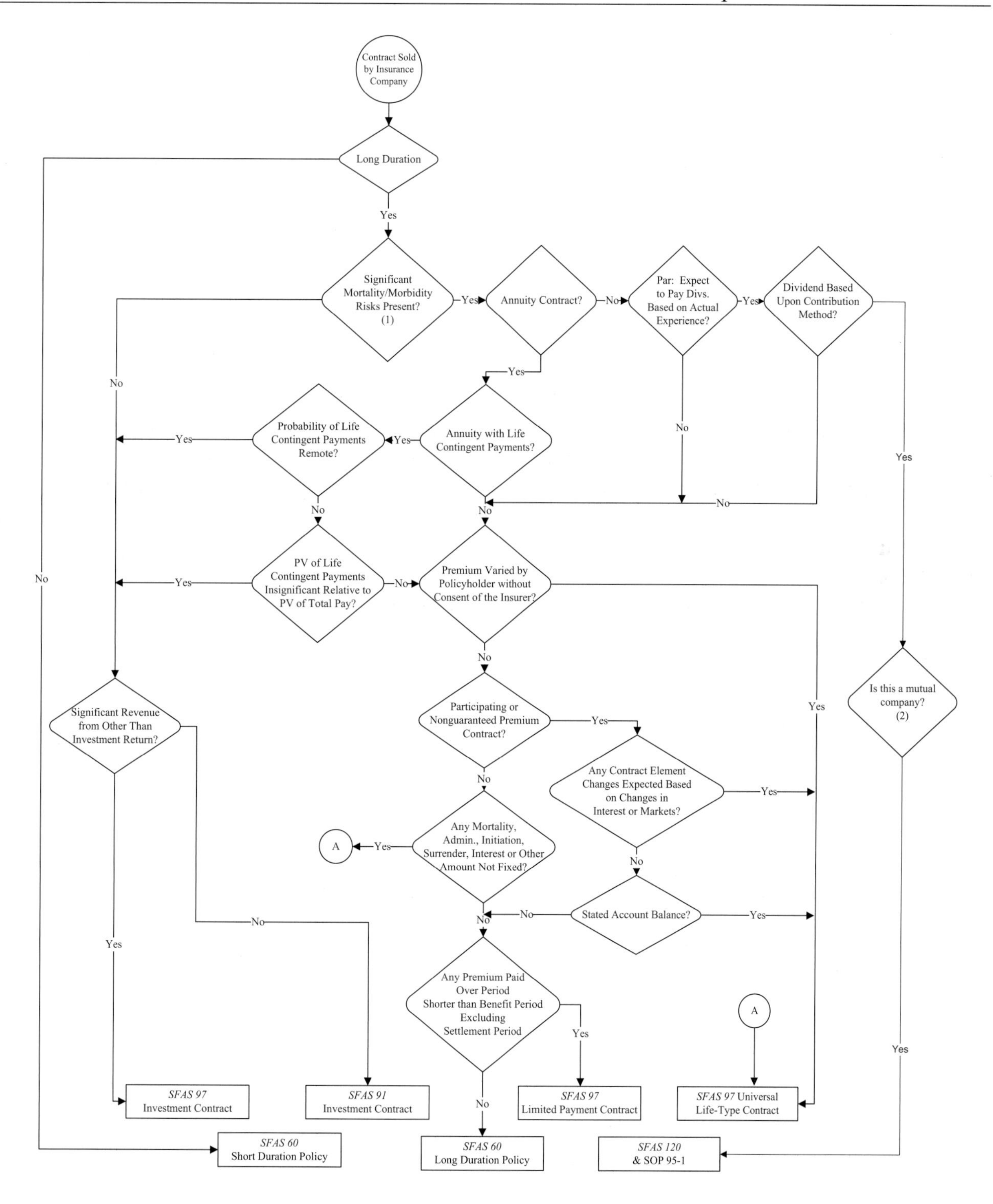

(1) For deferred annuities in the U.S., *SFAS 97*, in paragraphs 7 and 40, does not recognize annuity purchase options as creating "significant mortality/morbidity risk." Specific reference is made to "the right to purchase" a new contract upon the exercise of an annuity purchase option. Outside of the U.S. there are deferred annuity contracts that provide for the automatic application of amounts accumulated under the contract toward a life annuity benefit at maturity. The original deferred annuity contract is not terminated, with a new contract issued, as it generally is in the U.S. In these cases, the guaranteed annuity rate could contain significant mortality guarantees, which many would believe comprises a significant mortality risk for the duration of the contract. This would suggest *SFAS 97* limited pay contract treatment.

(2) Stock companies have the option of using either *SFAS 120* or *SFAS 60*/*SFAS 97* limited pay.

In using the chart, some issues arise. One of the primary differences between U.S. and non-U.S. stock companies is the existence of and treatment of the participating features of the policies.

16.2.2 Applicability of *SFAS 120* for Participating Business

As described in Chapter 5, *SFAS 120*, "Accounting and Reporting by Mutual Life Insurance Enterprises and by Insurance Enterprises for Certain Long-Duration Participating Contracts," applies to long-duration participating life insurance contracts that meet both of the following conditions:

(a) The contracts are long-duration participating contracts that are expected to pay dividends to policyholders based on the actual experience of the insurer.

(b) Annual policyholder dividends are paid in a manner that identifies divisible surplus and distributes that surplus in approximately the same proportion as the contracts are considered to have contributed to divisible surplus. (Paragraph 5)

It should be noted that references made to *SFAS 120*, in many cases, are considered to include *AICPA SOP 95-1*, "Accounting for Certain Insurance Activities of Mutual Life Insurance Enterprises," since this SOP provides the specific accounting guidance for *SFAS 120*.

Dividends on U.S. policies may be (a) paid in cash, (b) used in some way equivalent to receiving cash (for example, used to reduce premiums), or (c) used to buy additional benefits (for example, paid-up additions). For U.S. mutual companies or recently demutualized stock companies, the company identifies distributable surplus and distributes it approximately in proportion to the contribution made by each policy by identifying the contribution that each policy has made.

In many other parts of the world, policies are designed to provide a bonus, which is similar to a U.S. paid-up addition. The bonus is often calculated as a percentage increase in the sum assured; this percentage is the same across many lines of business. It can be argued that bonuses are based on the experience of the insurance enterprise and that divisible surplus is identified. However, the distribution of that surplus to individual policies may or may not be based on the contribution of each individual policy's contribution to divisible surplus. Four examples follow:

1. In some continental European countries, the policy of the insurer is to distribute profits on the participating policies in proportion to reserves. Divisible surplus is identified and a proportion determined such that policyholder sums insured are increased in a fair way to all policyholders. The reserves would be indicative of the policyholders' contribution to divisible surplus. Companies in countries such as Switzerland, France, Belgium, Spain, Portugal, and several others have taken this view and therefore have applied *SFAS 120* to nearly all of their participating policies. There are some companies that choose to distribute bonuses based on sums insured rather than reserves. Except in certain circumstances where policies are relatively homogeneous, this treatment is generally viewed as not satisfying the contribution principle.

2. In the United Kingdom, a portion of the total bonus payment is directly allocated to the policyholders in the form of an annual reversionary bonus while another part of the bonus is not distributed until the contract is terminated. This terminal bonus may represent greater than 50% of the payment at time of death, maturity, or surrender. The U.K. bonus treatment may follow the contribution principle over the entire life of

the policies, but it is generally accepted that this is not the case in the near term and therefore the contribution principle is not satisfied.

3. In Italy, a common type of participating product provides dividends or bonuses based on investment performance only. Any gains or losses from mortality, persistency, expenses, or other source are ignored. A strict interpretation of the contribution principle would say that these contracts do not receive dividends based on the U.S. contribution principle because they do not consider all elements of the divisible surplus. (It might even be appropriate to classify such products as interest sensitive and subject to *SFAS 97*). Some others may take a less strict interpretation on certain policies where the profits are materially investment return since the other components (mortality and expenses) can be offsetting. In this more liberal interpretation, *SFAS 120* may be considered appropriate after a thorough review and understanding of the terms and conditions of the specific policies.

4. With respect to reinsurance assumed, it is questionable as to whether *SFAS 120* should be considered. The reason is that bonuses are typically paid based on the ceding company's earnings and not on the divisible surplus of the reinsurer. It is thought that this invalidates the use of *SFAS 120* for reinsurers generally.

To conclude, every participating product must be assessed for applicability to *SFAS 120*. In the U.S. this is not a primary area of focus since there is usually no debate that *SFAS 120* applies to mutual companies. Most stock companies do use *SFAS 60* since that standard applied for many years prior to the issuance of *SFAS 120*. But outside of the U.S., participating business is significant to many stock insurers and reinsurers so they must assess whether or not the contribution principle is satisfied. It should also be pointed out that a stock company may satisfy the contribution principle and yet choose to use *SFAS 60*. Unlike mutual companies, stock companies have the choice as to whether they use *SFAS 120* or *SFAS 60*, assuming that they satisfy the contribution principle.

16.2.3 Applicability of *SFAS 60* for Participating Business

SFAS 60 states that policyholder dividends shall be accrued using an estimate of the amount to be paid. (Paragraph 41) It then distinguishes between insurance enterprises where there are restrictions on the amount of net income that may be distributed to shareholders and those where there are no restrictions.

16.2.3.1 Restricted Distribution to Shareholders

SFAS 60 continues:

> If limitations exist on the amount of net income from participating insurance contracts of life insurance enterprises that may be distributed to stockholders, the policyholders' share of net income on those contracts that cannot be distributed to stockholders shall be excluded from stockholders' equity by a charge to operations and a credit to a liability relating to participating policyholders' funds in a manner similar to the accounting for net income applicable to minority interests. Dividends declared or paid to participating policyholders shall reduce that liability; dividends declared or paid in excess of the liability shall be charged to operations. Income-based dividend provisions shall be based on net income that includes adjustments between general-purpose and statutory financial statements that will reverse and enter into future calculations of the dividend provision. (Paragraph 42)

This paragraph implies that wherever a restriction exists on shareholder dividend payments, the company should hold a liability to take into account valuation differences between U.S. GAAP and the dividend basis (most commonly the local statutory basis). More detail is provided in Chapter 4, where this liability is addressed as an undistributed participating policyholders' earnings account. In this chapter, this liability is referred to as the deferred bonus reserve (DBR). The DBR is a positive value. It would not be appropriate to have a negative liability because these policyholders do not owe the company this amount.

There are several countries outside the U.S. that have restrictions on payments to shareholders. For example, assume the restriction is policyholders are entitled to at least 90% of profits at termination of the policy. It may be the case that 40% is allocated immediately to the policyholders in the form of an annual reversionary bonus and the remaining 50% is placed in a bonus pool that will eventually be allocated, but for the time being represents unallocated policyholder funds.

In this situation, the DBR can be thought of as the sum of two parts:

(a) Unallocated bonus pool on a local statutory basis (presuming this is the dividend basis), and

(b) An adjustment for any GAAP-to-local-statutory timing differences.

There are several additional points to consider.

If policyholder allocations to the bonus pool exceed the restricted amount (for example, 95% instead of 90%), can the company establish full amount as the liability under U.S. GAAP? Generally, as long as the potential disbursements are guaranteed to be distributed to policyholders and are not disbursable at the discretion of the company, this liability may be held for U.S. GAAP. If there is discretion as to whether or not this money will be distributed to policyholders, only the restricted, guaranteed amounts should be considered qualifying as the liability under U.S. GAAP.

Further, in calculating the liability for part (b) above, is it necessary to employ the restricted percentages for recognizing timing differences? It is generally believed that these timing differences exist only to the extent that a restriction exists, and therefore it is inappropriate to consider anything above the restriction as eligible for this adjustment. It should be pointed out that there may be opposing views on the determination of (b), because some believe that a "best estimate" percent is appropriate and consistent with the treatment of dividends under *SFAS 60*.

16.2.3.2 Unrestricted Distribution to Shareholders

If there are no restrictions on shareholder dividends and the dividend scales are not related to actual net income, it is common practice to accrue the dividends anticipated at outset by including the projected dividend payments in the benefit stream when calculating the benefit net premium and the benefit reserve. Differences between actual dividend payments and payments anticipated at outset would flow through income.

16.2.4 Products that Span Accounting Models

Products that span accounting models is an issue that is not confined to non-U.S. products because many U.S. products contain characteristics that are governed by different standards.

If different features in a product are classified according to different standards, there are a number of approaches:

1. It might be possible to split each contract into its component parts and report each element separately.

2. One part of the contract might predominate and the standard governing that part might be used for the whole contract.

3. The predominant part of a block of business could determine the accounting standard.

16.3 Impact of Tax Systems

Benefit reserves, deferred acquisition costs (DAC) and value of business acquired (VOBA) under U.S. GAAP for life insurance and annuity contracts are prepared on a pre-tax basis. This approach is consistent with the U.S. tax system, which primarily taxes life insurance companies on profits.

The tax systems in other countries are often different. For example, the U.K. has historically taxed life insurance products on the basis of investment income minus total company expenses (I-E), which exists in a modified version in Australia.

This approach to taxation has a significant impact on product design and pricing. Consider term insurance, which generates little investment income. For a company with I-E close to zero, the expenses associated with term insurance will be offset by the overall investment income; the product may be priced on a net-of-tax basis. The term insurance premium rates in the marketplace reflect this phenomenon and are significantly lower than premium rates without the tax advantage.

If U.S. GAAP financial reporting for this product were prepared on a pre-tax basis, term business would be unprofitable. At the very least, a significant proportion of acquisition costs would not be deferrable and further loss recognition might be required. The result would be a loss at outset for the term business followed by zero profit or loss if experience followed the expected assumptions. There would be a mirror benefit for the business generating high investment income with lower expenses.

For a company where I = E, the tax is zero and the impact is to subsidize the low investment business by the high investment business. Other companies take this into account when pricing and reflect this effect. To avoid the result of term business being unprofitable and high premium business being too profitable, a company could prepare its U.S. GAAP reserves using the local pricing approach including the I–E tax as an expense. This expense is positive for high premium, high reserve contracts and negative for term insurance. However, care must be taken in preparing the results to make certain that the appropriate allowance is taken. If E exceeds I, the expenses may not be fully deductible and the products should not be reported on a U.S. GAAP basis as if they were. In practice, excess E may be carried forward indefinitely to offset future I. However, companies might not be able to use it in the foreseeable future.

An illustrative example follows.

Table 16-1
Assumptions for a Level 25-Year Temporary Insurance Policy

Item	Amount	Basis
Sum assured	100,000	Per policy
Monthly premium	15.00	Per policy
Set up cost	250.00	Per policy
Year 1 commission	60.00%	of premium
Marketing costs	100.00%	of commission
Ongoing cost	25.00	Per policy
Ongoing commission	2.50%	of premium
Bond yield	5.00%	
Inflation	2.50%	
Equity–dividend yield	3.00%	
Equity capital growth	4.50%	
Investment	80% bond; 20% equity	
Tax rate	20%	I – E
Gross investment income	5.500%	
Tax	1.00%	
Net investment income	4.500%	
Deferrable Expenses: U.S. GAAP		
Set-up cost	250.00	Per policy
Commission	57.50%	of premium
Marketing	0	
Deferrable Expenses: U.K. Tax		
Set up cost	250.00	Per policy
Commission	36.00%	of premium
Marketing	60.00%	of commission

The tax benefit on initial expenses as defined by the UK tax code is spread over seven years. Capitalized expenses under U.S. GAAP are defined by U.S. GAAP rules, which differ from U.K. tax rules. There is a tax offset to U.S. GAAP capitalized expenses, which occurs as a negative amount of capitalized expense in each of the first seven years of the book of business. This is demonstrated along with the usual cash flows in the following table.

Table 16-2

Development of Benefit Net Premium, Expense Net Premium and Deferred Expense Net Premium Percentages

Initial Cash Flows													Assumptions			
(1)	(2)	(3)	(4)	(5)	(6)	(7)	(8)	(9)	(10)	(11)	(12)	(13)	(14)	(15)	(16)	(17)
								GAAP								
Year	Policies In Force	Premium	Commission	Other	Tax Deferred Expenses	Deferred Tax Benefit	Tax Benefit	Pre-Tax Deferred Expenses	Outstanding Tax Benefit	Annual Tax Benefit	Net Expenses Deferred	Deaths	Mortality Rate	Lapses	Total Decement	Annual Premium
0			108,000	358,000	379,600	75,920	-	353,500	70,700		353,500					
1	1,000.0	170,521	(5,687)	23,683		65,074	(14,445)	(5,450)	60,600	10,100	(15,550)	40,600	0.000406	12.50%	0.125406	11.3681
2	874.6	149,135	3,728	21,231		54,229	(15,838)		50,500	10,100	(10,100)	37,345	0.000427	12.50%	0.125427	11.3680
3	764.9	130,429	3,261	19,032		43,383	(15,304)		40,400	10,100	(10,100)	34,267	0.000448	12.50%	0.125448	11.3679
4	668.9	114,065	2,852	17,060		32,537	(14,828)		30,300	10,100	(10,100)	32,310	0.000483	12.50%	0.125483	11.3677
5	585.0	99,750	2,494	15,292		21,691	(14,403)		20,200	10,100	(10,100)	30,713	0.000525	12.50%	0.125525	11.3675
6	511.6	87,227	2,181	13,707		10,846	(14,023)		10,100	10,100	(10,100)	29,722	0.000581	12.50%	0.125581	11.3673
7	447.3	76,271	1,907	12,285		-	(13,684)		-	10,100	(10,100)	28,495	0.000637	12.50%	0.125637	11.3670
8	391.1	66,687	1,667	11,010			(2,535)			-	0	27,926	0.000714	12.50%	0.125714	11.3666
9	342.0	58,301	1,458	9,866			(2,265)			-	0	27,288	0.000798	12.50%	0.125798	11.3663
10	298.9	50,965	1,274	8,840			(2,023)				0	26,785	0.000896	12.50%	0.125896	11.3658
11	261.3	44,547	1,114	7,920			(1,807)				0	26,522	0.001015	12.50%	0.126015	11.3653
12	228.4	38,931	973	7,095			(1,614)				0	26,058	0.001141	12.50%	0.126141	11.3647
13	199.6	34,018	850	6,354			(1,441)				0	25,704	0.001288	12.50%	0.126288	11.3640
14	174.4	29,720	743	5,690			(1,287)				0	25,387	0.001456	12.50%	0.126456	11.3632
15	152.3	25,960	649	5,095			(1,149)				0	25,162	0.001652	12.50%	0.126652	11.3623
16	133.0	22,670	567	4,560			(1,025)				0	24,769	0.001862	12.50%	0.126862	11.3613
17	116.1	19,792	495	4,081			(915)				0	24,391	0.002100	12.50%	0.127100	11.3602
18	101.4	17,275	432	3,651			(817)				0	24,059	0.002373	12.50%	0.127373	11.3590
19	88.5	15,072	377	3,265			(728)				0	23,595	0.002667	12.50%	0.127667	11.3576
20	77.2	13,146	329	2,919			(650)				0	23,176	0.003003	12.50%	0.128003	11.3561
21	67.3	11,462	287	2,609			(579)				0	22,706	0.003374	12.50%	0.128374	11.3544
22	58.7	9,989	250	2,330			(516)				0	22,214	0.003787	12.50%	0.128787	11.3525
23	51.1	8,701	218	2,080			(460)				0	21,714	0.004249	12.50%	0.129249	11.3504
24	44.5	7,575	189	1,856			(409)				0	21,150	0.004753	12.50%	0.129753	11.3480
25	38.7	6,590	165	1,656			(364)				0	20,575	0.005313	12.50%	0.130313	11.3455
NPV@	4.50%	1,009,449	123,502	517,141			(100,261)				287,328	430,164				

Benefit Net Premium =	42.6%	= NPV (13) / NPV (3)
Expense Net Premium =	53.5%	= NPV[(4) + (5) + (8)] / NPV (3)
Profit =	3.9%	= 100% – Benefit Net Premium – Expense Net Premium
Deferred ENP =	28.5%	= NPV (12) / NPV (3)

Legend:

(1), $(2)_1$ Given.

$(2)_t = (2)_{t-1} \times [1 - (16)_{t-1}]$.

$(3)_t = (2)_t \times (17)_t \times$ Monthly premium.

$(4)_0 =$ Initial commission rate $\times 12 \times$ Monthly premium $\times (2)_1$.

$(4)_1 =$ Initial commission rate $\times [(3)_1 - 12 \times$ Monthly premium $\times (2)_1]$.

$(4)_t = (3)_t \times$ Renewal commission rate for $t > 1$.

$(5)_0 =$ Marketing costs $+ (2)_1 \times$ set up costs.

$(5)_t =$ Initial ongoing costs $\times (2)_t \times (17)_t \times (1 +$ inflation$)$ ^ $(1)_{t-1}/12$.

$(6)_0 = (2)_1 \times$ Set up costs $+ 60\% \times [(4)_0 =$ Marketing costs$]$.

$(7)_t = (6)_0 \times$ Tax rate $\times (7 - (1)_t)/7$.

$(8)_t = -[(4)_t + (5)_t] \times$ Tax rate $+ (7)_t - (7)_{t-1}$.

$(9)_0 = (57.5\% \times 12 \times$ Monthly premium $+$ Set up costs$) \times (2)_1$.

$(9)_1 = 57.5\% \times [(3)_1 - 12 \times$ Monthly Premium $\times (2)_1]$.

$(10)_t = (9)_0 \times$ Tax rate $\times (7 - (1)_t)/7$, but not to exceed $(7)_t$.

$(11)_t = (10)_{t-1} - (10)_t$.

$(12) = (9) - (11)$.

$(13) = (2) \times (14) \times$ Sum assured.

(14) and (15) given.

$(16) = (14) + (15)$.

$(17) = 12 \times a$, where a is one year annuity factor payable monthly in advance.

The development of benefit reserves and DAC is shown in Table 16-3.

Table 16-3
Development of Benefit Reserve and DAC Factors

(1)	(2)	(3)	(4)	(5)	(6)	(7)	(8)
		Net Expenses		**Benefit**		**Factors per 1000**	
Year	**Premium**	**Deferred**	**Deaths**	**Reserve**	**DAC**	**Benefit Reserve**	**DAC**
		353,500			0		
1	170,521	(15,550)	40,600	32,779	303,894	0.37	3.47
2	149,135	(10,100)	37,345	61,044	263,850	0.80	3.45
3	130,429	(10,100)	34,267	85,578	227,448	1.28	3.40
4	114,065	(10,100)	32,310	106,090	194,169	1.81	3.32
5	99,750	(10,100)	30,713	122,921	163,557	2.40	3.20
6	87,227	(10,100)	29,722	136,066	135,212	3.04	3.02
7	76,271	(10,100)	28,495	146,286	108,779	3.74	2.78
8	66,687	0	27,926	153,371	94,270	4.49	2.76
9	58,301	0	27,288	157,775	81,548	5.28	2.73
10	50,965	0	26,785	159,695	70,388	6.11	2.69
11	44,547	0	26,522	159,174	60,594	6.97	2.65
12	38,931	0	26,058	156,659	51,993	7.85	2.61
13	34,018	0	25,704	152,251	44,434	8.73	2.55
14	29,720	0	25,387	146,097	37,786	9.59	2.48
15	25,960	0	25,162	138,258	31,933	10.39	2.40
16	22,670	0	24,769	129,035	26,773	11.11	2.31
17	19,792	0	24,391	118,529	22,219	11.69	2.19
18	17,275	0	24,059	106,794	18,193	12.07	2.06
19	15,072	0	23,595	94,045	14,626	12.19	1.90
20	13,146	0	23,176	80,312	11,459	11.93	1.70
21	11,462	0	22,706	65,707	8,639	11.20	1.47
22	9,989	0	22,214	50,307	6,121	9.84	1.20
23	8,701	0	21,714	34,164	3,865	7.68	0.87
24	7,575	0	21,150	17,380	1,835	4.49	0.47
25	6,590	0	20,575	(0)	(0)	-	-

Legend:
Benefit net premium and deferred ENP are calculated in Table 16-2.
(1), (2), (3) and (4) from Table 16-2.
$(5)_t = (5)_{t-1} \times (1 + i) + [(2)_t \times \text{benefit net premium} - (4)_{t}] \times (1 + i) ^\wedge .5$.
$(6)_1 = (3)_0 \times (1 + i) + [(3)_1 - (2)_1 \times \text{deferred ENP}] \times (1 + i) ^\wedge .5$.
$(6)_t = (6)_{t-1} \times (1 + i) + [(3)_t - (2)_t \times \text{deferred ENP}] \times (1 + i) ^\wedge .5$.
i = net investment yield.
(7) = 1000 × (5) / in force.
(8) = 1000 × (6) / in force.

This leads to the income statement presentation shown in Table 16-4.

Table 16-4
Cash Flows and GAAP Income Statement

(1) Year	(2) Premium	(3) Investment Income	(4) Commission	(5) Other	(6) Tax	(7) Deaths	(8) Change Benefit Reserve	(9) Change DAC	(10) GAAP Profit	(11) Benefit Reserve	(12) DAC
			108,000	358,000	-					-	-
1	170,521	(18,158)	(5,687)	23,683	(14,445)	40,600	32,779	303,894	(86,673)	32,779	303,894
2	149,135	(9,916)	3,728	21,231	(15,838)	37,345	28,265	(40,044)	24,444	61,044	263,850
3	130,429	(7,142)	3,261	19,032	(15,304)	34,267	24,534	(36,403)	21,094	85,578	227,448
4	114,065	(4,678)	2,852	17,060	(14,828)	32,310	20,511	(33,279)	18,203	106,090	194,169
5	99,750	(2,503)	2,494	15,292	(14,403)	30,713	16,831	(30,612)	15,709	122,921	163,557
6	87,227	(590)	2,181	13,707	(14,023)	29,722	13,146	(28,345)	13,559	136,066	135,212
7	76,271	1,090	1,907	12,285	(13,684)	28,495	10,220	(26,433)	11,707	146,286	108,779
8	66,687	2,325	1,667	11,010	(2,535)	27,926	7,085	(14,509)	9,349	153,371	94,270
9	58,301	3,148	1,458	9,866	(2,265)	27,288	4,404	(12,722)	7,977	157,775	81,548
10	50,965	3,788	1,274	8,840	(2,023)	26,785	1,920	(11,160)	6,797	159,695	70,388
11	44,547	4,259	1,114	7,920	(1,807)	26,522	(521)	(9,794)	5,783	159,174	60,594
12	38,931	4,579	973	7,095	(1,614)	26,058	(2,515)	(8,601)	4,912	156,659	51,993
13	34,018	4,767	850	6,354	(1,441)	25,704	(4,408)	(7,559)	4,166	152,251	44,434
14	29,720	4,834	743	5,690	(1,287)	25,387	(6,154)	(6,648)	3,526	146,097	37,786
15	25,960	4,790	649	5,095	(1,149)	25,162	(7,839)	(5,853)	2,978	138,258	31,933
16	22,670	4,647	567	4,560	(1,025)	24,769	(9,223)	(5,159)	2,510	129,035	26,773
17	19,792	4,418	495	4,081	(915)	24,391	(10,505)	(4,554)	2,110	118,529	22,219
18	17,275	4,110	432	3,651	(817)	24,059	(11,735)	(4,027)	1,769	106,794	18,193
19	15,072	3,733	377	3,265	(728)	23,595	(12,749)	(3,567)	1,478	94,045	14,626
20	13,146	3,293	329	2,919	(650)	23,176	(13,733)	(3,167)	1,231	80,312	11,459
21	11,462	2,797	287	2,609	(579)	22,706	(14,605)	(2,819)	1,021	65,707	8,639
22	9,989	2,250	250	2,330	(516)	22,214	(15,400)	(2,518)	843	50,307	6,121
23	8,701	1,658	218	2,080	(460)	21,714	(16,143)	(2,256)	693	34,164	3,865
24	7,575	1,025	189	1,856	(409)	21,150	(16,784)	(2,030)	566	17,380	1,835
25	6,590	356	165	1,656	(364)	20,575	(17,380)	(1,835)	460	(0)	(0)

Legend:

(1), (2), (4), (5), (6), and (7) from Table 16-2.

$(8)_t = (11)_t - (11)_{t-1}$.

$(9)_t = (12)_t - (12)_{t-1}$.

$(10)_t = (2)_t + (3)_t - (4)_t - (5)_t - (6)_t - (7)_t - (8)_t + (9)_t$.

$(11)_t = (5)_t$ from Table 16-3.

$(12)_t = (6)_t$ from Table 16-3.

The present value of the projected tax benefits significantly exceeds the present value of the GAAP profits. If the tax benefit were not included as a negative expense, the amount of acquisition costs that could be deferred would be restricted. A loss would be incurred at outset and, if experience followed the assumed, ongoing profits would be zero. Since such results may not appear reasonable, one could conclude that after-tax assumptions should be used in an "I-E" tax environment, subject to any caps or floors.

It should be noted that there are significant opposing views to this approach. Other practitioners have taken a more strict interpretation of U.S. GAAP and state that all assumptions should be pre-tax with no exceptions.

The first year loss in this table is due to the costs of non-deferrable acquisition expenses.

16.4 Impact of Realized and Unrealized Investment Gains

As discussed in Chapter 13, unrealized gains and losses only impact the income statement directly if the investments are classified as trading. In the United States, the majority of assets backing life insurance liabilities have been classified as available for sale. The proportion of U.S. life insurance company assets that are classified as trading is small.

The U.S. life insurance and annuity products usually offer a significant level of long-term guarantees. This, together with statutory capital requirements, compels U.S. companies to invest mainly in fixed income securities. Markets in other countries are not constrained in this way; consequently, companies have more freedom to invest in equity securities and real estate.

Historically, equity markets have outperformed fixed income markets. Companies with high equity portfolios often have high unrealized capital gains. For companies selling participating business in this environment (for example, in the U.K. market), bonuses may be declared using the unrealized gains. Unless the securities supporting this block are classified as trading, an earnings distortion due to timing differences could emerge under U.S. GAAP. When bonuses are declared they become a liability. However, the investment income cannot be recognized until the gain is realized. This problem can be partially eliminated in the restricted earnings (*SFAS 60*, paragraph 42) environment.

Revenues and expenses match if gains and losses are realized when the dividend liability is established or if the assets are classified as trading. This issue is constrained to the income statement since shadow adjustments tend to have a mitigating effect from a balance sheet perspective. See Chapter 15 for the discussion of shadow adjustments.

16.5 Product Classification Considerations in Specific Markets

The following sections address the European and Asian markets in general and certain specific countries. Products in other markets, such as South America, would undergo similar analyses for determining which standard governs the financial reporting of the product.

16.5.1 European Market in General

The European life business consists of endowment insurance, term insurance, immediate and deferred annuities, and disability contracts. These products can vary both in the term of the coverage period and the length of the premium paying period. Important riders are disability and accident riders, which exist for most of the major products. Most of the products are split into several tariff generations, i.e., products of the same type that sold in different issue eras are based on different mortality tables and different guaranteed interest rates. Endowment products represent the largest block of individual and group life business for most companies.

These products may have both annual dividends and terminal dividends. As discussed previously, because participating contracts may or may not satisfy the contribution principle, they must be evaluated on a case-by-case basis.

Unit-linked products are popular in the U.K. and in some continental European markets. Index-linked products exist as well.

16.5.2 United Kingdom

16.5.2.1 Participating Business

The U.K. market has an earnings distribution system such that most companies return at least 90% of distributable profits to the policyholders. Profits are calculated and then a certain discretionary amount is placed in the fund for future appropriations (FFA) on a U.K. GAAP basis. Distributable profits are those profits after the allocation to the FFA has been made. Bonus distribution takes the form of (a) an annual reversionary bonus that is directly allocated to the policyholders in the year in which the profit has occurred, plus (b) a significant terminal bonus that is not allocated to policyholders until termination at death, surrender, or maturity. This method of allocation and the discretion associated with it has been commonly accepted as a process that does not satisfy the contribution principle. Therefore, product classifications have been restricted to either *SFAS 60* or, where a policyholder account balance exists, *SFAS 97*.

For many companies, the 90%/10% split is considered a restriction on payment to the shareholders. While this restriction is not governed by law, many UK companies have the 90%/10% distribution written into their articles of association, which may only be changed by board approval. It is commonly viewed that if a company has this restriction as part of the articles, it may apply paragraph 42 of *SFAS 60*. However, if the restriction is subject to change by the board at its discretion, some practitioners might not consider the amounts restricted to be a liability.

16.5.2.2 Unit Linked Products

Unit-linked products have characteristics that are similar to variable contracts in the United States. A proportion of each premium is invested (actually or notionally) in units of an investment fund. This fund could be a separate unit trust or mutual fund or it could be a segregated account within the life insurance general account. The benefits paid to the policyholder depend upon the performance of the fund chosen. There is normally a choice of investment funds; the contract may permit investments in multiple funds and may permit transfers between funds. There might be a charge for transfers. There is often a 5% spread between the bid and offer price of the units.

Premiums and death benefits are usually fixed. Death benefits may or may not exceed the account balance. There is not normally a minimum guaranteed rate of return; however, some contracts do have minimum maturity guarantees.

Traditionally, unit-linked contracts were designed with significant front-end loads in the first two years and ongoing risk and expense charges. Under local basis accounting, the front-end loads were designed to cover acquisition expenses and include a significant profit contribution. In fact, under local basis accounting, most of the profit emerges during the first two years of the contract.

To mitigate the marketing disadvantage of high front-end loads, some regular premium contracts are designed with two types of units: accumulation units and capital units. Accumulation units are ones with normal market design and charge structure. Capital units provide an alternative mechanism to the high front-end load. They have a much higher than normal annual charge (possibly as high as 5%), and a surrender penalty applies if the contract is surrendered early. The surrender penalty is usually equal to the discounted value of the capital units.

A typical product could be designed so that premiums paid in the first year or two would purchase capital units. Subsequent premiums would purchase accumulation units. The policy owner would see a contract with an account value, part of which would have a higher annual charge as well as a significant surrender charge in the early policy years. Unit-linked contracts are classified as *SFAS 97* insurance or investment contracts and are usually accounted for using the universal life-type model. They have typically been accounted for as separate accounts. However, this has changed following the introduction of *SOP 03-1*, which disqualifies many funds as separate accounts. (See below) The benefit reserve is set equal to the account value, which is easily determined by multiplying the number of accumulation and capital units by their respective bid values. Appropriate acquisition costs (as described in Chapter 3) are deferred and amortized over estimated gross profits. In addition, excess front-end loads give rise to an unearned revenue liability ("URL") as described in Chapter 6.

Estimated gross profits (EGPs) are calculated as they are for universal life insurance as described in Chapter 6. If units are purchased from a separate legal entity, the spread will not belong to that company and therefore should not be part of the EGP.

One issue that occurs is that the present values of both acquisition costs and unearned revenue items may exceed the present value of EGPs. If the present value of acquisition costs less the present value of unearned revenue is not greater than the present value of EGPs, the normal formulas may be used without modification. If it is greater, it may not be possible to defer all of the acquisition costs.

In practice, acquisition costs for contracts with capital units that are expensed in the local currency are offset by higher charges from those capital units and protected by a surrender penalty. It can be demonstrated that this is equivalent to holding fewer capital units initially, which is the same as a front-end load. In order to cover the liability, the company only needs to hold the reduced number of units and would only hold more if required to do so by the regulators or if the company wanted to invest its own funds in the units. The current U.K. requirement permits funding of the reduced amount.

It should be noted that there are significant opposing views to this treatment. Many believe that the appropriate *SFAS 97* reserve is the unreduced account value since using the lower value is akin to reducing the account value for surrender charges, which is specifically disallowed by *SFAS 97*. In addition, if the reduced account value were held as the liability, the separate account liability would not equal the market value of assets. Both treatments are found in the UK.

Under *SFAS 97*, the basic benefit reserve is the account balance. Holding the full account balance rather than the funded account balance means that the company would be offsetting an asset (DAC) designated in the local currency with a unit liability (the units equivalent to the front-end load). Typically, units are invested in equity-type investments and can fluctuate widely in price. The DAC amortizes with investment earnings but does not vary in capital terms. This can lead to fluctuations in reported earnings. The effects are somewhat mitigated to the extent that there is an unearned revenue liability that amortizes over the same stream. One way to offset this is to employ paragraph 25 of *SFAS 97*, which allows for the most recent revised investment earnings rate to be used for amortization rather than the rate in effect at the inception of the book of business.

SOP 03-1 has had an impact on the treatment of the assets backing the unit-linked liabilities. Historically, a one line item for the value of the unit fund as held in a similar manner as a separate account in the US. *SOP 03-1* says that, to qualify for separate account treatment, the fund must satisfy the following conditions:

a. The separate account is legally recognized. That is, the separate account is established, approved, and regulated under special rules such as state insurance laws, federal securities laws, or similar foreign laws.

b. The separate account assets supporting the contract liabilities are legally insulated from the general account liabilities of the insurance enterprise (that is, the contract holder is not subject to insurer default risk to the extent of the assets held in the separate account).

c. The insurer must, as a result of contractual, statutory, or regulatory requirements, invest the contract holder's funds within the separate account as directed by the contract holder in designated investment alternatives or in accordance with specific investment objectives or policies.

d. All investment performance, net of contract fees and assessments, must as a result of contractual, statutory, or regulatory requirements be passed through to the individual contract holder. Contracts may specify conditions under which there may be a minimum guarantee, but not a ceiling, because a ceiling would prohibit all investment performance from being passed through to the contract holder.

Many UK unit-linked funds do not satisfy all of the above criteria, so that the assets must be reported as if they were assets of the general account. This could lead to an income statement mismatch if the assets are not designated as trading because then they would not be reported at fair value whereas the liabilities would be at fair value.

16.5.3 Germany

16.5.3.1 Life Business

Many of the participating contracts are endowment contracts or annuity contracts that appear to satisfy the contribution principle. The dividend distribution system for Germany (as well as for Austria) is somewhat unique in Europe in that the company's German statutory accounts have established a reserve for future dividends. Required contributions to this reserve have historically been based upon the after-tax gross profits for the company. Withdrawals from this reserve are the dividends actually allocated to the policyholders. Based upon the German regulatory restrictions upon how much of the after-tax gross profit may be left for shareholders, this exemplifies the restrictive dividend situation as described above. This reserve for future bonuses can only be used by the company to provide annual or terminal dividends, with a possible exception that the reserve may be used to support policyholder guarantees in the event of a company's severe financial crisis. Therefore, once money is contributed to this reserve, it belongs to policyholders even though it has not been allocated specifically to individual policyholders.

Many companies reporting under U.S. GAAP have elected to account for these life products according to *SFAS 120*; some companies have chosen to use *SFAS 60* accounting treatment for the benefit reserves and DAC.

16.5.3.2 Health Business

The German health business presents a unique contrast to the life business. The health insurance policies are generally guaranteed renewable medical or dental reimbursement policies that are highly specific to the German market. *SFAS 120* treatment for these contracts is not appropriate because the dividend distribution system does not follow the contribution principle. Although the divisible surplus is calculated based on the gross profits generated by the business, there are intergenerational subsidies, so that the rate increases for elderly policyholders are held down below what would be an equitable determination, with the understanding of the younger policyholders that as they age they would receive similar consideration. Therefore, *SFAS 60* is used. One approach that has been used is called "prospective unlocking." Using this method, at the point of each premium rate increase a new net premium is computed as a constant percentage of the new gross premium, with consideration given to the existing reserve balance. That is, the present value of future net premiums plus the existing GAAP reserve equals the present value of future benefits and maintenance expenses. Further detail is provided in Chapters 4 and 10.

16.5.4 Switzerland

16.5.4.1 Participating Business

The Swiss participating business is similar to Germany in that the participating contracts generally appear to follow the contribution principle. The critical difference from Germany is that there is no regulatory restriction on the amounts paid to policyholders. Swiss companies may be holding reserves to cover future expected bonus payments to policyholders, but this reserve tends to be discretionary and can be used to cover earnings shortfalls or to hold back excess earnings in the more profitable years. Therefore, it is unlikely that, in most scenarios, a Swiss company would be allowed to hold a DBR under *SFAS 60*, paragraph 42, unless there exists some type of contractual guarantee to policyholders. It is more likely that a life company in Switzerland would be eligible to use *SFAS 120*.

16.5.4.2 Group Pension Business

Group pension business is a group product expressed as a contract between the insurance company and an entity called a foundation. The foundation is formed to represent the company's employees. The contract is a product that is regulated, with provisions specified, by the BVG pension law in Switzerland.

The insurance company insures employees against death, disability, and other risks while building a cash surrender value to be used to fund a pension benefit. The exact benefits are determined at contract inception; the insurance company ensures that the provisions meet the standards in the law.

The insurance company calculates the premium for these benefits in total and charges the foundation this amount. The employer sponsoring the foundation must pay for at least 50% of the premiums. The remaining amount of the premium is collected from the employees. The premiums are not guaranteed beyond one year.

A surrender value accumulates within this contract in which a portion of the premiums, as determined in the contract, is set aside each year and grows at a 4% (defined by law) technical interest rate. This surrender value is made available to an employee upon transfer to another company or foundation. Upon contract cancellation, the sum of these transfer values less a surrender charge is paid to the foundation.

The contracts are participating insurance contracts. The form of profit participation is determined by the terms of the contract. Usually, the profit participation takes the form of either a premium reduction for the next year's premium or paid up additional retirement pension benefits.

The ultimate pension benefits covered by a contract are either defined by the formula with reference to the employees' salaries (defined benefit) or by reference to the amounts set aside each year to accumulate in the cash surrender value of the contract (defined contribution).

There is a risk portion and a savings portion to these contracts. These portions could be considered together or separately. The separate treatment would lead to different FAS classifications, though results would be similar no matter which classification was selected. The one dominating feature of such products is the lack of flexibility on the part of the insurance company. Many of the product characteristics are in fact dictated by law with very little opportunity for the insurance company to make amendments. This is true for both the defined benefit and defined contribution versions.

If the risk and savings elements are bifurcated, the risk part would be classified as *SFAS 60* and the savings portion of the contract would require deposit accounting under *SFAS 97* because it would be considered an investment contract.

If the contract is considered as one total contract, the transfer value can be viewed as an account balance, but the fixed and guaranteed nature of the transfer value appears different from the intent of an account value in the U.S. In the U.S., the account balance serves as the unbundled mechanism to allow for flexibility with respect to premiums, benefits, charges, and/or credits. It is this lack of true flexibility that causes the actuary to reflect on propriety of applying *SFAS 97*, because this standard's paragraph 10 discusses the universal life criteria that its terms not be fixed and guaranteed. The guaranteed nature aspects of the product could indicate that *SFAS 120* may be more appropriate.

This is an example of a type of business where there are arguments for one several classifications: *SFAS 60*, *SFAS 97*, or *SFAS 120*.

16.5.5 Italy

Participating business, often referred to as revaluable business, is similar to the tariff policies that are common in continental Europe. Initial premium rates are set according to the appropriate tariff. Bonuses are declared on a regular basis by giving an interest credit. Typically, the return would be calculated on designated assets. These assets represent a reasonable set of investments that could have been purchased by the premiums from these contracts. The bonus interest rate would be calculated as the excess of a percentage of that return over the tariff rate (a floor of zero is common). The percentage would typically be around 80%. The bonus would be calculated as an increase in the sum assured. Some revaluable products include an automatic premium increase, which may be at the same rate as the increase in the sum insured or at some lower rate.

For many Italian companies, the profit-sharing percentage is specified in the contract as a percent to be applied to investment earnings on a book value basis where 80% is by far the most common percent. This contractual restriction implies that a restricted environment (*SFAS 60*, paragraph 42) tends to exist in Italy. But one key difference between Italy and the UK and Germany is that policyholder distributions are typically allocated directly to the policyholder in the year in which they occur; there are no unallocated policyholder monies.

If contract terms provide for an excess interest benefit, consideration should be given to a *SFAS 97* universal life or investment contract classification. The contracts would be accounted for as universal life-type business and the benefit reserve would be the account balance or a proxy for the account balance.

Alternatively, if it is believed that the benefits are effectively fixed, with a modest potential bonus, it could be argued that *SFAS 60* applies. Benefit reserve and DAC would be calculated at outset and applied to the actual in force amounts.

16.5.6 Asian Market in General

Increasingly, U.S. GAAP is becoming more important to insurance companies in Asia, mainly due to:

- **Quest for external finance.** The world's largest capital markets are in the U.S. Non-US companies that register with the Securities and Exchange Commission (SEC) must file either full U.S. GAAP statements, or their annual local accounts, together with a reconciliation to U.S. GAAP. In either case, a full U.S. GAAP conversion is usually needed to carry out this reconciliation.

- **Use of US GAAP financial statements by multi-nationals.** The US parent companies of foreign subsidiaries may have to prepare US GAAP financial statements for those subsidiaries and include the results in their consolidated returns.

- **US GAAP as current de-facto International Accounting Standard.** The International Accounting Standards Committee is preparing an international approach to accounting for life insurance contracts. It is also uncertain, until the completion of the international standards, whether the SEC will approve of the subsequent international standards for listing in the U.S. In the meantime, U.S. GAAP will remain not only the required basis for financial statements in the U.S., but also the basis on which a company, looking to raise external finance from an international source, would consider producing its financials.

Predominantly, products sold in Asia have been traditional whole life, endowment, term assurance, and health-type contracts. Therefore, *SFAS 60* or *SFAS 120* is likely to act as the main accounting standard for most in-force business, with *SFAS 97* applying to limited payment products (*SFAS 97* LP). However, in recent years, products similar to U.S.-style variable life and UK-style unit-linked products have become increasingly popular in the prevailing low interest rate environment. This situation implies greater use of *SFAS 97*.

Where product design features, local regulations, and/or industry practices differ greatly from the U.S., classification issues become more complex. Generally, product classification should be performed on a case-by-case basis to ensure allowance for a company's specific experience. The following section looks at some examples from Asian markets, where products differ from those in the U.S. Many of the issues considered are not country-specific and will arise in other Asian countries.

16.5.7 Japan

While many new types of products have been introduced to Japan in recent years, most of the products in force and currently sold are traditional, such as whole life, endowment, and term. A common combination is to sell a whole life base product with a large amount of term rider. Riders that cover accidental death and disability, hospital and surgical benefits, and various other health coverages are also offered. Riders in Japan often have substantial profit margins. Therefore, greater attention should be paid to riders in this case than is often the practice in the U.S.

Life annuities are commonly sold in Japan. They may be sold as single- or regular-premium products. Typically annuities are very long-term with an accumulation period and then a payout phase. The latter may function as a life annuity or as an annuity certain.

Another feature common in the Japanese life market is the pre-payment of premiums. For example, a policyholder can put down a lump sum that will then be used to pay premiums in the future.

Japan's original 20 companies were predominantly mutual companies, so participating ("par") products are common. Two general types are offered. The first is the usual par product, which pays dividends based on a three-factor formula reflecting gains on mortality, interest, and expenses. The second type consists of semi-par products, which pay dividends based on gains from interest only.

One of the first decisions for implementing U.S. GAAP is whether the par products and the dividend practices followed by the relevant company qualify them for *SFAS 120* or *SFAS 60* (or *SFAS 97* LP) treatment. The key requirements for *SFAS 120* classification were discussed earlier in this chapter in the section "Applicability of *SFAS 120* for Participating Business" and apply similarly to Japan.

Generally, par products in Japan are of a long-term nature, in accordance with the definition of *SFAS 60*. Whether the company pays dividends based on the actual experience and contribution of each policy depends on its own practices. A semi-par product would be less likely to qualify for *SFAS 120* treatment, given that the contribution to the divisible surplus—from mortality and expense gains—is not reflected. Even for regular par products, it is fair to say that some companies may conclude that the business qualifies for *SFAS 120* treatment, while others will reflect *SFAS 60* treatment.

Stock companies have a choice as to whether to apply *SFAS 120* or *SFAS 60/97* LP. In general, stock companies in Japan have found *SFAS 60/97* LP easier to implement, although some have selected *SFAS 120* due to the added flexibility for DAC amortization.

An additional liability is required for terminal dividends under *SFAS 120*. Whereas one might expect the U.S. GAAP reserve to be less than the statutory reserve, the inclusion of a terminal dividend reserve may prompt a higher U.S. GAAP reserve.

The other classificatory issue to consider is whether any products should be treated as investment rather than insurance products. This is primarily an issue for annuities, where the mortality component can represent a relatively small portion of the total premium. Such a situation will require the testing of the products in question to determine the extent of the mortality benefits reflected in the premium.

An example of a test used in one specific situation in Japan is ascertaining that the present value of incremental death benefits did not exceed 5% of the present value of total benefits. "Incremental" is important because the return of cash values, as a part of a death benefit paid, should not be counted in this part of the calculation.

A related issue is how the pre-paid premiums should be treated. If they are not considered part of the base contract, they are likely seen as an investment contract.

Furthermore, some companies view the accumulation period for annuities as separate from the payout period. Others view it as one contract. While some have preferred to split the contract into accumulation and payout pieces, it is much more likely that the former will be treated as an investment contract.

On the other hand, if the payout benefit is a life annuity and the accumulation phase and payout phase are treated together, it is almost certain to be classified as an insurance contract.

16.5.8 Korea

16.5.8.1 Korean Traditional Business

Korean products can be broadly grouped into two categories—traditional and interest sensitive. The latter include variable life products, which have been available since July 2001. Such products are generally long duration and can be either participating or non-participating, although a general shift has occurred in recent years from participating to non-participating. The traditional products include significant amounts of mortality and/or morbidity risk, such that classification as investment contracts is not applicable.

Therefore, traditional products generally fall either into the *SFAS 60* classification (where the premium and benefit periods are equal), *SFAS 97* LP, or *SFAS 120*. Universal life products were introduced in early 2004 and are expected to follow the *SFAS 97* universal life classification to the extent that they have product features similar to such products in the U.S.

An interesting debate arises when deciding on which accounting standard to apply to Korean participating business—*SFAS 60* or *SFAS 120*. The question of *SFAS 120* classification relates to:

- Does the dividend scale follow the contribution principle?
- If so, could a stock company elect to follow *SFAS 60* anyway?

Regulatory guidelines specify that a minimum 90% of all pre-dividend profits on participating policies must be returned to policyholders. In total, the dividends clearly reflect the contribution principle. However, on an individual basis, it is questionable as to whether the dividend practices strictly follow the contribution principle. In fact, this issue could be argued either way. Although Korean participating business meets criteria for the application of *SFAS 120* (paragraph 5), it also seems possible to account for such contracts using *SFAS 60*, given the wording of *SFAS 120*.

Other considerations that influence the selection of *SFAS 120* or *SFAS 60* are:

- *SFAS 120* policyholder benefit liabilities are based on the net level premium method. In Korea, the statutory reserve is also based on the net level premium method. Therefore, this should be more comparable to calculate and analyze than *SFAS 60* reserves, which can allow for future dividends and withdrawals.

- The data requirements necessary to calculate historical gross margins for *SFAS 120* may not be readily available if the company did not keep these records.

- Assumptions required for *SFAS 60* should be those appropriate at the time of policy issuance. This data may also not be readily available. Note that this is not a problem with PGAAP accounting, which only requires assumptions from the date of purchase.

16.5.8.2 Korean Interest Sensitive Business

Prior to the introduction of variable life products in 2001, interest sensitive products (ISP) were typically based on a general investment account that produced a fund value as the roll-up of the premium received, less contractual loads. Interest credited to the ISPs is usually tied to an index, such as the company's policy loan rate or the one-year term deposit interest rate of the major banks in Korea.

The product is clearly an investment contract and therefore the question arises as to whether *SFAS 97* or *SFAS 91* applies. Practice Bulletin No. 8, an interpretive document issued by the American Institute of Certified Public Accountants, provides guidance in this area. For classification as an investment contract under *SFAS 97*, significant revenue sources, other than investment returns, must be present. Most Korean ISPs exhibit such a condition. For example, contracts may include a premium load for expenses, risk charges, and/or a surrender charge.

Within the *SFAS 97* classification, a choice exists between the *SFAS 97* Investment Contract (*SFAS 97* IC) and *SFAS 97* Universal Life Contract (*SFAS 97* UL) classification. Treatment as a universal life-type business under *SFAS 97* may be considered.

The criteria for *SFAS 97* UL classification (paragraph 10(b)) seems to be satisfied due to the mechanism whereby interest is usually credited to the business through an index, rather than being fixed by contract. For the majority of the ISPs that do not contain significant insurance risks, as required for *SFAS 97* UL, treatment as investment contracts would be appropriate. For ISPs with significant mortality or morbidity risks, treatment as universal life contracts is possible.

A suggested test for assessing the significance of mortality and morbidity risks is to identify what percentage of the total present value of future revenue sources at policy issuance is due to mortality and morbidity revenues. In practice, the level of significance can vary between 5% and 20%, depending on circumstances. This is for guidance purposes and is not actually prescribed.

16.5.9 Singapore and Malaysia

Participating business sold in Singapore has an earnings distribution system whereby most companies return at least 90% of distributable profits to policyholders. Malaysia has a similar structure whereby most companies return at least 80% of distributable profits to policyholders. This is similar to the system in the U.K. Consequently, some U.S. GAAP conversion issues will be more familiar because they are likely to have already been dealt with in the U.K.

The distribution of profits takes the form of:

a. An annual reversionary bonus, allocated to policyholders in the year in which the profits emerge, and

b. A terminal bonus, which is allocated only at maturity, death, or surrender. This portion of benefits is usually highly significant, especially at maturity.

This distribution has been commonly viewed as not following the contribution principle. For example, there may be cross-subsidies across generations of participating policyholders. Therefore, *SFAS 60* should apply. If participating profits are not restricted by law or company charter, policyholder dividends or bonuses are assumed to be policyholder benefits and are included in the calculation of US GAAP benefit reserves. Where there is a restriction on policyholder dividend payments, as in this case and the Korean example, then *SFAS 60* indicates that future bonuses be excluded from the benefit reserve calculations. An insurer in this situation would be required to hold an additional liability to take into account 90% of the valuation differences between the US GAAP and the local statutory basis. This is commonly known as the undistributed participating policyholders earnings account (UPPEA). The UPPEA can be thought of as a roll-up of the undistributed policyholders' share of surplus each year, less the dividends or bonuses awarded.

16.5.10 Taiwan

Products sold in Taiwan have mainly been traditional, predominantly savings type and long-term health. Unit-linked and variable life products were introduced in 2001.

Participating products in Taiwan can be split into two groups—the old style compulsory dividend products that were no longer allowed to be sold from 2004, but make up the bulk of current in-force business, and "true" participating products, which were allowed from 2003.

For old style compulsory dividend products, the Taiwanese Ministry of Finance (MoF) prescribes a dividend formula consisting of interest and mortality components. The interest component is based on a specified interest rate, less the assumed pricing interest rate, if positive. The specified interest rate is the average of the maximum 2-year term deposit rate of four specified financial institutions in Taiwan. The mortality dividend is based on the standard pricing mortality table, less the life industry experience rates as declared by MoF. The new style participating product allows the company to set the dividends, subject to certain regulations.

The old style form of profit distribution clearly does not follow the scope of *SOP 95-1*. For example, profit distribution does not account for the actual experience of the company, and it would be difficult to argue that it follows the contribution principle. Therefore, *SFAS 60* would apply.

The new style participating dividends allow companies a freer reign over the types of dividends paid. It is possible that a variety of policyholder dividend and bonus systems will be implemented in Taiwan, although they should trend towards those systems present elsewhere in the world, making product classification easier for newer contracts.

Taiwan applies various other taxes in addition to its corporate tax on profits, such as a "Gross Business Receipts Tax" (or premium tax), stamp duty, and a contribution to a "Stabilization Fund." These taxes, which do not depend on profits, are generally treated as variable maintenance expenses under U.S. GAAP and are usually not considered in the calculation of U.S. GAAP deferred taxes.

16.5.11 China

The majority of business sold in recent years contains an endowment savings element. Personal accident and medical riders have also been popular. Pure life insurance or protection coverage has proved less popular in the past, but sales are expected to increase in the future. These products are traditional in nature, and *SFAS 60* or *SFAS 97* LP would be deemed appropriate.

From 2000, most companies began to sell participating contracts with a requirement that at least 70% of the mortality and interest surpluses be distributed to par policyholders. Generally, the domestic companies have not distributed any expense surplus and therefore would find it difficult to classify their par products under *SFAS 120*. In order to demonstrate *SFAS 120* classification, it would be necessary to show that the two-factor dividend approach reflects surpluses from all sources, either due to the immateriality of other sources or their ability to offset each other. Those companies that do intend to distribute expense surplus would find it easier to argue that their products satisfy the *SFAS 120* requirements.

Unit-linked products were first launched in China in 1999. Such products are generally investment products with a small mortality component. They would be expected to satisfy the classification requirements of *SFAS 97*, with significant revenue sources other than investment returns, for example from premium loads for expenses and risk charges. Due to the early stage of development for unit-linked products in China, it is difficult to generalize, and it is important to determine the product classification criteria on a case-by-case basis.

16.5.12 Hong Kong

A variety of products are sold in Hong Kong. In-force products are mainly traditional par whole life or anticipated endowments. Unit-linked products are becoming increasingly popular, often with a simple front-end load or reduced allocation-charging structure. However, some more complex designs are also sold.

Many of the products sold in Hong Kong are based on U.S. designs, making classification relatively simple. Most par products have U.S.-style cash dividends, although some demonstrate the U.K.-style reversionary bonus system. Historically, dividend scales have been set relatively passively and not in accordance with the contribution approach. Therefore, *SFAS 60* classification is implied.

16.5.13 The Philippines

Significant amounts of pre-need plans are sold in the Philippines. The benefits are designed to meet a number of known future events, such as education fees, memorial benefits, and payments upon retirement. In return for premiums paid, benefits are guaranteed and, in some cases, inflationary increases are covered. Surrender values may be available for early terminations. The benefits payable on early death are, in general, modest.

Pension plans normally provide fixed payments on specific dates, usually at retirement. They do not provide pension payments contingent upon death. Likewise, education plans provide for fixed payments on specific dates. In both cases, the level of mortality and morbidity cover is small. Premium waivers on death or disability are common, but additional payments on death are usually limited to a return of premiums.

While the majority of life insurers consider pre-need products as life insurance, the industry is currently regulated by the Securities and Exchange Commission, not the insurance commissioner. However, a proposal has emerged to place regulation under the jurisdiction of the latter, implying the reclassification of pre-need plans from securities to insurance.

Each plan should be considered on its merits and classified according to the appropriate accounting standard. Contracts are normally long duration. Contract terms are usually fixed, both in terms of premium payments and benefits, so that it is unlikely that *SFAS 97* universal life would be appropriate. If there is a significant mortality or morbidity element, *SFAS 60* or *SFAS 97* limited pay would probably apply. However, if the mortality or morbidity risk is not significant, the contract should be accounted for as an investment contract under *SFAS 97*. For most education and pension plans, it appears that the mortality/morbidity benefit is minimal and that these contracts should be classified as investment contracts.

SFAS 97 paragraph 15 says that investment contracts should be "accounted for in a manner consistent with the accounting for interest-bearing, or other financial instruments." Further guidance is available in Practice Bulletin 8 issued by the American Institute of Certified Public Accountants. Paragraph 7 states that the *SFAS 97* UL method for amortizing acquisition costs should be used if there are significant surrender charges or if the contracts yield significant revenues from sources other than the investment of contract holder funds. This approach is normally used where there is a clearly defined account value (for example, in U.S. SPDA contracts).

Paragraph 7 also says that the alternative is to use an accounting method that recognizes acquisition and interest costs as expenses at a constant rate applied to net policy liabilities and that is consistent with the interest method under *SFAS 91*.

SFAS 91 was designed for non-refundable fees and costs associated with loans. The examples in Appendix B of the statement demonstrate that the methodology aims to (1) project future cash flows, (2) calculate the equivalent yield, such that the present value of future cash flows equals the initial cash outflow, (3) use this interest rate to calculate the carrying amount at subsequent reporting dates, and (4) set unamortized net fees at levels equal to the difference between the remaining principal and the carrying amount.

Applying this to long-duration contracts, subject to *SFAS 97*—Investment Contracts, leads to the following: (1) projection of future cash flows, (2) calculation of the equivalent yield, such that the present value of future cash flows equals the initial cash outflow, (3) use of this interest rate to calculate the net liability at subsequent reporting dates, and (4) establishment of unamortized DAC at a level equal to the difference between the benefit reserve and net liability. The difficulty lies in calculating the benefit reserve when no obvious account value is apparent.

Methods of establishing the benefit reserve are using a statutory reserve or determining a liability using the equivalent yield methodology, excluding deferrable acquisition costs. However, the important thing is to calculate the appropriate net liability with DAC as the balancing item.

16.6 Practical Issues

SFAS 60 requires assumptions to be set based on information as at policy issuance. For an in-force block of business, this may require data from over 30 years ago. The availability of historical information is likely to be a problem for most companies worldwide. Approximations would therefore be widely used. Any relevant data, such as historic financial statements and pricing bases, should be used to validate the approximations.

This is not an issue for PGAAP, which requires best estimate assumptions only as of the purchase date. However, recent experience data and studies are needed to derive these assumptions. One issue for Asian companies is whether these studies are available as well as having systems that are capable of producing the data required. For example, a company may have to produce quarterly U.S. GAAP financials, but its systems may only show interest credited on *SFAS 97* investment-type contracts at year-end. This data is required to produce estimated gross profits (EGPs).

Although *SFAS 97* and *SFAS 120* require current best estimate assumptions, historical data is required to derive outstanding DAC and unreleased profit reserve balances. The data required includes original acquisition costs, product loads, and historical EGPs and/or estimated gross margins (EGMs).

U.S. GAAP classifies expenses into four categories:

- Deferrable acquisition
- Non-deferrable acquisition
- Maintenance
- Overhead.

This type of expense analysis is likely to be new to many non-U.S. companies. Not only will an initial expense analysis be required for the initial U.S. GAAP financials, but annual expense studies thereafter will likely be required as well.

Companies will need to do additional analyses of their expenses to split them between acquisition and maintenance on the one hand and deferrable versus non-deferrable acquisition expenses on the other. *SFAS 60* gives guidance as to the classification of deferrable acquisition expenses—"costs that vary with and are primarily related to the acquisition of new and renewal insurance contracts." The U.S. GAAP definition of acquisition expenses versus maintenance expenses might differ from the definition used for local regulatory reporting.

For example, in Japan, head office expenses that support the acquisition of new business (such as underwriting) need to be reclassified from maintenance under the statutory guidelines to acquisition under U.S. GAAP. Similarly, there may be branch office expenses relating to the servicing of policies that need to be reclassified from acquisition expenses to maintenance expenses.

A particular challenge for Korean and Japanese insurance companies, with their traditional "sales lady" distribution channel, is the split between deferrable and non-deferrable remuneration and expenses. The system of compensating sales ladies is complex and it is difficult to determine which portions directly vary with production and which do not. This area will require significant analysis and judgment on the part of the actuaries and accountants implementing U.S. GAAP.

Traditionally, Asian asset valuations have been amortized cost valuations. U.S. GAAP also requires an amortized cost basis, but with some adjustments as demanded by *SFAS 115*—Accounting for Certain Investments in Debt and Equity Securities. Under U.S. GAAP, assets are to be classified as "available for sale," "trading," or "held to maturity."

For those classified in the first two categories, the adjustments relate to marketable securities (such as bonds, mortgage-backed securities, and equities) that are to be reported on a fair value (market value) basis.

Under PGAAP, all assets must be restated at fair value as of the purchase date. Certainly, in some countries in Asia, the need for such restatement will bring into question the quality of certain investments.

16.7 Impact of *SOP 03-1*

The AICPA introduced *Statement of Position 03-1*, "Accounting and Reporting for Certain Nontraditional Long-Duration Contracts and for Separate Accounts" ("*SOP 03-1*"), effective for fiscal years beginning after December 15, 2003.

16.7.1 Background

Since *SFAS 97* was introduced, there have been significant developments in the types of annuity and life insurance contracts offered for sale. Some of those products may combine fixed and variable features and may be sold as general account or separate account products. The features of these contracts are many and complex, and may be offered in different combinations, such that there are numerous variations of the same basic products being sold in the marketplace. Guaranteed minimum death and income benefits have become common features of variable annuities as well as different structures for charging for universal life and annuity contracts.

In addressing the appropriate accounting approach to these contracts, the AICPA also reviewed associated issues such as the definition of and accounting for separate accounts; sales inducements to contract holders; the significance of mortality and/or morbidity risks and the associated product classification; and accounting for certain death features, reinsurance, and annuitization features.

The *SOP* cannot be applied retroactively; cumulative effects are reported as a change in accounting principle. The *SOP* excludes benefits already fair valued under *SFAS 133*.

16.7.2 Definition of a Separate Account

Paragraph 11 of SOP 03-1 lists criteria required to qualify for separate account treatment. The criteria are:

- It must be a legally recognized separate account.
- It must be legally insulated from the general account.
- It must invest as directed by SA contract holder, and
- All investment performance must be passed through to the contract holder.

Many countries do not provide for the legal insulation of separate accounts, including the following:

- Czech Republic
- France (some contracts)
- Italy
- Japan
- Liechtenstein
- Netherlands
- Poland
- Slovakia.

In any country, it is important to obtain the appropriate legal opinion about qualification under the rules set out in *SOP 03-1*.

Many U.K. funds are notionally separate, but are really part of the general account and would not get separate account treatment. In the U.S., there are products that satisfy the first three criteria and pass on all of the investment performance up to a certain level but share it thereafter, which do not qualify.

Failure to meet all criteria results in "full" consolidation, which precludes a one line consolidation. Liabilities and assets are recorded on the appropriate line on the balance sheet. The liability is marked to market, and its change runs through the income statement. Assets designated as "trading" will also be marked to market and its change appears in the income statement. Assets designated as "available-for-sale" will be marked to market and their change is a component of other comprehensive income (OCI). Assets designated as "held-to-maturity" will be recorded at amortized cost. Thus a potential mismatch exists.

16.7.3 Seed Money

Prior to the SOP, seed money was recorded in other invested assets. It was treated as an equity investment and marked-to-market in OCI.

SOP 03-1 requires consolidation of seed money investments. If seed money exceeds 20% of total separate account assets, it is no longer a component of other invested assets, but is consolidated with other stocks and bonds. This situation frequently occurs where large multinational companies have funded start-up operations with an investment designed to cover a number of years of operation.

16.7.4 Valuation of liabilities

The *SOP* provides guidance for determining (1) the account balance for investment and universal life-type contracts, (2) the significance of mortality and morbidity risks, (3) any additional liability for death or other insurance features, (4) any additional liability for benefits available upon annuitization, and (5) any additional liability for sales inducements.

16.7.4.1 Account Balance

The *SOP* clarifies the definition of the accrued account balance referenced in paragraph 17.a. of *SFAS 97* as the sum of:

a. Deposit(s) net of withdrawals
b. Plus amounts credited pursuant to the contract
c. Less fees and charges assessed
d. Plus additional interest (for example, persistency bonus), and
e. Other adjustments.

There is to be no reduction for surrender charges or market value adjustments.

Items a, b, and c have not changed since the introduction of *SFAS 97*. However, d and e may be different from amounts held by some insurance companies.

Additional interest is a liability that has not yet been credited to the policyholder's account balance. It is accrued at the rate that would accrue to the balance available in cash, or its equivalent, at the earlier of the reset date (if any) or contract maturity.

When multiple account values exist, the highest account value available in cash or cash equivalent at contract maturity or the reset date should be held. There had been diversity in practice for "two-tiered annuities" and similar products.

16.7.4.2 Significance of Risk

Contracts are to be classified either as "insurance" or "investment." This assessment is performed at contract inception, and the classification does not change thereafter (except at the adoption of *SOP 03-1*). If the contract is classified as an investment contract, no additional liability is allowed.

For in-force contracts, a significance test is performed as of initial adoption of the *SOP*, using actual experience to date and expected experience prospectively.

The determination of the significance of risk is made by comparing the present value of future excess payments with the present value of future assessments under a full range of assumptions (which implies that stochastic analysis is appropriate, but is not required). Assessments include those charges for administration, mortality, expense, and surrender, as well as investment margins on fixed accounts. The assumptions must be consistent with those used in projecting EGPs for DAC amortization.

There is a rebuttable presumption that a contract has significant mortality risk where the additional insurance benefit would vary significantly with capital markets volatility.

Examples of products that qualify:

(1) An Italian equity indexed product that pays the single premium improved with interest at maturity plus 50% of the appreciation in the DAX50 stock index that also guarantees a return of premium at death. In this case the single premium for the death benefit (1%) is significant when compared to the total front-end load (10%).

(2) A French single premium unit-linked product that guarantees a return of premium at death. This qualifies under the rebuttable presumption that the benefit "would vary significantly with capital markets volatility."

(3) An example of a product that fails to qualify is a UK unit linked contract that pays a death benefit equal to 101% of the account value at death since the value of the benefit is insignificant when compared to the value of fees to be collected.

It should be noted that there is a significant incentive for European companies to qualify products as having significant mortality risk since this permits them to continue existing local accounting treatment under IFRS 4 for their 2005 International Accounting Standard compliance.

16.7.4.3 Additional Liability for *SFAS 97*— universal life-type contracts

For contracts classified as *SFAS 97* UL-type, a comparison must be made of the amounts assessed for and the expected payments from an insurance benefit feature (for example, death or disability). If the charges result in "profits in earlier years and losses in subsequent years," an additional liability must be held.

A full discussion of the approach to and determination of any liability is included in Chapter 6, sections 6.12 and 6.13.

A comparable process should be followed for reinsurance contracts. Depending on the significance to the reinsurer, the accounting may not necessarily follow that of the ceding company.

16.7.4.4 Contracts with Annuitization Benefits

The *SOP* covers potential benefits that are payable only upon annuitization and that are not valued under *SFAS 133*.

An additional liability must be established if the present value of the expected annuitization payments (plus related expenses) exceeds the expected account balance at the expected annuitization date. The additional liability is calculated using a similar approach to the retrospective accumulation liability for "Contracts with Death or Other Insurance Benefits."

The benefit ratio is the present value of the expected annuitization payments (plus related expenses) minus the expected account balance at the expected annuitization date divided by the present value of expected assessments during the accumulation phase of the contract.

The expected annuitization election rate is one of the assumptions that needs to be estimated. The additional liability can never be less than zero. The assumptions used should be consistent with those used in calculating EGPs, and the unlocking is comparable to DAC, where estimates are evaluated regularly and updated as warranted. The impact of changes to the liability is reported as a charge or credit to benefit expense and the changes in liability flow through DAC EGPs.

The excess annuitization considers the present value of the annuity purchased, not the value available to purchase an annuity.

Although this section is written using terms more often associated with *SFAS 97* products, it applies to other products as well. For contracts that have implicit charges (for example participating traditional contracts), assessments would be premiums plus investment income minus benefit payments (including dividends) minus expenses minus the change in liabilities plus the change in DAC.

In the U.K., many contracts were written with guaranteed annuity benefits available at retirement on both traditional and unit-linked retirement contracts. As interest and mortality rates have fallen, many of these options are currently in the money, and a liability must be established as described in the SOP.

Deferred annuity contracts in some countries, such as Italy, have guaranteed annuity purchase rates based upon the statutory life insurance mortality table used to value death benefits. Regulators (such as ISVAP in Italy) may require insurance companies to hold an additional statutory liability when contractual annuity purchase rate guarantees are more favorable than current purchase rates. The question then arises whether the statutory GMIB reserve can be used for GAAP purposes, and the answer requires a careful review of three key assumptions:

(1) Discount rate – GAAP best estimate may be higher than a conservative statutory valuation rate

(2) Annuity election rate – election rates are low, frequently in the 2% to 4% range, since customers may not understand the value equation

(3) Annuitant mortality – there is a tendency for regulatory conservatism

The greatest challenge is with the third assumption, expected annuitant mortality, since this is rarely studied. The local actuary may wish to refer to the SOA's Table Manager[1] in this case to develop a reasonable estimate of annuitant mortality. In the Italian case, the following logic was followed:

- Recent Swiss retiree mortality was similar to US retiree mortality, and the assumption was made that neighboring Italian mortality would be similar to US mortality

- A comparison of mortality improvement from Italian statutory mortality tables over the period from 1971 to 1992 to a US annuitant mortality projection scale indicated that the US projection scale was reasonable.

- A comparison of US individual annuity mortality against group annuity mortality indicated that individual selection increases the cost of an immediate annuity about 5%.[2]

Applying the mortality assumption derived in this manner and a realistic discount rate led to the conclusion that unique "best estimate" GAAP assumptions produce additional reserves lower than statutory reserves.

16.7.4.5 Sales Inducements to Policyholders

Sales inducements to policyholders include a day-one bonus, persistency bonus, and enhanced crediting rate bonus and should be included as a liability over the period for which the policyholder must stay in force to be eligible. If the criteria are met, the bonus is deferred and amortized using the same methodology and assumptions used to amortize DAC.

The unamortized sales inducement is booked as an asset separately from DAC. It is called the Deferred Sales Inducement. The amortization is to be recognized as a component of benefit expense.

16.7.5 Transition Rules

Insurers are to re-perform a mortality significance test on in-force contracts as of the initial application and should use actual experience since inception and current expectations for the future. The adjustment to liabilities and DAC from EGP adjustments should be reported as a change in accounting principle and the cumulative effect is reported through income. The cumulative changes in EGPs may also lead to adjustments to DAC.

---

[1] The SOA Table Manager is available for free at the SOA's web site at www.soa.org. Search for "table manager" to find it.

[2] Report of the Individual Annuity Experience Committee, "Mortality under Individual Immediate Annuities, Life Income Settlements, and Matured Deferred Annuities between 1976 and 1986 Anniversaries," Transactions of Society of Actuaries 1991-92 Reports.

Initial costs deferred prior to adoption are not adjusted, and the unamortized balances are to be amortized according to the *SOP* after implementation. Companies cannot retroactively capitalize sales inducements not previously deferred. This is prospective only; there are no cumulative effects.

Chapter 17 Reinsurance

17.1 Uses of Reinsurance

Reinsurance is a transaction whereby an insurance company transfers all or part of a risk that it has assumed during its insurance business. Insurers purchase reinsurance from other insurance companies in much the same manner as individuals purchase insurance coverages from insurers. The insurer purchasing reinsurance coverage is often called the ceding company. The insurer would expect to pay a premium or consideration to the company offering reinsurance (the reinsurer) in exchange for indemnification of specified losses.

This chapter describes GAAP accounting for reinsurance; however, certain aspects of statutory accounting influence the way reinsurance contracts are designed and operate. In particular, state insurance departments and rating agencies use an insurer's statutory financial results, particularly the level of statutory surplus, in monitoring, regulating, and rating a company's performance. Many reinsurance arrangements between life insurers are designed to provide insurance protection for the level of a company's current and future statutory surplus.

Mortality and morbidity are key insurance risks that life insurers bear. Reinsurance can be used to modify the distribution of expected mortality or morbidity costs that a company has to bear. Many reinsurance arrangements are designed to specifically limit how much mortality or morbidity risk an insurer retains on an individual or group of insureds. By limiting its retention on larger or more risky polices, an insurer can affect its level of surplus and expected pattern of profits. The use of reinsurance in performing risk transfer must of course be compared to the cost of purchasing such reinsurance protection.

Other major risks in life and health insurance contracts arise from policy lapsation and investments. Reinsurance treaties can be created that transfer these risks, in part or in total. Lapse risk is frequently a critical issue with policies that have large first-year total costs; investment risk is critical to most interest-sensitive policies.

One of the oldest uses of reinsurance is to increase a company's capacity to write new business. For small to mid-size insurers, reinsurance can be a vehicle enabling them to write insurance coverages or contracts that they might otherwise not be willing to accept independently. These same small to mid-size insurers can also gain access to underwriting, pricing, and claims evaluation expertise from reinsurance providers that they might not ever be able to develop adequately on their own.

Reinsurance can enable an insurer to expand into new markets. A reinsurance partner can provide entry to additional jurisdictions or other coverages. Insurers desiring to enter a new line of business may want to limit their risks at the outset of such ventures. In many cases, writing insurance coverages at a reduced profit margin (after the cost of reinsurance) is better than not writing at all.

A key use of reinsurance is to protect an insurer's statutory surplus. Statutory surplus is a primary consideration in a company's ratings with the key rating agencies. In addition, every life insurer's statutory surplus is reviewed regularly by state regulatory authorities to determine whether it exceeds specific risk-based capital (RBC) requirements. Failure to meet these RBC standards can result in a company being put into rehabilitation by state regulatory authorities.

Another use of reinsurance is to buy or sell blocks of business. An insurer can legally make a permanent transfer (i.e., sell) to another insurer of all risks and future gains and losses in a specific block of business through assumption reinsurance. Reinsurance arrangements can be constructed that transfer all the same risks and gains and losses that an assumption arrangement does. However, these other reinsurance arrangements do not result in a legal permanent transfer of risks and obligations from the ceding company to the reinsurer.

Insurers have used reinsurance as an element of tax-planning strategy. Regardless of contractual intent, reinsurance can have a material effect on the tax position of all companies involved in a treaty. In particular, reinsurance treaties can affect the amount of taxes currently payable for both the ceding company and the reinsurer.

17.2 Types of Reinsurance

Reinsurance treaties can be viewed as being proportional or nonproportional. In a proportional treaty, the portion of the benefit ceded to the reinsurer is defined at the time of the cession with a formula relating to the ceding company's retention limit. The standard forms of proportional reinsurance used by life insurers are yearly renewable term (YRT), coinsurance, and modified coinsurance (MODCO). In a nonproportional treaty, the amount ceded is not fixed in advance but depends on the amount of claims incurred during the contract period. The standard forms of nonproportional reinsurance used by life insurers are stop loss and catastrophe.

Proportional and nonproportional coverages are indemnity insurance coverages. This means that the ceding company is not relieved of its legal liability to the policyholders. As mentioned earlier, assumption reinsurance treaties, which are not indemnity reinsurance, provide for a legal replacement of one insurer by another.

Surplus relief occurs when a reinsurance treaty provides additional statutory surplus to the ceding company. Although it has been common to refer to certain reinsurance treaties as surplus relief treaties, the treaty providing the relief is generally written as one of or a combination of the indemnity treaty forms. Reinsurance treaties that have been written to provide surplus relief or to facilitate tax planning are also referred to as financial reinsurance.

17.2.1 Yearly Renewable Term

YRT reinsurance treaties are also called annual renewable term and risk premium reinsurance. When the ceding company purchases YRT reinsurance, the coverage purchased from the reinsurer is one-year term insurance on the reinsured portion of the contract. Only the basic mortality or morbidity risk is reinsured.

For reinsurance on life insurance contracts, the reinsured amount is the net amount of risk. The net amount at risk is the face amount reinsured less the related statutory policy reserves (or sometimes the cash value). For YRT on health coverages, the amount of coverage reinsured is not reduced by any related reserves. The premium rates used to determine the YRT reinsurance cost are determined by the reinsurer and are generally not related to the premium rates on the reinsured contracts. However, in some cases, the reinsurer may base the premium rates on the ceding company's premiums or cost of insurance charges.

YRT premium rates generally vary by age, sex, underwriting class, and policy duration. They may be discounted in the first year of a reinsurance treaty in order to recognize the acquisition expenses incurred by the ceding company. YRT rates usually increase by age and duration. Most reinsurance treaties contain maximum rate guarantees. The YRT rates currently being charged may themselves be guaranteed for a number of years. Otherwise, the reinsurer reserves the right to increase the rates at regular intervals, not to exceed the maximums stated in the reinsurance treaty.

17.2.2 Coinsurance

When reinsurance is purchased for an insurance contract on a coinsurance basis, the reinsurer participates, on a pro-rata basis, in all premiums and benefits from the underlying policy according to a fixed percentage. For ordinary life, these can include death benefits, surrenders, and policyholder dividends; rider benefits can be covered as well. The ceding company pays the reinsurer the gross premium on the reinsured portion of the policy at the rate the ceding company charges. Insurers also use coinsurance to cede coverage on annuity and health insurance.

The reinsurer pays the ceding company for its share of the covered benefits. It reimburses the ceding company for some proportion of the ceding company's commissions, expenses, and taxes. The reinsurer also maintains assets to support its proportionate share of reserves. Because the reinsurer generally controls the types of investments made with these assets, it will realize the effect of bearing its share of the investment risk.

Although premiums, expenses, reserves, and benefits are shared proportionally, expense reimbursements paid by the reinsurer are subject to negotiation. The incidence of expense reimbursements may or may not bear a reasonable relationship to the amount and incidence of expenses actually paid by the ceding company. For coinsurance purchased on seasoned blocks of profitable business, the expense allowances may be enhanced as a way for the ceding company to share in subsequent profits.

17.2.3 Modified Coinsurance

Modified coinsurance (MODCO) is coinsurance in which the ceding company never relinquishes the statutory reserves (and associated assets) on the business being reinsured. MODCO is frequently used when the ceding company wishes to keep control of the investment and management of the assets supporting the reserves. Except for the MODCO reserve adjustment, MODCO operates much like coinsurance. The MODCO reserve adjustment is the mechanism by which the reinsurer funds the reserve on the reinsured portion of the risk. It is needed to adjust for the financial effect of the ceding company holding the statutory reserves on the ceded coverage rather than the reinsurer.

MODCO can be characterized as coinsurance accompanied by a loan from the reinsurer to the ceding company in amount equal to these reserves. If the ceded reserves increase, the reinsurer loans the additional amount to the ceding company. As the ceded reserves decrease, the ceding company repays the decreased amount to the reinsurer. The loan accrues interest and is combined with the reserve increase/decrease in an annual settlement known as the MODCO adjustment. Although the actual contractual arrangement makes no mention of any loan, the substance of the transaction points to the need for financial adjustments between the ceding company and the reinsurer so that the effect of any sharing of reserves and investment income is properly recognized.

The interest rate charged by the reinsurer in the MODCO reserve adjustment is negotiated at the inception of the treaty. There are a number of ways to stipulate the MODCO interest rate; most MODCO treaties define the MODCO interest rate with reference to the actual interest earned by the ceding company on the underlying assets.

17.2.4 Stop-Loss

Stop-loss reinsurance provides protection against adverse claim experience on an entire block of policies. Generally written for only one year at a time, these treaties compensate when aggregate claims exceed some defined amount during a contract period. The stop-loss reinsurance treaty defines which policies are being reinsured, the defined amount (the attachment point) above which the reinsurer will pay on the covered claims, and the calendar period during which the reinsurance coverage is in force. If aggregate claims exceed the attachment point, the reinsurer usually pays some percentage of the excess up to a maximum amount. Stop-loss reinsurance of a block of health contracts may refer to aggregate losses in excess of an attachment point, or it may refer to the capping the loss of individual claims, sometimes called specific stop-loss. Other than the premiums paid by the ceding company and the claims reimbursed by the reinsurer, there are usually no other financial transactions between the ceding company and the reinsurer. Like YRT, stop-loss is pure loss coverage for a limited time. Unlike YRT, stop-loss is usually not guaranteed renewable; future premiums and coverage are generally subject to negotiation between the ceding company and the reinsurer.

17.2.5 Catastrophe

Catastrophe coverage provides reinsurance coverage when the ceding company's aggregate claims from a single accidental event exceed some defined amount. The reinsurance treaty defines the covered events, the minimum number of claims, the covered contracts, the maximum amount of claims covered, and the contractual period. As with stop-loss coverage, catastrophe coverage is pure loss coverage for a limited time.

17.2.6 Assumption Reinsurance

An assumption reinsurance arrangement provides for the legal replacement of one insurer by another. In most forms of reinsurance, the policyholder is unaware of the effect of any reinsurance on the policy. However, under an assumption reinsurance agreement, the assuming company notifies the policyholder of the reinsurance with a certification of assumption. In some states, the policyholder may be given a choice between consenting to the transfer of the policy to the reinsurer or refusing it and staying with the ceding company.

17.3 Special Aspects of Reinsurance

17.3.1 Experience Rating

Many reinsurance arrangements have special features that affect the timing and amount of cash flows between the ceding company and the reinsurer as well as the effective transfer of risk. One of these features is experience rating. This feature allows the reinsurer to remit to the ceding company a share of the reinsurer's profits by using an experience rating refund. The profits considered in the experience rating formulas are generally statutory profits. Because of the nature of statutory accounting, early-duration profits may be negative for a reinsured book of business. Many experience rating refund formulas contain a loss carryforward provision that aggregates several years' experience. Because the reinsurer may be incurring a proportional share of early-duration statutory losses, this may be a critical element in the calculation of the refund. Other features of experience rating formulas can dramatically affect the timing and amounts to be paid. Experience rating refunds have been used with all the indemnity-type reinsurance arrangements, although they are far less typical today than in the past.

17.3.2 Recapture

Many reinsurance arrangements permit the ceding company to increase (or recapture) the amount it retains on previously reinsured business. Recapture is generally limited under terms of the reinsurance arrangement and does not effect any residual amount of reinsurance coverage. Ceding companies are more likely to recapture reinsurance on direct coverage that may have stable, long-term profits. Recapture provisions are usually designed to discourage antiselection on the part of the ceding company. For example, recapture, if elected by the ceding company, is only permitted on an entire class of risks. The ceding company cannot select the specific cessions it wishes to recapture.

17.4 GAAP Summary

GAAP accounting for reinsurance ceded is governed by the requirements of *SFAS 113*, "Accounting and Reporting for Reinsurance of Short-Duration and Long-Duration Contracts." *SFAS 113* specifies different accounting treatment depending on whether the reinsurance is for short-duration or long-duration insurance contracts. Although not stated specifically, the definitions of short- and long-duration contracts in *SFAS 113* are the same as those in *SFAS 60*, *SFAS 97,* and *SFAS 120.*

Except for assumption reinsurance, *SFAS 113* does not permit the ceding company to report liabilities on reinsured contracts net of the effects of reinsurance. In particular, any unearned premium, claim, or benefit reserve credits arising from reinsurance are to be reported as reinsurance receivable assets by the ceding company for GAAP. Although *SFAS 113* does not permit the netting of liabilities, it does require that any items associated with the recovery of acquisition costs be used to reduce the ceding company's unamortized acquisition costs.

Because assumption reinsurance extinguishes the ceding company's legal responsibility to the policyholder, *SFAS 113* permits the ceding company to remove the assets and liabilities related to the reinsured contracts covered by the assumption from its financial statements. The ceding company is also permitted to immediately recognize the full amount of any gain associated with the assumption arrangement. If the ceding company incurs a loss due to the assumption arrangement, that loss must be recognized immediately as well.

SFAS 113 specifies risk transfer rules for determining whether a reinsurance arrangement provides indemnification of insurance risk and therefore can be reported as reinsurance for GAAP. These rules apply to both the ceding company and the reinsurer. These rules may or may not produce the same results as the risk transfer rules for similar decisions in other accounting bases, such as for tax or statutory accounting. Reinsurance on contracts classified as investment contracts for GAAP, such as single-premium deferred-annuity contracts, does not qualify for reinsurance accounting under *SFAS 113*.

Those reinsurance treaties that do not qualify for GAAP reinsurance accounting under *SFAS 113* are to be reported as deposits. The accounting treatment is the same as though the reinsurance arrangement was a financing transaction or a loan. In the typical case, the standard GAAP balance sheet and income statement adjustments for reinsurance would be reversed for both the ceding company and the reinsurer. Any assets transferred to the ceding company would be reported as deposit liabilities for the ceding company and deposit assets for the reinsurer. Any fees charged for the reinsurance would be reported as an expense to the ceding company and income to the reinsurer.

AICPA *Statement of Position 98-7*, "Deposit Accounting: Accounting for Insurance and Reinsurance Contracts That Do Not Transfer Insurance Risk," and *FASB Interpretation 39*, "Offsetting of Amounts Related to Certain Contracts," provide specific guidance for deposit accounting for reinsurance treaties that do not qualify for reinsurance accounting under *SFAS 113*.

Except for the risk transfer rules, *SFAS 113* is silent on GAAP accounting for reinsurance assumed. In general, an insurer accounts for reinsurance assumed in the same fashion as it does for business written directly.

In general, *SFAS 113* does not provide specific guidelines on the actuarial methods and assumptions to be used in calculating the appropriate accounting entries for reinsurance. However, *SFAS 113* does refer to the GAAP accounting requirements for the insurance contracts being reinsured for consistency in both methodology and assumptions. In particular, *SFAS 113*, which applies to all reinsurance contracts, states:

> Reinsurance receivables shall be recognized in a manner consistent with the liabilities (including estimated claims incurred but not reported and future policy benefits) relating to the underlying reinsured contracts. Assumptions used in estimating reinsurance receivables shall be consistent with those used in estimating the related liabilities. (Paragraph 20)

Further guidance on the choice of actuarial methods and assumptions to be used in developing GAAP for reinsurance is provided in *ASOP No. 11*, "The Treatment of Reinsurance Transactions in Life and Health Insurance Company Financial Statements," and in *ASOP No. 10*, "Methods and Assumptions for Use in Life Insurance Company Financial Statements Prepared in Accordance with GAAP."

17.5 Qualification as Reinsurance under *SFAS 113*

Depending on whether the insurance contracts being reinsured are short or long duration, *SFAS 113* provides for different standards in determining whether a reinsurance contract indemnifies the ceding company against insurance risk and therefore meets the conditions for reinsurance accounting.

17.5.1 Short-Duration Contracts

In order for reinsurance on short duration insurance contracts to meet the requirements for reinsurance accounting, *SFAS 113* requires that both of two basic conditions be met:

> 9a. The reinsurer assumes significant insurance risk under the reinsured portions of the underlying insurance contracts.
>
> 9b. It is reasonably possible that the reinsurer may realize a significant loss from a transaction. (Paragraph 9)

The 9a requirement of significant insurance risk is based upon the expected variability of both the amount and the timing of cash flows. Paragraph 9 further states:

> A reinsurer shall not be considered to have significant insurance risk under the reinsured contracts if the probability of a significant variation in either the amount or timing of payments by the reinsurer is remote.

SFAS 113 does not give any specific methods for determining whether requirement 9a is being met, but it does give an example of a situation that would suggest that the reinsurer is not assuming a significant insurance risk with regard to the timing of payments. The standard specifies:

> Contractual provisions that delay timely reimbursement to the ceding enterprise would prevent this condition from being met. (Paragraph 9)

In addition, *SFAS 113* adds the requirement that:

> ... both the amount and timing of the reinsurer's payments depend on and directly vary with the amount and timing of claims settled under the reinsured contracts. (Paragraph 62)

A reinsurance contract provision that permits the ceding company and the reinsurer to withhold payments until the net amounts owed by the ceding company reach a specified level is an example of a contract provision that affects the timing of payments to the ceding company. Such a provision might prevent a ceding company and reinsurer from meeting the *SFAS 113* conditions for reinsurance accounting. Treaties that are settled less frequently than once a year may present problems with timing risk as well.

Paragraph 9 does not give any examples of situations that might disqualify a reinsurance contract with regard to variability of the amounts to be reimbursed. However, paragraph 8 of *SFAS 113* does give some examples of those sorts of reinsurance contract provisions that may be used to limit the amount of insurance risk. These sorts of limitations may also limit the variability of the total amounts to be reimbursed by the reinsurer. Among the provisions mentioned are experience refunds and adjustable contract features. An example of an adjustable contract feature is one providing for commission or expense allowances payable to the ceding company by the reinsurer that vary in relation to the claims experience.

Overall, the requirements of paragraph 9a address whether the reinsured insurance risk demonstrates appropriate contingent behavior over the life of the reinsurance contract. If the actual operation of the reinsurance smoothes out or limits either the timing or the amounts to be paid by the reinsurer, *SFAS 113* suggests that the ceding company and the reinsurer may be unable to characterize the reinsured amounts as constituting an insurance risk.

Complying with the requirements of paragraph 9a requires a detailed reading of a reinsurance treaty. Both its business purpose and economic implications need to be analyzed. The facts and circumstances of each arrangement must be considered.

Although *SFAS 113* does not give any specific numerical methods for determining whether the requirements of 9a are being met, it does require that a specific method be used in testing for the requirements of paragraph 9b:

> The ceding enterprise's evaluation of whether it is reasonably possible for a reinsurer to realize a significant loss from the transaction shall be based on the present value of all cash flows between the ceding and assuming enterprises under reasonably possible outcomes, without regard to how the individual cash flows are characterized. (Paragraph 10)

Significance of loss shall be evaluated by comparing the present value of all cash flows, determined as described in paragraph 10, with the present value of the amounts to be paid or deemed to have been paid to the reinsurer. (Paragraph 11)

The paragraph 9b test just described suggests that there must be a reasonable probability of future outcomes that result in the reinsurer suffering a loss and that, when these losses occur, they must be significant. While *SFAS 113* does not give any guidance on what is a reasonable probability of loss for a reinsurer, a percentage of 10 or more is sometimes used. In calculating size of the losses, a value of 10% or greater of the present value of the amounts paid by the ceding company to the reinsurer has been assumed to be a significant loss. In practice, other percentages may be used. The paragraph 9b analysis may involve the review of specific future outcomes or it may be based upon a cumulative expected loss distribution.

Tables 17-1, 17-2, 17-3, and 17-4 examine whether a coinsurance treaty on a group health contract meets the requirements for reinsurance account as specified in paragraph 9b of *SFAS 113*. For the ceded expense allowance, two different formulas are presented.

Table 17-1 provides general information on the treaty.

Table 17-1
Information to Use in Testing for Qualification as Reinsurance under *SFAS 113*

Coinsurance on group health
Single year's exposure
Ceded annual premiums:$10 million
Expected loss ratio of reinsured business: 65%

Expected loss ratio distribution of reinsured business:

Loss ratio range:	Probability:
40% to 50%	10%
50% to 60%	20%
60% to 70%	40%
70% to 80%	20%
80% to 90%	10%

Expected loss payment run-off pattern pattern:

Year 1:	80%
Year 2:	15%
Year 3:	5%

Expense allowance as a percent of premiums
Example 1: 35% of ceded premium
Example 2: 1 – minimum of (loss ratio and 75%) but with tentative payment of 35% at beginning of first year and true-up at end of beginning of second year

Discount rate: 6.5%

Significant loss to reinsurer: 10% or more of ceded premium

Reasonable probability of reinsurer realizing significant loss: 10%

Tables 17-2 and 17-3 show the results of testing each of the two ceding expense allowances under the requirements of paragraph 9b of *SFAS 113*. In both Tables 17-2 and 17-3, the present value of expected losses to the reinsurer is estimated for specific ranges of loss ratio and compared to the reinsurer's premium.

Table 17-2
Testing for Qualification as Reinsurance Under *SFAS 113:* Details of Results by Loss Ratio for Example 1

(1) Policy Year$_t$	(2) Loss Ratio Range	(3) Assumed Loss Ratio	(4) Ceded Premium	(5) Ceded Claims Reimbursed	(6) Expense Allowance Received	(7) Reinsurer's Net Cash Flow	(8) Discount Rate	(9) Present Value of Net Cash Flow	(10) Present Value as Percentage of Premium
1	40% to 50%	0.45	10,000,000	3,600,000	3,500,000	2,900,000	6.50%	2,338,332	23.4%
2				675,000		(675,000)	6.50%	(832,176)	
3				225,000		(225,000)	6.50%	(211,268)	
1	50% to 60%	0.55	10,000,000	4,400,000	3,500,000	2,100,000	6.50%	1,413,517	14.1%
2				825,000		(825,000)	6.50%	(1,017,104)	
3				275,000		(275,000)	6.50%	(258,216)	
1	60% to 70%	0.65	10,000,000	5,200,000	3,500,000	1,300,000	6.50%	488,702	4.9%
2				975,000		(975,000)	6.50%	(1,202,032)	
3				325,000		(325,000)	6.50%	(305,164)	
1	70% to 80%	0.75	10,000,000	6,000,000	3,500,000	500,000	6.50%	(436,113)	-4.4%
2				1,125,000		(1,125,000)	6.50%	(1,386,960)	
3				375,000		(375,000)	6.50%	(352,113)	
1	80% to 90%	0.85	10,000,000	6,800,000	3,500,000	(300,000)	6.50%	(1,360,928)	-13.6%
2				1,275,000		(1,275,000)	6.50%	(1,571,888)	
3				425,000		(425,000)	6.50%	(399,061)	

Premiums and expense allowances paid at beginning of year.
Claims paid at end of year.

Legend:
(1) Policy year.
(2) Loss ratio range from Table 17-1.
(3) Assumed loss ratio (mid-point of range).
(4) Ceded premium from Table 17-1.
(5) Ceded claims reimbursed $(5)_t$ = assumed loss ratio times ceded premium times expected run-off factor from Table 17-1.
(6) Expense allowance $(6)_t = 0.35 \times (4)$.
(7) Reinsurer's net cash flow $(7)_t = (4)_t - (5)_t - (6)_t$.
(8) Discount rate from Table 17-1.
(9) Present value of net cash flows in (7) at rate in (8).
(10) Present value of net cash flows at beginning of first year as percent of premium in (4).

Table 17-3
Testing for Qualification as Reinsurance under *SFAS 113:* Details of Results by Loss Ratio for Example 2

(1) Policy Year, t	(2) Loss Ratio Range	(3) Assumed Loss Ratio	(4) Ceded Premium	(5) Ceded Claims Reimbursed	(6) Expense Allowance Received	(7) Reinsurer's Net Cash Flow	(8) Discount Rate	(9) Present Value of Net Cash Flow	(10) Present Value as Percentage of Premium
1	40% to 50%	0.45	10,000,000	3,600,000	3,500,000	2,900,000	6.50%	460,398	4.6%
2				675,000	2,000,000	(2,675,000)	6.50%	(2,832,176)	
3				225,000		(225,000)	6.50%	(211,268)	
1	50% to 60%	0.55	10,000,000	4,400,000	3,500,000	2,100,000	6.50%	474,550	4.7%
2				825,000	1,000,000	(1,825,000)	6.50%	(2,017,104)	
3				275,000		(275,000)	6.50%	(258,216)	
1	60% to 70%	0.65	10,000,000	5,200,000	3,500,000	1,300,000	6.50%	488,702	4.9%
2				975,000	0	(975,000)	6.50%	(1,202,032)	
3				325,000		(325,000)	6.50%	(305,164)	
1	70% to 80%	0.75	10,000,000	6,000,000	3,500,000	500,000	6.50%	502,854	5.0%
2				1,125,000	-1,000,000	(125,000)	6.50%	(386,960)	
3				375,000		(375,000)	6.50%	(352,113)	
1	80% to 90%	0.85	10,000,000	6,800,000	3,500,000	(300,000)	6.50%	(421,961)	-4.2%
2				1,275,000	-1,000,000	(275,000)	6.50%	(571,888)	
3				425,000		(425,000)	6.50%	(399,061)	

Premiums and expense allowances paid at beginning of year.
Claims paid at end of year.

Legend:
(1) Policy year.
(2) Loss ratio range from Table 17-1.
(3) Assumed loss ratio (mid-point of range).
(4) Ceded premium from Table 17-1.
(5) Ceded claims reimbursed $(5)_t$ = assumed loss ratio times ceded premium times expected run-off factor from Table 17-1.
(6) Expense allowance (6) = {1 – minimum of [(3) and .75]} × (4). Provisional allowance of 35% of $(4)_1$ with true-up at $t = 2$.
(7) Reinsurer's net cash flow $(7)_t = (4)_t - (5)_t - (6)_t$.
(8) Discount rate from Table 17-1.
(9) Present value of net cash flows in (7) at rate in (8).
(10) Present value of net cash flows at beginning of first year as percent of premium in (4).

Table 17-4 summarizes the results from Table 17-2 and 17-3.

Table 17-4
Testing for Qualification as Reinsurance under *SFAS 113:* Summary of Results

(1) **Loss Ratio Range**	(2) **Ceded Premium**	(3) **Present Value of Reinsurer's Net Cash Flow**	(4) **Present Value as Percentage of Premium**	(5) **Probablility of Loss Ratio**
Example 1. Expense Allowance Equal to 35% of Premium				
40% to 50%	10,000,000	2,338,332	23.4%	10%
50% to 60%	10,000,000	1,413,517	14.1%	20%
60% to 70%	10,000,000	488,702	4.9%	40%
70% to 80%	10,000,000	(436,113)	(4.4%)	20%
80% to 90%	10,000,000	(1,360,928)	(13.6%)	10%
Conclusion: there is a reasonable probability (10%) of a significant loss (13.6% >10%) and example 1 should be treated as reinsurance under *SFAS 113.*				
Example 2. Expense Allowance Equal to [1 – minimum of (loss ratio and 75%)] of Premium				
40% to 50%	10,000,000	460,398	4.6%	10%
50% to 60%	10,000,000	474,550	4.7%	20%
60% to 70%	10,000,000	488,702	4.9%	40%
70% to 80%	10,000,000	502,854	5.0%	20%
80% to 90%	10,000,000	(421,961)	(4.2%)	10%
Conclusion: there isn't a reasonable probability (10%) of a significant loss (4.2% < 10%) and example 2 should not be treated as reinsurance under *SFAS 113.*				

Legend:
(1) Loss ratio range from (2) in 17-2 and 17-3.
(2) Ceded premium from (4) in 17-2 and 17-3.
(3) Present value of reinsurer's net cash flow from (9) in 17-2 and 17-3.
(4) Present value as percent of premium from (10) in 17-2 and 17-3.
(5) Probability of loss ratio range from 17-1.

Based on the facts provided, the coinsurance treaty with a level ceding expense allowance appears to satisfy the requirements for reinsurance accounting under *SFAS 113* while the ceding expense allowance that changes as the loss ratio changes does not.

For certain reinsurance arrangements that do not qualify under the 9b test, *SFAS 113* gives a possible exception to the 9b requirements. In particular,

> If, based on this comparison [the paragraph 9b test], the reinsurer is not exposed to the reasonable possibility of significant loss, the ceding enterprise shall be considered indemnified against loss or liability relating to insurance risk only if substantially all of the insurance risk relating to the reinsured portions of the underlying insurance contracts has been assumed by the reinsurer. (Paragraph 11)

This exception may be critical for certain reinsurance contracts, especially for coinsurance, where the underlying block of business is expected to be profitable and the pattern of future experience is not expected to be volatile.

EITF 93-6, "Accounting for Multiple-Year Retrospectively Rated Contracts by Ceding and Assuming Enterprises," issued after *SFAS 113* became effective, addresses the accounting for reinsurance on short-duration insurance contracts in which the reinsurance has retrospective rating features that are measured over periods of more than one year. Although *EITF 93-6* was written primarily to address issues with reinsurance on property and casualty coverages, reinsurance treaties on life and health contracts having experience rating refunds with loss carryforward provisions may fall under the requirements of *EITF 93-6*.

For those reinsurance contracts covered by *EITF 93-6*, the requirements to qualify for reinsurance accounting under *SFAS 113* have been expanded. In particular, if any of the following conditions are not met, then both the ceding company and the reinsurer must use deposit accounting to account for the failing reinsurance treaty:

(1) the (reinsurance) contract must qualify as a short duration contract under paragraph 7(a) of statement 60,

(2) the contract must not contain features that prevent the risk transfer criteria in paragraphs 8 through 13 of Statement 113 from being reasonably applied (and those criteria must be met), and

(3) the ultimate premium expected to be paid or received under the (reinsurance) contract must be reasonably estimable and allocable in proportion to the reinsurance protection provided as required by paragraph 14(a) and (b) of Statement 60 and paragraph 21 of Statement 113.

Condition (1) specifies that the reinsurance contracts must themselves be short duration contracts as that term is normally understood. However, *EITF Topic D-35*, "FASB Staff Views on Issue No. 93-6," also states that:

> Reinsurance of short-duration contracts is inherently short duration. Contracts that reinsure short duration contract over a significantly longer period are, in substance, financing arrangements… (Answer 8)

Classifying reinsurance arrangements with retrospective rating features as short duration will be challenging to justify if the time period over which those features are to be contractually determined is substantially longer than the contractual terms of the underlying treaty.

Condition (2) contains the risk transfer requirements of *SFAS 113*. Condition (3) basically requires that the expected financial outcomes of the reinsurance arrangement be estimable. Because it would be difficult to demonstrate compliance with the *SFAS 113* risk transfer rules for these types of contracts [as specified in condition (2)] without reasonable projections of expected financial results, condition (3) should be met if condition (2) has already been satisfied.

For reinsurance arrangements meeting the conditions of *EITF 93-6* and thus qualifying for accounting as reinsurance under *SFAS 113*, there are a number of special conditions that relate to the accrual of liabilities and assets for the experience rated features by either the ceding company or the reinsurer. In general, *EITF 93-6* requires that these items be accrued under GAAP based upon experience to date, regardless of whether that experience has generated a current amount due under the terms of the reinsurance contract experience rating formula.

17.5.2 Long-Duration Contracts

In order for reinsurance on long-duration insurance contracts to meet the requirements for reinsurance accounting, *SFAS 113* states:

> Indemnification of the ceding enterprise against loss or liability relating to insurance risk in reinsurance of long duration contracts requires the reasonable possibility that the reinsurer may realize significant loss from assuming insurance risk as that concept is contemplated Statement 60 and FASB Statement No. 97. (Paragraph 12)

This paragraph 12 repeats the requirements of paragraph 9b for reinsurance on short-duration insurance contracts. It does not define significant insurance risk but does point to the requirements of *SFAS 60* and *SFAS 97* for insurance risk in long-duration contracts. A major requirement of *SFAS 97* is that long-duration contracts that do not subject the insurer to significant mortality or morbidity risk are deemed to be investment contracts. Because investment contracts are not insurance contracts as contemplated in *SFAS 97*, reinsurance on investment contracts does not qualify for reinsurance treatment under *SFAS 113*.

SFAS 113 does not provide any further guidance on how the requirements of paragraph 12 are to be applied in practice. One difficulty in applying paragraph 12 to reinsurance on long-duration insurance contracts is that there is no specific guidance in *SFAS 60* or *SFAS 97* as to what constitutes a reasonable possibility that the ceding company will realize a significant loss on the underlying direct business being reinsured. It is possible to analyze the risk transfer of reinsurance on long duration contracts with methods similar to those described in paragraphs 10 and 11 of *SFAS 113* for reinsurance on short-duration contracts. However, the expected financial results for most long-duration life and health insurance coverages are not as volatile as the analogous results for short-duration life and health coverages. Because of this reduced volatility, an argument can be made for reducing the theoretical thresholds used in considering what constitutes both a reasonable possibility and a significant loss for reinsurance on long-duration contracts.

In practice, most ceding companies and reinsurers use qualitative approaches to determine whether a reinsurance treaty on long-duration contracts satisfies the requirements of paragraph 12. In particular, if a reinsurance treaty on long-duration contracts satisfies the 9b exception for reinsurance on short-duration contracts (that is, it transfers substantially all the insurance risk on the reinsured portions of the underlying contracts to the reinsurer), most companies would assume that the reinsurance meets the *SFAS 113* requirements for reinsurance accounting. However, to the extent a reinsurance treaty contains any provisions that limit the reinsurance risk (for example, experience refunds), it will be more difficult to make the assertion that substantially all the insurance risk has been assumed by the reinsurer. These issues must be addressed on a treaty-by-treaty basis.

When it cannot be asserted unequivocally that a reinsurance treaty on long-duration contracts transfers substantially all relevant insurance risk, companies may need to use numerical techniques to demonstrate the level of risk transferred. Variations of the present value techniques described in paragraphs 10 and 11 of *SFAS 113* for testing reinsurance on short-duration contracts, as well as, methods used in the formal study of risk theory, can be employed. As suggested previously, the thresholds used to evaluate what constitutes both a reasonable possibility and a significant loss may be lower for reinsurance on insurance coverages whose expected financial results are less volatile.

17.6 Accounting Requirements for Reinsurance Ceded

17.6.1 Short-Duration Contracts

SFAS 113 requires different accounting treatment for reinsurance on short-duration contracts contingent on whether the reinsurance is prospective or retroactive. *SFAS 113* defines prospective reinsurance as:

> Reinsurance in which an assuming enterprise agrees to reimburse a ceding enterprise for losses that may be incurred as a result of future insurable events covered under contracts subject to the reinsurance. (Appendix C)

Most reinsurance on life and health coverages is prospective.

SFAS 113 defines retroactive reinsurance as:

> Reinsurance in which an assuming enterprise agrees to reimburse a ceding enterprise for liabilities incurred as a result of past insurable events covered under contracts subject to the reinsurance. (Appendix C)

A reinsurance arrangement in which a reinsurer accepts liability for a book of group long-term-care claims with a 100% coinsurance treaty is an example of retroactive reinsurance.

If a prospective reinsurance arrangement meets the conditions for reinsurance accounting, *SFAS 113* specifies that:

> Amounts paid ... shall be reported as prepaid insurance premiums and amortized over the remaining contract period in proportion to the amount of the insurance protection provided. If the amounts paid are subject to adjustment and can be reasonably estimated, the basis for amortization shall be the estimated ultimate amount to be paid. (Paragraph 21)

The definition of contract period in paragraph 21 is meant to be the contract period of the underlying reinsured contracts. The specific definition of contract period given in *SFAS 113* is "the period over which insured events that occur are covered by the reinsured contracts." Paragraph 21 is also specific in requiring that if the amounts paid by the ceding company for reinsurance are subject to adjustment (through such contractual features as experience rating refunds) and can be reasonably estimated, then the financial effect of those adjustments must be reflected in the deferral and amortization of the amounts paid.

At the inception of a retroactive contract, there may be a transfer of assets from the ceding company to the reinsurer. *SFAS 113* provides for different accounting treatment when the net amounts paid by the ceding company to the reinsurer (including any assets transferred) are greater or less than the recorded reserve liabilities that the ceding company is holding on the underlying reinsured contracts. In particular, when the amounts paid are less than the recorded liabilities, there is a gain to the ceding company. Paragraph 22 of *SFAS 113* requires that "reinsurance receivables shall be increased to reflect the difference" (in other words, the gain) and the gain shall be deferred and "amortized over the remaining settlement period."

SFAS 113 defines the settlement period as "the estimated period over which a ceding enterprise expects to recover substantially all amounts due from the reinsurer under the terms of the reinsurance contract." For the typical retroactive arrangement on life or health insurance, this will be the period over which the claim reserves run off.

In determining the amortization of any gain on a retroactive reinsurance arrangement, *SFAS 113* specifies that the ceding company use either the interest method or the recovery method. As defined in paragraph 22, the interest method entails the amortization of any gain over the estimated timing and amounts of the recoveries from the reinsurer based upon the "effective interest rate inherent in the amount paid to the reinsurer." In calculating the amortization of the deferred gain, most ceding companies use the same interest rate used in determining the recorded liabilities on the underlying reinsured contracts.

In most practical situations, the deferred gain at any time is a fixed percentage of the present value of the remaining claims to be reimbursed by the reinsurer. The fixed percentage used in the gain calculation is usually determined at initiation of the reinsurance and is equal to the gain divided by the present value of the amounts to be reimbursed. The use of the interest method assumes the timely reimbursement of claims by the reinsurer.

The recovery method is to be used when the amounts and timing of the reinsurance recoveries cannot be reasonably estimated. This could occur when the retrospective reinsurance arrangement contains experience rating provisions whose future financial effect is uncertain. The recovery method specifies that at any time the cumulative amortization of any gain should be in relation to "the proportion of actual recoveries to total estimated recoveries." Amortization of gains under the recovery method is a function of the actual timing and pattern of reimbursements from the reinsurer and the ceding company's estimate of future recoveries, which may change over time. The effect of interest is ignored.

For those retroactive arrangements in which the amounts paid to the reinsurer exceed the ceding company's recorded liabilities, *SFAS 113* requires that the excess be immediately added to the ceding company's recorded liabilities, be subtracted from their reinsurance receivables, or both. This situation can occur when the reinsurer estimates a higher level for claim reserves to be reinsured than the ceding company is currently holding. The excess amounts paid are therefore recognized as an expense by the ceding company at the time such amounts are paid.

For retroactive reinsurance on short duration contracts, *SFAS 113* further requires that:

> Changes in the estimated amount of the liabilities relating to the underlying reinsured contracts shall be recognized in earnings in the period of the change. Reinsurance receivables shall reflect the related change in the amount recoverable from the reinsurer, and a gain to be deferred and amortized, as described in paragraph 22, shall be adjusted or established as a result. When changes in the estimated amount recoverable from the reinsurer or in the timing of receipts related to that amount occur, a cumulative amortization adjustment shall be recognized in earnings in the period of the change so that the deferred gains reflects the balance that would have existed had the revised estimate been available at the inception of the reinsurance transaction. (Paragraph 24)

Paragraph 24 has a number of effects on the accounting for retroactive reinsurance on short-duration contracts. First, regardless of the terms of the reinsurance contract, the ceding company must recognize in earnings any changes in its estimate of the recorded liabilities on the underlying reinsured contracts. Second, to the extent that related changes in reinsurance receivables and recorded liabilities result in a gain to ceding company on a retroactive contract, the gain must be deferred and amortized using the interest or recovery method. However, if the result of the changes is a loss, footnote 6 of *SFAS 113* further states that the "loss shall not be deferred" and "the resulting differences shall be recognized in earnings immediately." Third, any changes in the estimated amount recoverable from a reinsurer must be reflected in the amortization of deferred gains on a retroactive reinsurance contract on a cumulative basis as though the additional gain was known at the inception of the contract. This cumulative catch-up provision is analogous to similar amortization provisions in *SFAS 97* and *SFAS 120*.

Tables 17-5, 17-6, 17-7, and 17-8 show the effect of coinsuring a block of group long-term disability claims with a retroactive reinsurance contract. Table 17-5 shows the development of the ceded claim reserves as well as the liability that the ceding company will use to amortize its gain on the treaty. The liability for the deferred gain has been calculated using the interest method.

Table 17-5
Detail for Retroactive Reinsurance on Group LTD

(1) Year, t	(2) Projected Paid Claims	(3) Discount Rate for Claim Reserves	(4) Direct Claim Reserves	(5) Amount Paid to Reinsurer	(6) Ceding Company's Gain	(7) Reserve for Unamortized Gain	(8) Ceded Claim Reserves
0			498,022	400,000	98,022	0	0
1	89,500	5.00%	433,423			85,307	(433,423)
2	82,300	5.00%	372,794			73,374	(372,794)
3	79,600	5.00%	311,833			61,376	(311,833)
4	78,400	5.00%	249,025			49,014	(249,025)
5	74,300	5.00%	187,176			36,840	(187,176)
6	72,000	5.00%	124,535			24,511	(124,535)
7	67,000	5.00%	63,762			12,550	(63,762)
8	39,000	5.00%	27,950			5,501	(27,950)
9	20,300	5.00%	9,048			1,781	(9,048)
10	9,500	5.00%	-			-	-

Coinsurance of group long term disability claims
100% of all claims ceded
No direct premiums or expenses are assumed
There are no more claim payments beyond end of 19th year

Legend:
(1) Time, in years.
(2) Projected paid claims.
(3) Discount rate used by ceding company to discount claim reserves.
(4) Direct claim reserves, $(4)_t$ = present value of (2) at rate in (3).
(5) Amount paid to reinsurer.
(6) Ceding company's gain, $(6)_0 = (4)_0 - (5)_0$.
(7) Reserve for unamortized gain (for $t > 0$), $(7)_t = [(6)_0 / (4)_0] \times (4)_t$.
(8) Ceded claim reserves (for $t > 0$), $(8)_t = -(7)_t$,

Present value at $t = 0$ of ceding company gain in (6) divided by present value of claims in (4) equals 19.68%.

Table 17-6 shows the expected income statement impacts to the ceding company for the treaty. The gain is amortized so that the profits are directly related to the ceded claim payments.

Table 17-6
Expected Policy Year Results for Retroactive Reinsurance on Group LTD

(1) Policy Year$_t$	(9) Projected Paid Claims	(10) Increase in Direct Claim Reserve	(11) Ceded Coinsurance Premiums Paid	(12) Morbidity Expense Reimbursed	(13) Increase in Reserve for Unamortized Gain	(14) Increase in Benefit Reserve for Reinsurance	(15) Investment Income	(16) GAAP Book Profit net of Reinsurance	(17) Profit as a Percentage of of Paid Claims
0									
1	89,500	(64,599)	400,000	89,500	85,307	(433,423)	4,901	17,616	19.68%
2	82,300	(60,629)		82,300	(11,933)	60,629	4,265	16,198	19.68%
3	79,600	(60,960)		79,600	(11,998)	60,960	3,669	15,667	19.68%
4	78,400	(62,808)		78,400	(12,362)	62,808	3,069	15,431	19.68%
5	74,300	(61,849)		74,300	(12,173)	61,849	2,451	14,624	19.68%
6	72,000	(62,641)		72,000	(12,329)	62,641	1,842	14,171	19.68%
7	67,000	(60,773)		67,000	(11,962)	60,773	1,226	13,187	19.68%
8	39,000	(35,812)		39,000	(7,049)	35,812	627	7,676	19.68%
9	20,300	(18,902)		20,300	(3,720)	18,902	275	3,995	19.68%
10	9,500	(9,048)		9,500	(1,781)	9,048	89	1,870	19.68%

Premiums paid at the beginning of the year.
Disability benefits paid at the end of the year
No direct premiums or expenses are assumed

Legend:
(1) Time, in years.
(9) Projected claim payments, $(9)_t = (2)_t$.
(10) Increase in direct claim reserve, $(10)_t = (4)_t - (4)_{t-1}$.
(11) Ceded coinsurance premiums paid, $(11)_t = (5)_t$.
(12) Morbidity expense reimbursed, $(12)_t = (2)_t$.
(13) Increase in reserve for unamortized gain, $(13)_t = (7)_t - (7)_{t-1}$.
(14) Increase in benefit reserve for reinsurance, $(14)_t = (8)_t - (8)_{t-1}$.
(15) Investment income, $(15)_t = (3)_t \times [(6)_t + (7)_t]$
(16) GAAP book profit net of reinsurance, $(16)_t = -(9)_t - (10)_t - (11)_t + (12)_t - (13)_t - (14)_t + (15)_t$
(17) Profit as a percent of paid claims, $(17)_t = (16)_t / (9)_t$

Table 17-7 shows the accounting adjustments that are required if the expected amount of ceded claims changes at the end of the fifth year. The ceded claim reserves are restated to reflect the new assessment of expected claims and the deferred gain is restated on a cumulative catch-up basis as required in paragraph 24 of *SFAS 113*.

Table 17-7
Detail for Retroactive Reinsurance on Group LTD with Change at End of Fifth Year

(1) Year$_t$	(18) Actual and Projected Paid Claims	(19) Discount Rate for Claim Reserves	(20) Restated Direct Claim Reserves	(21) Amount Paid to Reinsurer	(22) Restated Ceding Company's Gain	(23) Restated Reserve for Unamortized Gain	(24) Restated Ceded Reserves	(25) Booked Direct Claim Reserves	(26) Booked Reserve for Unamortized Gain	(27) Booked Ceded Claim Reserves
0			509,599	400,000	109,599			498,022	-	-
1	89,500	5.00%	445,579					433,423	85,307	(433,423)
2	82,300	5.00%	385,558					372,794	73,374	(372,794)
3	79,600	5.00%	325,236					311,833	61,376	(311,833)
4	78,400	5.00%	263,097					249,025	49,014	(249,025)
5	74,300	5.00%	201,952			43,434	(201,952)	201,952	43,434	(201,952)
6	**79,100**	5.00%	132,950			28,593	(132,950)	132,950	28,593	(132,950)
7	**72,000**	5.00%	67,597			14,538	(67,597)	67,597	14,538	(67,597)
8	**41,000**	5.00%	29,977			6,447	(29,977)	29,977	6,447	(29,977)
9	**21,000**	5.00%	10,476			2,253	(10,476)	10,476	2,253	(10,476)
10	**11,000**	5.00%	-			-	-	-	-	-

Change to projected paid claims recognized at end of fifth year
Revised projected paid claims shown in **BOLD**
No direct premiums or expenses are assumed
Claim reserves and reserve for unamortized are restated at end of 5th year on cumulative catch-up basis

Legend:
(1) Time, in years.
(18) Actual ($t = 1$ to 5) and projected claim payments ($t = 6$ to 10).
(19) Discount rate used by ceding company to discount claim reserves from Table 17-5.
(20) Restated direct claim reserves, $(20)_t$ = present value of (18) at rate in (19).
(21) Amount paid to reinsurer from Table 17-5.
(22) Restated ceding company's gain, $(22)_0 = (20)_0 - (21)_0$.
(23) Restated reserve for unamortized gain (for $t = 5$ to 10), $(23)_t = [(22)_0 / (21)_0] \times (21)_t$
(24) Restated ceded claim reserves (for $t = 5$ to 10), $(24)_t = -(20)_t$
(25) Booked direct claim reserves, $(25)_t = (4)_t$ for $t = 0$ to 4 and $(23)_t$ for $t = 5$ to 10.
(26) Booked reserve for unamortized gain, $(26)_t = (7)_t$ for $t = 0$ to 4 and $(26)_t$ for $t = 5$ to 10.
(27) Booked ceded claim reserves, $(27)_t = (8)_t$ for $t = 0$ to 4 and $(24)_t$ for $t = 5$ to 10.

Present value at $t = 0$ of restated ceding company gain in (22) divided by present value of restated claims in (20) equals 21.51%.

Table 17-8 shows the income statement with the changes as determined in 17-7. The information in 17-8 reflects actual experience for the first 5 years and revised experience for years 6 and subsequent.

Table 17-8

Policy Year Results for Retroactive Reinsurance on Group LTD with change at end of fifth year

(1) Policy Year, t	(28) Actual and Projected Paid Claims	(29) Increase in Claim Reserve	(30) Ceded Coinsurance Premiums Paid	(31) Morbidity Expense Reimbursed	(32) Increase in Reserve for Unamortized Gain	(33) Increase in Benefit Reserve for Reinsurance	(34) Investment Income	(35) GAAP Book Profit net of Reinsurance	(36) Profit as a Percentage of Paid Claims
0									
1	89,500	(64,598.92)	400,000	89,500	85,307	(433,423)	4,901	17,616	19.68%
2	82,300	(60,628.87)		82,300	(11,933)	60,629	4,265	16,198	19.68%
3	79,600	(60,960.31)		79,600	(11,998)	60,960	3,669	15,667	19.68%
4	78,400	(62,808.33)		78,400	(12,362)	62,808	3,069	15,431	19.68%
5	74,300	(47,072.83)		74,300	(5,580)	47,073	2,451	8,031	10.81%
6	79,100	(69,002.38)		79,100	(14,840)	69,002	2,172	17,012	21.51%
7	72,000	(65,352.50)		72,000	(14,055)	65,353	1,430	15,485	21.51%
8	41,000	(37,620.13)		41,000	(8,091)	37,620	727	8,818	21.51%
9	21,000	(19,501.13)		21,000	(4,194)	19,501	322	4,516	21.51%
10	11,000	(10,476.19)		11,000	(2,253)	10,476	113	2,366	21.51%

Premiums paid at the beginning of the year.
Disability benefits paid at the end of the year
No direct premiums or expenses are assumed
Results are actual for years 1 to 5 and projected for years 6 to 10

Legend:
(1) Time, in years.
(28) Actual (t = 1 to 5) and projected claim payments (t = 6 to 10) from (18).
(29) Increase in direct claim reserve, $(29)_t = (25)_t - (25)_{t-1}$.
(30) Ceded coinsurance premiums paid, $(30)_t = (5)_t$.
(31) Morbidity expense reimbursed, $(31)_t = (28)_t$.
(32) Increase in reserve for unamortized gain, $(32)_t = (26)_t - (26)_{t-1}$.
(33) Increase in benefit reserve for reinsurance, $(33)_t = (27)_t - (27)_{t-1}$.
(34) Investment income for t = 6 to 10, $(34)_t = [(19)_t \times (23)_t]$, for t = 1 to 5, $(34)_t = (15)_t$.
(35) GAAP book profit net of reinsurance, $(35)_t = -(28)_t - (29)_t - (30)_t + (31)_t - (32)_t - (33)_t + (34)_t$.
(36) Profit as a percent of paid claims, $(36)_t = (35)_t / (28)_t$.

17.6.2 Long-Duration Contracts

SFAS 113 requires different accounting treatment for the reinsurance depending on whether the reinsurance contract itself is classified as short duration or long duration. As elsewhere in *SFAS 113*, the definitions of short duration and long duration are consistent with the definitions of these terms as contemplated in *SFAS 60*, *SFAS 97*, and *SFAS 120*. Specifically, *SFAS 113* requires that the cost of reinsurance:

> ... shall be amortized over the remaining life of the underlying reinsured contracts if the reinsurance contract is long duration, or over the contract period of the reinsurance if the reinsurance is short duration. (Paragraph 26)

Paragraph 26 also states that the determination of whether a reinsurance arrangement is short or long duration is a "matter of judgment." In their most common form, YRT, coinsurance, and MODCO arrangements would be classified as long-duration contracts and stop-loss and catastrophe reinsurance would be classified as short-duration contracts. However, the presence of contractual features that limit the amount of reinsurance risk, such as experience rating refunds, may suggest that a reinsurance treaty normally classified as short duration is actually long duration. In addition, any reinsurance arrangement with a large first-year ceding commission allowance (or similarly, zero first-year reinsurance premiums) should not be classified as short duration because of the implied acquisition cost recovery expectation by the reinsurer.

SFAS 113 does not specifically define what constitutes the cost of reinsurance on long-duration contracts except to note that:

> The difference, if any, between amounts paid for a reinsurance contract and the amount of the liabilities for policy benefits relating to the underlying reinsured contracts is part of the estimated cost to be amortized. (Paragraph 26)

The effect of this sentence is to require that any cash gains or losses that occur at the inception of a reinsurance contract or due to its ongoing operation must be considered part of the cost of the reinsurance by the ceding company. Therefore, these gains and losses must be amortized over the life of the reinsurance contract (if short duration) or the life of the reinsured business (if long duration).

Except for the period of amortization, *SFAS 113* does not specify how the cost of reinsurance from long-duration reinsurance contracts is to be amortized. In practice, the determination of the cost of reinsurance and a method for its amortization will generally be no different than what is done for other benefit reserve and DAC balances in GAAP accounting. This is consistent with paragraph 20 of *SFAS 113*, which requires that reinsurance receivables be "recognized in a manner consistent with the liabilities (including estimated amounts for claims incurred but not reported and future policy benefits) relating to the underlying reinsured contracts."

There are net cash flows associated with the reinsurance that may, in total, result in a gain or a loss to the ceding company. All the cash flows associated with the reinsurance arrangement need to considered in determining the net cost of reinsurance. This includes amounts paid to the reinsurer (including assets transferred) and amounts reimbursed by the reinsurer (including any initial or renewal ceding commissions allowances).

The net cost of reinsurance should be recognized in income on a basis consistent with the way the benefits and expenses on the underlying reinsured contracts are recognized. This suggests the use of parallel accounting treatment for reinsurance and the underlying reinsured contracts. For example, reinsurance on insurance contracts reported under *SFAS 60* requirements would itself be reported under the requirements of *SFAS 60*. In other words, the reinsurance costs would be amortized as a constant percentage of premium income. For insurance products covered under *SFAS 97* or *SFAS 120*, the cost of reinsurance would be amortized as a constant percentage of expected gross profits or margins.

Although *SFAS 113* is silent on the methods to be used in amortizing the cost of reinsurance, it does insist that:

> The assumptions used in accounting for reinsurance contracts shall be consistent with those used for the reinsured contracts. (Paragraph 26)

This sentence does not require that exactly the same assumptions used in determining benefit reserves and DAC balances be used in the amortization of the cost of reinsurance. For example, the expected mortality on the portion of the insurance contracts being reinsured may be dramatically different than the mortality assumed for those insurance contracts in total. In this case, the mortality assumptions used to amortize the cost of reinsurance may be based upon the reinsured mortality risks only and not the total.

17.6.3 Examples

Following are a series of examples that display several aspects of accounting for reinsurance under GAAP. In all cases, the experience assumptions equal the assumptions used in establishing reserves. This was done so the reader can more readily observe profit patterns.

17.6.3.1 Coinsurance

Tables 17-9, 17-10, and 17-11 address a coinsurance treaty. The direct policy is the ten year endowment policy studied in Chapter 4.

Table 17-9 shows the calculation of DAC and benefit reserves for the coinsurance.

Table 17-9
Policy-Year Results for Coinsurance on 10-Year Endowment

(1) Policy Year, t	(2) Projected In Force	(3) Direct Premium Income	(4) Per-Premium Expense Allowances	(5) Investment Rate	(6) Expense Allowances Received	(7) Ceded DAC	(8) Direct Benefit Reserve	(9) Ceded Benefit Reserve
0	100,000					0.00	0.00	0.00
1	81,948	9,500.00	90.0%	7.00%	5,130.00	4957.54	8,576.57	(5,145.94)
2	72,060	7,785.09	12.0%	6.90%	560.53	5237.68	17,032.92	(10,219.75)
3	64,790	6,845.67	5.0%	6.80%	205.37	4976.49	25,660.06	(15,396.04)
4	58,891	6,155.01	5.0%	6.70%	184.65	4611.33	34,609.17	(20,765.50)
5	54,111	5,594.67	5.0%	6.50%	167.84	4130.04	43,916.49	(26,349.89)
6	50,252	5,140.51	5.0%	6.50%	154.22	3534.20	53,744.33	(32,246.60)
7	47,163	4,773.98	5.0%	6.50%	143.22	2821.08	64,187.79	(38,512.67)
8	44,725	4,480.45	5.0%	6.50%	134.41	1991.08	75,337.73	(45,202.64)
9	42,849	4,248.85	5.0%	6.50%	127.47	1048.16	87,273.98	(52,364.39)
10	0	4,070.70	5.0%	6.50%	122.12	0.00	0.00	0.00

Sample policy: male, age 35
Premium mode: annual
Units of coverage: 100.000
Direct results based upon Tables 4-4, 4-5, and 4-6.
Reinsurance: 60% coinsurance with schedule of ceding expense allowances.

Legend:
(1) Time, in years.
(2) Projected in force from Table 4-5.
(3) Direct premium income from Table 4-5.
(4) Ceding expense allowances as percentage of ceded premium.
(5) Investment income rate from Table 4-4.
(6) Expense allowances received, $(6)_t = (4)_t \times 0.6 \times (3)_t$
(7) Ceded expense reserve, $(7)_t = \{[(7)_{t-1} \times [(2)_{t-1} / (2)_0] + (6)_t - 0.2339 \times 0.6 \times (3)_t\} \times [1 + (5)_t] / [(2)_t / (2)_0]$
(8) Direct benefit reserve from Table 4-6
(9) Ceded benefit reserve, $(9)_t = -0.6 \times (8)_t$.

GAAP ceded expense premium percentage = present value of expense allowances received in (4) divided by present value of direct premium income in (3), discounted at the investment rate in (5) = 23.39%.

Table 17-10 displays the income statement elements of the coinsured business.

Table 17-10
Policy-Year Results for Coinsurance on 10-Year Endowment

(1) Policy Year$_t$	(10) Projected In Force	(11) Direct GAAP Book Profit	(12) Ceded Coinsurance Premiums Paid	(13) Expense Allowances Received	(14) Mortality Expense Reimbursed	(15) Surrender Expense Reimbursed	(16) Increase in Expense Reserve for Reinsurance	(17) Increase in Benefit Reserve for Reinsurance	(18) GAAP Book Profit net of Reinsurance
0	100,000								
1	81,948	803.73	5,700.00	5,130.00	37.80	0.00	4,062.62	(4,217.01)	387.32
2	72,060	658.02	4,671.06	560.53	37.37	589.58	(288.36)	(3,147.31)	317.11
3	64,790	578.08	4,107.40	205.37	42.80	907.05	(550.01)	(2,610.70)	278.58
4	58,891	519.27	3,693.00	184.65	44.32	1,118.29	(508.57)	(2,254.05)	250.24
5	54,111	471.11	3,356.80	167.84	45.23	1,213.96	(480.88)	(2,029.02)	227.03
6	50,252	432.87	3,084.31	154.22	45.45	1,225.51	(458.77)	(1,946.61)	208.60
7	47,163	402.00	2,864.39	143.22	47.64	1,174.05	(445.52)	(1,958.90)	193.73
8	44,725	377.29	2,688.27	134.41	50.37	1,073.39	(439.99)	(2,053.17)	181.82
9	42,849	357.78	2,549.31	127.47	53.94	931.98	(441.38)	(2,221.09)	172.42
10	0	342.78	2,442.42	122.12	57.59	25,652.10	(449.13)	22,437.87	165.19

Premiums paid at the beginning of the year.
Commissions and expenses paid at the beginning of the year.
Death benefits paid at the middle of the year.
Withdrawals paid at the end of the year.

Legend:
(1) Time, in years.
(10) Projected in force from Table 4-5.
(11) Direct GAAP book profit from Table 4-6.
(12) Ceded coinsurance premiums paid, $(12)_t = (3)_t \times 0.6$
(13) Expense allowances received, $(13)_t = (6)_t$.
(14) Mortality expense reimbursed, $(14)_t = 0.6 \times (20)_t$ of Table 4-5.
(15) Surrender expense reimbursed, $(15)_t = 0.6 \times (21)_t$ of Table 4-6.
(16) Increase in expense reserve, $(16)_t = [(10)_t / (10)_0] \times (7)_t - [(10)_{t-1} / (10)_0] \times (7)_{t-1}$.
(17) Increase in benefit reserve, $(17)_t = [(10)_t / (10)_0] \times (9)_t - [(10)_{t-1} / (10)_0] \times (9)_{t-2}$.
(18) GAAP profit net of reinsurance, $(18)_t = (11)_t - (12)_t + (13)_t + (14)_t + (15)_t - (16)_t - (17)_t + (5)_t \times \{[(10)_{t-1} \times (7)_{t-1}] + [(10)_{t-1} \times (9)_{t-1}] - (12)_t + (13)_t\} + [(1 + (5)_t)^{(.5)} - 1] \times (14)_t$.

Table 17-11 shows the emergence of earnings. The direct component displays its original profitability. The coinsured component itself displays profitability that is a level percentage of its premium stream. Profits net of reinsurance also display profit that is a level percentage of net premium. This is because both the direct and the reinsured business are level premium.

Table 17-11
Analysis of Profits for Coinsurance on 10-Year Endowment

(1) Policy Year$_t$	(19) Direct Premium Income	(20) Direct GAAP Book Profit	(21) Direct Profit as Percentage of Direct Premium	(22) Ceded Coinsurance Premiums	(23) Ceded GAAP Book Profit	(24) Ceded Profit as Percentage of Ceded Premium	(25) Premiums Net of Reinsurance	(26) GAAP Book Profit Net of Reinsurance	(27) Net Profit as Percentage of Net Premium
0									
1	9,500.00	803.73	7.91%	5,700.00	416.40	6.83%	3,800.00	387.32	9.53%
2	7,785.09	658.02	7.91%	4,671.06	340.92	6.83%	3,114.04	317.11	9.53%
3	6,845.67	578.08	7.91%	4,107.40	299.50	6.83%	2,738.27	278.58	9.53%
4	6,155.01	519.27	7.91%	3,693.00	269.03	6.83%	2,462.00	250.24	9.53%
5	5,594.67	471.11	7.91%	3,356.80	244.08	6.83%	2,237.87	227.03	9.53%
6	5,140.51	432.87	7.91%	3,084.31	224.27	6.83%	2,056.20	208.60	9.53%
7	4,773.98	402.00	7.91%	2,864.39	208.28	6.83%	1,909.59	193.73	9.53%
8	4,480.45	377.29	7.91%	2,688.27	195.47	6.83%	1,792.18	181.82	9.53%
9	4,248.85	357.78	7.91%	2,549.31	185.37	6.83%	1,699.54	172.42	9.53%
10	4,070.70	342.78	7.91%	2,442.42	177.59	6.83%	1,628.28	165.19	9.53%

Premiums paid at the beginning of the year.
Profits recognized at the end of the year

Legend:
(1) Time, in years.
(19) Direct premium income, $(19)_t = (3)_t$.
(20) Direct GAAP book profit, $(20)_t = (11)_t$.
(21) Direct GAAP book profit at beginning of the year as a percentage of direct premium income, $(21)_t = [(20)_t / (19)_t] / [1 + (5)_t]$.
(22) Coinsurance premiums paid, $(22)_t = (12)_t$.
(23) Ceded GAAP book profit, $(23)_t = (20)_t - (18)_t$.
(24) Ceded GAAP book profit at the beginning of the year as a percentage of ceded premiums, $(24)_t = [(23)_t / (22)_t] / [1 + (5)_t]$.
(25) Premiums, direct less ceded, $(25)_t = (19)_t - (22)_t$.
(26) GAAP book profit, direct less ceded, $(26)_t = (18)_t$.
(27) GAAP book profit, direct less ceded, at the beginning of the year as a percentage of net premiums, $(27)_t = [(26)_t / (25)_t] / [1 + (5)_t]$.

17.6.3.2 Yearly Renewable Term

Tables 17-12, 17-13, 17-14, and 17-15 look at the same direct policy but the treaty is now YRT. The initial face insured remains 60% of the face amount.

Table 17-12 shows the net amount at risk, YRT premium rates and expense allowances.

Table 17-12
Per-Policy Assumptions for YRT Reinsurance on 10-Year Endowment

(1) Policy Year$_t$	(2) Direct Gross Premium	(3) Direct Mortality Rate	(4) Direct Face Amount	(5) Direct Statutory Reserve	(6) Net Amount at Risk	(7) Amount Ceded	(8) YRT Rates Per $1,000	(9) Ceding Commission Allowance	(10) Investment Rate
0			1,000.00	0.00					
1	95.00	0.00063	1,000.00	100.00	1000.00	600.00	1.008	0.60	7.00%
2	95.00	0.00076	1,000.00	200.00	900.00	540.00	1.216	0.00	6.90%
3	95.00	0.00099	1,000.00	300.00	800.00	480.00	1.584	0.00	6.80%
4	95.00	0.00114	1,000.00	400.00	700.00	420.00	1.824	0.00	6.70%
5	95.00	0.00128	1,000.00	500.00	600.00	360.00	2.048	0.00	6.50%
6	95.00	0.00140	1,000.00	600.00	500.00	300.00	2.240	0.00	6.50%
7	95.00	0.00158	1,000.00	700.00	400.00	240.00	2.528	0.00	6.50%
8	95.00	0.00178	1,000.00	800.00	300.00	180.00	2.848	0.00	6.50%
9	95.00	0.00201	1,000.00	900.00	200.00	120.00	3.216	0.00	6.50%
10	95.00	0.00224	1,000.00	1,000.00	100.00	60.00	3.584	0.00	6.50%

Sample policy: male, age 35
Premium mode: annual
Units of coverage: 100.000
Direct results based upon Tables 4-4, 4-5 and 4-6.
Reinsurance: YRT on 60% of net amount at risk with first year expense allowance.

Legend:
(1) Time, in years.
(2) Direct gross premium from Table 4-4.
(3) Direct mortality rates from Table 4-4.
(4) Direct face amount from Table 4-4.
(5) Direct statutory reserve from Table 4-4.
(6) Net amount at risk, $(6)_t = (4)_{t-1} - (5)_{t-1}$.
(7) Amount ceded, $(7)_t = (6)_t \times 0.6$.
(8) YRT rates per $1,000, $(8)_t = (3)_t \times 1.6 \times 1{,}000$.
(9) Ceding commission allowance (year one only), $(9)_1 = [(8)_1 \times (7)_t] / 1{,}000$.
(9) Investment rate from Table 4-4.

Table 17-13 shows the YRT premium stream and the development of the ceded DAC and benefit reserves.

Table 17-13
YRT Reinsurance Transactions and Reserves on 10-Year Endowment

(1) Policy Year$_t$	(11) Projected In Force	(12) Ceded YRT Reinsurance Premiums Paid	(13) Expense Allowances Received	(14) Ceded Expense Reserve	(15) Mortality Expense Reimbursed	(16) Ceded Mortality Reserve
0	100,000			0.00		0.00
1	81,948	60.48	60.48	63.57	37.80	(0.06)
2	72,060	53.81	0.00	61.72	33.63	(0.11)
3	64,790	54.79	0.00	55.71	34.24	(0.15)
4	58,891	49.63	0.00	47.87	31.02	(0.16)
5	54,111	43.42	0.00	38.82	27.14	(0.13)
6	50,252	36.36	0.00	29.50	22.73	(0.10)
7	47,163	30.49	0.00	20.05	19.06	(0.07)
8	44,725	24.18	0.00	11.29	15.11	(0.04)
9	42,849	17.26	0.00	4.19	10.79	(0.01)
10	0	9.21	0.00	0.00	5.76	0.00

Premiums paid at the beginning of the year.
Commissions and expenses paid at the beginning of the year
Death Benefits paid at the middle of the year
Units of coverage: 100.000

Legend:
(1) Time, in years.
(11) Projected in force from Table 4-5.
(12) Ceded YRT reinsurance premiums paid, $(12)_t = 100 \times [(11)_{t-1} / (11)_0] \times (7)_t \times (8)_t / 1{,}000$.
(13) Expenses allowances received, $(13)_t = 100 \times [(11)_{t-1} / (11)_0] \times (9)_t$.
(14) Ceded expense reserve, $(14)_t = \{(14)_{t-1} \times [(11)_{t-1} / (11)_0] + (13)_t - 0.1949 \times (12)_t\} \times [1 + (10)_t)] / [(11)_t / (11)_0]$.
(15) Mortality expense reimbursed, $(15)_t = 100 \times [(11)_{t-1} / (11)_0] \times (7)_t \times (3)_t$.
(16) Ceded benefit reserve, $(16)_t = \{[(16)_{t-1} \times [(11)_{t-1} / (11)_0] - 0.6050 \times (12)_t] \times [1 + (10)_t] + (15)_t \times [(1 + (10)_t)^{0.5}]\} / [(11)_t / (11)_0]$.

GAAP ceded expense premium percentage = present value of expense allowances received in (13) divided by present value of ceded premium income in (12), discounted at the investment rate in (10) = 19.49%.

GAAP ceded benefit premium percentage = present value of mortality expense reimbursed in (15) divided by present value of ceded premium income in (12), discounted at the investment rate in (10) = 60.50%.

Table 17-14 displays the YRT ceded elements of the income statement.

Table 17-14
Book Profits for 10-Year Endowment with YRT Reinsurance

(1) Policy Year, t	(17) Projected In Force	(18) Direct GAAP Book Profit	(19) Ceded YRT Premiums Paid	(20) Expense Allowances Received	(21) Mortality Expense Reimbursed	(22) Increase in Expense Reserve for Reinsurance	(23) Increase in Benefit Reserve for Reinsurance	(24) GAAP Book Profit Net of Reinsurance
0	100,000							
1	81,948	803.73	60.48	60.48	37.80	52.10	(0.05)	790.78
2	72,060	658.02	53.81	0.00	33.63	(7.62)	(0.03)	646.51
3	64,790	578.08	54.79	0.00	34.24	(8.38)	(0.02)	566.37
4	58,891	519.27	49.63	0.00	31.02	(7.91)	0.00	508.67
5	54,111	471.11	43.42	0.00	27.14	(7.18)	0.02	461.86
6	50,252	432.87	36.36	0.00	22.73	(6.18)	0.02	425.12
7	47,163	402.00	30.49	0.00	19.06	(5.37)	0.02	395.51
8	44,725	377.29	24.18	0.00	15.11	(4.41)	0.02	372.13
9	42,849	357.78	17.26	0.00	10.79	(3.26)	0.01	354.11
10	0	342.78	9.21	0.00	5.76	(1.80)	0.01	340.82

Premiums paid at the beginning of the year.
Commissions and expenses paid at the beginning of the year.
Death benefits paid at the middle of the year.
Withdrawals paid at the end of the year.

Legend:
(1) Time, in years.
(17) Projected in force from Table 4-5.
(18) Direct GAAP book profit from Table 4-6.
(19) Ceded reinsurance premiums paid, $(19)_t = (12)_t$.
(20) Expense allowances received, $(19)_t = (13)_t$.
(21) Mortality expense reimbursed, $(20)_t = (15)_t$.
(22) Increase in expense reserve, $(22)_t = [(17)_t / (17)_0] \times (14)_t - [(17)_{t-1} / (17)_0] \times (14)_{t-1}$.
(23) Increase in benefit reserve, $(23)_t = [(17)_t / (17)_0] \times (16)_t - [(17)_{t-1} / (17)_0] \times (16)_{t-1}$.
(24) GAAP profit net of reinsurance, $(24)_t = (18)_t - (19)_t + (20)_t + (21)_t - (22)_t - (23)_t +$
$(10)_t \times \{[(17)_{t-1} \times (14)_{t-1}] + [(17)_{t-1} \times (16)_{t-1}] - (19)_t + (20)_t\} + \{[1 + (10)_t]^{.5} - 1\} \times (21)_t$.

Table 17-15 reveals the emergence of earnings for this block.

Table 17-15
Analysis of Profits for YRT Reinsurance on 10-Year Endowment

(1) Policy Year, t	(25) Direct Premium Income	(26) Direct GAAP Book Profit	(27) Direct Profit as Percentage of Direct Premium	(28) Ceded YRT Premiums	(29) Ceded GAAP Book Profit	(30) Ceded Profit as Percent of Ceded Premium	(31) Premiums Net of Reinsurance	(32) GAAP Book Profit net of Reinsurance	(33) Net Profit as Percentage of Net Premium
0									
1	9,500.00	803.73	7.91%	60.48	12.95	20.01%	9,439.52	790.78	7.83%
2	7,785.09	658.02	7.91%	53.81	11.51	20.01%	7,731.28	646.51	7.82%
3	6,845.67	578.08	7.91%	54.79	11.71	20.01%	6,790.89	566.37	7.81%
4	6,155.01	519.27	7.91%	49.63	10.60	20.01%	6,105.37	508.67	7.81%
5	5,594.67	471.11	7.91%	43.42	9.25	20.01%	5,551.25	461.86	7.81%
6	5,140.51	432.87	7.91%	36.36	7.75	20.01%	5,104.15	425.12	7.82%
7	4,773.98	402.00	7.91%	30.49	6.50	20.01%	4,743.49	395.51	7.83%
8	4,480.45	377.29	7.91%	24.18	5.15	20.01%	4,456.27	372.13	7.84%
9	4,248.85	357.78	7.91%	17.26	3.68	20.01%	4,231.59	354.11	7.86%
10	4,070.70	342.78	7.91%	9.21	1.96	20.01%	4,061.49	340.82	7.88%

Premiums paid at the beginning of the year.
Profits recognized at the end of the year.

Legend:
(1) Time, in years.
(25) Direct premium income from Table 4-5.
(26) Direct GAAP book profit, $(25)_t = (18)_t$.
(27) Direct GAAP book profit at beginning of the year as a percentage of direct premium income, $(27)_t = [(26)_t / (25)_t] / [1 + (10)_t]$.
(28) Coinsurance premiums paid, $(28)_t = (19)_t$.
(29) Ceded GAAP book profit, $(29)_t = (26)_t - (24)_t$
(30) Ceded GAAP book profit at the beginning of the year as a percentage of ceded premiums, $(30)_t = [(29)_t / (28)_t] / [1 + (10)_t]$.
(31) Premiums, direct less ceded, $(31)_t = (25)_t - (28)_t$.
(32) GAAP book profit, direct less ceded, $(32)_t = (24)_t$.
(33) GAAP book profit, direct less ceded, at the beginning of the year as a percentage of net premiums, $(33)_t = [(32)_t / (31)_t] / [1 + (10)_t]$.

The earnings for the direct component remain as if there were no reinsurance. The earnings for the YRT ceded are a level percentage of the YRT premium. However, when net earnings are viewed as a percentage of net premiums, the income does not emerge as a level percentage of the net premiums.

There is no definitive instruction for establishing YRT reinsurance reserves such that profits emerge in a specified pattern. In the example above, the cost of reinsurance has been amortized so that it is a level percentage of the ceded premium. As a result, profits after reinsurance do not emerge as a level percentage of premiums after reinsurance. It is possible that it may be more appropriate to amortize the cost of reinsurance so that emerging profits are a level percentage of the direct premium on the policies being reinsured. In such a case, profits net of reinsurance would emerge as a level percentage of premiums net of reinsurance (if actual experience equals the reserve assumptions). It is generally appropriate to consider that the issuance of the direct insurance policy and the arrangement for YRT reinsurance are not the same transaction. Also, the transactions are not necessarily linked initially or for the life of the underlying policy. The separate, stand-alone analysis may be appropriate.

The actuary may encounter a YRT reinsurance treaty where there is no first year premium. This is effectively analogous to having a stated premium and a 100% expense allowance. There is no explicit accounting guidance for this situation. Basing the reinsurance accounting on the economic substance of the transaction would suggest an extrapolated first year premium and a 100% expense allowance. A more direct reading of the reinsurance contract for what it does say rather than what may have been intended might result in assuming zero first year reinsurance premium and zero first year expense allowance, with reserves being based on such pattern.

17.6.3.3 Modified Coinsurance

Tables 17-16, 17-17, 17-18, and 17-19 revisit the coinsurance treaty from Tables 17-9, 17-10, and 17-11 and consider the treaty as modified coinsurance rather than coinsurance.

Table 17-16 repeats basic assumptions from the earlier direct and coinsurance examples.

Table 17-16
Modco Premium and Expense Reserve Development for 10-Year Endowment

(1) Policy Year$_t$	(2) Projected In Force	(3) Ceded Premium	(4) Per-Premium Expense Allowances	(5) Investment Rate	(6) Expense Allowances Received	(7) Ceded Expense Reserve
0	100,000					0.00
1	81,948	5,700.00	90.0%	7.00%	5,130.00	4,957.54
2	72,060	4,671.06	12.0%	6.90%	560.53	5,237.68
3	64,790	4,107.40	5.0%	6.80%	205.37	4,976.49
4	58,891	3,693.00	5.0%	6.70%	184.65	4,611.33
5	54,111	3,356.80	5.0%	6.50%	167.84	4,130.04
6	50,252	3,084.31	5.0%	6.50%	154.22	3,534.20
7	47,163	2,864.39	5.0%	6.50%	143.22	2,821.08
8	44,725	2,688.27	5.0%	6.50%	134.41	1,991.08
9	42,849	2,549.31	5.0%	6.50%	127.47	1,048.16
10	0	2,442.42	5.0%	6.50%	122.12	0.00

Sample policy: male, age 35.
Premium mode: annual.
Units of coverage: 100.000.
Direct results based upon Tables 4-4, 4-5, and 4-6.
Reinsurance: 60% modco with schedule of ceding expense allowances and modco interest rate.

Legend:
(1) Time, in years
(2) Projected in force from Table 4-5
(3) Ceded premium, $(3)_t$ = direct premium income from Table 4-5 × 0.6.
(4) Ceding expense allowances as percentage of ceded premium from column (4) of Table 17-9.
(5) Investment income rate from Table 4-4.
(6) Expense allowances received, $(6)_t$ = Column (6) of Table 17-9.
(7) Ceded expense reserve, $(7)_t$ = Column (7) of Table 17-9.

Table 17-17 develops the reserves for the MODCO block.

Table 17-17
Modco Transactions and Reserves on 10-Year Endowment

(1) Policy Year$_t$	(8) Projected In Force	(9) Modco Interest Rate	(10) Statutory Reserve	(11) Modco Reserve Adjustment Received	(12) Ceded Reserve Adjustment for Modco	(13) Ceded Benefit Reserve for Benefits	(14) Adjusted Ceded Benefit Reserve
0	100,000		0.00		0.00	0.00	0.00
1	81,948	6.75%	100.00	4,916.90	5,940.89	(5,145.94)	794.95
2	72,060	6.65%	200.00	3,403.29	11,890.17	(10,219.75)	1,670.42
3	64,790	6.55%	300.00	2,448.56	17,849.14	(15,396.04)	2,453.10
4	58,891	6.45%	400.00	1,719.58	23,819.28	(20,765.50)	3,053.78
5	54,111	6.25%	500.00	1,215.91	29,803.36	(26,349.89)	3,453.47
6	50,252	6.25%	600.00	843.11	35,803.35	(32,246.60)	3,556.75
7	47,163	6.25%	700.00	586.76	41,821.37	(38,512.67)	3,308.70
8	44,725	6.25%	800.00	421.55	47,859.28	(45,202.64)	2,656.64
9	42,849	6.25%	900.00	329.09	53,918.51	(52,364.39)	1,554.12
10	0	6.25%	1,000.00	(24,584.89)	0.00	0.00	0.00

Premiums paid at the beginning of the year.
Commissions and expenses paid at the beginning of the year.
Death benefits paid at the middle of the year.
Modco reserve adjustment paid at end of year.
Units of coverage: 100.000.

Legend:
(1) Time, in years.
(8) Projected in force from Table 4-5.
(9) Modco interest rate $(8)_t = (5)_t - 0.0025$.
(10) Statutory reserve per policy from Table 4-4.
(11) Modco reserve adjustment, $(11)_t = [100 \times 0.6 \times (10)_t \times (8)_t / (8)_0] - [1 + (9)_t] \times [100 \times 0.6 \times (10)_{t-1} \times (8)_{t-1} / (8)_0]$.
(12) Ceded reserve adjustment for modco, $(12)_t = \{[((12)_{t-1} \times [(8)_{t-1} / (8)_0] - 0.0079 \times (3)_t) \times (1 + (5)_t)] + (11)_t\} / [(8)_t / (8)_0]$.
(13) Ceded benefit reserve for benefits = Column (9) of Table 17-9.
(14) Ceded benefit reserve adjusted for modco, $(14)_t = (12)_t + (13)_t$.

GAAP benefit premium percentage for modco adjustment = present value of modco reserve adjustments received in (11) divided by present value of ceded premium income in (3), discounted at the investment rate in (5) = .79%.

Table 17-18 constructs the income statement. It starts with the direct component profits then displays each item for the MODCO elements.

Table 17-18
Policy Year Results for Modco on 10-Year Endowment

(1) Policy Year$_t$	(15) Projected In Force	(16) Direct GAAP Book Profit	(17) Ceded Coinsurance Premiums Paid	(18) Expense Allowances Received	(19) Mortality Expense Reimbursed	(20) Surrender Expense Reimbursed	(21) Modco Reserve Adjustment Received	(22) Increase in Expense Reserve for Reinsurance	(23) Increase in Benefit Reserve for Reinsurance	(24) GAAP Book Profit Net of Reinsurance
0	100,000									
1	81,948	803.73	5,700.00	5,130.00	37.80	0.00	4,916.90	4,062.62	651.45	435.76
2	72,060	658.02	4,671.06	560.53	37.37	589.58	3,403.29	(288.36)	552.25	356.76
3	64,790	578.08	4,107.40	205.37	42.80	907.05	2,448.56	(550.01)	385.65	313.42
4	58,891	519.27	3,693.00	184.65	44.32	1,118.29	1,719.58	(508.57)	209.05	281.53
5	54,111	471.11	3,356.80	167.84	45.23	1,213.96	1,215.91	(480.88)	70.29	255.42
6	50,252	432.87	3,084.31	154.22	45.45	1,225.51	843.11	(458.77)	(81.34)	234.69
7	47,163	402.00	2,864.39	143.22	47.64	1,174.05	586.76	(445.52)	(226.88)	217.96
8	44,725	377.29	2,688.27	134.41	50.37	1,073.39	421.55	(439.99)	(372.29)	204.55
9	42,849	357.78	2,549.31	127.47	53.94	931.98	329.09	(441.38)	(522.25)	193.98
10	0	342.78	2,442.42	122.12	57.59	25,652.10	(24,584.89)	(449.13)	(665.93)	185.85

Premiums paid at the beginning of the year.
Commissions and expenses paid at the beginning of the year.
Death Benefits paid at the middle of the year.
Withdrawals paid at the end of the year.
Modco reserve adjustment paid at end of year.

Legend:
(1) Time, in years.
(15) Projected inforce from Table 4-5.
(16) Direct GAAP book profit from Table 4-6.
(17) Ceded coinsurance premiums paid, $(17)_t = (3)_t$.
(18) Expense allowances received, $(18)_t = (6)_t$.
(19) Mortality expense reimbursed, $(19)_t = 0.6 \times (20)_t$ of Table 4-5.
(20) Surrender expense reimbursed, $(20)_t = 0.6 \times (21)_t$ of Table 4-6.
(21) Modco reserve adjustment received, $(21)_t = (11)_t$.
(22) Increase in expense reserve, $(22)_t = [(15)_t / (15)_0] \times (7)_t - [(15)_{t-1} / (15)_0] \times (7)_{t-1}$
(23) Increase in benefit reserve adjusted for modco, $(23)_t = [(15)_t / (15)_0] \times (14)_t - [(15)_{t-1} / (15)_0] \times (14)_{t-2}$.
(24) GAAP profit net of reinsurance, $(24)_t = (16)_t - (17)_t + (18)_t + (19)_t + (20)_t + (21)_t - (22)_t - (23)_t + (5)_t \times \{[(15)_{t-1} \times (7)_{t-1}] + [(15)_{t-1} \times (14)_{t-1}] - (17)_t + (18)_t\} + \{[1 + (5)_t]^{(.5)} - 1\} \times (19)_t$

Finally, table 17-19 displays profits as a percentage of premiums from the direct, reinsured and net viewpoints.

Table 17-19
Analysis of Profits for Modco on 10-Year Endowment

(1) Policy Year, t	(25) Direct Premium Income	(26) Direct GAAP Book Profit	(27) Direct Profit as Percentage of Direct Premium	(28) Ceded Modco Premiums	(29) Ceded GAAP Book Profit	(30) Ceded Profit as Percentage of Ceded Premium	(31) Premiums Net of Reinsurance	(32) GAAP Book Profit Net of Reinsurance	(33) Net Profit as Percentage of Net Premium
0									
1	9,500.00	803.73	7.91%	5,700.00	367.97	6.03%	3,800.00	435.76	10.72%
2	7,785.09	658.02	7.91%	4,671.06	301.26	6.03%	3,114.04	356.76	10.72%
3	6,845.67	578.08	7.91%	4,107.40	264.66	6.03%	2,738.27	313.42	10.72%
4	6,155.01	519.27	7.91%	3,693.00	237.74	6.03%	2,462.00	281.53	10.72%
5	5,594.67	471.11	7.91%	3,356.80	215.69	6.03%	2,237.87	255.42	10.72%
6	5,140.51	432.87	7.91%	3,084.31	198.18	6.03%	2,056.20	234.69	10.72%
7	4,773.98	402.00	7.91%	2,864.39	184.05	6.03%	1,909.59	217.96	10.72%
8	4,480.45	377.29	7.91%	2,688.27	172.73	6.03%	1,792.18	204.55	10.72%
9	4,248.85	357.78	7.91%	2,549.31	163.80	6.03%	1,699.54	193.98	10.72%
10	4,070.70	342.78	7.91%	2,442.42	156.94	6.03%	1,628.28	185.85	10.72%

Premiums paid at the beginning of the year.
Profits recognized at the end of the year

Legend:
(1) Time, in years.
(25) Direct premium income from Table 4-5.
(26) Direct GAAP book profit, $(20)_t = (16)_t$.
(27) Direct GAAP book profit at beginning of the year as a percentage of direct premium income, $(27)_t = [(26)_t / (25)_t] / [1 + (5)_t]$.
(28) Ceded premiums paid, $(22)_t = (3)_t$.
(29) Ceded GAAP book profit, $(29)_t = (26)_t - (24)_t$.
(30) Ceded GAAP book profit at the beginning of the year as a percentage of ceded premiums, $(30)_t = [(29)_t / (28)_t] / [1 + (5)_t]$.
(31) Premiums, direct less ceded, $(31)_t = (25)_t - (28)_t$.
(32) GAAP book profit, direct less ceded, $(32)_t = (24)_t$.
(33) GAAP book profit, direct less ceded, at the beginning of the year as a percent of net premiums, $(33)_t = [(32)_t / (31)_t] / [1 + (5)_t]$.

In the example above, the GAAP benefit reserves for reinsurance have been calculated to directly include the impact of the MODCO reserve adjustment. In practice, GAAP benefit reserves net of MODCO reinsurance have sometimes been set equal to the direct GAAP reserves reduced by the portion reinsured plus the statutory reserves relating to the ceded portion held by the ceding company. The use of this type of approximation for GAAP is only justified when the expected differences between the approximation and the more precise calculation are not material.

17.6.3.4 Post-Issue Reinsurance

A life insurer may reinsure an entire block of business in the middle of its lifetime rather from inception. While significant amounts of assets would not likely change hands at the time the treaty was enacted, there would likely be a significant impact on future cash flows.

Paragraph 26 of *SFAS 113* states "The cost shall be amortized over the remaining life of the underlying reinsured contracts if the reinsured contract is long duration, or over the contract period of the reinsurance if the reinsurance contract is short duration."

The following tables examine the accounting for a block of business that was significantly reinsured in the middle of its lifetime. Tables 17-20, 17-21, 17-22, and 17-23 trace the accounting for the block of ten year endowments as if they are 90% reinsured on a YRT basis at the beginning of year six.

Table 17-20 displays the net amount at risk, the YRT reinsurance rates and the then-best-estimate for earnings rates as of year six. The best estimate of all other assumptions did not change as of year six.

Table 17-20
Per-Policy Assumptions for Post-Issue YRT Reinsurance on 10-Year Endowment

(1) Policy Year$_t$	(2) Direct Gross Premium	(3) Direct Mortality Rate	(4) Direct Face Amount	(5) Direct Statutory Reserve	(6) Net Amount at Risk	(7) Amount Ceded	(8) YRT Rates Per $1,000	(9) Ceded Investment Rate	(10) Direct Investment Rate
0			1,000.00	0.00					
1	95.00	0.00063	1,000.00	100.00	1000.00				7.00%
2	95.00	0.00076	1,000.00	200.00	900.00				6.90%
3	95.00	0.00099	1,000.00	300.00	800.00				6.80%
4	95.00	0.00114	1,000.00	400.00	700.00				6.70%
5	95.00	0.00128	1,000.00	500.00	600.00				6.50%
6	95.00	0.00140	1,000.00	600.00	500.00	450.00	1.470	7.00%	6.50%
7	95.00	0.00158	1,000.00	700.00	400.00	360.00	1.580	6.75%	6.50%
8	95.00	0.00178	1,000.00	800.00	300.00	270.00	1.691	6.50%	6.50%
9	95.00	0.00201	1,000.00	900.00	200.00	180.00	1.809	6.25%	6.50%
10	95.00	0.00224	1,000.00	1,000.00	100.00	90.00	1.904	6.00%	6.50%

Sample policy: male, age 35.
Premium mode: annual.
Units of coverage: 100.000.
Direct results based upon Tables 4-4, 4-5 and 4-6.
Reinsurance: YRT on 90% of net amount at risk starting at beginning of sixth year.

Legend:
(1) Time, in years.
(2) Direct gross premium from Table 4-4.
(3) Direct mortality rates from Table 4-4.
(4) Direct face amount from Table 4-4.
(5) Direct statutory reserve from Table 4-4.
(6) Net amount at risk, $(6)_t = (4)_{t-1} - (5)_{t-1,}$ years 6 to 10 only.
(7) Amount ceded, $(7)_t = (6)_t \times 0.9$, years 6 to 10 only.
(8) YRT rates per $1,000, $(8)_t$ = rates negoitated between ceding company and reinsurer.
(9) Ceding investment income rate.
(10) Investment rate from Table 4-4.

Table 17-21 shows the expected ceded premiums and develops the benefit reserve for the ceded block.

Table 17-21
Post-Issue YRT Transactions and Reserves

(1) **Policy Year$_t$**	(11) **Projected In Force**	(12) **Ceded YRT Reinsurance Premiums Paid**	(13) **Mortality Expense Reimbursed**	(14) **Ceded Mortality Reserve**
0	100,000			
1	81,948			
2	72,060			
3	64,790			
4	58,891			
5	54,111			0.00
6	50,252	35.79	34.09	(2.61)
7	47,163	28.58	28.58	(3.54)
8	44,725	21.53	22.67	(2.98)
9	42,849	14.56	16.18	(1.47)
10	0	7.34	8.64	0.00

Premiums paid at the beginning of the year.
Death Benefits paid at the middle of the year.
Units of coverage: 100.000.
Reinsurance starts at the beginning of the sixth year.

Legend:
(1) Time, in years.
(11) Projected in force from Table 4-5.
(12) Ceded YRT reinsurance premiums paid, $(12)_t = 100 \times [(11)_{t-1} / (11)_0] \times (7)_t \times (8)_t / 1{,}000$.
(13) Mortality expense reimbursed, $(13)_t = 100 \times [(11)_{t-1} / (11)_0] \times (7)_t \times (3)_t$.
(14) Ceded benefit reserve, $(14)_t =$

$$\{[(14)_{t-1} \times [(11)_{t-1} / (11)_0] - 0.9841 \times (12)_t] \times [1 + (9)_t] + (13)_t \times [(1 + (9)_t)^{.5} - 1]\} / [(11)_t / (11)_0]$$

GAAP ceded benefit premium percentage = present value of mortality expense reimbursed in (13), divided by present value of ceded premium income in (12), discounted at the investment rate in (9) = 98.41%.

Table 17-22 develops profit for the block. It commences with the direct profit. It then presents the elements of the reinsurance treaty starting in year six and calculates the expected profit after reinsurance.

Table 17-22
Book Profits for 10-Year Endowment with Post-Issue YRT Reinsurance

(1) Policy Year$_t$	(15) Projected In Force	(16) Direct GAAP Book Profit	(17) Ceded YRT Premiums Paid	(18) Mortality Expense Reimbursed	(19) Increase in Benefit Reserve for Reinsurance	(20) GAAP Book Profit Net of Reinsurance
0	100,000					
1	81,948	803.73				
2	72,060	658.02				
3	64,790	578.08				
4	58,891	519.27				
5	54,111	471.11				
6	50,252	432.87	35.79	34.09	-1.31	432.26
7	47,163	402.00	28.58	28.58	-0.36	401.52
8	44,725	377.29	21.53	22.67	0.34	376.92
9	42,849	357.78	14.56	16.18	0.70	357.54
10	0	342.78	7.34	8.64	0.63	342.66

Premiums paid at the beginning of the year.
Commissions and expenses paid at the beginning of the year
Death benefits paid at the middle of the year
Withdrawals paid at the end of the year
Reinsurance starts at the beginning of the sixth year

Legend:

(1) Time, in years.
(15) Projected in force from Table 4-5.
(16) Direct GAAP book profit from Table 4-6.
(17) Ceded reinsurance premiums paid, $(17)_t = (12)_t$.
(18) Mortality expense reimbursed, $(18)_t = (13)_t$.
(19) Increase in benefit reserve, $(19)_t = [(15)_t / (15)_0] \times (14)_t - [(15)_{t-1} / (15)_0] \times (14)_{t-1}$.
(20) GAAP profit net of reinsurance, $(20)_t = (16)_t - (17)_t + (18)_t - (19)_t + (9)_t \times \{[(15)_{t-1} \times (14)_{t-1}] - (17)_t\} + \{[1 + (9)_t]^{.5} - 1\} \times (18)_t$.

Finally, Table 17-23 displays profits as a percentage of premiums from the direct, reinsured and net viewpoints.

Table 17-23
Analysis of Profits for Post-Issue YRT Reinsurance on 10-Year Endowment

(1) Policy $Year_t$	(21) Direct Premium Income	(22) Direct GAAP Book Profit	(23) Direct Profit as Percentage of Direct Premium	(24) Ceded YRT Premiums	(25) Ceded GAAP Book Profit	(26) Ceded Profit as Percentage of Ceded Premium	(27) Premiums Net of Reinsurance	(28) GAAP Book Profit Net of Reinsurance	(29) Net Profit as Percentage of Net Premium
0									
1	9,500.00	803.73	7.91%				9,500.00	803.73	7.91%
2	7,785.09	658.02	7.91%				7,785.09	658.02	7.91%
3	6,845.67	578.08	7.91%				6,845.67	578.08	7.91%
4	6,155.01	519.27	7.91%				6,155.01	519.27	7.91%
5	5,594.67	471.11	7.91%				5,594.67	471.11	7.91%
6	5,140.51	432.87	7.91%	35.79	0.61	1.59%	5,104.72	432.26	7.95%
7	4,773.98	402.00	7.91%	28.58	0.49	1.59%	4,745.40	401.52	7.94%
8	4,480.45	377.29	7.91%	21.53	0.37	1.59%	4,458.92	376.92	7.94%
9	4,248.85	357.78	7.91%	14.56	0.25	1.59%	4,234.29	357.54	7.93%
10	4,070.70	342.78	7.91%	7.34	0.12	1.59%	4,063.36	342.66	7.92%

Premiums paid at the beginning of the year.
Profits recognized at the end of the year
Reinsurance starts at the beginning of the sixth year

Legend:
(1) Time, in years.
(21) Direct premium income from Table 4-5.
(22) Direct GAAP book profit, $(22)_t = (16)_t$.
(23) Direct GAAP book profit at beginning of the year as a percentage of direct premium income, $(23)_t = [(22)_t / (21)_t] / [1 + (10)_t]$.
(24) Ceded premiums paid, $(24)_t = (17)_t$.
(25) Ceded GAAP book profit, $(25)_t = (22)_t - (20)_t$ (years 6 to 10 only).
(26) Ceded GAAP book profit at the beginning of the year as a percentage of ceded premiums, $(26)_t = [(25)_t / (24)_t] / [1 + (9)_t]$.
(27) Premiums, direct less ceded, $(27)_t = (21)_t - (24)_t$.
(28) GAAP book profit, direct less ceded, $(28)_t = (20)_t$.
(29) GAAP book profit, direct less ceded, at the beginning of the year as a percentage of net premiums, $(29)_t = \{[(22)_t / (1 + (10)_t] - [(25) / (1 + (9)_t]\} / (27)_t$.

17.6.3.5 Universal Life & Estimated Gross Profits

The examples in this section will show the accounting for YRT reinsurance on universal life contracts accounted for with *SFAS 97*. Two potential approaches to recognizing the cost of reinsurance are shown. The first approach, which utilizes a EGP net of reinsurance costs to amortize DAC, is shown in Tables 17-24 and 17-25.

Except for excess ceding expense allowances, the first approach treats the cost of reinsurance as other net costs to be recognized in the EGP. This derives from the requirements of item e) in paragraph 23 of *SFAS 97,* which states "Estimated gross profits ... shall include estimates of the following elements: ... e) Other expected assessments and credits, however characterized."

Table 17-24 develops post-reinsurance EGPs.

Table 17-24
Development of Universal Life EGPs with Reinsurance Ceded

(1) Year	(2) Direct Estimated Gross Profit	(3) Ceded YRT Premiums	(4) Ceded YRT Recoveries	(5) YRT Expense Allowance Deferred	(6) YRT Expense Allowance Not Deferred	(7) Estimated Gross Profits after YRT
1	396,147	40,149	15,672	32,120	4,015	375,685
2	513,758	36,341	18,549	0	3,634	499,600
3	435,723	35,086	21,065	0	3,509	425,211
4	375,177	32,482	22,302	0	3,248	368,245
5	342,773	31,535	22,653	0	3,154	337,044
6	320,750	30,675	23,338	0	3,068	316,480
7	311,100	29,911	24,152	0	2,991	308,332
8	320,684	30,189	24,686	0	3,019	318,200
9	335,700	30,258	24,891	0	3,026	333,359
10	346,931	30,146	25,353	0	3,015	345,153
11	360,728	29,291	26,484	0	2,929	360,851
12	376,056	29,584	28,547	0	2,958	377,978
13	395,590	30,678	30,576	0	3,068	398,555
14	412,476	30,573	31,708	0	3,057	416,668
15	432,977	30,458	32,019	0	3,046	437,583
16	452,887	29,297	31,923	0	2,930	458,443
17	477,919	32,908	35,898	0	3,291	484,200
18	502,059	37,791	41,180	0	3,779	509,226
19	519,299	42,349	47,165	0	4,235	528,350
20	530,114	47,528	53,792	0	4,753	541,131
Totals	8,158,848	667,232	581,954	32,120	66,723	8,140,294

Legend:
Reinsured amount is 30% of net amount at risk
First-year expense allowance is 90% of the YRT premium
Renewal expense allowance is 10% of the YRT premium

(1) Time t in years.
(2) From Table 6-8.
(3) From rates negotiated by direct and ceding companies.
(4) Best estimate of death claim recoveries.
(5) = 80% × (3) in year one.
(6) = 10% × (3) all years.
(7) = (2) – (3) + (4) + (6).

Table 17-25 presents the determination of deferrable costs and their subsequent amortization using EGPs from Table 17-24. Deferrable costs are net of any excess YRT expense allowance.

Table 17-25
Development of Universal Life DAC with Reinsurance Ceded

(1) Year	(2) Estimated Gross Profits after YRT	(3) Expenses Capitalized (Direct)	(4) YRT Expense Allowance Deferred	(5) Deferrable Expenses Net of YRT	(6) Interest on DAC	(7) Expenses Amortized	(8) DAC
1	375,685	2,442,500	32,120	2,410,380	132,571	233,813	2,309,139
2	499,600	178,038	0	178,038	136,795	310,933	2,313,038
3	425,211	71,128	0	71,128	131,129	264,636	2,250,660
4	368,245	64,625	0	64,625	127,341	229,182	2,213,443
5	337,044	59,345	0	59,345	125,003	209,764	2,188,027
6	316,480	55,075	0	55,075	123,371	196,966	2,169,507
7	308,332	51,649	0	51,649	122,164	191,895	2,151,425
8	318,200	48,936	0	48,936	121,020	198,036	2,123,344
9	333,359	46,595	0	46,595	119,347	207,470	2,081,816
10	345,153	44,587	0	44,587	116,952	214,810	2,028,544
11	360,851	10,774	0	10,774	112,162	224,580	1,926,900
12	377,978	10,408	0	10,408	106,552	235,240	1,808,621
13	398,555	10,048	0	10,048	100,027	248,046	1,670,650
14	416,668	9,693	0	9,693	92,419	259,319	1,513,443
15	437,583	9,342	0	9,342	83,753	272,336	1,334,203
16	458,443	-	0	-	73,381	285,318	1,122,266
17	484,200	-	0	-	61,725	301,349	882,642
18	509,226	-	0	-	48,545	316,924	614,264
19	528,350	-	0	-	33,785	328,826	319,223
20	541,131	-	0	-	17,557	336,780	0
Present Value at 5.5%	4,729,928	2,975,854	32,120	2,943,735			

Discount rate = 5.5%
k-factor = 0.622363 = Present Value of Column (5) / Present Value of Column (6)

Legend
(1) Time t in years
(2) = (7) From Table 17-24
(3) = (9) From Table 6-9
(4) = (5) From Table 17-24
(5) = (3) – (4)
(6) = $[(8)_{t-1} + (5)_t] \times 0.055$ where $(8)_0 = 0$
(7) = (2) × k-factor
(8) = $(8)_{t-1} + (5) + (6) - (7)$ where $(8)_0 = 0$

The second approach establishes a liability or an asset that will result in the recognition of the net cost of reinsurance as a function of the direct EGP. This second approach is shown in Table 17-26. With the values for net cost of reinsurance shown in 17-26, the liability is negative at most durations and may be reported as an asset. Related to the liability in Table 17-26, there is no contra DAC amount established for excess ceding expense allowances. DAC is reported on a gross basis and is amortized with the direct EGP.

Because the YRT treaty shown in Tables 17-24, 17-25 and 17-26 pays the ceding company an initial expense allowance and has a expected premium structure that is flatter than the expected claims recoveries, we have concluded the reinsurance treaty is long duration. As a result, we have amortized the net cost of reinsurance over the expected 20 year lifetime of underlying business. As required in *SFAS 113*:

> The cost shall be amortized over the remaining life of the underlying reinsured contracts if the reinsurance contract is long duration, or over the contract period of the reinsurance if the reinsurance contract is short duration. (Paragraph 26).

Table 17-26
Development of Liability for Net Cost of Reinsurance

(1) Year	(2) Direct Estimated Gross Profit	(3) Ceded YRT Premiums	(4) Ceded YRT Recoveries	(5) YRT Expense Allowance	(6) Net Cost Of Reinsurance	(7) Liability for Net Cost of Reinsurance
1	396,147	40,149	15,672	36,135	(11,657)	12,358
2	513,758	36,341	18,549	3,634	14,158	(211)
3	435,723	35,086	21,065	3,509	10,512	(9,964)
4	375,177	32,482	22,302	3,248	6,932	(16,780)
5	342,773	31,535	22,653	3,154	5,729	(22,826)
6	320,750	30,675	23,338	3,068	4,270	(27,784)
7	311,100	29,911	24,152	2,991	2,768	(31,529)
8	320,684	30,189	24,686	3,019	2,484	(35,180)
9	335,700	30,258	24,891	3,026	2,341	(38,863)
10	346,931	30,146	25,353	3,015	1,778	(42,165)
11	360,728	29,291	26,484	2,929	(122)	(43,723)
12	376,056	29,584	28,547	2,958	(1,922)	(43,541)
13	395,590	30,678	30,576	3,068	(2,966)	(42,271)
14	412,476	30,573	31,708	3,057	(4,192)	(39,673)
15	432,977	30,458	32,019	3,046	(4,606)	(36,483)
16	452,887	29,297	31,923	2,930	(5,556)	(32,133)
17	477,919	32,908	35,898	3,291	(6,281)	(26,774)
18	502,059	37,791	41,180	3,779	(7,168)	(20,191)
19	519,299	42,349	47,165	4,235	(9,051)	(11,331)
20	530,114	47,528	53,792	4,753	(11,017)	-
Totals	8,158,848	667,232	581,954	98,843	(13,565)	

Discount rate = 5.5%
k-factor = 0.0018 = Present Value of Column (5) / Present Value of Column (1)

Legend:
(1) Time t in years
(2) = (8) From Table 6-8
(3) From rates negotiated by direct and ceding companies
(4) Best estimate of death claim recoveries
(5) = 90% × (3) in year one and 10% × (3) in years 2 to 20
(6) = (3) – (4) – (5)
(7) = $(7)_{t-1}$ × (1.055) – (6) + 0.0018 × (2)

17.7 Accounting for Reinsurance under *SOP 03-1*

Statement of Position (SOP) 03-1 is effective for financial statements for fiscal years beginning after December 15, 2003. The *SOP* applies to all insurance products reported under *SFAS 60, SFAS 97* and *SFAS 120.* Complying with the *SOP* may result in a company holding reserve liabilities in addition to those already called for under the requirements of *SFAS 60, SFAS 97* and *SFAS 120.*

The additional reserve liabilities that can arise from the *SOP* requirements may relate to product features for death or other insurance benefits, annuitization benefits or sales inducements. At the same time, it may be permissible under the *SOP* to defer and amortize the build-up of additional liabilities for sales inducements. The determination of these accounting entries is described in detail in other chapters of this book.

In addition to the SOP, there are other documents related to the *SOP* that may provide guidance on the accounting for reinsurance. These other documents are a FASB staff position paper *(FSP) FAS 97-a* and AICPA Technical Practice Aids *(TPA) 6300.05 to 6300.10).*

Reinsurance is also subject to the requirements of the *SOP*. These additional requirements relate to the classification of reinsurance contracts by reinsurers as insurance or investment contracts. They also give guidance on how reinsurance related recoverables and DAC are to be accounted for when a ceding company has established additional liabilities under the requirements of the *SOP*.

In particular, a ceding company may need to calculate adjustments for reinsurance recoverables in a manner consistent with the requirements of the *SOP* for additional reserves on direct benefits. Although this issue is not directly addressed in the *SOP,* the AICPA issued a technical practice aid (*TPA*) for *SOP 03-1* that states:

> …the recoverable should be calculated using methods and assumptions consistent with those used to establish the direct contract holder's liability. Therefore, a benefit ratio using the same assumptions and scenarios used to establish the direct contract liability, as required in paragraph 26 of *SOP 03-1*, should be used to establish a reinsurance recoverable with excess benefit payments ceded under the terms of the reinsurance contract as the numerator and direct assessments as the denominator. (*TPA* Paragraph 6300.09)

The example following in Table 17-27 shows how a ceded reserve is to be calculated following the guidance in the *TPA* related to the additional *SOP* reserve in Table 6-20 of Chapter 6. It relates to a universal life contract in which the death benefit shows a pattern of gains followed by losses. The reinsurance treaty assumed is 30% pro-rata YRT with no ceding expense allowances. Although only a single scenario is shown, the actuary should consider if a range of scenarios would be appropriate as called for in the *SOP*.

Table 17-27 displays an *SOP* reserve for the ceded excess benefits has been determined as a function of total direct assessments. Although not shown in Table 17-27, the *SOP* reserves on both a direct and ceded basis are to be regularly restated to reflect actual experience as described in paragraph 27 of *SOP 03-1*.

Table 17-27
Example of SOP Reserve with Reinsurance

Contract Assumptions

Number of Policies	100	Average Face Amount	10,000	Target Premium	$25/1000

Year	COIs	Expected Mortality Rates	Expected Credited Rates	Expected Lapse Rates	Interest Spread	Expense Charges	Discount Rate	Percent Ceded	Ceded Premium Rates
1	0.00176	0.0007	8%	3%	0.50%	$10/pol	8%	30%	0.00091
2	0.00165	0.0008	8%	3%	0.50%	$10/pol	8%	30%	0.00104
3	0.00154	0.0009	8%	3%	0.50%	$10/pol	8%	30%	0.00117
4	0.00143	0.0010	8%	3%	0.50%	$10/pol	8%	30%	0.00130
5	0.00132	0.0011	8%	2%	0.50%	$10/pol	8%	30%	0.00143
6	0.00121	0.0012	8%	1%	0.50%	$10/pol	8%	30%	0.00156
7	0.00110	0.0013	8%	1%	0.50%	$10/pol	8%	30%	0.00169
8	0.00099	0.0014	8%	1%	0.50%	$10/pol	8%	30%	0.00182
9	0.00088	0.0015	8%	1%	0.50%	$10/pol	8%	30%	0.00195
10	0.00077	0.0016	8%	100%	0.50%	$10/pol	8%	30%	0.00208

	(1)	(2)	(3)	(4)	(5)	(6)	(7)	(8)	(9)	(10)	(11)	(12)
Year	Premium	Ceded YRT Premiums	Account Value EOP	Excess Death Benefits	Total Assessments	Discount Factor (8%)	Persistency Factor	Benefit Ratio (BR):	SOP Reserve	Ceded Excess Death Benefits	Ceded Benefit Ratio (BR):	Ceded SOP Reserve
1	25,000	262	26,171	671	2,797	0.962250	0.984530		184	201		55
2	24,613	289	53,158	742	2,738	0.890973	0.954305		291	223		87
3	23,858	305	80,607	783	2,649	0.824975	0.924913		336	235		101
4	23,123	317	108,555	813	2,577	0.763865	0.896333		330	244		99
5	22,408	324	138,456	831	2,521	0.707283	0.868547		287	249		86
6	21,714	331	171,046	848	2,506	0.654891	0.850220		219	254		66
7	21,256	336	205,338	862	2,531	0.606381	0.840698		139	259		42
8	21,017	337	241,677	865	2,575	0.561464	0.831198		63	259		19
9	20,780	334	280,194	856	2,636	0.519874	0.821722		9	257		3
10	20,543	325	-	834	2,717	0.481365	0.812272		(0)	250		0
PV				5,570	18,367			30.3%		1,671	9.1%	

Assumes premiums, interest credits, and expenses charges occur at start of year, deaths at mid year and surrenders at end of year

Legend:

(1) Equals $25 × 1,000 × $(6)_{t-1}$
(2) Equals ceded premium rate × percent ceded × [1,000,000 × $(7)_t - (3)_{t-1}$ × (1 + crediting rate) ^ 0.5]
(3) Equals [$(2)_{t-1}$ + (1)] × (1 – mortality rate – lapse rate) × (1 + credited rate)
(4) Equals mortality rate × [1,000,000 × $(7)_t - (3)_{t-1}$ × (1 + crediting rate) ^ 0.5]
(5) Column (8) from Table 6-20
(6) Equals $(6)_{t-1}$ / (1 + discount rate); Year 1 equals 1 / (1 + discount rate) ^ 0.5
(7) Equals $(7)_{t-1}$ × (1 – mortality rate – lapse rate); Year 1 equals (1 – mortality rate – lapse rate) ^ 0.5
(8) Equals PV (4) / PV (5)
(9) Equals $(9)_{t-1}$ × 1.08 + [((8) × $(5)_t$) – $(4)_t$] × 1.08 ^ 0.5
(10) Equals $(4)_t$ × Percent Ceded
(11) Equals PV (10) / PV (5)
(12) Equals $(12)_{t-1}$ × 1.08 + [((11) × $(5)_t$) – $(10)_t$] × 1.08 ^ 0.5

A ceding company may also have to adjust how the net cost of reinsurance is to be recognized if reinsurance covers excess benefits as defined in the *SOP*. The *SOP* does not give direct advice on this issue. Related to the issue of amortizing the net cost of reinsurance, the *TPA* states:

> The cost of reinsurance may be recognized based on total direct assessments or on another reasonable manner such as estimated gross profits. (*TPA* Paragraph 6300.09)

SFAS 113 does not define the net cost of reinsurance nor does it specify the methods to be used in amortizing the cost of reinsurance. Given the lack of guidance in *SFAS 113* and the *SOP*, there are a number of possible approaches that could be used for recognizing the net cost of reinsurance when ceding a ceding company has accrued additional liabilities under the *SOP*.

The example in Table 17-28 shows how DAC can be adjusted for the ceded *SOP* reserve from Table 17-27. It follows the first approach for recognizing the cost of reinsurance described in Section 17.6.3.5 for *SFAS 97* accounting and utilizes an EGP net of reinsurance costs to amortize DAC. There is a question as to how the ceded *SOP* reserves should be reflected in the EGP used for DAC amortization. With regards to the direct *SOP* reserves, Paragraph 29 of *SOP 03-1* requires:

> The estimated gross profits used for the amortization of deferred acquisition costs should be adjusted to reflect the recognition of the liability in accordance with paragraph 28 of this SOP.

Although the *SOP* requires that the EGP should be adjusted for the additional *SOP* liabilities, there is no specific requirement that the ceded reserve adjustment called for by the TPA should be included in the EGP. So there may be some variation in practice with the treatment of the ceded *SOP* reserve in determining DAC. For consistency, the changes in both the direct and ceded *SOP* reserves are reflected as adjustments to the EGP in Table 17-28.

The interest income on any assets backing the net *SOP* reserves has been ignored in the determination of EGP in Table 17-28. The *SOP* is silent on the potential of interest income on assets backing the *SOP* reserves although many practitioners believe that recognizing this interest as income in EGP is an acceptable practice.

Table 17-28
Impact of Direct and Ceded SOP Liability on DAC

DAC on a Direct Basis

Year	(1) Account Value EOP	(2) Deferrals	(3) EGPs	(4) Amortization Ratio (k)	(5) DAC Balance EOP	(6) DAC Amortization
1	26,171	5,000	2,126		4,537	831
2	53,158	-	1,996		4,089	780
3	80,607	-	1,867		3,659	729
4	108,555	-	1,764		3,235	689
5	138,456	-	1,690		2,808	660
6	171,046	-	1,658		2,359	648
7	205,338	-	1,670		1,870	652
8	241,677	-	1,710		1,325	668
9	280,194	-	1,780		708	696
10	-	-	1,883		-	736
PV		5,000	12,797	39.1%		

SOP 03-1 Reserve and revised DAC Balance

Year	(7) Account Value EOY	(8) Ceded YRT Premiums	(9) Ceded Excess Death Benefits	(10) SOP 03-1 Reserve	(11) Ceded SOP Reserve	(12) Revised EGPs	(13) Revised Amortization Ratio (k)	(14) Revised Amortization	(15) Revised DAC Balance
1	26,171	262	201	184	55	1,936		792	4,577
2	53,158	289	223	291	87	1,855		759	4,154
3	80,607	305	235	336	101	1,765		722	3,736
4	108,555	317	244	330	99	1,695		693	3,315
5	138,456	324	249	287	86	1,645		673	2,880
6	171,046	331	254	219	66	1,630		667	2,418
7	205,338	336	259	139	42	1,648		674	1,911
8	241,677	337	259	63	19	1,685		689	1,347
9	280,194	334	257	9	3	1,741		712	715
10	-	325	250	(0)	0	1,815		743	0
PV						12,221	40.9%		

Interest on assets backing net SOP liability has been ignored

Legend:

(1) Column (2) from Table 6-19
(2) Actual deferrals for DAC calculations
(3) Column (3) from Table 6-21
(4) PV of (2) / PV of (3)
(5) Equals $((5)_{t-1} \times 1.08) + (2) - ((6) \times 1.08 \wedge 0.5)$
(6) Equals (4) × (3)
(7) Equals (1)
(8) Column (2) of Table 17-27
(9) Column (10) from Table 17-27
(10) Column (9) from Table 17-27
(11) Column (12) from Table 17-27
(12) Equals $(3)_t - (8)_t + (9)_t - ((10)_t - (10)_{t-1}) + ((11)_t - (11)_{t-1})$
(13) PV of (2) / PV of (12)
(13) Equals $(13) \times (12)_t$
(14) Equals $((15)_{t-1} \times 1.08) + (2) - ((14)_t) \times 1.08 \wedge 0.5)$

17.8 Accounting for Reinsurance under *SFAS 133*

SFAS 133 was effective for fiscal years beginning after June 15, 2000, and has potential applications to accounting for reinsurance. Because of the complexity of *SFAS 133*, FASB also created a special Derivatives Implementation Group (DIG) to provide additional interpretations and guidance on the implementation of *SFAS 133*. There are several DIG issues that may impact GAAP accounting for reinsurance.

An important application of *SFAS 133* to reinsurance is described in *DIG Issue B36: Embedded Derivatives: Modified Coinsurance Arrangements and Debt Instruments That Incorporate Credit Risk Exposures That Are Unrelated or Only Partially Related to the Creditworthiness of the Obligor under Those Instruments*. In particular, as described in *B36*, MODCO and funds withheld reinsurance contracts may contain embedded derivatives requiring bifurcation as required in *SFAS 133*.

There are other situations in which reinsurance transactions may contain derivatives as defined in *SFAS 133*. One important issue in determining whether a reinsurance treaty has derivative features is whether the payment of claims under the treaty satisfies the net settlement provisions of *SFAS 133*. An example is a reinsurance contract covering guaranteed minimum income benefits or guaranteed minimum withdrawal benefits in which the payment of claims by the reinsurer under the treaty is made on a lump sum basis. There is no requirement that such a treaty would always be construed as containing derivative features, and the facts and circumstances may lead to a different conclusion.

17.8.1 *DIG B36*

DIG B36 (*B36*) was effective in the first quarter following September 15, 2003. Although MODCO and funds withheld reinsurance contracts are a major focus of *B36, B36* specifies that any debt instrument in which the return paid on the debt is based upon anything other than the debt issuer's own creditworthiness may contain an embedded derivative.

As an example, if a debt requires that the debt issuer (borrower) pay a total investment return based upon the interest income and realized gains and losses of a portfolio of other fixed income securities, then that debt may contain an embedded derivative as defined in *SFAS 133*. In this case, a key criterion in determining the need to bifurcate an embedded derivative is the use of an investment return to be paid on the debt unrelated to the borrower's own credit rating. In other words, if the investment return is based upon the credit rating of the issuers of the securities rather than the issuer of the debt, there may be an embedded derivative.

MODCO and funds withheld reinsurance permit the ceding company to withhold invested funds and repay them later. This feature of the reinsurance treaties generates a payable liability for the ceding company and a receivable asset for the reinsurer. At the same time, under most MODCO and funds withheld reinsurance treaties the ceding company pays a total investment return (interest income plus realized gains and losses and in some situations unrealized gains and losses) based upon either a specified portion of the ceding company's general account assets or a specified block of those assets.

B36 concludes that a MODCO treaty that pays the reinsurer a return based upon a portion of the ceding company's assets or a pool of those assets contains an embedded derivative. Although not spelled out in *B36*, this interpretation is based upon the *SFAS 133* definition of an embedded derivative contained in other contractual arrangements where those arrangements do not meet the definition of stand-alone derivatives. Embedded derivatives are:

> implicit or explicit terms that affect some or all of the cash flows or the value of other exchanges required by the contract in a manner similar to a derivative instrument. The effect of embedding a derivative instrument in another type of contract ("the host contract") is that some or all of the cash flows or other exchanges that otherwise would be required by the contract, whether unconditional or contingent upon the occurrence of a specified event, will be modified based on one or more underlyings. (Paragraph 12)

B36 indicates that for MODCO arrangements it may be the case that the host contract is determined to be the MODCO arrangement, including the funds-withheld receivable-payable but excluding the embedded derivative. The facts and circumstances may also indicate that the funds-withheld payable receivable itself, excluding the embedded derivative, is the host. The conclusion that there is an embedded derivative that must be separately valued applies in either case.

Under the requirements of *SFAS 133*, paragraph 12, an embedded derivative must be bifurcated and reported separately if three conditions are met. The condition that is most critical to *B36* is:

> The economic characteristics and risks of the embedded derivative instrument are not clearly and closely related to the economic characteristics and risks of the host contracts. (Paragraph 12a)

In the case of the MODCO treaty paying a return on the ceding company's general account assets, *B36* describes when the embedded derivative feature of the treaty satisfies the requirements of *SFAS 133* paragraph 12a:

> The risk exposure of the ceding company's return on its general account assets or its securities portfolio is not clearly and closely related to the risk exposure arising from the overall creditworthiness of the ceding company, which is also affected by other factors. Consequently, the economic characteristics and risks of the embedded derivative feature are not clearly and closely related to the economic characteristics and risks of the host contract and, accordingly, the criterion in paragraph 12(a) is met.

In addition to MODCO and funds withheld reinsurance, there are other reinsurance treaties that may contain embedded derivative features requiring bifurcation under the requirements of *B36*. For example, reinsurance treaties with experience rating refunds to be paid to the ceding company may contain an embedded derivative if the refund includes an investment element based upon the return of an investment portfolio.

17.8.2 Types of Credit Derivatives

There are a variety of credit derivatives that may be useful in analyzing the requirements of *B36*. The following will describe the most basic structures.

A credit default swap is a derivative contract under which the swap seller, in return for a premium, agrees to compensate the swap buyer for the financial loss that would occur to a reference asset as the result of specified credit events. As an example, a credit swap could cover the financial impact on the value of debt if the issuer of that debt defaults and is unable to pay the coupons or principal. When this occurs, the swap seller will pay the swap buyer an amount based upon the terms of the contract. This amount is frequently meant to represent the percentage decrease in the value of the reference asset specified in the swap arrangement. For this type of arrangement, the swap buyer has transferred only the credit risk of the specified securities to the swap seller.

In a total return swap, one party (the total return payer) transfers the economic risks and rewards associated with an underlying asset to another counterparty (the total return receiver). The total return payer will make periodic payments to the total return receiver consisting of the coupons/interest from the underlying asset and, either periodically or at maturity of the swap, an amount equivalent to the appreciation in the market value of the underlying asset.

If the value of the reference asset depreciates in a total return swap, a payment for the change in the market value of the assets would typically be made by the total return receiver to the total return payer. In contrast to a credit default swap, a total return swap transfers the credit risk and the other market risks associated with the underlying asset. In this context, market risk is generally assumed to cover risks from changes in interest rate and equity returns but also can include other risks impacting the value of assets, such as liquidity risk.

The economic effect for a total return receiver is equivalent to that derived from owning the asset. The total return receiver, however, does not incur the direct costs of funding the purchase of the underlying asset. The total return receiver makes a payment to the total return payer to compensate the latter for the funding costs. This payment, sometimes referred to as the premium or fee, is the other leg of the swap and usually consists of a one- or three-month LIBOR-based (or some other floating rate index) payment plus or minus a spread. The spread above or below the referenced interest rate index will be determined by the relative credit quality of the two counterparties as well as any collateral called for from a counterparty as part of the swap arrangement. The premium paid by the total return receiver may be based upon a fixed rate of return.

17.8.3 Determining the Nature of an Embedded Derivative under *DIG B36*

Determining if a contract contains an embedded derivative and whether that embedded derivative must be bifurcated can be a complicated process and must be based upon the relevant facts and circumstances. Based upon *B36*, the typical MODCO and funds withheld reinsurance treaty contains an embedded derivative that must be bifurcated for GAAP reporting under *SFAS 133*.

Although *B36* concludes that the typical MODCO or funds withheld reinsurance treaty contains an embedded derivative that must be bifurcated for GAAP reporting, it does not specify the nature of the embedded derivative nor does it specify how that embedded derivative is to be measured. The general requirements of *SFAS 133* and other DIG pronouncements must be followed. Comments from the SEC staff indicated that at a minimum, the embedded derivative would be a credit default swap and in other cases the company might conclude that the embedded derivative is a total return swap.

A company will need to review each reinsurance treaty for compliance with *SFAS 133* and the related DIG issue statements. In addition to the specific guidance in paragraph 12, which establishes criteria under which an embedded derivative instrument must be separated from the host contract, a company should consult paragraph 13 when determining the nature of the embedded derivative.

Characterizing the embedded derivative as described in *B36* as a credit default swap would imply a derivative incorporating only credit risk. If the derivative were characterized as a total return swap it would imply a derivative incorporating both market and credit risk. As mentioned above, market risk is generally meant to include interest rate risk but can also include other risks impacting the value of assets.

The determination of whether the embedded derivative is credit only or total return is based on whether the interest rate risk is clearly and closely related to the host contract. Paragraph 13 of *SFAS 133*, addresses the issue of when interest rate risk is clearly and closely related to a debt host and provides the relevant criteria. Paragraph 13 states:

> ...an embedded derivative instrument in which the underlying is an interest rate or interest rate index that alters net interest payments that otherwise would be paid or received on an interest-bearing host contract is considered to be clearly and closely related to the host contract unless either of the following conditions exist:
>
> a. The hybrid instrument can contractually be settled in such a way that the investor (holder) would not recover *substantially all* of its initial recorded investment.
>
> b. The embedded derivative could at least double the investor's initial rate of return on the host contract and could also result in a rate of return that is at least twice what otherwise would be the market return for a contract that has the same terms as the host contract and that involves a debtor with a similar credit quality.

Making the determination of whether the interest rate risk is or is not clearly related to the debt host will depend on the particular facts and circumstances of the MODCO or funds withheld reinsurance arrangement.

If it is determined that the embedded derivative is a total return swap, deciding whether the notional total return swap in a MODCO treaty has a fixed or floating rate leg is directly related to the assumed nature of the host contract. The provisions of *SFAS 133* do not provide explicit guidance regarding whether a debt host contract is required to be floating-rate or fixed rate. *DIG B19* addresses the characteristics of a debt host contract. It states that:

> The characteristics of a debt host contract generally should be based on the stated or implied substantive terms of the hybrid instrument. Those terms may include a fixed-rate, floating rate, zero coupon, discount or premium, or some combination thereof. In the absence of stated or implied term, an entity may make its own determination of whether to account for the host as a fixed rate, floating rate, or zero coupon bond. That determination requires the applications of judgment, which is appropriate because the circumstances surrounding each hybrid instrument containing an embedded derivative may be different. That is, in the absence of stated or implied terms, it is appropriate to consider the features of the hybrid instrument, the issuer, and the market in which the instrument is issued, as well as other factors, in order to determine the characteristics of the debt host contract.

A reinsurer may conclude differently from the ceding company as to the nature of the embedded derivative and the host contract. There is no requirement that the ceding company and reinsurer have the same classification of the embedded derivative under *B36.*

17.8.4 Examples of Embedded Derivative Valuation

Methods used to estimate the value of the embedded derivative will depend on the nature of the derivative and the facts and circumstances of the particular reinsurance arrangement. Several techniques have been used in the industry. It is important that any technique be consistent with the provisions of *SFAS 133* and relevant *DIG*s.

The following examples will illustrate one technique for valuing the embedded derivative in MODCO treaties requiring bifurcation as described in *SFAS 133* and *DIG B36*. Only the ceding company's position will be considered.

For all of the examples, the value of the embedded derivative is zero at time zero in the models. This follows the requirement of *DIG B20* that all non-option embedded derivatives should have a value of zero at inception of the hybrid instrument. The examples also assume that the market value of any related assets equals the book value of those assets at time zero. In practice, any difference between the market and book value of the assets may impact the value of the embedded derivatives under the total return approaches.

17.8.4.1 Total Return Swap with Floating Rate Leg

The value of a swap at any point in time is the difference between the present values of the future net cash flows to be exchanged under the terms of the swap arrangement. This net present value may be positive or negative depending size of the future cash flows from each counterparty and whether the value of the swap is being determined from the perspective of one or another of the counterparties.

Table 17-29 starts with a block of ceded reserves under a MODCO treaty. A swap is constructed on the assumption that a total return is paid by the ceding company on assets equaling the outstanding reserves at any point in time. This parallels the MODCO arrangement with the total return being paid to the reinsurer as part of reinsurance reserve adjustment. A floating rate (based upon LIBOR) applied to the outstanding reserves is assumed to be received as part of the swap.

Table 17-29 also assumes that the expected total market return will be a level rate for each period. The value of the swap at any time is the present value of the net swap cash flows discounted at LIBOR. At time zero, the value of the swap is zero. In the Table 17-29 example, the expected value of the swap at later durations is a negative liability, or asset, to the ceding company.

Table 17-29
***DIG B36* Total Return Swap with Floating Rate Leg**
Value of Swap Based Upon Present Value of Net Cash Flows

	(1)	(2)	(3)	(4)	(5)	(6)	(7)	(8)
Year	**Persistency**	**Remaining Ceded Statutory Reserves BOP**	**Floating Rate (LIBOR)**	**Expected Total Market Return**	**Projected Total Return Swap Payments**	**Projected Floating Rate Swap Payments**	**Net Liability Cash Flows for Ceding Company**	**Swap Liability to Ceding Company at BOP**
1	0.90000	1,000,000	3.00%	3.230%	32,299	30,000	2,299	(0)
2	0.60000	900,000	3.25%	3.230%	29,069	29,250	(181)	(2,299)
3	0.30000	540,000	3.50%	3.230%	17,442	18,900	(1,458)	(2,194)
4	0.00000	162,000	3.75%	3.230%	5,233	6,075	(842)	(812)
5		-						-

Legend:
(1) Annual peresistency rate of ceded business.
(2) Remaining ceded reserves $(2)_0 = 1{,}000{,}000$; $(2)_t = (2)_{t-1} \times (1)_{t-1}$.
(3) LIBOR rate curve.
(4) Expected market returns on invested modco or funds withheld assets.
(5) Projected total return swap payments $(5)_t = (4)_t \times (2)_t$.
(6) Projected floating rate swap payments $(6)_t = (3)_t \times (2)_t$.
(7) Projected net cash flows for ceding company $(7)_t = (6)_t - (7)_t$.
(8) Swap Liability at beginning of period $(8)_t = [(8)_{t+1} + (7)_t] / [(1 + (3)_t]$.

A practical approach to valuing the total return swap with a floating rate leg under *B36* is to assume that the value of the swap is the change in the fair value of the assets in the portfolio supporting the MODCO reserves but with the change in value due to any principal payments made during the measurement period being ignored. Table 17-30 estimates this market value of assets as the present values (at LIBOR) of principal payments equal to the remaining change in reserves and of total return payments equal to an assumed return times the outstanding reserves. This present value is then increased by the value of principal payments made since the last valuation date.

The values derived in Table 17-30 for the value of the swap are also still consistent with the principle of valuing a swap as the present value of the net cash flows as previously shown in Table 17-29.

Table 17-30
***DIG B36* Total Return Swap with Floating Rate Leg**
Value of Swap Based Upon Change in Market Value of Assets Paying Total Return

Year	(1) Remaining Ceded Statutory Reserves BOP	(2) Change in Statutory Reserves (Payment of Principal)	(3) Floating Rate (LIBOR)	(4) Expected Total Market Return	(5) Market Value of Assets at BOP	(6) Market Value of Assets at EOP before Principal Payment	(7) Change in Market Value Prior to Reset	(8) Swap Liability to Ceding Company at EOP
1	1,000,000	100,000	3.00%	3.230%	1,000,000	997,701	(2,299)	(2,299)
2	900,000	360,000	3.25%	3.230%	897,701	897,806	106	(2,194)
3	540,000	378,000	3.50%	3.230%	537,806	539,188	1,382	(812)
4	162,000	162,000	3.75%	3.230%	161,188	162,000	812	0

Legend:
Assets are assumed to have principal payments equal to change in statutory reserves.

(1) Remaining ceded reserves from Table 17-29.
(2) Change in reserves $(2)_t = (1)_t - (1)_{t+1}$.
(3) LIBOR rate curve.
(4) Expected market returns on invested modco or funds withheld assets.
(5) Market value of assets at BOP $(5)_t = [(5)_{t+1} + (2)_t + \{(4)_t \times (1)_t\}] / [1 + (3)_t]$.
(6) Market value of assets at EOP before principal repayment $(6)_t = (5)_{t+1} + (2)_t$.
(7) Change in market value before reset $(7)_t = (5)_t - (6)_t$.
(8) Swap liability to ceding company $(8)_t = (8)_{t-1} + (7)_t$.

Although the cash flows exchanged in a total return swap don't involve the payment of principal on any obligation, the valuation of swaps will sometime use values that assume that principal amounts are being exchanged by the counterparties as well as the specified investment returns. This technique can sometimes makes it easier to value the swap and assumes that the value of the exchanged principal payments nets to zero any final swap value.

Table 17-30 is based upon the approach that the swap can be viewed as the exchange of cash flows each including a principal payment. However, only the total return leg has been shown (i.e., the total value of the supporting assets). The floating rate leg is not shown because its value does not change between measurement dates when principal payments are ignored, which occurs because the interest rate used to value the swap is the same as the rate paid on the floating rate leg.

The floating rate approach implies that the host contract is a floating rate instrument. The host contract has principal payments equal to the change in statutory reserves. The value of this floating rate debt after any principal payment is made is equal to the outstanding principal payments, i.e., the remaining reserves.

Table 17-31 shows how the swap would be evaluated if the market value changed at the end of year two.

Table 17-31
***DIG B36* Total Return Swap with Floating Rate Leg**
Value of Swap Based Upon Change in Market Value of Assets Paying Total Return
Change in Market Return at End of Year Two

Year	(1) Remaining Ceded Statutory Reserves BOP	(2) Change in Statutory Reserves (Payment of Principal)	(3) Floating Rate (LIBOR)	(4) Expected Total Market Return	(5) Market Value of Assets at BOP	(6) Market Value of Assets at EOP before Principal Payment	(7) Change in Market Value Prior to Reset	(8) Swap Liability to Ceding Company at EOP
1	1,000,000	100,000	3.00%	3.230%	1,000,000	997,701	(2,299)	(2,299)
2	900,000	360,000	3.25%	3.230%	897,701	896,260	(1,441)	(3,740)
3	540,000	378,000	3.50%	3.000%	536,260	538,829	2,569	(1,171)
4	162,000	162,000	3.75%	3.000%	160,829	162,000	1,171	0

Legend:
Data for columns (1) to (5), years 1-2 and for columns (6) to (8), year 1: from Table 17-30.
Assets are assumed to have principal payments equal to change in statutory reserves.

(1) Remaining ceded reserves from Table 17-29.
(2) Change in reserves $(2)_t = (1)_t - (1)_{t+1}$.
(3) LIBOR rate curve.
(4) Expected market returns on invested modco or funds withheld assets.
(5) Market value of assets at BOP $(5)_t = [(5)_{t+1} + (2)_t + \{(4)_t \times (1)_t\}] / [1 + (3)_t]$.
(6) Market value of assets at EOP before principal repayment $(6)_t = (5)_{t+1} + (2)_t$.
(7) Change in market value before reset $(7)_t = (5)_t - (6)_t$.
(8) Swap liability to ceding company $(8)_t = (8)_{t-1} + (7)_t$.

The swap value identified in Tables 17-29 to 17-31 for the ceding company will be held in addition to any of the other accounting entries. In addition, if the block of business held is accounted for under *SFAS 97*, the change in the value of the swap should be recognized in the EGP used for DAC amortization.

Valuing a total return swap by using the change in the value of the supporting assets is based upon the assumption that the expected future cash flows from those assets reflect a reasonable approximation to the implied total return swap cash flows and the repayment of the notional principal payments from the host contract. This may not always be the case, and there may be other ways to analyze a swap structure. Companies should let any swap valuation under *B36* be guided by the relevant facts and circumstances.

17.8.4.2 Total Return Swap with Fixed Rate Leg

The swap from Tables 17-29 to 17-31 can also be analyzed as a total return swap with a fixed rate leg. Table 17-32 shows how this swap would be initially analyzed and a fixed rate leg would be determined. In this example, the fixed rate is such that the present value of the assumed host contract principal payments (the change in reserves) plus the fixed interest rate on the opening reserves in each year, discounted at LIBOR, equals the initial reserve balance at time zero.

Table 17-32
***DIG B36* Total Return Swap with Fixed Rate Leg**
Determination of Fixed Rate at Initiation of the Swap

Year	(1) Remaining Ceded Statutory Reserves BOP	(2) Change in Statutory Reserves (Payment of Principal)	(3) Floating Rate (LIBOR)	(4) Market Value of Assets at $t = 0$	(5) Implied Fixed Rated	(6) Expected Value of Fixed Rate Leg at BOP
1	1,000,000	100,000	3.00%	1,000,000	3.230%	1,000,000
2	900,000	360,000	3.25%		3.230%	897,701
3	540,000	378,000	3.50%		3.230%	537,806
4	162,000	162,000	3.75%		3.230%	161,188

Legend:
Assets are assumed to have principal payments equal to change in statutory reserves.

(1) Remaining ceded reserves from Table 17-29.
(2) Change in reserves $(2)_t = (1)_t - (1)_{t+1}$.
(3) LIBOR rate curve.
(4) Market value of assets at beginning of year 1.
(5) Implied fixed rate (5) such that $(1)_1 = 1{,}000{,}000 = \text{Sum}\ [(2)_t + \{(5) \times (1)_t\}] / [1 + (3)_t]$ across all t.
(6) Expected value of fixed rate leg $(6)_t = [(6)_{t+1} + (2)_t + \{(5)_t \times (1)_t\}] / [1 + (3)_t]$.

Table 17-33 shows the value of the swap if the market values of the supporting assets from Table 17-31 occur. The approach of assuming a principal repayment for both legs is also used in Table 17-31. Otherwise, there are no changes in expected reserve levels or LIBOR rates. If the reserve levels or expected LIBOR changed, the company would need to revalue the fixed leg.

Table 17-33
***DIG B36* Total Return Swap with Fixed Rate Leg**
Value of Swap Based Upon Difference in Value of Each Leg
Change in Market Return at End of Year Two

Year	(1) Remaining Ceded Statutory Reserves BOP	(2) Change in Statutory Reserves (Payment of Principal)	(3) Floating Rate (LIBOR)	(4) Market Value of Assets at BOP	(5) Implied Fixed Rated	(6) Value of Fixed Rate Leg at BOP	(7) Swap Liability to Ceding at EOP
1	1,000,000	100,000	3.00%	1,000,000	3.230%	1,000,000	-
2	900,000	360,000	3.25%	897,701	3.230%	897,701	(1,547)
3	540,000	378,000	3.50%	536,260	3.230%	537,806	(359)
4	162,000	162,000	3.75%	160,829	3.230%	161,188	-

Legend:
Assets are assumed to have principal payments equal to change in statutory reserves.

(1) Remaining ceded reserves from Table 17-29.
(2) Change in reserves $(2)_t = (1)_t - (1)_{t+1}$.
(3) LIBOR rate curve.
(4) Market value of assets at beginning of year from Table 17-30, column 5.
(5) Implied fixed rate from Table 17-32, column 5.
(6) Value of fixed rate leg $(6)_t = [(6)_{t+1} + (2)_t + \{(5)_t \times (1)_t\}] / [1 + (3)_t]$.
(7) Swap liability to ceding company at end of year $(6)_t = (4)_{t+1} - (6)_{t+1}$.

The fixed leg approach for the total return swap in Table 17-33 appears to result in smaller values than the floating rate approach in Table 17-31. In general, it can be expected a fixed rate approach will result in smaller and less volatile results than a floating rate approach. However, the fixed rate approach will require that both the supporting assets be tracked and the value of fixed rate leg be reestimated regularly.

The fixed rate assumption implies that the host contract is a fixed rate instrument. This host contract has principal payments equal to the change in statutory reserves. As with the floating rate host, the value of this fixed rate debt after any principal payment is made is equal to the outstanding principal payments, i.e., the remaining reserves.

As with the total return swap approach, if the block of business held is accounted for under *SFAS 97*, the change in the value of the swap should be recognized in the EGP used for DAC amortization. This swap value will be held in addition to any other accounting entries. The same warning made above in the discussion of the fixed rate approach applies here as well: the supporting assets need to reflect a reasonable approximation to the expected total return and principal payments implied in the *B36* swap structure.

17.8.4.3 Credit Default Swap

There are a large number of pricing models that have been developed to estimate the value of credit default swaps. A company may want to utilize one of those models if it has concluded that an embedded derivative requiring bifurcation under *B36* is a credit default swap. Some of these models incorporate a large number of assumptions, and in practice many of these assumptions will be calibrated in some fashion to current market conditions for other derivatives or securities.

The following examples will show a very simple approach that has been used in practice to estimate the value of credit default swaps for MODCO or funds withheld reinsurance arrangements. The analysis would normally be performed for each asset supporting the MODCO or funds withheld reserves but the following assumes a single bond structure to support the reinsured reserves.

Table 17-34 shows the determination of the credit default swap at initiation of the reinsurance. As with the other swap examples, the value of the initial credit default swap to the ceding company is zero. Although not shown in Table 17-34, it is implicitly equal to the present value of a premium (normally a fixed interest cost in each period) less the present value of the expected credit losses.

As part of the initial analysis in Table 17-34, there is a spread of market yield to maturity over a risk-free Treasury rate defined. The market value of the assets is based upon the market yield. Table 17-34 defines the initial credit spread on a yield to maturity basis.

Table 17-34
***DIG B36* Credit Default Swap**
Value at Initiation of Swap
Supporting Assets are Bonds Purchased at Par

Year	(1) Remaining Ceded Statutory Reserves BOP	(2) Change in Statutory Reserves (Payment of Principal)	(3) Treasury Yield to Maturity (YTM)	(4) Credit Spread	(5) Market Yield to Maturity (YTM)	(6) Market Value of Bonds with Initial Market YTM at BOP	(7) Market Value of Bonds at BOP	(8) Liability Value of Swap to Ceding Company
1	1,000,000	100,000	2.90%	0.330%	3.230%	1,000,000	1,000,000	-
2	900,000	360,000				900,000		
3	540,000	378,000				540,000		
4	162,000	162,000				162,000		

Legend:
Assets are assumed to have principal payments equal to change in statutory reserves.

(1) Remaining ceded reserves from Table 17-29.
(2) Change in reserves $(2)_t = (1)_t - (1)_{t+1.}$
(3) Current Treasury Yield to Maturity (YTM).
(4) Current Spread of Market YTM over Treasury YTM.
(5) Market YTM $(5)_1 = (3)_1 + (4)_{1.}$
(6) Market Value of Bonds with Initial Market YTM $(6)_t = [(2)_t + (6)_{t+1} + \{(5)_1 \times (1)_t\}] / [1 + (5)_1]$.
(7) Market Value of Bonds $(7)_1 = (6)_{1.}$
(8) Value of Credit Default Swap to Ceding Company $(8)_1 = (7)_1 - (6)_{1.}$

Table 17-34 and Table 17-35 value the credit default swap as the difference between the current market value of the related bonds less the same bonds revalued with a restated yield. At time zero there is no difference between these values.

At subsequent points in time the restated yield is the then-current treasury rate plus the initial credit spread. The current market value of the bonds will likely be different than the value of the bonds revalued with the restated yield.

Table 17-35 shows that the difference between these two assets values is a negative liability to the ceding company. The sign of this liability to the ceding company is consistent with the results in the examples above based upon total return swaps.

Table 17-35
***DIG B36* Credit Default Swap**
Value at End of Year 2

Year	(1) Remaining Ceded Statutory Reserves BOP	(2) Change in Statutory Reserves (Payment of Principal)	(3) Treasury YTM	(4) Initial Credit Spread	(5) Restated Market YTM	(6) Market Value of Bonds with Restated Initial Market YTM at BOP	(7) Market Value of Bonds at BOP	(8) Liability Value of Swap to Ceding Company at EOP
1	1,000,000	100,000						
2	900,000	360,000						(1,052)
3	540,000	378,000	3.30%	0.33%	3.630%	537,312	536,260	(546)
4	162,000	162,000				161,375	160,829	-

Legend:
Assets are assumed to have principal payments equal to change in statutory reserves.

(1) Remaining ceded reserves from Table 17-29.
(2) Change in reserves $(2)_t = (1)_t - (1)_{t+1}$.
(3) Current Treasury Yield to Maturity (YTM).
(4) Initial Spread of Market YTM over Treasury YTM = Table 17-34 Column (4).
(5) Market YTM $(5)_3 = (3)_3 + (4)_3$.
(6) Market Value of Bonds with Initial Market YTM $(6)_t = [(2)_t + (6)_{t+1} + \{(5)_3 \times (1)_t\}] / [1 + (5)_3]$.
(7) Market Value of Bonds $(7)_t$ = Table 17-33 Column $(6)_t$.
(8) Value of Credit Default Swap to Ceding Company $(8)_t = (7)_{t+1} - (6)_{t+1}$.

The example in Table 17-35 does not provide for a direct calculation of a credit default swap but instead assumes that the value of the swap is the difference between the current market value of a bond and that same bond revalued with a yield equal to the sum of the current risk-free Treasury rate and an initial credit spread.

The difference between the two bond values in Table 17-35 is the present value of the change in the expected value of the credit default losses. The approach in Table 17-35 also makes the simplifying assumption that the initial swap will have a value of approximately zero at all durations as long as the market does not change its value of the expected credit losses in the bond. Under these assumptions, the change in the expected value of the credit default losses is the value of the total credit default swap.

As with the floating rate leg approach, if the block of business held is accounted for under *SFAS 97*, the change in the value of the swap should be recognized in the EGP used for DAC amortization. The swap value will be held in addition to any other accounting entries.

17.9 Accounting for Special Aspects of Reinsurance

17.9.1 Experience Rating

The effects of experience refunds should be considered in all GAAP assets and liabilities. For example, if a YRT reinsurance contract covering universal life had an experience rating provision, the reinsurance costs, both historic and prospective, should include the actual or an estimate of the experience rating refunds.

17.9.2 Recapture

Recapture provisions, although a common provision is many reinsurance treaties, are generally not specifically provided for in GAAP liabilities or DAC. If the effect of possible recapture is not a consideration in the determination of GAAP liabilities and assets for reinsurance, there would generally be an accounting gain or loss at the time of recapture. If the effect of these gains or losses is expected to be material, the recaptures should be contemplated in the determination of GAAP liabilities and assets as though the recaptures had the effect of an additional policy termination.

17.10 Reinsurance Assumed

Except for the qualification for reinsurance accounting, paragraph 7 in *SFAS 113* does not "address or change the existing practice in accounting for reinsurance assumed, other than to provide guidance on indemnification against loss or liability relating to insurance risk in paragraphs 8-13…" For most reinsurers, accounting for reinsurance assumed under GAAP is no different than accounting for direct insurance coverages and is governed by the GAAP accounting standards applicable the coverages being assumed.

The reference to paragraphs 8-13 in paragraph 7 of *SFAS 113* requires that the ceding company and reinsurer use the same methods to analyze risk transfer and suggests that they should each reach the same conclusion as to whether a specific reinsurance treaty passes sufficient risk to be accounted for as reinsurance under *SFAS 113*. The GAAP assumptions chosen by the reinsurer (such as mortality or interest) are not expected to exactly match the ceding company's assumptions.

Prior to the *SOP 03-1*, there was no specific requirement for a reinsurer to classify reinsurance as an insurance or investment contract. The classification as insurance or investment contract by a reinsurer is to be performed at the inception of the reinsurance and is to follow the requirements of paragraph 24 and 25 of the *SOP*. Once this classification is established at inception, it does not change for the remaining lifetime of the reinsurance.

Paragraphs 24 and 25 of the *SOP* provide for additional guidance in testing whether a reinsurance contract meets the conditions for reinsurance accounting as under *SFAS 113*. For example, if a reinsurance contract has nominal risk from mortality or morbidity as determined under the test of significance in paragraph 25 of the *SOP*, then the reinsurance contract is deemed to be an investment contract and is not eligible for reinsurance accounting. This would be the conclusion even if the reinsurance contract otherwise appeared to pass risk under *SFAS 113*.

17.11 Recoverability and Loss Recognition

When applying the requirements in *SFAS 60*, *SFAS 97*, and *SFAS 120* for recoverability and loss recognition, the effects of reinsurance must be recognized. See Chapters 4–11 for specific applications.

Chapter 18 Other Topics

This chapter deals with topics important to the preparation financial statements according to GAAP but whose content is too concise to merit its own chapter. These topics comprise deferred taxes, riders, fair value, demutualizations & mutual holding companies, surplus notes and materiality.

18.1 Deferred Taxes

18.1.1 Differences Between Taxable Income and GAAP Income

The taxable income of a corporation for federal income tax purposes is determined under the *Internal Revenue Code*. Insurance companies are taxed as corporations and thus are subject to the general corporate tax provisions of the code. However, the code also includes specific provisions for the determination of insurance company taxable income. These specific provisions are set forth in Part I (life insurance companies) and Part II (property and casualty insurance companies) of Subchapter L.

In general, the starting point for the determination of insurance company taxable income is statutory gain from operations as set forth in the NAIC Annual Statement. However, Subchapter L of the code requires numerous adjustments to statutory income in determining taxable income, such as the following:

- Life insurance reserves must be determined under federally prescribed standards (Code Section 807).

- A life insurance company's policyholder dividend reserve is generally not deductible until the liability to make a payment to a given policyholder is fixed and determinable (Code Section 808). A portion of a mutual life insurance company's policyholder dividends may not be deductible at all (Code Section 809).

- A portion of policy acquisition expenses on "specified insurance contracts" must be capitalized and amortized (Code Section 848). These capitalized expenses are often referred to as "tax DAC."

- Certain unpaid losses and loss adjustment expenses are deductible only on a discounted basis (Code Section 846). Life insurance companies may not deduct unpaid loss adjustment expenses at all until they become fixed and determinable.

- A portion of interest income on state and municipal bonds is excluded from taxable income.

- A deduction is allowed for a portion of the dividends received on stocks of other corporations.

- Other accrued liabilities (e.g., deferred compensation, liability for post-retirement benefits) may not be deductible until paid.

- A net operating loss carryback or carryforward is allowed.

The determination of insurance company income for GAAP financial accounting and reporting purposes also differs from that for NAIC statutory purposes. Major differences between GAAP and statutory income include the following:

- Certain policy acquisition expenses are deferred and amortized against future income for GAAP purposes. These expenses are generally referred to as DAC.

- Different assumptions are used in determining life insurance reserves for GAAP purposes than for statutory purposes.

- Deferred and uncollected premiums generally are frequently recast as liability offsets for GAAP purposes.

- The concept of an interest maintenance reserve, which facilitates the realization of capital gains and losses, does not exist under GAAP.

- Provisions for possible asset default are not established in an asset valuation reserve by formula but rather considered and adjusted on an asset-by-asset basis.

In addition, unrealized gains and losses attributable to changes in market interest rates generally are currently recognized in the shareholders' equity section of the GAAP balance sheet.

18.1.2 *SFAS 109*

SFAS 109, "Accounting for Income Taxes," establishes standards of GAAP financial accounting and reporting for income taxes that are currently payable and for the tax consequences of:

- Revenues, expenses, gains, or losses that are included in taxable income in an earlier or later year than the year in which they are recognized in GAAP income (e.g., the calculation of life insurance reserves)

- Other events that create differences between the tax bases of assets and liabilities and their amounts for GAAP purposes (e.g., an acquisition of another company)

- Operating loss or tax credit carrybacks for refunds of taxes paid in prior years and carryforwards to reduce taxes payable in future years.

As stated in *SFAS 109*, one objective of accounting for income taxes is to recognize the amount of taxes payable or refundable for the current year. A second objective, the one which *SFAS 109* principally addresses, is to recognize deferred tax liabilities and assets for the future tax consequences of events that have been recognized in the company's GAAP financial statements or in its tax returns. To implement these objectives, the following basic principles are generally applied in GAAP accounting for income taxes:

- A current tax liability or asset is recognized for the estimated taxes payable or refundable on tax returns for the current year.

- A deferred tax liability is recognized for the estimated future tax effects attributable to temporary differences and to loss or credit carryforwards.

- The measurement of current and deferred tax liabilities and assets is based on provisions of enacted tax law; the effects of future changes in tax laws or rates are not anticipated.

- The measurement of deferred tax assets is reduced, if necessary, by the amount of any tax benefits that, based on available evidence, are not expected to be realized.

This chapter provides an overview of the major concepts of *SFAS 109*.

18.1.3 Glossary

The following (in alphabetic order) are definitions of certain terms or phrases used in *SFAS 109*; they are key to understanding the nature of accounting for income taxes.

- *Carrybacks.* Deductions or credits that cannot be utilized on the tax return during a year that may be carried back to reduce taxable income or taxes payable in a prior year.

- *Carryforwards.* Deductions or credits that cannot be utilized on the tax return during a year that may be carried forward to reduce taxable income or taxes payable in a future year.

- *Current tax expense or benefit.* The amount of income taxes paid or payable (or refundable) for a year as determined by applying the provisions of the enacted tax law to the taxable income or excess of deductions over revenues for that year.

- *Deductible temporary difference.* A temporary difference that results in tax deductible amounts in future years when the related asset is recovered or the related liability is settled. See also *temporary difference.*

- *Deferred tax asset.* The deferred tax consequences attributable to deductible temporary differences. A deferred tax asset is reduced by a valuation allowance if, based on the weight of evidence available, it is more likely than not that some portion or all of a deferred tax asset will not be realized.

- *Deferred tax consequences.* The future effects on income taxes as measured by the applicable enacted tax rate and provisions of the enacted tax law resulting from temporary differences and carryforwards at the end of the current year.

- *Deferred tax expense or benefit.* The change during the year in the company's deferred tax liabilities and assets. This expense or benefit is allocated among continuing operations, discontinued operations, extraordinary items, and items charged or credited directly to shareholders' equity.

- *Deferred tax liability.* The deferred tax consequences attributable to taxable temporary differences.

- *Income taxes.* Domestic and foreign federal, state, and local taxes based on income.

- *Income tax expense (benefit).* The sum of current tax expense (benefit) and deferred tax expense (benefit).

- *Taxable income.* The excess of taxable revenues over tax deductible expenses and exemptions for the year as defined by the governmental taxing authority.

- *Taxable temporary difference.* A temporary difference that results in taxable amounts in future years when the related asset is recovered or the related liability is settled. See also *temporary difference.*

- *Tax-planning strategy.* An action (including elections for tax purposes) that meets certain criteria and that would be implemented to realize a tax benefit for an operating loss or tax credit carryforward before it expires. Tax-planning strategies are considered when assessing the need for and amount of a valuation allowance for deferred tax assets.

- *Temporary difference.* A difference between the tax basis of an asset or liability and its reported amount in the GAAP financial statements that will result in taxable or tax-deductible amounts in future years when the reported amount of the asset or liability is recovered or settled, respectively. Some events recognized in financial statements do not have tax consequences. Certain revenues are exempt from taxation, and certain expenses are not deductible. Events that do not have tax consequences do not give rise to temporary differences.

18.1.4 The Asset and Liability Method

SFAS 109 adopts the asset and liability method of accounting for deferred taxes. That is, *SFAS 109* is concerned with the recognition of deferred tax assets and liabilities. Under this method the focus of accounting for income taxes is on the balance sheet. The objective of *SFAS 109* is to recognize deferred tax assets and liabilities for the *expected* future tax consequences of events that have been recognized in the financial statements or tax returns. Deferred tax assets and liabilities are calculated at the beginning and end of the year; the change in the sum of the deferred tax asset, valuation allowance, and deferred tax liability during the year generally is recognized as deferred tax expense or benefit. Deferred tax assets and liabilities are adjusted for changes in tax rates and other changes in the tax law when such changes are enacted.

The following example shows the application of bond discount.

- Insurance Company A acquires a bond with a par value of $100,000 for $90,000 on January 1, 2000. During 2000, Company A collects $6,000 of interest on the bond and records $1,000 of bond discount for financial reporting purposes. For federal income tax purposes, no bond discount is recognized. At December 31, 2000, the bond has a carrying amount of $91,000 for financial reporting purposes and a tax basis of $90,000. The $1,000 difference between the financial statement carrying amount and the tax basis of the bond will result in future taxable income when the financial statement carrying amount of $91,000 is recovered.

- Assuming that there are no other differences between the financial statement carrying amounts and the tax bases of assets and liabilities, and that the tax rate for 2000 and all future years is 35%, Company A would record a deferred tax liability of $350 (35% of $1,000) at December 31, 2000.

The following steps would be applied in the tax calculation under *SFAS 109*.

1. A current tax liability or asset and current tax expense or benefit are recognized for the estimated amount of income taxes payable or refundable based on the tax returns for the current year.

2. All temporary differences (i.e., differences between the financial statement carrying amounts and tax bases of assets and liabilities that will result in future taxable or deductible amounts) are identified and accumulated for each tax jurisdiction. Those temporary differences are segregated as *taxable* temporary differences (temporary differences that will result in taxable amounts in future years) and *deductible* temporary differences (temporary differences that will result in deductible amounts in future years).

3. Operating loss and tax credit carryforwards for tax purposes are identified.

4. A deferred tax liability is recognized for taxable temporary differences based on the enacted tax rate that is expected to apply when those differences are expected to reverse.

5. A deferred tax asset initially is recognized for deductible temporary differences and operating loss and tax credit carryforwards based on the enacted tax rate that is expected to apply when those differences are expected to reverse.

6. The potential deferred tax asset (step 5) is evaluated to determine whether that potential asset should be reduced by a valuation allowance. A valuation allowance is recognized to reduce that potential deferred tax asset if, based on an evaluation of all available evidence, it is *more likely than not* (i.e., a level of likelihood that is more than 50%) that all or some portion of that potential deferred tax asset will not be realized. The valuation allowance should reduce that potential deferred tax asset to the amount that *more likely than not* will be realized. The valuation allowance is based on the total potential deferred tax asset (the total amount calculated in step 5) and *not* on the net deferred tax asset (i.e., the deferred tax asset net of the deferred tax liability calculated in step 4).

7. The change in the sum of the deferred tax asset, valuation allowance, and deferred tax liability during the year is generally recognized as deferred tax expense or benefit.

8. If the balance sheet segregates current and noncurrent assets and liabilities, the deferred tax asset and liability are classified as current or noncurrent based on the classification of the related asset or liability for financial reporting purposes. The valuation allowance is allocated between the current and noncurrent deferred tax asset on a pro-rata basis.

A second example in Section 18.1.17 provides a simple illustration of the application of these steps to the tax calculation under *SFAS 109*.

18.1.5 Temporary Differences

Under *SFAS 109*, deferred tax assets and liabilities are recognized for temporary differences, i.e., those differences between the tax bases of assets and liabilities and their reported amounts in the financial statements that will result in taxable or deductible amounts in future years when the financial statement carrying amounts of the assets and liabilities are recovered and settled. Temporary differences are identified as *taxable* temporary differences (differences that will result in future taxable amounts) and *deductible* temporary differences (differences that will result in future deductible amounts).

Although the term *permanent difference* is not used in *SFAS 109*, the concept of permanent differences under *SFAS 109* is limited to events recognized in the financial statements that do not have tax consequences, such as tax-exempt interest. Those types of permanent differences will continue to affect the calculation of current tax expense under *SFAS 109*.

In most cases, the identification of all temporary differences requires the development of a tax-basis balance sheet. Temporary differences are then identified by comparing the financial statement carrying amounts of assets and liabilities with their tax bases.

18.1.6 Recognition of Deferred Tax Assets and Liabilities

A deferred tax liability is recognized for virtually all taxable temporary differences. A deferred tax asset initially is recognized for virtually all deductible temporary differences and operating loss and tax credit carryforwards.

SFAS 109 provides for certain specific exceptions to the basic recognition principle. For example, *SFAS 109* continues to apply the "indefinite reversal" criterion of *APB Opinion 23* to certain temporary differences, such as the policyholders' surplus account of life insurance companies that accumulated in taxable years prior to 1984. In addition, *SFAS 109* indicates that certain basis differences should not be treated as temporary differences if it is expected that the asset will be recovered or the liability will be settled without tax consequences. An example of the latter is the excess of a parent company's investment in the stock of a domestic subsidiary over its tax basis if the tax law provides a means to recover the investment tax-free and the parent company expects that it will ultimately use that means.

The likelihood of realizing the tax benefits related to a potential deferred tax asset is evaluated and a valuation allowance is recognized to reduce that deferred tax asset, if it is *more likely than not* that all or some portion of the deferred tax asset will not be realized. The remaining deferred tax asset, net of the valuation allowance, represents the portion of the deferred tax benefits that *more likely than not* will be realized. *More likely than not* is intended to mean a level of likelihood that is more than 50%.

18.1.7 Measurement of Deferred Tax Assets and Liabilities

Deferred tax assets and liabilities are measured under *SFAS 109* by using the enacted tax rate that is expected to apply to taxable income in the periods in which the deferred tax asset or liability is expected to be realized or settled. The effects of future changes in tax rates are not anticipated. When graduated tax rates are expected to have significant effects on future taxes, an average tax rate applicable to the estimated average annual taxable income is used to measure deferred tax assets and liabilities. Special deductions in future years, such as the small life insurance company deduction, generally are not anticipated in the measurement of deferred tax assets and liabilities under *SFAS 109*.

In addition, *SFAS 109* does not permit discounting future tax consequences in the measurement of deferred tax assets and liabilities. Thus, for example, the deferred tax liability in the first example is measured at 35% of $1,000, or $350, even though that $350 may not be paid until many years in the future. The implementation issues associated with discounting income taxes are numerous and complex. These issues include the selection of the discount rate(s) and determination of the future years in which amounts will become taxable or deductible. If deferred income taxes were discounted, a detailed analysis of the future reversals of temporary differences would be routinely required. This need for scheduling was a frequent criticism of *SFAS 96*, which was superseded by *SFAS 109*.

18.1.8 Recognition of Valuation Allowance on Deferred Tax Assets

The amount of the valuation allowance for deferred tax assets under *SFAS 109* may range from zero to the full amount of the potential deferred tax asset, not just the net deferred tax asset (net of any deferred tax liability). Although potential offsetting of deductible temporary differences against taxable temporary differences should be considered in the determination of the valuation allowance, offsetting deferred tax liabilities does not provide justification for recognizing a deferred tax asset (not recognizing a valuation allowance) if the future taxable and deductible amounts cannot be offset within the carryback and carryforward period under applicable tax law.

Realization of tax benefits of deductible temporary differences and operating loss or tax credit carryforwards depends on sufficient taxable income of an appropriate character within the carryback and carryforward periods. Sources of taxable income that may allow for the realization of those tax benefits are:

1. Taxable income in the current year or prior years that is available through carryback (potential recovery of taxes paid for the current year or prior years),

2. Future taxable income that will result from the reversal of existing taxable temporary differences (potential offsetting of deferred tax liabilities),

3. Future taxable income, exclusive of the reversal of existing temporary differences, that is generated by future operations.

In addition, tax-planning strategies may be available to accelerate taxable income or deductions, change the character of taxable income or deductions, or switch from tax-exempt to taxable investments so that there is sufficient taxable income of the appropriate character and in the appropriate periods to allow for realization of the tax benefits. The term character refers to whether income or loss is ordinary or capital in nature. Premiums and investment income are ordinary income, gain on the sale of a bond is capital income. Character is important because, while an ordinary loss may be offset against ordinary income or capital gain, a capital loss may be offset against capital gain income only.

A valuation allowance is required to reduce the potential deferred tax asset when it is *more likely than not* that all or some portion of the potential deferred tax asset will not be realized because of the lack of sufficient taxable income. All available evidence, both positive and negative, needs to be identified and considered in determining whether it is *more likely than not* that all or some portion of the deferred tax asset will not be realized. In applying the *more likely than not* criterion, positive evidence of sufficient quality and quantity must exist to counteract any negative evidence to support a conclusion that, based on the weight of all available evidence, a valuation allowance is not needed. The weight given to the potential effect of negative and positive evidence should be commensurate with the extent to which it can be objectively verified.

18.1.9 *APB Opinion 23* Differences

SFAS 109 revised and eliminated, on a prospective basis, the exceptions in *APB Opinion 23* to comprehensive recognition of deferred taxes on temporary differences related to undistributed earnings of *domestic* subsidiaries and *domestic* corporate joint ventures that arise in fiscal years beginning after December 15, 1992. The FASB decided to retain the exception to comprehensive recognition of deferred taxes for temporary differences related to undistributed earnings of *foreign* subsidiaries and *foreign* corporate joint ventures that meet the indefinite reversal criterion in *APB Opinion 23*. In addition, *SFAS 109* extends the exception to comprehensive recognition of deferred taxes to the entire amount of a temporary difference related to an investment in the stock of a *foreign* subsidiary or *foreign* corporate joint ventures without regard to the underlying causes.

Under pre-1984 tax law, life insurance companies were allowed to defer certain income into a policyholders' surplus account or (PSA). Amounts generally were subtracted from the PSA only if the life company made excessive distributions to shareholders or if its premiums or reserves fell below certain levels. A subtraction from the PSA resulted in taxable income to the life insurance company, the so-called Phase III tax. The Tax Reform Act of 1984 froze the balance of all PSAs at their December 31, 1983 levels but continued the rules for subtractions from the PSA.

Because subtractions from the PSA generally are within the control of the life insurance company, the indefinite reversal criterion of *APB Opinion 23* provided that no deferred tax liability need be established with respect to a PSA balance unless it becomes apparent that it will be brought into taxable income in the foreseeable future. *SFAS 109* continues this exception.

18.1.10 Changes in Tax Laws or Rates

Under the asset and liability method of accounting for income taxes, deferred tax assets and liabilities represent taxes to be recovered or settled in the future. Accordingly, deferred tax assets and liabilities are adjusted under *SFAS 109* to reflect the effects of enacted changes in tax rates or other provisions of the tax law. Future changes in tax laws or rates are not anticipated. For example, if it is anticipated that the corporate tax rate will be 30% instead of 35% when a taxable temporary difference reverses in the future, the deferred tax liability is measured by using the 35% rate. However, if a future corporate tax rate cut were actually passed by Congress and signed by the President and if such lower rates were expected to apply when an existing temporary difference reverse, then the deferred tax asset or liability related to such temporary difference would be measured at the lower tax rate. The effects of enacted changes in tax laws or rates are charged or credited to income from continuing operations as part of deferred tax expense or benefit of the period in which the changes are enacted.

The tax law allows a special deduction to a *small life insurance company* (generally, a company's whose assets (plus those of its affiliates) are less than $500 million). This small-life-insurance company deduction is equal to 60% of the first $3 million of taxable income and phases out ratably between $3 and $15 million of taxable income. *SFAS 109* provides that the tax benefit of the small life insurance company deduction should not be anticipated for purposes of offsetting a deferred tax liability for taxable temporary differences. Thus, even though a life company expects to be able to claim the small company deduction when a taxable temporary difference reverses, it must establish the deferred tax liability using the higher corporate tax rate. On the other hand, a valuation allowance may be needed against a small life company's deferred tax asset to reflect the fact that deductible temporary differences may not be realizable at the higher corporate rate.

18.1.11 Alternative Tax Systems

SFAS 109 indicates that the tax rate used in the deferred tax calculation for U.S. federal income tax purposes should be based on the regular tax system, and a potential deferred tax asset should be recognized for any available alternative minimum tax credit carryforward. That potential deferred tax asset should be reduced, if necessary, by a valuation allowance.

Scheduling the reversal of temporary differences under the alternative minimum tax system and calculating the minimum tax effects of the net taxable or deductible amount scheduled in each future year are not required under *SFAS 109*.

18.1.12 Scheduling

Although scheduling the reversal of temporary differences is not specifically required by *SFAS 109*, estimation of the periods of reversal may be necessary (1) to determine the valuation allowance on deferred tax assets, (2) to estimate the applicable tax rate when there is a phased-in change in tax rates, or (3) to determine the appropriate classification of certain deferred tax assets and liabilities that are not related to an asset or liability reported on the balance sheet.

18.1.13 Tax-Planning Strategies

Under *SFAS 109*, tax-planning strategies should be considered in determining the amount of the valuation allowance on deferred tax assets. Tax-planning strategies are defined in *SFAS 109* as actions (including elections under the tax law) that (1) are prudent and feasible, (2) ordinarily might not be taken by an enterprise but would be taken to prevent an operating loss or tax credit carryforward from expiring unused, and (3) would result in realization of deferred tax assets. Under *SFAS 109*, implementation of the tax-planning strategy must be primarily within the control of management, but need not be within management's unilateral control.

The amount of the deferred tax benefit that results from a tax-planning strategy (the reduction in the amount of the valuation allowance that otherwise would be recognized) should be reduced by the net-of-tax amount of any significant expenses necessary to implement that strategy and by any significant losses that would be recognized if that strategy were implemented.

18.1.14 Different Tax Jurisdictions

SFAS 109 generally requires separate tax calculations for each tax-paying component of the enterprise in each tax jurisdiction in which the enterprise is subject to income taxes. Accordingly, enterprises may need to identify temporary differences and perform separate deferred tax calculations for each tax-paying component in each tax jurisdiction, including federal, state, local, and foreign.

In some cases, the deferred tax calculations for certain tax jurisdictions can be combined if there are no significant differences in the temporary differences or tax laws in the different jurisdictions.

Because insurance companies pay premium taxes, they are subject to income taxes in only a few states. In many cases, the effect of state income taxes may be immaterial to the measurement of taxes under *SFAS 109*.

18.1.15 Purchase Business Combinations

SFAS 109 requires that deferred tax assets and liabilities be recognized on differences between the assigned values and tax bases of assets acquired and liabilities assumed in purchase business combinations, except for temporary differences related to the portion of goodwill for which amortization is not deductible for tax purposes, unallocated negative goodwill, and leveraged leases. Tax benefits are recognized at the date of acquisition for acquired deductible temporary differences and acquired carryforwards if realization is *more likely than not.* If a valuation allowance is recognized for acquired deductible temporary differences or acquired operating loss or tax credit carryforwards at the acquisition date, those tax benefits, when initially recognized, are applied to first reduce to zero any goodwill related to the acquisition, then to reduce to zero any noncurrent intangible assets related to the acquisition, and then to reduce income tax expense.

18.1.16 Effective Date

SFAS 109 became effective for fiscal years beginning after December 15, 1992.

The effect of initially applying *SFAS 109* (the change in the net deferred tax asset or liability), except for the effects of certain items that were required to be excluded from comprehensive income, was reported as the effect of a change in accounting principle in the income statement for the year of initial application. If the earliest year restated upon adoption of *SFAS 109* was not presented with the financial statements for that year, the effect of the change as of the earliest year presented was reported as an adjustment of beginning retained earnings for that year.

18.1.17 Illustrative Application of *SFAS 109*

The following is a second example showing the straightforward application of the principles of *SFAS 109.*

- A life insurance company had no temporary differences at the beginning of the year (2000).

- During the current year, the company had pretax accounting income of $500.

- At the end of the year, the company had the following two temporary differences:

	Financial Statement Carrying Amount	Tax Basis	Taxable (Deductible) Temporary Differences
GAAP DAC	$ 150	---	$ 150
Tax DAC	---	50	(50)
Reserves	(750)	(550)	(200)
Net temporary differences			$ (100)

- The GAAP DAC is expected to be amortized over the next 15 years.

- The tax DAC is expected to be amortized over the next 10 years.

- The temporary difference related to reserves is expected to reverse over the next 15 years.

- There are no operating loss or tax credit carryforwards.
- There are no permanent differences.
- The enacted tax rate for the current year and future years is 35%. There are no graduated tax rates. The tax law permits, for life insurance companies, 3-year carryback and 15-year carryforward periods for operating losses.

Based on the requirements in *SFAS 109*, the life insurance company would apply the following steps:

1. Current tax expense and a current tax liability of $210 would be recognized for taxes payable on taxable income for the current year.

Pretax accounting income	$500
Tax DAC vs. GAAP DAC	(100)
Tax reserves vs. GAAP reserves	200
Taxable income	600
Tax rate	35%
Current tax expense	$210

2. At the end of the year, the company has taxable temporary differences of $150 and deductible temporary differences of $250.

3. The company has no operating loss or tax credit carryforwards.

4. The company would recognize a deferred tax liability of $52.5 for the taxable temporary differences related to the GAAP DAC based on the enacted tax rate (35%).

   Deferred tax liability = $150 × 35% = $52.5

5. The company would recognize a potential deferred tax asset of $87.5 for the deductible temporary differences related to the tax DAC and reserves based on the enacted tax rate (35%).

   Deferred tax asset = $250 × 35% = $87.5

6. The company would recognize a valuation allowance on the potential deferred tax asset (step 5) if it is *more likely than not* that all or some portion of the deferred tax asset will not be realized. The potential valuation allowance would range from *zero to $87.5* depending on the circumstances. (The valuation allowance is based on the total deferred tax asset of $87.5, not on the net deferred tax asset of $35.) The valuation allowance should reduce the potential deferred tax asset of $87.5 to the amount of the tax benefit that *more likely than not* will be realized on the future tax deductions related to the deferred compensation contracts.

   Circumstances that would be considered in determining the amount, if any, of the valuation allowance include, but are not limited to, the following:

a. Taxable temporary differences related to GAAP DAC will result in taxable amounts over the period of years in which the deductible amounts related to the tax DAC and reserves will occur.

b. Realization of the tax benefits of the deductible amounts related to the tax DAC and reserves will depend on earning taxable income in the years 2001 through 2030 (15-year carryforward from 2015). Because realization of the potential deferred tax asset is dependent upon the company earning income in the future, all available evidence concerning the likelihood of future income should be considered. For example, consideration should be given to current income levels, expected changes in operations, and potential losses related to existing contingencies, and built-in gains on existing net assets (to the extent such gains are not reflected in GAAP carrying value).

7. Assuming that the company concludes that it is *more likely than not* that the full amount of the potential deferred tax asset of $87.5 will be realized, no valuation allowance would be recognized. In that case, a net deferred tax asset of $35 (deferred tax asset of $87.5 less deferred tax liability of $52.5) would be recognized. The deferred tax benefit for the current year would be $35, which is the difference between the sum of the deferred tax asset, valuation allowance, and deferred tax liability at the beginning of the year (zero) and the sum of the deferred tax asset, valuation allowance, and deferred tax liability at the end of the year ($35). Total tax expense would be $175 (current tax expense of $210 less deferred tax benefit of $35).

The following presents the balance sheet and income statement amounts under *SFAS 109*:

Balance Sheet	
Deferred tax asset	$ 87.5
Valuation allowance	-----
Deferred tax liability	(52.5)
Net deferred tax asset (liability)	$ 35.0

Income Statement	
Pretax income	$500
Tax expense	175*
Net income	$325
Effective tax rate	35%

*Current tax expense of $210 less deferred tax benefit of $35

18.1.18 Summary of *SFAS 109*

Tables 18-1 through 18-5 summarize the major principles and impacts of *SFAS 109.*

Table 18-1
General Aspects of Deferred Taxes

Concept	Impact
Method	Asset and liability method
Objective	Recognition of taxes payable or refundable for the current year and deferred taxes for the expected future consequences of events that have been recognized in the financial statements or tax returns.
Measurement	Measurement of deferred tax liabilities for taxable temporary differences and deferred tax assets for deductible temporary differences and operating loss carryforwards using enacted tax rates.
Focus	Balance sheet
Changes in tax law or rates	Balance sheet amounts adjusted to reflect the effects of changes in tax laws or rates.
Scheduling of temporary differences	Scheduling not specifically required but ay be necessary to determine (1) the valuation allowance for deferred tax assets, (2) the applicable tax rate when there is a phased-in change in enacted tax rates, or (3) the appropriate classification of deferred tax assets or liabilities that are not related to an asset or liability for financial reporting.
Recognition of deferred tax assets	Deferred tax assets recognized for all deductible temporary differences and reduced by a valuation allowance, if necessary, to the amount that more likely than not will be realized
Operating loss and tax credit carryforwards	Tax benefits of operating loss and tax credit carryforwards recognized as a deferred tax asset and reduced by a valuation allowance, if necessary, to the amount that more likely than not will be realized.
Tax-planning strategies	These are strategies that are prudent and feasible and would prevent an operating loss or tax credit carryforward from expiring. These are strategies that are considered in determining the amount of a valuation allowance for deferred tax assets. The effects of any significant expenses or losses to implement the strategy (net of any tax benefit of those expenses or losses) are included in the valuation allowance.
Alternative tax systems	In U.S. federal jurisdiction, deferred taxes measured using regular tax system and a deferred tax asset, reduced by any necessary valuation allowance, recognized for any alternative minimum tax credit carryforward.

Table 18-2
Purchase Business Combinations

Concept	Impact
Differences between assigned values and tax bases	Deferred tax assets and liabilities recognized for the tax effect of differences between assigned values and tax bases of assets and liabilities; however, recognition of deferred tax assets based on more likely than not criterion.
Subsequent recognition of the tax benefit of acquired operating loss or tax credit carryforwards and purchased excess tax basis	Positive goodwill and other noncurrent intangible assets reduced to zero, with any additional amounts creditied to income tax expense.
Goodwill in purchase business combinations	A deferred tax liability or asset recognized for a difference between the amount of goodwill for financial reporting purposes and its tax basis only if amortization of goodwill is deductible for tax purposes.

Table 18-3
Temporary Differences That are Not Timing Differences

Concept	Impact
Foreign nonmonetary assets and liabilities when the reporting currency is the functional currency	Recognition of deferred taxes prohibited for the difference between the foreign currency equivalent of the U.S. dollar financial statement carrying amount and the foreign currency tax basis; effects of indexing the tax basis eliminated in recognition of a deferred tax asset or liability for the difference between the historical foreign currency financial statement carrying amount and historical foreign currency tax basis.
Intercompany trasfer of assets between tax jurisdictions	Recognition of deferred taxes prohibited for the change in tax basis that results from an intercompany sale or transfer

Table 18-4
APB *Opinion 23* Differences

Concept	Impact
Undistributed earnings of domestic subsidiaries and domestic corporate joint ventures	Deferred tax liabilities recognized for those temporary differences that arise in fiscal years beginning after December 15, 1992, unless recovery of the investment in the subsidiary will be tax-free.
Undistributed earnings of foreign subsidiaries and foreign subsidiaries and foreign corporate joint ventures	Deferred taxes not recognized when the indefinite reversal criterion is met; exception extended to the entire basis difference related to the investment in the subsidiary.
Policyholders' surplus of stock life insurance companies	Deferred tax liability recognized for temporary differences that arise in fiscal years beginning after December 15, 1992.

Table 18-5 Other Aspects of Accounting for Income Taxes	
Basis differences that are not temporary differences	Certain basis differences are not temporary differences for which deferred taxes are recognized if the related asset or liability is expected to be recovered or settled without tax consequences
Small life insurance and other types of special deductions	Tax benefit of small life insurance company deduction and other types of special deductions in future years should not be anticipated for purposes of offsetting a deferred tax liability for taxable temporary differences at the end of the current year
Intraperiod tax allocations	The tax consequences of all items reported apart from continuing operations considered in determining the allocation of income tax expense or benefit to continuing operations
Disclosure	Disclosure requirements include, but are not limited to: • The types of temporary differences that comprise significant portions of deferred tax assets and liabilities • Income tax expense allocated between continuing operations, discontinued operations, extraordinary items, and certain other categories • Significant components of income tax expense allocated to continuing operations • Reconciliation of expected income tax expense attributable to continuing operations to the reported income tax expense • Tax carryforward amounts and expiration dates • The gross amounts of deferred tax assets and liabilities and the total valuation allowance recognized to reduce deferred tax assets • The portion of any valuation allowance for which subsequently recognized tax benefits will be allocated to reduce goodwill or other noncurrent intangible assets or directly credited to equity
Presentation and classification	Classification between current and noncurrent generally determined by classification of the related asset or liability that gives rise to the temporary difference
Intercorporate tax allocation	No prescribed method of allocation of consolidated income tax expense for a group among members of a group (certain allocation methods are expressly prohibited); however, required disclosure of the method used, the effect of any changes in that method and in determining related balances due to or from affiliates, the amount of current and deferred tax expense, and any tax-related balances due to or from affiliates

18.2 Riders

18.2.1 Definition & Types

A rider is a legal document attached to an insurance base policy. Riders have their own premiums or cost of insurance rates; riders have a defined set of benefits and possibly cash values. Riders are typically included at the time of issue of the base policy, but can be added after issue. Riders can be terminated by the policyholder or expire without terminating the base policy.

Riders can be attached to all forms of insurance policies; they cover a wide range of benefits that are used to supplement or enhance the benefits of a base policy. Common types of riders include benefits for accidental death, waiver of premium, spouse, and child benefits, return of premium, extra term benefit coverage for the base policy insured, disability income, and account value-type accumulation benefits.

18.2.2 Classifications

Accounting standards and actuarial assumptions apply to riders based on the rider features, provisions, and expectations. Riders can be classified as *SFAS 60*, *SFAS 97*, or *SFAS 120* and can have a different classification from the base policy to which they are attached. One example of this would be a deferred annuity rider attached to a traditional life contract. The rider would be accounted for under *SFAS 97* while, the base plan would be accounted for under *SFAS 60*.

18.2.3 Deferred Acquisition Costs

For per-policy deferred acquisition costs, incremental expenses to market, underwrite, and issue the riders are considered for deferral. Incremental refers to those expenses over and above the expenses incurred to issue the base policy.

For commissions, capitalization is based upon the premium and commission scales related to the rider without consideration of the base policy premiums and commissions. Deferred acquisition costs are amortized in accordance with the SFAS classification of the riders and do not typically consider the base policy classification and provisions. One special case involves a type of life insurance contract written by some mutual insurers. The participating base policy has a participating paid-up additions rider and a nonparticipating one-year term rider. These three coverages all interact to determine future face amounts. Because all three must be considered together to anticipate future death benefits, the margins from the base policy and the rider are combined to produce the *SFAS 120* estimated gross margins to amortize DAC.

18.2.4 Benefit Reserves

Reserves are developed based on the rider premiums, benefits, and features in accordance with the appropriate SFAS classification. Premiums, benefits, and features of the base policy are generally not combined with the rider to produce a single reserve. For example, for a *SFAS 60* base product with a *SFAS 60* rider, the mechanics of the GAAP reserve calculations are performed independently. The expected profit on the base plan emerges as a level percentage of the base policy premium, while the expected profit from the rider emerges as a level percentage of the rider premium.

18.2.5 Interdependency of Actuarial Assumptions

The attachment of a rider can affect the GAAP assumptions for the base policy. There may be additional antiselection or a lowering of risks. For example, a return-of-premium rider attached to a disability income policy may improve persistency because healthier policyholders may be attracted to this option. In this case, the base policy may have lower disability levels, but benefits under the rider would be increased. Also, the presence of a cost-of-living-adjustment rider to a base disability income plan may affect the overall claim termination (recovery) rates because benefits are increasing. In cases in which the rider contains large death benefits, the additional underwriting and antiselection could affect the mortality levels experienced by the base policies. Margins for adverse deviation should be used for rider reserves and the amortization of DAC for *SFAS 60* products.

18.2.6 Loss Recognition and Recoverability

Loss recognition and recoverability testing are generally applied to the base policies and riders combined.

18.2.7 Reinsurance

Should any portion of a rider be reinsured, offsets should be considered to the benefit reserves and DAC in accordance with assumptions and methods used for the direct rider. Reinsurance is discussed in detail in Chapter 17.

18.3 Fair Value Reporting

18.3.1 Background

SFAS 107, "Disclosures about Fair Value of Financial Instruments," requires disclosure of the fair values of both assets and liabilities. It involves only disclosure and does not affect the GAAP balance sheet value of assets or liabilities. The disclosure occurs in the body of the financial statements or the accompanying notes.

SFAS 115, "Accounting for Certain Investments in Debt and Equity Instruments," requires balance sheet determination and recognition of the fair value of bonds not held to maturity and all equity investments. *SFAS 133*, "Accounting for Derivative Instruments and Hedging Activities," requires derivative financial instruments (as defined in that standard) to be recorded in the financial statements at fair value. Changes in the fair value of derivative financial instruments may flow through the income statement or simply through Other Comprehensive Income depending on the nature and purpose of the derivative. When purchase accounting is applied, *SFAS 141*, "Business Combinations," requires that all of the assets and liabilities of the acquired entity be restated to their fair values, and *SFAS 142*, "Goodwill and Other Intangibles," uses fair value to evaluate the appropriateness of the carrying value of intangible assets. These standards are pertinent to insurance companies, and their requirements are discussed in more detail throughout this book. Other standards incorporate fair value concepts but are outside the scope of this textbook.

As evidenced by the various standards cited as well as many others, the FASB has concluded that fair value information is relevant. At the time of publication, the FASB is developing a Statement of Financial Accounting Standards that will establish a framework for applying the fair value measurement objective in U.S. GAAP. An exposure draft of this standard was released in June, 2004, with the final standard proposed to be effective for financial statements issued for fiscal years beginning after June 15, 2005. Somewhat different than other standards, this standard "Fair Value Measurements" discusses *how* to determine fair value rather than *what* to measure at fair value. The "what" will be addressed separately on a project-by-project basis.

The proposed standard defines fair value as "the price at which an asset or liability could be exchanged in a current transaction between knowledgeable, unrelated willing parties." The standard proposes specific guidance on how to measure fair value for various types of assets and liabilities. For example:

- The fair value of financial instruments traded in active dealer markets would be determined using bid prices for assets and asked prices for liabilities.

- The fair value of restricted securities would be based on the quoted price of an identical unrestricted security, adjusted for the effect of the restriction.

- In the absence of quoted prices, fair value would be estimated using multiple valuation techniques consistent with the market, income, or cost approach. The valuation techniques would emphasize relevant market inputs.

In February 2000, the FASB published *Concept Statement 7*, "Using Cash Flow Information and Present Value in Accounting Measurements." The proposed standard "Fair Value Measurements" clarifies and incorporates the guidance in *Concept Statement 7* and thereby broadens its applicability to all pronouncements in which present values are used to estimate fair value.

Insurance liabilities would generally fall under the category of instruments for which quoted prices are absent. Therefore, determining the fair value of insurance liabilities or related items (like embedded derivatives as defined by *SFAS 133*) would generally involve the application of various valuation techniques such as the market approach, the income approach, or the cost approach. Actuarial appraisal methods would generally be classified as in income approach. Since actuarial appraisal methods use cash flow information and present values, the guidance in *Concept Statement 7* is directly relevant.

The actuarial profession has also been active in developing standards with respect to the fair value of insurance liabilities. As yet, no Actuarial Standard of Practice has been developed. However, in September 2002, the American Academy of Actuaries (AAA) published a public policy monograph titled "Fair Valuation of Insurance Liabilities: Principles and Methods." Although the AAA monograph was published prior to the development of the FASB proposed standard, it is generally consistent with the proposed standard. The AAA monograph provides a more detailed discussion of the application to insurance contracts of the same fair value concepts as addressed in the proposed standard.

18.3.2 Fair Value and *SFAS 107*

> Fair value is currently defined by *SFAS 107* as the amount at which the instrument could be exchanged in a current transaction between willing parties, other than a forced or liquidation sale. If a quoted market price is available for an instrument, the fair value to be disclosed for that instrument is the product of the number of trading units of the instrument times that market price. (Paragraph 5)

SFAS 107 requires the disclosure of fair value for all financial instruments. The term *financial instrument* is defined by the standard as:

(1) Cash
(2) Evidence of an ownership interest in an entity
(3) A contract that both
  (a) Imposes on one entity a contractual obligation:
    (i) to deliver cash or another financial instrument to a second entity
    (ii) or to exchange other financial instruments on potentially unfavorable terms with the second entity.
  (b) And, conveys to that second entity a contractual right
    (i) to receive cash or another financial instrument from the first entity

(ii) or to exchange other financial instruments on potentially favorable terms with the first entity. (Paragraph 3).

All financial instruments require disclosure unless they are specifically excluded by the standard. In general, most invested assets, including policy loans, are considered financial instruments.

A complete list of financial instruments excluded is described in paragraph 8 of the standard. A summary of the list is as follows:

(1) Employers' obligations for pension benefits and other similar benefits
(2) Substantively extinguished debt
(3) Insurance contracts, other than financial guarantees and investment contracts as defined in *SFAS 60* and *SFAS 97*
(4) Lease contracts
(5) Warranty obligations and rights
(6) Unconditional purchase obligations
(7) Investments account for under the equity method of accounting
(8) Minority interests in consolidated subsidiaries
(9) Equity investments in consolidated subsidiaries
(10) Equity instruments issued by the entity.

Obligations under certain insurance contracts are exempt from the fair value disclosure requirement. Universal life and limited-payment contracts covered by *SFAS 97* and insurance contracts covered by *SFAS 60* and *SFAS 120* do not require disclosure. Contracts that are classified as investment contracts under *SFAS 97* and *SFAS 91* do require disclosure. The most common investment contracts are interest-sensitive deferred annuities. The FASB decided not to require disclosure for insurance contract obligations because definitional and valuation difficulties as well as disclosure of the component parts of the obligations needed additional consideration.

Some examples of other assets and liabilities not subject to the fair value disclosure requirements of *SFAS 107* are employers' obligations for pension and post-retirement benefits, lease contracts as described in *FASB Statement 13*, warranty obligations and rights, investments accounted for under the equity method in accordance with *APB Opinion 18*, minority interest in consolidated subsidiaries, and equity investments in consolidated subsidiaries.

The standard does make provision for instances in which it is not practicable to estimate the fair value of a particular financial instrument or class of financial instruments. Practicable is defined in terms of excessive costs. The materiality of the instrument to the company is relevant to determining if the costs associated with estimating its fair value are excessive. For example, it may be impracticable to estimate fair value on an individual instrument basis, but practicable on a portfolio basis. In addition, it may be impracticable to precisely estimate the fair value of a financial instrument but practicable to develop a reasonable estimate. In this case, determining the precision with which a fair value is estimated is based on both the cost and the materiality of the difference between different estimation techniques.

In those instances in which it is not practicable to make any estimate of fair value, the company is required to disclose:

(1) Information pertinent to estimating fair value such as carrying amount, effective interest rate, and maturity, and

(2) Reasons why it is not practicable to estimate fair value.

The use of the term *fair value* in *SFAS 107* was deliberate. In its original form, the standard used the term *market value* rather than *fair value*. Although market value had been defined to include financial instruments with and without an active market, the term *fair value* was chosen to avoid confusion. Fair value is a broader concept that includes prices and rates obtained from primary and secondary markets.

Paragraphs 5 and 6 of *SFAS 107* give the quoted price in the most active market as the preferred method for determining fair value for any given financial instrument. Other means of determining fair value should be used only when a satisfactory market value is not available. Paragraph 5 also requires that any transaction expense that would be incurred in selling an asset or liability not be considered in determining fair value.

When a market price does not exist for a financial instrument or a class of financial instruments, the market price of similar financial instruments can be used. In these instances, the similar market price is used as a benchmark for the instrument in question.

Present value of cash flows is another acceptable method of determining fair value. The choice of a discount rate is critical to this approach; judgment is required. A discount rate could be chosen that is commensurate with the credit risk, duration, and prepayment risk of the instrument. Another approach would be to choose a discount rate that reflects the effects of interest rate changes and then revise cash flow estimates for cash flows not expected to be collected due to credit risk. The methodology and significant assumptions used in the development of fair values should be disclosed. In instances in which it is not practicable to estimate fair value, a disclosure of pertinent descriptive information is required.

Deposit liabilities with no defined maturities are discussed in paragraph 12 of the standard. Fair value for these financial instruments is the amount payable on demand at the reporting date. There is no further definition of what constitutes a deposit liability. Insurance companies may have deposit liabilities with similar characteristics to banking institutions such as funds on deposit and dividend accumulations on deposits. It is reasonable to assume that these contracts should be considered deposit liabilities as defined by the standard.

Surrender values offer a third possibility for reporting fair value in instances in which observable market values do not exist. The argument can be made that each contract has a liquidation value equal to its current surrender value, taking into account market value adjustments and other applicable charges.

Fair values determination practices relating to various financial instruments for disclosure purposes are provided in Table 18-6.

Table 18-6
***SFAS 107* Requirements for Fair Value Disclosure**

Balance Sheet Item	Is Fair Value Disclosure Required?	Commonly-used Fair Value Method
SFAS 60 products	No	Not applicable
SFAS 120 products	No	Not applicable
SFAS 97 "Universal Life and Limited Pay Products"	No	Not applicable
SFAS 97 and *SFAS 91* "Investment Contracts"	Yes	Discounted future cash flows
Funds on deposit	Yes	Amounts payable on demand
Dividend accumulations on deposit	Yes	Amounts payable on demand
Deferred acquisition cost	No	Not applicable

18.3.3 *SFAS 133* and Fair Value

SFAS 133, "Accounting for Derivative Instruments and Hedging Activities," is a comprehensive standard addressing accounting for the broad group of investment contracts that meet the definition of a derivative in the standard. A complete discussion of the accounting requirements for derivatives is beyond the scope of this book. The reader is referred to a variety of sources for learning more about these requirements, such as the publications of the Derivatives Implementation Group (DIG) and "how to" guides published by accounting firms.

SFAS 133 recognizes that certain "hybrid contracts" may contain features that are in and of themselves a derivative. In these situations, the "hybrid" contract is said to be composed of a host contract and an embedded derivative. In addition to addressing how to account for free-standing derivative contracts, *SFAS 133* also addresses how to account for the embedded derivatives inside of hybrid contracts. So, while insurance contracts are excluded from the scope of *SFAS 133*, an insurance contract may, depending on its terms, be a hybrid contract. The embedded derivative within a hybrid insurance contract would need to be accounted for under the provisions of *SFAS 133*. Insurance companies also sell investment contracts (for example, variable annuities), and these contracts may also, depending on their terms, be considered hybrid contracts.

Paragraph 12 of *SFAS 113* describes when an embedded derivative is present. It reads, in part:

> Contracts that do not in their entirety meet the definition of a derivative instrument (refer to paragraphs 6-9), such as bonds, insurance policies, and leases, may contain "embedded" derivative instruments-implicit or explicit terms that affect some or all of the cash flows or the value of other exchanges required by the contract in a manner similar to a derivative instrument. The effect of embedding a derivative instrument in another type of contract ("the host contract") is that some or all of the cash flows or other exchanges that otherwise would be required by the host contract, whether

unconditional or contingent upon the occurrence of a specified event, will be modified based on one or more underlyings.

For example, an equity indexed deferred annuity is considered a hybrid contract. The portion of the contract that provides for a repayment, with interest, of the policyholder's net deposits would be the host contract, and the portion that provides an increase in the policyholder's interest based on the performance of an equity index would be considered an embedded derivative. *SFAS 133* may require that the embedded derivative be separated from the host contract and accounted for separately as a derivative. Separating a hybrid contract into its host contract and embedded derivative components is referred to as "bifurcation." Bifurcation of a hybrid contract is required if all of the following conditions are met:

a. The economic characteristics of the embedded derivative are not clearly and closely related to those of the host contract.

b. The hybrid contract (including the host and the embedded derivative) is not otherwise measured at fair value, with changes reported in earnings as they occur, and

c. A separate contract with the same terms as the embedded derivative would itself be classified as a derivative under the definition in *SFAS 133*.

Many contracts offered by insurance companies are hybrid contracts and contain embedded derivatives. For example, variable annuity contracts with guaranteed minimum withdrawal benefits or guaranteed minimum account balances are hybrid contracts, as are equity indexed annuities and variable life insurance contracts. In some of these situations, the hybrid contract must be bifurcated. A description of the means by which these hybrid contracts are bifurcated and the accounting for each component is provided in the chapter of this book addressing the specific product under consideration.

Under *SFAS 133*, derivatives and embedded derivatives are accounted for at fair value. There are differences in the accounting treatment of the changes in the fair value of these instruments depending on whether the instrument is part of a qualifying hedge. A hedge is an investment that reduces or cancels risk in another investment. A hedge relationship exists between the hedge investment and the other, or "hedged," investment. *SFAS 133* defines three types of hedges:

- Fair Value Hedge: When a derivative is purchased to reduce or cancel the impact of changes in the fair value of the hedged instrument

- Cash Flow Hedge: When a derivative is purchased to reduce or cancel the impact of changes in expected cash flows from an asset, a liability or a forecasted transaction (An example would be a fixed for floating interest rate swap.)

- Foreign Currency Hedge: When a derivative is purchased to reduce or cancel the impact of foreign currency denominated assets, liabilities, or cash flows.

If a derivative qualifies for hedge accounting, the changes in the fair value of the derivative contract affects only other comprehensive income and is not considered part of net income. The requirements for obtaining hedge accounting treatment for a derivative and the specific treatment of derivatives that are considered part of a qualifying hedge are discussed in *SFAS 133* and are outside the scope of this text.

18.3.4 *SFAS 142* and Fair Value

SFAS 142, "Goodwill and Other Intangible Assets," uses fair value as the basis for testing the impairment of both intangible assets and goodwill. Intangible assets arise as a result of a purchase of a business or a business combination. These intangible assets may be identifiable, such as the value of a contracted sales force or the value of a customer list, or may be considered goodwill. Goodwill is the excess of the purchase price for a business over the net fair value of the tangible and identifiable intangible assets acquired.

Under *SFAS 142*, an identifiable intangible asset is impaired if the carrying value of the intangible asset is greater than the fair value of the intangible asset. This standard, in its paragraph 24, also provides some guidance as to how to determine the fair value of an intangible asset.

Goodwill is recorded at the "reporting unit" level. A reporting unit is effectively an operating segment or a level below an operating segment, provided there is discrete financial information available for the reporting unit. A more detailed description of a reporting unit is provided in the standard's paragraphs 30 – 36.

Testing goodwill for impairment is a two-step process. The first step is to determine if the carrying value of a reporting unit is greater than the fair value of the reporting unit. If it is, the amount of the impairment to goodwill, if any, is determined by comparing the implied fair value of the goodwill to the carrying amount of goodwill for that reporting unit. *SFAS 142* provides guidance on determining the fair value of a reporting unit.

Purchase accounting and the methods used to identify and value intangible assets acquired are discussed in Chapter 15, Accounting for Business Combinations.

18.4 Accounting for Demutualizations and Mutual Holding Company Formations

18.4.1 Background

In January 1995 the FASB issued *SFAS 120*, "Accounting and Reporting by Mutual Life Insurance Enterprises and by Insurance Enterprises for Certain Long-Duration Participating Contracts." *SFAS 120* was effective with fiscal years beginning after December 15, 1995, and it applied the GAAP requirements of *SFAS 60*, *SFAS 97*, and *SFAS 113* to mutual life insurance enterprises, whereas previously these requirements applied only to stock insurance companies.

However, additional guidance was considered necessary for participating life insurance products of mutual insurance companies, because neither *SFAS 60* nor *SFAS 97* appeared to provide an appropriate accounting model. The additional guidance was prepared and released simultaneously with *SFAS 120*, as the AICPA *SOP 95-1*, "Accounting for Certain Insurance Activities of Mutual Life Insurance Enterprises." Treatment of participating products according to *SOP 95-1* was required of a mutual company and was optional for a stock company with participating contracts that met the criteria of *SOP 95-1*. Further guidance was needed for mutual companies that wanted to reorganize, either through a full demutualization or through the formation of a mutual insurance holding company. This guidance was released on December 15, 2000 as *SOP 00-3*, "Accounting by Insurance Enterprises for Demutualizations and Formations of Mutual Holding Companies and for Certain Long-Term Participating Policies." *SOP 00-3* also applies to stock life companies that have elected *SOP 95-1* for participating business.

SOP 95-1 applies to life insurance contracts that have both of the following characteristics:

a. They are long-duration participating contracts that are expected to pay dividends to policyholders based on actual experience of the insurance enterprise.

b. Annual policyholder dividends are paid in a manner that identifies divisible surplus and distributes that surplus in approximately the same proportion as the contracts are considered to have contributed to divisible surplus (commonly referred to in actuarial literature as the contribution principle). (Paragraph 5)

Mutual insurance companies have no stockholders and are in effect owned by policyholders. This form of organization limits the ability of such companies to raise external capital for accomplishing long-term strategic growth objectives. Many mutual insurance companies in the U.S. and Canada have addressed this issue by reorganizing, either through full demutualization or formation of a mutual insurance holding company.

In a full demutualization, eligible participating policyholders receive some form of consideration (e.g., additional policyholder benefits, cash, stock, or subscription rights) as payment for their membership interest. Nonparticipating policyholders may not receive any compensation, because they are not considered to have ownership interest in the mutual insurance company.

Another form of reorganization is the formation of a mutual insurance holding company (MIHC). For this type of reorganization, a MIHC is formed and the former mutual insurance company is converted to a downstream stock insurance company that operates as a subsidiary of the MIHC. The MIHC is issued all the common stock as part of the reorganization, and it must retain at least effective control of the enterprise. Thus, generally less than 50% of the stock is available for a public offering. The eligible participating policyholders have their membership interests transferred to the MIHC, but do not receive consideration in the form of cash, equity, or subscription rights, unless the MIHC is subsequently demutualized. The policyholder's contractual rights in their insurance policies and their annuity contracts remain with the stock insurance company.

The remainder of this section discusses the accounting issues that are addressed in *SOP 00-3*.

18.4.2 Establishment of the Closed Block

When a mutual insurance company is considering reorganization, whether a full demutualization or the formation of a MIHC, there is a concern by both regulatory authorities and the accounting rulemakers about how much of the profit of the company belongs to stockholders and how much belongs to policyholders.

The block of eligible participating policies in force and identified at the date of demutualization or formulation of a MIHC is commonly referred to as the closed block. There is generally a regulatory requirement that some methodology be adopted to protect the status of nonguaranteed elements on these policies. The mechanism chosen should be able to satisfy regulatory authorities that policyholder equity will be maintained regardless of form of ownership. A closed block mechanism is governed by the plan of reorganization, which must be approved by the regulatory authorities.

Alternatives to the closed block mechanism can be devised to achieve the same goal of the equitable treatment of existing eligible policyholders. These are generally written agreements with regulators that specify the assumptions and methods for calculating the various nonguaranteed elements for the covered policies, as well as addressing when the nonguaranteed elements are to be credited to the eligible policyholders.

Funding is generally based on an actuarial calculation that estimates future liability cash flows for the closed block. Assets sufficient to fund these future cash flows are designated as belonging to the closed block. The amount of assets required for the initial funding is calculated assuming that current experience for the block (mortality, persistency, and so on) continues for the future and assuming the current dividend scale is continued into the future. In many cases, expenses of the closed block are excluded from the funding calculation. Actual dividends paid may be higher or lower than what is assumed in the funding calculation, based on the future experience of the closed block. The selection of the amount and type of assets is subject to negotiations between the mutual insurance company and regulatory authorities.

If the experience of the closed block is more favorable than anticipated in the original funding, total dividends paid will be higher than those assumed initially. These net experience gains are available for equitable distribution to in-force closed block policyholders only.

If the experience of the closed block is less favorable than anticipated in the original funding, total dividends will be lower than those assumed initially. However, because the guaranteed policy benefits must still be provided, the insurance company may need to support the underlying policy guarantees in the event of net experience losses, potentially impacting distributions to stockholders.

18.4.3 Accounting for the Closed Block

The unamortized deferred acquisition costs and the liability for future policy benefits for the closed block subsequent to reorganization are calculated according to *SFAS 60*, *SFAS 97*, or *SOP 95-1*, as appropriate. However, *SOP 00-3* in paragraph 17 notes that:

> the segregation of undistributed accumulated earnings on participating contracts is meaningful in a stock life insurance company, because the objective of such presentation is to identify amounts that are not distributable to stockholders.

SOP 00-3 then concludes that, following reorganization, the company should apply provisions of *SFAS 60* as follows:

> Policyholder dividends shall be accrued using an estimate of the amount to be paid. (Paragraph 41)
>
> If limitations exist on the amount of net income from participating insurance contracts of life insurance enterprises that may be distributed to stockholders, the policyholders' share of net income on those contracts that cannot be distributed to stockholders shall be excluded from stockholders' equity by a charge to operations and a credit to a liability relating to participating policyholders' funds in a manner similar to the accounting for net income applicable to minority interests. Dividends declared or paid to participating policyholders shall reduce that liability; dividends declared or paid in excess of the liability shall be charged to operations. Income-based dividend provisions shall be based on net income that includes adjustments between general-purpose and statutory financial statements that will reverse and enter into future calculations of the dividend provision. (Paragraph 42)

The application of paragraph 42 of *SFAS 60* gives rise to the policyholder dividend obligation (PDO), or what some companies have also called the deferred dividend liability. That is, to the extent that there is an experience gain for the closed block, this gain should not be reflected in the net income to stockholders. Rather, it should be considered as belonging solely to the closed block policyholders. It represents experience gains that ultimately will be paid out equitably as higher dividends to the closed block policyholders. It is essentially a liability for future dividends or profit sharing for the closed block policyholders.

The actual PDO should be determined by comparing the amount of actual cumulative earnings of the closed block from the date of reorganization to the amount of expected cumulative earnings based on the initial actuarial calculation of the closed block funding including asset cash flows and liability cash flows. The PDO equals the excess of the actual cumulative earnings over the expected cumulative earnings.

The situation is therefore clear in the case of net experience gains; a liability should be established as the policyholder dividend obligation. This liability increases with the closed block policyholders' share of net income and decreases with the actual dividends paid.

However, consider the situation in which there is a net experience loss. This would lead the insurance company to consider reducing future dividends to closed block policyholders. Although the insurance company may have the ability and intent to decrease future dividends, *SOP 00-3* will not permit an asset to be carried. That is, if the situation arises in which the actual cumulative earnings on the closed block are less than the expected cumulative earnings, the PDO will be floored at zero, and no corresponding asset will be established. This effectively creates a loss, which is funded through the current operations of the insurance company.

SOP 00-3 provides for special treatment for unrealized gains and losses on the closed block. According to *SFAS 115*, if an asset is classified as "available for sale," unrealized gains and losses are normally reported in accumulated other comprehensive income. For computing the PDO, unrealized investment gains and losses that have arisen subsequent to reorganization should be part of the PDO rather than other comprehensive income. However, unrealized losses that would otherwise make the PDO negative should be recognized in other comprehensive income applicable to stockholders. Unrealized investment gains and losses and other items of accumulated other comprehensive income related to the closed block at the date of reorganization "should continue to be reported in accumulated other comprehensive income" until recognized in earnings, according to paragraph 16 of the SOP.

At the date of the reorganization, the GAAP liabilities on the closed block generally exceed the GAAP assets. The assets classified as *SFAS 115* "available for sale" are carried at fair value, with the unrealized gain or loss carried as part of the accumulated other comprehensive income. The reorganization is not considered a change in ownership that requires purchase accounting, so the unrealized gains and losses are realized in operating income over time.

Therefore, the amount of operating income for the closed block is known as a result of the calculation of the initial closed block funding. The future aggregate operating income from the closed block equals the net closed block liability as of the date of the reorganization, which is calculated as follows:

> Net closed block GAAP liability equals the GAAP value of liabilities, minus the GAAP value of assets, plus the accumulated net unrealized gains and losses in other comprehensive income.

The change in the net closed block liability over time represents the expected closed block GAAP contribution to the earnings to the stockholders of the insurer. The actuarial calculation of the asset cash flows and liability cash flows on a best-estimate basis (i.e., no provisions for adverse deviation) as of the date of reorganization provide the initial net closed block GAAP liability. This calculation also provides the expected changes in the net closed block GAAP liability over time, which, combined with adjustments for items in other comprehensive income, represents the GAAP earnings emergence over time. This pattern of earnings emergence is fixed, unless experience becomes so unfavorable that a negative PDO would develop that cannot be recognized in the financial statements of the insurer.

Any amounts of unamortized DAC for the closed block polices are part of the GAAP assets. The future DAC amortization is also effectively locked in at the date of reorganization, because no differences in actual versus expected experience for estimated gross margins can be used to accelerate or decelerate the amortization schedule.

To illustrate the principles just described, Table 18-7 presents a block of business that has been treated under *SOP 95-1*. The source of Table 18-7 is Table 5-7.

Table 18-7
Calculation of Estimated Gross Margins Prior to Reorganization

	(1)	(2)	(3)	(4)	(5)	(6)	(7)	(8)	(9)
Period	**Expected Premiums**	**Interest on NLP Reserve**	**Interest on Cash Flow**	**Benefits**	**Administration Costs**	**Nondeferred Acquisition Costs**	**Increase in NLP Reserve**	**Expected Dividends**	**Estimated Gross Margin**
1	95.00	-	6.34	3.60	2.50	1.90	66.44	-	26.90
2	80.46	4.65	5.37	3.39	2.12	1.61	55.61	0.44	27.32
3	72.12	8.54	4.81	5.05	1.90	1.44	55.49	1.23	20.37
4	68.22	12.43	4.55	8.31	1.80	1.36	52.08	2.02	19.63
5	64.49	16.07	4.31	11.37	1.70	1.29	48.86	2.79	18.86
6	60.95	19.49	4.07	14.24	1.60	1.22	45.83	3.57	18.05
7	57.58	22.70	3.84	17.02	1.52	1.15	42.98	4.32	17.14
8	54.37	25.71	3.63	19.62	1.43	1.09	40.30	5.07	16.21
9	51.32	28.53	3.43	22.07	1.35	1.03	37.77	5.79	15.27
10	48.43	31.18	3.23	505.12	1.27	0.97	(445.37)	6.51	14.33

Legend:
(1) Gross premiums expected in period.
(2) Interest earned at expected investment yield on net level premium reserve at beginning of period.
(3) Interest earned on cash flow elements over period, expected investment yield × [(1) – (5) – (6)].
(4) Death, surrender, and endowment benefits expected to be paid in period.
(5) Administrative expenses expected to be incurred in period.
(6) Acquisition costs not capitalized in period (ultimate renewal commission rate applied to expected premiums).
(7) Increase in the net level premium reserve expected for the period.
(8) Expected dividends in the period.
(9) Estimated gross margins = (1) + (2) + (3) – (4) – (5) – (6) – (7) – (8).

Consider a reorganization at the beginning of the third year of the illustration. Table 18-8 shows the calculation of the estimated gross margins after the reorganization. Note that expenses are assumed to be excluded from the calculation of the initial funding and are also excluded from this calculation of the estimated gross margin calculation.

Table 18-8 Calculation of Initial Estimated Gross Margins after Reorganization in Year 3									
Period	(1) Expected Premiums	(2) Interest on Closed Block Assets	(3) Interest on Cash Flow	(4) Benefits	(5) Increase in NLP Reserve	(6) Expected Dividends	(7) Estimated Gross Margin	(8) Increase in Policyholder Dividend Obligation	(9) Closed Block Initial Estimated Gross Margin
1	n/a	n/a	n/a	n/a	n/a	n/a	n/a	n/a	n/a
2	n/a	n/a	n/a	n/a	n/a	n/a	n/a	n/a	n/a
3	72.12	5.55	5.05	5.05	55.49	1.23	20.95	0	20.95
4	68.22	8.08	4.78	8.31	52.08	2.02	18.66	0	18.66
5	64.49	10.45	4.51	11.37	48.86	2.79	16.43	0	16.43
6	60.95	12.67	4.27	14.24	45.83	3.57	14.25	0	14.25
7	57.58	14.76	4.03	17.02	42.98	4.32	12.04	0	12.04
8	54.37	16.71	3.81	19.62	40.30	5.07	9.90	0	9.90
9	51.32	18.55	3.59	22.07	37.77	5.79	7.83	0	7.83
10	48.43	20.26	3.39	505.12	(445.37)	6.51	5.81	0	5.81

Legend:
(1) Gross premiums expected in period.
(2) Interest earned at expected investment yield on closed block assets at beginning of period.
(3) Interest on cash flow for closed block [same as (3) from Table 18-7, except neither administrative costs nor nondeferred acquisition costs included].
(4) Death, surrender, and endowment benefits expected to be paid in period.
(5) Increase in the net level premium reserve expected for the period.
(6) Expected dividends in the period.
(7) Estimated gross margin for closed block = (1) + (2) + (3) – (4) – (5) – (6)
(8) Increase in policyholder dividend obligation (at initial valuation for closed block; this is expected to be zero).
(9) Closed block initial estimated gross margin = (7) – (8)

The accounting for an experience gain occurring in the interest earned during period 3 of $0.56 is revealed by Table 18-9. This amount is also shown as an increase in the PDO, which is then paid out as additional dividends over the following two years.

Table 18-9 Calculation of Revised Estimated Gross Margins after Reorganization in Year 3									
Period	(1) Expected Premiums	(2) Interest on Closed Block Assets	(3) Interest on Cash Flow	(4) Benefits	(5) Increase in NLP Reserve	(6) Expected Dividends	(7) Estimated Gross Margin	(8) Increase in Policyholder Dividend Obligation	(9) Closed Block Initial Estimated Gross Margin
1	n/a	n/a	n/a	n/a	n/a	n/a	n/a	n/a	n/a
2	n/a	n/a	n/a	n/a	n/a	n/a	n/a	n/a	n/a
3	72.12	6.11	5.05	5.05	55.49	1.23	21.51	0.56	20.95
4	68.22	8.08	4.78	8.31	52.08	2.30	18.38	(0.28)	18.66
5	64.49	10.45	4.51	11.37	48.86	3.07	16.15	(0.28)	16.43
6	60.95	12.67	4.27	14.24	45.83	3.57	14.25	0	14.25
7	57.58	14.76	4.03	17.02	42.98	4.32	12.04	0	12.04
8	54.37	16.71	3.81	19.62	40.30	5.07	9.90	0	9.90
9	51.32	18.55	3.59	22.07	37.77	5.79	7.83	0	7.83
10	48.43	20.26	3.39	505.12	(445.37)	6.51	5.81	0	5.81

Legend:
(1) Gross premiums expected in period.
(2) Interest on closed block assets, reflecting interest gain in year 3 in excess of initial expected amount.
(3) Interest on cash flow for closed block (neither administrative costs nor nondeferred acquisition costs included).
(4) Death, surrender, and endowment benefits expected to be paid in period.
(5) Increase in the net level premium reserve expected for the period.
(6) Expected dividends in the period, revised to reflect the interest gain paid out over the following two years.
(7) Estimated gross margin for closed block = (1) + (2) + (3) – (4) – (5) – (6)
(8) Increase in policyholder dividend obligation (reflecting interest gain and its subsequent payout to policyholders).
(9) Closed block initial estimated gross margin = (7) – (8)

This example illustrates the point that because experience gains are put into the PDO, the calculation of estimated gross margins is not affected by the experience gains. That is, experience gains are expected to be paid out in the future except to the extent they are offset by future experience losses. The increase and decrease in the PDO can be considered as a way to absorb the experience gains and losses so that as long as a non-zero PDO exists, the earnings pattern is effectively fixed for the closed block. Some companies have referred to the earnings emergence as the glide path.

Prior to *SOP 00-3*, in presenting the closed block accounting, some companies chose to collapse the closed block into a single entry for assets, liabilities, and P&L. However, *SOP 00-3* ended this practice. Closed block assets, liabilities, revenues, and expenses should be displayed together with all the other assets, liabilities, revenues, and expenses of the insurance enterprise based on the nature of the particular item, with appropriate disclosures relating to the closed block.

18.4.4 Accounting for the Open Block

The block of participating policies not included in the closed block at the reorganization or sold subsequent to the date of demutualization or formation of a mutual holding company is referred to as the open block. Policyholder equity is a concern as well for the open block.

A stock insurance company can apply *SFAS 60*, *SFAS 97*, or *SOP 95-1* treatment to its participating business. However, *SOP 95-1* requires that if a stock company chooses to apply *SOP 95-1* treatment to any of its qualifying participating business, it should be applied to all business that qualifies. Therefore, in the general case of a mutual insurer that reorganizes, if *SOP 95-1* were applied prior to reorganization, it must be applied subsequent to reorganization to all contracts that qualify.

SOP 00-3 requires application of *SFAS 60*, paragraphs 41-42, for the open block if there are participating contracts and the requirements of *SOP 95-1* are met. Therefore, if there is a limitation on the amount of net income from participating contracts included in the open block that is available to stockholders, paragraph 17 of *SOP 00-3* indicates that "the policyholders' share of income on those contracts that may not be distributed to stockholders should be charged to operations with a corresponding credit to a liability" and that "dividends paid to participating policyholders reduce this liability."

18.5 Surplus Notes

Surplus debentures or notes are financial instruments issued by an insurance company that have characteristics of both debt and equity. The notes have debt-like features such as a fixed nominal value, a maturity date, and a stated rate of interest. The issuing company's state insurance department must approve the form and content of surplus notes. Surplus notes must also contain provisions that require them to be subordinate to all policyholder liabilities, claimant and beneficiary claims, and all other classes of creditor claims. In addition, each payment of interest and/or principal requires the prior approval of the commissioner of the issuing insurer's state of domicile.

All types of companies, stock, mutual, large and small, use surplus notes in a variety of circumstances. However, surplus notes have most often been used by mutual insurance companies as a source of capital because the mutuals have had limited access to capital other than through accumulated earnings. In some instances, surplus notes have been used as a tool to give regulators flexibility in dealing with companies that need to enhance surplus levels. The development of risk-based capital (RBC) standards in the 1990s gave regulators and investors a new tool for defining the adequacy of regulatory capital. Further, investors also believed the RBC standards would give regulators a tool, or basis, for making a decision when considering the approval of requests for payment of interest and principal on the surplus notes. As a result, access to capital increased and many large mutual insurance companies issued surplus notes through private placements with institutional investors.

For statutory reporting purposes, surplus notes are treated as surplus and not as a liability of the issuer. Under codification of statutory accounting principles, *SSAP 41* describes the accounting for both the issuer and holder of surplus notes. Proceeds from the notes must be in the form of cash or other admitted assets with sufficient liquidity to satisfy the insurance department. Interest, including interest in arrears, on surplus notes is not recorded as an expense or liability until the insurance department has approved the approval for payment of such interest. As of the date of approval of principal repayment by the insurance department, the issuer can reclassify such approved payments from surplus to liabilities.

Under GAAP, surplus notes are treated as a liability of the issuer. The distinction between a liability and equity instruments in GAAP is found in *SFAS 6*, "Elements of Financial Statements." Under GAAP, stockholders' equity, or net worth, is a measure of the amount of net assets available to stockholders after all other obligations have been satisfied. Surplus notes have characteristics of debt because the enterprise is obligated to distribute its assets to holders of surplus notes, which takes precedence over ownership interests. Thus, there is a significant difference between the regulatory reporting and GAAP reporting for surplus notes.

Specific guidance has been provided by the AICPA in *Practice Bulletin 15*, "Accounting by the Issuer of Surplus Notes."

Paragraph .07 of *PB 15* states "Surplus notes should be accounted for as debt instruments and presented as liabilities in the financial statements of the issuer." Paragraph .09 states "Interest should be accrued over the life of the surplus note, irrespective of the approval of interest and principal payments by the insurance commissioner, and recognized as an expense in the same manner as other debt."

18.6 Materiality

18.6.1 Concept

Materiality recognizes that some matters, either individually or in the aggregate, are important for the fair presentation of financial statements in conformity with GAAP. It also recognizes that other matters may not be important for a fair presentation.

Financial statements are materially misstated when they contain information whose effect, individually or in the aggregate, causes them not to be presented fairly in conformity with the basis of accounting under which they are presented. In addition, whenever actuaries are performing professional services, their work product should consider materiality in the context of the users or potential users. Misstatements can result from errors or fraud.

A common definition of materiality is "a misstatement in the financial statements can be considered material if knowledge of the misstatement would affect a decision of a reasonably intelligent user of the statements." A broader definition would substitute the word *information* for *financial statements.*

This definition is derived in part from FASB *Statement of Financial Accounting Concepts 2*, which states:

> The omission or misstatement of an item in a financial report is material if, in the light of surrounding circumstances, the magnitude of the item is such that it is probable that the judgment of a reasonable person relying upon the report would have been changed or influenced by the inclusion or correction of the item. Significant misstatements can be defined as omissions or misstatements that, when aggregated with other misstatements, may result in a material misstatement in the financial statements.

While the essence of this concept may be clear, the practical application of this materiality concept is difficult and requires significant judgment in practice. Quantitative rules of thumb such as 5% to 10% of net income historically have been applied to situations requiring materiality conclusions. But use of these rules of thumb has been challenged by the SEC. The SEC has focused on and criticized "earnings management" abuses, some of which have involved the inappropriate application of materiality concepts. These particular concerns about earnings management fall into two groupings:

- Use of arbitrary thresholds such as 5% to 10% of earnings without further evaluation of qualitative factors.

- Intentionally recording erroneous information or applying non-GAAP accounting principles within the financial statements. These actions have been "justified" by those carrying them out on the basis that the amounts involved are immaterial.

To the extent that the misuse of materiality considerations has resulted in financial reporting abuse, the SEC's comments are certainly justified. Given the definition of materiality for financial reporting purposes, it is easy to see that the use of quantitative thresholds without evaluation of qualitative factors can lead to incorrect conclusions. It is also difficult to reconcile the materiality justification for recording erroneous information or for the intentional misapplication of GAAP. If it is not material, why do it? There may be legitimate reasons, however. For example, if the amounts involved in a transaction are so clearly inconsequential that the cost of applying a GAAP principle clearly outweighs its benefit, then an alternative approach would be justifiable. In fact, many authoritative standards specifically state that the guidance need not be applied to immaterial items or transactions.

The evaluation of the qualitative factors is still the most difficult part of materiality judgment. Basically the preparer has to put him or herself in the shoes of all the reasonable people who may have a basis for reliance on the financial information presented. This can be quite a task considering the variety of individuals who review and rely on the financial information. Lenders, analysts, regulators, and "mom and pop" investors all may look at the same information with a somewhat different perspective. To some users, missing a quarterly earnings forecast by a penny per share may be material. A small change in earnings could make the difference between achieving or not achieving an employee bonus payout threshold; this could be material to owners and employees alike. Previously, overstatements of earnings were perceived as more unacceptable than understatements. Typically a higher threshold was applied in evaluating such understatements. This is no longer the case, overstatements and understatements are equally unacceptable.

The definition of materiality in the accounting literature is in substance identical to that used by the courts in interpreting the federal securities laws. The U.S. Supreme Court (TSC Industries v. Northway, Inc., 1976) has held that a fact is material if there is a substantial likelihood that the "... fact would have been viewed by the reasonable investor as having significantly altered the 'total mix' of information made available."

Thus, the consideration of materiality is a matter of professional judgment by those persons involved in the financial reporting process and is influenced by their perception of the needs of a reasonable person who will rely on the financial statements.

18.6.2 Judgment

In practice, deciding on actual materiality in a given situation is difficult. There are no simple, well-defined guidelines. Materiality is a relative rather than an absolute concept. Thus, it is not possible to establish specific dollar guidelines.

The definition of materiality emphasizes *reasonable* users; thus, the preparers must have knowledge of the likely users of the financial statements. The significance of an item to a particular entity (for example, investments versus inventories to an insurance company), the pervasiveness of the misstatement (such as whether it affects the amounts and presentation of numerous financial statement items), and the effect of the misstatement on the financial statements as a whole are all factors in judging materiality. Evaluating the effect of a misstatement on the financial statements as a whole may not be possible for certain preparers (such as accountants or actuaries) of limited portions of the financial statements. Misstatements of any magnitude should be documented by all preparers and sent to the appropriate designated staff responsible for evaluating materiality of all known items separately and in the aggregate.

When evaluating materiality, consideration should also be given to both quantitative and qualitative factors and the results of risk assessment of material misstatements due to fraud.

18.6.3 Quantitative Factors

When assessing the quantitative materiality of differences, preparers have historically used various types of numerical thresholds. Such thresholds have included percentages applied; for instance, amounts above 10% might be presumed as material; amounts less than 10% could be material; and amounts under 5%, not material. However, depending on the facts and circumstances, different thresholds of materiality can be used in evaluating individual line items and subtotals in the financial statements. When an entity's earnings are at or near breakeven or some other important threshold, other measures may be necessary for determining overall materiality. Numeric thresholds generally apply to net income and retained earnings in total, and not to an individual item.

In 1999, the SEC issued guidance in *SAB 99*, "Materiality" that called into question the use of strict numerical thresholds to define materiality. *SAB 99* emphasizes disclosure of differences (for example, to senior management, to the audit committee, and in footnotes in the financial statements). In this guidance, the SEC discouraged the use of universal quantitative thresholds as "rules of thumb" to assist in the preparation of the financial statements. In particular, one rule of thumb cited by the SEC was that a misstatement or omission of an item that falls under a 5% threshold is not material in the absence of particularly egregious circumstances, such as self-dealing or misappropriation by senior management. In its guidance, the SEC "reminded" registrants and the auditors of their financial statements that exclusive reliance on any percentage or numerical threshold has no basis in the accounting literature or the law. The SEC goes on to state that it does not object to such a "rule of thumb" as an initial step in assessing materiality. However, quantifying, in percentage terms, the magnitude of a misstatement is only the beginning of an analysis of materiality; it cannot appropriately be used as a substitute for a full analysis of all relevant considerations. Materiality concerns the significance of an item to users of a registrant's financial statements.

18.6.4 Qualitative Factors

The qualitative factors of misstatements center on the evaluation of cause and effect and other knowledge of the overall financial statements. Qualitative factors that may cause misstatements of quantitatively small amounts to be material include:

(1) Whether the misstatement arises from an item capable of precise measurement or whether it arises from an estimate and, if so, the degree of imprecision inherent in the estimate,

(2) Whether the misstatement masks a change in earnings or other trends,

(3) Whether the misstatement hides a failure to meet analysts' consensus expectations for the enterprise,

(4) Whether the misstatement changes a loss into income or vice versa,

(5) Whether the misstatement concerns a segment or other portion of the registrant's business that has been identified as playing a significant role in the registrant's operations or profitability,

(6) Whether the misstatement affects the registrant's compliance with regulatory requirements,

(7) Whether the misstatement affects the entity's compliance with loan covenants or other contractual requirements,

(8) Whether the misstatement has the effect of increasing management's compensation—for example, by satisfying requirements for the award of bonuses or other forms of incentive compensation,

(9) Whether the misstatement involves concealment of an unlawful transaction.

The SEC also indicated that the demonstrated volatility of the price of a registrant's securities in response to certain types of disclosures may also provide guidance whether investors regard quantitatively small misstatements as material. Consideration of potential market reaction to disclosure of a misstatement by itself is not sufficient in considering materiality. However, when management or the independent auditor expects (based, for example, on a pattern of market performance) that a known misstatement may result in a significant positive or negative market reaction, that expected reaction should be taken into account when considering materiality.

Although the intent of management does not render a misstatement material, it may provide significant evidence of materiality. The evidence may be particularly compelling in instances in which management has intentionally misstated items in the financial statements to "manage" reported earnings. In that instance, management presumably has done so believing that the resulting amounts and trends would be significant to users of the registrant's financial statements. The SEC believes that investors generally would regard as significant (or "material" in this context) a management practice to overstate or understate earnings up to an amount just short of a percentage threshold in order to "manage" earnings. Investors presumably also would regard as significant an accounting practice that, in essence, rendered all earnings figures subject to a management-directed margin of misstatement.

The materiality of a misstatement may also depend where it appears in the financial statements. For example, a misstatement may involve a segment of the registrant's operations. In that instance, in assessing materiality of a misstatement to the financial statements taken as a whole, registrants and their auditors should consider not only the size of the misstatement but also the significance of the segment information to the financial statements taken as a whole. The AICPA "Codification of Statements on Auditing Standards," Section 326.33 states:

> A misstatement of the revenue and operating profit of a relatively small segment that is represented by management to be important to the future profitability of the entity is more likely to be material to investors than a misstatement in a segment that management has not identified as especially important.

For example, if the mortality experience on an old established product "masked" a significant mortality loss versus expectation on an entity's new, rapidly expanding product line, such lack of disclosure could be material.

In assessing the materiality of misstatements in segment information, situations can arise in practice in which preparers or auditors conclude that a matter relating to segment information is qualitatively material even though, in their judgment, it is quantitatively immaterial to the financial statements taken as a whole.

As a result of the interaction of quantitative and qualitative considerations in materiality judgments, misstatements of relatively small amounts could have a material effect on the financial statements. For example, an improper payment of an otherwise immaterial amount could be material if there is a reasonable possibility that it could lead to a material contingent liability or a material loss of revenue.

Thus, the discussions of materiality in the literature recognize that such judgments are made in light of surrounding circumstances and necessarily involve both quantitative and qualitative considerations. Under the governing principles, an assessment of materiality requires that the facts be viewed in the context of the "surrounding circumstances," as the accounting literature puts it, or the "total mix" of information, in the words of the U.S. Supreme Court. In the context of a misstatement of a financial statement item, while the "total mix" includes the size in numerical or percentage terms of the misstatement, it also includes the factual context in which the user of financial statements would view the financial statement item. Briefly stated, company management and the auditor must consider both *quantitative* and *qualitative* factors in assessing an item's materiality. Court decisions, SEC rules and enforcement actions, and accounting and auditing literature have all considered *qualitative* factors in various contexts. *SAB 99* focuses on the responsibility of the registrants to keep accurate books and records, and, in particular, on whether a misstatement or omission indicates a failure to meet that responsibility. In addition, *SAB 99* affirms that intentional misstatements that are immaterial are not permitted and that authoritative literature takes precedence over industry practice.

18.6.5 Responsibility

Under AICPA standards, company management and its board of directors have the ultimate responsibility for the preparation of the company's financial statements. As a result, they are ultimately responsible for the determination of materiality with respect to such statements. In fact, company executive management executes a representation letter to the company's auditors that represents that the financial statements subject to audit are free of material misstatements including any unadjusted misstatements detected during the conduct of the audit. The company's auditors must then independently assess the qualitative and quantitative factors affecting materiality to ascertain whether they can render an unqualified opinion on such statements or whether adjustments to such statements are needed to keep such statements from being misleading.

18.6.6 Professional Standards

The financial reporting actuary may or may not be a member of the designated management staff responsible for determining the materiality of omissions and misstatements and deciding upon the appropriate reporting action.

To evaluate materiality, the actuary is required to assess qualitative and quantitative factors. Under *ASOP 23*, "Data Quality," an actuary is to select and obtain the appropriate data and information necessary for the intended purpose of the analysis (Section 5.1) and to make appropriate reliance on data supplied by others (Section 5.3).

The American Academy of Actuaries' "Financial Reporting Recommendations and Interpretations" provides guidance to the actuary on materiality. *Recommendation 9*, "Materiality," discusses utilizing methods or procedures which imply a degree of precision that may be unattainable due to the level of uncertainly contained in the actuarial assumptions employed. This recommendation also directs the actuary to identify the typical user of the actuary's work. Examples of such users are provided in *Interpretation 9-A*, "Materiality, Typical Users." *Interpretation 9-B*, 'Materiality, Quantitative Considerations," expands on the concept that materiality is determined by the net impact of a number of items which may be the responsibility of other actuaries or accountants. Finally, *Interpretation 9-C*, "Materiality, Qualitative Considerations," suggests the actuary consider documentation of the circumstances where items were judged to be not material.

For actuaries who are responsible for the delivery of professional services related to U.S. GAAP financial statements, the *Code of Professional Conduct* Precept 5 requires a disclosure of professional findings along with the required signature of the actuary responsible for the communication (Annotation 5-3). Actuaries should communicate in writing actuarial financial data and omissions or misstatements to designated accounting and financial staff for assembly of financial statements and to the management staff responsible for materiality decisions. In addition, actuaries should state whether they have evaluated the materiality of actuarial omissions and misstatements. Under Annotation 5-2, the actuary who makes an actuarial communication regarding professional services assumes responsibility for it except to the extent the actuary disclaims responsibility by stating appropriate reliances. Such communications should also cover any reliance on accounting interpretations and generally accepted accounting practices provided by other persons.

Because of the significant growth in holding companies, large numbers of insurance companies may be owned by a single registrant. This creates difficulties for actuaries and accountants at the subsidiary to determine materiality at the holding company level. In these cases, the actuary should be guided by Precept 5 previously described. These standards apply to actuaries who are company employees, consultants, and actuarial audit support actuaries. In addition, the *Securities and Exchange Act of 1934* states a broad level definition of responsibility:

- No person shall, directly or indirectly, falsify or cause to be falsified, any book, record or account subject to Section 13(b) (2) A of the *1934 Act*;

- No director or officer of an issuer shall directly or indirectly

- Make or cause to be made a materially false or misleading statement in connection with the preparation of required reports and documents,

- Omit to state, or cause another person to omit to state, any material fact necessary in order to make statements made, in light of the circumstances under which such statements are made, not misleading to an accountant in connection with (1) an audit of financial statements or (2) the preparation or filing of any document or report. (Regulation 13 B-2).

Chapter 19 Financial Statement Presentations

19.1 Purpose

In this chapter, a life insurance company and an operating environment are used to illustrate reporting under Generally Accepted Accounting Principles. Previous chapters addressed the accounting requirements at the product level and described procedures to reflect experience different than the assumptions used to develop the various accounting elements for each product.

The examples in this chapter display balance sheets and income statements at the product level. The actuary makes assumptions about future experience in order to calculate liabilities for future policyholder benefits, deferred acquisition costs (DAC), and various other related liabilities and assets. As time passes, experience unfolds that is different than the assumptions used to determine these balances; these variations impact different products in various ways. The examples in this chapter illustrate these differences. The examples give the reader a sense of the ongoing work necessary in a life insurance company environment in order to properly account for its operations.

Each example provides three balance sheets and two income statements. The results of each product segment over the two-year period are discussed, and an analysis of the impact of the company's experience on each balance is provided. While the results are supported by detailed calculations at the product level, the reader should consult with the appropriate product discussion in a previous chapter to understand these detailed calculations. The analysis in this chapter assumes that the reader is familiar with the product level mechanics provided in earlier chapters. For simplicity, taxes are not considered.

19.2 Company Description

The example company, Exco, is a shareholder-owned entity. However, it was formerly a mutual life insurance company, having demutualized at the end of the calendar year preceding the first balance sheet date (12/31/00). Exco is organized into nine product segments:

1. Participating Whole Life
2. Term Life
3. Universal Life
4. Variable Universal Life
5. Variable Deferred Annuity
6. Fixed Deferred Annuity
7. Equity Indexed Annuity
8. Immediate Annuity
9. Disability Income

Recently Exco has been selling products other than participating life insurance. Exco continues to sell participating life insurance contracts even though it has now demutualized. Exco's operations are exclusively in the United States.

19.3 Operating Environment

Year one has a low available new money rate, some high bond write-downs, and a poor equity market. Year two has a high available new money rate, little in the way of write-downs, and a strong equity market. While there are other changes in experience from one period to the next, these are the principal changes.

19.4 Product Segments

The following sections discuss and display the results of two years' performance for each product segment as if it were its own company.

19.4.1 Participating Whole Life

The participating whole life block balance sheets and income statements for the example period are displayed in Tables 19-1 and 19-2. Over this period, the participating whole life block assets grow from $632 million to $813 million. Operating income was $58.8 million in year one and $59.3 million in year two.

This is a participating whole life plan. Gross premium is $5,000 per policy with an average size of 100,000. Dividends are paid in cash. Commission is 55% of premium in policy year one grading down to 2% by policy year eleven.

The accounting model is *SFAS 120*. A policyholder dividend obligation (PDO) liability is established. The PDO is included on the balance sheet as "Policyholder dividends."

The PDO is positive in year one due to higher than expected lapses. This creates a larger than expected gain on surrender in the gross margins. Since the PDO is positive in year one, the earnings pattern is effectively fixed for the closed block. The DAC amortization pattern is essentially fixed.

In year two the PDO calculation produces a negative balance, which is floored at zero. Therefore the PDO is shown as zero in year two on the balance sheet. Consequently, the gross margins and DAC are recomputed (unlocked) in year two.

There are no sales in year two.

Table 19-1
Participating Whole Life Balance Sheet

	Year 0	Year 1	Year 2
ASSETS			
Invested Assets			
Held-to-maturity debt securities, at amortized cost	510,496	532,516	574,723
Total investments	510,496	532,516	574,723
Cash and cash Equivalents	45,944	93,431	145,139
Deferred policy acquisition costs	75,702	94,625	93,371
Total assets	632,142	720,572	813,233
LIABILITIES			
Policy liabilities and accruals*	526,100	555,708	589,137
Policyholder dividends		52	
Total liabilities	526,100	555,760	589,137
STOCKHOLDER'S EQUITY			
Common stock and additional paid-in capital	50,000	50,000	50,000
Accumulated income	56,042	114,812	174,096
Accumulated other comprehensive income			
Total stockholders' equity	106,042	164,812	224,096
Total liabilities and stockholders' equity	632,142	720,572	813,233
* Excludes liability for policyholder dividends			

Table 19-2
Participating Whole Life Income Statement and Comprehensive Income

	Year 1	Year 2
REVENUES		
Premiums	57,468	53,236
Investment income, net of expenses	47,486	51,707
Total revenues	104,954	104,943
BENEFITS AND EXPENSES		
Policy benefits, excluding policyholder dividends	36,078	39,041
Policyholder dividends	119	788
Policy acquisition costs amortization	(18,923)	1,254
Other operating expenses	28,910	4,576
Total benefits and expenses	46,184	45,659
Applicable income tax		
Net Income	58,770	59,284
COMPREHENSIVE INCOME		
Net Income	58,770	59,284
Other comprehensive income		
Comprehensive income	58,770	59,284

19.4.2 Term Life Insurance

The term balance sheets and income statements for the example period are displayed in Tables 19-3 and 19-4. Over this period, the term assets grow from $18.8 million to $32.5 million. Net income was $2.8 million in year one and $4.5 million in year two.

This is a non-participating ten year term plan. Gross premium is $600 per policy with an average size of 100,000. Commission is 80% of premium in policy year one grading down to 2% by policy year three.

This is a new block of business so polices are in the early durations. DAC has large relative benefit reserves in the early policy years. This relationship reverses in later policy years when benefit reserves exceed DAC. The DAC is recoverable as demonstrated by a GAAP net premium (including benefit premium, maintenance premium, and DAC premium) to gross premium ratio less than one hundred percent.

The accounting model is *SFAS 60*. Except for investment income, this block's income is relatively insensitive to the interest rate environment changes and the equity environment changes. The growth in income from year one to year two is due primarily to increased sales in year two.

Table 19-3
Term Life Balance Sheet

	Year 0	Year 1	Year 2
ASSETS			
Invested Assets			
Available-for-sale debt securities, at fair value	8,261	5,300	3,117
Total investments	8,261	5,300	3,117
Cash and cash Equivalents	744	474	315
Deferred policy acquisition costs	9,749	19,163	29,081
Total assets	18,754	24,937	32,513
LIABILITIES			
Policy liabilities and accruals	1,356	3,849	7,504
Total liabilities	1,356	3,849	7,504
STOCKHOLDERS' EQUITY			
Common stock and additional paid-in capital	15,000	15,000	15,000
Accumulated income	2,398	5,175	9,711
Accumulated other comprehensive income		913	298
Total stockholders' equity	17,398	21,088	25,009
Total liabilities and stockholders' equity	18,754	24,937	32,513

Table 19-4
Term Life Income Statement and Comprehensive Income

	Year 1	Year 2
REVENUES		
Premiums	10,600	15,946
Investment income, net of expenses	472	315
Total revenues	11,072	16,261
BENEFITS AND EXPENSES		
Policy benefits, excluding policyholder dividends	3,916	5,592
Policy acquisition costs amortization	(9,414)	(9,918)
Other operating expenses	13,793	16,051
Total benefits and expenses	8,295	11,725
Applicable income tax		
Net Income	2,777	4,536
COMPREHENSIVE INCOME		
Net Income	2,777	4,536
Other comprehensive income	913	(615)
Comprehensive income	3,690	3,921

Year one other comprehensive income is calculated as follows:

Unrealized gain:	
Fair value	5,300
Amortized cost	4,387
	913

There is no shadow DAC adjustment since the accounting model is *SFAS 60.*

19.4.3 Universal Life

The universal life balance sheets and income statements are displayed in Tables 19-5 and 19-6. Over this period, the universal life assets grew from $5.6 million to $18.9 million. Operating income was $0.1 million in year one and $0.7 million in year two.

The business is non-participating flexible premium universal life. There is a persistency bonus of 10% of the fund at the end of policy year ten. The initial credited interest rate is 5.5%. Policy average size is 250,000. Commission is 86% of premium in policy year one grading down to 1% by policy year sixteen.

The accounting model is *SFAS 97*. Under *SOP 03-1* a deferred sales inducement liability (SIL) is established for the persistency bonus. In addition, a sales inducement asset (SIA) is established due to the deferred sales inducement liability. The total liability is the sum of the policyholder deposit fund and the *SOP 03-1* SIL.

The assets for this block are all available-for-sale bonds purchased at par. No purchases or write-downs occur on these bonds during the two-year period.

This block's income is sensitive to the interest rate environment. The DAC, the SIL, and the SIA are recomputed due to changes in emerging history and due to projection assumption changes.

Year two income is positively affected by increased sales. Year two is also affected by unlocking. In addition to interest rate changes, prospective unlocking also occurs due to changes in lapse and mortality expectations. The combined effect of interest rate, lapse, and mortality changes is a higher DAC than originally forecasted.

In this example, the cash flows were not reinvested over the two-year period, so investment income is lower than credited interest.

Shadow DAC and shadow SIA are shown on the balance sheet. The primary DAC and primary SIA are calculated and used to compute operating income. In year 1 the difference in shadow DAC/SIA and primary DAC/SIA is shown in other comprehensive income along with the realized gain. In year 2 the difference between shadow DAC/SIA increase and the primary DAC/SIA increase is an element of other comprehensive income, along with the unrealized loss.

Table 19-5
Universal Life Balance Sheet

	Year 0	Year 1	Year 2
ASSETS			
Invested Assets			
Available-for-sale debt securities, at fair value	2,500	2,799	2,378
Total investments	2,500	2,799	2,378
Cash and cash Equivalents		1,697	5,220
Deferred policy acquisition costs	2,969	5,755	10,311
Accrued Sales Inducement	163	320	950
Total assets	5,632	10,571	18,859
LIABILITIES			
SIL	226	645	1,357
Policyholder deposit funds	2,309	6,660	13,495
Total liabilities	2,535	7,305	14,852
STOCKHOLDERS' EQUITY			
Common stock and additional paid-in capital	2,735	2,735	2,735
Accumulated income	362	442	1,181
Accumulated other comprehensive income		89	91
Total stockholders' equity	3,097	3,266	4,007
Total liabilities and stockholders' equity	5,632	10,571	18,859
FOOTNOTES			
Available-for-sale debt securities, at amortized cost	2,500	2,500	2,500
Deferred policy acquisition costs (primary)	2,969	5,924	10,143
Accrued Sales Inducement (primary)	163	361	906

Table 19-6
Universal Life Income Statement and Comprehensive Income

	Year 1	Year 2
REVENUES		
Insurance and investment product fees	1,532	2,103
Investment income, net of expenses	225	225
Total revenues	1,757	2,328
BENEFITS AND EXPENSES		
Policy benefits, excluding policyholder dividends	666	1,047
Interest Credited to Account Balances	348	932
Policy acquisition costs amortization	(2,955)	(4,219)
Net sales inducement cost	(198)	(545)
Other operating expenses	3,816	4,374
Total benefits and expenses	1,677	1,589
Net Income	80	739
COMPREHENSIVE INCOME		
Net Income	80	739
Other comprehensive income	89	2
Comprehensive income	169	741

Year 1 other comprehensive income is calculated as follows:

Unrealized gain (1):		
Fair value	2,799	
Amortized cost	2,500	
		299
DAC adjustment (2)		
DAC (shadow):	5,755	
DAC (primary):	5,924	
		(169)
SIA adjustment (3)		
SIA (shadow):	320	
SIA (primary):	361	
		(41)
Year 1 other comprehensive income (1) + (2) + (3):		89

19.4.4 Variable Universal Life

The variable universal life balance sheets and income statements are displayed in Tables 19-7 and 19-8. Over this period, the variable universal life assets grow from $69.3 million to $87.3 million. Operating income was $1.4 million in year one and $4.4 million in year two.

This is a non-participating flexible premium variable universal life plan. There is no persistency bonus. Policy average size is 250,000. The policyholder fund is entirely invested in a separate account. The same commission scale applies to both universal life and variable universal life.

The accounting model is *SFAS 97*. This block's income is sensitive to the equity environment. DAC is recomputed due to changes in emerging history and due to projection assumption changes. The discount rate for DAC and EGP is the variable funds rate prior to M&E.

Year two income is positively affected by increased sales. Year two is also affected by unlocking. In addition to equity rate changes, prospective unlocking also occurs due to changes in lapse and mortality expectations. The combined effect of interest rate, lapse, and mortality changes is a higher DAC than originally forecasted.

Year two income is also positively affected by increase M&E charges on larger account values due to a strong equity market.

Since all funds are in the separate account, there are no realized or unrealized gains or losses.

Table 19-7
Variable Universal Life Balance Sheet

	Year 0	Year 1	Year 2
ASSETS			
Invested Assets			
Total investments	0	0	0
Cash and cash Equivalents	11,631	7,747	4,400
Deferred policy acquisition costs	5,537	10,826	18,586
Separate account assets	52,147	45,572	64,322
Total assets	69,315	64,145	87,308
LIABILITIES			
Separate account liabilities	52,147	45,572	64,322
Total liabilities	52,147	45,572	64,322
STOCKHOLDERS' EQUITY			
Common stock and additional paid-in capital	15,000	15,000	15,000
Accumulated income	2,168	3,573	7,986
Accumulated other comprehensive income	0	0	0
Total stockholders' equity	17,168	18,573	22,986
Total liabilities and stockholders' equity	69,315	64,145	87,308

Table 19-8
Variable Universal Life Income Statement and Comprehensive Income

	Year 1	Year 2
REVENUES		
Insurance and investment product fees	4,195	6,022
Total revenues	4,195	6,022
BENEFITS AND EXPENSES		
Policy benefits, excluding policyholder dividends	448	622
Policy acquisition costs amortization	(5,289)	(7,760)
Other operating expenses	7,631	8,747
Total benefits and expenses	2,790	1,609
Applicable income tax		
Net Income before realized gains/losses	1,405	4,413
COMPREHENSIVE INCOME		
Net Income	1,405	4,413
Other comprehensive income		
Comprehensive income	1,405	4,413

19.4.5 Variable Annuity

The variable annuity balance sheets and income statements for the example period are provided in Tables 19-9 and 19-10. Over this period, the variable annuities assets grow from $61.9 million to $176.8 million. Net income was $0.4 million in year one and $3.1 million in year two.

This is a non-participating single premium deferred variable annuity. The single premium per policy is $50,000; the surrender charge period is seven years. There are GMDB and GMIB benefits. The policyholder fund is entirely invested in a separate account. Commission is 5% of premium.

The accounting model is *SFAS 97*. Under *SOP 03-1*, a liability is established for excess deaths and excess annuitizations. The discount rates for DAC and the *SOP 03-1* liability are a vector of historical and projected variable appreciation rates.

DAC unlocking in years one and two has minimal effects due to prospective changes in assumptions for equity returns. A mean reversion approach is used to set the future equity return assumption.

Income increases from year one to year two due to increased sales.

Table 19-9
Variable Deferred Annuity Balance Sheet

	Year 0	Year 1	Year 2
ASSETS			
Invested Assets			
Total investments			
Cash and cash Equivalents	8,357	7,444	6,964
Deferred policy acquisition costs	2,563	3,932	7,789
Separate account assets	51,010	82,810	162,031
Total assets	61,930	94,186	176,784
LIABILITIES			
Other general account liabilities	55	140	373
Separate account liabilities	51,010	82,810	162,031
Total liabilities	51,065	82,950	162,404
STOCKHOLDERS' EQUITY			
Common stock and additional paid-in capital	10,000	10,000	10,000
Accumulated income	865	1,236	4,380
Accumulated other comprehensive income			
Total stockholders' equity	10,865	11,236	14,380
Total liabilities and stockholders' equity	61,930	94,186	176,784

Table 19-10
Variable Deferred Annuity Income Statement and Comprehensive Income

	Year 1	Year 2
REVENUES		
Insurance and investment product fees	2,044	2,807
Total revenues	2,044	2,807
BENEFITS AND EXPENSES		
Policy benefits, excluding policyholder dividends	101	257
Policy acquisition costs amortization	(1,369)	(3,857)
Other operating expenses	2,941	3,263
Total benefits and expenses	1,673	(337)
Applicable income tax		
Net Income	371	3,144
COMPREHENSIVE INCOME		
Net Income	371	3,144
Other comprehensive income		
Comprehensive income	371	3,144

19.4.6 Fixed Deferred Annuities

The fixed deferred annuities balance sheets and income statements for the example period are displayed in Tables 19-11 and 19-12. Over this period, the fixed deferred annuities assets grow from $514 million to $562 million. Net income was $0.4 million in year one and $3.9 million in year two.

This is a non-participating single premium deferred annuity. The contract has a day one bonus of 2% of premium. The initial credited interest rate is 6.25%; interest is credited on a portfolio rate basis. Commission is 5% of premium.

The accounting model is *SFAS 97*. Under *SOP 03-1* an asset is established at issue for the day one bonus. This asset is written down over future years using the same basis as DAC.

Bonds support the fixed deferred annuities. Cash flows are reinvested in bonds each year at the current market rate.

Realized capital losses occur in year one due to a bond write-down. Most of these losses directly affect operating income. The remainder of the realized losses is spread into the future since the realized losses are included in the gross profits used to amortize DAC and the day one bonus.

In year two, the calculated shadow DAC would have exceeded the amount capitalized accrued with interest. The large unrealized loss in year two causes the calculated shadow DAC to exceed the amount capitalized accrued with interest. Therefore, the shadow DAC is capped at the amount capitalized with interest.

New sales for fixed deferred annuities are low and have little impact on earnings.

Table 19-11
Fixed Deferred Annuity Balance Sheet

	Year 0	Year 1	Year 2
ASSETS			
Invested Assets			
Available-for-sale debt securities, at fair value	445,720	497,860	471,471
Total investments	445,720	497,860	471,471
Cash and cash Equivalents	35,657	37,248	39,958
Deferred policy acquisition costs	24,139	19,925	33,289
Accrued Sales Inducement	8,962	7,398	17,612
Total assets	514,478	562,431	562,330
LIABILITIES			
Policyholder deposit funds	511,298	537,384	566,265
Total liabilities	511,298	537,384	566,265
STOCKHOLDERS' EQUITY			
Common stock and additional paid-in capital			
Accumulated income	3,180	3,583	7,508
Accumulated other comprehensive income		21,464	(11,443)
Total stockholders' equity	3,180	25,047	(3,935)
Total liabilities and stockholders' equity	514,478	562,431	562,330
FOOTNOTES			
Available-for-sale debt securities, at amortized cost	445,720	469,147	499,272
Deferred policy acquisition costs (primary)	24,139	25,212	25,190
Accrued Sales Inducement (primary)	8,962	9,361	9,352

Table 19-12
Fixed Deferred Annuity Income Statement and Comprehensive Income

	Year 1	Year 2
REVENUES		
Insurance and investment product fees	1,723	1,545
Investment income, net of expenses	37,247	39,959
Net realized investment gains	(5,000)	
Total revenues	33,970	41,504
BENEFITS AND EXPENSES		
Policy benefits, excluding policyholder dividends		
Interest Credited to Account Balances	33,513	35,889
Policy acquisition costs amortization	(1,073)	22
Net sales inducement cost	(399)	9
Other operating expenses	1,526	1,659
Total benefits and expenses	33,567	37,579
Net Income	403	3,925
COMPREHENSIVE INCOME		
Net Income	403	3,925
Other comprehensive income	21,464	(32,907)
Comprehensive income	21,867	(28,982)

19.4.7 Equity-Indexed Annuity

The equity-indexed annuities (EIA) balance sheets and income statements for the example period are presented in Tables 19-13 and 19-14. Over this period, the EIA assets declined from $54.7 million to $52.9 million. Operating income was approximately $0.9 million in year one and a loss of $0.3 million in year two.

This closed block of business comprises a single premium plan. Its base guarantee is defined as 90% of premium accumulated at 3% annual interest. The equity feature is a five-year European option on the S&P 500 with 50% participation and no cap. Commission is 5% of premium and a 25 basis point of fund trailer. Policy issue costs are $35; maintenance expenses are $25 annually.

The product is accounted under *SFAS 97* and *SFAS 133*.

The assets supporting the EIA are invested in bonds and derivatives. The derivative is a call option on the S&P 500 with characteristics (five-year Euro, 50% participation, and no cap) equal to those granted to the policyholder. Because the bonds have been declared trading securities, they are shown at fair value on the balance sheet and their realized gains included in net income. The derivatives are also shown at fair value with realized gains on the derivatives also included in net income.

Year one net income is negatively impacted by the poor equity market. The poor equity market causes a substantial decline in the value of the derivatives. In year two net income is positively impacted by the strong equity market. The strong equity market causes a substantial increase in the value of the options. These effects are seen in the investment income line of the income statement.

Year one net income is positively impacted by low interest rates. The low interest rates result in realized gains on the bonds. In year two, net income is negatively impacted by high interest rates. The high interest rates result in realized losses on the bonds since the bonds are classified as "trading" securities, which permits the insurer to avoid the separate accounting required for the unrealized gain/loss present if the bonds were classified as "available-for-sale" and held at amortized cost. As noted above, assets in the trading category are held at fair value instead of amortized cost, and any gains or losses are recognized immediately in income.

The changes in the value of the bonds and derivative assets are both included in the EGP used to amortize DAC.

Year two income is negatively impacted by the increased value of the embedded derivative. The embedded derivative increases in value at the end of year two due to the strong equity market.

Table 19-13
Equity-Indexed Annuity Balance Sheet

	Year 0	Year 1	Year 2
ASSETS			
Invested Assets			
Trading securities, at fair value	43,203	45,470	42,453
Available-for-sale equity securities, at fair value*	7,590	3,899	5,929
Total investments	50,793	49,369	48,382
Cash and cash Equivalents	1,898	2,219	2,230
Deferred policy acquisition costs	1,963	2,165	2,293
Total assets	54,654	53,753	52,905
LIABILITIES			
Host Contract	40,535	38,441	35,853
Value of Embedded Derivative	4,827	5,148	7,147
Total liabilities	45,362	43,589	43,000
STOCKHOLDERS' EQUITY			
Common stock and additional paid-in capital	2,000	2,000	2,000
Accumulated income	7,292	8,164	7,905
Accumulated other comprehensive income			
Total stockholders' equity	9,292	10,164	9,905
Total liabilities and stockholders' equity	54,654	53,753	52,905

* The fair value of the derivative asset

Table 19-14
Equity-Indexed Annuity Income Statement and Comprehensive Income

	Year 1	Year 2
REVENUES		
Insurance and investment product fees	130	113
Investment income, net of expenses	198	5,918
Net realized investment gains	2,268	(3,017)
Total revenues	2,596	3,014
BENEFITS AND EXPENSES		
Increase in Value of Embedded Derivative plus *SFAS 133* Excess Benefits	474	1,998
Interest on Host Contract	1,307	1,277
Policy benefits, excluding policyholder dividends	1,781	3,275
Policy acquisition costs amortization	(202)	(128)
Other operating expenses	145	126
Total benefits and expenses	1,724	3,273
Applicable income tax		
Net Income	872	(259)
COMPREHENSIVE INCOME		
Net Income	872	(259)
Other comprehensive income		
Comprehensive income	872	(259)

19.4.8 Immediate Annuity

The immediate annuities balance sheets and income statements for the example period are displayed in Tables 19-15 and 19-16. Over this period, the immediate annuities assets declined from $42.7 million to $38.4 million. Net income was $0.9 million in year one and $1.5 million in year two.

This is a nonparticipating single premium immediate annuity. The policy is life contingent; the payments continue until the policyholder dies. All policies were issued prior to the opening balance sheet; there is no new business.

The accounting models are *SFAS 60* and *SFAS 97* limited pay. This block's income is relatively insensitive to the interest rate environment changes and the equity environment changes.

The mortality experience in year one is poor (not enough annuitants died), leading to loss recognition. The company unlocked and increased the mortality assumption used to compute benefit reserves at the end of year one. The year one results reflect an increase in benefit reserves due to loss recognition. Consequently, the year two results reflect a lower change in reserve when compared to year one. This consequence is improved earnings in year two over those in year one.

Other comprehensive income is entirely unrealized gains or losses.

Table 19-15
Immediate Annuity Balance Sheet

	Year 0	Year 1	Year 2
ASSETS			
Invested Assets			
Available-for-sale debt securities, at fair value	39,217	43,149	35,051
Total investments	39,217	43,149	35,051
Cash and cash Equivalents	3,530	3,447	3,337
Total assets	42,747	46,596	38,388
LIABILITIES			
Policy liabilities and accurals	33,359	31,731	29,565
Other general account liabilities	8,010	7,498	6,986
Total liabilities	41,369	39,229	36,551
STOCKHOLDERS' EQUITY			
Common stock and additional paid-in capital	0	0	0
Accumulated income	1,378	2,257	3,726
Accumulated other comprehensive income	0	5,110	(1,889)
Total stockholders' equity	1,378	7,367	1,837
Total liabilities and stockholders' equity	42,747	46,596	38,388

Table 19-16
Immediate Annuity Income Statement and Comprehensive Income

	Year 1	Year 2
REVENUES		
Investment income, net of expenses	3,447	3,337
Total revenues	3,447	3,337
BENEFITS AND EXPENSES		
Policy benefits, excluding policyholder dividends	2,520	1,822
Other operating expenses	48	46
Total benefits and expenses	2,568	1,868
Applicable income tax		
Net Income	879	1,469
COMPREHENSIVE INCOME		
Net Income	879	1,469
Other comprehensive income	5,110	(6,999)
Comprehensive income	5,989	(5,530)

19.4.9 Disability Income

The disability income balance sheets and income statements for the example period are displayed in Tables 19-17 and 19-18. Over this period, the disability income assets grew from $6.6 million to $11.9 million. Operating income was $0.4 million in year one and $0.6 million in year two.

This is a non-participating disability income plan. The monthly benefit is $7,000 to age 65 with a 90-day elimination period issued to a 45-year-old male with a $2,000 annual premium. Commission is 60% of premium in policy year one, 5% in years two to ten and 2% thereafter.

The accounting model is *SFAS 60*. This block's income is relatively insensitive to the interest rate environment changes and the equity environment changes.

This is a new block of business so claims are relatively low for years one and two. The growth in income from year one to year two is due primarily to new sales in year two.

Table 19-17
Disability Income Balance Sheet

	Year 0	Year 1	Year 2
ASSETS			
Invested Assets			
Available-for-sale debt securities, at fair value	3,791	4,541	5,138
Total investments	3,791	4,541	5,138
Cash and cash Equivalents	341	365	492
Deferred policy acquisition costs	2,460	4,470	6,270
Total assets	6,592	9,376	11,900
LIABILITIES			
Policy liabilities and accruals	894	2,865	5,468
Total liabilities	894	2,865	5,468
STOCKHOLDERS' EQUITY			
Common stock and additional paid-in capital	5,000	5,000	5,000
Accumulated income	698	1,071	1,664
Accumulated other comprehensive income		440	(232)
Total stockholders' equity	5,698	6,511	6,432
Total liabilities and stockholders' equity	6,592	9,376	11,900

Table 19-18
Disability Income Income Statement and Comprehensive Income

	Year 1	Year 2
REVENUES		
Premiums	3,465	4,778
Investment income, net of expenses	363	490
Total revenues	3,828	5,268
BENEFITS AND EXPENSES		
Policy benefits, excluding policyholder dividends	2,182	3,039
Policy acquisition costs amortization	(2,010)	(1,800)
Other operating expenses	3,283	3,436
Total benefits and expenses	3,455	4,675
Applicable income tax		
Net Income	373	593
COMPREHENSIVE INCOME		
Net Income	373	593
Other comprehensive income	440	(672)
Comprehensive income	813	(79)

Appendix A Purchase Accounting

A.1 Introduction

The pursuit of merger and acquisition opportunity is a significant activity in all major business sectors, including insurance and other financial services. Yet authoritative literature providing definitive guidance for the accounting of business combinations has been relatively sparse over the years.

The principal guidance has been provided by the Accounting Principles Board (predecessor to FASB) in *Opinion 16*, "Business Combinations" (*APB 16*), and *Opinion 17*, "Intangible Assets" (*APB 17*), issued in 1970. Since then, there have been numerous AICPA and FASB interpretations of these opinions, many issues covered by the EITF, and a number of SEC Staff Accounting Bulletins and Accounting Series Releases. Actuarial guidance has not been particularly definitive. The most significant enlightenment appears in ASB *Interpretation 1-D* and *EITF 92-9*, discussed in greater detail later.

In 1999 the FASB decided to undertake a project to revisit existing guidance. As this textbook was being written, this draft standard was entitled "Business Combinations and Intangible Assets." This exposure draft did not address techniques for determining actuarially derived values. The most significant changes in this proposed SFAS call for the elimination of the pooling method (described in Section A.3) and major revisions in the accounting for goodwill.

A.2 Business Combination

According to *APB 16*, a business combination occurs when a corporation and one or more incorporated or unincorporated businesses are brought together into a single accounting entity. The single entity carries on the business activities of the previously separate, independent entities.

APB 16 defines two accounting methods for a business combination: the "pooling of interests" method (pooling) and the purchase method (also known as purchase GAAP, or PGAAP). Although both methods are acceptable in accounting for business combinations, they are not alternatives for the same transaction. Under the guidance, the characteristics of the business combination first would be tested against a list of criteria required for a pooling. If the transaction does not meet *all* the criteria, it must be accounted for as a purchase.

Most business combinations in the insurance industry involve the combination of stock companies or of a mutual company acquiring a stock company. The discussion in *APB 16* follows this approach but is silent about the combination of two mutual companies. This remains an issue in the U.S. and worldwide for mutual insurance companies that plan to merge into single entities. *SFAS 72*, "Accounting for Certain Acquisitions of Banking or Thrift Institutions", in paragraph 19, states that most of the mergers of mutual thrift institutions have been accounted for under PGAAP. It is believed that the merger of two mutual insurance companies could be treated similarly, although practice has varied on this issue.

Another form of business combination considered in this chapter is the acquisition of blocks of insurance business by another company. Block acquisitions generally involve reinsurance between the parties involved. Indemnity reinsurance is the most common because it does not require policyholder approval and contract novation, a costly and time-consuming process. Assumption reinsurance typically does require policyholders' approval.

A.3 The Pooling Method

The pooling method is defined as "the uniting of the ownership interests of two or more companies by exchange of equity securities" (*APB 16*, paragraph 12). It occurs when one entity exchanges all its voting common shares for substantially all the voting common shares of one or more other entities. Under a pooling, no new capital is invested and no assets are withdrawn from the combined entities. Instead, the net assets of the constituent shareholders remain intact and are combined.

APB 16 requires that to use the pooling method twelve specific criteria in three areas must all be satisfied:

1. Two criteria relate to the attributes of the combining companies (they must be autonomous in the two years prior to the transaction and must be independent of each other, with no more than 10% ownership in the other).

2. Seven relate to the manner in which the interests are combined (key criteria include a single transaction completed within one year; the exchange of one entity's voting shares for at least 90% of the other's voting shares with no cash involved; no dilution of any shareholders' voting interests from what they were prior to the transaction).

3. Three relate to the absence of certain planned transactions (for example, arrangements that would benefit the former shareholders are not allowed).

Under the pooling method, the recorded assets and liabilities of the separate entities generally become the recorded assets and liabilities of the combined companies. These historic cost-based amounts are recorded because the existing basis of accounting continues. The historic-based accounting is frequently abbreviated HGAAP. Where the separate entities may have used different methods of accounting, any desired change to conform the individual methods must be applied retroactively, restating the financial statements of prior periods.

The pooling method offers several advantages that have contributed to the flurry of pooling activity in the U.S. in the 1990s. The method has been especially popular in the technology and banking industries. One key advantage is no goodwill to amortize. This improves post-purchase earnings, relative to the purchase method, and allows for more aggressive price negotiation in transactions. Another advantage is that pooling is much easier to implement.

Among significant criticisms of the pooling method is the belief that it distorts the fair value exchanged in a business combination and does not allow investors to readily compare investment returns of similar transactions that in substance are not economically different. Another is that most other countries either do not allow poolings or make them extremely difficult to execute. The desire for global harmony in accounting standards would call for similar treatment in the U.S.

A.4 The Purchase Method

A.4.1 Description of Concept

All business combinations that fail any of the pooling criteria are to be accounted for under PGAAP. A purchase generally results in the acquisition of one entity by another and involves a "purchase price." It often involves transactions in which one company is clearly dominant and assumes control over the other. Structurally, a purchase may involve the distribution of assets, the incurral of liabilities, and/or the issuance of stock to obtain the assets or stock of the acquired entity. Per paragraph 70 of *APB 16*, for combinations involving an exchange of stock, the acquiring entity can be identified by evaluating the former common shareholders' interests of the combining entities that either retain or receive the larger portion of the voting rights in the combined entity.

Per *APB 16*, paragraph 67, the acquirer's new cost basis becomes the fair value of the acquired assets over the fair value of the liabilities. This is sometimes defined as the "net assets acquired." The excess of the purchase price, adjusted for the direct costs of the transaction, over the net assets acquired becomes an intangible asset. Costs of registering and issuing equity securities are a reduction of the determinable fair value of the securities. However, indirect and general expenses related to a purchase are deducted as incurred in determining net income.

Certain costs associated with a purchase business combination can be established as a liability assumed in the transaction and included in the allocation of the purchase price, in accordance with *APB 16*. These include the costs of a plan to exit an activity of the acquired entity and costs associated with the involuntary termination or relocation of employees of the acquired entity. *EITF 95-3* specifies certain conditions or criteria that must first be met to be able to record a liability. All other costs of integrating the acquired company's activities are considered indirect and general expenses related to the acquisition, to be expensed when incurred, as discussed in *APB 16*, paragraph 76.

A clear advantage of PGAAP is its emphasis on recording the fair value of the transaction at the date of business combination. This provides investors with a clear picture of the transaction's economics and helps them make informed judgments about the price paid versus the value received in a transaction. The key disadvantage is the required presentation of the excess purchase price as goodwill or other purchased intangible, which under current guidance (paragraph 31 of *APB 17*) must be amortized against earnings over a fixed period and proven to be recoverable from the expected future cash flow of the acquired entity.

The acquisition of a block of business executed under an indemnity or assumption reinsurance arrangement may also constitute the acquisition of a "business" as defined by SEC Regulation S-X item 210.11-01d. In such case, PGAAP concepts and disclosures can be applied. In general, equity of the acquiring entity is unaffected by the block purchase under PGAAP. However, if it is determined that the excess of the purchase price over the net assets acquired cannot be recovered from the expected future cash flows associated with the acquired block of business, then the acquiring company's equity would be reduced at purchase. If the reinsurance agreement does not, in essence, constitute an acquisition of a "business," then it should be accounted for as any other assumed reinsurance treaty (see Chapter 17). The accounting effect of the two approaches is generally similar; the major difference relates to disclosure requirements.

A.4.2 Initial PGAAP Balance Sheet

All assets and liabilities on the initial PGAAP balance sheet must be reported at fair value as of the purchase date, which is fair market value where available. Assets acquired for cash or other assets must be recorded at cost, that is, the amount of cash disbursed or the fair value of the other assets disbursed. Similarly, assets acquired by incurring liabilities are also recorded at cost (the present value of the amounts to be paid). Finally, assets acquired by issuing shares of stock of the acquiring entity must be recorded at the fair value of the consideration received for the stock.

In other words, the acquiring entity must allocate its cost for the transaction to the various assets acquired and liabilities assumed. To accomplish this, it first must assign a portion of the cost to each of the acquired assets (including identifiable intangible assets) and assumed liabilities, at their fair value as of the purchase date. Second, it must record as goodwill any positive excess of the cost of the acquired entity over the fair value of the net assets acquired. If such excess is negative, goodwill is forced to equal zero by first reducing any identifiable intangible assets and then if necessary by increasing liabilities. In general, negative balances are rare.

More specifically, for an acquired life insurance company, the general guidance for assigning amounts to individual acquired assets and assumed liabilities is as follows:

1. Marketable securities, such as publicly traded bonds, mortgage-backed securities, stock, cash and other cash equivalents, are established at current net realizable value.

2. Other investments, such as mortgage loans, properties, and private placements, are established at appraisal value, discounted cash flows, or other reasonable financial model result.

3. Receivables are established at the present value of amounts to be received determined at appropriate current interest rates, less allowances for uncollectibility and collection costs.

4. The present value of future profits from in-force business (an identifiable intangible asset), generally calculated at an appropriate risk discount rate, is established by using current best-estimate assumptions.

5. Other identifiable intangible assets, such as brand name and franchise value, are established at appraisal value.

6. Capital assets are established at the lower of replacement cost or their value in use after any existing accumulated depreciation has been eliminated.

7. Policyholder liabilities are established at the present value of all future benefits and expenses associated with the policies, by using current best-estimate assumptions [with provisions for adverse deviation (PAD), as necessary for *SFAS 60* and *SFAS 97* limited-pay business].

8. Deferred taxes are established at the undiscounted value of all temporary timing differences between the PGAAP and tax basis of the acquired assets and liabilities, multiplied by the appropriate tax rate.

9. Other liabilities and commitments are established at the present value of amounts to be determined at appropriate current interest rates.

Under PGAAP, the opening shareholders' equity of the acquired entity becomes the purchase price paid, net of certain costs of doing the transaction. Goodwill becomes the balancing item on the initial balance sheet.

Certain other adjustments are made to the acquired company's initial balance sheet, previously reported on an HGAAP basis. Deferred acquisition costs (DAC) are replaced by the pre-tax value of business acquired asset (VOBA), sometimes called the present value of future profits or PVP asset). Other deferred costs, intangibles, and prepaid expenses are eliminated to the extent that there is no future benefit to the acquiring company. HGAAP reserves for future policyholder benefits are replaced by PGAAP reserves and historic deferred income taxes are recalculated by using PGAAP temporary timing differences, as noted above. Certain asset items like reinsurance accounts receivable and accrued investment income can be carried forward, subject to collectibility.

It is worthwhile to emphasize that *APB 16* was written for general application to all entities and industries. In many cases, the formal guidance does not adequately address the complexities associated with the accounting for life insurance companies. As a result, considerable judgment and analysis may be required in selecting the appropriate accounting methodology for a business combination.

While this chapter is intended to provide practical methods of applying *APB 16* to purchase business combinations, it is not possible to cover all potential issues and fact situations. The overall purpose of purchase accounting is to report the balance sheet of the acquired entity on a fair value basis at the date of purchase and then to determine subsequent earnings of the acquired operations on a basis that reflects this fair valuation at purchase.

A.4.3 Comparison of PGAAP with HGAAP

As can be seen, there is considerably more work to be done in preparing the initial balance sheet on a purchase basis than for a pooling. Actuaries are generally involved with a number of these determinations, particularly PGAAP benefit reserves and the VOBA asset. Table A-1 provides a comparison of HGAAP and PGAAP in areas of interest to actuaries involved in the accounting for a business combination.

In summary, the primary involvement for actuaries in a PGAAP conversion and subsequent PGAAP reporting would include the determination of the initial VOBA asset and its subsequent amortization, the determination of post-acquisition DAC asset amounts, the restatement of policyholder liabilities, as necessary, and expense recoverability and the loss recognition analyses. Actuaries are also often involved with company efforts to prepare GAAP financial projections that include PGAAP values for planning, budgeting and other purposes.

Chart A-1
General Comparison of HGAAP and PGAAP

	HGAAP	PGAAP
Accounting models	*SFAS 60, 91, 97,* and *120*	*SFAS 60, 91, 97* and *120*
Basis for applying models	Product level	Product level
Asset valuation	Book values generally based on cost at the acquisition of the asset	Fair value at purchase date; becomes cost basis going forward
Basis of assumptions	Best estimate at date of issue (*SFAS 60* and *97* LP); current best estimate for other models	Best-estimate at date of purchase for acquired business; same as HGAAP for new business
PAD in assumptions	*SFAS 97* Limited Pay	*SFAS 97* Limited Pay
DAC asset	Yes for all models, based on *SFAS 60* criteria, amortized over period that revenues are recognized	Only for post-purchase business and future deferrable costs on acquired in force; amortization as for HGAAP
Discount rate for DAC amortization	GAAP earned rate for *SFAS 60, 97* LP, and *120*; assumed credited rate for *SFAS 97*; break-even rate for *SFAS 91*	GAAP earned rate for *SFAS 60, 97* LP, and *120*; assumed credited rate for *SFAS 97*; break-even rate for *SFAS 91*
VOBA asset	None	Yes replaces existing DAC at purchase
Discount rate for VOBA determination	Not applicable	Risk rate under EITF method, reflecting buyer's expectations or other criteria; same as for DAC amortization under DPR method
Discount rate for VOBA amortization	Not applicable	Same as for DAC one new business issued at time of purchase
Goodwill	None	Excess of purchase price over net assets acquired, including VOBA asset, at purchase
Policyholder liabilities	NLP basis, based on assumptions at issue (*SFAS 60* and *97* LP); AV or discounted CFs at assumed credited rate (*SFAS 91)*; AV (*SFAS 97* UL and IC); NLP basis, based on dividend basis assumptions (*SFAS 120)*	NLP basis, based on assumptions at purchase (*SFAS 60* and *97* LP); AV or discounted CFs at assumed credited rate (*SFAS 91*); AV (*SFAS 97* UL and IC); NLP basis, based on dividend basis assumptions (*SFAS 120*)
Deferred FIT	Yes, based on timing differences between HGAAP and tax basis	Yes, based on timing differences between PGAAP and tax basis

A.5 Policyholder Liabilities

A.5.1 General Approach

A general guiding principle is that the rules that define HGAAP also apply to PGAAP, regarding product classification, reserve methodology, and the inclusion of PAD. At purchase, the reserve for future policyholder benefits may require restatement depending on the product type, the underlying applicable accounting model, and the nature of the reserve. For example, to obtain a fair value estimate of reserve at the date of purchase, as required by *APB 16* in paragraph 87, restatement is required of products subject to *SFAS 60* and *SFAS 97* limited-pay contracts. However, in practice, for *SFAS 97* universal life-type contracts and investment contracts, the policyholder account value (AV) is generally carried over as the fair value estimate of the reserve. While the AV has been deemed to be the fair value liability at the acquisition date by many accountants, a different value based on the present value of expected product and expense cash flows using current best-estimate assumptions would probably be acceptable. The reserve for *SFAS 91* products would be either the account value (if available) or the discounted value of future benefit and maintenance expense cash flows at the assumed credited rate or the contract rate (for example, the rate on a fixed period payout annuity) at time of acquisition. The basic reserve for *SFAS 120* products would be the same net level premium (NLP) reserve defined for HGAAP reporting.

Each major reserve component is now described in more detail. Formulas are demonstrated in section A.6.4 and examples are given in section A.10.

A.5.2 Reserve Methods for *SFAS 60* and *SFAS 97* Limited-Pay

A.5.2.1 Historical Perspective

As indicated earlier, guidance for actuaries on how to restate policy liabilities to a fair value basis basically does not exist. *APB 16* calls for fair value liabilities but provides no guidance on methodology. As a result, a variety of methods have evolved over the years.

In 1977, the American Academy of Actuaries released *Interpretation 1-D,* "Purchase Accounting" in an attempt to provide some guidance to practicing actuaries. In 1981, the AICPA Purchase Accounting Task Force of the Insurance Companies Committee released a draft document titled "Calculation of Life Insurance Policy Reserves and Value of Acquired Insurance Inforce" (the AICPA Draft Paper). Although this document was never finalized, some actuaries used concepts identified there as a basis for formulating PGAAP reserves. In 1992, the FASB Emerging Issues Task Force released *EITF 92-9*, an abstract entitled "Accounting for the Present Value of Future Profits Resulting from the Acquisition of a Life Insurance Company." While the final abstract did not discuss reserves directly, certain documents contained in the *EITF 92-9 Minutes/Issues Summary* provide some definitive guidance. Of these sources, *Interpretation 1-D* is the most specific.

A.5.2.2 Methodology

Interpretation 1-D defines two approaches for calculating reserves for *SFAS 60* and *97* limited-pay contracts:

1. The defined initial reserve method (DIR)
2. The defined valuation premium method (DVP).

Under the DIR method, the reserve at purchase is taken as a predetermined amount, such as the HGAAP or statutory reserve at acquisition. By using this initial reserve and assumptions appropriate to the business, with PAD where applicable, valuation premiums are then calculated that may be used in subsequent valuations. Such valuation premiums would not be allowed to exceed the gross premium for large aggregations of business using assumptions appropriate to the business without PAD.

Under the DVP method, valuation premiums are taken as the gross premiums less a reasonable profit allowance for the risk assumed by the acquiring entity. Opening reserves are then calculated as the present value of future benefits and maintenance expenses less the present value of the future valuation premiums, using assumptions appropriate to the business with PAD. The profit allowance and PAD should be consistent with those that apply to current new business issued by the company that will be assuming future risk on the acquired business. This may be either the acquiring or purchased company, depending on whether the purchased company is continued as a separate entity or merged with the purchaser.

Under both methods, the "assumptions appropriate to the business" are based on current best estimates at the date of acquisition and reflect the acquired company's economic situation post-purchase. For example, the interest assumptions should reflect the revaluation of the acquired company's investment portfolio at fair value. Maintenance expense assumptions should reflect the company's current expense structure and future plans to reorganize. Decrements (mortality, morbidity, lapse) should reflect current and expected future experience, as influenced by the acquired company's historical experience.

The AICPA Draft Paper concluded that "the current and prospective valuation of acquired policy reserves should be based upon the expected receipt of that portion of the gross premium which is just sufficient to provide for future benefits and expenses" using prior experience and estimates of future experience appropriate at the time of purchase. The paper recognized the importance of the valuation premium in such calculation, calling for a net level premium that is calculated as of the original issue date of the contract, using assumptions that recognize actual past experience of the company (for expenses and decrements) and provide for reasonable future expectations. This guidance on assumptions is similar to that in *Interpretation 1-D* in that the interest rate assumption is to be based on the fair value of the underlying assets at purchase with reflection of future experience and the expense and decrement assumptions are to reflect actual past experience.

The minutes of a July 23, 1992 EITF meeting, which eventually led to the issuance of *EITF 92-9*, stated that "In determining the [*SFAS 60*] liability for policy benefits subsequent to the acquisition date, the actuary computes a net premium which is the portion of the gross premium necessary to support future benefits and costs using the liability at the acquisition date." Little is said about what assumptions to use, other than "the liability and the value of insurance in force are to be determined jointly."

Historically, many acquisitions have employed the DVP method to calculate *SFAS 60* and *SFAS 97* limited-pay reserves. The DIR method requires a recalculation of reserves post-acquisition for each plan, issue year, and issue age cell, hence a seriatim valuation, based on the redefined valuation premiums and best-estimate assumptions at the date of purchase.

While some companies employ valuation systems that can calculate reserves on a policy-by-policy basis, many companies use various aggregation (model office) techniques to simplify the process. One common technique is to consolidate (model) similar plan types into a "major" plan and to reduce the range of issue ages into a smaller number of representative ages (e.g., quinquennial, decennial, three, or five issue-age groups). Others use a single ratio to represent the average valuation premium as a percentage of the gross premium, at the major plan or business segment level.

One practical difficulty concerns how to define appropriate valuation premiums under the DVP method. Many actuaries agree that regardless of the modeling technique employed, the calculation should be made as of the date of original policy issuance. This is consistent with the guidance of the AICPA Draft Paper and is required by most projection and valuation systems.

Because most acquired policies are in "mid life" at the date of purchase, considering only future benefits and maintenance expenses would likely yield a nonsensical result (because it ignores the contribution of prior premiums to the reserve). In defining PGAAP valuation premiums measured from the original issue date of the policy, the actuary must select appropriate assumptions for the period from policy issuance to the purchase date. One common approach is to set the assumptions equal to those used for similar business currently being written by the acquiring or purchased company at the time of acquisition. Companies that use a single valuation premium ratio generally base it on a composite average of the valuation premium ratios for similar currently issued business and demonstrate its reasonableness through various validation techniques.

The reserve for paid-up policies and for limited pay policies in their paid up period should equal the present value of future benefits and maintenance expenses, using appropriate best-estimate assumptions as of the date of acquisition, with PAD.

A.5.3 Reserve Methods for Other *SFAS 97* Contracts

In general, the basic policy liability for *SFAS 97* universal life-type and investment contracts is not restated from the previous HGAAP basis, that is, the balance that accrues to the benefit of the policyholder at the financial statement date (the account value). This is supported by the discussion in paragraphs 4 and 5 of the July 23, 1992 EITF meeting minutes, referenced in Section A.5.2.2.

Some actuaries question whether indeed this is inconsistent with the *APB 16* requirement to restate liabilities on a fair value basis at the date of acquisition. They argue that a discounted present value of future product cash flows (including maintenance expenses), using current best-estimate assumptions and an interest rate that reflects the fair value of assets at the date of acquisition, provides a better proxy to a fair value policyholder liability. Nevertheless, the account value has been the result most commonly employed and is believed to be consistent with existing accounting literature. Thus, no change is generally required in going to PGAAP from an historic GAAP reporting basis.

Note that any premium deficiency reserve reported on the prior HGAAP balance sheet would be eliminated at purchase. New loss recognition tests would be completed at the purchase date to determine if a restated premium deficiency reserve is still required. Discussion of the unearned revenue liability and accrued bonus liability on *SFAS 97* contracts is included in Section A.5.6.

A.5.4 *SFAS 91* Reserve Methodology

Certain investment contracts do not involve mortality or morbidity risk and do not have significant revenue sources other than from investment return. Such contracts are subject to *SFAS 91*. Examples are payout annuities payable for a fixed period of years and deferred annuities with little or no surrender charges. Under PGAAP, current practice is to hold the account value, where one exists or is determinable, or a prospective reserve representing the present value of future contract cash flows (including maintenance expenses). Assumptions underlying the prospective reserve (related to surrenders, expenses, etc.) would be based upon current best estimates and would include the contract rate for discounting cash flows.

A.5.5 *SFAS 120* Reserve Methodology

SFAS 120 has been used mainly by mutual life insurance companies, which have not been subject to purchase business combinations (except as acquirers of other companies). Very few U.S. stock companies have sold significant volumes of participating business that are subject to *SFAS 120.*

Accordingly, *SFAS 120* has not been an issue in most prior U.S. acquisitions. However, many foreign stock life insurance companies that sell qualifying participating business and report on a U.S. GAAP basis have been involved in purchase business combinations. Similarly, as more and more of the U.S. mutual life insurance companies demutualize, it is likely that some will be acquired in the future and become subject to PGAAP accounting.

Under PGAAP, the net level premium reserve for death and endowment policy benefits is not restated from an HGAAP basis. The HGAAP liability for terminal dividends would likely be restated in a manner similar to the accrued bonus liability, under *SFAS 97* universal life-type contracts (see section 5.5.6). Any premium deficiency reserve recorded on the prior HGAAP balance sheet would be eliminated and recalculated, based on current best-estimate assumptions.

Companies that have closed blocks of participating business subject to *SFAS 120* should consider accounting for any undistributed accumulated earnings (to policyholders) in accordance with paragraphs 41 and 42 of *SFAS 60.* This was confirmed by the AICPA proposed statement of position (SOP) on the accounting for closed blocks, which was exposed in the spring of 2000. A similar liability would likely be required of acquired companies with closed blocks of qualifying participating business.

However, the proposed SOP does not address PGAAP situations and accordingly no current guidance exists. It is not clear whether the original "glide path" (see Chapter 18) of expected HGAAP earnings projected at the time of company demutualization would be carried forward under PGAAP or would be restated at purchase. Given that assets are to be restated to fair value at purchase and any DAC that appeared on the HGAAP balance sheet would be eliminated, it seems reasonable that the glide path would also change and that the accrual of any liability for undistributed earnings to policyholders would also be affected. The proposed SOP needs to provide definitive guidance to clarify this potential situation.

A.5.6 Other Actuarial Liabilities

An interesting question relates to the treatment on the PGAAP balance sheet of any outstanding HGAAP unearned revenue liability (URL) derived from excess front-end loads (FEL) on *SFAS 97* universal life-type or investment contracts, any outstanding HGAAP deferred profit liability (DPL) on *SFAS 97* limited-pay contracts, and any outstanding HGAAP accrued bonus liability on *SFAS 97* universal life-type and investment contracts. While not explicitly stated as such, accountants have generally interpreted paragraph 88 of *APB 16* as suggesting that identifiable assets and liabilities acquired in the transaction that result in no future benefit to or obligation upon the acquiring entity should be eliminated on the PGAAP balance sheet. This might suggest that the HGAAP balances for URL and DPL should be eliminated.

However, some companies have successfully argued that there are future profits to be derived from acquired blocks of paid-up business. Accordingly, a DPL should be established at purchase, based upon current best-estimate assumptions, for the discounted value of these future profits. Thus, two alternatives are found in practice:

a. Do not establish a DPL. In some cases, the PADs in the reserve assumptions are enhanced to more accurately reflect the future profitability of the business. Any residual value falls into goodwill.

b. Do establish a DPL. The DPL is based on current best-estimate assumptions, reflecting normal PADs in the reserve assumptions. This alternative is more often found in the accounting for the purchase of a block of business.

The liability for accrued bonuses would likely be carried over, restated as necessary to reflect assumption changes, because the company's responsibility to meet future contingent bonus payments clearly continues to exist.

Note that a new URL will accrue after the purchase date for any future residual excess FEL on the acquired business. Similarly, a DPL will accrue in the future for the restated percentage-of-premium profit margin on limited-pay business still in the premium paying period at purchase.

Little guidance exists about how to calculate the accrued bonus liability in a PGAAP environment. A reasonable approach would be to restate the existing accrued HGAAP liability at the date of purchase with an amount based on an estimate of actual past gross profits and future estimated gross profits, based on current best-estimate assumptions without PAD.

A.5.7 Special Issues Regarding Expense Assumptions

The basic policy liabilities for *SFAS 60* and *SFAS 97* limited-pay business and the prospective reserve, defined for certain *SFAS 91* products, are to include a provision for the expected cost of administering the business in the future. While practice has varied somewhat in this area, it is generally believed that only policy-related administrative expenses should be included, not overhead allocations and other expenses not related to the maintenance of the acquired business. Chapter 3 provides a more detailed discussion of the expenses that are included in each category.

The actuary should consider both prior expense levels and the expected future expense structure of the acquired company when setting best-estimate assumptions. Efforts to reorganize the operations of an acquired company following its acquisition can have a significant impact on future expected expense levels.

Excess commissions and commission-related expenses (such as bonuses) for business in the first or early policy years at acquisition will likely result in the accrual of a DAC asset on in-force business at the time of acquisition. Accordingly, such expenses should be excluded from consideration in defining the basic policy liability and in the determination of expected gross profits or margins under *SFAS 97* and *SFAS 120* respectively. More is said about this in the section defining the VOBA asset.

A.5.8 Special Considerations for Group, Credit and Individual Health

Group insurance—life, health and disability—is generally short duration, as defined by *SFAS 60.* The policyholder liability is generally limited to a provision for benefits expected to be incurred during the current period that coverage is provided or premiums are collected, plus any outstanding claim liabilities (see next section). In general, this liability is represented by the gross unearned premium at the financial statement date, and no restatement from the prior HGAAP basis is performed. Group pension and other accumulation contracts are generally long-duration contracts and are handled in a manner similar to that described earlier for investment contracts subject to *SFAS 97* or *SFAS 91* (accumulation phase) and for contracts in the payout phase subject to either *SFAS 97* for limited-pay contracts or *SFAS 91.*

Credit life and disability insurance has generally been regarded as short-duration business, subject to *SFAS 60.* The reserve is frequently the gross unearned premium calculated on the rule of

78 method for credit life and the mean of the rule of 78 and pro-rata methods for credit disability, (the same as under HGAAP). The liability for outstanding claims is established as well.

Individual health and disability coverage generally falls under *SFAS 60* as well. Most noncancelable (NC) and guaranteed renewable (GR) coverage is long duration. Cancelable coverage and products that are nonrenewable for stated reasons only are generally treated as short-duration products, with only a gross unearned premium reserve plus an outstanding claims liability being held.

For NC and GR products with a premium structure that is level or age banded, a *SFAS 60* net premium active life reserve is calculated for the duration of the period that coverage is guaranteed, reflecting the actual premium structure. At purchase, the reserve is generally calculated in a manner similar to that described above for *SFAS 60* and *SFAS 97* limited-pay life products. Current best-estimate assumptions with PAD for the entire period from policy issuance are used to obtain the valuation premiums.

On GR coverage where rate increases have occurred since policy issuance, the premium rates that are in effect at the date of purchase are generally used throughout, under the assumption that future premiums would increase to cover the impact of inflation on covered benefits and to preserve the current profit margin. However, some acquired blocks with historically high loss ratios may have rate increases anticipated in absence of any significant anticipated inflation. In this case, future premium increases might be anticipated in the purchase GAAP benefit reserve. Usually, the best-estimate assumptions would generally exclude the effect of future inflation on premiums and the morbidity decrements. See Chapter 10 for a more complete description of individual health and disability insurance reserves.

A.5.9 Claim Reserves

As discussed in Chapter 10, claim reserves (also called unpaid claim liabilities) represent the best estimate of a company's obligation, at the valuation date, for future payments on all life, health, and annuity claims incurred on or prior to that date, regardless of whether the claim has been reported to the company. Under both PGAAP and HGAAP, this best estimate should reflect current conditions as of the valuation date, along with the company's best estimate of future conditions that will affect future claims payments.

For claim reserves that are affected by the interest rate, PGAAP estimates can vary from HGAAP if there is a significant difference between the fair value and book value of the assets supporting the reserves. The best-estimate HGAAP interest rate is always based on asset book values, while the initial PGAAP interest rate (at purchase) is based on asset fair values. As stated earlier, fair value at purchase (i.e., cost basis) becomes the basis for restating asset book values in all subsequent reporting dates.

At purchase, there is no required *SFAS 115* shadow adjustment to the PGAAP claim reserves (see Chapter 14 for a more complete discussion). In subsequent valuations, the PGAAP claim reserves may require a shadow adjustment, depending on how much then current asset fair values move from the restated book value of the underlying assets.

A.6 The Value of Business Acquired Asset

A.6.1 Definition

The excess of the purchase price over the fair value of the net assets acquired is defined as goodwill in *APB 17* (paragraph 26). For this purpose, net assets acquired include both tangible and identifiable intangible assets; "fair value" at acquisition becomes the new cost basis for the acquired assets. An important identifiable intangible asset in life insurance company acquisitions is the value of business acquired asset, representing the pre-tax value of business acquired. Stated another way, the VOBA asset represents compensation to the selling entity for producing in-force business, after providing for all future benefits, administrative expenses, and claim settlement costs and after allowing for an element of profit to the acquiring entity. VOBA does not include the value of future business.

The AICPA Draft Paper states that

> ... in a purchase situation, once the acquired policy reserves have been determined, it remains necessary to determine that portion of the residual gross premium (the gross premium in excess of the benefit and maintenance valuation premiums) which is needed to recover the cost of acquiring the business. Any portion of the residual gross premium in excess of that amount would then be available to contribute to the gross profit of the acquiring company.

In this context, VOBA is defined as the cost of acquiring the business and the "profit element" is the residual gross premium that is profit to the acquiring entity.

Interpretation 1-D is more specific in its definition of the profit element. It states that

> ... in applying the DVP method, a determination of a reasonable profit allowance must be made. The profit allowance and the provision for adverse deviation used in determining the reserves should be consistent with those which apply to current new business issued by the company ... This may be either the acquiring company or the purchased company, depending on whether or not the purchased company is continued as a separate entity or merged with the purchaser.

The *EITF 92-9 Abstract* does not address the issue of how to calculate the initial amount of the VOBA asset at purchase nor does it directly address the profit element. However, in the July 23, 1992 EITF meeting minutes, reference is made to "an actuarial study" for calculating the initial VOBA derived from "all contractual cash flows [that] are projected for suitable policy groupings based on company or industry data. The cash flows include premiums, charges, claims, expenses and investment earnings." The profit element is implicit in the rate of interest used to discount the cash flows, a rate that will "reflect general market conditions and the inherent risk in the transaction."

Note that in defining the initial VOBA asset and its subsequent amortization, the general methodology and underlying assumptions should be the same or consistent with those used to calculate policyholder liabilities. This was confirmed in the AICPA Draft Paper and the July 23, 1992 EITF meeting minutes. Accordingly, the estimated future cash flows from the acquired business and the related accrual adjustments that relate to those cash flows are to reflect the accounting guidance of the applicable accounting standard (*SFAS 60*, *91*, *97*, or *120*).

Note that if the excess purchase price is negative, resulting in negative goodwill, adjustments are made to the opening PGAAP balance sheet to remove the negative goodwill, first by reducing or eliminating the VOBA asset and any other recorded identifiable intangible asset and then by increasing purchased liabilities. However, such occurrences are rare.

A.6.2 Methods for Deriving the Initial VOBA Asset

Various methods have been used over the years to define the initial amount of VOBA asset on the opening PGAAP balance sheet. Several techniques found in common usage were the use of the statutory appraisal value (used to price the transaction) and the use of a risk discount rate to calculate both the initial VOBA amount and its subsequent amortization. The latter method was particularly attractive to companies because it enabled the acquiring entity to realize a level return on its investment, more consistent with the original pricing of the transaction.

EITF 92-9 (described in Section A.6.3), issued in 1992, focused on the selection of the VOBA accrual rate. Since that time, two commonly employed methods have been: (1) the "discounted cash flows at a risk rate" method (referred to as the EITF method in this chapter), and (2) the "defined percentage of revenue" method (DPR). The first is broadly described in the July 23, 1992 EITF meeting minutes, a process that resulted in the release of *EITF 92-9.* The second is inherent in the AICPA Draft Paper and *Interpretation 1-D.* Of the two methods, the EITF method has been the most popular.

Under the EITF method, available revenues (cash flows) are discounted at a risk rate of return. There is no explicit profit margin defined. Instead, all the available revenues after adequate provision for future benefits, maintenance expenses, and deferrable costs are discounted at the risk rate. An implicit profit results, derived from the difference between the risk rate and the PGAAP rate (earned rate less a PAD for *SFAS 60* and *97* limited-pay contracts, credited rate for *SFAS 97* universal life-type and investment contracts, earned rate for *SFAS 120* and credited or contract rate for *SFAS 91*). Thus the initial VOBA asset is defined as the discounted value at the date of purchase of:

(i) Future premiums times (1 minus the valuation premium ratio) for *SFAS 60* and *SFAS 97* limited-pay contracts

(ii) Future estimated gross profits (EGP) for *SFAS 97* universal life-type and investment contracts

(iii) Future estimated gross margins (EGM) for *SFAS 120* contracts

(iv) Future investment spreads (assumed earned rate less the credited or contract rate) for *SFAS 91*.

In establishing the risk rate, key factors to consider are the yields generated on similar currently issued business, the cost of capital to the acquiring entity, the discount rate implicit in the seller's offering price, the general interest rate environment, and the potential impact of changes in the regulatory environment. (See also paragraph 6 of the July 23, 1992 EITF meeting minutes.)

Under the DPR method, revenue is defined to be premium for *SFAS 60* and *SFAS 97* limited-pay contracts, future EGP for *SFAS 97* universal life-type and investment contracts, future EGM for *SFAS 120* contracts, and the difference between expected future earned and credited or guaranteed interest for *SFAS 91* contracts. In each case, a portion (level percentage) of the expected future revenues is defined to be the profit element desired by the acquiring entity. The remaining portion of revenue not required for future policy benefits and maintenance expenses contributes to the VOBA asset.

Thus, for the DPR method for *SFAS 60* and *97* limited-pay products, the VOBA asset percentage is equal to 100% times (1 minus the valuation premium ratio minus the profit percentage). This is applied to the discounted value of future premiums at the purchase date, using the best-estimate future earned interest rate less a PAD, to obtain the initial VOBA asset. Note that the valuation premium should contain a provision for future deferrable costs. For *SFAS 97* universal life-type and investment contracts and *SFAS 120* products, it is equal to (1 minus the profit percentage) times the discounted value of future estimated EGP or EGM respectively. The EGP and EGM are based on best-estimate assumptions without PAD at purchase and the discount rate is the credited rate for EGP and the assumed earned rate for EGM.

Formulas for defining the initial VOBA asset are given in section A.6.4 and examples are provided in section A.10.

A.6.3 VOBA Amortization Procedures

Post-acquisition amortization of the VOBA asset generally follows the "matching principle" of U.S. GAAP and requires proportionality of the amounts written off each accounting period to generated revenue, in accordance with the applicable U.S. GAAP accounting model. *EITF 92-9* provides key guidance to the process.

EITF 92-9 draws three primary conclusions:

1. The PGAAP interest rate must be used in defining the amortization stream.

2. The normal HGAAP accounting guidance for *SFAS 97* business an the periodic true-up of assumptions for actual experience as it evolves and future assumptions unlocking continue to apply in defining the post-acquisition amortization pattern.

3. The VOBA asset is subject to both recoverability and loss recognition testing in accordance with *SFAS 60* and *97* rules.

Although *EITF 92-9* was released before *SFAS 120*, it is widely believed that the above criteria apply in a similar manner to *SFAS 97* products.

Note that *EITF 92-9* forbids the use of the risk rate of return in VOBA amortization for transactions that occur after the effective date. As noted earlier, this had been a common practice among companies involved in acquisitions prior to the effective date of the accounting pronouncement. Accordingly, for earlier transactions there may still be VOBA amortizing at a risk rate of return.

For companies using the EITF method to calculate the initial VOBA asset, PGAAP profits can no longer flow in accordance with the desired risk rate of return for acquisitions, after the effective date of *EITF 92-9*. Generally, the use of the PGAAP rate instead hastens the amortization process and delays profit recognition in the early years after the purchase date. Section A.10 provides examples of how VOBA amortization and pre-tax earnings affect both the EITF and DPR methods of defining the initial VOBA asset.

Note that while the VOBA asset amortizes over the remaining premium paying period for *SFAS 97* limited-pay products, the profit element is to be deferred and recognized in income over the entire remaining lifetime of the business, in a constant relationship with insurance in force (for life insurance contracts) and with the amount of expected future benefit payments (for income-paying annuity contracts). Thus, any DPL carried on the prior HGAAP balance sheet is eliminated and a new liability begins to accrue, post-purchase, as the profit element is realized. Section A.10 provides an example of how this works.

A.6.4 PGAAP Formulas

A.6.4.1 *SFAS 60* and *SFAS 97* LP

The following formulas demonstrate one common approach for developing the PGAAP reserve, the initial and post-purchase VOBA asset, and any post-purchase DAC incurred after the purchase date. A level annual premium plan is assumed. Appropriate adjustments can be made for other premium frequencies and a non-level-premium pattern.

A.6.4.1.1 Definitions

h = Time elapsed between the policy issue date and the purchase date

t = Policy duration since the purchase date

${}^{Ben}P_x$ = GAAP benefit premium for issue age x

${}^{Main}P_x$ = GAAP maintenance expense premium for issue age x

${}^{DAC}P_{x+h}$ = GAAP premium for post-purchase deferred acquisition costs, measured from age $x + h$

Note that ${}^{Ben}P_x$ and ${}^{Main}P_x$ are measured from the original issue date, using best-estimate assumptions with PAD, as of the date of purchase. ${}^{DAC}P_x$ considers only deferrable expenses incurred after the purchase date but, under most actuarial software systems, is also calculated by imputing back to the original issue date of the policy.

${}^{Marg}P_x^{(EITF)}$ = PGAAP margin for issue age x under the EITF method

${}^{AdjMarg}P_x^{(EITF)}$ = VOBA amortization premium for issue age x under the EITF method

${}^{VOBA}P_x^{(DPR)}$ = VOBA amortization premium for issue age x under DPR

$PM_x^{(DPR)}$ = Profit element for issue age x under DPR method

G_x = Gross premium for issue age x

Ann_{x+h+t} = Present value of an annuity of \$1 per year, starting at $x + h + t$

AE_{h+t} = Deferred acquisition costs incurred in year $h + t$

i_t = PGAAP earned rate in year t

r = Risk rate of return used to define the initial VOBA asset

${}_tp_x$ = Probability of survivorship at duration t for issue year x

$PVFB_{x+h+t}$ = Present value of future benefits for issue age x measured from t years after purchase date

$PVFE_{x+h+t}$ = Present value of future maintenance expenses for issue age x measured from t years after purchase date

PVP^{i} = Present value of future margins discounted at the GAAP earned rate as of the purchase date

PVP^{r} = Present value of future margins discounted at the risk rate of return as of the purchase date

Res_{x+h+t} = Reserve for future policy benefits and maintenance expenses as of t years after the purchase date for issue age x

DAC_{h+t} = DAC asset at end of year t for business in force at the purchase date

$VOBA_{h}$ = Value of business acquired as of the purchase date

$VOBA_{h+t}$ = Value of business acquired as of t years after the purchase date

A.6.4.1.2 Formulas

$${}^{Marg}P_x^{(EITF)} = G_x - {}^{Ben}P_x - {}^{Main}P_x - {}^{DAC}P_{x+h}$$

$${}^{VOBA}P_x^{(DPR)} = G_x - {}^{Ben}P_x - {}^{Main}P_x - {}^{DAC}P_{x+h} - PM_x^{(DPR)}$$

Note that the reserve, DAC, and VOBA formulas are per unit of insurance in force.

$$Res_{x+h+t} = PVFB_{x+h+t} + PVFE_{x+h+t} - ({}^{Ben}P_x + {}^{Main}P_x) \times Ann_{x+h+t}$$

$$DAC_{h+t} = (DAC_{h+t-1} + AE_{h+t} - {}^{DAC}P_{x+h}) \times (1 + i_t) \,/\, p_{x+h+t}$$

The VOBA asset formulas under the defined percentage of revenue method are as follows:

$VOBA_{h} = \sum {}^{VOBA}P_x^{(DPR)} \times {}_{h+s}p_x / {}_{h}p_x \times (1 + i_t)^{-s}$ for all s from purchase date to the end of the premium-paying period.

$$VOBA_{h+t} = \sum {}^{VOBA}P_x^{(DPR)} \times {}_{h+t+s}p_x / {}_{h+t}p_x \times (1 + i_t)^{-s}$$

for all s from purchase date to the end of the premium-paying period. VOBA can also be determined by using a retrospective formula.

$$VOBA_{h+t} = (VOBA_{h+t-1} - P_x^{(DPR)}) \times (1 + i_t)/p_{x+h+t}$$

The VOBA asset formulas under the EITF method are as follows:

$$PVP^{i} = \sum {}^{Marg}P_x^{(EITF)} \times {}_{h+s}p_x / {}_{h}p_x \times (1 + i_t)^{-s}$$

for all s from purchase date to the end of the premium-paying period.

$$PVP^{r} = \sum {}^{Marg}P_x^{(EITF)} \times {}_{h+s}p_x / {}_hp_x \times (1 + r)^{-s}$$

for all s from purchase date to the end of the premium-paying period.

$${}^{AdjMarg}P_x^{(EITF)} = PVP^{r}/PVP^{i} \times {}^{Marg}P_x^{(EITF)}$$

$$VOBA_h = PVP^{r}$$

$$VOBA_{h+t} = \sum {}^{AdjMarg}P_x^{(EITF)} \times {}_{h+t+s}p_x / {}_{h+t}p_x \times (1 + i_t)^{-s}$$

for all s from purchase date to the premium end of the paying period. It can also be determined by using a retrospective formula.

$$VOBA_{h+t} = (VOBA_{h+t-1} - {}^{AdjMarg}P_x^{(EITF)}) \times (1 + i_t) / p_{x+h+t}$$

For limited-pay business at the time of purchase, the following formulas can be used to obtain the deferred profit liability (DPL) each year. Note that the DPL results from spreading the profit element in the premium over the entire remaining benefit period, in accordance with *SFAS 97* for limited-pay contracts. This example assumes a life insurance product with a level face amount of insurance (FA).

DPL_{x+h} DPL at date of purchase; equals 0 as prior HGAAP DPL is first eliminated.

The DPL formulas under the DPR method are as follows:

${}^{DPL}P_{x+h}^{(DPR)}$ = premium to amortize (take into income) the DPL for issue age x under DPR method.

$$= G_x \times PM_x^{(DPR)} / FA_x \times (\sum {}_{h+s}p_x / {}_hp_x \times (1 + i_t)^{-s}) / (\sum {}_{h+u}p_x / {}_hp_x \times (1 + i_t)^{-u})$$

for all s from purchase date to the end of the premium period and u from purchase date to the end of the benefit period.

$$DPL_{x+h+t} = PM_x^{(DPR)} \times G_x \times {}_{t-1}p_{x+h} + (DPL_{x+h+t-1} - {}^{DPL}P_{x+h}^{(DPR)} \times FA_x \times {}_tp_{x+h}) \times (1 + i_t)$$

The DPL formulas under the EITF method are as follows:

$$PM_x^{(EITF)} = (G_x - {}^{Ben}P_x - {}^{Main}P_x - {}^{DAC}P_x - {}^{AdjMarg}P_x^{(EITF)}) / G_x$$

$DPLP_{x+h}^{(EITF)}$ = premium to amortize the DPL under the EITF method

$$= {}^{Marg}P_x^{(EITF)} / FA_x \times (\sum {}_{h+s}p_x / {}_hp_x \times (1 + i_t)^{-s}) / (\sum {}_{h+u}p_x / {}_hp_x \times (1 + i_t)^{-u})$$

for all s from purchase date to the end of the premium period and u from purchase date to the end of the benefit period.

$$DPL_{x+h+t} = PM_x^{(EITF)} \times G_x \times {}_{t-1}p_{x+h} + (DPL_{x+h+t-1} - {}^{DPL}P_{x+h}^{(EITF)} \times FA_x \times {}_tp_{x+h}) \times (1 + i_t)$$

A.6.4.2 *SFAS 97* Universal Life-Type and Investment Contract

The following formulas demonstrate one common approach for developing the initial and post-purchase VOBA asset and any post-purchase DAC incurred after the purchase date. No formula is given for the basic policy reserve because it is assumed to equal the policyholder account value. Definitions common to those included in the section above on formulas for *SFAS 60* and *SFAS 97* limited-pay contracts are not repeated here.

A.6.4.2.1 Definitions

h	Time elapsed between the policy issue date and the purchase date
t	Policy duration since the purchase date
EGP_{h+t}, AGP_{h+t}	Estimated and actual gross profits in t-th year after the purchase date; they are similar to those defined in Chapters 6 and 7; except under PGAAP, gross profits are measured from the purchase date. It is assumed that the current-year AGP_t value includes investment income earned on PGAAP cash flow to the end of the year. Each value already reflects the lapse, surrender, and death decrement rates.
${}^{VOBA}k_{h+t}^{(DPR)}$	VOBA amortization ratio in t-th year after the purchase date under the DPR method
${}^{VOBA}k_{h+t}^{(EITF)}$	VOBA amortization ratio in t-th year after the purchase date under the EITF method
${}^{DAC}k_{h+t}$	DAC amortization ratio in t-th year after the purchase date
i^{C}_{h+t}	Credited interest rate in the t-th year after the purchase date
${}_{h+t}p$	Probability of survivorship from the purchase date h to the end of year t; reflects policy lapse, surrender, and death rates for the aggregation of business under consideration.

A.6.4.2.2 Formulas

The formulas in this section are expressed for aggregations of business, such as all in-force universal life products or deferred annuity contracts subject to the *SFAS 97* investment contract guidance. This is in contrast to the formulas for *SFAS 60* and *97* limited-pay contracts, which were expressed at a cell level (issue age within plan within issue year) per unit of insurance in force. Thus it is assumed that the EGP, AGP, VOBA and DAC values are at the same aggregate level.

$${}^{DAC}k_h \quad = \quad [\textstyle\sum AE_{h+s} / \Pi(1+i^{C}_{p})^{-s}] / [\textstyle\sum EGP_s / \Pi(1+i^{C}_{v})^{-s}]$$

This is the initial amortization factor for all s from the purchase date until the end of the revenue period recognized in the calculation, for all p from purchase date to $s-1$ and for all v from 1 to s; additional deferred acquisition costs generally relate to heaped renewal commissions; an annual premium is assumed. In all subsequent years, the amortization factor is restated as follows:

$$^{DAC}k_{h+t} = \sum AE_{h+s} \;/\; \Pi(1+i^{C}_{h+p}) \;/\; \sum(AGP_{h+v} \;/\; \Pi\;(1+i^{C}_{h+v}) \;+\; \sum(EGP_{h+w} \;/\; \Pi\;(1+i^{C}_{h+w}))$$

for all s from 1 to the end of the revenue period, for all p from purchase date to $s - 1$, for all v from 1 to t and for all w from $t + 1$ to the end of the revenue period.

$$DAC_{h} = 0$$

$$DAC_{h+t} = (DAC_{h+t-1} + AE_{h+t}) \times (1 + i^{C}_{h+t}) - {}^{DAC}k_{h+t} \times AGP_{h+t}$$

The VOBA asset formulas under the DPR method are as follows:

$$^{VOBA}k_{h+t}{}^{(DPR)} = 1 - {}^{DAC}k_{h+t} - PM^{(DPR)}$$

In this case, the profit element ($PM^{(DPR)}$) is expressed as a constant percentage of the EGP/AGP stream.

$$VOBA_{h} = \text{the initial VOBA at purchase}$$

$$= \sum {}^{VOBA}k_{h}{}^{(DPR)} \times EGP_{h+s} \;/\; \Pi\;(1 + i^{C}_{h+v})$$

for all years s after the purchase date that amortization is assumed to take place and for all v from 1 to s.

$$VOBA_{h+t} = {}^{VOBA}k_{h+t}{}^{(DPR)} \times \sum EGP_{h+t+s} \;/\; \Pi\;(1 + i^{C}_{h+t+p})$$

for all future s after the end of the t-th year following the purchase date and all p from 1 to s. It can also be determined by using a retrospective formula.

$$VOBA_{h+t} = VOBA_{h+t-1} \times (1 + i^{C}_{h+t}) - {}^{VOBA}k_{h+t}{}^{(DPR)} \times AGP_{h+t}$$

The VOBA asset formulas under the EITF method are as follows:

$$PVP^{iC} = \sum(1 - {}^{DAC}k_{h}) \times EGP_{h+s} \;/\; \Pi\;(1 + i^{C}_{p})$$

for all s measured from the purchase date and for all p from 1 to s.

$$PVP^{r} = \sum(1 - {}^{DAC}k_{h}) \times EGP_{s} \times (1 + r)^{-s}$$

for all s measured from the purchase date.

$$^{VOBA}k_{h}{}^{(EITF)} = PVP^{r} \;/\; PVP^{iC}$$

$$VOBA_{h} = PVP^{r}$$

Note that after the purchase date, the amortization factor $^{VOBA}k_{h+t}{}^{(EITF)}$ will be revised to reflect actual prior gross profits and possible future assumption changes.

$$VOBA_{h+t} = {}^{VOBA}k_{h+t}{}^{(EITF)} \times \sum EGP_{h+t+s} \;/\; \Pi\;(1 + i^{C}_{h+t+p})$$

for all future s after the end of the t-th year following the purchase date. It can also be determined using a retrospective formula.

$$VOBA_{h+t} = VOBA_{h+t-1} \times (1 + i^{C}_{h+t}) - {}^{VOBA}k_{h+t}{}^{(EITF)} \times AGP_{h+t}$$

For *SFAS 91* and *120,* formulas similar to those for *SFAS 97* universal life-type and investment contracts can be developed but are excluded here.

A.7 Treatment of Goodwill

A.7.1 Identification and Amortization

Goodwill is the balancing item to a transaction's purchase price on the PGAAP balance sheet, after consideration of the cost of identifiable intangible assets, and is generally subject to *APB Opinion No. 17* guidance. This is true of both company acquisitions and the acquisition of blocks of business. In general, with insurance company transactions, the VOBA asset is the only identifiable intangible asset that is explicitly identified on the PGAAP balance sheet. Other identifiable intangible assets with economic benefit include the value of state license, the field force, customer lists, and favorable leases.

On the acquisition of a block of business, goodwill must relate to something other than the acquired block of business itself. Examples of such acquired intangibles are the value of an expanded administrative capacity that may accompany a block of business and the value of an agency force that may accompany the transaction, especially where the selling entity is exiting a line of business sold exclusively by that agency force.

All remaining excess purchase price is generally considered goodwill at the enterprise level and is to be amortized on a straight-line basis over an estimated useful lifetime of the intangibles contributing to enterprise goodwill, but not to exceed 40 years. Many insurance companies have used a shorter period such as 20 years to estimate useful lifetime.

Generally, in stock purchases, insurance companies have justified their selection of a useful lifetime of enterprise goodwill by pointing to the potential after-tax cash flows that are likely to be generated by their existing agency operations and other distribution networks. An after-tax basis is required because goodwill is shown on a gross-of-tax basis on the balance sheet and normally there is no goodwill element in the PGAAP deferred tax liability. Thus a company must demonstrate that the full amount of goodwill is recoverable from future available cash flows (after tax) from new business estimates.

Positive goodwill, gross of tax, can appear on the PGAAP balance sheet of an acquired company. Negative goodwill is eliminated by first reducing the value of identifiable intangible assets (generally the VOBA asset) and then by increasing the value of policyholder liabilities, so that no negative goodwill appears on the PGAAP balance sheet.

A.7.2 Goodwill Recoverability Issues

Paragraph 31 of *APB 17* requires companies to continually evaluate whether events and circumstances warrant revised estimates of the useful life of an intangible asset (including the VOBA asset) and a charge-off of all or a portion of the carrying amount, if it is not believed to be recoverable. However, *APB 17* does not specify a particular quantitative method for measuring the existence or extent of an impairment.

SFAS 121 provides a basis for testing insurance company goodwill for recoverability. The guidance "applies to long-lived assets, certain identifiable intangibles, and goodwill related to those assets to be held and used ..." (see paragraph 3). Impairment, in the context of *SFAS 121*, is defined in respect of the carrying value of a long-lived asset or identifiable intangible assets. However, the guidance does not clarify what identifiable intangibles are to include. Accordingly, it is not clear whether *SFAS 121* applies to insurance company enterprise goodwill, which is generally represented by the acquired company's marketing capability. Note that an acquired company's marketing capability does not have a carrying value on the U.S. GAAP balance sheet, as opposed to the VOBA asset, which does.

Paragraph 107 of *SFAS 121* states that goodwill that is not identified with impaired assets should continue to be accounted for under *APB 17*. Because *APB 17* lacks specificity in how to test for impairment, the SEC offered some clarification of this issue in its *Staff Accounting Bulletin No. 100* (*SAB 100*).

SFAS 121 provides a list of events and changes in circumstances that indicate when the recoverability of the carrying amount of an asset should be assessed. If the standard applies and an impairment is indicated, the remaining balance of the carrying value of an asset and its accompanying goodwill are compared with the sum of the expected future after-tax cash flows expected to arise from the asset. The cash flows cannot be discounted and interest charges cannot be made. If this sum is less than the asset's carrying value and its accompanying goodwill, then an impairment must be recognized by holding only the fair value of the asset, believed to be represented as the discounted value of the future after-tax cash flows at an earned or risk-free rate of return. Any write-down is first made to goodwill and then to the carrying value of the asset. In this context, cash flows refers to future after-tax U.S. GAAP earnings over the remaining goodwill amortization period on future business to be sold by the company's marketing capability over that same period.

By contrast, *SAB 100* indicates that several methods have evolved for measuring impairment of enterprise-level goodwill under *APB 17*. Three methods are cited and appear to be acceptable to the SEC:

1. A market value method, which compares the enterprise's net book value to the value indicated by the market price of its equity securities

2. An undiscounted cash flow approach, as defined for *SFAS 121* above, and

3. A discounted cash flow approach.

No guidance is given for selecting the discount rate for the third method. *SAB 100* states that if the acquired business is to be managed as a separate business unit, goodwill is to be evaluated at the business unit level and not at the level of the registrant as a whole.

SAB 100 suggests an order of preference for the three methods: the market value approach is favored, followed by the discounted cash flow approach, and finally the undiscounted cash flow approach. It also suggests that changes in the method used to evaluate the carrying value of goodwill can be made. However, while a company can change from the undiscounted approach to the discounted approach, it cannot do the reverse.

As a result, there appears to be some subjectivity in selecting an appropriate approach for testing the recoverability of an acquired entity's goodwill.

A.8 Tax Considerations

The taxation of a purchase business combination can have a significant impact on the price of a transaction. Similarly, the accounting for taxes on a U.S. GAAP basis is complex and is based on a number of considerations about the transaction that are beyond the scope of this text. Examples of these considerations are tax basis "step-up" under certain optional provisions of the tax code, operating loss and tax-credit carryforwards, and "valuation allowances" (the portion of any deferred tax asset for which it is more likely than not that a tax benefit will not be realized). *SFAS 109* applies. This section provides a simplified explanation of some considerations under PGAAP reporting.

Under PGAAP, the prior HGAAP deferred tax liability or asset is eliminated and replaced by a similar liability or asset for the tax effect of the deferred tax consequences of temporary differences between the tax basis of the insurance company's assets and liabilities and the PGAAP reporting basis. According to Appendix D of *SFAS 109*, temporary differences are those "that will result in taxable or deductible amounts in future years when the reported amount of the asset or liability is recovered or settled." The primary temporary differences relate to asset valuation, the difference between the VOBA asset and the tax-basis value of business acquired, and policy reserves. DAC tax liability created in reinsurance transactions is another example of a temporary difference.

The initial post-purchase deferred federal income tax balance is calculated as the tax rate in effect at the time of purchase times the difference between the GAAP and tax balance sheet items.

As stated earlier, fair value at the purchase date becomes the new cost basis of the assets going forward. As a result, the difference between this basis and the tax amortized or depreciated cost basis leads to revised deferred tax consequences. Similarly, the difference between the PGAAP reserve and the tax reserve also leads to deferred tax consequences. Often the largest deferred tax consequence relates to the difference between the pre-tax VOBA asset on a PGAAP basis and the tax-basis VOBA. For this purpose, the tax-basis VOBA generally results from acquisition costs required to be capitalized under Internal Revenue Code Section 848 (the so-called DAC-tax provision) and certain reinsurance commissions that are required to be capitalized for tax purposes.

The examples in Section A.10 demonstrate how the deferred tax liability or asset is defined at the purchase date under both positive and negative goodwill situations. In a negative goodwill situation, a recursive formula is required to eliminate negative goodwill by reallocating it on the PGAAP balance sheet. This is also demonstrated in the examples.

A.9 Post-Purchase Issues

After the purchase date, the GAAP financial statements for an acquired entity become a combination of the run-off of the PGAAP assets and liabilities and the application of normal HGAAP procedures to the assets and liabilities resulting from new business and other transactions occurring since the purchase date. Some of the considerations in this process are as follows:

1. The normal HGAAP rules for the amortization of discounts on bonds, depreciation of real estate, etc. apply to the purchased assets but each asset's fair value at the purchase date is used as the new cost basis.

2. *SFAS 115* rules for fair value reporting of certain marketable securities continue to apply to all assets. However, any shadow effect under the "available for sale"

classification for purchased assets is measured from the revised book value basis outlined in 1.

3. New business is to be accounted for under normal HGAAP rules, i.e., with a DAC asset, a URL where applicable, etc.

4. Consistent with the provisions of *EITF 92-9*, the VOBA asset and PGAAP policyholder balances are subject to loss recognition testing going forward, in the same manner as for DAC under HGAAP accounting.

5. Any remaining goodwill requires periodic testing for recoverability, as outlined in Section A.7.2.

6. Shareholders' equity, which starts with the purchase price for the acquired entity, accrues in the normal fashion, reflecting after-tax PGAAP and HGAAP gains and losses each year, goodwill amortization, shareholder dividends, changes in items of other comprehensive income, etc.

A.10 Examples

This section provides examples of the following concepts, regarding the accounting for a purchase business transaction of a life insurance company:

1. The PGAAP reserve and VOBA asset for a nonparticipatory 10-year endowment product (*SFAS 60*), showing income statement and balance sheet development.

2. The VOBA asset and DPL for a *SFAS 97* limited-pay plan, showing the balance sheet and income statement development.

3. The VOBA asset and goodwill for a *SFAS 97* universal life product, showing income statement development.

4. Initial PGAAP balance sheet, in comparison with HGAAP and statutory basis, with positive and negative initial goodwill and deferred tax implications.

5. Comparative 3-year pro-forma PGAAP income statement and balance sheet, measured from date of purchase, company level.

The intent is to demonstrate how PGAAP works under different situations.

A.10.1 *SFAS 60*

Table A-1 shows the reserve and VOBA development for a $10,000 10-year endowment policy issued to a male aged 45. The purchase is assumed to take place at the end of the policy's third year. Shown in the table are the cash flows and the PGAAP reserve and VOBA development in all applicable years. The first three years are based on actual experience while the subsequent years are expected values. Note that to obtain the initial PGAAP premium ratio for benefits and maintenance expenses, calculations are made from the original issue date of the policy, using assumptions appropriate for new business as of the date of purchase.

Table A-1
10 Year Non-Participating Endowment
PGAAP Calculations (*SFAS 60*)

	Year										
	0	**1**	**2**	**3**	**4**	**5**	**6**	**7**	**8**	**9**	**10**
GAAP Interest Rate		7.5%	7.5%	7.5%	7.5%	7.5%	7.5%	7.5%	7.5%	7.5%	7.5%
Investment Yield		8.0%	8.0%	8.0%	8.0%	8.0%	8.0%	8.0%	8.0%	8.0%	8.0%
Cash Flows											
Premium		850	722	656	602	559	524	496	475	459	448
Interest		48	91	133	174	213	252	292	336	384	437
Commission		170	29	26	12	11	10	10	9	9	9
Initial Expenses		43	0	0	0	0	0	0	0	0	0
Renewal Expenses		55	47	43	40	38	36	35	34	33	33
Deaths		10	13	15	17	18	18	19	20	21	23
Surrenders		123	128	159	173	176	169	152	128	95	0
Maturities		0	0	0	0	0	0	0	0	0	5,250
Premium Tax		14	12	11	10	9	9	8	8	8	7
Net Cash Flows (A)		483	584	535	524	520	533	564	612	677	(4,438)
Invested assets		483	1,067	1,601	2,141	2,660	3,194	3,758	4,370	5,046	609
Present Values (EOY)											
Premium	4,456	3,877	3,391	2,941	2,514	2,102	1,696	1,290	876	448	-
Maintenance Expenses	290	255	226	198	171	144	117	90	61	32	-
Claims	3,590	3,726	3,864	3,980	4,089	4,202	4,330	4,483	4,671	4,906	-
Premium Tax Only	74	64	56	49	41	35	28	21	14	7	-
Benefit & Expense Reserve	0	605	1,137	1,617	2,070	2,515	2,970	3,449	3,970	4,547	-

PV(Benefits & Expenses)/PV(Prem) at Original Issue	0.8874	Using the PGAAP rate of 7.5%
PV at date of purchase of PGAAP profit margins (pre-tax)	300	Initial pre-tax VOBA. Uses a 12% risk discount rate.
VOBA Amortization Factor	0.1019	Equals initial VOBA/PV future gross premiums, discounted at 7.5%

Development of PGAAP Values (EOY)	**3**	**4**	**5**	**6**	**7**	**8**	**9**	**10**
Initial VOBA	300							
Amortization in year		61	57	53	51	48	47	46
Interest on VOBA		18	15	12	9	6	3	0
EOY VOBA		256	214	173	131	89	46	0
Initial Reserve	1,617							
EOY Reserve		2,070	2,515	2,970	3,450	3,970	4,547	-
Decrease in VOBA Asset (B)		(44)	(42)	(41)	(41)	(42)	(44)	(46)
Increase in Reserve (C)		453	445	455	480	520	577	(4,547)
Pre-tax PGAAP gain in year		27	32	37	43	49	56	64

It is assumed that all decrements occur at the end of the year and that premiums are annual mode.
Maintenance expenses are assumed to be paid in the middle of the year.
At the purchase date, it is assumed, for purposes of calculating future earned investment income, that the initial invested assets equals the initial PGAAP reserve ($1,617), not the invested assets at the end of the third year ($1,601) shown in the cash flow section of the table.
The pre-tax PGAAP gain assumes no distributions of profits to shareholders.

The initial VOBA is calculated as the present value at the date of purchase of future PGAAP margins in the gross premiums, after subtracting the premium for benefits, maintenance expenses and future deferrable costs, discounted at an assumed risk discount rate of 12%. Thereafter, the VOBA is amortized as a percentage of premium by using the PGAAP rate of 7.5%. Note that this example has no future deferrable costs. If it did, a DAC asset would accrue in the normal fashion, but would be measured from the purchase date only.

Table A-1 also shows the pre-tax PGAAP profit each year before consideration of any goodwill amortization. Note that the increasing pattern of profits is due to the release of PAD in the assumptions, primarily the 0.5% PAD on the interest assumption. The PAD release increases each year as the endowment reserve increases.

A.10.2 *SFAS 97* Limited-Pay

Table A-2 provides an example of a 10-pay life policy, per $1,000 of face amount, for a male aged 35 at issue, assuming the company purchase takes place at the end of the fifth policy year. Two concepts are demonstrated here: the development of the VOBA asset and the development of the deferred profit liability (DPL). In this example, the benefit reserve is simply the present value of future expected benefits less 60% of the present value of future gross premiums, all discounted at the PGAAP earned rate of 6%. The 60% is assumed to be representative for all currently issued business of the same type.

Table A-2
Nonparticipating 10-Pay Whole Life Plan
VOBA and URL Calculations (*SFAS 97* Limited Pay)

(1) Years Since Purchase	(2) Premium	(3) Deaths	(4) Surrenders	(5) Total Benefits	(6) Discount Factor	(7) Benefit Reserve	(8) Percentage of Premium Profit	(9) VOBA	(10) PGAAP % of Premium Profit	(11) Survivors	(12) URL	(13) Pre-tax GAAP Profit
At purchase					1.00000	125.90		38.78		1.0000	-	
1	30.00	1.81	10.02	11.83	0.94340	140.71	12.00	30.76	2.24	0.9383	1.12	1.07
2	28.15	1.85	11.20	13.05	0.89000	154.01	11.26	22.91	2.11	0.8803	2.23	1.00
3	26.41	1.88	12.27	14.15	0.83962	165.89	10.56	15.18	1.98	0.8257	3.35	0.94
4	24.77	1.92	13.23	15.14	0.79209	176.46	9.91	7.55	1.85	0.7743	4.47	0.88
5	23.23	1.95	14.09	16.03	0.74726	185.79	9.29	0	1.74	0.7260	5.60	0.82
6	-	1.98	13.67	15.65	0.70496	181.29	-	0	-	0.6806	5.12	0.77
7	-	2.01	13.25	15.26	0.66506	176.90	-	0	-	0.6379	4.66	0.72
8	-	2.04	12.84	14.88	0.62741	172.64	-	0	-	0.5977	4.22	0.68
9	-	2.06	12.44	14.50	0.59190	168.50	-	0	-	0.5599	3.79	0.64
10	-	2.09	12.05	14.13	0.55839	164.47	-	0	-	0.5244	3.39	0.60
11	-	2.11	11.66	13.77	0.52679	160.58	-	0	-	0.4909	3.00	0.56
12	-	2.15	11.27	13.42	0.49697	156.79	-	0	-	0.4594	2.63	0.52
13	-	2.19	10.89	13.08	0.46884	153.12	-	0	-	0.4298	2.26	0.49
14	-	2.25	10.51	12.76	0.44230	149.54	-	0	-	0.4019	1.92	0.46
15	-	2.31	10.14	12.44	0.41727	146.07	-	0	-	0.3756	1.58	0.43
16	-	2.36	9.77	12.13	0.39365	142.71	-	0	-	0.3509	1.25	0.40
17	-	2.41	9.40	11.81	0.37136	139.46	-	0	-	0.3275	0.93	0.37
18	-	2.45	9.04	11.49	0.35034	136.33	-	0	-	0.3056	0.61	0.35
19	-	2.49	8.68	11.17	0.33051	133.34	-	0	-	0.2849	0.30	0.33
20	-	2.52	138.81	141.34	0.31180	-	-	0	-	0.0000	(0.00)	0.30

Assumptions:	
PGAAP interest rate	6.00%
Risk discount rate	12.00%
Initial gross premium (annual mode)	30.00
Benefit premium ratio (no expenses are assumed)	60.00%
Margin in premium for VOBA	40.00%
Purchase takes place at end of the 5th policy year.	
Issue age is 35 male.	
Policy surrenders for its cash value at the end of the 25th policy year.	
There are no future deferrable commissions.	
Experience mortality is 60% of 1980 CSO male ANB.	
Lapse rate is 6% in all years except the last, when it is 100%.	

Calculations:		
1	Present value of future gross premiums at 6% (col. 2 above)	119.26
2	Present value of future benefits at 6% (col. 5)	197.46
3	Present value of margins in premiums at 12% (initial VOBA) (col. 8)	38.78
4	VOBA amortization factor (= 3/1)	32.52%
5	Pre-tax PGAAP profit percentage of premiums (= 1 – 0.6 – 0.3252)	7.48%
6	Present value of PGAAP percent of premium profits at 6% (col. 10)	8.42
7	Present value of survivors (lx) at 6% (col. 11, using col. 6)	7.90
8	Amortization factor for URL (of the survivorship column) (= 6/7)	106.50%

Note that VOBA relates only to future premium margins of the policy and that the initial VOBA amount is based upon an assumed 12% risk discount rate. Note also that because the policy is limited pay, this profit margin must be spread over the entire remaining expected life of policy, using the amount of insurance (as represented by the survivorship factor in the example) as the basis for earnings recognition. Therefore, a DPL accrues during the remaining premium paying period and is released over the remaining lifetime of the policy in relation to the expected survivorship factor.

A.10.3 *SFAS 97*

The example in Table A-3 is for a company that sells only universal life business. It is assumed that, at purchase, only the next 25 years of future estimated gross profits are to be considered in calculating the initial VOBA asset. The purchase price is assumed to be $5,000 and goodwill is to be written off on a straight-line basis over 20 years. Other simplifying assumptions are given in the table.

The initial VOBA is the discounted value of the future EGPs at 12%. Subsequent amortization uses the 7% assumed credited rate. This leads to a deferral of PGAAP profits before goodwill amortization is considered, as shown in the second from last column of the exhibit. This is caused by the *EITF 92-9* requirement that amortization must use the GAAP discount rate (the credited rate) instead of the risk discount rate, used to calculate the initial VOBA amount. Note also the dampening effect on earnings of goodwill amortization and its impact on earnings.

Table A-3
Universal Life
VOBA and Goodwill Demonstration (*SFAS 97* Universal Life-Type Contract)

(1) Years Since Purchase	(2) Investment Gain: Interest Earned	(3) Investment Gain: Interest Credited	(4) Investment Gain: Net Gain	(5) Mortality Gain: COI Charges	(6) Mortality Gain: Claims Costs	(7) Mortality Gain: Net Gain	(8) Expense Gain: Policy Loads	(9) Expense Gain: Policy Expenses	(10) Expense Gain: Net Gain	(11) Surrender Net Gain	(12) Total EGP Stream	(13) EOY VOBA	(14) EOY Goodwill	(15) Deferred Tax Liability	(16) PGAAP Equity	(17) After-tax Earnings Before GW	(18) After-tax Earnings After GW	(19) PGAAP ROE Before GW	(20) PGAAP ROE After GW
At purchase												4,241	2,244	1,484	5,000				
1	1,100	860	240	499	264	235	137	178	(41)	183	617	4113	2131	1,440	4,805	318	206	6.37%	4.12%
2	1,236	967	269	501	273	228	129	167	(39)	138	596	3991	2019	1,397	4,614	308	196	6.42%	4.08%
3	1,362	1,066	296	504	281	224	121	157	(37)	92	575	3876	1907	1,357	4,426	299	186	6.47%	4.04%
4	1,477	1,156	321	508	287	220	113	148	(35)	45	552	3768	1795	1,319	4,244	288	176	6.52%	3.98%
5	1,582	1,238	344	513	302	211	106	139	(33)	-	521	3673	1683	1,286	4,070	277	165	6.54%	3.89%
6	1,677	1,313	364	516	321	195	99	131	(32)	-	528	3568	1570	1,249	3,890	274	162	6.74%	3.99%
7	1,762	1,379	382	519	341	178	93	123	(30)	-	531	3453	1458	1,208	3,703	270	158	6.95%	4.06%
8	1,838	1,439	399	519	361	158	87	116	(29)	-	528	3332	1346	1,166	3,512	264	152	7.14%	4.11%
9	1,905	1,492	413	516	381	135	81	108	(27)	-	521	3207	1234	1,122	3,318	258	145	7.33%	4.14%
10	1,964	1,538	426	512	402	110	76	102	(26)	-	511	3080	1122	1,078	3,124	250	138	7.53%	4.14%
11	2,014	1,577	437	507	425	82	71	95	(24)	-	495	2956	1010	1,035	2,931	241	129	7.70%	4.11%
12	2,055	1,610	446	499	421	79	66	89	(23)	-	501	2818	897	986	2,729	236	124	8.07%	4.24%
13	2,090	1,637	453	491	416	75	62	83	(22)	-	507	2667	785	934	2,519	231	119	8.47%	4.36%
14	2,117	1,658	459	481	410	72	57	78	(21)	-	510	2504	673	876	2,300	225	113	8.93%	4.48%
15	2,136	1,673	463	469	402	67	53	73	(19)	-	511	2328	561	815	2,074	218	106	9.47%	4.59%
16	2,149	1,683	466	453	390	63	50	68	(18)	-	510	2140	449	749	1,840	210	98	10.11%	4.70%
17	2,155	1,688	467	432	376	56	46	63	(17)	-	505	1943	337	680	1,599	200	88	10.87%	4.78%
18	2,154	1,688	466	405	357	49	43	59	(16)	-	499	1736	224	608	1,353	190	78	11.87%	4.85%
19	2,148	1,683	465	373	332	42	39	55	(15)	-	491	1520	112	532	1,100	179	67	13.23%	4.93%
20	2,137	1,675	462	336	299	37	36	51	(14)	-	485	1293	0	452	840	168	56	15.25%	5.05%
21	2,121	1,662	459	294	261	33	33	47	(13)	-	478	1054	0	369	685	156	156	18.57%	18.57%
22	2,100	1,646	454	251	221	31	31	43	(12)	-	472	804	0	281	522	144	144	21.00%	21.00%
23	2,074	1,626	448	195	174	21	28	40	(12)	-	457	546	0	191	355	130	130	24.79%	24.79%
24	2,045	1,604	441	135	120	15	26	36	(11)	-	446	278	0	97	180	115	115	32.55%	32.55%
25	2,012	1,578	434	74	65	8	23	33	(10)	-	432	0	0	(0)	(0)	101	101	55.69%	55.69%

Values and assumptions:

(A) Present value of future EGPs at 12% (initial VOBA) 4,241
(B) Present value of future EGPs at 7% 6,171
(C) VOBA amortization percentage 68.73%
(D) Assumed purchase price 5,000
(E) Assumed credited interest rate 7.0%
(F) Goodwill amortization period 20
(G) Goodwill amortization method Straight Line

(H) Tax rate 35%
(I) Assume tax reserves equals the account value which is the PGAAP reserve.
(J) Assume there is no IRC Section 848 tax (DAC tax).
(K) Assume only temporary difference for taxes is the VOBA asset, in all years.
(L) Assume all PGAAP profits are distributed at the end of each year.
(M) Considers only 25 years of future EGPs for VOBA purposes.

Formulas:

(13) = A in year 1; = PY (13) × (1 + E) – C × (12) thereafter
(14) = D – A + (15) at purchase, amortized over 20 years
(15) = H × (13)
(16) = D in year 1; = (13) + (14 – (15) thereafter
(17) = (1 – H) × [(12) + (13) – PY (13)]
(18) = (17) + (14) – PY (14)
(19) = (17) / PY (16)
(20) = (18) / PY (16)

Abbreviations:
VOBA = Value of Business Acquired
GW = Goodwill
ROE = Return on Equity
PY = Prior Year
COI = Cost of Insurance

A.10.4 Comparative Balance Sheets at the Purchase Date

Tables A-4 and A-5 provide simplified examples of an acquired life insurance company's balance sheet under three accounting bases—statutory, HGAAP, and PGAAP—all at the date of purchase. They demonstrate some of the more significant differences between the three accounting bases. The two examples are similar except the first involves a purchase price that yields positive goodwill and the second, a price that yields an initial negative goodwill.

Table A-4
Balance Sheet Comparisons
As of the Purchase Date
Situation of a Positive Goodwill Value

Balance Sheet Item	Statutory Basis	Historic GAAP	Purchase GAAP
Investments	$6,000	$5,800	$6,300
Other assets	200	125	125
Deferred acquisition costs	-	800	-
Value of business acquired (VOBA) asset	-	-	750
Goodwill	-	-	220
Total assets	6,200	6,725	7,395
Reserves	5,125	5,250	5,200
Other liabilities	375	150	150
Deferred income taxes	-	137	245
Shareholders' equity	700	1,188	1,800
Total liabilities and equity	6,200	6,725	7,395

Allocated Cost (Purchase Price)

	PGAAP	Tax Basis	Temporary Differences
Investments	$6,300	$6,000	$300
Other assets	125	125	-
Value of business acquired (VOBA) asset	750	150	600
Reserves	(5,200)	(5,000)	(200)
Other liabilities	(150)	(150)	-
Identifiable net assets	1,825	1,125	700

Reconciliation of Purchase Price	
Tangible assets (investments, other assets)	$6,425
VOBA asset	750
Reserves and other liabilities	(5,350)
Deferred tax liability	(245)
Goodwill	220
Purchase price	1,800

Table A-5
Balance Sheet Comparisons
As of the Purchase Date
Situation of a Negative Goodwill Value

Balance Sheet Item	Statutory Basis	Historic GAAP	Purchase GAAP
Investments	$6,000	$5,800	$6,300
Other assets	200	125	125
Deferred acquisition costs	-	800	-
Value of business acquired (VOBA) asset	-	-	581
Goodwill	-	-	-
Total Assets	6,200	6,725	7,006
Reserves	5,125	5,250	5,200
Other liabilities	375	150	150
Deferred income taxes	-	137	256
Shareholders' equity	700	1,188	1,400
Total liabilities and equity	6,200	6,725	7,006

Allocated Cost (Purchase Price)

	PGAAP	Tax Basis	Temporary Differences
Investments	$6,300	$6,000	$300
Other assets	125	125	-
Value of business acquired (VOBA) asset	581	150	431
Reserves	(5,200)	(5,000)	(200)
Other liabilities	(150)	(150)	-
Identifiable net assets	1,656	1,125	531

Calculations	
Initial negative goodwill – $1,825 (Exhibit 15.4) less $1,400 (purchase price)	(425)
Initial net temporary differences – $1,400 less $1,125 (tax basis)	275
Factor from simultaneous equation (Table A-6)	0.9309
Deferred tax liability – 0.9309 × 275	256
Reconciliation of Purchase Price	
Tangible assets (investments, other assets)	$6,425
VOBA asset	581
Reserves and other liabilities	(5,350)
Deferred tax liability	(256)
Goodwill	-
Purchase price	1,400

The examples include the effects of federal income taxes on a purchase business combination. The underlying tax calculations and references to appropriate tax laws are omitted from this discussion because of the complexity of these laws. The intent is to demonstrate that the tax aspects of a business combination can have a material effect on the PGAAP results.

A.10.4.1 Assumptions

Both examples use the same statutory and HGAAP balance sheets values. At the date of purchase, net investments were written down by $200 for HGAAP reporting purposes (from the statutory basis). "Other assets" reflect adjustments such as the removal of statutory net premiums. Under HGAAP, DAC is $800; reserves exceed statutory by $125; "other liabilities" reduce by $225 (reflecting the removal of the asset valuation reserve, the interest maintenance reserve and certain contingency reserves); and the deferred federal income tax liability is $137 (based on the temporary differences between the HGAAP and the tax return bases). This results in shareholders' equity of $1,188.

The purchase price in Tables A-4 and A-5 is assumed to be $1,800 and $1,400, respectively. Under both situations, the pre-tax VOBA is $750 and is calculated by using the EITF method. Investments at fair value are $6,300 and PGAAP reserves are $5,200. There are no changes in the "other assets" and "other liabilities" categories from a HGAAP basis. A 35% federal income tax rate applies for both income and capital gains.

A.10.4.2 Analysis of the Balance Sheets

In Table A-4, the higher purchase price leads to positive goodwill. Note in both examples that the HGAAP DAC value is eliminated and replaced by a VOBA asset and goodwill, if any. Note also that the purchase price becomes "shareholders' equity" at the date of purchase. (Both examples assume a 100% acquisition.) The HGAAP deferred tax liability is eliminated and replaced by a PGAAP value based upon PGAAP temporary differences.

The largest temporary difference in the two examples relates to the difference between the PGAAP and tax-basis VOBA. The tax-basis VOBA is assumed to result from the capitalization of acquisition costs under *IRC* Section 848 (the DAC tax provision) and certain reinsurance commissions that were capitalized for tax purposes (*IRC* Section 197). It is further assumed that the tax basis of investments is the statutory value, resulting in a $300 temporary difference at the purchase date. "Identifiable net assets" are defined as assets other than goodwill less liabilities other than the deferred tax liability.

In Table A-4, total temporary differences at the purchase date on the identifiable net assets are $700 and the resultant deferred tax liability is $245 (35% of $700). Goodwill, the balancing item, becomes $220.

The situation in Table A-2 is more complicated. The lower price leads to an initial negative goodwill, initially determined to be ($425). This is equal to the PGAAP identifiable net assets before considering any adjustments caused by negative goodwill (see Table A-4) less the purchase price. Under PGAAP, goodwill cannot be reported as a negative value. Thus, an allocation is needed to reduce the initial assigned values of non-current assets (VOBA, in this case). Any reduction to the VOBA asset also changes the temporary differences, which in turn change the deferred tax liability estimate. A simultaneous equation is required to develop a factor, which is applied to the restated temporary differences (see Table A-6) to get the reinstated VOBA and deferred tax amounts such that goodwill on a PGAAP basis is zero.

	Table A-6 **Derivation of Simultaneous Equation** **for Negative Goodwill Situation** **in Table A-5**	
1.	Tax rate on income	35%
2.	Tax rate on capital gains	35%
3.	Pre-tax VOBA, PGAAP basis	750
4.	Pre-tax VOBA, tax basis	150
5.	Purchase price	1,400
6.	PGAAP net identifiable assets (from Table 15-4)	1,825
7.	Tax-basis net identifiable assets	1,125
8.	Initial negative goodwill (5–6)	(425)
9.	Initial new temporary differences (5–7)	275

Let x = the required adjustment, which also represents the final deferred tax liability

Let y = the final adjusted VOBA

Let f = the adjustment factor to the initial temporary difference to get the required adjustment
$= x$ / the initial temporary difference; i.e., $f = x / 275$

then the PGAAP deferred tax liability, x, can be expressed as follows:

$x = 0.35 \times (y - 150) + 0.35 \times$ net capital gains (losses) on the revalued assets (300 from Table A-5)
$= 0.35 \times (y - 150) + 105$

Thus, the first equation is $x = 52.5 + 0.35y$

It is known that $y - x$ must equal the sum of the pre-tax VOBA and the initial negative goodwill, in order to generate a zero goodwill value for the PGAAP balance sheet.

Thus, $y - x = 325$. Now there are two equations and two unknowns.

Solving, $x = 256$, and $y = 581$

Therefore, $f = 0.9309$

Note that by offsetting the initial negative goodwill ($425) against the initial temporary differences of $700 (from Table A-4), we reduce the temporary differences to $275. Applying the factor of 0.9309 from Table A-6 to this value, we get an adjustment of $256, an amount that represents the new estimate for deferred taxes. This amount is also added to the adjusted initial estimate of VOBA, $325 ($750 less the $425 initial negative goodwill), to give a final adjusted VOBA value of $581. As a result, we have eliminated the negative goodwill value and preserved the purchase price as the PGAAP shareholders' equity.

These examples ignore any potential "valuation allowances" and assume that there are no net operating loss and tax-credit carryforwards. These latter items are often important elements of the consolidated tax return.

A.10.5 Comparative Income Statements

Table A-7 provides three years of pro-forma income statement and balance sheet data for an illustrative model representing a company with traditional life insurance, single-premium deferred annuities, and immediate annuities on its books at the point of sale. Both PGAAP and original HGAAP values are shown to illustrate the effect of a purchase on both the balance sheet and income statement. The illustration is for the runoff of the purchased in-force business only. To simplify the example, it was assumed that all investments on the HGAAP balance sheet were at fair value, after appropriate *SFAS 115* adjustments, and that no further *SFAS 115* adjustments are required after the purchase for the three-year period.

Table A-7
Illustrative Financial Statements for HGAAP with PGAAP
at Purchase and for Ensuing Three Years

	At Purchase		2001		2002		2003	
	HGAAP	PGAAP	HGAAP	PGAAP	HGAAP	PGAAP	HGAAP	PGAAP
Income Statement								
Premium income			91,308	91,308	80,477	80,477	76,484	76,484
Investment income			185,038	185,038	180,553	180,553	173,211	173,211
Interest credited			(109,699)	(109,699)	(105,306)	(105,306)	(98,417)	(98,417)
Surrender net income			1,174	1,174	1,073	1,073	872	872
Total income			167,821	167,821	156,797	156,797	152,150	152,150
Death benefits			8,247	8,247	8,426	8,426	9,087	9,087
Annuity benefits			8,942	8,942	8,842	8,842	8,733	8,733
Surrenders and maturities			24,302	24,302	8,663	8,663	9,939	9,939
Benefit reserve increase			(4,972)	12,360	23,283	24,881	21,494	22,813
Total benefits			36,519	53,851	49,214	50,812	49,253	50,572
DAC amortization			27,842		10,759		10,204	
VOBA amortization				34,501		30,995		29,015
Maintenance expenses			2,829	2,829	2,548	2,548	2,352	2,352
Overhead			1,886	1,886	1,699	1,699	1,568	1,568
Premium taxes			2,054	2,054	1,811	1,811	1,721	1,721
Total expenses			34,611	41,270	16,817	37,053	15,845	34,656
GAAP earnings before tax and goodwill amortization			96,691	72,700	90,766	68,932	87,052	66,922
Goodwill amortization				2,884		2,884		2,884
Current federal income tax			31,901	29,613	29,287	26,077	28,302	25,092
Deferred federal income tax			1,942	(8,316)	2,481	(5,718)	2,167	(5,893)
GAAP earnings after tax and goodwill amortization			62,848	48,519	58,998	45,689	56,583	44,839
Balance Sheet								
Total GAAP invested assets	2,384,593	2,384,593	2,331,112	2,331,112	2,260,739	2,260,739	2,133,497	2,133,497
DAC	159,198		140,367		133,131		125,910	
VOBA		374,237		339,737		308,742		279,727
Goodwill		72,103		69,219		66,335		63,451
Total GAAP assets	2,543,791	2,830,933	2,471,479	2,740,068	2,393,870	2,635,816	2,259,407	2,476,675
Benefit reserves	2,299,712	2,332,572	2,212,883	2,263,074	2,116,460	2,168,248	1,973,703	2,026,809
Deferred federal income taxes	19,458	98,362	21,399	90,046	23,881	84,328	26,047	78,435
Total GAAP liabilities	2,319,170	2,430,934	2,234,282	2,353,120	2,140,341	2,252,576	1,999,750	2,105,244
GAAP equity	224,622	400,000	233,986	395,035	247,109	394,851	250,027	386,026
Change in GAAP equity								
Beginning of year GAAP equity			224,622	400,000	233,986	395,035	247,109	394,851
Shareholder contributions (dividends)			(53,485)	(53,485)	(45,876)	(45,876)	(53,667)	(53,667)
Gain from operations			62,850	48,521	58,998	45,691	56,585	44,842
End-of-year GAAP equity			233,986	395,035	247,109	394,851	250,027	386,026
GAAP return on equity			28.0%	12.1%	25.2%	11.6%	22.9%	11.4%
Assumes no new business is sold.								
Purchase price is $400,000								

The purchase price was $400,000 for a 100% interest in a company with HGAAP equity at the time of sale of $224,622. Note the significant differences in the comparative HGAAP and PGAAP equity, earnings, return on equity (ROE), and deferred tax account. The considerably lower ROE is caused by a combination of a higher equity base, the need to amortize the VOBA asset (which is greater each year than the DAC amortization under HGAAP), and the dampening effect of goodwill amortization. In addition, current U.S. tax laws allow the company to receive a tax deduction over time for the cost of the transaction. This has a positive effect on PGAAP earnings.

A.11 Practice Variations

The discussion so far outlines methods and procedures applicable to life insurance company business combinations and block-of-business acquisitions that are believed to fully comply with existing accounting guidance. Because the existing guidance for purchase accounting is not entirely comprehensive, a number of practice variations have surfaced over the years regarding the definition of the initial VOBA asset, the manner in which the VOBA asset is amortized, and the way that PGAAP reserves are defined. In addition, a number of approximations have been made to simplify the process, especially where it was believed the results would not have a material impact on the acquiring entity. This section discusses two such variations: how the initial VOBA is defined and how it has been amortized. No conclusions are drawn about the propriety or acceptability of such variations.

Some practitioners believe that the VOBA asset is similar to the actuarial appraisal value of the acquired business (in other words, its embedded value), a result often used as an aid in pricing a transaction or in evaluating the asking price. Some companies have used the pre-tax appraisal value, with some modification, as the initial VOBA asset on their PGAAP balance sheets. They have justified this approach, stating that the actuarial appraisal value comprises future distributable profits and reflects the acquiring entity's expectations for future earnings.

Others have gone one step further and included the risk-based capital component of the appraisal value calculation in the initial VOBA amount as well, at a level consistent with the acquiring company's expectations for the acquired entity. They claim this helps refine the definition of distributable earnings. By casting VOBA in this fashion, the asset represents distributable profits of the acquired entity that the acquiring entity will never be able to realize as earnings under PGAAP.

Still others start with the appraisal value of the acquired business, add back deferred taxes, remove any cost of capital element, and adjust for the initial difference between the PGAAP reserves of the underlying business and the statutory reserves that underlie the appraisal value. They claim these adjustments appropriately adjust to a PGAAP basis for determining the initial VOBA asset.

Prior to the issuance of *EITF 92-9*, it was a fairly common practice to both calculate and amortize the VOBA asset by using a risk rate of return. As a result, PGAAP earnings were released in accordance with the desired risk rate, if experience equaled the assumptions. Because *EITF 92-9* did not require retroactively application, many companies still have some VOBA remaining that amortizes on this basis.

Other companies use various forms of simplifications to amortize the VOBA asset, depending on its significance to the acquiring company's financial statements, such as a straight-line amortization over a fixed period of years.

Appendix B Proposed Statement to Replace *SFAS 141*

B.1 Introduction

During the first half of the 2000 decade, the Financial Accounting Standards Board (FASB) and the International Accounting Standards Board (IASB) have worked toward developing a common set of exposure drafts of proposed accounting standards for business combinations. This is part of an ongoing process to converge the FASB's U.S. accounting standards with the IASB's international accounting standards. Such convergence is considered to become increasingly important in the global capital markets, especially among multinational entities involved in cross-border financial activities.

Early decisions reached by the respective Boards comprised Phase I of the business combinations project and resulted in the FASB's release of *SFAS 141*, Business Combinations (see Chapter 15) in June 2001 and the IASB's release of International Reporting Financial Standards *(IFRS) No. 3*, "Business Combinations," in March 2004.

Phase II efforts will result in two new exposure drafts being released in 2005 (on purchase method procedures and noncontrolling interests). They will incorporate more recent decisions reached by the Boards during deliberations of their joint purchase method procedures project. The intent is that any new standard and implementation guidance will differ only in instances where the Boards reach different decisions on the same issue.

B.2 Purpose

Chapter 15 discusses *SFAS 141* and *SFAS 142* issued in June 2001 and effective for fiscal years beginning after December 15, 2001. The FASB's latest exposure drafts, expected to be released in 2005, are intended to be issued as final Standards in 2006 and would likely apply to fiscal years beginning after December 15, 2006. The new accounting standards will replace *SFAS 141.* The exposure drafts are not considered to be authoritative. The process of exposure may result in material changes, delay in its issuance and effective dates, or, though not likely, abandonment. Therefore the reader of this text should refer to the final Standards and any amendments thereto for authoritative guidance.

In issuing the proposed standard on "Purchase Method Procedures," the FASB has expressed the following objectives:

1. **Reconsider and improve the consistency of the procedures used in accounting for an acquisition of a business**. The proposed standard requires the use of fair value (FV) in recognizing an acquired business. This assumes all assets and liabilities assumed as part of the business combination will be recognized and measured at their fair values.

2. **Improve the relevance and transparency of information provided to investors, creditors, and other users of the financial statements.** Examples given include (a) contingencies that meet the definition of assets or liabilities but not the current criteria for recognition would be separately recognized at FV rather than included in goodwill and (b) assets and liabilities of acquired businesses that are not wholly owned would be recognized at the full FV of

the acquired business rather than measured in part at FV, based on the percentage of ownership interest acquired.

3. **Improve international comparability.** This is part of a joint effort to achieve international convergence (FASB and IASB) of accounting and reporting for business combinations.

The proposed standard will be issued concurrent with the proposed *FASB Statement 1XX*, "Consolidated Financial Statements, including Accounting and Reporting of Noncontrolling Interests in Subsidiaries." *SFAS 1XX* will improve the procedures for preparing consolidated financial statements related to noncontrolling interests in subsidiaries (minority interests).

B.3 Summary of Key Differences

This section summarizes key differences between the proposed standard on "Purchase Method Procedures" and *SFAS 141*. It should be noted that the proposed standard will apply to the financial statements of all acquiring business enterprises, including mutual enterprises. Hence, mergers and other business combinations of mutual life insurance companies will be subject to the new standard after its effective date. The proposed standard, however, will still not apply to the formation of joint ventures, transactions between entities under common control, combinations between not-for-profit organizations, or the acquisition of a for-profit business by a not-for-profit organization.

Key differences with particular relevance and general applicability to life insurance entities include the following:

1. The proposed standard requires all business acquisition to be measured at fair value, rather than the cost-based provisions that *SFAS 141* carried forward, without reconsideration, from *APB No. 16*, "Business Combinations." This is consistent with the long-standing practice for exchange transactions, where FV of the business acquired may be measured based on the FV of the consideration given in exchange. Hence SFAS 141 would change as follows:

    (a) Transaction costs of the acquirer, incurred in connection with an acquisition, would be expensed when incurred rather than be included as part of the consideration exchanged for the acquired business. This includes finder's fees, advisory, legal, accounting, actuarial, and other professional fees related to negotiating and completing the transaction.

    (b) Obligations for contingent consideration for the business acquired would be recognized and measured at fair value at the acquisition date rather than as a post-combination adjustment in a subsequent period when the contingency is resolved. Estimation of fair value of the contingent payments should be based on the facts and circumstances existing at the acquisition date and may incorporate a probability-weighted approach as discussed in FASB *Concepts Statement No. 7*. Subsequent changes in the estimated value of the contingent consideration would be recognized in income in that subsequent period.

    (c) The fair value of equity securities of the acquiring company given as consideration would be measured as of the acquisition date rather than as of the agreement date.

2. Combinations between two or more mutual enterprises would be accounted for under the provisions of the new statement. Previously *SFAS 141* provided for a delayed effective date for such business combinations.

3. The new Standard would require the recognition and measurement of assets acquired and liabilities assumed at their fair value at the acquisition date rather than allocating the cost of an acquisition to those assets and liabilities.

   (a) Assets acquired and liabilities assumed for contingencies of the acquired business that meet the definitions in *FASB Concepts Statement No. 6* for assets and liabilities but did not meet the recognition criteria of FASB 5, Accounting for Contingencies, would be required to be recognized and measured at their fair value. *Concepts Statement No. 6* definitions for assets and liabilities are as follows:

      (i) Assets are probable future economic benefits obtained or controlled by a particular entity as a result of past transactions or events.

      (ii) Liabilities are probable future sacrifices of economic benefits arising from present obligations of a particular entity to transfer assets or provide services to other entities in the future as a result of past transactions or events.

   (b) Restructuring costs that do not meet the definition of liabilities at the acquisition date would no longer be recognized as part of the business combination.

   (c) In an acquisition of less than 100% of the acquired business, the assets and liabilities would be accounted for at their full fair value rather than a proportionate fair value calculation. The related noncontrolling interest in the equity of the subsidiary would reflect their portion of the net assets acquired.

4. Goodwill will continue to be measured as a residual and would now include the goodwill attributable to the noncontrolling interest in the partially owned subsidiary. In the event of a bargain purchase, the fair value of assets, other than goodwill, would no longer be reduced.

5. The accounting for acquisitions completed in more than one step would change. If an acquiring entity holds a previously acquired noncontrolling equity investment in an acquired business, that investment would be remeasured at fair value at the date of the business combination, and any unrealized holding gains or losses would be recognized in consolidated net income. Once a controlling interest is obtained, subsequent additional acquisitions of additional ownership interests of a subsidiary would no longer be accounted for as part of a business combination but rather as capital transactions.

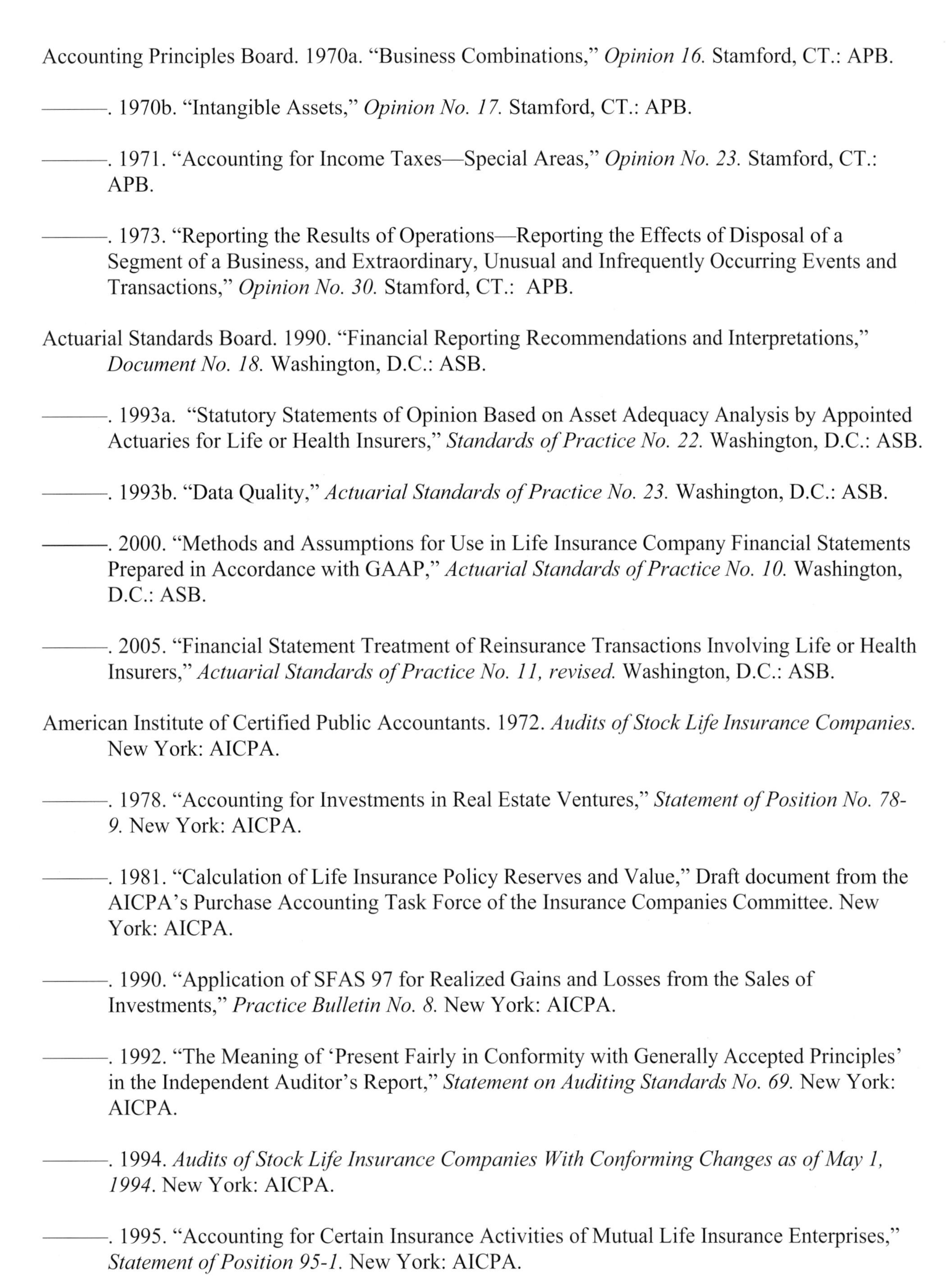

Bibliography

Accounting Principles Board. 1970a. "Business Combinations," *Opinion 16.* Stamford, CT.: APB.

———. 1970b. "Intangible Assets," *Opinion No. 17.* Stamford, CT.: APB.

———. 1971. "Accounting for Income Taxes—Special Areas," *Opinion No. 23.* Stamford, CT.: APB.

———. 1973. "Reporting the Results of Operations—Reporting the Effects of Disposal of a Segment of a Business, and Extraordinary, Unusual and Infrequently Occurring Events and Transactions," *Opinion No. 30.* Stamford, CT.: APB.

Actuarial Standards Board. 1990. "Financial Reporting Recommendations and Interpretations," *Document No. 18.* Washington, D.C.: ASB.

———. 1993a. "Statutory Statements of Opinion Based on Asset Adequacy Analysis by Appointed Actuaries for Life or Health Insurers," *Standards of Practice No. 22.* Washington, D.C.: ASB.

———. 1993b. "Data Quality," *Actuarial Standards of Practice No. 23.* Washington, D.C.: ASB.

———. 2000. "Methods and Assumptions for Use in Life Insurance Company Financial Statements Prepared in Accordance with GAAP," *Actuarial Standards of Practice No. 10.* Washington, D.C.: ASB.

———. 2005. "Financial Statement Treatment of Reinsurance Transactions Involving Life or Health Insurers," *Actuarial Standards of Practice No. 11, revised.* Washington, D.C.: ASB.

American Institute of Certified Public Accountants. 1972. *Audits of Stock Life Insurance Companies.* New York: AICPA.

———. 1978. "Accounting for Investments in Real Estate Ventures," *Statement of Position No. 78-9.* New York: AICPA.

———. 1981. "Calculation of Life Insurance Policy Reserves and Value," Draft document from the AICPA's Purchase Accounting Task Force of the Insurance Companies Committee. New York: AICPA.

———. 1990. "Application of SFAS 97 for Realized Gains and Losses from the Sales of Investments," *Practice Bulletin No. 8.* New York: AICPA.

———. 1992. "The Meaning of 'Present Fairly in Conformity with Generally Accepted Principles' in the Independent Auditor's Report," *Statement on Auditing Standards No. 69.* New York: AICPA.

———. 1994. *Audits of Stock Life Insurance Companies With Conforming Changes as of May 1, 1994.* New York: AICPA.

———. 1995. "Accounting for Certain Insurance Activities of Mutual Life Insurance Enterprises," *Statement of Position 95-1.* New York: AICPA.

———. 1997a. "Accounting by Insurance and Other Enterprises for Insurance-Related Assessments," *Statement of Position 97-3.* New York: AICPA.

———. 1997b. "Accounting by the Issuer of Surplus Notes," *Practice Bulletin 15.* New York: AICPA.

———. 1998a. "Accounting for the Costs of Computer Software Developed or Obtained for Internal Use," *Statement of Position 98-1.* New York: AICPA.

———. 1998b, April 3. "Reporting on the Costs of Start-Up Activities," *Statement of Position 98-5.* New York: AICPA.

———. 1998c. "Deposit Accounting: Accounting for Insurance and Reinsurance Contracts That Do Not Transfer Insurance Risk," *Statement of Position No. 98-7.* New York: AICPA.

———. 2000. *AICPA Audit and Accounting Guide, Life and Health Insurance Entities, New Edition as of June 15, 2000.* New York: AICPA.

———. 2003. "Accounting and Reporting by Insurance Enterprises for Certain Nontraditional Long-Duration Contracts and for Separate Accounts," *Statement of Position 03-1.* New York: AICPA.

———. Issued annually. "AICPA Codification of Statements on Auditing." New York: AICPA.

Becker, D. N., and Kitsos, T. J. 1985. "Mortality and Lapse Assumptions in Renewable Term Insurance," *Lincoln National Reinsurance Reporter, No. 104*, August, 9-14.

Bluhm, W. 1982. "Cumulative Anti-Selection Theory," *Transactions of the Society of Actuaries XXXIV,* 215–231.

Cloninger, K. 1981. "GAAP for Non-Guaranteed Premium Life Insurance," *Transactions of the Society of Actuaries XXXIII,* 498–510.

Dukes, J., and McDonald, A. 1980. "Pricing a Select and Ultimate Renewable Term Policy," *Transactions of the Society of Actuaries XXXII,* 547–565.

Financial Accounting Standards Board. 1975a. "Accounting for Contingencies," *Statement of Financial Accounting Standard No. 5.* Norwalk, CT: FASB.

———. 1975b. "Reasonable Estimation of the Amount of a Loss: An Interpretation of FASB Statement No. 5," *Interpretation No. 14.* Norwalk, CT: FASB.

———. 1978, November. "Objectives of Financial Reporting by Business Enterprises," *Statement of Financial Accounting Concept No. 1.* Norwalk, CT: FASB.

———. 1980, May. "Qualitative Characteristics of Accounting Information," *Statement of Financial Accounting Concept No. 2.* Norwalk, CT: FASB.

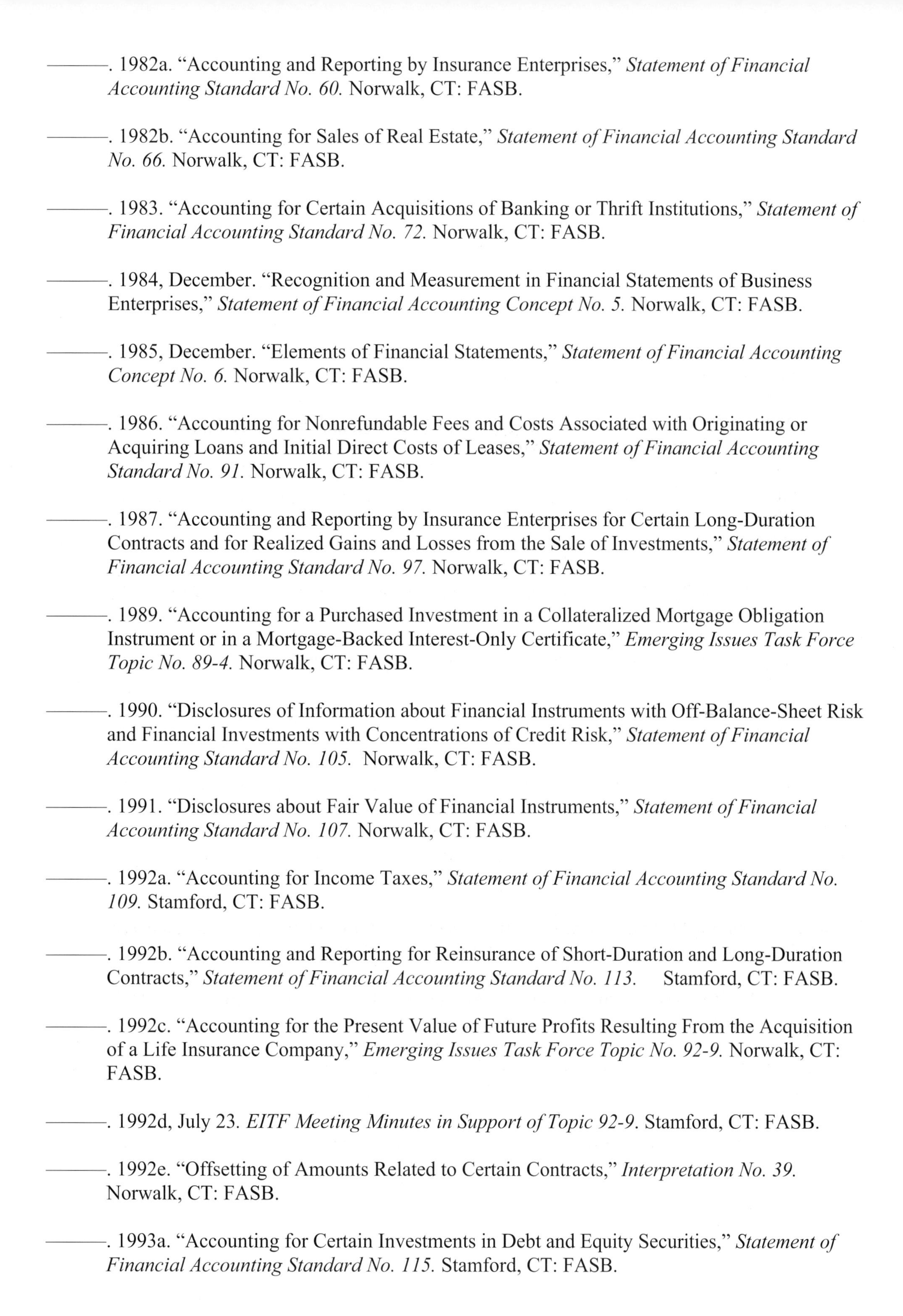

———. 1982a. "Accounting and Reporting by Insurance Enterprises," *Statement of Financial Accounting Standard No. 60.* Norwalk, CT: FASB.

———. 1982b. "Accounting for Sales of Real Estate," *Statement of Financial Accounting Standard No. 66.* Norwalk, CT: FASB.

———. 1983. "Accounting for Certain Acquisitions of Banking or Thrift Institutions," *Statement of Financial Accounting Standard No. 72.* Norwalk, CT: FASB.

———. 1984, December. "Recognition and Measurement in Financial Statements of Business Enterprises," *Statement of Financial Accounting Concept No. 5.* Norwalk, CT: FASB.

———. 1985, December. "Elements of Financial Statements," *Statement of Financial Accounting Concept No. 6.* Norwalk, CT: FASB.

———. 1986. "Accounting for Nonrefundable Fees and Costs Associated with Originating or Acquiring Loans and Initial Direct Costs of Leases," *Statement of Financial Accounting Standard No. 91.* Norwalk, CT: FASB.

———. 1987. "Accounting and Reporting by Insurance Enterprises for Certain Long-Duration Contracts and for Realized Gains and Losses from the Sale of Investments," *Statement of Financial Accounting Standard No. 97.* Norwalk, CT: FASB.

———. 1989. "Accounting for a Purchased Investment in a Collateralized Mortgage Obligation Instrument or in a Mortgage-Backed Interest-Only Certificate," *Emerging Issues Task Force Topic No. 89-4.* Norwalk, CT: FASB.

———. 1990. "Disclosures of Information about Financial Instruments with Off-Balance-Sheet Risk and Financial Investments with Concentrations of Credit Risk," *Statement of Financial Accounting Standard No. 105.* Norwalk, CT: FASB.

———. 1991. "Disclosures about Fair Value of Financial Instruments," *Statement of Financial Accounting Standard No. 107.* Norwalk, CT: FASB.

———. 1992a. "Accounting for Income Taxes," *Statement of Financial Accounting Standard No. 109.* Stamford, CT: FASB.

———. 1992b. "Accounting and Reporting for Reinsurance of Short-Duration and Long-Duration Contracts," *Statement of Financial Accounting Standard No. 113.* Stamford, CT: FASB.

———. 1992c. "Accounting for the Present Value of Future Profits Resulting From the Acquisition of a Life Insurance Company," *Emerging Issues Task Force Topic No. 92-9.* Norwalk, CT: FASB.

———. 1992d, July 23. *EITF Meeting Minutes in Support of Topic 92-9*. Stamford, CT: FASB.

———. 1992e. "Offsetting of Amounts Related to Certain Contracts," *Interpretation No. 39.* Norwalk, CT: FASB.

———. 1993a. "Accounting for Certain Investments in Debt and Equity Securities," *Statement of Financial Accounting Standard No. 115.* Stamford, CT: FASB.

———. 1993b. "Accounting for Multiple-Year Retrospectively Rated Contracts by Ceding and Assuming Enterprises," *Emerging Issues Task Force Topic No. 93-6.* Norwalk, CT: FASB.

———. 1993c. "Applicability of GAAP to Mutual Life Insurance and Other Enterprises," *Interpretation No. 40.* Norwalk, CT: FASB.

———. 1993d. "FASB Staff Views on Issue No. 93-6," *EITF Topic D-35.* Norwalk, CT: FASB.

———. 1993e. "Recognition of Impairment for an Investment in a Collateralized Mortgage Obligation Instrument or in a Mortgage-Backed Interest-Only Certificate," *Emerging Issues Task Force Topic No. 93-18.* Norwalk, CT: FASB.

———. 1994. "Adjustments in Assets and Liabilities for Holding Gains and Losses as Related to the Implementation of SFAS No. 115," *Emerging Issues Task Force Topic No. D-41.* Norwalk, CT: FASB.

———. 1995a. "Accounting and Reporting by Mutual Life Insurance Enterprises and by Insurance Enterprises for Certain Long-Duration Participating Contracts," *Statement of Financial Accounting Standard No. 120.* Stamford, CT: FASB.

———. 1995b. "Accounting for the Impairment of Long-Lived Assets and for Long-Lived Assets to be Disposed of," *Statement of Financial Accounting Standard No. 121.* Stamford, CT: FASB.

———. 1995c. "Recognition of Liabilities in Connection with a Business Combination," *Emerging Issues Task Force Topic No. 95-3.* Stamford, CT: FASB.

———. 1997. "Reporting Comprehensive Income," *Statement of Financial Accounting Standard No. 130.* Stamford, CT: FASB.

———. 1998. "Accounting for Derivative Instruments and Hedging Activities," *Statement of Financial Accounting Standard No. 133.* Stamford, CT: FASB.

———. 1999. September 7. "Business Combinations and Intangible Assets," Proposed Statement of Financial Accounting Standard. Stamford, CT: FASB.

———. 2000. "Accounting for Certain Derivative Instruments and Certain Hedging Activities—An Amendment of FASB Statement No. 133," *Statement of Financial Accounting Standard No. 138.* Stamford, CT: FASB.

———. 2001. "Business Combinations," *Statement of Financial Accounting Standard No. 141.* Stamford, CT: FASB.

———. 2001. "Goodwill and Other Intangible Assets," *Statement of Financial Accounting Standard No. 142.* Stamford, CT: FASB.

Halpern, E. 1979. "Approach to the Pricing of a Social Insurance Supplement to Disability Income Policies," *Transactions of the Society of Actuaries XXXI,*533-542.

Horn, R. G. 1971. "Life Insurance Earnings and the Release from Risk Policy Reserve System," *Transactions of the Society of Actuaries XXII,* 391-399.

McLaughlin, S.M. 1987. "A Comparison of Alternate Generally Accepted Accounting Principles (GAAP) Methodologies for Universal Life," *Transactions of the Society of Actuaries XXXIX,* 131–167.

Raws, A. 1990. "GAAP for Medicare Supplement Policies," *Transactions of the Society of Actuaries XLII,* 339–369.

Robbins, E. 1994, March. "Dealing with the New 'Shadow DAC'," *The Financial Reporter,* Number 22, 7.

———. 1995, March. "Implementation Issues of the 'Shadow DAC'," *The Financial Reporter*, Number 25, 9–10.

Securities and Exchange Commission. 1986. "Discounting by Property-Casualty Insurance Companies," *Staff Accounting Bulletin 62.* Washington, D.C.: U.S. Government Printing Office.

———. 1999a. "Materiality," *Staff Accounting Bulletin 99.* Washington, D.C.: U.S. Government Printing Office.

———. 1999b. "Restructuring and Impairment Change," *Staff Accounting Bulletin 100.* Washington, D.C.: U.S. Government Printing Office.

Index

A

accident and health insurance (A&H). *See* health insurance (individual)
accidental death and dismemberment (ADD), 364, 383
account balance products, 165–170
account value, 72, 165
Accounting by Stock Life Insurance Companies for Annuities, Universal Life Insurance and Related Products and Accounting for Nonguaranteed-Premium Contracts, 161
Accounting for Universal Life, 161
accounting information, 4–5
accounting literature, 29–30. *See also* specific titles of publications
Accounting Principles Board (APB) Opinions, 19, 30. *See also* specific titles beginning *APB*
Accounting Research Bulletins (ARBs), 19, 30
Accounting Standards Executive Committee (AcSec), 30, 34
accumulation funds, 165–170
acquisition dates, 458–459
acquisitions. *See also* business combinations
  accounting, 461–462, 484–487
  cost allocation, 460–461
  costs, 38, 44–47, 172
  expenses, 37–40, 84–86, 129, 333 (*See also* expenses and capitalization)
  generally, 25, 28
actuarial appraisal method, 474–476
Actuarial Standards Board (ASB), 31
Actuarial Standards of Practice (ASOPs), 30–31
ADD. *See* accidental death and dismemberment (ADD)
adverse deviation, 86–89, 90, 348–351
advertising expenses, 50
AFS. *See* available for sale (AFS) securities
agents, 49, 50
AICPA. *See* American Institute of Certified Public Accountants (AICPA)
alternative discount rates, 157–159
alternative tax systems, 583
American Academy of Actuaries, 30–31
American Institute of Certified Public Accountants (AICPA), 3–4, 18–23, 30, 34. *See also* specific titles of publications
American Institute of Certified Public Accountants Issue Papers, 30
amortization. *See also* deferred acquisition costs (DAC)
  of acquisition expenses, 171–186
  choice of crediting rate, 189–190
  DAC and DSI amortization under *SFAS 97,* 211–217
  methods, 130–132
  of persistency bonuses, 170
  ratios, 157–159
  under *SFAS 91,* 217–218
  true-up and unlocking, 138–141
  of unearned revenue liability, 269
  universal life insurance, 173–175, 175–184
  of VOBA, 477–478
  worksheet approaches to calculation, 78–80

A&H. *See* health insurance (individual)
annual renewable term reinsurance. *See* yearly renewable term (YRT)
annuities. *See also* deferred annuities
  background, 311
  contract classification, 311–312
  conversion of policy-year factors to calendar-year factors, 319–320
  equity-indexed, 290–294
  immediate, 626–627
  investment contracts, 312–317
  life, 203
  limited payment contracts, 317–319
  retirement, 203–205
  variable, 430–435, 620–621
  variable deferred, 233–234, 258–263
  variable payout, 234, 264–270
annuitization guarantees, 394–397
APB. *See* Accounting Principles Board (APB) Opinions
APB Opinion 16, "Business Combinations," 19, 460, 631–633
APB Opinion 17, "Intangible Assets," 19
APB Opinion 20, 15
APB Opinion 23, "Accounting for Income Taxes – Special Areas," 582, 588
APB Opinion 30, "Reporting the Results of Operations – Reporting the Effects of Disposal of a Segment of a Business, and Extraordinary, Unusual and Infrequently Occurring Events and Transactions," 65–66
apportionment ratios, 53–54
appraisal value method, 476–477
Asian market, 508–509
ASOP 10, "Methods and Assumptions for Use in Life Insurance Company Financial Statements Prepared in Accordance with GAAP," 31, 87, 93, 114–117
ASOP 22, "Statutory Statements of Opinion Based on Asset Adequacy Analysis by Appointed Actuaries for Life or Health Insurers," 58
assessment, defined, 190–191
assessment enterprises. *See* mutual life insurance enterprises
assessment of public companies, 20, 33–34
asset groups, 66
assets and liabilities
  deferred taxes, 580–581
  deposit liabilities, 594
  discounting liabilities, 378–379
  generally, 1, 5–7
  method of accounting for deferred taxes, 577–581
  method of accounting for reporting units, 459
  from sales inducements, 72–78
  unearned premium, 121–122
assumption reinsurance, 526, 574
assumptions
  alternative contract rates, 271–276
  best-estimate, 87, 155–156
  for business combinations, 487
  deferred annuities, 218–219
  five-year average method, 273–276
  health insurance (individual), 342–351

level prospective approach, 271–276
limited payment contracts, 318–319
purchase accounting, 659–660
riders, 590
traditional life insurance, 85–93, 114–117, 133–138
universal life insurance, 182–184
variable products, 238–244
Audit and Accounting Guide, 370–372
Audit and Accounting Guide, Life and Health Entities, 56–57, 81, 88–93, 114
audits of insurance companies
auditor's role, 32–34
authorities, 17, 20, 608
life and health insurance companies, 81, 87–88, 94
stock life insurance companies, 37–38
Audits of Stock Life Insurance Companies (Audit Guide), 17, 37–38, 81, 87–88, 94
authorities
accounting by analogy, 32
American Institute of Certified Public Accountants (AICPA), 3–4, 18–23
congressional and regulatory involvement, 32–34
Financial Accounting Standards Board (FASB), 23–29, 34
GAAP hierarchy, 29–31
historical perspective, 17
role of the auditor, 32
Securities and Exchange Commission (SEC), 31–34
available for sale (AFS) securities, 405–406, 442

B

backdating policies, 47
bail-out provisions, 204
balance sheets, 58–60, 660–661
Becker, David, 90
benefit reserves
assumptions, 133–134
categorization of expenses, 37–39
coinsurance, 542
deferred annuities, 208–210
defined, 10–11
development of, 94–105, 110–113
factor approaches, 332
health insurance (individual), 331–332, 336–340, 345, 350
measurement methods and estimates, 13–14
methodology, 82–83
reserve factors, 92
reserve formula selection, 118–122
riders, 590
universal life insurance, 168–170
yearly renewable term reinsurance, 545
benefits
coordination of, 389
disability, 365
guaranteed maturity death benefits (GMDB), 243, 247–248, 276–285
guaranteed maturity income benefits (GMIB), 209–210, 243, 248, 467–468

guaranteed minimum accumulation benefits (GMAB), 234, 243–244, 248–250, 286–289
guaranteed minimum death benefits (GMDB), 233
guaranteed minimum income benefits (GMIB), 233
guaranteed minimum withdrawal benefits (GMWB), 234, 243–244, 248–250
health insurance (individual), 322–323, 331–332
indemnity, 322–324, 326
managed care, 383
partial disability, 365
policyholders, 129, 134, 146–148
reserves, 114–115
social security, 365
special, 188–189
waiver-of-premium, 383
best-estimate assumptions, 87, 155–156
Black-Scholes calculations, 277, 294–295, 299–300
block of business, defined, 94, 598–603
bond discount, 578–579
bonds, 407–412. *See also* equity-indexed annuities
bonuses, 49, 67, 166, 188–189. *See also* persistency bonuses
book profits, 60–61
business combinations
accounting, 19, 484–487
acquisition accounting compared with HGAAP, 461–462
acquisition cost allocation, 460–461
assumptions, selecting, 487
background, 455
date of acquisition, 458–459
defined, 457–458
disclosures, 489–490
goodwill, 456–457, 479–484
identifying intangible assets, 469–471
intangible assets other than goodwill, 456–457, 471–479
policyholder liabilities, 463–469
post-purchase issues, 488–489
purchase accounting, 631–632
reporting units, 459–460
SFAS 141 and *SFAS 142* decisions, 456–457
taxes, 488, 584
business overhead policies, 327

C

calendar-year conversion from policy-year, 319–320
cancellation of policies, 322
capital gains, 5–6, 141–143
capitalization. *See* expenses and capitalization
carrybacks and carryforwards, 577
cash flow hedge, 596
cash surrender value, 165
catastrophe coverage, 526
categorization of costs, 41–48
census development, 287
certain annuities, 203, 465

China, 513
CIDA. *See* Commissioners Individual Disability table (85CIDA)
circulatory issue, 200–202
claim reserves
  credit insurance coverage, 376–379
  health insurance (individual), 358–363
  life and health insurance (group), 385–386
  policyholder liabilities, 468
  and purchase accounting, 642
claim settlement expenses, 363
claim triangle method. *See* lag tables
closed block of participating policies, 598–603
CMO. *See* collateralized mortgage obligations (CMO)
Code of Professional Conduct, 609
Codification of Statements on Auditing Standards, 608
COI. *See* cost of insurance (COI) charges
coinsurance, 438–439, 525, 542–543, 548–551, 562–563
COLA
  See cost-of-living adjustment (COLA)
collateralized mortgage obligations (CMO), 404, 412–418
Commissioners Individual Disability table (85CIDA), 361, 377–378
commissions
  assumptions, 91–92, 347
  deferrability, 38, 49
  overrides, 50
  timing, 54–55
  trailers, 49
Committee of Sponsoring Organizations (COSO), 33
company rollup
  background and company description, 611
  disability income, 628–629
  equity-indexed annuities, 624–625
  fixed deferred annuities, 622–623
  immediate annuities, 626–627
  operating environment, 611–612
  participating whole life, 612–613
  term life, 614–615
  universal life, 616–617
  variable annuities, 620–621
  variable universal life, 618–619
completion factor method. *See* lag tables
"component of an entity," 66
comprehensive income, 6–8
computer hardware and software, 39
concept statements. *See* Statements of Financial Accounting Concepts (SFAC)
Constant Yield Method, 313–317
contingencies, 6, 13, 24–25, 359, 460
contract administration costs, 40, 171
contracts
  administration costs, 40, 171
  analysis, 428–439
  backdating, 47

cancellation, 322
issue expenses, 50
renewability, 321–322, 330
reserves (*See* benefit reserves)
riders, 150–151, 172
coordination of benefits, 389
corridor factor, 250, 252
COSO. *See* Committee of Sponsoring Organizations (COSO)
cost of insurance (COI) charges, 67, 71, 166, 187–188
cost-of-living adjustment (COLA), 365
costs. *See also* expenses and capitalization
categorization of, 41–48
outsourcing, 470, 478
credit default swaps, 571–573
credit insurance coverage, 376–379, 468
credit life and disability insurance, 641–642
credited rate, 69, 71, 165, 173, 189–190
currency, foreign, 438
current tax expense or benefit, 577
customer relationships, 470, 478

D

DA contracts. *See* deposit administration (DA) contracts
DAC. *See* deferred acquisition costs (DAC)
date of acquisition, 458–459
day-one bonuses, 67, 188
debt securities
bonds, 407–412
collateralized mortgage obligations, 412–418
generally, 404–407
deductible temporary difference, 577
deferred acquisition costs (DAC). *See also* shadow adjustments
coinsurance, 542
credit insurance coverage, 374–375
deferred annuities, 210–218, 221–226
defined, 11–12, 37, 38
determination of, 48–50
equity-indexed annuities, 291–294
expenses and capitalization, 78–80, 215–217
and front end load considerations, 210
health insurance (individual), 335–342
interest method, 398–399
on internal replacements, 22–23
investment contracts, 314–317
margin for adverse deviation in assumptions, 87–88
measurement methods, 13–14
nondeferrable acquisition costs, 38, 44–47, 172
pension liabilities, 397–400
percentage (k-factor), 446
reserves, 336–340
riders, 590
SOP liability, 197–199

and tax, 92
terminal dividend liabilities, 148–150
timing of deferrability, 51–56
true-up and unlocking, 138–141, 183–186
UL method, 398–399
unamortized acquisition costs, 85
universal life insurance, 167, 173–175, 175–184
variable products, 238–242, 244–247, 262, 267–268
worksheet approaches to calculation, 78–80
deferred annuities
accounting model classification, 205–208
assumptions, selection of, 218–219
background and products, 203–205
benefit reserves, 208–210
contract classification, 235–237
DAC amortization under *SFAS 91,* 217–218
DAC and DSI amortization under *SFAS 97,* 211–217
DAC and front end loads, 210–211
DAC and URL amortization examples, 221–226
fixed, 203–205, 622–623
flexible-premium (FPDAs), 204
income statement presentations, 226–227
loss recognition tests, 219–220
market-value-adjusted annuities, 228–230
pension contracts, 391–392
temporary, 203
two-tiered, 205, 209–210
unearned revenue liability, accrual of, 218
variable, 430–435, 620–621
deferred dividend liability. *See* policyholder dividend obligation (PDO)
deferred policy acquisition costs (DPAC), 37, 85, 385
deferred profit liability (DPL), 110–113, 318, 333–335, 640–641
deferred sales inducements (DSI), 211
deferred taxes
alternative tax systems, 583
APB Opinion 23 differences, 582
assets and liabilities, 577–581
glossary, 577–578
jurisdictions, 583
law and rate changes, 582
purchase business combinations, 584
SFAS 109, 576–577, 584–586
tax planning, 583
taxable income *vs.* GAAP income, 575–576
temporary differences, 579–580
valuation allowance, 581
defined initial reserve (DIR) method, 637
defined valuation premium (DVP) method, 637–638
demutualizations, 464, 597, 599–600
deposit administration (DA) contracts, 392
deposit liabilities, 594
Derivative Implementation Group (DIG), 27, 29, 427. *See also* specific titles beginning DIG

derivatives
credit, 563–564
embedded, 290–293, 301–302, 563–573, 595–596
equity-indexed annuities, 290–294
investment accounting, 427–428
development method. *See* lag tables
DI. *See* disability income (DI)
DIG. *See* Derivative Implementation Group (DIG)
DIG B6, "Embedded Derivatives: Allocating the Basis of a Hybrid Instrument to the Host Contract and the Embedded Derivative," 291
DIG B19, 565
DIG B29, "Embedded Derivatives: Equity-Indexed Contracts with Embedded Derivatives," 291
DIG B30, "Embedded Derivatives: Application of Statement 97 and Statement 133 to Equity-Indexed Annuity Contracts," 291
DIG B36, 562–573
DIG Issue B8, 236–237
DIG Issue B25, 238
DIR method. *See* defined initial reserve (DIR) method
direct maintenance costs, 39, 43–44
disability, defined, 321
disability benefits
residual, 365
disability continuance table, 361, 377–378
disability income (DI), 323, 326–327, 361–363, 628–629
disability insurance, 641–642
disability table (85CIDA), 361, 377–378
disclosures, 15–16, 489–490
discontinued operations, 65–66
discount rates, 241–242
discounted cash flows, 400, 644
discounting liabilities, 362–363, 378–379
distribution of surplus, 41
distribution systems, 470, 478
dividends
and benefits reserves, 114–115
defined, 126–127
as distribution of surplus, 41
estimates of future gross margins, 135–136
net level premiums as different, 152–154
terminal, 129, 143–144, 150
dollar-cost averaging (DCA) bonuses, 67
DPAC. *See* deferred policy acquisition costs (DPAC)
DPL. *See* deferred profit liability (DPL)
DSI. *See* deferred sales inducements (DSI)
dual entry accounting, 10
Dukes, Jeffrey, 90
DVP method. *See* defined valuation premium (DVP) method

E

earnings for life insurers, 9–13
earnings management, 605
EGP. *See* estimated gross profits (EGPs)

EIAs. *See* equity-indexed annuities (EIAs)
EITF. *See* Emerging Issues Task Force (EITF)
EITF 92-9, "Accounting for the Present Value of Future Profits Resulting from the Acquisition of a Life Insurance Company," 644–646
EITF Issue No. 03-1, "The Meaning of Other-Than-Temporary Impairment and Its Application to Certain Investments," 406–407
EITF Issue No. 96-12, 437
EITF Topic D-35, "FASB Staff Views on Issue No.93-6," 534
EITF Topic D-41, "Adjustments in Assets and Liabilities for Holding Gains and Losses as Related to the Implementation of SFAS No. 115," 443–448
embedded derivatives, 290–293, 301–302, 563–573, 595–596
Emerging Issues Task Force (EITF), 24, 29, 30. *See also* specific titles beginning EITF
endowment contracts, 82
equity in the unearned premium (EUEP), 338
equity-indexed annuities (EIAs)
  accounting for derivatives, 290–291
  background, 231
  company rollup, 624–625
  GAAP methodologies for DAC and reserves, 291–294
  investment accounting, 436–438
  nature of product, 289–290
  point-to-point design products, 277, 292, 294–299, 436
  policyholder liabilities, 466
  ratchet design products, 299–309, 436
  sample assumptions, 277–279
  sample balance sheet and income statement, 280–281
equity-indexed life insurance, 435–436
estimated gross margins (EGMs)
  and amortization methods, 130–132
  assumptions, 134–137
  DAC and terminal dividend liabilities, 148–150
  policy riders, 151
  realized capital gains, 141–143
  recoverability and loss recognition, 143–144
  true-up and unlocking, 138–141
estimated gross profits (EGPs)
  capitalization and amortization of acquisition expenses, 171–174, 175–184
  contract interest rates, 239–241
  defined, 211–218, 238
  determination, 278–279, 282–283, 285
  reinsurance, 555–558, 560–561
  sales inducements, 68–70, 73–78, 171–174
EUEP. *See* equity in the unearned premium (EUEP)
European market, 502–503
expense charges (loads), 186, 210–211, 218, 253–254, 257
expense reserves, 92, 94–105, 110–113, 120–122, 333. *See also* maintenance expense reserves
expenses and capitalization
  acquisition expenses, 37–40, 84–86, 129, 171–186, 333
  advertising, 50
  assumptions, 62, 136, 346–347, 469, 641
  background, 35–37
  categorization by *SFAS 60,* 37–39

categorization under other pronouncements, 39–41
DAC calculation, 78–80, 215–217
deferrability of acquisition costs, 48–56
defined, 6
discontinued operations, 65–66
internal replacements, 62–63
life and health insurance (group), 384–385
line of business and category analysis, 41–48
overhead, 39, 43–44
purchase accounting, 64–65
recoverability testing and loss recognition, 56–61
reimbursements, 50
reinsurance, 63–64
relation of GAAP expense assumptions to pricing expense assumptions, 62
sales inducements, 66–78
experience rating, 526, 573

F

Fackler formula, 341–342
Fair Valuation of Insurance Liabilities: Principles and Methods, 592
fair value accounting
actuarial appraisal method, 474–476
background, 591–592
pension liabilities, 400
SFAS 107, 592–595
SFAS 133, 595–596
SFAS 142, 597
fair value hedge, 596
FASB. *See* Financial Accounting Standards Board (FASB)
FASB Concepts Statement No. 7, "Using Cash Flow Information and Present Value in Accounting Measurements," 483–484
FASB Interpretation No. 14, "Reasonable Estimation of the Amount of a Loss: an interpretation of FASB Statement No. 5," 359, 377
FASB Interpretations (FIN), 23
FASB Staff Positions (FSPs), 24, 29. *See also* specific titles beginning *FSP*
FASB Standards, 24–25. *See also* specific titles beginning *SFAS*
FASB Technical Bulletins (FTBs), 24, 30
federal income tax (FIT), 92, 183, 348, 488, 576–586
federal laws and regulations, 32–33. *See also* title of specific laws
FEL. *See* front-end loads (FEL)
Financial Accounting Foundation, 18
Financial Accounting Standards Board (FASB), 23–29, 34
financial instruments, 592–593
Financial Reporting Recommendations and Interpretations, 609
financial statements
accounting information, 4–5
assumptions, 87, 93, 114–117
background, 1–4
basic elements of, 5–7
coinsurance, 543
comprehensive income, 7–8
disclosures, 15–16, 489–490

earnings for life insurers, 9–13
expenses and capitalization, 35–37
footnotes, 15–16
interrelationship of income statement and balance sheet, 12–13
material misstatements, 60, 604
measurement methods, estimates and materiality, 8–9, 13–14
mutual life insurers, 16
recognition of elements, 8–9
required reports, 31–32
riders, 589–591
FIT. *See* federal income tax (FIT)
five-year average method, 273–276
fixed deferred annuities, 203–205, 622–623
fixed rate leg, 569–571
flexible-premium deferred annuities (FPDAs), 204. *See also* deferred annuities
floating rate leg, 566–569
footnotes in financial statements, 15–16
foreign currency, 438
foreign currency hedge, 596
foreign tax systems, 497–502
FPDAs. *See* flexible-premium deferred annuities (FPDAs)
fraternal benefit societies. *See* mutual life insurance enterprises
front-end loads (FEL), 186, 210–211, 218, 253–254, 257
FSP staff position FAS97-a, 162, 186–187, 191
FTBs. *See* FASB Technical Bulletins (FTBs)
fund balance, 165
fund value, 165
fund-based sales compensation, 49
funding agreements, 390–391
future deferrable expenses, 55–56
future events, 14
future value or utility, 12, 39

G

GAAP. *See* Generally Accepted Accounting Principles (GAAP)
gains and losses, 6–7, 451–452
Generally Accepted Accounting Principles (GAAP)
assumptions, 62, 86
concepts defined, 1–4
DAC and reserves, 291–294
GAAP income *vs.* taxable income, 575–576
hierarchy, 29–31, 34
illustration of reporting, 611–629
objectives of, 1–16
reinsurance, 527–528, 542–558
GICs. *See* guaranteed investment contracts (GICs)
glidepaths, 464
GMAB. *See* guaranteed minimum accumulation benefits (GMAB)
GMDB. *See* guaranteed maturity death benefits (GMDB)
GMIB. *See* guaranteed maturity income benefits (GMIB)
GMWB. *See* guaranteed minimum withdrawal benefits (GMWB)
goodwill

acquisition cost allocation, 460–461
allocation of, 480
impairment, 481–482
implementation issues, 482–484
market impact, 484
negative, 471
and purchase accounting, 651–652, 656–662
reporting units, 480, 481
SFAS 142, 28–29
SFAS 142 requirement, 479–480, 597
Governmental Accounting Standards Board (GASB), 30
"gross cash flows," 74
gross premiums, 58–61
gross profits, 7, 211–212. *See also* estimated gross profits (EGPs)
group insurance, 381. *See also* life and health insurance (group); pension contracts
group survivorship income, 383
guaranteed investment contracts (GIC), 389–391, 429–430, 465
guaranteed maturity death benefits (GMDB), 243, 247–248, 276–285
guaranteed maturity income benefits (GMIB), 209–210, 243, 248, 467–468
guaranteed minimum accumulation benefits (GMAB), 234, 243–244
guaranteed minimum income benefits (GMIB), 233
guaranteed minimum withdrawal benefits (GMWB), 234, 243–244, 248–250

H

health insurance (group). *See* life and health insurance (group)
health insurance (individual)
benefit, maintenance and DAC reserves, 335–342
benefits, 322–323, 331–332
characteristics of the business, 321–325
claim reserves, 358–363
contractual terms, 321–322
insurable events, 321
policy types, 325–328
policyholder liabilities, 468
premiums, 323–325
product classification, 328–330
recoverability and loss recognition, 356–358
reinsurance, 364
reserve methods, 330–335
reserving after a premium increase, 352–356
riders, 364–367
selection of assumptions, 342–351
Health Insurance Protection and Availability Act (HIPAA), 326
hedging activities, 27, 427–428, 596
held to maturity (HTM) securities, 405–406, 442
HGAAP. *See* historic generally accepted accounting principles (HGAAP)
high lapse rates, 340–342
HIPAA. *See Health Insurance Protection and Availability Act (HIPAA)*
historic generally accepted accounting principles (HGAAP), 460–462, 635–636, 657–659
holding companies, 16, 597–603
home office expenses, 50

Hong Kong, 513
HTM securities. *See* held to maturity (HTM) securities

I

IBNR claims. *See* incurred but not reported (IBNR) claims
identifiable intangible assets (IIAs). *See also* goodwill
  actuarial appraisal method, 474–476
  amortizable, 472–473
  determining useful life, 472
  examples, 470–471
  nonamortizable, 473
  value of business acquired, 473–478
  valuing IIAs other than VOBA, 478–479
immediate annuities, 626–627
immediate participation guarantee (IPG) contracts, 393
impairments, 406–407
income
  comprehensive, 7–8, 442
  other comprehensive (OCI), 8, 442
  replacement policies, 327
  statutory, 575–576
  taxes, 577 (*See also* federal income tax (FIT); taxes)
income statement presentations, 226–227, 661–662
income tax expense (benefit), 578
income-pay annuities, 203
incurred but not reported (IBNR) claims, 359–360, 377–378
indemnity benefits, 322–324, 326
indeterminate premium products, 116–118
individual health insurance. *See* health insurance (individual)
Industry Audit and Accounting Guides, 20, 30. *See also* specific titles
inflation and assumptions, 85
initial bonus interest, 67
initiation fees, 186
insurance companies
  audits, 32–34
  ratings, 476, 523
insurance-related assessments, 20
intangible assets
  acquisition cost allocation, 460–461
  and fair value, 597
  and financial statements, 5
  identifying, 469–471
  other than goodwill, 471–479
  other than VOBA, 478–479
  and *SFAS 142,* 28–29
interest
  additional, 168–170
  assumptions, 89, 134–135, 345–346
  on surplus, 60–61
interest method, 398–399, 536–537
interest only strips (IOs), 404
interest rate bonuses, 188

interest-sensitive-whole-life (ISWL), 166
internal replacements, 22–23, 62–63
Internal Revenue Code, 575
International Accounting Standards, 30, 34, 491, 508
Interpretation 1-D, "Purchase Accounting," 637–639, 643
Interpretation 40, "Applicability of Generally Accepted Accounting Principles to Mutual Life Insurance and Other Enterprises," 16, 123
investment accounting. *See also SFAS 97*
  background, 403
  bonds, 407–412
  collateralized mortgage obligations, 412–418
  contract analysis under *SFAS 133,* 428–439
  debt securities, 404–418
  derivative and hedging activities, 427–428
  mortgage loans, 420
  partnerships, 426
  policy loans, 426
  real estate, 421–426
  short-term investments, 426
  stocks, 418–420
  typical life insurer investments, 403–404
investment facility contracts, 393
investments
  accounting of, 25–27
  contracts, 39, 208–209
  earnings, 89, 171–172
  expenses, 39, 44, 46
  impact of gains, 502
investors, needs of, 17
IPG contracts. *See* immediate participation guarantee (IPG) contracts
Italy, 507–508

J

Japan, 509–510

K

401(k) plans, 391
k-factor, 174, 184–186, 213–216, 446
Kitsos, Theodore, 90
Korea, 510–511

L

LAE reserves. *See* loss adjustment expense (LAE) reserves
lag tables, 360
lapse rates, 90–91, 136, 346, 523
leases, 25. *See also SFAS 91,* "Accounting for Nonrefundable Fees and Costs Associated with Originating or Acquiring Loans and Initial Direct Costs of Leases"
level of aggregation for recoverability testing, 57–58
level prospective approach, 271–276
liabilities
  fair value reporting, 592
  future policy benefits, 83

pension plans, 394–397
from sales inducements, 71–72
under *SOP 03-1,* 191–192, 196–202
valuation of, 517–520
LIBOR. *See* London Inter-Bank Overnight Rates (LIBOR)
life and health insurance (group)
active life and unearned premium reserves, 384
expense capitalization, 384–385
general characteristics, 381–383
policyholder liabilities, 468
purchase accounting special considerations, 641–642
reserves, 385–386, 386–387, 388
stop-loss reinsurance, 388–389
life annuities, 203
life insurance. *See* traditional life insurance *(SFAS 60 & SFAS 97);* traditional life insurance *(SFAS 120);* universal life insurance
life-contingent payments, 312
limited-payment contracts, 109–110
line of business allocation, 41–48, 57–58
literature, 29–30. *See also* specific titles
loading, 83
loads (expense charges), 253–254, 257
loans, 25, 40. *See also* investments
lock-in, 92
lock-in concept, 343, 353
London Inter-Bank Overnight Rates (LIBOR), 390, 566–570
long-duration contracts. *See also SFAS 97; SFAS 120; SOP 03-1;* universal life insurance
nontraditional, 20–22
participating life insurance, 494–495
reinsurance, 534–535, 540–541
SFAS 113, 123, 527–541, 557
traditional life insurance, 82–83
long-term care (LTC) policies, 328, 383
loss adjustment expense (LAE) reserves, 363, 376–379
loss recognition
credit insurance, 376
deferred annuities, 219–220
expenses and capitalization, 56–61
health insurance (individual), 356–358
pension liabilities, 400
reinsurance, 574
riders, 591
traditional life insurance, 92–94, 143–146
universal life insurance, 189
losses, defined, 6–7, 57, 190–196
LTC policies. *See* long-term care (LTC) policies

M

maintenance expense reserves, 44, 92, 314–319, 332–333, 336–339. *See also* expense reserves
Malaysia, 511–512
managed care benefits, 383
market value, 594. *See also* fair value accounting

marketing expenses, 50
marketing information, 470
market-value-adjusted (MVA) annuities, 204, 228–230, 435
materiality
background, 604–605
generally, 14
judgment, 606
professional standards, 609–610
qualitative factors, 607–608
quantitative factors, 606
responsibility, 608–609
McDonald, Andrew, 90
measurement methods and estimates, 13–14, 44–47
medical coverages, 322, 326
Medicare supplement policies, 328, 383
MGDB. *See* minimum guaranteed death benefit (MGDB)
MIHC. *See* mutual insurance holding companies (MIHC)
minimum guaranteed death benefit (MGDB), 467–468
Missouri trusts, 322
modified coinsurance, 438–439, 525, 548–551, 562–567
morbidity, defined, 321
Mortality and Lapse Assumptions in Renewable Term Insurance, 90
mortality and morbidity
assumptions, 344–345
deferred annuities, 207, 235–236
and reinsurance, 523
traditional life insurance, 89–90, 133, 134
universal life insurance, 163–164, 171, 190
mortality rates, 242
mortgage loans
investment accounting, 420
mutual insurance holding companies (MIHC)
background, 597–598
closed block accounting, 599–603
closed block establishment, 598–599
generally, 16
open block accounting, 603
mutual life insurance enterprises. *See also SFAS 120; SOP 95-1*
accounting, 20, 27, 123
expenses and capitalization, 41
financial statements, 16
MVA annuities. *See* market-value-adjusted (MVA) annuities

N

negative goodwill, 471
negative gross profits, 175
net assets. *See* assets
net GAAP reserve, 83
net level-premium method, 146–148, 152–154
new ventures, 48
no lapse guarantees, 466
nominal account value, 400

nondeferrable acquisition costs, 38, 44–47, 172
non-monetary assets, 1
non-recurring expenses, 48
nonrefundable fees, 25
nontraditional long-duration contracts, 20–22
non-U.S. products, 491–521
  Asian market in general, 508–509
  background, 491–492
  China, 513
  European market in general, 502–503
  Hong Kong, 513
  investment gains, 502
  Italy, 507–508
  Japan, 509–510
  Korea, 510–511
  The Philippines, 513–514
  practical issues, 514–516
  product classification issues, 492–497, 502–514
  Singapore and Malaysia, 511–512
  SOP 03-1, 516–521
  Switzerland, 506–507
  Taiwan, 512
  tax systems, 497–502
  United Kingdom, 503–505
Northway, Inc., TSC Industries v., 605

O

open block of participating policies, 603
optionally renewable (OR) contracts, 330
order of adjustments to the balance sheet, 58–60
other comprehensive income (OCI), 8, 442
outsourcing of costs, 470, 478
overhead expenses, 39, 43–44

P

PAD. *See* provisions for adverse deviation (PAD)
paid-up additions (PUAs), 151
partial disability benefits, 365
participating products, 114–116
participating whole life, 612–613
partnerships, 426
payout annuities, 203, 234, 237–238, 264–270
PB. *See* Practice Bulletins (PB)
PDO. *See* policyholder dividend obligation (PDO)
pension contracts
  annuitization guarantees, 394–397
  deferred acquisition cost, 397–400
  fair value accounting, 400
  general characteristics, 389–390
  GICs and funding agreements, 390–391
  group master contract pension plans, 391–394
  implications of *SFAS 133,* 400–401

participating contracts, 393
plan closeout, 393–394
pension fund investment contracts (PICs), 393
"per application" basis, 46
performance guarantees, 394
permanent difference, 580
"per-policy issued" basis, 46
persistency bonuses, 49–50, 67–77, 168–170, 188–189
The Philippines, 513–514
PIC. *See* pension fund investment contracts (PICs)
PO. *See* principal only strips (POs)
point-to-point EIA products, 277, 292, 294–299, 436
policies. *See* contracts
policy loans, 426
policyholder dividend obligation (PDO), 599–602
policyholders
benefits, 129, 134, 146–148
liabilities, 463–469
purchase accounting, 636–642
sales inducements, 520
surplus, 7
policy-year conversion to calendar-year, 319–320
pooling method, 632
pooling of interests, 19
Practice Bulletin 8
deferred annuities, 207–208, 210, 212, 220
expenses and capitalization, 37, 40, 63
health insurance (individual), 334–335
investment contracts, 316–317
pension liabilities, 397–398
Practice Bulletins (PB), 19–20
Practice Note on Anticipated Common Practices Relating to SOP 03-1, 70–78
premium deficiencies
credit insurance, 376
expenses and capitalization, 56–59
health insurance (individual), 335
life and health insurance (group), 386–387
traditional life insurance, 93–94, 144–147
premium expense allocation, 42
premium products, 116–118
premium reserves, 335, 384
premium taxes, 40, 92
premiums
attrition, 40
gross, 58–61
health insurance (individual), 323–325
indeterminate, 116–118
and liabilities, 9–12
reserving after increase, 352–356
traditional life insurance, 129
universal life insurance, 165–166
present value of cash flows, 594

present value of future profits (PVP). *See* value of business acquired (VOBA)
pre-tax net income, 7
Pricing a Select and Ultimate Renewable Term Policy, 90
principal only strips (POs), 404
probable loss, defined, 57
"profits followed by losses" test, 190–196
Prospective Deposit Method, 313–317
prospective reinsurance, 535–536
prospective unlocking method, 117–118
provisions for adverse deviation (PAD), 344–345, 348–351, 640–641
PUA. *See* paid-up additions (PUAs)
public companies assessment, 33–34
Public Company Accounting Oversight Board, 33–34
purchase accounting
  assumptions, 659–660
  background, 631
  balance sheet analysis, 660–661
  business combinations, 631–632
  comparative balance sheets at the purchase date, 657–659
  comparative income statements, 661–662
  expenses and capitalization, 64–65
  and goodwill, 651–652
  policyholder liabilities, 636–642
  pooling method, 632
  post-purchase issues, 653–654
  practice variations, 662–663
  purchase method, 633–635
  SFAS 60, 654–655
  SFAS 97, 655–656
  tax considerations, 653
  value of business acquired assets, 643–651
purchase generally accepted accounting principles (PGAAP), 634–635, 646–650, 657–659
purchase of business, 19. *See also* acquisitions
PVP. *See* value of business acquired (VOBA)

R

ratchet contracts, 292, 299–309
rate assumptions. *See* assumptions
ratings of insurance companies, 476, 523
RBC. *See* risk-based capital (RBC) requirements
real estate as investments, 421–426
realized capital gains, 5–6, 141–143
recapture provisions, 527, 574
recognition of loss. *See* loss recognition
recoverability
  credit insurance coverage, 376
  expenses and capitalization, 56–61, 84
  goodwill, 651–652
  health insurance (individual), 356–358
  life and health insurance (group), 386–387
  reinsurance, 574
  riders, 591

traditional life insurance, 143–146
universal life insurance, 189
recovery method, 536–537
recruiting allowances, 50
Regulation SX, 31
reinsurance
assumption reinsurance, 526, 574
as business combination, 458
catastrophe coverage, 526
ceded, 535–558
coinsurance, 525, 542–543
credit insurance coverage, 379
expenses and capitalization, 63–64
experience rating, 526, 573
GAAP accounting, 527–528
health insurance (individual), 364
as identifiable intangible asset, 470, 478
life and health insurance (group), 388–389
long-duration contracts, 534–535, 540–541
modified coinsurance, 548–551
post-issue, 551–555
prospective, 535–536
qualification under *SFAS 113,* 528–535
recapture, 527, 574
recoverability and loss recognition, 574
retroactive, 536–540
riders, 591
SFAS 113, 26
SFAS 133, 562–573
short-duration contracts, 528–534, 535–540
SOP 03-1, 558–561
stop-loss, 388–389, 526
traditional life insurance *(SFAS 120),* 152
universal life and estimated gross profits, 555–558
uses of, 523–524
yearly renewable term, 524–525, 544–547
renewability of contracts, 321–322, 330
reporting units (RU), 459–460, 479–484
reserve methods
health insurance (individual), 330–335, 352–356, 365
policyholder liabilities, 463–464
SFAS 60 and *SFAS 97* limited pay, 637–639
reserves. *See also* assumptions
accrued experience refunds, 388
after premium increase, 352–356
contingency, 13
for experience refunds, 388
factors, 51
formula selection, 118–122, 469
generally, 7
premium, 335, 384
residual disability benefits, 365

retirement annuities, 203–205
retroactive reinsurance, 536–540
retrospective deposit method, 166, 168
return of premium riders (ROP), 366–367
revenues, defined, 6
riders
  financial statement preparation, 589–591
  health insurance (individual), 364–367
  traditional life insurance, 150–151
risk
  pricing, 207
  and *SFAS 113, 528–529*
  significance of, 518
risk premium reinsurance. *See* yearly renewable term (YRT)
risk-based capital (RBC) requirements, 523, 603
ROP. *See* return of premium riders (ROP)
RU. *See* reporting units (RU)
rule of 78 method, 371–373
rule-making authorities. *See* authorities

S

SAB. *See* Staff Accounting Bulletins (SABs)
SAB 62, "Discounting by Property-Casualty Insurance Companies," 362–363, 378–379
SAB 100, "Restructuring and Impairment Change," 652
salary expenses, 43, 50
sale of investments, 25–26. *See also SFAS 97*
sales compensation, 49
sales inducement assets (SIA), 69, 72–78
sales inducement liability (SIL), 69–70
sales inducements
  and annuities, 205
  capitalization and amortization, 68–69
  deferred, 211
  defined, 22
  definition and classification, 66–68
  interpretation of authoritative guidance, 70–78
  policyholder liabilities, 467–468, 520
  transitional rules, 70
Sarbanes-Oxley Act of 2002, 33–34
SEC Regulation S-K, 15
securities
  available for sale (AFS), 405–406, 442
  bonds, 407–412, 578–579
  stocks, 418–420
Securities Act of 1933, 31
Securities and Exchange Commission (SEC), 31–34, 491
Securities Exchange Act of 1934, 31, 609–610
securities investments, 26–27
seed money, 517
self-insured plans, 383, 388–389
separate accounts, 20–21, 48, 516–517. *See also SOP 03-1*
service agreements, 47–48, 470, 478

SFAC. *See* Statements of Financial Accounting Concepts (SFAC)
SFAC 1, "Objectives of Financial Reporting by Business Enterprises," 4
SFAC 2, "Qualitative Characteristics of Accounting Information," 604
SFAC 5, "Recognition and Measurement in Financial Statements of Business Enterprises," 35
SFAC 6, "Elements of Financial Statements," 5–7, 36, 442
SFAS. *See* Statements of Financial Accounting Standards (SFAS)
SFAS 1, "Objectives of Financial Reporting by Business Enterprises," 2
SFAS 5, "Accounting for Contingencies," 6, 13, 24–25, 359
SFAS 38, "Accounting for Preacquisition Contingencies of Purchased Enterprises," 460
SFAS 60, "Accounting and Reporting by Insurance Enterprises"
  credit insurance, 376–379
  deferred annuities, 205–206, 226–227
  expenses and capitalization, 36–39, 43–44, 51, 56–60, 63–64
  generally, 25
  health insurance (individual), 328–330, 342–343, 353, 358–359, 363
  life and health insurance (group), 384–385
  participating business applicability, 495–496
  PGAAP formulas, 646–648
  and purchase accounting, 654–655
  reserve methods, 637–639
  traditional life insurance, 81–108, 114–122, 114–123, 128–129
  universal life insurance, 161, 167, 173, 189
SFAS 66, "Accounting for Sales of Real Estate," 421–426
SFAS 91, "Accounting for Nonrefundable Fees and Costs Associated with Originating or Acquiring Loans and Initial Direct Costs of Leases"
  deferred annuities, 206–209, 217–218, 224–226
  expenses and capitalization, 37, 39–40
  generally, 25
  investment contracts, 313
  reserve methods, 639
SFAS 97, "Accounting and Reporting by Insurance Enterprises for Certain Long-Duration Contracts and for Realized Gains and Losses from the Sale of Investments"
  annuities in payment status, 311–313
  credited rate determination, 241
  deferral of capital gains or losses, 5–6
  deferred annuities, 206–214, 219–220, 226–227, 235–238
  expenses and capitalization, 36–37, 39–40, 59–60, 62–63
  generally, 22, 25–26
  health insurance (individual), 329, 334–335
  investment contracts, 22, 649–651
  limited-payment contracts, 109–113, 317–318
  non-U.S. products, 514, 518–519
  PGAAP formulas, 646–648
  purchase accounting, 649–651, 655–657
  reserve methods, 637–639
  shadow adjustments, 446–448
  shadow adjustments *(SFAS 115),* 451–452
  traditional life insurance, 81, 123–124, 127–128
  universal life insurance, 161–168, 171–175, 182, 186, 189–191
SFAS 107, "Disclosures about Fair Value of Financial Instruments," 592–595
SFAS 109, "Accounting for Income Taxes," 576–586

SFAS 113, "Accounting and Reporting for Reinsurance of Short-Duration and Long-Duration Contracts," 26, 123, 527–541, 557
SFAS 115, "Accounting for Certain Investments in Debt and Equity Securities," 8, 26–27, 442–443
SFAS 120, "Accounting and Reporting by Mutual Life Insurance Enterprises and by Insurance Enterprises for Certain Long-Duration Participating Contracts"
  expenses and capitalization, 37, 41, 59–60, 70–71
  GAAP requirements, 597
  generally, 27
  participating business applicability, 494–495
  reserve methods, 639–640
  shadow adjustments, 451–452
  traditional life insurance, 123–159
SFAS 121, "Accounting for the Impairment of Long-Lived Assets and for Long-Lived Assets to be Disposed of," 652
SFAS 130, "Reporting Comprehensive Income," 7, 442
SFAS 133, "Accounting for Derivative Instruments and Hedging Activities"
  assumptions for variable products, 243–244
  contract analysis, 428–439
  equity-indexed annuities, 290–294
  fair value accounting, 595–596
  generally, 27
  guaranteed investment contracts, 400–401
  investment accounting, 428–439
  pension liabilities, 400–401
  reinsurance, 562–573
SFAS 138, "Accounting for Certain Derivative Instruments and Certain Hedging Activities an amendment of FASB Statement 133," 27
SFAS 141, "Business Combinations"
  acquisition cost allocation, 460–461
  decisions, 456
  determining control, 457–458
  generally, 27–28
  proposed statement to replace, 665–667
SFAS 142, "Goodwill and Other Intangible Assets"
  accounting requirements, 479–480, 483–484
  decisions, 456–457
  disclosures, 490
  fair value accounting, 597
  generally, 28–29
SFAS 144, "Accounting for the Impairment or Disposal of Long-Lived Assets," 66
shadow adjustments
  background, 441
  calculations, 448–451, 452–453
  contracts governed by *SFAS 97* and *SFAS 120,* 451–452
  EITF Topic D-41, 443–448
  group pension contracts, 400
  SFAS 115 requirements, 441–443
shareholder dividends, 495–496
short-duration contracts
  reinsurance, 535–540
  SFAS 113, 26, 123, 527–541, 557
  traditional life insurance, 81–82

short-term medical insurance, 322
SIA. *See* sales inducement assets (SIA)
significance test, 164–165
SIL. *See* sales inducement liability (SIL)
Singapore, 511–512
single-premium deferred annuities (SPDAs), 204, 465–466
Social Security Administration (SSA) benefits, 365
SOP. *See* Statements of Position (SOP)
SOP 00-3, "Accounting by Insurance Enterprises for Demutualizations and Formations of Mutual Insurance Holding Companies and for Certain Long-Duration Participating Contracts," 464, 599–600
SOP 03-1, "Accounting and Reporting by Insurance Enterprises for Certain Nontraditional Long-Duration Contracts and for Separate Accounts"
  assumptions for variable products, 243
  deferred annuities, 205–212
  expenses and capitalization, 66–78
  generally, 20–22
  GMDB liability, 247–248
  interaction with unearned revenue liability, 191–192, 196–202
  non-U.S. products, 516–521
  pension liabilities, 394–395
  policyholder liabilities, 467–468
  reinsurance, 558–561
  universal life insurance, 162–163, 168, 189–191, 196–202
  variable universal life, 235–237
SOP 95-1, "Accounting for Certain Insurance Activities of Mutual Life Insurance Enterprises"
  expenses and capitalization, 41
  generally, 20
  mutual companies, 597–598
  traditional life insurance, 123–128, 130, 135, 146–151
SOP 97-3, "Accounting by Insurance and Other Enterprises for Insurance-Related Assessments," 20
SOP 98-5, "Reporting on the Costs of Start-Up Activities," 39, 385–387
source-of-earnings approach, 348
SPDA. *See* single-premium deferred annuities (SPDAs)
special benefits, 188–189
specific and aggregate stop-loss reinsurance (S&A), 388–389
SSA benefits. *See* Social Security Administration (SSA) benefits
Staff Accounting Bulletins (SABs), 31. *See also* specific titles beginning *SAB*
standard setters, 3–4, 18–29. *See also* authorities
state approved insurance products, 471
state licenses, 471, 479
Statement on Auditing Standards 1, "Subsequent Events," 15–16
Statement on Auditing Standards 69, 29–30
Statements of Financial Accounting Concepts (SFAC), 4, 23, 30, 35. *See also* specific titles beginning *SFAC*
Statements of Financial Accounting Standards (SFAS), 23, 30, 36–37. *See also* specific titles beginning *SFAS*
Statements of Position (SOP), 20–23, 30. *See also* specific title beginning *SOP*
statutory basis of accounting, 657–659
statutory income, 575–576
step-rated variable costs, 50
stochastic-type technique, 240–241

stock investments. *See also* equity-indexed annuities
accounting, 405–406, 418–420
Stock Option Accounting and Reform Act, 32–33
stockholders, 114–115
stop-loss reinsurance, 388–389, 526
subrogation, 389
subsidiaries, 1
surplus, 7, 12, 475–476, 523
surplus notes, 60, 603–604
surrender values, 165, 172, 400, 594
swap arrangements, 566–571
Switzerland, 506–507

T

Taiwan, 512
tangible assets, 5
target surplus, 475–476
taxable income, defined, 578
taxable income *vs.* GAAP income, 575–576
taxes. *See also* federal income tax (FIT)
alternative systems, 583
changes in laws or rates, 582
deferred taxes, 576–583
jurisdictions, 583
non-U.S. systems, 497–502
planning strategies, 578, 583
on premium, 40, 92
on premiums, 92, 348
purchase accounting considerations, 653
Technical Information Service Inquiries and Replies, 30
Technical Practice Aids, 30
temporary annuities, 203
temporary differences, 578, 579–588
term life contracts, 82, 90, 614–615
terminal dividends, 129, 143–144, 150
terminal funding case, 393–394
termination rates, 90–91
TPA 6300.05 to 6300.10, 162, 190–191
trade names and trademarks, 470, 478
trading securities, 405–406
traditional life insurance *(SFAS 60 & SFAS 97)*
background, 81–82
benefit reserve methodology, 82–83
expense recognition, 83–86
implications of reserve formula selection, 118–122
intermediate premium products, 116–118
limited-payment contracts, 109–110
lock-in, 92
loss recognition, 92–94
participating products, 114–116
product features, 82
selection of assumptions, 86–92

SFAS 60 numerical examples, 94–108
SFAS 97 limited pay numerical example, 110–113
traditional life insurance *(SFAS 120)*
alternative discount rates, 157–159
amortization methods, 130–132
background, 123–125
DAC and terminal dividend liabilities, 148–150
dividend fund different than net level premium reserve, 152–154
experience different than best-estimate assumptions, 155–156
overview of accounting model, 128–129
policy riders, 150–151
policyholder benefit liabilities, 146–148
realized capital gains, 141–143
recoverability and loss recognition, 143–146
reinsurance, 152
scope and applicability, 125–128
selection of assumptions, 133–138
true-up and unlocking, 138–141
training allowances, 50
transitional rules for sales inducements, 70, 520–521
Treadway Commission, 33
true-up, 51–54, 138–141, 183–184, 415
trusts, 322
TSC Industries v. Northway, Inc., 605
two-tiered annuities, 205, 209–210, 467–468

U

UEP. *See* unearned premium assets (UEP)
UER. *See* unearned revenue (UER)
UHG&L. *See* unrealized holding gains and losses (UHG&Ls)
UL method, 398–399
unamortized acquisition costs (UAC), 37, 85
unamortized expense assets (UEA), 37
underwriting expenses, 38, 46
undistributed participating policyholders' earnings account (UPPEA), 114–116, 512
unearned premium assets (UEP), 121–122
unearned premium reserves (UPR), 333, 338, 370–374, 384
unearned profit reserve, 110–113
unearned revenue liability (URL), 218, 269, 444, 447–448
unearned revenue (UER)
deferred annuities, 218
traditional life insurance, 111–113
transitional rules, 71
universal life insurance, 167, 186–188, 191–192, 200–202
variable universal life, 253, 256
United Kingdom, 503–505
unitization of expenses, 44–47
units of measurement, 44–47
universal life insurance
accounting under *SFAS 97,* 127–128
applicability, 162–163
background, 161–162

benefit reserves, 168–170
bonuses and other special benefits, 188–189
company rollup, 616–617
computation and amortization of acquisition expenses, 171–186
credit rating in DAC amortization, 189–190
deferral of unearned revenue, 186–188
defined, 163–165
establishment of liabilities under SOP 03-1, 196–202
income statement presentation, 166–167
nontraditional long-duration contracts, 22
policyholder liabilities, 466
product designs, 165–166
profits followed by losses, 190–196
recoverability and loss recognition, 189
reinsurance, 555–558
significance test, 164–165
UL method, 398–399
unlocking, 117–118, 138–141, 183–186, 197
unpaid claims liability. *See* claim reserves
unrealized holding gains and losses (UHG&Ls), 442–448, 451–453
unreleased profit reserve, 110–113
unrestricted stockholder profits, 115
UPPEA. *See* undistributed participating policyholders' earnings account (UPPEA)
UPR. *See* unearned premium reserves (UPR)
URL. *See* unearned revenue liability (URL)

V

valuation allowance, 581, 585–586
valuation of liabilities, 517–520
value of business acquired (VOBA)
appraisal value method, 476–477
as intangible asset, 470, 473–479
present value techniques, 483–484
and purchase accounting, 643–651
shadow adjustments, 444–448
variable annuity contracts, 430–435, 620–621
variable deferred annuity contracts
examples of accounting, 258–263
product description, 233–234
variable payout annuity contracts, 234, 264–270
variable products
assumptions, 238–244
background, 231
contract classification, 234–238
examples of accounting, 250–289
methods of accounting, 244–250
product descriptions, 232–234
variable universal life (VUL) contracts
company rollup, 618–619
contract classification, 234–235
examples of accounting, 250–257
no-lapse premium guarantee liability, 248

product description, 232–233
VEBAs. *See* voluntary employer benefit associations (VEBAs)
VOBA. *See* value of business acquired (VOBA)
volume bonuses, 49
voluntary employer benefit associations (VEBAs), 322
VUL. *See* variable universal life (VUL) contracts

W

waiver-of-premium benefit, 383
whole life contracts, 82, 612–613
withdrawal rates, 90–91
worksheet approaches, 322

Y

yearly renewable term (YRT) reinsurance, 524–525, 544–547